The Legal and E-Commerce Environment Today 4ᵀᴴ EDITION

Business in Its Ethical, Regulatory, and International Setting

Roger LeRoy Miller
Institute for University Studies
Arlington, Texas

Frank B. Cross
Herbert D. Kelleher
Centennial Professor in Business Law
University of Texas at Austin

THOMSON ™

SOUTH-WESTERN

WEST

Australia · Canada · Mexico · Singapore · Spain · United Kingdom · United States

THOMSON

SOUTH-WESTERN

WEST

The Legal and E-Commerce Environment Today
Business in Its Ethical, Regulatory, and International Setting
FOURTH EDITION

Roger LeRoy Miller
Institute for University Studies
Arlington, Texas

Frank B. Cross
Herbert D. Kelleher
Centennial Professor in Business Law
University of Texas at Austin

Vice President and Editorial Director:
Jack Calhoun

Vice President and Editor-in-Chief:
George Werthman

Publisher, Business Law and Accounting:
Rob Dewey

Sr. Developmental Editor:
Jan Lamar

Marketing Manager:
Steve Silverstein

Production Manager:
Bill Stryker

Media Developmental Editor:
Christine A. Wittmer

Media Production Editor:
Amy Wilson

Manufacturing Coordinator:
Rhonda Utley

Compositor:
Parkwood Composition
New Richmond, WI

Printer:
Quebecor World Versailles

Sr. Design Project Manager:
Michelle Kunkler

Internal Designer:
Bill Stryker

Cover Designer:
Ramsdell Design
Cincinnati, OH

Library of Congress Control Number: 2003116141

ISBN 0-324-27057-7

The Legal and E-Commerce Environment Today

Today's Legal Environment ...
in Print, on CD-ROM, and Online

Dear Student:

Today's legal environment brings challenges not only to business leaders—chief executive officers and chief financial officers—but also to the business community in general. Recent legislation calls for heightened accountability and ethical behavior, and new laws continue to have a direct effect on the regulation of e-commerce.

This text covers the new changes affecting the legal environment of business today and also presents fundamental principles of the traditional legal environment. You can count on *The Legal and E-Commerce Environment Today* to deliver:

- **Currency in ethics and e-commerce.** The focus of this text is on new legislation and cases affecting the legal environment of business as well as e-commerce. In addition to the latest legislative coverage, all chapters have at least one 2003 court decision and other case updates, such as 2003 cases used in our end-of-chapter *Case Problems*.

- **Business applications to engage students.** The law can be compelling when presented with interesting features, cases, and unrivaled assessment tools.

- **Videos, CD-ROM, and Internet research tools.** Our technology offerings, which are specifically designed to engage the students, range from a complete video library, to interactive quizzes, to access to the best research tool available to undergraduates—Westlaw® Campus.

The Legal and E-Commerce Environment Today has been designed to help you connect law with today's business and e-commerce world. We hope you find this edition the best yet.

Sincerely,

ROGER MILLER　　　　　　**FRANK CROSS**

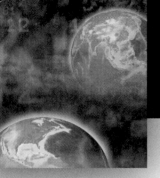

Full coverage of the new legal

Changing legal environment, new laws, changes on the Internet, ethics

- **THE *LEGAL E-NVIRONMENT* FEATURE EXPLORES** how traditional legal concepts or newly enacted laws apply to specific, real-world disputes relating to online transactions.

- **E-COMMERCE** has been integrated throughout the text to illustrate how this emerging form of commerce relates to traditional business law concepts.

- **LANDMARK AND CLASSIC CASES** are set off with a special heading. A concluding *Comment* section helps students understand the relevance of these cases to today's world.

18   UNIT ONE   THE FOUNDATIONS

LEGAL *e*-NVIRONMENT

International Jurisdiction and the Internet

www.FindLaw.com

As you will learn in Chapter 4, *jurisdiction* is an important legal concept that relates to the authority of a court to hear and decide a case. Within the United States, there is a federal court system, which has jurisdiction over specific types of cases. There are also fifty state court systems, each having jurisdiction over certain types of cases. In today's interconnected world, the issue of jurisdiction has become critical. Specifically, businesses using the Internet can reach individuals in any part of the world. Does that mean that every court everywhere has jurisdiction over, say, an [...] in Chicago?

of any jurisdiction in which it targets customers for its products.[a] Businesses may even be sued under another nation's laws for different reasons. For example, consider a case brought against Dow Jones & Company, the U.S. publisher of the *Wall Street Journal*. The *Wall Street Journal* has a Web site that contains articles written by its reporters. One such article included information about an American businessperson, Joseph Gutnick, living in Melbourne, Australia. Gutnick decided to sue the *Wall Street Journal* for defamation in an Australian court. (As you will read in Chapter 8, defamation is a *tort*, or civil wrong, that is committed when one makes a false statement that harms the good reputation of another.)

Dow Jones argued that the Australian court could not exercise jurisdiction over its U.S. servers [...]

CHAPTER 13

E-Contracts

CONTENTS

FORMING
CONTRACTS ONLINE

E-SIGNATURES

PARTNERING AGREEMENTS

THE UNIFORM ELECTRONIC
TRANSACTIONS ACT

CHAPTER OBJECTIVES

After reading this chapter, you should be able to answer the following questions:

1. What are some important clauses to include when making offers to form electronic contracts, or e-contracts?

2. What are shrink-wrap agreements and click-on agreements? How have traditional laws been applied to such agreements? What problems arise in the application of traditional laws to [...]

for wheat and thus could have a substantial effect on interstate commerce.[...]

The following landmark case involved a challenge to the scope of the national government's constitutional authority to regulate local activities.

3. 317 U.S. 111, 63 S.Ct. 82, 87 L.Ed. 122 (1942).

LANDMARK AND CLASSIC CASES

CASE 5.1   Heart of Atlanta Motel v. United States

Supreme Court of the United States, 1964.
379 U.S. 241,
85 S.Ct. 348,
13 L.Ed.2d 258.
http://supct.law.cornell.edu/supct/
cases/name.htm[a]

HISTORICAL AND SOCIAL SETTING *In the first half of the twentieth century, state governments sanctioned segregation on the basis of race. In 1954, the United States Supreme Court decided that racially segregated school systems violated the Constitution. In*

the following decade, the Court ordered an end to racial segregation imposed by the states in other public facilities, such as beaches, golf courses, buses, parks, auditoriums, and courtroom seating. Privately owned facilities that excluded or segregated African Americans and others on the basis of race were not subject to the same constitutional restrictions, however. Congress passed the Civil Rights Act of 1964 to prohibit racial discrimination in "establishments affecting interstate commerce." These facilities included "places of public accommodation."

a. This is the "Historic Supreme Court Decisions—by Party Name" page within the "Caselists" collection of the Legal Information Institute available at its site on the Web. Click on the "H" link or scroll down the list of cases to the entry for the *Heart of Atlanta* case. Click on the [...] on one of the choices to read the "Syllabus," the "Full Decision," or the "Edited Decision."

environment of business

CHAPTER 2

Ethics and Social Responsibility

CHAPTER OBJECTIVES

...this chapter you should be able to answer...

gious services, the Court has viewed this effect as an incidental, not a primary, purpose of Sunday closing laws. ●

ETHICAL ISSUE

Do religious displays on public property violate the establishment clause?

The thorny issue of whether religious displays on public property violate the establishment clause often arises during the holiday season. Time and again, the courts have wrestled with this issue, but it has never been resolved in a way that satisfies everyone. In a 1984 case, the United States Supreme Court decided that a city's official Christmas display, which included a crèche (Nativity scene), did not violate the establishment clause because it was just one part of a larger holiday display that featured secular symbols, such as reindeer and candy canes.[33] In a later case, the Court held that the presence of a crèche within a county courthouse violated the establishment clause because it was not in close proximity to nonreligious ~~symbols~~ ... ~~were located outside, on the~~

INTERNATIONAL PERSPECTIVE

International Guidelines for Business Conduct

In today's global marketplace, conflicts and misunderstandings often arise due to different

forth international standards of business conduct that governments, businesses, and other groups can voluntarily implement to prevent misunderstandings and build an atmosphere of predictability. Over time, the guidelines have been updated to address new ... For example, the 2000

business conduct are now available, the guidelines constitute the only multilaterally endorsed and comprehensive code that governments are committed to promoting.

FOR CRITICAL ANALYSIS

Why might an American corporation comply with the

be commenced after the expiration of the time limited and within six months after the termination of the first action unless the termination resulted from voluntary discontinuance or from dismissal for failure or neglect to prosecute.

(4) This section does not alter the law on tolling of the statute of limitations nor does it apply to causes of action which have accrued before this Act becomes effective.

Article 2 Amendments (Excerpts)[1]

Part 1 Short Title, General Construction and Subject Matter

* * * *

§ 2–103. Definitions and Index of Definitions.

(1) In this article unless the context otherwise requires

* * * *

sonal, family, or household purposes.

(d) "Consumer contract" means a contract between a merchant seller and a consumer.

* * * *

(j) "Good faith" means honesty in fact and the observance of reasonable commercial standards of fair dealing.

(k) "Goods" means all things that are movable at the time of identification to a contract for sale. The term includes future goods, specially manufactured goods, the unborn young of animals, growing crops, and other identified things attached to realty as described in Section 2–107. The term does not include information, the money in which the price is to be paid, investment securities under Article 8, the subject matter of foreign exchange transactions, and choses in action.

* * * *

(m) "Record" means information that is inscribed on a tangible medium or that is stored in an electronic or other medium and is retrievable in perceivable form.

ARTICLE 2 AMENDMENTS (E...

● **CHAPTER 2, "ETHICS AND SOCIAL RESPONSIBILITY,"** has been substantially rewritten and now presents a more practical, real-world approach to ethical issues in the legal environment, including a case study of Enron. Discussions on the Sarbanes-Oxley Act of 2002 are found in Chapter 2 and again in Chapter 23 in the context of securities law.

● **IN ADDITION TO ETHICAL TOPICS** integrated throughout the text, most chapters contain at least one *Ethical Issue* addressing an ethical dimension of the topic under discussion.

● **WITH THE *INTERNATIONAL PERSPECTIVE* FEATURE,** students gain an awareness of the global legal environment. The feature indicates how international laws or the laws of other nations deal with specific legal topics.

● **UP-TO-THE-MINUTE COVERAGE** of the 2003 amendments to Article 2 of the Uniform Commercial Code are included in this newest edition.

Engage students with law

Practical applications for future managers

● **THE *INSIDE THE LEGAL ENVIRONMENT* FEATURE** emphasizes managerial issues and offers practical and instructive examples of how the law applies to real-world business situations. A concluding *For Critical Analysis* section in each feature presents a question that requires the student to think critically about a specific aspect of the feature topic.

INSIDE THE LEGAL ENVIRONMENT

Mandatory Arbitration—A Problematic Issue for Managers

Arbitration is normally simpler, speedier, and less costly than litigation. For that reason, business owners and managers today often include arbitration clauses in their contracts, including employment contracts. What happens, though, if a job candidate whom you wish to hire (or an existing employee whose contract is being renewed) objects

held that arbitration clauses in employment contracts should not be enforced if they are too one sided and unfair to the employee.

In one case, court held that to be not have to subnary arbitration bec were so one sid law."**b** possible purpo the neutrality According to t biased rules cr**ps, 173** system unwort name of arbitr**ies' 6, 279 F.3d** **Ninth** **the** **wed the**

Stores, Inc. (see Case 3.2), another federal appellate court refused to enforce a provision in a mandatory arbitration

FOR CRITICAL ANALYSIS

Why might victims of employment discrimination prefer to litigate their claims in a judicial forum rather than having them arbitrated, even assuming that arbitration proceedings would be unbiased and would not violate due process rights?

● **NEW CASES HAVE BEEN SELECTED** to interest students while also illustrating key legal points.

CASE 5.2 Interactive Digital Software Association v. St. Louis County, Missouri

United States Court of Appeals, Eighth Circuit, 2003. 329 F.3d 954.

BACKGROUND AND FACTS
St. Louis County, Missouri, passed an ordinance that made it unlawful for any person knowingly to sell, rent, or make available "graphically violent" video games to minors or to "permit the free play of" such games by minors without a parent' or guardian's consent.**a** Interactive Digital Software Association and other firms that create or provide the public with video games and related software filed a suit against the county in a federal district court. The plaintiffs asserted that the ordi-

nance violated the First Amendment, and filed a motion for summary judgment. The county argued that the ordinance forwarded the compelling state interest of protecting the "psychological well-being of minors" by reducing the harm suffered by children who play violent video games. A psychologist, a high school principal, and others offered their conclusions that playing violent video games leads to aggressive behavior, but the county did not provide proof of a link between the games and psychological harm. The court denied the plaintiffs' motion and dismissed the case. The plaintiffs appealed to the U.S. Court of Appeals for the Eighth Circuit.

IN THE WORDS OF THE COURT . . .

MORRIS SHEPPARD ARNOLD, Circuit Judge.
  *   *   *   *

*   *   * If the First Amendment is versatile enough to shield the painting of Jackson Pollock, music of Arnold Schoenberg, or Jabberwocky verse of Lewis Carroll, we see no reason why the pictures, graphic design, concept art, sounds, music, stories, and narrative present in video games are not entitled to protection. The mere fact that they appear in a novel medium is

● **THE *LANDMARK IN THE LEGAL ENVIRONMENT* FEATURE** concludes with a section titled *Application to Today's World* that shows the relevance of the landmark law or case being discussed to the contemporary legal environment of business.

LANDMARK IN THE LEGAL ENVIRONMENT

Gibbons v. Ogden (1824)

The commerce clause, which is found in Article I, Section 8, of the U.S. Constitution, gives Congress the power "[t]o regulate Commerce with foreign Nations, and among the several States, and with the Indian Tribes." What exactly does "to regulate commerce" mean? What does "commerce" entail? These questions came before the United States Supreme Court in 1824 in the case of *Gibbons v. Ogden.***a**

BACKGROUND   In 1803, Robert Fulton, inventor [. . .]ton, who was

advocate of a strong national government. In his decision, Marshall defined the word *commerce* as used in the commerce clause to mean all commercial intercourse—that is, all business dealings that affect more than one state. The Court ruled against Ogden's monopoly, reversing the injunction against Gibbons. Marshall used this opportunity not only to expand the definition of commerce but also to validate and increase the power of the national legislature to regulate commerce. Said Marshall, "What is this power? It is the power . . . to prescribe the rule by which commerce is to be governed." Marshall held that the power to regulate interstate commerce was an exclusive power of the national government.

relevant to their careers

ONLINE LEGAL RESEARCH EXERCISES

Go to **http://leet.westbuslaw.com**, the Web site that accompanies this text. Select "Interactive Study Center," and then click on "Chapter 4." There you will find the following Internet research exercises that you can perform to learn more about topics covered in this chapter.

Activity 4–1: HISTORICAL PERSPECTIVE—The Judiciary's Role in American Government
Activity 4–2: MANAGEMENT PERSPECTIVE—Small Claims Courts
Activity 4–3: TECHNOLOGICAL PERSPECTIVE—Virtual Courtrooms

BEFORE THE TEST

Go to **http://leet.westbuslaw.com**, the Web site that accompanies this text. Select "Interactive Quizzes." You will find at least twenty interactive questions relating to this chapter.

Westlaw® Campus

If your textbook provided for a subscription to Westlaw® Campus, or if you ⋯⋯⋯ Westlaw Campus database, you can ⋯⋯⋯ by using your Westlaw

● **AT THE END OF EACH CHAPTER,** a section titled *Online Legal Research Exercises* provides students with an opportunity to explore Web resources relating to topics covered in the chapter.

Critical-Thinking Social Question

5–12. The Bay City Council adopts a dress code for cab drivers that requires them, while driving a cab, to wear shoes (no sandals) and dark pants to ankle length, or a dark skirt or dress, and a solid white or light blue shirt or blouse with sleeves and a folded collar. If a hat is worn, it must be a baseball-style cap with a Bay City or taxicab theme. Is this dress code rationally related to a legitimate government objective?

INTERACTING WITH THE INTERNET

For updated links to resources available on the Web, as well as a variety of other materials, visit this text's Web site at

http://leet.westbuslaw.com

For an online version of the Constitution that provides hypertext links to amendments and other changes, as well as the history of the document, go to

http://www.constitutioncenter.org

For discussions of current issues involving the rights and liberties contained ⋯⋯ f Rights, go to the Web site of the American Civil Liberties U⋯

● **AS IN PAST EDITIONS, THERE IS A** range of chapter-ending materials. This edition includes a revised series of critical-thinking questions that are designed to bring more relevance to student assignments.

3–9. Arbitration. Alexander Little worked for Auto Stiegler, Inc., an automobile dealership in Los Angeles County, California, eventually becoming the service manager. While employed, Little signed an arbitration agreement that required the submission of all employment-related disputes to arbitration. The agreement also provided that any award over $50,000 could be appealed to a second arbitrator. Little was later demoted and terminated. Alleging that these actions were in retaliation for investigating and reporting warranty fraud and thus were in violation of public policy, Little filed a suit in a California state court against Auto Stiegler. The defendant filed a motion with the court to compel arbitration. Little responded that the arbitration agreement should not be enforced, in part because the appeal provision was unfairly one sided. Is this provision enforceable? Should the court grant Auto Stiegler's motion? Why or why not? [*Little v. Auto Stiegler, Inc.*, 29 Cal.4th 1064, 63 P.3d 979, 130 Cal.Rptr.2d 892 (2003)]

2. Should the fact that reviewing courts rarely set aside arbitrators' awards have any bearing on the arbitrability of certain types of claims, such as those brought under Title VII?

Case Briefing Assignment

3–11. Examine Case A.1 [*Rodriguez de Quijas v. Shearson/American Express, Inc.*, 490 U.S. 477, 109 S.Ct. 1917, 104 L.Ed.2d 379 (1989)] in Appendix A. The case has been excerpted there in great detail. Review and then brief the case, making sure that your brief answers the following questions.

1. What is the legislative policy "embodied in the Arbitration Act"?
2. How did the Court reconcile the protections afforded investors under the Securities Act and the legislative policy advanced by the Arbitration Act? Did the Court believe that by submitting to arbitration⋯⋯

● **CASE BRIEFING ASSIGNMENTS** appear in the *Questions and Case Problems* section of selected chapters. One chapter in each unit contains one of these useful assignments.

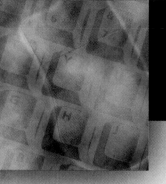

Great classroom and assignment

The Legal and E-Commerce Environment Today is the only legal environment text on the market today that comes with an interactive CD-ROM that completely maps the links between the text and assessment tools, videos, interactive exercises, and other elements. The Product Support Web Site offers online quizzes, research activities, videos, legal links, and more.

- ● **THE LEGAL AND E-COMMERCE** Environment Today Interactive CD-ROM, which is available at an additional cost and can be purchased separately or with the text, allows users to review a chapter or pursue a topic in depth. This CD includes the textbook, the study guide, quizzes, video clips, reference materials, full cases, and links to resources on the Web.

The Legal and
E-Commerce Environment Today

INCLUDES:
- Textbook
- Study guide
- Quizzes
- Video clips
- Reference materials
- Full cases
- Links to Web resources

INTERACTIVE CD-ROM

- ● **ONE END-OF-CHAPTER CASE** problem, set off by a special logo, directs students to text's Web site to view a sample answer to the problem.

Case Problem with Sample Answer

3–5. Arbitration. Phillip Beaudry, who suffered from mental illness, worked in the Department of Income Maintenance for the state of Connecticut. Beaudry was fired from his job when it was learned that he had misappropriated approximately $1,640 in state funds. Beaudry filed a complaint with his union, Council 4 of the American Federation of State, County, and Municipal Employees (AFSCME), and eventually the dispute was submitted to an arbitrator. The arbitrator concluded that Beaudry had been dismissed without "just cause," because Beaudry's acts were caused by his mental illness and were not "within his capacity to control." Because Beaudry had a disability, the employer was required, under state law, to transfer him to a position that he was competent to hold. The arbitrator awarded Beaudry reinstatement, back pay, seniority, and other benefits. The state appealed the decision to a court. What public policies must the court weigh in making its decision? How should the court rule? [*State v. Council 4, AFSCME,* 27 Conn.App. 635, 608 A.2d 718 (1992)]

was notified, and if the grievance was not resolved with in thirty days, the dispute was to be submitted to arbitration. Prince reported to the union, which told CNY, that she was being sexually harassed by her supervisors, Michael Drake and Leonard Erlanger. When no action was taken and Prince was subjected to retaliatory behavior by Drake and Erlanger, she filed a complaint with the Equal Employment Opportunity Commission. The supervisors retaliated again by ordering her to leave the workplace and "stay home." Prince filed a suit in a federal district court against CNY and the supervisors, alleging, among other things, violations of federal antidiscrimination law. CNY responded that its agreement with the union required Prince to submit her claim to arbitration. Is CNY right? In whose favor should the court rule? Why? [*Prince. v. Coca-Cola Bottling Co. of New York, Inc.,* 37 F.Supp.2d 289 (S.D.N.Y. 1999)]

3–8. Arbitration. New York State revised its New Car Lemon Law to allow consumers who complained of purchasing a "lemon" to have their disputes arbitrated before a professional arbitrator appointed by the New York attorney general. Before this revision, the Lemon Law allowed for arbitration of disputes, but the forum in which arbitration took place was sponsored by trade associations within the automobile industry, and consumers often complained of unfair awards. The revised law also provided that consumers could choose between two options: arbitration before a professional arbitrator and suing the manufacturer in court. Manufacturers, however, were compelled to arbitrate claims, if a consumer

support with the best technology

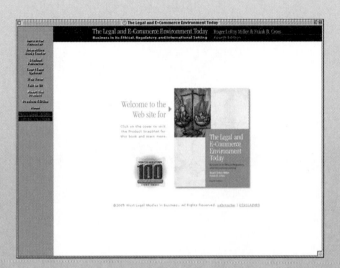

● **INTERACTIVE QUIZZES GIVE**
students an opportunity to check
their comprehension of topics
covered in the chapters. At the
end of each chapter, students are
referred to the text's Web site
where they will find at least twenty
interactive quizzes for that chapter.

4–9. Jurisdiction. Kazaa BV was a company formed under the
laws of the Netherlands. Kazaa distributed the Kazaa Media
Desktop (KMD) software that enabled users to exchange, via
a peer-to-peer transfer network, digital media, including
movies and music. Kazaa also operated the Kazaa.com Web
site, through which it distributed the KMD software to millions of California residents and other users. Metro-Goldwyn-
Mayer Studios, Inc., and other parties in the entertainment
industries based in California filed a suit in a federal district
court against Kazaa and others, alleging copyright infringement. Kazaa filed a counterclaim, but while legal action was
pending, the firm passed its assets and its Web site to Sharman
Networks, Ltd., a company organized under the laws of
Vanuatu (an island republic east of Australia) and doing business principally in Australia. Sharman explicitly disclaimed
the assumption of any of Kazaa's liabilities. When the plaintiffs added Sharman as a defendant, Sharman filed a motion
to dismiss on the ground that the court did not have jurisdiction. Would it be fair to subject Sharman to suit in this case?
Explain. [*Metro-Goldwyn-Mayer Studios, Inc. v. Grokster,
Ltd.*, 243 F.Supp.2d 1073 (C.D.Cal.2003)]

A Question of Ethics & Social Responsibility

4–10. The state of Alabama, on behalf
of _____ (T.B.) brought a paternity
_____ (T.B.) of

Critical-Thinking Legal Question

4–11. A dispute arises between Haru
Koto, a resident of California, and
Maria Mendez, a resident of Texas, over
the ownership of the *Fairweather*, a sailboat in dry dock in San Diego,
California. Can a California state court
exercise jurisdiction in the dispute?

Video Question

4–12. Go to this text's Web site at
http://leet.westbuslaw.com and select
"Video Questions." Click on "Chapter
4" and view the video titled *Jurisdiction
in Cyberspace*. Then answer the following questions.

1. What standard would a court apply to determine
   whether it has jurisdiction over the out-of-state computer firm in the video?
2. What factors is a court likely to consider in assessing
   whether sufficient contacts existed when the only connection to the jurisdiction is through a Web site?
3. How do you think the court would resolve the issue in
   this case?

● **IN SELECTED CHAPTERS, THE**
Questions and Case Problems
section concludes with a *Video
Question.* The student is directed
to the text's Web site to view a
specific video and then answer a
series of questions about it. The
videos and questions allow
students to engage in critical
thinking and to apply the legal
concepts learned in the chapter to
the real-world situations portrayed
in the videos.

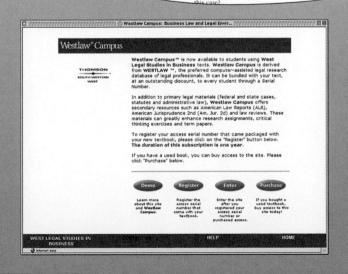

● **AVAILABLE ONLY WITH TEXTS**
from West Legal Studies in
Business, Westlaw® Campus, the
academic version of the leading
computer-assisted legal research
tool, Westlaw®, can be accessed at
a minimal charge for students.
Westlaw Campus contains cases,
statutes, and administrative
regulations, as well as American
Law Reports, American
Jurisprudence 2d, law reviews,
journals, and more.

Contents in Brief

Contents

UNIT THREE The Private
Environment   233

CHAPTER 8
Torts and Cyber Torts   234

Chapter 9

Strict Liability and Product Liability   268

Preface

It is no exaggeration to say that today's legal environment is changing at a pace never before experienced. In many instances, technology is both driving and facilitating this change. The expanded use of the Internet for both business and personal transactions has led to new ways of doing business, and, consequently, to a changing legal environment for the twenty-first century. In the midst of this evolving environment, however, one thing remains certain: for those entering the business world, an awareness of the legal and regulatory environment of business is critical.

The Fourth Edition of *The Legal and E-Commerce Environment Today: Business in Its Ethical, Regulatory, and International Setting* is designed to bring this awareness to your students. They will learn not only about the traditional legal environment but also about some of the most significant recent developments in the e-commerce environment. They will also be motivated to learn more through our use of high-interest pedagogical features that explore real-life situations and legal challenges facing businesspersons and consumers. We believe that teaching the legal environment can be enjoyable and so, too, can learning about it.

EMPHASIS ON ETHICS AND CORPORATE ACCOUNTABILITY

For the Fourth Edition of *The Legal and E-Commerce Environment Today,* we have included a significantly revised and updated chapter on ethics and social responsibility (Chapter 2). The chapter now presents a more practical approach to this topic, including a case study examining the scandal surrounding the Enron Corporation's actions in the early 2000s. In addition to this chapter on ethics, most chapters contain at least one *Ethical Issue* addressing an ethical dimension of the topic under discussion in the chapter. Moreover, in the *Questions and Case Problems* section of each chapter is a special question entitled *A Question of Ethics and Social Responsibility.*

In the Fourth Edition, we also refer to the Sarbanes-Oxley Act of 2002 and the corporate scandals that led to the passage of that legislation. For example, in Chapter 2, which focuses on ethics and social responsibility, we refer to the requirements of the Sarbanes-Oxley Act relating to confidential reporting systems. In Chapter 23, we again look at some of the key provisions of the act relating to corporate accountability with respect to securities transactions.

Finally, a special Web project focusing on Enron, entitled "Inside Look," can be accessed (at an additional cost) on the Web at **http://insidelook.westbuslaw. com**. There you will find in-depth articles and expert analysis concerning the events leading to Enron's collapse and the continuing investigation of that company. Inside Look provides analysis from all angles by using an interdisciplinary approach emphasizing accounting, business law, and management disciplines.

EMPHASIS ON INTERNET LAW

We have spent considerable time and effort to make sure that the Fourth Edition of *The Legal and E-Commerce Environment Today* reflects the most significant developments in e-commerce and cyberlaw. For example, in Chapter 10, which focuses on intellectual property, we point out how traditional laws—and some newly enacted laws—are being applied to online issues relating to *copyrights, trademarks, patents,* and *trade secrets.* Other chapters in the text include sections on *privacy rights* in the online world, *jurisdictional issues* as they arise in cyberspace, *cyber torts* and *cyber crimes, online securities offerings,* and a number of other topics relating to the online legal environment. We have also included an entire chapter (Chapter 13) devoted solely to the topic of *electronic contracts,* or e-contracts.

THE WEB CONNECTION

In addition to incorporating Internet law throughout the basic text of this book, the Fourth Edition offers several other components focusing on technology.

The Legal and E-Commerce Environment Today Web Site

When your students visit our Web site at <u>http://leet.westbuslaw.com</u>, you will find a broad array of teaching/learning resources, including the following:

- *Instructor's Course Planning Guide and Media Handbook* (accessible only to instructors who adopt this text).
- *Videos* referenced in the video questions that appear in selected chapters of this text. (Students can select "Video Questions" on the Web site to view the videos as well as the questions for each video.)
- *Interactive quizzes* for every chapter in this text (at least twenty questions per chapter).
- *Internet exercises* for every chapter in the text (at least two per chapter), located in the "Interactive Study Center" of the Web site.
- *Answers* for each *Case Problem with Sample Answer* presented in the text (one per chapter), located in the "Interactive Study Center."
- *Case updates* from various legal publications, all linked to this text.
- A *"Statutes" page* that offers links to the full text of selected statutes referenced in the text.
- *Links to other important legal resources* available for free on the Web.
- A *"Talk to the Authors" feature* that allows you to e-mail your questions about *The Legal and E-Commerce Environment Today,* Fourth Edition, to the authors.

Westlaw® Campus

Westlaw® Campus is now available to students using West Legal Studies in Business texts. Westlaw Campus is derived from Westlaw®, the preferred computer-assisted legal research database of legal professionals. It can be bundled with your text, at a significant discount, for every student through a passcode. (Students who buy used books may purchase access to Westlaw Campus at http://campus.westbuslaw.com.)

In addition to primary legal materials (federal and state cases, statutes, and administrative law), Westlaw Campus offers secondary resources such as *American Law Reports* (ALR), *American Jurisprudence 2d* (Am.Jur.2d), and law reviews. These materials can greatly enhance research assignments, critical-thinking exercises, and term papers.

West's Digital Video Library

For this edition of *The Legal and E-Commerce Environment Today,* we have added special new *Video Questions* at the ends of selected chapters. Each of these questions directs students to the text's Web site (at http://leet.westbuslaw. com) to view a video relevant to a topic covered in the chapter. This instruction is followed by a series of questions based on the video. The questions are again repeated on the Web site, when the student accesses the video. An access code for the videos accompanies each new copy of this textbook. (Students who buy used books may purchase access to the digital video library at http://digitalvideolibrary.westbuslaw.com.)

These videos can be used as homework assignments, discussion starters, or classroom demonstrations. By viewing a video and answering the questions, students will gain an understanding of how the legal concepts they have studied in the chapter apply to the real-life situation portrayed in the video. **Suggested answers for all of the video questions are given in both the *Instructor's Manual* and the *Answers Manual* that accompany this text.** The videos are part of the *West's Digital Video Library,* a compendium of fifty-five video scenarios and explanations.

Online Legal Research Guide

With every new book, your students will receive a free copy of the *Online Legal Research Guide*. This is the most complete brief guide to using the Internet that exists today. Text co-author Roger LeRoy Miller developed and wrote this supplement, which has been updated for the Fourth Edition of *The Legal and E-Commerce Environment Today*. The guide even includes an appendix on how to evaluate information obtained from the Internet.

Online Features and Pedagogy

The following features and pedagogy in the Fourth Edition of *The Legal and E-Commerce Environment Today* are designed to acquaint your students with online trends in the study of the legal environment of business, as well as with the broad selection of legal resources available on the Web.

- *Legal E-nvironment*—Nearly every chapter in the Fourth Edition contains one of these features. Each feature explores how traditional legal concepts or newly enacted laws have been applied to a specific real-world dispute relating to an online transaction. A concluding *For Critical Analysis* section asks the student to think critically about some aspect of the issue explored in the feature. **Suggested answers to these questions are included in both the *Instructor's Manual* and the *Answers Manual* that accompany this text.**

- *Video Questions*—As described earlier.

- *Case Problem with Sample Answer*—At the end of each chapter, we include one case problem, titled *Case Problem with Sample Answer*, for which students can find the answer by going to the text's companion Web site at **http://leet.westbuslaw.com**. This problem-answer set, which is new to this edition, is designed to help your students learn how to answer case problems by acquainting them with model answers to selected problems.

- *URLs for Cases*—Whenever possible, we have included URLs that can be used to access the cases presented in the text. When a URL is available, it appears just below the case citation.

- *Interacting with the Internet*—Each chapter concludes with this section, which presents URLs for specific Web sites at which students can access information related to topics covered in the chapter. This section also includes the Internet exercises and online quizzes discussed next.

- *Online Legal Research Exercises*—To familiarize your students with online legal resources while introducing them to additional information on topics covered in the chapters, we have included within the *Interacting with the Internet* section a subsection titled *Online Legal Research Exercises*. The subsection refers students to the Internet activities presented on the text's companion Web site (located in the "Interactive Study Center"). There are at least two exercises for each chapter in the text.

- *Before the Test*—Also included in the *Interacting with the Internet* section is a subsection titled *Before the Test*. Here, students are again directed to the text's Web site to access at least twenty interactive questions relating to the topics covered in the chapter.

AN INTERACTIVE CD-ROM EDITION

For this edition of *The Legal and E-Commerce Environment Today,* we have included in the supplements package a CD-ROM edition of the text. Instead of just placing the entire text on the CD-ROM, however, we have gone several steps further. The CD-ROM not only includes video segments, audio clips, and the like but also organizes the information in a very appropriate, pedagogically sound manner. Your students will find sections on *Content, Chapters,* and *Applications.* No other legal environment text offers such advanced learning capacity.

OTHER FEATURES AND PEDAGOGY

In addition to the components of the teaching/learning package accompanying *The Legal and E-Commerce Environment Today,* Fourth Edition, that we have described above, the text offers a number of other special features and pedagogy.

Features

In addition to the *Legal E-nvironment* feature, which we have already discussed, most of the chapters in this text have one or more of the special features listed below. These features are designed to both instruct and pique the interest of the student.

- *Landmark in the Legal Environment*—This special feature presents a case, statute, or other law that has become a landmark in the legal environment of business. For the Fourth Edition, we have added a special section titled *Application to Today's World,* indicating how the landmark law applies to the contemporary legal environment of business, including the online world.
- *Inside the Legal Environment*—This feature, which emphasizes managerial issues, offers practical and instructive examples of how the law applies to real-world business situations.
- *Ethical Issues*—Each of these features, which are closely integrated with the text, opens with a question addressing an ethical dimension of the topic under discussion. The *Ethical Issues* are numbered so that they can easily be located for review or discussion.
- *International Perspectives*—These features give students an awareness of the global legal environment by indicating how international laws or the laws of other nations deal with specific legal topics being discussed in the text.
- *Highlighted, numbered examples*—Throughout each chapter, we have included numbered examples, highlighted in color, to illustrate important points of law.

Case Presentation

In each chapter, we present cases that have been selected to illustrate principles of law discussed in the text. The cases are numbered sequentially for easy referencing in class discussions, homework assignments, and examinations. In selecting the cases to be included in this edition, our goal has been to choose cases that reflect the most current law or that represent a significant precedent in case law.

A Special Case Format Each case is presented in a special format, which begins with the case title and citation (including parallel citations). Whenever possible, we also include a URL, just below the case citation, that can be used to access the case online. Whenever a URL is presented, a footnote to the URL explains how students can navigate the site accessed to find the specific case. Following the citations for the case, we present sections giving the background and facts of the case, excerpts from the court opinion showing the court's reasoning on the issue, and the decision and remedy in the case.

In addition, many of the cases are preceded by a *Company Profile,* which provides background information on a party to the case, or a *Historical and Social [or other] Setting.* These settings, along with case-concluding *For Critical Analysis* questions, address the AACSB's curriculum requirements by focusing on how particular aspects o f the dispute or the court's decision relate to ethical, international, technological, cultural, or other types of issues.

Landmark Cases For the Fourth Edition of *The Legal and E-Commerce Environment Today,* we have given special emphasis to landmark and classic cases by setting these off with a unique heading and logo. Additionally, a *Comment* section at the end of each landmark or classic case stresses the importance of the court's decision in the case to the evolution of the law concerning the issue addressed by the court.

Additional Pedagogical Devices

The Legal and E-Commerce Environment Today, Fourth Edition, offers a number of additional pedagogical devices, including those listed below.

Pedagogical Devices in the Text

- *Chapter Objectives* (a series of brief questions at the beginning of each chapter designed to provide a framework for the student as he or she reads through the chapter).
- *Contents* (listing the first-level heads within the chapter).
- *Margin Definitions.*
- *Margin Reminders and Instructional Notes.*
- *Quotations.*
- *Exhibits and Forms.*
- *Photographs* (with critical-thinking questions).

Chapter-Ending Pedagogy

- *Key Terms* (with appropriate page references).
- *Chapter Summary* (in graphic format with page references).
- *For Review* (the questions set forth in the chapter-opening *Chapter Objectives* section are again presented to aid the student in reviewing the chapter).
- *Questions and Case Problems* (including hypotheticals as well as problems based on actual cases, many of which are from the early 2000s).
- *A Question of Ethics and Social Responsibility* (discussed previously).
- *Case Briefing Assignment* (instructing students to brief selected cases contained in Appendix A of this book; one of these assignments has been included for each unit of the text).
- *Critical-Thinking Managerial [or other] Question* (asking the students to think critically about a specific hypothetical situation and how the law covered in the chapter should apply to that situation).
- *Video Question* (directing the students to view a specific video on the text's Web site and then answer a series of questions about the video; the questions require the students to apply the legal concepts that they have learned in the chapter to the real-world situations portrayed in the videos).
- *Interacting with the Internet*—(providing URLs for specific legal resource materials on the Web; as already noted, this section also directs students to the Web site for online research exercises and quizzes that they can perform to learn more about topics covered in the chapter and to review chapter materials prior to tests).

Unit-Ending Cumulative Questions

At the end of the final chapter in each unit, we present a *Cumulative Business Hypothetical*. The problem introduces a hypothetical business firm and then asks a series of questions about how the law applies to various actions taken by the firm. To answer the questions, the student must consider the laws discussed throughout the unit. Suggested answers to these questions are included in the *Answers Manual*.

Appendices

To help students learn how to find published primary sources of law, including those cited in footnotes throughout this text, we have included a special appendix at the end of Chapter 1. There your students will find information, including an exhibit, on how to read citations to cases, statutes, and agency regulations.

Because the majority of students keep their legal environment texts as a reference source, we have also included at the end of the book a full set of appendices. For the Fourth Edition, we have added URLs that can be used to access the U.S. Constitution online and the full text of each statute for which excerpts are given in the appendices.

SUPPLEMENTS

The Legal and E-Commerce Environment Today, Fourth Edition, is accompanied by an expansive array of teaching and learning supplements, including those listed below. For further information on the elements contained in the teaching/learning package, contact your local West sales representative or go to the Web site that accompanies this text at **http://leet.westbuslaw.com**.

Supplements for Instructors

- *Instructor's Resource CD-ROM*—Includes the following supplements: Instructor's Course Planning Guide and Media Handbook, Instructor's Manual, Answers Manual, Test Bank, ExamView, Case Printouts. Case-Problem Cases, and PowerPoint Slides.

- *Instructor's Course Planning Guide and Media Handbook*—Also available on the Instructor's Resource CD-ROM (IRCD) as well as on the text's Web site.

- **Instructor's Manual**—Includes additional cases on point with at least one case summary per chapter, as well as answers to all *For Critical Analysis* questions in the features and answers for the *Video Questions* that conclude selected chapters. Also available on the IRCD.

- *Test Bank*—Also available on the IRCD.

- *ExamView*—Also available on the IRCD.

- *Answers Manual (Answers to Questions and Case Problems and Alternate Problem Sets with Answers)*—Includes answers to the *Questions and Case*

Problems, answers to the *For Critical Analysis* questions in the features, answers for the *Video Questions* that conclude selected chapters, and alternate problem sets with answers. Also available on the IRCD.

- *Web Tutor on WebCT*—Features chat, discussion groups, testing, student progress tracking, and business law course materials.
- *Case Printouts*—Available only on the IRCD.
- *PowerPoint Slides*—Also available on the IRCD.
- *Transparency Acetates.*
- *Westlaw*®—Ten free hours to qualified instructors.
- *Video Library*—Including CourtTV®, the *Legal Conflicts in Business* videos, and the *Drama of the Law* video series. (For further information on video supplements, go to <u>http://videos.westbuslaw.com</u>. Students who buy used books may purchase access to the digital video library mentioned earlier in this preface at <u>http://digitalvideolibrary.westbuslaw.com</u>.)
- *Instructor's Manual* for the *Drama of the Law* video series.

Supplements for Students

- *Online Legal Research Guide* (free with every new copy of this text).
- *Study Guide.*
- *Handbook of Landmark Cases and Statutes in Business Law and the Legal Environment.*
- *Guide to Personal Law.*
- *Handbook on Critical Thinking and Writing in Business Law and the Legal Environment.*
- *Westlaw*® *Campus*—As described earlier.

FOR USERS OF THE THIRD EDITION

We thought that those of you who have been using the Third Edition of this book would like to know some of the major changes that have been made for the Fourth Edition. This new edition continues the coverage of the essential legal environment topics covered in the previous edition, but we think that we have improved it greatly, thanks in part to the many letters, telephone calls, and reviews that we have received.

Expanded Coverage of Internet Law

For the Fourth Edition of *The Legal and E-Commerce Environment Today,* we have expanded the coverage of cyberlaw as it relates to topics covered in the chapters. The text now includes more material on jurisdictional issues in cyberspace, a thoroughly updated discussion of intellectual property rights in the online environment, new sections examining online securities offerings and online securities fraud, an expanded discussion of privacy rights in the employment context, an updated chapter on e-contracts, and more.

An Improved Presentation of Ethics and Corporate Accountability

As noted earlier in this preface, the chapter on ethics and social responsibility has been significantly revised for the Fourth Edition. The chapter now presents a more practical, real-world approach to ethical issues in the legal environment, including a case study of the Enron Corporation and the consequences for that firm resulting from its unethical actions. Congress responded to the ethical scandals of the early 2000s by passing the Sarbanes-Oxley Act of 2002. We discuss this act and some of its key provisions in Chapter 2, in the context of ethics, and again in Chapter 23, in the context of securities transactions.

New Pedagogy

Each *Legal E-nvironment* and *Inside the Legal Environment* feature is either new or has been largely rewritten for the Fourth Edition of this text. In particular, the *Inside the Legal Environment* features are now approached from a managerial perspective. In addition, we have added the following special new elements:

- An *Application to Today's World* section concluding each *Landmark in the Legal Environment* feature.
- A *Comment* section concluding each landmark and classic case.
- *Case Problem with Sample Answer* (in the *Questions and Case Problems* section).
- *Critical-Thinking Managerial [or other] Question* (in the *Questions and Case Problems* section).
- *Video Question* (in the *Questions and Case Problems* section of selected chapters).

Significantly Revised Chapters

Each chapter of the Fourth Edition has been revised as necessary to incorporate recent developments in the law or to streamline the presentations. A number of new trends in the legal environment of business are also addressed in the cases and special features of the Fourth Edition. Other major changes and additions made for this edition include those described below.

- **Chapter 1 (The Legal and International Foundations)**—The section entitled "The Nature of Law" has been revised and now includes discussions of the historical school and the sociological school.
- **Chapter 2 (Ethics and Social Responsibility)**—As noted earlier in this preface, this chapter has been extensively revised to address ethical concerns in today's legal environment. The chapter now includes sections on how to set an ethical tone in a business environment, the Enron scandal, and the requirements of the Sarbanes-Oxley Act of 2002 with respect to corporate compliance. Generally, the revised chapter offers a more practical approach to business and ethical decision making.
- **Chapter 3 (Legal Representation and Alternative Dispute Resolution)**—This chapter, which appeared as Chapter 4 in the Third Edition, has been

repositioned for the Fourth Edition so that it is presented, more logically, before the chapter covering the court system. The chapter now includes a discussion of the latest developments with respect to mandatory arbitration in the employment context, including the Supreme Court's recent decision on this topic and how subsequent cases have dealt with the issue. Also included in the chapter are new sections on online dispute resolution (ODR) and alternative dispute resolution in the international context.

- **Chapter 4 (The American Court System)**—This chapter now includes a discussion of the types of jurisdictional issues that have been raised by Internet transactions, including international transactions, and how the courts have dealt with these issues.

- **Chapter 5 (Constitutional Authority to Regulate Business)**—A discussion of the dormant commerce clause has been added, and the section discussing unprotected speech has been updated to reflect recent court decisions concerning online speech.

- **Chapter 7 (Criminal Law and Cyber Crimes)**—As indicated by the chapter title, a section on cyber crimes has been added to this chapter for the Fourth Edition. The section discusses cyber theft (including identity theft), cyber-stalking, hacking, cyber terrorism, and the difficulty of prosecuting cyber crimes.

- **Chapter 8 (Torts and Cyber Torts)**—A final section in the chapter now covers cyber torts, including defamation online and spamming.

- **Chapter 10 (Intellectual Property and Internet Law)**—The materials on intellectual property rights in the online environment have been thoroughly revised and updated. They have also been integrated into the discussions of each form of intellectual property covered in the chapter.

- **Chapter 13 (E-Contracts)**—This chapter has been thoroughly revised. It now opens with a discussion of what should be included in online offers and the nature of online acceptances. Because of its significance in today's legal environment, the coverage of the Uniform Electronic Transactions Act has been greatly expanded.

- **Chapter 14 (Business Organizations) and Chapter 15 (Creditors' Rights and Bankruptcy)**—These two chapters have been repositioned for the Fourth Edition to streamline the presentation of these two topics. The dollar amounts for the exemptions under bankruptcy law have been updated, and a *Landmark in the Legal Environment* feature looks at the bankruptcy reform legislation that is currently pending before Congress.

- **Chapter 16 (Employment Relationships)**—The section on employee privacy rights has been rewritten to bring it up to date with respect to contemporary electronic monitoring practices. A new *Legal E-nvironment* feature addresses employment issues relating to the virtual workplace.

- **Chapter 17 (Equal Employment Opportunities)**—This chapter has been extensively updated to incorporate the latest United States Supreme Court decisions relating to disability-based discrimination and affirmative action.

- **Chapter 19 (Consumer Protection)**—The chapter now includes an expanded discussion of online marketing and online deceptive practices.

- **Chapter 20 (Protecting the Environment)**—A new *Inside the Legal Environment* feature focuses on "environmental takings," and the chapter now concludes with a discussion of international environmental issues.

- **Chapter 21 (Land-Use Control and Real Property)**—A new *Inside the Legal Environment* feature looks at the topic of "taking" real property for private developments.
- **Chapter 23 (Investor Protection and Online Securities Offerings)**—The chapter was revised as necessary to reflect the relevant provisions of the Sarbanes-Oxley Act of 2002. Also included is a full-page exhibit describing some of the key provisions of this act that relate to corporate accountability with respect to securities transactions. The chapter now concludes with sections discussing online securities offerings and online securities fraud.

What Else Is New?

In addition to the changes noted above, you will find a number of other new items or features in *The Legal and E-Commerce Environment Today,* Fourth Edition, as listed below.

- An expanded number of Internet exercises—there are now at least two of these exercises for each chapter, most of which have been newly created.
- New cases—including at least one 2003 case in each chapter.
- New case problems—many of which are from 2002 or 2003.
- New exhibits.
- New photos (with critical-thinking questions).
- URLs for the statutes excerpted in the appendices.
- New cases on point accompanying selected case summaries in the *Instructor's Manual.*
- Answers to the *For Critical Analysis* questions in the features and to the *Video Questions* in both the *Instructor's Manual* and the *Answers Manual.*
- Westlaw® Campus.
- A *Statutes* page on the text's Web site offering links to selected statutes referenced in the text.

ACKNOWLEDGMENTS

We owe a debt of extreme gratitude to the numerous individuals at West who worked on this project. We especially wish to thank Rob Dewey and Jan Lamar for their helpful advice and guidance during all of the stages of this new edition. Jan Lamar also assisted us in making sure that we addressed all reviewers' criticisms and suggestions, and she was instrumental in ensuring that the supplements came out on time. Christine Wittmer and Amy Wilson deserve a special note of appreciation for their incredibly masterful work on the Web site, the CD-ROM Edition, and just about everything else relating to technology for this text. Our long-time production editor at West, Bill Stryker, made sure that we came out with an error-free edition on time. We will always be in his debt. Additionally, we thank Ann Borman, also at West, for her assistance.

We also extend our thanks to a number of other people who worked directly with us on this project. We wish to thank Lavina Leed Miller for her management of the project, as well as for the application of her superb research, editorial, and proofreading skills. We must especially thank William Eric Hollowell, co-author of the *Instructor's Manual, Study Guide, Test Bank,* and *Instructor's Course Planning Guide and Media Handbook,* for his excellent research and writing efforts. Our appreciation also goes to Suzie DeFazio and Beverly Peavler, whose copyediting and proofreading skills, respectively, will not go unnoticed. We also thank Roxanna Lee and Gregory Scott for their proofreading services and other contributions, and Suzanne Jasin for her valuable help on the project.

Finally, numerous careful and conscientious users of previous editions have been kind enough to offer us their comments and suggestions on how to improve this text. We are particularly indebted to these reviewers, whom we list below. With their help, we have been able to make this book even more useful for professors and students alike.

Acknowledgments for Previous Editions

Jane Bennett
Orange Coast College

Penelope L. Herickhoff
Mankato State University

Susan Key
University of Alabama
at Birmingham

Tom Moore
Georgia College and State University

Mark Phelps
University of Oregon

Gary Sambol
Rutgers, the State University of New Jersey, Camden Campus

Martha Sartoris
North Hennepin Community College

Gwen Seaquist
Ithaca College

Acknowledgements for the Fourth Edition

Teri Elkins
University of Houston

Gary Greene
Manatee Community College

Karrin Klotz
University of Washington

Y. S. Lee
Oakland University

Michael J. O'Hara
University of Nebraska at Omaha

G. Keith Roberts
University of Redlands

Dawn R. Swink
University of St. Thomas

We know that we are not perfect. If you or your students find something that you don't like or want us to change, write or e-mail us your thoughts. That is how we can make *The Legal and E-Commerce Environment Today,* Fourth Edition, an even better book in the future.

Roger LeRoy Miller
Frank B. Cross

Dedication

To my wife, Francette.
May the joy that you give me
every day be reciprocal.
R.L.M.

To my parents and sisters.
F.B.C.

UNIT ONE
The Foundations

CHAPTER **1**

The Legal and International Foundations

CONTENTS

CHAPTER OBJECTIVES

After reading this chapter, you should be able to answer the following questions:

1. What are the major schools of jurisprudential thought?

2. What are the sources of American law?

3. What is the common law tradition?

4. What is a precedent? When might a court depart from precedent?

5. What are some important differences between civil law and criminal law?

Lord Balfour's assertion in the quotation below emphasizes the underlying theme of every page in this book—that law is of interest to all persons, not just to lawyers. Those entering the world of business will find themselves subject to numerous laws and government regulations. A basic knowledge of these laws and regulations is beneficial—if not essential—to anyone contemplating a successful career in business today.

In this introductory chapter, we first look at the nature of law and at some concepts that have significantly influenced how jurists (those skilled in the law, including judges, lawyers, and legal scholars) view the nature and function of law. We then examine some of the major sources of American law and the common law tradition of the United States. The chapter concludes with a discussion of various classifications of law.

> **"The law is of as much interest to the layman as it is to the lawyer."**
> Lord Balfour, 1848–1930
> (British prime minister, 1902–1905)

THE NATURE OF LAW

There have been and will continue to be different definitions of law. Although the definitions vary in their particulars, they all are based on the general observation that, at a minimum, law consists of *enforceable rules governing relationships among individuals and between individuals and their society.* These "enforceable rules" may consist of unwritten principles of behavior established by a nomadic tribe. They may be set forth in an ancient or a modern law code. They may consist of written laws and court decisions created by modern legislative and judicial bodies, as in the United States. Regardless of how such rules are created, they all have one thing in common: they establish rights, duties, and privileges that are consistent with the values and beliefs of their society or its ruling group.

Those who embark on a study of law will find that these broad statements leave unanswered some important questions concerning the nature of law. **Jurisprudence** refers to the science or philosophy of law. Part of the study of law involves learning about different schools of jurisprudential thought and discovering how each school's approach to law can affect judicial decision making.

You may think that legal philosophy is far removed from the practical study of business law and the legal environment. In fact, it is not. As you will learn in the chapters of this text, how judges apply the law to specific disputes, including disputes relating to the business world, depends in part on their philosophical approaches to law. We look now at some of the significant schools of legal, or jurisprudential, thought that have evolved over time.

The Natural Law Tradition

An age-old question about the nature of law has to do with the finality of a nation's laws, such as the laws of the United States at the present time. For example, what if a particular law is deemed to be a "bad" law by a substantial number of that nation's citizens? Must a citizen obey the law if it goes against his or her conscience to do so? Is there a higher or universal law to which individuals can appeal? One who adheres to the natural law tradition would answer this question in the affirmative. **Natural law** denotes a system of moral and ethical principles that are inherent in human nature and that people can discover through the use of their inborn intelligence.

The natural law tradition is one of the oldest and most significant schools of jurisprudence. It dates back to the days of the Greek philosopher Aristotle (384–322 B.C.E.), who distinguished between natural law and the laws governing a particular nation. According to Aristotle, natural law applies universally to all humankind.

The notion that people have "natural rights" stems from the natural law tradition. Those who claim that a specific foreign government is depriving certain citizens of their human rights are implicitly appealing to a higher law that has universal applicability. The question of the universality of basic human rights also comes into play in the context of international business affairs. For example, U.S. companies that have operations abroad often hire foreign workers as employees. Should the same laws protecting U.S. employees apply to these foreign employees? This question is rooted implicitly in a concept of universal rights that has its origins in the natural law tradition.

LAW
A body of enforceable rules governing relationships among individuals and between individuals and their society.

JURISPRUDENCE
The science or philosophy of law.

NATURAL LAW
The belief that government and the legal system should reflect universal moral and ethical principles that are inherent in human nature. The natural law school is the oldest and one of the most significant schools of legal thought.

"An individual who breaks a law that his conscience tells him is unjust, . . . in order to arouse the conscience of the community over its injustices, is in reality expressing the highest respect for the law."

MARTIN LUTHER KING, JR.,
1929–1968
(American civil rights leader)

Legal Positivism

POSITIVE LAW
The body of conventional, or written, law of a particular society at a particular point in time.

LEGAL POSITIVISM
A school of legal thought centered on the assumption that there is no law higher than the laws created by the government. Laws must be obeyed, even if they are unjust, to prevent anarchy.

In contrast, **positive law,** or national law (the written law of a given society at a particular point in time), applies only to the citizens of that nation or society. Those who adhere to **legal positivism** believe that there can be no higher law than a nation's positive law. According to the positivist school, there is no such thing as "natural rights." Rather, human rights exist solely because of laws. If the laws are not enforced, anarchy will result. Thus, whether a law is "bad" or "good" is irrelevant. The law is the law and must be obeyed until it is changed—in an orderly manner through a legitimate lawmaking process. A judge with positivist leanings probably would be more inclined to defer to an existing law than would a judge who adheres to the natural law tradition.

The Historical School

HISTORICAL SCHOOL
A school of legal thought that emphasizes the evolutionary process of law and that looks to the past to discover what the principles of contemporary law should be.

The **historical school** of legal thought emphasizes the evolutionary process of law by concentrating on the origin and history of the legal system. Thus, this school looks to the past to discover what the principles of contemporary law should be. The legal doctrines that have withstood the passage of time—those that have worked in the past—are deemed best suited for shaping present laws. Hence, law derives its legitimacy and authority from adhering to the standards that historical development has shown to be workable. Adherents of the historical school are more likely than those of other schools to strictly follow decisions made in past cases.

Legal Realism

LEGAL REALISM
A school of legal thought of the 1920s and 1930s that generally advocated a less abstract and more realistic approach to the law, an approach that takes into account customary practices and the circumstances in which transactions take place. The school left a lasting imprint on American jurisprudence.

SOCIOLOGICAL SCHOOL
A school of legal thought that views the law as a tool for promoting justice in society.

In the 1920s and 1930s, a number of jurists and scholars, known as legal realists, rebelled against the historical approach to law. **Legal realism** is based on the idea that law is just one of many institutions in society and that it is shaped by social forces and needs. The law is a human enterprise, and judges should take social and economic realities into account when deciding cases. Legal realists also believe that the law can never be applied with total uniformity. Given that judges are human beings with unique personalities, value systems, and intellects, obviously different judges will bring different reasoning processes to the same case.

Legal realism strongly influenced the growth of what is sometimes called the **sociological school** of jurisprudence. This school views law as a tool for promoting justice in society. In the 1960s, for example, the justices of the United States Supreme Court played a leading role in the civil rights movement by upholding long-neglected laws calling for equal treatment for all Americans, including African Americans and other minorities. Generally, jurists who adhere to the sociological school are more likely to depart from past decisions than are those jurists who adhere to the other schools of legal thought.

> "Law cannot stand aside from the social changes around it."
>
> WILLIAM J. BRENNAN, JR.,
> 1906–1997
> (Associate justice of the United States
> Supreme Court, 1956–1990)

BUSINESS ACTIVITIES AND THE LEGAL ENVIRONMENT

As those entering the world of business will learn, laws and government regulations affect virtually all business activities—from hiring and firing decisions, to workplace safety, to the manufacturing and marketing of products, to busi-

CHAPTER 1   THE LEGAL AND INTERNATIONAL FOUNDATIONS

ness financing, and so on. To make good business decisions, a basic knowledge of the laws and regulations governing these activities is beneficial—if not essential. Realize also that in today's world a knowledge of "black-letter" law is not enough. Businesspersons are also expected to make ethical decisions. Thus, the study of business law necessarily involves an ethical dimension.

Many Different Laws May Affect a Single Business Transaction

As you will note, each chapter in this text covers a specific area of the law and shows how the legal rules in that area affect business activities. Though compartmentalizing the law in this fashion promotes conceptual clarity, it does not indicate the extent to which a number of different laws may apply to just one transaction.

● EXAMPLE 1 Suppose that you are the president of NetSys, Inc., a company that creates and maintains computer network systems for its clients, including business firms. NetSys also markets software for customers who need an internal computer network but cannot afford an individually designed intranet. One day, Janet, an operations officer for Southwest Distribution Corporation (SDC), contacts you by e-mail about a possible contract concerning SDC's computer network. In deciding whether to enter into a contract with SDC, you need to consider, among other things, the legal requirements for an enforceable contract. Are there different requirements for a contract for services and a contract for products? What are your options if SDC fails to perform the contract? The answers to these questions are part of contract law and sales law.

Other questions might concern payment under the contract. What can you do if SDC refuses to pay NetSys? Answers to such questions can be found in the laws that relate to creditors' rights. Also, a dispute may occur over the rights to NetSys's software, or there may be a question of liability if the software is defective. There may be an issue as to whether you and Janet have the authority to make the deal in the first place. Resolutions of these questions may be found in areas of the law that relate to intellectual property, e-commerce, torts, product liability, agency, and business organizations. Finally, if any dispute cannot be resolved amicably, then the laws and the rules concerning courts and court procedures spell out the steps of a lawsuit. ●

Exhibit 1–1 on the following page illustrates the areas of law covered in this text that may influence business decision making.

Ethics and the Legal Environment

Merely knowing the areas of law that may affect a business decision is not sufficient in today's world of commerce. Businesspersons must also take ethics into account. As you will learn in Chapter 2, *ethics* is generally defined as the study of what constitutes right or wrong behavior. In today's world, business decision makers need to consider not just whether a decision is profitable and legal, but also whether it is ethical.

Throughout this text, you will learn about the relationship between the law and ethics, as well as about some of the types of ethical questions that often arise in the business context. For example, Chapter 2 offers a detailed look at the importance of ethical considerations in business decision making. Various

EXHIBIT 1-1   AREAS OF THE LAW THAT MAY
AFFECT BUSINESS DECISION MAKING

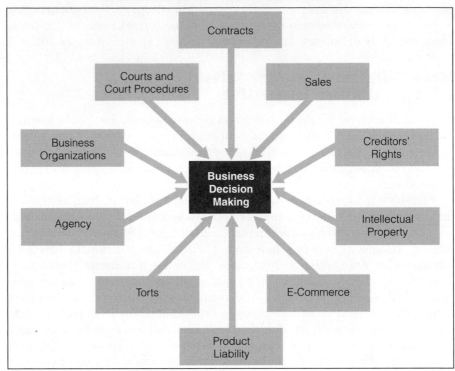

other elements in this text, such as the *Ethical Issues* interspersed throughout
the text and the ethical questions that conclude each chapter, are designed to
introduce you to ethical aspects of specific cases involving real-life situations.

SOURCES OF AMERICAN LAW

PRIMARY SOURCE OF LAW
A document that establishes the law
on a particular issue, such as a
constitution, a statute, an
administrative rule, or a court
decision.

There are numerous sources of American law. **Primary sources of law,** or
sources that establish the law, include the following:

- The U.S. Constitution and the constitutions of the various states.
- Statutes, or laws, passed by Congress and by state legislatures.
- Regulations created by administrative agencies, such as the federal Food
  and Drug Administration.
- Case law (court decisions).

We describe each of these important primary sources of law in the following
pages. (See the appendix at the end of this chapter for a discussion of how to
find statutes, regulations, and case law.)

SECONDARY SOURCE OF LAW
A publication that summarizes or
interprets the law, such as a legal
encyclopedia, a legal treatise, or an
article in a law review.

Secondary sources of law are books and articles that summarize and clarify
the primary sources of law. Legal encyclopedias, compilations (such as
Restatements of the Law—to be discussed later in this chapter), official comments to statutes, treatises, articles in law reviews published by law schools,
and articles in other legal journals are examples of secondary sources of law.

Young students view the U.S. Constitution on display in Washington, D.C.
Can a law be in violation of the Constitution and still be enforced? Why or why not?

Courts often refer to secondary sources of law for guidance in interpreting and applying the primary sources of law discussed here.

Constitutional Law

The federal government and the states have separate written constitutions that set forth the general organization, powers, and limits of their respective governments. **Constitutional law** is the law as expressed in these constitutions.

The U.S. Constitution is the supreme law of the land. As such, it is the basis of all law in the United States. A law in violation of the Constitution, no matter what its source, will be declared unconstitutional and will not be enforced. Because of its paramount importance in the American legal system, we discuss the U.S. Constitution at length in Chapter 5 and present the complete text of the Constitution in Appendix B.

The Tenth Amendment to the U.S. Constitution, which defines the powers of and limitations on the federal government, reserves all powers not granted to the federal government to the states. Each state in the union has its own constitution. Unless they conflict with the U.S. Constitution or a federal law, state constitutions are supreme within their respective borders.

CONSTITUTIONAL LAW
Law based on the U.S. Constitution and the constitutions of the various states.

Statutory Law

Statutes enacted by legislative bodies at any level of government make up another source of law, which is generally referred to as **statutory law.**

Federal Statutes Federal statutes are laws that are enacted by the U.S. Congress. As mentioned, any law—including a federal statute—that violates the U.S. Constitution will be held unconstitutional.

STATUTORY LAW
The body of law enacted by legislative bodies (as opposed to constitutional law, administrative law, or case law).

Federal statutes that affect business operations include statutes prohibiting employment discrimination (discussed in Chapter 17), consumer protection statutes (discussed in Chapter 19), and laws regulating the purchase and sale of securities (corporate stocks and bonds—discussed in Chapter 23). Whenever a particular statute is mentioned in this text, we usually provide a footnote showing its **citation** (a reference to a publication in which a legal authority—such as a statute or a court decision—or other source can be found). In the appendix following this chapter, we explain how you can use these citations to find statutory law.

State and Local Statutes and Ordinances   State statutes are laws enacted by state legislatures. Any state law that is found to conflict with the U.S. Constitution, with federal laws enacted by Congress, or with the state's constitution will be deemed unconstitutional. Statutory law also includes the ordinances passed by cities and counties, none of which can violate the U.S. Constitution, the relevant state constitution, or federal or state laws.

State statutes include state criminal statutes (discussed in Chapter 7), state corporation statutes (discussed in Chapter 14), state deceptive trade practices acts (referred to in Chapter 19), and state versions of the Uniform Commercial Code (to be discussed shortly). Local ordinances include zoning ordinances and local laws regulating housing construction and such matters as the overall appearance of a community.

A federal statute, of course, applies to all states. A state statute, in contrast, applies only within the state's borders. State laws thus vary from state to state.

Uniform Laws   The differences among state laws were particularly notable in the 1800s, when conflicting state statutes frequently created problems for the rapidly developing trade and commerce among the states. To counter these difficulties, a group of legal scholars and lawyers formed the National Conference of Commissioners on Uniform State Laws (NCCUSL) in 1892 to draft uniform ("model") statutes for adoption by the states. The NCCUSL still exists today and continues to issue uniform statutes.

BE CAREFUL Even though uniform laws are intended to be adopted without changes, states often modify them to suit their particular needs.

Adoption of a uniform law is a state matter, and a state may reject all or part of the statute or rewrite it as the state legislature wishes. Hence, even when a uniform law is said to have been adopted in many states, those states' laws may not be entirely "uniform." Once adopted by a state legislature, a uniform act becomes a part of the statutory law of that state.

The earliest uniform law, the Uniform Negotiable Instruments Law, was completed by 1896 and was adopted in every state by the early 1920s (although not all states used exactly the same wording). Over the following decades, other acts were drawn up in a similar manner. In all, over two hundred uniform acts have been issued by the NCCUSL since its inception. Recent uniform acts issued by the NCCUSL include the Uniform Electronic Transactions Act. This act, which addresses some of the specific legal needs created by e-commerce, will be discussed at length in Chapter 13, in the context of electronic contracts. The most ambitious uniform act of all, however, was the Uniform Commercial Code.

The Uniform Commercial Code (UCC)   The Uniform Commercial Code (UCC), which was created through the joint efforts of the NCCUSL and the American

Law Institute,[1] was first issued in 1952. The UCC has been adopted in all fifty states,[2] the District of Columbia, and the Virgin Islands. The UCC facilitates commerce among the states by providing a uniform, yet flexible, set of rules governing commercial transactions. The UCC assures businesspersons that their contracts, if validly entered into, normally will be enforced.

Because of its importance in the area of commercial law, we cite the UCC frequently in this text. We also present Article 2 of the UCC in Appendix D.

Administrative Law

Another important source of American law consists of **administrative law**—the rules, orders, and decisions of administrative agencies. An **administrative agency** is a federal, state, or local government agency established to perform a specific function. Administrative law and procedures, which will be examined in detail in Chapter 6, constitute a dominant element in the legal environment of business. Rules issued by various administrative agencies now affect virtually every aspect of a business's operations, including the firm's capital structure and financing, its hiring and firing procedures, its relations with employees and unions, and the way it manufactures and markets its products.

At the national level, numerous **executive agencies** exist within the cabinet departments of the executive branch. For example, the Food and Drug Administration is within the Department of Health and Human Services. Executive agencies are subject to the authority of the president, who has the power to appoint and remove officers of federal agencies. There are also major **independent regulatory agencies** at the federal level, including the Federal Trade Commission, the Securities and Exchange Commission, and the Federal Communications Commission. The president's power is less pronounced in regard to independent agencies, whose officers serve for fixed terms and cannot be removed without just cause.

There are administrative agencies at the state and local levels as well. Commonly, a state agency (such as a state pollution-control agency) is created as a parallel to a federal agency (such as the Environmental Protection Agency). Just as federal statutes take precedence over conflicting state statutes, so do federal agency regulations take precedence over conflicting state regulations. Because the rules of state and local agencies vary widely, we focus here exclusively on federal administrative law.

Case Law and Common Law Doctrines

The body of law that was first developed in England and that is still used today in the United States consists of the rules of law announced in court decisions. These rules of law include interpretations of constitutional provisions, of statutes enacted by legislatures, and of regulations created by administrative agencies. Today, this body of law is referred to variously as the common law, judge-made law, or **case law.** Because of the importance of the common law in our legal system, we look next at the origins and characteristics of the common law tradition in some detail.

ADMINISTRATIVE LAW
The body of law created by administrative agencies (in the form of rules, regulations, orders, and decisions) in order to carry out their duties and responsibilities.

ADMINISTRATIVE AGENCY
A federal or state government agency established to perform a specific function. Administrative agencies are authorized by legislative acts to make and enforce rules to administer and enforce the acts.

EXECUTIVE AGENCY
An administrative agency within the executive branch of government. At the federal level, executive agencies are those within the cabinet departments.

INDEPENDENT REGULATORY AGENCY
An administrative agency that is considered part of the government's executive branch but is not under the direction of the president. Independent agency officials cannot be removed without cause.

CASE LAW
The rules of law announced in court decisions. Case law includes the aggregate of reported cases that interpret judicial precedents, statutes, regulations, and constitutional provisions.

---

1. This institute was formed in the 1920s and consists of practicing attorneys, legal scholars, and judges.
2. Louisiana has adopted only Articles 1, 3, 4, 5, 7, 8, and 9.

THE COMMON LAW TRADITION

How jurists view the law is particularly important in a legal system in which judges play a paramount role, as they do in the American legal system. Because of our colonial heritage, much of American law is based on the English legal system. A knowledge of this tradition is necessary to an understanding of the nature of our legal system today.

Early English Courts of Law

After the Normans conquered England in 1066, William the Conqueror and his successors began the process of unifying the country under their rule. One of the means they used to this end was the establishment of the king's courts, or *curiae regis*. Before the Norman Conquest, disputes had been settled according to the local legal customs and traditions in various regions of the country. The king's courts sought to establish a uniform set of rules for the country as a whole. What evolved in these courts was the beginning of the **common law**—a body of general legal principles that eventually was applied throughout the entire English realm.

Courts developed the common law rules from the principles underlying judges' decisions in actual legal controversies. Judges attempted to be consistent, and whenever possible, they based their decisions on the principles suggested by earlier cases. They sought to decide similar cases in a similar way and considered new cases with care, because they knew that their decisions would make new law. Each interpretation became part of the law on the subject and served as a legal **precedent**—that is, a decision that furnished an example or authority for deciding subsequent cases involving similar legal principles or facts.

In the early years of the common law, there was no single place or publication where court opinions, or written decisions, could be found. Beginning in the late thirteenth and early fourteenth centuries, however, each year portions of significant decisions of that year were gathered together and recorded in *Year Books*. The *Year Books* were useful references for lawyers and judges. In the sixteenth century, the *Year Books* were discontinued, and other reports of cases became available. (See the appendix to this chapter for a discussion of how cases are reported, or published, in the United States today.)

Stare Decisis

The practice of deciding new cases with reference to former decisions, or precedents, eventually became a cornerstone of the English and American judicial systems. The practice forms a doctrine called *stare decisis*[3] ("to stand on decided cases").

The Importance of Precedents in Judicial Decision Making   The doctrine of *stare decisis* means that once a court has set forth a principle of law as being applicable to a certain set of facts, that court and courts of lower rank must adhere to that principle and apply it in future cases involving similar fact patterns.

---

3. Pronounced *ster*-ay dih-*si*-ses.

COMMON LAW
That body of law developed from custom or judicial decisions in English and U.S. courts, not attributable to a legislature.

PRECEDENT
A court decision that furnishes an example or authority for deciding subsequent cases involving identical or similar facts.

STARE DECISIS
A common law doctrine under which judges are obligated to follow the precedents established in prior decisions.

● EXAMPLE 2 Suppose that the lower state courts in California have reached conflicting conclusions on whether drivers are liable for accidents they cause while merging into freeway traffic, even though the drivers looked and did not see any oncoming traffic and even though witnesses (passengers in their cars) testified to that effect. To settle the law on this issue, the California Supreme Court decides to review a case involving this fact pattern. The court rules that in such a situation, the driver who is merging into traffic is liable for any accidents caused by the driver's failure to yield to freeway traffic, regardless of whether the driver looked carefully and did not see an approaching vehicle. The California Supreme Court's decision on the matter will influence the outcome of all future cases on this issue brought before the California state courts. ●

Similarly, a decision on a given issue by the United States Supreme Court (the nation's highest court) is binding on all inferior courts. Controlling precedents in a jurisdiction (an area in which a court or courts have the power to apply the law—see Chapter 4) are referred to as binding authorities. A **binding authority** is any source of law that a court must follow when deciding a case. Binding authorities include constitutions, statutes, and regulations that govern the issue being decided, as well as court decisions that are controlling precedents within the jurisdiction.

Stare Decisis **and Legal Stability** The doctrine of *stare decisis* helps the courts to be more efficient, because if other courts have carefully reasoned through a similar case, their legal reasoning and opinions can serve as guides. *Stare decisis* also makes the law more stable and predictable. If the law on a given subject is well settled, someone bringing a case to court can usually rely on the court to make a decision based on what the law has been. Sometimes, however, a court will depart from the rule of precedent if it decides that a given precedent should no longer be followed.

BINDING AUTHORITY
Any source of law that a court must follow when deciding a case. Binding authorities include constitutions, statutes, and regulations that govern the issue being decided, as well as court decisions that are controlling precedents within the jurisdiction.

ETHICAL ISSUE

Why do courts depart from precedent?

As you have just read, courts are obligated to follow binding authorities, including controlling precedents within a court's jurisdiction. The importance of precedent was underscored in 1997 in a case decided by a federal appellate court. The court noted that the last pronouncement on the issue under consideration was a Supreme Court decision of 1875. Despite the age of the precedent, the court stated that it was "duty bound to follow the law given to us by the Supreme Court unless and until it is changed."[4]

Nonetheless, courts do depart from the rule of precedent on occasion. If a court decides that a precedent is simply incorrect or that technological or social changes have rendered the precedent inapplicable, the court might rule contrary to the precedent. Sometimes, departures from precedent reflect changing ethical values or legal philosophy on the part of the judges hearing the cases. In *Brown v. Board of Education of Topeka,*[5] for example, the

---

4. *Korczak v. United States,* 124 F.3d 227 (Fed.Cir. 1997). (See the appendix at the end of this chapter for an explanation of how to read legal citations.)
5. 347 U.S. 483, 74 S.Ct. 686, 98 L.Ed. 873 (1954).

Supreme Court expressly overturned precedent when it concluded that separate educational facilities for whites and blacks, which had been upheld as constitutional in numerous previous cases, were inherently unequal. The Supreme Court's departure from precedent in this case received a tremendous amount of publicity as people began to realize the ramifications of this change in the law.

When There Is No Precedent   At times, courts hear cases for which there are no precedents within their jurisdictions on which to base their decisions. When hearing such cases, called "cases of first impression," courts often look to precedents set in other jurisdictions for guidance. Precedents from other jurisdictions, because they are not binding on the court, are referred to as **persuasive authorities.** A court may also consider a number of factors, including legal principles and policies underlying previous court decisions or existing statutes, fairness, social values and customs, public policy, and data and concepts drawn from the social sciences.

Equitable Remedies and Courts of Equity

A **remedy** is the means given to a party to enforce a right or to compensate for the violation of a right. ● EXAMPLE 3 Suppose that Shem is injured because of Rowan's wrongdoing. A court may order Rowan to compensate Shem for the harm by paying Shem a certain amount of money.●

In the early king's courts of England, the kinds of remedies that could be granted were severely restricted. If one person wronged another, the king's courts could award as compensation either money or property, including land. These courts became known as *courts of law,* and the remedies were called *remedies at law.* Even though this system introduced uniformity in the settling of disputes, when plaintiffs wanted a remedy other than economic compensation, the courts of law could do nothing, so "no remedy, no right."

Remedies in Equity   *Equity* refers to a branch of the law, founded in justice and fair dealing, that seeks to supply a fair and adequate remedy when no remedy is available at law. In medieval England, when individuals could not obtain an adequate remedy in a court of law, they petitioned the king for relief. Most of these petitions were decided by an adviser to the king called the *chancellor.* The chancellor was said to be the "keeper of the king's conscience." When the chancellor thought that the claim was a fair one, new and unique remedies were granted. In this way, a new body of rules and remedies came into being, and eventually formal *chancery courts,* or *courts of equity,* were established. The remedies granted by these courts were called *remedies in equity.* Thus, two distinct court systems were created, each having a different set of judges and a different set of remedies.

Plaintiffs (those bringing lawsuits) had to specify whether they were bringing an "action at law" or an "action in equity," and they chose their courts accordingly. ● EXAMPLE 4 A plaintiff might ask a court of equity to order a **defendant** (a person against whom a lawsuit is brought) to perform within the terms of a contract. A court of law could not issue such an order, because its remedies were limited to payment of money or property as compensation for damages. A court of equity, however, could issue a decree for *specific*

PERSUASIVE AUTHORITY
Any legal authority or source of law that a court may look to for guidance but on which it need not rely in making its decision. Persuasive authorities include cases from other jurisdictions and secondary sources of law.

REMEDY
The relief given to an innocent party to enforce a right or compensate for the violation of a right.

PLAINTIFF
One who initiates a lawsuit.

DEFENDANT
One against whom a lawsuit is brought; the accused person in a criminal proceeding.

The court of chancery in the reign of George I. Early English court decisions formed the basis of what type of law?

performance—an order to perform what was promised. A court of equity could also issue an *injunction*, directing a party to do or refrain from doing a particular act. In certain cases, a court of equity could allow for the *rescission* (cancellation) of the contract so that the parties would be returned to the positions that they held prior to the contract's formation.● Equitable remedies will be discussed in greater detail in Chapter 12.

The Merging of Law and Equity   Today, in most states, the courts of law and equity are merged, and thus the distinction between the two courts has largely disappeared. A plaintiff may now request both legal and equitable remedies in the same action, and the trial court judge may grant either form—or both forms—of relief. The merging of law and equity, however, does not diminish the importance of distinguishing legal remedies from equitable remedies. To request the proper remedy, a businessperson (or his or her attorney) must know what remedies are available for the specific kinds of harms suffered. Today, as a rule, courts will grant an equitable remedy only when the remedy at law (money damages) is inadequate. Exhibit 1–2 summarizes the procedural differences (applicable in most states) between an action at law and an action in equity.

REMEMBER Even though, in most states, courts of law and equity have merged, the principles of equity still apply.

Equitable Principles and Maxims   Over time, a number of **equitable principles and maxims** evolved that have since guided the courts in deciding whether plaintiffs should be granted equitable relief. Because of their importance, both historically and in our judicial system today, these principles and maxims are set forth in this chapter's *Landmark in the Legal Environment* feature on page 14.

EQUITABLE PRINCIPLES AND MAXIMS
General propositions or principles of law that have to do with fairness (equity).

The Common Law Today

The common law—the doctrines and principles embodied in case law—continues to govern all areas not covered by statutory law (or agency regulations issued to implement various statutes). ● EXAMPLE 5   In disputes concerning contracts for the sale of goods, the Uniform Commercial Code (statutory law) applies when one of its provisions supersedes the common law of contracts. Similarly, in a dispute concerning a particular employment practice, a statute regulating that practice will apply rather than the common law doctrine governing employment relationships that applied prior to the enactment of the statute.●

EXHIBIT 1–2 PROCEDURAL DIFFERENCES BETWEEN AN ACTION AT LAW AND AN ACTION IN EQUITY

PROCEDURE	ACTION AT LAW	ACTION IN EQUITY
Initiation of lawsuit	By filing a complaint	By filing a petition
Decision	By jury or judge	By judge (no jury)
Result	Judgment	Decree
Remedy	Monetary damages	Injunction, specific performance, or rescission

LANDMARK IN THE LEGAL ENVIRONMENT

Equitable Principles and Maxims

In medieval England, courts of equity had the responsibility of using discretion in supplementing the common law. Even today, when the same court can award both legal and equitable remedies, such discretion is exercised. Courts often invoke equitable principles and maxims when making their decisions. Here are some of the most significant equitable principles and maxims:

1. *Whoever seeks equity must do equity.* (Anyone who wishes to be treated fairly must treat others fairly.)

2. *Where there is equal equity, the law must prevail.* (The law will determine the outcome of a controversy in which the merits of both sides are equal.)

3. *One seeking the aid of an equity court must come to the court with clean hands.* (Plaintiffs must have acted fairly and honestly.)

4. *Equity will not suffer a wrong to be without a remedy.* (Equitable relief will be awarded when there is a right to relief and there is no adequate remedy at law.)

5. *Equity regards substance rather than form.* (Equity is more concerned with fairness and justice than with legal technicalities.)

6. *Equity aids the vigilant, not those who rest on their rights.* (Equity will not help those who neglect their rights for an unreasonable period of time.)

The last maxim has become known as the *equitable doctrine of laches.* The doctrine arose to encourage people to bring lawsuits while the evidence was fresh; if they failed to do so, they would not be allowed to bring a lawsuit. What constitutes a reasonable time, of course, varies according to the circumstances of the case. Time periods for different types of cases are now usually fixed by *statutes of limitations.* After the time allowed under a statute of limitations has expired, no action can be brought, no matter how strong the case was originally.

Application to Today's World

The equitable maxims listed above underlie many of the legal rules and principles that are commonly applied by the courts today—and that you will read about in this book. For example, in Chapter 11 you will read about the doctrine of promissory estoppel. *Under this doctrine, a person who has reasonably and substantially relied on the promise of another may be able to obtain some measure of recovery, even though no enforceable contract, or agreement, exists. The court will* estop *(bar, or impede) the one making the promise from asserting the lack of a valid contract as a defense. The rationale underlying the doctrine of promissory estoppel is similar to that expressed in the fourth and fifth maxims above.*

The Relationship between the Common Law and Statutory Law   The body of statutory law has expanded greatly since the beginning of this nation, and this expansion has resulted in a proportionate reduction in the applicability of common law doctrines. Nonetheless, there is a significant overlap between statutory law and the common law, and thus common law doctrines remain a significant source of legal authority.

Many statutes essentially codify existing common law rules, so the courts, in interpreting the statutes, often rely on the common law as a guide to what the legislators intended. Additionally, how the courts interpret a particular statute determines how that statute will be applied. Thus, if you wanted to learn about the coverage and applicability of a particular statute, for example, you would, of course, need to locate the statute and study it. You would also need to see how the courts in your jurisdiction have interpreted the statute—in other words, what precedents have been established in regard to that statute. Often, the applicability of a newly enacted statute does not become clear until a body of case law develops to clarify how, when, and to whom the statute applies.

Restatements of the Law   The American Law Institute (ALI) drafted and published compilations of the common law called *Restatements of the Law,* which generally summarize the common law rules followed by most states. There are *Restatements of the Law* in many areas of the law, including contracts, torts, agency, trusts, property, restitution, security, judgments, and conflict of laws. Although the *Restatements,* like other secondary sources of law, do not in themselves have the force of law, they are an important source of legal analysis and opinion on which judges often rely in making their decisions.

The ALI periodically revises the *Restatements,* and many of them are now in their second or third editions. For instance, as you will read in Chapter 9, the ALI has recently published the first volume of the third edition of the *Restatement of the Law of Torts.*

We refer to the Restatements frequently in subsequent chapters of this text, indicating in parentheses the edition to which we are referring. For example, we refer to the second edition of the *Restatement of the Law of Contracts* simply as the *Restatement (Second) of Contracts.*

> **BE AWARE** *Restatements of the Law* are authoritative sources, but they do not have the force of law.

CLASSIFICATIONS OF LAW

The huge body of the law may be broken down according to several classification systems. For example, one classification system divides law into **substantive law** (all laws that define, describe, regulate, and create legal rights and obligations) and **procedural law** (all laws that establish the methods of enforcing the rights established by substantive law). Other classification systems divide law into federal law and state law, private law (concerning relationships between persons) and public law (addressing the relationship between persons and their governments), and so on.

We look below at two broad classifications. One divides the law into criminal and civil law; the other divides the law into national law and international law. Following that, we mention an emerging body of law regulating transactions in cyberspace, informally characterized as "cyberlaw."

> **SUBSTANTIVE LAW**
> Law that defines, describes, regulates, and creates legal rights and obligations.
>
> **PROCEDURAL LAW**
> Law that establishes the methods of enforcing the rights established by substantive law.

Civil Law and Criminal Law

Civil law spells out the rights and duties that exist between persons and between persons and their governments, and the relief available when a person's rights are violated. Typically, in a civil case, a private party sues another private party (although the government can also sue a party for a civil law violation) to make that other party comply with a duty or pay for the damage caused by the failure to comply with a duty. ● **EXAMPLE 6** If a seller fails to perform a contract with a buyer, the buyer may bring a lawsuit against the seller. The purpose of the lawsuit will be either to compel the seller to perform as

> **CIVIL LAW**
> The branch of law dealing with the definition and enforcement of all private or public rights, as opposed to criminal matters.

promised or, more commonly, to obtain money damages for the seller's failure to perform.●

Much of the law that we discuss in this text is civil law. Contract law, for example, which we discuss in Chapters 11 through 13, is civil law. The whole body of tort law (see Chapter 8) is civil law. Note that *civil law* is not the same as a *civil law system*. As you will read shortly, in the subsection discussing international law, a civil law system is a legal system based on a written code of laws.

Criminal law has to do with wrongs committed against society for which society demands redress (see Chapter 7). Criminal acts are proscribed by local, state, or federal government statutes. Criminal defendants are thus prosecuted by public officials, such as a district attorney (D.A.), on behalf of the state, not by their victims or other private parties. Whereas in a civil case the object is to obtain remedies (such as money damages) to compensate the injured party, in a criminal case the object is to punish the wrongdoer in an attempt to deter others from similar actions. Penalties for violations of criminal statutes consist of fines and/or imprisonment—and, in some cases, death. We will discuss the differences between civil and criminal law in greater detail in Chapter 7.

National and International Law

Although the focus of this book is U.S. business law, increasingly businesspersons in this country engage in transactions that extend beyond our national borders. In these situations, the laws of other nations or the laws governing relationships among nations may come into play. For this reason, those who pursue a career in business today should have an understanding of the global legal environment.

National Law   The law of a particular nation, such as the United States or Sweden, is **national law.** National law, of course, varies from country to country, because each nation's law reflects the interests, customs, activities, and values that are unique to its particular culture. Even though the laws and legal systems of various countries differ substantially, broad similarities do exist.

Basically, there are two legal systems in today's world. One of these systems is the common law system of England and the United States, which we have already discussed. The other system is based on Roman civil law, or "code law." The term *civil law,* as used here, refers not to civil as opposed to criminal law but to codified law—an ordered grouping of legal principles enacted into law by a legislature or governing body. In a **civil law system,** the primary source of law is a statutory code, and case precedents are not judicially binding, as they normally are in a common law system. Although judges in a civil law system commonly refer to previous decisions as sources of legal guidance, they are not bound by precedent; in other words, the doctrine of *stare decisis* does not apply.

Exhibit 1–3 lists selected countries that today follow either the common law system or the civil law system. Generally, those countries that were once colonies of Great Britain retained their English common law heritage after they achieved their independence. Similarly, the civil law system, which is followed in most of the continental European countries, was retained in the Latin American, African, and Asian countries that were once colonies of those nations. Japan and South Africa also have civil law systems, and ingredients of

---

CRIMINAL LAW
Law that defines and governs actions that constitute crimes. Generally, criminal law has to do with wrongful actions committed against society for which society demands redress.

NATIONAL LAW
Law that pertains to a particular nation (as opposed to international law).

CIVIL LAW SYSTEM
A system of law derived from that of the Roman Empire and based on a code rather than case law; the predominant system of law in the nations of continental Europe and the nations that were once their colonies. In the United States, Louisiana, because of its historical ties to France, has in part a civil law system.

EXHIBIT 1-3   THE LEGAL SYSTEMS OF SELECTED COUNTRIES

CIVIL LAW		COMMON LAW	
Argentina	Indonesia	Australia	Nigeria
Austria	Iran	Bangladesh	Singapore
Brazil	Italy	Canada	United Kingdom
Chile	Japan	Ghana	United States
China	Mexico	India	Zambia
Egypt	Poland	Israel	
Finland	South Korea	Jamaica	
France	Sweden	Kenya	
Germany	Tunisia	Malaysia	
Greece	Venezuela	New Zealand	

the civil law system are found in the Islamic courts of predominantly Muslim countries. In the United States, the state of Louisiana, because of its historical ties to France, has in part a civil law system. The legal systems of Puerto Rico, Québec, and Scotland are similarly characterized as having elements of the civil law system.

International Law   In contrast to national law, international law applies to more than one nation. **International law** can be defined as a body of written and unwritten laws observed by independent nations and governing the acts of individuals as well as governments. International law is an intermingling of rules and constraints derived from a variety of sources, including the laws of individual nations, the customs that have evolved among nations in their relations with one another, and treaties and international organizations. In essence, international law is the result of centuries-old attempts to reconcile the traditional need of each country to be the final authority over its own affairs with the desire of nations to benefit economically from trade and harmonious relations with one another.

> **INTERNATIONAL LAW**
> The law that governs relations among nations. National laws, customs, treaties, and international conferences and organizations are generally considered to be the most important sources of international law.

   The key difference between national law and international law is that national law can be enforced by government authorities. If a nation violates an international law, however, the most that other countries or international organizations can do (if persuasive tactics fail) is to resort to coercive actions against the violating nation. Coercive actions range from the severance of diplomatic relations and boycotts to, at the last resort, war. We examine the laws governing international business transactions in greater detail in Chapter 24.

Cyberlaw

Increasingly, traditional laws are being applied to new legal issues stemming from the use of the Internet. (For a discussion of one such issue, see this chapter's *Legal E-nvironment* feature on the next page.) Additionally, new laws are being created to deal specifically with such issues. Frequently, people use the term **cyberlaw** to refer to the emerging body of law (consisting of court decisions,

> **CYBERLAW**
> An informal term used to refer to all laws governing electronic communications and transactions, particularly those conducted via the Internet.

LEGAL *e*-NVIRONMENT

International Jurisdiction and the Internet

As you will learn in Chapter 4, *jurisdiction* is an important legal concept that relates to the authority of a court to hear and decide a case. Within the United States, there is a federal court system, which has jurisdiction over specific types of cases. There are also fifty state court systems, each having jurisdiction over certain types of cases. In today's interconnected world, the issue of jurisdiction has become critical. Specifically, businesses using the Internet can reach individuals in any part of the world. Does that mean that every court everywhere has jurisdiction over, say, an Internet-based company in Chicago?

The Minimum-Contacts Requirement

Domestically, jurisdiction over individuals and businesses is based on the requirement of minimum contacts (see Chapter 4). Essentially, this requirement means that a business must have a minimum level of contacts with residents of a particular state for that state's courts to exercise jurisdiction over the firm. In the context of the Internet, most courts have *not* viewed the mere existence of a *passive* Web site as sufficient minimum contacts to exercise jurisdiction over a person or entity located out of state. Rather, a site must offer some degree of interactivity (such as allowing a person to order goods from the site) to meet the minimum-contacts requirement.

International Jurisdictional Problems

Internationally, the courts of other countries are applying the requirement of minimum contacts as developed by the U.S. courts. As a result, a business in the United States offering products for sale via its Web site may be required to comply with the laws of any jurisdiction in which it targets customers for its products.[a] Businesses may even be sued under another nation's laws for different reasons. For example, consider a case brought against Dow Jones & Company, the U.S. publisher of the *Wall Street Journal*. The *Wall Street Journal* has a Web site that contains articles written by its reporters. One such article included information about an American businessperson, Joseph Gutnick, living in Melbourne, Australia. Gutnick decided to sue the *Wall Street Journal* for defamation in an Australian court. (As you will read in Chapter 8, defamation is a *tort,* or civil wrong, that is committed when one makes a false statement that harms the good reputation of another.)

Dow Jones argued that the Australian court could not exercise jurisdiction over its U.S. servers, which were located in New Jersey, but the Australian judge rejected this argument. The judge claimed that the event (libel) had occurred in the place where the article was viewed or downloaded—in this case, of course, Australia. Therefore, the Australian court could exercise jurisdiction.[b] If the Australian decision is upheld on appeal, any U.S. company with an Internet presence could potentially become subject to worldwide jurisdiction for defamation and other alleged torts.

FOR CRITICAL ANALYSIS

Would extending the jurisdiction of courts to include any company that uses the Internet— regardless of where that company is located—have a "chilling" effect on the growth of Internet commerce, as well as on the dissemination of ideas?

a. See, for example, the case brought in France against Yahoo! Inc., which we present in Chapter 4 as Case 4.2. (Note, though, that a U.S. federal district court refused to enforce the French court's order—as we point out in a *Comment* section at the end of that case.)
b. *Gutnick v. Dow Jones & Co., Inc.,* VSC 305 (August 28, 2001).

newly enacted or amended statutes, and so on) that governs cyberspace transactions. Note that cyberlaw is not really a classification of law; rather, it is an informal term used to describe how traditional classifications of law, such as civil law and criminal law, are being applied to online activities.

Realize, too, that cyberlaw is not a new *type* of law. For the most part, it consists of traditional legal principles that have been modified and adapted to fit situations that are unique to the online world. Of course, in some areas new statutes have been enacted, at both the federal and state levels, to cover specific types of problems stemming from online communications.

Anyone preparing to enter today's business world will find it useful to know how old and new laws are being applied to activities conducted online, such as advertising, contracting, filing documents with the courts or government agencies, employment relations, and a variety of other transactions. For that reason, many sections in this text are devoted to this topic. Special features throughout the book also focus on how the law is evolving to govern specific legal issues that continue to emerge in the online environment.

> "Science and technology revolutionize our lives, but memory, tradition, and myth frame our response."
>
> ARTHUR SCHLESINGER, JR., 1917–
> (American historian)

KEY TERMS

administrative agency   9
administrative law   9
binding authority   11
case law   9
citation   8
civil law   15
civil law system   16
common law   10
constitutional law   7
criminal law   16
cyberlaw   17
defendant   12

equitable principles and
   maxims   13
executive agency   9
historical school   4
independent regulatory agency   9
international law   17
jurisprudence   3
law   3
legal positivism   4
legal realism   4
national law   16
natural law   3

persuasive authority   12
plaintiff   12
positive law   4
precedent   10
primary source of law   6
procedural law   15
remedy   12
secondary source of law   6
sociological school   4
stare decisis   10
statutory law   7
substantive law   15

CHAPTER SUMMARY THE LEGAL AND INTERNATIONAL FOUNDATIONS

The Nature of Law (See pages 3–4.)	Law can be defined as a body of rules of conduct with legal force and effect, prescribed by the controlling authority (the government) of a society. Important schools of legal thought, or legal philosophies, include the following: 1. *Natural law tradition*—One of the oldest and most significant schools of legal thought. Those who believe in natural law hold that there is a universal law applicable to all human beings and that this law is of a higher order than positive, or conventional, law. 2. *Legal positivism*—A school of legal thought centered on the assumption that there is no law higher than the laws created by the government. Laws must be obeyed, even if they are unjust, to prevent anarchy. 3. *The historical school*—A school of legal thought that stresses the evolutionary nature of law and that looks to doctrines that have withstood the passage of time for guidance in shaping present laws.

(continued)

CHAPTER SUMMARY THE LEGAL AND INTERNATIONAL
FOUNDATIONS—Continued

The Nature of Law—continued	4. *Legal realism*—A school of legal thought, popular during the 1920s and 1930s, that advocated a less abstract and more realistic approach to the law, an approach that would take into account customary practices and the circumstances in which transactions take place. Legal realism strongly influenced the growth of the *sociological school* of jurisprudence, which views law as a tool for promoting social justice.
Business Activities and the Legal Environment (See pages 4–6.)	1. *Many different laws may affect a single business transaction*—The laws covered in this text frequently overlap and interact. Often, a number of different laws will apply to just one business transaction. See, for example, Exhibit 1–1 on page 6.
	2. *Ethics and the legal environment*—In today's legal environment, business decision makers need to consider not just whether a decision is profitable and legal, but also whether it is ethical.
Sources of American Law (See pages 6–9.)	1. *Constitutional law*—The law as expressed in the U.S. Constitution and the various state constitutions. The U.S. Constitution is the supreme law of the land. State constitutions are supreme within state borders to the extent that they do not violate the U.S. Constitution or a federal law.
	2. *Statutory law*—Laws or ordinances created by federal, state, and local legislatures and governing bodies. None of these laws can violate the U.S. Constitution or (if they are state statutes) the relevant state constitutions. Uniform laws, when adopted by a state legislature, become statutory law in that state.
	3. *Administrative law*—The rules, orders, and decisions of federal or state government administrative agencies.
	4. *Case law and common law doctrines*—Judge-made law, including interpretations of constitutional provisions, of statutes enacted by legislatures, and of regulations created by administrative agencies.
The Common Law Tradition (See pages 10–15.)	1. *Common law*—Law that originated in medieval England with the creation of the king's courts, or *curiae regis,* and the development of a body of rules that were common to (or applied throughout) the land.
	2. *Stare decisis*—A doctrine under which judges "stand on decided cases"—or follow the rule of precedent—in deciding cases. *Stare decisis* is the cornerstone of the common law tradition.
	3. *Remedies—*
	a. Remedies at law—Money or something else of value.
	b. Remedies in equity—Remedies that are granted when the remedies at law are unavailable or inadequate. Equitable remedies include specific performance, an injunction, and contract rescission (cancellation).
	4. *The common law today*—The doctrines and principles embodied in case law govern all areas not covered by statutory law (or agency regulations issued to implement various statutes).
Classifications of Law (See pages 15–19.)	The law may be broken down according to several classification systems, such as substantive or procedural law, federal or state law, and private or public law. Two broad classifications are civil and criminal law, and national and international law. Cyberlaw is not really a classification of law but a term that is applied to the growing body of case law and statutory law that applies to Internet transactions.

FOR REVIEW

1. What are the major schools of jurisprudential thought?
2. What are the sources of American law?
3. What is the common law tradition?
4. What is a precedent? When might a court depart from precedent?
5. What are some important differences between civil law and criminal law?

QUESTIONS AND CASE PROBLEMS

1–1. Philosophy of Law. After World War II, which ended in 1945, an international tribunal of judges convened at Nuremberg, Germany. The judges convicted several Nazi war leaders of "crimes against humanity." Assuming that the Nazis who were convicted had not disobeyed any law of their country and had merely been following their government's (Hitler's) orders, what law had they violated? Explain.

1–2. Legal Systems. What are the key differences between a common law system and a civil law system? Why do some countries have common law systems and others have civil law systems?

1–3. Reading Citations. First read the appendix to this chapter. Assume that you want to read the entire court opinion in the case of *Kelly v. Arriba Soft Corp.*, 280 F.3d 934 (9th Cir. 2002). The case considers whether a photographer's images could be legally displayed on another person's Web site. Explain specifically where you would find the court's opinion.

1–4. Sources of American Law. This chapter discussed a number of sources of American law. Which source of law takes priority in the following situations, and why?

   (a) A federal statute conflicts with the U.S. Constitution.

   (b) A federal statute conflicts with a state constitution.

   (c) A state statute conflicts with the common law of that state.

   (d) A state constitutional amendment conflicts with the U.S. Constitution.

   (e) A federal administrative regulation conflicts with a state constitution.

1–5. *Stare Decisis.* In the text of this chapter, we stated that the doctrine of *stare decisis* "became a cornerstone of the English and American judicial systems." What does *stare decisis* mean, and why has this doctrine been so fundamental to the development of our legal tradition?

1–6. Court Opinions. Read through the section entitled "Case Titles and Terminology" in the appendix following this chapter. What is the difference between a concurring opinion and a majority opinion? Between a concurring opinion and a dissenting opinion? Why do judges and justices write concurring and dissenting opinions, given the fact that these opinions will not affect the outcome of the case at hand, which has already been decided by majority vote?

1–7. Statute of Limitations. The equitable principle "Equity aids the vigilant, not those who rest on their rights" means that courts will not aid those who do not pursue a cause of action while the evidence is fresh and while the true facts surrounding the issue can be discovered. State statutes of limitations are based on this principle. Under Article 2 of the Uniform Commercial Code, which has been adopted by virtually all of the states, the statute of limitations governing sales contracts says that parties must bring an action for the breach of a sales contract within four years, although the parties (the seller and the buyer) can reduce this period by agreement to only one year. Which party (the seller or the buyer) would benefit more by a one-year period, and which would benefit more by a four-year period? Discuss.

1–8. Binding versus Persuasive Authority. A county court in Illinois is deciding a case involving an issue that has never been addressed before in that state's courts. The Iowa Supreme Court, however, recently decided a case involving a very similar fact pattern. Is the Illinois court obligated to follow the Iowa Supreme Court's decision on the issue? If the United States Supreme Court had decided a similar case, would that decision be binding on the Illinois court? Explain.

A Question of Ethics & Social Responsibility

1–9. On July 5, 1884, Dudley, Stephens, and Brooks—"all able-bodied English seamen"—and an English teenage boy were cast adrift in a lifeboat following a storm at sea. They had no water with them in the boat, and all they had for sustenance were two one-pound tins of turnips. On July 24, Dudley proposed that one of the four in the lifeboat be sacrificed to save the others. Stephens agreed with Dudley, but Brooks refused to consent—and the boy was never asked for his opinion. On July 25, Dudley killed the boy, and the three men then fed on the boy's body and blood. Four days later, the men were rescued by a passing vessel. They were taken to

England and tried for the murder of the boy. If the men had not fed on the boy's body, they would probably have died of starvation within the four-day period. The boy, who was in a much weaker condition, would likely have died before the rest. [*Regina v. Dudley and Stephens,* 14 Q.B.D. (Queen's Bench Division, England) 273 (1884)]

1. The basic question in this case was whether the survivors should be subject to penalties under English criminal law, given the men's unusual circumstances. You be the judge, and decide the issue. Give the reasons for your decisions.
2. Should judges ever have the power to look beyond the written "letter of the law" in making their decisions? Why or why not?

Critical-Thinking Legal Question

1-10. John's company is involved in a lawsuit with a customer, Beth. John argues that for fifty years, in cases involving circumstances similar to those in this one, judges have ruled in a way that indicates that the judge in this case should rule in favor of John's company. Is this a valid argument? If so, does the judge in this case have to rule as those other judges have? What argument could Beth use to counter John's reasoning?

INTERACTING WITH THE INTERNET

Today, business law professors and students can go online to access information on virtually every topic covered in this text. A good point of departure for online legal research is the Web site for *The Legal and E-Commerce Environment Today,* Fourth Edition, at

http://leet.westbuslaw.com

There you will find numerous materials relevant to this text and to the legal environment of business generally, including links to various legal resources on the Web. Additionally, every chapter in this text ends with an *Interacting with the Internet* feature that contains selected Web addresses.

You can access many of the sources of law discussed in Chapter 1 at the FindLaw Web site, which is probably the most comprehensive source of free legal information on the Internet. Go to

http://www.findlaw.com

The Legal Information Institute (LII) at Cornell Law School, which offers extensive information about U.S. law, is also a good starting point for legal research. The URL for this site is

http://www.law.cornell.edu

The Library of Congress offers numerous links to state and federal government resources at

http://www.loc.gov

The Virtual Law Library Index, created and maintained by the Indiana University School of Law, provides an index of legal sources categorized by subject at

http://www.law.indiana.edu/v-lib/index.html

ONLINE LEGAL RESEARCH EXERCISES

Go to **http://leet.westbuslaw.com**, the Web site that accompanies this text. Select "Interactive Study Center," and then click on "Chapter 1." There you will find the following Internet research exercises that you can perform to learn more about some important sources of law discussed in Chapter 1 and other useful legal sites on the Web.

Activity 1–1: MANAGEMENT PERSPECTIVE—Internet Sources of Law
Activity 1–2: REGULATORY PERSPECTIVE—Online Assistance from
                Government Agencies

BEFORE THE TEST

Go to **http://leet.westbuslaw.com**, the Web site that accompanies this text. Select "Interactive Quizzes." You will find at least twenty interactive questions relating to this chapter.

Westlaw® Campus

If your textbook provided for a subscription to Westlaw® Campus, or if you have otherwise purchased access to the Westlaw Campus database, you can access any of the cases presented or cited in this chapter by using your Westlaw Campus account.

CHAPTER 1

Appendix

FINDING AND ANALYZING THE LAW

The statutes, agency regulations, and case law referred to in this text establish the rights and duties of businesspersons engaged in various types of activities. The cases presented in the following chapters provide you with concise, real-life illustrations of how the courts interpret and apply these laws. Because of the importance of knowing how to find statutory, administrative, and case law, this appendix offers a brief introduction to how these laws are published and to the "shorthand" employed in referencing these legal sources.

FINDING STATUTORY AND ADMINISTRATIVE LAW

When Congress passes laws, they are collected in a publication titled *United States Statutes at Large*. When state legislatures pass laws, they are collected in similar state publications. Most frequently, however, laws are referred to in their codified form—that is, the form in which they appear in the federal and state codes.

In these codes, laws are compiled by subject. The *United States Code* (U.S.C.) arranges all existing federal laws of a public and permanent nature by subject. Each of the fifty subjects into which the U.S.C. arranges the laws is given a title and a title number. For example, laws relating to commerce and trade are collected in Title 15, which is titled "Commerce and Trade." Titles are subdivided by sections. A citation to the U.S.C. includes title and section numbers. Thus, a reference to "15 U.S.C. Section 1" means that the statute can be found in Section 1 of Title 15. ("Section" may also be designated by the symbol §, and "Sections" by §§.)

Sometimes a citation includes the abbreviation *et seq.*—as in "15 U.S.C. Sections 1 *et seq.*" The term is an abbreviated form of *et sequitur*, which in Latin means "and the following"; when used in a citation, it refers to sections that concern the same subject as the numbered section and follow it in sequence.

State codes follow the U.S.C. pattern of arranging law by subject. The state codes may be called codes, revisions, compilations, consolidations, general statutes, or statutes, depending on the preference of the states. In some codes, subjects are designated by number. In others, they are designated by name. For example, "13 Pennsylvania Consolidated Statutes Section 1101" means that the statute can be found in Title 13, Section 1101, of the Pennsylvania code. "California Commercial Code Section 1101" means that the statute can be found under the subject heading "Commercial Code" of the California code in Section 1101. Abbreviations may be used. For example, "13 Pennsylvania

Consolidated Statutes Section 1101" may be abbreviated "13 Pa. C.S. § 1101," and "California Commercial Code Section 1101" may be abbreviated "Cal. Com. Code § 1101."

Rules and regulations adopted by federal administrative agencies are compiled in the *Code of Federal Regulations* (C.F.R.). Like the U.S.C., the C.F.R. is divided into fifty titles. Rules within each title are assigned section numbers. A full citation to the C.F.R. includes title and section numbers. For example, a reference to "17 C.F.R. Section 230.504" means that the rule can be found in Section 230.504 of Title 17.

Commercial publications of these laws and regulations are available and are widely used. For example, West Group publishes the *United States Code Annotated* (U.S.C.A.). The U.S.C.A. contains the complete text of laws included in the U.S.C., as well as notes of court decisions that interpret and apply specific sections of the statutes, plus the text of presidential proclamations and executive orders. The U.S.C.A. also includes research aids, such as cross-references to related statutes, historical notes, and library sources. A citation to the U.S.C.A. is similar to a citation to the U.S.C.: "15 U.S.C.A. Section 1."

FINDING CASE LAW

Before discussing the case reporting system, we need to look briefly at the court system (which will be discussed in detail in Chapter 4). There are two types of courts in the United States, federal courts and state courts. Both the federal and state court systems consist of several levels, or tiers, of courts. *Trial courts,* in which evidence is presented and testimony given, are on the bottom tier (which also includes lower courts handling specialized issues). Decisions from a trial court can be appealed to a higher court, which commonly would be an intermediate *court of appeals,* or an *appellate court.* Decisions from these intermediate courts of appeals may be appealed to an even higher court, such as a state supreme court or the United States Supreme Court.

State Court Decisions

Most state trial court decisions are not published. Except in New York and a few other states that publish selected opinions of their trial courts, decisions from state trial courts are merely filed in the office of the clerk of the court, where the decisions are available for public inspection. Written decisions of the appellate, or reviewing, courts, however, are published and distributed. As you will note, most of the state court cases presented in this book are from state appellate courts. The reported appellate decisions are published in volumes called *reports* or *reporters,* which are numbered consecutively. State appellate court decisions are found in the state reporters of that particular state.

Additionally, state court opinions appear in regional units of the National Reporter System, published by West Group. Most lawyers and libraries have the West reporters because they report cases more quickly and are distributed more widely than the state-published reports. In fact, many states have eliminated their own reporters in favor of West's National Reporter System. The National Reporter System divides the states into the following geographic areas: *Atlantic* (A. or A.2d), *South Eastern* (S.E. or S.E.2d), *South Western* (S.W., S.W.2d, or S.W.3d), *North Western* (N.W. or N.W.2d), *North Eastern*

(N.E. or N.E.2d), *Southern* (So. or So.2d), and *Pacific* (P., P.2d, or P.3d). (The *2d* and *3d* in the abbreviations refer to *Second Series* and *Third Series,* respectively.) The states included in each of these regional divisions are indicated in Exhibit 1A–1, which illustrates West's National Reporter System.

After appellate decisions have been published, they are normally referred to (cited) by the name of the case; the volume, name, and page number of the state's official reporter (if different from West's National Reporter System); the volume, unit, and page number of the *National Reporter;* and the volume, name, and page number of any other selected reporter. This information is included in the *citation.* (Citing a reporter by volume number, name, and page number, in that order, is common to all citations.) When more than one reporter is cited for the same case, each reference is called a *parallel citation.* For example, consider the following case: *Tiberino v. Spokane County,* 103 Wash.App. 680, 13 P.3d 1104 (2000). We see that the opinion in this case may be found in Volume 103 of the official *Washington Appellate Reports,* on page 680. The parallel citation is to Volume 13 of the *Pacific Reporter, Third Series,* page 1104. In presenting appellate opinions in this text, in addition to the reporter, we give the name of the court hearing the case and the year of the court's decision.

A few states—including those with intermediate appellate courts, such as California, Illinois, and New York—have more than one reporter for opinions issued by their courts. Sample citations from these courts, as well as others, are listed and explained in Exhibit 1A–2 on page 28.

Federal Court Decisions

Federal district court decisions are published unofficially in West's *Federal Supplement* (F.Supp. or F.Supp.2d), and opinions from the circuit courts of appeals (federal reviewing courts) are reported unofficially in West's *Federal Reporter* (F., F.2d, or F.3d). Cases concerning federal bankruptcy law are published unofficially in West's *Bankruptcy Reporter* (Bankr.). The official edition of United States Supreme Court decisions is the *United States Reports* (U.S.), which is published by the federal government. Unofficial editions of Supreme Court cases include West's *Supreme Court Reporter* (S.Ct.) and the *Lawyers' Edition of the Supreme Court Reports* (L.Ed. or L.Ed.2d). Sample citations for federal court decisions are also listed and explained in Exhibit 1A–2.

Unpublished Opinions

Many court opinions that are not yet published or that are not intended for publication can be accessed through Westlaw® (abbreviated in citations as "WL"), an online legal database maintained by West Group. When no citation to a published reporter is available for cases cited in this text, we give the WL citation (see Exhibit 1A–2 on page 28 for an example).

Old Case Law

On a few occasions, this text cites opinions from old, classic cases dating to the nineteenth century or earlier; some of these are from the English courts. The citations to these cases appear not to conform to the descriptions given above, because the reporters in which they were published have since been replaced.

EXHIBIT 1A–1 WEST'S NATIONAL REPORTER SYSTEM—REGIONAL/FEDERAL

Regional Reporters	Coverage Beginning	Coverage
Atlantic Reporter (A. or A.2d)	1885	Connecticut, Delaware, Maine, Maryland, New Hampshire, New Jersey, Pennsylvania, Rhode Island, Vermont, and District of Columbia.
North Eastern Reporter (N.E. or N.E.2d)	1885	Illinois, Indiana, Massachusetts, New York, and Ohio.
North Western Reporter (N.W. or N.W.2d)	1879	Iowa, Michigan, Minnesota, Nebraska, North Dakota, South Dakota, and Wisconsin.
Pacific Reporter (P., P.2d, or P.3d)	1883	Alaska, Arizona, California, Colorado, Hawaii, Idaho, Kansas, Montana, Nevada, New Mexico, Oklahoma, Oregon, Utah, Washington, and Wyoming.
South Eastern Reporter (S.E. or S.E.2d)	1887	Georgia, North Carolina, South Carolina, Virginia, and West Virginia.
South Western Reporter (S.W., S.W.2d, or S.W.3d)	1886	Arkansas, Kentucky, Missouri, Tennessee, and Texas.
Southern Reporter (So. or So.2d)	1887	Alabama, Florida, Louisiana, and Mississippi.

Federal Reporters	Coverage Beginning	Coverage
Federal Reporter (F., F.2d, or F.3d)	1880	U.S. Circuit Courts from 1880 to 1912; U.S. Commerce Court from 1911 to 1913; U.S. District Courts from 1880 to 1932; U.S. Court of Claims (now called U.S. Court of Federal Claims) from 1929 to 1932 and since 1960; U.S. Courts of Appeals since 1891; U.S. Court of Customs and Patent Appeals since 1929; and U.S. Emergency Court of Appeals since 1943.
Federal Supplement (F.Supp. or F.Supp.2d)	1932	U.S. Court of Claims from 1932 to 1960; U.S. District Courts since 1932; and U.S. Customs Court since 1956.
Federal Rules Decisions (F.R.D.)	1939	U.S. District Courts involving the Federal Rules of Civil Procedure since 1939 and Federal Rules of Criminal Procedure since 1946.
Supreme Court Reporter (S.Ct.)	1882	U.S. Supreme Court since the October term of 1882.
Bankruptcy Reporter (Bankr.)	1980	Bankruptcy decisions of U.S. Bankruptcy Courts, U.S. District Courts, U.S. Courts of Appeals, and U.S. Supreme Court.
Military Justice Reporter (M.J.)	1978	U.S. Court of Military Appeals and Courts of Military Review for the Army, Navy, Air Force, and Coast Guard.

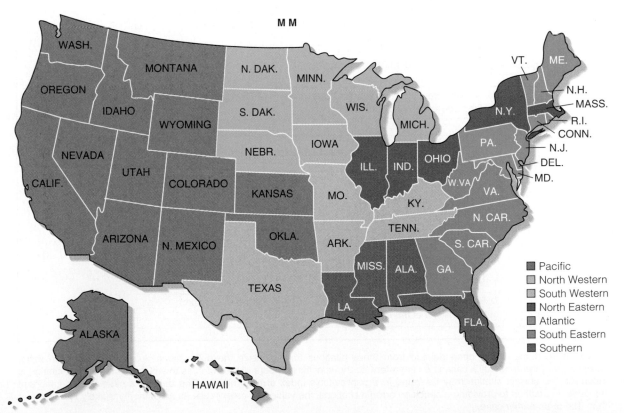

EXHIBIT 1A–2 HOW TO READ CITATIONS

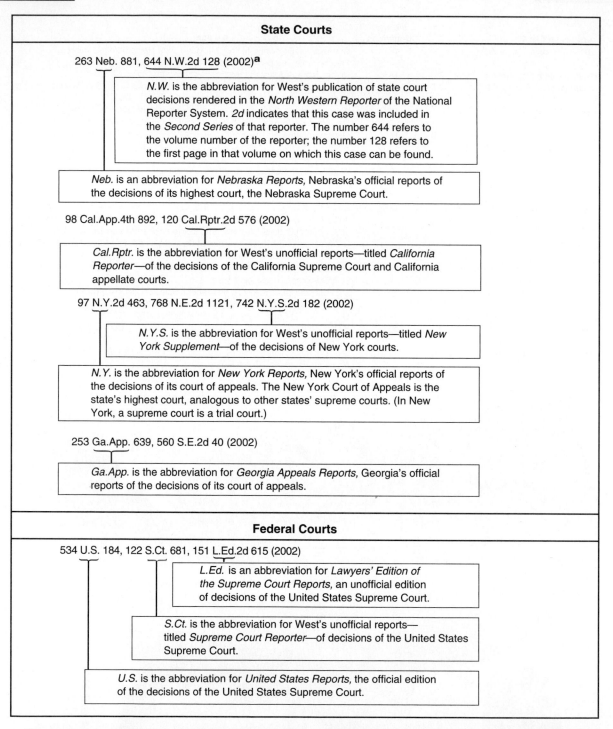

State Courts

263 Neb. 881, 644 N.W.2d 128 (2002)**a**

N.W. is the abbreviation for West's publication of state court decisions rendered in the *North Western Reporter* of the National Reporter System. *2d* indicates that this case was included in the *Second Series* of that reporter. The number 644 refers to the volume number of the reporter; the number 128 refers to the first page in that volume on which this case can be found.

Neb. is an abbreviation for *Nebraska Reports,* Nebraska's official reports of the decisions of its highest court, the Nebraska Supreme Court.

98 Cal.App.4th 892, 120 Cal.Rptr.2d 576 (2002)

Cal.Rptr. is the abbreviation for West's unofficial reports—titled *California Reporter*—of the decisions of the California Supreme Court and California appellate courts.

97 N.Y.2d 463, 768 N.E.2d 1121, 742 N.Y.S.2d 182 (2002)

N.Y.S. is the abbreviation for West's unofficial reports—titled *New York Supplement*—of the decisions of New York courts.

N.Y. is the abbreviation for *New York Reports,* New York's official reports of the decisions of its court of appeals. The New York Court of Appeals is the state's highest court, analogous to other states' supreme courts. (In New York, a supreme court is a trial court.)

253 Ga.App. 639, 560 S.E.2d 40 (2002)

Ga.App. is the abbreviation for *Georgia Appeals Reports,* Georgia's official reports of the decisions of its court of appeals.

Federal Courts

534 U.S. 184, 122 S.Ct. 681, 151 L.Ed.2d 615 (2002)

L.Ed. is an abbreviation for *Lawyers' Edition of the Supreme Court Reports,* an unofficial edition of decisions of the United States Supreme Court.

S.Ct. is the abbreviation for West's unofficial reports—titled *Supreme Court Reporter*—of decisions of the United States Supreme Court.

U.S. is the abbreviation for *United States Reports,* the official edition of the decisions of the United States Supreme Court.

a. The case names have been deleted from these citations to emphasize the publications. It should be kept in mind, however, that the name of a case is as important as the specific numbers of the volumes in which it is found. If a citation is incorrect, the correct citation may be found in a publication's index of case names. The date of a case is also important because, in addition to providing a check on error in citations, the value of a recent case as an authority is likely to be greater than that of an earlier case.

EXHIBIT 1A–2 HOW TO READ CITATIONS—CONTINUED

Federal Courts (continued)

287 F.3d 122 (2d Cir. 2002)

> *2d Cir.* is an abbreviation denoting that this case was decided in the United States Court of Appeals for the Second Circuit.

187 F.Supp.2d 1288 (D.Colo. 2002)

> *D.Colo.* is an abbreviation indicating that the United States District Court for the District of Colorado decided this case.

English Courts

9 Exch. 341, 156 Eng.Rep. 145 (1854)

> *Eng.Rep.* is an abbreviation for *English Reports, Full Reprint,* a series of reports containing selected decisions made in English courts between 1378 and 1865.

> *Exch.* is an abbreviation for *English Exchequer Reports*, which included the original reports of cases decided in England's Court of Exchequer.

Statutory and Other Citations

18 U.S.C. Section 1961(1)(A)

> *U.S.C.* denotes *United States Code,* the codification of *United States Statutes at Large.* The number 18 refers to the statute's U.S.C. title number and 1961 to its section number within that title. The number 1 refers to a subsection within the section and the letter A to a subdivision within the subsection.

UCC 2–206(1)(b)

> *UCC* is an abbreviation for *Uniform Commercial Code.* The first number 2 is a reference to an article of the UCC and 206 to a section within that article. The number 1 refers to a subsection within the section and the letter b to a subdivision within the subsection.

Restatement (Second) of Contracts, Section 162

> *Restatement (Second) of Contracts* refers to the second edition of the American Law Institute's *Restatement of the Law of Contracts.* The number 162 refers to a specific section.

17 C.F.R. Section 230.505

> *C.F.R.* is an abbreviation for *Code of Federal Regulations,* a compilation of federal administrative regulations. The number 17 designates the regulation's title number, and 230.505 designates a specific section within that title.

EXHIBIT 1A–2 HOW TO READ CITATIONS—CONTINUED

Westlaw® Citations[b]

2005 WL 10238

WL is an abbreviation for Westlaw®. The number 2005 is the year of the document that can be found with this citation in the Westlaw database. The number 10238 is a number assigned to a specific document. A higher number indicates that a document was added to the Westlaw database later in the year.

Uniform Resource Locators (URLs)

http://www.westlaw.com[c]

The suffix *com* is the top level domain (TLD) for this Web site. The TLD *com* is an abbreviation for "commercial," which means that normally a for-profit entity hosts (maintains or supports) this Web site.

westlaw is the host name—the part of the domain name selected by the organization that registered the name. In this case, West Group registered the name. This Internet site is the Westlaw database on the Web.

www is an abbreviation for "World Wide Web." The Web is a system of Internet servers that support documents formatted in *HTML* (hypertext markup language). HTML supports links to text, graphics, and audio and video files.

http://www.uscourts.gov

This is "The Federal Judiciary Home Page." The host is the Administrative Office of the U.S. Courts. The TLD *gov* is an abbreviation for "government." This Web site includes information and links from, and about, the federal courts.

http://www.law.cornell.edu/index.html

This part of a URL points to a Web page or file at a specific location within the host's domain. This page is a menu with links to documents within the domain and to other Internet resources.

This is the host name for a Web site that contains the Internet publications of the Legal Information Institute (LII), which is a part of Cornell Law School. The LII site includes a variety of legal materials and links to other legal resources on the Internet. The TLD *edu* is an abbreviation for "educational institution" (a school or a university).

http://www.ipl.org/ref

ref is an abbreviation for "Internet Public Library Reference Center," which is a map of the topics into which the links at this Web site have been categorized.

ipl is an abbreviation for Internet Public Library, which is an online service that provides reference resources and links to other information services on the Web. The IPL is supported chiefly by the School of Information at the University of Michigan. The TLD *org* is an abbreviation for "organization" (normally nonprofit).

---

b. Many court decisions that are not yet published or that are not intended for publication can be accessed through Westlaw®, an online legal database.

c. The basic form for a URL is "service://hostname/path." The Internet service for all of the URLs in this text is *http* (hypertext transfer protocol). Most Web browsers will add this prefix automatically when a user enters a host name or a hostname/path.

READING AND UNDERSTANDING CASE LAW

The cases in this text have been condensed from the full text of the courts' opinions and paraphrased by the authors. For those wishing to review court cases for future research projects or to gain additional legal information, the following sections will provide useful insights into how to read and understand case law.

Case Titles and Terminology

The title of a case, such as *Adams v. Jones,* indicates the names of the parties to the lawsuit. The *v.* in the case title stands for *versus,* which means "against." In the trial court, Adams was the plaintiff—the person who filed the suit. Jones was the defendant. If the case is appealed, however, the appellate court will sometimes place the name of the party appealing the decision first, so the case may be called *Jones v. Adams.* Because some reviewing courts retain the trial court order of names, it is often impossible to distinguish the plaintiff from the defendant in the title of a reported appellate court decision. You must carefully read the facts of each case to identify the parties.

The following terms and phrases are frequently encountered in court opinions and legal publications. Because it is important to understand what these terms and phrases mean, we define and discuss them here.

Plaintiffs and Defendants   As mentioned in Chapter 1, the plaintiff in a lawsuit is the party that initiates the action. The defendant is the party against which a lawsuit is brought. Lawsuits frequently involve more than one plaintiff and/or defendant.

Appellants and Appellees   The *appellant* is the party that appeals a case to another court or jurisdiction from the court or jurisdiction in which the case was originally brought. Sometimes, an appellant that appeals a judgment is referred to as the *petitioner.* The *appellee* is the party against which the appeal is taken. Sometimes, the appellee is referred to as the *respondent.*

Judges and Justices   The terms *judge* and *justice* are usually synonymous and represent two designations given to judges in various courts. All members of the United States Supreme Court, for example, are referred to as justices. Justice is also the formal title usually given to judges of appellate courts, although this is not always the case. In New York, a justice is a judge of the trial court (which is called the Supreme Court), and a member of the Court of Appeals (the state's highest court) is called a judge. The term *justice* is commonly abbreviated to J., and *justices* to JJ. A Supreme Court case might refer to Justice O'Connor as O'Connor, J., or to Chief Justice Rehnquist as Rehnquist, C.J.

Decisions and Opinions   Most decisions reached by reviewing, or appellate, courts are explained in written *opinions.* The opinion contains the court's reasons for its decision, the rules of law that apply, and the judgment. When all judges or justices unanimously agree on an opinion, the opinion is written for the entire court and can be deemed a *unanimous opinion.* When there is not a unanimous opinion, a *majority opinion* is written, outlining the views of the majority of the judges or justices deciding the case.

Often, a judge or justice who feels strongly about making or emphasizing a point that was not made or emphasized in the unanimous or majority opinion will write a *concurring opinion*. That means the judge or justice agrees (concurs) with the judgment given in the unanimous or majority opinion but for different reasons. In other than unanimous opinions, a *dissenting opinion* is usually written by a judge or justice who does not agree with the majority. The dissenting opinion is important because it may form the basis of the arguments used years later in overruling the precedential majority opinion. Occasionally, a court issues a *per curiam* (Latin for "of the court") opinion, which does not indicate which judge or justice authored the opinion.

A Sample Court Case

To illustrate the various elements contained in a court opinion, we present in Exhibit 1A–3, starting on page 34, an annotated court opinion. The opinion is from an actual case decided by the Virginia Supreme Court in 2003. Dominion Technology Partners, L.L.C.,[1] initiated a suit against Donald

---

1. *L.L.C.* is an abbreviation for *limited liability company,* which is a particular form of business enterprise that limits the liability of its owners for the firm's debts and other obligations. See Chapter 14.

The Supreme Court building in Washington, D.C. In what reporters are Supreme Court opinions published?

Williams, claiming in part that Williams breached a fiduciary duty (a duty to act primarily for another's benefit, such as the duty of loyalty owed by employees to their employers) that he owed to Dominion as its employee. The court ruled in Dominion's favor on this claim, and Williams appealed. The question before the Virginia Supreme Court was whether the trial court erred in its conclusion that Williams breached a duty of loyalty to Dominion.

You will note that triple asterisks (* * *) and quadruple asterisks (* * * *) frequently appear in the opinion. The triple asterisks indicate that we have deleted a few words or sentences from the opinion for the sake of readability or brevity. Quadruple asterisks mean that an entire paragraph (or more) has been omitted. Additionally, when the opinion cites another case or legal source, the citation to the case or other source has been omitted to save space and to improve the flow of the text. These editorial practices are continued in the other court opinions presented in this text. In addition, whenever we present a court opinion that includes a term or phrase that may not be readily understandable, a bracketed definition or paraphrase has been added.

Knowing how to read and understand court opinions and the legal reasoning used by the courts is an essential step in undertaking accurate legal research. Yet a further step is "briefing," or summarizing, the case. Legal researchers routinely brief cases by reducing the texts of the opinions to their essential elements. Instructions on how to brief a case are given in Appendix A, which also includes a briefed version of the sample court case presented in Exhibit 1A–3 on the following pages.

EXHIBIT 1A-3 A SAMPLE COURT CASE

Williams v. Dominion Technology Partners, L.L.C.

Virginia Supreme Court, 2003.

576 S.E.2d 752

> LAWRENCE L. KOONTZ, JR., Justice.
>
> * * *

This line gives the name of the judge who authored the opinion of the court.

> **Background**
>
> * * *

The court divides the opinion into three parts. The first part of the opinion summarizes the factual background of the case.

Dominion Technology Partners, L.L.C. * * * is an employment firm specializing in recruiting qualified computer consultants and placing them * * * on a temporary basis with various companies. Sometime in late 1998 or early 1999, Dominion learned that Stihl, Inc. (Stihl), a power tool manufacturing firm, was seeking a computer consultant to oversee the installation of a new software package on computer systems at Stihl's facilities in Virginia Beach.

Dominion recruited Donald Williams as a possible candidate to fill the position at Stihl. * * * Dominion offered to employ Williams as an **at-will employee,** paying Williams $80 per hour. * * * Williams [agreed].

Employment at will is a common law doctrine under which an employer or an employee may terminate their relationship at any time for any reason, unless a contract specifies otherwise.

* * * On January 22, 1999, Stihl entered into a **contract** * * * to employ Williams for an initial period of three months. * * *

* * * *

An agreement that can be enforced in court; formed by two or more parties, each of which agrees to perform, or to refrain from performing, some act now or in the future.

* * * Williams was responsible for the installation of a new software package related to Stihl's computer word processing, production and materials planning, and customer shipment functions. * * * The installation was completed on time, and Stihl decided to **retain** Williams in "a support and maintenance role" for an indeterminate period * * * on "a monthly basis * * * ."

To keep; to engage the services of a party.

* * * *

[More than a year later, when] Stihl was considering a further software upgrade to its computer systems * * * , Williams indicated that he would prefer to continue working at Stihl under a direct agreement * * * .

* * * *

" " " In a letter dated March 4, 2000, Williams formally tendered his resignation as an at-will employee of Dominion to be effective April 14, 2000. * * *

Unconditionally offered to perform an act (in this case, to quit employment).

* * * In May 2000, Dominion learned that Williams had continued working at Stihl * * * [for which he was] paid $115 per hour * * * .

On July 11, 2000, Dominion filed a [suit in a Virginia state court] against Williams alleging * * * breach of **fiduciary duty** [among other things].

A duty, imposed on a party by virtue of his or her position, to act primarily for another's benefit.

* * * *

* * * [T]he trial court entered **judgment** [in favor of Dominion.] * * * [W]e awarded Williams this appeal.

Final order or decision.

Discussion

The second major section of the opinion analyzes the issue before the court.

* * * *

We have long recognized that under the common law an employee, including an employee-at-will, owes a fiduciary duty of loyalty to his employer during his employment. Subsumed within this general duty of loyalty is the more specific duty that the employee not compete with his employer during his employment. Nonetheless, in the absence of a contract restriction regarding this duty of loyalty, an employee has the right to make arrangements during his employment to compete with his employer after resigning his post. * * *

* * * *

Allegations; declarations; statements claimed to be true.

* * * [T]he essence of Dominion's **assertions** against Williams * * * is that Williams, * * * while still an employee of Dominion, arranged [to continue working for Stihl] effective upon his resignation from Dominion.

A question a final answer to which will resolve a controversy.

The **dispositive question** * * * is whether this conduct * * * was sufficient to constitute a breach of Williams' fiduciary duty of loyalty to Dominion. * * *

A general designation of the remedy that a complainant seeks from a court.

A loss or injury of any kind to any person resulting from any cause. Courts do not grant relief for all harms.

A contractual promise to refrain from competing with another party for a certain period of time and within a reasonable geographic area. Also called a covenant not to compete.

To be added as increase or profit.

Information; knowledge of the existence of a fact.

Design, resolve, or determination; the state of mind with which an act is done or omitted. Intent should not be confused with *motive,* which is what prompts a person to act or fail to act.

The final section of the opinion, in which the court gives its order.

* * * [T]hat particular conduct of an employee caused harm to his employer does not establish that the conduct breached any duty to the employer. This is so because the law will not provide **relief** to every disgruntled player in the rough-and-tumble world comprising the competitive marketplace, especially where, through more prudent business practices, the **harm** complained of could easily have been avoided.

* * * *

* * * Dominion had not sought a **noncompete agreement** from Williams * * * . In such circumstances, it cannot be said that Williams' conduct to safeguard his own interests was either disloyal or unfair to Dominion. Rather, we are of the opinion that Dominion's contracts provided it with nothing more than a subjective belief or hope that the business relationships would continue and merely a possibility that future economic benefit would **accrue** to it.

* * * [B]y providing reasonable **notice** of his **intent** to resign his post * * * , Williams allowed Dominion to receive all the benefits for which it had bargained. Dominion's disappointment that its hopes did not bear the expected additional benefit it might have obtained under a different contractual agreement * * * does not translate into a breach of any fiduciary duty Williams owed to Dominion.

Conclusion

* * * Accordingly, we will reverse the judgment in favor of Dominion, and enter final judgment for Williams.

CHAPTER 2

Ethics and Social Responsibility

CONTENTS

CHAPTER OBJECTIVES

After reading this chapter, you should be able to answer the following questions:

1. What is ethics? What is business ethics? Why is business ethics important?

2. What steps can business leaders take to ensure that their companies act ethically?

3. How do duty-based ethical standards differ from outcome-based ethical standards?

4. What is corporate social responsibility? What are some different theories of social responsibility?

5. What is the difference between maximum profits and optimum profits?

Business owners and managers traditionally have had to ensure that their profit-making activities do not exceed the ethical boundaries established by society. In the past, though, these boundaries were often regarded as being coterminous with the law—that is, if something was legal, it was ethical. Shady business dealings were regarded as "just business" more often than not.

In the last few decades, however, the ethical boundaries within which business firms must operate have narrowed significantly. As the chapter-opening quotation below indicates, "New occasions teach new duties," and in the rights-conscious world of today, a business firm that decides it has no duties other than those prescribed by law may find it difficult to survive.

Consider the business scandals of the early 2000s. Certainly, those responsible for grossly inflating the reported profits at WorldCom, Inc., ended up not only destroying shareholder value in a great company but also facing possible prison terms. Those officers and directors at Enron Corporation who utilized a system of complicated off-the-books

"New occasions teach new duties."

James Russell Lowell, 1819–1891
(American editor, poet, diplomat)

transactions to inflate current earnings saw their company go bankrupt—one of the largest bankruptcies in U.S. history. They harmed not only their employees and shareholders but also the communities in which they worked—and themselves (some of them may be serving prison sentences when you read this). The officers and directors of Tyco International who used corporate funds to pay for lavish personal lifestyles also ended up in court. The shareholders of that company suffered dearly, too.

Ethical business decision making is not just theory. It is practical, useful, and essential. While a good understanding of business law and the legal environment is critical, it is not enough. Understanding how one should act in her or his business dealings is equally—if not more—important in today's business arena. How one should act in business is the focus of this chapter on business ethics.

BUSINESS ETHICS

ETHICS
Moral principles and values applied to social behavior.

Before we look at business ethics, we need to discuss what is meant by ethics generally. **Ethics** can be defined as the study of what constitutes right or wrong behavior. It is the branch of philosophy that focuses on morality and the way in which moral principles are derived or the way in which a given set of moral principles applies to one's conduct in daily life. Ethics has to do with questions relating to the fairness, justness, rightness, or wrongness of an action. What is fair? What is just? What is the right thing to do in this situation? These are essentially ethical questions.

What Is Business Ethics?

BUSINESS ETHICS
Ethics in a business context; a consensus of what constitutes right or wrong behavior in the world of business and the application of moral principles to situations that arise in a business setting.

Business ethics focuses on what constitutes right or wrong behavior in the business world and on how moral and ethical principles are applied by businesspersons to situations that arise in their daily activities in the workplace. Note that business ethics is not a separate *kind* of ethics. The ethical standards that guide our behavior as, say, mothers, fathers, or students apply equally well to our activities as businesspersons. Business decision makers, though, must often address more complex ethical issues and conflicts in the workplace than they face in their personal lives.

Why Is Business Ethics Important?

Why is business ethics important? The answer to this question is clear from this chapter's introduction. A keen and in-depth understanding of business ethics is important to the long-run viability of a corporation. A thorough knowledge of business ethics is also important to the well-being of the individual officers and directors of the corporation, as well as to the welfare of the firm's employees.

Later in this chapter, you will read about corporate social responsibility and the duties that a corporation owes to various "stakeholders" in the entity's well-being. Certainly, corporate decisions and activities can significantly affect not only those who own, operate, or work for the company but also such groups as suppliers, the community, and society as a whole.

Note that questions concerning ethical and responsible behavior are not confined to the corporate context. Business ethics applies to *all* businesses, regardless of their organizational forms. In a business partnership, for example, partners owe a fiduciary duty to each other and to their firm. (A *fiduciary* is a party who, because of some action that he or she has undertaken, has a duty to act primarily for another's benefit.) This duty can sometimes conflict with what a partner sees as his or her own best interest. Partners who act solely in their own interests may violate their duties to the other partners and the firm, however. By violating this duty, they may end up paying steep penalties—as the following case illustrates.

CASE 2.1   Time Warner Entertainment Co. v. Six Flags Over Georgia, L.L.C.

Georgia Court of Appeals, 2002.
254 Ga.App. 598,
563 S.E.2d 178.

BACKGROUND AND FACTS   The Six Flags Over Georgia theme park in Atlanta, Georgia, was developed in 1967 as a limited partnership known as Six Flags Over Georgia, L.L.C. (Flags). The sole limited partner was Six Flags Fund, Limited (Fund). The general partner was Six Flags Over Georgia, Inc. (SFOG). In 1991, Time Warner Entertainment Company (TWE) became the majority shareholder of SFOG. The next year, TWE secretly bought 13.7 acres of land next to the park, limiting the park's expansion opportunities. Over the next couple of years, using confidential business information from the park, TWE began plans to develop a competing park. Meanwhile, TWE installed no major new attractions at the park, deferred basic maintenance, withheld financial information from Fund (the limited partner), and began signing future employment contracts with SFOG officers. TWE also charged Flags for unrelated expenses, including over $4 million for lunches in New York City and luxury automobiles for TWE officers. Flags and Fund filed a suit in a Georgia state court against TWE and SFOG, alleging, among other things, breach of fiduciary duty. A jury awarded the plaintiffs $197,296,000 in compensatory damages and $257,000,000 in punitive damages.[a] TWE appealed to a state intermediate appellate court, alleging in part that the amount of the punitive damages was excessive.

IN THE WORDS OF THE COURT . . .

Ellington, Judge.
*   *   *   *

We begin our analysis by examining the degree of reprehensibility [degree of wrongfulness] of appellants' conduct in this case. *In examining the degree of reprehensibility of a defendant's conduct, [there are] a number of aggravating factors [to consider], including whether the harm was more than purely economic in nature, and whether the defendant's behavior evinced indifference to or reckless disregard for the health and safety of others.* Here, although the harm to Flags and Fund was primarily economic, it was caused by conduct we find especially reprehensible. Appellants' intentional breach of its fiduciary duty revealed a callous indifference to the financial well-being of its limited partners and their individual investors. [Emphasis added.]

*   *   * [T]he evidence adduced supported the jury's conclusion that appellants acted in concert to breach SFOG's fiduciary duty to its business partners. *   *   * [T]his evidence clearly and convincingly supported an award of punitive damages *   *   * because the evidence showed that the appellants withheld vital business information from Fund and Flags, undertook to compete with them, took money belonging to them, and carried out a plan to depress the value of their investment, the Six Flags Over Georgia Park. Moreover, the jury found a specific intent to cause harm *   *   *.

---
a. Damages that are intended to punish the wrongdoer and deter others from similar wrongdoing—see Chapter 8.

(continued)

CASE 2.1—Continued

Appellants' conduct toward its partners and those who invested in the limited partnership was part of a premeditated plan surreptitiously [secretly] executed over a period of years. Appellants' conduct was deceitful, self-serving, and financially damaging. More importantly, however, appellants' conduct was a breach of fiduciary duty, a violation of a confidential relationship of trust requiring the utmost in good faith. * * * Appellants' conduct was, in short, the kind of behavior we find deserving of reproof [disapproval], rebuke, or censure; blameworthy—the very definition of reprehensible. * * * *Trickery and deceit are reprehensible wrongs, especially when done intentionally through affirmative acts of misconduct.* * * * [Emphasis added.]

* * * *

In this case, the ratio of compensatory to punitive damages is 1 to 1.3. We see no shocking disparity inherent in this figure. Nor does it appear to approach that fuzzy line suggesting the bounds of constitutional impropriety. More importantly, however, given the amount of intentional economic damage inflicted by the appellants, corporate entities with collective assets measured in billions of dollars, we believe the award of punitive damages was reasonably calculated to punish them and to deter such conduct in the future.

DECISION AND REMEDY The state intermediate appellate court affirmed the judgment of the lower court, finding that the award of punitive damages was not excessive, considering the defendants' financial status and "reprehensible" conduct toward the plaintiffs.

FOR CRITICAL ANALYSIS—Ethical Consideration *If TWE had proceeded with its plans to build a competing park but had not otherwise acted "reprehensibly" with regard to Flags and Fund, would the decision in this case likely have been different?*

SETTING THE RIGHT ETHICAL TONE

Many unethical business decisions are made simply because they *can* be made. In other words, the decision makers not only have the opportunity to make such decisions but also are not too concerned about being seriously sanctioned for their unethical actions. Perhaps one of the most difficult challenges for business leaders today is to create the right "ethical tone" in their workplaces so as to deter unethical conduct.

The Importance of Ethical Leadership

Talking about ethical business decision making means nothing if management does not set standards. Moreover, managers must apply those standards to themselves and to the employees in the company.

> "What you do speaks so loudly that I cannot hear what you say."
> RALPH WALDO EMERSON,
> 1803–1882
> (American poet and essayist)

Attitude of Top Management One of the most important factors in creating and maintaining an ethical workplace is the attitude of top management. Managers who are not totally committed to maintaining an ethical workplace will rarely succeed in creating one. Surveys of business executives indicate that management's behavior, more than anything else, sets the ethical tone of a firm. In other words, employees take their cue from management. ● **EXAMPLE 1** If a firm's managers adhere to obvious ethical norms in their business dealings, employees will likely follow their example. In contrast, if managers act unethically, employees will see no reason not to do so themselves. For instance, if an employee observes a manager cheating on her expense account, the employee quickly understands that such behavior is acceptable.●

Looking the Other Way A manager who looks the other way when he knows about an employee's unethical behavior also sets an example—one indicating that ethical transgressions will be accepted. Managers must show that they will not tolerate unethical business behavior. Although this may seem harsh, managers have found that discharging even one employee for ethical reasons has a tremendous impact as a deterrent to unethical behavior in the workplace.

Creating Realistic Goals Helps Managers can reduce the probability that employees will act unethically by setting realistic production or sales goals. If a sales quota, for example, can be met only through high-pressure, unethical sales tactics, employees trying to act "in the best interests of the firm" may think that management is implicitly asking them to behave unethically.

Periodic Evaluation Some companies require their managers to meet individually with employees and to grade them on their ethical (or unethical) behavior. ● EXAMPLE 2 One company asks its employees to fill out ethical checklists each week and return them to their supervisors. This practice serves two purposes: First, it demonstrates to employees that ethics matters. Second, employees have an opportunity to reflect on how well they have measured up in terms of ethical performance.●

Ethical Codes of Conduct

One of the most effective ways of setting a tone of ethical behavior within an organization is to create an ethical code of conduct. A well-written code of ethics explicitly states a company's ethical priorities.

Costco—An Example This chapter includes a pull-out exhibit showing a code of ethics created by Costco Wholesale Corporation, a large warehouse-club retailer with over 42 million "members." This code of conduct indicates Costco's commitment to legal compliance, as well as to the welfare of its members (those who purchase its goods), its employees, and its suppliers. The code also details some specific ways in which the interests and welfare of these different groups will be protected. If you look closely at this exhibit, you will also see that Costco acknowledges that by protecting these groups' interests, it will realize its "ultimate goal"—rewarding its shareholders with maximum shareholder value.

Another Necessity—Clear Communication to Employees For an ethical code to be effective, its provisions must be clearly communicated to employees. Most large companies have implemented ethics training programs, in which management discusses with employees on a face-to-face basis the firm's policies and the importance of ethical conduct. Some firms hold periodic ethics seminars during which employees can openly discuss any ethical problems that they may be experiencing and learn how the firm's ethical policies apply to those specific problems.

Johnson & Johnson—An Example of Web-Based Ethics Training   Creating a code of conduct and implementing it are two different activities. In many companies, codes of conduct are simply documents that have very little relevance to day-to-day operations. When Johnson & Johnson wanted to do "better" than other companies with respect to ethical business decision making, it created a Center for Legal and Credo Awareness. (Its code of ethical conduct is called its credo.)

The center created a Web-based set of instructions designed to enhance the corporation's efforts to train employees in the importance of its code of conduct. Given that Johnson & Johnson has over 120,000 employees throughout the world, reinforcing its code of conduct and its values has not been easy, but Web-based training has helped. The company established a Web-based legal and compliance center, which consists of a set of interactive modules to train employees in areas of law and ethics.

Corporate Compliance Programs

In large corporations, ethical codes of conduct are usually just one part of a comprehensive corporate compliance program. Other components of such a program, some of which were already mentioned, include a corporation's ethics committee, ethical training programs, and internal audits to monitor compliance with applicable laws and the company's standards of ethical conduct.

The Sarbanes-Oxley Act and Web-Based Reporting Systems   The Sarbanes-Oxley Act of 2002[1] requires that companies set up confidential systems so that employees and others may "raise red flags" about suspected illegal or unethical auditing and accounting practices. The act required publicly traded companies to have such systems in place by April 2003. At least one Web-based reporting system was put in place in 2002. Employees can click on an icon on their computer that anonymously links them with Ethicspoint, an organization based in Vancouver, Washington. Through Ethicspoint, employees may report suspicious accounting practices, sexual harassment, and other possibly unethical behavior. Ethicspoint, in turn, alerts management personnel or the audit committee at the designated company to the possible problem. Those who have used the system say that it is less inhibiting than calling a company's 800 number.

Compliance Programs Must Be Integrated   To be effective, a compliance program must be integrated throughout the firm. For large corporations, such integration is essential. Ethical policies and programs need to be coordinated and monitored by a committee that is separate from various corporate departments. Otherwise, unethical behavior in one department can easily escape the attention of those in control of the corporation or the corporate officials responsible for implementing and monitoring the company's compliance program.

Conflicts and Trade-Offs

BE CAREFUL Ethical concepts about what is right and wrong can change.

Management constantly faces ethical trade-offs, some of which may lead to legal problems. As mentioned earlier, firms have implied ethical (and legal) duties to a number of groups, including shareholders and employees.

---

1. 15 U.S.C. Sections 7701 *et. seq.* This act, which became effective on August 29, 2002, will be discussed in Chapter 23.

When a company decides to reduce costs by downsizing and restructuring, the decision may benefit shareholders, but it will harm those employees who are laid off or fired. When downsizing occurs, which employees should be laid off first? Cost-cutting considerations might dictate firing the most senior employees, who generally have higher salaries, and retaining less senior employees, whose salaries are much lower. A company does not necessarily act illegally when it does so. Yet the decision to be made by management clearly involves an important ethical question: Which group's interests—those of the shareholders or those of employees who have been loyal to the firm for a long period of time—should take priority in this situation?

Selling information can bolster a company's profits, which may satisfy the firm's duty to its owners, but when the data is personal, its sale may violate an ethical or legal duty. In what circumstances might a party who sells information about someone else have a duty to that other party with respect to the sale of the information? This question arose in the following case.

CASE 2.2   Remsburg v. Docusearch, Inc.

New Hampshire Supreme Court, 2003.
816 A.2d 1001.
http://www.courts.state.nh.us/supreme/opinions/index.htm[a]

BACKGROUND AND FACTS Docusearch, Inc., operates Docusearch.com, an Internet-based investigation and information service. In July 1999, Liam Youens, a resident of New Hampshire, contacted Docusearch through its Web site and requested information about Amy Boyer, another New Hampshire resident. Youens provided his name, address, and phone number, and paid Docusearch's fee by credit card. Docusearch provided Boyer's home address, birth date, and Social Security number. Youens asked for Boyer's

workplace address. To obtain this information, Michele Gambino, a Docusearch subcontractor, placed a "pretext" phone call to Boyer. Gambino lied about who she was and the purpose of her call. On October 15, Youens drove to Boyer's workplace and fatally shot her, and then shot and killed himself. The police discovered Youens's Web site, which referred to stalking and killing Boyer. Helen Remsburg, Boyer's mother, filed a suit in a federal district court against Docusearch and others, claiming the defendants acted wrongfully. The court asked the New Hampshire Supreme Court whether, under the state's common law, a person who sells information about another has a duty to the other party with respect to the sale.

IN THE WORDS OF THE COURT . . .

DALIANIS, J. [Justice]
*   *   *   *

*   *   * [A] party who realizes or should realize that his conduct has created a condition which involves an unreasonable risk of harm to another has a duty to exercise reasonable care to prevent the risk from occurring. *The exact occurrence or precise injuries need not have been foreseeable. Rather, where the defendant's conduct has created an unreasonable risk of criminal misconduct, a duty is owed to those foreseeably endangered.* [Emphasis added.]

Thus, if a private investigator or information broker's *   *   * disclosure of information to a client creates a foreseeable risk of criminal misconduct against the third person whose information was disclosed, the investigator

---

a. Select "February 2003." In the "February 18, 2003" section, click on the name of the case to access the opinion. This is a page within a Web site maintained by the judicial branch of the state of New Hampshire.

(continued)

CASE 2.2—Continued

owes a duty to exercise reasonable care not to subject the third person to an unreasonable risk of harm. In determining whether the risk of criminal misconduct is foreseeable to an investigator, we examine two risks of information disclosure implicated by this case: stalking and identity theft.

It is undisputed that stalkers, in seeking to locate and track a victim, sometimes use an investigator to obtain personal information about the victim.

Public concern about stalking has compelled all fifty States to pass some form of legislation criminalizing stalking. * * * Stalking is a crime that causes serious psychological harm to the victim, and often results in the victim experiencing post-traumatic stress disorder, anxiety, sleeplessness, and sometimes, suicidal ideations. Not only is stalking itself a crime, but it can lead to more violent crimes, including assault, rape or homicide.

Identity theft, *i.e.,* the use of one person's identity by another, is an increasingly common risk associated with the disclosure of personal information * * * . Armed with one's [Social Security number, for example,] an unscrupulous individual could obtain a person's welfare benefits or Social Security benefits, order new checks at a new address on that person's checking account, obtain credit cards, or even obtain the person's paycheck.

Like the consequences of stalking, the consequences of identity theft can be severe. * * * Victims of identity theft risk the destruction of their good credit histories. This often destroys a victim's ability to obtain credit from any source and may, in some cases, render the victim unemployable or even cause the victim to be incarcerated.

The threats posed by stalking and identity theft lead us to conclude that the risk of criminal misconduct is sufficiently foreseeable so that an investigator has a duty to exercise reasonable care in disclosing a third person's personal information to a client. And we so hold. This is especially true when, as in this case, the investigator does not know the client or the client's purpose in seeking the information. [Emphasis added.]

DECISION AND REMEDY The New Hampshire Supreme Court held that an information broker who sells to a client information about a third person has a duty to exercise reasonable care in disclosing the information. The court reasoned that the risk of criminal misconduct is sufficiently foreseeable to impose this duty, in light of threats posed by stalking and identity theft.

FOR CRITICAL ANALYSIS—Technological Consideration *What might the defendants in this case have done to satisfy their legal and ethical duties?*

DEFYING THE RULES: THE ENRON CASE

For years to come, the Enron debacle—at that time, the single largest bankruptcy in the history of U.S. business—will remain a symbol of the cost of unethical behavior to management, employees, suppliers, shareholders, the community, society, and indeed the world. Shareholders lost $62 billion of value in a very short period of time in the early 2000s. This case study of "cooking the books," conflicts of interest, and deviation from accepted ethical standards of business has all of the trappings of an epic novel. Unfortunately, for the thousands of employees who lost millions of dollars and for the millions of shareholders who lost billions of dollars, the Enron story was not fiction.

The Growth of Enron in a Nutshell

In the 1990s, two gas-pipeline companies, Houston Natural Gas Corporation and InterNorth, Inc., merged to create a very large energy trading company, Enron Corporation. It was a "first mover" in a deregulated electricity market and enjoyed impressive growth. By 1998, Enron was the largest energy trader in the world. Then it entered the online energy trading market. By December 2000, its shares were selling at $85. Most Enron employees had a large part or even all of their retirement packages tied up in the company's stock.

When competition in energy trading increased, Enron diversified into water, power plants in Brazil and India, and finally fiber optics and high-speed Internet transmission.

Accounting Issues

According to the rules of the Financial Accounting Standards Board, energy traders such as Enron could include in *current* earnings profits that they *anticipated* on energy contracts. Herein lay the beginning of a type of accounting "fudging" that increased over time as the company struggled to improve its reported current earnings. By 2000, 50 percent of Enron's $1.4 billion of reported pretax profits consisted of "anticipated" future earnings on energy contracts.

Because Enron's managers received bonuses based on whether they met earnings goals, they had an incentive to inflate the anticipated earnings on such contracts. Some of the contracts extended as long as twenty years in the future. In retrospect, the temptation to management was too great, and common norms of both ethical and legal business decision making were violated as managers overestimated future earnings in order to inflate current earnings.

Kenneth Lay, a former executive of Enron Corporation, is sworn in during a congressional hearing into Enron's financial affairs in 2002. What legislation did Congress pass in 2002 in an attempt to curb unethical and deceptive accounting practices?

Off-the-Books Transactions

To artificially maintain and even increase its reported earnings, Enron also created a complex network of subsidiaries that enabled it to move losses from the core company to the subsidiaries—companies that did not show up on Enron's books. When it created the subsidiaries, Enron transferred assets to them, assigning a value to the assets that was much greater than their actual market value. The effect was to increase Enron's apparent net worth. Consider one example: Enron sold its unused fiber optic cable capacity to a subsidiary for $30 million in cash and a $70 million promissory note. This transaction added $53 million to Enron's reported earnings for just one quarter. The value of the unused fiber optic cable would soon be negligible, however.

For several years, Enron transferred assets from its books, along with the accompanying debt, to partnerships outside the main corporation. Many of these transactions were carried out in the Cayman Islands, a haven for those seeking corporate secrecy as well as a means for avoiding federal income taxes.

Self-Dealing

Enron's chief executive officer (CEO) frequently did business with companies owned by his son and his daughter. The son created a company that was later bought by Enron. The son was then hired as an executive with a guaranteed pay package of $1 million over three years as well as 20,000 Enron stock options. The CEO's daughter owned a Houston travel agency that received over $10 million—50 percent of the agency's total revenues—from Enron during a three-year period.

The Corporate Culture

The many transgressions just described could not have happened without a corporate culture that fostered unethical and, in many instances, illegal business decision making. This case study of unethical behavior is sufficiently important that West Legal Studies in Business has created a project titled "Inside Look," accessible on the Web at http://insidelook.westbuslaw.com. There you will discover how, on numerous occasions, Enron management was apprised, both by insiders and outsiders, that a "house of cards" had been created. Nonetheless, upper management more often than not refused to investigate and reveal to the public (or to shareholders and employees) the financial improprieties that had occurred over the previous three years.

BUSINESS ETHICS AND THE LAW

MORAL MINIMUM
The minimum degree of ethical behavior expected of a business firm, which is usually defined as compliance with the law.

Today, legal compliance is regarded as a **moral minimum**—the minimum acceptable standard for ethical business behavior. Had Enron Corporation strictly complied with existing laws and generally accepted accounting practices, very likely the "Enron scandal" would never have happened. Simply obeying the law does not fulfill all business ethical obligations, however. In the interests of preserving personal freedom, as well as for practical reasons, the law does not—and cannot—codify all ethical requirements. No law says, for example, that it is illegal to lie to one's family, but it may be unethical to do so.

It may seem that determining the legality of a given action should be simple. Either something is legal or it is not. In fact, one of the major challenges businesspersons face is that the legality of a particular action is not always clear. In part, this is because there are so many laws regulating business that a firm may violate one of them without realizing it. The law also contains numerous "gray areas," making it difficult to predict with certainty how a court will apply a given law to a particular action.

Laws Regulating Business

Today's business firms are subject to extensive government regulation. Virtually every action a firm undertakes—from the initial act of going into business, to hiring and firing personnel, to selling products in the marketplace—is subject to statutory law and to numerous rules and regulations issued by administrative agencies. Furthermore, these rules and regulations are changed or supplemented frequently.

Determining whether a planned action is legal thus requires that decision makers keep abreast of the law. Normally, large business firms have attorneys on their staffs to assist them in making key decisions. Small firms must also seek legal advice before making important business decisions because the consequences of just one violation of a regulatory rule may be costly.

Ignorance of the law will not excuse a business owner or manager from liability for violating a statute or regulation. ● **EXAMPLE 3** In one case the court imposed criminal fines, as well as imprisonment, on a company's supervisory employee for violating a federal environmental act—even though the employee was completely unaware of what was required under the provisions of that act.[2] ●

"Gray Areas" in the Law

In many situations, business firms can predict with a fair amount of certainty whether a given action would be legal. Certainly, firing an employee solely because of that person's race or gender would clearly violate federal laws prohibiting employment discrimination. In some situations, though, the legality of a particular action may be less clear.

● **EXAMPLE 4** Suppose that a firm decides to launch a new advertising campaign. How far can the firm go in making claims for its products or services? Federal and state laws prohibit firms from engaging in "deceptive advertising." At the federal level, the test for deceptive advertising normally used by the Federal Trade Commission is whether an advertising claim would deceive a "reasonable consumer."[3] At what point, though, would a reasonable consumer be deceived by a particular ad? ●

In short, business decision makers need to proceed with caution and evaluate an action and its consequences from an ethical perspective. Generally, if a company can demonstrate that it acted in good faith and responsibly in the circumstances, it has a better chance of successfully defending its action in court or before an administrative law judge.

ETHICAL ISSUE

How can a business decide whether a warning is "adequate"?

One of the "gray areas" in the law has to do with product misuse. As you will read in Chapter 9, product liability laws require manufacturers and sellers to warn consumers of the kind of injuries that might result from the foreseeable misuse of their products. An exception to this rule is made when a risk associated with a product is "open and obvious." Sharp knives, for example, can obviously injure their users. Sometimes, however, a business has no way of predicting how a court might rule in deciding whether a particular risk is open and obvious or whether consumers should be warned of the risk. If consumers should be warned, a further question arises: What constitutes an adequate warning? Even the courts often disagree on such matters.

In one case, for example, a company sold small aerosol cans of butane, a fuel for cigarette lighters. On each can was the warning "DO NOT BREATHE SPRAY." Nonetheless, twenty-year-old Stephen Pavlik died from intentionally inhaling the contents of one of the cans. In the lawsuit that followed, brought

---

2. *United States v. Hanousek,* 176 F.3d 1116 (9th Cir. 1999). This case is presented in Chapter 7 as Case 7.1.

3. See Chapter 19 for a discussion of the Federal Trade Commission's role in regulating deceptive trade practices, including misleading advertising.

by Pavlik's father, the trial court and the appellate court came to different conclusions. The trial court reasoned that Pavlik must have been aware of the dangers of inhaling butane and that a more specific warning would not have affected his conduct. The appellate court, though, concluded that the warning gave Pavlik "no notice of the serious nature of the danger posed by inhalation, intentional or otherwise."[4] Cases such as this send a clear message to businesspersons: never assume that a risk that may seem open and obvious to you will necessarily be open and obvious to a court.

Technological Developments and Legal Uncertainties

Uncertainties concerning how particular laws may apply to specific factual situations have been compounded in the cyber age. The widespread use of the Internet has given rise to situations never before faced by the courts.

The case presented next is illustrative. The case involved an airline pilot who claimed that defamatory, gender-based messages made by her co-workers in an online forum created a hostile working environment. As will be discussed in Chapter 17, federal law prohibits harassment in the workplace, including "hostile-environment harassment," which occurs when an employee is subjected to sexual conduct or comments that he or she perceives as offensive. Generally, employers are expected to take immediate and appropriate corrective action in response to employees' complaints of sexual harassment or abuse. Otherwise, they may be held liable for the harassing actions of an employee's co-workers or supervisors. At issue in the case was whether the online forum could be considered part of the "workplace" over which the employer had control.

---

4. *Pavlik v. Lane Ltd./Tobacco Exporters International,* 135 F.3d 876 (3d Cir. 1998).

CASE 2.3   Blakey v. Continental Airlines, Inc.

New Jersey Supreme Court, 2000.
751 A.2d 538.
http://lawlibrary.rutgers.edu/search.shtml [a]

pilots and assistant chief pilots, who are considered management at Continental. Technical assistance is provided by system operators (SYSOPS), who are volunteer crew members.

HISTORICAL AND TECHNOLOGICAL SETTING *CompuServe, Inc., a subsidiary of America Online, Inc., is the Internet service provider for Continental Airlines, Inc. CompuServe provides Continental's pilots and other crew members with online access to their flight schedules. As part of the service, CompuServe makes a "Crew Members Forum" available for the online exchange of ideas and information. Through customized software, any individual with a Continental pilot or crew member identification number can access the forum. This includes chief*

BACKGROUND AND FACTS Tammy Blakey, a pilot for Continental Airlines since 1984, was the airline's first female captain—and one of only five Continental pilots—to fly an Airbus A300 aircraft. Shortly after qualifying to be a captain on the A300, Blakey complained about pornographic photos and vulgar gender-based comments directed at her in her plane's cockpit and other work areas by her male co-employees. Blakey pursued claims against Continental with the Equal Employment Opportunity Commission, the agency that administers federal laws prohibiting

---

a. This page contains the database of the recent opinions of the New Jersey state courts. In the search box, type "Blakey" and click on the "Search" link. When the results appear, scroll down the list and click on the *Blakey* case name to access the opinion. This Web site is maintained by Rutgers School of Law in Camden, New Jersey.

CASE 2.3—Continued

employment discrimination, and in a federal district court.[b] Meanwhile, Continental pilots published a series of harassing, gender-based, defamatory messages about Blakey on the forum. When the court refused to consider these messages, Blakey filed a complaint against Continental and others in a New Jersey state court. She alleged, in part, gender-based harassment arising from a hostile work environment. Continental filed a motion for summary judgment[c] on this claim, which the court granted. A state intermediate appellate court upheld the summary judgment, and Blakey appealed to the New Jersey Supreme Court.

IN THE WORDS OF THE COURT . . .

O'HERN, J. [Justice]

*   *   *   *

*   *   * When an employer knows or should know of the harassment and fails to take effective measures to stop it, the employer has joined with the harasser in making the working environment hostile. The employer, by failing to take action, sends the harassed employee the message that the harassment is acceptable and that the management supports the harasser. *"Effective" remedial measures are those reasonably calculated to end the harassment.* *   *   * [Emphasis added.]

*   *   *   *

*   *   * Continental's liability [depends] on whether the Crew Members Forum was such an integral part of the workplace that harassment on the Crew Members Forum should be regarded as a continuation or extension of the pattern of harassment that existed in the Continental workplace.

Our common experience tells us how important are the extensions of the workplace where the relations among employees are cemented or sometimes sundered [destroyed]. If an "old boys' network" continued, in an after-hours setting, the belittling conduct that edges over into harassment, what exactly is the outsider (whether black, Latino, or woman) to do? Keep swallowing the abuse or give up the chance to make the team? We believe that severe or pervasive harassment in a work-related setting that continues a pattern of harassment on the job is sufficiently related to the workplace that an informed employer who takes no effective measures to stop it, sends the harassed employee the message that the harassment is acceptable and that the management supports the harasser. *   *   *

*   *   *   *

CompuServe's role may *   *   * be analogized to that of a company that builds an old-fashioned bulletin board. If the maker of an old-fashioned bulletin board provided a better bulletin board by setting aside space on it for employees to post messages, we would have little doubt that messages on the company bulletin board would be part of the workplace setting. Here, the Crew Members Forum is an added feature to the company bulletin board.

DECISION AND REMEDY The New Jersey Supreme Court reversed the judgment of the lower court and remanded the case (sent it back to the lower court) for further proceedings. The state supreme court indicated that the trial court was to determine, among other things, which messages were harassing, whether Continental had notice of those messages, and the severity or pervasiveness of the harassing conduct.

FOR CRITICAL ANALYSIS—Social Consideration *Does the ruling in the* Blakey *case mean that employers have a duty to monitor their employees' e-mail and other online communications?*

b. In 1997, the federal court ruled in favor of Blakey on a claim of gender-based harassment, awarding her $480,000 in back pay, $15,000 in front pay, and $250,000 for emotional distress, pain, and suffering. The court also found that Blakey had failed to mitigate damages (reduce her damages—by finding other work, for example) and subtracted $120,000 from her back pay award.
c. A motion requesting the court to enter a judgment without proceeding to trial—see Chapter 4.

SOURCES OF ETHICAL STANDARDS

Each individual, when faced with a particular ethical dilemma, engages in *ethical reasoning*—that is, a reasoning process in which the individual examines the situation at hand in light of her or his moral convictions or ethical standards. Businesspersons do likewise when making decisions with ethical implications.

How do business decision makers decide whether a given action is the "right" one for their firms? What ethical standards should be applied? Broadly speaking, ethical reasoning relating to business traditionally has been characterized by two fundamental approaches. One approach defines ethical behavior in terms of duty, which also implies certain rights. The other approach determines what is ethical in terms of the consequences, or outcome, of any given action. We examine each of these approaches here.

Duty-Based Ethics

Duty-based ethical standards often are derived from revealed truths, such as religious precepts. They can also be derived through philosophical reasoning.

Religious Ethical Standards   In the Judeo-Christian tradition, which is the dominant religious tradition in the United States, the Ten Commandments of the Old Testament establish fundamental rules for moral action. Other religions have their own sources of revealed truth. Religious rules generally are absolute with respect to the behavior of their adherents. ● EXAMPLE 5 The commandment "Thou shalt not steal" is an absolute mandate for a person, such as a Jew or a Christian, who believes that the Ten Commandments reflect revealed truth. Even a benevolent motive for stealing (such as Robin Hood's) cannot justify the act because the act itself is inherently immoral and thus wrong.●

Ethical standards based on religious teachings also involve an element of *compassion*. Therefore, for example, even though it might be profitable for a firm to lay off an employee who is not as productive as others, if that employee would find it difficult to find employment elsewhere and his or her family would suffer as a result, this potential suffering would be given substantial weight by the decision makers. Compassionate treatment of others is also mandated—to a certain extent, at least—by the Golden Rule of the ancients ("Do unto others as you would have them do unto you"), which has been adopted by most religions.

Kantian Ethics   Duty-based ethical standards may also be derived solely from philosophical reasoning. The German philosopher Immanuel Kant (1724–1804), for example, identified some general guiding principles for moral behavior based on what he believed to be the fundamental nature of human beings. Kant held that it is rational to assume that human beings are qualitatively different from other physical objects occupying space. Persons are endowed with moral integrity and the capacity to reason and conduct their affairs rationally. Therefore, their thoughts and actions should be respected. When human beings are viewed merely as a means to an end, they are being viewed as the equivalent of objects and are being denied their basic humanity.

A central postulate in Kantian ethics is that individuals should evaluate their actions in light of the consequences that would follow if *everyone* in society acted in the same way. This **categorical imperative** can be applied to any action. ● EXAMPLE 6 Suppose that you are deciding whether to cheat on an examination. If you have adopted Kant's categorical imperative, you will decide not to cheat because if everyone cheated, the examination would be meaningless.●

The Principle of Rights   Because a duty cannot exist without a corresponding right, duty-based ethical standards imply that human beings have basic rights. For example, the commandment "Thou shalt not kill" implies that individuals have a right to live. Additionally, religious ethics may involve a rights component because of the belief—characteristic of some religions—that an individual is "made in the image of God." This belief confers on the individual great dignity as a person. For one who holds this belief, not to respect that dignity—and the rights and status that flow from it—would be morally wrong. Kantian ethics also implies fundamental rights based on the personal dignity of each individual. Just as individuals have a duty not to treat others as a means to an end, so individuals have a right to have their status and moral integrity as human beings treated with respect.

The principle that human beings have certain fundamental rights (to life, freedom, and the pursuit of happiness, for example) is deeply embedded in Western culture. As discussed in Chapter 1, the natural law tradition embraces the concept that certain actions (such as killing another person) are morally wrong because they are contrary to nature (the natural desire to continue living). Those who adhere to this **principle of rights,** or "rights theory," believe that a key factor in determining whether a business decision is ethical is how that decision affects the rights of others. These others include the firm's owners, its employees, the consumers of its products or services, its suppliers, the community in which it does business, and society as a whole.

Which Rights Are Most Important?   A potential dilemma for those who support rights theory, however, is that they may disagree on which rights are most important. When considering all those affected by a business decision, for example, how much weight should be given to employees relative to shareholders, customers relative to the community, or employees relative to society as a whole?

In general, rights theorists believe that whichever right is stronger in a particular circumstance takes precedence. ● EXAMPLE 7 Suppose that a firm can either shut down a plant to avoid dumping pollutants in a river that would affect the health of thousands of people or save the jobs of the twelve workers in the plant. In this situation, a rights theorist can easily choose which group to favor. (Not all choices are so clear-cut, however.)●

Outcome-Based Ethics: Utilitarianism

"Thou shalt act so as to generate the greatest good for the greatest number." This is a paraphrase of the major premise of the utilitarian approach to ethics. **Utilitarianism** is a philosophical theory developed by Jeremy Bentham (1748–1832) and then advanced, with some modifications, by John Stuart Mill (1806–1873)—both British philosophers. In contrast to duty-based ethics, utilitarianism is outcome oriented. It focuses on the consequences of an action, not on the nature of the action itself or on any set of preestablished moral values or religious beliefs.

CATEGORICAL IMPERATIVE
A concept developed by the philosopher Immanuel Kant as an ethical guideline for behavior. In deciding whether an action is right or wrong, or desirable or undesirable, a person should evaluate the action in terms of what would happen if everybody else in the same situation, or category, acted the same way.

PRINCIPLE OF RIGHTS
The principle that human beings have certain fundamental rights (to life, freedom, and the pursuit of happiness, for example). Those who adhere to this "rights theory" believe that a key factor in determining whether a business decision is ethical is how that decision affects the rights of various groups. These groups include the firm's owners, its employees, the consumers of its products or services, its suppliers, the community in which it does business, and society as a whole.

UTILITARIANISM
An approach to ethical reasoning that evaluates behavior not on the basis of any absolute ethical or moral values but on the basis of the consequences of that behavior for those who will be affected by it. In utilitarian reasoning, a "good" decision is one that results in the greatest good for the greatest number of people affected by the decision.

COST-BENEFIT ANALYSIS
A decision-making technique that involves weighing the costs of a given action against the benefits of that action.

Under a utilitarian model of ethics, an action is morally correct, or "right," when, among the people it affects, it produces the greatest amount of good for the greatest number. When an action affects the majority adversely, it is morally wrong. Applying the utilitarian theory thus requires (1) a determination of which individuals will be affected by the action in question; (2) a **cost-benefit analysis,** which involves an assessment of the negative and positive effects of alternative actions on these individuals; and (3) a choice among alternative actions that will produce maximum societal utility (the greatest positive net benefits for the greatest number of individuals).

The utilitarian approach to decision making commonly is employed by businesses, as well as by individuals. Weighing the consequences of a decision in terms of its costs and benefits for everyone affected by it is a useful analytical tool in the decision-making process. At the same time, utilitarianism is often criticized because its objective, calculated approach to problems tends to reduce the welfare of human beings to plus and minus signs on a cost-benefit worksheet and to "justify" human costs that many find totally unacceptable.

CORPORATE SOCIAL RESPONSIBILITY

CORPORATE SOCIAL RESPONSIBILITY
The concept that corporations can and should act ethically and be accountable to society for their actions.

At one time businesses had few ethical requirements other than complying with the law. Generally, if an action was legal, it was regarded as ethical—no more, no less. By the 1960s, however, this attitude had begun to change significantly. Groups concerned with civil rights, employee safety and welfare, consumer protection, environmental preservation, and other causes began to pressure corporate America to behave in a more responsible manner with respect to these causes. Thus was born the concept of **corporate social responsibility**—the idea that corporations can and should act ethically and be accountable to society for their actions.

Since the advent of the Internet, the actions of business firms have been even more closely scrutinized by the media and various interest groups. "Corporate watch" groups routinely report on their Web sites any corporate activities that the groups deem unethical. Usually, the groups also urge those who access the site to take action—by printing out and sending a prepared letter to the offending firm, for example. Numerous Web sites today have been set up to protest against specific companies' products or services. (For a further discussion of this issue, see this chapter's *Legal E-nvironment* feature.)

Views on Corporate Social Responsibility

"Never doubt that a small group of committed citizens can change the world; indeed, it is the only thing that ever has."
MARGARET MEAD, 1901–1978
(American anthropologist)

Just what constitutes corporate social responsibility has been debated for some time. No one contests the claim that corporations have duties to their shareholders, employees, and product or service users (consumers). Many of these duties are written into law—that is, they are legal duties. The nature of a corporation's duties to other groups and to society at large, however, is not so clear. Today, there are a number of views on this issue, including those discussed in the following subsections.

Profit Maximization   Corporate directors and officers have a duty to act in the shareholders' interest. Because of the nature of the relationship between corporate directors and officers and the shareholder-owners, the law holds

LEGAL *e*-NVIRONMENT

Cybergriping

In today's online world, a recurring challenge for businesses is how to deal with cybergripers—those who complain in cyberspace about corporate products, services, or activities. For trademark owners, the issue becomes particularly thorny when cybergriping sites add the word "sucks" or "stinks" or some other disparaging term to the domain name of particular companies. These sites, sometimes referred to collectively as "sucks" sites, are established solely for the purpose of criticizing the products or services sold by the companies that own the marks. Can businesses do anything to ward off these cyber attacks on their reputations and goodwill?

Trademark Protection versus Free Speech Rights

A number of companies have sued the owners of "sucks" sites for trademark infringement in the hope that a court or an arbitrating panel will order the owner of that site to cease using the domain name. To date, however, companies have had little success pursuing this alternative. In one case, for example, Bally Total Fitness Holding Corporation sued Andrew Faber, who had established a "Bally sucks" site for the purpose of criticizing Bally's health clubs and business practices. Bally claimed that Faber had infringed on its trademark. The court did not agree, holding that the "speech"— consumer commentary—on Faber's Web site was protected by the First Amendment. According to the court, "The explosion of the Internet is not without its growing pains. It is an efficient means for business to disseminate information, but it also affords critics of those businesses an equally efficient means of disseminating commentary." In short, Bally could not look to trademark law for a remedy against cyber critics.[a]

Generally, the courts have been reluctant to hold that the use of a business's domain name for a "sucks" site infringes on the trademark owner's rights. After all, one of the primary reasons trademarks are protected under U.S. law is to prevent customers from becoming confused over the origins of the goods for sale—and a cybergriping site would certainly not create such confusion. Furthermore, American courts give extensive protection to free speech rights, including the right to express opinions about companies and their products.

Preventive Tactics

Many businesses have concluded that while they cannot control what people say about them, they can make it more difficult for it to be said—by buying up insulting domain names before the cybergripers can register them. For example, United Parcel Service (UPS) recently bought UPSstinks.com, IHateUPS.com, UPSBites.com, and a number of similar names. This has now become standard procedure for many firms. Indeed, a study by Company Sleuth of domain name registrations revealed that in just one month (August 2000), nearly 250 companies had registered domain names containing "stinks," "bites," "sucks," or similarly disparaging words. Wal-Mart alone registered more than two hundred anti–Wal-Mart names.[b]

FOR CRITICAL ANALYSIS

Do you believe that cybergriping sites help to improve the ethical performance of the businesses they criticize?

---

a. *Bally Total Fitness Holding Corp. v. Faber*, 29 F.Supp.2d 1161 (C.D.Cal. 1998).
b. David Streitfeld, "Making Bad Names for Themselves: Firms Preempt Critics with Nasty Domains," *The Washington Post*, September 8, 2000, p. A1.

directors and officers to a high standard of care in business decision making (see Chapter 14).

In the traditional view, this duty to shareholders takes precedence over all other corporate duties, and the primary goal of corporations should be profit maximization. Milton Friedman, the Nobel Prize–winning economist and a proponent of the profit-maximization view, sees "one and only one" social responsibility of a corporation: "to use its resources and engage in activities designed to increase its profits, so long as it stays within the rules of the game, which is to say, engages in open and free competition without deception and fraud."[5]

Those who accept this position argue that a firm can best contribute to society by generating profits. Society benefits because a firm realizes profits only when it markets products or services that are desired by society. These products and services enhance the standard of living, and the profits accumulated by successful business firms generate national wealth. Our laws and court decisions promoting trade and commerce reflect the public policy that the fruits of commerce (income and wealth) are desirable and good. Because our society regards income and wealth as ethical goals, corporations, by contributing to income and wealth, automatically are acting ethically.

The Stakeholder Approach   Another view of corporate social responsibility stresses that a corporation's duty to its shareholders should be weighed against its duties to other groups affected by corporate decisions. Corporate decision makers should consider not only the welfare of shareholders but also the welfare of other *stakeholders*—employees, customers, creditors, suppliers, and the community in which the corporation operates. The reasoning behind this "stakeholder view" of corporate social responsibility is that in some circumstances, one or more of these other groups may have a greater stake in company decisions than the shareholders do.

● **EXAMPLE 8** A heavily indebted corporation is facing imminent bankruptcy. The shareholder-investors have little to lose in this situation because their stock is already next to worthless. The corporation's creditors will be first in line for any corporate assets remaining. Thus, in this situation the creditors have the greatest "stake" in the corporation. Therefore, under the stakeholder view, corporate directors and officers should give greater weight to the creditors' interests than to those of the shareholders.●

Corporate Citizenship   Another theory of social responsibility argues that corporations should actively promote goals that society deems worthwhile and take positive steps toward solving social problems. Because so much of the wealth and power of this country is controlled by business, business in turn has a responsibility to society to use that wealth and power in socially beneficial ways. To be sure, since the nineteenth century and the emergence of large business enterprises in America, corporations have generally contributed some of their shareholders' wealth to meet social needs. Indeed, virtually all large corporations today have established nonprofit foundations for this purpose. Yet corporate citizenship requires more than just making donations to worthwhile causes. Under a corporate citizenship view of social responsibility, companies

"Next to doing the right thing, the most important thing is to let people know you are doing the right thing."
JOHN D. ROCKEFELLER, 1839–1897
(American industrialist and philanthropist)

5. Milton Friedman, "Does Business Have Social Responsibility?" *Bank Administration*, April 1971, pp. 13–14.

are also judged on how they conduct their affairs with respect to employment discrimination, human rights, environmental concerns, and so on.

Critics of this view believe that it is inappropriate to use the power of the corporate business world to fashion society's goals by promoting social causes. Determinations as to what exactly is in society's best interest involve questions that are essentially political; therefore, the public, through the political process, should have a say in making those determinations. The legislature—not the corporate board room—is thus the appropriate forum for such decisions.

Maximum versus Optimum Profits

Today's corporate decision makers are, in a sense, poised on a fulcrum between profitability and ethical responsibility. If they emphasize profits at the expense of perceived ethical responsibilities to other groups, they may become the target of negative media exposure and even lawsuits. If they go too far in the other direction (keep an unprofitable plant open so that the employees do not lose their jobs, invest too heavily in charitable works or social causes, and so on), their profits will suffer, and they may have to go out of business.

Striking the right balance on this fulcrum is difficult, and usually some profits must be sacrificed in the process. Instead of maximum profits, many firms today aim for **optimum profits**—the maximum profits a firm can realize while staying within legal *and* ethical limits.

OPTIMUM PROFITS
The amount of profits that a business can make and still act ethically, as opposed to maximum profits, defined as the amount of profits a firm can make if it is willing to disregard ethical concerns.

ETHICS IN THE GLOBAL CONTEXT

Given the varied cultures and religions of the world's nations, one should not be surprised that frequent conflicts in ethics arise between foreign and U.S. businesspersons. ● EXAMPLE 9 In some countries, the consumption of alcohol and certain foods is forbidden for religious reasons. It would be thoughtless and imprudent to invite a native business contact out for a drink in these locales.●

The role played by women in other countries may also present some difficult ethical problems for firms doing business internationally. Equal employment opportunity is a fundamental public policy in the United States, and Title VII of the Civil Rights Act of 1964 prohibits discrimination against women in the employment context (see Chapter 17). Some other nations, however, offer little protection for women against gender discrimination in the workplace, including sexual harassment.

We look here at how laws governing workers in other countries, particularly in developing nations, have created some especially difficult ethical problems for U.S. sellers of goods manufactured in foreign countries. First, though, we examine some of the ethical ramifications of a U.S. law that prohibits American businesspersons from bribing foreign officials to obtain favorable business contracts.

The Foreign Corrupt Practices Act

Another ethical problem in international business dealings has to do with the legitimacy of certain side payments to government officials. In the United States, the majority of contracts are formed within the private sector. In many

International Guidelines for Business Conduct

In today's global marketplace, conflicts and misunderstandings often arise due to different languages, business customs, national policies, and legal requirements. In 1976, the Organization for Economic Cooperation and Development (OECD), to which twenty-six of the world's leading industrialized nations belong, issued its Guidelines for Multinational Enterprises. The guidelines set forth international standards of business conduct that governments, businesses, and other groups can voluntarily implement to prevent misunderstandings and build an atmosphere of predictability. Over time, the guidelines have been updated to address new concerns. For example, the 2000 revision of the guidelines included recommendations relating to the elimination of child and forced labor, environmental performance, human rights, combating corruption, and protecting consumer interests. Although many public codes of business conduct are now available, the guidelines constitute the only multilaterally endorsed and comprehensive code that governments are committed to promoting.

FOR CRITICAL ANALYSIS

Why might an American corporation comply with the guidelines, which are recommendations only, if compliance would be more costly to the corporation than noncompliance?

REMEMBER Changing ethical notions about social responsibility often motivate lawmakers to enact or repeal laws.

foreign countries, however, decisions on most major construction and manufacturing contracts are made by government officials because of extensive government regulation and control over trade and industry. Side payments to government officials in exchange for favorable business contracts are not unusual in such countries; nor are such payments considered to be unethical—although this is now changing, as you will read shortly.

In the 1970s, the U.S. press, and government officials as well, uncovered a number of business scandals involving large side payments by American corporations to foreign representatives for the purpose of securing advantageous international trade contracts. In response to this unethical behavior, Congress passed the Foreign Corrupt Practices Act (FCPA) in 1977, which prohibits American businesspersons from bribing foreign officials to secure advantageous contracts. The act, which is the subject of this chapter's *Landmark in the Legal Environment* feature, made it difficult for American companies to compete as effectively as they otherwise might have in the global marketplace.

Monitoring the Employment Practices of Foreign Suppliers

Many U.S. businesses now contract with companies in developing nations to produce goods, such as shoes and clothing, because the wage rates in those nations are significantly lower than in the United States. Yet what if a foreign company exploits its workers—by hiring women and children at below-minimum-wage rates, for example, or by requiring its employees to work long

LANDMARK IN THE LEGAL ENVIRONMENT

The Foreign Corrupt Practices Act of 1977

The Foreign Corrupt Practices Act (FCPA) of 1977 is divided into two major parts. The first part applies to all U.S. companies and their directors, officers, shareholders, employees, and agents. This part of the FCPA prohibits the bribery of most officials of foreign governments if the purpose of the payment is to get the official to act in his or her official capacity to provide business opportunities.

PERMISSIBLE PAYMENTS   The FCPA does not prohibit payment of substantial sums to minor officials whose duties are ministerial. These payments are often referred to as "grease," or facilitating payments. They are meant to ensure that administrative services that might otherwise be performed at a slow pace are sped up. Thus, for example, if a firm makes a payment to a minor official to speed up an import licensing process, the firm has not violated the FCPA. Generally, the act, as amended, permits payments to foreign officials if such payments are lawful in the foreign country. The act also does not prohibit payments to private foreign companies or other third parties unless the American firm knows that the payments will be passed on to a foreign government in violation of the FCPA.

ACCOUNTING DUTIES   The second part of the FCPA is directed toward accountants because in the past bribes were often concealed in corporate financial records. All companies must keep detailed records that "accurately and fairly" reflect the company's financial activities. In addition, all companies must have an accounting system that provides "reasonable assurance" that all transactions entered into by the company are accounted for and legal. These requirements assist in detecting illegal bribes. The FCPA further prohibits any person from making false statements to accountants or false entries in any record or account.

In 1988, the FCPA was amended to provide that business firms that violate the act may be fined up to $2 million. Individual officers or directors who violate the FCPA may be fined up to $100,000 (the fine cannot be paid by the company) and may be imprisoned for up to five years.

Application to Today's World

The FCPA did not change international trade practices in other countries, but it effectively tied the hands of American firms trying to secure foreign contracts. For twenty years, the FCPA remained the only law of its kind in the world, despite attempts by U.S. political leaders to convince other nations to pass similar legislation. The international ethical landscape has changed significantly, however, and today other nations besides the United States regard payments to public officials in return for favorable contracts as unethical. Indeed, in 1997 the twenty-six member nations of the Organization for Economic Cooperation and Development signed a convention (treaty) that made the bribery of foreign public officials a serious crime. Each signatory was obligated to enact domestic legislation in accordance with the treaty.

hours in a workplace full of health hazards? What if the company's supervisors routinely engage in workplace conduct that is offensive to women?

Given today's global communications network, few companies can assume that their actions in other nations will go unnoticed by "corporate watch" groups that discover and publicize unethical corporate behavior. As a result, U.S. businesses today usually take steps to avoid such adverse publicity—either by refusing to deal with certain suppliers or by making arrangements to monitor their suppliers' workplaces to make sure that the workers are not being mistreated.

REMEMBER There is a constant tension among ethics, social forces, profits, and the law.

KEY TERMS

business ethics   38

categorical imperative   51

corporate social responsibility   52

cost-benefit analysis   52

ethics   38

moral minimum   46

optimum profits   55

principle of rights   51

utilitarianism   51

CHAPTER SUMMARY   ETHICS AND SOCIAL RESPONSIBILITY

Business Ethics (See pages 38–40.)	Ethics can be defined as the study of what constitutes right or wrong behavior. Business ethics focuses on how moral and ethical principles are applied in the business context.
Setting the Right Ethical Tone (See pages 40–44.)	1. *Role of management*—Management commitment and behavior are essential in creating an ethical workplace. Most large firms have ethical codes or policies and corporate compliance programs to help staff members determine whether certain actions are ethical. 2. *Ethical trade-offs*—Management constantly faces ethical trade-offs because firms have ethical and legal duties to a number of groups, including shareholders and employees.
Defying the Rules: The Enron Case (See pages 44–46.)	The Enron debacle—the largest bankruptcy in U.S. history—can serve as a case study of a corporate culture that fostered unethical and, in part, illegal business decision making.
Business Ethics and the Law (See pages 46–49.)	1. *The moral minimum*—Lawful behavior is a moral minimum. The law has its limits, though, and some actions may be legal but not ethical. 2. *Legal uncertainties*—It may be difficult to predict with certainty whether particular actions are legal given the numerous and frequently changing laws regulating business and the "gray areas" in the law.
Sources of Ethical Standards (See pages 50–52.)	1. *Duty-based ethics*—Ethics based on religious beliefs; philosophical reasoning, such as that of Immanuel Kant; and the basic rights of human beings (the principle of rights). 2. *Outcome-based ethics (utilitarianism)*—Ethics based on philosophical reasoning, such as that of John Stuart Mill.
Corporate Social Responsibility (See pages 52–55.)	Corporate social responsibility means that corporations can and should act ethically and be accountable to society for their actions. Different views on what constitutes social responsibility include the following: 1. *Profit maximization*—The view that the only concern of corporations should be to maximize profits while operating within legal limits so that the shareholders and society in general benefit from increased wealth. 2. *Stakeholder view*—The view that a corporation has other stakeholders besides shareholders (including employees, consumers of the corporation's product, suppliers, creditors, and so on) and that the interests of shareholders should be balanced against the interests of these other stakeholders in corporate decision making. 3. *Corporate citizenship*—The view that corporations, through philanthropy and their own conduct, should promote social goals (promote equal opportunity for women, minority groups, and persons with disabilities; protect the human rights of employees; and so on).
Ethics in the Global Context (See pages 55–57.)	There are many cultural, religious, and legal differences among nations. Notable differences relate to the role of women in society, employment laws governing workplace conditions, and the practice of giving side payments to foreign officials to secure favorable contracts.

...rently working in our warehouses, depots, buying offices, u........ departments, as well as in our home offices.

To that end, we are committed to these principles:

- Provide a safe work environment.

- Pay a fair wage.

- Make every job challenging, but make it fun!

- Consider the loss of any employee as a failure on the part of the company and a loss to the organization.

- Teach our people how to do their jobs and how to improve personally and professionally.

- Promote from within the company to achieve the goal of a minimum of 80% of management positions being filled by current employees.

- Create an "open door" attitude at all levels of the company that is dedicated to "fairness and listening."

RESPECT OUR VENDORS

Our vendors are our partners in business and for us to prosper as a company, they must prosper with us. It is important that our vendors understand that we will be tough negotiators, but fair in our treatment of them.

- Treat all vendors and their representatives as you would expect to be treated if visiting their places of business.

- Pay all bills within the allocated time frame.

- Honor all commitments.

- Protect all vendor property assigned to Costco as though it were our own.

- Always be thoughtful and candid in negotiations.

- Provide a careful review process with at least two levels of authorization before terminating business with an existing vendor of more than two years.

- Do not accept gratuities of any kind from a vendor

These guidelines are exactly that - guidelines, some common sense rules for the conduct of our business. Intended to simplify our jobs, not complicate our lives, these guidelines will not answer every question or solve every problem. At the core of our philosophy as a company must be the implicit understanding that not one of us is required to lie or cheat on behalf of PriceCostco. In fact, dishonest conduct will not be tolerated. To do any less would be unfair to the overwhelming majority of our employees who support and respect Costco's commitment to ethical business conduct.

If you are ever in doubt as to what course of action to take on a business matter that is open to varying ethical interpretations, take the high road and do what is right.

- Avoid all conflict of interest issues with public officials.

- Comply with all disclosure and reporting requirements.

- Comply with safety and security standards for all products sold.

- Exceed ecological standards required in every community where we do business.

- Comply with all applicable wage and hour laws.

- Comply with all applicable anti-trust laws.

- Protect "inside information" that has not been released to the general public.

TAKE CARE OF OUR MEMBERS

The member is our key to success. If we don't keep our members happy, little else that we do will make a difference.

- Provide top-quality products at the best prices in the market.

- Provide a safe shopping environment in our warehouses.

- Provide only products that meet applicable safety and health standards.

- Sell only products from manufacturers who comply with "truth in advertising/packaging" standards.

- Provide our members with a 100% satisfaction guaranteed warranty on every product and service we sell, including their membership fee.

- Assure our members that every product we sell is authentic in make and in representation of performance.

- Make our shopping environment a pleasant experience by making our members feel welcome as our guests.

- Provide products to our members that will be ecologically sensitive.

Our member is our reason for being. If they fail to show up, we cannot survive. Our members have extended a "trust" to Costco by virtue of paying a fee to shop with us. We can't let them down or they will simply go away. We must always operate in the following manner when dealing with our members:
Rule #1 – The member is always right.
Rule #2 – In the event the member is ever wrong, refer to rule #1.

There are plenty of shopping alternatives for our members. We will succeed only if we do not violate the trust that they have extended to us. We must be committed at every level of our company, with every ounce of energy and grain of creativity we have, to constantly strive to "bring goods to market at a lower price."

If you want our help, we are always available for advice and counsel. That's our job. We welcome your questions or comments.

Our continued success depends on you. We thank each of you for your contribution to our past success and for the high standards you have insisted upon in our company.

9380322

Accepting "gratuities" from a vendor might be interpreted as accepting a bribe. This can be a crime (see Chapter 7). In an international context, a bribe can be a violation of the Foreign Corrupt Practices Act (see Chapter 2). Other international laws are discussed in Chapter 24.

If the company fails to honor one of its commitments, it may be sued for breach of contract. Breach of contract and its remedies are discussed in Chapter 12.

Failing to pay bills when they become due could subject the company to creditors' remedies. The company might even be forced into involuntary bankruptcy (see Chapter 15).

Promotions and other benefits of employment cannot be granted or withheld on the basis of discrimination. This is against the law. Employment discrimination is the subject of Chapter 17.

Safety standards for the work environment are governed by the Occupational Safety and Health Act and other statutes. Laws regulating safety in the workplace are discussed in Chapter 13.

If we do these four things throughout our organization, we will realize our ultimate goal, which is to REWARD OUR SHAREHOLDERS.

"Truth in advertising/packaging" legal standards are part of the statutes and regulations that are discussed in Chapter 19, which deals with consumer law.

If the company did not provide products that comply with safety and health standards, it could be held liable in civil suits on legal grounds that are classified as torts (see Chapters 8 and 9).

Disclosure of "inside information" that constitutes *trade secrets* could subject an employee to civil liability or criminal prosecution (see Chapters 7 and 10).

Antitrust laws apply to illegal restraints of trade—an agreement between competitors to set prices, for example, or an attempt by one company to control an entire market. Antitrust laws are discussed in Chapter 22.

Failure to comply with "ecological" standards could be a violation of environmental laws (see Chapter 20).

Costco Background

Costco Wholesale Corporation operates a chain of cash-and-carry membership warehouses that sell high-quality, nationally branded, and selected private-label merchandise at low prices. Its target markets include both businesses that buy goods for commercial use or resale and individuals who are employees of specific organizations. The company tries to reach high sales volume and fast inventory turnover by offering a limited choice of merchandise in many product groups at competitive prices.

The company takes a strong position on behaving ethically in all transactions and relationships. It expects employees to behave ethically. For example, no one can accept gratuities from vendors. The company also expects to behave ethically, according to domestic ethical standards, in any country in which it operates.

COSTCO

CODE OF ETHICS

B y   J i m   S i n e g a l

OBEY THE LAW

The law is irrefutable! Absent a moral imperative to challenge a law, we must conduct our business in total compliance with the laws of every community where we do business.

- Comply with all statutes.
- Cooperate with authorities.
- Respect all public officials and their positions.

TAKE CARE OF OUR EMPLOYEES

To claim "people are our most important asset" is true and an understatement. Each employee has been hired for a very important job. Jobs such as stocking the shelves, ringing members' orders, buying products, and paying our bills are jobs we would all choose to perform because of their importance. The employees hired to perform these jobs are performing as management's "alter egos." Every employee, whether they are in a Costco warehouse, or whether they work in the regional or corporate offices, is a Costco ambassador trained to give our members professional, courteous treatment.

Today we have warehouse managers who were once stockers and callers, and vice presidents who were once in clerical positions for Costco. We believe that Costco's future executive officers are currently...

FOR REVIEW

1. What is ethics? What is business ethics? Why is business ethics important?
2. What steps can business leaders take to ensure that their companies act ethically?
3. How do duty-based ethical standards differ from outcome-based ethical standards?
4. What is corporate social responsibility? What are some different theories of social responsibility?
5. What is the difference between maximum profits and optimum profits?

QUESTIONS AND CASE PROBLEMS

2-1. Business Ethics. Some business ethicists maintain that whereas personal ethics has to do with right or wrong behavior, business ethics is concerned with appropriate behavior. In other words, ethical behavior in business has less to do with moral principles than with what society deems to be appropriate behavior in the business context. Do you agree with this distinction? Do personal and business ethics ever overlap? Should personal ethics play any role in business ethical decision making?

2-2. Business Ethics and Public Opinion. Assume that you are a high-level manager for a shoe manufacturer. You know that your firm could increase its profit margin by producing shoes in Indonesia, where you could hire women for $100 a month to assemble them. You also know, however, that a competing shoe manufacturer recently was accused by human rights advocates of engaging in exploitative labor practices because the manufacturer sold shoes made by Indonesian women for similarly low wages. You personally do not believe that paying $100 a month to Indonesian women is unethical, because you know that in their country, $100 a month is a better-than-average wage rate. Assuming that the decision is yours to make, should you have the shoes manufactured in Indonesia and make higher profits for your company? Should you instead avoid the risk of negative publicity and the consequences of that publicity for the firm's reputation and subsequent profits? Are there other alternatives? Discuss fully.

2-3. Business Ethics and Public Opinion. In recent years, human rights groups, environmental activists, and other interest groups concerned with unethical business practices have conducted publicity campaigns against various corporations that those groups feel have engaged in unethical practices. Do you believe that a small group of well-organized activists should dictate how a major corporation conducts its affairs? Discuss fully.

2-4. Ethical Decision Making. Shokun Steel Co. owns many steel plants. One of its plants is much older than the others. Equipment at that plant is outdated and inefficient, and the

costs of production are twice as high as at any of Shokun's other plants. The company cannot raise the price of steel because of competition, both domestic and international. The plant is located in Twin Firs, Pennsylvania, which has a population of about 45,000, and currently employs over a thousand workers. Shokun is contemplating whether to close the plant. What factors should the firm consider in making its decision? Will the firm violate any ethical duties if it closes the plant? Analyze these questions from the two basic perspectives on ethical reasoning discussed in this chapter.

Case Problem with Sample Answer

2-5. Consumer Welfare. Isuzu Motors America, Inc., does not warn its customers of the danger of riding unrestrained in the cargo beds of its pickup trucks. Seventeen-year-old Donald Josue was riding unrestrained in the bed of an Isuzu truck driven by Iaone Frias. When Frias lost control of the truck, it struck a concrete center divider. Josue was ejected and his consequent injuries rendered him a paraplegic. Josue filed a suit in a Hawaii state court against Isuzu, asserting a variety of legal claims based on its failure to warn of the danger of riding in the bed of the truck. Should Isuzu be held liable for Josue's injuries? Why or why not? [*Josue v. Isuzu Motors America, Inc.,* 87 Haw. 413, 958 P.2d 535 (1998)]

To view a sample answer for this case problem, go to this book's Web site at http://leet.westbuslaw.com and click on "Interactive Study Center."

2-6. Ethical Conduct. Richard and Suzanne Weinstein owned Elm City Cheese Co. Elm City sold its products to three major customers that used the cheese as a "filler" to blend into their cheeses. In 1982, Mark Federico, a certified public accountant, became Elm City's accountant and the Weinsteins' personal accountant. The Weinsteins had known Federico since he was seven years old, and even before he became their accountant, he knew the details of Elm City's business. Federico's duties went beyond typical accounting work, and when the Weinsteins were absent, Federico was put in charge of operations. In 1992, Federico was made a vice president of the company, and a year later he was placed in charge of day-to-day operations. He also continued to serve as Elm City's accountant. The relationship between Federico and the Weinsteins deteriorated, and in 1995, he resigned as Elm City's employee and as its accountant. Less than two years later, Federico opened Lomar Foods, Inc., to make the same products as Elm City by the same process and to sell the products to the same customers. Federico located Lomar closer to Elm City's suppliers. Elm City filed a suit in a Connecticut state court against Federico and Lomar, alleging, among other things, misappropriation of trade secrets. Elm City argued that it was entitled to punitive damages because Federico's conduct was "willful and malicious." Federico responded in part that he did not act willfully and maliciously because he did not know that Elm City's business details were trade secrets. Were Federico's actions "willful and malicious"? Were they ethical? Explain. [*Elm City Cheese Co. v. Federico,* 251 Conn. 59, 752 A.2d 1037 (1999)]

2–7. Cybergriping. Lockheed Corp. has used the name "Lockheed" since the 1930s. In 1995, Lockheed merged with Martin Marietta Corp., another large company with an international reputation, to form Lockheed Martin Corp. Lockheed Martin, one of the world's largest and best-known aerospace, electronics, and advanced materials manufacturers, continued to use the Lockheed name. In 1998, Dan Parisi registered the domain names "lockheedsucks.com" and "lockheedmartinsucks.com." Parisi used the names to point to a Web site that offered visitors an opportunity to vent their views on Lockheed and other companies. Lockheed demanded that Parisi transfer the names to it. Parisi refused. Lockheed filed a complaint with a provider of arbitration services—the World Intellectual Property Organization Arbitration and Mediation Center (WIPO Center)—asking it to transfer the names. Lockheed contended in part that the names were "confusingly similar" to Lockheed's trademarks. Parisi responded that "no one would reasonably believe [Lockheed] operates a website that appends the word 'sucks' to its name and then uses it to criticize corporate America." In whose favor should the WIPO Center rule, and why? [*Lockheed Martin Corp. v. Parisi,* WIPO Case No. D2000-1015 (2000)]

2–8. Ethical Conduct. Richard Fraser was an "exclusive career insurance agent" under a contract with Nationwide Mutual Insurance Co. Fraser leased computer hardware and software from Nationwide for his business. During a dispute between Nationwide and the Nationwide Insurance Independent Contractors Association, an organization representing Fraser and other exclusive career agents, Fraser prepared a letter to Nationwide's competitors asking whether they were interested in acquiring the represented agents' policyholders. Nationwide obtained a copy of the letter and searched its electronic file server for e-mail indicating that the letter had been sent. It found a stored e-mail that Fraser had sent to a co-worker indicating that the letter had been sent to at least one competitor. The e-mail was retrieved from the co-worker's file of already received and discarded messages stored on the receiver. When Nationwide canceled its contract with Fraser, he filed a suit in a federal district court against the firm, alleging, among other things, violations of various federal laws that prohibit the interception of electronic communications during transmission. In whose favor should the court rule, and why? In any case, did Nationwide act ethically in retrieving the e-mail? [*Fraser v. Nationwide Mutual Insurance Co.,* 135 F.Supp.2d 623 (E.D.Pa. 2001)]

2–9. Ethical Conduct. EF Cultural Travel BV is a travel agency whose principal clients are students. EF requires some employees to sign an agreement that prohibits them from using confidential information obtained during their employment to compete with EF. In the spring of 2000, several former EF employees started Explorica, Inc., to compete with EF. Explorica hired Zefer Corp. to build a scraper to "scrape" EF's prices from its Web site. (A scraper is a computer program that accesses information contained in a succession of Web pages and downloads it to the user's computer.) At the time, there was no statement on EF's site restricting the use of scrapers. After receiving the data from Zefer, Explorica set its prices to undersell EF. When EF discovered Explorica's use of the scraper, EF filed a suit in a federal district court against Zefer and others, seeking in part an injunction against the use of the scraper. Have any of the defendants violated an ethical or legal duty? In particular, on what basis might Zefer be ordered to stop scraping EF's site? Explain. [*EF Cultural Travel BV v. Zefer Corp.,* 318 F.3d 58 (1st Cir. 2003)]

A Question of Ethics & Social Responsibility

2–10. Hazen Paper Co. manufactured paper and paperboard for use in such products as cosmetic wrap, lottery tickets, and pressure-sensitive items. Walter Biggins, a chemist hired by Hazen in 1977, developed a water-based paper coating that was both environmentally safe and of superior quality. By the mid-1980s, the company's sales had increased dramatically as a result of its extensive use of "Biggins Acrylic." Because of this, Biggins thought he deserved a substantial raise in salary, and from 1984 to 1986, Biggins's persistent requests for a raise became a bone of contention between him and his employers. Biggins ran a business on the side, which involved cleaning up hazardous wastes for various companies. Hazen told Biggins that unless he signed a "confidentiality agreement" promising to restrict his outside activities during the time he was employed by Hazen and for a limited time afterward, he would be fired. Biggins said he would sign the agreement only if Hazen raised his salary to $100,000. Hazen refused to do so, fired Biggins, and hired a younger man to replace him. At the time of his discharge in 1986, Biggins was sixty-two years old, had worked for the company nearly ten years, and was just a few weeks away from being entitled to pension rights worth about $93,000. In view of these circumstances, evaluate and answer the following questions. [*Hazen Paper Co. v. Biggins*, 507 U.S. 604, 113 S.Ct. 1701, 123 L.Ed.2d 338 (1993)]

1. Did the company owe an ethical duty to Biggins to increase his salary, given that its sales increased dramatically as a result of Biggins's efforts and ingenuity in developing the coating? If you were one of the company's executives, would you have raised Biggins's salary? Why or why not?
2. Generally, what public policies come into conflict in cases involving employers who, for reasons of cost and efficiency of operations, fire older, higher-paid workers and replace them with younger, lower-paid workers? If you were an employer facing the need to cut back on personnel to save costs, what would you do, and on what ethical premises would you justify your decision?

Critical-Thinking Ethical Question

2-11. The sales of some of Delta Corporation's products are at an all-time low. Delta sets up Eagle, Inc., a new company, and convinces employees who are involved with the poorly selling products to transfer their retirement benefits to Eagle. Delta anticipates that Eagle will fail within two years. Would it be legal for Delta to keep its expectations for Eagle secret from the employees? Would it be ethical to do so?

Video Question

2-12. Go to this text's Web site at http://leet.westbuslaw.com and select "Video Questions." Click on "Chapter 2" and view the video titled *Ethics: Business Ethics an Oxymoron?* Then answer the following questions.

1. According to the instructor in the video, what is the primary reason why businesses act ethically?
2. Which of the two approaches to ethical reasoning that were discussed in the chapter seems to have had more influence on the instructor in the discussion of how business activities are related to societies? Explain your answer.
3. The instructor asserts that "[i]n the end, it is the unethical behavior that becomes costly, and conversely ethical behavior creates its own competitive advantage." Do you agree with this statement? Why or why not?

INTERACTING WITH THE INTERNET

For updated links to resources available on the Web, as well as a variety of other materials, visit this text's Web site at

http://leet.westbuslaw.com

As mentioned earlier in this chapter, West's Legal Studies in Business offers an "Inside Look" at Enron at

http://insidelook.westbuslaw.com

You can find articles on issues relating to shareholders and corporate accountability at the Corporate Governance Web site. Go to

http://www.corpgov.net

For an example of an online group that focuses on corporate activities from the perspective of corporate social responsibility, go to

http://www.corpwatch.org

Global Exchange offers information on global business activities, including some of the ethical issues stemming from those activities, at

http://www.globalexchange.org

ONLINE LEGAL RESEARCH EXERCISES

Go to **http://leet.westbuslaw.com**, the Web site that accompanies this text. Select "Interactive Study Center," and then click on "Chapter 2." There you will find the following Internet research exercises that you can perform to learn more about topics covered in this chapter.

Activity 2–1: ETHICAL PERSPECTIVE—**Ethics in Business**
Activity 2–2: MANAGEMENT PERSPECTIVE—**Environmental Self-Audits**

BEFORE THE TEST

Go to **http://leet.westbuslaw.com**, the Web site that accompanies this text. Select "Interactive Quizzes." You will find at least twenty interactive questions relating to this chapter.

Westlaw® Campus

If your textbook provided for a subscription to Westlaw® Campus, or if you have otherwise purchased access to the Westlaw Campus database, you can access any of the cases presented or cited in this chapter by using your Westlaw Campus account.

CHAPTER 3

Legal Representation and Alternative Dispute Resolution

CONTENTS

ATTORNEY
A person who has received a law
degree and has been licensed by
one or more states to practice law.

LITIGATION
The process of resolving a dispute
through the court system.

CHAPTER OBJECTIVES

*After reading this chapter, you should be able to answer
the following questions:*

1. What role do attorneys play in the dispute-resolution process?

2. What are the differences between litigation and the other
   forms of dispute resolution?

3. How do the processes of negotiation and mediation differ?

4. What are the steps in the arbitration process?

5. What are the differences between voluntary arbitration and
   court-annexed arbitration?

When a person has suffered an injury for which he or she seeks legal redress
or compensation, he or she may wish to seek the advice of an attorney,
or lawyer. An **attorney** is a person who has received a law degree and has been
licensed by one or more states to practice law. Despite Jeremy Bentham's sen-
timents to the contrary in the quotation below, all persons, *including* attorneys,
are expected to know the law in order to conduct themselves in an appropriate manner. In the first part of this chapter, we look at the role of attorneys in
the dispute-resolution process.

Litigation (the process of working a lawsuit through the court system) is
expensive and time consuming. As the cost and complexity of litigation have
grown, businesspersons and other individuals have resorted to alternative forms
of dispute resolution. Indeed, only about 5 to 10 percent of lawsuits filed actually go to trial. Most cases are settled by the parties or dismissed long before the
parties enter a courtroom. Today,
alternative methods of dispute resolution include the online dispute-
resolution process. We look at recent
developments concerning this area in
the final pages of this chapter.

> "Lawyers are the only persons
> in whom ignorance of the law is
> not punished."
> Jeremy Bentham, 1748–1832
> (British philosopher)

ATTORNEYS AND DISPUTE RESOLUTION

An attorney is often hired to represent the interests of a client in a legal proceeding or to review particular legal documents, such as a contract to purchase or lease a home. Despite the diversity of legal issues that attorneys may confront on a day-to-day basis, they share a common approach to the law because their education always involves an in-depth study of basic legal principles and concepts, rather than a memorization of existing laws (which frequently change). Consequently, all attorneys use similar research and analytical techniques.

The Roles of an Attorney

An attorney must fulfill several different roles to represent the interests of a client effectively. Although law school training provides a general background from which to approach a given legal matter and research the law, attorneys also research the extent to which the client's position is supported by that law. The attorney must also verify that the facts support the client's position. In a legal matter involving illegal activities, the attorney may uncover evidence that contradicts the client's position or even directly implicates the client in criminal conduct. In such cases, the attorney is not required to disclose the client's complicity, but the attorney may not knowingly assist the client in any way that would facilitate the perpetration of a crime.

Adviser If a client comes to an attorney for advice on how to avoid a particular problem in the future, the attorney will counsel the client as to what practices should be changed and what measures should be taken to head off potential problems. Here the attorney will find it necessary to practice **preventive law** and play the role of adviser, spotting possible legal land mines before they harm the client. Because there is more than one way to deal with most legal problems, the attorney will have to investigate the full range of possible solutions and then suggest a preferred alternative.

● **EXAMPLE 1** Primo Electronics wants to buy fifty Adco computers from Wadel Wholesalers, Inc. Wadel is willing to sell. Wadel agrees to ship the computers to Primo, but Wadel does not want to pay for any damage to the computers that may occur while they are in transit. Wadel's attorney might suggest that Wadel obtain insurance to cover the risk of any damage to the computers. The attorney might alternatively suggest that a clause be included in the contract under which Primo agrees to assume the risk of damage.●

PREVENTIVE LAW
The law that an attorney practices when he or she plays the role of an adviser for a client, spotting possible legal problems and suggesting preventive measures before the problems harm the client.

Drafter In handling a client's legal affairs, the attorney may be called on to draft documents and instruments ranging from leases and contracts to promissory notes and mortgages. Words are the lawyer's tools. Most attorneys find that they must familiarize themselves with several areas of the law to draft documents competently. The form of a document, particularly the extent to which it complies with certain legal formalities, may be as important as the document's content. Yet an attorney cannot draft a document for a client without knowing something about the content and the client's goals and objectives. In the case of a corporate client, the attorney often finds that he or she can draft a more effective document by becoming familiar with the corporation's operations and future plans.

● **EXAMPLE 2** Wadel's attorney can draft a more effective contract by knowing that Wadel wishes to avoid liability for any damage to the Adco computers while they are being shipped to Primo. If the attorney knows that Wadel wishes to avoid liability in all similar future transactions, he or she might draft a basic contract form that Wadel could use in the Primo deal and in future dealings. ●

Negotiator An attorney is often required to negotiate the terms of a particular agreement or settlement on behalf of his or her client. Negotiation is the art of persuasion. The attorney must marshal the strongest arguments in favor of the client and bring them to bear on the opposing side to produce the most favorable results. Most transactions involving significant sums of money are preceded by lengthy negotiations in which the terms of the deal and any accompanying details are worked out. Although the client may choose to conduct certain business negotiations without the attorney present, the client will want to confer with the attorney throughout the course of the negotiations. A properly negotiated contract can prevent many legal disputes and costs in the future.

Advocate Sometimes a lawyer must represent a client in court. If two parties are unable to resolve their dispute over a particular matter—such as whether the delivery of a defective item should obligate the buyer to pay for that item—then they may wish to solve their problem in court. Both parties will usually hire attorneys to present their respective positions to a jury. This advocacy role is perhaps the most demanding one for attorneys to fulfill because the litigation of even minor claims requires that the attorney be prepared to deal with a myriad of potential difficulties, ranging from witnesses who knowingly offer false testimony to a last-minute revelation of damaging evidence. A court proceeding, particularly one that involves high stakes, can be mentally and

An attorney advises her client. Does an attorney's skill as an advocate and an adviser have a significant effect on the outcome of a client's case?

emotionally draining. The successful advocate will maintain the necessary presence of mind to deal with or minimize any problems that may arise.

The Attorney-Client Relationship

For many individuals and businesses, relationships with attorneys last for decades. Thus, it is important that clients seek attorneys who are knowledgeable in the areas of the law that are needed to address their concerns. The client and attorney should communicate well—the attorney should perceive which issues are of foremost concern to the client and focus on those issues. The attorney should keep the client informed of developments in the law that affect the client's concerns. Most important, the attorney should advise the client of possible actions to take and then act according to the client's choice.

Selecting an Attorney In some situations, attorneys are allowed to include information about their areas of specialization in advertisements aimed at the general public. Also, a person interested in pursuing a legal claim should ask friends or relatives to recommend an attorney. If they cannot suggest an attorney who practices in the desired area of law, the individual can call the local or state bar association to obtain the names of several lawyers. If this approach proves unsatisfactory, the local telephone directory may be scanned for possible selections. If all these steps are unsuccessful, a professional directory should be consulted. Most libraries have copies of the *Martindale-Hubbell Law Directory,* which features professional biographies of nearly all the attorneys engaged in private practice throughout the country; the listings also include areas of concentration, as well as bank references and representative clients. The *Martindale-Hubbell Law Directory* and other sources for selecting an attorney can also be found on the Internet.

Establishing the Relationship Having selected an attorney, the client should make an appointment to see the attorney as soon as possible. Even a company that maintains an in-house attorney usually seeks outside counsel when the matter involves a particular area of expertise beyond the range of the company attorney. Undue delay may cost the client the opportunity of pursuing legal action or may, alternatively, increase the potential liability of the client. Although it is preferable that a client consult a lawyer before becoming involved in a legal dispute, many people put off the decision to hire a lawyer until the matter has become aggravated. In many cases, this procrastination prevents a simple, relatively inexpensive solution to the matter.

Once the decision to hire an attorney has been made, the client must disclose any relevant information so that the attorney can formulate the strongest possible plan of attack or the best defense.

The Attorney-Client Privilege Attorneys can best serve their clients only when they know all the relevant facts. The **attorney-client privilege** protects any relevant confidential communications from compelled disclosure—that is, courts and other government institutions cannot require that the communications be divulged. The privilege protects communications between an attorney and client made for the purpose of furnishing or obtaining professional legal advice or assistance. Thus, as long as the client's present legal matters are being discussed, the attorney cannot reveal the contents of these discussions even if, for

ATTORNEY-CLIENT PRIVILEGE
Protected communications between an attorney and client made for the purpose of furnishing or obtaining professional legal advice or assistance. Courts and other government institutions cannot require disclosure of the communications.

example, the client confesses to having committed a string of robberies in the past. This privilege may be waived only by the client.

Note that privileged information is *confidential* information. If confidential information is disclosed to others, it is no longer confidential and can no longer be considered privileged. Thus, if an attorney-client conversation is overheard by a third party, such as a janitor or someone walking down a hall, the information exchanged in the conversation is no longer confidential and thus no longer privileged. The presence of the client's spouse will not affect the attorney-client privilege, however, even if he or she is not a part of the discussion. Similarly, this privilege will continue to exist if the attorney's paralegal or other staff member hears the conversation, because the staff member will assist the attorney in preparing the client's case. (See this chapter's *Legal E-nvironment* feature on the next page for an examination of whether e-mail communications between attorneys and their clients are confidential.)

The Role of the Court

The adversarial nature of our legal system pits the attorneys for the opposing parties against each other; the assumption is that the search for the truth will best be facilitated by the presentation of competing arguments and evidence. The dispute must be a real one, however, in which a tangible injury has been suffered or there is an immediate threat of harm; the courts will not consider hypothetical questions. ● **EXAMPLE 3** A court will hear a dispute between you and your neighbor over whether his weekend barbecues constitute a nuisance that should be stopped. The court will not entertain questions of law relating to nuisances from two persons who are interested purely in discussing the law's theoretical implications. ●

Although the courts allow attorneys great leeway in defining the issues and presenting the relevant evidence, the court itself is responsible for making sure that the trial is conducted in a proper and dignified manner. The court does not usually interview witnesses or ask many questions about particular evidence, but it will prevent the parties from straying too far from the issues being litigated. It will also monitor the methods used by the attorneys in questioning witnesses and rule on various motions made by the attorneys regarding, for example, the introduction of new evidence. Although the role of the jury is to determine the relevant facts in a case, the judge—by virtue of the instructions that he or she gives to the jury members before they begin deliberating their formal decision, called a **verdict**—determines in part whether those facts support the position of the plaintiff or the defendant.

The Decision to File a Lawsuit

Before an individual or a company decides to file a complaint and thus initiate legal proceedings against a defendant, it must be determined, in consultation with an attorney, (1) whether the law provides an adequate remedy for the claim, (2) who can reasonably be expected to prevail in the lawsuit, and (3) whether the expected benefit is sufficient to compensate for any costs and expenses as well as any lost business.

In deciding whether to pursue a legal claim or right, the prospective **litigant** must consider a number of questions that relate not only to the desirability of the suit itself but also to whether such an action will help or hinder the

A judge listens as an attorney appeals to the jury during a trial. Can a judge in a jury trial influence the outcome of the case? If so, in what way? Should an individual or a company consider such factors when deciding whether to file a lawsuit?

VERDICT
A formal decision made by a jury.

LITIGANT
A party to a lawsuit.

LEGAL *e*-NVIRONMENT

The Confidentiality of E-Mail

An attorney who breaches his or her duty to preserve the confidentiality of client information may face serious consequences, including liability to the client for damages caused by the breach and the possibility of disciplinary action by the state bar association. The widespread use of the Internet by lawyers to communicate with their clients has thus raised a significant question: Does communicating with a client via e-mail constitute a violation of the confidentiality rule?

State Bar Associations Consider the Issue

The problem with using e-mail to communicate with clients is that there is an increased risk that an unauthorized person will intercept (and read) the e-mail. When state bar associations first considered whether e-mail communications violate the duty of confidentiality, most concluded that lawyers should not use e-mail for sensitive client communications unless the e-mail is encrypted (encoded using some type of encryption software). In 1997, however, a number of states reached the opposite conclusion—finding that unencrypted e-mail communications with clients do not violate an attorney's ethical obligations, at least under normal circumstances. Some states, such as Vermont, went on to say that while encryption is not required, it may be prudent to use encryption in situations in which the message being conveyed is "of a very sensitive nature."

The ABA Takes a Stand

In 1999, the American Bar Association (ABA) issued an opinion on the matter. According to the ABA's Standing Committee on Ethics and Professional Responsibility, "a lawyer may transmit information relating to the representation of a client by unencrypted e-mail" without violating the ABA's rules governing attorney conduct. The committee went on to state that plain, unencrypted e-mail "affords a reasonable expectation of privacy from a technological and legal standpoint."

Attorneys Remain Concerned

Notwithstanding the ABA's opinion, attorneys remain concerned. Although the ABA's opinions wield considerable influence, it is entirely possible that a court may arrive at a different conclusion. For this reason, many attorneys remain cautious when communicating with clients over the Internet. Encrypting e-mail and files that are transmitted over the Internet is one way to avoid confidentiality problems. Another is to add disclaimers to e-mail indicating that the communications may not be secure. Finally, some legal ethicists suggest that lawyers should discuss the issue with their clients and let the clients decide on how sensitive information should be exchanged.

FOR CRITICAL ANALYSIS

In terms of privacy and confidentiality, what is the difference between cell phone conversations and e-mail communications?

person's long-term objectives. Filing a lawsuit may permanently rupture a long-standing personal or business relationship, so careful attention will have to be given to whether the expected gains resulting from a successful court case outweigh the potential costs. Any such cost-benefit analysis is further muddied when both parties have strong legal support for their particular positions. In such cases, the verdict may turn on a party's demeanor or some other irrelevant factor. Although an attorney will take all reasonable measures to present the strongest possible case on behalf of a client, there are other factors, such as the client's appearance or voice, that are beyond the control of even the most talented attorney.

Adequacy of the Remedy The fact that a company has been adversely affected by the actions of a competitor will not necessarily give rise to a claim for **damages,** because the law grants remedies only for certain types of conduct. In general, the courts will not grant a particular type of relief simply because a company wishes to be insulated from the pressures of a competitive market.

● **EXAMPLE 4** Suppose that the Sparkling Cola Company tries to convince Red Castle, a nationwide chain of fast-food restaurants, to use its cola products instead of those offered by Red Castle's long-time supplier, the Effervescent Cola Company. Sparkling succeeds in its efforts, largely because of favorable consumer taste tests and its willingness to undersell Effervescent. Effervescent will probably not be able to sue Sparkling for interfering with its contractual relationship with Red Castle simply because it lost a customer to a competitor having a better product. In contrast, if Sparkling convinces Red Castle to stop using Effervescent's products by spreading false rumors about the quality of the products or labor problems at Effervescent's manufacturing plants, Effervescent can seek to recover damages from Sparkling based on a variety of legal theories, including defamation and wrongful interference with a contractual relationship (discussed in Chapter 8). In such a situation, it would clearly be in Effervescent's interest to seek damages, because Sparkling might otherwise continue spreading false rumors about its products to Effervescent's remaining customers. ●

Chances of Winning the Suit Once a party, such as Effervescent, has determined that there is a remedy for the particular injury it has suffered, the next factor to consider is the likelihood that the company will be able to win the lawsuit. Although jury trials always have an element of unpredictability (jurors may disregard important facts and give undue weight to trivial facts), any assessment by the company of its chances of prevailing in court will depend on the applicable laws and the outcomes of any factually similar cases. The client company and its attorney will also have to consider whether there is enough evidence to convince a court to rule in its favor and whether the other party can offer any **defenses,** or excuses, to justify its actions. Finally, the company will have to consider whether its own actions could significantly reduce its chances of prevailing in court.

Value of the Remedy Assuming that the client and the client's attorney have determined that they stand a very good chance of winning their suit against the defendant, they will then have to decide whether the relief that they would probably receive is worth the time and expense of the litigation.

Legal Fees. One factor to be considered is, of course, the cost of the attorney's time—the legal fees that the client will have to pay to collect damages from the defendant. Attorneys base their fees on such factors as the difficulty of a matter, the amount of time involved, the experience and skill of the attorney in the particular area of the law, and the cost of doing business. In the United States, legal fees range from $75 per hour to $500 per hour (the average fee per hour is between $150 and $170). Not included in attorneys' fees are such expenses as court filing charges and other costs directly related to a case.

A particular legal matter may include one or a combination of several types of fees. *Fixed fees* may be charged for the performance of such services as drafting a simple will. *Hourly fees* may be computed for matters that involve

DAMAGES
Money sought as a remedy for a breach of contract or for a tortious act.

DEFENSE
That which a defendant offers and alleges in an action or suit as a reason why the plaintiff should not recover or establish what he or she seeks.

"A lawyer's opinion is worth nothing unless paid for."

(Proverb)

an indeterminate period of time. Any case brought to trial, for example, may entail an expenditure of time that cannot be precisely estimated in advance. *Contingent fees* are fixed as a percentage (between 25 and 40 percent) of a client's recovery in certain types of lawsuits, such as personal injury. If the lawsuit is unsuccessful, the attorney receives no fee. The client will, however, have to pay the court fees and any other expenses incurred by the attorney (such as travel expenses, copying fees, and so on—often called out-of-pocket costs) on the client's behalf.

Many state and federal statutes allow for an award of attorneys' fees in certain legal actions, such as probate matters. In these cases, a judge sets the amount of the fee, based on such factors as the results obtained by the attorney and the fee customarily charged for similar services. In some cases, a client may receive an award of attorneys' fees as part of his or her recovery.

Settlement Consideration. A client's decision regarding how much he or she can afford to invest in the resolution of a particular legal problem is frequently the most important factor in determining the extent to which an attorney will pursue a resolution. If a client decides that he or she can afford a lengthy trial and one or more appeals, an attorney may pursue those actions. Often, once a client learns the extent of the costs involved in litigating a claim, he or she will be more willing to settle the case instead of going to trial.

● EXAMPLE 5   If the litigation is expected to be extremely costly, then in our earlier example, Effervescent may wish to consider alternative approaches, such as settling with Sparkling out of court, submitting the dispute to a third party (not a member of the judiciary), or doing nothing at all. Effervescent will also have to decide whether Sparkling has the financial resources to satisfy a court judgment and whether the enforcement of the judgment will be excessively expensive.●

The Decision to Defend against a Lawsuit

The plaintiff is not the only one that must consider the merits of becoming involved in a lawsuit. The defendant does not usually wish to be embroiled in a lawsuit, and there are a number of issues that the defendant must consider before deciding to battle the plaintiff in court. These issues include (1) whether the relationship it has with the plaintiff is too valuable to risk by becoming involved in an adversarial proceeding, (2) whether the publicity surrounding a trial would appreciably damage its reputation or image, and (3) whether the claim can be settled in a less costly manner.

Value of a Business Relationship In some cases, the defendant will not have to worry about the potential disruption of any business relationship because it has no commercial association with the plaintiff. But even in the case of a competitor, a company might be reluctant to become involved in litigation because of the effect a court battle might have on possible joint ventures or mutually beneficial research and development programs.

● EXAMPLE 6 Because Sparkling is highly competitive with Effervescent, it is not likely to place a very great value on the effect a vigorous courtroom defense will have on their relationship. Consequently, Sparkling will be more inclined to consider litigation as a viable strategy for resolving the dispute. The story might be very different if the suit were filed by Bob's Beef Wagon, a regional restaurant chain and long-time purchaser of Sparkling products. In that situation, Sparkling would consider the value of Bob's business very seriously and investigate alternative solutions before deciding to become involved in a court trial. ●

Potential Damage to a Company's Reputation Because trials are public proceedings, they may be covered, if the case is sufficiently noteworthy, by newspaper, magazine, radio, and television journalists. This means that any statements made by either side, as well as any testimony or evidence, may be publicized by the media. ● EXAMPLE 7 If the case between Effervescent and Sparkling involves numerous unflattering allegations regarding unethical business practices and poor product quality, then Sparkling will have to consider the likelihood that these charges will be publicized throughout the country. Sparkling's attorney may also remind the company that the charges themselves—rather than the actual truth of the charges—will dominate the media coverage. Furthermore, Sparkling will have to consider the harm to its image as a model corporate citizen that might result from a verdict for the plaintiff (Effervescent). ● In general, the cost of satisfying a judgment might understate the true cost of the legal dispute, because the publicity might negate the positive public image that Sparkling has achieved through its advertising campaigns.

Other Forms of Resolution Even though a defendant may have been served with a complaint by the plaintiff's attorney, this does not preclude the defendant from exploring alternative methods of settling the dispute. One of these methods is an out-of-court settlement. The attractiveness of an out-of-court settlement may be directly related to the amount of publicity given to the case and its effect on public attitudes toward the company. Because the terms of out-of-court settlements are normally not made available to the public, they provide a means by which a company may "buy" its way out of a lawsuit and avoid the attendant publicity.

● EXAMPLE 8 Sparkling's receptiveness to an out-of-court settlement will depend on its own perception about the strength of its case. If it believes that Effervescent has filed the lawsuit merely to harass it, then it might prefer to risk litigating the claims. Alternatively, Sparkling might propose to Effervescent that they submit the matter to arbitration. In *arbitration,* which will be discussed more fully later in this chapter, the parties agree to let a neutral third party decide the issue. Both parties might prefer arbitration as a solution for avoiding the incessant delays and higher costs of courtroom litigation. Because the terms of the arbitration agreement would not be released to the public, both companies could avoid having their images sullied by the press. ●

THE SEARCH FOR ALTERNATIVES TO LITIGATION

A number of solutions have been proposed, and some have been implemented, to reduce the congestion in our court system and to reduce the litigation costs facing all members of society. The enforcement of arbitration clauses, the use of court-referred arbitration and mediation, and the emergence of an increasing number of private forums for dispute resolution have all helped to reduce the caseload of the courts.

The parties to a controversy and their attorneys negotiate to resolve the dispute. When should a third party be brought in to mediate?

Another solution to the problem involves putting caps on damage awards, particularly for pain and suffering. Without the probability of obtaining multimillion-dollar judgments for pain and suffering, some potential litigants will be deterred from undertaking lawsuits to obtain damages. Another avenue of attack is to penalize those who bring frivolous lawsuits. Currently, a procedural rule used in federal courts (see Chapter 4) allows for disciplinary sanctions against lawyers and litigants who bring frivolous lawsuits.

Many courts require mediation or arbitration before a case goes to trial. There are proposals to reduce delay and expenses in federal civil cases further, and suggestions are being considered by the states as well. Some of the proposals can be viewed as case management plans. One suggested program, for example, would require each federal district court to implement procedures for placing cases on different tracks, with simple cases being handled more quickly than complex ones.

Politics and Law

Because reforms of any system affect individuals and groups differently, they seldom are accomplished easily and quickly. Reform of the court system is a prime example. At the federal level, members of Congress long have been interested in bringing court costs and delays under control. These concerns led to the passage of legislation in the early 1990s that required the federal courts to develop a plan to cut costs and reduce delay within the federal judicial system.

Alternative Methods of Dispute Settlement

The search for alternative means to resolve disputes has produced several distinct methods and arrangements. These range from neighbors' sitting down over a cup of coffee to work out their differences to huge multinational corporations' agreeing to resolve a dispute through a formal hearing before a panel of experts. All of these alternatives to traditional litigation make up what is broadly termed alternative dispute resolution.

Alternative dispute resolution (ADR) describes any procedure or device for resolving disputes other than the traditional judicial process. ADR is normally a less expensive and less time-consuming procedure than formal litigation. In some cases, it also has the advantage of being more private. Except in cases involving court-annexed arbitration (discussed later in this chapter), no public record of ADR proceedings is created; only the parties directly involved are privy to the information presented during the process. This is a particularly important consideration in many business disputes, because such cases may involve sensitive commercial information.

ALTERNATIVE DISPUTE RESOLUTION (ADR)
The resolution of disputes in ways other than those involved in the traditional judicial process. Negotiation, mediation, and arbitration are forms of ADR.

NEGOTIATION AND MEDIATION

Alternative dispute resolution methods differ in the degree of formality involved and the extent to which third parties participate in the process. Generally, negotiation is the least formal method and involves no third parties. Mediation may be similarly informal but does involve the participation of a third party.

Negotiation

In the process of **negotiation,** the parties come together informally, with or without attorneys to represent them. Within this informal setting, the parties air their differences and try to reach a settlement or resolution without the involvement of independent third parties. Because no third parties are involved and because of the informal setting, negotiation is the simplest form of ADR. Even if a lawsuit has been initiated, the parties may continue to negotiate their differences at any time during the litigation process and settle their dispute. Less than 10 percent of all corporate lawsuits, for example, end up in trial—the rest are settled beforehand.

NEGOTIATION
In regard to dispute settlement, a process in which parties, with or without attorneys to represent them, attempt to settle their dispute without going to court.

Preparation for Negotiation Because so many disputes are settled through negotiation, in spite of the informality of this means of dispute resolution, each party must carefully prepare his or her side of the case. The elements of the dispute should be considered, documents and other evidence should be collected, and witnesses should be prepared to testify. Negotiating from a well-prepared position improves the odds of obtaining a favorable result. Even if a dispute is not resolved through negotiation, preparation for negotiation will reduce the effort required to get ready for the next step in the dispute-resolution process.

"Assisted Negotiation" To facilitate negotiation, various forms of what might be called "assisted negotiation" have been employed. Forms of ADR associated with the negotiation process include mini-trials and early neutral case evaluation. Another form of assisted negotiation—the summary jury trial—is discussed later in this chapter.

A **mini-trial** is a private proceeding in which each party's attorney briefly argues the party's case before the other party. Typically, a neutral third party, who acts as an adviser and an expert in the area being disputed, is also present.

MINI-TRIAL
A private proceeding in which each party to a dispute argues its position before the other side and vice versa. A neutral third party may be present and act as an adviser if the parties fail to reach an agreement.

If the parties fail to reach an agreement, the adviser renders an opinion as to how a court would likely decide the issue. The proceeding helps the parties determine whether they should negotiate a settlement of the dispute or take it to court.

In **early neutral case evaluation,** the parties select a neutral third party (generally an expert in the subject matter of the dispute) to evaluate their respective positions. The parties explain their positions to the case evaluator however they wish. The evaluator then assesses the strengths and weaknesses of the parties' viewpoints, and this evaluation forms the basis for negotiating a settlement.

Disputes may also be resolved in a friendly, nonadversarial manner through **conciliation,** in which a third party aids parties to a dispute in reconciling their differences. The conciliator helps to schedule negotiating sessions and carries offers back and forth between the parties when they refuse to face each other in direct negotiations. Technically, conciliators are not supposed to recommend solutions. In practice, however, they often do. In contrast, a mediator is expected to propose solutions.

Mediation

Mediation is similar to negotiation. In the mediation process, as in negotiation, the parties themselves must reach agreement about their dispute. The major difference between negotiation and mediation is that the latter involves a third party, called a mediator. The **mediator** assists the parties in reaching a mutually acceptable agreement. The mediator talks face to face with the parties and allows them to discuss their disagreement, usually in an informal environment. The mediator's role, however, is limited to assisting the parties. The mediator does not decide a controversy; he or she only facilitates the process by helping the parties more quickly find common ground on which they can begin to reach an agreement for themselves.

Advantages of Mediation Few procedural rules are involved in the mediation process—far fewer than in a courtroom setting. The proceedings can be tailored to fit the needs of the parties—the mediator can be told to maintain a diplomatic role or be asked to express an opinion about the dispute, lawyers can be excluded from the proceedings, and the exchange of a few documents can replace the more expensive and time-consuming process of pretrial discovery. Disputes are often settled much more quickly in mediation than in formal litigation.[1]

There are other benefits. Because the parties reach agreement by mutual consent, the bitterness that often flows from the winner-take-all outcome of a formal trial decision is avoided. Hard feelings are also minimized by the less stressful environment provided by mediation; the absence of the formal rules and adversarial tone of courtroom proceedings lessens the hostility the parties may feel toward one another. Minimizing hard feelings can be very important when the parties have to go on working with one another while the controversy is being resolved or after it has been settled. This is frequently the case when two businesses—say, a supplier and a purchaser—have a long-standing, mutually beneficial relationship that they would like to preserve despite their

EARLY NEUTRAL CASE EVALUATION
A form of alternative dispute resolution in which a neutral third party evaluates the strengths and weaknesses of the disputing parties' positions; the evaluator's opinion forms the basis for negotiating a settlement.

CONCILIATION
A form of alternative dispute resolution in which the parties reach an agreement themselves with the help of a neutral third party, called a conciliator, who facilitates the negotiations.

MEDIATION
A method of settling disputes outside of court by using the services of a neutral third party, called a mediator. The mediator acts as a communicating agent between the parties and suggests ways in which the parties can resolve their dispute.

MEDIATOR
A person who attempts to reconcile the differences between two or more parties.

---

1. In Florida alone, as many as fifty thousand disputes that might have ended up in court are instead resolved through mediation each year.

disagreement. Similar considerations are found in the context of management and labor disputes; employee disciplinary matters and grievances are subjects that invite mediation as an alternative to formal litigation.

Another important benefit of mediation is that the mediator is selected by the parties. In litigation, the parties have no control over the selection of a judge. In mediation, the parties may choose a mediator on the basis of expertise in a particular field as well as for fairness and impartiality. To the degree that the mediator has these attributes, he or she will more effectively aid the parties in reaching an agreement over their dispute.

Disadvantages of Mediation Mediation is not without disadvantages. A mediator is likely to charge a fee. (This can be split between the parties, though, and thus may represent less expense than would both sides' hiring lawyers.)

Informality and the absence of a third party referee can also be a detriment. (Remember that a mediator can only help the parties reach a decision, not make a decision for them.) Without a deadline hanging over the parties' heads, and without the threat of sanctions if they fail to negotiate in good faith, they may be less willing to make concessions or otherwise strive honestly and diligently to reach a settlement. This can slow the process or even cause it to fail.

ARBITRATION

A third method of dispute resolution combines the advantages of third party decision making—as provided by judges and juries in formal litigation—with the speed and flexibility inherent in rules of procedure and evidence less rigid than those governing courtroom litigation. This is the process of **arbitration**— the settling of a dispute by an impartial third party (other than a court) who renders a legally binding decision. The third party who renders the decision is called an **arbitrator.**

When a dispute arises, the parties can agree to settle their differences informally through arbitration rather than formally through the court system. Alternatively, the parties may agree ahead of time that, if a dispute should arise, they will submit to arbitration rather than bring a lawsuit. Both parties are obligated to follow the arbitrator's decision regardless of whether or not they agree with it; this is what is meant by saying the decision is legally binding.

The federal government and many state governments favor arbitration over litigation. The federal policy favoring arbitration is embodied in the Federal Arbitration Act (FAA) of 1925.[2] The FAA requires that courts give deference to all voluntary arbitration agreements in cases governed by federal law. Virtually any dispute can be the subject of arbitration. A voluntary agreement to arbitrate a dispute normally will be enforced by the courts if the agreement does not compel an illegal act or contravene public policy.

ARBITRATION
The settling of a dispute by submitting it to a disinterested third party (other than a court), who renders a decision. The decision may or may not be legally binding.

ARBITRATOR
A disinterested party who, by prior agreement of the parties submitting their dispute to arbitration, has the power to resolve the dispute and (generally) bind the parties.

The Federal Arbitration Act

The Federal Arbitration Act does not establish a set arbitration procedure. The parties themselves must agree on the manner of resolving their dispute. The FAA provides the means for enforcing the arbitration procedure that the parties have established for themselves.

2. 9 U.S.C. Sections 1–15.

INTERNATIONAL PERSPECTIVE

ADR in Japan and China

The United States is not the only country that encourages mediation, arbitration, and other forms of ADR. Japan, for example, has recently authorized the establishment of neutral panels to act as mediators in product liability suits (suits brought by plaintiffs who have allegedly been injured by a seller's

defective product—see Chapter 9). Several industries, including those manufacturing and selling housing materials, automobiles, and appliances, have set up such panels, which follow guidelines published by the Japanese Ministry of International Trade and Industry.

Since the mid-1990s, China has also made it simpler for disputes to be settled through ADR. Under Chinese law, although most disputes can be arbitrated, family matters (such

as those relating to marriage, adoption, and financial support) cannot be submitted for arbitration. Such disputes will continue to be handled by the relevant administrative agencies of the Chinese government.

FOR CRITICAL ANALYSIS

Do you see any reason why certain types of disputes, such as those involving family matters, should not be decided by arbitration?

Section 4 of the FAA allows a party to petition a federal district court for an order compelling arbitration under an agreement to arbitrate a dispute. If the judge is "satisfied that the making of the agreement for arbitration or the failure to comply therewith is not in issue, the court shall make an order directing the parties to proceed with arbitration in accordance with the terms of the agreement."

Under Section 9 of the FAA, the parties to the arbitration may agree to have the arbitrator's decision confirmed in a federal district court. Through confirmation, one party obtains a court order directing another party to comply with the terms of the arbitrator's decision. Section 10 establishes the grounds by which the arbitrator's decision may be set aside (canceled). The grounds for setting aside a decision are limited to misconduct, fraud, corruption, or abuse of power in the arbitration process itself; a court will not review the merits of the dispute or the arbitrator's judgment.

The FAA covers any arbitration clause in a contract that involves interstate commerce. Business activities that have even remote connections or minimal effects on commerce between two or more states are considered to be included. Thus, arbitration agreements involving transactions only slightly connected to the flow of interstate commerce may fall under the FAA, even if the parties, at the time of contracting, did not expect their arbitration agreement to involve interstate commerce.[3]

One of the issues being debated in the early 2000s was whether the FAA applied to employment contracts. Some lower courts had claimed that when Congress passed the FAA it intended to exempt such contracts from coverage. In the following case, the United States Supreme Court addressed this issue.

---

3. *Allied-Bruce Terminix Cos., Inc. v. Dobson,* 513 U.S. 265, 115 S.Ct. 834, 130 L.Ed.2d 753 (1995).

CASE 3.1 Circuit City Stores, Inc. v. Adams

Supreme Court of the United States, 2001.
532 U.S. 105,
121 S.Ct. 1302,
149 L.Ed.2d 234.
http://supct.law.cornell.edu/
supct/index.html[a]

BACKGROUND AND FACTS Saint Clair Adams applied for a job at Circuit City Stores, Inc. Adams signed an employment application that contained a clause requiring the arbitration of any employment-related disputes, including claims under federal and state law. Adams was hired as a sales counselor in a Circuit City store in Santa Rosa, California. Two years later, Adams filed a suit in a California state court against Circuit City, alleging employment discrimination in violation of state law. Circuit City immediately filed a

suit against Adams in a federal district court, asking the court to compel arbitration of Adams's claim. Adams argued that Section 1 of the Federal Arbitration Act (FAA), which excludes from coverage "contracts of employment of seamen, railroad employees, or any other class of workers engaged in foreign or interstate commerce," excluded all employment contracts. The court entered an order in favor of Circuit City. Adams appealed to the U.S. Court of Appeals for the Ninth Circuit, which held that the arbitration agreement between Adams and Circuit City was contained in a "contract of employment" and thus was not subject to the FAA. The court interpreted the language in Section 1 to exclude all employment contracts. Circuit City appealed to the United States Supreme Court.

IN THE WORDS OF THE COURT . . .

Justice *KENNEDY* delivered the opinion of the Court.

* * * *

* * * Most Courts of Appeals conclude the [FAA's] exclusion provision is limited to transportation workers, defined, for instance, as those workers "actually engaged in the movement of goods in interstate commerce." * * *

* * * *

Respondent [Adams], endorsing the reasoning of the Court of Appeals for the Ninth Circuit that the provision excludes all employment contracts, relies on the asserted breadth of the words "contracts of employment of * * * any other class of workers engaged in * * * commerce." * * * [R]espondent contends [Section] 1's interpretation should have a like reach, thus exempting all employment contracts. The two provisions, it is argued, are coterminous; under this view the "involving commerce" provision brings within the FAA's scope all contracts within the Congress' commerce power, and the "engaged in * * * commerce" language in [Section] 1 in turn exempts from the FAA all employment contracts falling within that authority.

This reading of [Section] 1, however, runs into an immediate and, in our view, insurmountable textual obstacle [a problem in interpreting the text of Section 1 of the FAA]. * * * [T]he words "any other class of workers engaged in * * * commerce" constitute a residual phrase, following, in the same sentence, explicit reference to "seamen" and "railroad employees." *Construing the residual phrase to exclude all employment contracts fails to give independent effect to the statute's enumeration of the specific categories of workers which precedes it;* there would be no need for Congress to use the phrases "seamen" and "railroad employees" if those same classes of workers were subsumed within the meaning of the "engaged in * * * commerce" residual clause. The wording of [Section] 1 calls for the application of * * *

a. In the "Search" box, type in "Circuit City Stores" and then click on "Submit." In the result, click on the name of the case to access the opinion. The Legal Information Institute of Cornell Law School in Ithaca, New York, maintains this Web site.

(continued)

CASE 3.1—Continued

the statutory canon that "[w]here general words follow specific words in a statutory enumeration, the general words are construed to embrace only objects similar in nature to those objects enumerated by the preceding specific words." Under this rule of construction the residual clause should be read to give effect to the terms "seamen" and "railroad employees," and should itself be controlled and defined by reference to the enumerated categories of workers which are recited just before it; the interpretation of the clause pressed by respondent fails to produce these results. [Emphasis added.]

* * * *

In sum, the text of the FAA forecloses the construction of [Section] 1 followed by the Court of Appeals * * * *.

DECISION AND REMEDY The United States Supreme Court reversed the judgment of the lower court and remanded the case, holding that the FAA applies to most employment contracts (excluding only those involving interstate transportation workers).

FOR CRITICAL ANALYSIS—Cultural Consideration *What does the decision in this case indicate about the courts' interpretation of the phrases used in statutes?*

State Arbitration Statutes

Virtually all states follow the federal approach to voluntary arbitration. Thirty-four states and the District of Columbia have adopted the Uniform Arbitration Act, which was drafted by the National Conference of Commissioners on Uniform State Laws in 1955. Those states that have not adopted the uniform act nonetheless follow many of the practices specified in it.

Under the uniform act, the basic approach is to give full effect to voluntary agreements to arbitrate disputes between private parties. The act supplements private arbitration agreements by providing explicit procedures and remedies for enforcing arbitration agreements. The uniform act does not, however, dictate the terms of the agreement. Moreover, under both federal and state statutes, the parties are afforded considerable latitude in deciding the subject matter of the arbitration and the methods for conducting the arbitration process. In the absence of a controlling statute, the rights and duties of the parties are established and limited by their agreement.

The Arbitration Process

SUBMISSION
An agreement by two or more parties to refer any disputes they may have under their contract to a disinterested third party, such as an arbitrator, who has the power to render a binding decision.

The arbitration process begins with a *submission*. **Submission** is the act of referring a dispute to an arbitrator. The next step is the *hearing*, in which evidence and arguments are presented to the arbitrator. The process culminates in an *award*, which is the decision of the arbitrator.

The right to appeal the award to a court of law is limited. If the award was made under a voluntary arbitration agreement, a court normally will not set it aside even if it was the result of an erroneous determination of fact or an incorrect interpretation of law by the arbitrator.

This limitation is based on at least two grounds. First, if an award is not treated as final, rather than speeding up the dispute-resolution process, arbitration would merely add one more layer to the process of litigation. Second, the basis of arbitration—the freedom of parties to agree among themselves how to settle a controversy—supports treating an award as final. Having had the opportunity to frame the issues and to set out the manner for resolving the

INTERNATIONAL PERSPECTIVE

International Arbitration

International standards for the recognition of arbitration agreements and awards were set by the United Nations Convention on the Recognition and Enforcement of Foreign Arbitral Awards,[a] which has been

a. June 10, 1958, 21 U.S.T. 2517 (also known as the New York Convention).

signed by 126 countries, including the United States. Article V(2) of the convention creates an exception to enforcement of arbitration clauses that are "contrary to the public policy" of the relevant country. Thus, the resolution of a case will depend on the strength of a public policy in a given nation. International organizations that handle arbitration matters include the United Nations Commission on International Trade Laws, the

London Court of International Arbitration, the Euro-Arab Chamber of Commerce, the International Chamber of Commerce in Paris, and the International Trademark Association.

FOR CRITICAL ANALYSIS

Should businesspersons evaluate the policies of different countries before deciding where to arbitrate their disputes?

dispute, one party should not complain if the result was not what that party had hoped it would be.

Submission The parties may agree to submit questions of fact, questions of law, or both to the arbitrator. The parties may even agree to leave the interpretation of the arbitration agreement to the arbitrator. The submission typically states the identities of the parties, the nature of the dispute to be resolved, the monetary amounts involved in the controversy, the place at which the arbitration is to take place, and the intention of the parties to be bound by the arbitrator's award. Exhibit 3–1 on the following page contains a sample submission form.

Most states require that an agreement to submit a dispute to arbitration be in writing. Moreover, because the goal of arbitration is speed and efficiency in resolving controversies, most states require that matters be submitted within a definite period of time, generally six months from the date on which the dispute arises.

The Hearing Because the parties are free to construct the method by which they want their dispute resolved, they must state the issues that will be submitted and the powers that the arbitrator will exercise. The arbitrator may be given power at the outset of the process to establish rules that will govern the proceedings. Typically, these rules are much less restrictive than those governing formal litigation. Regardless of who establishes the rules, the arbitrator will apply them during the course of the hearing.

Restrictions on the kind of evidence and the manner in which it is presented may be less rigid in arbitration, partly because the arbitrator is likely to be an expert in the subject matter involved in the controversy. Restrictions may also be less stringent because there is less fear that the arbitrator will be swayed by improper evidence. In contrast, evidence in a jury trial must sometimes be presented twice: once to the judge, outside the presence of the jury, to determine

EXHIBIT 3–1   SAMPLE SUBMISSION FORM

American Arbitration Association

Submission to Dispute Resolution

Date: _____

The named parties hereby submit the following dispute for resolution under the _____
_____ Rules* of the American Arbitration Association:

Procedure Selected: ☐ Binding arbitration   ☐ Mediation settlement

                          ☐ Other _____
                                              (Describe)

THE NATURE OF THE DISPUTE

THE CLAIM OR RELIEF SOUGHT (the Amount, if Any):

TYPE OF BUSINESS: Claimant _____ Respondent _____

PLACE OF HEARING: _____

We agree that, if binding arbitration is selected, we will abide by and perform any award rendered hereunder and that a judgment may be entered on the award.

To Be Completed by the Parties

Name of Party	Name of Party
Address	Address
City, State, and ZIP Code	City, State, and ZIP Code
( ) _____ Telephone Fax	( ) _____ Telephone Fax
Signature†	Signature†
Name of Representative for Party	Name of Representative for Party
Name of Firm (if Applicable)	Name of Firm (if Applicable)
Representative's Address	Representative's Address
City, State, and ZIP Code	City, State, and ZIP Code
( ) _____ Telephone Fax	( ) _____ Telephone Fax
Signature†	Signature†

Please file three copies with the AAA.

* *If you have a question as to which rules apply, please contact the AAA.*
† *Signatures of all parties are required for arbitration.*
1997-W
© 2002 American Arbitration Association. All Rights Reserved.

if the evidence may be heard by the jury, and—depending on the judge's ruling—again, to the jury.

In the typical hearing format, the parties begin as they would at trial by presenting opening arguments to the arbitrator and stating what remedies should or should not be granted. After the opening statements have been made, evidence is presented. Witnesses may be called and examined by both sides. After all the evidence has been presented, the parties give their closing arguments. On completion of the closing arguments, the arbitrator closes the hearing.

The Award After each side has had an opportunity to present evidence and to argue its case, the arbitrator reaches a decision. The final decision of the arbitrator is called an **award,** even if no money is conferred on a party as a result of the proceedings. Under most statutes, the arbitrator must render an award within thirty days of the close of the hearing.

AWARD
In the context of arbitration, the arbitrator's decision. In the context of litigation, the amount of money awarded to a plaintiff in a civil lawsuit as damages.

In most states, the award need not state the arbitrator's findings regarding factual questions in the case. Nor must the award state the conclusions that the arbitrator reached on any questions of law that may have been presented. All that is required for the award to be valid is that it completely resolve the controversy.

Most states do, however, require that the award be in writing, regardless of whether any conclusions of law or findings of fact are included. If the arbitrator does state his or her legal conclusions and factual findings, a letter or an opinion will be drafted containing the basis for the award. Even when there is no statutory requirement that the arbitrator state the factual and legal basis for the award, the parties may impose the requirement in their submission or in their predispute agreement to arbitrate.

Enforcement of Agreements to Submit to Arbitration

The role of the courts in the arbitration process is limited. One important role is played at the prearbitration stage. A court may be called on to order one party to an arbitration agreement to submit to arbitration under the terms of the agreement. The court in this role is essentially interpreting a contract. The court must determine to what the parties have committed themselves before ordering that they submit to arbitration.

The Issue of Arbitrability When a dispute arises as to whether the parties have agreed in an arbitration clause to submit a particular matter to arbitration, one party may file suit to compel arbitration. The court before which the suit is brought will not decide the basic controversy but must rule on the issue of arbitrability—that is, whether the matter is one that must be resolved through arbitration. If the court finds that the subject in controversy is covered by the agreement to arbitrate, a party may be compelled to arbitrate the dispute involuntarily.

REMEMBER Litigation—even of a dispute over whether a particular matter should be submitted to arbitration—can be time consuming and expensive.

Although the parties may agree to submit the issue of arbitrability to an arbitrator, the agreement must be explicit; a court will never *infer* an agreement to arbitrate. Unless a court finds an *explicit* agreement to have the arbitrator decide whether a dispute is arbitrable, the court will decide the issue. This is an important initial determination, because no party will be ordered to submit to arbitration unless the court is convinced that the party has consented to do so.

A payroll manager looks over a job application with a person attending a Boston job fair in January 2003. If a job applicant signs an application form that requires him or her to arbitrate any future dispute with the employer if the applicant is hired, is the agreement enforceable?

Compulsory Arbitration Are violations of rights granted by statutes appropriate subjects for arbitration? For example, should a court order the arbitration of a claim involving an alleged violation of a federal statute protecting an employee from employment discrimination?

In one important case, the United States Supreme Court held that a claim brought under the Age Discrimination in Employment Act (ADEA) of 1967 (discussed in Chapter 17) could be subject to compulsory arbitration. The plaintiff in the case, Robert Gilmer, had been discharged from his employment at the age of sixty-two. Gilmer sued his employer, claiming that he was a victim of age discrimination. The employer argued that Gilmer had to submit the dispute to arbitration because he had agreed, as part of a required registration application to be a securities representative with the New York Stock Exchange, to arbitrate "any dispute, claim, or controversy" relating to his employment. The Supreme Court held that Gilmer, by agreeing to arbitrate any dispute, had waived his right to sue.[4] (For a further discussion of compulsory arbitration in the employment context, see this chapter's *Inside the Legal Environment* feature on page 84.)

Compulsory arbitration agreements often spell out the rules for a mandatory proceeding. For example, an agreement may address in detail the amount and payment of filing fees and other expenses. Some courts have overturned provisions in employment-related agreements that require the parties to split the costs on the basis of an individual worker's ability to pay. The court in the following case took this reasoning a step further.

---

4. *Gilmer v. Interstate/Johnson Lane Corp.,* 500 U.S. 20, 111 S.Ct. 1647, 114 L.Ed.2d 26 (1991).

CASE 3.2   Morrison v. Circuit City Stores, Inc.

United States Court of Appeals,
Sixth Circuit, 2003.
317 F.3d 646.
**http://pacer.ca6.uscourts.gov/
opinions/main.php**[a]

BACKGROUND AND FACTS Lillian Morrison, an African American woman with a bachelor's degree in engineering from the U.S. Air Force Academy and a master's degree in administration from Central Michigan University, applied for a managerial position at a Circuit City store in Cincinnati, Ohio. As part of the job application, Morrison was required to sign an agreement that mandated arbitration for any employment-related dispute. The employee was to pay one-half of the costs of the arbitration, unless the arbitrator decided otherwise.

An employee's share might be limited to either $500 or 3 percent of her most recent annual salary, but all charges were to be paid within ninety days of the issuance of an award. Morrison was hired in 1995, but two years later, she was terminated. She filed a suit in an Ohio state court against Circuit City, alleging in part that the employer had discriminated against her on the basis of her race and gender.[b] The case was moved to a federal district court, which ordered the parties to proceed to arbitration. Morrison appealed to the U.S. Court of Appeals for the Sixth Circuit, arguing in part that the cost-splitting provision of the arbitration agreement was unenforceable. Meanwhile, the arbitration proceeded, and as part of the award, the arbitrator did not require Morrison to pay any of the costs.

---

a. This a page within the Web site of the U.S. Court of Appeals for the Sixth Circuit. In the left-hand column, click on "Opinions Search." In the "Short Title contains" box, type "Morrison" and click "Submit Query." In the "Opinion" box corresponding to the name of the case, click on the number to access the opinion.
b. Employment discrimination is discussed in detail in Chapter 17.

CASE 3.2—Continued

IN THE WORDS
OF THE COURT . . .

KAREN NELSON MOORE, Circuit Judge.

* * * *

* * * Circuit City argues that Morrison could have avoided having to pay half of the cost of the arbitration * * * if she could have arranged to pay the greater of $500 or 3 percent of her annual salary (in this case, 3 percent of $54,060, or $1,622) within ninety days of the arbitrator's award. * * *

In the abstract, this sum may not appear prohibitive, but it must be considered from the vantage point of the potential litigant in a case such as this. Recently terminated, the potential litigant must continue to pay for housing, utilities, transportation, food, and the other necessities of life in contemporary society despite losing her primary, and most likely only, source of income. Unless she is exceedingly fortunate, the potential litigant will experience at least a brief period of unemployment. Turning to the arbitration agreement with her employer, the potential litigant finds that * * * she will be obligated to pay half the costs of any arbitration which she initiates.

Minimal research will reveal that the potential costs of arbitrating the dispute easily reach thousands, if not tens of thousands, of dollars, far exceeding the costs that a plaintiff would incur in court. Courts charge plaintiffs initial filing fees, but they do not charge extra for in-person hearings, discovery requests, routine motions, or written decisions, costs that are all common in the world of private arbitrators. * * * Based on these considerations, along with the evidence that Morrison presented regarding her previous salary, we conclude that *the default cost-splitting rule in the Circuit City arbitration agreement would deter a substantial percentage of potential litigants from bringing their claims in the arbitral forum.* [Emphasis added.]

The provision reducing the (former) employee's exposure to the greater of $500 or 3 percent of her annual compensation presents a closer issue. However, a potential litigant considering arbitration would still have to arrange to pay 3 percent of her most recent salary, in this case, $1,622, within a three-month period, or risk incurring her full half of the costs * * * . Faced with this choice—which really boils down to risking one's scarce resources in the hopes of an uncertain benefit—it appears to us that a substantial number of similarly situated persons would be deterred from seeking to vindicate their statutory rights under these circumstances.

Based on this reasoning, we hold that Morrison has satisfied her burden in the present case in demonstrating that * * * the cost-splitting provision in the agreement was unenforceable with respect to her claims.

DECISION AND REMEDY The U.S. Court of Appeals for the Sixth Circuit held that the cost-splitting provision in Circuit City's mandatory arbitration agreement was unenforceable because, regardless of an individual employee's ability to pay those costs, the provision would deter "similarly situated individuals" from exercising their rights.[c]

FOR CRITICAL ANALYSIS—Economic Consideration *Does the court's ruling in this case mean that cost-splitting provisions in compulsory arbitration agreements are always unenforceable?*

c. The court also concluded that the provision could be severed from the agreement, which meant that the rest of the agreement could be enforced. Because the arbitration in this case had already occurred, and Morrison had not been required to pay any share of the costs, the court affirmed the lower court's order compelling arbitration, "on these different grounds."

INSIDE THE LEGAL ENVIRONMENT

Mandatory Arbitration—A Problematic Issue for Managers

Arbitration is normally simpler, speedier, and less costly than litigation. For that reason, business owners and managers today often include arbitration clauses in their contracts, including employment contracts. What happens, though, if a job candidate whom you wish to hire (or an existing employee whose contract is being renewed) objects to one or more of the provisions in an arbitration clause? If you insist that signing the agreement to arbitrate future disputes is a mandatory condition of employment, will such a clause be enforceable?

What the Courts Say

As mentioned elsewhere in this chapter, the United States Supreme Court has consistently taken the position that because the Federal Arbitration Act (FAA) favors the arbitration of disputes, arbitration clauses in employment contracts should generally be enforced. Nonetheless, some courts have

held that arbitration clauses in employment contracts should not be enforced if they are too one sided and unfair to the employee.

In one case, for example, a court held that an employee did not have to submit her claim to arbitration because "the rules were so one sided that their only possible purpose is to undermine the neutrality of the proceeding." According to the court, the biased rules created "a sham system unworthy even of the name of arbitration" in violation of the parties' contract to arbitrate.[a]

In another case, the U.S. Court of Appeals for the Ninth Circuit refused to enforce an arbitration clause on the ground that the agreement was *unconscionable*— so one sided and unfair as to be unenforceable under "ordinary principles of state contract law."[b] In *Morrison v. Circuit City*

---

a. *Hooters of America, Inc. v. Phillips,* 173 F.3d 933 (4th Cir. 1999).
b. *Circuit City Stores, Inc. v. Adams,* 279 F.3d 889 (9th Cir. 2002). (This was the Ninth Circuit's decision, on remand, after the United States Supreme Court reviewed the case—see Case 3.1.)

Stores, Inc. (see Case 3.2), another federal appellate court refused to enforce a provision in a mandatory arbitration agreement on the ground that it was unfair to the employee.

The Need for Caution

Although the United States Supreme Court has made it clear that arbitration clauses in employment contracts are enforceable under the FAA, business owners and managers would be wise to exercise caution when drafting such clauses. It is especially important to make sure that the terms of the agreement are not so one sided that a court could declare the entire agreement unconscionable.

FOR CRITICAL ANALYSIS

Why might victims of employment discrimination prefer to litigate their claims in a judicial forum rather than having them arbitrated, even assuming that arbitration proceedings would be unbiased and would not violate due process rights?

Setting Aside an Arbitration Award

After the arbitration has been concluded, the losing party may appeal the arbitrator's award to a court, or the winning party may seek a court order compelling the other party to comply with the award. The scope of review in either situation is much more restricted than in an appellate court's review of a trial court decision. The court does not look at the merits of the underlying dispute, and the court will not add to or subtract from the remedies provided by the award. The court's role is limited to determining whether there exists a valid award. If so, the court will order the parties to comply with the terms. The general view is that because the parties were free to frame the issues and set the powers of the arbitrator at the outset, they cannot complain about the result.

Fact Findings and Legal Conclusions The arbitrator's fact findings and legal conclusions are normally final. That the arbitrator may have erred in a ruling during the hearing or made an erroneous fact finding is normally no basis for setting aside an award: the parties agreed that the arbitrator would be the judge of the facts. Similarly, no matter how obviously the arbitrator was mistaken in a conclusion of law, the award is normally nonetheless binding: the parties agreed to accept the arbitrator's interpretation of the law. A court will not look at the merits of the dispute, the sufficiency of the evidence presented, or the arbitrator's reasoning in reaching a particular decision.

This approach is consistent with the underlying view of all voluntary arbitration—that its basis is really contract law. If the parties freely contract with one another, courts will not interfere simply because one side feels that it received a bad bargain. Any party challenging an award must face the presumption that a final award is valid.

Public Policy and Illegality In keeping with contract law principles, no award will be enforced if compliance with the award would result in the commission of a crime or would conflict with **public policy**—a government policy based on widely held societal values and (usually) expressed or implied in laws or regulations. A court will not overturn an award, however, simply because the arbitrator was called on to resolve a dispute involving a matter of significant public concern.[5] For an award to be set aside, it must call for some action on the part of the parties that would conflict with or in some way undermine public policy.[6]

PUBLIC POLICY
A government policy based on widely held societal values and (usually) expressed or implied in laws or regulations.

Defects in the Arbitration Process There are some bases for setting aside an award when there is a defect in the arbitration process. These bases are typified by those set forth in the Federal Arbitration Act. Section 10 of the act provides four grounds on which an arbitration award may be set aside:

1. The award was the result of corruption, fraud, or other "undue means."
2. The arbitrator exhibited bias or corruption.
3. The arbitrator refused to postpone the hearing despite sufficient cause, refused to hear evidence pertinent and material to the dispute, or otherwise acted to substantially prejudice the rights of one of the parties.
4. The arbitrator exceeded his or her powers or failed to use them to make a mutual, final, and definite award.

The first three bases for setting aside the award include actions or decisions that are more than simply mistakes in judgment. Each requires some "bad faith" on the part of the arbitrator. Bad faith actions or decisions are ones that affect the integrity of the arbitration process. The honesty and impartiality, rather than the judgment, of the arbitrator are called into question.

---

5. See, for example, *Faherty v. Faherty,* 97 N.J. 99, 477 A.2d 1257 (1984).
6. See, for example, *Meehan v. Nassau Community College,* 647 N.Y.S.2d 865 (App.Div. 2 Dept. 1996).

Sometimes it is difficult to make the distinction between honest mistakes in judgment and actions or decisions made in bad faith. A bribe is clearly the kind of "undue means" included in the first basis for setting aside an award. Letting only one side argue its case is likewise a clear violation of the second basis.

Meetings between the arbitrator and one party outside the presence of the other party also taint the arbitration process. Although meetings might not involve the kind of corruption that results from taking a bribe, they do affect the integrity of the process; the third basis for setting aside an award is meant to protect against this.

Not every refusal by an arbitrator to admit certain evidence is grounds for setting aside an award under the third basis. As noted, to provide a basis for overturning an award, the arbitrator's decision must be more than an error in judgment, no matter how obviously incorrect that judgment might appear to another observer. The decision must be so obviously wrong or unfair as to imply bias or corruption. Otherwise, the decision normally cannot be a basis for setting aside an award.

The fourth basis for setting aside an award is that the arbitrator exceeded his or her powers in arbitrating the dispute. This issue involves the question of arbitrability. An arbitrator exceeds his or her powers and authority by attempting to resolve an issue that is not covered by the agreement to submit to arbitration.

In the following case, a party to an arbitration proceeding asked a court to set aside the award.

CASE 3.3 · Major League Baseball Players Association v. Garvey

Supreme Court of the United States, 2001.
532 U.S. 1015,
121 S.Ct. 1724,
149 L.Ed.2d 740.
http://supct.law.cornell.
edu/supct/index.php [a]

BACKGROUND AND FACTS In 1986, 1987, and 1988, the Major League Baseball Players Association complained that the Major League Baseball Clubs had engaged in collusion to underpay some of the players. The grievance was submitted to arbitration before a panel chaired by Thomas Roberts. During a hearing in 1986, Ballard Smith, the president of the San Diego Padres, testified that there had been no collusion. Roberts's panel rejected this testimony as false. The Association and the Clubs entered into a settlement agreement, under which the Clubs set up a fund of $280 million to be distributed to players who suffered

losses due to the collusion and the Association established a framework for evaluating each player's claim. A player could challenge the Association's recommendation in binding arbitration. Steve Garvey, who had played for the Padres between 1983 and 1987 under a contract, filed a claim for damages, alleging that the Padres would have extended his contract for the 1988 and 1989 seasons but for the collusion. Roberts, the arbitrator in Garvey's case, denied the claim. Roberts cited Smith's testimony in the 1986 hearing that the Padres were not interested in extending Garvey's contract. Roberts rejected Smith's admission, in a 1996 letter, that he had not told the truth during those hearings and that he had made Garvey an offer that was withdrawn due to the collusion. Garvey filed a suit in a federal district court against Roberts and the Association to have the arbitrator's award set aside. The court ruled in the defendants' favor. Garvey appealed to the U.S. Court of

---

a. In the "Search" box, type "Garvey." In the pull-down menu, select "all current and historic decisions" and click on "submit." In the result, click on the first item that includes the name of the case to access the opinion. The Legal Information Institute of Cornell Law School in Ithaca, New York, maintains this Web site.

CASE 3.3—Continued

Appeals for the Ninth Circuit, which reversed the ruling of the lower court and remanded the case with direc-

tions to set aside the arbitrator's award. The defendants appealed to the United States Supreme Court.

IN THE WORDS
OF THE COURT . . .

PER CURIAM [by the whole court].

* * * *

* * * Courts are not authorized to review the arbitrator's decision on the merits despite allegations that the decision rests on factual errors or misinterprets the parties' agreement. * * * [I]f an arbitrator is even arguably construing or applying the contract and acting within the scope of his authority, the fact that a court is convinced he committed serious error does not suffice to overturn his decision. It is only when the arbitrator strays from interpretation and application of the agreement and effectively dispenses his own brand of * * * justice that his decision may be unenforceable. * * *

* * * Even in the very rare instances when an arbitrator's procedural aberrations rise to the level of affirmative misconduct, as a rule the court must not foreclose further proceedings by settling the merits according to its own judgment of the appropriate result. That step * * * would improperly substitute a judicial determination for the arbitrator's decision that the parties bargained for in their agreement. Instead, the court should simply vacate the award, thus leaving open the possibility of further proceedings if they are permitted under the terms of the agreement.

To be sure, the Court of Appeals here recited these principles, but its application of them is nothing short of baffling. The substance of the Court's discussion reveals that it overturned the arbitrator's decision because it disagreed with the arbitrator's factual findings, particularly those with respect to credibility. The Court of Appeals, it appears, would have credited Smith's 1996 letter, and found the arbitrator's refusal to do so at worst irrational and at best bizarre. *But even serious error on the arbitrator's part does not justify overturning his decision, where, as here, he is construing a contract and acting within the scope of his authority.* [Emphasis added.]

* * * [The court] both rejected the arbitrator's findings and went further, resolving the merits of the parties' dispute based on the court's assessment of the record before the arbitrator. For that reason, the court found further arbitration proceedings inappropriate. But again, established law ordinarily precludes a court from resolving the merits of the parties' dispute on the basis of its own factual determinations, no matter how erroneous the arbitrator's decision. Even when the arbitrator's award may properly be vacated, the appropriate remedy is to remand the case for further arbitration proceedings. * * * The Court of Appeals usurped the arbitrator's role by resolving the dispute and barring further proceedings.

DECISION AND REMEDY The United States Supreme Court reversed the judgment of the lower court and remanded the case for further proceedings. The Court held that the appellate court "usurped the arbitrator's role" when the court rejected the arbitrator's findings and resolved the dispute on the basis of its own assessment of the record.

FOR CRITICAL ANALYSIS—Ethical Consideration *The Supreme Court noted that "established law ordinarily precludes a court from resolving the merits of the parties' dispute on the basis of its own factual determinations, no matter how erroneous the arbitrator's decision." Why do courts allow erroneous arbitrators' decisions to stand?*

Waiver Although a defect in the arbitration process is sufficient grounds for setting aside an award, a party sometimes forfeits the right to challenge an award by failing to object to the defect in a timely manner. The party must object when he or she learns of the problem. After making the objection, the party can still proceed with the arbitration process and still challenge the award in court after the arbitration proceedings have concluded. If, however, a party makes no objection and proceeds with the arbitration process, then a later court challenge to the award may be denied on the ground that the party *waived* the right to challenge the award on the basis of the defect.

Frequently, a waiver occurs when a party fails to object that an arbitrator is exceeding his or her powers in resolving a dispute because the subject matter is not arbitrable or because the party did not agree to arbitrate the dispute. The question of arbitrability is one for the courts to decide. If a party does not object on this ground at the first demand for arbitration, however, a court may consider the objection waived.

Conflicts of Law Parties are afforded wide latitude in establishing the manner in which their disputes will be resolved. Nevertheless, an agreement to arbitrate may be governed by the Federal Arbitration Act (FAA) or one of the many state arbitration acts, even though the parties do not refer to a statute in their agreement. Recall that the FAA covers any arbitration clause in a contract that involves interstate commerce. Frequently, however, transactions involving interstate commerce also have substantial connections to particular states, which may in turn have their own arbitration acts. In such situations, unless the FAA and state arbitration law are nearly identical, the acts may conflict. How are these conflicts to be resolved?

As a general principle, the supremacy clause and the commerce clause of the U.S. Constitution are the bases for giving federal law preeminence; when there is a conflict, state law is preempted by federal law. Thus, in cases of arbitration, the strong federal policy favoring arbitration can override a state's laws that might be more favorable to normal litigation.

Choice of Law Notwithstanding federal preemption of conflicting state laws, the Federal Arbitration Act has been interpreted as allowing the parties to choose a particular state law to govern their arbitration agreement. The parties may choose to have the laws of a specific state govern their agreement by including in the agreement a *choice-of-law clause*. The FAA does not mandate any particular set of rules that parties must follow in arbitration; the parties are free to agree on the manner best suited to their needs. Consistent with this view that arbitration is at heart a contractual matter between private parties, the United States Supreme Court has upheld arbitration agreements containing choice-of-law provisions.

Disadvantages of Arbitration

Arbitration has some disadvantages. The result in any particular dispute can be unpredictable, in part because arbitrators do not need to conform to precedent in any previous cases in rendering their decisions. Unlike judges, arbitrators do not have to issue written opinions or facilitate a participant's appeal to a court. Arbitrators must decide disputes according to whatever rules have been provided by the parties, regardless of how unfair those rules may be. In some cases, arbitration can be nearly as expensive as litigation. In part, this is because both sides must prepare their cases for presentation before a third party decision maker, just as they would have to do to appear in court. Discovery is usually not available in arbitration, however, which means that during the hearing the parties must take the time to question witnesses whom, in a lawsuit, they would not need to call.[7]

THE INTEGRATION OF ADR AND FORMAL COURT PROCEDURES

Because of the congestion within the judicial system, many jurisdictions at both the state and federal levels are integrating alternative dispute resolution into the formal legal process. Utilizing methods such as arbitration and mediation within the traditional framework may relieve the logjams afflicting most of the nation's court systems.

Court-Annexed ADR

Today, many courts require that parties attempt to settle their differences through some form of ADR before proceeding to trial. Less than 10 percent of the cases referred for arbitration ever go to trial. About half of all federal courts have now adopted formal rules regarding the use of ADR, and many other courts without such rules use ADR procedures.

Most states have adopted programs that allow them to refer certain types of cases for negotiation, mediation, or arbitration. Typically—as in California and Hawaii—court systems have adopted mandatory mediation or nonbinding arbitration programs for certain types of disputes, usually involving less than a specified threshold dollar amount.[8] Only if the parties fail to reach an agreement, or if one of the parties disagrees with the decision of a third party mediating or arbitrating the dispute, will the case be heard by a court.

Court-annexed arbitration differs significantly from the voluntary arbitration process discussed previously. There are some disputes that courts will not allow to go to arbitration. Most states, for example, do not allow court-annexed arbitration in disputes involving title to real estate or in cases in which a court's equity powers are involved.

A Fundamental Difference The fundamental difference between voluntary arbitration and court-annexed arbitration is the finality and reviewability of the award. With respect to court-annexed arbitration, either party may reject the award for any reason. In the event that one of the parties does reject the award, the case will proceed to trial, and the court will hear the case *de novo*—that is, the court will reconsider all the evidence and legal questions as though no arbitration had occurred.

Everyone who has a recognizable cause of action or against whom such an action is brought is entitled to have the issue decided in a court of law. Because court-annexed arbitration is not voluntary, there must be some safeguard

---

7. One notable dispute concerning computer chip technology lasted more than seven years and cost the participants more than $100 million. See *Advanced Micro Devices, Inc. v. Intel Corp.,* 9 Cal.4th 362, 885 P.2d 994, 36 Cal.Rptr.2d 581 (1994).

8. Hawaii, for example, has a program of mandatory, nonbinding arbitration for disputes involving less than $150,000.

against using it in a way that denies an individual his or her day in court. This safeguard is provided by permitting either side to reject the award regardless of the reason for so doing.

The party rejecting the award may be penalized, however. Many statutes providing for court-annexed arbitration impose court costs and fees on a party who rejects an arbitration award but does not improve his or her position by going to trial. Thus, for example, if a party rejects an arbitration award, and the award turns out to be more favorable to that party than the subsequent jury verdict, the party may be compelled to pay the costs of the arbitration or some fee for the costs of the trial.

The Role of the Arbitrator Notwithstanding the differences between voluntary and court-annexed arbitration, the role of the arbitrator is essentially the same in both types of proceedings. The arbitrator determines issues of both fact and law. The arbitrator also makes all decisions concerning applications of the rules of procedure and evidence during the hearing.

Discovery of Evidence In court-annexed arbitration, discovery of evidence occurs before the hearing. After the hearing has commenced, a party seeking to discover new evidence must usually secure approval from the court that mandated the arbitration. This is intended to prevent the parties from using arbitration as a means of previewing each other's cases and then rejecting the arbitrator's award.

Rules of Evidence Regarding the rules of evidence, there are differences among the states. Most states impose the same rules of evidence on an arbitration hearing as on a trial. Other states, such as New Jersey, allow all evidence relevant to the dispute regardless of whether the evidence would be admissible at trial. Still other jurisdictions, such as Washington, leave it to the arbitrator to decide what evidence is admissible.

Waiver Once a court directs that a dispute is to be submitted to court-annexed arbitration, the parties must proceed to arbitration. As noted above, either side may reject the award that results from the arbitration for any reason. If a party fails to appear at or participate in the arbitration proceeding as directed by the court, however, that failure constitutes a waiver of the right to reject the award.

Court-Related Mediation

Mediation is proving to be more popular than arbitration as a court-related method of ADR. No federal court has adopted an arbitration program since 1991, while mediation programs continue to increase in number in both federal and state courts. Today, more court systems offer or require mediation, rather than arbitration, as an alternative to litigation.

Mediation is often used in disputes relating to employment law, environmental law, product liability, and franchises. One of the most important business advantages of mediation is its lower cost, which can be 25 percent (or less) of the expense of litigation. Another advantage is the speed with which a dispute can go through mediation (possibly one or two days) compared with arbitration (possibly months) or litigation (potentially years).

Part of the popularity of mediation is that its goal, unlike that of litigation and some other forms of ADR, is for opponents to work out a resolution that benefits both sides. The rate of participants' satisfaction with the outcomes in mediated disputes is high. In New Hampshire, for example, where mediation is mandatory for all civil cases in most state trial courts, as many as 70 percent of the participants report satisfaction with the results.

Summary Jury Trials

Another means by which the courts have integrated alternative dispute resolution methods into the traditional court process is through the use of summary jury trials. A **summary jury trial** is a mock trial that occurs in a courtroom before a judge and jury. Evidence is presented in an abbreviated form, along with each side's major contentions. The jury then presents a verdict.

The fundamental difference between a traditional trial and a summary jury trial is that in the latter, the jury's verdict is only advisory. The goal of a summary jury trial is to give each side an idea of how it would fare in a full-blown jury trial with a more elaborate and detailed presentation of evidence and arguments. At the end of the summary jury trial, the presiding judge normally meets with the parties and encourages them to settle their dispute without going through a standard jury trial.

SUMMARY JURY TRIAL
A method of settling disputes in which a trial is held, but the jury's verdict is not binding. The verdict acts only as a guide to both sides in reaching an agreement during the mandatory negotiations that immediately follow the summary jury trial.

ADR and Mass Torts

A *tort* is a civil wrong that does not arise from a breach of contract. (Torts are discussed in detail in Chapter 8. Breach of contract is discussed in Chapter 12.) *Mass tort* is the term applied to civil lawsuits that share such features as scientific or technological complexity and a large number of participants. Such cases often feature a high degree of emotional involvement on the part of the claimants, who may suffer from severe or life-threatening injuries, and on the part of the defendants, whose financial existence may be at stake. Examples of mass torts include litigation involving Agent Orange, the Dalkon Shield, the prescription drug DES, heart valves, and asbestos.

Since the 1990s, an explosion in the number of mass torts has been overwhelming our civil justice system. In attempts to clear the courts, some judges in mass tort cases turn to methods of alternative dispute resolution, including mediation, arbitration, mini-trials, and summary jury trials. ADR may be used to assess the validity or the value of the claims or to sort out or resolve the scientific, technological, or medical issues involved. ADR may be utilized to settle large numbers of claims in a speedy, efficient, cost-effective manner. Once a settlement is reached, a neutral third party may coordinate payments to claimants. There may even be provision for an ADR appeals process.

ADR FORUMS AND SERVICES

Services facilitating dispute resolution outside the courtroom are provided by both government agencies and private organizations.

Nonprofit Organizations

The major source of private arbitration services is the American Arbitration Association (AAA). Most of the largest law firms in the nation are members of this association. Founded in 1926, the AAA now settles more than 200,000 disputes a year and has offices in every state. Cases brought before the AAA are heard by an expert or a panel of experts—of whom about half are usually lawyers—in the area relating to the dispute. To cover its costs, this nonprofit organization charges a fee, paid by the party filing the claim. In addition, each party to the dispute pays a price for each hearing day, as well as a special additional fee in cases involving personal injuries or property loss.

In addition to the AAA, hundreds of other state and local nonprofit organizations provide arbitration services. For example, the Arbitration Association of Florida provides ADR services in that state. The Better Business Bureau offers ADR programs to aid in the resolution of certain types of disagreements. Many industries—including the insurance, automobile, and securities industries—also now have mediation or arbitration programs to facilitate timely and inexpensive settlement of claims.

For-Profit Organizations

Those who seek to settle their disputes quickly can turn to private, for-profit organizations to act as mediators or arbitrators. The leading firm in this private system of justice is JAMS/Endispute, which is based in Santa Ana, California. The private system of justice includes hundreds of firms throughout the country offering dispute-resolution services by hired judges. Procedures in these private courts are fashioned to meet the desires of the clients seeking their services. For example, the parties might decide on the date of the hearing, the presiding judge, whether the judge's decision will be legally binding, and the site of the hearing—which could be a conference room, a law school office, or a leased courtroom. The judges may follow procedures similar to those of the federal courts and use comparable rules. Each party to the dispute may pay a filing fee and a designated fee for a half-day hearing session or a special, one-hour settlement conference.

There are also international organizations, such as the International Chamber of Commerce, that provide forums for the arbitration of disputes between parties to international contracts. These organizations, as well as some of the advantages and disadvantages of arbitrating disputes in the international context, will be discussed in Chapter 24.

Online Forums

ONLINE DISPUTE RESOLUTION (ODR)
The resolution of disputes with the assistance of organizations that offer dispute-resolution services via the Internet.

An increasing number of companies and organizations are offering dispute-resolution services using the Internet. The settlement of disputes in these online forums is known as **online dispute resolution (ODR)**. To date, the disputes resolved in these forums have most commonly involved disagreements over the rights to domain names (Web site addresses—see Chapter 10) and disagreements over the quality of goods sold via the Internet, including goods sold through Internet auction sites.

Currently, ODR may be best for resolving small- to medium-sized business liability claims, which may not be worth the expense of litigation or traditional methods of alternative dispute resolution. Rules being developed in online forums, however, may ultimately become a code of conduct for everyone who does business in cyberspace. Most online forums do not automatically apply the law of any specific jurisdiction. Instead, results are often based on general, more universal legal principles. As with offline methods of dispute resolution, any party may appeal to a court at any time.

Negotiation and Mediation Services The online negotiation of a dispute is generally simpler and more practical than litigation. Typically, one party files a complaint, and the other party is notified by e-mail. Password-protected access is possible twenty-four hours a day, seven days a week. Fees are sometimes nominal and otherwise low (often 2 to 4 percent, or less, of the disputed amount).

CyberSettle.com, Inc., clickNsettle.com, and other Web-based firms offer online forums for negotiating monetary settlements. The parties to a dispute may agree to submit offers; if the offers fall within a previously agreed-on range, they will end the dispute, and the parties will split the difference. Special software keeps secret any offers that are not within the range. If there is no agreed-on range, typically an offer includes a deadline within which the other party must respond before the offer expires. The parties can drop the negotiations at any time.

Mediation providers are also resolving disputes online. SquareTrade, one of the mediation providers that has been used by eBay, the online auction site, mediates disputes involving $100 or more between eBay customers, currently for no charge. SquareTrade, which also resolves disputes among other parties, uses Web-based software that walks participants through a five-step e-resolution process. Negotiation between the parties occurs on a secure page within SquareTrade's Web site. If the parties prefer, they may consult a mediator. The entire process takes as little as ten to fourteen days, and there is no fee unless the parties use a mediator.

Arbitration Programs A number of organizations and companies offer online arbitration programs. The Internet Corporation for Assigned Names and Numbers (ICANN), a nonprofit corporation set up by the federal government to oversee the distribution of domain names, has issued special rules for the resolution of domain name disputes.[9] ICANN has also authorized several organizations to arbitrate domain name disputes in accordance with its rules. Additionally, the American Arbitration Association now provides technology-based arbitration services as well.

Resolution Forum, Inc. (RFI), a nonprofit organization associated with the Center for Legal Responsibility at South Texas College of Law, offers arbitration services through its CAN-WIN conferencing system. Using standard browser software and an RFI password, the parties to a dispute access an online conference room. When multiple parties are involved, private communications and breakout sessions are possible via private messaging facilities. RFI also offers mediation services.

The Virtual Magistrate Project (VMAG) is affiliated with the American Arbitration Association, Chicago-Kent College of Law, Cyberspace Law Institute, National Center for Automated Information Research, and other organizations. VMAG offers arbitration for disputes involving users of online systems; victims of wrongful messages, postings, and files; and system operators subject to complaints or similar demands. VMAG also arbitrates intellectual property, personal property, real property, and tort disputes related to online contracts. VMAG attempts to resolve a dispute within seventy-two

---

9. ICANN's Rules for Uniform Domain Name Dispute Resolution Policy are online at **http://www.icann.org/udrp/udrp-rules-24oct99.htm**. Domain names will be discussed in more detail in Chapter 10, in the context of trademark law.

hours. The proceedings occur in a password-protected online news group setting, and private e-mail among the participants is possible. A VMAG arbitrator's decision is issued in a written opinion. A party may appeal the outcome to a court.

INTERNATIONAL DISPUTE RESOLUTION

Businesspersons who engage in international business transactions normally take special precautions to protect themselves in the event that a party with whom they are dealing in another country breaches an agreement. Often, parties to international contracts include special clauses in their contracts providing for how any disputes arising under the contracts will be resolved.

Forum-Selection and Choice-of-Law Clauses

As you will read in Chapter 24, parties to international contracts often include forum-selection and choice-of-law clauses in their agreements. These clauses designate the jurisdiction (court or country) where any dispute arising under the contract will be litigated and which nation's law will be applied. If no forum-selection and choice-of-law clauses have been included in an international contract, legal proceedings will be more complex and attended by much more uncertainty. For example, litigation may take place in two or more countries, with each country applying its own national law to the particular transactions involved.

Furthermore, even if a plaintiff wins a favorable judgment in a lawsuit litigated in the plaintiff's country, there is no guarantee that the court's judgment will be enforced by judicial bodies in the defendant's country. As will be discussed in Chapter 24, for reasons of courtesy, the judgment may be enforced in the defendant's country, particularly if the defendant's country is the United States and the foreign court's decision is consistent with U.S. national law and policy. Other nations, however, may not be as accommodating as the United States, and the plaintiff may be left empty-handed.

Arbitration Clauses

In an attempt to prevent such problems, parties to international contracts often include arbitration clauses in their contracts, requiring that any contract disputes be decided by a neutral third party. In international arbitration proceedings, the third party may be a neutral entity (such as the International Chamber of Commerce), a panel of individuals representing both parties' interests, or some other group or organization. The United Nations Convention on the Recognition and Enforcement of Foreign Arbitral Awards[10]—which has been implemented in more than fifty countries, including the United States—assists in the enforcement of arbitration clauses, as do provisions in specific treaties among nations. The American Arbitration Association provides arbitration services for international as well as domestic disputes.

---

10. June 10, 1958, 21 U.S.T. 2517, T.I.A.S. No. 6997 (the "New York Convention").

KEY TERMS

alternative dispute
  resolution (ADR) 73
arbitration 75
arbitrator 75
attorney 63
attorney-client privilege 66
award 81
conciliation 74

damages 69
defense 69
early neutral case evaluation 74
litigant 67
litigation 63
mediation 74
mediator 74
mini-trial 73

negotiation 73
online dispute
  resolution (ODR) 92
preventive law 64
public policy 85
submission 78
summary jury trial 91
verdict 67

CHAPTER SUMMARY LEGAL REPRESENTATION AND ALTERNATIVE DISPUTE RESOLUTION

Attorneys and Dispute Resolution (See pages 64–71.)	1. *Roles of an attorney*—Adviser (advises a client on steps to take to avoid possible legal problems), drafter (writes contracts and other documents for clients), negotiator (persuades, argues, or settles with another party on a client's behalf), and advocate (presents a client's position in court).
	2. *Attorney-client relationship*—A client must disclose all relevant information to his or her attorney so the attorney can determine the best course of action. The attorney must keep the information confidential—the attorney-client privilege prevents a court or other government bodies from compelling disclosure of the information.
	3. *Decision to file a lawsuit*—Factors include whether the law provides a remedy, whether the person can expect to prevail, and whether the expected benefit will compensate for expenses and other costs, including any business lost as a result of the lawsuit and accompanying publicity.
	4. *Decision to defend against a lawsuit*—Factors include whether the relationship with the plaintiff is too valuable to risk, whether the publicity surrounding a trial would damage the defendant's reputation or image, and whether the dispute could be resolved in a less costly manner.
Alternative Dispute Resolution (ADR) (See pages 71–94.)	ADR is a less costly, less time-consuming, and increasingly attractive alternative to litigation in the courts. Forms of ADR include the following:
	1. *Negotiation*—The parties come together, with or without attorneys to represent them, and try to reach a settlement without the involvement of a third party.
	2. *Mediation*—The parties themselves reach an agreement with the help of a third party, called a mediator, who proposes solutions.
	3. *Arbitration*—A more formal method of ADR in which the parties submit their dispute to a neutral third party, the arbitrator, who renders a decision, which may or may not be legally binding, depending on the circumstances. Some courts refer certain cases for arbitration before allowing the cases to proceed to trial; in most cases, this kind of arbitration is nonbinding on the parties.
	4. *Summary jury trial*—A kind of trial in which litigants present their arguments and evidence and the jury renders a nonbinding verdict.

(continued)

CHAPTER SUMMARY LEGAL REPRESENTATION AND ALTERNATIVE DISPUTE RESOLUTION—Continued

Alternative Dispute Resolution (ADR)—continued	5. *Mini-trial*—A private proceeding in which each party's attorney argues the party's case before the other party. Often, a neutral third party acts as an adviser and renders an opinion on how a court would likely decide the issue.
	6. *ADR forums*—Both government agencies and private firms provide ADR services. Private firms include both nonprofit and for-profit organizations. A number of organizations and firms are now offering negotiation, mediation, and arbitration services through online forums. To date, these forums have been a practical alternative for the resolution of domain name disputes and e-commerce disputes in which the amount in controversy is relatively small.
	7. *International Dispute Resolution*—Persons engaging in international business transactions often include special clauses—including forum-selection, choice-of-law, and arbitration clauses—in their contracts. These clauses are designed to clarify where and how disputes will be resolved and what law will be applied.

FOR REVIEW

1. What role do attorneys play in the dispute-resolution process?
2. What are the differences between litigation and the other forms of dispute resolution?
3. How do the processes of negotiation and mediation differ?
4. What are the steps in the arbitration process?
5. What are the differences between voluntary arbitration and court-annexed arbitration?

QUESTIONS AND CASE PROBLEMS

3–1. Arbitration. In an arbitration proceeding, the arbitrator need not be a judge or even a lawyer. How, then, can the arbitrator's decision have the force of law and be binding on the parties involved?

3–2. Choice of Law. Two private U.S. corporations enter into a joint-venture agreement to conduct mining operations in the newly formed Middle Eastern nation of Euphratia. As part of the agreement, the companies include an arbitration clause and a choice-of-law provision. The first states that any controversy arising out of the performance of the agreement will be settled by arbitration. The second states that the agreement is to be governed by the laws of the location of the venture, Euphratia. A dispute arises, and the parties discontinue operations. One of the parties claims sole ownership to the Euphratian mines and orders the other party to remove its equipment from the mines. The other party disputes the claim of sole ownership and seeks an order from a U.S. federal court compelling the parties to submit to arbitration over the ownership issue and alleged breaches of the joint-venture agreement. How should the court rule if the laws of

Euphratia state that, whereas arbitration agreements are to be enforced generally, matters of ownership of natural resources can only be resolved in a Euphratian court of law? Does it matter that two U.S. companies engaged in international commerce would be governed by the Federal Arbitration Act?

3–3. Confirmation of Award. Two brothers, both of whom are certified public accountants (CPAs), form a professional association to provide tax-accounting services to the public. They also agree, in writing, that any disputes that arise between them over matters concerning the association will be submitted to an independent arbitrator, whom they designate to be their father, who is also a CPA. A dispute arises, and the matter is submitted to the father for arbitration. During the course of arbitration, which occurs over several weeks, the father asks the older brother, who is visiting one evening, to explain a certain entry in the brothers' association accounts. The younger brother learns of the discussion at the next meeting for arbitration; he says nothing about it, however. The arbitration is concluded in favor of the older brother, who seeks a court order compelling the younger brother to comply with the award. The younger brother seeks to set aside the award, claiming that the arbitration process was tainted by bias because "Dad always liked my older brother best." The younger brother also seeks to have the award set aside on the basis of improper conduct in that matters subject to arbitration were discussed between the father and older brother without the younger brother's being present. Should a court confirm the award or set it aside? Why?

3–4. Calculation of Award. After resolving their dispute, the two brothers encountered in Problem 3–3 above decide to resume their tax-accounting practice according to the terms of their original agreement. Again a dispute arises, and again it is decided by the father (now retired except for numerous occasions on which he acts as an arbitrator) in favor of the older brother. The older brother files a petition to enforce the award. The younger brother seeks to set aside the award and offers evidence that the father, as arbitrator, made a gross error in calculating the accounts that were material to the dispute being arbitrated. If the court is convinced that the father erred in the calculations, should the award be set aside? Why?

Case Problem with Sample Answer

3–5. Arbitration. Phillip Beaudry, who suffered from mental illness, worked in the Department of Income Maintenance for the state of Connecticut. Beaudry was fired from his job when it was learned that he had misappropriated approximately $1,640 in state funds. Beaudry filed a complaint with his union, Council 4 of the American Federation of State, County, and Municipal Employees (AFSCME), and eventually the dispute was submitted to an arbitrator. The arbitrator concluded that Beaudry had been dismissed without "just cause," because Beaudry's acts were caused by his mental illness and were not "within his capacity to control." Because Beaudry had a disability, the employer was required, under state law, to transfer him to a position that he was competent to hold. The arbitrator awarded Beaudry reinstatement, back pay, seniority, and other benefits. The state appealed the decision to a court. What public policies must the court weigh in making its decision? How should the court rule? [*State v. Council 4, AFSCME,* 27 Conn.App. 635, 608 A.2d 718 (1992)]

To view a sample answer for this case problem, go to this book's Web site at http://leet.westbuslaw.com and click on "Interactive Study Center."

3–6. Arbitration. Randall Fris worked as a seaman on an Exxon Shipping Co. oil tanker for eight years without incident. One night, he boarded the ship for duty while intoxicated, in violation of company policy. This policy also allowed Exxon to discharge employees who were intoxicated

and thus unfit for work. Exxon discharged Fris. Under a contract with Fris's union, the discharge was submitted to arbitration. The arbitrators ordered Exxon to reinstate Fris on an oil tanker. Exxon filed a suit against the union, challenging the award as contrary to public policy, which opposes having intoxicated persons operate seagoing vessels. Can a court set aside an arbitration award on the ground that the award violates public policy? Should the court set aside the award in this case? Explain. [*Exxon Shipping Co. v. Exxon Seamen's Union,* 11 F.3d 1189 (3d Cir. 1993)]

3–7. Arbitration. Stephanie Prince was an employee of Coca-Cola Bottling Co. of New York, Inc. (CNY), and a member of the Soft Drink and Brewery Workers Union. An agreement between CNY and the union set out a procedure to follow in the event of a dispute between an employee and CNY relating to "any matter whatsoever, including the meaning, interpretation, application or violation of this Agreement." In this context, the agreement mentioned some employment laws but did not mention federal antidiscrimination laws. After the union was notified, and if the grievance was not resolved within thirty days, the dispute was to be submitted to arbitration. Prince reported to the union, which told CNY, that she was being sexually harassed by her supervisors, Michael Drake and Leonard Erlanger. When no action was taken and Prince was subjected to retaliatory behavior by Drake and Erlanger, she filed a complaint with the Equal Employment Opportunity Commission. The supervisors retaliated again by ordering her to leave the workplace and "stay home." Prince filed a suit in a federal district court against CNY and the supervisors, alleging, among other things, violations of federal antidiscrimination law. CNY responded that its agreement with the union required Prince to submit her claim to arbitration. Is CNY right? In whose favor should the court rule? Why? [*Prince. v. Coca-Cola Bottling Co. of New York, Inc.,* 37 F.Supp.2d 289 (S.D.N.Y. 1999)]

3–8. Arbitration. New York State revised its New Car Lemon Law to allow consumers who complained of purchasing a "lemon" to have their disputes arbitrated before a professional arbitrator appointed by the New York attorney general. Before this revision, the Lemon Law allowed for arbitration of disputes, but the forum in which arbitration took place was sponsored by trade associations within the automobile industry, and consumers often complained of unfair awards. The revised law also provided that consumers could choose between two options: arbitration before a professional arbitrator and suing the manufacturer in court. Manufacturers, however, were compelled to arbitrate claims, if a consumer chose to do so, and could not resort to the courts. Trade associations representing automobile manufacturers and importers brought an action seeking a declaration that the alternative arbitration mechanism of the Lemon Law was unconstitutional because it deprived them of their right to trial by jury. How will the court decide? Discuss. [*Motor Vehicle Manufacturers Association of the United States v. State,* 75 N.Y.2d 175, 550 N.E.2d 919, 551 N.Y.S.2d 470 (1990)]

3–9. Arbitration. Alexander Little worked for Auto Stiegler, Inc., an automobile dealership in Los Angeles County, California, eventually becoming the service manager. While employed, Little signed an arbitration agreement that required the submission of all employment-related disputes to arbitration. The agreement also provided that any award over $50,000 could be appealed to a second arbitrator. Little was later demoted and terminated. Alleging that these actions were in retaliation for investigating and reporting warranty fraud and thus were in violation of public policy, Little filed a suit in a California state court against Auto Stiegler. The defendant filed a motion with the court to compel arbitration. Little responded that the arbitration agreement should not be enforced, in part because the appeal provision was unfairly one sided. Is this provision enforceable? Should the court grant Auto Stiegler's motion? Why or why not? [*Little v. Auto Stiegler, Inc.,* 29 Cal.4th 1064, 63 P.3d 979, 130 Cal.Rptr.2d 892 (2003)]

A Question of Ethics & Social Responsibility

3–10. Linda Bender, in her application for registration as a stockbroker with A. G. Edwards & Sons, Inc., agreed to submit any disputes with her employer to arbitration. Bender later sued her supervisor and employer (the defendants) for sexual harassment in violation of Title VII of the Civil Rights Act of 1964, which prohibits, among other things, employment discrimination based on gender. The defendants asked the court to compel arbitration. The district court judge refused to do so, holding that Bender could not be forced to waive her right to adjudicate Title VII claims in a federal court. The appellate court reversed, ruling that Title VII claims are arbitrable. The court held that compelling Bender to submit her claim for arbitration did not deprive her of the right to a judicial forum, because if the arbitration proceedings were somehow legally deficient, she could still take her case to a federal court for review. [*Bender v. A. G. Edwards & Sons, Inc.,* 971 F.2d 698 (11th Cir. 1992)]

1. Does the right to a postarbitration judicial forum equate to the right to initial access to a judicial forum in employment disputes?

2. Should the fact that reviewing courts rarely set aside arbitrators' awards have any bearing on the arbitrability of certain types of claims, such as those brought under Title VII?

Case Briefing Assignment

3–11. Examine Case A.1 [*Rodriguez de Quijas v. Shearson/American Express, Inc.,* 490 U.S. 477, 109 S.Ct. 1917, 104 L.Ed.2d 379 (1989)] in Appendix A. The case has been excerpted there in great detail. Review and then brief the case, making sure that your brief answers the following questions.

1. What is the legislative policy "embodied in the Arbitration Act"?

2. How did the Court reconcile the protections afforded investors under the Securities Act and the legislative policy advanced by the Arbitration Act? Did the Court believe that by submitting to arbitration, investors forgo "substantive rights" given under the Securities Act?

Critical-Thinking Legal Question

3–12. Suppose that a state statute requires that all civil lawsuits involving damages of less than $50,000 be arbitrated and that the case could be tried in court only if a party was dissatisfied with the arbitrator's decision. Suppose further that the statute also provides that if a trial does not result in an improvement of more than 10 percent in the position of the party who demanded the trial, that party must pay the costs of the arbitration proceeding. Would such a statute violate litigants' rights of access to the courts and to trial by jury? Would it matter if the statute was part of a pilot program and affected only a few judicial districts in the state?

INTERACTING WITH THE INTERNET

For updated links to resources available on the Web, as well as a variety of other materials, visit this text's Web site at

http://leet.westbuslaw.com

For information on alternative dispute resolution, go to the American Arbitration Association's Web site at

http://www.adr.org

To learn more about online dispute resolution, go to the following Web sites:

http://clicknsettle.com

http://cybersettle.com

http://SquareTrade.com

You can find links to information about various forms of ADR, ADR statutes, and ADR techniques at

http://www.adrlawinfo.com/state.html

ONLINE LEGAL RESEARCH EXERCISES

Go to **http://leet.westbuslaw.com**, the Web site that accompanies this text. Select "Interactive Study Center," and then click on "Chapter 3." There you will find the following Internet research exercises that you can perform to learn more about topics covered in this chapter.

Activity 3–1: SOCIAL PERSPECTIVE—Alternative Dispute Resolution
Activity 3–2: MANAGEMENT PERSPECTIVE—Resolve a Dispute Online

BEFORE THE TEST

Go to **http://leet.westbuslaw.com**, the Web site that accompanies this text. Select "Interactive Quizzes." You will find at least twenty interactive questions relating to this chapter.

Westlaw® Campus

If your textbook provided for a subscription to Westlaw® Campus, or if you have otherwise purchased access to the Westlaw Campus database, you can access any of the cases presented or cited in this chapter by using your Westlaw Campus account.

CHAPTER 4

The American Court System

CONTENTS

CHAPTER OBJECTIVES

After reading this chapter, you should be able to answer the following questions:

1. What is judicial review? How and when was the power of judicial review established?

2. Before a court can hear a case, it must have jurisdiction. Over what must it have jurisdiction? How are the courts applying traditional jurisdictional concepts to cases involving Internet transactions?

3. What is the difference between a trial court and an appellate court?

4. In a lawsuit, what are the pleadings? What is discovery? What is electronic filing?

5. What steps are involved in an appeal?

As Chief Justice John Marshall remarked in the quotation below, ultimately, we are all affected by what the courts say and do. This is particularly true in the business world—nearly every businessperson faces either a potential or an actual lawsuit at some time or another in her or his career. For this reason, anyone contemplating a career in business will benefit from an understanding of American court systems, including the mechanics of lawsuits.

In this chapter, after examining the judiciary's overall role in the American governmental scheme, we discuss some basic requirements that must be met before a party may bring a lawsuit before a particular court. We then look at the court systems of the United States in some detail and, to clarify judicial procedures, follow a hypothetical case through a state

"The Judicial Department comes home in its effects to every man's fireside: it passes on his property, his reputation, his life, his all."

John Marshall, 1755–1835
(Chief justice of the United States Supreme Court, 1801–1835)

court system. Even though there are fifty-two court systems—one for each of the fifty states, one for the District of Columbia, plus a federal system—similarities abound. Keep in mind that the federal courts are not superior to the state courts; they are simply an independent system of courts, which derives its authority from Article III, Section 2, of the U.S. Constitution.

Note that technological developments are affecting court procedures just as they are affecting all other areas of the law. In this chapter, we will also indicate how court doctrines and procedures are being adapted to the needs of a cyber age.

"I am unaware that any nation of the globe has hitherto organized a judicial power in the same manner as the Americans .... A more imposing judicial power was never constituted by any people."

ALEXIS DE TOCQUEVILLE, 1805–1859
(French historian and statesman)

THE JUDICIARY'S ROLE IN AMERICAN GOVERNMENT

As you learned in Chapter 1, the body of American law includes the federal and state constitutions, statutes passed by legislative bodies, administrative law, and the case decisions and legal principles that form the common law. These laws would be meaningless, however, without the courts to interpret and apply them. This is the essential role of the judiciary—the courts—in the American governmental system: to interpret and apply the law.

Judicial Review

As the branch of government entrusted with interpreting the laws, the judiciary can decide, among other things, whether the laws or actions of the other two branches are constitutional. The process for making such a determination is known as **judicial review.** The power of judicial review enables the judicial

JUDICIAL REVIEW
The process by which a court decides on the constitutionality of legislative enactments and actions of the executive branch.

INTERNATIONAL PERSPECTIVE

Judicial Review in Other Nations

The concept of judicial review was pioneered by the United States. Some maintain that one of the reasons the doctrine was readily accepted in this country was that it fit well with the checks and balances designed by the founders. Today, all established constitutional democracies have some form of judicial review—the power to rule on the constitutionality of laws—but its form varies from country to country.

For example, Canada's Supreme Court can exercise judicial review but is barred from doing so if a law includes a provision explicitly prohibiting such review. France has a Constitutional Council that rules on the constitutionality of laws *before* the laws take effect. Laws can be referred to the council for prior review by the president, the prime minister, and the heads of the two chambers of parliament. Prior review is also an option in Germany and Italy, if requested by the national or a regional government. In contrast, the United States Supreme Court does not give advisory opinions;

there must be an actual dispute concerning an issue before the Supreme Court will render a decision on the matter.

FOR CRITICAL ANALYSIS

In any country in which a constitution sets forth the basic powers and structure of government, some government body has to decide whether laws enacted by government are consistent with that constitution. Is this task best handled by the courts? Can you think of a better alternative?

branch to act as a check on the other two branches of government, in line with the system of checks and balances established by the U.S. Constitution.

The Origins of Judicial Review in the United States

The power of judicial review was not mentioned in the Constitution, but the concept was not new at the time the nation was founded. Indeed, prior to 1789 state courts had already overturned state legislative acts that conflicted with state constitutions. Additionally, many of the founders expected the United States Supreme Court to assume a similar role with respect to the federal Constitution. Alexander Hamilton and James Madison both emphasized the importance of judicial review in their essays urging the adoption of the new Constitution. The doctrine of judicial review was not legally established, however, until 1803, when the United States Supreme Court rendered its decision in *Marbury v. Madison*.[1] Details of this case are offered in this chapter's *Landmark in the Legal Environment* feature.

BASIC JUDICIAL REQUIREMENTS

Before a court can hear a lawsuit, certain requirements must first be met. These requirements relate to jurisdiction, venue, and standing to sue. We examine each of these important concepts here.

Jurisdiction

In Latin, *juris* means "law," and *diction* means "to speak." Thus, "the power to speak the law" is the literal meaning of the term **jurisdiction.** Before any court can hear a case, it must have jurisdiction over the person against whom the suit is brought or over the property involved in the suit. The court must also have jurisdiction over the subject matter.

JURISDICTION
The authority of a court to hear and decide a specific action.

Jurisdiction over Persons Generally, a court can exercise personal jurisdiction (*in personam* jurisdiction) over residents of a certain geographic area. A state trial court, for example, normally has jurisdictional authority over residents of a particular area of the state, such as a county or district. A state's highest court (often called the state supreme court)[2] has jurisdictional authority over all residents within the state.

In some cases, under the authority of a state **long arm statute,** a court can exercise personal jurisdiction over nonresident defendants as well. Before a court can exercise jurisdiction over a nonresident under a long arm statute, though, it must be demonstrated that the nonresident had sufficient contacts, or *minimum contacts,* with the state to justify the jurisdiction.[3] ● EXAMPLE 1 If an individual has committed a wrong within the state, such as causing an automobile injury or selling defective goods, a court can usually exercise

LONG ARM STATUTE
A state statute that permits a state to obtain personal jurisdiction over nonresident defendants. A defendant must have certain "minimum contacts" with that state for the statute to apply.

---

1. 5 U.S. (1 Cranch) 137, 2 L.Ed. 60 (1803).
2. As will be discussed shortly, a state's highest court is often referred to as the state supreme court, but there are exceptions. For example, in New York, the supreme court is a trial court.
3. The minimum-contacts standard was established in *International Shoe Co. v. State of Washington,* 326 U.S. 310, 66 S.Ct. 154, 90 L.Ed. 95 (1945).

LANDMARK IN THE LEGAL ENVIRONMENT

Marbury v. Madison (1803)

In the edifice of American law, the *Marbury v. Madison* decision in 1803 can be viewed as the keystone of the constitutional arch. The facts of the case were as follows. John Adams, who had lost his bid for reelection to Thomas Jefferson in 1800, feared the Jeffersonians' antipathy toward business and toward a powerful central government. Adams thus worked feverishly to "pack" the judiciary with loyal Federalists (those who believed in a strong national government) by appointing what came to be called "midnight judges" just before Jefferson took office. All of the fifty-nine judicial appointment letters had to be certified and delivered, but Adams's secretary of state (John Marshall) had succeeded in delivering only forty-two of them by the time Jefferson took over as president. Jefferson, of course, refused to order his secretary of state, James Madison, to deliver the remaining commissions.

MARSHALL'S DILEMMA William Marbury and three others to whom the commissions had not been delivered sought a writ of *mandamus* (an order directing a government official to fulfill a duty) from the United States Supreme Court, as authorized by Section 13 of the Judiciary Act of 1789. As fate would have it, John Marshall had stepped down as Adams's secretary of state only to become chief justice of the Supreme Court. Marshall faced a dilemma: If he ordered the commissions delivered, the new secretary of state (Madison) could simply refuse to deliver them—and the Court had no way to compel action, because it had no police force. At the same time, if Marshall simply allowed the new administration to do as it wished, the Court's power would be severely eroded.

MARSHALL'S DECISION Marshall masterfully fashioned his decision. On the one hand, he enlarged the power of the Supreme Court by affirming the Court's power of judicial review. He stated, "It is emphatically the province and duty of the Judicial Department to say what the law is. . . . If two laws conflict with each other, the courts must decide on the operation of each. . . . So if the law be in opposition to the Constitution . . . [t]he Court must determine which of these conflicting rules governs the case. This is the very essence of judicial duty."

On the other hand, his decision did not require anyone to do anything. He stated that the highest court did not have the power to issue a writ of *mandamus* in this particular case. Marshall pointed out that although the Judiciary Act of 1789 specified that the Supreme Court could issue writs of *mandamus* as part of its original jurisdiction, Article III of the Constitution, which spelled out the Court's original jurisdiction, did not mention writs of *mandamus*. Because Congress did not have the right to expand the Supreme Court's jurisdiction, this section of the Judiciary Act of 1789 was unconstitutional—and thus void. The decision still stands today as a judicial and political masterpiece.

Application to Today's World

Since the Marbury v. Madison *decision, the power of judicial review has remained unchallenged. Today, this power is exercised by both federal and state courts. This power clearly acts as a restraint on Congress today. For example, as you will read in Chapter 5, Congress has passed a number of laws in an attempt to protect minors from pornographic materials on the Internet. Several of these laws have been held unconstitutional by the courts—in some cases, by the United States Supreme Court—on the ground that they violate constitutional provisions, such as freedom of speech. If the courts did not have the power of judicial review, the constitutionality of these acts of Congress could not be challenged in court—a congressional statute would remain law until changed by Congress.*

James Madison. If Madison had delivered the commissions of the Federalist judges, would the U.S. Supreme Court today have the power of judicial review?

jurisdiction even if the person causing the harm is located in another state. Similarly, a state may exercise personal jurisdiction over a nonresident defendant who is sued for breaching a contract that was formed within the state.●

In regard to corporations,[4] the minimum-contacts requirement is usually met if the corporation does business within the state. ● EXAMPLE 2 Suppose that a corporation incorporated under the laws of Maine and headquartered in that state has a branch office or manufacturing plant in Georgia. Does this corporation have sufficient minimum contacts with the state of Georgia to allow a Georgia court to exercise jurisdiction over the Maine corporation? Yes, it does. If the Maine corporation advertises and sells its products in Georgia, those activities may suffice to meet the minimum-contacts requirement.●

In the following case, the issue was whether phone calls and letters constituted sufficient minimum contacts to give a court jurisdiction over a nonresident defendant.

---

4. In the eyes of the law, corporations are "legal persons"—entities that can sue and be sued. See Chapter 14.

CASE 4.1   Cole v. Mileti

United States Court of Appeals, Sixth Circuit, 1998.
133 F.3d 433.
http://www.law.emory.edu/6circuit/jan98/index.html[a]

HISTORICAL AND ECONOMIC SETTING *A movie production company is costly to operate. Over the several years it can take to produce a film, there are many expenses, including maintaining an office and hiring professionals of all kinds. Newcomers to the industry make many of the same wrong moves that are the pitfalls of all businesses. For a novice producer or investor, there is the uncertainty of not knowing what you are doing and the danger of being outnegotiated by those who prey on a novice's ignorance. Finally, once a film is made, there is the audience, which may not choose to see it.*

BACKGROUND AND FACTS Nick Mileti, a resident of California, co-produced a movie called *Streamers* and organized a corporation, Streamers International Distributors, Inc., to distribute the film. Joseph Cole, a resident of Ohio, bought two hundred shares of Streamers stock. Cole also lent the firm $475,000, which he borrowed from Equitable Bank of Baltimore. The film was unsuccessful. Mileti agreed to repay Cole's loan in a contract arranged through phone calls and correspondence between California and Ohio. When Mileti did not repay the loan, the bank sued Cole, who in turn filed a suit against Mileti in a federal district court in Ohio. The court entered a judgment against Mileti. He appealed to the U.S. Court of Appeals for the Sixth Circuit, arguing in part that the district court's exercise of jurisdiction over him was unfair.

IN THE WORDS OF THE COURT . . .

MERRITT, Circuit Judge.
    *   *   *   *
    *   *   * [There is] a three-part test to determine whether specific jurisdiction exists over a nonresident defendant like Mileti. First, the defendant must purposefully avail himself of the privilege of conducting activities within the forum state; second, the cause of action must arise from the defendant's activities there; and third, the acts of the defendant or consequences caused by the defendant must have a substantial enough connection with the forum state to make its exercise of jurisdiction over the defendant fundamentally fair.

---

a. This is a page at the Web site of the Emory University School of Law that lists the published opinions of the U.S. Court of Appeals for the Sixth Circuit for January 1998. Scroll down the list of cases to the *Cole* case. To access the opinion, click on the case name.

CASE 4.1—Continued

If, as here, a nonresident defendant transacts business by negotiating and executing a contract via telephone calls and letters to an Ohio resident, then the defendant has purposefully availed himself of the forum by creating a continuing obligation in Ohio. Furthermore, if the cause of action is for breach of that contract, as it is here, then the cause of action naturally arises from the defendant's activities in Ohio. Finally, when we find that a defendant like Mileti purposefully availed himself of the forum and that the cause of action arose directly from that contact, we presume the specific assertion of personal jurisdiction was proper.

DECISION AND REMEDY The U.S. Court of Appeals for the Sixth Circuit held that the district court could exercise personal jurisdiction over Mileti. The appellate court reasoned that a federal district court in Ohio can exercise personal jurisdiction over a resident of California who does business in Ohio via phone calls and letters.

FOR CRITICAL ANALYSIS—Economic Consideration *Why might a defendant prefer to be sued in one state rather than in another?*

Jurisdiction over Property A court can also exercise jurisdiction over property that is located within its boundaries. This kind of jurisdiction is known as *in rem* jurisdiction, or "jurisdiction over the thing." ● EXAMPLE 3 Suppose that a dispute arises over the ownership of a boat in dry dock in Fort Lauderdale, Florida. The boat is owned by an Ohio resident, over whom a Florida court normally cannot exercise personal jurisdiction. The other party to the dispute is a resident of Nebraska. In this situation, a lawsuit concerning the boat could be brought in a Florida state court on the basis of the court's *in rem* jurisdiction.●

Jurisdiction over Subject Matter Jurisdiction over subject matter is a limitation on the types of cases a court can hear. In both the federal and state court systems, there are courts of *general* (unlimited) *jurisdiction* and courts of *limited jurisdiction*. An example of a court of general jurisdiction is a state trial court or a federal district court. An example of a state court of limited jurisdiction is a probate court. **Probate courts** are state courts that handle only matters relating to the transfer of a person's assets and obligations after that person's death, including matters relating to the custody and guardianship of children. An example of a federal court of limited subject-matter jurisdiction is a bankruptcy court. **Bankruptcy courts** handle only bankruptcy proceedings, which are governed by federal bankruptcy law (discussed in Chapter 15). In contrast, a court of general jurisdiction can decide a broad array of cases.

A court's jurisdiction over subject matter is usually defined in the statute or constitution creating the court. In both the federal and state court systems, a court's subject-matter jurisdiction can be limited not only by the subject of the lawsuit but also by the amount of money in controversy, by whether a case is a felony (a more serious type of crime) or a misdemeanor (a less serious type of crime), or by whether the proceeding is a trial or an appeal.

Original and Appellate Jurisdiction The distinction between courts of original jurisdiction and courts of appellate jurisdiction normally lies in whether the case is being heard for the first time. Courts having original jurisdiction are courts of the first instance, or trial courts—that is, courts in which lawsuits begin, trials take place, and evidence is presented. In the federal court system,

PROBATE COURT
A state court of limited jurisdiction that conducts proceedings relating to the settlement of a deceased person's estate.

BANKRUPTCY COURT
A federal court of limited jurisdiction that handles only bankruptcy proceedings. Bankruptcy proceedings are governed by federal bankruptcy law.

the *district courts* are trial courts. In the various state court systems, the trial courts are known by various names, as will be discussed shortly.

The key point here is that, normally, any court having original jurisdiction is known as a trial court. Courts having appellate jurisdiction act as reviewing courts, or appellate courts. In general, cases can be brought before appellate courts only on appeal from an order or a judgment of a trial court or other lower court.

Jurisdiction of the Federal Courts Because the federal government is a government of limited powers, the jurisdiction of the federal courts is limited. Article III of the U.S. Constitution establishes the boundaries of federal judicial power. Section 2 of Article III states that "[t]he judicial Power shall extend to all Cases, in Law and Equity, arising under this Constitution, the Laws of the United States, and Treaties made, or which shall be made, under their Authority."

Whenever a plaintiff's cause of action is based, at least in part, on the U.S. Constitution, a treaty, or a federal law, then a **federal question** arises, and the case comes under the judicial power of the federal courts. Any lawsuit involving a federal question can originate in a federal court. People who claim that their rights under the U.S. Constitution have been violated can begin their suits in a federal court.

Federal district courts can also exercise original jurisdiction over cases involving **diversity of citizenship.** Such cases may arise between (1) citizens of different states, (2) a foreign country and citizens of a state or of different states, or (3) citizens of a state and citizens or subjects of a foreign country. The amount in controversy must be more than $75,000 before a federal court can take jurisdiction in such cases. For purposes of diversity jurisdiction, a corporation is a citizen of both the state in which it is incorporated and the state in which its principal place of business is located. A case involving diversity of citizenship can be filed in the appropriate federal district court, or, if the case starts in a state court, it can sometimes be transferred to a federal court. A large percentage of the cases filed in federal courts each year are based on diversity of citizenship.

Note that in a case based on a federal question, a federal court will apply federal law. In a case based on diversity of citizenship, however, a federal court will apply the relevant state law (which is often the law of the state in which the court sits).

Exclusive versus Concurrent Jurisdiction When both federal and state courts have the power to hear a case, as is true in suits involving diversity of citizenship, **concurrent jurisdiction** exists. When cases can be tried only in federal courts or only in state courts, **exclusive jurisdiction** exists. Federal courts have exclusive jurisdiction in cases involving federal crimes, bankruptcy, patents, and copyrights; in suits against the United States; and in some areas of admiralty law (law governing transportation on the seas and ocean waters). States also have exclusive jurisdiction in certain subject matters—for example, in divorce and adoption. The concepts of exclusive and concurrent jurisdiction are illustrated in Exhibit 4–1.

When concurrent jurisdiction exists, a party has a choice of whether to bring a suit in, for example, a federal or a state court. The party's lawyer will consider several factors in counseling the party as to which choice is more desirable. The lawyer may prefer to litigate the case in a state court because he or

FEDERAL QUESTION
A question that pertains to the U.S. Constitution, acts of Congress, or treaties. A federal question provides a basis for federal jurisdiction.

DIVERSITY OF CITIZENSHIP
Under Article III, Section 2, of the Constitution, a basis for federal district court jurisdiction over a lawsuit between (1) citizens of different states, (2) a foreign country and citizens of a state or of different states, or (3) citizens of a state and citizens or subjects of a foreign country. The amount in controversy must be more than $75,000 before a federal district court can take jurisdiction in such cases.

CONCURRENT JURISDICTION
Jurisdiction that exists when two different courts have the power to hear a case. For example, some cases can be heard in a federal or a state court.

EXCLUSIVE JURISDICTION
Jurisdiction that exists when a case can be heard only in a particular court or type of court.

EXHIBIT 4-1   EXCLUSIVE AND CONCURRENT JURISDICTION

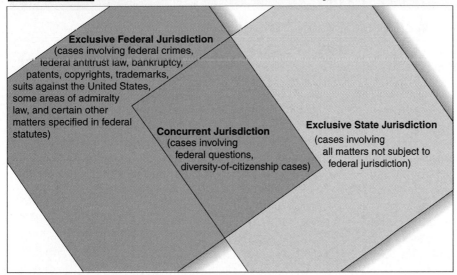

Exclusive Federal Jurisdiction
(cases involving federal crimes,
federal antitrust law, bankruptcy,
patents, copyrights, trademarks,
suits against the United States,
some areas of admiralty
law, and certain other
matters specified in federal
statutes)

Concurrent Jurisdiction
(cases involving
federal questions,
diversity-of-citizenship cases)

Exclusive State Jurisdiction
(cases involving
all matters not subject to
federal jurisdiction)

she is more familiar with the state court's procedures, or perhaps the attorney believes that the state's judge or jury would be more sympathetic to the client and the case. Alternatively, the lawyer may advise the client to sue in federal court. Perhaps the state court's **docket** (the court's schedule listing the cases to be heard) is crowded, and the case could be brought to trial sooner in a federal court. Perhaps some feature of federal practice or procedure could offer an advantage in the client's case. Other important considerations include the law in an available jurisdiction, how that law has been applied in the jurisdiction's courts, and what the results in similar cases have been in that jurisdiction.

DOCKET
The list of cases entered on a court's calendar and thus scheduled to be heard by the court.

Jurisdiction in Cyberspace

The Internet's capacity to bypass political and geographic boundaries undercuts the traditional basic limitations on a court's authority to exercise jurisdiction. These limits include a party's contacts with a court's geographic jurisdiction. As already discussed, for a court to compel a defendant to come before it, there must be at least minimum contacts—the presence of a salesperson within the state, for example. Are there sufficient minimum contacts if the only connection to a jurisdiction is an ad on the Web originating from a remote location?

The "Sliding-Scale" Standard   Gradually, the courts are developing a standard—called a "sliding-scale" standard—for determining when the exercise of jurisdiction over an out-of-state defendant is proper. In developing this standard, the courts have identified three types of Internet business contacts: (1) substantial business conducted via the Internet (with contracts, sales, and so on); (2) some interactivity through a Web site; and (3) passive advertising. Jurisdiction is proper for the first category, improper for the third, and may or may not be appropriate for the second.[5] (For a discussion of whether a single e-mail can constitute "minimum contacts," see this chapter's *Legal E-nvironment* feature on the following page.)

---

5. For a leading case on this issue, see *Zippo Manufacturing Co. v. Zippo Dot Com, Inc.,* 952 F.Supp. 1119 (W.D.Pa. 1997).

LEGAL *e*-NVIRONMENT

Web Contacts and Jurisdiction

In virtually every area of the law, the use of the Internet to conduct business activities has raised new legal questions—or, more often, new variations on old questions. This is certainly true with respect to jurisdiction. To be sure, the courts are coming to some consensus as to when jurisdiction over a Web site owner or operator in another state is proper. Yet cases continue to come before the courts that do not readily "fit" into the categories and rules being developed by case law.

Consider a case that came before a federal court sitting in Mississippi. The case involved a lawsuit brought by Internet Doorway, Inc., an Internet service provider based in Mississippi, against Connie Davis, a Texas resident. Internet Doorway alleged that Davis had sent an unsolicited e-mail message, advertising a pornographic Web site, to persons all over the world, including Mississippi residents. The problem for Internet Doorway was that Davis had falsified the "from" header to make the e-mail appear to have been sent from an Internet Doorway account. In its suit, Internet Doorway claimed that Davis had committed the tort (civil wrong—see Chapter 8) of trespass to chattels, or personal property—the property in this case consisting of Internet Doorway's name and Internet accounts. Internet Doorway claimed that its reputation and goodwill in the community had been harmed as a result of Davis's action. Davis asked the court to dismiss the case for lack of personal jurisdiction.

The Minimum-Contacts Requirement

Years ago, in *International Shoe Co. v. State of Washington*,[a] the United States Supreme Court made it clear that before a state can exercise jurisdiction over a nonresident, the nonresident must have some minimum contacts with the state. If there were no minimum-contacts requirement, the exercise of personal jurisdiction "would offend traditional notions of fair play and substantial justice" mandated by the due process clause of the Fourteenth Amendment (see Chapter 5.) Generally, the courts have concluded that a defendant's conduct in connection with the forum state (the state in which a lawsuit is initiated) must be such that she or he should reasonably anticipate "being haled into court" in that state.

Does One E-Mail Constitute "Minimum Contacts"?

In determining whether jurisdiction over Davis was proper, the federal court in Mississippi had to decide, among other things, whether Davis's single e-mail to Mississippi residents satisfied the minimum-contacts requirement for jurisdiction over an out-of-state defendant. The court held that "even a single contact" could satisfy the minimum-contacts requirement in certain situations, including this one.

In its reasoning, the court distinguished between "active" and "passive" Internet communications. In this case, the message was not posted on a "passive" Web site, which people would have to voluntarily access in order to read the message. Rather, the message was sent via "active" e-mail to specific recipients. The court further noted that exercising jurisdiction over Davis did not offend any notions of fair play and substantial justice. The court concluded that Davis, by sending her e-mail solicitation "to the far reaches of the earth," had done so "at her own peril." She should reasonably have expected that she could be "haled into court in a distant jurisdiction to answer for the ramifications of that [e-mail]."[b]

FOR CRITICAL ANALYSIS

What if Internet Doorway had never become aware of Davis's action? Davis would still have committed a tort, but who would file a suit?

---

a. 326 U.S. 310, 66 S.Ct. 154, 90 L.Ed. 95 (1945).

b. *Internet Doorway, Inc. v. Parks,* 138 F.Supp.2d 773 (S.D.Miss. 2001).

International Jurisdictional Issues Because the Internet is international in scope, international jurisdictional issues understandably have come to the fore. We have already looked at one of these issues in the *Legal E-nvironment* feature in Chapter 1. What seems to be emerging in the world's courts is a standard that echoes the requirement of "minimum contacts" applied by the U.S. courts. Most courts are indicating that minimum contacts—doing business within the jurisdiction, for example—are enough to compel a defendant to appear and that a physical presence is not necessary.[6] The effect of this standard is that a business firm may have to comply with the laws in any jurisdiction in which it targets customers for its products.

The question then arises as to whether, in light of current technology, it is possible to do business over the Internet in one jurisdiction but not in another. If a company provides a link on its Web site through which a person in one country can do business with the firm, is it technically possible for that company to block access to persons in other countries? This question was one of the issues in the following widely publicized case.

---

6. Currently under negotiation is the Hague Convention on Jurisdiction, an international treaty that is intended to make civil judgments enforceable across national borders. One issue in the negotiations is whether to require that all disputes be settled in the country of the seller or the country of the buyer. It has also been suggested that mandatory jurisdiction provisions be left out of the treaty.

CASE 4.2   International League Against Racism and Antisemitism v. Yahoo! Inc.

Tribunal de Grande Instance de Paris, 2000.

HISTORICAL AND TECHNOLOGICAL SETTING *The Internet is a combination of several hundred million computer networks and associated sites that are interconnected throughout the world. Between 1973 and 1980, the U.S. Department of Defense defined a set of procedures by which the networks connected to the Internet could communicate. These procedures are known as Transmission Control Protocol/Internet Protocol, or TCP/IP. Each unit connected to the Internet must have what is known as an IP address, which is a series of numbers. For convenience, the numbers are associated with names, which are referred to as domain names (see Chapter 10).*

BACKGROUND AND FACTS Yahoo! Inc. operates a "Yahoo Auctions" Web site (at **http://auctions.**

yahoo.com) that is directed principally at customers in the United States. Items offered for sale have included objects representing symbols of Nazi ideology. In France, the act of displaying such objects is a crime and is also subject to civil liability. The International League Against Racism and Antisemitism and others filed a suit in the Tribunal de Grande Instance de Paris (a French court) against Yahoo and others, seeking an injunction and damages. The court ordered Yahoo to, among other things, "take all necessary measures to dissuade and make impossible any access [by persons in France or French territory] via yahoo.com to the auction service for Nazi merchandise as well as to any other site or service that may be construed as an apology for Nazism or contesting the reality of Nazi crimes." Two months later, Yahoo returned to the court, arguing in part that the court did not have jurisdiction and that even if it did, Yahoo was not technically able to do what the court ordered.

IN THE WORDS OF THE COURT . . .   [*JEAN-JACQUES GOMEZ*] the Presiding Justice.

*   *   *   *

*   *   * YAHOO is aware that it is addressing French parties because upon making a connection to its auctions site from a terminal located in France it responds by transmitting advertising banners written in the French language[.]

(continued)

CASE 4.2—Continued

* * * [A] sufficient basis is thus established in this case for a connecting link with France, which renders our jurisdiction perfectly competent to rule in this matter[.]

* * * *

* * * [I]t emerges from the [findings of the panel of consultants whom the court appointed to consider technical solutions] that it is possible to determine the physical location of a surfer from the IP address[.]

* * * *

* * * [I]t should be borne in mind that YAHOO Inc. already carries out geographical identification of French surfers or surfers operating out of French territory and visiting its auctions site, insofar as it routinely displays advertising banners in the French language targeted at these surfers, in respect of whom it therefore has means of identification * * * .

* * * [A] request [can] be made to surfers whose IP address is ambiguous * * * to provide a declaration of nationality, which in effect amounts to a declaration of the surfer's geographical origin, which YAHOO could ask for when the home page is reached, or when a search is initiated for Nazi objects * * * immediately before the request is processed by the search engine[.]

* * * [A] combination of [the] two procedures, namely geographical identification and declaration of nationality, would enable a filtering success rate approaching 90% to be achieved[.]

* * * *

* * * [E]ven if YAHOO [is] unable to identify with certainty the surfer's geographical origin, in this case France, it would know the place of delivery, and would be in a position to prevent the delivery from taking place if the delivery address was located in France[.]

DECISION AND REMEDY The court affirmed the injunction, reasoning that the "combination of technical measures at [Yahoo's] disposal" rendered compliance possible. The court gave Yahoo three months to comply, after which it would be fined 100,000 francs (approximately $14,000) for each day that it failed to do so. The court also ordered Yahoo to pay each plaintiff 10,000 francs.

FOR CRITICAL ANALYSIS—Technological Consideration *With this case in mind, how is the technology that underlies the Internet likely to change?*

COMMENT *Subsequent to this decision, Yahoo filed a suit in a U.S. federal court, arguing that the French court's order was not enforceable in the United States on the ground that the order presented a "real and immediate threat" to Yahoo's constitutional right to free speech. The federal court agreed and refused to recognize the French court's order. See* Yahoo! Inc. v. La Ligue Contre le Racisme et l'Antisemitisme, *169 F.Supp.2d 1181 (N.D.Cal. 2001).*

Venue

VENUE
The geographic district in which an action is tried and from which the jury is selected.

Jurisdiction has to do with whether a court has authority to hear a case involving specific persons, property, or subject matter. **Venue**[7] is concerned with the most appropriate location for a trial. Two state courts (or two federal courts) may have the authority to exercise jurisdiction over a case, but it may be more appropriate or convenient to hear the case in one court than in the other.

Basically, the concept of venue reflects the policy that a court trying a suit should be in the geographic neighborhood (usually the county) where the inci-

---

7. Pronounced *ven*-yoo.

dent leading to the lawsuit occurred or where the parties involved in the lawsuit reside. Pretrial publicity or other factors, though, may require a change of venue to another community, especially in criminal cases in which the defendant's right to a fair and impartial jury has been impaired.

Standing to Sue

Before a person can bring a lawsuit before a court, the party must have **standing to sue,** or a sufficient "stake" in a matter to justify seeking relief through the court system. In other words, a party must have a legally protected and tangible interest at stake in the litigation in order to have standing. The party bringing the lawsuit must have suffered a harm, or have been threatened by a harm, as a result of the action about which she or he complained. At times, a person will have standing to sue on behalf of another person. ● EXAMPLE 4 Suppose that a child suffered serious injuries as a result of a defectively manufactured toy. Because the child is a minor, a lawsuit could be brought on his or her behalf by another person, such as the child's parent or legal guardian.●

Standing to sue also requires that the controversy at issue be a **justiciable**[8] **controversy**—a controversy that is real and substantial, as opposed to hypothetical or academic. ● EXAMPLE 5 In the above example, the child's parent could not sue the toy manufacturer merely on the ground that the toy was defective. The issue would become justiciable only if the child had actually been injured due to the defect in the toy as marketed. In other words, the parent normally could not ask the court to determine, for example, what damages might be obtained if the child had been injured, because this would be merely a hypothetical question.●

At issue in the following case was whether an unsuccessful bidder for a broadband license had standing to challenge a federal agency's award of that license to a different bidder.

STANDING TO SUE
The requirement that an individual must have a sufficient stake in a controversy before he or she can bring a lawsuit. The plaintiff must demonstrate that he or she has been either injured or threatened with injury.

JUSTICIABLE CONTROVERSY
A controversy that is not hypothetical or academic but real and substantial; a requirement that must be satisfied before a court will hear a case.

---

8. Pronounced jus-*tish*-uh-bul.

CASE 4.3   High Plains Wireless, Limited Partnership v. Federal Communications Commission

United States Court of Appeals,
District of Columbia Circuit, 2002.
276 F.3d 599.
**http://www.cadc.uscourts.gov/opinions/
opinions.asp**[a]

**HISTORICAL AND TECHNOLOGICAL
SETTING** *Broadband personal communications services (PCS) comprise a group of technologies that allow mobile communication using the electromagnetic spectrum. Cell phones, portable fax machines,*

and other methods of wireless communication are based on broadband PCS. Recognizing the commercial potential of these technologies, the Federal Communications Commission (FCC) requires that before a party can use the spectrum for these services, it must get a license from the FCC. In 1993, Congress directed the FCC to choose between mutually exclusive applications for a license through competitive bidding. In 1996 and 1997, the FCC auctioned off these licenses.[b]

---

a. This is a page within the Web site of the U.S. Court of Appeals for the District of Columbia Circuit. In the "Please select from the following menu to find opinions by date of issue" section, select "January" in the month menu and "2002" in the year menu, and click on "Go." On the page that appears, click on the docket number next to the name of the case to access the opinion.

b. Each auction was open, simultaneous, and ascending. That the auction was *open* meant that, in contrast to a sealed-bid auction, each participant was aware of every other participant's bid as it was cast. The auction was *simultaneous* in that all of the licenses were open for bidding at the same time, and the auction were *ascending* in the sense that bidding on the licenses continued through successive rounds until no new high bid was cast. Because the bidding was open, any bidder could send the other bidders a message encoded in the digits of its bid.

(continued)

CASE 4.3—Continued

BACKGROUND AND FACTS Mercury PCS II, Limited Liability Company, and High Plains Wireless, Limited Partnership, bid on broadband PCS licenses for Lubbock and Amarillo, Texas.[c] Mercury used reflexive bidding to dissuade High Plains from bidding on the license for Lubbock. Specifically, Mercury made the last three digits of its bids for the licenses in Lubbock and Amarillo the same as the FCC's numbers designated for those cities. In one round of the auction, for example, Mercury bid $1,375,013 on the Lubbock license, "013" being the number for Amarillo. After High Plains bid again for the Lubbock license, Mercury bid $1,615,264 on the Amarillo license, "264" being the number for Lubbock. By repeatedly encoding its bids, Mercury was warning High Plains that if High Plains did not stop bidding, Mercury would drive up the price of the Amarillo license. High Plains stopped bidding for the Lubbock license but was the successful bidder for the Amarillo license. The FCC awarded Mercury all thirty-two licenses for which it was the high bidder, including the Lubbock license. High Plains asked the FCC to review that order. The FCC investigated but declined to punish Mercury. High Plains appealed this decision to the U.S. Court of Appeals for the District of Columbia Circuit. The FCC and Mercury argued that High Plains lacked standing to challenge this decision.

IN THE WORDS OF THE COURT . . .

GINSBURG, Chief Judge:

*   *   *   *

The irreducible constitutional minimum that High Plains must show for standing to maintain this appeal is that it suffered an injury in fact, that the conduct of which it complains caused the injury, and that a favorable decision of this court would redress the injury. This court has had occasion in prior cases to tailor the application of these prerequisites specifically to complaints arising from the Commission's [FCC's] auctions of spectrum. We have held that a bidder in a government auction has a right to a legally valid procurement process [and that] a party allegedly deprived of this right asserts a cognizable injury. *A disappointed bidder need not show that it would be successful if the license were auctioned anew, but only that it was able and ready to bid and that the decision of the Commission prevented it from doing so on an equal basis.* The bidder may satisfy the requirement of redressability by showing that it is ready, willing, and able to participate in a new auction should it prevail in court. [Emphasis added.]

Insofar as the appellant [High Plains] challenges the award to Mercury of the *   *   * license for Lubbock, it meets these requirements. High Plains complains that it was injured because the Commission awarded the license to Mercury, *   *   * instead of holding a new auction in which High Plains could bid free of the illicit influence of reflexive bidding. Further, High Plains has expressed its willingness to bid in a *   *   * [new public sale] for the *   *   * license in Lubbock; and it is obvious that the court could redress High Plains' injuries by ordering the Commission to auction the license anew. *   *   * Accordingly, High Plains has standing to appeal the Commission's award to Mercury of the *   *   * license for Lubbock.

The Commission contends separately that High Plains does not have standing to challenge the award of the 31 other licenses that Mercury acquired in the *   *   * auction *   *   * . We agree with the Commission *   *   * . High Plains did not compete against Mercury for those licenses. Nor does it allege that the award of those licenses somehow deprived it of a valid auction process with respect to the lots for which it did bid. It follows that denying those 31 licenses to Mercury will not redress the injury that High Plains suffered in its attempt to acquire the *   *   * license in Lubbock. Accordingly, we hold that High Plains' challenge to the award of licenses other than the *   *   * license in Lubbock is not within the jurisdiction of this court.

---

c. Limited liability companies and limited partnerships are discussed in Chapter 14.

CASE 4.3—Continued

DECISION AND REMEDY The U.S. Court of Appeals for the District of Columbia Circuit held that High Plains had standing to appeal the FCC's decision not to punish Mercury. The court ruled, however, that High Plains did not show that the award of the Lubbock license to Mercury was arbitrary or irrational; therefore, the court affirmed the FCC's order.

FOR CRITICAL ANALYSIS—Legal Consideration *Suppose that High Plains had been the successful bidder for the Lubbock license. Would it then have had standing to appeal the FCC's decision not to punish Mercury?*

THE STATE AND FEDERAL COURT SYSTEMS

As mentioned earlier in this chapter, each state has its own court system. Additionally, there is a system of federal courts. Although state court systems differ, Exhibit 4–2 illustrates the basic organizational structure characteristic of the court systems in many states, as well as the federal court system. The exhibit also shows how federal and state administrative agencies relate to the judicial structure. As you will read in Chapter 6, decisions made during adjudication by federal administrative agencies may be appealed to a federal court. Similarly, decisions rendered by state administrative agencies may be appealed to a state court. We turn now to an examination of the state and federal court systems, beginning with the state courts.

State Court Systems

Typically, a state court system will include several levels, or tiers, of courts. As indicated in Exhibit 4–2, state courts may include (1) trial courts of limited jurisdiction, (2) trial courts of general jurisdiction, (3) appellate courts, and (4) the state's highest court (often called the state supreme court). Generally, any person who is a party to a lawsuit has the opportunity to plead the case before a trial court and then, if he or she loses, before at least one level of appellate court. Finally, if a federal statute or federal constitutional issue is

> "The perfect judge fears nothing—he could go front to front before God."
>
> WALT WHITMAN, 1819–1892
> (American poet)

EXHIBIT 4-2 FEDERAL COURTS AND STATE COURT SYSTEMS

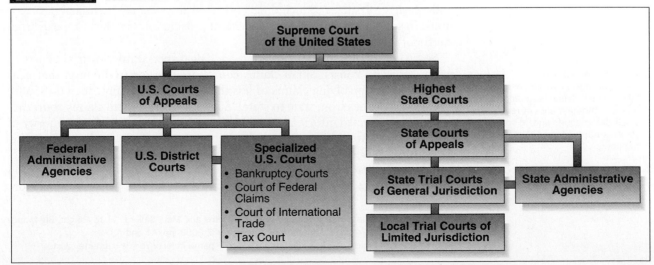

involved in the decision of the state supreme court, that decision may be further appealed to the United States Supreme Court.

Judges in the state court system are usually elected by the voters for a specified term. In contrast, as you will read shortly, judges in the federal court system are appointed by the president of the United States and, if they are confirmed by the Senate, hold office for life—unless they engage in blatantly illegal conduct.

ETHICAL ISSUE

Are state court systems too political?

Judges in the federal court system, because they are appointed, do not have to worry about reelection and, consequently, can make rulings on specific issues without having to take public opinion into account. Although some state judges are appointed (the procedures vary widely from state to state), in most states at least some judges are elected. To gain (or retain) their seats, those judges usually must conduct political campaigns—and obtain funds to pay for those campaigns. In some judicial races, campaign contributions have exceeded $5 million. Typically, a substantial portion of those funds has come from trial lawyers, many of whom argue cases before the very judges whose campaigns they help to finance. In 2000, affiliates of the U.S. Chamber of Commerce spent close to $10 million on ads in state judicial races in support of or against specific judges. Because of increasing influence of campaign contributions on state judicial elections, some have advocated legal reforms that include placing caps on contributions to state judicial candidates.[9]

Trial Courts Trial courts are exactly what their name implies—courts in which trials are held and testimony taken. State trial courts have either general or limited jurisdiction. Trial courts that have general jurisdiction as to subject matter may be called county, district, superior, or circuit courts.[10] The jurisdiction of these courts is often determined by the size of the county in which the court sits. State trial courts of general jurisdiction have jurisdiction over a wide variety of subjects, including both civil disputes and criminal prosecutions. In some states, trial courts of general jurisdiction may hear appeals from courts of limited jurisdiction.

Some courts of limited jurisdiction are called special inferior trial courts or minor judiciary courts. **Small claims courts** are inferior trial courts that hear only civil cases involving claims of less than a certain amount, such as $5,000 (the amount varies from state to state). Suits brought in small claims courts are generally conducted informally, and lawyers are not required. In a minority of states, lawyers are not even allowed to represent people in small claims courts for most purposes. Another example of an inferior trial court is a local municipal court that hears mainly traffic cases. Decisions of small claims courts and municipal courts may be appealed to a state trial court of general jurisdiction.

SMALL CLAIMS COURT
A special court in which parties may litigate small claims (such as $5,000 or less). Attorneys are not required in small claims courts and, in some states, are not allowed to represent the parties.

9. For further information on this issue, see Emily Heller and Mark Ballard, "Hard-Fought, Big-Money Judicial Races," *The National Law Journal,* November 6, 2000, pp. A1 and A8.
10. The name in Ohio is court of common pleas; the name in New York is supreme court.

Other courts of limited jurisdiction as to subject matter include probate courts, as mentioned earlier, and domestic relations courts, which handle only certain types of cases, including divorce actions and child-custody cases.

Courts of Appeals Every state has at least one court of appeals (appellate court, or reviewing court), which may be an intermediate appellate court or the state's highest court. About three-fourths of the states have intermediate appellate courts. Generally, courts of appeals do not conduct new trials, in which evidence is submitted to the court and witnesses are examined. Rather, an appellate court panel of three or more judges reviews the record of the case on appeal, which includes a transcript of the trial proceedings, and determines whether the trial court committed an error.

Usually, appellate courts do not look at questions of *fact* (such as whether a party did, in fact, commit a certain action, such as burning a flag) but at questions of *law* (such as whether the act of flag-burning is a form of speech protected by the First Amendment to the Constitution). Only a judge, not a jury, can rule on questions of law. Appellate courts normally defer to a trial court's findings on questions of fact because the trial court judge and jury were in a better position to evaluate testimony—by directly observing witnesses' gestures, demeanor, and nonverbal behavior during the trial. At the appellate level, the judges review the written transcript of the trial, which does not include these nonverbal elements.

An appellate court will challenge a trial court's finding of fact only when the finding is clearly erroneous (that is, when it is contrary to the evidence presented at trial) or when there is no evidence to support the finding. ● EXAMPLE 6 If a jury concluded that a manufacturer's product harmed the plaintiff but no evidence was submitted to the court to support that conclusion, the appellate court would hold that the trial court's decision was erroneous.● The options exercised by appellate courts will be further discussed later in this chapter.

State Supreme (Highest) Courts The highest appellate court in a state is usually called the supreme court but may be called by some other name. For example, in both New York and Maryland, the highest state court is called the court of appeals. The decisions of each state's highest court on all questions of state law are final. Only when issues of federal law are involved can a decision made by a state's highest court be overruled by the United States Supreme Court.

The Federal Court System

The federal court system is basically a three-tiered model consisting of (1) U.S. district courts (trial courts of general jurisdiction) and various courts of limited jurisdiction, (2) U.S. courts of appeals (intermediate courts of appeals), and (3) the United States Supreme Court.

Unlike state court judges, who are usually elected, federal court judges—including the justices of the Supreme Court—are appointed by the president of the United States and confirmed by the U.S. Senate. All federal judges receive lifetime appointments (because under Article III they "hold their offices during Good Behavior").

U.S. District Courts At the federal level, the equivalent of a state trial court of general jurisdiction is the district court. There is at least one federal district

A mother talks with a social worker after a court awarded the mother custody of her child. Are child-custody matters decided by federal or state courts?

BE AWARE The decisions of a state's highest court are final on questions of state law.

court in every state. The number of judicial districts can vary over time, primarily owing to population changes and corresponding caseloads. Currently, there are ninety-four federal judicial districts.

U.S. district courts have original jurisdiction in federal matters. Federal cases typically originate in district courts. There are other courts with original, but special (or limited), jurisdiction, such as the federal bankruptcy courts and others shown in Exhibit 4–2 on page 113.

U.S. Courts of Appeals In the federal court system, there are thirteen U.S. courts of appeals—also referred to as U.S. circuit courts of appeals. The federal courts of appeals for twelve of the circuits, including the U.S. Court of Appeals for the District of Columbia Circuit, hear appeals from the federal district courts located within their respective judicial circuits. The Court of Appeals for the Thirteenth Circuit, called the Federal Circuit, has national appellate jurisdiction over certain types of cases, such as cases involving patent law and cases in which the U.S. government is a defendant.

The decisions of the circuit courts of appeals are final in most cases, but appeal to the United States Supreme Court is possible. Exhibit 4–3 shows the geographic boundaries of the U.S. circuit courts of appeals and the boundaries of the U.S. district courts within each circuit.

The United States Supreme Court The highest level of the three-tiered model of the federal court system is the United States Supreme Court. According to

EXHIBIT 4–3   U.S. COURTS OF APPEALS AND U.S. DISTRICT COURTS

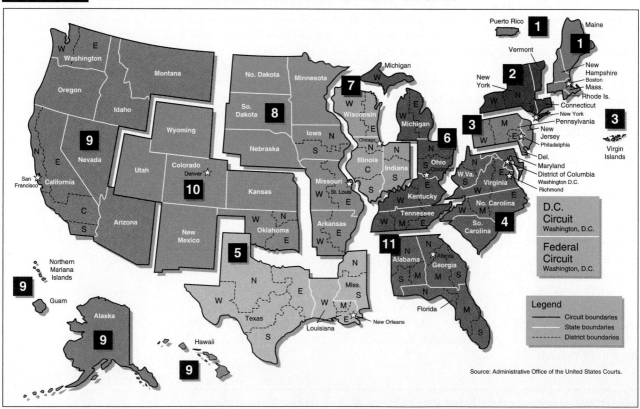

Source: Administrative Office of the United States Courts.

The justices of the U.S. Supreme Court (as of early 2004) are, seated left to right, Antonin Scalia, John Paul Stevens, Chief Justice William H. Rehnquist, Sandra Day O'Connor, and Anthony M. Kennedy; and standing left to right, Ruth Bader Ginsburg, David H. Souter, Clarence Thomas, and Stephen Breyer. Does the fact that these justices are appointed for life have any effect on the decisions they reach in the cases they hear?

the language of Article III of the U.S. Constitution, there is only one national Supreme Court. All other courts in the federal system are considered "inferior." Congress is empowered to create other inferior courts as it deems necessary. The inferior courts that Congress has created include the second tier in our model—the U.S. courts of appeals—as well as the district courts and any other courts of limited, or specialized, jurisdiction.

The United States Supreme Court consists of nine justices. Although the Supreme Court has original, or trial, jurisdiction in rare instances (set forth in Article III, Section 2), most of its work is as an appeals court. The Supreme Court can review any case decided by any of the federal courts of appeals, and it also has appellate authority over some cases decided in the state courts.

Appeals to the Supreme Court. To bring a case before the Supreme Court, a party requests the Court to issue a writ of *certiorari.* A **writ of *certiorari***[11] is an order issued by the Supreme Court to a lower court requiring the latter to send it the record of the case for review. The Court will not issue a writ unless at least four of the nine justices approve of it. This is called the **rule of four.** Whether the Court will issue a writ of *certiorari* is entirely within its discretion. The Court is not required to issue one, and most petitions for writs are denied. (Thousands of cases are filed with the Supreme Court each year, yet it hears, on average, fewer than one hundred of these cases.)[12] A denial is not a decision on the merits of a case, nor does it indicate agreement with the lower court's opinion. Furthermore, a denial of the writ has no value as a precedent.

Petitions Granted by the Court. Typically, the petitions granted by the Court involve cases that raise important constitutional questions or cases that conflict with other state or federal court decisions. Similarly, if federal appellate

> "We are not final because we are infallible, but we are infallible only because we are final."
>
> ROBERT H. JACKSON,
> 1892–1954
> (Associate justice of the United States Supreme Court, 1941–1954)

WRIT OF *CERTIORARI*
A writ from a higher court asking the lower court for the record of a case.

RULE OF FOUR
A rule of the United States Supreme Court under which the Court will not issue a writ of *certiorari* unless at least four justices approve of the decision to issue the writ.

11. Pronounced sur-shee-uh-*rah*-ree.
12. From the mid-1950s through the early 1990s, the Supreme Court reviewed more cases per year than it has in the last few years. In the Court's 1982–1983 term, for example, the Court issued opinions in 151 cases. In contrast, in its 2002–2003 term, the Court issued opinions in only 80 cases.

courts are rendering inconsistent opinions on an important issue, the Supreme Court may review the case and issue a decision to define the law on the matter. The justices, however, never explain their reasons for hearing certain cases and not others, so it is difficult to predict which type of case the Court might select.

Certainly, many legal scholars were surprised when the Court, in the confusing aftermath of the 2000 presidential elections, decided to review the Florida Supreme Court's decision that the votes in selected Florida counties could be manually recounted. Many observers had predicted that, given the Court's tendency to support states' rights and its traditional reluctance to get involved in "political questions," it would deny *certiorari* in that case. The Court, however, concluded that the case raised an important constitutional question—whether manually counting votes in some counties but not others violated the equal protection clause—and thus reviewed (and overturned) the Florida court's decision.[13]

FOLLOWING A STATE COURT CASE

To illustrate the procedures that would be followed in a civil lawsuit brought in a state court, we present a hypothetical case and follow it through the state court system. The case involves an automobile accident in which Kevin Anderson, driving a Mercedes, struck Lisa Marconi, driving a Ford Taurus. The accident occurred at the intersection of Wilshire Boulevard and Rodeo Drive in Beverly Hills, California. Marconi suffered personal injuries, incurring medical and hospital expenses as well as lost wages for four months. Anderson and Marconi are unable to agree on a settlement, and Marconi sues Anderson. Marconi is the plaintiff, and Anderson is the defendant. Both are represented by lawyers.

During each phase of the litigation, Marconi and Anderson will be required to observe strict procedural requirements. A large body of law—procedural law—establishes the rules and standards for determining disputes in courts. Procedural rules are very complex, and they vary from court to court. There is a set of federal rules of procedure, as noted in Chapter 3, as well as various sets of rules for state courts. Additionally, the applicable procedures will depend on whether the case is a civil or criminal proceeding. Generally, the Marconi-Anderson civil lawsuit will involve the procedures discussed in the following subsections. Keep in mind that attempts to settle the case may be ongoing throughout the trial.

PLEADINGS
Statements made by the plaintiff and the defendant in a lawsuit that detail the facts, charges, and defenses involved in the litigation; the complaint and answer are part of the pleadings.

COMPLAINT
The pleading made by a plaintiff alleging wrongdoing on the part of the defendant; the document that, when filed with a court, initiates a lawsuit.

The Pleadings

The complaint and answer (and the counterclaim and reply)—all of which are discussed below—taken together are called the **pleadings.** The pleadings inform each party of the other's claims and specify the issues (disputed questions) involved in the case.

The Plaintiff's Complaint Marconi's suit against Anderson commences when her lawyer files a **complaint** with the appropriate court. The complaint con-

---

13. *Bush v. Gore,* 531 U.S. 98, 121 S.Ct. 525, 148 L.Ed.2d 388 (2000).

tains a statement alleging (asserting to the court, in a pleading) the facts necessary for the court to take jurisdiction, a brief summary of the facts necessary to show that the plaintiff is entitled to a remedy, and a statement of the remedy the plaintiff is seeking. Exhibit 4–4 illustrates how the complaint might read in the Marconi Anderson case. Complaints may be lengthy or brief, depending on the complexity of the case.

EXHIBIT 4–4   EXAMPLE OF A TYPICAL COMPLAINT

IN THE LOS ANGELES MUNICIPAL COURT
FOR THE LOS ANGELES JUDICIAL DISTRICT

CIVIL NO. 8–1026

Lisa Marconi
_____
       Plaintiff

              v.
                                                    COMPLAINT

Kevin Anderson
_____
       Defendant

Comes now the plaintiff and for her cause of action against the defendant alleges and states as follows:

1. The jurisdiction of this court is based on Section 86 of the California Civil Code.
2. This action is between plaintiff, a California resident living at 1434 Palm Drive, Anaheim, California, and defendant, a California resident living at 6950 Garrison Avenue, Los Angeles, California.
3. On September 10, 2001, plaintiff, Lisa Marconi, was exercising good driving habits and reasonable care in driving her car through the intersection of Rodeo Drive and Wilshire Boulevard when defendant, Kevin Anderson, negligently drove his vehicle through a red light at the intersection and collided with plaintiff's vehicle. Defendant was negligent in the operation of the vehicle as to:

   a. Speed,
   b. Lookout,
   c. Management and control.

4. As a result of the collision plaintiff suffered severe physical injury that prevented her from working and property damage to her car. The costs she incurred included $10,000 in medical bills, $9,000 in lost wages, and $5,000 for automobile repairs.

WHEREFORE, plaintiff demands judgment against the defendant for the sum of $24,000 plus interest at the maximum legal rate and the costs of this action.

By _____ _Robert Harrington_ _____
Robert Harrington
Attorney for the Plaintiff
800 Orange Avenue
Anaheim, CA 91426

SUMMONS
A document informing a defendant that a legal action has been commenced against him or her and that the defendant must appear in court on a certain date to answer the plaintiff's complaint. The document is delivered by a sheriff or any other person so authorized.

DEFAULT JUDGMENT
A judgment entered by a court against a defendant who has failed to appear in court to answer or defend against the plaintiff's claim.

ANSWER
Procedurally, a defendant's response to the plaintiff's complaint.

COUNTERCLAIM
A claim made by a defendant in a civil lawsuit against the plaintiff. In effect, the defendant is suing the plaintiff.

REPLY
Procedurally, a plaintiff's response to a defendant's answer.

MOTION TO DISMISS
A pleading in which a defendant asserts that the plaintiff's claim fails to state a cause of action (that is, has no basis in law) or that there are other grounds on which a suit should be dismissed.

MOTION FOR JUDGMENT ON THE PLEADINGS
A motion by either party to a lawsuit at the close of the pleadings requesting the court to decide the issue solely on the pleadings without proceeding to trial. The motion will be granted only if no facts are in dispute.

After the complaint has been filed, the sheriff, a deputy of the county, or another *process server* (one who delivers a complaint and summons) serves a **summons** and a copy of the complaint on defendant Anderson. The summons notifies Anderson that he must file an answer to the complaint with both the court and the plaintiff's attorney within a specified time period (usually twenty to thirty days). The summons also informs Anderson that failure to answer may result in a **default judgment** for the plaintiff, meaning the plaintiff will be awarded the damages alleged in her complaint.

The Defendant's Answer The defendant's **answer** either admits the statements or allegations set forth in the complaint or denies them and outlines any defenses that the defendant may have. If Anderson admits to all of Marconi's allegations in his answer, the court will enter a judgment for Marconi. If Anderson denies any of Marconi's allegations, the litigation will go forward.

Anderson can deny Marconi's allegations and set forth his own claim that Marconi was in fact negligent and therefore owes him money for damages to his Mercedes. This is appropriately called a **counterclaim.** If Anderson files a counterclaim, Marconi will have to answer it with a pleading, normally called a **reply,** which has the same characteristics as an answer.

Anderson can also admit the truth of Marconi's complaint but raise new facts that may result in dismissal of the action. This is called *raising an affirmative defense.* For example, Anderson could assert the expiration of the time period under the relevant statute of limitations (a state or federal statute that sets the maximum time period during which a certain action can be brought or rights enforced) as an affirmative defense.

Motion to Dismiss A **motion to dismiss** requests the court to dismiss the case for stated reasons. A defendant often makes a motion to dismiss before filing an answer to the plaintiff's complaint. Grounds for dismissal of a case include improper delivery of the complaint and summons, improper venue, and the plaintiff's failure to state a claim for which a court could grant relief (a remedy). For example, if Marconi had suffered no injuries or losses as a result of Anderson's negligence, Anderson could move to have the case dismissed because Marconi had not stated a claim for which relief could be granted.

If the judge grants the motion to dismiss, the plaintiff generally is given time to file an amended complaint. If the judge denies the motion, the suit will go forward, and the defendant must then file an answer. Note that if Marconi wishes to discontinue the suit because, for example, an out-of-court settlement has been reached, she can likewise move for dismissal. The court can also dismiss the case on its own motion.

Pretrial Motions

Either party may attempt to get the case dismissed before trial through the use of various pretrial motions. We have already mentioned the motion to dismiss. Two other important pretrial motions are the motion for judgment on the pleadings and the motion for summary judgment.

At the close of the pleadings, either party may make a **motion for judgment on the pleadings,** or on the merits of the case. The judge will grant the motion only when there is no dispute over the facts of the case and the only issue to be resolved is a question of law. In deciding on the motion, the judge may consider only the evidence contained in the pleadings.

In contrast, in a **motion for summary judgment** the court may consider evidence outside the pleadings, such as sworn statements (affidavits) by parties or witnesses or other documents relating to the case. A motion for summary judgment can be made by either party. As with the motion for judgment on the pleadings, a motion for summary judgment will be granted only if there are no genuine questions of fact and the only question is a question of law.

Discovery

Before a trial begins, each party can use a number of procedural devices to obtain information and gather evidence about the case from the other party or from third parties. The process of obtaining such information is known as **discovery**. Discovery includes gaining access to witnesses, documents, records, and other types of evidence.

The Federal Rules of Civil Procedure and similar rules in the states set forth the guidelines for discovery activity. The rules governing discovery are designed to make sure that a witness or a party is not unduly harassed, that privileged material (communications that need not be presented in court) is safeguarded, and that only matters relevant to the case at hand are discoverable.

Discovery prevents surprises at trial by giving parties access to evidence that might otherwise be hidden. This allows both parties to learn as much as they can about what to expect at a trial before they reach the courtroom.[14] It also serves to narrow the issues so that trial time is spent on the main questions in the case.

Depositions and Interrogatories Discovery can involve the use of depositions or interrogatories, or both. **Depositions** are sworn testimony by a party to the lawsuit or any witness. The person being deposed (the deponent) answers questions asked by the attorneys, and the questions and answers are recorded by an authorized court official and sworn to and signed by the deponent. (Occasionally, written depositions are taken when witnesses are unable to appear in person.) The answers given to depositions will, of course, help the attorneys prepare their cases. They can also be used in court to impeach (challenge the credibility of) a party or a witness who changes testimony at the trial. In addition, the answers given in a deposition can be used as testimony if the witness is not available at trial.

Interrogatories are written questions for which written answers are prepared and then signed under oath. The main difference between interrogatories and written depositions is that interrogatories are directed to a party to the lawsuit (the plaintiff or the defendant), not to a witness, and the party can prepare answers with the aid of an attorney. The scope of interrogatories is broader, because parties are obligated to answer questions, even if it means disclosing information from their records and files.

Other Information A party can serve a written request to the other party for an admission of the truth of matters relating to the trial. Any matter admitted under such a request is conclusively established for the trial. For example, Marconi can ask Anderson to admit that he was driving at a speed of forty-five

MOTION FOR SUMMARY JUDGMENT
A motion requesting the court to enter a judgment without proceeding to trial. The motion can be based on evidence outside the pleadings and will be granted only if no facts are in dispute.

DISCOVERY
A phase in the litigation process during which the opposing parties may obtain information from each other and from third parties prior to trial.

DEPOSITION
The testimony of a party to a lawsuit or a witness taken under oath before a trial.

INTERROGATORIES
A series of written questions for which written answers are prepared, usually with the assistance of the party's attorney, and then signed under oath by a party to a lawsuit.

---

14. This is particularly evident in the 1993 revision of the Federal Rules of Civil Procedure. The revised rules provide that each party must disclose to the other, on an ongoing basis, the types of evidence that will be presented at trial, the names of witnesses that may or will be called, and so on.

miles an hour. A request for admission saves time at trial, because the parties will not have to spend time proving facts on which they already agree.

A party can also gain access to documents and other items not in her or his possession in order to inspect and examine them. Likewise, a party can gain "entry upon land" to inspect the premises. Anderson's attorney, for example, normally can gain permission to inspect and duplicate Marconi's car repair bills.

When the physical or mental condition of one party is in question, the opposing party can ask the court to order a physical or mental examination. If the court is willing to make the order, which it will do only if the need for the information outweighs the right to privacy of the person to be examined, the opposing party can obtain the results of the examination.

Electronic Discovery and Compliance Costs   Under the Federal Rules of Civil Procedure, any relevant material may be the object of a discovery request, and generally, the party responding must pay the expense to comply. A court can limit the scope of a request, however, if compliance would be too burdensome or the cost would be too high.

As individuals and businesses have increased their use of computers to create and store documents, make deals, and exchange e-mail, the universe of discoverable material has expanded exponentially. The more information there is to discover, however, the more expensive it is to uncover all the relevant data.

Some courts have balanced these competing principles by shifting the cost of discovery to the requesting party. The point of contention has been when this "cost-shifting" should occur. In the following case, involving the discovery of electronic data, the court developed a new set of factors for determining when discovery costs should be shifted to the requester.

CASE 4.4   Zubulake v. UBS Warburg, LLC

United States District Court,
Southern District of New York, 2003.
__ F.Supp.2d __.

HISTORICAL AND TECHNOLOGICAL SETTING
UBS Warburg, LLC, is an investment sales firm. Each UBS salesperson receives nearly two hundred e-mails each day. UBS maintains e-mail files in three forms: active user e-mail files, archived e-mails on optical disks, and back-up data stored on tapes. The active data are the most accessible: it is online data that resides on an active server and can be accessed immediately. The optical disk data are only slightly less accessible; the disks need to be located and read, but the system is configured to make searching simple and automated once they are located. E-mail stored on back-up tape is indexed, which makes finding a specific message relatively easy, but restoring a message stored on tape takes five days.

BACKGROUND AND FACTS   UBS hired Laura Zubulake in August 1999 as a director and senior salesperson in a department managed by Dominic Vail. At the time, Zubulake was told that she would be considered for Vail's position if it became vacant. In December 2000, however, when the position opened, she was not considered—UBS hired Matthew Chapin instead. Less than eight months later, Zubulake filed a charge with the Equal Employment Opportunity Commission, alleging that Chapin had, among other things, excluded her from work-related activities with male co-workers and clients.[a] Less than eight weeks later, she was fired. She filed a suit in a federal district court against UBS, alleging violations of discrimination laws. As part of a discovery request, Zubulake asked UBS for "[a]ll documents concerning any communication by or between UBS employees concerning Plaintiff," including "without limitation, electronic or computerized data compilations." UBS produced one hundred pages of e-mail but refused to search further, claiming that the cost would be too high.

---

a. This allegation and Zubulake's other charges relate to employment discrimination, which is discussed in detail in Chapter 17.

CASE 4.4—Continued

IN THE WORDS
OF THE COURT . . .

SCHEINDLIN, J. [Judge]

The world was a far different place in 1849, when Henry David Thoreau opined [thought, suggested] * * * that "[t]he process of discovery is very simple." That hopeful maxim has given way to rapid technological advances, requiring new solutions to old problems. The issue presented here is one such problem, recast in light of current technology: To what extent is inaccessible electronic data discoverable, and who should pay for its production?

* * * *

* * * [D]eciding disputes regarding the scope and cost of discovery of electronic data requires a three-step analysis:

First, it is necessary to thoroughly understand the responding party's computer system, both with respect to active and stored data. For data that is kept in an accessible format, the usual rules of discovery apply: the responding party should pay the costs of producing responsive data. A court should consider cost-shifting *only* when electronic data [are] relatively inaccessible, such as in back-up tapes.

Second, because the cost-shifting analysis is so fact-intensive, it is necessary to determine what data may be found on the inaccessible media. Requiring the responding party to restore and produce responsive documents from a small sample of the requested back-up tapes is a sensible approach in most cases.

Third, and finally, in conducting the cost-shifting analysis, the following factors should be considered, weighted more-or-less in the following order:

1. The extent to which the request is specifically tailored to discover relevant information;
2. The availability of such information from other sources;
3. The total cost of production, compared to the amount in controversy;
4. The total cost of production, compared to the resources available to each party;
5. The relative ability of each party to control costs and its incentive to do so;
6. The importance of the issues at stake in the litigation; and
7. The relative benefits to the parties of obtaining the information.

Accordingly, UBS is ordered to produce *all* responsive e-mails that exist on its optical disks or on its active servers * * * at its own expense. UBS is also ordered to produce, at its expense, responsive e-mails from any *five* back-up tapes selected *by Zubulake.* UBS should then prepare an affidavit detailing the results of its search, as well as the time and money spent. After reviewing the contents of the back-up tapes and UBS's [affidavit], the Court will conduct the appropriate cost-shifting analysis.

DECISION AND REMEDY The court issued a new seven-factor test for determining when the cost of discovery of electronic data should be shifted to the requesting party. Based on this test, the court ordered UBS to retrieve all data from easily accessible media at its own expense. The court also ordered the defendant to retrieve, from a "relatively inaccessible" medium (the back-up tapes), certain sample data, the expense and content of which the court would review to decide whether the plaintiff should pay the cost to retrieve more.

FOR CRITICAL ANALYSIS—Economic Consideration *Should cost-shifting be considered in every case involving the discovery of electronic data?*

Pretrial Conference

Either party or the court can request a pretrial conference, or hearing. Usually, the hearing consists of an informal discussion between the judge and the opposing attorneys after discovery has taken place. The purpose of the hearing is to explore the possibility of a settlement without trial and, if this is not possible, to identify the matters that are in dispute and to plan the course of the trial.

Jury Selection

A trial can be held with or without a jury. The Seventh Amendment to the U.S. Constitution guarantees the right to a jury trial for cases in federal courts when the amount in controversy exceeds $20. Most states have similar guarantees in their own constitutions (although the threshold dollar amount is higher than $20). The right to a trial by jury does not have to be exercised, and many cases are tried without a jury. In most states and in federal courts, one of the parties must request a jury, or the right is presumed to be waived.

Before a jury trial commences, a jury must be selected. The jury-selection process is known as *voir dire*.[15] In most jurisdictions, *voir dire* consists of oral questions that attorneys for the plaintiff and the defendant ask prospective jurors to determine whether a potential jury member is biased or has any connection with a party to the action or with a prospective witness.

During *voir dire*, a party may challenge a certain number of prospective jurors *peremptorily*—that is, ask that an individual not be sworn in as a juror without providing any reason. Alternatively, a party may challenge a prospective juror *for cause*—that is, provide a reason why an individual should not be sworn in as a juror. If the judge grants the challenge, the individual is asked to step down. A prospective juror may not be excluded from the jury by the use of discriminatory challenges, however, such as those based on racial criteria[16] or gender.[17]

VOIR DIRE
Old French verbs that mean "to speak the truth." In jury trials, the phrase refers to the process in which the attorneys question prospective jurors to determine whether they are biased or have any connection with a party to the action or with a prospective witness.

TAKE NOTE A prospective juror cannot be excluded solely on the basis of his or her race or gender.

At the Trial

At the beginning of the trial, the attorneys present their opening arguments, setting forth the facts that they expect to provide during the trial. Then the plaintiff's case is presented. In our hypothetical case, Marconi's lawyer would introduce evidence (relevant documents, exhibits, and the testimony of witnesses) to support Marconi's position. The defendant has the opportunity to challenge any evidence introduced and to cross-examine any of the plaintiff's witnesses.

At the end of the plaintiff's case, the defendant's attorney has the opportunity to ask the judge to direct a verdict for the defendant on the ground that the plaintiff has presented no evidence that would justify the granting of the

---

15. Pronounced vwahr *deehr*.
16. *Batson v. Kentucky,* 476 U.S. 79, 106 S.Ct. 1712, 90 L.Ed.2d 69 (1986).
17. *J.E.B. v. Alabama ex rel. T.B.,* 511 U.S. 127, 114 S.Ct. 1419, 128 L.Ed.2d 89 (1994). (*Ex rel.* is Latin for *ex relatione.* The phrase refers to an action brought on behalf of the state, by the attorney general, at the instigation of an individual who has a private interest in the matter.) This case is the subject of this chapter's "Question of Ethics and Social Responsibility" on page 133.

plaintiff's remedy. This is called a **motion for a directed verdict** (known in federal courts as a *motion for judgment as a matter of law*). If the motion is not granted (it seldom is), the defendant's attorney then presents the evidence and witnesses for the defendant's case. At the conclusion of the defendant's case, the defendant's attorney has another opportunity to make a motion for a directed verdict. The plaintiff's attorney can challenge any evidence introduced and cross-examine the defendant's witnesses.

After the defense concludes its presentation, the attorneys present their closing arguments, each urging a verdict in favor of her or his client. The judge instructs the jury in the law that applies to the case (these instructions are often called *charges*), and the jury retires to the jury room to deliberate a verdict. In the Marconi-Anderson case, the jury will not only decide for the plaintiff or for the defendant but, if it finds for the plaintiff, will also decide on the amount of the **award** (the money to be paid to her).

Posttrial Motions

After the jury has rendered its verdict, either party may make a posttrial motion. If Marconi wins, and Anderson's attorney has previously moved for a directed verdict, Anderson's attorney may make a **motion for judgment *n.o.v.*** (from the Latin *non obstante veredicto,* which means "notwithstanding the verdict"—called a *motion for judgment as a matter of law* in the federal courts) in Anderson's favor on the ground that the jury verdict in favor of Marconi was unreasonable and erroneous. If the judge decides that the jury's verdict was reasonable in light of the evidence presented at trial, the motion will be denied. If the judge agrees with Anderson's attorney, then he or she will set the jury's verdict aside and enter a judgment in favor of Anderson.

Alternatively, Anderson could make a **motion for a new trial,** requesting the judge to set aside the adverse verdict and to hold a new trial. The motion will be granted if the judge is convinced, after looking at all the evidence, that the jury was in error but does not feel it is appropriate to grant judgment for the other side. A new trial may also be granted on the ground of newly discovered evidence, misconduct by the participants or the jury during the trial, or error by the judge.

The Appeal

Assume here that any posttrial motion is denied and that Anderson appeals the case. (If Marconi wins but receives a smaller money award than she sought, she can appeal also.) A notice of appeal must be filed with the clerk of the trial court within a prescribed time. Anderson now becomes the appellant, or petitioner, and Marconi becomes the appellee, or respondent.

Filing the Appeal Anderson's attorney files with the appellate court the record on appeal, which includes the pleadings, the trial transcript, the judge's rulings on motions made by the parties, and other trial-related documents. Anderson's attorney will also provide a condensation of the record, known as an abstract, which is filed with the reviewing court along with the brief. The **brief** is a formal legal document outlining the facts and issues of the case, the judge's rulings or jury's findings that should be reversed or modified, the applicable law, and arguments on Anderson's behalf (citing applicable statutes and relevant cases as precedents).

MOTION FOR A DIRECTED VERDICT
In a jury trial, a motion for the judge to take the decision out of the hands of the jury and direct a verdict for the party who filed the motion on the ground that the other party has not produced sufficient evidence to support her or his claim.

AWARD
The amount of money awarded to a plaintiff in a civil lawsuit as damages.

MOTION FOR JUDGMENT *N.O.V.*
A motion requesting the court to grant judgment in favor of the party making the motion on the ground that the jury verdict against him or her was unreasonable and erroneous.

MOTION FOR A NEW TRIAL
A motion asserting that the trial was so fundamentally flawed (because of error, newly discovered evidence, prejudice, or other reason) that a new trial is necessary to prevent a miscarriage of justice.

BRIEF
A formal legal document submitted by the attorney for the appellant or the appellee (in answer to the appellant's brief) to an appellate court when a case is appealed. The appellant's brief outlines the facts and issues of the case, the judge's rulings or jury's findings that should be reversed or modified, the applicable law, and the arguments on the client's behalf.

Marconi's attorney will file an answering brief. Anderson's attorney can file a reply to Marconi's brief, although it is not required. The reviewing court then considers the case.

Appellate Review As mentioned earlier, a court of appeals does not hear evidence. Rather, it reviews the record for errors of law. Its decision concerning a case is based on the record on appeal, the abstracts, and the attorneys' briefs. The attorneys can present oral arguments, after which the case is taken under advisement. In general, appellate courts do not reverse findings of fact unless the findings are unsupported or contradicted by the evidence.

If the reviewing court believes that an error was committed during the trial or that the jury was improperly instructed, the judgment will be *reversed.* Sometimes the case will be *remanded* (sent back to the court that originally heard the case) for a new trial.

A case may be remanded for several reasons. ● **EXAMPLE 7** If the appellate court decides that a judge improperly granted summary judgment, the case will be remanded for trial. If the appellate court decides that the trial judge erroneously applied the law, the case will be remanded for a new trial, with instructions to the trial court to apply the law as clarified by the appellate court. If the appellate court decides that the trial jury's award of damages was too high, the case will be remanded with instructions to reduce the damages award. ● In most cases, the judgment of the lower court is *affirmed,* resulting in the enforcement of the court's judgment or decree.

As noted earlier in this text, in the appendix following Chapter 1, most of the state court opinions presented in this book are from state appellate courts. In part, this is because most state trial court decisions are not published in reporters and are thus not readily available. Also important, however, is the fact that appellate courts decide questions of law, and all trial courts within that jurisdiction will be obligated to follow the appellate court's opinion with respect to a particular issue. Thus, appellate court decisions have a broader reach and more final authority than decisions rendered by trial courts. Even when a case is remanded to a trial court for further proceedings, the appellate court normally spells out how the relevant law should be interpreted and applied to the case. Thus, you may not learn about the ultimate disposition of a case after it has been remanded, but you will discover the relevant legal principles and laws that apply to the case.

Appeal to a Higher Appellate Court If the reviewing court is an intermediate appellate court, the losing party normally may appeal to the state supreme court (the highest state court). Such a petition corresponds to a petition for a writ of *certiorari* from the United States Supreme Court. If the petition is granted (in some states, a petition is automatically granted), new briefs must be filed before the state supreme court, and the attorneys may be allowed or requested to present oral arguments. Like the intermediate appellate courts, the supreme court may reverse or affirm the appellate court's decision or remand the case. At this point, unless a federal question is at issue, the case cannot be appealed further.

Enforcing the Judgment

The uncertainties of the litigation process are compounded by the lack of guarantees that any judgment will be enforceable. Even if a plaintiff wins an award of damages in court, the defendant may not have sufficient assets or insurance to cover that amount. Usually, one of the factors considered before a lawsuit is initiated is whether the defendant has sufficient assets to cover the amount of damages sought, should the plaintiff win the case.

THE COURTS ADAPT TO THE ONLINE WORLD

We have already mentioned how the courts have attempted to adapt traditional jurisdictional concepts to the online world. Not surprisingly, the Internet has also brought about changes in court procedures and practices, including new methods for filing pleadings and other documents and issuing decisions and opinions. Several courts are experimenting with electronic delivery, such as via the Internet or CD-ROM. Some jurisdictions are exploring the possibility of cyber courts, in which legal proceedings could be conducted totally online.

Electronic Filing

The federal court system first experimented with an electronic filing system in January 1996, in an asbestos case heard by the U.S. District Court for the Northern District of Ohio. Currently, a number of federal courts permit attorneys to file documents electronically in certain types of cases. At last count, more than 7 million cases had been filed electronically in federal courts. The Administrative Office of the U.S. Courts expects that electronic filing will be available for all federal courts by 2005.

State and local courts are also setting up electronic court filing systems. Since the late 1990s, the court system in Pima County, Arizona, has been accepting pleadings via e-mail. The supreme court of the state of Washington also now accepts online filings of litigation documents. In addition, electronic filing projects are being developed in other states, including California, Idaho, Kansas, Maryland, Michigan, Mississippi, Texas, Utah, and Virginia. Notably, the judicial branch of the state of Colorado recently implemented the first statewide court e-filing system in the United States. In a number of other states, court clerks offer docket information and other searchable databases online.

Typically, when electronic filing is made available, it is optional. In 2001, however, a trial court judge in the District of Columbia launched a pilot project that *required* attorneys to file electronically all documents relating to certain types of civil cases.

ETHICAL ISSUE

How will electronic filing affect privacy?

From a practical perspective, trial court records, although normally available to the public, remain obscure. Because the decisions of most state trial courts (and some federal courts) are not published, someone must be strongly motivated to go to the trouble of traveling to the relevant courthouse in person to access the documents. If electronic filing becomes the norm, however, this "practical obscurity," as lawyers call it, may soon disappear. Electronic filing on a nationwide basis would open up all federal trial court documents to anyone with an Internet connection and a

Web browser. Utilizing special "data-mining" software, anyone could go online and within just a few minutes access information—ranging from personal health records to financial reports to criminal violations—from hundreds of courts. This means that serious privacy issues are at stake if courts nationwide adopt electronic filing. Should the courts restrict public access to certain types of documents, such as bankruptcy records or documents containing personal information that is not directly related to the legal issue being decided? Clearly, finding solutions to the privacy issues raised by electronic filing will not be easy.

Courts Online

Most courts today have sites on the Web. Of course, it is up to each court to decide what to make available at its site. Some courts display only the names of court personnel and office phone numbers. Others add court rules and forms. Some include judicial decisions, although generally the sites do not feature archives of old decisions. Instead, decisions are available online for only a limited time. For example, California keeps opinions online for only sixty days.

Appellate court decisions are often posted online immediately after they are rendered. Recent decisions of the U.S. courts of appeals, for example, are available online at their Web sites. The United States Supreme Court has also launched an official Web site and publishes its opinions there immediately after they are announced to the public.

Cyber Courts and Proceedings

Someday, litigants may be able to use cyber courts, in which judicial proceedings take place only on the Internet. The parties to a case could meet online to make their arguments and present their evidence. This might be done with e-mail submissions, through video cameras, in designated "chat rooms," at closed sites, or through the use of other Internet facilities. These courtrooms could be efficient and economical. We might also see the use of virtual lawyers, judges, and juries—and possibly the replacement of court personnel with computers or software.

The governor of Michigan recently proposed that separate cyber courts be created for cases involving technology and high-tech businesses. In these courts, everything would be done via computer and the Internet, rather than in a courtroom. The state of Maryland is also planning a separate judicial division for cases involving high-tech businesses. Many lawyers predict that other states will do likewise.

The courts may also use the Internet in other ways. In a ground-breaking decision in early 2001, for example, a Florida county court granted "virtual" visitation rights in a couple's divorce proceeding. Although the court granted custody rights to the father of the couple's ten-year-old daughter, the court also ordered each parent to buy a computer and a videoconferencing system so that the mother could "visit" with her child via the Internet at any time.[18]

Michigan governor John Engler signs legislation in 2001 creating the Michigan Cyber Court. What are some of the advantages of using cyber courts, instead of traditional courts, to resolve disputes? Are there any disadvantages?

18. For a discussion of this case, see Shelley Emling, "After the Divorce, Internet Visits?" *Austin American-Statesman*, January 30, 2001, pp. A1 and A10.

KEY TERMS

answer   120
award   125
bankruptcy court   105
brief   125
complaint   118
concurrent jurisdiction   106
counterclaim   120
default judgment   120
deposition   121
discovery   121
diversity of citizenship   106
docket   107
exclusive jurisdiction   106

federal question   106
interrogatories   121
judicial review   101
jurisdiction   102
justiciable controversy   111
long arm statute   102
motion for a directed verdict   125
motion for a new trial   125
motion for judgment *n.o.v.*   125
motion for judgment on the
   pleadings   120
motion for summary
   judgment   121

motion to dismiss   120
pleadings   118
probate court   105
reply   120
rule of four   117
small claims court   114
standing to sue   111
summons   120
venue   110
voir dire   124
writ of *certiorari*   117

CHAPTER SUMMARY   THE AMERICAN COURT SYSTEM

The Judiciary's Role in American Government (See pages 101–102.)	The role of the judiciary—the courts—in the American governmental system is to interpret and apply the law. Through the process of judicial review—determining the constitutionality of laws—the judicial branch acts as a check on the executive and legislative branches of government.
Basic Judicial Requirements (See pages 102–113.)	1. *Jurisdiction*—Before a court can hear a case, it must have jurisdiction over the person against whom the suit is brought or the property involved in the suit, as well as jurisdiction over the subject matter. a. Limited versus general jurisdiction—Limited jurisdiction exists when a court is limited to a specific subject matter, such as probate or divorce. General jurisdiction exists when a court can hear any kind of case. b. Original versus appellate jurisdiction—Original jurisdiction exists with courts that have authority to hear a case for the first time (trial courts). Appellate jurisdiction exists with courts of appeals, or reviewing courts; generally, appellate courts do not have original jurisdiction. c. Federal jurisdiction—Arises (1) when a federal question is involved (when the plaintiff's cause of action is based, at least in part, on the U.S. Constitution, a treaty, or a federal law) or (2) when a case involves diversity of citizenship (citizens of different states, for example) and the amount in controversy exceeds $75,000. d. Concurrent versus exclusive jurisdiction—Concurrent jurisdiction exists when two different courts have authority to hear the same case. Exclusive jurisdiction exists when only state courts or only federal courts have authority to hear a case. 2. *Jurisdiction in cyberspace*—Because the Internet does not have physical boundaries, traditional jurisdictional concepts have been difficult to apply in cases involving activities conducted via the Web. Gradually, the courts are developing standards to use in determining when jurisdiction over a Web owner or operator in another state is proper.

(continued)

CHAPTER SUMMARY THE AMERICAN COURT SYSTEM—Continued

Basic Judicial Requirements— continued	3. *Venue*—Venue has to do with the most appropriate location for a trial, which is usually the geographic area where the event leading to the dispute took place or where the parties reside. 4. *Standing to sue*—A requirement that a party must have a legally protected and tangible interest at stake sufficient to justify seeking relief through the court system. The controversy at issue must also be a justiciable controversy—one that is real and substantial, as opposed to hypothetical or academic.

The State and Federal Court Systems (See pages 113–118.)	1. *Trial courts*—Courts of original jurisdiction, in which legal actions are initiated.
	
	  a. State—Courts of general jurisdiction can hear any case; courts of limited jurisdiction include divorce courts, probate courts, traffic courts, small claims courts, and so on.
	
	  b. Federal—The federal district court is the equivalent of the state trial court. Federal courts of limited jurisdiction include the U.S. Tax Court, the U.S. Bankruptcy Court, and the U.S. Court of Federal Claims.
	
	2. *Intermediate appellate courts*—Courts of appeals, or reviewing courts; generally without original jurisdiction. Many states have an intermediate appellate court; in the federal court system, the U.S. circuit courts of appeals are the intermediate appellate courts.
	
	3. *Supreme (highest) courts*—Each state has a supreme court, although it may be called by some other name, from which appeal to the United States Supreme Court is possible only if a federal question is involved. The United States Supreme Court is the highest court in the federal court system and the final arbiter of the Constitution and federal law.

Following a State Court Case (See pages 118–127.)	Rules of procedure prescribe the way in which disputes are handled in the courts. Rules differ from court to court, and separate sets of rules exist for federal and state courts, as well as for criminal and civil cases. A sample civil court case in a state court would involve the following procedures:
	
	1. *The pleadings*—
	
	  a. Complaint—Filed by the plaintiff with the court to initiate the lawsuit; served with a summons on the defendant.
	
	  b. Answer—Admits or denies allegations made by the plaintiff; may assert a counterclaim or an affirmative defense.
	
	  c. Motion to dismiss—A request to the court to dismiss the case for stated reasons, such as the plaintiff's failure to state a claim for which relief can be granted.
	
	2. *Pretrial motions (in addition to the motion to dismiss)*—
	
	  a. Motion for judgment on the pleadings—May be made by either party; will be granted if the parties agree on the facts and the only question is how the law applies to the facts. The judge bases the decision solely on the pleadings.
	
	  b. Motion for summary judgment—May be made by either party; will be granted if the parties agree on the facts. The judge applies the law in rendering a judgment. The judge can consider evidence outside the pleadings when evaluating the motion.
	
	3. *Discovery*—The process of gathering evidence concerning the case. Discovery involves depositions (sworn testimony by a party to the lawsuit or any witness), interrogatories (written questions and answers to these questions made by parties to the action with the aid of their attorneys), and various requests (for admissions, documents, medical examination, and so on).

CHAPTER SUMMARY   THE AMERICAN COURT SYSTEM—Continued

Following a State Court Case— continued	4. *Pretrial conference*—Either party or the court can request a pretrial conference to identify the matters in dispute after discovery has taken place and to plan the course of the trial.
	5. *Trial*—Following jury selection (*voir dire*), the trial begins with opening statements from both parties' attorneys. The following events then occur:
	a. The plaintiff's introduction of evidence (including the testimony of witnesses) supporting the plaintiff's position. The defendant's attorney can challenge evidence and cross-examine witnesses.
	b. The defendant's introduction of evidence (including the testimony of witnesses) supporting the defendant's position. The plaintiff's attorney can challenge evidence and cross-examine witnesses.
	c. Closing arguments by attorneys in favor of their respective clients, the judge's instructions to the jury, and the jury's verdict.
	6. *Posttrial motions*—
	a. Motion for judgment *n.o.v.* ("notwithstanding the verdict")—Will be granted if the judge is convinced that the jury was in error.
	b. Motion for a new trial—Will be granted if the judge is convinced that the jury was in error; can also be granted on the grounds of newly discovered evidence, misconduct by the participants during the trial, or error by the judge.
	7. *Appeal*—Either party can appeal the trial court's judgment to an appropriate court of appeals. After reviewing the record on appeal, the abstracts, and the attorneys' briefs, the appellate court holds a hearing and renders its opinion.
The Courts Adapt to the Online World (See pages 127–128.)	A number of state and federal courts now allow parties to file litigation-related documents via the Internet or other electronic means. The federal courts are gradually implementing electronic filing systems in all federal district courts. Virtually every court now has a Web page offering information about the court and its procedures, and an increasing number of courts publish their opinions online. In the future, we may see "cyber courts," in which all trial proceedings are conducted online.

FOR REVIEW

  1. What is judicial review? How and when was the power of judicial review established?

  2. Before a court can hear a case, it must have jurisdiction. Over what must it have jurisdiction? How are the courts applying traditional jurisdictional concepts to cases involving Internet transactions?

  3. What is the difference between a trial court and an appellate court?

  4. In a lawsuit, what are the pleadings? What is discovery? What is electronic filing?

  5. What steps are involved in an appeal?

QUESTIONS AND CASE PROBLEMS

4–1. Courts of Appeals. Appellate courts normally see only written transcripts of trial proceedings when they are reviewing cases. Today, in some states, videotapes are being used as the official trial reports. If the use of videotapes as official reports continues, will this alter the appellate process? Should it? Discuss fully.

4–2. Discovery. In the past, the rules of discovery were very restrictive, and trials often turned on elements of surprise. For example, a plaintiff would not necessarily know until the trial what the defendant's defense was going to be. Within the last twenty-five years, however, new rules of discovery have substantially changed all this. Now each attorney can discover practically all the evidence that the other will be presenting at trial, with the exception of certain information—namely, the opposing attorney's work product. *Work product* is not a clear concept. Basically, it includes all the attorney's thoughts on the case. Can you see any reason why such information should not be made available to the opposing attorney? Discuss fully.

4–3. Motions. When and for what purpose are each of the following motions made? Which of them would be appropriate if a defendant claimed that the only issue between the parties was a question of law and that the law was favorable to the defendant's position?

    (a) A motion for judgment on the pleadings.
    (b) A motion for a directed verdict.
    (c) A motion for summary judgment.
    (d) A motion for judgment *n.o.v.*

4–4. Peremptory Challenges. During *voir dire,* the parties or their attorneys select those persons who will serve as jurors during the trial. The parties are prohibited, however, from excluding potential jurors on the basis of race or other discriminatory criteria. An issue concerns whether the prohibition against discrimination extends to potential jurors who have physical or mental disabilities. Federal law prohibits discrimination against an otherwise qualified person with a disability when that person could be accommodated without too much difficulty. Should this law also apply to the jury selection process? For example, should parties be prohibited from excluding blind persons, through either challenges for cause or peremptory challenges, from serving on juries? Discuss.

4–5. Jurisdiction. Marya Callais, a citizen of Florida, was walking near a busy street in Tallahassee, Florida, one day when a large crate flew off a passing truck and hit her, resulting in numerous injuries. She incurred a great deal of pain and suffering, plus significant medical expenses, and she could not work for six months. She wants to sue the trucking firm for $300,000 in damages. The firm's headquarters are in Georgia, although the company does business in Florida. In what court might Callais bring suit—a Florida state court, a Georgia state court, or a federal court? What factors might influence her decision?

Case Problem with Sample Answer

4–6. Jury Selection. Ms. Thompson filed a suit in a federal district court against her employer, Altheimer & Gray, seeking damages for alleged racial discrimination in violation of federal law. During *voir dire,* the judge asked the prospective jurors whether "there is something about this kind of lawsuit for money damages that would start any of you leaning for or against a particular party." Ms. Leiter, one of the prospective jurors, raised her hand and explained that she had "been an owner of a couple of businesses and am currently an owner of a business, and I feel that as an employer and owner of a business that will definitely sway my judgment in this case." She explained, "I am constantly faced with people that want various benefits or different positions in the company or better contacts or, you know, a myriad of issues that employers face on a regular basis, and I have to decide whether or not that person should get them." Asked by Thompson's lawyer whether "you believe that people file lawsuits just because they don't get something they want," Leiter answered, "I believe there are some people that do." In answer to another question, she said, "I think I bring a lot of background to this case, and I can't say that it's not going to cloud my judgment. I can try to be as fair as I can, as I do every day." Thompson filed a motion to strike Leiter for cause. Should the judge grant the motion? Explain. [*Thompson v. Altheimer & Gray*, 248 F.3d 621 (7th Cir. 2001)]

To view a sample answer for this case problem, go to this book's Web site at http://leet.westbuslaw.com and click on "Interactive Study Center."

4–7. E-Jurisdiction. American Business Financial Services, Inc. (ABFI), a Pennsylvania firm, sells and services loans to businesses and consumers. First Union National Bank, with its principal place of business in North Carolina, provides banking services. Alan Boyer, an employee of First Union, lives in North Carolina and has never been to Pennsylvania. In the course of his employment, Boyer learned that the bank was going to extend a $150 million line of credit to ABFI. Boyer then attempted to manipulate the stock price of ABFI for personal gain by sending disparaging e-mails to ABFI's independent auditors in Pennsylvania. Boyer also posted negative statements about ABFI and its management on a Yahoo bulletin board. ABFI filed a suit in a Pennsylvania state court against Boyer, First Union, and others, alleging wrongful interference with a contractual relationship, among other things. Boyer filed a motion to dismiss the complaint for lack of personal jurisdiction. Could the court exercise jurisdiction over Boyer? Explain. [*American Business Financial Services, Inc. v. First Union National Bank,* __ A.2d __ (Pa.Comm.Pl. 2002)]

4–8. Motion for a Directed Verdict. Gerald Adams worked as a cook for Uno Restaurants, Inc., at Warwick Pizzeria Uno Restaurant & Bar in Warwick, Rhode Island. One night, shortly after Adams's shift began, he noticed that the kitchen floor was saturated with a foul smelling liquid coming from the drains and backing up onto the floor. He complained of illness and went home, where he contacted the state health department. A department representative visited the restaurant and closed it for the night, leaving instructions to sanitize the kitchen and clear the drains. Two days later, in the restaurant, David Badot, the manager, shouted at Adams in the presence of other employees. When Adams shouted back, Badot fired Adams and had him arrested. Adams filed a suit in a Rhode Island state court against Uno, alleging that he had been unlawfully terminated for contacting the health department. Arguing that Adams had been fired for threatening Badot, Uno filed a motion for a directed verdict. What does a court weigh in considering whether to grant such a motion? Should the court grant the motion in this case? Why or why not? [*Adams v. Uno Restaurants, Inc.,* 794 A.2d 489 (R.I. 2002)]

4–9. Jurisdiction. Kazaa BV was a company formed under the laws of the Netherlands. Kazaa distributed the Kazaa Media Desktop (KMD) software that enabled users to exchange, via a peer-to-peer transfer network, digital media, including movies and music. Kazaa also operated the Kazaa.com Web site, through which it distributed the KMD software to millions of California residents and other users. Metro-Goldwyn-Mayer Studios, Inc., and other parties in the entertainment industries based in California filed a suit in a federal district court against Kazaa and others, alleging copyright infringement. Kazaa filed a counterclaim, but while legal action was pending, the firm passed its assets and its Web site to Sharman Networks, Ltd., a company organized under the laws of Vanuatu (an island republic east of Australia) and doing business principally in Australia. Sharman explicitly disclaimed the assumption of any of Kazaa's liabilities. When the plaintiffs added Sharman as a defendant, Sharman filed a motion to dismiss on the ground that the court did not have jurisdiction. Would it be fair to subject Sharman to suit in this case? Explain. [*Metro-Goldwyn-Mayer Studios, Inc. v. Grokster, Ltd.,* 243 F.Supp.2d 1073 (C.D.Cal.2003)]

A Question of Ethics & Social Responsibility

4–10. The state of Alabama, on behalf of a mother (T.B.), brought a paternity suit against the alleged father (J.E.B.) of T.B.'s child. During jury selection, the state, through peremptory challenges, removed nine of the ten prospective male jurors. J.E.B.'s attorney struck the final male from the jury pool. As a result of these peremptory strikes, the final jury consisted of twelve women. When the jury returned a verdict in favor of the mother, the father appealed. The father argued that eliminating men from the jury constituted gender discrimination and violated his rights to equal protection and due process (see Chapter 5). The father requested the court to extend the principle enunciated in *Batson v. Kentucky* (cited in footnote 16 of this chapter), which prohibited peremptory strikes based solely on race, to include gender-based strikes. The appellate court refused to do so. [*J.E.B. v. Alabama ex rel. T.B.,* 511 U.S. 127, 114 S.Ct. 1419, 128 L.Ed.2d 89 (1994)]

1. Do you agree with J.E.B. that the state's exercise of its peremptory challenges violated his right to equal protection and due process? Why or why not?
2. If you were the judge, how would you rule?
3. The late Supreme Court Justice Thurgood *Marshall* urged, when the Court was reviewing the *Batson* case, that peremptory challenges be banned entirely. Do you agree with this proposal? Discuss.

Critical-Thinking Legal Question

4–11. A dispute arises between Haru Koto, a resident of California, and Maria Mendez, a resident of Texas, over the ownership of the *Fairweather,* a sailboat in dry dock in San Diego, California. Can a California state court exercise jurisdiction in the dispute?

Video Question

4–12. Go to this text's Web site at **http://leet.westbuslaw.com** and select "Video Questions." Click on "Chapter 4" and view the video titled *Jurisdiction in Cyberspace.* Then answer the following questions.

1. What standard would a court apply to determine whether it has jurisdiction over the out-of-state computer firm in the video?
2. What factors is a court likely to consider in assessing whether sufficient contacts existed when the only connection to the jurisdiction is through a Web site?
3. How do you think the court would resolve the issue in this case?

INTERACTING WITH THE INTERNET

For updated links to resources available on the Web, as well as a variety of other materials, visit this text's Web site at

http://leet.westbuslaw.com

For the decisions of the United States Supreme Court, as well as information about the Supreme Court, go to

http://supremecourtus.gov

Another Web site offering information about the United States Supreme Court, including information on the justices and links to opinions they have authored, can be accessed at

http://oyez.nwu.edu

The Web site for the federal courts offers information on the federal court system and links to all federal courts at

http://www.uscourts.gov

The National Center for State Courts (NCSC) offers links to the Web pages of all state courts. Go to

http://www.ncsconline.org

If you are interested in learning more about the Federal Rules of Civil Procedure (FRCP) and the Federal Rules of Evidence (FRE), go to the following Web site and click on "Constitutions and Codes" on the left-hand side of the screen:

http://www.law.cornell.edu

The American Bar Association maintains a gateway to information on legal topics, including the court systems and court procedures, at

http://www.ABALawinfo.org

On January 9, 2002, the state of Michigan launched the nation's first "cyber court." For information about this virtual court and how it is designed to operate, go to

http://www.michigancybercourt.net

ONLINE LEGAL RESEARCH EXERCISES

Go to **http://leet.westbuslaw.com**, the Web site that accompanies this text. Select "Interactive Study Center," and then click on "Chapter 4." There you will find the following Internet research exercises that you can perform to learn more about topics covered in this chapter.

Activity 4–1: HISTORICAL PERSPECTIVE—The Judiciary's Role in American Government

Activity 4–2: MANAGEMENT PERSPECTIVE—Small Claims Courts

Activity 4–3: TECHNOLOGICAL PERSPECTIVE—Virtual Courtrooms

BEFORE THE TEST

Go to **http://leet.westbuslaw.com**, the Web site that accompanies this text. Select "Interactive Quizzes." You will find at least twenty interactive questions relating to this chapter.

Westlaw® Campus

If your textbook provided for a subscription to Westlaw® Campus, or if you have otherwise purchased access to the Westlaw Campus database, you can access any of the cases presented or cited in this chapter by using your Westlaw Campus account.

UNIT ONE   Cumulative Business Hypothetical

Joan owns and operates an antique furniture store in Eugene, Oregon. During the five years since she opened the store, the business has thrived. Initially, her customers were from Eugene and other Oregon communities. Today, through her Web site, she sells furniture to buyers around the country.

1. Joan learns that a charming older building that would be an ideal location for her business is being offered for sale. For some time, she has looked for the perfect building for her operations, and now, she realizes, she has finally found it. She forms a contract with the seller of the property to buy the premises. The seller then backs out of the deal and refuses to sell. If Joan sues the seller for breach of contract, would she be entitled to seek the equitable remedy of specific performance? Why or why not?

2. Joan contracts with a furniture manufacturer in Maine to purchase five replicas of an early American dresser from the "federal period." The manufacturer promised her that they would be delivered to Joan's store by March 1. Joan has already formed contracts with three of her customers to sell them the dressers, promising them that the dressers will arrive on March 1. In fact, the dressers are never delivered, despite the manufacturer's continuing promises that they will be completed and shipped "any day now." If Joan decides to sue the manufacturer for breach of contract, can an Oregon state court exercise jurisdiction over the dispute, or will she have to bring her lawsuit in a Maine court? Could she sue the manufacturer in a federal court located in Oregon? Explain.

3. One of Joan's customers, who lives in Kansas, ordered an antique hutch via Joan's Web site. After the customer receives the hutch, he calls Joan and complains that she misrepresented the quality of the hutch in her Web site ads. Joan contends that she did not engage in any deceptive advertising on her Web site

and that the customer has no claim against her. Eventually, the customer sues Joan in a Kansas state court. Joan moves to dismiss the case, alleging that the Kansas court lacks jurisdiction. After all, her business is physically located in Oregon, she has no sales representatives in Kansas, and her only contacts with Kansas are through her Web site. Will the court dismiss the suit on the ground that the "minimum-contacts" requirement for jurisdiction over an out-of-state defendant has not been met? Discuss.

4. With respect to the dispute in question 3 above, Joan is certain that the customer does not have a valid claim against her. At the same time, she wants to avoid the expense of litigation. What alternative dispute-resolution methods might Joan suggest to the customer to avoid having to resolve the matter in court? What might Joan have done in the first place to avoid the possibility of having to resolve disputes with customers in court?

5. Rebecca has been Joan's office manager for over five years. For most of those years she was a good worker and a loyal, dependable employee. In fact, Joan has come to rely on Rebecca and her skills extensively. Lately, however, Joan has noticed that Rebecca frequently comes to work late, leaves the office early, and takes time off to tend to matters that, in Joan's mind, do not seem all that important. On several occasions, Joan has talked to Rebecca about her performance, but to no effect. In the meantime, because of Rebecca's negligence, customer orders have been overlooked or mishandled, and Joan is receiving complaints. Joan also notices that some of the employees under Rebecca's supervision have begun to show a similar indifference to work schedules. Joan is thinking about firing Rebecca. Does Joan have an ethical duty to keep Rebecca on the payroll because of Rebecca's past loyalty and good performance record? Or should Joan think about the profits that she could lose if the inefficiency in the office operations continues and fire Rebecca? Would your answer be different if you knew that Rebecca was a single parent who depended on her income from this job and who could never find such a high-paying position elsewhere?

UNIT TWO
The Public Environment

CHAPTER 5

Constitutional Authority to Regulate Business

CONTENTS

CHAPTER OBJECTIVES

After reading this chapter, you should be able to answer the following questions:

1. What is the basic structure of the U.S. government?

2. What constitutional clause gives the federal government the power to regulate commercial activities among the various states?

3. What constitutional clause allows laws enacted by the federal government to take priority over conflicting state laws?

4. What is the Bill of Rights? What freedoms are guaranteed by the First Amendment?

5. Where in the Constitution can the due process clause be found?

The U.S. Constitution is brief.[1] It consists of only about seven thousand words, which is less than one-third of the number of words in the average state constitution. Perhaps its brevity explains why it has proved to be so "marvelously elastic," as Franklin Roosevelt pointed out in the quotation below, and why it has survived for over two hundred years—longer than any other written constitution in the world.

Laws that govern business have their origin in the lawmaking authority granted by this document, which is the supreme law in this country. As mentioned in Chapter 1, neither Congress nor any state may pass a law that conflicts with the Constitution.

In this chapter, we first look at some basic constitutional concepts and clauses and their significance for

> "The United States Constitution has proved itself the most marvelously elastic compilation of rules of government ever written."
>
> Franklin D. Roosevelt, 1882–1945
> (Thirty-second president of
> the United States, 1933–1945)

1. See Appendix B for the full text of the U.S. Constitution.

business. Then we examine how certain fundamental freedoms guaranteed by the Constitution affect businesspersons and the workplace.

THE CONSTITUTIONAL POWERS OF GOVERNMENT

Following the Revolutionary War, the states created a *confederal* form of government. The Articles of Confederation, which went into effect in 1781, established a confederation of independent states and a central (national) government that could exercise only very limited powers. The sovereign power, or supreme authority to govern, rested largely with the states. The limitation on the central government's powers reflected a basic tenet of the American Revolution—that a national government should not have unlimited power that could be used to tyrannize the states.

The confederation, however, faced serious problems. For one thing, laws passed by the various states hampered national commerce and foreign trade by preventing the free movement of goods and services. By 1784, the nation faced a serious economic depression. Many who could not afford to pay their debts were thrown into "debtors' prisons." By 1786, a series of uprisings by farmer debtors were proving difficult to control because the national government did not have the authority to demand revenues (by levying taxes, for example) to support a militia.

Because of these difficulties, a national convention was called to amend the Articles of Confederation. Instead of amending the articles, however, the delegates to the convention, now called the Constitutional Convention, wrote the U.S. Constitution. This document, after its ratification by the states in 1789, became the basis for an entirely new form of government. Many of the provisions of the Constitution, including those discussed in the following pages, were shaped by the delegates' experiences during the confederal era (1781–1789).

A Federal Form of Government

The new government created by the Constitution reflected a series of compromises made by the convention delegates on various issues. Some delegates wanted sovereign power to remain with the states; others wanted the national government alone to exercise sovereign power. The end result was a compromise—a **federal form of government** in which the national government and the states *share* sovereign power.

The Constitution sets forth specific powers that can be exercised by the national government and provides that the national government has the implied power to undertake actions necessary to carry out its expressly designated powers. All other powers are "reserved" to the states. The broad language of the Constitution, though, has left much room for debate over the specific nature and scope of these powers. Generally, it has been the task of the courts to determine where the boundary line between state and national powers should lie—and that line changes over time. For most of the twentieth century, for example, the national government met little resistance from the courts when extending its regulatory authority over broad areas of social and economic life. Today, in contrast, the courts, and particularly the United States Supreme Court, are more willing to interpret the Constitution in such a way as to curb the national government's regulatory powers.

FEDERAL FORM OF GOVERNMENT
A system of government in which the states form a union and the sovereign power is divided between a central government and the member states.

Should the EU Create a Federal Form of Government?

Today, the European Union (EU) consists of fifteen nations. Numerous other countries have applied for membership in the union. In 2000, the European University Institute in Florence, Italy, at the request of the European Commission, drafted a model constitution for the EU that essentially would establish a federal form of government. The preamble of the model constitution states, among other things, that "[t]his Constitution shall prevail over other European and national law, including Treaties of the Union, should conflict arise."[a] This is similar to the U.S. constitutional provision that if a state or local law conflicts with a national law, the national law will take precedence.

Just as delegates to the Constitutional Convention in the United States were reluctant to forfeit state sovereign powers, so are European nations. In the United States in the 1780s, at the time of the Constitutional Convention, the independent status of the states was relatively new. In contrast, most European nations have been in existence for centuries, making it even more difficult for them to part with any sovereign powers. Many other controversial issues remain. Some believe that signatory member states should have the right to leave the EU at any time. In the United States, we fought a civil war over that issue.

FOR CRITICAL ANALYSIS

Why might an existing EU member nation agree to give up any of its sovereignty?

a. As cited in "Our Constitution for Europe," *The Economist,* October 28, 2000, p. 18.

The Separation of Powers

To make it difficult for the national government to use its power arbitrarily, the Constitution divided the national government's powers among the three branches of government. The legislative branch makes the laws, the executive branch enforces the laws, and the judicial branch interprets the laws. Each branch performs a separate function, and no branch may exercise the authority of another branch.

Additionally, a system of **checks and balances** allows each branch to limit the actions of the other two branches, thus preventing any one branch from exercising too much power. Some examples of these checks and balances are the following:

CHECKS AND BALANCES
The national government is composed of three separate branches: the executive, the legislative, and the judicial branches. Each branch of the government exercises a check on the actions of the others.

1. The legislative branch (Congress) can enact a law, but the executive branch (the president) has the constitutional authority to veto that law.
2. The executive branch is responsible for foreign affairs, but treaties with foreign governments require the advice and consent of the Senate.
3. Congress determines the jurisdiction of the federal courts and the president appoints federal judges, with the advice and consent of the Senate, but the judicial branch has the power to hold actions of the other two branches unconstitutional.[2]

2. This judicial power was asserted in *Marbury v. Madison,* 5 U.S. (1 Cranch) 137, 2 L.Ed. 60 (1803). See the *Landmark in the Legal Environment* feature in Chapter 4 on page 103.

The Commerce Clause

To prevent states from establishing laws and regulations that would interfere with trade and commerce among the states, the Constitution expressly delegated to the national government the power to regulate interstate commerce. Article I, Section 8, of the U.S. Constitution expressly permits Congress "[t]o regulate Commerce with foreign Nations, and among the several States, and with the Indian Tribes." This clause, referred to as the **commerce clause,** has had a greater impact on business than any other provision in the Constitution.

For some time, the commerce power was interpreted as being limited to *interstate* commerce (commerce among the states) and not applicable to *intrastate* commerce (commerce within the states). In 1824, however, in *Gibbons v. Ogden* (see this chapter's *Landmark in the Legal Environment* feature on page 143), the United States Supreme Court held that commerce within states could also be regulated by the national government as long as the commerce *substantially affected* commerce involving more than one state.

The Commerce Clause and the Expansion of National Powers As the nation grew and faced new kinds of problems, the commerce clause became a vehicle for the additional expansion of the national government's regulatory powers. Even activities that seemed purely local came under the regulatory reach of the national government if those activities were deemed to substantially affect interstate commerce. ● **EXAMPLE 1** In 1942, in *Wickard v. Filburn,*[3] the Supreme Court held that wheat production by an individual farmer intended wholly for consumption on his own farm was subject to federal regulation. The Court reasoned that the home consumption of wheat reduced the demand for wheat and thus could have a substantial effect on interstate commerce. ●

The following landmark case involved a challenge to the scope of the national government's constitutional authority to regulate local activities.

COMMERCE CLAUSE
The provision in Article I, Section 8, of the U.S. Constitution that gives Congress the power to regulate interstate commerce.

> "We are under a Constitution, but the Constitution is what judges say it is."
>
> CHARLES EVANS HUGHES, 1862–1948
> (Chief justice of the United States
> Supreme Court, 1930–1941)

---

3. 317 U.S. 111, 63 S.Ct. 82, 87 L.Ed. 122 (1942).

LANDMARK AND CLASSIC CASES

CASE 5.1   Heart of Atlanta Motel v. United States

Supreme Court of the United States, 1964.
379 U.S. 241,
85 S.Ct. 348,
13 L.Ed.2d 258.
**http://supct.law.cornell.edu/supct/
cases/name.htm**[a]

HISTORICAL AND SOCIAL SETTING *In the first half of the twentieth century, state governments sanctioned segregation on the basis of race. In 1954, the United States Supreme Court decided that racially segregated school systems violated the Constitution. In*

the following decade, the Court ordered an end to racial segregation imposed by the states in other public facilities, such as beaches, golf courses, buses, parks, auditoriums, and courtroom seating. Privately owned facilities that excluded or segregated African Americans and others on the basis of race were not subject to the same constitutional restrictions, however. Congress passed the Civil Rights Act of 1964 to prohibit racial discrimination in "establishments affecting interstate commerce." These facilities included "places of public accommodation."

---

a. This is the "Historic Supreme Court Decisions—by Party Name" page within the "Caselists" collection of the Legal Information Institute available at its site on the Web. Click on the "H" link or scroll down the list of cases to the entry for the *Heart of Atlanta* case. Click on the case name. When the link opens, click on one of the choices to read the "Syllabus," the "Full Decision," or the "Edited Decision."

(continued)

CASE 5.1—Continued

BACKGROUND AND FACTS The owner of the Heart of Atlanta Motel, in violation of the Civil Rights Act of 1964, refused to rent rooms to African Americans. The motel owner brought an action in a federal district court to have the Civil Rights Act declared unconstitutional, alleging that Congress had exceeded its constitutional authority to regulate commerce by enacting the act. The owner argued that his motel was not engaged in inter-state commerce but was "of a purely local character."

The motel, however, was accessible to state and inter-state highways. The owner advertised nationally, maintained billboards throughout the state, and accepted convention trade from outside the state (75 percent of the guests were residents of other states). The court sustained the constitutionality of the act and enjoined (prohibited) the owner from discriminating on the basis of race. The owner appealed. The case ultimately went to the United States Supreme Court.

IN THE WORDS OF THE COURT . . .

Mr. Justice *CLARK* delivered the opinion of the Court.

* 　 * 　 * 　 *

While the Act as adopted carried no congressional findings, the record of its passage through each house is replete with evidence of the burdens that discrimination by race or color places upon interstate commerce * 　 * 　 * . This testimony included the fact that our people have become increasingly mobile with millions of all races traveling from State to State; that Negroes in particular have been the subject of discrimination in transient accommodations, having to travel great distances to secure the same; that often they have been unable to obtain accommodations and have had to call upon friends to put them up overnight. * 　 * 　 * These exclusionary practices were found to be nationwide, the Under Secretary of Commerce testifying that there is "no question that this discrimination in the North still exists to a large degree" and in the West and Midwest as well * 　 * 　 * . This testimony indicated a qualitative as well as quantitative effect on interstate travel by Negroes. The former was the obvious impairment of the Negro traveler's pleasure and convenience that resulted when he continually was uncertain of finding lodging. As for the latter, there was evidence that this uncertainty stemming from racial discrimination had the effect of discouraging travel on the part of a substantial portion of the Negro community * 　 * 　 * . We shall not burden this opinion with further details since the voluminous testimony presents overwhelming evidence that discrimination by hotels and motels impedes interstate travel.

* 　 * 　 * 　 *

It is said that the operation of the motel here is of a purely local character. But, assuming this to be true, "if it is interstate commerce that feels the pinch, it does not matter how local the operation that applies the squeeze." * 　 * 　 * Thus the power of Congress to promote interstate commerce also includes the power to regulate the local incidents thereof, including local activities in both the States of origin and destination, which might have a substantial and harmful effect upon that commerce.

DECISION AND REMEDY The United States Supreme Court upheld the constitutionality of the Civil Rights Act of 1964. The power of Congress to regulate interstate commerce permitted the enactment of legislation that could halt local discriminatory practices.

COMMENT *If the Supreme Court had invalidated the Civil Rights Act of 1964, the legal landscape of the United States would be much different today. The act*

prohibited discrimination based on race, color, national origin, religion, or gender in all "public accommodations" as well as discrimination in employment based on these criteria. Although state laws now prohibit many of these forms of discrimination as well, the protections available vary from state to state—and it is not certain when (and if) such laws would have been passed had the 1964 federal Civil Rights Act been deemed unconstitutional.

LANDMARK IN THE LEGAL ENVIRONMENT

Gibbons v. Ogden (1824)

The commerce clause, which is found in Article I, Section 8, of the U.S. Constitution, gives Congress the power "[t]o regulate Commerce with foreign Nations, and among the several States, and with the Indian Tribes." What exactly does "to regulate commerce" mean? What does "commerce" entail? These questions came before the United States Supreme Court in 1824 in the case of *Gibbons v. Ogden.*[a]

BACKGROUND In 1803, Robert Fulton, inventor of the steamboat, and Robert Livingston, who was then American minister to France, secured a monopoly on steam navigation on the waters in the state of New York from the New York legislature. Fulton and Livingston licensed Aaron Ogden, a former governor of New Jersey and a U.S. senator, to operate steam-powered ferryboats between New York and New Jersey. Thomas Gibbons, who had obtained a license from the U.S. government to operate boats in interstate waters, competed with Ogden without New York's permission. Ogden sued Gibbons. The New York state courts granted Ogden's request for an injunction—an order prohibiting Gibbons from operating in New York waters. Gibbons appealed the decision to the United States Supreme Court.

MARSHALL'S DECISION Sitting as chief justice on the Supreme Court was John Marshall, an advocate of a strong national government. In his decision, Marshall defined the word *commerce* as used in the commerce clause to mean all commercial intercourse—that is, all business dealings that affect more than one state. The Court ruled against Ogden's monopoly, reversing the injunction against Gibbons. Marshall used this opportunity not only to expand the definition of commerce but also to validate and increase the power of the national legislature to regulate commerce. Said Marshall, "What is this power? It is the power . . . to prescribe the rule by which commerce is to be governed." Marshall held that the power to regulate interstate commerce was an exclusive power of the national government.

Application to Today's World

Marshall's broad definition of the commerce power established the foundation for the expansion of national powers in the years to come. Today, the national government continues to rely on the commerce clause for its constitutional authority to regulate business activities. Marshall's conclusion that the power to regulate interstate commerce was an exclusive power of the national government has also had significant consequences. By implication, this means that a state cannot regulate activities that extend beyond its borders, such as out-of-state online gambling operations that affect the welfare of in-state citizens. It also means that state regulations over in-state activities normally will be invalidated if the regulations substantially burden interstate commerce.

---

a. 22 U.S. (9 Wheat.) 1, 6 L.Ed. 23 (1824).

The Commerce Power Today Today, at least theoretically, the power over commerce authorizes the national government to regulate every commercial enterprise in the United States. Federal (national) legislation governs virtually every major activity conducted by businesses—from hiring and firing decisions to workplace safety, competitive practices, and financing.

In the last decade, however, the Supreme Court has begun to curb somewhat the national government's regulatory authority under the commerce clause. In 1995, the Court held—for the first time in sixty years—that Congress had exceeded its regulatory authority under the commerce clause.

The Court stated that the Gun-Free School Zones Act of 1990, which banned the possession of guns within one thousand feet of any school, was unconstitutional because it attempted to regulate an area that had "nothing to do with commerce."[4]

Two years later, in 1997, the Court struck down portions of the Brady Handgun Violence Prevention Act of 1993, which obligated state and local law enforcement officers to do background checks on prospective handgun buyers until a national instant check system could be implemented. The Court stated that Congress lacked the power to "dragoon" state employees into federal service through an unfunded mandate of this kind.[5] In 2000, the Court invalidated key portions of the federal Violence Against Women Act of 1994, which allowed women to sue in federal court when they were victims of gender-motivated violence, such as rape. According to the Court, the commerce clause did not justify national regulation of noneconomic, criminal conduct.[6] The commerce clause, however, continues to serve as the constitutional backbone for national laws regulating a broad number of activities. (See, for example, Case 5.3 later in this chapter.)

The Regulatory Powers of the States As part of their inherent sovereignty, state governments have the authority to regulate affairs within their borders. This authority stems in part from the Tenth Amendment to the Constitution, which reserves all powers not delegated to the national government to the states. State regulatory powers are often referred to as **police powers.** The term encompasses not only criminal law enforcement but also the right of state governments to regulate private activities to protect or promote the public order, health, safety, morals, and general welfare. Fire and building codes, antidiscrimination laws, parking regulations, zoning restrictions, licensing requirements, and thousands of other state statutes covering virtually every aspect of life have been enacted pursuant to a state's police powers. Local governments, including cities, also exercise police powers.[7]

POLICE POWERS
Powers possessed by states as part of their inherent sovereignty. These powers may be exercised to protect or promote the public order, health, safety, morals, and general welfare.

The "Dormant" Commerce Clause The United States Supreme Court has interpreted the commerce clause to mean that the national government has the *exclusive* authority to regulate commerce that substantially affects trade and commerce among the states. This express grant of authority to the national government, which is often referred to as the "positive" aspect of the commerce clause, implies a negative aspect—that the states do *not* have the authority to regulate interstate commerce. This negative aspect of the commerce clause is often referred to as the "dormant" (implied) commerce clause.

RECALL Any law in violation of the U.S. Constitution will not be enforced.

The dormant commerce clause comes into play when state regulations impinge on interstate commerce. In this situation, the courts normally weigh the state's interest in regulating a certain matter against the burden that the state's regulation places on interstate commerce. ● EXAMPLE 2 In one case, the United States Supreme Court considered state regulations that, in the interest of promoting traffic safety, limited the length of trucks traveling on the state's

4. *United States v. Lopez,* 514 U.S. 549, 115 S.Ct. 1624, 131 L.Ed.2d 626 (1995).
5. *Printz v. United States,* 521 U.S. 898, 117 S.Ct. 2365, 138 L.Ed.2d 914 (1997).
6. *United States v. Morrison,* 529 U.S. 598, 120 S.Ct. 1740, 146 L.Ed.2d 658 (2000).
7. Local governments derive their authority to regulate their communities from the state, because they are creatures of the state. In other words, they cannot come into existence unless authorized by the state to do so.

State and local governments, as part of their police powers, have the power to condemn unsafe buildings. What other powers can be exercised by state and local governments as part of their constitutional powers?

highways. The Court invalidated the regulations, concluding that although they imposed a "substantial burden on interstate commerce," they failed to "make more than the most speculative contribution to highway safety."[8]• Because courts balance the interests involved, it is extremely difficult to predict the outcome in a particular case.

An emerging issue related to state laws that impinge on interstate commerce involves the Internet. For some examples of how commerce clause principles are being applied in cases involving the sale of wine via the Internet, see this chapter's *Legal E-nvironment* feature on the next page.

The Supremacy Clause

Article VI of the Constitution provides that the Constitution, laws, and treaties of the United States are "the supreme Law of the Land." This article, commonly referred to as the **supremacy clause,** is important in the ordering of state and federal relationships. When there is a direct conflict between a federal law and a state law, the state law is rendered invalid. Because some powers are *concurrent* (shared by the federal government and the states), however, it is necessary to determine which law governs in a particular circumstance.

SUPREMACY CLAUSE
The provision in Article VI of the Constitution that provides that the Constitution, laws, and treaties of the United States are "the supreme Law of the Land." Under this clause, state and local laws that directly conflict with federal law will be rendered invalid.

8. *Raymond Motor Transportation, Inc. v. Rice,* 434 U.S. 429, 98 S.Ct. 787, 54 L.Ed.2d 664 (1978).

LEGAL *e*-NVIRONMENT

Internet Wine Sales and the Constitution

In the past decade, the Internet has come to be widely used for direct sales to consumers, including direct sales of wine. Yet a number of state statutes effectively prohibit consumers from purchasing and receiving wine directly from out-of-state sellers. In a series of recent cases, plaintiffs have alleged that such statutes violate the commerce clause of the Constitution. As mentioned elsewhere, the commerce clause implies a negative, or "dormant," aspect: the states do *not* have the authority to regulate interstate commerce. Here we look at how the dormant commerce clause applies to state regulations affecting the sale and purchase of wine via the Internet.

For example, in *Dickerson v. Bailey*[a] the plaintiffs—Texas residents who wanted to receive wine shipments directly from out-of-state suppliers—claimed that a Texas statute prohibiting such purchases violated the dormant commerce clause. The statute prohibited Texans from importing for their personal use more than three gallons of wine without a permit unless the resident "personally accompan[ies] the wine or liquor as it enters the state." A federal court held that the statute violated the dormant commerce clause. In effect, the law discriminated against interstate commerce by prohibiting out-of-state wineries from shipping wines to Texas residents while allowing local Texas wineries or retailers to do so.

Enter the Twenty-First Amendment

In the Texas case, and in other cases involving the same issue, one of the arguments made by state authorities is that their liquor regulations are justified by Section 2 of the Twenty-first Amendment.[b] That section reads, "The transportation or importation into any State, Territory, or possession of the United States for delivery or use therein of intoxicating liquors, *in violation of the laws thereof,* is hereby prohibited." [Emphasis added.]

a. 87 F.Supp.2d 691 (S.D.Tex. 2000).

b. Section 1 of the Twenty-first Amendment (ratified in 1933) repealed the Eighteenth Amendment (ratified in 1919), which had made the manufacture, sale, or transportation of alcoholic beverages illegal. Section 2 of the Twenty-first Amendment effectively left the regulation of such activity up to the states.

PREEMPTION
A doctrine under which certain federal laws preempt, or take precedence over, conflicting state or local laws.

Preemption occurs when Congress chooses to act exclusively in a concurrent area. In this circumstance, a valid federal statute or regulation will take precedence over a conflicting state or local law or regulation on the same general subject. ● **EXAMPLE 3** The federal Controlled Substances Act[9] of 1970 strictly prohibits the manufacture and distribution of marijuana. When California legalized the use of marijuana for medical purposes, by a ballot initiative in 1996, the law was challenged as unconstitutional because it conflicted with the federal law. Ultimately, the United States Supreme Court ruled that the law was preempted by the 1970 federal act. The defendant in the case (an Oakland cooperative producing and distributing marijuana for medical purposes) had argued that the 1970 act provided for a "medical necessity" exception. The Supreme Court, however, held that there was no such exception, and thus the California law was preempted by the federal act.[10] ●

9. This is the popular name for the Comprehensive Drug Abuse Prevention and Control Act of 1970, 21 U.S.C. Sections 801 *et seq.*

10. *United States v. Oakland Cannabis Buyers' Co-op*, 532 U.S. 483, 121 S.Ct. 1711, 149 L.Ed.2d 722 (2001).

Internet Wine Sales and the Constitution (Continued)

Does the Twenty-First Amendment Trump the Dormant Commerce Clause?

Does the Twenty-first Amendment create an exception to the normal operation of the commerce clause? The courts are giving different answers to this question. In the Texas case, for example, the court held that the amendment did not create such an exception. The court did note that substantial deference is given to a state's power to regulate the sale and distribution of liquor within its boundaries when the goal of the regulation is "to combat the perceived evils of an unrestricted traffic in liquor." The court concluded, however, that no temperance (abstinence from alcohol) goal was served by the Texas statute because residents of that state could "become as drunk on local wines" as they could on wines that were effectively "kept out of the state by the statute." Because the goal of the Texas law was primarily to protect the economic interests of in-state wine producers and distributors, the law was not entitled to such deference and violated the commerce clause.

The first federal appellate court to rule on this issue reached a different conclusion. In *Bridenbaugh v. Freeman-Wilson,*[c] Indiana residents challenged the constitutionality of a state statute making it unlawful for persons in another state or country to ship alcoholic beverages directly to Indiana residents. The court concluded that the primary purpose of the Twenty-first Amendment was not necessarily to promote temperance; rather, it was designed to close a "loophole" created by the dormant commerce clause. This loophole allowed direct shipments from out-of-state sellers to consumers to "bypass state regulatory (and tax) systems." The Indiana statute did not involve any substantial discrimination against interstate commerce; it merely enabled the state "to collect its excise tax equally from in-state and out-of-state sellers."

FOR CRITICAL ANALYSIS

Suppose that a state passed a law prohibiting direct sales of tobacco products via the Internet to in-state consumers. Would such a law necessarily violate the commerce clause? Why or why not?

c. 227 F.3d 848 (7th Cir. 2000).

Often, it is not clear whether Congress, in passing a law, intended to preempt an entire subject area. In these situations, it is left to the courts to determine whether Congress intended to exercise exclusive power over a given area. No single factor is decisive as to whether a court will find preemption. Generally, congressional intent to preempt will be found if a federal law regulating an activity is so pervasive, comprehensive, or detailed that the states have no room to regulate in that area. Also, when a federal statute creates an agency—such as the National Labor Relations Board—to enforce the law, matters that may come within the agency's jurisdiction will likely preempt state laws.

The Taxing and Spending Powers

Article I, Section 8, provides that Congress has the "Power to lay and collect Taxes, Duties, Imposts, and Excises." Section 8 further provides that "all Duties, Imposts and Excises shall be uniform throughout the United States." The requirement of uniformity refers to uniformity among the states, and thus Congress may not tax some states while exempting others.

Traditionally, if Congress attempted to regulate indirectly, by taxation, an area over which it had no authority, the tax would be invalidated by the courts. Today, however, if a tax measure bears some reasonable relationship to revenue production, it is generally held to be within the national taxing power. Moreover, the expansive interpretation of the commerce clause almost always provides a basis for sustaining a federal tax.

Under Article I, Section 8, Congress has the power "to pay the Debts and provide for the common Defence and general welfare of the United States." Through the spending power, Congress disposes of the revenues accumulated from the taxing power. Congress can spend revenues not only to carry out its enumerated powers but also to promote any objective it deems worthwhile, so long as it does not violate the Constitution or its amendments. For example, Congress could not condition welfare payments on the recipients' political views. The spending power necessarily involves policy choices, with which taxpayers may disagree.

BUSINESS AND THE BILL OF RIGHTS

BILL OF RIGHTS
The first ten amendments to the U.S. Constitution.

The importance of a written declaration of the rights of individuals eventually caused the first Congress of the United States to submit twelve amendments to the Constitution to the states for approval. The first ten of these amendments, commonly known as the **Bill of Rights,** were adopted in 1791 and embody a series of protections for the individual against various types of interference by the federal government.[11] Some constitutional protections apply to business entities as well. For example, corporations exist as separate legal entities, or legal persons, and enjoy many of the same rights and privileges as natural persons do. Summarized here are the protections guaranteed by these ten amendments (see the Constitution in Appendix B for the complete text of each amendment):

1. The First Amendment guarantees the freedoms of religion, speech, and the press and the rights to assemble peaceably and to petition the government.
2. The Second Amendment guarantees the right to keep and bear arms.
3. The Third Amendment prohibits, in peacetime, the lodging of soldiers in any house without the owner's consent.
4. The Fourth Amendment prohibits unreasonable searches and seizures of persons or property.
5. The Fifth Amendment guarantees the rights to indictment by grand jury, to due process of law, and to fair payment when private property is taken for public use. The Fifth Amendment also prohibits compulsory self-incrimination and double jeopardy (trial for the same crime twice).
6. The Sixth Amendment guarantees the accused in a criminal case the right to a speedy and public trial by an impartial jury and with counsel. The accused has the right to cross-examine witnesses against him or her and to solicit testimony from witnesses in his or her favor.
7. The Seventh Amendment guarantees the right to a trial by jury in a civil case involving at least twenty dollars.[12]

---

11. One of these proposed amendments was ratified 203 years later (in 1992) and became the Twenty-seventh Amendment to the Constitution. See Appendix B.
12. Twenty dollars was forty days' pay for the average person when the Bill of Rights was written.

8. The Eighth Amendment prohibits excessive bail and fines, as well as cruel and unusual punishment.

9. The Ninth Amendment establishes that the people have rights in addition to those specified in the Constitution.

10. The Tenth Amendment establishes that those powers neither delegated to the federal government nor denied to the states are reserved for the states.

As originally intended, the Bill of Rights limited only the powers of the national government. Over time, however, the Supreme Court "incorporated" most of these rights into the protections against state actions afforded by the Fourteenth Amendment to the Constitution. That amendment, passed in 1868 after the Civil War, provides in part that "[n]o State shall . . . deprive any person of life, liberty, or property, without due process of law." Starting in 1925, the Supreme Court began to define various rights and liberties guaranteed in the national Constitution as constituting "due process of law," which was required of state governments under the Fourteenth Amendment. Today, most of the rights and liberties set forth in the Bill of Rights apply to state governments as well as the national government.

We will look closely at several of the amendments in the above list in Chapter 7, in the context of criminal law and procedures. Here we examine two important guarantees of the First Amendment—freedom of speech and freedom of religion. These and other First Amendment freedoms (of the press, assembly, and petition) have all been applied to the states through the due process clause of the Fourteenth Amendment. As you read through the following pages, keep in mind that none of these (or other) constitutional freedoms confers an absolute right. Ultimately, it is the United States Supreme Court, as the final interpreter of the Constitution, that gives meaning to these rights and determines their boundaries.

> "The Constitution is not neutral. It was designed to take the government off the backs of people."
> WILLIAM O. DOUGLAS, 1898–1980
> (Associate justice of the United States Supreme Court, 1939–1975)

BE CAREFUL Although most of these rights apply to actions of the states, some of them apply only to actions of the federal government.

Police search a crack house in Florida. Do the owners and occupants of such houses receive protection from unreasonable searches and seizures under the U.S. Constitution? Should they?

The First Amendment—Freedom of Speech

Freedom of speech is the most prized freedom that Americans have. Indeed, it forms the basis for our democratic form of government, which could not exist if people were unable to express their political opinions freely and criticize government actions or policies. Because of its importance, the courts traditionally have protected this right to the fullest extent possible.

The courts also protect **symbolic speech**—gestures, movements, articles of clothing, and other forms of nonverbal expressive conduct. ● **EXAMPLE 4**   In 1989, the Supreme Court held that the burning of the American flag to protest government policies is a constitutionally protected form of expression.[13] In a subsequent case, the Supreme Court ruled that a city statute banning bias-motivated disorderly conduct was an unconstitutional restriction of speech.[14]●

SYMBOLIC SPEECH
Nonverbal expressions of beliefs. Symbolic speech, which includes gestures, movements, and articles of clothing, is given substantial protection by the courts.

REMEMBER The First Amendment guarantee of freedom of speech applies only to *government* restrictions on speech.

Corporate Political Speech   Political speech by corporations also falls within the protection of the First Amendment. ● **EXAMPLE 5**   In *First National Bank of Boston v. Bellotti,*[15] national banking associations and business corporations sought United States Supreme Court review of a Massachusetts statute that prohibited corporations from making political contributions or expenditures that individuals were permitted to make. The Court ruled that the Massachusetts law was unconstitutional because it violated the right of corporations to freedom of speech.● Similarly, the Court has held that a law prohibiting a corporation from using bill inserts to express its views on controversial issues violates the First Amendment.[16] Although a more conservative Supreme Court subsequently reversed this trend somewhat,[17] corporate political speech continues to be given significant protection under the First Amendment.

Commercial Speech—Advertising   The courts also give substantial protection to "commercial" speech, which consists of speech and communications—primarily advertising—made by business firms. The protection given to commercial speech under the First Amendment is not as extensive as that afforded to noncommercial speech, however. A state may restrict certain kinds of advertising, for example, in the interest of protecting consumers from being misled by the advertising practices. States also have a legitimate interest in the beautification of roadsides, and this interest allows states to place restraints on billboard advertising.

Generally, a restriction on commercial speech will be considered valid as long as it meets the following three criteria: (1) it must seek to implement a substantial government interest, (2) it must directly advance that interest, and (3) it must go no further than necessary to accomplish its objective. ● **EXAMPLE 6** The South

Nike, Inc., came under criticism by activists, including those shown in this photo, for allegedly using underpaid Indonesian workers ("sweatshop labor") to create Nike shoes and apparel. When Nike defended its actions in a series of press releases and newspaper ads, it was sued by a San Francisco activist for making false and misleading statements in violation of California law. The California Supreme Court concluded that Nike's statements constituted commercial speech. As commercial speech, are Nike's statements fully protected under the First Amendment?

---

13. See *Texas v. Johnson,* 491 U.S. 397, 109 S.Ct. 2533, 105 L.Ed.2d 342 (1989).

14. *R.A.V. v. City of St. Paul, Minnesota,* 505 U.S. 377, 112 S.Ct. 2538, 120 L.Ed.2d 305 (1992).

15. 435 U.S. 765, 98 S.Ct. 1407, 55 L.Ed.2d 707 (1978).

16. *Consolidated Edison Co. v. Public Service Commission,* 447 U.S. 530, 100 S.Ct. 2326, 65 L.Ed.2d 319 (1980).

17. *See Austin v. Michigan Chamber of Commerce,* 494 U.S. 652, 110 S.Ct. 1391, 108 L.Ed.2d 652 (1990), in which the Court upheld a state law prohibiting corporations from using general corporate funds for independent expenditures in state political campaigns.

Carolina Supreme Court recently held that a state statute banning ads for video gambling violated the First Amendment because the statute did not directly advance a substantial government interest. Although the court acknowledged that the state had a substantial interest in minimizing gambling, there was no evidence that a reduction in video gambling ads would result in a reduction in gambling.[18] ●

The court in the following case applied these principles to determine the constitutionality of a county ordinance that regulated video games based on their content—the ordinance applied only to "graphically violent" video games.

18. *Evans v. State*, 344 S.C. 60, 543 S.E.2d 547 (2001).

CASE 5.2 · Interactive Digital Software Association v. St. Louis County, Missouri

United States Court of Appeals,
Eighth Circuit, 2003.
329 F.3d 954.

BACKGROUND AND FACTS

St. Louis County, Missouri, passed an ordinance that made it unlawful for any person knowingly to sell, rent, or make available "graphically violent" video games to minors or to "permit the free play of" such games by minors without a parent' or guardian's consent.[a] Interactive Digital Software Association and other firms that create or provide the public with video games and related software filed a suit against the county in a federal district court. The plaintiffs asserted that the ordinance violated the First Amendment, and filed a motion for summary judgment. The county argued that the ordinance forwarded the compelling state interest of protecting the "psychological well-being of minors" by reducing the harm suffered by children who play violent video games. A psychologist, a high school principal, and others offered their conclusions that playing violent video games leads to aggressive behavior, but the county did not provide proof of a link between the games and psychological harm. The court denied the plaintiffs' motion and dismissed the case. The plaintiffs appealed to the U.S. Court of Appeals for the Eighth Circuit.

IN THE WORDS OF THE COURT . . .

MORRIS SHEPPARD ARNOLD, Circuit Judge.

* * * *

* * * If the First Amendment is versatile enough to shield the painting of Jackson Pollock, music of Arnold Schoenberg, or Jabberwocky verse of Lewis Carroll, we see no reason why the pictures, graphic design, concept art, sounds, music, stories, and narrative present in video games are not entitled to a similar protection. The mere fact that they appear in a novel medium is of no legal consequence. Our review of the record convinces us that these violent video games contain stories, imagery, age-old themes of literature, and messages, even an ideology, just as books and movies do. * * *

We recognize that while children have in the past experienced age-old elemental violent themes by reading a fairy tale or an epic poem, or attending a Saturday matinee, the interactive play of a video game might present different difficulties. The County suggests in fact that with video games, the story lines are incidental and players may skip the expressive parts of the game and proceed straight to the player-controlled action. But the same could be said of

---

a. St. Louis County Revised Ordinances Sections 602.425 through 602.460.

(continued)

CASE 5.2—Continued

action-packed movies like "The Matrix" or "Charlie's Angels"; any viewer with a videocassette or DVD player could simply skip to and isolate the action sequences. * * *

We note, moreover, that *there is no justification for disqualifying video games as speech simply because they are constructed to be interactive;* indeed, literature is most successful when it draws the reader into the story, makes him identify with the characters, invites him to judge them and quarrel with them, to experience their joys and sufferings as the reader's own. In fact, some books, such as the pre-teen oriented "Choose Your Own Nightmare" series (in which the reader makes choices that determine the plot of the story, and which lead the reader to one of several endings, by following the instructions at the bottom of the page) can be every bit as interactive * * * . [Emphasis added.]

Whether we believe the advent of violent video games adds anything of value to society is irrelevant; *guided by the First Amendment, we are obliged to recognize that they are as much entitled to the protection of free speech as the best of literature.* * * * [Emphasis added.]

* * * * *

* * * [To] constitutionally restrict the speech at issue here, the County must come forward with empirical support for its belief that violent video games cause psychological harm to minors. In this case, * * * the County has failed to present the substantial supporting evidence of harm that is required before an ordinance that threatens protected speech can be upheld. * * * [T]he County may not simply surmise that it is serving a compelling state interest because "[s]ociety in general believes that continued exposure to violence can be harmful to children." Where First Amendment rights are at stake, the Government must present more than anecdote and supposition.

DECISION AND REMEDY The U.S. Court of Appeals for the Eighth Circuit reversed the judgment of the lower court and remanded the case for the entry of an injunction against the county's enforcement of its ordinance. Video games are entitled to the same First Amendment protection as other types of speech, and the defendants failed to present the required evidence of harm to uphold a law threatening protected speech.

FOR CRITICAL ANALYSIS—Political Consideration *In determining whether a medium of speech is entitled to constitutional protection, should a court consider the messages communicated by that medium?*

Unprotected Speech The United States Supreme Court has made it clear that certain types of speech will not be given any protection under the First Amendment. Speech that harms the good reputation of another, or defamatory speech (see Chapter 8), will not be protected. Speech that violates criminal laws (such as threatening speech) is not constitutionally protected. Other unprotected speech includes "fighting words," or words that are likely to incite others to respond violently.

The Supreme Court has also held that obscene speech is not protected by the First Amendment. The Court has grappled from time to time with the problem of trying to establish an objective definition of obscene speech. In a

1973 case, *Miller v. California*,[19] the Supreme Court created a test for legal obscenity, which involved a set of requirements that must be met for material to be legally obscene. Under this test, material is obscene if (1) the average person finds that it violates contemporary community standards; (2) the work taken as a whole appeals to a prurient interest in sex; (3) the work shows patently offensive sexual conduct; and (4) the work lacks serious redeeming literary, artistic, political, or scientific merit.

Because community standards vary widely, the *Miller* test has had inconsistent applications, and obscenity remains a constitutionally unsettled issue. Numerous state and federal statutes make it a crime to disseminate obscene materials, however, and such laws have often been upheld by the Supreme Court, including laws prohibiting the sale and possession of child pornography.[20]

Online Obscenity A significant problem facing the courts and lawmakers today is how to control obscenity and child pornography that are disseminated via the Internet. Congress first attempted to protect minors from pornographic materials on the Internet by passing the Communications Decency Act (CDA) of 1996. The CDA made it a crime to make available to minors online any "obscene or indecent" message that "depicts or describes, in terms patently offensive as measured by contemporary community standards, sexual or excretory activities or organs."[21]

The act was immediately challenged by civil rights groups as an unconstitutional restraint on speech, and ultimately the United States Supreme Court ruled that portions of the act were unconstitutional. The Court held that the terms *indecent* and *patently offensive* covered large amounts of nonpornographic material with serious educational or other value. Moreover, said the Court, "the 'community standards' criterion as applied to the Internet means that any communication available to a nationwide audience will be judged by the standards of the community most likely to be offended by the message."[22]

Some of Congress's later attempts to curb pornography on the Internet have also encountered constitutional stumbling blocks. For example, the Child Online Protection Act (COPA)[23] of 1998 banned material "harmful to minors" distributed without an age-verification system to separate adult and minor users. In 2002, the Supreme Court upheld a lower court's injunction suspending the COPA.[24] In 2000, Congress enacted the Children's Internet Protection Act (CIPA),[25] which requires public schools and libraries to block adult content from access by children by installing **filtering software.** Such software is designed to prevent persons from viewing certain Web sites by responding to a site's Internet address or its **meta tags,** or key words. The CIPA was also challenged on constitutional grounds, but in 2003 the United States Supreme Court held that the act did not violate the First Amendment. The Court concluded that because libraries can disable the filters for any patrons who ask, the system was reasonably flexible and did not burden free speech to an unconstitutional extent.[26]

FILTERING SOFTWARE
A computer program that includes a pattern through which data are passed. When designed to block access to certain Web sites, the pattern blocks the retrieval of a site whose address or key words are on a list within the program.

META TAG
A key word in a document that can serve as an index reference to the document. On the Web, search engines return results based, in part, on the tags in Web documents.

19. 413 U.S. 15, 93 S.Ct. 2607, 37 L.Ed.2d 419 (1973).
20. For example, see *Osborne v. Ohio,* 495 U.S. 103, 110 S.Ct. 1691, 109 L.Ed.2d 98 (1990).
21. 47 U.S.C. Section 223(a)(1)(B)(ii).
22. *Reno v. American Civil Liberties Union,* 521 U.S. 844, 117 S.Ct. 2329, 138 L.Ed.2d 874 (1997).
23. 47 U.S.C. Section 231.
24. *Ashcroft v. American Civil Liberties Union,* 535 U.S. 564, 122 S.Ct. 1700, 152 L.Ed.2d 771 (2002).
25. 17 U.S.C. Sections 1701–1741.
26. *United States v. American Library Association,* ___U.S.___, 123 S.Ct. 2297, 156 L.Ed.2d. 221 (2003).

ETHICAL ISSUE

Should "virtual" pornography be deemed a crime?

In 2002, the United States Supreme Court reviewed a case challenging the constitutionality of another federal act attempting to protect minors in the online environment—the Child Pornography Prevention Act (CPPA) of 1996. This act made it illegal to distribute or possess computer-generated images that appear to depict minors engaging in lewd and lascivious behavior. At issue in the case before the Court was a question with significant ethical and legal implications: Should digital child pornography be considered a crime? Clearly, child pornography laws are meant to protect children, in particular those who are involved in actual child pornography. Yet no actual children are involved in digital child pornography. Before the case reached the Supreme Court, the U.S. Court of Appeals for the Ninth Circuit had held that the CPPA was unconstitutional. That court emphasized that the government can place significant restraints on free speech rights only if the restraints are necessary to promote a compelling government interest. In the court's eyes, the government has a compelling interest only in protecting children from actual, not "fake," child pornography. The United States Supreme Court agreed and affirmed the lower court's ruling.[27] Some contend, nonetheless, that there is little difference, in effect, between digital and real pornography.

Other Forms of Online Speech On the Internet, extreme hate speech is known as *cyber hate speech*. Racist materials and Holocaust denials on the Web, for example, are cyber hate speech. Can the federal government restrict this type of speech? Should it? Are there other forms of speech that the government should restrict?[28] Content restrictions generally amount to censorship and can be difficult to enforce. Even if it were possible to enforce content restrictions online, U.S. federal law is only "local" law in cyberspace—less than half of the users of the Internet are in the United States. Speech that may be legal in one country may not be legal in another, thus making it extremely difficult for any one nation to regulate Internet speech. In 2001, a federal district court found that French laws banning the display of Nazi memorabilia could not be enforced against Yahoo!, Inc., in the United States.[29]

The First Amendment—Freedom of Religion

The First Amendment states that the government may neither establish any religion nor prohibit the free exercise of religious practices. The first part of this constitutional provision is referred to as the **establishment clause,** and the second part is known as the **free exercise clause.** Government action, both federal and state, must be consistent with this constitutional mandate.

The Establishment Clause The establishment clause prohibits the government from establishing a state-sponsored religion, as well as from passing laws that promote (aid or endorse) religion or that show a preference for one religion

ESTABLISHMENT CLAUSE
The provision in the First Amendment to the Constitution that prohibits Congress from creating any law "respecting an establishment of religion."

FREE EXERCISE CLAUSE
The provision in the First Amendment to the Constitution that prohibits Congress from making any law "prohibiting the free exercise" of religion.

---

27. *Ashcroft v. Free Speech Coalition,* 535 U.S. 234, 122 S.Ct. 1389, 152 L.Ed.2d 403 (2002).
28. The content of some speech is regulated to a certain extent by tort law, copyright law, trademark law, and other laws discussed in later chapters of this text.
29. *Yahoo! Inc. v. La Ligue Contre le Racisme et l'Antisemitisme,* 169 F.Supp.2d 1181 (N.D.Cal. 2001). The original case against Yahoo, tried in a French court, was presented in Chapter 4.

over another. The establishment clause does not require a complete separation of church and state, however. On the contrary, it requires the government to accommodate religions.[30]

The establishment clause covers all conflicts about such matters as the legality of state and local government support for a particular religion, government aid to religious organizations and schools, the government's allowing or requiring school prayers, and the teaching of evolution versus fundamentalist theories of creation. The Supreme Court has held that for a government law or policy to be constitutional, it must be secular in aim, must not have the primary effect of advancing or inhibiting religions, and must not create "an excessive government entanglement with religion."[31] Generally, federal or state regulation that does not promote religion or place a significant burden on religion is constitutional even if it has some impact on religion.

● EXAMPLE 7 "Sunday closing laws" make the performance of some commercial activities on Sunday illegal. These statutes, also known as "blue laws" (from the color of the paper on which an early Sunday law was written), have been upheld on the ground that it is a legitimate function of government to provide a day of rest. The United States Supreme Court has held that the closing laws, although originally of a religious character, have taken on the secular purpose of promoting the health and welfare of workers.[32] Even though Sunday closing laws admittedly make it easier for Christians to attend religious services, the Court has viewed this effect as an incidental, not a primary, purpose of Sunday closing laws. ●

ETHICAL ISSUE

Do religious displays on public property violate the establishment clause?

The thorny issue of whether religious displays on public property violate the establishment clause often arises during the holiday season. Time and again, the courts have wrestled with this issue, but it has never been resolved in a way that satisfies everyone. In a 1984 case, the United States Supreme Court decided that a city's official Christmas display, which included a crèche (Nativity scene), did not violate the establishment clause because it was just one part of a larger holiday display that featured secular symbols, such as reindeer and candy canes.[33] In a later case, the Court held that the presence of a crèche within a county courthouse violated the establishment clause because it was not in close proximity to nonreligious symbols, including a Christmas tree, which were located outside, on the building's steps. The presence of a menorah (a nine-branched candelabrum used in celebrating Chanukah) on the building's steps, however, did not violate the establishment clause because the menorah was situated in close proximity to the Christmas tree.[34] The courts continue to apply this reasoning in cases involving similar issues.

---

30. *Zorach v. Clauson,* 343 U.S. 306, 72 S.Ct. 679, 96 L.Ed. 954 (1952).
31. *Lemon v. Kurtzman,* 403 U.S. 602, 91 S.Ct. 2105, 29 L.Ed.2d 745 (1971).
32. *McGowan v. Maryland,* 366 U.S. 420, 81 S.Ct. 1101, 6 L.Ed.2d 393 (1961).
33. *Lynch v. Donnelly,* 465 U.S. 668, 104 S.Ct. 1355, 79 L.Ed.2d 604 (1984).
34. See, for example, *County of Allegheny v. American Civil Liberties Union,* 492 U.S. 573, 109 S.Ct. 3086, 106 L.Ed.2d 472 (1989).

The Free Exercise Clause The free exercise clause guarantees that a person can hold any religious belief that she or he wants or a person can have no religious belief. When religious *practices* work against public policy and the public welfare, however, the government can act. For example, regardless of a child's or parent's religious beliefs, the government can require certain types of vaccinations. Similarly, although children of Jehovah's Witnesses are not required to say the Pledge of Allegiance at school, their parents cannot prevent them from accepting medical treatment (such as blood transfusions) if in fact their lives are in danger. Additionally, public school students can be required to study from textbooks chosen by school authorities.

For business firms, an important issue involves the accommodation that businesses must make for the religious beliefs of their employees. For example, if an employee's religion prohibits him or her from working on a certain day of the week or at a particular type of job, the employer must make a reasonable attempt to accommodate these religious requirements. Employers must reasonably accommodate an employee's religious beliefs even if the beliefs are not based on the tenets or dogma of a particular church, sect, or denomination. The only requirement is that the belief be religious in nature and sincerely held by the employee. (We will look further at this issue in Chapter 17, in the context of employment discrimination.)

DUE PROCESS AND EQUAL PROTECTION

Two other constitutional guarantees of great significance to Americans are mandated by the due process clauses of the Fifth and Fourteenth Amendments and the equal protection clause of the Fourteenth Amendment.

Due Process

Both the Fifth and the Fourteenth Amendments provide that no person shall be deprived "of life, liberty, or property, without due process of law." The **due process clause** of each of these constitutional amendments has two aspects— procedural and substantive.

DUE PROCESS CLAUSE
The provisions of the Fifth and Fourteenth Amendments to the Constitution that guarantee that no person shall be deprived of life, liberty, or property without due process of law. Similar clauses are found in most state constitutions.

Procedural Due Process Procedural due process requires that any government decision to take life, liberty, or property must be made fairly. For example, fair procedures must be used in determining whether a person will be subjected to punishment or have some burden imposed on him or her. Fair procedure has been interpreted as requiring that the person have at least an opportunity to object to a proposed action before a fair, neutral decision maker (which need not be a judge). Thus, for example, if a driver's license is construed as a property interest, some sort of opportunity to object to its suspension or termination by the state must be provided.

"What is due process of law depends on circumstances. It varies with the subject-matter and necessities of the situation."

OLIVER WENDELL HOLMES, JR.,
1841–1935
(Associate justice of the United States
Supreme Court, 1902–1932)

Substantive Due Process Substantive due process focuses on the content, or substance, of legislation. If a law or other governmental action limits a *fundamental right*, it will be held to violate substantive due process unless it promotes a compelling or overriding state interest. Fundamental rights include interstate travel, privacy, voting, and all First Amendment rights. Compelling state interests could include, for example, the public's safety. ● EXAMPLE 8

Laws designating speed limits may be upheld even though they affect interstate travel, if they are shown to reduce highway fatalities, because the state has a compelling interest in protecting the lives of its citizens.●

In situations not involving fundamental rights, a law or action does not violate substantive due process if it rationally relates to any legitimate governmental end. It is almost impossible for a law or action to fail the "rationality" test. Under this test, virtually any business regulation will be upheld as reasonable—the United States Supreme Court has sustained insurance regulations, price and wage controls, banking controls, and controls of unfair competition and trade practices against substantive due process challenges.

● EXAMPLE 9 If a state legislature enacted a law imposing a fifteen-year term of imprisonment without a trial on all businesspersons who appeared in their own television commercials, the law would be unconstitutional on both substantive and procedural grounds. Substantive review would invalidate the legislation because it abridges freedom of speech. Procedurally, the law is unfair because it imposes the penalty without giving the accused a chance to defend her or his actions.● The lack of procedural due process will cause a court to invalidate any statute or prior court decision. Similarly, a denial of substantive due process requires courts to overrule any state or federal law that violates the Constitution.

Equal Protection

Under the Fourteenth Amendment, a state may not "deny to any person within its jurisdiction the equal protection of the laws." The United States Supreme Court has used the due process clause of the Fifth Amendment to make the **equal protection clause** applicable to the federal government as well. Equal protection means that the government must treat similarly situated individuals in a similar manner.

Both substantive due process and equal protection require review of the substance of the law or other governmental action rather than review of the procedures used. When a law or action limits the liberty of all persons to do something, it may violate substantive due process; when a law or action limits the liberty of some persons but not others, it may violate the equal protection clause. ● EXAMPLE 10 If a law prohibits all persons from buying contraceptive devices, it raises a substantive due process question; if it prohibits only unmarried persons from buying the same devices, it raises an equal protection issue.●

Basically, in determining whether a law or action violates the equal protection clause, a court will consider questions similar to those previously noted as applicable in a substantive due process review. Under an equal protection inquiry, when a law or action distinguishes between or among individuals, the basis for the distinction—that is, the classification—is examined. Depending on the classification, the courts apply different levels of scrutiny, or "tests," to determine whether the law or action violates the equal protection clause.

Minimal Scrutiny—The "Rational Basis" Test Generally, laws regulating economic and social matters are presumed to be valid and are subject to only minimal scrutiny. A classification will be considered valid if there is any conceivable "rational basis" on which the classification might relate to any *legitimate government interest*. It is almost impossible for a law or action to fail the rational basis test.

EQUAL PROTECTION CLAUSE
The provision in the Fourteenth Amendment to the Constitution that guarantees that no state will "deny to any person within its jurisdiction the equal protection of the laws." This clause mandates that the state governments treat similarly situated individuals in a similar manner.

"When one undertakes to administer justice, . . . what is done for one, must be done for everyone in equal degree."
THOMAS JEFFERSON, 1743–1826
(Third president of the United States, 1801–1809)

● EXAMPLE 11 A city ordinance that in effect prohibits all pushcart vendors except a specific few from operating in a particular area of the city will be upheld if the city proffers a rational basis—perhaps regulation and reduction of traffic in the particular area—for the ordinance. In contrast, a law that provides unemployment benefits only to people over six feet tall would violate the guarantee of equal protection. There is no rational basis for determining the distribution of unemployment compensation on the basis of height. Such a distinction could not further any legitimate government objective. ●

Intermediate Scrutiny A harder standard to meet, that of "intermediate scrutiny," is applied in cases involving discrimination based on gender or legitimacy. Laws using these classifications must be substantially related to *important government objectives.* ● EXAMPLE 12 An important government objective is preventing illegitimate teenage pregnancies. Because males and females are not similarly situated in this circumstance—only females can become pregnant—a law that punishes men but not women for statutory rape will be upheld. A state law requiring illegitimate children to bring paternity suits within six years of their births, however, will be struck down if legitimate children are allowed to seek support from their parents at any time. ●

Strict Scrutiny The most difficult standard to meet is that of "strict scrutiny." Very few cases survive strict-scrutiny analysis. Strict scrutiny is applied when a law or action inhibits some persons' exercise of a fundamental right or is based on a suspect trait (such as race, national origin, or citizenship status). Strict scrutiny means that the court will examine the law or action involved very closely, and the law or action will be allowed to stand only if it is necessary to promote a *compelling government interest.*

● EXAMPLE 13 Suppose that a city gives preference to minority applicants in awarding construction contracts. Because the policy is based on suspect traits (race and national origin), it will violate the equal protection clause unless it is necessary to promote a compelling state interest. Courts have often held that states have a compelling interest in remedying past unconstitutional or illegal discrimination. The Supreme Court has declared, however, that such programs must be narrowly tailored. In other words, the city must identify the past unconstitutional or illegal discrimination against minority construction firms that it is attempting to correct, go no further than necessary to correct the problem, and change or drop its program once it has succeeded in correcting the problem.[35] ●

PRIVACY RIGHTS

In today's information age, it is understandable that issues relating to privacy rights have come to the fore. One question relates to the public's belief that personal information collected by government agencies, including the Federal Bureau of Investigation (FBI), poses a threat to individual privacy. Civil rights groups and others have been particularly concerned with how the war on terrorism following the terrorist attacks of September 11, 2001, will ultimately affect our privacy rights. Other privacy issues concern personal information

35. *Adarand Constructors, Inc. v. Peña,* 515 U.S. 200, 115 S.Ct. 2097, 132 L.Ed.2d 158 (1995).

collected by organizations in the private sector, such as banks, insurance companies, and health-care providers. One of the major concerns of individuals in recent years has been the increasing value of personal information for online marketers—who are willing to pay a high price to those who collect and sell them such information—and how to protect privacy rights in cyberspace.

In this section, we look at the protection of privacy rights under the U.S. Constitution and various federal statutes. Note that state constitutions and statutes also protect individuals' privacy rights, often to a significant degree. Privacy rights are also protected under tort law (see Chapter 8). Additionally, the Federal Trade Commission has played an active role in protecting the privacy rights of online consumers (see Chapter 19). The protection of employees' privacy rights, particularly with respect to electronic monitoring practices, is another area of growing concern (see Chapter 16).

Constitutional Protection of Privacy Rights

The U.S. Constitution does not explicitly mention a general right to privacy, and only relatively recently have the courts regarded the right to privacy as a constitutional right. In a 1928 Supreme Court case, *Olmstead v. United States,*[36] Justice Louis Brandeis stated in his dissent that the right to privacy is "the most comprehensive of rights and the right most valued by civilized men." The majority of the justices at that time did not agree, and it was not until the 1960s that a majority on the Supreme Court endorsed the view that the Constitution protects individual privacy rights.

In a landmark 1965 case, *Griswold v. Connecticut,*[37] the Supreme Court invalidated a Connecticut law that effectively prohibited the use of contraceptives. The Court held that the law violated the right to privacy. Justice William O. Douglas formulated a unique way of reading this right into the Bill of Rights. He claimed that "emanations" from the rights guaranteed by the First, Third, Fourth, Fifth, and Ninth Amendments formed and gave "life and substance" to "penumbras" (partial shadows) around these guaranteed rights. These penumbras included an implied constitutional right to privacy.

When we read these amendments, we can see the foundation for Justice Douglas's reasoning. Consider the Fourth Amendment. By prohibiting unreasonable searches and seizures, the amendment effectively protects individuals' privacy. Consider also the words of the Ninth Amendment: "The enumeration in the Constitution of certain rights, shall not be construed to deny or disparage others retained by the people." In other words, just because the Constitution, including its amendments, does not specifically mention the right to privacy does not mean that this right is denied to the people. Indeed, in a recent survey of America Online subscribers, respondents ranked privacy second behind freedom of speech and ahead of freedom of religion as the most important rights guaranteed by the Constitution. A Harris poll showed that almost 80 percent of those questioned believed that if the framers were writing the Constitution today, they would add privacy as an important right.[38]

---

36. 277 U.S. 438, 48 S.Ct. 564, 72 L.Ed. 944 (1928).

37. 381 U.S. 479, 85 S.Ct. 1678, 14 L.Ed.2d 510 (1965).

38. *Public Perspective,* November/December 2000, p. 9.

Federal Statutes Protecting Privacy Rights

In the last several decades, Congress has enacted a number of statutes that protect the privacy of individuals in various areas of concern. (See Exhibit 5–1 on pages 162 and 163 for a list and description of these statutes.) One of the most significant federal laws in this area, the Health Insurance Portability and Accountability Act (HIPAA)[39] of 1996, became effective on April 14, 2003. This act, which was passed in response to concerns over the privacy of health data, defines and limits the circumstances in which an individual's "protected health information" may be used or disclosed.

The HIPAA requires health-care providers and health-care plans, including certain employers who sponsor health plans, to inform patients of their privacy rights and of how their personal medical information may be used. The act also generally states that a person's medical records may not be used for purposes unrelated to health care—such as marketing, for example—or disclosed to others without the individual's permission. Covered entities must formulate written privacy policies, designate privacy officials, limit access to computerized health data, physically secure medical records with lock and key, train employees and volunteers on their privacy policies, and sanction those who violate those policies. These protections are intended to assure individuals that their health information, including genetic data, will be properly protected and not used for purposes that the patient did not know about or authorize.

As mentioned earlier, the federal government's constitutional authority to regulate activities on a national level, including activities that may jeopardize privacy rights, is rooted primarily in the commerce clause. At issue in the following case was whether Congress had exceeded its constitutional authority when it passed the Driver's Privacy Protection Act (DPPA) of 1994.

---

39. The HIPAA was enacted as Pub. L. No. 104-191 (1996) and is codified in 29 U.S.C. Sections 1181 *et seq.*

CASE 5.3　Reno v. Condon

Supreme Court of the United States, 2000.
528 U.S. 141,
120 S.Ct. 666,
145 L.Ed.2d 587.
**http://supct.law.cornell.edu/
supct/cases/name.htm**[a]

HISTORICAL AND TECHNOLOGICAL SETTING *In 1994, Congress passed the Driver's Privacy Protection Act (DPPA) when it learned that states were selling information obtained by state motor vehicle departments to commercial database suppliers. As a result, personal information given by those who applied for driver's licenses or vehicle registrations was finding its way to Web sites that anyone*

could access. This information included people's names, addresses, telephone numbers, vehicle descriptions, Social Security numbers, medical information, and photographs. Congress was pressured to take action after an actress, Rebecca Schaeffer, was killed by a stalker who obtained her address—which was not published in any phone book—from state driver's license records. Subsequent congressional investigation unearthed many similar incidents in which motor vehicle files were used to locate women trying to escape domestic abuse, as well as other victims, who were subsequently threatened or harmed. The 1994 act prevents states from disclosing or selling a driver's personal information without the driver's consent.

---

a. This is the "Historic Supreme Court Decisions—by Party Name" page within the "Caselists" collection of Cornell University's Legal Information Institute. Click on the "R" link or scroll down the list of cases to the entry for the *Reno* case.

Plaintiff Condon

CASE 5.3—Continued

BACKGROUND AND FACTS Each state's Department of Motor Vehicles (DMV) requires drivers and automobile owners to provide personal information, including a name, address, telephone number, and Social Security number, as a condition of obtaining a driver's license or registering an automobile. Many states sell this information to individuals and businesses.[b] Under the DPPA, before a state can sell the information, a driver must consent to its release, or, in other words, choose to "opt in." In contrast, under South Carolina state law, information in DMV records is available to anyone who promises not to use it for telemarketing. The state can sell the data unless a South Carolina driver affirmatively "opts out." Charles Condon, the attorney general of South Carolina, filed a suit in a federal district court against Janet Reno, the attorney general of the United States, alleging that the DPPA violated the Constitution. The court granted an injunction to prevent the DPPA's enforcement, and the U.S. Court of Appeals for the Fourth Circuit upheld the order. Reno appealed to the United States Supreme Court.

IN THE WORDS OF THE COURT . . .

Chief Justice *REHNQUIST* delivered the opinion of the Court.

* * * *

The United States asserts that the DPPA is a proper exercise of Congress's authority to regulate interstate commerce under the Commerce Clause. The United States bases its Commerce Clause argument on the fact that the personal, identifying information that the DPPA regulates is a "thin[g] in interstate commerce," and that the sale or release of that information in interstate commerce is therefore a proper subject of congressional regulation. We agree with the United States' contention. The motor vehicle information which the States have historically sold is used by insurers, manufacturers, direct marketers, and others engaged in interstate commerce to contact drivers with customized solicitations. The information is also used in the stream of interstate commerce by various public and private entities for matters related to interstate motoring. *Because drivers' information is, in this context, an article of commerce, its sale or release into the interstate stream of business is sufficient to support congressional regulation.* * * * [Emphasis added.]

But the fact that drivers' personal information is, in the context of this case, an article in interstate commerce does not conclusively resolve the constitutionality of the DPPA. In [other cases] we held federal statutes invalid * * * because those statutes violated the principles of federalism contained in the Tenth Amendment.[c] * * * While Congress has substantial powers to govern the Nation directly, including in areas of intimate concern to the States, *the Constitution has never been understood to confer upon Congress the ability to require the States to govern according to Congress's instructions.* [Emphasis added.]

* * * Congress cannot compel the States to enact or enforce a federal regulatory program. * * * Congress cannot circumvent that prohibition by conscripting the States' officers directly. The Federal Government may neither issue directives requiring the States to address particular problems, nor command the States' officers, or those of their political subdivisions, to administer or enforce a federal regulatory program.

* * * * *

---

b. Wisconsin's DMV, for example, receives approximately $8 million each year from the sale of this information.
c. Under the Tenth Amendment to the U.S. Constitution, "[t]he powers not delegated to the United States by the Constitution, nor prohibited by it to the States, are reserved to the States respectively, or to the people."

(continued)

CASE 5.3—Continued

* * * [However, the] DPPA does not require the States in their sovereign capacity to regulate their own citizens. The DPPA regulates the States as the owners of databases. It does not require the South Carolina Legislature to enact any laws or regulations, and it does not require state officials to assist in the enforcement of federal statutes regulating private individuals. We accordingly conclude that the DPPA is consistent with the constitutional principles * * * .

DECISION AND REMEDY The United States Supreme Court reversed the judgment of the U.S. Court of Appeals for the Fourth Circuit. The Supreme Court held that the DPPA was a proper exercise of Congress's power under the commerce clause and did not violate other constitutional provisions.

FOR CRITICAL ANALYSIS—Ethical Consideration *Are there any ethical reasons why a state should keep private its drivers' personal information?*

EXHIBIT 5–1 FEDERAL LEGISLATION RELATING TO PRIVACY

TITLE	PROVISIONS CONCERNING PRIVACY
Freedom of Information Act (1966)	Provides that individuals have a right to obtain access to information about them collected in government files.
Fair Credit Reporting Act (1970)	Provides that consumers have the right to be informed of the nature and scope of a credit investigation, the kind of information that is being compiled, and the names of the firms or individuals who will be receiving the report.
Crime Control Act (1973)	Safeguards the confidentiality of information amassed for certain state criminal systems.
Family and Educational Rights and Privacy Act (1974)	Limits access to computer-stored records of education-related evaluations and grades in private and public colleges and universities.
Privacy Act (1974)	Protects the privacy of individuals about whom the federal government has information. Specifically, the act provides as follows: 1. Agencies originating, using, disclosing, or otherwise manipulating personal information must ensure the reliability of the information and provide safeguards against its misuse. 2. Information compiled for one purpose cannot be used for another without the concerned individual's permission. 3. Individuals must be able to find out what data concerning them are being compiled and how the data will be used. 4. Individuals must be given a means by which to correct inaccurate data.
Tax Reform Act (1976)	Preserves the privacy of personal financial information.
Right to Financial Privacy Act (1978)	Prohibits financial institutions from providing the federal government with access to customers' records unless a customer authorizes the disclosure.
Electronic Fund Transfer Act (1978)	Prohibits the use of a computer without authorization to retrieve data in a financial institution's or consumer reporting agency's files.
Cable Communications Policy Act (1984)	Regulates access to information collected by cable service operators on subscribers to cable services.

EXHIBIT 5-1 FEDERAL LEGISLATION RELATING TO PRIVACY (CONTINUED)

TITLE	PROVISIONS CONCERNING PRIVACY
Electronic Communications Privacy Act (1986)	Prohibits the interception of information communicated by electronic means.
Driver's Privacy Protection Act (1994)	Prevents states from disclosing or selling a driver's personal information without the driver's consent.
Children's Online Privacy Protection Act (1998)	Requires operators of Web sites aimed at children under the age of thirteen to clearly provide notice about the information being collected and how it will be used; requires verifiable parental consent for certain types of information about children.
Financial Services Modernization Act (Gramm-Leach-Bliley Act) (1999)	Requires all financial institutions to provide customers with information on their privacy policies and practices; prohibits the disclosure of nonpublic personal information about a consumer to an unaffiliated third party unless strict disclosure and opt-out requirements are met. Final rules under the act, issued by the Federal Trade Commission, became mandatory on July 1, 2001.
Health Insurance Portability and Accountability Act (1996, effective April 14, 2003)	Requires providers of health care and health-care plans to inform patients of their privacy rights and of how their personal medical information may be used; prohibits the disclosure of a person's medical information without the person's permission.

KEY TERMS

Bill of Rights   148

checks and balances   140

commerce clause   141

due process clause   156

equal protection clause   157

establishment clause   154

federal form of government   139

filtering software   153

free exercise clause   154

meta tag   153

police powers   144

preemption   146

supremacy clause   145

symbolic speech   150

CHAPTER SUMMARY CONSTITUTIONAL AUTHORITY TO REGULATE BUSINESS

The Constitutional Powers of Government (See pages 139–140.)	The U.S. Constitution established a federal form of government, in which government powers are shared by the national government and the state governments. At the national level, government powers are divided among the legislative, executive, and judicial branches.
The Commerce Clause (See pages 141–145.)	1. *The expansion of national powers*—The commerce clause expressly permits Congress to regulate commerce. Over time, courts expansively interpreted this clause, thereby enabling the national government to wield extensive powers over the economic life of the nation.
	2. *The commerce power today*—Today, the commerce power authorizes the national government, at least theoretically, to regulate every commercial enterprise in the United States. In recent years, the Supreme Court has reined in somewhat the national government's regulatory powers under the commerce clause.

(continued)

CHAPTER SUMMARY CONSTITUTIONAL AUTHORITY TO
REGULATE BUSINESS—Continued

The Commerce Clause—continued	3. *The regulatory powers of the states*—The Tenth Amendment reserves all powers not expressly delegated to the national government to the states. Under their police powers, state governments may regulate private activities to protect or promote the public order, health, safety, morals, and general welfare.
	4. *The "dormant" commerce clause*—If state regulations substantially interfere with interstate commerce, they will be held to violate the "dormant" commerce clause of the U.S. Constitution. The commerce clause, which gives the national government the exclusive authority to regulate interstate commerce, implies a "dormant" aspect of the clause—that the states do not have this power.
The Supremacy Clause (See pages 145–147.)	The U.S. Constitution provides that the Constitution, laws, and treaties of the United States are "the supreme Law of the Land." Whenever a state law directly conflicts with a federal law, the state law is rendered invalid.
The Taxing and Spending Powers (See pages 147–148.)	The U.S. Constitution gives Congress the power to impose uniform taxes throughout the United States and to spend revenues accumulated from the taxing power. Congress can spend revenues to promote any objective it deems worthwhile, so long as it does not violate the Bill of Rights.
Business and the Bill of Rights (See pages 148–156.)	The Bill of Rights, which consists of the first ten amendments to the U.S. Constitution, was adopted in 1791 and embodies a series of protections for individuals—and, in some cases, business entities—against various types of interference by the federal government. Freedoms guaranteed by the First Amendment that affect businesses include the following:
	1. *Freedom of speech*—Speech, including symbolic speech, is given the fullest possible protection by the courts. Corporate political speech and commercial speech also receive substantial protection under the First Amendment. Certain types of speech, such as defamatory speech and lewd or obscene speech, are not protected under the First Amendment. Government attempts to regulate unprotected forms of speech in the online environment have, to date, met with little success.
	2. *Freedom of religion*—Under the First Amendment, the government may neither establish any religion (the establishment clause) nor prohibit the free exercise of religion (the free exercise clause).
Due Process and Equal Protection (See pages 156–158.)	1. *Due process*—Both the Fifth and the Fourteenth Amendments provide that no person shall be deprived of "life, liberty, or property, without due process of law." Procedural due process requires that any government decision to take life, liberty, or property must be made fairly, using fair procedures. Substantive due process focuses on the content of legislation. Generally, a law that conflicts with a fundamental right or that involves a suspect characteristic (such as race) violates substantive due process unless the law promotes a compelling state interest, such as public safety.
	2. *Equal protection*—Under the Fourteenth Amendment, a state may not "deny to any person within its jurisdiction the equal protection of the laws." A law or action that limits the liberty of some persons but not others may violate the equal protection clause. Such a law may be deemed valid, however, if there is a rational basis for the discriminatory treatment of a given group or if the law substantially relates to an important government objective.
Privacy Rights (See pages 158–163.)	Americans are increasingly becoming concerned over privacy issues in today's information age. The Constitution does not contain a specific guarantee of a right to privacy, but such a right has been derived from guarantees found in several constitutional amendments. A number of federal statutes protect privacy rights. Privacy rights are also protected by many state constitutions and statutes, as well as under tort law.

FOR REVIEW

1. What is the basic structure of the U.S. government?
2. What constitutional clause gives the federal government the power to regulate commercial activities among the various states?
3. What constitutional clause allows laws enacted by the federal government to take priority over conflicting state laws?
4. What is the Bill of Rights? What freedoms are guaranteed by the First Amendment?
5. Where in the Constitution can the due process clause be found?

QUESTIONS AND CASE PROBLEMS

5–1. Government Powers. The framers of the Constitution feared the twin evils of tyranny and anarchy. Discuss how specific provisions of the Constitution and the Bill of Rights reflect these fears and protect against both of these extremes.

5–2. Commercial Speech. A mayoral election is about to be held in a large U.S. city. One of the candidates is Luis Delgado, and his campaign supporters wish to post campaign signs on lampposts and utility posts throughout the city. A city ordinance, however, prohibits the posting of any signs on public property. Delgado's supporters contend that the city ordinance is unconstitutional, because it violates their rights to free speech. What factors might a court consider in determining the constitutionality of this ordinance?

5–3. Commerce Clause. Suppose that Georgia enacts a law requiring the use of contoured rear-fender mudguards on trucks and trailers operating within its state lines. The statute further makes it illegal for trucks and trailers to use straight mudguards. In thirty-five other states, straight mudguards are legal. Moreover, in the neighboring state of Florida, straight mudguards are explicitly required by law. There is some evidence suggesting that contoured mudguards might be a little safer than straight mudguards. Discuss whether this Georgia statute would violate the commerce clause of the U.S. Constitution.

Not 1st Amd (but civil rights act)

5–4. Freedom of Religion. A business has a backlog of orders, and to meet its deadlines, management decides to run the firm seven days a week, eight hours a day. One of the employees, Marjorie Tollens, refuses to work on Saturday on religious grounds. Her refusal to work means that the firm may not meet its production deadlines and may therefore suffer a loss of future business. The firm fires Tollens and replaces her with an employee who is willing to work seven days a week. Tollens claims that her employer, in terminating her employment, violated her constitutional right to the free exercise of her religion. Do you agree? Why or why not?

5–5. Equal Protection. With the objectives of preventing crime, maintaining property values, and preserving the qual-

ity of urban life, New York City enacted an ordinance to regulate the locations of commercial establishments that featured adult entertainment. The ordinance expressly applied to female, but not male, topless entertainment. Adele Buzzetti owned the Cozy Cabin, a New York City cabaret that featured female topless dancers. Buzzetti and an anonymous dancer filed a suit in a federal district court against the city, asking the court to block the enforcement of the ordinance. The plaintiffs argued in part that the ordinance violated the equal protection clause. Under the equal protection clause, what standard applies to the court's consideration of this ordinance? Under this test, how should the court rule? Why? [*Buzzetti v. City of New York,* 140 F.3d 134 (2d Cir. 1998)]

5–6. Free Speech. The city of Tacoma, Washington, enacted an ordinance that prohibited the playing of car sound systems at a volume that would be "audible" at a distance greater than fifty feet. Dwight Holland was arrested and convicted for violating the ordinance. The conviction was later dismissed, but Holland filed a civil suit in a Washington state court against the city. He claimed in part that the ordinance violated his freedom of speech under the First Amendment. On what basis might the court conclude that this ordinance is constitutional? (Hint: In playing a sound system, was Holland actually expressing himself?) [*Holland v. City of Tacoma,* 90 Wash.App. 533, 954 P.2d 290 (1998)]

Case Problem with Sample Answer

5–7. Freedom of Religion. Thomas worked in the nonmilitary operations of a large firm that produced both military and nonmilitary goods. When the company discontinued the production of nonmilitary goods, Thomas was transferred to a plant producing military equipment. Thomas left his job, claiming that it violated his religious principles to participate in the manufacture of goods to be used in destroying life. In effect, he argued, the transfer to the war-materials plant forced him to quit his job. He was denied unemployment compensation by the state because he had not been effectively "discharged" by the employer but had voluntarily terminated his employment. Did the state's denial of unemployment benefits to Thomas violate the free exercise clause of the First Amendment? Explain. [*Thomas v. Review Board of the Indiana Employment Security Division,* 450 U.S. 707, 101 S.Ct. 1425, 67 L.Ed.2d 624 (1981)]

To view a sample answer for this case problem, go to this book's Web site at http://leet.westbuslaw.com and click on "Interactive Study Center."

5–8. Freedom of Speech. The members of Greater New Orleans Broadcasting Association, Inc., operate radio and television stations in New Orleans. They wanted to broadcast ads for private, for-profit casinos that are legal in Louisiana. A federal statute banned casino advertising, but other federal statutes exempted ads for tribal, government, nonprofit, and "occasional and ancillary" commercial casinos. The association filed a suit in a federal district court against the federal government, asking the court to hold that the statute, as it applied to the Louisiana casinos' ads, violated the First Amendment. The government argued that the ban should be upheld because, "[u]nder appropriate conditions, some broadcast signals from Louisiana broadcasting stations may be heard in neighboring states including Texas and Arkansas," where private casino gambling is unlawful. What is the test for whether a regulation of commercial speech violates the First Amendment? How might it apply in this case? How should the court rule? [*Greater New Orleans Broadcasting Association, Inc. v. United States,* 527 U.S. 173, 119 S.Ct. 1923, 144 L.Ed.2d 161 (1999)]

5–9. Freedom of Speech. The Telephone Consumer Protection Act (TCPA) of 1991 made it unlawful for any person "to use any telephone facsimile machine, computer, or other device to send an unsolicited advertisement to a telephone facsimile machine." In enacting the TCPA, Congress did not consider any studies or empirical data estimating the cost of receiving a fax or the number of unsolicited fax ads that an average business receives in a day. American Blast Fax, Inc. (ABFI), provides fax ad services in Missouri. Between July 2000 and June 2001, the office of Jeremiah Nixon, the Missouri attorney general, received 229 unsolicited faxes, some of which were ads. Nixon filed a suit in a federal district court against ABFI and others, alleging in part violations of the TCPA. ABFI filed a motion to dismiss, asserting that the TCPA provision on unsolicited fax ads was unconstitutional. Nixon claimed that the ads shifted costs from advertisers to recipients and tied up recipients' fax machines, but he offered no evidence of the cost in money or time. What is the test for considering a restriction on commercial speech? Is the TCPA provision valid? Explain. [*Missouri v. American Blast Fax, Inc.,* 323 F.3d 649 (8th Cir. 2003)]

A Question of Ethics & Social Responsibility

5–10. In 1999, in an effort to reduce smoking by children, the attorney general of Massachusetts issued comprehensive regulations governing the advertising and sale of tobacco products. Among other things, the regulations banned cigarette advertisements within one thousand feet of any elementary school, secondary school, or public playground and required retailers to post any advertising in their stores at least five feet off the floor, out of the immediate sight of young children. A group of tobacco manufacturers and retailers filed suit against the state, claiming that the regulations were preempted by the federal Cigarette Labeling and Advertising Act (FCLAA) of 1965, as amended. That act sets uniform labeling requirements and bans broadcast advertising for cigarettes. Ultimately, the case reached the United States Supreme Court, which held that the federal law on cigarette ads preempted the cigarette advertising restrictions adopted by Massachusetts. The only portion of the Massachusetts regulatory package to survive was the requirement that retailers had to place tobacco products in an area accessible only by the sales staff. In view of these facts, consider the following questions. [*Lorillard Tobacco Co. v. Reilly,* 533 U.S. 525, 121 S.Ct. 2404, 69 L.Ed.2d 532 (2001)]

1. Some argue that having a national standard for tobacco regulation is more important than allowing states to set their own standards for tobacco regulation. Do you agree? Why or why not?
2. According to the Court in this case, the federal law does not restrict the ability of state and local governments to adopt general zoning restrictions that apply to cigarettes, as long as those restrictions are "on equal terms with other products." How would you argue in support of this reasoning? How would you argue against it?

Case Briefing Assignment

5–11. Examine Case A.2 [*Austin v. Berryman,* 878 F.2d 786 (4th Cir. 1989)] in Appendix A. The case has been excerpted there in great detail. Review and then brief the case, making sure that you include answers to the following questions in your brief.

1. Who were the plaintiff and defendant in this action?
2. Why did Austin claim that she had been forced to leave her job?
3. Why was Austin refused state unemployment benefits?
4. Did the state's refusal to give Austin unemployment compensation violate her rights under the free exercise clause of the First Amendment?
5. What logic or reasoning did the court employ in arriving at its conclusion?

Critical-Thinking Social Question

5-12. The Bay City Council adopts a dress code for cab drivers that requires them, while driving a cab, to wear shoes (no sandals) and dark pants to ankle length, or a dark skirt or dress, and a solid white or light blue shirt or blouse with sleeves and a folded collar. If a hat is worn, it must be a baseball-style cap with a Bay City or taxicab theme. Is this dress code rationally related to a legitimate government objective?

INTERACTING WITH THE INTERNET

For updated links to resources available on the Web, as well as a variety of other materials, visit this text's Web site at

http://leet.westbuslaw.com

For an online version of the Constitution that provides hypertext links to amendments and other changes, as well as the history of the document, go to

http://www.constitutioncenter.org

For discussions of current issues involving the rights and liberties contained in the Bill of Rights, go to the Web site of the American Civil Liberties Union at

http://www.aclu.org

ONLINE LEGAL RESEARCH EXERCISES

Go to **http://leet.westbuslaw.com**, the Web site that accompanies this text. Select "Interactive Study Center" and then click on "Chapter 5." There you will find the following Internet research exercises that you can perform to learn more about topics covered in this chapter.

Activity 5–1: MANAGEMENT PERSPECTIVE—Commercial Speech
Activity 5–2: TECHNOLOGICAL PERSPECTIVE—Privacy Rights in Cyberspace

BEFORE THE TEST

Go to **http://leet.westbuslaw.com**, the Web site that accompanies this text. Select "Interactive Quizzes." You will find at least twenty interactive questions relating to this chapter.

Westlaw® Campus

If your textbook provided for a subscription to Westlaw® Campus, or if you have otherwise purchased access to the Westlaw Campus database, you can access any of the cases presented or cited in this chapter by using your Westlaw Campus account.

CHAPTER 6

Powers and Functions of Administrative Agencies

CONTENTS

CHAPTER OBJECTIVES

After reading this chapter, you should be able to answer the following questions:

1. How are federal administrative agencies created?

2. What are the three basic functions of most administrative agencies?

3. What sequence of events must normally occur before an agency rule becomes law?

4. How do administrative agencies enforce their rules?

5. How do the three branches of government limit the power of administrative agencies?

As the quotation below suggests, government agencies established to administer the law have a tremendous impact on the day-to-day operation of the government and the economy. In the early years of our nation, the United States had a relatively simple, nonindustrial economy that required little regulation. Because administrative agencies often create and enforce such regulations, there were relatively few such agencies. Today, however, there are rules covering virtually every aspect of a business's operation. Consequently, agencies have multiplied. At the federal level, the Securities and Exchange Commission regulates a firm's capital structure and financing, as well as its financial reporting. The National Labor Relations Board oversees relations between a firm and any unions with which it may deal. The Equal Employment Opportunity Commission also regulates employment relationships. The Environmental Protection Agency and the Occupational Safety and Health Administration affect the way a firm manufactures the firm's products. The Federal Trade Commission influences the way it markets these products.

> "[P]erhaps more values today are affected by [administrative] decisions than by those of all the courts."
>
> Robert H. Jackson, 1892–1954
> (Associate justice of the United States Supreme Court, 1941–1954)

Added to this layer of federal regulation is a second layer of state regulation that, when not preempted by federal legislation, may cover many of the same activities or regulate independently those activities not covered by federal regulation. Finally, agency regulations at the county and municipal levels also affect certain types of business activities.

Administrative agencies issue rules, orders, and decisions. These regulations make up the body of *administrative law.* You were introduced briefly to some of the main principles of administrative law in Chapter 1. In the following pages, these principles are presented in much greater detail.

AGENCY CREATION AND POWERS

Congress creates federal administrative agencies. Because Congress cannot possibly oversee the actual implementation of all of the laws it enacts, it must delegate such tasks to others, particularly when the issues relate to highly technical areas, such as air and water pollution. By delegating some of its authority to make and implement laws, Congress can monitor indirectly a particular area in which it has passed legislation without becoming bogged down in the details relating to enforcement—details that are often best left to specialists.

Enabling Legislation

To create an administrative agency, Congress passes **enabling legislation,** which specifies the name, composition, purpose, functions, and powers of the agency being created. Federal administrative agencies can exercise only those powers that Congress has delegated to them in enabling legislation. Through similar enabling acts, state legislatures create state administrative agencies.

For example, Congress created the Federal Trade Commission (FTC) in the Federal Trade Commission Act of 1914.[1] The act prohibits unfair and deceptive trade practices. It also describes the procedures that the agency must follow to charge persons or organizations with violations of the act, and it provides for judicial review of agency orders. The act grants the FTC the power to

- Create rules and regulations for the purpose of carrying out the act.
- Conduct investigations of business practices.
- Obtain reports from interstate corporations concerning their business practices.
- Investigate possible violations of federal antitrust statutes.[2]
- Publish findings of its investigations.
- Recommend new legislation.
- Hold trial-like hearings to resolve certain kinds of trade disputes that involve FTC regulations or federal antitrust laws.

The commission that heads the FTC is composed of five members, each of whom the president appoints, with the advice and consent of the Senate, for a

ENABLING LEGISLATION
Statutes enacted by Congress that authorize the creation of an administrative agency and specify the name, composition, purpose, functions, and powers of the agency being created.

---

1. 15 U.S.C. Sections 41–58.
2. Antitrust statutes are designed to promote competition in the marketplace—see Chapter 22. The FTC shares this task with the Antitrust Division of the U.S. Department of Justice.

term of seven years. The president designates one of the commissioners to be chairperson. Various offices and bureaus of the FTC undertake different administrative activities for the agency. The organization of the FTC is illustrated in Exhibit 6–1.

Types of Agencies

There are two basic types of administrative agencies: executive agencies and independent regulatory agencies. Federal **executive agencies** include the cabinet departments of the executive branch, which were formed to assist the president in carrying out executive functions, and the subagencies within the cabinet departments. The Occupational Safety and Health Administration, for example, is a subagency within the Department of Labor. Exhibit 6–2 lists the cabinet departments and their most important subagencies.

All administrative agencies are part of the executive branch of government, but **independent regulatory agencies** are outside the major executive departments. The Federal Trade Commission and the Securities and Exchange Commission are examples of independent regulatory agencies. These and other selected independent regulatory agencies, as well as their principal functions, are listed in Exhibit 6–3 on page 172.

The significant difference between the two types of agencies lies in the accountability of the regulators. Agencies that are considered part of the executive branch are subject to the authority of the president, who has the power to appoint and remove federal officers. In theory, this power is less pronounced in regard to independent agencies, whose officers serve for fixed terms and cannot be removed without just cause. In practice, however, the president's power to exert influence over independent agencies is often considerable.

Agency Powers and the Constitution

Administrative agencies occupy an unusual niche in the American legal scheme, because they exercise powers that are normally divided among the three branches

EXECUTIVE AGENCY
An administrative agency that is either a cabinet department or a subagency within a cabinet department. Executive agencies fall under the authority of the president, who has the power to appoint and remove federal officers.

INDEPENDENT REGULATORY AGENCY
An administrative agency that is not considered part of the government's executive branch and is not subject to the authority of the president. Agency officials cannot be removed without cause.

EXHIBIT 6–1 ORGANIZATION OF THE FEDERAL TRADE COMMISSION

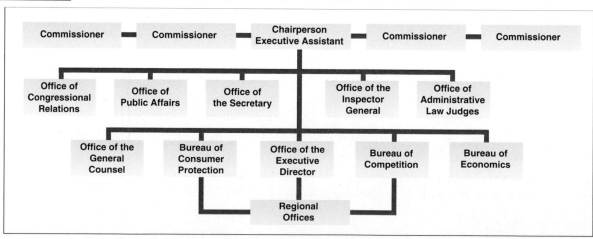

EXHIBIT 6-2   EXECUTIVE DEPARTMENTS AND SELECTED SUBAGENCIES

DEPARTMENT	DATE FORMED	SELECTED SUBAGENCIES
State	1789	Passport Office; Bureau of Diplomatic Security; Foreign Service; Bureau of Human Rights and Humanitarian Affairs; Bureau of Consular Affairs; Bureau of Intelligence and Research
Treasury	1789	Internal Revenue Service; U.S. Mint
Interior	1849	U.S. Fish and Wildlife Service; National Park Service; Bureau of Indian Affairs; Bureau of Land Management
Justice	1870[a]	Federal Bureau of Investigation; Drug Enforcement Administration; Bureau of Prisons; U.S. Marshals Service
Agriculture	1889	Soil Conservation Service; Agricultural Research Service; Food Safety and Inspection Service; Forest Service
Commerce	1913[b]	Bureau of the Census; Bureau of Economic Analysis; Minority Business Development Agency; U.S. Patent and Trademark Office; National Oceanic and Atmospheric Administration
Labor	1913[b]	Occupational Safety and Health Administration; Bureau of Labor Statistics; Employment Standards Administration; Office of Labor-Management Standards; Employment and Training Administration
Defense	1949[c]	National Security Agency; Joint Chiefs of Staff; Departments of the Air Force, Navy, Army; service academies
Housing and Urban Development	1965	Office of Community Planning and Development; Government National Mortgage Association; Office of Fair Housing and Equal Opportunity
Transportation	1967	Federal Aviation Administration; Federal Highway Administration; National Highway Traffic Safety Administration; Federal Transit Administration
Energy	1977	Office of Civilian Radioactive Waste Management; Office of Nuclear Energy; Energy Information Administration
Health and Human Services	1980[d]	Food and Drug Administration; Centers for Medicare and Medicaid Services; Centers for Disease Control; National Institutes of Health
Education	1980[d]	Office of Special Education and Rehabilitation Services; Office of Elementary and Secondary Education; Office of Postsecondary Education; Office of Vocational and Adult Education
Veterans' Affairs	1989	Veterans Health Administration; Veterans Benefits Administration; National Cemetery System
Homeland Security	2002	Bureau of Citizenship and Immigration Services; Directorate of Border and Transportation Services; U.S. Coast Guard; Federal Emergency Management Agency

a. Formed from the Office of the Attorney General (created in 1789).
b. Formed from the Department of Commerce and Labor (created in 1903).
c. Formed from the Department of War (created in 1789) and the Department of the Navy (created in 1798).
d. Formed from the Department of Health, Education, and Welfare (created in 1953).

EXHIBIT 6-3 SELECTED INDEPENDENT REGULATORY AGENCIES

NAME	DATE FORMED	PRINCIPAL DUTIES
Federal Reserve System Board of Governors (Fed)	1913	Determines policy with respect to interest rates, credit availability, and the money supply.
Federal Trade Commission (FTC)	1914	Prevents businesses from engaging in unfair trade practices; stops the formation of monopolies in the business sector; protects consumer rights.
Securities and Exchange Commission (SEC)	1934	Regulates the nation's stock exchanges, in which shares of stock are bought and sold; enforces the securities laws, which require full disclosure of the financial profiles of companies that wish to sell stock and bonds to the public.
Federal Communications Commission (FCC)	1934	Regulates all communications by telegraph, cable, telephone, radio, satellite, and television.
National Labor Relations Board (NLRB)	1935	Protects employees' rights to join unions and bargain collectively with employers; attempts to prevent unfair labor practices by both employers and unions.
Equal Employment Opportunity Commission (EEOC)	1964	Works to eliminate discrimination in employment based on religion, gender, race, color, disability, national origin, or age; investigates claims of discrimination.
Environmental Protection Agency (EPA)	1970	Undertakes programs aimed at reducing air and water pollution; works with state and local agencies to help fight environmental hazards.
Nuclear Regulatory Commission (NRC)	1975	Ensures that electricity-generating nuclear reactors in the United States are built and operated safely; regularly inspects operations of such reactors.

LEGISLATIVE RULE
An administrative agency rule that carries the same weight as a congressionally enacted statute.

DELEGATION DOCTRINE
A doctrine based on Article I, Sections 1 and 8, of the U.S. Constitution, which have been construed to allow Congress to delegate some of its power to make and implement laws to administrative agencies.

of government. ● **EXAMPLE 1** In the FTC's enabling legislation discussed above, the FTC's grant of power incorporates functions associated with the legislature (rulemaking), the executive branch (enforcement of the rules), and the courts (adjudication, or the formal resolution of disputes).●

The constitutional principle of *checks and balances* allows each branch of government to act as a check on the actions of the other two branches. Furthermore, the Constitution authorizes only the legislative branch to create laws. Yet administrative agencies, to which the Constitution does not specifically refer, make **legislative rules,** or *substantive rules,* that are as legally binding as laws that Congress passes.

Courts generally hold that Article I of the U.S. Constitution authorizes delegating such powers to administrative agencies. In fact, courts generally hold that Article I is the basis for all administrative law. Section 1 of that article grants all legislative powers to Congress and requires Congress to oversee the implementation of all laws. Article I, Section 8, gives Congress the power to make all laws necessary for executing its specified powers. The courts interpret these passages, under what is known as the **delegation doctrine,** as granting Congress the power to establish administrative agencies that can create rules for implementing those laws.

The three branches of government exercise certain controls over agency powers and functions, as is discussed later in this chapter, but in many ways administrative agencies function independently. For this reason, administrative agencies, which constitute the **bureaucracy,** are sometimes referred to as the "fourth branch" of the American government.

BUREAUCRACY
The organizational structure, consisting of government bureaus and agencies, through which the government implements and enforces the laws.

ETHICAL ISSUE

Do *administrative agencies exercise too much authority?*

As mentioned, administrative agencies, such as the Federal Trade Commission, combine functions normally divided among the three branches of government in a single governmental entity. The broad range of authority that agencies exercise sometimes poses questions of fairness. After all, agencies create rules that are as legally binding as the laws passed by Congress—the only federal government institution authorized by the Constitution to make laws. To be sure, arbitrary rulemaking by agencies is checked by the procedural requirements set forth in the Administrative Procedure Act, or APA (discussed next), as well as by the courts, to which agency decisions may be appealed. Yet some people claim that these checks are not enough.

Consider that in addition to legislative rules, which are subject to the procedural requirements of the APA, agencies also create *interpretive rules—* rules that specify how the agency will interpret and apply its regulations. The APA does not apply to interpretive rulemaking. Additionally, although a firm that challenges an agency's rule may be able to appeal the agency's decision in the matter to a court, the policy of the courts is generally to defer to agency rules, including interpretive rules, and to agency decisions.

ADMINISTRATIVE PROCESS

The three functions mentioned previously—rulemaking, enforcement, and adjudication—make up what is called the administrative process. **Administrative process** involves the administration of law by administrative agencies, in contrast to **judicial process,** which involves the administration of law by the courts.

The Administrative Procedure Act (APA) of 1946[3] imposes procedural requirements that all federal agencies must follow in their rulemaking, adjudication, and other functions. The APA is such an integral part of the administrative process that we examine its application as we go through the basic functions carried out by administrative agencies.

ADMINISTRATIVE PROCESS
The procedure used by administrative agencies in the administration of law.

JUDICIAL PROCESS
The procedures relating to, or connected with, the administration of justice through the judicial system.

Rulemaking

A major function of an administrative agency is **rulemaking**—the formulation of new regulations. In an agency's enabling legislation, Congress confers the agency's power to make rules. ● **EXAMPLE 2** The Occupational Safety and Health Act of 1970 authorized the Occupational Health and Safety Administration (OSHA) to

RULEMAKING
The actions undertaken by administrative agencies when formally adopting new regulations or amending old ones. Under the Administrative Procedure Act, rulemaking includes notifying the public of proposed rules or changes and receiving and considering the public's comments.

---

3. 5 U.S.C. Sections 551–706.

develop and issue rules governing safety in the workplace. In 1991, OSHA deemed it in the public interest to issue a new rule regulating the health-care industry to prevent the spread of such diseases as acquired immune deficiency syndrome (AIDS). OSHA created a rule specifying various standards—on how contaminated instruments should be handled, for example—with which employers in that industry must comply.●

In formulating rules, administrative agencies follow specific rulemaking procedures required under the APA. We look here at the most common rulemaking procedure, called **notice-and-comment rulemaking**. This procedure involves three basic steps: notice of the proposed rulemaking, a comment period, and the final rule.

NOTICE-AND-COMMENT RULEMAKING
A procedure in agency rulemaking that requires (1) notice, (2) opportunity for comment, and (3) a published draft of the final rule.

Notice of the Proposed Rulemaking　When a federal agency decides to create a new rule, the agency publishes a notice of the proposed rulemaking proceedings in the *Federal Register,* a daily publication of the executive branch that prints government orders, rules, and regulations. The notice states where and when the proceedings will be held, the agency's legal authority for making the rule (usually its enabling legislation), and the terms or subject matter of the proposed rule.

Comment Period　Following the publication of the notice of the proposed rulemaking proceedings, the agency must allow ample time for persons to comment on the proposed rule. The purpose of this comment period is to give interested parties the opportunity to express their views on the proposed rule in an effort to influence agency policy. The comments may be in writing or, if a hearing is held, may be given orally. The agency need not respond to all comments, but it must respond to any significant comments that bear directly on the proposed rule. The agency responds by either modifying its final rule or explaining, in a statement accompanying the final rule, why it did not make any changes. In some circumstances, particularly when the procedure being used in a specific instance is less formal, an agency may accept comments after the comment period is closed. The agency should summarize these *ex parte* (private, off-the-record) comments for possible review.

"In some respects matters of procedure constitute the very essence of ordered liberty under the Constitution."
WILEY B. RUTLEDGE, 1894–1949
(Associate justice of the United States Supreme Court, 1943–1949)

The Final Rule　After the agency reviews the comments, it drafts the final rule and publishes it in the *Federal Register.* The final rule is later compiled with the rules and regulations of other federal administrative agencies in the Code of Federal Regulations (C.F.R.). Final rules have binding legal effect unless the courts later overturn them.

Investigation

Administrative agencies conduct investigations of the entities that they regulate. Agencies investigate a wide range of activities, including coal mining, automobile manufacturing, and the industrial discharge of pollutants into the environment. A typical agency investigation occurs during the rulemaking process to obtain information about a certain individual, firm, or industry. The purpose of such an investigation is to avoid issuing a rule that is arbitrary and capricious and instead to issue a rule based on a consideration of relevant factors. After final rules are issued, agencies conduct investigations to monitor compliance with those rules. A typical agency investigation of this kind might begin when a citizen reports a possible violation.

Inspections and Tests Many agencies gather information through on-site inspections. Sometimes, inspecting an office, a factory, or some other business facility is the only way to obtain the evidence needed to prove a regulatory violation. At other times, an inspection or test is used in place of a formal hearing to show the need to correct or prevent an undesirable condition. Administrative inspections and tests cover a wide range of activities, including safety inspections of underground coal mines, safety tests of commercial equipment and automobiles, and environmental monitoring of factory emissions. An agency may also ask a firm or individual to submit certain documents or records to the agency for examination.

Normally, business firms comply with agency requests to inspect facilities or business records because it is in any firm's interest to maintain a good relationship with regulatory bodies. In some instances, however, such as when a firm thinks an agency's request is unreasonable and may be detrimental to the firm's interest, the firm may refuse to comply with the request. In such situations, an agency may resort to the use of a *subpoena* or a *search warrant*.

Subpoenas There are two basic types of subpoenas. The subpoena *ad testificandum* ("to testify") is an ordinary subpoena. It is a writ, or order, compelling a witness to appear at an agency hearing. The subpoena *duces tecum* ("bring it with you") compels an individual or organization to hand over books, papers, records, or documents to the agency. An administrative agency may use either type of subpoena.

There are limits on what an agency can demand. To determine whether an agency is abusing its discretion in its pursuit of information as part of an investigation, a court may consider such factors as the following:

- *The purpose of the investigation.* An investigation must have a legitimate purpose. An improper purpose is, for example, harassment.

- *The relevancy of the information being sought.* Information is relevant if it reveals that the law is being violated or if it assures the agency that the law is not being violated.

- *The specificity of the demand for testimony or documents.* A subpoena must, for example, adequately describe the material being sought.

- *The burden of the demand on the party from whom the information is sought.* In responding to a request for information, a party must bear the costs of, for example, copying the documents that must be handed over, but a business is generally protected from revealing such information as trade secrets.

In addition, a subpoena might not be enforced when the subject matter of an investigation is not within the authority of the agency to investigate. The issue in the following case was whether the subject matter of certain subpoenas issued by the Federal Trade Commission had exceeded the agency's statutory authority.

CASE 6.1   Federal Trade Commission v. Ken Roberts Co.

United States Court of Appeals,
District of Columbia Circuit, 2001.
276 F.3d 583.

BACKGROUND AND FACTS Ken Roberts Company, Ken Roberts Institute, Inc., United States Chart Company, and Ted Warren Corporation (collectively, Roberts) sell instructional materials that claim to teach would-be investors how to make money investing. In 1999, the Federal Trade Commission (FTC) began investigating whether a variety of online businesses were engaged in deceptive marketing practices in violation of the Federal Trade Commission Act. Aiming at high-risk, high-yield investment activity and suspicious Internet advertising, the FTC soon focused on Roberts. The FTC issued subpoenas that required Roberts to produce documents and answer written questions relating to the companies' business practices. Roberts refused to respond to most of the requests. The FTC asked a federal district court to enforce the subpoenas. When the court ordered Roberts to comply, Roberts appealed to the U.S. Court of Appeals for the District of Columbia Circuit. Roberts argued that other federal statutes, including the Investment Advisers Act (IAA), preempted the FTC's authority to investigate Roberts's practices.

IN THE WORDS OF THE COURT . . .

HARRY T. EDWARDS, Circuit Judge:

    *   *   *   *

Subpoena enforcement power is not limitless * * * . *[A] subpoena is proper only where the inquiry is within the authority of the agency, the demand is not too indefinite, and the information sought is reasonably relevant.* Accordingly, there is no doubt that a court asked to enforce a subpoena will refuse to do so if the subpoena exceeds an express statutory limitation on the agency's investigative powers. Thus, a court must assure itself that the subject matter of the investigation is within the statutory jurisdiction of the subpoena-issuing agency. * * * [Emphasis added.]

    *   *   *   *

On its own terms, the FTC Act gives the FTC ample authority to investigate and, if deceptive practices are uncovered, to regulate appellants' advertising practices. Therefore, the FTC is entitled to have its subpoenas enforced unless some other source of law patently [clearly] undermines these broad powers. * * *

    *   *   *   *

[Appellants], whose businesses involve securities * * * , assert that the comprehensive scope of the Investment Advisers Act of 1940 preempts the FTC's jurisdiction to regulate the fraudulent practices of "investment advisers" such as themselves. * * *

    * * * [T]he IAA contains no express exclusive jurisdiction provision. * * * [But] where intended by Congress, a precisely drawn, detailed statute preempts more general remedies. This can occur either where the two enactments are in irreconcilable conflict or where the latter was clearly meant to serve as a substitute for the former. Appellants contend that the antifraud provision of the IAA, which prohibits investment advisers from engaging "in any transaction, practice, or course of business which operates as a fraud or deceit upon any client or prospective client," stands as just such a specific remedy that displaces the more general coverage of the FTC Act.

    *   *   *   *

Because we live in an age of overlapping and concurring regulatory jurisdiction, a court must proceed with the utmost caution before concluding that one agency may not regulate merely because another may. In this case, while

CASE 6.1—Continued

it may be true that the IAA and the FTC Act employ different verbal formulae to describe their antifraud standards, it hardly follows that they therefore impose conflicting or incompatible obligations. Undoubtedly, entities in appellants' position can—and of course should—refrain from engaging in both "unfair and deceptive acts or practices" *and* "any transaction, practice, or course of business which operates as a fraud or deceit upon a client or prospective client." The proscriptions of the IAA are not diminished or confused merely because investment advisers must also avoid that which the FTC Act proscribes. And, because these statutes are capable of co-existence, it becomes the *duty* of this court to regard each as effective—at least absent clear congressional intent to the contrary.

Appellants can point to nothing in the background or history of the IAA that demonstrates (or even hints at) a congressional intent to preempt the antifraud jurisdiction of the FTC over those covered by the new statute. Nor does the subsequent case law interpreting these statutes contain such declarations.

DECISION AND REMEDY The U.S. Court of Appeals for the District of Columbia Circuit affirmed the lower court's decision. The appellate court held that the FTC was entitled to the enforcement of its subpoenas against Roberts. The Investment Advisers Act does not preempt the FTC's authority to investigate possibly deceptive advertising and marketing practices merely because those practices relate to the investment business.

FOR CRITICAL ANALYSIS—Social Consideration *The FTC has never undertaken to adjudicate deceptive conduct in the sale and purchase of securities (stocks and bonds). On this basis, should it be concluded that the agency does not have that power?*

Search Warrants The Fourth Amendment protects against unreasonable searches and seizures by requiring that a search warrant be obtained prior to a search, at least in most instances. An agency's search warrant is an order directing law enforcement officials to search a specific place for a specific item and present it to the agency. Although it was once thought that administrative inspections were exempt from the warrant requirement, the United States Supreme Court held in *Marshall v. Barlow's, Inc.,*[4] that the requirement does apply to the administrative process.

Agencies can conduct warrantless searches in several situations. Warrants are not required to conduct searches in highly regulated industries. Firms that sell firearms or liquor, for example, are automatically subject to inspections without warrants. Sometimes, a statute permits warrantless searches of certain types of hazardous operations, such as coal mines. Also, a warrantless inspection in an emergency situation is normally considered reasonable.

Adjudication

After conducting an investigation of a suspected rule violation, an agency may begin to take administrative action against an individual or organization. Most administrative actions are resolved through negotiated settlements at

---

4. 436 U.S. 307, 98 S.Ct. 1816, 56 L.Ed.2d 305 (1978).

ADJUDICATION
The act of rendering a judicial decision. In administrative process, the proceeding in which an administrative law judge hears and decides on issues that arise when an administrative agency charges a person or a firm with violating a law or regulation enforced by the agency.

their initial stages, without the need for formal **adjudication** (the resolution of the dispute through a hearing conducted by the agency).

Negotiated Settlements Depending on the agency, negotiations may take the form of a simple conversation or a series of informal conferences. Whatever form the negotiations take, their purpose is to rectify the problem to the agency's satisfaction and eliminate the need for additional proceedings. Settlement is an appealing option to firms for two reasons. First, regulated industries often do not want to appear to the regulating agency to be uncooperative. Second, litigation can be very expensive. To conserve their own resources and avoid formal actions, administrative agencies devote a great deal of effort to giving advice and negotiating solutions to problems.

Formal Complaints If a settlement cannot be reached, the agency may issue a formal complaint against the suspected violator. ● **EXAMPLE 3** The Environmental Protection Agency (EPA) finds that Acme Manufacturing, Inc., is polluting groundwater in violation of federal pollution laws. The EPA issues a complaint against the violator in an effort to bring the plant into compliance with federal regulations.● This complaint is a public document, and a press release may accompany it. The party charged in the complaint responds by filing an answer to the allegations. If the charged party and the agency cannot agree on a settlement, the case will be adjudicated. Agency adjudication may involve a trial-like setting before an **administrative law judge (ALJ)**. The formal adjudication process is described next and illustrated graphically in Exhibit 6–4.

ADMINISTRATIVE LAW JUDGE (ALJ)
One who presides over an administrative agency hearing and who has the power to administer oaths, take testimony, rule on questions of evidence, and make determinations of fact.

The Role of the Administrative Law Judge The ALJ presides over the hearing and has the power to administer oaths, take testimony, rule on questions of evidence, and make determinations of fact. Although formally the ALJ works for the agency prosecuting the case, the law requires an ALJ to be an unbiased adjudicator (judge).

Certain safeguards prevent bias on the part of the ALJ and promote fairness in the proceedings. For example, the Administrative Procedure Act requires that the ALJ be separate from the agency's investigative and prosecutorial staff. The APA also prohibits *ex parte* (private) communications between the ALJ and any party to an agency proceeding, including a party charged with a complaint and the agency itself. Finally, provisions of the APA protect the ALJ from agency disciplinary actions unless the agency can show good cause for such an action.

Hearing Procedures Hearing procedures vary widely from agency to agency. Administrative agencies generally can exercise substantial discretion over the type of hearing procedures that will be used. Frequently, disputes are resolved through informal adjudication proceedings. ● **EXAMPLE 4** The Federal Trade Commission (FTC) charges Good Foods, Inc., with deceptive advertising. Representatives of Good Foods and of the FTC, their counsel, and the ALJ meet at a table in a conference room to resolve the dispute informally.●

A formal adjudicatory hearing, in contrast, resembles a trial in many respects. Prior to the hearing, the parties are permitted to undertake extensive discovery proceedings (involving depositions, interrogatories, and requests for documents or other information, as described in Chapter 4). During the hearing, the parties may give testimony, present other evidence, and cross-examine adverse witnesses.

EXHIBIT 6–4   THE PROCESS OF FORMAL ADMINISTRATIVE ADJUDICATION

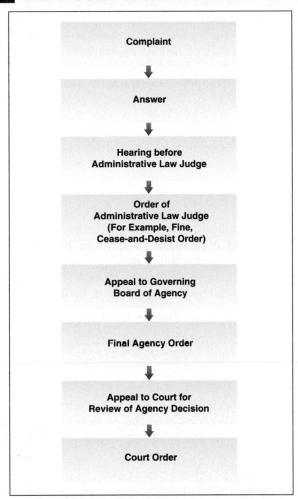

A significant difference between a trial and an administrative agency hearing, though, is that normally, much more information, including hearsay (secondhand information), can be introduced as evidence during an administrative hearing.

Agency Orders Following a hearing, the ALJ renders an **initial order,** or decision, on the case. Either party can appeal the ALJ's decision to the board or commission that governs the agency. ● EXAMPLE 5 National Warehouse Corporation is charged with violations of the Occupational Safety and Health Act, and an ALJ from the Occupational Safety and Health Administration (OSHA) imposes penalties on National Warehouse. If the firm is dissatisfied with the ALJ's decision, it can appeal the decision to the commission that governs OSHA. If the firm is dissatisfied with the commission's decision, it can appeal the decision to a federal court of appeals.● If no party appeals the case, the ALJ's decision becomes the **final order** of the agency. If a party does appeal the case, the final order comes from the commission's decision or that of the reviewing court. If a party appeals and the commission and the court decline to review the case, the ALJ's decision also becomes final.

INITIAL ORDER
In the context of administrative law, an agency's disposition in a matter other than a rulemaking. An administrative law judge's initial order becomes final unless it is appealed.

FINAL ORDER
The final decision of an administrative agency on an issue. If no appeal is taken, or if the case is not reviewed or considered anew by the agency commission, the administrative law judge's initial order becomes the final order of the agency.

LIMITATIONS ON AGENCY POWERS

Combining the functions normally divided among the three branches of government into an administrative agency concentrates considerable power in a single organization. Because of this concentration of authority, one of the major policy objectives of the government is to control the risks of arbitrariness and overreaching by administrative agencies without hindering the effective use of agency power to deal with particular problem areas, as Congress intended.

The judicial branch of the government exercises control over agency powers through the courts' review of agency actions. The executive and legislative branches also exercise control over agency authority.

Judicial Controls

The APA provides for judicial review of most agency decisions. As discussed above, if a charged party is dissatisfied with an agency's order, it can appeal the decision to a federal appeals court. Agency actions are not automatically subject to judicial review, however. Parties seeking review must demonstrate that they meet certain requirements, including those listed here:

- The action must be *reviewable* by the court. The APA creates a presumption that agency actions are reviewable, making this requirement easy to satisfy.

- The party must have *standing to sue* the agency (the party must have a direct stake in the outcome of the judicial proceeding).

- The party must have *exhausted all possible administrative remedies.* Each agency has its chain of review, and the party must follow agency appeal procedures before a court will deem that administrative remedies have been exhausted.

- There must be an *actual controversy* at issue. Courts will not review cases before it is necessary to decide them.

Recall from Chapter 4 that appellate courts normally defer to the decisions of trial courts on questions of fact. In reviewing administrative actions, the courts are similarly reluctant to review the factual findings of agencies. In most cases, the courts accept the facts as found in the agency proceedings. Normally, when a court reviews an administrative agency decision, the court considers the following types of issues:

- Whether the agency has exceeded its authority under its enabling legislation.

- Whether the agency has properly interpreted laws applicable to the agency action under review.

- Whether the agency has violated any constitutional provisions.

- Whether the agency has acted in accordance with procedural requirements of the law.

- Whether the agency's actions were arbitrary, capricious, or an abuse of discretion.

- Whether any conclusions drawn by the agency are not supported by substantial evidence.

"Absolute discretion . . . is more destructive of freedom than any of man's other inventions."

WILLIAM O. DOUGLAS, 1898–1980
(Associate justice of the United States
Supreme Court, 1939–1975)

In the following case, the Cellular Telecommunications & Internet Association and others asked a court to review an order of the Federal Communications Commission (FCC) relating to the enforcement of an FCC rule. The court considered how the FCC interpreted and applied a phrase in the Telecommunications Act of 1996 when the agency issued its order.

CASE 6.2 | Cellular Telecommunications & Internet Association v. Federal Communications Commission

United States Court of Appeals,
District of Columbia Circuit, 2003.
330 F.3d 502.
**http://www.findlaw.com/
casecode/courts/dc.html**[a]

HISTORICAL AND TECHNOLOGICAL SETTING *Congress enacted the Telecommunications Act of 1996 to "promote competition and reduce regulation in order to secure lower prices and higher quality services for American telecommunications consumers and encourage the rapid deployment of new telecommunications technologies." The act directs the Federal Communications Commission (FCC) to "forbear from applying any regulation * * * if the [FCC] determines that * * * enforcement * * * is not necessary for the protection of consumers."[b] At the time, a wireless telephone customer who wished to switch from one wireless service provider to another also had to change phone numbers.*

BACKGROUND AND FACTS In 1996, the FCC issued rules that required wireless service providers to

offer, by June 30, 1999, number portability.[c] In 1999, the FCC granted a request from the Cellular Telecommunications & Internet Association (CTIA) and others that the FCC temporarily refrain from enforcing these rules and extended the deadline to November 24, 2002 (and later extended again to November 24, 2003), partly because the industry needed more time to develop its technology. The FCC issued an order refusing to permanently refrain from enforcing the rules, however, on finding that consumers would otherwise be "forced to stay with carriers with whom they may be dissatisfied," due to price, service, or coverage, "because the cost of giving up their wireless phone number in order to move to another carrier is too high." The CTIA and others filed a suit against the FCC in the U.S. Court of Appeals for the District of Columbia Circuit for a review of this order. The plaintiffs argued, in part, that the FCC misinterpreted and misapplied the statutory phrase requiring the agency to forbear (refrain) from enforcing its regulations if "enforcement * * * is not necessary for the protection of consumers."

IN THE WORDS OF THE COURT . . .

HARRY T. EDWARDS, Circuit Judge.
* * * *

Petitioners' challenge to the Commission's [order] centers on the meaning of the statutory term "necessary." Petitioners contend that * * * the Commission erred in failing to construe "necessary" to mean "absolutely required," "indispensable," or "essential." Petitioners' position is that the Commission must forbear from enforcement of its wireless number portability rules if enforcement is not *absolutely required* to protect consumers. Petitioners argue that enforcement of the wireless number portability rules is not absolutely required to protect consumers * * * .
* * * *

[In the context of this case], *application of petitioners' definition of "necessary" would lead to an absurd result, because it is difficult to imagine a*

---

a. In the "By Date" section, select "2003" and "June." Click on "search." In the list of results, click on "Cell Telecom v. FCC" to access the opinion.
b. 47 U.S.C. Section 160(a).
c. *Number portability* is the ability of consumers to retain their phone numbers when they switch carriers.

(continued)

CASE 6.2—Continued

regulation whose enforcement is absolutely required or indispensable to protect consumers. Indeed, when counsel for petitioners was questioned about this, he could not give a viable example of a "necessary" regulation. None. In the forbearance context, we think that it would defy common sense to adopt a construction of "necessary" that results in a criterion that can never be met. What would follow is that every regulation would, strictly speaking, be "not necessary for the protection of consumers." *   *   * The Commission always would be required to forbear from enforcement *   *   * . [Emphasis added.]

Adopting petitioners' rigid construction of "necessary" in the forbearance context would result in a further absurdity. Under petitioners' view, the FCC, which is permitted to promulgate regulations *   *   * , could be required, the very next day, to forbear from enforcement of the same regulations, because the unattainable criterion of "necessary" cannot be met. *   *   *

*   *   *   *

*   *   * [W]e find the Commission's interpretation of "necessary" eminently reasonable. In the forbearance context, for the reasons already stated, it is reasonable to construe "necessary" as referring to the existence of a strong connection between what the agency has done by way of regulation and what the agency permissibly sought to achieve with the disputed regulation. In other words, the number portability rules are required to achieve the desired goal of consumer protection. That is essentially the definition of "necessary" that the Commission embraced and applied in its Order. We therefore find that deference to the agency's reasonable interpretation *   *   * is appropriate.

DECISION AND REMEDY The U.S. Court of Appeals for the District of Columbia Circuit dismissed the plaintiffs' challenge to the FCC's decision not to forbear from enforcing its number portability rules. The court concluded that the FCC's interpretation of the term *necessary* was reasonable. The FCC applied this interpretation to find that the number portability rules were required to achieve the goal of consumer protection.

FOR CRITICAL ANALYSIS—Social Consideration *On what basis might an agency decide that a temporary forbearance from the enforcement of a rule is justified while a permanent forbearance is not?*

Executive Controls

The executive branch of government exercises control over agencies both through the president's powers to appoint federal officers and through the president's veto powers. The president can veto enabling legislation presented by Congress or congressional attempts to modify an existing agency's authority.

Legislative Controls

Congress also exercises authority over agency powers. Through enabling legislation, Congress gives power to an agency. Of course, an agency cannot exceed the power that Congress delegates to it. Through subsequent legislation, Congress can take away that power or even abolish an agency altogether. Legislative authority is required to fund an agency, and enabling legislation usually sets certain time and monetary limits relating to the funding of particular programs. Congress can always revise these limits.

In addition to its power to create and fund agencies, Congress has the authority to investigate agencies and how they are implementing the laws. Individual legislators may also affect agency policy through their casework activities, which involve attempts to help their constituents deal with agencies.

Congress also has the power to "freeze" the enforcement of most federal regulations before the regulations take effect. Under the Small Business Regulatory Enforcement Fairness Act of 1996,[5] all federal agencies must submit final rules to Congress before the rules become effective. If, within sixty days, Congress passes a joint resolution of disapproval concerning a rule, enforcement of the regulation is frozen while the rule is reviewed by congressional committees.

Other legislative checks on agency actions include the Administrative Procedure Act, discussed earlier in this chapter, and the laws discussed in the next section.

PUBLIC ACCOUNTABILITY

As a result of growing public concern over the powers exercised by administrative agencies, Congress passed several laws to make agencies more accountable through public scrutiny. We discuss here the most significant of these laws.

Freedom of Information Act

Enacted in 1966, the Freedom of Information Act (FOIA)[6] requires the federal government to disclose certain records to any person on request, even without any reason being given for the request. The FOIA exempts certain types of records. For other records, though, a request that complies with the FOIA procedures need only contain a reasonable description of the information sought. An agency's failure to comply with such a request can be challenged in a federal district court. The media, industry trade associations, public-interest groups, and even companies seeking information about competitors rely on these FOIA provisions to obtain information from government agencies.

Government-in-the-Sunshine Act

Congress passed the Government-in-the-Sunshine Act,[7] or open meeting law, in 1976. It requires that "every portion of every meeting of an agency" be open to "public observation." The act also requires procedures to ensure that the public is provided with adequate advance notice of the agency's scheduled meeting and agenda. Like the FOIA, the Sunshine Act contains certain exceptions. Closed meetings are permitted when (1) the subject of the meeting concerns accusing any person of a crime, (2) open meetings would frustrate implementation of future agency actions, or (3) the subject of the meeting involves matters relating to future litigation or rulemaking. Courts interpret these exceptions to allow open access whenever possible.

> **"Law . . . is a human institution, created by human agents to serve human ends."**
> HARLAN F. STONE, 1872–1946
> (Chief justice of the United States Supreme Court, 1941–1946)

---

5. 5 U.S.C. Sections 801–808.
6. 5 U.S.C. Section 552.
7. 5 U.S.C. Section 552b.

Regulatory Flexibility Act

Concern over the effects of regulation on the efficiency of businesses, particularly smaller ones, led Congress to pass the Regulatory Flexibility Act in 1980.[8] Under this act, whenever a new regulation will have a "significant impact upon a substantial number of small entities," the agency must conduct a regulatory flexibility analysis. The analysis must measure the cost that the rule would impose on small businesses and must consider less burdensome alternatives. The act also contains provisions to alert small businesses about forthcoming regulations. The act relieved small businesses of some record-keeping burdens, especially with regard to hazardous waste management.

Small Business Regulatory Enforcement Fairness Act

The Small Business Regulatory Enforcement Fairness Act (SBREFA) of 1996 allows Congress to review new federal regulations for at least sixty days before they take effect. This period gives opponents of the rules time to present their arguments to Congress.

The SBREFA also authorizes the courts to enforce the Regulatory Flexibility Act. This helps to ensure that federal agencies, such as the Internal Revenue Service, consider ways to reduce the economic impact of new regulations on small businesses. Federal agencies are required to prepare guides that explain in plain English how small businesses can comply with federal regulations.

At the Small Business Administration, the SBREFA set up the National Enforcement Ombudsman to receive comments from small businesses about their dealings with federal agencies. Based on these comments, Regional Small Business Fairness Boards rate the agencies and publicize their findings.

Finally, the SBREFA allows small businesses to recover their expenses and legal fees from the government when an agency makes demands for fines or penalties that a court considers excessive.

STATE ADMINISTRATIVE AGENCIES

Although much of this chapter deals with federal administrative agencies, state agencies also play a significant role in regulating activities within the states. Many of the factors that encouraged the proliferation of federal agencies also fostered the growing presence of state agencies. For example, reasons for the expansion of administrative agencies at all levels of government include the inability of Congress and state legislatures to oversee the actual implementation of their laws and the greater technical competence of the agencies.

Parallel Agencies

Commonly, a state creates an agency as a parallel to a federal agency to provide similar services on a more localized basis. • EXAMPLE 6 The Pennsylvania Department of Public Welfare shoulders some of the same responsibilities at the state level as the Social Security Administration does at the federal level. The New York Department of Taxation and Finance performs, on a statewide basis, duties that resemble those performed by the Internal Revenue Service on

---

8. 5 U.S.C. Sections 601–612.

a nationwide basis. The Minnesota Pollution Control Agency parallels the federal Environmental Protection Agency.● Not all federal agencies have parallel state agencies, however. For example, the Central Intelligence Agency has no parallel agency at the state level.

Conflicts between Parallel Agencies

If the actions of parallel state and federal agencies conflict, the actions of the federal agency will prevail. ● EXAMPLE 7 The Federal Aviation Administration (FAA) specifies the hours during which airplanes may land at and depart from airports. A California state agency issues inconsistent regulations governing the same activities. In a proceeding initiated by Interstate Distribution Corporation, an air transport company, to challenge the state rules, the FAA regulations would be held to prevail.● The priority of federal law over conflicting state laws is based on the supremacy clause of the U.S. Constitution. This clause, which is found in Article VI of the Constitution, states that the Constitution and "the Laws of the United States which shall be made in Pursuance thereof . . . shall be the supreme Law of the Land."

Judicial Review of State Agency Actions

Most state agency decisions are subject to judicial review by state courts, provided that the parties seeking that review first meet certain requirements. Once a petition for review is granted, state courts, like their federal counterparts, consider such issues as whether a state or local agency exceeded its authority.

The following case provides an example of a state supreme court's review of a state agency decision. The court was asked to determine whether the agency's decision in a certain case was "[a]rbitrary, capricious, an abuse of discretion or otherwise not in accordance with law."

CASE 6.3   Swift v. Sublette County Board of County Commissioners

Wyoming Supreme Court, 2002.
2002 WY 32,
40 P.3d 1235.

BACKGROUND AND FACTS Joe's Concrete and Lumber, Inc., operates a gravel pit on agricultural land near Boulder, Wyoming, at the intersection of State Highway 187 and Sublette County Road 353. The Zoning and Development Regulations Resolutions of Sublette County allow gravel pits in agricultural districts under certain conditions. Gravel pits and "associated extraction activities" are permissible on issuance of a conditional use permit and compliance with specific development standards. In June 2000, Joe's applied for a conditional use permit to add a batch plant to its site.[a] Adjacent landowners Sara Swift and Circle Nine Ranch, Inc., opposed the application. They objected to the increased traffic, noise, and dust associated with a batch plant. The Sublette County Board of County Commissioners approved the permit. Swift and Circle Nine petitioned for a review of this decision with a Wyoming state court, which certified the dispute to the Wyoming Supreme Court.[b]

---

a. A batch plant mixes gravel with sand, water, and cement to produce concrete.
b. *Certification* in this context is a procedure by which the lower court abstained from deciding the question in this dispute until the state supreme court had an opportunity to rule on it.

(continued)

CASE 6.3—Continued
IN THE WORDS
OF THE COURT . . .

HILL, Justice.

*   *   *   *

*   *   * [T]he crux of [this] dispute is over whether or not [a batch plant] is an "associated extraction" activity. The root of "associated" has several different meanings depending upon the context in which the word is used and whether it is used as an adjective, verb, or noun. The word is used in the Zoning Regulations as a modifier of "activity." In that context, the plain meaning of the word can easily be discerned [according to *Merriam-Webster's Collegiate Dictionary* (10th ed. 1998)]:

> Associate—**1:** closely connected (as in function or office) with another **2:** closely related esp. in the mind.

"Extraction" is the process of extracting something:

> Extract—**1** *   *   * **b:** to pull or take out forcibly *   *   * **2:** to withdraw (as a juice or fraction) by physical or chemical process; *also:* to treat with a solvent so as to remove a soluble substance **3:** to separate (a metal) from an ore.

Putting the plain meaning of the words together, the Zoning Regulations define gravel pit operations to include activities closely connected or related to the process of withdrawing the gravel from the ground. The question now is whether a concrete batch plant fits within that plain meaning.

*   *   * *There is nothing in the record to indicate that the batch plant bears any relation to the actual physical extraction of the gravel from the ground.* There is no indication that a batch plant refines or processes the gravel in a manner that removes or separates the gravel from other substances. The batch plant processes the gravel with other ingredients to create a product—concrete—it does not extract or assist in the extraction of the gravel from the ground. This conclusion is supported by reference to the Zoning Regulations where cement and concrete manufacturing is an authorized use in a heavy industrial district but is noticeably absent from the list of authorized uses for agricultural districts. This evidences intent on the part of the drafters of the Zoning Regulations to treat concrete manufacturing distinctly from gravel pit operations. There is no rational argument to support a finding that the batch plant is "closely connected or related to the process of withdrawing the gravel." [Emphasis added.]

DECISION AND REMEDY The Wyoming Supreme Court reversed the decision of the local board granting a conditional use permit to Joe's. The court concluded that a batch plant is not an "associated extraction" activity that is closely connected to a gravel pit operation. The agency's interpretation of the phrase was inconsistent with the plain meaning of the words in the regulation.

FOR CRITICAL ANALYSIS—Social Consideration *Suppose that the regulation in this case had not used the word* extraction *and had allowed permits for any "associated" activity. Would the plaintiffs have been successful?*

KEY TERMS

adjudication   178

administrative
   law judge (ALJ)   178

administrative process   173

bureaucracy   173

delegation doctrine   172

enabling legislation   169

executive agency   170

final order   179

CHAPTER SUMMARY POWERS AND FUNCTIONS OF ADMINISTRATIVE AGENCIES

Agency Creation and Powers (See pages 169–173.)	1. Under the U.S. Constitution, Congress can delegate the task of implementing its laws to government agencies. By delegating the task, Congress can indirectly monitor an area in which it has passed legislation without becoming bogged down in details relating to enforcement of the legislation.
	2. Administrative agencies are created by enabling legislation, which usually specifies the name, composition, and powers of the agency.
	3. Administrative agencies exercise enforcement, rulemaking, and adjudicatory powers.
Administrative Process—Rulemaking (See pages 173–174.)	1. Agencies are authorized to create new regulations—their rulemaking function. This power is conferred on an agency in the enabling legislation.
	2. Agencies can create legislative rules, which are as important as formal acts of Congress.
	3. Notice-and-comment rulemaking is the most common rulemaking procedure. It begins with the publication of the proposed regulation in the *Federal Register.* Publication of the notice is followed by a comment period to allow private parties to comment on the proposed rule.
Administrative Process— Investigation (See pages 174–177.)	1. Administrative agencies investigate the entities that they regulate. Investigations are conducted during the rulemaking process to obtain information and after rules are issued to monitor compliance.
	2. The most important investigative tools available to an agency are the following:
	a. *Inspections and tests*—Used to gather information and to correct or prevent undesirable conditions.
	b. *Subpoenas*—Orders that direct individuals to appear at a hearing or to hand over specified documents.
	3. Limits on administrative investigations include the following:
	a. The investigation must be for a legitimate purpose.
	b. The information sought must be relevant, and the investigative demands must be specific and not unreasonably burdensome.
	c. The Fourth Amendment protects companies and individuals from unreasonable searches and seizures by requiring search warrants in most instances.
Administrative Process— Adjudication (See pages 177–179.)	1. After a preliminary investigation, an agency may initiate an administrative action against an individual or organization by filing a complaint. Most such actions are resolved at this stage before they go through the formal adjudicatory process.
	2. If there is no settlement, the case is presented to an administrative law judge (ALJ) in a proceeding similar to a trial.

(continued)

CHAPTER SUMMARY **POWERS AND FUNCTIONS OF
ADMINISTRATIVE AGENCIES—Continued**

Administrative Process—Adjudication—continued	3. After a case is concluded, the ALJ renders an initial order, which can be appealed by either party to the board or commission that governs the agency and ultimately to a federal appeals court. If no appeal is taken or the case is not reviewed, then the order becomes the final order of the agency. The charged party may be ordered to pay damages or to stop carrying on some specified activity.
Limitations on Agency Powers (See pages 180–183.)	1. *Judicial controls*—Administrative agencies are subject to the judicial review of the courts. A court may review whether—
	a. An agency has exceeded the scope of its enabling legislation.
	b. An agency has properly interpreted the laws.
	c. An agency has violated the U.S. Constitution.
	d. An agency has complied with all applicable procedural requirements.
	e. An agency's actions are arbitrary, capricious, or an abuse of discretion.
	f. An agency's conclusions are not supported by substantial evidence.
	2. *Executive controls*—The president can control administrative agencies through appointments of federal officers and through vetoes of legislation creating or affecting agency powers.
	3. *Legislative controls*—Congress can give power to an agency, take it away, increase or decrease the agency's funding, or abolish the agency. The Administrative Procedure Act of 1946 also limits agencies.
Public Accountability (See pages 183–184.)	1. *Freedom of Information Act of 1966*—Requires the government to disclose certain records to any person on request.
	2. *Government-in-the-Sunshine Act of 1976*—Requires the following:
	a. "[E]very portion of every meeting of an agency" must be open to "public observation."
	b. Procedures must be implemented to ensure that the public is provided with adequate advance notice of the agency's scheduled meeting and agenda.
	3. *Regulatory Flexibility Act of 1980*—Requires a regulatory flexibility analysis whenever a new regulation will have a "significant impact upon a substantial number of small entities."
	4. *Small Business Regulatory Enforcement Fairness Act of 1996*—Allows Congress to review new federal regulations. Requires federal agencies to explain in plain English how to comply with regulations. Established Regional Small Business Fairness Boards to rate agencies from a small-business perspective. Provides for the recovery of expenses and fees when an agency imposes an excessive penalty.
State Administrative Agencies (See pages 184–186.)	1. States create agencies that parallel federal agencies to provide similar services on a more localized basis.
	2. If the actions of parallel state and federal agencies conflict, the actions of the federal agency will prevail.

FOR REVIEW

1. How are federal administrative agencies created?

2. What are the three basic functions of most administrative agencies?

3. What sequence of events must normally occur before an agency rule becomes law?

4. How do administrative agencies enforce their rules?

5. How do the three branches of government limit the power of administrative agencies?

QUESTIONS AND CASE PROBLEMS

6–1. Rulemaking Procedures. Assume that the Securities and Exchange Commission (SEC) has a policy not to enforce rules prohibiting insider trading except when the insiders make monetary profits for themselves. Then the SEC modifies this policy by a determination that the agency has the statutory authority to bring an enforcement action against an individual even if he or she does not personally profit from the insider trading. In modifying the policy, the SEC does not conduct a rulemaking but simply announces its new decision. A securities organization objects and says that the policy was unlawfully developed without opportunity for public comment. In a lawsuit challenging the new policy, should the policy be overruled under the Administrative Procedure Act? Discuss.

6–2. Rulemaking Procedures. Assume that the Food and Drug Administration (FDA), using proper procedures, adopts a rule describing its future investigations. This new rule covers all future cases in which the FDA wants to regulate food additives. Under the new rule, the FDA says that it will not regulate food additives without giving food companies an opportunity to cross-examine witnesses. Some time later, the FDA wants to regulate methylisocyanate, a food additive. In doing so, the FDA undertakes an informal rulemaking procedure, without cross-examination, and regulates methylisocyanate. Producers protest, saying that the FDA promised cross-examination. The FDA responds that the Administrative Procedure Act does not require such cross-examination and that it can freely withdraw the promise made in its new rule. If the producers challenge the FDA in a court, on what basis would the court rule in their favor?

6–3. Rulemaking and Adjudication Powers. For decades, the Federal Trade Commission (FTC) resolved fair trade and advertising disputes through individual adjudications. In the 1960s, the FTC began promulgating rules that defined fair and unfair trade practices. In cases involving violations of these rules, the due process rights of participants were more limited and did not include cross-examination. This was because, although anyone found violating a rule would receive a full adjudication, the legitimacy of the rule itself could not be challenged in the adjudication. Any party charged with violating a rule was almost certain to lose the adjudication. Affected parties complained to a court, arguing that their rights before the FTC were unduly limited by the new rules. What will the court examine to determine whether to uphold the new rules?

6–4. Executive Controls. In 1982, the president of the United States appointed Matthew Chabal, Jr., to the position of U.S. marshal. U.S. marshals are assigned to the federal courts. In the fall of 1985, Chabal received an unsatisfactory annual performance rating, and he was fired shortly thereafter by the president. Given that U.S. marshals are assigned to the federal courts, are these appointees members of the executive branch? Did the president have the right to fire Chabal without consulting Congress about the decision? [*Chabal v. Reagan,* 841 F.2d 1216 (3d Cir. 1988)]

6–5. Agency Investigations. A state statute required vehicle dismantlers—persons whose business includes dismantling automobiles and selling the parts—to be licensed and to keep records regarding the vehicles and parts in their possession. The statute also authorized warrantless administrative inspections; that is, without first obtaining a warrant, agents of the state department of motor vehicles or police officers could inspect a vehicle dismantler's license and records, as well as vehicles on the premises. Pursuant to this statute, police officers entered an automobile junkyard and asked to see the owner's license and records. The owner replied that he did not have the documents. The officers inspected the premises and discovered stolen vehicles and parts. Charged with possession of stolen property and unregistered operation as a vehicle dismantler, the junkyard owner argued that the warrantless inspection statute was unconstitutional under the Fourth Amendment. The trial court disagreed, reasoning that the junkyard business was a highly regulated industry. On appeal, the highest state court concluded that the statute had no truly administrative purpose and impermissibly authorized searches only to discover stolen property. The state appealed to the United States Supreme Court. Should the Court uphold the statute? Discuss. [*New York v. Burger,* 482 U.S. 691, 107 S.Ct. 2636, 96 L.Ed.2d 601 (1987)]

6-6. Arbitrary and Capricious Test. In 1977, the Department of Transportation (DOT) adopted a passive-restraint standard (known as Standard 208) that required new cars to have either air bags or automatic seat belts. By 1981, it had become clear that all the major auto manufacturers would install automatic seat belts to comply with this rule. The DOT determined that most purchasers of cars would detach their automatic seat belts, thus making them ineffective. Consequently, the department repealed the regulation. State Farm Mutual Automobile Insurance Co. and other insurance companies sued in the District of Columbia Circuit Court of Appeals for a review of the DOT's repeal of the regulation. That court held that the repeal was arbitrary and capricious because the DOT had reversed its rule without sufficient support. The motor vehicle manufacturers then appealed this decision to the United States Supreme Court. What was the result? Discuss. [*Motor Vehicle Manufacturers Association v. State Farm Mutual Automobile Insurance Co.*, 463 U.S. 29, 103 S.Ct. 2856, 77 L.Ed.2d 443 (1983)]

6-7. Judicial Review. American Message Centers (AMC) provides answering services to retailers. Calls to a retailer are automatically forwarded to AMC, which pays for the calls. AMC obtains telephone service at a discount from major carriers, including Sprint. Sprint's tariff (a public document setting out rates and rules relating to Sprint's services) states that the "subscriber shall be responsible for the payment of all charges for service." When AMC learned that computer hackers had obtained the access code for AMC's lines and had made nearly $160,000 in long-distance calls, it asked Sprint to absorb the cost. Sprint refused. AMC filed a complaint with the Federal Communications Commission (FCC), claiming in part that Sprint's tariff was vague and ambiguous, in violation of the Communications Act of 1934 and FCC rules. These laws require that a carrier's tariff "clearly and definitely" specify any "exceptions or conditions which in any way affect the rates named in the tariff." The FCC rejected AMC's complaint. AMC appealed the FCC's decision to a federal appellate court, claiming that the FCC's decision to reject AMC's complaint was arbitrary and capricious. What should the court decide? Discuss fully. [*American Message Centers v. Federal Communications Commission*, 50 F.3d 35 (D.C.Cir. 1995)]

Case Problem with Sample Answer

6-8. Arbitrary and Capricious Test. Lion Raisins, Inc., is a family-owned, family-operated business that grows and markets raisins to private enterprises. In the 1990s, Lion also successfully bid on more than fifteen contracts awarded by the U.S. Department of Agriculture (USDA). In May 1999, a USDA investigation reported that Lion appeared to have falsified inspectors' signatures, given false moisture content, and changed the grade of raisins on three USDA raisin certificates issued between 1996 and 1998. Lion was subsequently awarded five more USDA contracts. Then, in November 2000, the company was the low bidder on two new USDA contracts for school lunch programs. In January 2001, however, the USDA awarded these contracts to other bidders and, on the basis of the May 1999 report, suspended Lion from participating in government contracts for one year. Lion filed a suit in the U.S. Court of Federal Claims against the USDA, seeking, in part, lost profits on the school lunch contracts on the ground that the USDA's suspension was arbitrary and capricious. On what basis might the court grant a summary judgment in Lion's favor? [*Lion Raisins, Inc. v. United States*, 51 Fed.Cl. 238 (2001)]

To view a sample answer for this case problem, go to this book's Web site at http://leet.westbuslaw.com and click on "Interactive Study Center."

6-9. Investigation. Maureen Droge began working for United Air Lines, Inc. (UAL), as a flight attendant in 1990. In 1995, she was assigned to Paris, France, where she became pregnant. Because UAL does not allow its flight attendants to fly during their third trimester of pregnancy, Droge was placed on involuntary leave. She applied for temporary disability benefits through the French social security system, but her request was denied because UAL does not contribute to the French system on behalf of its U.S.–based flight attendants. Droge filed a charge of discrimination with the U.S. Equal Employment Opportunity Commission (EEOC), alleging that UAL had discriminated against her and other Americans. The EEOC issued a subpoena, asking UAL to detail all benefits received by all UAL employees living outside the United States. UAL refused to provide the information in part on the grounds that it was irrelevant and compliance would be unduly burdensome. The EEOC filed a suit in a federal district court against UAL. Should the court enforce the subpoena? Why or why not? [*Equal Employment Opportunity Commission v. United Air Lines, Inc.*, 287 F.3d 643 (7th Cir. 2002)]

6-10. Judicial Controls. Under federal law, when accepting bids on a contract, an agency must hold "discussions" with all offerors. An agency may ask a single offeror for "clarification" of its proposal, however, without holding "discussions" with the others. Regulations define "clarifications" as "limited exchanges." In March 2001, the U.S. Air Force asked for bids on a contract. The winning contractor would examine, assess, and develop means of integrating national intelligence assets with the U.S. Department of Defense space systems, to enhance the capabilities of the Air Force's Space Warfare Center. Among the bidders were Information Technology and Applications Corp. (ITAC) and RS Information Systems, Inc. (RSIS). The Air Force asked the parties for more information on their subcontractors but did not allow them to change their proposals. Determining that there were weaknesses in ITAC's bid, the Air Force awarded the contract to RSIS. ITAC filed a suit in the U.S. Court of Federal Claims against the government, contending that the postproposal requests to RSIS, and its responses, were improper "discussions." Should the court rule in ITAC's favor? Why or why not? [*Information Technology & Applications Corp. v. United States,* 316 F.3d 1312 (Fed. Cir. 2003)]

A Question of Ethics & Social Responsibility

6-11. The Marine Mammal Protection Act was enacted in 1972 to reduce incidental killing and injury of marine mammals during commercial fishing operations. Under the act, commercial fishing vessels are required to allow an employee of the National Oceanic and Atmospheric Administration (NOAA) to accompany the vessels to conduct research and observe operations. In December 1986, after NOAA had adopted a new policy of recruiting female as well as male observers, NOAA notified Caribbean Marine Services Co. that female observers would be assigned to accompany two of the company's fishing vessels on their next voyages. The owners and crew members of the ships (the plaintiffs) moved for an injunction against the implementation of the NOAA directive. The plaintiffs contended that the presence of a female on board a fishing vessel would be very awkward, because the female would have to share the crew's quarters, and crew members enjoyed little or no privacy with respect to bodily functions. Further, they alleged that the presence of a female would be disruptive to fishing operations, because some of the crew members were "crude" men with little formal education who might harass or sexually assault a female observer, and the officers would therefore have to devote time to protecting the female from the crew. Finally, the plaintiffs argued that the presence of a female observer could destroy morale and distract the crew, thus affecting the crew's efficiency and decreasing the vessel's profits. [*Caribbean Marine Services Co. v. Baldrige,* 844 F.2d 668 (9th Cir. 1988)]

1. In general, do you think that the public policy of promoting equal employment opportunity should override the concerns of the vessel owners and crew? If you were the judge, would you grant the injunction? Why or why not?

2. The plaintiffs pointed out that fishing voyages could last three months or longer. Would the length of a particular voyage affect your answer to the preceding question?

3. The plaintiffs contended that even if the indignity of sharing bunk rooms and toilet facilities with a female observer could be overcome, the observer's very presence in the common areas of the vessel, such as the dining area, would unconstitutionally infringe on the crew members' right to privacy in these areas. Evaluate this claim.

Critical-Thinking Managerial Question

6-12. Natalie is a director of the First National Bank when it is declared insolvent. As part of an investigation into the bank's finances, the Federal Deposit Insurance Corporation (FDIC) issues a subpoena to Natalie for her personal financial records relating to gains and losses in her assets. She objects that the subpoena intrudes on her privacy. The FDIC says that it needs to determine whether she used bank funds for her personal benefit and asks a court to enforce the subpoena. Will the court enforce the subpoena? Why or why not?

INTERACTING WITH THE INTERNET

For updated links to resources available on the Web, as well as a variety of other materials, visit this text's Web site at

http://leet.westbuslaw.com

To view the text of the Administrative Procedure Act of 1946, go to

http://www.archives.gov/federal_register/public_laws/acts.htm

The Internet Law Library contains links to federal and state regulatory materials, including the *Code of Federal Regulations.* This page can be found at

http://www.lawguru.com/ilawlib

ONLINE LEGAL RESEARCH EXERCISES

Go to **http://leet.westbuslaw.com**, the Web site that accompanies this text. Select "Interactive Study Center," and then click on "Chapter 6." There you will find the following Internet research exercises that you can perform to learn more about topics covered in this chapter.

Activity 6–1: SOCIAL PERSPECTIVE—The Freedom of Information Act
Activity 6–2: MANAGEMENT PERSPECTIVE—Agency Inspections

BEFORE THE TEST

Go to **http://leet.westbuslaw.com**, the Web site that accompanies this text. Select "Interactive Quizzes." You will find at least twenty interactive questions relating to this chapter.

Westlaw® Campus

If your textbook provided for a subscription to Westlaw® Campus, or if you have otherwise purchased access to the Westlaw Campus database, you can access any of the cases presented or cited in this chapter by using your Westlaw Campus account.

CHAPTER 7

Criminal Law and Cyber Crimes

CHAPTER OBJECTIVES

After reading this chapter, you should be able to answer the following questions:

1. What two elements must exist before a person can be held liable for a crime? Can a corporation be liable for crimes?

2. What are five broad categories of crimes? What is white-collar crime?

3. What defenses might be raised by criminal defendants to avoid liability for criminal acts?

4. What constitutional safeguards exist to protect persons accused of crimes? What are the basic steps in the criminal process?

5. What is cyber crime? What laws apply to crimes committed in cyberspace?

Society uses various sanctions to ensure that individuals engaging in business can compete and flourish. These sanctions include damages for various types of tortious conduct (as discussed in Chapter 8), damages for breach of contract (to be discussed in Chapter 12), and the equitable remedies discussed in Chapter 1. Additional sanctions are imposed under criminal law. Many statutes regulating business provide for criminal as well as civil sanctions. Therefore, criminal law joins civil law as an important element in the legal environment of business.

In this chapter, following a brief summary of the major differences between criminal and civil law, we look at how crimes are classified and what elements must be present for

> **"No State shall . . . deprive any person of life, liberty, or property without due process of law, nor deny to any person within its jurisdiction the equal protection of the laws."**
> Fourteenth Amendment to the
> U. S. Constitution, July 28, 1868

criminal liability to exist. We then examine various categories of crime, the defenses that can be raised to avoid liability for criminal actions, and criminal procedural law. Criminal procedural law attempts to ensure that a criminal defendant's right to the Fourteenth Amendment's guarantee of "due process of law" (see the quotation on the previous page) is enforced.

Since the advent of computer networks and, more recently, the Internet, new types of crimes and new variations of traditional crimes have been committed in cyberspace. Such crimes are often referred to as **cyber crimes.** Generally, the term *cyber crime* refers to the way particular crimes are committed rather than denoting a new category of crimes. We devote the concluding pages of this chapter to a discussion of this increasingly significant area of criminal activity.

CYBER CRIME
A crime that occurs online, in the virtual community of the Internet, as opposed to the physical world.

CIVIL LAW AND CRIMINAL LAW

Remember from Chapter 1 that *civil law* spells out the duties that exist between persons or between persons and their governments, excluding the duty not to commit crimes. Contract law, for example, is part of civil law. The whole body of tort law, which deals with the infringement by one person on the legally recognized rights of another, is also an area of civil law.

Criminal law, in contrast, has to do with crime. A **crime** can be defined as a wrong against society proclaimed in a statute and punishable by society through fines and/or imprisonment—and, in some cases, death. As mentioned in Chapter 1, because crimes are *offenses against society as a whole,* they are prosecuted by a public official, such as a district attorney, not by victims.

CRIME
A wrong against society proclaimed in a statute and punishable by society through fines and/or imprisonment—and, in some cases, death.

Key Differences between Civil Law and Criminal Law

Because the state has extensive resources at its disposal when prosecuting criminal cases, numerous procedural safeguards have been put in place to protect the rights of defendants. One of these safeguards is the higher standard of proof that applies in a criminal case.

As you can see in Exhibit 7–1, which summarizes some of the key differences between civil law and criminal law, in a civil case the plaintiff usually must prove his or her case by a *preponderance of the evidence.* Under this standard, the plaintiff must convince the court that, based on the evidence presented by both parties, it is more likely than not that the plaintiff's allegation is true.

BEYOND A REASONABLE DOUBT
The standard of proof used in criminal cases. If there is any reasonable doubt that a criminal defendant committed the crime with which she or he has been charged, then the verdict must be "not guilty."

In a criminal case, in contrast, the state must prove its case **beyond a reasonable doubt.** Every juror in a criminal case must be convinced, beyond a reasonable doubt, of the defendant's guilt. The higher standard of proof in criminal cases reflects a fundamental social value—a belief that it is worse to convict an innocent individual than to let a guilty person go free. We will look at other safeguards later in the chapter, in the context of criminal procedure.

Civil Liability for Criminal Acts

Those who commit crimes may be subject to both civil and criminal liability.
● EXAMPLE 1 Joe is walking down the street, minding his own business, when suddenly a person attacks him. In the ensuing struggle, the attacker stabs Joe

EXHIBIT 7-1   CIVIL AND CRIMINAL LAW COMPARED

ISSUE	CIVIL LAW	CRIMINAL LAW
Area of concern	Rights and duties between persons and between persons and their government	Offenses against society as a whole
Wrongful act	Harm to a person or to a person's property	Violation of a statute that prohibits some type of activity
Party who brings suit	Person who suffered harm	The state
Standard of proof	Preponderance of the evidence	Beyond a reasonable doubt
Remedy	Damages to compensate for the harm or a decree to achieve an equitable result	Punishment (fine, removal from public office, imprisonment, or death)

several times, seriously injuring him. A police officer restrains and arrests the wrongdoer. In this situation, the attacker may be subject both to criminal prosecution by the state and to a tort lawsuit brought by Joe.● Exhibit 7–2 on the following page illustrates how the same act can result in both a tort action and a criminal action against the wrongdoer.

CLASSIFICATION OF CRIMES

Depending on their degree of seriousness, crimes are classified as felonies or misdemeanors. **Felonies** are serious crimes punishable by death or by imprisonment in a federal or state penitentiary for more than a year. The Model Penal Code[1] provides for four degrees of felony: (1) capital offenses, for which the maximum penalty is death; (2) first degree felonies, punishable by a maximum penalty of life imprisonment; (3) second degree felonies, punishable by a maximum of ten years' imprisonment; and (4) third degree felonies, punishable by a maximum of five years' imprisonment.

Under federal law and in most states, any crime that is not a felony is considered a **misdemeanor**. Misdemeanors are crimes punishable by a fine or by confinement for up to a year. If incarcerated (imprisoned), the guilty party goes to a local jail instead of a prison. Disorderly conduct and trespass are common misdemeanors. Some states have different classes of misdemeanors. For example, in Illinois misdemeanors are either Class A (confinement for up to a year), Class B (not more than six months), or Class C (not more than thirty days). Whether a crime is a felony or a misdemeanor can also determine

FELONY
A crime—such as arson, murder, rape, or robbery—that carries the most severe sanctions, which range from one year in a state or federal prison to the death penalty.

MISDEMEANOR
A lesser crime than a felony, punishable by a fine or incarceration in jail for up to one year.

---

1. The American Law Institute issued the Official Draft of the Model Penal Code in 1962. The Model Penal Code contains four parts: (1) general provisions, (2) definitions of special crimes, (3) provisions concerning treatment and corrections, and (4) provisions on the organization of corrections. The Model Penal Code is not a uniform code, however. Because of our federal structure of government, each state has developed its own set of laws governing criminal acts. Types of crimes and prescribed punishments may differ in each jurisdiction.

EXHIBIT 7-2   TORT LAWSUIT AND CRIMINAL PROSECUTION FOR THE SAME ACT

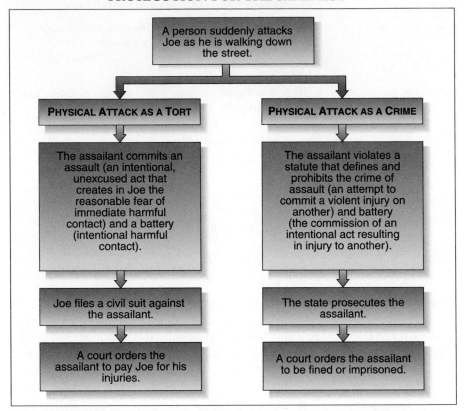

whether the case is tried in a magistrate's court (for example, by a justice of the peace) or in a general trial court.

In most jurisdictions, **petty offenses** are considered to be a subset of misdemeanors. Petty offenses are minor violations, such as disturbing the peace and violations of building codes. Even for petty offenses, however, a guilty party can be put in jail for a few days, fined, or both, depending on state or local law.

PETTY OFFENSE
In criminal law, the least serious kind of criminal offense, such as a traffic or building-code violation.

CRIMINAL LIABILITY

Two elements must exist simultaneously for a person to be convicted of a crime: (1) the performance of a prohibited act and (2) a specified state of mind or intent on the part of the actor. Every criminal statute prohibits certain behavior. Most crimes require an act of *commission;* that is, a person must *do* something in order to be accused of a crime. This is called the *guilty act*.[2] In some cases, an act of *omission* can be a crime, but only when a person has a legal duty to perform the omitted act. Failure to file a tax return is an example of an act that is a crime by omission.

The guilty act requirement is based on one of the premises of criminal law—that a person is punished for harm done to society. Thinking about killing

---

2. Called the *actus reus* (pronounced *ak*-tuhs *ray*-uhs), or "guilty act."

someone or about stealing a car may be morally wrong, but the thoughts do no harm until they are translated into action. Of course, a person can be punished for attempting murder or robbery, but normally only if he or she took substantial steps toward the criminal objective.

A *wrongful mental state*[3] is as necessary as a wrongful act in establishing criminal liability. What constitutes such a mental state varies according to the wrongful action. For murder, the act is the taking of a life, and the mental state is the intent to take life. For theft, the guilty act is the taking of another person's property, and the mental state involves both the knowledge that the property belongs to another and the intent to deprive the owner of it.

Criminal liability typically arises for actions that violate state criminal statutes. Federal criminal jurisdiction is limited to crimes that occur outside the jurisdiction of any state, crimes involving interstate commerce or communications, crimes that interfere with the operation of the federal government or its agents, and crimes directed at citizens or property located outside the United States. Federal jurisdiction also exists if a federal law or a federal government agency (such as the U.S. Department of Justice or the federal Environmental Protection Agency) defines a certain type of action as a crime. Today, businesspersons are subject to criminal penalties under numerous federal laws and regulations. We will examine many of these laws in later chapters of this text.

> "I haven't committed a crime. What I did was fail to comply with the law."
>
> DAVID DINKINS, 1927–
> (Mayor of New York City, 1990–1994)

CORPORATE CRIMINAL LIABILITY

At one time, it was thought that a corporation could not incur criminal liability because, although a corporation is a legal person, it can act only through its agents (corporate directors, officers, and employees). Therefore, the corporate entity itself could not "intend" to commit a crime. Under modern criminal law, however, a corporation may be held liable for crimes. Obviously, corporations cannot be imprisoned, but they can be fined or denied certain legal privileges (such as a license). Today, corporations are normally liable for the crimes committed by their agents and employees within the course and scope of their employment.

In addition, corporate directors and officers are personally liable for the crimes they commit, regardless of whether the crimes were committed for their personal benefit or on the corporation's behalf. Corporate directors and officers may also be held liable for the actions of employees under their supervision. Under what has become known as the "responsible corporate officer" doctrine, a court may impose criminal liability on a corporate officer regardless of whether she or he participated in, directed, or even knew about a given criminal violation.

● **EXAMPLE 2** In *United States v. Park,*[4] the chief executive officer of a national supermarket chain was held personally liable for sanitation violations in corporate warehouses, in which the food was exposed to contamination by rodents. The court imposed personal liability on the corporate officer not because he intended the crime or even knew about it but because he was in a "responsible relationship" to the corporation and had the power to prevent the violation. ● Since the *Park* decision, courts have applied this "responsible

---

3. Called the *mens rea* (pronounced mehns *ray*-uh), or "evil intent."
4. 421 U.S. 658, 95 S.Ct. 1903, 44 L.Ed.2d 489 (1975).

corporate officer" doctrine on a number of occasions to hold corporate officers liable for their employees' statutory violations. The following case illustrates that corporate officers and supervisors who oversee operations causing environmental harm may be held liable under the criminal provisions of environmental statutes.

CASE 7.1	United States v. Hanousek

United States Court of Appeals,
Ninth Circuit, 1999.
176 F.3d 1116.
http://www.ca9.uscourts.gov [a]

BACKGROUND AND FACTS Edward Hanousek worked for Pacific & Arctic Railway and Navigation Company (P&A) as a roadmaster of the White Pass & Yukon Railroad in Alaska. Hanousek was responsible "for every detail of the safe and efficient maintenance and construction of track, structures and marine facilities of the entire railroad," including special projects. One project was a rock quarry, known as "6-mile," above the Skagway River. Next to the quarry, and just beneath the surface, ran a high-pressure oil pipeline owned by Pacific & Arctic Pipeline, Inc., P&A's sister company. Hanousek halted several procedures to pro-

tect the pipeline that had been implemented by the previous manager. When the quarry's backhoe operator punctured the pipeline, an estimated 1,000 to 5,000 gallons of oil were discharged into the river. Hanousek was charged with, among other things, negligently discharging a harmful quantity of oil into a navigable water of the United States in violation of the criminal provisions of the Clean Water Act (CWA). After a trial in a federal district court, a jury convicted Hanousek, and the court imposed a sentence of six months' imprisonment, six months in a halfway house, six months' supervised release, and a fine of $5,000. Hanousek appealed to the U.S. Court of Appeals for the Ninth Circuit, arguing in part that the statute under which he was convicted violated his right to due process because he was not aware of what the CWA required.

IN THE WORDS OF THE COURT . . .

DAVID R. THOMPSON, Circuit Judge.

    *   *   *   *

The criminal provisions of the CWA [Clean Water Act] constitute public welfare legislation. Public welfare legislation is designed to protect the public from potentially harmful or injurious items and may render criminal a type of conduct that a reasonable person should know is subject to stringent public regulation and may seriously threaten the community's health or safety.

It is well established that a public welfare statute may subject a person to criminal liability for his or her ordinary negligence without violating due process. [Emphasis added.]

    *   *   * [W]here *   *   * dangerous or deleterious devices or products or obnoxious waste materials are involved, the probability of regulation is so great that anyone who is aware that he is in possession of them or dealing with them must be presumed to be aware of the regulation.

Hanousek argues that *   *   * he was simply the roadmaster of the White Pass & Yukon railroad charged with overseeing a rock-quarrying project and was not in a position to know what the law required under the CWA. *   *   * In the context of a public welfare statute, as long as a defendant knows he is dealing with a dangerous device of a character that places him in responsible relation to a public danger, he should be alerted to the probability of strict regulation. *   *   * Hanousek *   *   * does not dispute that he was aware that

---

a. The U.S. Court of Appeals for the Ninth Circuit maintains this Web site. Click on the "OPINIONS" box. From that page, click on the "1999" icon, and when the menu opens, click on "March." Scroll down to "USA V HANOUSEK" and click on the case name to access the case.

CASE 7.1—Continued

a high-pressure petroleum products pipeline owned by Pacific & Arctic's sister company ran close to the surface next to the railroad tracks at 6-mile, and does not argue that he was unaware of the dangers a break or puncture of the pipeline by a piece of heavy machinery would pose. Therefore, Hanousek should have been alerted to the probability of strict regulation.

In light of [the fact] that the criminal provisions of the CWA constitute public welfare legislation, and the fact that a public welfare statute may impose criminal penalties for ordinary negligent conduct without offending due process, we conclude that [the CWA] does not violate due process by permitting criminal penalties for ordinary negligent conduct.

DECISION AND REMEDY The U.S. Court of Appeals for the Ninth Circuit affirmed Hanousek's conviction. A corporate manager who has responsibility for operations with the potential to cause harm can be held criminally liable for harm that results even if he or she does not actually know of the specific statute under which liability may be imposed.

FOR CRITICAL ANALYSIS—Environmental Consideration *If corporate actors were able to avoid responsibility for violations of environmental statutes of which they were unaware, what might result?*

TYPES OF CRIMES

The number of acts that are defined as criminal is nearly endless. Federal, state, and local laws provide for the classification and punishment of hundreds of thousands of different criminal acts. Traditionally, though, crimes have been grouped into five broad categories, or types: violent crime (crimes against persons), property crime, public order crime, white-collar crime, and organized crime. Cyber crime—which consists of crimes committed in cyberspace with the use of computers—is, as mentioned earlier in this chapter, less a category of crime than a new way to commit crime. We will examine cyber crime later in this chapter.

Violent Crime

Crimes against persons, because they cause others to suffer physical harm or death, are referred to as *violent crimes*. Murder is a violent crime. So is sexual assault, or rape. Assault and battery, which will be discussed in Chapter 8 in the context of tort law, are also classified as violent crimes. Robbery—defined as the taking of money, personal property, or any other article of value from a person by means of force or fear—is a violent crime as well. Typically, states have more severe penalties for *aggravated robbery*—robbery with the use of a deadly weapon.

Each of these violent crimes is further classified by degree, depending on the circumstances surrounding the criminal act. These circumstances include the intent of the person committing the crime, whether a weapon was used, and (in cases other than murder) the level of pain and suffering experienced by the victim.

ROBBERY
The act of forcefully and unlawfully taking personal property of any value from another; force or intimidation is usually necessary for an act of theft to be considered a robbery.

Property Crime

The most common type of criminal activity is property crime—a crime in which the goal of the offender is some form of economic gain or the damaging of property. Robbery is a form of property crime, as well as a violent crime, because the offender seeks to gain the property of another. We look here at a number of other crimes that fall within the general category of property crime.

BURGLARY
The unlawful entry or breaking into a building with the intent to commit a felony. (Some state statutes expand this to include the intent to commit any crime.)

Burglary Traditionally, **burglary** was defined under the common law as breaking and entering the dwelling of another at night with the intent to commit a felony. Originally, the definition was aimed at protecting an individual's home and its occupants. Most state statutes have eliminated some of the requirements found in the common law definition. The time at which the breaking and entering occurs, for example, is usually immaterial. State statutes frequently omit the element of breaking and often do not require that the building be a dwelling. Aggravated burglary, which is defined as burglary with the use of a deadly weapon, burglary of a dwelling, or both, incurs a greater penalty.

LARCENY
The wrongful taking and carrying away of another person's personal property with the intent to permanently deprive the owner of the property. Some states classify larceny as either grand or petit, depending on the property's value.

Larceny Any person who wrongfully or fraudulently takes and carries away another person's personal property is guilty of **larceny**. Larceny includes the fraudulent intent to deprive an owner permanently of property. Many business-related larcenies entail fraudulent conduct. Whereas robbery involves force or fear, larceny does not. Therefore, picking pockets is larceny. Similarly, taking company products and supplies home for personal use, if one is not authorized to do so, is larceny.

In most states, the definition of property that is subject to larceny statutes has expanded. Stealing computer programs may constitute larceny even though the "property" consists of magnetic impulses. Stealing computer time can also constitute larceny. So, too, can the theft of natural gas. Trade secrets can be subject to larceny statutes. Obtaining another's phone-card number and then using that number, without authorization, to place long-distance calls is a form of property theft. These types of larceny are covered by "theft of services" statutes in many jurisdictions.

The common law distinguishes between grand and petit larceny depending on the value of the property taken. Many states have abolished this distinction, but in those that have not, grand larceny is a felony and petit larceny, a misdemeanor.

Obtaining Goods by False Pretenses It is a criminal act to obtain goods by means of false pretenses—for example, buying groceries with a check, knowing that one has insufficient funds to cover it. Statutes dealing with such illegal activities vary widely from state to state.

Receiving Stolen Goods It is a crime to receive stolen goods. The recipient of such goods need not know the true identity of the owner or the thief. All that is necessary is that the recipient knows or should have known that the goods are stolen, which implies an intent to deprive the owner of those goods.

ARSON
The intentional burning of another's dwelling. Today, arson statutes have been extended to cover any real property regardless of ownership and the destruction of property by other means—for example, by explosion.

Arson The willful and malicious burning of a building (and in some states, personal property) owned by another is the crime of **arson**. At common law, arson traditionally applied only to burning down another person's house. The law was designed to protect human life. Today, some arson statutes have been extended to cover the destruction of any building, regardless of ownership, by fire or explosion.

Every state has a special statute that covers a person's burning a building for the purpose of collecting insurance. ● EXAMPLE 3 If Smith owns an insured apartment building that is falling apart and sets fire to it himself or pays someone else to do so, he is guilty not only of arson but also of defrauding insurers, which is an attempted larceny.● Of course, the insurer need not pay the claim when insurance fraud is proved.

Forgery The fraudulent making or altering of any writing in a way that changes the legal rights and liabilities of another is **forgery.** ● EXAMPLE 4 If, without authorization, Severson signs Bennett's name to the back of a check made out to Bennett, Severson is committing forgery.● Forgery also includes changing trademarks, falsifying public records, counterfeiting, and altering a legal document.

Public Order Crime

Historically, societies have always outlawed activities that are considered to be contrary to public values and morals. Today, the most common public order crimes include prostitution, illegal gambling, and illegal drug use. These crimes are sometimes referred to as victimless crimes because they normally harm only the offender. From a broader perspective, however, they are deemed detrimental to society as a whole because they might create an environment that gives rise to property and violent crimes.

White-Collar Crime

Crimes that typically occur only in the business context are commonly referred to as **white-collar crimes.** Although there is no official definition of white-collar crime, the term is popularly used to mean an illegal act or a series of acts committed by an individual or business entity using some nonviolent means. Usually, this kind of crime is committed in the course of a legitimate occupation. Corporate crimes fall into this category.

Embezzlement When a person entrusted with another person's property or money fraudulently appropriates it, **embezzlement** occurs. Typically, embezzlement involves an employee who steals funds. Banks face this problem, and so do a number of businesses in which corporate officers or accountants "jimmy" the books to cover up the fraudulent conversion of funds for their own benefit. Embezzlement is not larceny, because the wrongdoer does not physically take the property from the possession of another, and it is not robbery, because force or fear is not used.

It does not matter whether the accused takes the funds from the victim or from a third person. ● EXAMPLE 5 If, as the financial officer of a large corporation, Saunders pockets a certain number of checks from third parties that were given to her to deposit into the corporate account, she is embezzling.●

Often, an embezzler who returns what has been taken will not be prosecuted, because the owner usually will not bother to report the crime, thus avoiding having to give depositions and appear in court. That the accused intended eventually to return the embezzled property, however, does not constitute a sufficient defense to the crime of embezzlement.

Mail and Wire Fraud One of the most potent weapons against white-collar criminals is the Mail Fraud Act of 1990.[5] Under this act, it is a federal crime

---

5. 18 U.S.C. Sections 1341–1342.

> "A large number of houses deserve to be burnt."
> H. G. WELLS, 1866–1946
> (English author)

FORGERY
The fraudulent making or altering of any writing in a way that changes the legal rights and liabilities of another.

WHITE-COLLAR CRIME
Nonviolent crime committed by individuals or corporations to obtain a personal or business advantage.

EMBEZZLEMENT
The fraudulent appropriation of funds or other property by a person to whom such items have been entrusted.

(mail fraud) to use the mails to defraud the public. Illegal use of the mails must involve (1) mailing or causing someone else to mail a writing—something written, printed, or photocopied—for the purpose of executing a scheme to defraud and (2) a contemplated or an organized scheme to defraud by false pretenses. ● **EXAMPLE 6** If Johnson advertises by mail the sale of a cure for cancer that he knows to be fraudulent because it has no medical validity, he can be prosecuted for fraudulent use of the mails. ●

Federal law also makes it a crime (wire fraud) to use wire (for example, the telephone), radio, or television transmissions to defraud.[6] Violators may be fined up to $1,000, imprisoned for up to five years, or both. If the violation affects a financial institution, the violator may be fined up to $1 million, imprisoned for up to thirty years, or both.

> **"[It is] very much better to bribe a person than kill him."**
>
> SIR WINSTON CHURCHILL, 1874–1965
> (British prime minister,
> 1940–1945, 1951–1955)

Bribery Basically, three types of bribery are considered crimes: bribery of public officials, commercial bribery, and bribery of foreign officials. The attempt to influence a public official to act in a way that serves a private interest is a crime. As an element of this crime, intent must be present and proved. The bribe can be anything the recipient considers to be valuable. Realize that *the crime of bribery occurs when the bribe is offered.* It does not matter whether the person to whom the bribe is offered accepts the bribe or agrees to perform whatever action is desired by the person offering the bribe. *Accepting a bribe* is a separate crime.

Typically, people make commercial bribes to obtain proprietary information, cover up an inferior product, or secure new business. Industrial espionage sometimes involves commercial bribes. ● **EXAMPLE 7** A person in one firm may offer an employee in a competing firm some type of payoff in exchange for trade secrets or pricing schedules. ● So-called kickbacks, or payoffs for special favors or services, are a form of commercial bribery in certain situations.

Bribing foreign officials to obtain favorable business contracts is a crime. The Foreign Corrupt Practices Act of 1977, which was presented as the *Landmark in the Legal Environment* feature in Chapter 2, was passed to curb the use of bribery by American businesspersons in securing foreign contracts.

Bankruptcy Fraud Today, federal bankruptcy law (see Chapter 15) allows individuals and businesses to be relieved of oppressive debt through bankruptcy proceedings. Numerous white-collar crimes can be committed during the many phases of a bankruptcy proceeding. ● **EXAMPLE 8** A creditor, for example, may file a false claim against the debtor, which is a crime. Also, a debtor may fraudulently transfer assets to favored parties before or after the petition for bankruptcy is filed. For instance, a company-owned automobile may be "sold" at a bargain price to a trusted friend or relative. ● Closely related to the crime of fraudulent transfer of property is the crime of fraudulent concealment of property, such as hiding gold coins.

The Theft of Trade Secrets As will be discussed in Chapter 10, trade secrets constitute a form of property that for many businesses can be extremely valuable. The Economic Espionage Act of 1996[7] made the theft of trade secrets a federal crime. The act also made it a federal crime to buy or possess trade

---

6. 18 U.S.C. Section 1343.
7. 18 U.S.C. Sections 1831–1839.

secrets of another person, knowing that the trade secrets were stolen or otherwise acquired without the owner's authorization.

Violations of the act can result in steep penalties. An individual who violates the act can be imprisoned for up to ten years and fined up to $500,000. If a corporation or other organization violates the act, it can be fined up to $5 million. Additionally, the law provides that any property acquired as a result of the violation and any property used in the commission of the violation are subject to criminal *forfeiture*—meaning that the government can take the property. A theft of trade secrets conducted via the Internet, for example, could result in the forfeiture of every computer, printer, and other device used to commit or facilitate the violation.

Insider Trading An individual who obtains "inside information" about the plans of a publicly listed corporation can often make stock-trading profits by using the information to guide decisions relating to the purchase or sale of corporate securities (corporate stocks and bonds). **Insider trading** is a violation of securities law and will be considered more fully in Chapter 23. At this point, it can be said that one who possesses inside information and who has a duty not to disclose it to outsiders may not profit from the purchase or sale of securities based on those facts until the information is available to the public.

INSIDER TRADING
The purchase or sale of securities on the basis of inside information (information that has not been made available to the public).

Organized Crime

As mentioned, white-collar crime takes place within the confines of the legitimate business world. *Organized crime,* in contrast, operates *illegitimately* by, among other things, providing illegal goods and services. For organized crime, the traditional preferred markets are gambling, prostitution, illegal narcotics, and loan sharking (lending money at higher-than-legal interest rates), along with more recent ventures into counterfeiting and credit-card scams.

Money Laundering The profits from illegal activities amount to billions of dollars a year, particularly the profits from illegal drug transactions and, to a lesser extent, from racketeering, prostitution, and gambling. Under federal law, banks, savings and loan associations, and other financial institutions are required to report currency transactions involving more than $10,000. Consequently, those who engage in illegal activities face difficulties in depositing their cash profits from illicit transactions.

As an alternative to simply storing cash from illegal transactions in a safe-deposit box, wrongdoers and racketeers have invented ways to make "dirty" money "clean." This **money laundering** is done through legitimate businesses. ● **EXAMPLE 9** Matt, a successful drug dealer, becomes a partner with a restaurateur. Little by little, the restaurant shows an increasing profit. As a partner in the restaurant, Matt is able to report the "profits" of the restaurant as legitimate income on which he pays federal and state taxes. He can then spend those monies without worrying that his lifestyle may exceed the level possible with his reported income. ●

The Federal Bureau of Investigation estimates that organized crime has invested tens of billions of dollars in as many as a hundred thousand business establishments in the United States for the purpose of money laundering. Globally, it is estimated that more than $500 billion in illegal money moves through the world banking system every year.

MONEY LAUNDERING
Falsely reporting income that has been obtained through criminal activity as income obtained through a legitimate business enterprise—in effect, "laundering" the "dirty money."

The Racketeer Influenced and Corrupt Organizations Act In 1970, in an effort to curb the apparently increasing entry of organized crime into the legitimate business world, Congress passed the Racketeer Influenced and Corrupt Organizations Act (RICO).[8] The act, which was enacted as part of the Organized Crime Control Act, makes it a federal crime to (1) use income obtained from racketeering activity to purchase any interest in an enterprise, (2) acquire or maintain an interest in an enterprise through racketeering activity, (3) conduct or participate in the affairs of an enterprise through racketeering activity, or (4) conspire to do any of the preceding activities.

Racketeering activity is not a new type of substantive crime created by RICO; rather, RICO incorporates by reference twenty-six separate types of federal crimes and nine types of state felonies[9] and declares that if a person commits two of these offenses, he or she is guilty of "racketeering activity." Additionally, RICO is often used today as an effective tool in attacking white-collar crimes rather than organized crime.

In the event of a violation, the statute permits the government to seek civil penalties, including the divestiture of a defendant's interest in a business (called forfeiture) and the dissolution of the business. Perhaps the most controversial aspect of RICO is that, in some cases, private individuals are allowed to recover three times their actual losses (treble damages), plus attorneys' fees, for business injuries caused by a violation of the statute. Under criminal provisions of RICO, any individual found guilty of a violation is subject to a fine of up to $25,000 per violation, imprisonment for up to twenty years, or both. Additionally, the statute provides that those who violate RICO may be required to forfeit (give up) any assets, in the form of property or cash, that were acquired as a result of the illegal activity or that were "involved in" or an "instrumentality of" the activity.

DEFENSES TO CRIMINAL LIABILITY

Among the most important defenses to criminal liability are infancy, intoxication, insanity, mistake, consent, duress, justifiable use of force, entrapment, and the statute of limitations. Many of these defenses involve assertions that the intent requirement for criminal liability is lacking. Also, in some cases, defendants are given immunity and thus relieved, at least in part, of criminal liability for crimes they committed. We look at each of these defenses here.

Note that procedural violations, such as obtaining evidence without a valid search warrant, may operate as defenses as well. As you will read later in this chapter, evidence obtained in violation of a defendant's constitutional rights normally may not be admitted in court. If the evidence is suppressed, there may be no basis for prosecuting the defendant.

Infancy

The term *infant*, as used in the law, refers to any person who has not yet reached the age of majority (see Chapter 11). In all states, certain courts handle cases involving children who are alleged to have violated the law. In some states, juvenile courts handle children's cases exclusively. In other states, how-

8. 18 U.S.C. Sections 1961–1968.
9. See 18 U.S.C. Section 1961(1)(A).

ever, courts that handle children's cases may also have jurisdiction over other matters.

Originally, juvenile court hearings were informal, and lawyers were rarely present. Since 1967, however, when the United States Supreme Court ordered that a child charged with delinquency must be allowed to consult with an attorney before being committed to a state institution,[10] juvenile court hearings have become more formal. In most states, a child may be treated as an adult and tried in a regular court if she or he is above a certain age (usually fourteen) and is charged with a felony, such as rape or murder.

Intoxication

The law recognizes two types of intoxication, whether from drugs or from alcohol: *involuntary* and *voluntary*. Involuntary intoxication occurs when a person either is physically forced to ingest or inject an intoxicating substance or is unaware that a substance contains drugs or alcohol. Involuntary intoxication is a defense to a crime if its effect was to make a person incapable of obeying the law or incapable of understanding that the act committed was wrong. Voluntary intoxication is rarely a defense, but it may be effective in cases in which the defendant was *extremely* intoxicated when committing the wrong.

Insanity

Just as a child is often judged incapable of the state of mind required to commit a crime, so also may be someone suffering from a mental illness. Thus, insanity may be a defense to a criminal charge. The courts have had difficulty deciding what the test for legal insanity should be, however, and psychiatrists as well as lawyers are critical of the tests used. Almost all federal courts and some states use the relatively liberal standard set forth in the Model Penal Code:

> A person is not responsible for criminal conduct if at the time of such conduct as a result of mental disease or defect he lacks substantial capacity either to appreciate the wrongfulness of his conduct or to conform his conduct to the requirements of the law.

Some states use the *M'Naghten* test,[11] under which a criminal defendant is not responsible if, at the time of the offense, he or she did not know the nature and quality of the act or did not know that the act was wrong. Other states use the irresistible-impulse test. A person operating under an irresistible impulse may know an act is wrong but cannot refrain from doing it.

Mistake

Everyone has heard the saying, "Ignorance of the law is no excuse." Ordinarily, ignorance of the law or a mistaken idea about what the law requires is not a valid defense. In some states, however, that rule has been modified. Criminal defendants who claim that they honestly did not know that they were breaking a law may have a valid defense if (1) the law was not published or reasonably

Fourteen-year-old Lionel Tate walks into the courtroom for a hearing at a courthouse in Fort Lauderdale, Florida. Tate, who was convicted of murdering his playmate when he was only thirteen years old, is now serving a life sentence. Should a juvenile who commits a criminal act be tried in a regular court, or should a juvenile be entitled to the protections associated with juvenile courts?

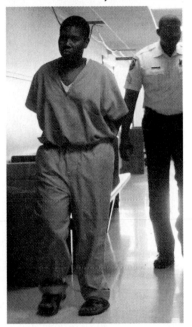

"Insanity is often the logic of an accurate mind overtaxed."

OLIVER WENDELL HOLMES, JR., 1841–1935
(Associate justice of the United States Supreme Court, 1902–1932)

COMPARE "Ignorance" is a lack of information. "Mistake" is a confusion of information.

---

10. *In re Gault,* 387 U.S. 1, 87 S.Ct. 1428, 18 L.Ed.2d 527 (1967).
11. A rule derived from *M'Naghten's Case,* 8 Eng.Rep. 718 (1843).

Andrea Yates, who allegedly drowned her five children, pleaded not guilty to the crime by reason of insanity. How could the court decide whether she was insane when she committed the crime?

CONSENT
The voluntary agreement to a proposition or an act of another; a concurrence of wills.

DURESS
Unlawful pressure brought to bear on a person, causing the person to perform an act that she or he would not otherwise have performed.

SELF-DEFENSE
The legally recognized privilege to protect oneself or one's property against injury by another. The privilege of self-defense protects only acts that are reasonably necessary to protect oneself, one's property, or another person.

made known to the public or (2) the defendant relied on an official statement of the law that was erroneous.

A *mistake of fact,* as opposed to a *mistake of law,* operates as a defense if it negates the mental state necessary to commit a crime. ● **EXAMPLE 10** If Oliver Wheaton mistakenly walks off with Julie Tyson's briefcase because he thinks it is his, there is no theft. Theft requires knowledge that the property belongs to another. (If Wheaton's act causes Tyson to incur damages, however, Wheaton may be subject to liability for trespass to personal property or conversion, torts that will be discussed in Chapter 8.)●

Consent

What if a victim consents to a crime or even encourages the person intending a criminal act to commit it? The law allows **consent** as a defense if the consent cancels the harm that the law is designed to prevent. In each case, the question is whether the law forbids an act that was committed against the victim's will or forbids the act without regard to the victim's wish. The law forbids murder, prostitution, and drug use regardless of whether the victim consents to it. Also, if the act causes harm to a third person who has not consented, there is no escape from criminal liability. Consent or forgiveness given after a crime has been committed is not really a defense, though it can affect the likelihood of prosecution. Consent operates most successfully as a defense in crimes against property.

Duress

Duress exists when the *wrongful threat* of one person induces another person to perform an act that she or he would not otherwise have performed. In such a situation, duress is said to negate the mental state necessary to commit a crime. For duress to qualify as a defense, the following requirements must be met:

1. The threat must be of serious bodily harm or death.
2. The harm threatened must be greater than the harm caused by the crime.
3. The threat must be immediate and inescapable.
4. The defendant must have been involved in the situation through no fault of his or her own.

Justifiable Use of Force

Probably the most well-known defense to criminal liability is **self-defense**—the protection of one's self or property against injury by another. Other situations, however, also justify the use of force: the defense of one's dwelling, the defense of other property, and the prevention of a crime. In all of these situations, it is important to distinguish between the use of deadly and nondeadly force. *Deadly force* is likely to result in death or serious bodily harm. *Nondeadly force* is force that reasonably appears necessary to prevent the imminent use of criminal force.

Generally speaking, people can use the amount of nondeadly force that seems necessary to protect themselves, their dwellings, or other property or to prevent the commission of a crime. Deadly force can be used in self-defense if there is a *reasonable belief* that imminent death or serious bodily harm will otherwise result, if the attacker is using unlawful force (as opposed to lawful force, such as that exerted by a police officer), and if the defender has not initiated or provoked the attack. Deadly force normally can be used to defend a dwelling only if the unlawful entry is violent and the person believes deadly force is necessary to prevent imminent death or great bodily harm or—in some jurisdictions—if the person believes deadly force is necessary to prevent the commission of a felony (such as arson) in the dwelling.

Entrapment

Entrapment is a defense designed to prevent police officers and other government agents from encouraging crimes in order to apprehend persons wanted for criminal acts. In the typical entrapment case, an undercover agent *suggests* that a crime be committed and somehow pressures or induces an individual to commit it. The agent then arrests the individual for the crime.

For entrapment to be considered a defense, both the suggestion and the inducement must take place. The defense is intended not to prevent law enforcement agents from setting a trap for an unwary criminal but rather to prevent them from pushing the individual into it. The crucial issue is whether a person who committed a crime was predisposed to commit the crime or did so because the agent induced it.

ENTRAPMENT
In criminal law, a defense in which the defendant claims that he or she was induced by a public official—usually an undercover agent or police officer—to commit a crime that he or she would otherwise not have committed.

Statute of Limitations

Recall from Chapter 1 that *statutes of limitations* establish time periods within which actions against parties for committing civil wrongs can be brought. With some exceptions, such as for the crime of murder, statutes of limitations apply to crimes just as they do to civil wrongs. In other words, criminal cases must be prosecuted within a certain number of years. If a criminal action is brought after the statutory time period has expired, the accused person can raise the statute of limitations as a defense.

Immunity

At times, the state may wish to obtain information from a person accused of a crime. Accused persons are understandably reluctant to give information if it will be used to prosecute them, and they cannot be forced to do so. The privilege against self-incrimination is granted by the Fifth Amendment to the Constitution, which reads, in part, "nor shall [any person] be compelled in any criminal case to be a witness against himself."

In cases in which the state wishes to obtain information from a person accused of a crime, the state can grant *immunity* from prosecution or agree to prosecute for a less serious offense in exchange for the information. Once immunity is given, the person can no longer refuse to testify on Fifth Amendment grounds because he or she now has an absolute privilege against self-incrimination.

Often, a grant of immunity from prosecution for a serious crime is part of a **plea bargain** between the defendant and the prosecuting attorney. The defendant may be convicted of a lesser offense, while the state uses the defendant's testimony to prosecute accomplices for serious crimes carrying heavy penalties.

PLEA BARGAIN
A negotiated agreement between a criminal defendant and the prosecutor in a criminal case that usually involves the defendant's pleading guilty to a lesser offense in return for a lighter sentence.

CONSTITUTIONAL SAFEGUARDS AND CRIMINAL PROCEDURES

Criminal law brings the power of the state, with all its resources, to bear against the individual. Criminal procedures are designed to protect the constitutional rights of individuals and to prevent the arbitrary use of power on the part of the government.

The U.S. Constitution provides specific safeguards for those accused of crimes. Most of these safeguards protect individuals not only against federal government actions but also, by virtue of the due process clause of the Fourteenth Amendment, against state government actions. These safeguards are set forth in the Fourth, Fifth, Sixth, and Eighth Amendments.

Fourth Amendment Protections

The Fourth Amendment protects the "right of the people to be secure in their persons, houses, papers, and effects." Before searching or seizing private property, law enforcement officers must obtain a **search warrant**—an order from a judge or other public official authorizing the search or seizure.

SEARCH WARRANT
An order granted by a public authority, such as a judge, that authorizes law enforcement personnel to search particular premises or property.

PROBABLE CAUSE
Reasonable grounds for believing that a person should be arrested or searched.

Search Warrants and Probable Cause To obtain a search warrant, the officers must convince a judge that they have reasonable grounds, or **probable cause,** to believe a search will reveal a specific illegality. Probable cause requires law enforcement officials to have trustworthy evidence that would convince a reasonable person that the proposed search or seizure is more likely justified than not. Furthermore, the Fourth Amendment prohibits general warrants. It requires a particular description of that which is to be searched or seized. General searches through a person's belongings are impermissible. The search cannot extend beyond what is described in the warrant.

There are exceptions to the requirement of a search warrant, as when it is likely that the items sought will be removed before a warrant can be obtained. For example, if a police officer has probable cause to believe an automobile contains evidence of a crime and it is likely that the vehicle will be unavailable by the time a warrant is obtained, the officer can search the vehicle without a warrant.

Searches and Seizures in the Business Context Constitutional protection against unreasonable searches and seizures is important to businesses and professionals. As federal and state regulation of commercial activities increased during the twentieth century, frequent and unannounced government inspections were conducted to ensure compliance with the regulations. Such inspections were extremely disruptive at times. In *Marshall v. Barlow's, Inc.,*[12] the United States Supreme Court held that government inspectors do not have the right to enter business premises without a warrant, although the standard of probable cause is not the same as that required in nonbusiness contexts. The existence of a general and neutral enforcement plan will justify issuance of the warrant.

Lawyers and accountants frequently possess the business records of their clients, and inspecting these documents while they are out of the hands of their true owners also requires a warrant. No warrant is required, however, for seizures of spoiled or contaminated food. Nor are warrants required for searches of businesses in such highly regulated industries as liquor, guns, and strip mining. General manufacturing is not considered to be one of these highly regulated industries, however.

Of increasing concern to many employers is how to maintain a safe and efficient workplace without jeopardizing the Fourth Amendment rights of employees

---

12. 436 U.S. 307, 98 S.Ct. 1816, 56 L.Ed.2d 305 (1978).

"to be secure in their persons." Requiring employees to undergo random drug tests, for example, may be held to violate the Fourth Amendment. In Chapter 16, we discuss Fourth Amendment issues in the employment context, as well as the privacy rights of employees in general, in detail.

Fifth Amendment Protections

The Fifth Amendment offers significant protections for accused persons. One is the guarantee that no one can be deprived of "life, liberty, or property without due process of law." Two other important Fifth Amendment provisions protect persons against double jeopardy and self-incrimination.

Due Process of Law Remember from Chapter 5 that *due process of law* has both procedural and substantive aspects. Procedural due process requirements underlie criminal procedures. Basically, the law must be carried out in a fair and orderly way. In criminal cases, due process means that defendants should have an opportunity to object to the charges against them before a fair, neutral decision maker, such as a judge. Defendants must also be given the opportunity to confront and cross-examine witnesses and accusers and to present their own witnesses.

Double Jeopardy The Fifth Amendment also protects persons from **double jeopardy**—being tried twice for the same criminal offense. The prohibition against double jeopardy means that once a criminal defendant is acquitted (found "not guilty") of a particular crime, the government may not reindict the person and retry him or her for the same crime.

The prohibition against double jeopardy does not preclude the crime victim from bringing a civil suit against the same person to recover damages, however. Additionally, a state's prosecution of a crime will not prevent a separate federal prosecution relating to the same activity, and vice versa. ● **EXAMPLE 11** A person found "not guilty" of assault and battery in a criminal case may be sued by the victim in a civil tort case for damages. A person who is prosecuted for assault and battery in a state court may be prosecuted in a federal court for civil rights violations resulting from the same action.●

Self-Incrimination The Fifth Amendment guarantees that no person "shall be compelled in any criminal case to be a witness against himself." Thus, in any criminal proceeding, an accused person cannot be compelled to give testimony that might subject her or him to any criminal prosecution.

The Fifth Amendment's guarantee against **self-incrimination** extends only to natural persons. Because a corporation is a legal entity and not a natural person, the privilege against self-incrimination does not apply to it. Similarly, the business records of a partnership do not receive Fifth Amendment protection. When a partnership is required to produce these records, it must do so even if the information incriminates the persons who constitute the business entity. Sole proprietors and sole practitioners (those who fully own their businesses) who have not incorporated cannot be compelled to produce their business records. These individuals have full protection against self-incrimination, because they function in only one capacity; there is no separate business entity (see Chapter 14).

DOUBLE JEOPARDY
A situation occurring when a person is tried twice for the same criminal offense; prohibited by the Fifth Amendment to the Constitution.

SELF-INCRIMINATION
The giving of testimony that may subject the testifier to criminal prosecution. The Fifth Amendment to the Constitution protects against self-incrimination by providing that no person "shall be compelled in any criminal case to be a witness against himself."

BE AWARE The Fifth Amendment protection against self-incrimination does not cover partnerships or corporations.

INTERNATIONAL PERSPECTIVE

The Death Penalty

The United States is now the only economically advanced Western democracy that uses the death penalty. All twenty-five countries of the European Union have banned its use and are actively promoting its abolition elsewhere. The United Nations Commission on Human Rights has called for its restriction and eventual abolition on a global level. When President George W. Bush visited Pope John Paul II in July 2001, the Pope urged him to put an end to this practice in the United States. Nonetheless, in the United States, thirty-eight states and the federal government continue to allow for the death penalty. Although polls indicate that public support for the death penalty has started to decline, it still remains high—about two-thirds of Americans favor the death penalty.

Some proponents of capital punishment believe that it functions as a deterrent to crime. In their view, it prevents future violence by showing how serious the consequences of violent criminal behavior can be. Critics of capital punishment maintain that it violates the Eighth Amendment's prohibition against cruel and unusual punishment. They also point out that despite the use of the death penalty, the various states within the United States have the highest murder rates in the industrialized world, and those rates are highest in the southern states, such as Texas, where the most executions occur. In contrast, in the European countries that have abolished the death penalty, murder rates are far lower than in the United States.

FOR CRITICAL ANALYSIS

The objectives of our criminal justice system include both punishment and rehabilitation. How can the concept of rehabilitation of wrongdoers be reconciled with the death penalty?

Protections under the Sixth and Eighth Amendments

The Sixth Amendment guarantees several important rights for criminal defendants: the right to a speedy trial, the right to a jury trial, the right to a public trial, the right to confront witnesses, and the right to counsel. The Eighth Amendment prohibits excessive bail and fines, as well as cruel and unusual punishment.

The Exclusionary Rule and the *Miranda* Rule

Two other procedural protections for criminal defendants are the exclusionary rule and the *Miranda* rule.

EXCLUSIONARY RULE
In criminal procedure, a rule under which any evidence that is obtained in violation of the accused's constitutional rights guaranteed by the Fourth, Fifth, and Sixth Amendments, as well as any evidence derived from illegally obtained evidence, will not be admissible in court.

The Exclusionary Rule Under what is known as the **exclusionary rule,** all evidence obtained in violation of the constitutional rights spelled out in the Fourth, Fifth, and Sixth Amendments normally must be excluded from the trial, as well as all evidence derived from the illegally obtained evidence. Evidence derived from illegally obtained evidence is known as the "fruit of the poisonous tree." For example, if a confession is obtained after an illegal arrest, the arrest is "the poisonous tree," and the confession, if "tainted" by the arrest, is the "fruit."

The purpose of the exclusionary rule is to deter police from conducting warrantless searches and from engaging in other misconduct. The rule is sometimes criticized because it can lead to injustice. Many a defendant has "gotten off on a technicality" because law enforcement personnel failed to observe procedural requirements. Even though a defendant may be obviously guilty, if the evidence of that guilt was obtained improperly (without a valid search warrant, for example), it normally cannot be used against the defendant in court.

In the following case, the court considered whether certain evidence had been obtained improperly and should be excluded as "fruit of the poisonous tree."

> "A search is not to be made legal by what it turns up."
>
> ROBERT H. JACKSON, 1892–1954
> (Associate justice of the United States
> Supreme Court, 1941–1954)

CASE 7.2   People v. McFarlan

New York Supreme Court, 2002.[a]
191 Misc.2d 531,
744 N.Y.S.2d 287.

HISTORICAL AND SOCIAL SETTING *In 1999, the state of New York adopted the Electronic Signatures and Records Act (ESRA).[b] ESRA concerns the use and legal admissibility in New York state courts of records that are stored by electronic means. Under rules issued pursuant to ESRA, an electronic record has the same force and effect as a record not produced or maintained by electronic means. Those rules state that ESRA's purpose is to "ensure that persons who voluntarily elect to use . . . electronic records can do so with confidence that they carry the same force and effect of non-electronic . . . records."*

BACKGROUND AND FACTS   In May 2001, Lisa Kordes saw two men picking pockets on a Lexington Avenue bus in Manhattan, in New York City. Based on Kordes's description of the men, a police department computer produced a six-photo array of possible suspects. Kordes selected a photo of Kevin McFarlan as one of the men she had seen. Five days later, on a bus, Neal Ariano, a police officer, arrested McFarlan after seeing him bump an elderly woman while placing his hand near her pocketbook. At the police station, Kordes viewed a lineup including McFarlan and identified him as the man she had seen on the Lexington Avenue bus. McFarlan was charged in a New York state court with various crimes. The printout of the computer-generated photo array that Kordes had been shown was lost, but the "People" (the state of New York) introduced into evidence a second printout to show what Kordes had seen. McFarlan argued, among other things, that the first printout was the original photo array and that because that printout had been lost, the court should presume the photo-array procedure had been illegal. Thus, McFarlan's arrest and Kordes's identification of him in the lineup should be excluded as "fruit of the poisonous tree." The court considered the application of ESRA in this context.

IN THE WORDS OF THE COURT . . .

LEWIS BART STONE, J. [Judge]
* * * *

Since the advent of the computer and the growth of the electronic storage of information, there has been a growing appreciation of the need to rearticulate rules of law relating to what is a writing, and in such context, what is an original document. There now seems [to be] a consensus embodied in recent proposed and enacted legislation that *for the pre-computer concept of "writing" the term "record" should now be substituted to accommodate this new reality.* * * * [Emphasis added.]

Under this concept, the record is electronic information which is retrievable in usable form. As no reported New York decision has yet cited or construed

---

a. In New York, a supreme court is a trial court.
b. New York Technology Law Sections 101–109.

(continued)

CASE 7.2—Continued

ESRA * * * , this is generally a case of first impression [a case presenting a legal issue that has not been addressed by the court's jurisdiction], and especially as to whether such law applies in the context of a criminal proceeding or trial. ESRA itself makes no distinction between civil and criminal proceedings, and was designed to be generally applicable and to change prior ways of doing business, superseding all other statutes, cases and rules. The only reason that a criminal or civil context might lead to a different result is, if in some way, an important constitutional protection of a criminal defendant would be lost by applying ESRA in a criminal proceeding. Thus, the issue here is whether the maintenance of a record in electronic form, and the use of a manifestation of the record, either as a printout or as a screen or other display, in connection with the arrest, prosecution and possible conviction of a criminal defendant, could violate constitutional rules.

Here, as both printouts were generated in the same format, there can be no prejudice from the fact that the defendant was selected from the first printout and that a second identical printout was later [introduced into evidence]. Each is identical and conveys the full recoverable information. To decide * * * to the contrary * * * is absurd. Where, for example, a witness is shown only the screen display, what must the People [public prosecutor] keep? For on such an analysis the printout of the screen could not be the "original." The purpose of requiring the preservation of a record is clear. Concern for the integrity of information has always led the Courts to prefer the original, and have led to many rules to bar or limit the use of non-"original" material. Here the original array was in electronic form in the computer memory, the testimony was unequivocal that [both] printout[s] * * * were generated in the same manner. * * * [A]s a result, defendant's argument crumbles.

DECISION AND REMEDY The New York state court held that the second printout of the photo array was not "fruit of the poisonous tree" and could be properly accepted into evidence. While acknowledging that the first printout was lost, the court reasoned that this did not indicate that the photo-array procedure had been illegal because the first printout was not the original photo array. The original photo array was the electronic record in the computer.

FOR CRITICAL ANALYSIS—Technological Consideration *When a record is stored on a computer, which should be considered the "original" record—the version on the computer or a printout of the computer rendition?*

The *Miranda* Rule In *Miranda v. Arizona,* a case decided in 1966, the United States Supreme Court established the rule that individuals who are arrested must be informed of certain constitutional rights, including their Fifth Amendment right to remain silent and their Sixth Amendment right to counsel. If the arresting officers fail to inform a criminal suspect of these constitutional rights, any statements the suspect makes normally will not be admissible in court. Because of its importance in criminal procedure, the *Miranda* case is presented as this chapter's *Landmark in the Legal Environment* feature.

The Supreme Court's *Miranda* decision was controversial, and in 1968 Congress attempted to overrule the decision when it enacted Section 3501 of the Omnibus Crime Control Act of that year. Essentially, Section 3501 reinstated the rule that had been in effect for 180 years before *Miranda*—namely,

REMEMBER Once a suspect has been informed of his or her rights, anything that person says can be used as evidence in a trial.

LANDMARK IN THE LEGAL ENVIRONMENT

Miranda v. Arizona (1966)

The United States Supreme Court's decision in *Miranda v. Arizona*[a] has been cited in more court decisions than any other case in the history of American law. Through television shows and other media, the case has also become familiar to most of America's adult population.

The case arose after Ernesto Miranda was arrested in his home, on March 13, 1963, for the kidnapping and rape of an eighteen-year-old woman. Miranda was taken to a Phoenix, Arizona, police station and questioned by two police officers. Two hours later, the officers emerged from the interrogation room with a written confession signed by Miranda.

RULINGS BY THE LOWER COURTS The confession was admitted into evidence at the trial, and Miranda was convicted and sentenced to prison for twenty to thirty years. Miranda appealed the decision, claiming that he had not been informed of his constitutional rights. He did not claim that he was innocent of the crime or that his confession was false or made under duress. He only claimed that he would not have confessed to the crime if he had been advised of his right to remain silent and to have an attorney. The Supreme Court of Arizona held that Miranda's constitutional rights had not been violated and affirmed his conviction. In forming its decision, the court emphasized the fact that Miranda had not specifically requested an attorney.

THE SUPREME COURT'S DECISION The *Miranda* case was subsequently consolidated with three other cases involving similar issues and reviewed by the United States Supreme Court. In its decision, the Supreme Court stated that whenever an individual is taken into custody, "the following measures are required: He must be warned prior to any questioning that he has the right to remain silent, that anything he says can be used against him in a court of law, that he has the right to the presence of an attorney, and that if he cannot afford an attorney one will be appointed for him prior to any questioning if he so desires." If the accused waives his or her rights to remain silent and to have counsel present, the government must be able to demonstrate that the waiver was made knowingly, intelligently, and voluntarily.

Application to Today's World

Today, both on television and in the real world, police officers routinely advise suspects of their "Miranda rights" on arrest. When Ernesto Miranda himself was later murdered, the suspected murderer was "read his Miranda rights." Despite Congress's attempt to overrule the Miranda decision through legislation in 1968, the requirements continue to exist and, as noted in this chapter, were affirmed by the Supreme Court in 2000 as constitutional.

a. 384 U.S. 436, 86 S.Ct. 1602, 16 L.Ed.2d 694 (1966).

that statements by defendants can be used against them as long as the statements are made voluntarily. The U.S. Justice Department immediately disavowed Section 3501 as unconstitutional, however, and the section has never been enforced. Although the U.S. Court of Appeals for the Fourth Circuit attempted to enforce the provision in 1999, the court's decision was reversed by the United States Supreme Court in 2000. The Supreme Court held that the *Miranda* rights enunciated by the Court in the 1966 case were constitutionally based and thus could not be overruled by a legislative act.[13]

13. *Dickerson v. United States,* 530 U.S. 428, 120 S.Ct. 2326, 147 L.Ed.2d 405 (2000).

Police officers take a suspect into custody. Why must a criminal suspect be informed of his or her legal rights?

Exceptions to the *Miranda* Rule Over time, as part of a continuing attempt to balance the rights of accused persons against the rights of society, the United States Supreme Court has carved out numerous exceptions to the *Miranda* rule. In 1984, for example, the Court recognized a "public safety" exception to the *Miranda* rule. The need to protect the public warranted the admissibility of statements made by the defendant (in this case, indicating where he had placed a gun) as evidence at trial, even though the defendant had not been informed of his *Miranda* rights.[14]

In 1985, the Supreme Court further held that a confession need not be excluded even though the police failed to inform a suspect in custody that his attorney had tried to reach him by telephone.[15] In an important 1991 decision, the Court stated that a suspect's conviction will not be overturned solely on the ground that the suspect was coerced by law enforcement personnel into making a confession. If other, legally obtained evidence admitted at trial is strong enough to justify the conviction without the confession, then the fact that the confession was obtained illegally can be, in effect, ignored.[16]

In yet another case, in 1994, the Supreme Court ruled that a suspect must unequivocally and assertively request to exercise his or her right to counsel in order to stop police questioning. Saying, "Maybe I should talk to a lawyer" during an interrogation after being taken into custody is not enough. The Court held that police officers are not required to decipher the suspect's intentions in such situations.[17]

---

14. *New York v. Quarles,* 467 U.S. 649, 104 S.Ct. 2626, 81 L.Ed.2d 550 (1984).
15. *Moran v. Burbine,* 475 U.S. 412, 106 S.Ct. 1135, 89 L.Ed.2d 410 (1985).
16. *Arizona v. Fulminante,* 499 U.S. 279, 111 S.Ct. 1246, 113 L.Ed.2d 302 (1991).
17. *Davis v. United States,* 512 U.S. 452, 114 S.Ct. 2350, 129 L.Ed.2d 362 (1994).

ETHICAL ISSUE

Are there too many exceptions to the Miranda *rule?*

As mentioned, the Supreme Court's decision in *Miranda* has always been controversial. Initially, many were concerned that the *Miranda* requirements would hamper efforts by law enforcement officials to bring criminals to justice. After all, even obviously guilty persons could "get off on a technicality" if their *Miranda* rights were violated. Over time, these criticisms lessened as the courts carved out various exceptions to the *Miranda* rule. As a result of these decisions, some legal scholars now contend that there are too many exceptions to the rule. David Steinberg, the director of the Thomas Jefferson School of Law's Center for Law and Social Justice in San Diego, argues that "the current patchwork of exceptions to *Miranda* is confusing and costly." Steinberg believes that the Supreme Court should either create a "standard rule," under which the *Miranda* rule would be strictly applied in all cases, or "deregulate confessions." Under the latter approach, it would be left to the courts to decide whether a confession had been coerced by the police and should be excluded.[18] Others have suggested abandoning *Miranda* entirely and requiring instead that all custodial interrogations be recorded using digital video cameras.

CRIMINAL PROCESS

As mentioned, a criminal prosecution differs significantly from a civil case in several respects. These differences reflect the desire to safeguard the rights of the individual against the state. Exhibit 7–3 on page 216 summarizes the major steps in processing a criminal case. We discuss three phases of the criminal process—arrest, indictment or information, and trial—in more detail below, and we then describe guidelines for sentencing those convicted of crimes.

Arrest

Before a warrant for arrest can be issued, there must be probable cause for believing that the individual in question has committed a crime. As discussed earlier, *probable cause* can be defined as a substantial likelihood that the person has committed or is about to commit a crime. Note that probable cause involves a likelihood, not just a possibility. Arrests may sometimes be made without a warrant if there is no time to get one, as when a police officer observes a crime taking place, but the action of the arresting officer is still judged by the standard of probable cause.

Indictment or Information

Individuals must be formally charged with having committed specific crimes before they can be brought to trial. If issued by a grand jury, this charge is called an **indictment.**[19] A **grand jury** does not determine the guilt or innocence

INDICTMENT
The formal written accusation of a crime, made by a grand jury and presented to a court for prosecution against the accused person.

GRAND JURY
A group of citizens called to decide, after hearing the state's evidence, whether a reasonable basis (probable cause) exists for believing that a crime has been committed and whether a trial ought to be held. Grand juries usually include more jurors than ordinary trial juries.

---

18. David Steinberg, *"Miranda* No Longer Works," *The National Law Journal,* August 14, 2000, p. A18.
19. Pronounced in-*dyte*-ment.

EXHIBIT 7-3 MAJOR PROCEDURAL STEPS IN A CRIMINAL CASE

ARREST

Police officer takes suspect into custody. Most arrests are made without a warrant. After the arrest, the officer searches the suspect, who is then taken to the police station.

BOOKING

At the police station, the suspect is searched again, photographed, fingerprinted, and allowed at least one telephone call. After the booking, charges are reviewed, and if they are not dropped, a complaint is filed and a magistrate reviews the case for probable cause.

INITIAL APPEARANCE

The suspect appears before the magistrate, who informs the suspect of the charges and of his or her rights. If the suspect requests a lawyer and cannot afford one, a lawyer is appointed. The magistrate sets bail (conditions under which a suspect can obtain release pending disposition of the case).

GRAND JURY

A grand jury determines if there is probable cause to believe that the defendant committed the crime. The federal government and about half of the states require grand jury indictments for at least some felonies.

PRELIMINARY HEARING

In a court proceeding, a prosecutor presents evidence, and the judge determines if there is probable cause to hold the defendant over for trial.

INDICTMENT

An indictment is the charging instrument issued by the grand jury.

INFORMATION

An information is the charging instrument issued by the prosecutor.

ARRAIGNMENT

The suspect is brought before the trial court, informed of the charges, and asked to enter a plea.

PLEA BARGAIN

A plea bargain is a prosecutor's promise to make concessions (or promise to seek concessions) in return for a suspect's guilty plea. Concessions may include a reduced charge or a lesser sentence.

GUILTY PLEA

In many jurisdictions, most cases that reach the arraignment stage do not go to trial but are resolved by a guilty plea, often as a result of a plea bargain. The judge sets the case for sentencing.

TRIAL

Generally, most felony trials are jury trials, and most misdemeanor trials are bench trials (trials before judges). If the verdict is "guilty," the judge sets the case for sentencing. Everyone convicted of a crime has the right to an appeal.

of an accused party; rather, its function is to determine, after hearing the state's evidence, whether a reasonable basis (probable cause) exists for believing that the suspect has committed a crime and should be held for trial.

Usually, grand juries are called in cases involving serious crimes, such as murder. For lesser crimes, an individual may be formally charged by what is called an **information,** or criminal complaint. An information will be issued by a government prosecutor if the prosecutor determines that there is sufficient evidence to justify bringing the individual to trial.

INFORMATION
A formal accusation or complaint made by a government prosecutor without a grand jury indictment.

Trial

At a criminal trial, the accused person does not have to prove anything; the entire burden of proof is on the prosecutor (the state). As mentioned earlier, the prosecution must show that, based on all the evidence presented, the defendant's guilt is established *beyond a reasonable doubt.* If there is any reasonable doubt as to whether a criminal defendant did, in fact, commit the crime with which she or he has been charged, then the verdict must be "not guilty." Note that giving a verdict of "not guilty" is not the same as stating that the defendant is innocent; it merely means that not enough evidence was properly presented to the court to prove guilt beyond a reasonable doubt.

Courts have complex rules about what types of evidence may be presented and how the evidence may be brought out in criminal cases, especially in jury trials. These rules are designed to ensure that evidence in trials is relevant, reliable, and not prejudicial against the defendant.

Sentencing Guidelines

Traditionally, persons convicted of the same crime might receive very different sentences, depending on the judge hearing the case, the jurisdiction in which it was heard, and many other factors. Today, however, court judges typically must consider state or federal guidelines when sentencing convicted persons.

At the federal level, the Sentencing Reform Act created the U.S. Sentencing Commission, which was charged with the task of standardizing sentences for federal crimes. The commission fulfilled its task, and since 1987 its sentencing guidelines have been applied by federal court judges. The guidelines establish a range of possible penalties for each federal crime. Depending on the defendant's criminal record, the seriousness of the offense, and other factors specified in the guidelines (see this chapter's *Legal E-nvironment* feature on the next page for a factor considered in one case), federal judges must select a sentence from within this range.

The commission also created specific guidelines for the punishment of crimes committed by corporate employees (white-collar crimes). These guidelines established stiffer penalties for criminal violations of securities laws (see Chapter 23),[20] antitrust laws (see Chapter 22), employment laws (see Chapters 16 through 18), mail and wire fraud, commercial bribery, and kickbacks and money laundering. The guidelines allow federal judges to take into consideration a number of factors when selecting from the range of possible penalties for a specified crime. These factors include the defendant company's history of past violations, the extent of management's cooperation with federal investigators,

---

20. The Sarbanes-Oxley Act of 2002 directed the Sentencing Commission to revise the guidelines to reflect the stiffer penalties imposed by the act for corporate securities fraud—see Chapter 23.

LEGAL *e*-NVIRONMENT

Web Site Ads and the Sentencing Guidelines

The Internet is a boon for advertisers. Ads offering goods for sale can be disseminated quickly and inexpensively to hundreds of millions of people throughout the world. Yet the same characteristics that make the Internet a valuable tool in today's commerce also allow unscrupulous individuals to reap profits by defrauding innocent victims. As you will read shortly, attempts to prosecute cyber crimes have raised new types of questions—including questions related to sentencing offenders convicted of cyber fraud.

A Case of Wire Fraud

Consider, for example, a case that came before the U.S. Court of Appeals for the Ninth Circuit. Michael Pirello posted a series of ads on a Web site known as *Excite Classifieds* offering computers for sale. In the ads, Pirello described the computers at great length, including details about their operating systems, monitors, memory capacities, modems, weights, processors, and the like. In fact, the ads were part of a fraudulent scheme whereby Pirello would induce prospective buyers to send him money for computers that he never intended to deliver. Over the course of three months, Pirello received checks totaling more than $4,000 for the nonexistent computers.

Ultimately, Pirello was convicted of, among other things, three counts of wire fraud. For this crime, the U.S. Sentencing Guidelines instruct district courts to enhance a defendant's sentence by two levels if the offense was committed through "mass-marketing." The guidelines define mass-marketing as "a plan, program, promotion, or campaign that is conducted through *solicitation by* telephone, mail, *the Internet,* or other means to

induce a large number of persons to . . . purchase goods or services." (Emphasis added.) The judge concluded that Pirello's fraud was committed through mass-marketing and applied the enhanced penalty.

Does Advertising on a Web Site Constitute "Mass-Marketing"?

One of Pirello's arguments on appeal was that his actions could not have constituted mass-marketing because his ads did not amount to "solicitation by . . . the Internet." Mass-marketing in the Internet context, claimed Pirello, occurs only where the seller actively solicits a large number of purchasers by circulating mass e-mail to a purchased list of e-mail addresses. The appellate court did not agree. The court noted that Pirello's use of a classified ad arguably enabled him to solicit even more people than would have been possible with a mass e-mail. While mass e-mail is sent to a finite number of people, there is no similar limitation on the number of people who can be exposed to an ad on a Web site accessible by the public.

One of the appellate court judges dissented from this reasoning. According to the dissenting judge, solicitation involves more than simply advertising goods for sale and suggests "some sort of one-on-one importuning [requesting or demanding]." Pirello's passive placement of an ad on a Web site did not, in this judge's mind, constitute the "solicitation by . . . the Internet" required by the sentencing guidelines for the enhanced penalty.[a]

FOR CRITICAL ANALYSIS

The outcome of this case clearly hinged on how the court interpreted the phrase "solicitation by . . . the Internet." Do you agree with the majority's interpretation of the phrase or with the dissenting judge's interpretation? Explain.

---

a. *United States v. Pirello,* 255 F.3d 728 (9th Cir. 2001).

---

and the extent to which the firm has undertaken specific programs and procedures to prevent criminal activities by its employees.

In imposing a sentence, a judge may depart from the guidelines only if the defendant has some notice of this possibility and thus can prepare to argue against it. Does the same notice requirement apply to unusual conditions of supervised release, or probation? That was the question in the following case.

CASE 7.3 **United States v. Scott**

United States Court of Appeals,
Seventh Circuit, 2003.
316 F.3d 733.

BACKGROUND AND FACTS Todd Scott was charged in a federal district court with fraud and pleaded guilty. Based on his conduct and previous crimes, the court imposed the maximum sentence—twenty-four months' imprisonment followed by three years' supervised release. During the sentencing, the prosecutor suggested that because a police search of a computer in Scott's office turned up a few images of child pornography, Scott's access to the Internet should be limited as part of the supervised release. The court agreed, and ordered that Scott "shall be prohibited from access to any Internet Services without prior approval of the probation officer." Scott appealed this order to the U.S. Court of Appeals for the Seventh Circuit, contending in part that he should have received notice of this condition so that at the sentencing, he could have offered an alternative.

IN THE WORDS
OF THE COURT . . .

EASTERBROOK, Circuit Judge.
       *   *   *   *

    *   *   * [T]he surprise addition of the Internet-access condition made it impossible for Scott's lawyer to formulate [alternative] proposals in time. And there were other possibilities. Scott obtained the pictures from a newsgroup on the Usenet, one of many services available on the Internet. The district judge might have prohibited Scott from accessing newsgroups, as opposed to the entire Internet. Or the judge might have required Scott to install filtering software that would block access to sexually oriented sites, and to permit the probation officer unannounced access to verify that the filtering software was functional. Filtering software is imperfect and may block access to some sites that lack the attributes sought to be put off limits *   *   * but is less restrictive than blocking the whole Internet *   *   * .

    Knowledge that a condition of this kind was in prospect would have enabled the parties to discuss such options intelligently. *Notice also would have afforded defense counsel time to* *   *   * *remind the district judge* *   *   * *that special conditions of supervised release must entail no greater deprivation of liberty than is reasonably necessary for the purposes of sentencing* *   *   * . If Scott had used the Internet extensively to commit the crime of conviction, then perhaps a ban might be justified. But here the only justification was misbehavior that neither resulted in a conviction nor was treated as relevant conduct, making an outright ban difficult to justify. *   *   * [Emphasis added.]
     *   *   *   *

    *   *   * [A defendant is entitled to] notice of terms that are out of the ordinary, and thus unexpected—and the United States does not contend that Scott should have foreseen that Internet access would be a subject of discussion at sentencing. So Scott is entitled to a new proceeding, at which he can offer alternatives to a flat ban *   *   * .
     *   *   *   *

    *   *   * The Internet is a vast repository, offering books, newspapers, magazines, and research tools along with smut. A judge who would not forbid Scott to enter a video rental store (which may have an adult-video section) also

(continued)

CASE 7.3—Continued

should not forbid Scott to enter the Internet, even though Disney's web site coexists with others offering filthy pictures or audio files circulated in violation of the copyright laws. A judge who would not forbid a defendant to send or receive postal mail or use the telephone should not forbid that person to send or receive e-mail or to order books at Amazon.com. Scott does not have a record of extensive abuse of digital communications that could justify an outright ban. *　*　* What conditions short of a ban may be appropriate in this case is a subject for the district judge to address in the first instance.

DECISION AND REMEDY The U.S. Court of Appeals for the Seventh Circuit vacated the judgment of the lower court and remanded the case for a new sentencing proceeding at which the defendant could offer alternatives to a total ban on his postimprisonment access to the Internet.

FOR CRITICAL ANALYSIS—Technological Consideration *Are limitations on a convicted criminal's access to the Internet ever justified?*

CYBER CRIME

COMPUTER CRIME
Any act that is directed against computers and computer parts, that uses computers as instruments of crime, or that involves computers and constitutes abuse.

BE AWARE Technological change is one of the primary factors leading to new types of crime.

Some years ago, the American Bar Association defined **computer crime** as any act that is directed against computers and computer parts, that uses computers as instruments of crime, or that involves computers and constitutes abuse. Today, because much of the crime committed with the use of computers occurs in cyberspace, many computer crimes fall under the broad label of cyber crime.

As mentioned earlier, most cyber crimes are not "new" crimes. Rather, they are existing crimes in which the Internet is the instrument of wrongdoing. The challenge for law enforcement is to apply traditional laws—which were designed to protect persons from physical harm or to safeguard their physical property—to crimes committed in cyberspace. Here we look at several activities that constitute cyber crimes against persons or property. Other cyber crimes will be discussed in later chapters of this text as they relate to particular topics.

Cyber Theft

In cyberspace, thieves are not subject to the physical limitations of the "real" world. A thief with dial-in access can steal data stored in a networked computer from anywhere on the globe. Only the speed of the connection and the thief's computer equipment limit the quantity of data that can be stolen.

Financial Crimes Computer networks provide opportunities for employees to commit crimes that can involve serious economic losses. For example, employees of a company's accounting department can transfer funds among accounts with little effort and often with less risk than that involved in transactions evidenced by paperwork.

Generally, the dependence of businesses on computer operations has left firms vulnerable to sabotage, fraud, embezzlement, and the theft of proprietary data, such as trade secrets and other intellectual property. As will be noted in Chapter 10, the piracy of intellectual property via the Internet is one of the most serious legal challenges facing lawmakers and the courts today.

Identity Theft A form of cyber theft that has become particularly troublesome in recent years is **identity theft.** Identity theft occurs when the wrongdoer steals a form of identification—such as a name, date of birth, or Social Security number—and uses the information to access the victim's financial resources. This crime existed to a certain extent before the widespread use of the Internet. Thieves would "steal" calling-card numbers by watching people using public telephones, or they would rifle through garbage to find bank account or credit-card numbers. The identity thieves would then use the calling-card or credit-card numbers or would withdraw funds from the victims' accounts.

The Internet, however, has turned identity theft into perhaps the fastest-growing financial crime in the United States. From the identity thief's perspective, the Internet provides an easy medium for using items such as stolen credit-card numbers or e-mail addresses while remaining protected by anonymity. An estimated 500,000 Americans are victims of identity theft each year.

Cyber Stalking

California enacted the first stalking law in 1990, in response to the murders of six women—including Rebecca Schaeffer, a television star—by men who had harassed them. The law made it a crime to harass or follow a person while making a "credible threat" that puts that person in reasonable fear for his or her safety or the safety of his or her immediate family.[21] **Cyber stalkers,** however, commit their crimes in cyberspace, finding their victims through Internet chat rooms, newsgroups or other bulletin boards, or e-mail. To close this "loophole" in existing stalking laws, more than three-fourths of the states now have laws specifically designed to combat cyber stalking and other forms of online harassment.

Note that cyber stalking can be even more threatening than physical stalking in some respects. While it takes a great deal of effort to physically stalk someone, it is relatively easy to harass a victim with electronic messages. Furthermore, the possibility of personal confrontation may discourage a stalker from actually following a victim. This disincentive is removed in cyberspace. Finally, there is always the possibility that a cyber stalker will eventually pose a physical threat to her or his target.

Hacking

Persons who use one computer to break into another are sometimes referred to as **hackers.** Hackers who break into computers without authorization often commit cyber theft. Sometimes, however, their principal aim is to prove how smart they are by gaining access to others' password-protected computers and causing random data errors or making unpaid-for telephone calls.[22]

The Computer Crime and Security Survey polled 538 companies and large government institutions and found that 85 percent had experienced security breaches through computer-based means in 2000. It is difficult to know, however, just how frequently hackers succeed in breaking into databases across the United States. The Federal Bureau of Investigation (FBI) estimates

---

21. Cal. Penal Code Section 646.9.
22. The total cost of crime on the Internet is estimated to be several billion dollars annually, but two-thirds of that total is said to consist of unpaid-for toll calls.

that only 25 percent of all corporations that suffer such security breaches report the incident to a law enforcement agency. Corporations do not want it to become publicly known that the security of their data has been breached. Admitting to a breach would be admitting to a certain degree of incompetence, which could damage their reputations.

Cyber Terrorism

CYBER TERRORIST
A hacker whose purpose is to exploit a target computer to create a serious impact, such as corrupting a program to sabotage a business.

Cyber terrorists are hackers who, rather than trying to gain attention, strive to remain undetected so that they can exploit computers to create a serious impact. Just as terrorists destroyed the World Trade Center towers and a portion of the Pentagon in September 2001, cyber terrorists might explode "logic bombs" to shut down central computers. Such activities can pose a danger to national security. After an American surveillance airplane collided with a Chinese military jet in 2001, hackers from China bombarded American Web sites with messages such as "Hack the USA" and "For our pilot Wang." Over a period of several weeks, these hackers were able to destroy or deface hundreds of Web sites, including some from the White House, the FBI, and NASA.

Businesses may also be targeted by cyber terrorists. The goals of a hacking operation might include a wholesale theft of data, such as a merchant's customer files, or the monitoring of a computer to discover a business firm's plans and transactions. A cyber terrorist might also insert false codes or data. For example, the processing control system of a food manufacturer could be changed to alter the levels of ingredients so that consumers of the food would become ill. A cyber terrorist attack on a major financial institution such as the New York Stock Exchange or a large bank could leave securities or money markets in flux and seriously affect the daily lives of millions of citizens. Similarly, any prolonged disruption of computer, cable, satellite, or telecommunications systems due to the actions of expert hackers would have serious repercussions on business operations—and national security—on a global level. Computer viruses are another tool that can be used by cyber terrorists to cripple communications networks.

Prosecuting Cyber Crimes

The location of cyber crime—cyberspace—has raised new issues in the investigation of crimes and the prosecution of offenders. A threshold issue is, of course, jurisdiction. A person who commits an act against a business in California, where the act is a cyber crime, might never have set foot in California but might instead reside in New York, or even in Canada, where the act may not be a crime. If the crime was committed via e-mail, the question arises as to whether the e-mail would constitute sufficient "minimum contacts" (see Chapter 4) for the victim's state to exercise jurisdiction over the perpetrator.

Identifying the wrongdoers can also be difficult. Cyber criminals do not leave physical traces, such as fingerprints or DNA samples, as evidence of their crimes. Even electronic "footprints" can be hard to find and follow. For example, e-mail may be sent through a remailer, an online service that guarantees that a message cannot be traced to its source.

For these reasons, laws written to protect physical property are difficult to apply in cyberspace. Nonetheless, state and federal governments have taken significant steps toward controlling cyber crime, both by applying existing criminal statutes and by enacting new laws that specifically address wrongs committed in cyberspace.

The Computer Fraud and Abuse Act Perhaps the most significant federal statute specifically addressing cyber crime is the Counterfeit Access Device and Computer Fraud and Abuse Act of 1984 (commonly known as the Computer Fraud and Abuse Act, or CFAA). This act, as amended by the National Information Infrastructure Protection Act of 1996,[23] provides, among other things, that a person who accesses a computer online, without authority, to obtain classified, restricted, or protected data, or attempts to do so, is subject to criminal prosecution. Such data could include financial and credit records, medical records, legal files, military and national security files, and other confidential information in government or private computers.

The crime has two elements: accessing a computer without authority and taking the data. If data are taken, a theft occurs. This theft is a felony if it is committed for a commercial purpose or for private financial gain or if the value of the stolen data (or computer time) exceeds $5,000. Penalties include fines and imprisonment for up to twenty years. A victim of computer theft can also bring a civil suit against the violator to obtain damages, an injunction, or other relief.

The CFAA defines *damage* as a "loss aggregating at least $5,000 in value during any one-year period to one or more individuals." At issue in the following case was whether the term *individuals* in this definition included a corporation.

---

23. 18 U.S.C. Section 1030.

CASE 7.4	United States v. Middleton

United States Court of Appeals, Ninth Circuit, 2000. 231 F.3d 1207.

BACKGROUND AND FACTS Nicholas Middleton worked as the personal computer administrator for Slip.net, an Internet service provider. His responsibilities included installing software and hardware on the company's computers and providing technical support to its employees. He had extensive knowledge of Slip.net's internal computer system. Dissatisfied with his job, Middleton quit. Through various subterfuges, he obtained access to a computer that the company had named "Lemming." Slip.net used Lemming to perform internal administrative functions and to host customers' Web sites. Lemming also contained the software for a new billing system. Middleton changed all the administrative passwords, altered the computer's registry, and deleted the entire billing system and two internal databases. To correct the damage cost Slip.net more than 150 worker-hours, in addition to the expense of an outside consultant and new software. Middleton was convicted of intentionally causing damage to a "protected computer" without authorization, in violation of the CFAA. He appealed to the U.S. Court of Appeals for the Ninth Circuit, arguing that the term *individuals,* as used in the statute, did not include a corporation.

IN THE WORDS OF THE COURT . . .

GRABER, Circuit Judge:

* * * * *

In 1996, Congress amended [the CFAA] to its current form, using the term "protected computer" and * * * expanding the number of computers that the statute "protected." The 1996 amendments also altered the definition of

(continued)

CASE 7.4—Continued

damage to read, "loss aggregating at least $5,000 in value during any one-year period to one or more individuals." We have found no explanation for this change. We do not believe, however, that this change evidences an intent to limit the statute's reach.

To the contrary, Congress has consciously broadened the statute consistently since its original enactment. The Senate Report on the 1996 amendments notes:

> As intended when the law was originally enacted, the Computer Fraud and Abuse statute facilitates addressing in a single statute the problem of computer crime. * * * *As computers continue to proliferate in businesses and homes, and new forms of computer crimes emerge, Congress must remain vigilant to ensure that the Computer Fraud and Abuse statute is up-to-date and provides law enforcement with the necessary legal framework to fight computer crime.* [Emphasis added.]

The report instructs that "the definition of 'damage' is amended to be sufficiently broad to encompass the types of harm against which people should be protected." The report notes that the interaction between the provision that prohibits conduct causing damage and the provision that defines damage will prohibit a hacker from stealing passwords from an existing log-on program, when this conduct requires "all system users to change their passwords, *and requires the system administrator to devote resources to resecuring the system.* * * * If the loss to the victim meets the required monetary threshold, the conduct should be criminal, and the victim should be entitled to relief." The reference to a "system administrator" suggests that a corporate victim is involved. That is, if Congress intended to limit the definition of the crime to conduct causing financial damage to a natural person only, its report would not use the example of a "system administrator" devoting resources to fix a computer problem as illustrative of the "damage" to be prevented and criminalized. The Senate Report's reference to the proliferation of computers in businesses as well as homes provides additional evidence of the Senate's intent to extend the statute's protections to corporate entities. [Emphasis added.]

DECISION AND REMEDY The U.S. Court of Appeals for the Ninth Circuit concluded that the CFAA's term *individual* included a corporation. The court affirmed Middleton's conviction. He was sentenced to three years' probation, subject to a condition of 180 days in community confinement, and ordered to pay $9,147 in restitution.

FOR CRITICAL ANALYSIS—Technological Consideration *How might Middleton's employer have avoided the damage to its computer systems?*

Other Federal Statutes The federal wire fraud statute, the Economic Espionage Act of 1996, and RICO, all of which were discussed earlier in this chapter, extend to crimes committed in cyberspace as well. Other federal statutes that may apply include the Electronic Fund Transfer Act of 1978, which makes unauthorized access to an electronic fund transfer system a crime; the Anticounterfeiting Consumer Protection Act of 1996, which increased penalties for stealing copyrighted or trademarked property; and the National Stolen Property Act of 1988, which concerns the interstate transport of stolen property. Recall from Chapter 5 that the federal government has also enacted laws (many of which have been challenged on constitutional grounds) to protect minors from online pornographic materials. In later chapters of this text, you will read about other federal statutes and regulations that are designed to address wrongs committed in cyberspace in specific areas of the law.

KEY TERMS

CHAPTER SUMMARY CRIMINAL LAW AND CYBER CRIMES

Civil Law and Criminal Law (See pages 194–195.)	1. *Civil law*—Spells out the duties that exist between persons or between citizens and their governments, excluding the duty not to commit crimes.
	2. *Criminal law*—Has to do with crimes, which are defined as wrongs against society proclaimed in statutes and punishable by society through fines, removal from public office, and/or imprisonment—and, in some cases, death. Because crimes are *offenses against society as a whole,* they are prosecuted by a public official, not by victims.
	3. *Key differences*—An important difference between civil and criminal law is that the standard of proof is higher in criminal cases (see Exhibit 7–1 for other differences between criminal and civil law).
	4. *Civil liability for criminal acts*—A criminal act may give rise to both criminal liability and tort liability (see Exhibit 7–2 for an example of criminal and tort liability for the same act).
Classification of Crimes (See pages 195–196.)	1. *Felonies*—Serious crimes punishable by death or by imprisonment in a penitentiary for more than one year.
	2. *Misdemeanors*—Under federal law and in most states, any crimes that are not felonies.
Criminal Liability (See pages 196–197.)	1. *Guilty act*—In general, some form of harmful act must be committed for a crime to exist.
	2. *Intent*—An intent to commit a crime, or a wrongful mental state, is required for a crime to exist.
Corporate Criminal Liability (See pages 197–199.)	1. *Liability of corporations*—Corporations normally are liable for the crimes committed by their agents and employees within the course and scope of their employment. Corporations cannot be imprisoned, but they can be fined or denied certain legal privileges.

(continued)

CHAPTER SUMMARY   CRIMINAL LAW AND CYBER CRIMES—Continued

Corporate Criminal Liability— continued	2. *Liability of corporate officers and directors*—Corporate directors and officers are personally liable for the crimes they commit and may be held liable for the actions of employees under their supervision.
Types of Crimes (See pages 199–204.)	1. *Violent crime*—Crimes that cause others to suffer physical harm or death. Examples include murder, assault and battery, rape, and robbery. 2. *Property crime*—Crimes in which the goal of the offender is some form of economic gain or the damaging of property. Examples include burglary, larceny, arson, receiving stolen goods, forgery, and obtaining goods by false pretenses. 3. *Public order crime*—Crimes contrary to public values and morals. Examples include public drunkenness, prostitution, gambling, and illegal drug use. 4. *White-collar crime*—Nonviolent crimes committed in the course of a legitimate occupation to obtain a personal or business advantage. Examples include embezzlement, mail and wire fraud, bribery, bankruptcy fraud, insider trading, and the theft of trade secrets. 5. *Organized crime*—Crime committed by groups operating illegitimately to satisfy the public's demand for illegal goods and services (such as narcotics and gambling). Often, organized crime involves *money laundering*—the establishment of legitimate enterprises through which "dirty" money obtained through criminal activities can be "laundered" and made to appear as legitimate income. The Racketeer Influenced and Corrupt Organizations Act (RICO) of 1970, which prohibits racketeering activity, was passed, in part, to control organized crime.
Defenses to Criminal Liability (See pages 204–207.)	1. *Infancy.* 6. *Duress.* 2. *Intoxication.* 7. *Justifiable use of force.* 3. *Insanity.* 8. *Entrapment.* 4. *Mistake.* 9. *Statute of limitations.* 5. *Consent.* 10. *Immunity.*
Constitutional Safeguards and Criminal Procedures (See pages 207–215.)	1. *Fourth Amendment*—Provides protection against unreasonable searches and seizures and requires that probable cause exist before a warrant for a search or an arrest can be issued. 2. *Fifth Amendment*—Requires due process of law, prohibits double jeopardy, and protects against self-incrimination. 3. *Sixth Amendment*—Provides guarantees of a speedy trial, a trial by jury, a public trial, the right to confront witnesses, and the right to counsel. 4. *Eighth Amendment*—Prohibits excessive bail and fines and cruel and unusual punishment. 5. *Exclusionary rule*—A criminal procedural rule that prohibits the introduction at trial of all evidence obtained in violation of constitutional rights, as well as any evidence derived from the illegally obtained evidence. 6. *Miranda rule*—A rule set forth by the Supreme Court in *Miranda v. Arizona* that individuals who are arrested must be informed of certain constitutional rights, including their right to counsel.

(continued)

CHAPTER SUMMARY CRIMINAL LAW AND CYBER CRIMES—Continued

Criminal Process (See pages 215–220.)	1. *Arrest, indictment, and trial*—Procedures governing arrest, indictment, and trial for a crime are designed to safeguard the rights of the individual against the state. See Exhibit *1–3* for the steps involved in prosecuting a criminal case. 2. *Sentencing guidelines*—Both the federal government and the states have established sentencing laws or guidelines. The federal sentencing guidelines indicate a range of penalties for each federal crime; federal judges must abide by these guidelines when imposing sentences on those convicted of federal crimes.
Cyber Crime (See pages 220–225.)	Cyber crime is any crime that occurs in cyberspace. Examples include cyber theft (financial crimes committed with the aid of computers, as well as identity theft), cyber stalking, hacking, and cyber terrorism. Significant federal statutes addressing cyber crimes include the Electronic Fund Transfer Act of 1978 and the Counterfeit Access Device and Computer Fraud and Abuse Act of 1984, as amended by the National Information Infrastructure Protection Act of 1996.

FOR REVIEW

1. What two elements must exist before a person can be held liable for a crime? Can a corporation be liable for crimes?
2. What are five broad categories of crimes? What is white-collar crime?
3. What defenses might be raised by criminal defendants to avoid liability for criminal acts?
4. What constitutional safeguards exist to protect persons accused of crimes? What are the basic steps in the criminal process?
5. What is cyber crime? What laws apply to crimes committed in cyberspace?

QUESTIONS AND CASE PROBLEMS

7–1. Criminal versus Civil Trials. In criminal trials, the defendant must be proved guilty beyond a reasonable doubt, whereas in civil trials, the defendant need only be proved guilty by a preponderance of the evidence. Discuss why a higher standard of proof is required in criminal trials.

7–2. Types of Crimes. The following situations are similar (all involve the theft of Makoto's television set), yet they represent three different crimes. Identify the three crimes, noting the differences among them.

(a) While passing Makoto's house one night, Sarah sees a portable television set left unattended on Makoto's lawn. Sarah takes the television set, carries it home, and tells everyone she owns it.

(b) While passing Makoto's house one night, Sarah sees Makoto outside with a portable television set. Holding Makoto at gunpoint, Sarah forces him to give up the set. Then Sarah runs away with it.

(c) While passing Makoto's house one night, Sarah sees a portable television set in a window. Sarah breaks the front-door lock, enters, and leaves with the set.

7–3. Types of Crimes. Which, if any, of the following crimes necessarily involve illegal activity on the part of more than one person?

(a) Bribery.
(b) Forgery.
(c) Embezzlement.
(d) Larceny.
(e) Receiving stolen property.

7–4. Double Jeopardy. Armington, while robbing a drugstore, shot and seriously injured Jennings, a drugstore clerk. Armington was subsequently convicted in a criminal trial of armed robbery and assault and battery. Jennings later brought a civil tort suit against Armington for damages.

Armington contended that he could not be tried again for the same crime, as that would constitute double jeopardy, which is prohibited by the Fifth Amendment to the Constitution. Is Armington correct? Explain.

7–5. Receiving Stolen Property. Rafael stops Laura on a busy street and offers to sell her an expensive wristwatch for a fraction of its value. After some questioning by Laura, Rafael admits that the watch is stolen property, although he says he was not the thief. Laura pays for and receives the wristwatch. Has Laura committed any crime? Has Rafael? Explain.

7–6. Defenses to Criminal Liability. The Child Protection Act of 1984 makes it a crime to receive knowingly through the mails sexually explicit depictions of children. After this act was passed, government agents found Keith Jacobson's name on a bookstore's mailing list. (Jacobson previously had ordered and received from a bookstore two *Bare Boys* magazines containing photographs of nude preteen and teenage boys.) To test Jacobson's willingness to break the law, government agencies sent mail to him, through five fictitious organizations and a bogus pen pal, over a period of two and a half years. Many of these "organizations" claimed that they had been founded to protect sexual freedom, freedom of choice, and so on. Jacobson eventually ordered a magazine. He testified at trial that he ordered the magazine because he was curious about "all the trouble and the hysteria over pornography and I wanted to see what the material was." When the magazine was delivered, he was arrested for violating the 1984 act. What defense discussed in this chapter might Jacobson raise to avoid criminal liability under the act? Explain fully. [*Jacobson v. United States*, 503 U.S. 540, 112 S.Ct. 1535, 118 L.Ed.2d 174 (1992)]

7–7. Searches and Seizures. The city of Ferndale enacted an ordinance regulating massage parlors. Among other things, the ordinance provided for periodic inspections of the establishments by "[t]he chief of police or other authorized inspectors from the City." Operators and employees of massage parlors in Ferndale filed a suit in a Michigan state court against the city. The plaintiffs pointed out that the ordinance did not require a warrant to conduct a search and argued in part that this was a violation of the Fourth Amendment. On what ground might the court uphold the ordinance? Do massage parlors qualify on this ground? Why or why not? [*Gora v. City of Ferndale*, 456 Mich. 704, 576 N.W.2d 141 (1998)]

7–8. Fifth Amendment. The federal government was investigating a corporation and its employees. The alleged criminal wrongdoing, which included the falsification of corporate books and records, occurred between 1993 and 1996 in one division of the corporation. In 1999, the corporation pleaded guilty and agreed to cooperate in an investigation of the individuals who might have been involved in the improper corporate activities. "Doe I," "Doe II," and "Doe III" were officers of the corporation during the period when the illegal activities occurred and worked in the division where the

wrongdoing took place. They were no longer working for the corporation, however, when, as part of the subsequent investigation, the government asked them to provide specific corporate documents in their possession. All three asserted the Fifth Amendment privilege against self-incrimination. The government asked a federal district court to order the three to produce the records. Corporate employees can be compelled to produce corporate records in a criminal proceeding because they hold the records as representatives of the corporation, to which the Fifth Amendment privilege against self-incrimination does not apply. Should *former* employees also be compelled to produce corporate records in their possession? Why or why not? [*In re Three Grand Jury Subpoenas* Duces Tecum *Dated January 29, 1999*, 191 F.3d 173 (2d Cir. 1999)]

Case Problem with Sample Answer

7–9. Computer Fraud. The District of Columbia Lottery Board licensed Soo Young Bae, a Washington, D.C., merchant, to operate a terminal that prints and dispenses lottery tickets for sale. Bae used the terminal to generate tickets with a face value of $525,586, for which he did not pay. The winning tickets among these had a total redemption value of $296,153, of which Bae successfully obtained all but $72,000. Bae pleaded guilty to computer fraud, and the court sentenced him to eighteen months in prison. In sentencing a defendant for fraud, a federal court must make a reasonable estimate of the victim's loss. The court determined that the value of the loss due to the fraud was $503,650—the market value of the tickets less the commission Bae would have received from the lottery board had he sold those tickets. Bae appealed, arguing that "[a]t the instant any lottery ticket is printed," it is worth whatever value the lottery drawing later assigns to it; that is, losing tickets have no value. Bae thus calculated the loss at $296,153, the value of his winning tickets. Should the U.S. Court of Appeals for the District of Columbia Circuit affirm or reverse Bae's sentence? Why? [*United States v. Bae*, 250 F.3d 774 (D.C.Cir. 2001)]

To view a sample answer for this case problem, go to this book's Web site at http://leet.weswtbuslaw.com and click on "Interactive Study Center."

7–10. Theft of Trade Secrets. Four Pillars Enterprise Co. is a Taiwanese company owned by Pin Yen Yang. Avery Dennison, Inc., a U.S. corporation, is one of Four Pillars's chief competitors in the manufacture of adhesives. In 1989, Victor Lee, an Avery employee, met Yang and Yang's daughter Hwei Chen. They agreed to pay Lee $25,000 a year to serve as a consultant to Four Pillars. Over the next eight years, Lee supplied the Yangs with confidential Avery reports, including information that Four Pillars used to make a new adhesive that had been developed by Avery. The Federal Bureau of Investigation (FBI) confronted Lee, and he agreed to cooperate in an operation to catch the Yangs. When Lee next met the Yangs, he showed them documents provided by the FBI. The documents bore "confidential" stamps, and Lee said that they were Avery's confidential property. The FBI arrested the Yangs with the documents in their possession. The Yangs and Four Pillars were charged with, among other crimes, the attempted theft of trade secrets. The defendants argued in part that it was impossible for them to have committed this crime because the documents were not actually trade secrets. Should the court acquit them? Why or why not? [*United States v. Yang*, 281 F.3d 534 (6th Cir. 2002)]

the murder. [*Illinois v. Perkins*, 496 U.S. 292, 110 S.Ct. 2394, 110 L.Ed.2d 243 (1990)]

1. Review the discussion of *Miranda v. Arizona* in this chapter's *Landmark in the Legal Environment* feature. Should Perkins's statements be suppressed—that is, not be treated as admissible evidence at trial—because he was not "read his rights," as required by the *Miranda* decision, prior to making his self-incriminating statements? Does *Miranda* apply to Perkins's situation?

2. Do you think that it is fair for the police to resort to trickery and deception to bring those who have committed crimes to justice? Why or why not? What rights or public policies must be balanced in deciding this issue?

A Question of Ethics & Social Responsibility

7-11. A troublesome issue concerning the constitutional privilege against self-incrimination has to do with "jail plants"—that is, undercover police officers placed in cells with criminal suspects to gain information from the suspects. For example, in one case the police placed an undercover agent, Parisi, in a jail cell block with Lloyd Perkins, who had been imprisoned on charges unrelated to the murder that Parisi was investigating. When Parisi asked Perkins if he had ever killed anyone, Perkins made statements implicating himself in the murder. Perkins was then charged with

Critical-Thinking Legal Question

7-12. Ray steals a purse from an unattended car at a gas station. Because the purse contains money and a handgun, Ray is convicted of grand theft of property (cash) and grand theft of a firearm. On appeal, Ray claims that he is not guilty of grand theft of a firearm because he did not know that the purse contained a gun. Can Ray be convicted of the crime of grand theft of a firearm even though he did not know that a gun was in the purse?

INTERACTING WITH THE INTERNET

For updated links to resources available on the Web, as well as a variety of other materials, visit this text's Web site at

http://leet.westbuslaw.com

The Bureau of Justice Statistics in the U.S. Department of Justice offers an impressive collection of statistics on crime at the following Web site:

http://www.ojp.usdoj.gov/bjs

For summaries of famous criminal cases and documents relating to these trials, go to Court TV's Web site at

http://www.courttv.com/index.html

If you would like to learn more about criminal procedures, the following site offers an "Anatomy of a Murder: A Trip through Our Nation's Legal Justice System":

http://library.thinkquest.org/2760/home.htm

At this site, you can also find a glossary of terms used in criminal law, view actual forms that are filled out during the course of an arrest, and learn about some controversial issues in criminal law.

Many state criminal codes are now online. To find your state's code, go to

http://www.findlaw.com

and select "State" under the link to "Laws: Cases and Codes."

You can learn about some of the constitutional questions raised by various criminal laws and procedures by going to the Web site of the American Civil Liberties Union at

http://www.aclu.org

The following Web site, which is maintained by the U.S. Department of Justice, offers information ranging from the various types of cyber crime to a description of how computers and the Internet are being used to prosecute cyber crime:

http://www.cybercrime.gov

ONLINE LEGAL RESEARCH EXERCISES

Go to **http://leet.westbuslaw.com**, the Web site that accompanies this text. Select "Interactive Study Center," and then click on "Chapter 7." There you will find the following Internet research exercises that you can perform to learn more about topics covered in this chapter.

Activity 7–1: SOCIAL PERSPECTIVE—Revisiting *Miranda*
Activity 7–2: MANAGEMENT PERSPECTIVE—Hackers
Activity 7–3: INTERNATIONAL PERSPECTIVE—Fighting Cyber Crime Worldwide

BEFORE THE TEST

Go to **http://leet.westbuslaw.com**, the Web site that accompanies this text. Select "Interactive Quizzes." You will find at least twenty interactive questions relating to this chapter.

Westlaw® Campus

If your textbook provided for a subscription to Westlaw® Campus, or if you have otherwise purchased access to the Westlaw Campus database, you can access any of the cases presented or cited in this chapter by using your Westlaw Campus account.

UNIT TWO   Cumulative Business Hypothetical

Jonatron, Inc., a battery manufacturer, has its headquarters in New Carlisle, Indiana.

1. Suppose that Jonatron, Inc., does business only within the state of Indiana. A Jonatron employee claims that the company has violated a federal employment law. Jonatron argues that it is not liable because the law applies only to employees of companies that are engaged in interstate commerce. What might a court decide? Discuss fully.

2. The Occupational Safety and Health Administration (OSHA) has proposed a new safety rule governing the handling of certain materials in the workplace, including those used by Jonatron in its manufacturing operations. Jonatron concludes that the rule, which will involve substantial compliance costs, will not significantly increase workplace safety. Jonatron sends a let-ter to OSHA indicating its objections to the proposed rule and enclosing research reports and other data supporting those objections. Does OSHA have any obligation to consider these objections? What procedures must OSHA follow when it makes new rules, such as this one?

3. The head of Jonatron's accounting department, Roy Olson, has to pay his daughter's college tuition within a week, or his daughter will not be able to continue taking classes. The payment due is over $20,000. Roy would be able to make the payment in two months, but cannot do so until then. The college refuses to wait that long. In desperation, Roy—through a fictitious bank account and some clever accounting—"borrows" funds from Jonatron. Before Roy can pay back the borrowed funds, an auditor discovers what Roy did. Jonatron's president alleges that Roy has "stolen" company funds and informs the police of the theft. Has Roy committed a crime? If so, what crime did he commit? Explain.

UNIT THREE
The Private Environment

CHAPTER **8**

Torts and Cyber Torts

CONTENTS

CHAPTER OBJECTIVES

After reading this chapter, you should be able to answer the following questions:

1. What is a tort?

2. What is the purpose of tort law? What are two basic categories of torts?

3. What are the four elements of negligence?

4. What defenses may be raised against claims of negligence?

5. What is a cyber tort, and how are tort theories being applied in cyberspace?

TORT
A civil wrong not arising from a breach of contract. A breach of a legal duty that proximately causes harm or injury to another.

BUSINESS TORT
The wrongful interference with another's business rights.

As Scott Turow's statement in the quotation below indicates, **torts** are wrongful actions.[1] Through tort law, society compensates those who have suffered injuries as a result of the wrongful conduct of others. Although some torts, such as assault and trespass, originated in the English common law, the field of tort law continues to expand. As new ways to commit wrongs are discovered, such as the use of the Internet to commit wrongful acts, the courts are extending tort law to cover these wrongs.

You will see in later chapters of this book that many of the lawsuits brought by or against business firms are based on the tort theories discussed in this chapter. Some of the torts examined here can occur in any context, including the business environment. Others traditionally have been referred to as **business torts**, which are defined as wrongful interferences with the business rights of others. Included in business torts are such vaguely worded concepts as *unfair competition* and *wrongfully*

> "'Tort' more or less means 'wrong' . . . . One of my friends [in law school] said that Torts is the course which proves that your mother was right."
> Scott Turow, 1949–
> (American lawyer and author)

---

1. The word *tort* is French for "wrong."

interfering with the business relations of others. Torts committed via the Internet are sometimes referred to as **cyber torts.** We look at how the courts have applied traditional tort law to wrongful actions in the online environment in the concluding pages of this chapter.

CYBER TORT
A tort committed via the Internet.

THE BASIS OF TORT LAW

Two notions serve as the basis of all torts: wrongs and compensation. Tort law recognizes that some acts are wrong because they cause injuries to others. In a tort action, one person or group brings a personal suit against another person or group to obtain compensation (money damages) or other relief for the harm suffered.

Generally, the purpose of tort law is to provide remedies for the invasion of various *protected interests.* Society recognizes an interest in personal physical safety, and tort law provides remedies for acts that cause physical injury or that interfere with physical security and freedom of movement. Society recognizes an interest in protecting real and personal property, and tort law provides remedies for acts that cause destruction or damage to property. Society also recognizes an interest in protecting certain intangible interests, such as personal privacy, family relations, reputation, and dignity, and tort law provides remedies for invasion of these protected interests.

There are two broad classifications of torts: *intentional torts* and *unintentional torts* (torts involving negligence). The classification of a particular tort depends largely on how the tort occurs (intentionally or negligently) and the surrounding circumstances.

INTENTIONAL TORTS AGAINST PERSONS

An **intentional tort,** as the term implies, requires *intent.* The **tortfeasor** (the one committing the tort) must intend to commit an act, the consequences of which interfere with the personal or business interests of another in a way not permitted by law. An evil or harmful motive is not required—in fact, the actor may even have a beneficial motive for committing what turns out to be a tortious act. In tort law, intent means only that the actor intended the consequences of his or her act or knew with substantial certainty that specific consequences would result from the act. The law generally assumes that individuals intend the *normal* consequences of their actions. Thus, forcefully pushing another—even if done in jest and without any evil motive—is an intentional tort (if injury results), because a person who is forcefully pushed can ordinarily be expected to fall down.

This section discusses intentional torts against persons, which include assault and battery, false imprisonment, infliction of emotional distress, defamation, invasion of the right to privacy, appropriation, misrepresentation, and wrongful interference.

INTENTIONAL TORT
A wrongful act knowingly committed.

TORTFEASOR
One who commits a tort.

Assault and Battery

Any intentional, unexcused act that creates in another person a reasonable apprehension or fear of immediate harmful or offensive contact is an **assault.** Apprehension is not the same as fear. If a contact is such that a reasonable

ASSAULT
Any word or action intended to make another person fearful of immediate physical harm; a reasonably believable threat.

person would want to avoid it, and if there is a reasonable basis for believing that the contact will occur, then the plaintiff suffers apprehension whether or not he or she is afraid. The interest protected by tort law concerning assault is the freedom from having to expect harmful or offensive contact. The occurrence of apprehension is enough to justify compensation.

The *completion* of the act that caused the apprehension, if it results in harm to the plaintiff, is a **battery,** which is defined as an unexcused and harmful or offensive physical contact *intentionally* performed. ● EXAMPLE 1 For example, suppose that Ivan threatens Jean with a gun, then shoots her. The pointing of the gun at Jean is an assault; the firing of the gun (if the bullet hits Jean) is a battery. ● The interest protected by tort law concerning battery is the right to personal security and safety. The contact can be harmful, or it can be merely offensive (such as an unwelcome kiss). Physical injury need not occur. The contact can involve any part of the body or anything attached to it—for example, a hat or other item of clothing, a purse, or a chair or an automobile in which one is sitting. Whether the contact is offensive or not is determined by the *reasonable person standard.*[2] The contact can be made by the defendant or by some force the defendant sets in motion—for example, a rock thrown, food poisoned, or a stick swung.

BATTERY
The unprivileged, intentional touching of another.

Compensation If the plaintiff shows that there was contact, and the jury agrees that the contact was offensive, the plaintiff has a right to compensation. There is no need to show that the defendant acted out of malice; the person could have just been joking or playing around. The underlying motive does not matter, only the intent to bring about the harmful or offensive contact to the plaintiff. In fact, proving a motive is never necessary (but is sometimes relevant). A plaintiff may be compensated for the emotional harm or loss of reputation resulting from a battery, as well as for physical damage.

Defenses to Assault and Battery A number of legally recognized **defenses** (reasons why plaintiffs should not obtain what they are seeking) can be raised by a defendant who is sued for assault, battery, or both:

DEFENSE
Reasons that a defendant offers in an action or suit as to why the plaintiff should not obtain what he or she is seeking.

1. *Consent.* When a person consents to the act that damages her or him, there is generally no liability (legal responsibility) for the damage done.
2. *Self-defense.* An individual who is defending his or her life or physical well-being can claim self-defense. In situations of both *real* and *apparent* danger, a person may use whatever force is *reasonably* necessary to prevent harmful contact.
3. *Defense of others.* An individual can act in a reasonable manner to protect others who are in real or apparent danger.
4. *Defense of property.* Reasonable force may be used in attempting to remove intruders from one's home, although force that is likely to cause death or great bodily injury can never be used just to protect property.

BE AWARE Some of these same four defenses can be raised by a defendant who is sued for torts other than assault and battery.

False Imprisonment

False imprisonment is defined as the intentional confinement or restraint of another person's activities without justification. False imprisonment interferes with the freedom to move without restraint. The confinement can be accom-

---

2. The *reasonable person standard* is a test of how a reasonable person would have acted under the same circumstances. See "The Duty of Care and Its Breach" later in this chapter.

plished through the use of physical barriers, physical restraint, or threats of physical force. Moral pressure or threats of future harm do not constitute false imprisonment. In addition, it is essential that the person being restrained not willingly comply with the restraint.

Businesspersons are often confronted with suits for false imprisonment after they have attempted to confine a suspected shoplifter for questioning. Under the "privilege to detain" granted to merchants in some states, a merchant can use the defense of *probable cause* to justify delaying a suspected shoplifter. Probable cause exists when there is sufficient evidence to support the belief that a person is guilty. Although laws governing false imprisonment vary from state to state, generally they require that any detention be conducted in a *reasonable* manner and for only a *reasonable* length of time.

Infliction of Emotional Distress

The tort of *infliction of emotional distress* can be defined as an intentional act that amounts to extreme and outrageous conduct resulting in severe emotional distress to another. • EXAMPLE 2 A prankster telephones an individual and says that the person's spouse has just been in a horrible accident. As a result, the individual suffers intense mental pain or anxiety. The caller's behavior is deemed to be extreme and outrageous conduct that exceeds the bounds of decency accepted by society and is therefore **actionable** (capable of serving as the ground for a lawsuit). •

The tort of infliction of emotional distress poses several problems for the courts. One concern is the difficulty of proving the existence of emotional suffering. For this reason, courts in many jurisdictions require that the emotional distress be evidenced by some physical symptom or illness or some emotional disturbance that can be documented by a psychiatric consultant or other medical professional.

Another problem is that emotional distress claims must be subject to some limitation, or they could flood the courts with lawsuits. A society in which individuals are rewarded if they are unable to endure the normal emotional stresses of day-to-day living is obviously undesirable. Therefore, the law usually holds that indignity or annoyance alone is not enough to support a lawsuit based on infliction of emotional distress. Repeated annoyances (such as those experienced by a person who is being stalked), however, coupled with threats, are enough. In the business context, the repeated use of extreme methods to collect a delinquent account may be actionable.

Defamation

Defamation of character involves wrongfully hurting a person's good reputation. The law has imposed a general duty on all persons to refrain from making false, defamatory statements about others. Breaching this duty orally involves the tort of **slander;** breaching it in writing (or other permanent medium, such as a digital recording) involves the tort of **libel.** The tort of defamation also arises when a false statement is made about a person's product, business, or title to property. We deal with these torts later in the chapter.

The common law has traditionally defined four types of false utterances that are considered slander *per se* (meaning that no proof of injury or harm is required for these false utterances to be actionable):

1. A statement that another has a loathsome communicable disease.

ACTIONABLE
Capable of serving as the basis of a lawsuit. An actionable claim can be pursued in a lawsuit or other court action.

DEFAMATION
Anything published or publicly spoken that causes injury to another's good name, reputation, or character.

SLANDER
Defamation in oral form.

LIBEL
Defamation in writing or other permanent form (such as a digital recording) having the quality of permanence.

2. A statement that another has committed improprieties while engaging in a profession or trade.

3. A statement that another has committed or has been imprisoned for a serious crime.

4. A statement that a woman is unchaste.

The Publication Requirement The basis of the tort of defamation is the publication of a statement or statements that hold an individual up to contempt, ridicule, or hatred. *Publication* here means that the defamatory statements are communicated to persons other than the defamed party. ● **EXAMPLE 3** If Thompson writes Andrews a private letter accusing him of embezzling funds, the action does not constitute libel. If Peters calls Gordon dishonest, unattractive, and incompetent when no one else is around, the action does not constitute slander. In neither case was the message communicated to a third party.●

The courts have generally held that even dictating a letter to an assistant constitutes publication, although the publication may be privileged (privileged communications will be discussed shortly). Moreover, if a third party overhears defamatory statements by chance, the courts usually hold that this constitutes publication. Defamatory statements made via the Internet are also actionable. Further, any individual who republishes or repeats defamatory statements is liable even if that person reveals the source of the statements.

Defenses against Defamation Truth is normally an absolute defense against a defamation charge. In other words, if the defendant in a defamation suit can prove that his or her allegedly defamatory statements were true, the defendant will not be liable.

Another defense that is sometimes raised is that the statements were **privileged** communications, and thus the defendant is immune from liability. Privileged communications are of two types: absolute and qualified. Only in judicial proceedings and certain legislative proceedings is *absolute* privilege granted. For example, statements made in the courtroom by attorneys and judges during a trial are absolutely privileged. So are statements made by government officials during legislative floor debate, even if the officials make such statements maliciously—that is, knowing them to be untrue. An absolute privilege is granted in these situations because judicial and legislative personnel deal with matters that are so much in the public interest that the parties involved should be able to speak out fully and freely without restriction.

In general, false and defamatory statements that are made about *public figures* (public officials who exercise substantial governmental power and any persons in the public limelight) and that are published in the press are privileged if they are made without **actual malice**.[3] To be made with actual malice, a statement must be made with either *knowledge of falsity* or *a reckless disregard of the truth*. Statements made about public figures, especially when they are made via a public medium, are usually related to matters of general public interest; they are made about people who substantially affect all of us. Furthermore, public figures generally have some access to a public medium for answering disparaging falsehoods about themselves; private individuals do not. For these reasons, public figures have a greater burden of proof in defamation cases (they must prove actual malice) than do private individuals.

---

3. *New York Times Co. v. Sullivan,* 376 U.S. 254, 84 S.Ct. 710, 11 L.Ed.2d 686 (1964).

"Reputation, reputation, reputation! Oh, I have lost my reputation! I have lost the immortal part of myself, and what remains is bestial."

WILLIAM SHAKESPEARE,
1564–1616
(English dramatist and poet)

PRIVILEGE
In tort law, the ability to act contrary to another person's right without that person's having legal redress for such acts. Privilege may be raised as a defense to defamation.

ACTUAL MALICE
Real and demonstrable evil intent. In a defamation suit, a statement made about a public figure normally must be made with actual malice (with either knowledge of its falsity or a reckless disregard of the truth) for liability to be incurred.

Invasion of the Right to Privacy

A person has a right to solitude and freedom from prying public eyes—in other words, to privacy. As discussed in Chapter 5, the Supreme Court has held that a fundamental right to privacy is also implied by various amendments to the U.S. Constitution. Some state constitutions explicitly provide for privacy rights. In addition, a number of federal and state statutes have been enacted to protect individual rights in specific areas. Tort law also safeguards these rights through the tort of *invasion of privacy.* Four acts qualify as an invasion of privacy:

1. *The use of a person's name, picture, or other likeness for commercial purposes without permission.* This tort, which is usually referred to as the tort of *appropriation,* will be examined shortly.
2. *Intrusion in an individual's affairs or seclusion.* For example, invading someone's home or illegally searching someone's briefcase is an invasion of privacy. The tort has been held to extend to eavesdropping by wiretap, the unauthorized scanning of a bank account, compulsory blood testing, and window peeping.
3. *Publication of information that places a person in a false light.* This could be a story attributing to the person ideas not held or actions not taken by the person. (Publishing such a story could involve the tort of defamation as well.)
4. *Public disclosure of private facts about an individual that an ordinary person would find objectionable.* A newspaper account of a private citizen's sex life or financial affairs could be an actionable invasion of privacy.

A pressing issue in today's online world has to do with the privacy rights of Internet users. This is particularly true with respect to personal information collected not only by government agencies but also by online merchants. Internet users face significant privacy issues in the employment context as well. In the following case, for example, a state government agency threatened to disclose to the media the personal e-mail messages that an employee had sent or received over the Internet from her work computer. The rules concerning public disclosure by government agencies do not apply in the context of private employment. The case illustrates, however, the problems associated with sending and receiving personal e-mail in any workplace where it is prohibited. (See Chapter 16 for a more detailed examination of privacy rights in the employment context.)

CASE 8.1   Tiberino v. Spokane County

Court of Appeals of Washington,
Division 3, 2000.
103 Wash.App. 680,
13 P.3d 1104.

BACKGROUND AND FACTS In August 1998, Gina Tiberino was hired as a secretary in the Prosecuting Attorney's Office in Spokane County, Washington. The county provided her with a personal computer with e-mail access. According to county policy, Tiberino was told that her employer could monitor all e-mail, that she was not to put anything into an e-mail message that she would not want on the front page of

a newspaper, and that county equipment was not for personal use. In October, Tiberino's co-workers complained that she was using her computer to send personal e-mail over the Internet. Her supervisor reminded her that county computers were not to be used for personal business. In November, she was discharged for unsatisfactory work performance related to her use of e-mail for personal matters. When she threatened to sue the county, her ex-employer printed out all of her e-mail. Of 551 items, 467 were personal

(continued)

CASE 8.1—Continued

messages. When the media asked the prosecutor's office to release copies of the e-mail (more than 3,700 pages), Tiberino filed a suit in a Washington state court against the county to stop the release. The court concluded that the messages were "public records" and

refused to grant her request. On Tiberino's appeal, the state intermediate appellate court agreed that the messages were public records. The court then considered whether, under a state statutory exception, their disclosure would violate her right to privacy.

IN THE WORDS OF THE COURT . . .

KURTZ, C.J. [Chief Judge]

*   *   *   *

A person's right to privacy is violated only if disclosure of information about the person: (1) [w]ould be highly offensive to a reasonable person, and (2) is not of legitimate concern to the public. *   *   *

*   *   *   *

Ms. Tiberino argues that the purely personal nature of her e-mails to her mother, sister and friends makes it clear that public disclosure would be highly offensive to any reasonable person. Ms. Tiberino's e-mails contain intimate details about her personal and private life and do not discuss specific instances of misconduct. *An individual has a privacy interest whenever information which reveals unique facts about those named is linked to an identifiable individual.* *   *   * Any reasonable person would find disclosure of Ms. Tiberino's e-mails to be highly offensive. [Emphasis added.]

*   *   *   *

For the e-mails to be exempt from disclosure, Ms. Tiberino must also show that the public has no legitimate concern requiring release of the e-mails. Ms. Tiberino contends that the disclosure of private e-mails could decrease the efficiency and morale of government employees. The County argues that the County employees were on notice that the computers should not be used for personal business, so the disclosure of their e-mail would not affect the efficient administration of government.

*   *   *   *

Generally, records of governmental agency expenditures for employee salaries, including vacation and sick leave, and taxpayer-funded benefits are of legitimate public interest and therefore not exempt from disclosure. Certainly, there exists a reasonable concern by the public that government conduct itself fairly and use public funds responsibly.

*   *   *   *

However, *   *   * [t]he content of Ms. Tiberino's e-mails is personal and is unrelated to governmental operations. Certainly, the public has an interest in seeing that public employees are not spending their time on the public payroll pursuing personal interests. But it is the amount of time spent on personal matters, not the content of personal e-mails or phone calls or conversations, that is of public interest. The fact that Ms. Tiberino sent 467 e-mails over a 40 working-day time frame is of significance in her termination action and the public has a legitimate interest in having that information. But what she said in those e-mails is of no public significance. The public has no legitimate concern requiring release of the e-mails and they should be exempt from disclosure.

DECISION AND REMEDY The state intermediate appellate court reversed the judgment of the lower court. The appellate court concluded that Tiberino's e-mail messages were "public records" but that they were exempt from public disclosure as personal information.

FOR CRITICAL ANALYSIS—Social Consideration *Instead of giving rise to a lawsuit, as in the* Tiberino *case, how might an employer's monitoring of employees' e-mail prevent litigation?*

Appropriation

The use by one person of another person's name, likeness, or other identifying characteristic, without permission and for the benefit of the user, constitutes the tort of **appropriation.** Under the law, an individual's right to privacy normally includes the right to the exclusive use of her or his identity.

● **EXAMPLE 4** Vanna White, the hostess of the popular television game show *Wheel of Fortune,* brought a case against Samsung Electronics America, Inc. Without White's permission, Samsung included in an advertisement for its videocassette recorders a depiction of a robot dressed in a wig, gown, and jewelry, posed in a scene that resembled the *Wheel of Fortune* set, in a stance for which White is famous. The court held in White's favor, holding that the tort of appropriation does not require the use of a celebrity's name or likeness. The court stated that Samsung's robot ad left "little doubt" as to the identity of the celebrity whom the ad was meant to depict.[4]●

Cases of wrongful appropriation, or misappropriation, may also involve the rights of those who invest time and money in the creation of a special system, such as a method of broadcasting sports events. In addition, commercial misappropriation may occur when a person takes and uses the property of another for the sole purpose of capitalizing unfairly on the goodwill or reputation of the property owner.

APPROPRIATION
In tort law, the use by one person of another person's name, likeness, or other identifying characteristic without permission and for the benefit of the user.

Misrepresentation (Fraud)

A misrepresentation leads another to believe in a condition that is different from the condition that actually exists. This is often accomplished through a false or an incorrect statement. Misrepresentations may be innocently made by someone who is unaware of the existing facts, but the tort of **fraudulent misrepresentation,** or fraud, involves intentional deceit for personal gain. The tort includes several elements:

1. Misrepresentation of facts or conditions with knowledge that they are false or with reckless disregard for the truth.
2. Intent to induce another to rely on the misrepresentation.
3. Justifiable reliance by the deceived party.
4. Damages suffered as a result of the reliance.
5. Causal connection between the misrepresentation and the injury suffered.

FRAUDULENT MISREPRESENTATION
Any misrepresentation, either by misstatement or by omission of a material fact, knowingly made with the intention of deceiving another and on which a reasonable person would and does rely to his or her detriment.

For fraud to occur, more than mere **puffery,** or *seller's talk,* must be involved. Fraud exists only when a person represents as a fact something he or she knows is untrue. For example, it is fraud to claim that a building does not leak when one knows that it does. Facts are objectively ascertainable, whereas seller's talk is not. "I am the best accountant in town" is seller's talk. The speaker is not trying to represent something as fact, because the term *best* is a subjective, not an objective, term.

Normally, the tort of misrepresentation or fraud occurs only when there is reliance on a *statement of fact.* Sometimes, however, reliance on a *statement of opinion* may involve the tort of misrepresentation if the individual making the statement of opinion has a superior knowledge of the subject matter. For example, when a lawyer makes a statement of opinion about the law in a state in which the lawyer is licensed to practice, a court would construe reliance on

PUFFERY
A salesperson's exaggerated claims concerning the quality of items offered for sale. Such claims involve opinions rather than facts and are not considered to be legally binding promises or warranties.

---

4. *White v. Samsung Electronics America, Inc.,* 971 F.2d 1395 (9th Cir. 1992).

such a statement to be equivalent to reliance on a statement of fact. We examine fraudulent misrepresentation in further detail in Chapter 12, in the context of contract law.

Wrongful Interference

Business torts involving wrongful interference are generally divided into two categories: wrongful interference with a contractual relationship and wrongful interference with a business relationship.

Wrongful Interference with a Contractual Relationship A landmark case relating to *intentional interference with a contractual relationship* involved an opera singer, Joanna Wagner, who was under contract to sing for a man named Lumley for a specified period of years. A man called Gye, who knew of this contract, nonetheless "enticed" Wagner to refuse to carry out the agreement, and Wagner began to sing for Gye. Gye's action constituted a tort because it wrongfully interfered with the contractual relationship between Wagner and Lumley.[5] (Note that Wagner's refusal to carry out the agreement also entitled Lumley to sue Wagner for breach of contract—see Chapter 12.)

Three elements are necessary for wrongful interference with a contractual relationship to occur:

> **REMEMBER** It is the intent to do an act that is important in tort law, not the motive behind the intent.

1. A valid, enforceable contract must exist between two parties.
2. A third party must know that this contract exists.
3. The third party must *intentionally* cause either of the two parties to breach the contract.

The contract may be between a firm and its employees or a firm and its customers. Sometimes a competitor of a firm draws away one of the firm's key employees. If the original employer can show that the competitor induced the breach—that is, that the former employee would not otherwise have broken the contract—damages can be recovered from the competitor.

The following case illustrates the elements of the tort of wrongful interference with a contractual relationship in the context of a contract between an independent sales representative and his agent (agency relationships are discussed in Chapter 16). The case was complicated by the existence of a second contract between the sales representative and the third party.

---

5. *Lumley v. Gye,* 118 Eng.Rep. 749 (1853).

CASE 8.2   Mathis v. Liu

United States Court of Appeals, Eighth Circuit, 2002.
276 F.3d 1027.

BACKGROUND AND FACTS

Ching and Alex Liu own Pacific Cornetta, Inc. In 1997, Pacific Cornetta entered into a contract with Lawrence Mathis, under which Mathis agreed to solicit orders for Pacific Cornetta's products from Kmart Corporation for a commission of 5 percent on net sales. Under the terms, either party could terminate the contract at any time. The next year, Mathis entered into a one-year contract with John Evans, under which Evans agreed to serve as Mathis's agent to solicit orders from Kmart for the product lines that Mathis represented, including Pacific Cornetta, for a commission of 1 percent on net sales. Under the terms of this contract, either party

CASE 8.2—Continued

could terminate it only on written notice of six months. A few months later, Pacific Cornetta persuaded Evans to break his contract with Mathis and enter into a contract with Pacific Cornetta to be its sales representative to Kmart. Evans terminated his contract with Mathis without notice. Two days later, Pacific Cornetta terminated its contract with Mathis. Mathis filed a suit in a federal district court against the Lius and Pacific Cornetta, alleging in part wrongful interference with a contractual relationship. The court issued a judgment that included a ruling in Mathis's favor on this claim, but Mathis appealed the amount of damages to the U.S. Court of Appeals for the Eighth Circuit.

IN THE WORDS OF THE COURT . . .

MORRIS SHEPHARD ARNOLD, Circuit Judge.

* * * *

* * * *[A] defendant is liable for tortious interference only if the defendant's interference with some relevant advantage was improper. [The] courts [look at several considerations] to determine whether a defendant's interference is improper.* These considerations include the nature of the actor's conduct[,] * * * the actor's motive[,] * * * the interests of the other with which the actor's conduct interferes[,] * * * the interests sought to be advanced by the actor[,] * * * the social interests in protecting the freedom of action of the actor and the contractual interests of the other[,] * * * the proximity or remoteness of the actor's conduct to the interference[,] and * * * the relations between the parties. [Emphasis added.]

We conclude that Mr. Mathis made out a * * * case on this element of his claim. If Mr. Evans's agency arrangement with Mr. Mathis had been purely at-will [a legal doctrine under which a contractual relationship can be terminated at any time by either party for any or no reason], we do not believe that Pacific Cornetta's successful effort to hire Mr. Evans * * * would have risen to the level of impropriety necessary to make out a case for tortious interference. That is because a party's interference with an at-will contract is primarily an interference with the future relation between the parties, and *when an at-will contract is terminated there is no breach of it.* In such circumstances, the interfering party is free for its own competitive advantage, to obtain the future benefits for itself by causing the termination, provided it uses suitable means. [Emphasis added.]

Mr. Evans's contract with Mr. Mathis, however, did not create a simple at-will arrangement because Mr. Evans could terminate it only after giving Mr. Mathis six months' notice of his intention to do so. In these circumstances, we think that the jury was entitled to conclude that Pacific Cornetta's blandishments [flattering statements] were improper, especially since *inducing a breach of contract absent compelling justification is, in and of itself, improper.* [Emphasis added.]

* * * *

Mr. Mathis asked for damages for the loss of anticipatory profits on his tortious interference claim. He argues that the damages that the jury awarded were supported by Mr. Evans's sales of * * * Pacific Cornetta products to Kmart [after Pacific Cornetta terminated the firm's contract with Mathis].

* * * *

We reject this theory * * * . Mr. Mathis's losses on these sales were a result of Pacific Cornetta exercising its right to terminate its contract with him at will, not Pacific Cornetta's tortious interference, and the losses were therefore not recoverable under a theory of tortious interference.

(continued)

CASE 8.2—Continued

DECISION AND REMEDY The U.S. Court of Appeals for the Eighth Circuit affirmed the judgment of the lower court. The appellate court concluded that the defendants had committed wrongful interference with Mathis's contract with Evans. Evans's sales of Pacific Cornetta products after Pacific Cornetta terminated its contract with Mathis could not furnish a basis for an award of damages on this claim, however, because the firm's contract with Mathis was terminable at will.

FOR CRITICAL ANALYSIS—Ethical Consideration *Does the ruling in this case mean that Mathis is entirely without recourse? Could he sue Evans for anything?*

PREDATORY BEHAVIOR
Business behavior that is undertaken with the intention of unlawfully driving competitors out of the market.

"Anyone can win unless there happens to be a second entry."

GEORGE ADE,
1866–1944
(American humorist)

REMEMBER What society and the law consider permissible often depends on the circumstances.

Wrongful Interference with a Business Relationship Businesspersons devise countless schemes to attract customers, but they are forbidden by the courts to interfere unreasonably with another's business in their attempts to gain a share of the market. There is a difference between competitive methods and **predatory behavior**—actions undertaken with the intention of unlawfully driving competitors completely out of the market.

The distinction usually depends on whether a business is attempting to attract customers in general or to solicit only those customers who have shown an interest in a similar product or service of a specific competitor. If a shopping center contains two shoe stores, an employee of Store A cannot be positioned at the entrance of Store B for the purpose of diverting customers to Store A. This type of activity constitutes the tort of wrongful interference with a business relationship, which is commonly considered to be an unfair trade practice. If this type of activity were permitted, Store A would reap the benefits of Store B's advertising.

Defenses to Wrongful Interference A person will not be liable for the tort of wrongful interference with a contractual or business relationship if it can be shown that the interference was justified, or permissible. Bona fide competitive behavior is a permissible interference even if it results in the breaking of a contract. ●**EXAMPLE 5** If Antonio's Meats advertises so effectively that it induces Beverly's Restaurant Chain to break its contract with Otis Meat Company, Otis Meat Company will be unable to recover against Antonio's Meats on a wrongful interference theory. After all, the public policy that favors free competition in advertising outweighs any possible instability that such competitive activity might cause in contractual relations.●

INTENTIONAL TORTS AGAINST PROPERTY

Intentional torts against property include trespass to land, trespass to personal property, conversion, and disparagement of property. These torts are wrongful actions that interfere with individuals' legally recognized rights with regard to their land or personal property. The law distinguishes real property from personal property (see Chapter 21). *Real property* is land and things "permanently" attached to the land. *Personal property* consists of all other items, which are basically movable. Thus, a house and lot are real property, whereas the furniture inside a house is personal property. Money and stocks and bonds are also personal property.

Trespass to Land

A **trespass to land** occurs whenever a person, without permission, enters onto, above, or below the surface of land that is owned by another; causes anything to enter onto the land; remains on the land; or permits anything to remain on it. Actual harm to the land is not an essential element of this tort because the tort is designed to protect the right of an owner to exclusive possession of his or her property. Common types of trespass to land include walking or driving on the land, shooting a gun over the land, throwing rocks at a building that belongs to someone else, building a dam across a river and thus causing water to back up on someone else's land, and placing part of one's building on an adjoining landowner's property.

Trespass Criteria, Rights, and Duties Before a person can be a trespasser, the owner of the real property (or other person in actual and exclusive possession of the property) must establish that person as a trespasser. For example, "posted" trespass signs expressly establish as a trespasser a person who ignores these signs and enters onto the property. A guest in your home is not a trespasser—unless she or he has been asked to leave but refuses. Any person who enters onto your property to commit an illegal act (such as a thief entering a lumberyard at night to steal lumber) is established impliedly as a trespasser, without posted signs.

At common law, a trespasser is liable for damages caused to the property and generally cannot hold the owner liable for injuries sustained on the premises. This common law rule is being abandoned in many jurisdictions in favor of a "reasonable duty of care" rule that varies depending on the status of the parties; for example, a landowner may have a duty to post a notice that the property is patrolled by guard dogs. Furthermore, under the "attractive nuisance" doctrine, children do not assume the risks of the premises if they are attracted to the premises by some object, such as a swimming pool, an abandoned building, or a sand pile. Trespassers normally can be removed from the premises through the use of reasonable force without the owner's being liable for assault and battery.

Defenses against Trespass to Land Trespass to land involves wrongful interference with another person's real property rights. If it can be shown that the trespass was warranted, however, as when a trespasser enters to assist someone in danger, a defense exists. Another defense exists when the trespasser can show that he or she had a license to come onto the land. A *licensee* is one who is invited (or allowed to enter) onto the property of another for the licensee's benefit. A person who enters another's property to read an electric meter, for example, is a licensee. When you purchase a ticket to attend a movie or sporting event, you are licensed to go onto the property of another to view that movie or event. Note that licenses to enter onto another's property are *revocable* by the property owner. If a property owner asks a meter reader to leave and the meter reader refuses to do so, the meter reader at that point becomes a trespasser.

Trespass to Personal Property

Whenever any individual unlawfully harms the personal property of another or otherwise interferes with the personal property owner's right to exclusive possession and enjoyment of that property, **trespass to personal property—**

A sign warns trespassers. Should a trespasser be allowed to recover from a landowner for injuries sustained on the premises?

TRESPASS TO LAND
The entry onto, above, or below the surface of land owned by another without the owner's permission or legal authorization.

TRESPASS TO PERSONAL PROPERTY
The unlawful taking or harming of another's personal property; interference with another's right to the exclusive possession of his or her personal property.

also called *trespass to personalty*[6]—occurs. If a student takes another student's business law book as a practical joke and hides it so that the owner is unable to find it for several days prior to a final examination, the student has engaged in a trespass to personal property.

If it can be shown that trespass to personal property was warranted, then a complete defense exists. Most states, for example, allow automobile repair shops to hold a customer's car (under what is called an *artisan's lien*, discussed in Chapter 15) when the customer refuses to pay for repairs already completed.

Conversion

CONVERSION
The act of wrongfully taking or retaining possession of a person's personal property and placing it in the service of another.

Whenever personal property is wrongfully taken from its rightful owner or possessor and placed in the service of another, the act of **conversion** occurs. Conversion is defined as any act depriving an owner of personal property without that owner's permission and without just cause. Conversion is the civil side of crimes related to theft. A store clerk who steals merchandise from the store commits a crime and engages in the tort of conversion at the same time. When conversion occurs, the lesser offense of trespass to personal property usually occurs as well. If the initial taking of the property was unlawful, there is trespass; retention of that property is conversion. If the initial taking of the property was permitted by the owner or if for some other reason the taking was not a trespass, failure to return the property may still be conversion.

Even if a person mistakenly believed that she or he was entitled to the property, a tort of conversion may occur. In other words, good intentions are not a defense against conversion; in fact, conversion can be an entirely innocent act. Someone who buys stolen goods, for example, is guilty of conversion even if he or she did not know that the goods were stolen. If the true owner brings a tort action against the buyer, the buyer must either return the property to the owner or pay the owner the full value of the property, despite having already paid the thief.

A successful defense against the charge of conversion is that the purported owner does not in fact own the property or does not have a right to possess it that is superior to the right of the holder. Necessity is another possible defense against conversion. ● **EXAMPLE 6** If Abrams takes Mendoza's cat, Abrams is guilty of conversion. If Mendoza sues Abrams, Abrams must return the cat or pay damages. If, however, the cat has rabies and Abrams took the cat to protect the public, Abrams has a valid defense—necessity (and perhaps even self-defense, if he can prove that he was in danger because of the cat).●

Conversion was one of the claims in the following case.

---

6. Pronounced *per*-sun-ul-tee.

CASE 8.3	Pearl Investments, LLC v. Standard I/O, Inc.

United States District Court,
District of Maine, 2003.
257 F.Supp.2d 326.

BACKGROUND AND FACTS Pearl Investments, LLC, operates automated stock-trading computer systems (ATSs) in Portland, Maine. Standard

I/O, Inc., provides custom software-programming services. Jesse Chunn owns Standard. In April 2000, Pearl hired Standard to develop software for Pearl's ATSs. Standard installed the software on several of Pearl's servers, including one Pionex server, at a computer facility maintained by On-Site Trading, Inc., in New

CASE 8.3—Continued

York. In March 2001, with Pearl's consent, Chunn opened an account with On-Site. Chunn bought and delivered a Pionex server to On-Site and told it to maintain the server apart from Pearl's equipment. In November, On-Site sold its assets to A. B. Watley, Inc. (ABW). Pearl asked ABW to install a new operating system on Pearl's Pionex server, but ABW mistakenly installed the system on Chunn's server, which ABW found connected to Pearl's network. Dennis Daudelin,

Pearl's chief executive officer, took the server from ABW's facility. After repeated demands, Daudelin returned the server on January 9, 2002, and its hard disk drive on October 24. Pearl filed a suit in a federal district court against Standard and Chunn, alleging, among other things, misappropriation of trade secrets. Chunn filed a counterclaim against Pearl, alleging conversion.

IN THE WORDS OF THE COURT . . .

HORNBY, District Judge.

* * * *

In * * * his counterclaim, Chunn asserts that Daudelin, acting on behalf of and in concert with Pearl, wrongfully converted to his own use property owned by Chunn without Chunn's knowledge or consent. Chunn, Daudelin and Pearl [filed motions] for summary judgment as to this [counterclaim].

* * * *The necessary elements to make out a claim for conversion are: (1) a showing that the person claiming that his property was converted has a property interest in the property; (2) that he had the right to possession at the time of the alleged conversion; and (3) that the party with the right to possession made a demand for its return that was denied by the holder.* * * * [C]onversion is defined as the unauthorized assumption and exercise of the right of ownership over goods belonging to another to the exclusion of the owner's rights. [Emphasis added.]

It is undisputed that Daudelin seized Chunn's server from ABW without Chunn's knowledge or permission and that Daudelin and Pearl were unwilling to return the server, despite demand, without certain conditions that evidently were unacceptable to Chunn. Daudelin and Pearl emphasize that the server was discovered to have been connected to Pearl's [network] without its authorization and that Daudelin's intent was solely to preserve evidence for any later claim against whomever owned the server.

* * * *[W]rongful intent is not a necessary element of a claim of conversion (and, conversely, good faith is not a defense).* [Emphasis added.]

To the extent that Pearl and Daudelin suggest that, rather than having been "mistaken," they were privileged to act as they did (for example, to prevent spoliation of evidence), they fail to develop the argument, citing no authority for any claimed privilege. They thereby effectively waive the point.

Nor is summary judgment staved off by Pearl's and Daudelin's contention that Chunn fails to show damages—an assertion that Chunn disputes.

Chunn accordingly is entitled to summary judgment as to liability with respect to * * * his counterclaim, with damages to be determined by a trier of fact.

DECISION AND REMEDY The court denied the plaintiffs' motions for summary judgment and granted a summary judgment to Chunn on his counterclaim for conversion against Pearl. The court ordered a trial for a determination as to the amount of damages. The court also ordered that other issues, including some of the plaintiffs' claims, be submitted for trial, adding, however, that Pearl could not base any claim on the contents of Chunn's server.

FOR CRITICAL ANALYSIS—Technological Consideration *How might Daudelin and Pearl successfully assert necessity as a defense to Chunn's charge?*

Disparagement of Property

Disparagement of property occurs when economically injurious false statements are made not about another's reputation but about another's product or property. Disparagement of property is a general term for torts that can be more specifically referred to as *slander of quality* or *slander of title*.

Slander of Quality Publication of false information about another's product, alleging that it is not what its seller claims, constitutes the tort of **slander of quality,** or **trade libel.** The plaintiff must prove that actual damages proximately resulted from the slander of quality. In other words, the plaintiff must show not only that a third person refrained from dealing with the plaintiff because of the improper publication but also that there were associated damages. The economic calculation of such damages—they are, after all, conjectural—is often extremely difficult.

An improper publication may be both a slander of quality and a defamation. For example, a statement that disparages the quality of a product may also, by implication, disparage the character of the person who would sell such a product.

During the 1990s, at least thirteen states enacted special statutes to protect against disparagement of perishable food products. Food producers began to push for such laws in 1991 after Washington state apple growers, using traditional libel and product-disparagement laws, failed to win a lawsuit against CBS News for a *60 Minutes* broadcast on the growth regulator Alar. Food-disparagement laws received national media attention when a group of Texas cattle ranchers sued talk-show host Oprah Winfrey for saying on one of her shows that the fear of "mad cow" disease "stopped her cold from eating a hamburger." The ranchers claimed that Winfrey had defamed their product, beef, in violation of the Texas food-disparagement statute. In 1998, the federal judge hearing the case held that the cattle ranchers had failed to make a case under the Texas statute. In 2000, this ruling was affirmed on appeal.[7]

Slander of Title When a publication denies or casts doubt on another's legal ownership of any property, and when this results in financial loss to that property's owner, the tort of **slander of title** occurs. Usually, this tort arises in situations in which someone knowingly publishes an untrue statement about property with the intent of discouraging a third person from dealing with the person slandered. For example, it would be difficult for a car dealer to attract customers after competitors published a notice that the dealer's stock consisted of stolen autos.

UNINTENTIONAL TORTS (NEGLIGENCE)

The tort of **negligence** occurs when someone suffers injury because of another's failure to live up to a required *duty of care*. In contrast to an intentional tort, a tort involving negligence is committed by a tortfeasor who neither wishes to bring about the consequences of the act nor believes that they will occur. The actor's conduct merely creates a *risk* of such consequences. If no risk is created, there is no negligence.

---

7. *Texas Beef Group v. Winfrey*, 201 F.3d 680 (5th Cir. 2000).

Drawing by Maslin; © 1990 The New Yorker Magazine, Inc.

"To answer your question. Yes, if you shoot an arrow into the air and it falls to earth you should know not where, you could be liable for any damage it may cause."

Many of the actions discussed in the section on intentional torts constitute negligence if the element of intent is missing. ● **EXAMPLE 7** If Juarez intentionally shoves Natsuyo, who falls and breaks an arm as a result, Juarez will have committed the intentional tort of assault and battery. If Juarez carelessly bumps into Natsuyo, however, and she falls and breaks an arm as a result, Juarez's action will constitute negligence. In either situation, Juarez has committed a tort.●

In examining a question of negligence, one should ask four questions:

1. Did the defendant owe a duty of care to the plaintiff?
2. Did the defendant breach that duty?
3. Did the plaintiff suffer a legally recognizable injury as a result of the defendant's breach of the duty of care?
4. Did the defendant's breach cause the plaintiff's injury?

Each of these elements of negligence is discussed in this section.

The Duty of Care and Its Breach

The concept of a **duty of care** arises from the notion that if we are to live in society with other people, some actions can be tolerated, and some cannot; some actions are right, and some are wrong; and some actions are reasonable, and some are not. The basic principle underlying the duty of care is that people are free to act as they please so long as their actions do not infringe on the interests of others.

DUTY OF CARE
The duty of all persons, as established by tort law, to exercise a reasonable amount of care in their dealings with others. Failure to exercise due care, which is normally determined by the "reasonable person standard," constitutes the tort of negligence.

When someone fails to comply with the duty of exercising reasonable care, a potentially tortious act may have been committed. Failure to live up to a standard of care may be an act (setting fire to a building) or an omission (neglecting to put out a campfire). It may be a careless act or a carefully performed but nevertheless dangerous act that results in injury. Courts consider the nature of the act (whether it is outrageous or commonplace), the manner in which the act is performed (cautiously versus carelessly), and the nature of the injury (whether it is serious or slight) in determining whether the duty of care has been breached.

REASONABLE PERSON STANDARD
The standard of behavior expected of a hypothetical "reasonable person." The standard against which negligence is measured and that must be observed to avoid liability for negligence.

The Reasonable Person Standard Tort law measures duty by the **reasonable person standard.** In determining whether a duty of care has been breached, the courts ask how a reasonable person would have acted in the same circumstances. The reasonable person standard is said to be (though in an absolute sense it cannot be) objective. It is not necessarily how a particular person would act. It is society's judgment on how a particular person *should* act. If the so-called reasonable person existed, he or she would be careful, conscientious, even tempered, and honest. This hypothetical reasonable person is frequently used by the courts in decisions relating to other areas of law as well. (For an example of how courts may impose a duty of care on parties to a lawsuit to act reasonably and preserve evidence, see this chapter's *Inside the Legal Environment* feature.)

That individuals are required to exercise a reasonable standard of care in their activities is a pervasive concept in business law, and many of the issues dealt with in subsequent chapters of this text have to do with this duty. What constitutes reasonable care varies, of course, with the circumstances.

ETHICAL ISSUE

Does a person's duty of care include a duty to come to the aid of a stranger in peril?

Suppose you are walking down a city street and notice that a pedestrian is about to step directly in front of an oncoming bus. Do you have a legal duty to warn that individual? No. Although most people would probably concede that in this situation, the observer has an ethical or moral duty to warn the other, tort law does not impose a general duty to rescue others in peril. People involved in special relationships, however, have been held to have a duty to rescue other parties within the relationship. A person has a duty to rescue his or her child or spouse if either is in danger, for example. Other special relationships, such as those between teachers and students or hiking and hunting partners, may also give rise to a duty to rescue. In addition, if a person who has no duty to rescue undertakes to rescue another, then the rescuer is charged with a duty to follow through with due care on the rescue attempt.

The Duty of Landowners Landowners are expected to exercise reasonable care to protect persons coming onto their property from harm. As mentioned earlier, in some jurisdictions, landowners are held to owe a duty to protect

A Caution to Business Managers: Preserve the Evidence

According to an age-old legal maxim, when a party loses or destroys evidence relating to a lawsuit, the presumption arises that the evidence was harmful to the "spoliator"—the party that lost or destroyed the evidence. As a practical matter, business owners and managers should take great care to preserve any evidence that may be necessary to bring or defend against a lawsuit.

Sanctions for Evidence Spoliation

Courts may impose sanctions— including fines, the dismissal of a lawsuit, and the entry of a default judgment for the opposing party—for evidence spoliation. In addition, some states now allow the injured party to file a separate tort action against the spoliator to recover money damages. Traditionally, courts have imposed sanctions for evidence spoliation only when evidence is *intentionally* destroyed.

Increasingly, however, courts are imposing sanctions even when the evidence was *accidentally* destroyed. In one case, for example, a federal court of appeals sanctioned the plaintiff by dismissing his lawsuit because, through no fault of his own, the plaintiff had failed to preserve evidence (a defective landing gear) for the defendant's inspection.[a]

Some state courts are going even further to punish those who destroy or lose evidence. For example, during a posttrial proceeding, a plaintiff discovered evidence indicating that the defendant's employees had given false and misleading testimony during depositions prior to trial and that certain documents (weekly accident reports) were not produced. The plaintiff filed another tort action for spoliation. Ultimately, the Ohio Supreme Court[b] held that "[c]oncealing,

---

a. *Miller v. Mid-Continent Aircraft Service, Inc.,* 139 F.3d 912 (10th Cir. 1998).
b. *Davis v. Wal-Mart Stores, Inc.,* 93 Ohio St.3d 488, 756 N.E.2d 657 (2001).

destroying, misrepresenting or intentionally interfering with evidence" during a trial may give rise to a separate tort action if the evidence spoliation is not discovered until after the conclusion of the trial.

The Need for Caution

Keep in mind that courts may impose sanctions even if evidence was lost or destroyed accidentally, or by someone else who was working for you. Moreover, in some states losing or destroying evidence may subject you to tort liability and even punitive damages. Businesspersons should also be aware that failure to produce documents and evidence during the discovery process may be interpreted by some courts as evidence spoliation.

FOR CRITICAL ANALYSIS

Is it fair to impose severe sanctions, such as the dismissal of a case, on those who inadvertently lose or destroy evidence relevant to a lawsuit?

---

even trespassers against certain risks. Landowners who rent or lease premises to tenants (see Chapter 21) are expected to exercise reasonable care to ensure that the tenants and their guests are not harmed in common areas, such as stairways, entryways, laundry rooms, and the like.

Retailers and other firms that explicitly or implicitly invite persons to come onto their premises are usually charged with a duty to exercise reasonable care to protect those persons, who are considered **business invitees**. For example, suppose you entered a supermarket, slipped on a wet floor, and sustained injuries as a result. The owner of the supermarket would be liable for damages if, when you slipped, there was no sign warning that the floor was wet. A court

BUSINESS INVITEE
A person, such as a customer or a client, who is invited onto business premises by the owner of those premises for business purposes.

would hold that the business owner was negligent because the owner failed to exercise a reasonable degree of care in protecting the store's customers against foreseeable risks about which the owner knew or *should have known*. That a patron might slip on the wet floor and be injured as a result was a foreseeable risk, and the owner should have taken care to avoid this risk or to warn the customer of it. The landowner also has a duty to discover and remove any hidden dangers that might injure a customer or other invitee.

Some risks, of course, are so obvious that the owner need not warn of them. For instance, a business owner does not need to warn customers to open a door before attempting to walk through it. Other risks, however, even though they may seem obvious to a business owner, may not be so in the eyes of another, such as a child. For example, a hardware store owner may not think it is necessary to warn customers that a stepladder leaning against the back wall of the store could fall down and harm them. It is possible, though, that a child could tip the ladder over and be hurt as a result and that the store could be held liable.

In the following case, the court had to decide whether a store owner should be held liable for a customer's injury on the premises. The question was whether the owner had notice of the condition that led to the customer's injury.

| **CASE 8.4** | Martin v. Wal-Mart Stores, Inc. |

United States Court of Appeals, Eighth Circuit, 1999. 183 F.3d 770. **http://www.findlaw.com/ casecode/courts/8th.html**[a]

BACKGROUND AND FACTS Harold Martin was shopping in the sporting goods department of a Wal-Mart store. There was one employee in the department at that time. In front of the sporting goods section, in the store's main aisle (which the employees referred to as "action alley"), was a large display of stacked cases of shotgun shells. On top of the cases were individual boxes of shells. Shortly after the sporting goods employee walked past the display, Martin did so, but Martin slipped on some loose shotgun shell pellets and fell to the floor. He immediately lost feeling in, and control of, his legs. Sensation and control returned, but during the next week, he lost the use of his legs several times for periods of ten to fifteen minutes. Eventually, sensation and control did not return to the front half of his left foot. Doctors diagnosed the condition as permanent. Martin filed a suit against Wal-Mart in a federal district court, seeking damages for his injury. The jury found in his favor, and the court denied Wal-Mart's motion for a directed verdict. Wal-Mart appealed to the U.S. Court of Appeals for the Eighth Circuit.

IN THE WORDS OF THE COURT . . .

BEAM, Circuit J. [Judge]

*   *   *   *

*   *   *   [T]he traditional rule *   *   * required a plaintiff in a slip and fall case to establish that the defendant store had either actual or constructive notice of the dangerous condition. The defendant store [was] deemed to have actual notice if it [was] shown that an employee created or was aware of the hazard. Constructive notice could be established by showing that the dangerous condition had existed for a sufficient length of time that the defendant should reasonably have known about it.

---

a. This URL will take you to a Web site maintained by FindLaw, which is now a part of West Group. When you access the site, enter "Wal-Mart" in the "Party Name Search" box and then click on "Search." Scroll down the list on the page that opens and select the link to "Harold Martin v. Wal-Mart Stores."

CASE 8.4—Continued

* * * *

* * * [R]etail store operations have evolved since the traditional liability rules were established. In modern self-service stores, customers are invited to traverse the same aisles used by the clerks to replenish stock, they are invited to retrieve merchandise from displays for inspection, and to place it back in the display if the item is not selected for purchase. Further, a customer is enticed to look at the displays, thus reducing the chance that the customer will be watchful of hazards on the floor. * * * [C]ustomers may take merchandise into their hands and may then lay articles that no longer interest them down in the aisle. * * * The risk of items creating dangerous conditions on the floor, previously created by employees, is now created by other customers as a result of the store's decision to employ the self-service mode of operation. * * * *Thus, in slip and fall cases in self-service stores, the inquiry of whether the danger existed long enough that the store should have reasonably known of it (constructive notice) is made in light of the fact that the store has notice that certain dangers arising through customer involvement are likely to occur, and the store has a duty to anticipate them.* [Emphasis added.]

* * * *

Wal-Mart * * * claims that Martin * * * failed to establish that Wal-Mart had actual or constructive notice of the pellets in the action aisle. We disagree. We find there is substantial evidence of constructive notice in the record. Martin slipped on shotgun shell pellets on the floor which were next to a large display of shotgun shells immediately abutting the sporting goods department. The chance that merchandise will wind up on the floor (or merchandise will be spilled on the floor) in the department in which that merchandise is sold or displayed is exactly the type of foreseeable risk [that is part of the self-service exception to the traditional rule]. Under [this exception], Wal-Mart has notice that merchandise is likely to find its way to the floor and create a dangerous condition, and *it must exercise due care to discover this hazard and warn customers or protect them from the danger.* * * * Even assuming that the hazard was created by a customer, a jury could easily find, given that it had notice that merchandise is often mishandled or mislaid by customers in a manner that can create dangerous conditions, that, had Wal-Mart exercised due care under the circumstances, it would have discovered the shotgun pellets on the floor. [Emphasis added.]

DECISION AND REMEDY The U.S. Court of Appeals for the Eighth Circuit affirmed the judgment of the lower court. There was sufficient evidence for a jury to find that Wal-Mart had constructive notice of the pellets on the floor in the main aisle.

FOR CRITICAL ANALYSIS—Ethical Consideration *Why do the courts impose constructive notice requirements on owners of self-service stores but not on owners of other stores?*

The Duty of Professionals If an individual has knowledge, skill, or intelligence superior to that of an ordinary person, the individual's conduct must be consistent with that status. Professionals—including physicians, dentists, psychiatrists, architects, engineers, accountants, lawyers, and others—are required to have a standard minimum level of special knowledge and ability. Therefore, in determining what constitutes reasonable care in the case of professionals, their

MALPRACTICE
Professional misconduct or lack of the requisite degree of skill as a professional. Negligence—the failure to exercise due care—on the part of a professional, such as a physician, is commonly referred to as malpractice.

training and expertise are taken into account. In other words, an accountant cannot defend against a lawsuit for negligence by stating, "But I was not familiar with that principle of accounting."

If a professional violates her or his duty of care toward a client, the professional may be sued for **malpractice**. For example, a patient might sue a physician for *medical malpractice*. A client might sue an attorney for *legal malpractice*.

The Injury Requirement and Damages

For a tort to have been committed, the plaintiff must have suffered a *legally recognizable* injury. To recover damages (receive compensation), the plaintiff must have suffered some loss, harm, wrong, or invasion of a protected interest. Essentially, the purpose of tort law is to compensate for legally recognized injuries resulting from wrongful acts. If no harm or injury results from a given negligent action, there is nothing to compensate—and no tort exists.

● **EXAMPLE 8** If you carelessly bump into a passerby, who stumbles and falls as a result, you may be liable in tort if the passerby is injured in the fall. If the person is unharmed, however, there normally could be no suit for damages, because no injury was suffered. Although the passerby might be angry and suffer emotional distress, few courts recognize negligently inflicted emotional distress as a tort unless it results in some physical disturbance or dysfunction.●

COMPENSATORY DAMAGES
A money award equivalent to the actual value of injuries or damages sustained by the aggrieved party.

PUNITIVE DAMAGES
Money damages that may be awarded to a plaintiff to punish the defendant and deter future similar conduct.

As already mentioned, the purpose of tort law is not to punish people for tortious acts but to compensate the injured parties for damages suffered. Occasionally, however, damages awarded in tort lawsuits include both **compensatory damages** (which are intended to reimburse a plaintiff for actual losses—to make the plaintiff whole) and **punitive damages** (which are intended to punish the wrongdoer and deter others from similar wrongdoing).

Causation

Another element necessary to a tort is *causation*. If a person fails in a duty of care and someone suffers injury, the wrongful activity must have caused the harm for a tort to have been committed. In deciding whether there is causation, the court must address two questions:

CAUSATION IN FACT
An act or omission without which an event would not have occurred.

1. *Is there causation in fact?* Did the injury occur because of the defendant's act, or would it have occurred anyway? If an injury would not have occurred without the defendant's act, then there is causation in fact. **Causation in fact** can usually be determined by the use of the *but for* test: "but for" the wrongful act, the injury would not have occurred. Theoretically, causation in fact is limitless. One could claim, for example, that "but for" the creation of the world, a particular injury would not have occurred. Thus, as a practical matter, the law has to establish limits, and it does so through the concept of proximate cause.

PROXIMATE CAUSE
Legal cause; exists when the connection between an act and an injury is strong enough to justify imposing liability.

2. *Was the act the proximate cause of the injury?* **Proximate cause**, or legal cause, exists when the connection between an act and an injury is strong enough to justify imposing liability. ● **EXAMPLE 9** Ackerman carelessly leaves a campfire burning. The fire not only burns down the forest but also sets off an explosion in a nearby chemical plant that spills chemicals into a river, killing all the fish for a hundred miles downstream and ruining the

NOTE Proximate cause can be thought of as a question of social policy. Should the defendant be made to bear the loss instead of the plaintiff?

Tort Liability and Damages in Other Nations

In contrast to U.S. courts, courts in Europe generally limit damages to compensatory damages; punitive damages are virtually unheard of in European countries. Even when plaintiffs do win compensatory damages, they generally receive much less than would be awarded in a similar case brought in the United States. In part, this is because governments in Europe usually provide for health care and have relatively generous Social Security payments. Yet it is also because European courts tend to view the

duty of care and the concept of risk differently than U.S. courts do. In the United States, if a swimmer is injured from falling off a high diving board, a court may decide that the pool owner should be held liable, given that such a fall is a foreseeable risk. If punitive damages are awarded, they could total millions of dollars. In a similar situation in Europe, a court might hold that the plaintiff, not the pool owner, was responsible for the injury.

Tort laws in other nations also differ in the way damages are calculated. For example, under Swiss law and Turkish law, a court is permitted to reduce damages if an award of full damages would cause undue hardship for a party

who was found negligent. In some nations of northern Africa, different amounts of damages are awarded depending on the type of tortious action committed and the degree of intent involved. In the United States, in contrast, the calculation of compensatory damages does not depend on whether the tort was negligent or intentional—although they are most often awarded in cases involving intentional torts.

FOR CRITICAL ANALYSIS

Punitive damages are an important element in American tort litigation. Why is this? What do awards of punitive damages achieve?

economy of a tourist resort. Should Ackerman be liable to the resort owners? To the tourists whose vacations were ruined? These are questions of proximate cause that a court must decide.●

Probably the most cited case on proximate cause is the *Palsgraf* case, discussed in this chapter's *Landmark in the Legal Environment* feature on the following page. In determining the issue of proximate cause, the court addressed the following question: Does a defendant's duty of care extend only to those who may be injured as a result of a foreseeable risk, or does it extend also to a person whose injury could not reasonably have been foreseen?

Defenses to Negligence

Defendants often defend against negligence claims by asserting that the plaintiffs failed to prove the existence of one or more of the required elements for negligence. Additionally, there are three basic *affirmative* defenses in negligence cases (defenses that defendants can use to avoid liability even if the facts are as the plaintiffs state): (1) assumption of risk, (2) superseding cause, and (3) contributory negligence.

Assumption of Risk A plaintiff who voluntarily enters into a risky situation, knowing the risk involved, will not be allowed to recover. This is the defense

LANDMARK IN THE LEGAL ENVIRONMENT

Palsgraf v. Long Island Railroad Co. (1928)

In 1928, the New York Court of Appeals (that state's highest court) issued its decision in *Palsgraf v. Long Island Railroad Co.,*[a] a case that has become a landmark in negligence law with respect to proximate cause.

THE FACTS OF THE CASE   The plaintiff, Palsgraf, was waiting for a train on a station platform. A man carrying a small package wrapped in newspaper was rushing to catch a train that had begun to move away from the platform. As the man attempted to jump aboard the moving train, he seemed unsteady and about to fall. A railroad guard on the train car reached forward to grab him, and another guard on the platform pushed him from behind to help him board the train. In the process, the man's package fell on the railroad tracks and exploded, because it contained fireworks. The repercussions of the explosion caused scales at the other end of the train platform to fall on Palsgraf, who was injured as a result. She sued the railroad company for damages in a New York state court.

THE QUESTION OF PROXIMATE CAUSE
At the trial, the jury found that the railroad guards were negligent in their conduct. On appeal, the question before the New York Court of Appeals was whether the conduct of the railroad guards was the proximate cause of Palsgraf's injuries. In other words, did the guards' duty of care extend to Palsgraf, who was outside the zone of danger and whose injury could not reasonably have been foreseen?

The court stated that the question of whether the guards were negligent *with respect to Palsgraf* depended on whether her injury was *reasonably foreseeable* to the railroad guards. Although the guards may have acted negligently with respect to the man boarding the train, this has no bearing on the question of their negligence with respect to Palsgraf. This is not a situation in which a person commits an act so potentially harmful (for example, firing a gun at a building) that he or she would be held responsible for any harm that resulted. The court stated that here, "there was nothing in the situation to suggest to the most cautious mind that the parcel wrapped in newspaper would spread wreckage through the station." The court thus concluded that the railroad guards were not negligent with respect to Palsgraf because her injury was not reasonably foreseeable.

Application to Today's World

The Palsgraf *case established* foreseeability *as the test for proximate cause. Today, the courts continue to apply this test in determining proximate cause — and thus tort liability for injuries. Generally, if the victim of a harm or the consequences of a harm done are unforeseeable, there is no proximate cause. Note, though, that in the online environment, distinctions based on physical proximity, such as the "zone of danger" cited by the court in this case, are largely inapplicable.*

a. 248 N.Y. 339, 162 N.E. 99 (1928).

ASSUMPTION OF RISK
A doctrine whereby a plaintiff may not recover for injuries or damages suffered from risks he or she knew of and voluntarily assumed.

of **assumption of risk.** The requirements of this defense are (1) knowledge of the risk and (2) voluntary assumption of the risk.

The risk can be assumed by express agreement, or the assumption of risk can be implied by the plaintiff's knowledge of the risk and subsequent conduct. For example, a driver entering a race knows that there is a risk of being killed or injured in a crash. Of course, the plaintiff does not assume a risk different from or greater than the risk normally carried by the activity. In our example, the race driver would not assume the risk that the banking in the curves of the racetrack will give way during the race because of a construction defect.

Risks are not deemed to be assumed in situations involving emergencies. Neither are they assumed when a statute protects a class of people from harm and a member of the class is injured by the harm. For example, employees are protected by statute from dangerous working conditions and therefore do not assume the risks associated with the workplace. If an employee is injured, he or she will generally be compensated regardless of fault under state workers' compensation statutes (discussed in Chapter 16).

Superseding Cause An unforeseeable intervening event may break the connection between a wrongful act and an injury to another. If so, it acts as a *superseding cause*—that is, it relieves a defendant of liability for injuries caused by the intervening event. ● **EXAMPLE 10** Suppose that Derrick keeps a can of gasoline in the trunk of his car. The presence of the gasoline creates a foreseeable risk and is thus a negligent act. If Derrick's car skids and crashes into a tree, causing the gasoline can to explode, Derrick will be liable for injuries sustained by passing pedestrians because of his negligence. If the explosion had been caused by lightning striking the car, however, the lightning would supersede Derrick's original negligence as a cause of the damage, because the lightning was not foreseeable. ●

Contributory Negligence All individuals are expected to exercise a reasonable degree of care in looking out for themselves. In a few jurisdictions, recovery for injury resulting from negligence is prevented if the plaintiff was also negligent (failed to exercise a reasonable degree of care). This is the defense of **contributory negligence.** Under the common law doctrine of contributory negligence, no matter how insignificant the plaintiff's negligence is relative to the defendant's negligence, the plaintiff will be precluded from recovering any damages.

An exception to the doctrine of contributory negligence may apply if the defendant failed to take advantage of an opportunity to avoid causing the damage. Under the "last clear chance" rule, the plaintiff may recover full damages despite her or his own negligence. (Note that in those states that have adopted the comparative negligence rule, discussed next, the last clear chance doctrine does not apply.) ● **EXAMPLE 11** Murphy is walking across the street against the light, and Lewis, a motorist, sees her in time to avoid hitting her but hits her anyway. In this situation, Lewis (the defendant) is not permitted to use Murphy's (the plaintiff's) prior negligence as a defense. The defendant negligently missed the opportunity to avoid injuring the plaintiff. ●

The majority of states now allow recovery based on the doctrine of **comparative negligence.** This doctrine enables both the plaintiff's and the defendant's negligence to be computed and the liability for damages distributed accordingly. Some jurisdictions have adopted a "pure" form of comparative negligence that allows the plaintiff to recover even if the extent of his or her fault is greater than that of the defendant. For example, if the plaintiff was 80 percent at fault and the defendant 20 percent at fault, the plaintiff can recover

A bungee jumper leaps from a platform. If the jumper is injured and sues the operator of the jump for negligence, what defenses might the operator use to avoid liability?

CONTRIBUTORY NEGLIGENCE
A theory in tort law under which a complaining party's own negligence contributed to or caused his or her injuries. Contributory negligence is an absolute bar to recovery in a minority of jurisdictions.

NOTE The concept of superseding cause is not a question of physics but is, like proximate cause, a question of responsibility.

COMPARATIVE NEGLIGENCE
A theory in tort law under which the liability for injuries resulting from negligent acts is shared by all persons who were guilty of negligence (including the injured party), on the basis of each person's proportionate carelessness.

20 percent of his or her damages. Many states' comparative negligence statutes, however, contain a "50 percent" rule by which the plaintiff recovers nothing if she or he was more than 50 percent at fault.

Special Negligence Doctrines and Statutes

A number of special doctrines and statutes apply to negligence. We examine a few of them here.

Res Ipsa Loquitur Generally, in lawsuits involving negligence, the plaintiff has the burden of proving that the defendant was negligent. In certain situations, however, when negligence is very difficult or impossible to prove, the courts may infer that negligence has occurred; then the burden of proof rests on the defendant—to prove he or she was not negligent. The inference of the defendant's negligence is known as the doctrine of *res ipsa loquitur,*[8] which translates as "the facts speak for themselves."

This doctrine is applied only when the event creating the damage or injury is one that ordinarily would occur only as a result of negligence. ● EXAMPLE 12 If a person undergoes knee surgery and following the surgery has a severed nerve in the knee area, that person can sue the surgeon under a theory of *res ipsa loquitur.* In this case, the injury would not have occurred but for the surgeon's negligence.[9] ● For the doctrine of *res ipsa loquitur* to apply, the event must have been within the defendant's power to control, and it must not have been due to any voluntary action or contribution on the part of the plaintiff.

Negligence *Per Se* Certain conduct, whether it consists of an action or a failure to act, may be treated as **negligence *per se*** (*per se* means "in or of itself"). Negligence *per se* may occur if an individual violates a statute or an ordinance providing for a criminal penalty and that violation causes another to be injured. The injured person must prove (1) that the statute clearly sets out what standard of conduct is expected, when and where it is expected, and of whom it is expected; (2) that he or she is in the class intended to be protected by the statute; and (3) that the statute was designed to prevent the type of injury that he or she suffered. The standard of conduct required by the statute is the duty that the defendant owes to the plaintiff, and a violation of the statute is the breach of that duty.

● EXAMPLE 13 A statute may require a landowner to keep a building in safe condition and may also subject the landowner to a criminal penalty, such as a fine, if the building is not kept safe. The statute is meant to protect those who are rightfully in the building. Thus, if the owner, without a sufficient excuse, violates the statute and a tenant is thereby injured, a majority of courts will hold that the owner's unexcused violation of the statute conclusively establishes a breach of a duty of care—that is, that the owner's violation is negligence *per se.* ●

---

8. Pronounced *rayz ihp*-suh *low*-kwuh-tuhr.
9. *Edwards v. Boland,* 41 Mass.App.Ct. 375, 670 N.E.2d 404 (1996).

RES IPSA LOQUITUR
A doctrine under which negligence may be inferred simply because an event occurred, if it is the type of event that would not occur in the absence of negligence. Literally, the term means "the facts speak for themselves."

NEGLIGENCE *PER SE*
An action or failure to act in violation of a statutory requirement.

"Danger Invites Rescue" Doctrine Typically, in cases in which an individual takes a defensive action, such as swerving to avoid an oncoming car, and an injury results, the original wrongdoer will not be relieved of liability even though the injury actually resulted from the attempt to escape harm. The same is true under the "danger invites rescue" doctrine. Under this doctrine, if Lemming commits an act that endangers Salter, and Yokem sustains an injury trying to protect Salter, then Lemming will be liable for Yokem's injury, as well as for any injuries Salter may sustain. Rescuers can injure themselves, or the person rescued, or even a stranger, but the original wrongdoer will still be liable.

Special Negligence Statutes A number of states have enacted statutes prescribing duties and responsibilities in certain circumstances. For example, most states now have what are called **Good Samaritan statutes.**[10] Under these statutes, persons who are aided voluntarily by others cannot turn around and sue the "Good Samaritans" for negligence. These laws were passed largely to protect physicians and medical personnel who voluntarily render their services in emergency situations to those in need, such as individuals hurt in car accidents.

Many states have also passed **dram shop acts,** under which a tavern owner or bartender may be held liable for injuries caused by a person who became intoxicated while drinking at the bar or who was already intoxicated when served by the bartender. In some states, statutes impose liability on *social hosts* (persons hosting parties) for injuries caused by guests who became intoxicated at the hosts' homes. Under these statutes, it is unnecessary to prove that the tavern owner, bartender, or social host was negligent.

> **"No one would remember the Good Samaritan if he'd only had good intentions—he had money, too."**
> MARGARET THATCHER, 1925–
> (British prime minister, 1979–1990)

GOOD SAMARITAN STATUTE
A state statute stipulating that persons who rescue or provide emergency services to others in peril—unless they do so recklessly, thus causing further harm—cannot be sued for negligence.

DRAM SHOP ACT
A state statute that imposes liability on tavern owners and bartenders for injuries resulting from accidents caused by intoxicated persons when the sellers or servers of alcoholic drinks contributed to the intoxication.

CYBER TORTS

A significant issue that has come before the courts in recent years relates to the question of who should be held liable for *cyber torts,* or torts committed in cyberspace. For example, who should be held liable when someone posts a defamatory message online? Should an Internet service provider (ISP) be liable for the remark if the ISP was unaware that it was being made?

Other questions involve issues of proof. How, for example, can it be proved that an online defamatory remark was "published" (which requires that a third party see or hear it)? How can the identity of the person who made the remark be discovered? Can an ISP be forced to reveal the source of an anonymous comment? We explore some of these questions in this section, as well as some of the legal issues that have arisen with respect to bulk e-mail advertising. In the *Ethical Issue* on the following page we look at yet another topic: the legal questions raised by computer viruses.

---

10. These laws derive their name from the Good Samaritan story in the Bible. In the story, a traveler who had been robbed and beaten lay along the roadside, ignored by those passing by. Eventually, a man from the country of Samaria (the "Good Samaritan") stopped to render assistance to the injured person.

ETHICAL ISSUE

Who should be held liable for computer viruses?

As everybody knows, viruses sent into cyberspace can cause significant damage to the computer systems they "infect." To date, adapting tort law to virus-caused damages has been difficult because it is not all that clear who should be held liable for these damages. For example, who should be held liable for damages caused by the "Blaster.worm" that spread around the globe in 2003 and caused, it is estimated, billions of dollars in damages? Of course, the person who wrote the virus is responsible. But what about the producer of the e-mail software that the virus utilized to spread itself so rapidly? What about the antivirus software companies? Were they negligent in failing to market products that were capable of identifying and disabling the virus before damage occurred? Should the users themselves share part of the blame? After all, even after the virus had received widespread publicity, users continued to open e-mail attachments containing the virus.

Generally, determining what tort duties apply in cyberspace and the point at which one of those duties is breached continues to be a pressing issue for today's courts.

Defamation Online

Online forums allow anyone—customers, employees, or crackpots—to complain about a business firm's personnel, policies, practices, or products. Regardless of whether the complaint is justified or whether it is true, it might have an impact on the business of the firm. One of the early questions in the online legal arena was whether the providers of such forums could be held liable for defamatory statements made in those forums.

Liability of Internet Service Providers Newspapers, magazines, and television and radio stations may be held liable for defamatory remarks that they disseminate, even if those remarks are prepared or created by others. Under the Communications Decency Act of 1996, however, ISPs are not liable for such material.[11] An ISP typically provides access to the Internet through a local phone number and may provide other services, including access to databases available only to the ISP's subscribers. (See this chapter's *Legal E-nvironment* feature for a further discussion of the immunity of ISPs.)

Piercing the Veil of Anonymity A threshold barrier to anyone who seeks to bring an action for online defamation is discovering the identity of the person who posted the defamatory message online. ISPs can disclose personal information about their customers only when ordered to do so by a court. Because of this, businesses and individuals are increasingly resorting to lawsuits against "John Does." Then, using the authority of the courts, they can obtain from the ISPs the identities of the persons responsible for the messages.

---

11. 47 U.S.C. Section 230.

LEGAL *e*-NVIRONMENT
Internet Service Providers and Tort Liability

Recall from the discussion of defamation earlier in this chapter that one who repeats or otherwise republishes a defamatory statement is subject to liability as if he or she had originally published it. Thus, publishers generally can be held liable for defamatory contents in the books and periodicals that they publish.

Prior to the passage of the Communications Decency Act (CDA) of 1996, the courts grappled on several occasions with the question of whether Internet service providers (ISPs) should be regarded as publishers and thus held liable for defamatory messages made by users of their services. The CDA resolved the issue by stating that "[n]o provider or user of an interactive computer service shall be treated as the publisher or speaker of any information provided by another information content provider." Although portions of the CDA were held unconstitutional by the United States Supreme Court (the provisions prohibiting the transmission of materials harmful to minors—see Chapter 5), the provision regarding the liability of ISPs was not.

The CDA Shields ISPs from Liability

In a number of key cases, the ISP provisions of the CDA have been invoked to shield ISPs from liability for defamatory postings on their bulletin boards. In a leading case, decided the year after the CDA was enacted, America Online, Inc. (AOL), was not held liable even though it did not promptly remove defamatory messages of which it had been made aware. In upholding a district court's ruling in AOL's favor, a federal appellate court stated that the CDA "plainly immunizes computer service providers like AOL from liability for information that originates with third parties." The court explained that the purpose of the statute is "to maintain the robust nature of Internet communication and, accordingly, to keep government interference in the medium to a minimum." The court added, "None of this means, of course, that the original culpable party who posts defamatory messages would escape accountability."[a]

Extending CDA Immunity to Online Auction Services

Most of the cases concerning ISP immunity under the CDA have involved bulletin boards and other forums provided by ISPs. In 2000, however, a California state court extended the CDA further into the realm of e-commerce when it ruled that eBay, the online auction house, could not be held liable for the sale of pirated sound recordings on its Web site. In *Stoner v. eBay, Inc.,*[b] the plaintiff alleged that eBay had knowingly reaped "massive profits" from the sale of pirated sound recordings in violation of a California statute prohibiting unfair business practices. A California state court, however, concluded that there was nothing to indicate that eBay's function should be transformed from that of an interactive service provider to that of a seller responsible for items sold on the site. The court noted that "a principal objective of the immunity provision [of the CDA] is to encourage commerce over the Internet by ensuring that interactive computer service providers are not held responsible for how third parties use their services."

FOR CRITICAL ANALYSIS

Although publishers traditionally have been held liable for defamatory contents in the books and periodicals that they publish, distributors (libraries, bookstores, newsstands, and the like) have not—unless it can be shown that a distributor was aware of the defamatory nature of a particular work and distributed it anyway. Can you think of any reason why the drafters of the CDA decided to grant virtually total immunity to ISPs instead of treating them as "distributors"? Explain.

a. *Zeran v. America Online, Inc.,* 129 F.3d 327 (4th Cir. 1997); cert. denied, 524 U.S. 934, 118 S.Ct. 2341, 141 L.Ed.2d 712 (1998).
b. Cal.Super.Ct. 2000. For further details on this unpublished decision, see "California Judge Finds eBay Immune under CDA," *e-commerce Law & Strategy,* November 2000, p. 9.

In one case, for example, Eric Hvide, a former chief executive of a company called Hvide Marine, sued a number of "John Does" who had posted allegedly defamatory statements about his company on various online message boards. Hvide, who eventually lost his job, sued the John Does for libel in a Florida court. The court ruled that Yahoo and AOL had to reveal the identities of the defendant Does.[12]

In another case, however, discovering the identity of the person who had posted an online defamatory message was more difficult. The case involved a physician, Dr. Sam D. Graham, Jr., who at the time was the chair of the Department of Urology at Emory University's School of Medicine. A posting on a Yahoo message board suggested that Graham had taken kickbacks from a urology company after giving his department's pathology business to the company. Graham resigned from his position and sued the anonymous poster for libel. Because the person posting the message was not actually a Yahoo customer, an extensive investigation and, according to Graham's attorney, a lot of "dumb luck" were required to learn the person's identity. The case went to trial, and a federal district court ordered the person who posted the message to pay Graham $675,000 in damages.[13]

Spam

SPAM
Bulk, unsolicited ("junk") e-mail.

Bulk, unsolicited e-mail ("junk" e-mail) is often called **spam**.[14] Typical spam consists of a product ad sent to all the users on an e-mailing list or all the members of a newsgroup.

Spam can waste user time and network bandwidth (the amount of data that can be transmitted within a certain time). It can also impose a burden on an ISP's equipment. ● EXAMPLE 14 In a leading case on this issue, Cyber Promotions, Inc., sent bulk e-mail to subscribers of CompuServe, Inc., an ISP. CompuServe subscribers complained to the service about ads, and many canceled their subscriptions. Handling the ads also placed a tremendous burden on CompuServe's equipment. CompuServe told Cyber Promotions to stop using CompuServe's equipment to process and store the ads—in effect, to stop sending the ads to CompuServe subscribers. Ignoring the demand, Cyber Promotions stepped up the volume of its ads. After CompuServe attempted unsuccessfully to block the flow with screening software, it filed a suit against Cyber Promotions in a federal district court, seeking an injunction on the ground that the ads constituted trespass to personal property. The court agreed and ordered Cyber Promotions to stop sending its ads to e-mail addresses maintained by CompuServe.[15] ●

Because of the problems associated with spam, some states have taken steps to prohibit or regulate its use. For example, a few states, such as Washington, prohibit unsolicited e-mail that is promoting goods, services, or real estate for sale or lease. In California, an unsolicited e-mail ad must state in its subject line that it is an ad ("ADV:"). The ad must also include a toll-free phone number or return e-mail address through which the recipient can contact the

---

12. *Does v. Hvide*, 770 So.2d 1237 (Fla.App.3d 2000).

13. *Graham v. Oppenheimer* (E.D.Va. 2000). For details on this unpublished decision, see "Net Libel Verdict Is Upheld," *The National Law Journal*, December 25, 2000, p. A19.

14. The term *spam* is said to come from a Monty Python song with the lyrics, "Spam spam spam spam, spam spam spam spam, lovely spam, wonderful spam." Like these lyrics, spam online is often considered to be a repetition of worthless text.

15. *CompuServe, Inc. v. Cyber Promotions, Inc.*, 962 F.Supp.1015 (S.D.Ohio 1997).

sender to request that no more ads be e-mailed.[16] An ISP can bring a successful suit in a California state court against a spammer who violates the ISP's policy prohibiting or restricting unsolicited e-mail ads. The court can award damages of up to $25,000 per day.[17] The Internet is a public forum, however. Thus, free speech issues may be involved—see Chapter 5.

16. Ca. Bus. & Prof. Code Section 17538.4.
17. Ca. Bus. & Prof. Code Section 17538.45.

KEY TERMS

CHAPTER SUMMARY TORTS AND CYBER TORTS

Intentional Torts against Persons (See pages 235–244.)	1. *Assault and battery*—An assault is an unexcused and intentional act that causes another person to be apprehensive of immediate harm. A battery is an assault that results in physical contact.
	2. *False imprisonment*—The intentional confinement or restraint of another person's movement without justification.
	3. *Infliction of emotional distress*—An intentional act that amounts to extreme and outrageous conduct resulting in severe emotional distress to another.
	4. *Defamation (libel or slander)*—A false statement of fact, not made under privilege, that is communicated to a third person and that causes damage to a person's reputation. For public figures, the plaintiff must also prove actual malice.
	5. *Invasion of the right to privacy*—The use of a person's name or likeness for commercial purposes without permission, wrongful intrusion into a person's private activities, publication of information that places a person in a false light, or disclosure of private facts that an ordinary person would find objectionable.
	6. *Appropriation*—The use of another person's name, likeness, or other identifying characteristic, without permission and for the benefit of the user.

(continued)

CHAPTER SUMMARY   TORTS AND CYBER TORTS—Continued

Intentional Torts against Persons—continued	7. *Misrepresentation (fraud)*—A false representation made by one party, through the misstatement or omission of material facts, with the intention of deceiving another and on which the other reasonably relies to his or her detriment.
	8. *Wrongful interference*—The knowing, intentional interference by a third party with an enforceable contractual relationship or an established business relationship between other parties for the purpose of advancing the economic interests of the third party.
Intentional Torts against Property (See pages 244–248.)	1. *Trespass to land*—The invasion of another's real property without consent or privilege. Specific rights and duties apply once a person is expressly or impliedly established as a trespasser.
	2. *Trespass to personal property*—Unlawfully damaging or interfering with the owner's right to use, possess, or enjoy his or her personal property.
	3. *Conversion*—A wrongful act in which personal property is taken from its rightful owner or possessor and placed in the service of another.
	4. *Disparagement of property*—Any economically injurious false statement that is made about another's product or property; an inclusive term for the torts of *slander of quality* and *slander of title*.
Unintentional Torts—Negligence (See pages 248–259.)	1. *Negligence*—The careless performance of a legally required duty or the failure to perform a legally required act. Elements that must be proved are that a legal duty of care exists, that the defendant breached that duty, and that the breach caused damage or injury to another.
	2. *Defenses to negligence*—The basic affirmative defenses in negligence cases are (a) assumption of risk, (b) superseding cause, and (c) contributory negligence.
	3. *Special negligence doctrines and statutes*—
	a. *Res ipsa loquitur*—A doctrine under which a plaintiff need not prove negligence on the part of the defendant because "the facts speak for themselves."
	b. Negligence *per se*—A type of negligence that may occur if a person violates a statute or an ordinance providing for a criminal penalty and the violation causes another to be injured.
	c. Special negligence statutes—State statutes that prescribe duties and responsibilities in certain circumstances, the violation of which will impose civil liability. Dram shop acts and Good Samaritan statutes are examples of special negligence statutes.
Cyber Torts (See pages 259–263.)	General tort principles are being extended to cover cyber torts, or torts that occur in cyberspace, such as online defamation and spamming (which may constitute trespass to personal property). Federal and state statutes may also apply to certain forms of cyber torts. For example, under the federal Communications Decency Act of 1996, Internet service providers are not liable for defamatory messages posted by their subscribers. Some states restrict the use of "junk" e-mail, or spam. Certain types of online wrongs, such as the transmission of computer viruses, pose unique legal challenges.

FOR REVIEW

1. What is a tort?
2. What is the purpose of tort law? What are two basic categories of torts?
3. What are the four elements of negligence?
4. What defenses may be raised against claims of negligence?
5. What is a cyber tort, and how are tort theories being applied in cyberspace?

QUESTIONS AND CASE PROBLEMS

8–1. Defenses to Negligence. Corinna was riding her bike on a city street. While she was riding, she frequently looked back to verify that the books that she had fastened to the rear part of her bike were still attached. On one occasion while she was looking behind her, she failed to notice a car that was entering an intersection just as she was crossing it. The car hit her, causing her to sustain numerous injuries. Three eyewitnesses stated that the driver of the car had failed to stop at the stop sign before entering the intersection. Corinna sued the driver of the car for negligence. What defenses might the defendant driver raise in this lawsuit? Discuss fully.

8–2. Liability to Business Invitees. Kim went to Ling's Market to pick up a few items for dinner. It was a rainy, windy day, and the wind had blown water through the door of Ling's Market each time the door opened. As Kim entered through the door, she slipped and fell in the approximately one-half inch of rainwater that had accumulated on the floor. The manager knew of the weather conditions but had not posted any sign to warn customers of the water hazard. Kim injured her back as a result of the fall and sued Ling's for damages. Can Ling's be held liable for negligence in this situation? Discuss.

8–3. Negligence. In which of the following situations will the acting party be liable for the tort of negligence? Explain fully.

(a) Mary goes to the golf course on Sunday morning, eager to try out a new set of golf clubs she has just purchased. As she tees off on the first hole, the head of her club flies off and injures a nearby golfer.

(b) Mary's doctor gives her some pain medication and tells her not to drive after she takes it as the medication induces drowsiness. In spite of the doctor's warning, Mary decides to drive to the store while on the medication. Owing to her lack of alertness, she fails to stop at a traffic light and crashes into another vehicle, injuring a passenger.

8–4. Causation. Ruth carelessly parks her car on a steep hill, leaving the car in neutral and failing to engage the parking brake. The car rolls down the hill, knocking down an electric line. The sparks from the broken line ignite a grass fire. The fire spreads until it reaches a barn one mile away. The barn houses dynamite, and the burning barn explodes, causing part of the roof to fall on and injure a passing motorist, Jim. Can Jim recover from Ruth? Why or why not?

8–5. Wrongful Interference. Jennings owns a bakery shop. He has been trying to obtain a long-term contract with the owner of Julie's Tea Salon for some time. Jennings starts a local advertising campaign on radio and television and in the newspaper. The campaign is so persuasive that Julie decides to break the contract she has had for several years with Orley's Bakery so that she can patronize Jennings's bakery. Is Jennings liable to Orley's Bakery for the tort of wrongful interference with a contractual relationship? Is Julie liable for this tort? For anything?

8–6. Duty of Care. As pedestrians exited at the close of an arts and crafts show, Jason Davis, an employee of the show's producer, stood near the exit. Suddenly and without warning, Davis turned around and collided with Yvonne Esposito, an eighty-year-old woman. Esposito was knocked to the ground, fracturing her hip. After hip-replacement surgery, she was left with a permanent physical impairment. Esposito filed a suit in a federal district court against Davis and others, alleging negligence. What are the factors that indicate whether Davis owed Esposito a duty of care? What do those factors indicate in these circumstances? [*Esposito v. Davis,* 47 F.3d 164 (5th Cir. 1995)]

8–7. Duty to Business Invitees. Flora Gonzalez visited a Wal-Mart store. While walking in a busy aisle from the store's cafeteria toward a refrigerator, Gonzalez stepped on some macaroni that came from the cafeteria. She slipped and fell, sustaining injuries to her back, shoulder, and knee. She filed a suit in a Texas state court against Wal-Mart, alleging that the store was negligent. She presented evidence that the macaroni had "a lot of dirt" and tracks through it and testified that the macaroni "seemed like it had been there awhile." What duty does a business have to protect its patrons from dangerous conditions? In Gonzalez's case, should Wal-Mart be held liable for a breach of that duty? Why or why not? [*Wal-Mart Stores, Inc. v. Gonzalez,* 968 S.W.2d 934 (Tex.Sup. 1998)]

8–8. Misappropriation. The United States Golf Association (USGA) was founded in 1894. In 1911, the USGA developed the Handicap System, which was designed to enable individual golfers of different abilities to compete fairly with one another. The USGA revised the system and implemented new handicap formulas between 1987 and 1993. The USGA permits any entity to use the system free of charge as long as it complies with the USGA's procedure for peer review through authorized golf associations of the handicaps issued to individual golfers. In 1991, Arroyo Software Corp. began marketing software known as EagleTrak, which incorporated the USGA's system, and used the USGA's name in the software's ads without permission. Arroyo's EagleTrak did not incorporate any means for obtaining peer review of handicap computations. The USGA filed a suit in a California state court against Arroyo, alleging, among other things, misappropriation. The USGA asked the court to stop Arroyo's use of its system. Should the court grant the injunction? Why or why not? [*United States Golf Association v. Arroyo Software Corp.,* 69 Cal.App.4th 607, 81 Cal.Rptr.2d 708 (1999)]

Case Problem with Sample Answer

8–9. Cyber Torts. America Online, Inc. (AOL), provides services to its customers (members), including the transmission of e-mail to and from other members and across the Internet. To become a member, a person must agree not to use AOL's computers to send bulk, unsolicited, commercial e-mail (spam). AOL uses filters to block spam, but bulk e-mailers sometimes use other software to thwart the filters. National Health Care Discount, Inc. (NHCD), sells discount optical and dental service plans. To generate leads for NHCD's products, sales representatives, who included AOL members, sent more than 300 million pieces of spam through AOL's computer system. Each item cost AOL an estimated $.00078 in equipment expenses. Some of the spam used false headers and other methods to hide the source. After receiving more than 150,000 complaints, AOL asked NHCD to stop. When the spam continued, AOL filed a suit in a federal district court against NHCD, alleging in part trespass to chattels—an unlawful interference with another's rights to possess personal property. AOL asked the court for a summary judgment on this claim. Did the spamming constitute trespass to chattels? Explain. [*America Online, Inc. v. National Health Care Discount, Inc.,* 121 F.Supp.2d 1255 (N.D.Iowa 2000)]

To view a sample answer for this case problem, go to this book's Web site at http://leet.westbuslaw.com and click on "Interactive Study Center."

8–10. Invasion of Privacy. During the spring and summer of 1999, Edward and Geneva Irvine received numerous "hang up" phone calls, including three calls in the middle of the night. With the help of their local phone company, the Irvines learned that many of the calls were from the telemarketing department of the *Akron Beacon Journal* in Akron, Ohio. The Beacon's sales force was equipped with an automatic dialing machine. During business hours, the dialer was used to maximize productivity by calling multiple phone numbers at once and connecting a call to a sales representative only after it was answered. After business hours, the dialer was used to dial a list of disconnected numbers to determine whether they had been reconnected. If the dialer detected a ring, it recorded the information and dropped the call. If the automated dialing system crashed, which it did frequently, it redialed the entire list. The Irvines filed a suit in an Ohio state court against the *Beacon* and others, alleging in part an invasion of privacy. In whose favor should the court rule, and why? [*Irvine v. Akron Beacon Journal,* 147 Ohio App.3d 428, 770 N.E.2d 1105 (9 Dist. 2002)]

A Question of Ethics & Social Responsibility

8–11. Patsy Slone, while a guest at the Dollar Inn, a hotel, was stabbed in the thumb by a hypodermic needle concealed in the tube of a roll of toilet paper. Slone, fearing that she might have been exposed to the virus that causes acquired immune deficiency syndrome (AIDS), sued the hotel for damages to compensate her for the emotional distress she suffered after the needle stab. An Indiana trial court held for Slone and awarded her $250,000 in damages. The hotel appealed, and one of the issues before the court was whether Slone had to prove that she was actually exposed to AIDS to recover for emotional distress. The appellate court held that she did not and that her fear of getting AIDS was reasonable in these circumstances. [*Slone v. Dollar Inn, Inc.,* 695 N.E.2d 185 (Ind.App. 1998)]

1. Should the plaintiff in this case have been required to show that she was actually exposed to the AIDS virus in order to recover for emotional distress? Should she have been required to show that she actually acquired the AIDS virus as a result of the needle stab?
2. In some states, plaintiffs are barred from recovery in emotional distress cases unless the distress is evidenced by some kind of physical symptoms. Is this fair?

Critical-Thinking Managerial Question

8–12. Brian, an experienced all-terrain-vehicle (ATV) rider, purchases a new ATV manufactured by your company. Without putting on his helmet, Brian takes the ATV for a drive. The ATV flips over, and Brian strikes his head, causing severe injuries. Brian files a suit against your company. During the trial, it is proved that Brian's failure to wear a helmet was responsible for essentially all of his injuries. The relevant state law provides for a "50 percent" rule. Under these circumstances, will your company be liable for any of the damages sustained?

Video Question

8–13. Go to this text's Web site at http://leet.westbuslaw.com and select "Video Questions." Click on "Chapter 8" and view the video titled *Negligence and Assumption of Risk.* Then answer the following questions.

1. According to the chapter, what standard of care does the supermarket in the video owe to Maria?
2. Did Vinny, the employee of the supermarket, act as a reasonable person would have acted under the circumstances? Why or why not? Why is this determination important?
3. What was the proximate cause of Maria's injuries? Should the supermarket be liable for damages?
4. What defenses, other than assumption of risk, might be raised in this scenario?

INTERACTING WITH THE INTERNET

For updated links to resources available on the Web, as well as a variety of other materials, visit this text's Web site at

http://leet.westbuslaw.com

You can find cases and articles on torts, including business torts, in the tort law library at the Internet Law Library's Web site. Go to

http://www.lawguru.com/ilawlib

ONLINE LEGAL RESEARCH EXERCISES

Go to **http://leet.westbuslaw.com**, the Web site that accompanies this text. Select "Interactive Study Center," and then click on "Chapter 8." There you will find the following Internet research exercises that you can perform to learn more about topics covered in this chapter.

Activity 8–1: ECONOMIC PERSPECTIVE—Negligence and the *Titanic*
Activity 8–2: MANAGEMENT PERSPECTIVE—Legal and Illegal Uses of Spam

BEFORE THE TEST

Go to **http://leet.westbuslaw.com**, the Web site that accompanies this text. Select "Interactive Quizzes." You will find at least twenty interactive questions relating to this chapter.

Westlaw® Campus

If your textbook provided for a subscription to Westlaw® Campus, or if you have otherwise purchased access to the Westlaw Campus database, you can access any of the cases presented or cited in this chapter by using your Westlaw Campus account.

CHAPTER **9**

Strict Liability and Product Liability

CONTENTS

CHAPTER OBJECTIVES

After reading this chapter, you should be able to answer the following questions:

1. What is meant by strict liability?

2. What types of warranties may arise in a sales or lease transaction?

3. How can negligence and misrepresentation provide a basis for a product liability action?

4. What are the requirements for an action in strict product liability?

5. What defenses can be raised against product liability claims?

PRODUCT LIABILITY
The legal liability of manufacturers, sellers, and lessors of goods to consumers, users, and bystanders for injuries or damages that are caused by the goods.

Product liability refers to the liability incurred by manufacturers and sellers of products when product defects cause injury or property damage to consumers, users, or bystanders (people in the vicinity of the product). Product liability encompasses the tort theories of negligence and misrepresentation, which were discussed in Chapter 8. For example, as indicated in the quotation below, if a product is defective because of the manufacturer's negligence, an injured user of the product can sue the manufacturer for negligence in a product liability suit.

If a user is injured by a product as a result of the seller's fraudulent misrepresentation of the nature of that product, the basis of the product liability suit is fraud. In the last several decades, the doctrine of *strict liability* often has been applied in product liability suits. Product liability can also be based on warranty law. In this chapter, we examine each of these bases for product liability.

> "If the nature of a thing is such that it is reasonably certain to place life and limb in peril when negligently made, it is then a thing of danger."
>
> Benjamin N. Cardozo, 1870–1938
> (Associate justice of the United States Supreme Court, 1932–1938)

THE DOCTRINE OF STRICT LIABILITY

An important doctrine in tort law is **strict liability**, or *liability without fault*. Intentional torts and torts of negligence involve acts that depart from a reasonable standard of care and cause injuries. Under the doctrine of strict liability, liability for injury is imposed for reasons other than fault. Strict liability for damages proximately caused by an abnormally dangerous or exceptional activity is one application of this doctrine. Courts apply the doctrine of strict liability in such cases because of the extreme risk of the activity. ● EXAMPLE 1 Even if blasting with dynamite is performed with all reasonable care, there is still a risk of injury. Balancing that risk against the potential for harm, it seems reasonable to ask the person engaged in the activity to pay for injuries caused by that activity. Although there is no fault, there is still responsibility because of the dangerous nature of the undertaking.●

There are other applications of the strict liability principle. Persons who keep dangerous animals, for example, are strictly liable for any harm inflicted by the animals. In the business context, a significant application of strict liability is in the area of product liability. We will discuss what is known as *strict product liability* later in this chapter.

STRICT LIABILITY
Liability regardless of fault. In tort law, strict liability is imposed on a merchant who introduces into commerce a good that is unreasonably dangerous when in a defective condition.

WARRANTY LAW

Today, warranty law is an important part of the entire spectrum of laws relating to product liability. Most goods are covered by some type of warranty designed to protect consumers. The concept of warranty is based on the seller's assurance to the buyer that the goods will meet certain standards. Because a warranty imposes a duty on the seller, a breach of the warranty is a breach of the seller's promise.

The Uniform Commercial Code (UCC) designates five types of warranties that can arise in a contract for the sale of goods. These include express and implied warranties.

Express Warranties

A seller can create an **express warranty** by making a representation concerning the quality, condition, description, or performance potential of goods at such a time that the buyer could have relied on the representation when he or she agreed to the contract. These representations may be made in advertisements or by a salesperson.

Realize that sellers are allowed to "huff and puff" their wares as they like. Sellers' statements of opinion (such as "this car is a gem") are known as *puffery*, as noted in Chapter 8 in the discussion of the tort of misrepresentation. Normally, a seller's statement of *opinion* does not constitute an express warranty. If a seller makes a statement of *fact*, however, such as "this car has a new engine," this may create an express warranty if the statement goes to the "basis of the bargain"—that is, was essential to the buyer's decision to

EXPRESS WARRANTY
A promise, ancillary to an underlying sales agreement, that is included in the written or oral terms of the sales agreement under which the promisor assures the quality, description, or performance of the goods.

purchase the car. The line distinguishing puffery from statements that constitute express warranties is often blurred.

Implied Warranties

An **implied warranty of merchantability** that goods are "reasonably fit for the ordinary purposes for which such goods are used" arises automatically in a sale of goods by a merchant who deals in such goods. An **implied warranty of fitness for a particular purpose** arises when any seller—merchant or non-merchant—knows the particular purpose for which a buyer will use the goods and knows that the buyer is relying on the seller's skill and judgment to select suitable goods.

Liability for Breach of Warranty

Consumers, purchasers, and even users of goods can recover *from any seller* for losses resulting from breach of implied and express warranties. A manufacturer is a *seller*. Therefore, a person who purchases goods from a retailer can recover from the retailer or the manufacturer if the goods are not merchantable, because in most states *privity of contract* (the legal connection that exists between contracting parties) is no longer a prerequisite for recovery for personal injuries for a breach of warranty; that is, a product purchaser may sue not only the firm from which he or she purchased a product but also a third party—the manufacturer of the product—in product liability.

The UCC does permit warranties to be disclaimed or limited by specific and unambiguous language, provided that this is done in a manner that protects the buyer or lessee from surprise. Therefore, a written disclaimer in language that is clear and conspicuous, and called to a buyer's or lessee's attention, could negate all oral express warranties not included in the written sales contract. Generally speaking, unless circumstances indicate otherwise, the implied warranties of merchantability and fitness are disclaimed by the expressions "as is," "with all faults," and other similar phrases that in common understanding call the buyer's or lessee's attention to the fact that there are no implied warranties. (Disclaimers of warranties, both express and implied, are frequently contained in contracts formed online. For a discussion of one such warranty disclaimer, see this chapter's *Legal E-nvironment* feature.)

PRODUCT LIABILITY BASED ON NEGLIGENCE

In Chapter 8, *negligence* was defined as the failure to exercise the degree of care that a reasonable, prudent person would have exercised under the circumstances. If a manufacturer fails to exercise "due care" to make a product safe, a person who is injured by the product may sue the manufacturer for negligence.

Due Care Must Be Exercised

Due care must be exercised in designing the product, selecting the materials, using the appropriate production process, assembling the product, and placing

IMPLIED WARRANTY OF MERCHANTABILITY
A presumed promise by a merchant seller of goods that the goods are reasonably fit for the general purpose for which they are sold, are correctly packaged and labeled, and are of proper quality.

IMPLIED WARRANTY OF FITNESS FOR A PARTICULAR PURPOSE
A presumed promise made by a merchant seller of goods that the goods are fit for the particular purpose for which the buyer will use the goods. The seller must know the buyer's purpose and be aware that the buyer is relying on the seller's skill and judgment to select suitable goods.

RECALL The elements of negligence include a duty of care, a breach of the duty, and an injury to the plaintiff proximately caused by the breach.

LEGAL *e*-NVIRONMENT

Online Warranty Disclaimers

All too often, purchasers of goods or services fail to read the "fine print" of contracts. This is a problem not only with respect to traditional (paper) contracts but also with contracts formed online. Indeed, parties may be more likely to overlook contract provisions when the terms of the contract appear on a computer screen. Consider a case that came before a New York court.

Web Site Representations

The plaintiffs in the case were a group of subscribers to a DSL (digital subscriber line) service offered by Bell Atlantic Corporation. The subscribers claimed that Bell Atlantic had misrepresented the quality of its DSL service in statements made on its Web site. The representations at issue stated that subscribers would have "high-speed Internet access service up to 126 times faster than your 56K modem" and that the service was dedicated: "You're always connected—no dialing in and no busy signals, ever!" When the subscribers became dissatisfied with the actual connection speed and the fact that they sometimes had difficulty accessing Web sites, they sued Bell Atlantic for, among other things, breach of warranty. Bell Atlantic moved to dismiss the case on the ground that it had disclaimed all warranties in its online terms and conditions agreement.

It's All in the Contract— Including the Warranty Disclaimer

The court had little difficulty in granting Bell Atlantic's motion to dismiss the case. For one thing, stated the court, the plaintiffs had misunderstood the representations made by Bell Atlantic on its Web site. The representation as to high-speed service set forth a maximum possible speed, not the standard speed at which the service would operate. The representation regarding the dedicated connection referred to the fact that the connection need not be dialed up, not that the connection was infallible and would never be interrupted for any reason. The court also noted that the subscribers were given thirty days to try out the service and, if they were dissatisfied, to cancel it and receive a full refund.

Finally, Bell Atlantic's online terms and conditions agreement stated, in boldface, large capital letters, that the service was provided on an "as is" or "as available" basis and that "any and all warranties for the services, whether express or implied, including but not limited to the implied warranties of merchantability and fitness for a particular purpose" were disclaimed. In response to the plaintiffs' argument that it was possible to use the service without having read the terms and conditions, the court simply stated that this "does not impair the enforcement of the agreement."[a]

FOR CRITICAL ANALYSIS

If Bell Atlantic had promised on its Web site that DSL subscribers would have maximum-speed Internet access, would the subscribers have had a cause of action for breach of warranty? Why or why not?

---

a. *Scott v. Bell Atlantic Corp.,* 726 N.Y.S.2d 60 (N.Y.A.D. 1st Dept. 2001).

adequate warnings on the label informing the user of dangers of which an ordinary person might not be aware. The duty of care also extends to the inspection and testing of any purchased products that are used in the final product sold by the manufacturer.

ETHICAL ISSUE

Should gun manufacturers be required to warn of the dangers associated with gun use?

Across the nation, numerous plaintiffs have sued gun manufacturers for negligence. One of the allegations in many of these suits is that gun manufacturers have a duty to warn users of the dangers associated with gun use. The gun manufacturers counter that such dangers are "open and obvious" and that under negligence law there is no duty to warn of such dangers (see Chapter 8). In one of the first appellate court decisions addressing this issue, an Ohio appellate court ruled in favor of the gun manufacturer. Said the court, "Knives are sharp, bowling balls are heavy, bullets cause puncture wounds in flesh. The law has long recognized that obvious dangers are an excluded class." "Were we to decide otherwise," concluded the court, "we would open a Pandora's box." The Supreme Court of Ohio, however, reversed that decision and remanded the case.[1] Some other appellate courts are helping to make sure that "Pandora's box" stays closed. New York's highest court, for example, has held that a gun manufacturer's duty of care does not extend to those who are injured by the illegal use of handguns.[2]

Privity of Contract Not Required

A product liability action based on negligence does not require privity of contract between the injured plaintiff and the negligent defendant manufacturer. Section 395 of the *Restatement (Second) of Torts* states as follows:

> A manufacturer who fails to exercise reasonable care in the manufacture of a chattel [movable good] which, unless carefully made, he should recognize as involving an unreasonable risk of causing physical harm to those who lawfully use it for a purpose for which the manufacturer should expect it to be used and to those whom he should expect to be endangered by its probable use, is subject to liability for physical harm caused to them by its lawful use in a manner and for a purpose for which it is supplied.

In other words, a manufacturer is liable for its failure to exercise due care to any person who sustains an injury proximately caused by a negligently made (defective) product, regardless of whether the injured person is in privity of contract with the negligent defendant manufacturer or lessor. Relative to the long history of the common law, this exception to the privity requirement is a fairly recent development, dating to the early part of the twentieth century. A leading case in this respect is *MacPherson v. Buick Motor Co.*, which we present as this chapter's *Landmark in the Legal Environment* feature.

"The assault upon the citadel of privity [of contract] is proceeding in these days apace."

BENJAMIN CARDOZO, 1870–1938
(Associate justice of the United States Supreme Court, 1932–1938)

PRODUCT LIABILITY BASED ON MISREPRESENTATION

When a fraudulent misrepresentation has been made to a user or consumer, and that misrepresentation ultimately results in an injury, the basis of liability may be the tort of fraud. For example, the intentional mislabeling of packaged

1. *Cincinnati v. Beretta U.S.A. Corp.,* 95 Ohio St.3d 416, 768 N.E.2d 1136 (2002).
2. *Hamilton v. Beretta U.S.A. Corp.,* 96 N.Y.2d 222, 750 N.E.2d 1055, 727 N.Y.S.2d 7 (2001).

LANDMARK IN THE LEGAL ENVIRONMENT

MacPherson v. Buick Motor Co. (1916)

In the landmark case of *MacPherson v. Buick Motor Co.*,[a] the New York Court of Appeals—New York's highest court—dealt with the liability of a manufacturer that failed to exercise reasonable care in manufacturing a finished product.

CASE BACKGROUND   The case was brought by Donald MacPherson, who suffered injuries while riding in a Buick automobile that suddenly collapsed because one of the wheels was made of defective wood. The spokes crumbled into fragments, throwing MacPherson out of the vehicle and injuring him.

MacPherson had purchased the car from a Buick dealer, but he brought suit against the manufacturer, Buick Motor Company. The wheel itself had not been made by Buick; Buick bought it from another manufacturer. Evidence showed, however, that the defects could have been discovered by reasonable inspection by Buick and that no such inspection had taken place. MacPherson charged Buick with negligence for putting a human life in imminent danger.

THE ISSUE BEFORE THE COURT AND THE COURT'S RULING   The major issue before the court was whether Buick owed a duty of care to anyone except the immediate purchaser of the car (that is, the Buick dealer). In deciding the issue, Justice Benjamin Cardozo stated that "[i]f the nature of a thing is such that it is reasonably certain to place life and limb in peril when negligently made, it is then a thing of danger. . . . If to the element of danger there is added knowledge that the thing will be used by persons other than the purchaser, and used without new tests, then, irrespective of contract, the manufacturer of this thing of danger is under a duty to make it carefully."

The court concluded that "[b]eyond all question, the nature of an automobile gives warning of probable danger if its construction is defective. This automobile was designed to go 50 miles an hour. Unless its wheels were sound and strong, injury was almost certain." Although Buick had not manufactured the wheel itself, the court held that Buick had a duty to inspect the wheels and that Buick "was responsible for the finished product." Therefore, Buick was liable to MacPherson for the injuries he sustained when he was thrown from the car.

Application to Today's World

This landmark decision was a significant step toward the world we live in today—in which it is common for an automobile manufacturer to be held liable when its negligence causes a product user to be injured. As is often the situation, technological developments had necessitated changes in the law. Had the courts continued to require privity of contract in product liability cases, today's legal landscape would be quite different indeed. Certainly, fewer product liability cases would be pending before the courts; and just as certainly, many purchasers of products, including automobiles, would have less recourse for obtaining legal redress for injuries caused by those products.

a. 217 N.Y. 382, 111 N.E. 1050 (1916).

---

cosmetics and the intentional concealment of a product's defects would constitute fraudulent misrepresentation. Nonfraudulent misrepresentation, which occurs when a merchant *innocently* misrepresents the character or quality of goods, can also provide a basis of liability. In this situation, the plaintiff does not have to prove that the misrepresentation was made knowingly.

Whether fraudulent or nonfraudulent, the misrepresentation must be of a material fact (a fact concerning the quality, nature, or appropriate use of the product on which a normal buyer may be expected to rely). There must also

> "One may smile, and smile, and be a villain."
>
> WILLIAM SHAKESPEARE, 1564–1616
> (English dramatist and poet)

have been an intent to induce the buyer's reliance on the misrepresentation. Misrepresentation on a label or advertisement is enough to show an intent to induce the reliance of anyone who may use the product. The buyer also must rely on the misrepresentation. If the buyer is not aware of the misrepresentation or if it does not influence the transaction, there is no liability.

STRICT PRODUCT LIABILITY

Under the doctrine of strict liability, discussed earlier in this chapter, people may be liable for the results of their acts regardless of their intentions or their exercise of reasonable care. Under this doctrine, liability does not depend on privity of contract. The injured party does not have to be the buyer or a third party beneficiary, as required under contract warranty theory. Indeed, this type of liability in law is not governed by the provisions of the UCC because it is a tort doctrine, not a principle of the law relating to sales contracts.

Strict Product Liability and Public Policy

Strict product liability is imposed by law as a matter of public policy. This policy rests on the threefold assumption that (1) consumers should be protected against unsafe products; (2) manufacturers and distributors should not escape liability for faulty products simply because they are not in privity of contract with the ultimate user of those products; and (3) manufacturers, sellers, and lessors of products are generally in a better position than consumers to bear the costs associated with injuries caused by their products—costs that they can ultimately pass on to all consumers in the form of higher prices.

California was the first state to impose strict product liability in tort on manufacturers. In the landmark decision that follows, the California Supreme Court sets out the reason for applying tort law rather than contract law to cases in which consumers are injured by defective products.

LANDMARK AND CLASSIC CASES

CASE 9.1   Greenman v. Yuba Power Products, Inc.

Supreme Court of California, 1962.
59 Cal.2d 57,
377 P.2d 897,
27 Cal.Rptr. 697.

BACKGROUND AND FACTS The plaintiff, Greenman, wanted a Shopsmith—a combination power tool that could be used as a saw, drill, and wood lathe—after seeing a Shopsmith demonstrated by a retailer and studying a brochure prepared by the manufacturer. The plaintiff's wife bought and gave him one for Christmas. More than a year later, a piece of wood flew out of the lathe attachment of the Shopsmith while the plaintiff was using it, inflicting serious injuries on him. About ten and a half months later, the plaintiff filed a suit in a California state court against both the retailer and the manufacturer for breach of warranties and negligence. The trial court jury found for the plaintiff. The case was ultimately appealed to the Supreme Court of California.

IN THE WORDS
OF THE COURT . . .

TRAYNOR, Justice.
     *   *   *   *

Plaintiff introduced substantial evidence that his injuries were caused by defective design and construction of the Shopsmith. * * * The jury could

CASE 9.1—Continued

therefore reasonably have concluded that the manufacturer negligently constructed the Shopsmith. The jury could also reasonably have concluded that statements in the manufacturer's brochure were untrue, that they constituted express warranties, and that plaintiff's injuries were caused by their breach.

* * * *

[But] to impose strict liability on the manufacturer under the circumstances of this case, it was not necessary for plaintiff to establish an express warranty * * *. *A manufacturer is strictly liable in tort when an article he places on the market, knowing that it is to be used without inspection for defects, proves to have a defect that causes injury to a human being.* * * * [Emphasis added.]

* * * *

* * * The purpose of such liability is to insure that the costs of injuries resulting from defective products are borne by the manufacturers * * * rather than by the injured persons who are powerless to protect themselves.

DECISION AND REMEDY The Supreme Court of California upheld the verdict for the plaintiff.

COMMENT *From the earliest days of the common law, English courts applied a doctrine of strict liability. Often, persons whose conduct resulted in injuries to others were held liable for damages, even if they had not intended to injure anyone and had exercised reasonable care. This approach was abandoned around 1800 in favor of a fault-based approach, in which an action was considered tortious only if it was wrongful or blameworthy in some respect. Strict liability began to be reapplied to manufactured goods in several landmark cases in the 1960s, a decade when many traditional assumptions were being challenged. The case just presented is considered a landmark in U.S. law not only because it revived the doctrine of strict liability for defective products but also because it enunciated a compelling reason for doing so—protecting "injured persons who are powerless to protect themselves."*

Requirements for Strict Liability

Section 402A of the *Restatement (Second) of Torts* indicates how it was envisioned that the doctrine of strict liability should be applied. It was issued in 1964, and during the decade following its release it became a widely accepted statement of the liabilities of sellers of goods (including manufacturers, processors, assemblers, packagers, bottlers, wholesalers, distributors, retailers, and lessors). Section 402A states as follows:

(1) One who sells any product in a defective condition unreasonably dangerous to the user or consumer or to his property is subject to liability for physical harm thereby caused to the ultimate user or consumer or to his property, if
    (a) the seller is engaged in the business of selling such a product, and
    (b) it is expected to and does reach the user or consumer without substantial change in the condition in which it is sold.
(2) The rule stated in Subsection (1) applies although
    (a) the seller has exercised all possible care in the preparation and sale of his product, and
    (b) the user or consumer has not bought the product from or entered into any contractual relation with the seller.

The Six Requirements for Strict Liability The bases for an action in strict liability is set forth in Section 402A of the *Restatement (Second) of Torts*. The

If a child is injured by a toy, does he or she (through his or her parents) have a cause of action against the manufacturer?

doctrine, as it came to be commonly applied, can be summarized as a series of six requirements, which are listed here.

1. The product must be in a defective condition when the defendant sells it.
2. The defendant must normally be engaged in the business of selling (or otherwise distributing) that product.
3. The product must be unreasonably dangerous to the user or consumer because of its defective condition (in most states).
4. The plaintiff must incur physical harm to self or property by use or consumption of the product.
5. The defective condition must be the proximate cause of the injury or damage.
6. The goods must not have been substantially changed from the time the product was sold to the time the injury was sustained.

Unreasonably Dangerous Products Under the requirements just listed, in any action against a manufacturer, seller, or lessor, the plaintiff does not have to show why or in what manner the product became defective. To recover damages, however, the plaintiff must show that the product was so "defective" as to be "unreasonably dangerous"; that the product caused the plaintiff's injury; and that at the time the injury was sustained, the condition of the product was essentially the same as when it left the hands of the defendant manufacturer, seller, or lessor.

   A court could consider a product so defective as to be an **unreasonably dangerous product** if either (1) the product was dangerous beyond the expectation of the ordinary consumer or (2) a less dangerous alternative was eco-

UNREASONABLY DANGEROUS PRODUCT
A product that is defective to the point of threatening a consumer's health and safety. A product will be considered unreasonably dangerous if it is dangerous beyond the expectation of the ordinary consumer or if a less dangerous alternative was economically feasible for the manufacturer but the manufacturer failed to produce it.

nomically feasible for the manufacturer, but the manufacturer failed to produce it. As will be discussed in the next section, a product may be unreasonably dangerous due to a flaw in the manufacturing process, a design defect, or an inadequate warning.

Product Defects

Because Section 402A of the *Restatement (Second) of Torts* did not clearly define such terms as "defective" and "unreasonably dangerous," these terms have been subject to different interpretations by different courts. In 1997, to address these concerns, the American Law Institute (ALI) issued the *Restatement (Third) of Torts: Products Liability.* The *Restatement* defines the three types of product defects that have traditionally been recognized in product liability law—manufacturing defects, design defects, and warning defects.

Manufacturing Defects According to Section 2(a) of the latest *Restatement,* a product "contains a manufacturing defect when the product departs from its intended design even though all possible care was exercised in the preparation and marketing of the product." This statement imposes liability on the manufacturer (and on the wholesaler and retailer) regardless of whether the manufacturer acted "reasonably." This is strict liability, or liability without fault.

Design Defects A determination that a product has a design defect (or a warning defect, to be discussed shortly) can affect all of the units of a product. A product "is defective in design when the foreseeable risks of harm posed by the product could have been reduced or avoided by the adoption of a reasonable alternative design by the seller or other distributor, or a predecessor in the commercial chain of distribution, and the omission of the alternative design renders the product not reasonably safe."[3]

To succeed in a product liability suit alleging a design defect, a plaintiff must show that there is a reasonable alternative design. In other words, a manufacturer or other defendant is liable only when the harm was *reasonably* preventable. According to the Official Comments accompanying the *Restatement (Third) of Torts: Products Liability,* factors that a court may consider on this point include

> the magnitude and probability of the foreseeable risks of harm, the instructions and warnings accompanying the product, and the nature and strength of consumer expectations regarding the product, including expectations arising from product portrayal and marketing. The relative advantages and disadvantages of the product as designed and as it alternatively could have been designed may also be considered. Thus, the likely effects of the alternative design on production costs; the effects of the alternative design on product longevity, maintenance, repair, and esthetics; and the range of consumer choice among products are factors that may be taken into account.

Note that "consumer expectations," instead of being the entire test, are only one factor taken into consideration. Another factor is the warning that accompanies a product. Can a warning insulate a manufacturer from liability for the harm caused by a design defect? That was the issue in the following case.

---

3. *Restatement (Third) of Torts: Products Liability,* Section 2(b).

CASE 9.2   Rogers v. Ingersoll-Rand Co.

United States Court of Appeals,
District of Columbia Circuit, 1998.
144 F.3d 841.
http://laws.lp.findlaw.com/
DC/ 977131A.html[a]

COMPANY PROFILE *Ingersoll-Rand Company is a manufacturer of air compressors, construction and mining equipment, bearings and precision components, tools, locks and architectural hardware, and industrial machinery. The company also makes Bobcat skid-steer loaders, Blaw-Knox pavers, Club Car golf carts and light utility vehicles, and Thermo King transport temperature control systems. In joint ventures with other firms, Ingersoll-Rand is a supplier of pumps and hydrocarbon processing equipment and services. Ingersoll-Rand distributes its products in more than one hundred countries. Forty percent of its sales are outside the United States.*

BACKGROUND AND FACTS Among the equipment that Ingersoll-Rand makes is a milling machine. In the maintenance manual that accompanies the machine are warnings that users should stay ten feet away from the rear of the machine when it is operating, verify that the back-up alarm is working, and check the area for the presence of others. There is also a sign on the machine that tells users to stay ten feet away. While using the machine to strip asphalt from a road being repaved, Terrill Wilson backed up. The alarm did not sound, and Cosandra Rogers, who was standing with her back to the machine, was run over and maimed. Rogers filed a suit in a federal district court against Ingersoll-Rand, alleging in part strict liability on the basis of a design defect. The jury awarded Rogers $10.2 million in compensatory damages and $6.5 million in punitive damages. Ingersoll-Rand appealed, emphasizing the adequacy of its warnings.

**IN THE WORDS
OF THE COURT . . .**

SENTELLE, Justice.

*   *   *   *

*   *   * Under [a risk-utility balancing] test [in a defective design case], a plaintiff must show the risks, costs and benefits of the product in question and alternative designs, and that the magnitude of the danger from the product outweighed the costs of avoiding danger. *   *   *

[Ingersoll-Rand argues that] the adequacy of its warnings [should be] the sole consideration in the risk-utility analysis. As Ingersoll-Rand would have it, once the jury evaluates the milling machine's warnings and finds them adequate, its job is over; it "should find for [the] defendant." *   *   * [T]he "warnings" defense would have instructed the jury that adequate warnings trump all other factors—including the "magnitude of the danger from the product" *   *   * .

*   *   *   *

We do not mean to dispute that warnings may tip the balance in a manufacturer's favor in individual cases. On the other hand, warnings need not be the [decisive] factor in every case. Here, for example, it seems reasonably foreseeable that a worker with her back to a milling machine would be in no position to "heed" a sign on the machine instructing her to keep ten feet away. Under these circumstances, a manufacturer may have a heightened responsibility to incorporate additional safety features to guard against foreseeable harm.

DECISION AND REMEDY The U.S. Court of Appeals for the District of Columbia Circuit upheld the jury's award. The court held that an adequate warning cannot immunize a manufacturer from any liability caused by a defectively designed product.

FOR CRITICAL ANALYSIS—Technological Consideration *What other safety features might a manufacturer use in these circumstances?*

---

a. This is a page within the Web site of FindLaw (now a part of West Group), an Internet site offering legal sources.

Warning Defects A product may also be deemed defective because of inadequate instructions or warnings. A product "is defective because of inadequate instructions or warnings when the foreseeable risks of harm posed by the product could have been reduced or avoided by the provision of reasonable instructions or warnings by the seller or other distributor, or a predecessor in the commercial chain of distribution, and the omission of the instructions or warnings renders the product not reasonably safe."[4]

Important factors for a court to consider under the *Restatement (Third) of Torts: Products Liability* include the risks of a product, the "content and comprehensibility" and "intensity of expression" of warnings and instructions, and the "characteristics of expected user groups."[5] For example, children would likely respond readily to bright, bold, simple warning labels, whereas educated adults might need more detailed information.

Obvious Risks. There is no duty to warn about risks that are obvious or commonly known. Warnings about such risks do not add to the safety of a product and could even detract from it by making other warnings seem less significant. The obviousness of a risk and a user's decision to proceed in the face of that risk may be a defense in a product liability suit based on a warning defect. (Defenses to product liability will be discussed later in the chapter.)

ETHICAL ISSUE

Do pharmacists have a duty to warn customers about the side effects of drugs?

Clearly, manufacturers of pharmaceuticals have a duty to disclose and warn users of any side effects associated with their products.

Typically, these disclosures and warnings are given to physicians, and many pharmacies today include a list of possible side effects with the drugs that they dispense. What if a pharmacist does not disclose the potential side effects of a drug being sold? Should the pharmacy be held liable if a purchaser suffers harms from a drug's side effects? This question, which has both legal and ethical implications, has come before several courts in recent years—and the courts have reached different conclusions.

In one case, for example, an Illinois court held that a pharmacist had a duty to warn his customer about a potentially fatal drug reaction to a prescribed medication. The court reasoned that the duty existed because the pharmacist knew of the customer's allergies, knew that the prescribed medication should not be taken by a person with those allergies, and knew that injury or death was substantially certain to result.[6] In another case, however, a Texas appellate court reached the opposite conclusion. The court held that imposing such a duty on pharmacists would necessarily interfere with the physician-patient relationship because pharmacies seeking to avoid liability would "question the propriety of every prescription they fill."[7] Clearly, the arguments put forth in both cases have merit, and as yet the courts have not reached a consensus on the issue.

---

4. *Restatement (Third) of Torts: Products Liability*, Section 2(c).
5. *Restatement (Third) of Torts: Products Liability*, Section 2, Comment h.
6. *Happel v. Wal-Mart Stores, Inc.*, 193 Ill.2d 586, 744 N.E.2d 284, 253 Ill.Dec. 2 (2001).
7. *Morgan v. Wal-Mart Stores, Inc.*, 30 S.W.3d 455 (Tex.App.–Austin 2001).

Foreseeable Misuses. Generally, a seller must warn those who purchase its product of the harm that can result from the foreseeable misuse of the product as well. The key is the foreseeability of the misuse. According to the Official Comments accompanying the *Restatement (Third) of Torts: Products Liability,* sellers "are not required to foresee and take precautions against every conceivable mode of use and abuse to which their products might be put."

Market-Share Liability

Generally, in all cases involving product liability, a plaintiff must prove that the defective product that caused his or her injury was the product of a specific defendant. In the last decade or so, in cases in which plaintiffs could not prove which of many distributors of a harmful product supplied the particular product that caused the plaintiffs' injuries, courts have dropped this requirement.

● EXAMPLE 2 Market-share liability has been imposed in several product liability cases involving DES (diethylstilbestrol), a drug administered in the past to prevent miscarriages. DES's harmful character was not realized until, a generation later, daughters of the women who had taken DES developed health problems, including vaginal carcinoma, that were linked to the drug. Partly because of the passage of time, a plaintiff-daughter often could not prove which pharmaceutical company—out of as many as three hundred—had marketed the DES her mother had ingested. In these cases, some courts applied market-share liability, holding that all firms that manufactured and distributed DES during the period in question were liable for the plaintiffs' injuries in proportion to the firms' respective shares of the market.[8] ●

Market-share liability has also been applied in other situations. ● EXAMPLE 3 In one case, a plaintiff who was a hemophiliac received injections of a blood protein known as antihemophiliac factor (AHF) concentrate. The plaintiff later tested positive for the AIDS (acquired immune deficiency syndrome) virus. Because it was not known which manufacturer was responsible for the particular AHF received by the plaintiff, the court held that all of the manufacturers of AHF could be held liable under a market-share theory of liability.[9] ●

Other Applications of Strict Liability

Although the drafters of the *Restatement (Second) of Torts,* Section 402A, did not take a position on bystanders, all courts extend the strict liability of manufacturers and other sellers to injured bystanders. The rule of strict liability also is applicable to suppliers of component parts. ● EXAMPLE 4 General Motors buys brake pads from a subcontractor and puts them in Chevrolets without changing their composition. If those pads are defective, both the supplier of the brake pads and General Motors will be held strictly liable for the damages caused by the defective parts. ●

---

8. See, for example, *Martin v. Abbott Laboratories,* 102 Wash.2d 581, 689 P.2d 368 (1984).
9. *Smith v. Cutter Biological, Inc.,* 72 Haw. 416, 823 P.2d 717 (1991).

DEFENSES TO PRODUCT LIABILITY

There are several defenses that manufacturers, sellers, or lessors can raise to avoid liability for harms caused by their products. We look at some of these defenses here.

Assumption of Risk

Assumption of risk can sometimes be used as a defense in a product liability action. For example, if a buyer fails to heed a product recall by the seller, a court might conclude that the buyer assumed the risk caused by the defect that led to the recall. To establish such a defense, the defendant must show that (1) the plaintiff knew and appreciated the risk created by the product defect and (2) the plaintiff voluntarily assumed the risk, even though it was unreasonable to do so. (See Chapter 8 for a more detailed discussion of assumption of risk.)

BE CAREFUL A defendant cannot successfully claim that the plaintiff assumed a risk different from or greater than the risk normally associated with the product.

Product Misuse

Similar to the defense of voluntary assumption of risk is that of misuse of the product. Here, the injured party *does not know that the product is dangerous for a particular use* (contrast this with assumption of risk), but the use is not the one for which the product was designed. The courts have severely limited this defense, however. Even if the injured party does not know about the inherent danger of using the product in a wrong way, if the misuse is foreseeable, the seller must take measures to guard against it.

Comparative Negligence

Developments in the area of comparative negligence (discussed in Chapter 8) have even affected the doctrine of strict liability—the most extreme theory of product liability. Whereas previously the plaintiff's conduct was not a defense to strict liability, today many jurisdictions consider the negligent or intentional actions of both the plaintiff and the defendant in the apportionment of liability and damages. This means that even if a product was misused by the plaintiff, the plaintiff may nonetheless be able to recover at least some damages for injuries caused by the defendant's defective product.

Commonly Known Dangers

The dangers associated with certain products (such as sharp knives and guns) are so commonly known that manufacturers need not warn users of those dangers. If a defendant succeeds in convincing the court that a plaintiff's injury resulted from a *commonly known danger,* the defendant normally will not be liable.

● EXAMPLE 5 A classic case on this issue involved a plaintiff who was injured when an elastic exercise rope that she had purchased slipped off her foot and struck her in the eye, causing a detachment of the retina. The plaintiff claimed that the manufacturer should be liable because it had failed to warn users that the exerciser might slip off a foot in such a manner. The court stated that to hold the manufacturer liable in these circumstances "would go beyond the reasonable dictates of justice in fixing the liabilities of manufacturers." After all, stated the court, "[a]lmost every physical object can be inherently dangerous or potentially dangerous in a sense. . . . A manufacturer cannot manufacture a knife that will not cut or a hammer that will not mash a thumb or a stove that will not burn a finger. The law does not require [manufacturers] to warn of such common dangers."[10]●

A related defense is the *knowledgeable user* defense. If a particular danger (such as electrical shock) is or should be commonly known by particular users of the product (such as electricians), the manufacturer of electrical equipment need not warn these users of the danger.

The following case was the first of its kind. As the defendants argued, and the court acknowledged, the outcome of the case "could spawn thousands of similar 'McLawsuits' against restaurants. Even if limited to that ilk of fare dubbed 'fast food,' the potential for lawsuits is great."

---

10. *Jamieson v. Woodward & Lothrop*, 247 F.2d 23, 101 D.C.App. 32 (1957).

CASE 9.3   Pelman v. McDonald's Corp.

United States District Court,
Southern District of New York, 2003.
237 F.Supp.2d 512.

HISTORICAL AND SOCIAL
SETTING *Americans spend more than $110 billion on fast food each year, and on any given day in the United States, almost one in four adults visits a fast-food restaurant. Today, there are nearly twice as many overweight children and almost three times as many overweight adolescents as there were in 1980. In 2004, an estimated 60 percent of U.S. adults were overweight or obese. Compared to the normal-weight population, obese individuals have a 50 to 100 percent increased risk of premature death.*

BACKGROUND AND FACTS McDonald's
Corporation has its main administrative office in Oak Brook, Illinois, but does business throughout the world,

serving nearly 46 million customers each day. McDonald's, with about 13,000 restaurants in the United States, has a 43 percent share of the U.S. fast-food market. McDonald's of New York has its principal place of business in Albany, New York, but owns and operates fast-food outlets throughout the state. Ashley Pelman, a New York resident, and other teenagers who often ate at the McDonald's outlets, became overweight and developed adverse health effects. Their parents filed a suit in a New York state court against McDonald's and others, alleging that, among other things, the defendants failed to warn of the quantities, qualities, and levels of cholesterol, fat, salt, sugar, and other ingredients in their products, and that a diet high in fat, salt, sugar, and cholesterol could lead to obesity and health problems. The suit was transferred to a federal district court. The defendants filed a motion to dismiss the complaint.

IN THE WORDS
OF THE COURT . . .

SWEET, District Judge.

*   *   *   *

This opinion is guided by the principle that *legal consequences should not attach to the consumption of hamburgers and other fast food fare unless consumers are unaware of the dangers of eating such food. *   *   * If consumers know (or reasonably should know) the potential ill health effects of eating at McDonald's, they cannot blame McDonald's if they, nonetheless, choose to satiate their appetite with a surfeit of supersized McDonald's products. On the

CASE 9.3—Continued

other hand, consumers cannot be expected to protect against a danger that was solely within McDonald's knowledge. Thus, one necessary element of any potentially viable claim must be that McDonald's products involve a danger that is not within the common knowledge of consumers. * * * [Emphasis added.]

* * * *

[Among other things, the plaintiffs assert] that McDonald's failed to post nutritional labeling on the products and at points of purchase. * * *

* * * *

* * * Plaintiffs admit that McDonald's has made its nutritional information available online and do not contest that such information is available upon request. Unless McDonald's has specifically promised to provide nutritional information on all its products and at all points of purchase, plaintiffs do not state a claim.

* * * *

[Or] in order to state a claim, the Complaint must allege * * * that the attributes of McDonald's products are so extraordinarily [unhealthful] that they are outside the reasonable contemplation of the consuming public * * * . The Complaint—which merely alleges that the foods contain high levels of cholesterol, fat, salt and sugar, and that the foods are therefore [unhealthful]—fails to reach this bar. It is well-known that fast food in general, and McDonald's products in particular, contain high levels of cholesterol, fat, salt, and sugar, and that such attributes are bad for one.

* * * If a person knows or should know that eating copious orders of supersized McDonald's products is [unhealthful] and may result in weight gain (and its [attending] problems) because of the high levels of cholesterol, fat, and salt, it is not the place of the law to protect them from their own excesses. Nobody is forced to eat at McDonald's. * * * Even more pertinent, nobody is forced to supersize their meal or choose less healthy options on the menu.

DECISION AND REMEDY The court dismissed the plaintiffs' complaint, because it failed to allege that the products consumed by the plaintiffs were dangerous in any way other than that which was open and obvious to a reasonable consumer.

FOR CRITICAL ANALYSIS—Social Consideration *Where should the line be drawn between an individual's responsibility to take care of himself or herself and society's responsibility to protect that individual?*

Other Defenses

A defendant can also defend against product liability by showing that there is no basis for the plaintiff's claim. Suppose that a plaintiff alleges that a seller breached an implied warranty. If the seller can prove that he or she effectively disclaimed all implied warranties, the plaintiff cannot recover. Similarly, in a product liability case based on negligence, a defendant who can show that the plaintiff has not met the requirements (such as causation) for an action in negligence will not be liable. In regard to strict product liability, a defendant could claim that the plaintiff failed to meet one of the requirements for an action in strict liability. If the defendant establishes that the goods have been subsequently altered, the defendant will not be held liable.

Statutes of Limitations and Repose

As discussed earlier in this text, *statutes of limitations* restrict the time within which an action may be brought. A typical statute of limitations provides that an action must be brought within a specified period of time after the cause of action accrues. Generally, a cause of action is held to accrue when some damage occurs. Sometimes, the running of the prescribed period is *tolled* (that is, suspended) until the party suffering an injury has discovered it or should have discovered it.

Many states have passed laws, called **statutes of repose,** placing outer time limits on some claims so that the defendant will not be left vulnerable to lawsuits indefinitely. These statutes may limit the time within which a plaintiff can file a product liability suit. Typically, a statute of repose begins to run at an earlier date and runs for a longer time than a statute of limitations. For example, a statute of repose may require that claims must be brought within twelve years from the date of sale or manufacture of the defective product. It is immaterial that the product is defective or causes an injury if the injury occurs *after* this statutory period has lapsed. In addition, some of these legislative enactments have limited the application of the doctrine of strict liability only to new goods.

STATUTES OF REPOSE
Laws that place time limits on some claims so that defendants will not be vulnerable to lawsuits indefinitely.

KEY TERMS

express warranty   269
implied warranty of fitness for a
   particular purpose   270
implied warranty of
   merchantability   270

product liability   268
statutes of repose   284
strict liability   269

unreasonably dangerous
   product   276

CHAPTER SUMMARY   STRICT LIABILITY AND PRODUCT LIABILITY

The Doctrine of Strict Liability (See page 269.)	Under the doctrine of strict liability, a person may be held liable, regardless of the degree of care exercised, for damages or injuries caused by his or her product or activity. Strict liability includes liability for harms caused by abnormally dangerous activities, by wild animals, and by defective products (product liability).
Warranty Law (See pages 269–270.)	Under the Uniform Commercial Code, certain warranties can arise in a contract for a sale of goods. These include express warranties, an implied warranty of merchantability, and an implied warranty of fitness for a particular purpose. Consumers and others can recover from any seller for losses resulting from a breach of these warranties.
Product Liability Based on Negligence (See pages 270–272.)	1. Due care must be used by the manufacturer in designing the product, selecting materials, using the appropriate production process, assembling and testing the product, and placing adequate warnings on the label or product.
	2. Privity of contract is not required. A manufacturer is liable for failure to exercise due care to any person who sustains an injury proximately caused by a negligently made (defective) product.

CHAPTER SUMMARY STRICT LIABILITY AND PRODUCT LIABILITY—Continued

Product Liability Based on Misrepresentation (See pages 272–274.)	Fraudulent misrepresentation of a product may result in product liability based on the tort of fraud.
Strict Liability— Requirements (See pages 275–277.)	1. The defendant must sell the product in a defective condition. 2. The defendant must normally be engaged in the business of selling that product. 3. The product must be unreasonably dangerous to the user or consumer because of its defective condition (in most states). 4. The plaintiff must incur physical harm to self or property. 5. The defective condition must be the proximate cause of the injury or damage. 6. The goods must not have been substantially changed from the time the product was sold to the time the injury was sustained.
Strict Liability— Product Defects (See pages 277–280.)	There are three basic ways in which a product may be defective: 1. In its manufacture. 2. In its design. 3. In the instructions or warnings that come with it.
Market-Share Liability (See page 280.)	In cases in which plaintiffs cannot prove which of many distributors of a defective product supplied the particular product that caused the plaintiffs' injuries, some courts have applied market-share liability. All firms that manufactured and distributed the harmful product during the period in question are then held liable for the plaintiffs' injuries in proportion to the firms' respective shares of the market, as directed by the court.
Other Applications of Strict Liability (See page 280.)	1. Manufacturers and other sellers are liable for harms suffered by injured bystanders due to defective products. 2. Suppliers of component parts are strictly liable for defective parts that, when incorporated into a product, cause injuries to users.
Defenses to Product Liability (See pages 281–284.)	1. *Assumption of risk*—The user or consumer knew of the risk of harm and voluntarily assumed it. 2. *Product misuse*—The user or consumer misused the product in a way unforeseeable by the manufacturer. 3. *Comparative negligence and liability*—Liability may be distributed between plaintiff and defendant under the doctrine of comparative negligence if the plaintiff's misuse of the product contributed to the risk of injury. 4. *Commonly known dangers*—If a defendant succeeds in convincing the court that a plaintiff's injury resulted from a commonly known danger, such as the danger associated with using a sharp knife, the defendant will not be liable. 5. *Other defenses*—A defendant can also defend against a strict liability claim by showing that there is no basis for the plaintiff's claim (that the plaintiff has not met the requirements for an action in negligence). 6. *Statutes of repose*—Many states have passed statutes of repose, which limit the time within which a plaintiff can file a product liability suit.

FOR REVIEW

1. What is meant by strict liability?
2. What types of warranties may arise in a sales or lease transaction?
3. How can negligence and misrepresentation provide a basis for a product liability action?
4. What are the requirements for an action in strict product liability?
5. What defenses can be raised against product liability claims?

QUESTIONS AND CASE PROBLEMS

9–1. Product Liability. Carmen buys a television set manufactured by AKI Electronics. She is going on vacation, so she takes the set to her mother's house for her mother to use. Because the set is defective, it explodes, causing considerable damage to her mother's home. Carmen's mother sues AKI for the damages to her house. Discuss the theories under which Carmen's mother can recover from AKI.

9–2. Failure to Warn. A water pipe burst, flooding a company's switchboard and tripping the switchboard circuit breakers. Company employees assigned to reactivate the switchboard included an electrical technician with twelve years of on-the-job training, a licensed electrician, and an electrical engineer who had studied power engineering in college and had twenty years of experience. The employees attempted to switch one of the circuit breakers back on without testing for short circuits, which they later admitted they knew how to do and should have done. The circuit breaker failed to engage but ignited an explosive fire. The company sued the supplier of the circuit breakers for damages, alleging that the supplier had failed to give adequate warnings and instructions regarding the circuit breakers. How might the supplier defend against this claim? Discuss.

9–3. Product Liability. Colt manufactures a new pistol. The firing of the pistol depends on an enclosed high-pressure device. The pistol has been thoroughly tested in two laboratories in the Midwest, and its design and manufacture are in accord with current technology. Wayne purchases one of the new pistols from Hardy's Gun and Rifle Emporium. When he uses the pistol in the high altitude of the Rockies, the difference in pressure causes the pistol to misfire, resulting in serious injury to Wayne. Colt can prove that all due care was used in the manufacturing process, and it refuses to pay for Wayne's injuries. Discuss Colt's liability in tort.

9–4. Product Liability. Baxter manufactures electric hair dryers. Julie purchases a Baxter dryer from her local Ace Drugstore. Cox, a friend and guest in Julie's home, has taken a shower and wants to dry her hair. Julie tells Cox to use the new Baxter hair dryer that she has just purchased. As Cox plugs in the dryer, sparks fly out from the motor, and sparks continue to fly as she operates it. Despite this, Cox begins drying her hair. Suddenly, the entire dryer ignites into flames, severely burning Cox's scalp. Cox sues Baxter on the basis of negligence and strict liability in tort. Baxter admits the dryer was defective but denies liability, particularly because Cox was not the person who purchased the dryer. In other words, Cox had no contractual relationship with Baxter. Discuss the validity of Baxter's defense. Are there any other defenses that Baxter might assert to avoid liability? Discuss fully.

9–5. Product Liability. Gina is standing on a street corner waiting for a ride to work. Gomez has just purchased a new car manufactured by Optimal Motors. He is driving down the street when suddenly the steering mechanism breaks, causing him to run over Gina. Gina suffers permanent injuries. Gomez's total income per year has never exceeded $15,000. Thus, instead of suing Gomez, Gina files suit against Optimal under the theory of strict liability in tort. Optimal claims that it is not liable because (1) due care was used in the manufacture of the car, (2) Optimal is not the manufacturer of the steering mechanism (Smith is), and (3) strict product liability applies only to users or consumers, and Gina is neither. Discuss the validity of the defenses claimed by Optimal.

9–6. Failure to Warn. When Mary Bresnahan drove her Chrysler LeBaron, she sat very close to the steering wheel—less than a foot away from the steering-wheel enclosure of the driver's side air bag. At the time, Chrysler did not provide any warning that a driver should not sit close to the air bag. In an accident with another car, Bresnahan's air bag deployed. The bag caused her elbow to strike the windshield pillar and fracture in three places, resulting in repeated surgery and physical therapy. Bresnahan filed a suit in a California state court against Chrysler to recover for her injuries, alleging in part that they were caused by Chrysler's failure to warn consumers about sitting near the air bag. At the trial, an expert testified that the air bag was not intended to prevent arm injuries, which were "a predictable, incidental consequence" of the bag's deploying. Should Chrysler pay for Bresnahan's injuries? Why or why not? [*Bresnahan v. Chrysler Corp.,* 76 Cal.Rptr.2d 804, 65 Cal.App.4th 1149 (1998)]

9–7. Product Liability. New England Ecological Development, Inc. (NEED), a recycling station in Rhode Island, needed a conveyor belt system and gave the specifications to Colmar Belting Co. Colmar did not design or make belts but distributed the component parts. For this system, Emerson Power Transmission Corp. (EPT) manufactured the wing pulley, a component of the nip point (the point at which a belt moves over the stationary part of the system). Kenneth Butler, a welder, assembled the system with assistance from Colmar. Neither Colmar nor EPT recommended the use of a protective shield to guard the nip point, and as finally built, NEED's system did not have a shield. Later, as Americo Buonanno, a NEED employee, was clearing debris from the belt, his arm was pulled into the nip point. The arm was severely crushed and later amputated at the elbow. Buonanno filed a suit in a Rhode Island state court against Colmar and EPT, alleging in part strict liability. The defendants filed a motion for summary judgment, arguing that as sellers of component parts, they had no duty to ensure the proper design of the final product. On what grounds might the court deny the motion? [*Buonanno v. Colmar Belting Co.*, 733 A.2d 712 (R.I. 1999)]

Case Problem with Sample Answer

9–8. Design Defect. In May 1995, Ms. McCathern and her daughter, together with McCathern's cousin, Ms. Sanders, and her daughter, were riding in Sanders's 1994 Toyota 4Runner. Sanders was driving, McCathern was in the front passenger seat, and the children were in the back seat. Everyone was wearing a seat belt. While the group was traveling south on Oregon State Highway 395 at a speed of approximately 50 miles per hour, an oncoming vehicle veered into Sanders's lane of travel. When Sanders tried to steer clear, the 4Runner rolled over and landed upright on its four wheels. During the rollover, the roof over the front passenger seat collapsed, and as a result, McCathern sustained serious, permanent injuries. McCathern filed a suit in an Oregon state court against Toyota Motor Corp. and others, alleging in part that the 1994 4Runner "was dangerously defective and unreasonably dangerous in that the vehicle, as designed and sold, was unstable and prone to rollover." What is the test for product liability based on a design defect? What would McCathern have to prove to succeed under that test? [*McCathern v. Toyota Motor Corp.*, 332 Or. 59, 23 P.3d 320 (2001)]

To view a sample answer for this case problem, go to this book's Web site at http://leet.westbuslaw.com and click on "Interactive Study Center."

9–9. Liability to Third Parties. Lee Stegemoller was a union member who insulated large machinery between 1947 and 1988. During his career, he worked for a number of different companies, including ACandS, Inc. Stegemoller primarily worked with asbestos insulation, which was used on industrial boilers, engines, furnaces, and turbines. After he left a

work site, some of the asbestos dust always remained on his clothing. His wife Ramona, who laundered his work clothes, was also exposed to the dust on a daily basis. Allegedly as a result of this contact, she was diagnosed with colon cancer, pulmonary fibrosis, and pleural thickening in April 1998. The Stegemollers filed a suit in an Indiana state court against ACandS and thirty-three others, contending, among other things, that the asbestos originated from products attributable to some of the defendants and from the premises of other defendants. Several defendants filed a motion to dismiss the complaint, asserting that Ramona was not a "user or consumer" of asbestos because she was not in the vicinity of the product when it was used. Should the court dismiss the suit on this basis? Explain. [*Stegemoller v. ACandS, Inc.*, 767 N.E.2d 974 (Ind. 2002)]

A Question of Ethics & Social Responsibility

9–10. On July 1, 1993, Gian Luigi Ferri entered the offices of a law firm against which he had a grudge. Using two semiautomatic assault weapons (TEC-9 and TEC-DC9) manufactured and distributed by Navegar, Inc., he killed eight persons and wounded six others before killing himself. The survivors and the families of some of those who had died sued Navegar, based in part on negligence. They claimed that Navegar had a duty not to create risks to the public beyond those inherent in the lawful use of firearms. They offered evidence that Navegar knew or should have known that the assault guns had "no legitimate sporting or self-defense purpose" and that the guns were "particularly well adapted to military-style assault on large numbers of people." They also claimed that the TEC-DC9 advertising "targets a criminal clientele," further increasing the risk of harm. A California trial court granted summary judgment in Navegar's favor. The appellate court reversed, ruling that the case should go to trial. The court stated that "the likelihood that a third person would make use of the TEC-DC9 in the kind of criminal rampage Ferri perpetrated is precisely the hazard that would support a determination that Navegar's conduct was negligent." Navegar appealed the decision to the California Supreme Court. In view of these facts, consider the following questions. [*Merrill v. Navegar, Inc.*, 26 Cal.4th 465, 28 P.3d 116, 110 Cal.Rptr.2d 370 (2001)]

1. Do you agree with the appellate court that Navegar could be held negligent in marketing the TEC-DC9? What should the California Supreme Court decide? (Before answering this question, you may wish to review the elements of negligence in Chapter 8.)

2. Should gun manufacturers ever be held liable for deaths caused by nondefective guns? Why or why not?

3. Generally, do you believe that policy decisions regarding the liability of gun manufacturers should be made by the courts, whose job is to interpret the law, or by Congress and state legislatures, whose job is to make the law?

4. In your opinion, have Congress and state legislatures gone far enough in regulating the use of firearms? Have they gone too far? Explain.

scribes the drug for a patient, who develops an addiction that turns out to be fatal. Can the manufacturer be held liable in these circumstances?

Critical-Thinking Legal Question

9-11. Suppose that a pharmaceutical company innocently represents to the medical profession that a prescription medication the company manufactures is not physically addictive. Relying on this information, a physician pre-

INTERACTING WITH THE INTERNET

For updated links to resources available on the Web, as well as a variety of other materials, visit this text's Web site at

http://leet.westbuslaw.com

The law firm of Horvitz & Levy offers a review of recent judicial decisions in the area of product liability at

http://www.horvitzlevy.com/annrev/yirtoc4b.html

For information on product liability suits against tobacco companies and recent settlements, go to the Web site of the Library & Center for Knowledge Management (maintained by the University of California, San Francisco) at

http://library.ucsf.edu/tobacco/litigation

You can find articles, cases, and other information on litigation in the area of product liability by going to the following Web site and selecting "products liability" on the pull-down menu titled "Choose a Practice Area":

http://www.law.com/jsp/pc/litlaw.jsp

ONLINE LEGAL RESEARCH EXERCISES

Go to **http://leet.westbuslaw.com**, the Web site that accompanies this text. Select "Interactive Study Center," and then click on "Chapter 9." There you will find the following Internet research exercises that you can perform to learn more about topics covered in this chapter.

Activity 9–1: SOCIAL PERSPECTIVE—Product Liability Litigation
Activity 9–2: MANAGEMENT PERSPECTIVE—The Duty to Warn
Activity 9–3: ECONOMIC PERSPECTIVE—Class-Action Lawsuits

BEFORE THE TEST

Go to **http://leet.westbuslaw.com**, the Web site that accompanies this text. Select "Interactive Quizzes." You will find at least twenty interactive questions relating to this chapter.

Westlaw® Campus

If your textbook provided for a subscription to Westlaw® Campus, or if you have otherwise purchased access to the Westlaw Campus database, you can access any of the cases presented or cited in this chapter by using your Westlaw Campus account.

CHAPTER **10**

Intellectual Property and Internet Law

CONTENTS

INTELLECTUAL PROPERTY
Property resulting from intellectual, creative processes.

CHAPTER OBJECTIVES

After reading this chapter, you should be able to answer the following questions:

1. What is intellectual property?

2. Why are trademarks and patents protected by the law?

3. What laws protect authors' rights in the works they generate?

4. What are trade secrets, and what laws offer protection for this form of intellectual property?

5. What steps have been taken to protect intellectual property rights in today's digital age?

Of significant concern to businesspersons today is the need to protect their rights in intellectual property. **Intellectual property** is any property resulting from intellectual, creative processes—the products of an individual's mind. Although it is an abstract term for an abstract concept, intellectual property is nonetheless familiar to virtually everyone. The information contained in books and computer files is intellectual property. The software you use, the movies you see, and the music you listen to are all forms of intellectual property. In fact, in today's information age, it should come as no surprise that the value of the world's intellectual property now exceeds the value of physical property, such as machines and houses.

The need to protect creative works was voiced by the framers of the U.S. Constitution over two hundred years ago: Article I, Section 8, of the Constitution authorized Congress "[t]o promote the Progress

> "The Internet, by virtue of its ability to mesh what will be hundreds of millions of people together, . . . is . . . a profoundly different capability that by and large human beings have not had before."
>
> Tony Rutkowski, 1943–
> (Executive director of the Internet Society, 1994–1996)

of Science and useful Arts, by securing for limited Times to Authors and Inventors the exclusive Right to their respective Writings and Discoveries." Laws protecting patents, trademarks, and copyrights are explicitly designed to protect and reward inventive and artistic creativity. Exhibit 10–1 on pages 293 and 294 offers a comprehensive summary of these forms of intellectual property, as well as intellectual property that consists of trade secrets.

An understanding of intellectual property law is important because intellectual property has taken on increasing significance, not only in the United States but globally as well. Today, ownership rights in intangible intellectual property are more important to the prosperity of many U.S. companies than are their tangible assets. As you will read in this chapter, protecting these assets in today's online world has proved particularly challenging. This is because, as indicated in the quotation on the previous page, the Internet's capability is "profoundly different" from anything we have had in the past.

> "The protection of trademarks is the law's recognition of the psychological function of symbols. If it is true that we live by symbols, it is no less true that we purchase goods by them."
>
> FELIX FRANKFURTER, 1882–1965
> (Associate justice of the United States Supreme Court, 1939–1962)

TRADEMARKS AND RELATED PROPERTY

A **trademark** is a distinctive mark, motto, device, or emblem that a manufacturer stamps, prints, or otherwise affixes to the goods it produces so that they can be identified on the market and their origin vouched for. At common law, the person who used a symbol or mark to identify a business or product was protected in the use of that trademark. Clearly, by using another's trademark, a business could lead consumers to believe that its goods were made by the other business. The law seeks to avoid this kind of confusion. In the following classic case concerning Coca-Cola, the defendants argued that the Coca-Cola trademark was entitled to no protection under the law, because the term did not accurately represent the product.

TRADEMARK
A distinctive mark, motto, device, or emblem that a manufacturer stamps, prints, or otherwise affixes to the goods it produces so that they can be identified on the market and their origins made known. Once a trademark is established (under the common law or through registration), the owner is entitled to its exclusive use.

LANDMARK AND CLASSIC CASES

CASE 10.1 The Coca-Cola Co. v. Koke Co. of America

Supreme Court of the United States, 1920.
254 U.S. 143,
41 S.Ct. 113,
65 L.Ed. 189.
http://www.findlaw.com/ casecode/supreme.html[a]

Mexico. Candler continued to sell Coke aggressively and to open up new markets, reaching Europe before 1910. In doing so, however, he attracted numerous competitors, some of whom tried to capitalize directly on the Coke name.

COMPANY PROFILE *John Pemberton, an Atlanta pharmacist, invented a caramel-colored, carbonated soft drink in 1886. His bookkeeper, Frank Robinson, named the beverage Coca-Cola after two of the ingredients, coca leaves and kola nuts. Asa Candler bought the Coca-Cola Company in 1891, and within seven years, he made the soft drink available in all of the United States, as well as in parts of Canada and*

BACKGROUND AND FACTS The Coca-Cola Company brought an action in a federal district court to enjoin (prevent) other beverage companies from using the words "Koke" and "Dope" for the defendants' products. The defendants contended that the Coca-Cola trademark was a fraudulent representation and that Coca-Cola was therefore not entitled to any help

---

a. This is the "U.S. Supreme Court Opinions" page within the Web site of the "FindLaw Internet Legal Resources" database. This page provides several options for accessing an opinion. Because you know the citation for this case, you can go to the "Citation Search" box, type in the appropriate volume and page numbers for the *United States Reports* ("254" and "143," respectively, for the *Coca-Cola* case), and click on "Get It."

(continued)

CASE 10.1—Continued

from the courts. By use of the Coca-Cola name, the defendants alleged, the Coca-Cola Company represented that the beverage contained cocaine (from coca leaves). The district court granted the injunction, but the federal appellate court reversed. The Coca-Cola Company appealed to the United States Supreme Court.

IN THE WORDS OF THE COURT . . .

Mr. Justice *HOLMES* delivered the opinion of the court.

    *   *   *   *

    *   *   * Before 1900 the beginning of [Coca-Cola's] good will was more or less helped by the presence of cocaine, a drug that, like alcohol or caffeine or opium, may be described as a deadly poison or as a valuable item of the pharmacopœa [collection of pharmaceuticals] according to the [purposes of the speaker]. *   *   * [A]fter the Food and Drug Act of June 30, 1906, if not earlier, long before this suit was brought, it was eliminated from the plaintiff's compound. *   *   *

    *   *   * Since 1900 the sales have increased at a very great rate corresponding to a like increase in advertising. The name now characterizes a beverage to be had at almost any soda fountain. It means a single thing coming from a single source, and well known to the community. It hardly would be too much to say that the drink characterizes the name as much as the name the drink. In other words Coca-Cola probably means to most persons the plaintiff's familiar product to be had everywhere rather than a compound of particular substances. *   *   * [B]efore this suit was brought the plaintiff had advertised to the public that it must not expect and would not find cocaine, and had eliminated everything tending to suggest cocaine effects except the name and the picture of the leaves and nuts, which probably conveyed little or nothing to most who saw it. It appears to us that it would be going too far to deny the plaintiff relief against a palpable fraud because possibly here and there an ignorant person might call for the drink with the hope for incipient cocaine intoxication. The plaintiff's position must be judged by the facts as they were when the suit was begun, not by the facts of a different condition and an earlier time.

DECISION AND REMEDY The United States Supreme Court upheld the district court's injunction. The competing beverage companies were enjoined from calling their products "Koke." The Court did not prevent them, however, from calling their products "Dope."

COMMENT *In this classic case, the United States Supreme Court made it clear that trademarks and trade names (and nicknames for those marks and names, such as the nickname "Coke" for "Coca-Cola") that are in common use receive protection under the common law. This holding is significant historically because the federal statute later passed to protect trademark rights (the Lanham Act of 1946, to be discussed shortly) in many ways represented a codification of common law principles governing trademarks.*

Statutory Protection of Trademarks

Statutory protection of trademarks and related property is provided at the federal level by the Lanham Act of 1946.[1] The Lanham Act was enacted in part to protect manufacturers from losing business to rival companies that used confusingly similar trademarks. The Lanham Act incorporates the common

---

1. 15 U.S.C. Sections 1051–1128.

EXHIBIT 10-1   FORMS OF INTELLECTUAL PROPERTY

	PATENT	COPYRIGHT	TRADEMARK (SERVICE MARK, TRADE DRESS)	TRADE SECRET
Definition	A grant from the government that gives an inventor exclusive rights to an invention.	An intangible property right granted to authors and originators of a literary work or artistic production that falls within specified categories.	Any distinctive word, name, symbol, or device (image or appearance), or combination thereof, that an entity uses to identify and distinguish its goods or services from those of others.	Any information (including formulas, patterns, programs, devices, techniques, and processes) that a business possesses and that gives the business an advantage over competitors who do not know the information or processes.
Requirements	An invention must be: 1. Novel. 2. Not obvious. 3. Useful.	Literary or artistic works must be: 1. Original. 2. Fixed in a durable medium that can be perceived, reproduced, or communicated. 3. Within a copyrightable category.	Trademarks, service marks, and trade dresses must be sufficiently distinctive (or must have acquired a secondary meaning) to enable consumers and others to distinguish the manufacturer's, seller's, or business user's products or services from those of competitors.	Information and processes that have commercial value, that are not known or easily ascertainable by the general public or others, and that are reasonably protected from disclosure.
Types or Categories	1. Utility (general). 2. Design. 3. Plant (flowers, vegetables, and so on).	1. Literary works (including computer programs). 2. Musical works. 3. Dramatic works. 4. Pantomime and choreographic works. 5. Pictorial, graphic, and sculptural works. 6. Films and audiovisual works. 7. Sound recordings.	1. Strong, distinctive marks (such as fanciful, arbitrary, or suggestive marks). 2. Marks that have acquired a secondary meaning by use. 3. Other types of marks, including certification marks and collective marks. 4. Trade dress (such as a distinctive decor, menu, or style or type of service).	1. Customer lists. 2. Research and development. 3. Plans and programs. 4. Pricing information. 5. Production techniques. 6. Marketing techniques. 7. Formulas. 8. Compilations.
How Acquired	By filing a patent application with the U.S. Patent and Trademark Office and receiving that office's approval.	Automatic (once in tangible form).	1. At common law, ownership is created by use of mark. 2. Registration (either with the U.S. Patent and Trademark Office or with the appropriate state office)	Through the originality and development of information and processes that are unique to a business, that are unknown by others, and that would

(continued)

EXHIBIT 10-1   FORMS OF INTELLECTUAL PROPERTY (CONTINUED)

	PATENT	COPYRIGHT	TRADEMARK (SERVICE MARK, TRADE DRESS)	TRADE SECRET
How Acquired—continued			gives constructive notice of date of use. 3. Federal registration is permitted if the mark is currently in use *or* if the applicant intends use within six months (period can be extended to three years). 4. Federal registration can be renewed between the fifth and sixth years and, thereafter, every ten years.	be valuable to competitors if they knew of the information and processes.
Rights	An inventor has the right to make, use, sell, assign, or license the invention during the duration of the patent's term. The first to invent has patent rights.	The author or originator has the exclusive right to reproduce, distribute, display, license, or transfer a copyrighted work.	The owner has the right to use the mark or trade dress and to exclude others from using it. The right of use can be licensed or sold (assigned) to another.	The owner has the right to sole and exclusive use of the trade secrets and the right to use legal means to protect against misappropriation of the trade secrets by others. The owner can license or assign a trade secret.
Duration	Twenty years from the date of application; for design patents, fourteen years.	1. For authors: the life of the author plus 70 years. 2. For publishers: 95 years after the date of publication or 120 years after creation.	Unlimited, as long as it is in use. To continue notice by registration, the registration must be renewed by filing.	Unlimited, as long as not revealed to others. (Once revealed to others, they are no longer trade secrets.)
Civil Remedies for Infringement	Monetary damages, which include reasonable royalties and lost profits, *plus* attorneys' fees. (Treble [triple] damages are available for intentional infringement.)	Actual damages plus profits received by the infringer *or* statutory damages of not less than $500 and not more than $20,000 ($100,000, if infringement is willful), *plus* costs and attorneys' fees in either case.	1. Injunction prohibiting future use of mark. 2. Actual damages plus profits received by the infringer (can be increased to three times the actual damages under the Lanham Act). 3. Impoundment and destruction of infringing articles. 4. *Plus* costs and attorneys' fees.	Monetary damages for misappropriation (the Uniform Trade Secrets Act permits punitive damages up to twice the amount of actual damages for willful and malicious misappropriation), *plus* costs and attorneys' fees.

law of trademarks and provides remedies for owners of trademarks who wish to enforce their claims in federal court. Many states also have trademark statutes.

In 1995, Congress amended the Lanham Act by passing the Federal Trademark Dilution Act,[2] which expanded the protection available to trademark owners by creating a federal cause of action for trademark *dilution*. Until the passage of this amendment, federal trademark law only prohibited the unauthorized use of the same mark on competing—or on noncompeting but "related"—goods or services when such use would likely confuse consumers as to the origin of those goods and services. Trademark dilution laws, which about half of the states have also enacted, protect "distinctive" or "famous" trademarks (such as Jergens, McDonald's, RCA, and Macintosh) from certain unauthorized uses of the marks *regardless* of a showing of competition or a likelihood of confusion.

A famous mark may be diluted not only by the use of an *identical* mark but also by the use of a *similar* mark. ● **EXAMPLE 1** Ringling Bros.–Barnum & Bailey, Combined Shows, Inc., brought a suit against the state of Utah, claiming that Utah's use of the slogan "The Greatest Snow on Earth"—to attract visitors to the state's recreational and scenic resorts—diluted the distinctiveness of the circus's famous trademark, "The Greatest Show on Earth." Utah moved to dismiss the suit, arguing that the 1995 provisions protect owners of famous trademarks only against the unauthorized use of identical marks. A federal court disagreed and refused to grant Utah's motion to dismiss the case.[3] ●

Trademark Registration

Trademarks may be registered with the state or with the federal government. To register for protection under federal trademark law, a person must file an application with the U.S. Patent and Trademark Office in Washington, D.C. Under current law, a mark can be registered (1) if it is currently in commerce or (2) if the applicant intends to put the mark into commerce within six months.

In special circumstances, the six-month period can be extended by thirty months, giving the applicant a total of three years from the date of notice of trademark approval to make use of the mark and file the required use statement. Registration is postponed until the mark is actually used. Nonetheless, during this waiting period, any applicant can legally protect his or her trademark against a third party who previously has neither used the mark nor filed an application for it. Registration is renewable between the fifth and sixth years after the initial registration and every ten years thereafter (every twenty years for trademarks registered before 1990).

Trademark Infringement

Registration of a trademark with the U.S. Patent and Trademark Office gives notice on a nationwide basis that the trademark belongs exclusively to the registrant. The registrant is also allowed to use the symbol ® to indicate that the

A billboard and theater marquee in New York City. Why are trademarks protected by the law?

---

2. 15 U.S.C. Section 1125.
3. *Ringling Bros.–Barnum & Bailey, Combined Shows, Inc. v. Utah Division of Travel Development*, 935 F.Supp. 763 (E.D.Va. 1996).

The purple and orange colors displayed on FedEx envelopes, packets, and delivery vehicles, including this airplane, are a distinctive feature of that company. If a start-up company specializing in courier delivery services used those same colors, would the new company be infringing on FedEx's trademark?

mark has been registered. Whenever that trademark is copied to a substantial degree or used in its entirety by another, intentionally or unintentionally, the trademark has been *infringed* (used without authorization). When a trademark has been infringed, the owner of the mark has a cause of action against the infringer. A person need not have registered a trademark in order to sue for trademark infringement, but registration does furnish proof of the date of inception of the trademark's use.

Only trademarks that are deemed sufficiently distinctive from all competing trademarks will be protected. The trademarks must be sufficiently distinct to enable consumers to identify the manufacturer of the goods easily and to differentiate among competing products.

Strong Marks Fanciful, arbitrary, or suggestive trademarks are generally considered to be the most distinctive (strongest) trademarks, because they are normally taken from outside the context of the particular product and thus provide the best means of distinguishing one product from another. ● EXAMPLE 2 Fanciful trademarks include invented words, such as "Xerox" for one manufacturer's copiers and "Kodak" for another company's photographic products. Arbitrary trademarks include actual words that have no literal connection to the product, such as "English Leather" used as a name for an after-shave lotion (and not for leather processed in England). Suggestive trademarks are those that suggest something about a product without describing the product directly. For example, "Dairy Queen" suggests an association between the company's products and milk, but it does not directly describe ice cream. ●

Secondary Meaning Descriptive terms, geographic terms, and personal names are not inherently distinctive and do not receive protection under the law until they acquire a secondary meaning. A secondary meaning may arise when customers begin to associate a specific term or phrase, such as "London Fog," with specific trademarked items (coats with "London Fog" labels). Whether a secondary meaning becomes attached to a term or name usually depends on how extensively the product is advertised, the market for the product, the number of sales, and other factors. The United States Supreme Court has held that even a color can qualify for trademark protection in this way.[4] Once a secondary meaning is attached to a term or name, the term or name is considered distinctive and is protected.

Generic Terms Generic terms (general, commonly used terms that refer to an entire class of products, such as *bicycle* and *computer*) receive no protection, even if they acquire secondary meanings. A particularly thorny problem arises when a trademark acquires generic use. For example, *aspirin* and *thermos* were originally trademarked products, but today the words are used generically. Other examples are *escalator, trampoline, raisin bran, dry ice, lanolin, linoleum, nylon,* and *corn flakes.*

As noted, a generic term will not be protected under trademark law even if the term has acquired a secondary meaning. ● EXAMPLE 3 In one case, America Online, Inc. (AOL), sued AT&T Corporation, claiming that AT&T's use of "You Have Mail" on its WorldNet Service infringed AOL's trademark rights in the same phrase. The court ruled, however, that because each of the three words in the phrase was a generic term, the phrase as a whole was generic. Although the phrase had become widely associated with AOL's e-mail notification service, and thus may have acquired a secondary meaning, this issue was of no significance in the case. The court stated that it would not consider whether the mark had acquired any secondary meaning because "generic marks with secondary meaning are still not entitled to protection."[5] ●

Service, Certification, and Collective Marks

A **service mark** is similar to a trademark but is used to distinguish the services of one person or company from those of another. For example, each airline has a particular mark or symbol associated with its name. Titles and character names used in radio and television are frequently registered as service marks.

Other marks protected by law include certification marks and collective marks. A *certification mark* is used by one or more persons other than the owner to certify the region, materials, mode of manufacture, quality, or accuracy of the owner's goods or services. When used by members of a cooperative, association, or other organization, such a mark is referred to as a *collective mark.* ● EXAMPLE 4 Certification marks include such marks as "Good Housekeeping Seal of Approval" and "UL Tested." Collective marks appear at the ends of the credits of movies to indicate the various associations and organizations that participated in making the movie. The union marks found on the tags of certain products are also collective marks. ●

A UL certification mark. How does a certification mark differ from a trademark?

SERVICE MARK
A mark used in the sale or advertising of services to distinguish the services of one person or company from those of others.

---

4. *Qualitex Co. v. Jacobson Products Co.,* 514 U.S. 159, 115 S.Ct. 1300, 131 L.Ed.2d 248 (1995).
5. *America Online, Inc. v. AT&T Corp.,* 243 F.3d 812 (4th Cir. 2001).

Trade Names

Trademarks apply to *products*. The term **trade name** is used to indicate part or all of a business's *name,* whether the business is a sole proprietorship, a partnership, or a corporation. Generally, a trade name is directly related to a business and its goodwill. Trade names may be protected as trademarks if the trade name is the same as the company's trademarked product—for example, Coca-Cola. Unless also used as a trademark or service mark, a trade name cannot be registered with the federal government. Trade names are protected under the common law, however. As with trademarks, words must be unusual or fancifully used if they are to be protected as trade names. The word *Safeway,* for example, was held by the courts to be sufficiently fanciful to obtain protection as a trade name for a food-store chain.[6]

Trade Dress

The term **trade dress** refers to the image and overall appearance of a product. Basically, trade dress is subject to the same protection as trademarks. ● **EXAMPLE 5** The distinctive decor, menu, layout, and style of service of a particular restaurant may be regarded as the restaurant's trade dress. Similarly, if a golf course is distinguished from other golf courses by prominent features, those features may be considered the golf course's trade dress.● In cases involving trade dress infringement, as in trademark infringement cases, a major consideration is whether consumers are likely to be confused by the allegedly infringing use.

CYBER MARKS

In cyberspace, trademarks are sometimes referred to as **cyber marks.** We turn now to a discussion of trademark-related issues in cyberspace and how new laws and the courts are addressing these issues. One concern relates to the rights of a trademark's owner to use the mark as part of a domain name (Internet address). Other issues have to do with cybersquatting, meta tags, and trademark dilution on the Web. The use of licensing as a way to avoid liability for infringing on another's intellectual property rights in cyberspace will be discussed later in this chapter.

Domain Names

In the real world, one business can often use the same name as another without causing any conflict, particularly if the businesses are small, their goods or services are different, and the areas where they do business are separate. In the online world, however, there is only one area of business—cyberspace. Thus, disputes between parties over which one has the right to use a particular domain name have become common. A **domain name** is the core part of an Internet address—for example, "westlaw.com." It includes at least two parts. The top level domain (TLD) is the part of the name to the right of the period, such as *com* or *gov.* The second level (the part of the name to the left of the period) is chosen by the business entity or individual registering the domain name.

---

6. *Safeway Stores v. Suburban Foods,* 130 F.Supp. 249 (E.D.Va. 1955).

Conflicts over rights to domain names emerged during the 1990s as e-commerce expanded on a worldwide scale. As e-commerce expanded, the *com* TLD came to be widely used by businesses on the Web. Competition among firms with similar names and products for the words preceding the *com* TLD led, understandably, to numerous disputes over domain name rights. By using the same, or a similar, domain name, parties have attempted to profit from the goodwill of a competitor, to sell pornography, to offer for sale another party's domain name, and to otherwise infringe on others' trademarks.

As noted in Chapter 3, the Internet Corporation for Assigned Names and Numbers (ICANN) is a nonprofit corporation set up by the federal government to oversee the distribution of domain names. ICANN has played a leading role in facilitating the settlement of domain name disputes worldwide.

Anticybersquatting Legislation

In the late 1990s, Congress passed legislation prohibiting another practice that had given rise to numerous disputes over domain names: cybersquatting. **Cybersquatting** occurs when a person registers a domain name that is the same as, or confusingly similar to, the trademark of another and then offers to sell the domain name back to the trademark owner. During the 1990s, cybersquatting became a contentious issue and led to much litigation. Often in dispute in these cases was whether cybersquatting constituted a commercial use of the mark so as to violate federal trademark law. Additionally, it was not always easy to separate cybersquatting from legitimate business activity. Although no clear rules emerged from this litigation, many courts held that cybersquatting violated trademark law.[7]

In 1999, Congress addressed this issue by passing the Anticybersquatting Consumer Protection Act (ACPA), which amended the Lanham Act—the federal law protecting trademarks, discussed earlier in this chapter. The ACPA makes it illegal for a person to "register, traffic in, or use" a domain name (1) if the name is identical or confusingly similar to the trademark of another and (2) if the one registering, trafficking in, or using the domain name has a "bad faith intent" to profit from that trademark. The act does not define what constitutes bad faith. Instead, it lists several factors that courts can consider in deciding whether bad faith exists. Some of these factors are the trademark rights of the other person, whether there is an intent to divert consumers in a way that could harm the goodwill represented by the trademark, whether there is an offer to transfer or sell the domain name to the trademark owner, and whether there is an intent to use the domain name to offer goods and services.

The ACPA applies to all domain name registrations of trademarks, even domain names registered before the passage of the act. Successful plaintiffs in suits brought under the act can collect actual damages and profits or they can elect to receive statutory damages of from $1,000 to $100,000. The question in the following case—which was an appeal from the first decision on the issue—was whether the ACPA applied to reregistrations of domain names containing family names that were initially registered before the effective date of the act.

> "It was not so very long ago that people thought semiconductors were part-time orchestra leaders and microchips were very small snack foods."
>
> GERALDINE FERRARO, 1935–
> (American politician; Democratic candidate for vice president in 1984)

CYBERSQUATTING
An act that occurs when a person registers a domain name that is the same as, or confusingly similar to, the trademark of another and offers to sell the domain name back to the trademark owner.

---

7. See, for example, *Panavision International, L.P. v. Toeppen,* 141 F.3d 1316 (9th Cir. 1998).

CASE 10.2 | Schmidheiny v. Weber

United States Court of Appeals,
Third Circuit, 2003.
319 F.3d 581.

HISTORICAL AND SOCIAL

SETTING *Domain name registrars are organizations that keep track of Internet domain names and ensure that only one party controls a specific name at any time. To register a name, the party interested in its exclusive use—the registrant—contracts with a registrar. In exchange for the right to use the name for a particular period of time, the registrant pays a fee and agrees to certain other conditions. Originally Network Solutions, Inc., was the only registrar, but today there are dozens.*

BACKGROUND AND FACTS In February 1999, Steven Weber registered the domain name

schmidheiny.com. The Anticybersquatting Consumer Protection Act (ACPA) took effect nine months later, on November 29. Weber reregistered the name on behalf of Famology.com, Inc., in June 2000, with a different registrar. Weber is the president and treasurer of Famology.com and the administrative and technical contact for the *schmidheiny.com* domain. The following November, Weber sent an e-mail to Stephan Schmidheiny, offering to sell him the name. With a net worth of $3.1 billion, Schmidheiny is among the wealthiest individuals in the world. Schmidheiny filed a suit in a federal district court against Weber and Famology.com, alleging violations of the ACPA. The court granted a summary judgment to the defendants. Schmidheiny appealed to the U.S. Court of Appeals for the Third Circuit.

IN THE WORDS
OF THE COURT . . .

NYGAARD, Circuit Judge.

* * * *

The District Court decided that the registration of *schmidheiny.com* was not covered by the Anticybersquatting Act because the domain name was *first* registered several months before the date when the statute became effective, and "the statute references only 'registrations,' not 'reregistrations.'" The District Court stressed that "Congress made a clear legislative choice that [the Anticybersquatting Act] is not to be applied retroactively," and focused on the "creation date" of *schmidheiny.com*—the date when the domain name was initially created. "[T]o consider a reregistration to be a registration," the District Court stated, "would [blur the date clearly] established by the Act * * * ." According to the District Court, "the plain meaning of the word 'registration' as used by Congress imparts to us no other meaning but the initial registration of the domain name."

We disagree. *We do not consider the "creation date" of a domain name to control whether a registration is subject to the Anticybersquatting Act, and we believe that the plain meaning of the word "registration" is not limited to "creation registration."* [Emphasis added.]

The words "initial" and "creation" appear nowhere in [the ACPA] and Congress did not add an exception for "noncreation registrations" * * * . The District Court's rationale that "if Congress chose to treat reregistrations as registrations, it could have used words appropriate to impart that definition," is not a sufficient reason for courts to infer the word "initial." Instead, we conclude that the language of the statute does not limit the word "registration" to the narrow concept of "creation registration."

Here, in March 2000, the named registrant for *schmidheiny.com* was "Weber Net" and the domain name registrar was Network Solutions, Inc. In June 2000, a new registrant, Famology.com, contractually bound itself in a new registration agreement with a new registrar, Internet Names Worldwide, to secure the *schmidheiny.com* domain name for a new one-year period. We

CASE 10.2—Continued   hold that the word "registration" includes a new contract at a different registrar and to a different registrant. In this case, with respect to Famology.com—
that occurs after the effective date of the Anticybersquatting Act.

To conclude otherwise would permit the domain names of living persons to
be sold and purchased without the living persons' consent, *ad infinitum*, so
long as the name was first registered before the effective date of the Act.

DECISION AND REMEDY The U.S. Court of
Appeals for the Third Circuit concluded that a domain
name's reregistration qualifies as a "registration" for
purposes of the ACPA. The court reversed the judgment of the lower court and remanded the case for
further proceedings consistent with this opinion.

FOR CRITICAL ANALYSIS—Social
Consideration *Should all legislation be presumed to
apply retroactively?*

Meta Tags

Search engines compile their results by looking through a Web site's key-words
field. Various key words, or *meta tags,* can be inserted into this field to
increase the frequency of a site's inclusion in search engine results, even though
the site has nothing to do with the inserted words. Using this technique, one
site can appropriate the key words of other sites with more frequent hits, so
that the appropriating site is included in the same search engine results as the
more popular sites. Using another's trademark in a meta tag without the
owner's permission, however, constitutes trademark infringement.

• **EXAMPLE 6** An early case concerning meta tags involved Calvin Designer
Label's use of "Playboy," "Playboy magazine," and "Playmate"—marks that
were owned by Playboy Enterprises, Inc. (PEI)—as meta tags for its Web sites
on the Internet. As tags, the terms were invisible to viewers (they were in black
type on a black background), but they caused the Web sites to be returned at
the top of the list of a search engine query for "Playboy" or "Playmate." PEI
sued Calvin Designer Label, alleging, among other things, trademark infringement. The court granted PEI's motion for summary judgment and ordered
Calvin Designer Label to stop using PEI's trademarks.[8] •

Dilution in the Online World

As discussed earlier, trademark dilution occurs when a trademark is used, without authorization, in a way that diminishes the distinctive quality of the mark.
Unlike the situation with trademark infringement, a cause of action involving
dilution does not require proof that consumers are likely to be confused by a
connection between the unauthorized use and the mark. For this reason, the
products involved do not have to be similar. In the first case alleging dilution
on the Web, for example, a court ruled that "candyland.com" could not be
used as the URL for an adult site. The suit was brought by the maker of the
"Candyland" children's game and owner of the "Candyland" mark.[9]

---

8. *Playboy Enterprises, Inc. v. Calvin Designer Label,* 985 F.Supp.2d 1220 (N.D.Cal. 1997).
9. *Hasbro, Inc. v. Internet Entertainment Group, Ltd.,* 1996 WL 84853 (W.D.Wash. 1996).

In another case, a court issued an injunction on the ground that spamming under another's logo constitutes trademark dilution. In that case, Hotmail Corporation provided free e-mail services and worked to dissociate itself from spam. Van$ Money Pie, Inc., and others spammed thousands of e-mail customers, using Hotmail as a return address. The court ordered the defendants to stop.[10]

PATENTS

PATENT
A government grant that gives an inventor the exclusive right or privilege to make, use, or sell his or her invention for a limited time period.

A **patent** is a grant from the government that gives an inventor the exclusive right to make, use, and sell an invention or a design for a limited time period. For inventions, this period is twenty years from the date of filing the application for a patent; for designs, the period is fourteen years. For either type of patent, the applicant must demonstrate to the satisfaction of the U.S. Patent and Trademark Office that the invention, discovery, process, or design is genuine, novel, useful, and not obvious in light of current technology. A patent holder gives notice to all that an article or design is patented by placing on it the word *Patent* or *Pat.* plus the patent number. In contrast to patent law in other countries, in the United States patent protection is given to the first person to invent a product or process, even though someone else may have been the first to file for a patent on that product or process.

At one time, it was difficult for developers and manufacturers of software to obtain patent protection because many software products simply automate procedures that can be performed manually. In other words, the computer programs do not meet the "novel" and "not obvious" requirements previously mentioned. Also, the basis for software is often a mathematical equation or formula, which is not patentable. In 1981, however, the United States Supreme Court held that it is possible to obtain a patent for a *process* that incorporates a computer program—providing, of course, that the process itself is patentable.[11] Since then, many patents have been issued for software-related inventions.

> "The patent system . . . added the fuel of interest to the fire of genius."
> ABRAHAM LINCOLN, 1809–1865
> (Sixteenth president of the United States, 1861–1865)

A significant development relating to patents is the availability online of the world's patent databases. The Web site of the U.S. Patent and Trademark Office provides searchable databases covering U.S. patents granted since 1976. The Web site of the European Patent Office maintains databases covering all patent documents in sixty-five nations and the legal status of patents in twenty-two of those countries.

Patent Infringement

If a firm makes, uses, or sells another's patented design, product, or process without the patent owner's permission, it commits the tort of patent infringement. Patent infringement may exist even though the patent owner has not put the patented product in commerce. Patent infringement may also occur even though not all features or parts of an invention are copied. (With respect to a patented process, however, all steps or their equivalent must be copied for infringement to exist.)

Often, litigation for patent infringement is so costly that the patent holder will instead offer to sell to the infringer a license to use the patented design,

---

10. *Hotmail Corp. v. Van$ Money Pie, Inc.,* 47 U.S.P.Q.2d 1020 (N.D.Cal. 1998).
11. *Diamond v. Diehr,* 450 U.S. 175, 101 S.Ct. 1048, 67 L.Ed.2d 155 (1981).

product, or process (licensing is discussed later in this chapter). Indeed, in many cases the costs of detection, prosecution, and monitoring are so high that patents are of little value to their owners; the owners cannot afford to protect them.

Business Process Patents

Traditionally, patents have been granted to inventions that are "new and useful processes, machines, manufactures, or compositions of matter, or any new and useful improvements thereof." The U.S. Patent and Trademark Office routinely rejected computer systems and software applications because they were deemed not to be useful processes, machines, articles of manufacture, or compositions of matter. They were simply considered to be mathematical algorithms, abstract ideas, or "methods of doing business." In a landmark 1998 case, however, *State Street Bank & Trust Co. v. Signature Financial Group, Inc.,*[12] the U.S. Court of Appeals for the Federal Circuit ruled that only three categories of subject matter will always remain unpatentable: (1) the laws of nature, (2) natural phenomena, and (3) abstract ideas. This decision meant, among other things, that business processes were patentable.

After this decision, numerous technology firms applied for business process patents. Walker Digital, for example, applied for a business process patent for its "Dutch auction" system, which allowed consumers to make offers for airline tickets on the Internet and led to the creation of Priceline.com. Amazon.com obtained a business process patent for its "one-click" ordering system, a method of processing credit-card orders securely without asking for the customer's card number or other personal information, such as the customer's name and address, more than once. Indeed, since the State Street decision, the number of Internet-related patents issued by the U.S. Patent and Trademark Office has increased more than 800 percent.

ETHICAL ISSUE

Will business process patents have a chilling effect on e-commerce?

Business process patents have raised some troublesome legal and ethical questions with respect to Internet commerce. Some argue that venture capitalists are more inclined to invest in Internet and high-tech companies if they believe that such start-ups can obtain patents for their business processes. Others believe that business process patents will have a chilling effect on Internet businesses. This group points out that Internet firms have obtained business process patents for processes that are neither new nor nonobvious. For example, the Dutch auction system, which Walker Digital patented for use by Priceline.com, is simply the electronic version of a system that has been around for centuries. Some argue that the more patents are granted for some of the building blocks of e-commerce, the more those involved in e-commerce will have to pay licensing fees to use those building blocks. Consider an analogy: had an airline obtained a business process patent for the granting of frequent flyer miles, then all other airlines would have to pay a license fee to implement such programs.

---

12. 149 F.3d 1368 (Fed. Cir. 1998).

COPYRIGHTS

COPYRIGHT
The exclusive right of authors to publish, print, or sell an intellectual production for a statutory period of time. A copyright has the same monopolistic nature as a patent or trademark, but it differs in that it applies exclusively to works of art, works of literature, and other works of authorship (including computer programs).

A **copyright** is an intangible property right granted by federal statute to the author or originator of certain literary or artistic productions. Currently, copyrights are governed by the Copyright Act of 1976,[13] as amended. Works created after January 1, 1978, are automatically given statutory copyright protection for the life of the author plus 70 years. For copyrights owned by publishing houses, the copyright expires 95 years from the date of publication or 120 years from the date of creation, whichever is first. For works by more than one author, the copyright expires 70 years after the death of the last surviving author.[14]

Copyrights can be registered with the U.S. Copyright Office in Washington, D.C. A copyright owner no longer needs to place a © or *Copr.* or *Copyright* on the work, however, to have the work protected against infringement. Chances are that if somebody created it, somebody owns it.

What Is Protected Expression?

BE CAREFUL If a creative work does not fall into a certain category, it may not be copyrighted, but it may be protected by other intellectual property law.

Works that are copyrightable include books, records, films, artworks, architectural plans, menus, music videos, product packaging, and computer software. To obtain protection under the Copyright Act, a work must be original and fall into one of the following categories: (1) literary works; (2) musical works; (3) dramatic works; (4) pantomimes and choreographic works; (5) pictorial, graphic, and sculptural works; (6) films and other audiovisual works; and (7) sound recordings. To be protected, a work must be "fixed in a durable medium" from which it can be perceived, reproduced, or communicated. Protection is automatic. Registration is not required.

Section 102 of the Copyright Act specifically excludes copyright protection for any "idea, procedure, process, system, method of operation, concept, principle, or discovery, regardless of the form in which it is described, explained, illustrated, or embodied." Note that it is not possible to copyright an *idea*. The underlying ideas embodied in a work may be freely used by others. What *is* copyrightable is the particular way in which an idea is *expressed*. Whenever an idea and an expression are inseparable, the expression cannot be copyrighted.

Generally, anything that is not an original expression will not qualify for copyright protection. Facts widely known to the public are not copyrightable. Page numbers are not copyrightable, because they follow a sequence known to everyone. Mathematical calculations are not copyrightable.

Compilations of facts, however, are copyrightable. Section 103 of the Copyright Act defines a compilation as "a work formed by the collection and assembling of preexisting materials of data that are selected, coordinated, or arranged in such a way that the resulting work as a whole constitutes an original work of authorship." The key requirement for the copyrightability of a compilation is originality. ● EXAMPLE 7 The White Pages of a telephone directory do not qualify for copyright protection when the information that makes up the directory (names, addresses, and telephone numbers) is not selected, coordi-

---

13. 17 U.S.C. Sections 101 *et seq.*
14. These time periods reflect the extensions set forth in the Sonny Bono Copyright Term Extension Act of 1998.

nated, or arranged in an original way.[15] In one case, even the Yellow Pages of a telephone directory did not qualify for copyright protection.[16]●

Copyright Infringement

Whenever the form or expression of an idea is copied, an infringement of copyright occurs. The reproduction does not have to be exactly the same as the original, nor does it have to reproduce the original in its entirety.

Penalties or remedies can be imposed on those who infringe copyrights. These range from actual damages (damages based on the actual harm caused to the copyright holder by the infringement) or statutory damages (damages provided for under the Copyright Act, not to exceed $100,000) to criminal proceedings for willful violations (which may result in fines and/or imprisonment).

An exception to liability for copyright infringement is made under the "fair use" doctrine. In certain circumstances, a person or organization can reproduce copyrighted material without obtaining the permission of the copyright holder. Section 107 of the Copyright Act provides as follows:

> [T]he fair use of a copyrighted work, including such use by reproduction in copies or phonorecords or by any other means specified by [Section 106 of the Copyright Act,] for purposes such as criticism, comment, news reporting, teaching (including multiple copies for classroom use), scholarship, or research, is not an infringement of copyright. In determining whether the use made of a work in any particular case is a fair use the factors to be considered shall include—
>
> (1) the purpose and character of the use, including whether such use is of a commercial nature or is for nonprofit educational purposes;
> (2) the nature of the copyrighted work;
> (3) the amount and substantiality of the portion used in relation to the copyrighted work as a whole; and
> (4) the effect of the use upon the potential market for or value of the copyrighted work.

Because these guidelines are very broad, the courts determine whether a particular use is fair on a case-by-case basis. Thus, anyone reproducing copyrighted material may be subject to a violation.

Copyright Protection for Software

In 1980, Congress passed the Computer Software Copyright Act, which amended the Copyright Act of 1976 to include computer programs in the list of creative works protected by federal copyright law. The 1980 statute, which classifies computer programs as "literary works," defines a computer program as a "set of statements or instructions to be used directly or indirectly in a computer in order to bring about a certain result."

Because of the unique nature of computer programs, the courts have had many problems applying and interpreting the 1980 act. Generally, though, the courts have held that copyright protection extends not only to those parts of

---

15. *Feist Publications, Inc. v. Rural Telephone Service Co.*, 499 U.S. 340, 111 S.Ct. 1282, 113 L.Ed.2d 358 (1991).
16. *Bellsouth Advertising & Publishing Corp. v. Donnelley Information Publishing, Inc.*, 999 F.2d 1436 (11th Cir. 1993).

a computer program that can be read by humans, such as the high-level language of a source code, but also to the binary-language object code of a computer program, which is readable only by the computer.[17] Additionally, such elements as the overall structure, sequence, and organization of a program have been deemed copyrightable.[18] The courts have disagreed on the issue of whether the "look and feel"—the general appearance, command structure, video images, menus, windows, and other screen displays—of computer programs should also be protected by copyright. The courts have tended, however, not to extend copyright protection to look-and-feel aspects of computer programs.

COPYRIGHTS IN DIGITAL INFORMATION

Copyright law is probably the most important form of intellectual property protection on the Internet. This is because much of the material on the Internet consists of works of authorship (including multimedia presentations, software, and database information), which are the traditional focus of copyright law. Copyright law is also important because the nature of the Internet requires that data be "copied" to be transferred online. Copies play a significant part in the traditional controversies arising in this area of the law. (For an example of one such controversy, see this chapter's *Legal E-nvironment* feature.)

The Copyright Act of 1976

When Congress drafted the principal U.S. law governing copyrights, the Copyright Act of 1976, cyberspace did not exist for most of us. The threat to copyright owners was posed not by computer technology but by unauthorized *tangible* copies of works and the sale of rights to movies, television, and other media.

Some issues that were unimagined when the Copyright Act was drafted have posed thorny questions for the courts. For example, to sell a copy of a work, permission of the copyright holder is necessary. Because of the nature of cyberspace, however, difficulties arise in determining the point at which an intangible, electronic "copy" of a work has been made. The courts have held that loading a file or program into a computer's random access memory, or RAM, constitutes the making of a copy for purposes of copyright law.[19] RAM is a portion of a computer's memory into which a file, for example, is loaded so that it can be accessed (read or written over). Thus, a copyright is infringed when a party downloads software into RAM without owning the software or otherwise having a right to download it.[20]

---

17. See *Stern Electronics, Inc. v. Kaufman*, 669 F.2d 852 (2d Cir. 1982); and *Apple Computer, Inc. v. Franklin Computer Corp.*, 714 F.2d 1240 (3d Cir. 1983).
18. *Whelan Associates, Inc. v. Jaslow Dental Laboratory, Inc.*, 797 F.2d 1222 (3d Cir. 1986).
19. *MAI Systems Corp. v. Peak Computer, Inc.*, 991 F.2d 511 (9th Cir. 1993).
20. *DSC Communications Corp. v. Pulse Communications, Inc.*, 170 F.3d 1354 (Fed. Cir. 1999).

LEGAL *e*-NVIRONMENT

Free Speech Rights versus Encryption Technology—The Courts Speak

A major legal controversy today pits free speech rights against encryption technology. There is an ongoing tension between movie studios, which are encrypting their DVDs, and "hackers" who have posted code-cracking programs on the Internet so that DVDs can be copied numerous times.

Almost as soon as encryption technology was developed to safeguard the contents of DVDs, its code was cracked by a group of hackers, including nineteen-year-old Norwegian Jon Johansen. His decryption program, called DeCCS, was quickly made available at various sites on the Internet, including 2600.com, owned by Ed Corley. Almost immediately after DeCCS was posted, a group of movie companies, including Disney and Twentieth Century Fox, filed suit.

Violation of the Digital Millennium Copyright Act

In what was seen as a victory for the motion picture industry, a federal district court ruled that DeCCS violated the Digital Millennium Copyright Act of 1998. As you will read elsewhere in this chapter, this act essentially prohibits individuals from breaking encryption programs put in place to protect digital versions of intellectual property such as movies, music, and the like.

The defendants argued that software programs designed to break encryption schemes were simply a form of constitutionally protected speech. The court, however, rejected the free speech argument. "Computer code is not purely expressive any more than the assassination of a political figure is purely a political statement. . . . The Constitution, after all, is a framework for building a just and democratic

society. It is not a suicide pact," stated the court. The court's decision was affirmed on appeal.[a]

Further Decisions

A California appellate court took a different approach in a case brought by a trade association of movie industry businesses against Internet Web site operators who made DeCCS programs available from their Web sites. The trade association asked the court to enjoin the defendants from copying, distributing, publishing, or otherwise marketing the DeCCS program because, by doing so, the defendants were, by necessity, disclosing or using the trade secrets contained in the encryption programs.

The California appellate court weighed in on the side of free speech and refused to grant the injunction. In contrast to the *Universal City Studios* decision, the court reasoned that the DeCCS program was a form of "pure speech." Furthermore, stated the court, the "scope of protection of trade secrets does not override the protection offered by the First Amendment." Subsequently, however, the California Supreme Court reversed this ruling, holding that the injunction did not violate the Web site operators' free speech rights.[b]

FOR CRITICAL ANALYSIS

At issue in the twenty-first century is the trade-off between the necessity for writers, musicians, artists, and movie studios to profit from their work and the free flow of ideas for the public's benefit. Is it possible to strike an appropriate balance between the rights of both groups on this issue?

---

a. *Universal City Studios, Inc. v. Corley,* 273 F.3d 429 (2d Cir. 2001).
b. *DVD Copy Control Association v. Bunner,* 31 Cal.4th 864, 75 P.3d 1, 4 Cal.Rptr.3d 69 (2003).

Other rights, including those relating to the revision of "collective works" such as magazines, were acknowledged thirty years ago but were considered to have only limited economic value. Today, technology has made some of those rights vastly more significant. How does the old law apply to these rights? That was one of the questions in the following case.

CASE 10.3   New York Times Co. v. Tasini

Supreme Court of the United States, 2001.
533 U.S. 483,
121 S.Ct. 2381,
150 L.Ed.2d 500.
http://supct.law.cornell.edu/supct[a]

BACKGROUND AND FACTS Magazines and newspapers, including the *New York Times,* buy and publish articles written by freelance writers. Besides circulating hard copies of their periodicals, these publishers sell the contents to e-publishers for inclusion in online and other electronic databases. Jonathan Tasini and other freelance writers filed a suit in a federal district court against the New York Times Company and other publishers, including the e-publishers, contending that the e-publication of the articles violated the Copyright Act. The publishers claimed, among other things, that the Copyright Act gave them a right to produce "revisions" of their publications. The writers argued that the Copyright Act did not cover electronic "revisions." The court granted a summary judgment in the publishers' favor, which was reversed on the writers' appeal to the U.S. Court of Appeals for the Second Circuit. The publishers appealed to the United States Supreme Court.

IN THE WORDS OF THE COURT . . .

Justice *GINSBURG* delivered the opinion of the Court.

*   *   *   *

[Under the Copyright Act, a] newspaper or magazine publisher is *   *   * privileged to reproduce or distribute an article contributed by a freelance author, absent a contract otherwise providing, only "as part of" any (or all) of three categories of collective works: (a) "that collective work" to which the author contributed her work, (b) "any revision of that collective work," or (c) "any later collective work in the same series." In accord with Congress' prescription, a publishing company could reprint a contribution from one issue in a later issue of its magazine, and could reprint an article from a 1980 edition of an encyclopedia in a 1990 revision of it; *the publisher could not revise the contribution itself or include it in a new anthology or an entirely different magazine or other collective work.* [Emphasis added.]

*   *   *   *

In determining whether the Articles have been reproduced and distributed "as part of" a "revision" of the collective works in issue, we focus on the Articles as presented to, and perceptible by, the user of the Databases. In this case, the three Databases present articles to users clear of the context provided either by the original periodical editions or by any revision of those editions. The Databases first prompt users to search the universe of their contents: thousands or millions of files containing individual articles from thousands of collective works (i.e., editions), either in one series (the *Times,* in NYTO) or in scores of series (the sundry titles in NEXIS and GPO). When the user conducts a search, each article appears as a separate item within the search result. In NEXIS and NYTO, an article appears to a user without the graphics, formatting, or other articles with which the article was initially published. In GPO, the article appears with the other materials published on the same page or pages, but without any material published on other pages of the original periodical. In either circumstance, we cannot see how the Database perceptibly reproduces and distributes the article "as part of" either the original edition or a "revision" of that edition.

One might view the articles as parts of a new compendium—namely, the entirety of works in the Database. In that compendium, each edition of each

---

a. In the "search" section, type in the name of the case and click on "submit."

CASE 10.3—Continued   periodical represents only a minuscule fraction of the ever-expanding Database. The Database no more constitutes a "revision" of each constituent edition than a 400-page novel quoting a sonnet in passing would represent a "revision" of that poem.

DECISION AND REMEDY The United States Supreme Court affirmed the appellate court's judgment. The Supreme Court remanded the case for a determination as to how the writers should be compensated.

FOR CRITICAL ANALYSIS—Economic Consideration *When technology creates a situation in which rights such as those in this case become more valuable, should the law be changed to redistribute the economic benefit of those rights?*

Further Developments in Copyright Law

In the last several years, Congress has enacted legislation designed specifically to protect copyright holders in a digital age. For example, prior to 1997 criminal penalties under copyright law could be imposed only if unauthorized copies were exchanged for financial gain. Yet much piracy of copyrighted materials was "altruistic" in nature; that is, unauthorized copies were made and distributed not for financial gain but simply for reasons of generosity—to share the copies with others.

To combat altruistic piracy and for other reasons, Congress passed the No Electronic Theft (NET) Act of 1997, which amended several sections of the Copyright Act of 1976. The act extends criminal liability for the piracy of copyrighted materials to persons who exchange unauthorized copies of copyrighted works, such as software, even though they realize no profit from the exchange. The act also imposes penalties on those who make unauthorized electronic copies of books, magazines, movies, or music for *personal* use, thus altering the traditional "fair use" doctrine. The criminal penalties for violating the act are steep; they include fines as high as $250,000 and incarceration for up to five years.

The following year, Congress passed further legislation to protect copyright holders—the Digital Millennium Copyright Act of 1998.[21] Because of its significance in protecting against the piracy of copyrighted materials in the online environment, this act is presented as this chapter's *Landmark in the Legal Environment* feature on the following page.

MP3 and File-Sharing Technology

At one time, music fans swapped compact disks (CDs) and recorded songs from others' CDs onto their own cassettes. This type of "file-sharing" was awkward at best. Soon after the Internet became popular, a few enterprising programmers created software to compress large data files, particularly those associated with music. The reduced file sizes make transmitting music over the Internet feasible. The most widely known compression and decompression system is MP3, which enables music fans to download songs or entire CDs onto their computers or onto a portable listening device, such as Rio or iPod. The MP3 system also made it possible for music fans to access other music fans' files by engaging in file-sharing via the Internet.

---

21. 17 U.S.C. Sections 512, 1201–1205, 1301–1332; 28 U.S.C. Section 4001.

LANDMARK IN THE LEGAL ENVIRONMENT

The Digital Millennium Copyright Act of 1998

The United States leads the world in the production of creative products, including books, films, videos, recordings, and software. In fact, the creative industries are becoming increasingly more important to the U.S. economy than the traditional product industries are. Exports of U.S. creative products, for example, surpass those of every other U.S. industry in value. Creative industries are growing at nearly three times the rate of the economy as a whole.

Steps have been taken, both nationally and internationally, to protect ownership rights in intellectual property, including copyrights. As you will read later in this chapter, to curb unauthorized copying of copyrighted materials, the World Intellectual Property Organization (WIPO) enacted a treaty in 1996 to upgrade global standards of copyright protection, particularly for the Internet.

IMPLEMENTING THE WIPO TREATY In 1998, Congress implemented the provisions of the WIPO treaty by updating U.S. copyright law. The new law—the Digital Millennium Copyright Act of 1998—is a landmark step in the protection of copyright owners and, because of the leading position of the United States in the creative industries, serves as a model for other nations. Among other things, the act created civil and criminal penalties for anyone who circumvents (bypasses, or gets around—using decryption techniques, for example) encryption software or other technological antipiracy protection. Also prohibited are the manufacture, import, sale, and distribution of devices or services for circumvention.

The act provides for exceptions to fit the needs of libraries, scientists, universities, and others. In general, the law does not restrict the fair use of circumvention methods for educational and other noncommercial purposes. For example, circumvention is allowed in order to test computer security, to conduct encryption research, to protect personal privacy, and to enable parents to monitor their children's use of the Internet. The exceptions are to be reconsidered every three years.

LIMITING THE LIABILITY OF INTERNET SERVICE PROVIDERS The 1998 act also limited the liability of Internet service providers (ISPs). Under the act, an ISP is not liable for any copyright infringement by its customer *unless* the ISP is aware of the subscriber's violation. An ISP may be held liable only if it fails to take action to shut the subscriber down after learning of the violation. A copyright holder must act promptly, however, by pursuing a claim in court, or the subscriber will have the right to be restored to online access.

Application to Today's World

Notwithstanding the passage of the Digital Millennium Copyright Act of 1998, copyright owners continue to have a difficult time obtaining legal redress against those who, without authorization, decrypt and/or reproduce copyrighted materials. The music recording industry's crusade to thwart unauthorized use of copyrighted musical works on the Internet is ongoing. So is the film industry's attempt to curb the production and distribution of software that allows users to copy DVDs without authorization. To date, there is no clear end in sight to these legal battles.

PEER-TO-PEER (P2P) NETWORKING
A technology that allows Internet users to access files on other users' computers.

Peer-to-Peer (P2P) Networking File-sharing via the Internet is accomplished through what is called **peer-to-peer (P2P) networking**. The concept is simple. Rather than going through a central Web server, P2P involves numerous personal computers (PCs) connected to the Internet. Files stored on one PC can be accessed by others who are members of the same network. Sometimes this is called a **distributed network** because parts of the network may be distributed all over the country or the world. File-sharing offers an unlimited number of uses for distributed networks. Currently, for example, many researchers allow their home computers' computing power to be accessed through file-sharing software so that very large mathematical problems can be solved quickly. Additionally, persons scattered throughout the country or the world can work together on the same project by using file-sharing programs.

Sharing Stored Music Files File-sharing clearly offers many advantages. When file-sharing is used to download others' stored music files, however, copyright issues arise. Recording artists and their labels stand to lose large amounts of royalties and revenues if relatively few CDs are purchased and then made available on distributed networks, from which everyone can get them for free. In the following widely publicized case, several firms in the recording industry sued Napster, Inc., the owner of the then-popular Napster Web site. The firms alleged that Napster was contributing to copyright infringement by those who downloaded CDs from other computers in the Napster file-sharing system. At issue was whether Napster could be held vicariously liable for the infringement.[22]

DISTRIBUTED NETWORK
A network that can be used by persons located (distributed) around the country or the globe to share computer files.

---

22. Vicarious (indirect) liability exists when one person is subject to liability for another's actions. A common example occurs in the employment context, when an employer is held vicariously liable by third parties for torts committed by employees in the course of their employment.

CASE 10.4 A&M Records, Inc. v. Napster, Inc.

United States Court of Appeals, Ninth Circuit, 2001.
239 F.3d 1004.
http://guide.lp.findlaw.com/ casecode/courts/9th.html[a]

HISTORICAL AND TECHNOLOGICAL SETTING *In 1987, the Moving Picture Experts Group set a standard file format for the storage of audio recordings in a digital format called MPEG-3, abbreviated as MP3. Digital MP3 files are created through a process called ripping. Ripping software allows a computer owner to copy an audio compact disk (CD) directly onto a computer's hard drive by compressing the audio information on the CD into the MP3 format. The MP3's compressed format allows for rapid transmission of digital audio files from one computer to another by e-mail or any other file-transfer protocol.*

BACKGROUND AND FACTS Napster, Inc. (**http://www.napster.com**), facilitated the transmis-

sion of MP3 files among the users of its Web site through peer-to-peer file-sharing. Napster allowed users to transfer exact copies of the contents of MP3 files from one computer to another via the Internet. This was made possible by Napster's MusicShare software, available free of charge from Napster's site, and Napster's network servers and server-side software. Napster also provided technical support. A&M Records, Inc., and others engaged in the commercial recording, distribution, and sale of copyrighted musical compositions and sound recordings filed a suit in a federal district court against Napster, alleging copyright infringement. The court issued a preliminary injunction ordering Napster to stop "facilitating others in copying, downloading, uploading, transmitting, or distributing plaintiffs' copyrighted musical compositions and sound recordings, * * * without express permission of the rights owner." Napster appealed to the U.S. Court of Appeals for the Ninth Circuit.

---

a. This URL will take you to a Web site maintained by FindLaw, which is now a part of West Group. When you access the site, enter "Napster" in the "Party Name Search" box and then click on "Search." Select the first *Napster* case in the list (dated "02/12/2001") on the page that opens.

(continued)

CASE 10.4—Continued

IN THE WORDS
OF THE COURT . . .

BEEZER, Circuit Judge:

* * * *

* * * In the context of copyright law, vicarious liability extends * * * to cases in which a defendant has the right and ability to supervise the infringing activity and also has a direct financial interest in such activities.

* * * *

The ability to block infringers' access to a particular environment for any reason whatsoever is evidence of the right and ability to supervise. Here, plaintiffs have demonstrated that Napster retains the right to control access to its system. Napster has an express reservation of rights policy, stating on its website that it expressly reserves the "right to refuse service and terminate accounts in [its] discretion, including, but not limited to, if Napster believes that user conduct violates applicable law * * * or for any reason in Napster's sole discretion, with or without cause."

To escape imposition of vicarious liability, the reserved right to police must be exercised to its fullest extent. *Turning a blind eye to detectable acts of infringement for the sake of profit gives rise to liability.* [Emphasis added.]

The district court correctly determined that Napster had the right and ability to police its system and failed to exercise that right to prevent the exchange of copyrighted material. * * *

Napster, however, has the ability to locate infringing material listed on its search indices, and the right to terminate users' access to the system. The file name indices, therefore, are within the "premises" that Napster has the ability to police. We recognize that the files are user-named and may not match copyrighted material exactly (for example, the artist or song could be spelled wrong). For Napster to function effectively, however, file names must reasonably or roughly correspond to the material contained in the files, otherwise no user could ever locate any desired music. As a practical matter, Napster, its users and the record company plaintiffs have equal access to infringing material by employing Napster's "search function."

Our review of the record requires us to accept the district court's conclusion that plaintiffs have demonstrated a likelihood of success on the merits of the vicarious copyright infringement claim. Napster's failure to police the system's "premises," combined with a showing that Napster financially benefits from the continuing availability of infringing files on its system, leads to the imposition of vicarious liability.

DECISION AND REMEDY The U.S. Court of Appeals for the Ninth Circuit affirmed the lower court's decision that Napster was obligated to police its own system and had likely infringed the plaintiffs' copyrights. Holding that the injunction was "overbroad," however, the appellate court remanded the case for a clarification of Napster's responsibility to determine whether music on its Web site was copyrighted.

FOR CRITICAL ANALYSIS—Technological Consideration *How might a system such as*

Napster's be put to commercially significant but non-infringing uses?

COMMENT *Napster later filed for bankruptcy. Bertelsmann sought to purchase Napster's assets, but the bankruptcy court denied Bertelsmann's bid. There are a number of sites similar to Napster's on the Web today.*

TRADE SECRETS

Some business processes and information that are not or cannot be patented, copyrighted, or trademarked are nevertheless protected against appropriation by a competitor as trade secrets. **Trade secrets** consist of customer lists, plans, research and development, pricing information, marketing techniques, production methods, and generally anything that makes an individual company unique and that would have value to a competitor.

Unlike copyright and trademark protection, protection of trade secrets extends to both ideas and their expression. (For this reason, and because a trade secret involves no registration or filing requirements, trade secret protection may be well suited for software.) Of course, the secret formula, method, or other information must be disclosed to some persons, particularly to key employees. Businesses generally attempt to protect their trade secrets by having all employees who use the process or information assent in their contracts, or in confidentiality agreements, never to divulge it.

TRADE SECRETS
Information or processes that give a business an advantage over competitors who do not know the information or processes.

State and Federal Law on Trade Secrets

Under Section 757 of the *Restatement of Torts,* "One who discloses or uses another's trade secret, without a privilege to do so, is liable to the other if (1) he discovered the secret by improper means, or (2) his disclosure or use constitutes a breach of confidence reposed in him by the other in disclosing the secret to him." The theft of confidential business data by industrial espionage, as when a business taps into a competitor's computer, is a theft of trade secrets.

Until recently, virtually all law with respect to trade secrets was common law. In an effort to reduce the unpredictability of the common law in this area, a model act, the Uniform Trade Secrets Act, was presented to the states for adoption in 1979. Parts of the act have been adopted in more than twenty states. Typically, a state that has adopted parts of the act has adopted only those sections that encompass its own existing common law. Additionally, in 1996 Congress passed the Economic Espionage Act, which made the theft of trade secrets a federal crime. We examined the provisions and significance of this act in Chapter 7, in the context of crimes related to business.

Does a trade secret lose its protection under the Uniform Trade Secrets Act when an employee commits it to memory rather than taking it in written form? That was the question in the following case.

CASE 10.5 Ed Nowogroski Insurance, Inc. v. Rucker

Supreme Court of Washington, 1999.
137 Wash.2d 427,
971 P.2d 936.

BACKGROUND AND FACTS Jerry Kiser, Darwin Rieck, and Michael Rucker worked for Ed Nowogroski Insurance, Inc., an insurance agency, as sales and service representatives. When friction developed between the agency and Kiser, Rieck, and Rucker, the three quit to go to work for Potter, Leonard and Cahan, Inc., a competing insurance firm. During their employment with Potter, the former Nowogroski employees used Nowogroski customer lists to attract business. Kiser and Rucker used written client information that they had copied from their ex-employer's files. Rieck worked chiefly from memory. The Nowogroski agency filed a suit in a Washington state court against its former employees and their new

(continued)

CASE 10.5—Continued

employer, alleging misappropriation of trade secrets. The court concluded that the client information fit the definition of a trade secret under the Uniform Trade Secrets Act and issued a judgment in the plaintiff's favor. The court decided, however, that only the written information was protected and did not award damages for the use of the memorized data. Nowogroski appealed to an intermediate state appellate court, which held that there is no distinction between written and memorized information and ordered a recalculation of the damages. The defendants appealed to the Washington Supreme Court.

IN THE WORDS OF THE COURT . . .

HILTON, J. [Judge]

*   *   *   *

The Uniform Trade Secrets Act does not distinguish between written and memorized information. The Act does not require a plaintiff to prove actual theft or conversion of physical documents embodying the trade secret information to prove misappropriation. The Washington Uniform Trade Secrets Act defines a "trade secret" to include compilations of information which have certain characteristics without regard to the form that such information might take. The definition of "misappropriation" includes unauthorized "disclosure or use." *   *   * [T]wo types of information mentioned in the Uniform Trade Secrets Act as examples of trade secrets include "method" and "technique"; these do not imply the requirement of written documents.

*   *   *   *

The form of information, whether written or memorized, is immaterial under the trade secrets statute; the Uniform Trade Secrets Act makes no distinction about the form of trade secrets. Whether the information is on a CD, a blueprint, a film, a recording, a hard paper copy or memorized by the employee, the inquiry is whether it meets the definition of a trade secret under the Act and whether it was misappropriated. Absent a contract to the contrary, an employee is free to compete against his or her former employer, and a former employee may use *general* knowledge, skills and experience acquired during the prior employment in competing with a former employer. However, an employee may not use or disclose trade secrets belonging to the former employer to actively solicit customers from a confidential customer list. In this case, the former employees actively solicited customers from the employer's customer lists, which the trial court found to be of independent value because unknown and subject to reasonable efforts to keep secret. *   *   * [W]e conclude the Court of Appeals was correct in holding that there is no legal distinction between written and memorized information under the Uniform Trade Secrets Act and in remanding for a recalculation of damages. [Emphasis added.]

DECISION AND REMEDY The Washington Supreme Court affirmed the judgment of the state intermediate appellate court. Under the Uniform Trade Secrets Act, there is no legal distinction between written and memorized information.

FOR CRITICAL ANALYSIS—Economic Consideration *Suppose that you own a firm whose success has been due to a formula or process that you have kept secret from your competitors. What steps might you take to ensure that your employees will not pass on this trade secret to your competitors or use it to set up a competing business?*

Trade Secrets in Cyberspace

Computer technology can undercut a business firm's ability to protect its confidential information, including trade secrets.[23] For example, a dishonest employee could e-mail trade secrets in a company's computer to a competitor or a future employer. If e-mail is not an option, the employee might walk out with the information on a CD-ROM. Dissatisfied former employees have resorted to other options as well. ● EXAMPLE 8 In one case, a former employee of Intel Corporation, Ken Hamidi, using a list of employees that he had obtained from a company directory, sent massive quantities of e-mail to current Intel employees. Unable to block the disruptive messages, Intel sued Hamidi for trespass to personal property. The court refused to grant Intel an injunction, however, because Intel failed to show that the e-mail damaged or impaired the functioning of its computer system.[24]●

LICENSING

One way to make use of another's trademark, copyright, patent, or trade secret, while avoiding litigation, is to obtain a license to do so. A license in this context is basically an agreement to permit the use of a trademark, copyright, patent, or trade secret for certain purposes.

Licensing Contracts

Licensing agreements are essentially contracts and are thus governed by contract law. A licensing agreement with a firm calls for a payment of royalties on some basis—such as so many cents per unit produced or a certain percentage of the profits from units sold in a particular geographic territory. ● EXAMPLE 9 The Coca-Cola Bottling Company licenses firms worldwide to use (and keep confidential) its secret formula for the syrup used in its soft drink, in return for a percentage of the income gained from the sale of Coca-Cola by those companies.● As with all contracts, licensing contracts must be carefully drafted— see, for example, this chapter's *Inside the Legal Environment* feature on page 317.

Benefits of Licensing Arrangements

The licensing of intellectual property rights benefits all parties to the transaction. The firm that receives the license can take advantage of an established reputation for quality. The company that grants the license receives income from the sales of its products. In the global marketplace, licensing also allows a business to establish its reputation worldwide. Once a firm's trademark is known around the world, the demand for other products manufactured or sold by that firm may also increase, which is another advantage of licensing.

---

23. Note that in one case, the court indicated that customers' e-mail addresses may constitute trade secrets. See *T-N-T Motorsports, Inc. v. Hennessey Motorsports, Inc.,* 965 S.W.2d 18 (Tex.App.–Hous. [1 Dist.] 1998), rehearing overruled (1998), petition dismissed (1998).
24. *Intel Corp. v. Hamidi,* 30 Cal.4th 1342, 71 P.3d 296, 1 Cal.Rptr.3d 32 (2003).

Setting Global Standards for Copyright Protection

Technology, particularly the Internet, offers new outlets for creative products. It also makes them easier to steal—copyrighted works can be pirated and distributed around the world quickly and efficiently. To curb this crime, in 1996 the World Intellectual Property Organization (WIPO) enacted the WIPO Copyright Treaty, a special agreement under the 1886 Berne Convention (see below). The purpose was to upgrade global standards of copyright protection, particularly for the Internet.

Special provisions of the WIPO treaty relate to rights in digital data. The treaty strengthens some rights for copyright owners, in terms of their application in cyberspace, but leaves other questions unresolved. For example, the treaty does not make clear what constitutes the making of a copy in electronic form for purposes of international law. The United States signed the WIPO treaty in 1996 and, as mentioned earlier in this chapter's *Landmark in the Legal Environment* feature on page 310, implemented its terms in the Digital Millennium Copyright Act of 1998.

FOR CRITICAL ANALYSIS

Is there any practical way to prevent the piracy of digital data via the Internet?

In 1999, the National Conference of Commissioners on Uniform State Laws approved the Uniform Computer Information Transactions Act (UCITA) and submitted it to the states for adoption. The act was drafted to address problems unique to electronic contracting and to the purchase and sale (licensing) of computer information, such as software. As you will read in Chapter 13, however, very few states have adopted this act.

INTERNATIONAL PROTECTION FOR INTELLECTUAL PROPERTY

For many years, the United States has been a party to various international agreements relating to intellectual property rights. For example, the Paris Convention of 1883, to which about ninety countries are signatory, allows parties in one country to file for patent and trademark protection in any of the other member countries. Other international agreements include the Berne Convention and the Trade-Related Aspects of Intellectual Property Rights (TRIPS) agreement.

The Berne Convention

The Berne Convention of 1886 is an international copyright agreement. Under the Berne Convention, if a citizen of a country that has signed the agreement writes a book, her or his copyright in the book must be recognized by every country that has signed this agreement. Also, if a citizen of a country that has not signed the convention first publishes a book in a country that has signed it, all other countries that have signed it must recognize that author's copyright. Copyright notice is not needed to gain protection under the Berne Convention for works published after March 1, 1989.

INSIDE THE LEGAL ENVIRONMENT

Copyright Law and Electronic Books

Traditionally, owners and managers of publishing houses purchased an *exclusive license* from the author (the owner of the copyright) to print, publish, and sell the original work and any revisions of that work. As noted elsewhere in this chapter, the Internet has changed the face of copyright law by raising new issues about what constitutes a revision of a printed article or book. These changes will dramatically affect industry practice in the drafting of licensing contracts.

Applying the Copyright Act

In *New York Times Co. v. Tasini*,[a] presented earlier in this chapter as Case 10.3, the United States Supreme Court held that the provision of the Copyright

Act granting licensees (publishers) the right to make revisions of original works did not give publishers the right to reprint the authors' articles online without permission from (or payment to) the authors. The decision was based entirely on the wording of the Copyright Act.

Applying State Law

Another dispute involving online publishing arose in *Random House, Inc. v. Rosetta Books, LLC*.[b] Several well-known authors (including Kurt Vonnegut) had previously given Random House an exclusive license to "print, publish and sell the [specific] work[s] in book form." The authors then individually contracted with Rosetta Books, giving Rosetta Books a license to print exactly the same text as electronic books, or e-books. When the e-books came out in 2001, Random House sued Rosetta Books, alleging copyright infringement and asking the court for an injunction to prohibit Rosetta from offering these works in digital form.

The federal district court stated that the law of contracts under New York law, rather than federal copyright law, governed what rights the publisher had under the licensing agreement. The court thus focused on the specific language of the licensing agreement. The court interpreted the phrase "in book form," which is standard in many licensing contracts, to mean only books in the traditional sense— printed sheets of paper bound together with a cover. Concluding that the contracts did not give Random House the right to publish the authors' books as e-books, the court denied Random House's request for an injunction. The court noted that its approach in this case placed the burden on the parties to negotiate for language that clearly indicates their intentions. The trial court's ruling was upheld on appeal.

FOR CRITICAL ANALYSIS

What are the implications of the court's decision in the Rosetta Books *case for publishers and authors when negotiating licensing contracts?*

a. See also *Greenberg v. National Geographic Society*, 244 F.3d 1267 (11th Cir. 2001), in which the court held that a magazine could not include photographs from past articles on a CD-ROM without violating the Copyright Act.

b. 283 F.3d 490 (2d Cir. 2002).

This convention and other international agreements have given some protection to intellectual property on a worldwide level. None of them, however, has been as significant and far-reaching in scope as the agreement on Trade-Related Aspects of Intellectual Property Rights, or, more simply, TRIPS.

The TRIPS Agreement

The TRIPS agreement was signed by representatives from more than one hundred nations in 1994. The agreement established, for the first time, standards for the international protection of intellectual property rights, including patents, trademarks, and copyrights for movies, computer programs, books, and music.

Prior to the agreement, U.S. sellers of intellectual property in the international market faced difficulties because many other countries either had no laws protecting intellectual property rights or failed to enforce existing laws. To address this problem, the TRIPS agreement provides that each member country must include in its domestic laws broad intellectual property rights and effective remedies (including civil and criminal penalties) for violations of those rights.

Generally, the TRIPS agreement provides that no member nation is to discriminate (in the administration, regulation, or adjudication of intellectual property rights) against foreign owners of such rights. In other words, a member nation cannot give its own nationals (citizens) favorable treatment without offering the same treatment to nationals of all member countries. ● EXAMPLE 10 If a U.S. software manufacturer brings a suit for the infringement of intellectual property rights under a member nation's national laws, the U.S. manufacturer is entitled to receive the same treatment as a domestic manufacturer.● Each member nation must also ensure that legal procedures are available for parties who wish to bring actions for infringement of intellectual property rights. In a related document, a mechanism was established for settling disputes among member nations.

Particular provisions of the TRIPS agreement refer to patent, trademark, and copyright protection for intellectual property. The agreement specifically provides copyright protection for computer programs by stating that compilations of data or databases are "intellectual creations" and that they are to be protected as copyrightable works. Other provisions relate to trade secrets and the rental of computer programs and cinematographic works.

KEY TERMS

copyright   304
cyber mark   298
cybersquatting   299
distributed network   311
domain name   298

intellectual property   290
patent   302
peer-to-peer (P2P)
   networking   310
service mark   297

trade dress   298
trade name   298
trade secret   313
trademark   291

CHAPTER SUMMARY INTELLECTUAL PROPERTY AND INTERNET LAW

Trademarks and Related Property (See pages 291–298.)	1. A *trademark* is a distinctive mark, motto, device, or emblem that a manufacturer stamps, prints, or otherwise affixes to the goods it produces so that they may be identified on the market and their origin vouched for.
	2. The major federal statutes protecting trademarks and related property are the Lanham Act of 1946 and the Federal Trademark Dilution Act of 1995. Generally, to be protected, a trademark must be sufficiently distinctive from all competing trademarks.

CHAPTER SUMMARY INTELLECTUAL PROPERTY AND INTERNET LAW—Continued

Trademarks and Related Property—continued	3. *Trademark infringement* occurs when one uses a mark that is the same as, or confusingly similar to, the protected trademark, service mark, trade name, or trade dress of another without permission when marketing goods or services.
Cyber Marks (See pages 298–302.)	A *cyber mark* is a trademark in cyberspace. Trademark infringement in cyberspace occurs when one person uses a name that is the same as, or confusingly similar to, the protected mark of another in a domain name or in meta tags.
Patents (See pages 302–303.)	1. A *patent* is a grant from the government that gives an inventor the exclusive right to make, use, and sell an invention for a period of twenty years from the date of filing the application for a patent. To be patentable, an invention (or a discovery, process, or design) must be genuine, novel, useful, and not obvious in light of current technology. Computer software may be patented. 2. *Patent infringement* occurs when one uses or sells another's patented design, product, or process without the patent owner's permission.
Copyrights (See pages 304–312.)	1. A *copyright* is an intangible property right granted by federal statute to the author or originator of certain literary or artistic productions. Computer software may be copyrighted. 2. *Copyright infringement* occurs whenever the form or expression of an idea is copied without the permission of the copyright holder. An exception applies if the copying is deemed a fair use. 3. Copyrights are governed by the Copyright Act of 1976, as amended. To protect copyrights in digital information, Congress passed the No Electronic Theft Act of 1997 and the Digital Millennium Copyright Act of 1998.
Trade Secrets (See pages 313–315.)	*Trade secrets* include customer lists, plans, research and development, pricing information, and so on. Trade secrets are protected under the common law and, in some states, under statutory law against misappropriation by competitors. The Economic Espionage Act of 1996 made the theft of trade secrets a federal crime (see Chapter 7).
Licensing (See pages 315–316.)	In the context of intellectual property rights, a *license* is an agreement in which the owner of a trademark, copyright, patent, or trade secret permits another person or entity to use that property for certain purposes.
International Protection for Intellectual Property (See pages 316–318.)	International protection for intellectual property exists under various international agreements. A landmark agreement is the 1994 agreement on Trade-Related Aspects of Intellectual Property Rights (TRIPS), which provides for enforcement procedures in all countries signatory to the agreement.

FOR REVIEW

1. What is intellectual property?
2. Why are trademarks and patents protected by the law?
3. What laws protect authors' rights in the works they generate?
4. What are trade secrets, and what laws offer protection for this form of intellectual property?
5. What steps have been taken to protect intellectual property rights in today's digital age?

QUESTIONS AND CASE PROBLEMS

10–1. Copyright Infringement. In which of the following situations would a court likely hold Maruta liable for copyright infringement?

(a) At the library, Maruta photocopies ten pages from a scholarly journal relating to a topic on which she is writing a term paper.

(b) Maruta makes leather handbags and sells them in her small leather shop. She advertises her handbags as "Vutton handbags," hoping that customers might mistakenly assume that they were made by Vuitton, the well-known maker of high-quality luggage and handbags.

(c) Maruta owns a video store. She purchases one copy of all the latest videos from various video manufacturers. Then, using blank videotapes, she makes copies to rent or sell to her customers.

(d) Maruta teaches Latin American history at a small university. She has a videocassette recorder (VCR) and frequently tapes television programs relating to Latin America. She then takes the videos to her classroom so that her students can watch them.

10–2. Trademark Infringement. Alpha Software, Inc., announced a new computer operating system to be marketed under the name McSoftware. McDonald's Corp. wrote Alpha a letter stating that the use of this name infringed on the McDonald's family of trademarks characterized by the prefix "Mc" attached to a generic term. Alpha claimed that "Mc" had come into generic use as a prefix and therefore McDonald's had no trademark rights to the prefix itself. Alpha filed an action seeking a declaratory judgment from the court that the mark McSoftware did not infringe on any of the federally registered trademarks or common law rights to the marks belonging to McDonald's and would not constitute an unfair trade practice. What factors must the court consider in deciding this issue? What will be the probable outcome of the case? Explain.

10–3. Patent Infringement. John and Andrew Doney invented a hard-bearing device for balancing rotors. Although they registered their invention with the U.S. Patent and Trademark Office, it was never used as an automobile wheel balancer. Some time later, Exetron Corp. produced an automobile wheel balancer that used a hard-bearing device with a support plate similar to that of the Doneys. Given the fact that the Doneys had not used their device for automobile wheel balancing, does Exetron's use of a similar hard-bearing device infringe on the Doneys' patent?

10–4. Copyright Infringement. Max plots a new Batman adventure and carefully and skillfully imitates the art of DC Comics to create an authentic-looking Batman comic. Max is not affiliated with the owners of the copyright to Batman. Can Max publish the comic without infringing on the owners' copyright?

10–5. Trademark Infringement. Elvis Presley Enterprises, Inc. (EPE), owns all of the trademarks of the Elvis Presley estate. None of these marks is registered for use in the restaurant business. Barry Capece registered "The Velvet Elvis" as a service mark for a restaurant and tavern with the U.S. Patent and Trademark Office. Capece opened a nightclub called "The Velvet Elvis" with a menu, décor, advertising, and promotional events that evoked Elvis Presley and his music. EPE filed a suit in a federal district court against Capece and others, claiming, among other things, that "The Velvet Elvis" service mark infringed on EPE's trademarks. During the trial, witnesses testified that they thought the bar was associated with Elvis Presley. Should Capece be ordered to stop using "The Velvet Elvis" mark? Why or why not? [*Elvis Presley Enterprises, Inc. v. Capece,* 141 F.3d 188 (5th Cir. 1998)]

10–6. Copyrights. Webbworld operates a Web site called Neptics, Inc. The site accepts downloads of certain images from third parties and makes these images available to any user who accesses the site. Before being allowed to view the images, however, the user must pay a subscription fee of $11.95 per month. Over a period of several months, images were available that were originally created by or for Playboy Enterprises, Inc. (PEI). The images were displayed at Neptics's site without PEI's permission. PEI filed a suit in a federal district court against Webbworld, alleging copyright infringement. Webbworld argued in part that it should not be held liable because, like an Internet service provider that furnishes access to the Internet, it did not create or control the content of the information available to its subscribers. Do you agree with Webbworld? Why or why not? [*Playboy Enterprises, Inc. v. Webbworld,* 968 F.Supp. 1171 (N.D.Tex. 1997)]

10–7. Trademark Infringement. A&H Sportswear, Inc., a swimsuit maker, obtained a trademark for its MIRACLESUIT in 1992. The MIRACLESUIT design makes the wearer appear slimmer. The MIRACLESUIT was widely advertised and discussed in the media. The MIRACLESUIT was also sold for a brief time in the Victoria's Secret (VS) catalogue, which is published by Victoria's Secret Catalogue, Inc. In 1993, Victoria's Secret Stores, Inc., began selling a cleavage-enhancing bra, which was named THE MIRACLE BRA and for which a trademark was obtained. The next year, THE MIRACLE BRA swimwear debuted in the VS catalogue and stores. A&H filed a suit in a federal district court against VS Stores and VS Catalogue, alleging in part that THE MIRACLE BRA mark, when applied to swimwear, infringed on the MIRACLESUIT mark. A&H argued that there was a "possibility of confusion" between the marks. The VS entities contended that the appropriate standard was "likelihood of confusion" and that, in this case, there was no likelihood of confusion. In whose favor will the court rule, and why? [*A&H Sportswear, Inc. v. Victoria's Secret Stores, Inc.,* 166 F.3d 197 (3d Cir. 1999)]

10-8. Domain Name Disputes. In 1999, Steve and Pierce Thumann and their father, Fred, created Spider Webs, Ltd., a partnership, to, according to Steve, "develop Internet address names." Spider Webs registered nearly two thousand Internet domain names for an average of $70 each, including the names of cities, the names of buildings, names related to a business or trade (such as air conditioning or plumbing), and the names of famous companies. It offered many of the names for sale on its Web site and through eBay.com. Spider Webs registered the domain name "ERNESTANDJULIOGALLO. COM" in Spider Webs name. E. and J. Gallo Winery filed a suit against Spider Webs, alleging, in part, violations of the Anticybersquatting Consumer Protection Act (ACPA). Gallo asked the court for, among other things, statutory damages. Gallo also sought to have the domain name at issue transferred to Gallo. During the suit, Spider Webs published anticorporate articles and opinions, and discussions of the suit, at the URL "ERNESTANDJULIOGALLO.COM." Should the court rule in Gallo's favor? Why or why not? [*E. & J. Gallo Winery v. Spider Webs, Ltd.*, 129 F.Supp.2d 1033 (S.D.Tex. 2001)]

To view a sample answer for this case problem, go to this book's Web site at http://leet.westbuslaw.com and click on "Interactive Study Center."

10-9. Fair Use Doctrine. Leslie Kelly is a professional photographer who has copyrighted many of his images of the American West. Some of the images can be seen on Kelly's Web site or other sites with which Kelly has a contract. Arriba Soft Corp. operates an Internet search engine that displays its results in the form of small pictures (thumbnails) rather than text. The thumbnails consist of images copied from other sites and reduced in size. By clicking on one of the thumbnails, a user can view a large version of the picture within the context of an Arriba Web page. Arriba displays the large picture by inline linking (importing the image from the other site without copying it onto Arriba's site). When Kelly discovered that his photos were displayed through Arriba's site without his permission, he filed a suit in a federal district court against Arriba, alleging copyright infringement. Arriba claimed that its use of Kelly's images was a "fair use." Considering the factors courts use to determine whether a use is fair, do Arriba's thumbnails qualify? Does Arriba's use of the larger images infringe on Kelly's copyright? Explain. [*Kelly v. Arriba Soft Corp.*, 280 F.3d 934 (9th Cir. 2002)]

A Question of Ethics & Social Responsibility

10-10. Texaco, Inc., conducts research to develop new products and technology in the petroleum industry. As part of the research, Texaco employees routinely photocopy articles from scientific and medical journals without the permission of the copyright holders. The publishers of the journals brought a copyright infringement action against Texaco in a federal district court. The court ruled that the copying was not a fair use. The U.S. Court of Appeals for the Second Circuit affirmed this ruling "primarily because the dominant purpose of the use is 'archival'—to assemble a set of papers for future reference, thereby serving the same purpose for which additional subscriptions are normally sold, or . . . for which photocopying licenses may be obtained." [*American Geophysical Union v. Texaco, Inc.*, 37 F.3d 881 (2d Cir. 1994)]

1. Do you agree with the court's decision that the copying was not a fair use? Why or why not?
2. Do you think that the law should impose a duty on every person to obtain permission to photocopy or reproduce any article under any circumstance? What would be some of the implications of such a duty for society? Discuss fully.

Critical-Thinking Managerial Question

10-11. Delta Computers, Inc., makes computer-related products under the brand name "Delta," which the company registers as a trademark. Without Delta's permission, E-Product Corp. embeds the Delta mark in E-Product's Web site, in black type on a blue background. This tag causes the E-Product site to be returned at the top of the list of results on a search engine query for "Delta." Does E-Product's use of the Delta mark as a meta tag without Delta's permission constitute trademark infringement? Explain.

Video Question

10-12. Go to this text's Web site at **http://leet.westbuslaw.com** and select "Video Questions." Click on "Chapter 10" and view the video titled *Choosing a Business Name and a Domain Name.* Then answer the following questions.

1. Which form of intellectual property is a domain name?
2. Can a Web-based business register and use a domain name that is identical to the business name of a firm located in a distant state?
3. If Caleb and Anna in the video chose to use the name "Wizard for Hire" and were sued for infringement, would it make any difference to the court whether a consumer was likely to be confused between the two computer businesses? What would the court focus on in analyzing infringement in this situation?

INTERACTING WITH THE INTERNET

For updated links to resources available on the Web, as well as a variety of other materials, visit this text's Web site at

http://leet.westbuslaw.com

An excellent overview of the laws governing various forms of intellectual property is available at FindLaw's Web site. Go to

http://profs.lp.findlaw.com

You can find much information about trademark and patent law—and links to registration forms, statutes, international patent and trademark offices, and numerous other related materials—at the Web site of the U.S. Patent and Trademark Office. Go to

http://www.uspto.gov

You can also access information on patent law at the following Internet site:

http://www.patents.com

For information on copyrights, go to the U.S. Copyright Office at

http://www.loc.gov/copyright

You can find extensive information on copyright law—including United States Supreme Court decisions in this area and the texts of the Berne Convention and other international treaties on copyright issues—at the Web site of the Legal Information Institute at Cornell University's School of Law. Go to

http://www.law.cornell.edu/topics/copyright.html

Law.com's Web site offers articles, case decisions, and other information concerning intellectual property at

http://www.law.com/jsp/pc/iplaw.jsp

ONLINE LEGAL RESEARCH EXERCISES

Go to **http://leet.westbuslaw.com**, the Web site that accompanies this text. Select "Interactive Study Center," and then click on "Chapter 10." There you will find the following Internet research exercises that you can perform to learn more about topics covered in this chapter.

Activity 10–1: MANAGEMENT PERSPECTIVE—Unwarranted Legal Threats
Activity 10–2: INTERNATIONAL PERSPECTIVE—Protecting Intellectual Property across Borders
Activity 10–3: TECHNOLOGICAL PERSPECTIVE—File-Sharing

BEFORE THE TEST

Go to **http://leet.westbuslaw.com**, the Web site that accompanies this text. Select "Interactive Quizzes." You will find at least twenty interactive questions relating to this chapter.

Westlaw® Campus

If your textbook provided for a subscription to Westlaw® Campus, or if you have otherwise purchased access to the Westlaw Campus database, you can access any of the cases presented or cited in this chapter by using your Westlaw Campus account.

CHAPTER **11**

Contract Formation

CONTENTS

CHAPTER OBJECTIVES

After reading this chapter, you should be able to answer the following questions:

1. What does the term *contract* mean, and how do contracts function in our society?

2. Which types of contracts are subject to Article 2 of the Uniform Commercial Code?

3. What are the four basic requirements for a valid contract?

4. What are the contractual rights and duties of minors?

5. How might third parties acquire rights in contracts?

As Roscoe Pound—an eminent jurist—observed in the quotation below, "keeping promises" is important to a stable social order. Contract law deals with, among other things, the formation and keeping of promises.

Like other types of law, contract law reflects our social values, interests, and expectations at a given point in time. It shows, for example, what kinds of promises our society thinks should be legally binding. It shows what excuses our society accepts for breaking such promises. Additionally, it shows what promises are considered to be contrary to public policy and therefore legally void. If a promise goes against the interests of society as a whole, it will be invalid. Also, if it was made by a child or a mentally incompetent person, or on the basis of false information, a question will arise as to whether the promise should be enforced. Resolving such questions is the essence of contract law. In business law and the legal environment of business, questions and disputes concerning contracts arise daily.

> **"The social order rests upon the stability and predictability of conduct, of which keeping promises is a large item."**
> Roscoe Pound, 1870–1964
> (American jurist)

THE LAW GOVERNING CONTRACTS

A **contract** is an agreement that can be enforced in court. It is formed by parties who agree to perform or to refrain from performing some act now or in the future. Although aspects of contract law vary from state to state, much of it is based on the common law.

CONTRACT
An agreement that can be enforced in court; formed by two or more parties who agree to perform or to refrain from performing some act now or in the future.

The Common Law of Contracts

In 1932, the American Law Institute compiled the *Restatement of the Law of Contracts*. This work is a nonstatutory, authoritative exposition of the present law on the subject of contracts and is presently in its second edition (although a third edition is in the process of being drafted). Throughout the following chapters on contracts, we will refer to the second edition of the *Restatement of the Law of Contracts* as simply the *Restatement (Second) of Contracts*.

Contracts for the Sale of Goods

The Uniform Commercial Code (UCC), which governs **sales contracts,** or contracts for the sale of goods, and lease contracts, occasionally departs from common law contract rules. Generally, the different treatment of contracts falling under the UCC stems from the general policy of encouraging commerce. Some of the ways in which the UCC changes common law contract rules are discussed in this chapter and in Chapter 12.

SALES CONTRACT
A contract for the sale of goods under which the ownership of goods is transferred from a seller to a buyer for a price.

The Relationship between Article 2 and the Common Law To facilitate commercial transactions, Article 2 modifies some of the common law contract requirements that are discussed in this chapter. To the extent that it has not been modified by the UCC, however, the common law of contracts also applies to sales contracts. For example, the common law requirements for a valid contract—agreement (offer and acceptance), consideration, capacity, and legality—that we discuss in this chapter are applicable to sales contracts as well. In general, the rule is that whenever there is a conflict between a common law contract rule and the UCC, the UCC controls. In other words, when a UCC provision addresses a certain issue, the UCC governs; when the UCC is silent, the common law governs.

The Scope of Article 2 In regard to Article 2, you should keep in mind two things. First, Article 2 deals with the sale of *goods;* it does not deal with real property (real estate), services, or intangible property such as stocks and bonds. Thus, if the subject matter of a dispute is goods, the UCC governs. If it is real estate or services, the common law applies. The relationship between general contract law and the law governing sales of goods is illustrated in Exhibit 11–1 on the following page. Second, in some cases, the rules may vary quite a bit, depending on whether the buyer or the seller is a *merchant*.

In 2003, the National Conference of Commissioners on Uniform State Laws (NCCUSL) and the American Law Institute adopted amendments to Article 2 (and Article 2A, which covers leases of goods). For the most part, the amendments mark an attempt to update Article 2 to accommodate electronic commerce. Among other things, the amendments include revised definitions of various terms to make the definitions consistent with those given in the

EXHIBIT 11-1 LAW GOVERNING CONTRACTS

This exhibit graphically illustrates the relationship between general contract law and the law governing contracts for the sale of goods. Sales contracts are not governed exclusively by Article 2 of the Uniform Commercial Code but also by general contract law whenever it is relevant and has not been modified by the UCC.

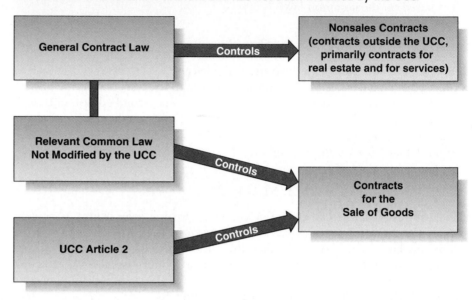

Uniform Electronic Transactions Act and the federal Electronic Signatures in Global and National Commerce Act. (See Chapter 13 for a discussion of these acts.)

Because of its importance in the legal environment of sales transactions, the full text of Article 2 of the UCC is included at the end of this text as Appendix D. The appendix also includes selected provisions from the 2003 amendments to Article 2.

THE FUNCTION OF CONTRACTS

PROMISOR
A person who makes a promise.

PROMISEE
A person to whom a promise is made.

OFFEROR
A person who makes an offer.

OFFEREE
A person to whom an offer is made.

Contract law assures the parties to private agreements that the promises they make will be enforceable. Clearly, many promises are kept because of a moral obligation to do so or because keeping a promise is in the mutual self-interest of the parties involved, not because the **promisor** (the person making the promise) or the **promisee** (the person to whom the promise is made) is conscious of the rules of contract law. Nevertheless, the rules of contract law are often followed in business agreements to avoid potential problems.

Every contract involves at least two parties. The **offeror** is the party making the offer. The **offeree** is the party to whom the offer is made. The offeror always promises to do or not to do something and thus is also a promisor. Generally, contract disputes arise when there is a promise of future performance. If the contractual promise is not fulfilled, the party who made it is subject to the sanctions of a court (see Chapter 12). That party may be required to pay money damages for failing to perform; in a limited number of instances, the party may be required to perform the promised act.

Today, online shoppers can form contracts online in a matter of minutes. Do such contracts constitute unilateral contracts, or are they bilateral contracts? What is the difference between these two types of contracts?

TYPES OF CONTRACTS

There are numerous types of contracts. The categories into which contracts are placed involve legal distinctions as to formation, enforceability, or performance. The best method of explaining each type of contract is to compare one type with another.

Bilateral versus Unilateral Contracts

Whether a contract is classified as *unilateral* or *bilateral* depends on what the offeree must do to accept the offer and to bind the offeror to a contract.

If to accept the offer the offeree must only *promise* to perform, the contract is a **bilateral contract.** Hence, a bilateral contract is a "promise for a promise." An example of a bilateral contract is a contract in which one person agrees to buy another person's automobile for a specified price. No performance, such as the payment of money or delivery of goods, need take place for a bilateral contract to be formed. The contract comes into existence at the moment the promises are exchanged.

If the offer is phrased so that the offeree can accept only by completing the contract performance, the contract is a **unilateral contract.** Hence, a unilateral contract is a "promise for an act." ● **EXAMPLE 1** Joe says to Celia, "If you walk across the Brooklyn Bridge, I'll give you $10." Joe promises to pay only if Celia walks the entire span of the bridge. Only on Celia's complete crossing does she fully accept Joe's offer to pay $10. If she chooses not to undertake the walk, there are no legal consequences. ● Contests, lotteries, and other competitions in which prizes are awarded are also examples of offers for unilateral contracts. If a person complies with the rules of the contest—such as by submitting the right lottery number at the right place and time—a unilateral contract is formed, binding the organization offering the prize to a contract to perform as promised in the offer.

Can a school's, or an employer's, letter of tentative acceptance to a prospective student, or a possible employee, qualify as a unilateral contract? That was the issue in the following case.

CASE 11.1   Ardito v. City of Providence

United States District Court,
District of Rhode Island, 2003.
263 F.Supp.2d 358.

BACKGROUND AND FACTS In 2001, the City of Providence, Rhode Island, decided to begin hiring police officers to fill vacancies in its police department. Because only individuals who graduated from the Providence Police Academy were eligible, the city also decided to conduct two training sessions, the "60th and 61st Police Academies." To be admitted, an applicant had to pass a series of tests and be deemed qualified by members of the department after an interview. The applicants judged most qualified were sent a letter informing them that they had been selected to attend if they successfully completed a medical checkup and a psychological examination. The letter to the applicants to the 61st Academy, dated October 15, stated that it was "a conditional offer of employment." Meanwhile, a new chief of police, Dean Esserman, decided to revise the selection process, which caused some of those who had received the letter to be rejected. Derek Ardito and thirteen other newly rejected applicants filed a suit in a federal district court against the city, seeking a halt to the 61st Academy unless they were allowed to attend. They alleged in part that the city was in breach of contract.

IN THE WORDS OF THE COURT . . .

ERNEST C. TORRES, Chief District Judge.

*   *   *   *

*   *   * *[T]he October 15 letter *   *   * is a classic example of an offer to enter into a unilateral contract.* The October 15 letter expressly stated that it was a "conditional offer of employment" and the message that it conveyed was that the recipient would be admitted into the 61st Academy if he or she successfully completed the medical and psychological examinations, requirements that the City could not lawfully impose unless it was making a conditional offer of employment. [Emphasis added.]

Moreover, the terms of that offer were perfectly consistent with what applicants had been told when they appeared [for their interviews]. At that time, [Police Major Dennis] Simoneau informed them that, if they "passed" the [interviews], they would be offered a place in the Academy provided that they also passed medical and psychological examinations.

The October 15 letter also was in marked contrast to notices sent to applicants by the City at earlier stages of the selection process. Those notices merely informed applicants that they had completed a step in the process and remained eligible to be considered for admission into the Academy. Unlike the October 15 letter, the prior notices did not purport to extend a "conditional offer" of admission.

The plaintiffs accepted the City's offer of admission into the Academy by satisfying the specified conditions. Each of the plaintiffs submitted to and passed lengthy and intrusive medical and psychological examinations. In addition, many of the plaintiffs, in reliance on the City's offer, jeopardized their standing with their existing employers by notifying the employers of their anticipated departure, and some plaintiffs passed up opportunities for other employment.

CASE 11.1—Continued   *   *   *   *

> The City argues that there is no contract between the parties because the plaintiffs have no legally enforceable right to employment. The City correctly points out that, even if the plaintiffs graduate from the Academy and there are existing vacancies in the Department, they would be required to serve a one-year probationary period during which they could be terminated without cause *   *   * . That argument misses the point. The contract that the plaintiffs seek to enforce is not a contract that they will be appointed as permanent Providence police officers; rather, it is a contract that they would be admitted to the Academy if they passed the medical and psychological examinations.

DECISION AND REMEDY The court issued an injunction to prohibit the city from conducting the 61st Police Academy unless the plaintiffs were included. The October 15 letter was a unilateral offer that the plaintiffs had accepted by passing the required medical and psychological examinations.

FOR CRITICAL ANALYSIS—Social Consideration *How might the city have phrased the letter to avoid its being considered a unilateral contract?*

Express versus Implied Contracts

An **express contract** is one in which the terms of the agreement are fully and explicitly stated in words, oral or written. A signed lease for an apartment or a house is an express written contract. ● **EXAMPLE 2** If a classmate calls you on the phone and agrees to buy your textbooks from last semester for $50, an express oral contract has been made. ●

An **implied-in-fact contract,** or an implied contract, differs from an express contract in that the *conduct* of the parties, rather than their words, creates and defines at least some of the terms of the contract. ● **EXAMPLE 3** Suppose that you need an accountant to fill out your tax return this year. You look through the Yellow Pages and find an accounting firm located in your neighborhood. You drop by the firm's office, explain your problem to an accountant, and learn what fees will be charged. The next day you return, giving the receptionist all of the necessary information and documents, such as canceled checks, W-2 forms, and other documents. You say nothing expressly to the receptionist; rather, you walk out the door. In this situation, you have entered into an implied-in-fact contract to pay the accountant the usual and reasonable fees for the accounting services. The contract is implied by your conduct. The accountant expects to be paid for completing your tax return. By bringing in the records the accountant will need to do the work, you have implied an intent to pay for the services. ●

EXPRESS CONTRACT
A contract in which the terms of the agreement are fully and explicitly stated in words, oral or written.

IMPLIED-IN-FACT CONTRACT
A contract formed in whole or in part from the conduct of the parties (as opposed to an express contract).

"Outward actions are a clue to hidden secrets."
(LEGAL MAXIM)

BE AWARE An implied-in-fact contract is as legally binding as an express contract.

Quasi Contracts—Contracts Implied in Law

Quasi contracts, or contracts *implied in law,* are wholly different from actual contracts. Express contracts and implied-in-fact contracts are actual, or true, contracts. Quasi contracts, as their name suggests, are not true contracts. They do not arise from any agreement, express or implied, between the parties themselves. Rather, quasi contracts are fictional contracts imposed on parties

QUASI CONTRACT
A fictional contract imposed on parties by a court in the interests of fairness and justice; usually, quasi contracts are imposed to avoid the unjust enrichment of one party at the expense of another.

What determines whether a contract for accounting, tax preparation, or any other service is an express contract or an implied-in-fact contract?

REMEMBER Quasi contract is an equitable concept, but most courts can apply the doctrine, because in most states, courts of law and equity have merged.

by courts in the interests of fairness and justice. Quasi contracts are therefore equitable, rather than contractual, in nature. Usually, quasi contracts are imposed to avoid the *unjust enrichment* of one party at the expense of another.

● EXAMPLE 4 Suppose that a vacationing doctor is driving down the highway and encounters Emerson, who is lying unconscious on the side of the road. The doctor renders medical aid that saves Emerson's life. Although the injured, unconscious Emerson did not solicit the medical aid and was not aware that the aid had been rendered, Emerson received a valuable benefit, and the requirements for a quasi contract were fulfilled. In such a situation, the law normally will impose a quasi contract, and Emerson will have to pay the doctor for the reasonable value of the medical services rendered.●

Executed versus Executory Contracts

Contracts are also classified according to their state of performance. A contract that has been fully performed on both sides is called an **executed contract.** A contract that has not been fully performed on either side is called an **executory contract.** If one party has fully performed but the other has not, the contract is said to be executed on the one side and executory on the other, but the contract is still classified as executory.

EXECUTED CONTRACT
A contract that has been completely performed by both parties.

EXECUTORY CONTRACT
A contract that has not as yet been fully performed.

● EXAMPLE 5 Assume that you agree to buy ten tons of coal from the Western Coal Company. Further assume that Western has delivered the coal to your steel mill, where it is now being burned. At this point, the contract is an executory contract—it is executed on the part of Western and executory on your part. After you pay Western for the coal, the contract will be executed on both sides.●

Valid, Void, and Voidable Contracts

A **valid contract** has the elements necessary for contract formation. Those elements consist of (1) an agreement (offer and an acceptance) (2) supported by legally sufficient consideration (3) for a legal purpose and (4) made by parties who have the legal capacity to enter into the contract. We will discuss each of these elements in this chapter.

A **void contract** is no contract at all. The terms *void* and *contract* are contradictory. A void contract produces no legal obligations on the part of any of the parties. ● EXAMPLE 6 A contract can be void because one of the parties was adjudged by a court to be legally insane (and thus lacked the legal capacity to enter into a contract) or because the purpose of the contract was illegal.●

A **voidable contract** is a *valid* contract but one that can be avoided at the option of one or both of the parties. The party having the option can elect either to avoid any duty to perform or to *ratify* (make valid) the contract. If the contract is avoided, both parties are released from it. If it is ratified, both parties must fully perform their respective legal obligations.

As a general rule, contracts made by minors are voidable at the option of the minor. Contracts entered into under fraudulent conditions are voidable at the option of the defrauded party. In addition, contracts entered into under legally defined duress or undue influence are voidable.

VALID CONTRACT
A contract that results when elements necessary for contract formation (agreement, consideration, legal purpose, and contractual capacity) are present.

VOID CONTRACT
A contract having no legal force or binding effect.

VOIDABLE CONTRACT
A contract that may be legally avoided (canceled, or annulled) at the option of one of the parties.

Unenforceable Contracts

An **unenforceable contract** is one that cannot be enforced because of certain legal defenses against it. It is not unenforceable because a party failed to satisfy a legal requirement of the contract; rather, it is a valid contract rendered unenforceable by some statute or law. ● EXAMPLE 7 Certain contracts must be in writing, and if they are not, they will not be enforceable except in certain exceptional circumstances.●

UNENFORCEABLE CONTRACT
A valid contract rendered unenforceable by some statute or law.

REQUIREMENTS OF A CONTRACT

The four requirements that constitute what are known as the elements of a contract are (1) agreement, (2) consideration, (3) capacity, and (4) legality. We discuss the element of agreement first.

Agreement

An essential element for contract formation is **agreement**—the parties must agree on the terms of the contract. Ordinarily, agreement is evidenced by two events: an *offer* and an *acceptance*. One party offers a certain bargain to another party, who then accepts that bargain.

In determining whether a contract has been formed, the element of intent is of prime importance, as will be discussed shortly. In contract law, intent is determined by what is referred to as the *objective theory of contracts*, not by the personal or subjective intent, or belief, of a party. The theory is that a party's intention to enter into a contract is judged by outward, objective facts as interpreted by a reasonable person, rather than by the party's own secret, subjective intentions. Objective facts include (1) what the party said when

AGREEMENT
A meeting of two or more minds in regard to the terms of a contract; usually broken down into two events—an offer by one party to form a contract and an acceptance of the offer by the person to whom the offer is made.

A worker takes apart machinery. If the worker makes a design modification that the manufacturer incorporates into later models of the machine, should the worker be compensated if there is no contract covering the work?

OFFER
A promise or commitment to perform or refrain from performing some specified act in the future.

BE CAREFUL An opinion is not an offer and not a contract term. Goods or services can be "perfect" in one party's opinion and "inferior" in another's.

entering into the contract,[1] (2) how the party acted or appeared, and (3) the circumstances surrounding the transaction. As discussed earlier, in the section on express versus implied contracts, intent to form a contract may be manifested not only in words, oral or written, but also by conduct.

Requirements of the Offer An **offer** is a promise or commitment to perform or refrain from performing some specified act in the future. Three elements are necessary for an offer to be effective:

1. There must be a *serious, objective intention* by the offeror.
2. The terms of the offer must be reasonably *certain*, or *definite*, so that the parties and the court can ascertain the terms of the contract.
3. The offer must be communicated to the offeree.

Once an effective offer has been made, the offeree has the power to accept the offer. If the offeree accepts, the offer is translated into an agreement (and into a contract, if other essential elements of a contract are present).

Intention. The first requirement for an effective offer to exist is a serious, objective intention on the part of the offeror. Intent is not determined by the *subjective* intentions, beliefs, or assumptions of the offeror. Rather, it is determined by what a reasonable person in the offeree's position would conclude the offeror's words and actions meant. Offers made in obvious anger, jest, or undue excitement do not meet the serious-and-objective-intent test. Because these offers are not effective, an offeree's acceptance does not create an agreement.

An expression of opinion is not an offer or a promise. It does not evidence an intention to enter into a binding agreement. ● **EXAMPLE 8** In *Hawkins v. McGee,*[2] Hawkins took his son to McGee, a doctor, and asked McGee to operate on the son's hand. McGee said that the boy would be in the hospital three or four days and that the hand would *probably* heal a few days later. The son's hand did not heal for a month, but nonetheless the father did not win a suit for breach of contract. The court held that McGee did not make an offer to heal the son's hand in three or four days. He merely expressed an opinion as to when the hand would heal. ● Similarly, a *statement of intention* is not an offer. ● **EXAMPLE 9** If Ari says "I *plan* to sell my stock in Novation, Inc., for $150 per share," a contract is not created if John "accepts" and tenders the $150 per share for the stock. ●

Preliminary negotiations must also be distinguished from an offer. A request or invitation to negotiate is not an offer; it only expresses a willingness to discuss the possibility of entering into a contract. Examples are statements such as "Will you sell Forest Acres?" and "I wouldn't sell my car for less than $1,000." A reasonable person in the offeree's position would not conclude that such a statement evidenced an intention to enter into a binding obligation. Likewise, when the government and private firms need to have construction work done, contractors are invited to submit bids. The *invitation* to submit

1. As Judge Learned Hand once said, a court will give words their usual meaning even if "it were proved by twenty bishops that they intended something else." *Hotchkiss v. National City Bank of New York,* 200 F. 287 (2d Cir. 1911), aff'd 231 U.S. 50, 34 S.Ct. 20, 58 L.Ed. 115 (1913). (The term *aff'd* is an abbreviation for *affirmed;* an appellate court can affirm a lower court's judgment, decree, or order, thereby declaring that it is valid and must stand as rendered.)
2. 84 N.H. 114, 146 A. 641 (1929).

INTERNATIONAL PERSPECTIVE

How Intent to Form a Contract Is Measured in Other Countries

U.S. courts routinely adhere to the objective theory of contracts. Courts in some nations, however, give more weight to subjective intentions. Under French law, for example, when there is a conflict between an objective interpretation and a subjective interpretation of a contract, the French civil law code prefers the subjective construction. Other nations that have civil law codes take this same approach. French courts, nonetheless, will look to writings and other objective evidence to determine a party's subjective intent. In operation, the difference between the French and U.S. approaches is therefore perhaps not as significant as it may seem at first blush.

FOR CRITICAL ANALYSIS

What problems may arise when a court attempts to look at the subjective basis of a contract?

bids is not an offer, and a contractor does not bind the government or private firm by submitting a bid. (The bids that the contractors submit are offers, however, and the government or private firm can bind the contractor by accepting the bid.) In general, advertisements, mail-order catalogues, price lists, and circular letters (meant for the general public) are treated not as offers to contract but as invitations to negotiate.[3]

Lucy v. Zehmer, presented next, is a classic case in the area of contractual agreement. The case involves a business transaction in which boasts, brags, and dares "after a few drinks" resulted in a contract to sell certain property. The sellers claimed that the offer had been made in jest and that, in any event, the contract was voidable at their option because they were intoxicated when the offer was made and thus lacked contractual capacity (discussed later in this chapter). The court looked to the words and actions of the parties—not their secret intentions—to determine whether a contract had been formed.

---

3. *Restatement (Second) of Contracts,* Section 26, Comment b.

LANDMARK AND CLASSIC CASES

CASE 11.2 Lucy v. Zehmer

Supreme Court of Appeals of Virginia, 1954.
196 Va. 493,
84 S.E.2d 516.

BACKGROUND AND FACTS Lucy and Zehmer had known each other for fifteen or twenty years. For some time, Lucy had been wanting to buy Zehmer's farm. Zehmer had always told Lucy that he was not interested in selling. One night, Lucy stopped in to visit with the Zehmers at a restaurant they operated. Lucy said to Zehmer, "I bet you wouldn't take $50,000 for that place." Zehmer replied, "Yes, I would, too; you wouldn't give fifty." Throughout the evening, the conversation returned to the sale of the farm. At the same time, the parties were drinking whiskey. Eventually, Zehmer wrote up an agreement, on the back of a restaurant check, for the sale of the farm, and he asked his wife to sign it—which she did. When Lucy brought an action in a Virginia state court to enforce the agreement, Zehmer argued that he had been "high

(continued)

Capacity

CASE 11.2—Continued

as a Georgia pine" at the time and that the offer had been made in jest: "two doggoned drunks bluffing to see who could talk the biggest and say the most." Lucy claimed that he had not been intoxicated and did not think Zehmer had been, either, given the way Zehmer handled the transaction. The trial court ruled in favor of the Zehmers, and Lucy appealed.

IN THE WORDS OF THE COURT . . .

BUCHANAN, J. [Justice] delivered the opinion of the court.

* * * *

The appearance of the contract, the fact that it was under discussion for forty minutes or more before it was signed; Lucy's objection to the first draft because it was written in the singular, and he wanted Mrs. Zehmer to sign it also; the rewriting to meet that objection and the signing by Mrs. Zehmer; the discussion of what was to be included in the sale, the provision for the examination of the title, the completeness of the instrument that was executed, the taking possession of it by Lucy with no request or suggestion by either of the defendants that he give it back, are facts which furnish persuasive evidence that the execution of the contract was a serious business transaction rather than a casual, jesting matter as defendants now contend.

* * * *

In the field of contracts, as generally elsewhere, *"We must look to the outward expression of a person as manifesting his intention rather than to his secret and unexpressed intention.* 'The law imputes to a person an intention corresponding to the reasonable meaning of his words and acts.' " [Emphasis added.]

DECISION AND REMEDY The Supreme Court of Virginia determined that the writing was an enforceable contract and reversed the ruling of the lower court. The Zehmers were required by court order to carry through with the sale of the farm to the Lucys.

COMMENT *This is a classic case in contract law because it illustrates so clearly the objective theory of contracts with respect to determining whether an offer* *was intended. Today, the objective theory of contracts continues to be applied by the courts, and* Lucy v. Zehmer *is routinely cited as a significant precedent in this area. Note that in cases involving contracts formed online, the issue of contractual intent rarely arises. Perhaps this is because an online offer is, by definition, "objective" in the sense that it consists of words only— the offeror's physical actions and behavior are not evidenced.*

> **"**[Contracts] must not be the sports of an idle hour, mere matters of pleasantry and badinage, never intended by the parties to have any serious effect whatever.**"**
>
> WILLIAM STOWELL, 1745–1836
> (English jurist)

Definiteness. The second requirement for an effective offer involves the definiteness of its terms. An offer must have reasonably definite terms so that a court can determine if a breach has occurred and give an appropriate remedy.[4] ● **EXAMPLE 10** You offer to sell "some" of your textbooks to a friend, and the friend accepts your offer. No contract was formed by your friend's acceptance because the term *some* is too indefinite.●

An offer may invite an acceptance to be worded in such specific terms that the contract is made definite. ● **EXAMPLE 11** Suppose that Marcus Business Machines contacts your corporation and offers to sell "from one to ten MacCool copying machines for $1,600 each; state number desired in acceptance." Your corporation agrees to buy two copiers. Because the quantity is specified in the acceptance, the terms are definite, and the contract is enforceable.●

---

4. *Restatement (Second) of Contracts,* Section 33.

For contracts for the sale of goods, Article 2 of the UCC relaxes considerably the common law requirement of definiteness of terms. Section 2–204 of the UCC provides that a contract will not fail for indefiniteness even if one or more terms are left open as long as the parties intended to make a contract and there is a reasonably certain basis for the court to grant an appropriate remedy. A seller and buyer of goods can thus create an enforceable contract even if several terms, including terms relating to price, payment, and delivery, are left unspecified. For example, if the price term is left open, Article 2 provides that the price will be "a reasonable price at the time of delivery" [UCC 2–305(1)]. If the payment term is left open, Article 2 states that "payment is due at the time and place at which the buyer is to receive the goods" [UCC 2–310(a)]. Under Article 2, the only term that normally must be specified is the quantity term; otherwise, the court will have no basis for determining a remedy.

If the essential terms are spelled out, then, a court may find that an enforceable contract exists even though the parties failed to specify other terms. The following case illustrates this point.

CASE 11.3   Satellite Entertainment Center, Inc. v. Keaton

Superior Court of New Jersey,
Appellate Division, 2002.
347 N.J.Super. 268,
789 A.2d 662.

BACKGROUND AND FACTS In 1993, John Keaton decided to open a barbecue restaurant in Jersey City, New Jersey, and entered into a six-year lease with George Williams to occupy a portion of Williams's building. After Williams died, Morris Winograd, the owner of Satellite Entertainment Center, Inc., bought the building that included Keaton's restaurant. Winograd planned to renovate the entire premises to open a new restaurant and bar. In September 1995, Winograd asked Keaton how much it would cost to buy his business. Keaton named a price of $175,000. Keaton later claimed, as corroborated by witnesses, that Winograd said he would pay that amount, that he wanted Keaton out by the end of the year, and that he wanted Keaton to manage the new enterprise. Keaton vacated the premises by December. In January, Winograd began paying Keaton a salary but did not pay him the $175,000, despite repeated requests. In April 1997, Winograd terminated Keaton. In a subsequent claim in a New Jersey state court against Satellite and Winograd, Keaton sought the $175,000. Winograd denied agreeing to pay Keaton anything. The court ruled in Keaton's favor. Winograd appealed to a state intermediate appellate court, claiming in part that the alleged agreement should not be enforced because it did not include the essential terms of an enforceable contract.

IN THE WORDS OF THE COURT . . .

LESEMANN, J.A.D. [Judge, Appellate Division]

*   *   *   *

We *   *   * reject the claim that Winograd's contractual undertaking to pay $175,000 to Keaton should be invalidated for lack of specificity concerning the terms of the contract. The basic terms of this very simple agreement were clear.

First, the price was firm: it was $175,000. So too was the description of what Winograd was purchasing. He was buying all of Keaton's business, including whatever tangible assets, inventory or "good will" might be involved. However, *   *   * none of those assets were particularly significant to Winograd. Thus, it is not surprising that the parties did not, for example, itemize with specificity the inventory or the furniture of Keaton's business

(continued)

CASE 11.3—Continued

which was to be turned over to Winograd. To Winograd, those details were unimportant. The critical point, and the real reason for Winograd's payment of $175,000, was Keaton's agreement to vacate the property by the end of 1995, which he did.

Winograd also argues that the contract was too vague for enforcement because there was no description of the interest rate or the due date of the * * * payment for the business. Keaton concedes that [there was] no provision for interest, and thus he had no right to interest. He claims further that without a specified due date, the [payment] should be regarded as due on demand.

It is a settled principle that when the essential parts of a contract are spelled out, a court will not refuse to enforce that contract because some of its less critical terms have not been articulated. In such a case, the court will imply a reasonable missing term or, if necessary, will receive evidence to provide a basis for such an implication. And that is particularly true when there has been part performance of the contract, or—as here—where one of the parties (Keaton) has fully performed his part of the bargain. [Emphasis added.]

In support of his claim of invalidity because of vagueness, Winograd relies on a number of cases in which critical, essential parts of a contract were missing and the contract was so vague or indefinite that it could not realistically be enforced. * * * Here, * * * the heart of the contract is the dollar amount to be paid to Keaton and Keaton's obligation to vacate the premises for Winograd's use. The incidental terms of the [interest and the date for] payment were just that: incidental terms, which do not bar enforcement of the essential agreement between the parties.

DECISION AND REMEDY The state intermediate appellate court affirmed the judgment of the lower court on Keaton's claim for $175,000. The essential terms of the agreement for the sale of Keaton's business could be determined, and thus there was an enforceable contract between the parties.

FOR CRITICAL ANALYSIS—Social Consideration *Suppose that Keaton had not yet performed (vacated the premises by the end of the year) under the contract. Would this have affected the court's decision in any way?*

Communication. A third requirement for an effective offer is communication, resulting in the offeree's knowledge of the offer. ● **EXAMPLE 12** Suppose that Tolson advertises a reward for the return of her lost cat. Dirlik, not knowing of the reward, finds the cat and returns it to Tolson. Ordinarily, Dirlik cannot recover the reward, because an essential element of a reward contract is that the one who claims the reward must have known that it was offered. A few states would allow recovery of the reward, but not on contract principles—Dirlik would be allowed to recover on the basis that it would be unfair to deny him the reward just because he did not know about it.●

Termination of the Offer The communication of an effective offer to an offeree gives the offeree the power to transform the offer into a binding, legal obligation (a contract) by an acceptance. This power of acceptance, however, does not continue forever. It can be terminated by *action of the parties* or by *operation of law.*

Termination by Action of the Offeror. An offer can be terminated by the action of the parties in any of three ways: by revocation, by rejection, or by counteroffer. The offeror's act of withdrawing an offer is referred to as **revocation.** Unless an offer is irrevocable, the offeror usually can revoke the offer (even if he or she has promised to keep the offer open), as long as the revocation is communicated to the offeree before the offeree accepts. Revocation may be accomplished by express repudiation of the offer (for example, with a statement such as "I withdraw my previous offer of October 17") or by performance of acts inconsistent with the existence of the offer, which are made known to the offeree.

Termination of Action of the Offeree. The offer may be rejected by the offeree, in which case the offer is terminated. A rejection is ordinarily accomplished by words or by conduct evidencing an intent not to accept the offer. As with revocation, rejection of an offer is effective only when it is actually received by the offeror or the offeror's agent. A **counteroffer** is a rejection of the original offer and the simultaneous making of a new offer. ● EXAMPLE 13 Suppose that Burke offers to sell his home to Lang for $270,000. Lang responds, "Your price is too high. I'll offer to purchase your house for $250,000." Lang's response is termed a counteroffer because it rejects Burke's offer to sell at $270,000 and creates a new offer by Lang to purchase the home at a price of $250,000.●

At common law, the **mirror image rule** requires that the offeree's acceptance match the offeror's offer exactly. In other words, the terms of the acceptance must "mirror" those of the offer. If the acceptance materially changes or adds to the terms of the original offer, it will be considered not an acceptance but a counteroffer—which, of course, need not be accepted. The original offeror can, however, accept the terms of the counteroffer and create a valid contract. The mirror image rule has been greatly modified in regard to contracts for the sale of goods. Section 2–207 of the UCC provides, with some exceptions, that a contract is formed if the offeree makes a definite expression of acceptance (such as signing the form in the appropriate location), even though the terms of the acceptance modify or add to the terms of the original offer.

Termination by Operation of Law. The offeree's power to transform an offer into a binding, legal obligation can be terminated by operation of law if any of four conditions occur. First, an offer terminates automatically by law when the period of time specified in the offer has passed. ● EXAMPLE 14 Jane offers to sell her boat to Jonah if he accepts within twenty days. Jonah must accept within the twenty-day period, or the offer will lapse (terminate).● If no time for acceptance is specified in the offer, the offer terminates at the end of a *reasonable* period of time. A reasonable period of time is determined by the subject matter of the contract, business and market conditions, and other relevant circumstances. An offer to sell farm produce, for example, will terminate sooner than an offer to sell farm equipment, because farm produce is perishable and subject to greater fluctuations in market value.

Second, an offer is automatically terminated if the specific subject matter of the offer is destroyed before the offer is accepted. If Bekins offers to sell his cow to Yatsen, but the cow dies before Yatsen can accept, the offer is automatically terminated. Third, an offeree's power of acceptance is terminated when the offeror or offeree dies or is deprived of legal capacity to enter into

REVOCATION
In contract law, the withdrawal of an offer by an offeror; unless the offer is irrevocable, it can be revoked at any time prior to acceptance without liability.

BE CAREFUL The way in which a response to an offer is phrased can determine whether the offer is accepted or rejected.

COUNTEROFFER
An offeree's response to an offer in which the offeree rejects the original offer and at the same time makes a new offer.

MIRROR IMAGE RULE
A common law rule that requires, for a valid contractual agreement, that the terms of the offeree's acceptance adhere exactly to the terms of the offeror's offer.

the proposed contract, unless the offer is irrevocable.[5] Finally, a statute or court decision that makes an offer illegal will automatically terminate the offer. ● EXAMPLE 15 If Acme Finance Corporation offers to lend Jack $20,000 at 10 percent annually, and a state statute is enacted prohibiting loans at interest rates greater than 8 percent before Jack can accept, the offer is automatically terminated. (If the statute is enacted after Jack accepts the offer, a valid contract is formed, but the contract may still be unenforceable.)●

ACCEPTANCE
A voluntary act by the offeree that shows assent, or agreement, to the terms of an offer; may consist of words or conduct.

Acceptance An **acceptance** is a voluntary act by the offeree that shows assent, or agreement, to the terms of an offer. The offeree's act may consist of words or conduct. Generally, a third person cannot substitute for the offeree and effectively accept the offer. After all, the identity of the offeree is as much a condition of a bargaining offer as any other term contained therein. Thus, except in special circumstances, only the person to whom the offer is made or that person's agent can accept the offer and create a binding contract. For example, Lottie makes an offer to Paul. Paul is not interested, but Paul's friend José accepts the offer. No contract is formed.

Unequivocal Acceptance. To exercise the power of acceptance effectively, the offeree must accept unequivocally. This is the *mirror image rule* previously discussed. If the acceptance is subject to new conditions or if the terms of the acceptance materially change the original offer, the acceptance may be deemed a counteroffer that implicitly rejects the original offer.

DON'T FORGET When an offer is rejected, it is terminated.

Certain terms, when added to an acceptance, will not qualify the acceptance sufficiently to constitute rejection of the offer. ● EXAMPLE 16 Suppose that in response to a person offering to sell a painting by a well-known artist, the offeree replies, "I accept; please send a written contract." The offeree is requesting a written contract but is not making it a condition for acceptance. Therefore, the acceptance is effective without the written contract. If the offeree replies, "I accept if you send a written contract," however, the acceptance is expressly conditioned on the request for a writing, and the statement is not an acceptance but a counteroffer. (Notice how important each word is!)●

If an offeror expressly authorizes acceptance of his or her offer by first-class mail or express delivery, can the offeree accept by a faster means, such as by fax?

As noted earlier, in regard to sales contracts, the UCC provides that an acceptance may still be valid even if some terms are added. The new terms are simply treated as proposals for additions to the contract, or become part of the contract [UCC 2–207(2)].

Communication of Acceptance. Whether the offeror must be notified of the acceptance depends on the nature of the contract. In a bilateral contract, communication of acceptance is necessary, because acceptance is in the form of a promise (not performance), and the contract is formed when the promise is made (rather than when the act is performed). The offeree must communicate the acceptance to the offeror. Communication of acceptance is not necessary, however, if the offer dispenses with the requirement. Also, if the offer can be accepted by silence, no communication is necessary. Note that under the UCC, an order or other offer to buy goods that are to be promptly shipped may be treated as an offer and can be accepted by a promise to ship or by actual shipment [UCC 2–206 (1)(b)].

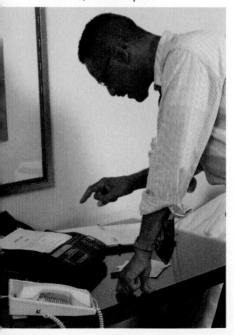

5. *Restatement (Second) of Contracts,* Section 48. If the offer is irrevocable, it is not terminated when the offeror dies. Also, if the offer is such that it can be accepted by the performance of a series of acts, and those acts began before the offeror died, the offeree's power of acceptance is not terminated.

Because in a unilateral contract the full performance of some act is called for, acceptance is usually evident, and notification is therefore unnecessary. Exceptions do exist, however. When the offeror requests notice of acceptance or has no adequate means of determining whether the requested act has been performed, or when the law requires such notice of acceptance, then notice is necessary.

Mode and Timeliness of Acceptance. The general rule is that acceptance in a bilateral contract is timely if it is effected within the duration of the offer. Problems arise, however, when the parties involved are not dealing face to face. In such cases, the offeree may use an authorized mode of communication. Acceptance takes effect, thus completing formation of the contract, at the time the offeree sends the communication via the mode expressly or impliedly authorized by the offeror. This is the so-called **mailbox rule,** also called the "deposited acceptance rule," which the majority of courts uphold. Under this rule, if the authorized mode of communication is the mail, then an acceptance becomes valid when it is dispatched—not when it is received by the offeror.

Technology and Acceptances. Clearly, some of the traditional rules governing acceptance do not seem to apply to an age in which acceptances are commonly delivered via electronic means, such as by fax or e-mail. For example, the mailbox rule does not apply to online acceptances, which typically are communicated instantaneously to the offeror. Nonetheless, the traditional rules—and the principles that underlie those rules—provide a basis for understanding what constitutes a valid acceptance in today's online environment. This is because, as in other areas of the law, much of the law governing online offers and acceptances consists of adaptations of traditional law to a new environment.

You will learn about online offers and acceptances in Chapter 13. It should be noted here, though, that while online offers are not significantly different from traditional offers contained in paper documents, online acceptances have posed some unusual problems for the court.

MAILBOX RULE
A rule providing that an acceptance of an offer becomes effective on dispatch (on being placed in a mailbox), if mail is, expressly or impliedly, an authorized means of communication of acceptance to the offeror.

Consideration

In every legal system, some promises will be enforced, and some promises will not be enforced. The simple fact that a party has made a promise, then, does not mean that the promise is enforceable. Under the common law, a primary basis for the enforcement of promises is consideration.

Elements of Consideration Consideration is usually defined as the value given in return for a promise. Often, consideration is broken down into two parts: (1) something of *legally sufficient value* must be given in exchange for the promise, and (2) there must be a *bargained-for* exchange.

Legal Value. The "something of legally sufficient value" may consist of (1) a promise to do something that one has no prior legal duty to do (to pay money on receipt of certain goods, for example), (2) the performance of an action that one is otherwise not obligated to undertake (such as providing accounting services), or (3) the refraining from an action that one has a legal right to undertake (known as *forbearance*).

CONSIDERATION
Generally, the value given in return for a promise. The consideration, which must be present to make the contract legally binding, must result in a detriment to the promisee (something of legally sufficient value and bargained for) or a benefit to the promisor.

Consideration in bilateral contracts normally consists of a promise in return for a promise. ● **EXAMPLE 17** In a contract for a sale of goods, a seller promises to ship specific goods to the buyer, and the buyer promises to pay for those goods when they are received. Each of these promises constitutes consideration for the contract.● In contrast, unilateral contracts involve a promise in return for a performance. ● **EXAMPLE 18** Suppose that Anita says to her neighbor, "When you finish painting the garage, I will pay you $100." Anita's neighbor paints the garage. The act of painting the garage is the consideration that creates Anita's contractual obligation to pay her neighbor $100.●

What if, in return for a promise to pay, a person forbears to pursue harmful habits, such as the use of tobacco and alcohol? Does such forbearance create consideration for the contract? This was the issue before the court in *Hamer v. Sidway,* a classic case concerning consideration, which we present in this chapter's *Landmark in the Legal Environment* feature.

Bargained-for Exchange. The second element of consideration is that it must provide the basis for the bargain struck between the contracting parties. The consideration given by the promisor must induce the promisee to offer a return promise, performance, or forbearance, and the promisee's promise, performance, or forbearance must induce the promisor to make the promise. This element of bargained-for exchange distinguishes contracts from gifts.

Adequacy of Consideration As mentioned, consideration involves the requirement that consideration be something of value in the eyes of the law. Adequacy of consideration involves "how much" consideration is given. Essentially, adequacy of consideration concerns the fairness of the bargain. On the surface, fairness would appear to be an issue when the values of items exchanged are unequal. In general, however, courts do not question the adequacy of consideration if the consideration is legally sufficient. Under the doctrine of freedom of contract, parties are usually free to bargain as they wish. If people could sue merely because they had entered into an unwise contract, the courts would be overloaded with frivolous suits.

In extreme cases, however, a court of law may look to the amount or value (the adequacy) of the consideration, because apparently inadequate consideration can indicate that fraud, duress, or undue influence was involved or that a gift was made (if a father "sells" a $100,000 house to his daughter for only $1, for example). Additionally, in cases in which the consideration is grossly inadequate, the courts may declare the contract unenforceable on the ground that it is unconscionable[6]—that is, generally speaking, it is so one sided under the circumstances as to be overly unfair. (Unconscionability will be discussed later in this chapter.)

Contracts That Lack Consideration Sometimes, one of the parties (or both parties) to a contract may think that the parties have exchanged consideration when in fact they have not. Here we look at some situations in which the parties' promises or actions do not qualify as contractual consideration.

Preexisting Duty. Under most circumstances, a promise to do what one already has a legal duty to do does not constitute legally sufficient considera-

---

"It is the essence of a consideration, that, by the terms of the agreement, it is given and accepted as the motive or inducement of the promise."
OLIVER WENDELL HOLMES, JR.,
1841–1935
(Associate justice of the United States Supreme Court, 1902–1932)

BE AWARE A consumer's signature on a contract does not always guarantee that the contract will be enforced. Ultimately, the terms must be fair.

---

6. Pronounced un-*kon*-shun-uh-bul.

LANDMARK IN THE LEGAL ENVIRONMENT

Hamer v. Sidway (1891)

In *Hamer v. Sidway,*[a] the issue before the court arose from a contract created in 1869 between William Story, Sr., and his nephew, William Story II. The uncle promised his nephew that if the nephew refrained from drinking alcohol, using tobacco, and playing billiards and cards for money until he reached the age of twenty-one, the uncle would pay him $5,000 (about $75,000 in today's dollars). The nephew, who indulged occasionally in all of these "vices," agreed to refrain from them and did so for the next six years. Following his twenty-first birthday in 1875, the nephew wrote to his uncle that he had performed his part of the bargain and was thus entitled to the promised $5,000. A few days later, the uncle wrote the nephew a letter stating, "[Y]ou shall have the five thousand dollars, as I promised you." The uncle said that the money was in the bank and that the nephew could "consider this money on interest."

THE ISSUE OF CONSIDERATION   The nephew left the money in the care of his uncle, who held it for the next twelve years. When the uncle died in 1887, however, the executor of the uncle's estate refused to pay the $5,000 claim brought by Hamer, a third party to whom the promise had been *assigned.* (As you will read later in this chapter, the law allows parties to assign, or transfer, rights in contracts to third parties.) The executor, Sidway, contended that the contract was invalid because there was insufficient consideration to support it. The uncle had received nothing, and the nephew had actually benefited by fulfilling the uncle's wishes. Therefore, no contract existed.

THE COURT'S CONCLUSION   Although a lower court upheld Sidway's position, the New York Court of Appeals reversed and ruled in favor of the plaintiff, Hamer. "The promisee used tobacco, occasionally drank liquor, and he had a legal right to do so," the court stated. "That right he abandoned for a period of years upon the strength of the promise of the testator [one who makes a will] that for such forbearance he would give him $5,000. We need not speculate on the effort which may have been required to give up the use of those stimulants. It is sufficient that he restricted his lawful freedom of action within certain prescribed limits upon the faith of his uncle's agreement."

Application to Today's World

Although this case was decided over a century ago, the principles enunciated in the case remain applicable to contracts formed today, including online contracts. For a contract to be valid and binding, consideration must be given, and that consideration must be something of legally sufficient value.

a. 124 N.Y. 538, 27 N.E. 256 (1891).

tion.[7] The preexisting legal duty may be imposed by law or may arise out of a previous contract. A sheriff, for example, cannot collect a reward for information leading to the capture of a criminal if the sheriff already has a legal duty to capture the criminal. Likewise, if a party is already bound by contract to perform a certain duty, that duty (the consideration given in the contract) cannot serve as consideration for a second contract.

7. See *Foakes v. Beer,* 9 App.Cas. 605 (1884).

● EXAMPLE 19 Suppose that Bauman-Bache, Inc., begins construction on a seven-story office building and after three months demands an extra $75,000 on its contract. If the extra $75,000 is not paid, it will stop working. The owner of the land, having no one else to complete construction, agrees to pay the extra $75,000. The agreement is not enforceable, because it is not supported by legally sufficient consideration; Bauman-Bache had a preexisting contractual duty to complete the building.●

The rule regarding preexisting duty is meant to prevent extortion and the so-called holdup game. What happens, though, when an honest contractor, who has contracted with a landowner to build a house, runs into extraordinary difficulties that were totally unforeseen at the time the contract was formed? In the interests of fairness and equity, the courts sometimes allow exceptions to the preexisting duty rule. In the example just mentioned, if the landowner agrees to pay extra compensation to the contractor for overcoming the unforeseen difficulties (such as having to use dynamite and special equipment to remove an unexpected rock formation in order to build a basement), the court may refrain from applying the preexisting duty rule and enforce the agreement. When the "unforeseen difficulties" that give rise to a contract modification are the types of risks ordinarily assumed in business, however, the courts will usually assert the preexisting duty rule.

Article 2 of the UCC significantly modifies the preexisting duty rule with respect to sales contracts. Under Article 2, any agreement modifying a contract needs no consideration to be binding [UCC 2–209(1)].

Past Consideration. Promises made in return for actions or events that have already taken place are unenforceable. These promises lack consideration in that the element of bargained-for exchange is missing. In short, you can bargain for something to take place now or in the future but not for something that has already taken place. Therefore, **past consideration** is no consideration.

● EXAMPLE 20 Suppose that Elsie, a real estate agent, does her friend Judy a favor by selling Judy's house and not charging any commission. Later, Judy says to Elsie, "In return for your generous act, I will pay you $3,000." This promise is made in return for past consideration and is thus unenforceable; in effect, Judy is stating her intention to give Elsie a gift.●

Illusory Promises. If the terms of the contract express such uncertainty of performance that the promisor has not definitely promised to do anything, the promise is said to be *illusory*—without consideration and unenforceable.
● EXAMPLE 21 The president of Tuscan Corporation says to his employees, "All of you have worked hard, and if profits continue to remain high, a 10 percent bonus at the end of the year will be given—if management thinks it is warranted." This is an *illusory promise,* or no promise at all, because performance depends solely on the discretion of the president (the management). There is no bargained-for consideration. The statement declares merely that management may or may not do something in the future.●

Promises Enforceable without Consideration—Promissory Estoppel Sometimes individuals rely on promises, and such reliance may form a basis for contract

PAST CONSIDERATION
An act done before the contract is made, which ordinarily, by itself, cannot be consideration for a later promise to pay for the act.

rights and duties. Under the doctrine of **promissory estoppel** (also called *detrimental reliance*), a person who has reasonably relied on the promise of another can often hope to obtain some measure of recovery. When the doctrine of promissory estoppel is applied, the promisor (the offeror) is *estopped* (barred, or impeded) from revoking the promise. For the doctrine of promissory estoppel to be applied, the following elements are required:

1. There must be a clear and definite promise.
2. The promisee must justifiably rely on the promise.
3. The reliance normally must be of a substantial and definite character.
4. Justice will be better served by the enforcement of the promise.

● **EXAMPLE 22** Your uncle tells you, "I'll pay you $150 a week so you won't have to work anymore." In reliance on your uncle's promise, you quit your job, but your uncle refuses to pay you. Under the doctrine of promissory estoppel, you may be able to enforce such a promise.[8] Now your uncle makes a promise to give you $10,000 with which to buy a car. If you buy the car and he does not pay you, you may once again be able to enforce the promise under this doctrine.●

An issue that has come before several courts is whether promises of employment can be enforced under the doctrine of promissory estoppel when the job candidate has relied on the employment offer to his or her detriment. (See this chapter's *Inside the Legal Environment* feature on the next page.)

Capacity

The third element required for the formation of a contract (after agreement and consideration) is **contractual capacity**—the legal ability to enter into a contractual relationship. Courts generally presume the existence of contractual capacity, but there are some situations in which capacity is lacking or may be questionable. A person *adjudged by a court* to be mentally incompetent, for example, cannot form a legally binding contract with another party. In other situations, a party may have the capacity to enter into a valid contract but also have the right to avoid liability under it. For example, minors usually are not legally bound by contracts.

Minors Today, in virtually all states, the *age of majority* (when a person is no longer a minor) for contractual purposes is eighteen years for both genders.[9] In addition, some states provide for the termination of minority on marriage. Subject to certain exceptions, the contracts entered into by a minor are voidable at the option of that minor.

The general rule is that a minor can enter into any contract an adult can, provided that the contract is not one prohibited by law for minors (for example, the sale of alcoholic beverages). Although minors have the right to avoid their contracts, there are exceptions.

PROMISSORY ESTOPPEL
A doctrine that applies when a promisor makes a clear and definite promise on which the promisee justifiably relies; such a promise is binding if justice will be better served by the enforcement of the promise.

"To break an oral agreement which is not legally binding is morally wrong."
THE TALMUD, Bava Metzi'a

CONTRACTUAL CAPACITY
The threshold mental capacity required by the law for a party who enters into a contract to be bound by that contract.

---

8. *Ricketts v. Scothorn,* 57 Neb. 51, 77 N.W. 365 (1898).
9. The age of majority may still be twenty-one for other purposes, such as the purchase and consumption of alcohol. The word *infant* is usually used synonymously with the word *minor.*

INSIDE THE LEGAL ENVIRONMENT

Promissory Estoppel and Employment Contracts

Today, approximately 85 percent of American workers have the legal status of "at-will employees." Under this common law employment doctrine, which applies in all states but Montana, an employer may fire an employee for any reason or no reason. The at-will doctrine, however, does not apply to any employee who has an employment contract or who falls under the protection of a state or federal statute (such as a law prohibiting discrimination)—which is, of course, a large number of employees.

Exceptions to the At-Will Doctrine

Even when an employee is subject to the employment-at-will doctrine, the courts sometimes make exceptions to the doctrine based on tort theory or contract principles, or on the ground that a termination violates an established public policy. These exceptions to the at-will doctrine, however, apply only when a current employee's employment is *terminated*. Should they also apply when a company fails to *hire* a job candidate after promising to do so?

Consider an example. Suppose that a job candidate, relying on a company's offer of employment, quits his or her present job, moves to another city, and rents

or buys housing in the new location. Then the firm decides not to hire the candidate after all. Given the employee's detrimental reliance on the company's job offer, should the company be prevented from revoking its offer under the doctrine of promissory estoppel? This question has come before a number of courts. As yet, however, the courts have not reached a consensus on this issue. Some jurisdictions allow the doctrine of promissory estoppel to be applied; others do not.

Should Promissory Estoppel Be Applied?

Many jurisdictions believe that reliance on a prospective employer's promise of at-will employment is unreasonable as a matter of law. Courts in these jurisdictions reason that an employee should know that, even if she or he is hired, the employer could terminate the employment at any time for any reason without liability. According to these courts, it would be contrary to reason to allow an employee who has not yet begun work to recover damages under a theory of promissory estoppel, given that the same employee could be terminated without liability one day after beginning work.[a]

A number of other jurisdictions have held that an employee can recover damages incurred as a result of resigning from a former job in reliance on an offer of at-will employment. These jurisdictions have determined that when a prospective employer knows or should know that a promise of employment will induce the future employee to leave his or her current job, the employer should be responsible for the prospective employee's damages. After all, without the offer from the prospective employer, the prospective employee would have continued to work in his or her prior position. As one court reasoned, "[A] cause of action for promissory estoppel is based upon a promise which the promisor should reasonably expect to induce action or forbearance on the part of the promisee [and] which does in fact induce such action or forbearance."[b]

FOR CRITICAL ANALYSIS

Which of these two approaches taken by the courts has greater merit, in your opinion? Why?

---

a. For an example of this approach, see *Thompson v. Bridgeport Hospital,* 2001 WL 823130 (Conn.Super. 2001).

b. *Goff-Hamel v. Obstetricians & Gynecologists, P.C.,* 256 Neb. 19, 588 N.W.2d 798 (1999).

Two young men discuss the sale of a car. When a minor disaffirms a contract, such as a contract to buy a car, most states require the minor to return only whatever consideration he or she received, if it is within his or her control. Why do some states require more?

Disaffirmance. For a minor to exercise the option to avoid a contract, he or she need only manifest an intention not to be bound by it. The minor "avoids" the contract by disaffirming it. The technical definition of **disaffirmance** is the legal avoidance, or setting aside, of a contractual obligation. Words or conduct may serve to express this intent. The contract can ordinarily be disaffirmed at any time during minority or for a reasonable time after the minor comes of age. In some states, however, when there is a contract for the sale of land by a minor, the minor cannot disaffirm the contract until he or she reaches the age of majority. When a minor disaffirms a contract, all property that he or she has transferred to the adult as consideration can be recovered, even if it is then in the possession of a third party.[10]

Note that an adult who enters into a contract with a minor cannot avoid his or her contractual duties on the ground that the minor can do so. Unless the minor exercises the option to disaffirm the contract, the adult party normally is bound by it.

Minor's Obligations on Disaffirmance. All state laws permit minors to disaffirm contracts (with certain exceptions—to be discussed shortly), including executed contracts. States differ, however, on the extent of a minor's obligations on disaffirmance. Courts in a majority of states hold that the minor need only return the goods (or other consideration) subject to the contract, provided the goods are in the minor's possession or control. ● EXAMPLE 23 Suppose that Jim Garrison, a seventeen-year-old, purchases a computer from Radio Shack. While transporting the computer to his home, Garrison, through no fault of his own, is involved in a car accident. As a result of the accident, the plastic casing of the

DISAFFIRMANCE
The legal avoidance, or setting aside, of a contractual obligation.

---

10. Section 2–403(1) of the UCC allows an exception if the third party is a "good faith purchaser for value." Such a purchaser is one who buys goods, for consideration, without notice of any circumstance that would make a person of ordinary prudence suspect that the seller did not have valid title to the goods being sold.

computer is broken. The next day, he returns the computer to Radio Shack and disaffirms the contract. Under the majority view, this return fulfills Garrison's duty even though the computer is now damaged.●

A minor who enters into a contract for necessaries may disaffirm the contract but remains liable for the reasonable value of the goods. **Necessaries** are basic needs, such as food, clothing, shelter, and medical services, at a level of value required to maintain the minor's standard of living or financial and social status. Thus, what will be considered a necessary for one person may be a luxury for another.

Generally, to qualify as a contract for necessaries, (1) the item contracted for must be necessary to the minor's existence, (2) the value of the necessary item may be up to a level required to maintain the minor's standard of living or financial and social status, and (3) the minor must not be under the care of a parent or guardian who is required to supply this item. Unless these three criteria are met, the minor can disaffirm the contract *without* being liable for the reasonable value of the goods used.

Ratification. In contract law, **ratification** is the act of accepting and giving legal force to an obligation that previously was not enforceable. A minor who has reached the age of majority can ratify a contract expressly or impliedly.

Express ratification occurs when the minor expressly states, orally or in writing, that he or she intends to be bound by the contract. Implied ratification exists when the conduct of the minor is inconsistent with disaffirmance (as when the minor enjoys the benefits of the contract) or when the minor fails to disaffirm an executed (fully performed) contract within a reasonable time after reaching the age of majority. If the contract is still executory (not yet performed or only partially performed), however, failure to disaffirm the contract will not necessarily imply ratification.

Generally, the courts base their determination on whether the minor, after reaching the age of majority, has had ample opportunity to consider the nature of the contractual obligations he or she entered into as a minor and the extent to which the adult party to the contract has performed.

Intoxicated Persons Another situation in which contractual capacity becomes an issue is when a contract is formed by a person who claims to have been intoxicated at the time the contract was made. The general rule is that if a person who is sufficiently intoxicated to lack mental capacity enters into a contract, the contract is voidable at the option of the intoxicated person. This is true even if the intoxication was purely voluntary. For the contract to be voidable, it must be proved that the intoxicated person's reason and judgment were impaired to the extent that he or she did not comprehend the legal consequences of entering into the contract. If the person was intoxicated but understood these legal consequences, the contract is enforceable.

Simply because the terms of the contract are foolish or are obviously favorable to the other party does not mean the contract is voidable (unless the other party fraudulently induced the person to become intoxicated). Problems often arise in determining whether a party was sufficiently intoxicated to avoid legal duties. Generally, contract avoidance on the ground of intoxication is rarely permitted.

NECESSARIES
Necessities required for life, such as food, shelter, clothing, and medical attention; may include whatever is believed to be necessary to maintain a person's standard of living or financial and social status.

BE AWARE A minor's station in life (financial and social status, lifestyle, and so on) is important in determining whether an item is a necessary or a luxury. For example, clothing is a necessary, but if a minor from a low-income family contracts for the purchase of a $2,000 coat, a court may deem the coat a luxury. In this situation, the contract would not be for "necessaries."

RATIFICATION
The act of accepting and giving legal force to an obligation that previously was not enforceable.

BE CAREFUL A contract will almost always be enforced if both parties knew what they were signing.

Mentally Incompetent Persons If a person has been adjudged mentally incompetent by a court of law and a guardian has been appointed, any contract made by the mentally incompetent person is *void*—no contract exists. Only the guardian can enter into a binding contract on behalf of the mentally incompetent person.

If a mentally incompetent person not previously so adjudged by a court enters into a contract, the contract may be *voidable* if the person does not know he or she is entering into the contract or lacks the mental capacity to comprehend its nature, purpose, and consequences. A contract entered into by a mentally incompetent person (but not previously so adjudged by a court) may also be deemed valid and enforceable if the contract was formed during a lucid interval. For such a contract to be valid, it must be shown that the person was able to comprehend the nature, purpose, and consequences of the contract *at the time the contract was formed.*

Legality

To this point, we have discussed three of the requirements for a valid contract to exist—agreement, consideration, and contractual capacity. Now we examine a fourth—legality. For a contract to be valid and enforceable, it must be formed for a legal purpose. A contract to do something that is prohibited by federal or state statutory law is illegal and, as such, void from the outset and thus unenforceable. Additionally, a contract to commit a tortious act or to commit an action that is contrary to public policy is illegal and unenforceable.

Contracts Contrary to Statute Statutes sometimes prescribe the terms of contracts. In some instances, the laws are specific, even providing for the inclusion of certain clauses and their wording. Other statutes prohibit certain contracts on the basis of their subject matter, the time at which they are entered into, or the status of the contracting parties. We examine here several ways in which contracts may be contrary to a statute and thus illegal.

Usury. Today, most states have statutes that set the maximum rate of interest that can be charged for different types of transactions, including ordinary loans. A lender who makes a loan at an interest rate above the lawful maximum commits **usury**. The maximum rate of interest varies from state to state.

USURY
Charging an illegal rate of interest.

Gambling. In general, gambling contracts are illegal and thus void. All states have statutes that regulate gambling—defined as any scheme that involves the distribution of property by chance among persons who have paid valuable consideration for the opportunity (chance) to receive the property.[11] Gambling is the creation of risk for the purpose of assuming it. In some states, certain forms of gambling, such as casino gambling or horse racing, are legal. The majority of states also have legalized state-operated lotteries, as well as lotteries (such as bingo) arranged for charitable purposes. A number of states also allow gambling on Indian reservations.

---

11. See *Wishing Well Club v. Akron,* 66 Ohio Law Abs. 406, 112 N.E.2d 41 (1951).

ETHICAL ISSUE

How can states enforce gambling laws in the age of the Internet?

One of the problems in regulating online gambling is jurisdictional in nature. For example, in those states that do not allow casino gambling or off-track betting, what can a state government do if residents of the state place bets online? After all, as you read in Chapter 5, states have no constitutional authority to regulate activities that occur in other states. Another issue in regulating online gambling involves determining where the physical act of placing a bet on the Internet occurs. Is it where the gambler is located or where the gambling site is based? For example, suppose that a resident of New York places bets via the Internet at a gambling site located in Antigua. Is the actual act of gambling taking place in New York or in Antigua?

When this exact question came before a New York court, the court, in a precedent-setting decision, concluded that the act of gambling occurred in New York. According to the court, "if the person engaged in gambling is located in New York, then New York is the location where the gambling occurred." Significantly, the U.S. Court of Appeals for the Second Circuit upheld the New York court's decision.[12]

BLUE LAWS
State or local laws that prohibit the performance of certain types of commercial activities on Sunday.

Sabbath (Sunday) Laws. Statutes called Sabbath (Sunday) laws prohibit the formation or performance of certain contracts on a Sunday. Under the common law, such contracts are legal in the absence of this statutory prohibition. Under some state and local laws, all contracts entered into on a Sunday are illegal. Laws in other states or municipalities prohibit only the sale of certain types of merchandise, such as alcoholic beverages, on a Sunday.

These laws, which date back to colonial times, are often called **blue laws.** Blue laws get their name from the blue paper on which New Haven, Connecticut, printed its new town ordinance in 1781. The ordinance prohibited all work on Sunday and required all shops to close on the "Lord's Day." A number of states and municipalities enacted laws forbidding the carrying on of "all secular labor and business on the Lord's Day." Exceptions to Sunday laws permit contracts for necessities (such as food) and works of charity. A fully performed (executed) contract that was entered into on a Sunday normally cannot be rescinded (canceled).

RECALL Under the First Amendment, the government cannot promote or place a significant burden on religion.

Sunday laws are often not enforced, and some of these laws have been held to be unconstitutional on the ground that they are contrary to the freedom of religion. Nonetheless, as a precaution, business owners contemplating doing business in a particular locality should check to see if any Sunday statutes or ordinances will affect their business activities.

Licensing Statutes. All states require that members of certain professions obtain licenses allowing them to practice. Physicians, lawyers, real estate brokers, architects, electricians, and stockbrokers are but a few of the people who must be licensed. Some licenses are obtained only after extensive schooling and examinations, which indicate to the public that a special skill has been acquired. Others require only that the particular person be of good moral character.

---

12. *United States v. Cohen,* 260 F.3d. 68 (2d Cir. 2001).

Adults gamble at a casino in Las Vegas, where casino gambling is legal. Would this same activity be illegal if it were conducted online? If so. could it be prevented? How?

Generally, business licenses provide a means of regulating and taxing certain businesses and protecting the public against actions that could threaten the general welfare. For example, in nearly all states, a stockbroker must be licensed and must file a bond with the state to protect the public from fraudulent transactions in stock. Similarly, a plumber must be licensed and bonded to protect the public against incompetent plumbers and to protect the public health. Only persons or businesses possessing the qualifications and complying with the conditions required by statute are entitled to licenses. Typically, for example, an owner of a saloon or tavern is required to sell food as a condition of obtaining a license to sell liquor for consumption on the premises.

When a person enters into a contract with an unlicensed individual, the contract may still be enforceable, depending on the nature of the licensing statute. Some states expressly provide that the lack of a license in certain occupations bars the enforcement of work-related contracts. If the statute does not expressly state this, one must look to the underlying purpose of the licensing requirements for a particular occupation. If the purpose is to protect the public from unauthorized practitioners, a contract involving an unlicensed individual is illegal and unenforceable. If, however, the underlying purpose of the statute is to raise government revenues, a contract with an unlicensed practitioner is enforceable—although the unlicensed person is usually fined.

Contracts Contrary to Public Policy Although contracts involve private parties, some are not enforceable because of the negative impact they would have on society. These contracts are said to be *contrary to public policy*. Examples include a contract to commit an immoral act (such as a surrogate-parenting contract, which several courts and state statutes equate with "baby selling") and a contract that prohibits marriage. ● EXAMPLE 24 Suppose that Everett offers a young man $500 if he refrains from marrying Everett's daughter. If the young man accepts, no contract is formed (the contract is void) because it is contrary to public policy. Thus, if the man marries Everett's daughter, Everett cannot sue him for breach of contract. ● Business contracts that may be contrary to public policy include contracts in restraint of trade and unconscionable contracts or clauses.

Contracts in Restraint of Trade. Contracts in restraint of trade (anticompetitive agreements) usually adversely affect the public, which favors competition in the economy. Typically, such contracts also violate one or more federal or state statutes.[13] An exception is recognized when the restraint is reasonable and it is *ancillary* to (is a subsidiary part of) a contract, such as a contract for the sale of a business or an employment contract. Many such exceptions involve a type of restraint called a *covenant not to compete,* or a restrictive covenant.

Covenants not to compete are often contained in contracts concerning the sale of an ongoing business. A covenant not to compete is created when a seller agrees not to open a new store in a certain geographical area surrounding the old store. Such an agreement, when it is ancillary to a sales contract and reasonable in terms of time and geographic area, enables the seller to sell, and the purchaser to buy, the "goodwill" and "reputation" of an ongoing business. If, for example, a well-known merchant sells his or her store and opens a competing business a block away, many of the merchant's customers will likely do business at the new store. This renders valueless the good name and reputation sold to the other merchant for a price. If a covenant not to compete was not ancillary to a sales agreement, however, it would be void, because it unreasonably restrains trade and is contrary to public policy.

Agreements not to compete can also be contained in employment contracts. It is common for many people in middle-level and upper-level management positions to agree not to work for competitors or not to start a competing business for a specified period of time after terminating employment. Such agreements are generally legal so long as the specified period of time is not excessive in duration and the geographical restriction is reasonable. Basically, the restriction on competition must be reasonable—that is, not any greater than necessary to protect a legitimate business interest. The following case illustrates this point. (For a discussion of what constitutes "reasonable" restrictions in the context of Web-based employment, see this chapter's *Legal E-nvironment* feature on page 353.)

> "Public policy is in its nature so uncertain and fluctuating, varying with the habits of the day, . . . that it is difficult to determine its limits with any degree of exactness."
>
> JOSEPH STORY, 1779–1845
> (Associate justice of the United States Supreme Court, 1811–1845)

---

13. Such as the Sherman Antitrust Act, the Clayton Act, and the Federal Trade Commission Act (see Chapter 22).

CASE 11.4   Moore v. Midwest Distribution, Inc.

Court of Appeals of
Arkansas, 2002.
76 Ark.App. 397,
65 S.W.3d 490.
http://courts.state.ar.us/
opinions/opinions.html[a]

BACKGROUND AND FACTS Ronnie Moore began working in the product display business in

1997 for Hubb Group (HG), in Memphis, Tennessee. In 1999, HG terminated his contract. Moore moved to Fort Smith, Arkansas, to work for Midwest Distribution, Inc., which also set up product displays as a contractor for HG. Midwest asked Moore to sign a "Service Work for Hire Agreement" under which Moore agreed that, for one year after the termination of his employment, he would not "provide, or solicit

---

a. In the "Search Cases by Party Name" section, enter "Moore" in the "Party Name" box and select "Search by Date Range." For the date range, choose "From January 2002" and "To February 2002," and click on "Search." From the list of results, click on the name of the case that includes the term "Reversed" to access the opinion. The Arkansas Judiciary maintains this Web site.

CASE 11.4—Continued

or offer to provide to any present or former Customer of Contractor, or become directly or indirectly interested in any person or entity which provides, or solicits or offers to provide, any services to such Customers." The agreement applied "to those geographical areas in which the Contractee acts as independent contractor including, but not limited to, the State of Arkansas, Illinois, Iowa, Kansas, Missouri, Nebraska, New Mexico, Oklahoma, Texas, and any

other state that contractor has granted a contract or agreement within." Moore quit this job to work for Jay Godwin in Oklahoma, who also contracted with HG. Midwest Distribution filed a suit in an Arkansas state court against Moore, seeking to enjoin (prevent) him from providing services to Godwin. The court issued a temporary injunction. Moore appealed to a state intermediate appellate court.

IN THE WORDS OF THE COURT . . .

TERRY CRABTREE, Judge.

* * * *

* * * The test of reasonableness of contracts in restraint of trade is that the restraint imposed upon one party must not be greater than is reasonably necessary for the protection of the other and not so great as to injure a public interest. *Where a covenant not to compete grows out of an employment relationship, the courts have found an interest sufficient to warrant enforcement of the covenant only in those cases where the covenantee provided special training, or made available trade secrets, confidential business information or customer lists, and then only if it is found that the covenantee was able to use information so obtained to gain an unfair competitive advantage.* [Emphasis added.]

In the present case, appellee's [Midwest Distribution's] president, Kevin Barrett, testified that appellant [Moore] had been provided with no special training. In addition, he stated that appellant had not been provided with any trade secrets, confidential business information, or customer lists. Further, Mr. Barrett testified that appellant was not using information he obtained from appellee to gain an unfair advantage over appellee, except how to install "fixtures and stuff." We hold that appellant did not use any information to gain an unfair competitive advantage over appellee. As such, we hold that appellee did not have a legitimate interest to be protected by the agreement.

We are also persuaded that the geographical area included in the agreement is too broad. The geographical area in a covenant not to compete must be limited in order to be enforceable. The restraint imposed upon one party must not be greater than is reasonably necessary for protecting the other party. In determining whether the geographic restriction is reasonable, the trade area of the former employer is viewed. Where a geographic restriction is greater than the trade area, the restriction is too broad and the covenant not to compete is void.

In the case at bar [before the court], the agreement precluded appellant from working in the trade of setting up displays in any of the nine states listed. The agreement included the state of Oklahoma. However, appellee did not conduct any business in Oklahoma. We find that it is not reasonable to restrict appellant from working in a state he never worked in before. By including in the scope of the non-compete agreement's geographic restriction a state that appellant has never worked in, appellee more broadly limited appellant's working than is reasonably necessary to protect appellee's trade area.

(continued)

CASE 11.4—Continued

DECISION AND REMEDY The state intermediate appellate court reversed the judgment of the lower court. The appellate court concluded that the covenant not to compete was unenforceable because it did not protect a legitimate interest of Midwest Distribution and the geographic scope of the agreement was unreasonably broad.

FOR CRITICAL ANALYSIS—Social Consideration *Suppose that Midwest Distribution had given Moore special training and provided him with a customer list, which he used when he worked for Godwin. Would the result in this case have been different? If so, how?*

UNCONSCIONABLE CONTRACT (OR UNCONSCIONABLE CLAUSE)
A contract or clause that is void on the basis of public policy because one party, as a result of his or her relative lack of bargaining power, is forced to accept terms that are unfairly burdensome and that unfairly benefit the dominating party.

ADHESION CONTRACT
A standard-form contract, such as that between a large retailer and a consumer, in which the stronger party dictates the terms.

EXCULPATORY CLAUSE
A clause that releases the contractual party from liability in the event of a monetary or physical injury, no matter who is at fault.

Unconscionable Contracts or Clauses. Ordinarily, a court does not look at the fairness or equity of a contract; in other words, it does not inquire into the adequacy of consideration. Persons are assumed to be reasonably intelligent, and the court does not come to their aid just because they have made unwise or foolish bargains. In certain circumstances, however, bargains are so oppressive that the courts relieve innocent parties of part or all of their duties. Such a bargain is called an **unconscionable contract** (or **unconscionable clause**). Both the Uniform Commercial Code (UCC) and the Uniform Consumer Credit Code (UCCC) embody the unconscionability concept—the former with regard to the sale of goods and the latter with regard to consumer loans and the waiver of rights.[14] The concept is now applied to common law contracts as well.

Contracts entered into because of one party's vastly superior bargaining power may be deemed unconscionable. These situations usually involve an **adhesion contract,** which is a contract drafted by the dominant party and then presented to the other—the adhering party—on a "take-it-or-leave-it" basis.[15]

Exculpatory Clauses. Often closely related to the concept of unconscionability are **exculpatory clauses,** defined as clauses that release a party from liability in the event of monetary or physical injury, *no matter who is at fault.* Indeed, some courts refer to such clauses in terms of unconscionability. ● **EXAMPLE 25** Suppose that Madison Manufacturing Company hires a laborer and has him sign a contract containing the following clause:

> Said employee hereby agrees with employer, in consideration of such employment, that he will take upon himself all risks incident to his position and will in no case hold the company liable for any injury or damage he may sustain, in his person or otherwise, by accidents or injuries in the factory, or which may result from defective machinery or carelessness or misconduct of himself or any other employee in service of the employer.

This contract provision attempts to remove Madison's potential liability for injuries occurring to the employee, and it would usually be held contrary to public policy.[16]●

Generally, an exculpatory clause will not be enforced if the party seeking its enforcement is involved in a business that is important to the public interest. These businesses include public utilities, common carriers, and banks. Because of the essential nature of these services, the companies offering them have an

---

14. See, for example, UCC Sections 2–302 and 2–719 (and UCCC Sections 5.108 and 1.107).
15. See, for example, *Henningsen v. Bloomfield Motors, Inc.,* 32 N.J. 358, 161 A.2d 69 (1960).
16. For a classic case with similar facts, see *Little Rock & Fort Smith Railway Co. v. Eubanks,* 48 Ark. 460, 3 S.W. 808 (1887). In such a case, the exculpatory clause may also be illegal on the basis of a violation of a state workers' compensation law.

LEGAL *e*-NVIRONMENT
Covenants Not to Compete in the Internet Context

For some companies today, particularly those in high-tech industries, trade secrets are their most valuable assets. Often, to prevent departing employees from disclosing trade secrets to competing employers, business owners and managers have their key employees sign covenants not to compete. In such a covenant, the employee typically agrees not to set up a competing business or work for a competitor in a specified geographic area for a certain period of time.

An Issue Facing Managers Today

A serious issue facing management today is whether time and geographic restrictions that have been deemed reasonable in the past serve as a guide to what might constitute reasonable limits in today's changing legal landscape. After all, in the Internet environment there are no physical borders, so geographical restrictions are no longer relevant. Similarly, given the rapid pace of development within the information technology industry, restricting an employee from working in the area for one year could seriously affect the employee's career.

Little Case Guidance

There is little case law to guide management on this issue. At least one court, however, has indicated that a time restriction of one year, which has traditionally been regarded as reasonable, may not be in the context of Internet employment. The case involved Mark Schlack, who worked as a Web site manager for EarthWeb, Inc., in New York. Schlack signed a covenant stating that, on termination of his employment, he would not work for any competing company for one year. When he resigned and accepted an offer from a company in Massachusetts to design a Web site, EarthWeb sued to enforce the covenant not to compete.

The court refused to enforce the covenant, in part because there was no evidence that Schlack had misappropriated any of EarthWeb's trade secrets or clients. The court also stated that because the Internet lacks physical borders, a covenant prohibiting an employee from working for a competitor anywhere in the world for one year is excessive in duration.[a]

FOR CRITICAL ANALYSIS

For Web-based work, the geographical restriction can be worldwide in scope. Does this mean that the time restriction in a covenant not to compete should be narrowed considerably to compensate for the extensive geographical restriction?

a. *EarthWeb, Inc. v. Schlack,* 71 F.Supp.2d 299 (S.D.N.Y. 1999).

advantage in bargaining strength and could insist that anyone contracting for their services agree not to hold them liable. This would tend to relax their carefulness and increase the number of injuries. Imagine the results, for example, if all exculpatory clauses in contracts between airlines and their passengers were enforced.

Exculpatory clauses may be enforced, however, when the parties seeking their enforcement are not involved in businesses considered important to the public interest. These businesses have included health clubs, amusement parks, horse-rental concessions, golf-cart concessions, and skydiving organizations. Because these services are not essential, the firms offering them are sometimes considered to have no relative advantage in bargaining strength, and anyone contracting for their services is considered to do so voluntarily.

The Effect of Illegality In general, an illegal contract is void: the contract is deemed never to have existed, and the courts will not aid either party. In most illegal contracts, both parties are considered to be equally at fault—*in pari delicto*. The general rule is that neither party to an illegal bargain can sue for breach and neither can recover for performance rendered. There are some exceptions to this rule, however, which we look at here.

Justifiable Ignorance of the Facts. When one of the parties to a contract is relatively innocent (has no knowledge or any reason to know that the contract is illegal), that party can often obtain restitution or recovery of benefits conferred in a partially executed contract. The courts do not enforce the contract but do allow the parties to return to their original positions. It is also possible for an innocent party who has fully performed under the contract to enforce the contract against the guilty party.

    • EXAMPLE 26 Gillespie contracts with a trucking company to carry goods to a specific destination for a normal fee of $1,000. The trucker delivers the goods and later finds out that the contents of the shipped crates were illegal. Although the law specifies that the shipment, use, and sale of the goods were illegal, the trucker, being an innocent party, can still legally collect the $1,000 from Gillespie.•

Members of Protected Classes. When a statute protects a certain class of people, a member of that class can enforce an illegal contract even though the other party cannot. For example, there are statutes that prohibit certain employees (such as flight attendants) from working more than a specified number of hours per month. These employees thus constitute a class protected by statute. An employee who is required to work more than the maximum can recover for those extra hours of service.

Fraud, Duress, or Undue Influence. Whenever a plaintiff has been induced to enter into an illegal bargain as a result of fraud, duress, or undue influence, he or she can either enforce the contract or recover for its value.

THIRD PARTY RIGHTS

A valid contract—that is, a contract that meets the four requirements for a valid contract just discussed—creates certain rights and duties. If one party fails to fulfill a contractual promise, the other party is entitled to a remedy, a topic examined in Chapter 12. Because a contract is a private agreement between the parties who have entered into it, it is fitting that these parties alone should have rights and liabilities under the contract. This concept is referred to as *privity of contract*, and it establishes the basic principle that third parties have no rights in contracts to which they are not parties.

    There are two important exceptions to the rule of privity of contract. One exception allows a party to a contract to transfer the rights arising from the contract to another or to free himself or herself from the duties of a contract by having another person perform them. Legally, the first of these actions is referred to as an *assignment of rights* and the second, as a *delegation of duties*. A second exception to the rule of privity of contract involves a *third party beneficiary* contract. Here, the rights of a third party against the promisor arise from the original contract, as the parties to the original contract normally make it with the intent to benefit the third party.

Assignments

In a bilateral (mutual) contract, the two parties have corresponding rights and duties. One party has a right to require the other to perform some task, and the other has a duty to perform it. The transfer of *rights* to a third person is known as an **assignment.** When rights under a contract are assigned unconditionally, the rights of the *assignor* (the party making the assignment) are extinguished.[17] The third party (the *assignee,* or party receiving the assignment) has a right to demand performance from the other original party to the contract (the *obligor*). The assignee takes only those rights that the assignor originally had.

ASSIGNMENT
The act of transferring to another all or part of one's rights arising under a contract.

As a general rule, all rights can be assigned. Exceptions are made, however, in special circumstances. If a statute expressly prohibits assignment, the particular right in question cannot be assigned. When a contract is *personal* in nature, the rights under the contract cannot be assigned unless all that remains is a money payment.[18] A right cannot be assigned if assignment will materially increase or alter the risk or duties of the obligor.[19] If a contract stipulates that the right cannot be assigned, then *ordinarily* it cannot be assigned.

There are several exceptions to the fourth restriction. These exceptions are as follows:

1. A contract cannot prevent an assignment of the right to receive money. This exception exists to encourage the free flow of money and credit in modern business settings.
2. The assignment of rights in real estate often cannot be prohibited, because such a prohibition is contrary to public policy. Prohibitions of this kind are called restraints against **alienation** (transfer of land ownership).
3. The assignment of *negotiable instruments* (checks and certain other financial items) cannot be prohibited.
4. In a contract for the sale of goods, the right to receive damages for breach of contract or for payment of an account owed may be assigned even though the sales contract prohibits such assignment.[20]

ALIENATION
A term used to define the process of transferring land out of one's possession (thus "alienating" the land from oneself).

Delegations

Just as a party can transfer rights to a third party through an assignment, a party can also transfer duties. Duties are not assigned, however; they are *delegated.* Normally, a **delegation of duties** does not relieve the party making the delegation (the *delegator*) of the obligation to perform in the event that the party to whom the duty has been delegated (the *delegatee*) fails to perform. No special form is required to create a valid delegation of duties. As long as the delegator expresses an intention to make the delegation, it is effective; the delegator need not even use the word *delegate.*

DELEGATION OF DUTIES
The act of transferring to another all or part of one's duties arising under a contract.

---

17. *Restatement (Second) of Contracts,* Section 317.
18. *Restatement (Second) of Contracts,* Sections 317 and 318.
19. See UCC 2–210(2).
20. See UCC 2–210(2).

As a general rule, any duty can be delegated. There are, however, some exceptions to this rule. Delegation is prohibited in the following circumstances:

1. When performance depends on the *personal* skill or talents of the obligor.
2. When special trust has been placed in the obligor.
3. When performance by a third party will vary materially from that expected by the obligee (the one to whom performance is owed) under the contract.
4. When the contract expressly prohibits delegation.

If a delegation of duties is enforceable, the *obligee* (the one to whom performance is owed) must accept performance from the delegatee (the one to whom the duties are delegated). The obligee can legally refuse performance from the delegatee only if the duty is one that cannot be delegated. A valid delegation of duties does not relieve the delegator of obligations under the contract. Thus, if the delegatee fails to perform, the delegator is still liable to the obligee.

Third Party Beneficiaries

To have contractual rights, a person normally must be a party to the contract. In other words, privity of contract must exist. As mentioned earlier in this chapter, an exception to the doctrine of privity exists when the original parties to the contract intend at the time of contracting that the contract performance directly benefit a third person. In this situation, the third person becomes a **third party beneficiary** of the contract. As an **intended beneficiary** of the contract, the third party has legal rights and can sue the promisor directly for breach of the contract.

The benefit that an **incidental beneficiary** receives from a contract between two parties is unintentional. Therefore, an incidental beneficiary cannot enforce a contract to which he or she is not a party. ● **EXAMPLE 27** Ed contracts with Ona to build a recreational facility on Ona's land. Once the facility is constructed, it will greatly enhance the property values in the neighborhood. If Ed subsequently refuses to build the facility, Tandy, Ona's neighbor, cannot enforce the contract against Ed.●

ETHICAL ISSUE

Should third party beneficiaries be able to recover from attorneys on the basis of negligence?

A question that periodically comes before the courts concerns the responsibility of attorneys who draw up legal documents involving designated beneficiaries. Suppose, for example, that an attorney's negligence in handling a land transfer causes loss to the designated beneficiary of a deed. Can the beneficiary sue the attorney? This can be a significant issue when the party who signed the deed is no longer living and thus cannot rectify the problem. A similar problem arises occasionally when intended beneficiaries under a will do not receive what the will's maker intended them to receive because of the attorney's negligence.

Traditionally, the rule was that third party beneficiaries could not sue the attorneys in these situations because they were not in privity of contract with the attorneys; that is, an attorney's duty of care extends only to his or her clients, and thus third parties do not have standing to sue the attorneys for negligence.

COMPARE In an assignment, the assignor's original contract rights are extinguished after assignment. In a delegation, the delegator remains liable for performance under the contract if the delegatee fails to perform.

THIRD PARTY BENEFICIARY
One for whose benefit a promise is made in a contract but who is not a party to the contract.

INTENDED BENEFICIARY
A third party for whose benefit a contract is formed; an intended beneficiary can sue the promisor if such a contract is breached.

INCIDENTAL BENEFICIARY
A third party who incidentally benefits from a contract but whose benefit was not the reason the contract was formed; an incidental beneficiary has no rights in a contract and cannot sue to have the contract enforced.

Clearly, restricting suits against attorneys in these situations can have harsh results for intended beneficiaries. Although some courts continue to adhere to the traditional rule, increasingly courts are allowing third party beneficiaries to sue attorneys in these circumstances.[21]

---

21. See, for example, *Passell v. Watts,* 794 So.2d 651 (Fla.App. 2 Dist. 2001).

KEY TERMS

acceptance 338	executory contract 330	quasi contract 329
adhesion contract 352	express contract 329	ratification 346
agreement 331	implied-in-fact contract 329	revocation 337
alienation 355	incidental beneficiary 356	sales contract 325
assignment 355	intended beneficiary 356	third party beneficiary 356
bilateral contract 327	mailbox rule 339	unconscionable contract (or
blue law 348	mirror image rule 337	unconscionable clause) 352
consideration 339	necessaries 346	unenforceable contract 331
contract 325	offer 332	unilateral contract 327
contractual capacity 343	offeree 326	usury 347
counteroffer 337	offeror 326	valid contract 331
delegation of duties 355	past consideration 342	void contract 331
disaffirmance 345	promisee 326	voidable contract 331
exculpatory clause 352	promisor 326	
executed contract 330	promissory estoppel 343	

CHAPTER SUMMARY **CONTRACT FORMATION**

The Law Governing Contracts (See pages 325–326.)	1. *Common law*—Governs many aspects of contract law. In applying the common law to contracts, courts often are guided by the *Restatement (Second) of Contracts,* which is a nonstatutory, authoritative exposition of the common law of contracts.
	2. *Article 2 of the Uniform Commercial Code (UCC)*—Modifies the common law for contracts for the sale of goods (sales contracts). If the common law has not been modified by Article 2, then the common law governs; when the common law has been modified by Article 2, then Article 2 governs.
The Function of Contracts (See page 326.)	Contract law establishes what kinds of promises will be legally binding and supplies procedures for enforcing legally binding promises, or agreements.
Types of Contracts (See pages 327–331.)	1. *Bilateral*—A promise for a promise.
	2. *Unilateral*—A promise for an act (acceptance is the completed—or substantial—performance of the act).
	3. *Express*—Formed by words (oral, written, or a combination).
	4. *Implied in fact*—Formed by the conduct of the parties.
	5. *Quasi contract (contract implied in law)*—Imposed by law to prevent unjust enrichment.

(continued)

CHAPTER SUMMARY CONTRACT FORMATION—Continued

Types of Contracts—continued	6. *Executed*—A fully performed contract.
	7. *Executory*—A contract not yet fully performed.
	8. *Valid*—The contract has the necessary contractual elements of offer and acceptance, consideration, parties with legal capacity, and having been made for a legal purpose.
	9. *Void*—No contract exists, or there is a contract without legal obligations.
	10. *Voidable*—One party has the option of avoiding or enforcing the contractual obligation.
	11. *Unenforceable*—A contract exists, but it cannot be enforced because of a legal defense.

AGREEMENT

Requirements of the Offer (See pages 332–336.)	1. *Intent*—There must be a serious, objective intention by the offeror to become bound by the offer. Nonoffer situations include (a) expressions of opinion; (b) statements of intention; (c) preliminary negotiations; and (d) generally, advertisements, catalogues, and circulars.
	2. *Definiteness*—The terms of the offer must be sufficiently definite to be ascertainable by the parties or by a court.
	3. *Communication*—The offer must be communicated to the offeree.
Termination of the Offer (See pages 336–338.)	1. *By action of the parties*—An offer can be revoked or rejected at any time before acceptance without liability. A counteroffer is a rejection of the original offer and the making of a new offer.
	2. *By operation of law*—An offer can terminate by (a) lapse of time, (b) destruction of the specific subject matter of the offer, (c) death or incompetence of the parties, or (d) supervening illegality.
Acceptance (See pages 338–339.)	1. Can be made only by the offeree or the offeree's agent.
	2. Must be unequivocal. Under the common law (mirror image rule), if new terms or conditions are added to the acceptance, it will be considered a counteroffer.

CONSIDERATION

Elements of Consideration (See pages 339–340.)	Consideration is broken down into two parts: (1) something of *legally sufficient value* must be given in exchange for the promise, and (2) there must be a *bargained-for exchange*. To be legally sufficient, consideration must consist of (1) a promise to do something that one has no prior legal duty to do, (2) the performance of an action that one is otherwise not obligated to undertake, or (3) the refraining from an action that one has a legal right to undertake.
Adequacy of Consideration (See page 340.)	Adequacy of consideration relates to "how much" consideration is given and whether a fair bargain was reached. Courts will inquire into the adequacy of consideration (if the consideration is legally sufficient) only when fraud, undue influence, duress, a gift, or unconscionability may be involved.
Contracts That Lack Consideration (See pages 340–342.)	Consideration is lacking in the following situations:
	1. *Preexisting duty*—Consideration is not legally sufficient if one is either by law or by contract under a preexisting duty to perform the action being offered as consideration for a new contract.
	2. *Past consideration*—Actions or events that have already taken place do not constitute legally sufficient consideration.
	3. *Illusory promises*—When the nature or extent of performance is too uncertain, the promise is rendered illusory (without consideration and unenforceable).

CHAPTER SUMMARY   CONTRACT FORMATION—Continued

Promissory Estoppel (See page 343.)	When a promisor reasonably expects a promise to induce definite and substantial action or forbearance by the promisee, and the promisee does act in reliance on the promise, the promise is binding if injustice can be avoided only by enforcement of the promise.

CAPACITY

Minors (See pages 343–346.)	Contracts with minors are voidable at the option of the minor. When disaffirming executed contracts, the minor has a duty to return received goods if they are still in the minor's control or (in some states) to pay their reasonable value.
Intoxicated Persons (See page 346.)	1. A contract entered into by an intoxicated person is voidable at the option of the intoxicated person if the person was sufficiently intoxicated to lack mental capacity, even if the intoxication was voluntary. 2. A contract with an intoxicated person is enforceable if, despite being intoxicated, the person understood the legal consequences of entering into the contract.
Mentally Incompetent Persons (See page 347.)	1. A contract made by a person adjudged by a court to be mentally incompetent is void. 2. A contract made by a mentally incompetent person not adjudged by a court to be mentally incompetent is voidable at the option of the mentally incompetent person.

LEGALITY

Contracts Contrary to Statute (See pages 347–349.)	1. *Usury*—Occurs when a lender makes a loan at an interest rate above the lawful maximum. The maximum rate of interest varies from state to state. 2. *Gambling*—Gambling contracts that contravene (go against) state statutes are deemed illegal and thus void. 3. *Sabbath (Sunday) laws*—Laws prohibiting the formation or the performance of certain contracts on Sunday. Such laws vary widely from state to state, and many states do not enforce them. 4. *Licensing statutes*—Contracts entered into by persons who do not have a license, when one is required by statute, will not be enforceable *unless* the underlying purpose of the statute is to raise government revenues (and not to protect the public from unauthorized practitioners).
Contracts Contrary to Public Policy (See pages 349–353.)	1. *Contracts in restraint of trade*—Contracts to reduce or restrain free competition are illegal. An exception is a *covenant not to compete*. It is usually enforced by the courts if the terms are ancillary to a contract (such as a contract for the sale of a business or an employment contract) and are reasonable as to time and area of restraint. 2. *Unconscionable contracts and clauses*—When a contract or contract clause is so unfair that it is oppressive to one party, it can be deemed unconscionable; as such, it is illegal and cannot be enforced. 3. *Exculpatory clauses*—An exculpatory clause is a clause that releases a party from liability in the event of monetary or physical injury, no matter who is at fault. In certain situations, exculpatory clauses may be contrary to public policy and thus unenforceable.

THIRD PARTY RIGHTS

Assignments (See page 355.)	1. An assignment is the transfer of rights under a contract to a third party. The party assigning the rights is the *assignor,* and the party to whom the rights are assigned is the *assignee.* The assignee has a right to demand performance from the other original party to the contract.

(continued)

CHAPTER SUMMARY CONTRACT FORMATION—Continued

Assignments—continued	2. Generally, all rights can be assigned, although there are some exceptions to this rule, such as when assignment is expressly prohibited by statute (for example, workers' compensation benefits).
Delegation (See pages 355–356.)	A delegation is the transfer of duties under a contract to a third party (the delegatee), who then assumes the obligation of performing the contractual duties previously held by the one making the delegation (the delegator). A valid delegation of duties does not relieve the delegator of obligations under the contract. If the delegatee fails to perform, the delegator is still liable to the obligee.
Third Party Beneficiaries (See pages 356–357.)	A third party beneficiary contract is one made for the purpose of benefiting a third party. 1. *Intended beneficiary*—One for whose benefit a contract is created. When the promisor (the one making the contractual promise that benefits a third party) fails to perform as promised, the third party can sue the promisor directly. 2. *Incidental beneficiary*—A third party who indirectly (incidentally) benefits from a contract but for whose benefit the contract was not specifically intended. Incidental beneficiaries have no rights to the benefits received and cannot sue to have the contract enforced.

FOR REVIEW

1. What does the term *contract* mean, and how do contracts function in our society?
2. Which types of contracts are subject to Article 2 of the Uniform Commercial Code?
3. What are the four basic requirements for a valid contract?
4. What are the contractual rights and duties of minors?
5. How might third parties acquire rights in contracts?

QUESTIONS AND CASE PROBLEMS

11–1. Express versus Implied Contracts. Suppose that McDougal, a local businessperson, is a good friend of Krunch, the owner of a nearby candy store. Every day on his lunch hour McDougal goes into Krunch's candy store and spends about five minutes looking at the candy. After examining Krunch's candy and talking with Krunch, McDougal usually buys one or two candy bars. One afternoon, McDougal goes into Krunch's candy shop, looks at the candy, and picks up a $1 candy bar. Seeing that Krunch is very busy, he waves the candy bar at Krunch without saying a word and walks out. Is there a contract? If so, classify it within the categories presented in this chapter.

11–2. Contract Classification. Jennifer says to her neighbor, Gordon, "On completion of mowing my lawn, I'll pay you $25." Gordon orally accepts her offer. Is there a contract? Is

Jennifer's offer intended to create a bilateral or a unilateral contract? What is the legal significance of the distinction?

11–3. Consideration. Ben hired Lewis to drive his racing car in a race. Tuan, a friend of Lewis, promised to pay Lewis $3,000 if he won the race. Lewis won the race, but Tuan refused to pay the $3,000. Tuan contended that no legally binding contract had been formed, because he had received no consideration from Lewis for his promise to pay the $3,000. Lewis sued Tuan for breach of contract, arguing that winning the race was the consideration given in exchange for Tuan's promise to pay the $3,000. What rule of law discussed in this chapter supports Tuan's claim? Explain.

11–4. Acceptance. On Saturday, Arthur mailed Tanya an offer to sell his car to her for $2,000. On Monday, having changed his mind and not having heard from Tanya, Arthur sent her a letter revoking his offer. On Wednesday, before she had received Arthur's letter of revocation, Tanya mailed a letter of acceptance to Arthur. When Tanya demanded that Arthur sell his car to her as promised, Arthur claimed that no contract existed because he had revoked his offer prior to Tanya's acceptance. Is Arthur correct? Explain.

11–5. Contracts by Minors. Kalen is a seventeen-year-old minor who has just graduated from high school. He is attending a university two hundred miles from home and has contracted to rent an apartment near the university for one year at $500 per month. He is working at a convenience store to earn enough money to be self-supporting. After Kalen has lived in the apartment and paid monthly rent for four months, a dispute arises between him and the landlord. Kalen, still a minor, moves out and returns the key to the landlord. The landlord wants to hold Kalen liable for the balance of the payments due under the lease. Discuss fully Kalen's liability in this situation.

11–6. Bilateral versus Unilateral Contracts. D.L. Peoples Group (D.L.) placed an ad in a Missouri newspaper to recruit admissions representatives, who were hired to recruit Missouri residents to attend D.L.'s college in Florida. Donald Hawley responded to the ad, his interviewer recommended him for the job, and he signed, in Missouri, an "Admissions Representative Agreement," which was mailed to D.L.'s president, who signed it in his office in Florida. The agreement provided in part that Hawley would devote exclusive time and effort to the business in his assigned territory in Missouri and that D.L. would pay Hawley a commission if he successfully recruited students for the school. While attempting to make one of his first calls on his new job, Hawley was accidentally shot and killed. On the basis of his death, a claim was filed in Florida for workers' compensation. (Under Florida law, when an accident occurs outside Florida, workers' compensation benefits are payable only if the employment contract was made in Florida.) Is this admissions representative agreement a bilateral or a unilateral contract? What are the consequences of the distinction in this case? Explain. [*D.L. Peoples Group, Inc. v. Hawley*, 804 So.2d 561 (Fla.App. 1 Dist. 2002)]

11–7. Definiteness of Terms. Southwick Homes, Ltd., develops and markets residential subdivisions. William McLinden and Ronald Coco are the primary owners of Southwick Homes. Coco is also the president of Mutual Development Co. Whiteco Industries, Inc., wanted to develop lots and sell homes in Schulien Woods, a subdivision in Crown Point, Indiana. In September 1996, Whiteco sent McLinden a letter enlisting Southwick Homes to be the project manager for developing and marketing the finished lots (lots where roads had been built and on which utility installation and connections to water and sewer lines were complete); the letter set out the roles and expectations of each of the parties, including the terms of payment. In October 1997, Whiteco sent Coco a letter naming Mutual Development the developer and general contractor for the houses to be built on the finished lots. A few months later, Coco told McLinden that he would not share the profits from the construction of the houses. McLinden and others filed a suit in an Indiana state court against Coco and others, claiming, in part, a breach of fiduciary duty. The defendants responded that the letter to McLinden lacked such essential terms as to render it unenforceable. What terms must an agreement include to be an enforceable contract? Did the McLinden letter include these terms? In whose favor should the court rule? Explain. [*McLinden v. Coco*, 765 N.E.2d 606 (Ind.App. 2002)]

11–8. Unconscionability. Frank Rodziewicz was driving a Volvo tractor-trailer on Interstate 90 in Lake County, Indiana, when he struck a concrete barrier. His tractor-trailer became stuck on the barrier, and the Indiana State Police contacted Waffco Heavy Duty Towing, Inc., to assist in the recovery of the truck. Before beginning work, Waffco told Rodziewicz that it would cost $275 to tow the truck. There was no discussion of labor or any other costs. Rodziewicz told Waffco to take the truck to a local Volvo dealership. Within a few minutes, Waffco pulled the truck off the barrier and towed it to Waffco's nearby towing yard. Rodziewicz was soon notified that, in addition to the $275 towing fee, he would have to pay $4,070 in labor costs and that Waffco would not release the truck until payment was made. Rodziewicz paid the total amount. Disputing the labor charge, however, he filed a suit in an Indiana state court against Waffco, alleging in part breach of contract. Was the towing contract unconscionable? Would it make a difference if the parties had discussed the labor charge before the tow? Explain. [*Rodziewicz v. Waffco Heavy Duty Towing, Inc.*, 763 N.E.2d 491 (Ind.App. 2002)]

11–9. Third Party Beneficiary. Acciai Speciali Terni USA, Inc. (AST), hired a carrier to ship steel sheets and coils from Italy to the United States on the *M/V Berane*. The ship's receipt for the goods included a forum-selection clause, which stated that any dispute would be "decided in the country where the carrier has his principal place of business." The receipt also contained a "Himalaya" clause, which extended "every right, exemption from liability, defense and immunity" that the carrier enjoyed to those acting on the carrier's behalf. Transcom Terminals, Ltd., was the U.S. stevedore—that is, Transcom off-loaded the vessel and stored the cargo for eventual delivery to AST. Finding the cargo damaged, AST filed a suit in a federal district court against Transcom and others, charging in part negligence in the off-loading. Transcom filed a motion to dismiss on the basis of the forum-selection clause. Transcom argued that it was an intended third party beneficiary of this provision through the Himalaya clause. Is Transcom correct? What should the court rule? Explain. [*Acciai Speciali Terni USA, Inc. v. M/V Berane*, 181 F.Supp.2d 458 (D.Md. 2002)]

Case Problem with Sample Answer

11–10. Covenants Not to Compete. In 1993, Mutual Service Casualty Insurance Co. and its affiliates (collectively, MSI) hired Thomas Brass as an insurance agent. Three years later, Brass entered into a career agent's contract with MSI. This contract contained provisions regarding Brass's activities after termination. These provisions stated that, for a period of not less than one year, Brass could not solicit any MSI customers to "lapse, cancel, or replace" any insurance contract in force with MSI in an effort to take that business to a competitor. If he did, MSI could at any time refuse to pay the commissions that it otherwise owed him. The contract also restricted Brass from working for American National Insurance Co. for three years after termination. In 1998, Brass quit MSI and immediately went to work for American National, soliciting MSI customers. MSI filed a suit in a Wisconsin state court against Brass, claiming that he had violated the noncompete terms of his MSI contract. Should the court enforce the covenant not to compete? Why or why not? [*Mutual Service Casualty Insurance Co. v. Brass,* 625 N.W.2d 648 (Wis.App. 2001)]

To view a sample answer for this case problem, go to this book's Web site at http://leet.westbuslaw.com and click on "Interactive Study Center."

A Question of Ethics & Social Responsibility

11–11. Nancy Levy worked for Health Care Financial Enterprises, Inc., and signed a noncompete agreement in June 1992. When Levy left Health Care and opened her own similar business in 1993, Health Care brought a court action in a Florida state court to enforce the covenant not to compete. The trial court concluded that the noncompete agreement prevented Levy from working in too broad a geographic area and thus refused to enforce the agreement. A Florida appellate court, however, reversed the trial court's ruling and remanded the case with instructions that the trial court modify the geographic area to make it reasonable and then enforce the covenant. In view of these facts, consider the following questions. [*Health Care Financial Enterprises, Inc. v. Levy,* 715 So.2d 341 (Fla.App.4th 1998)]

1. At one time in Florida, under the common law, noncompete covenants were illegal, although modern Florida statutory law now allows such covenants to be enforced. Generally, what interests are served by refusing to enforce covenants not to compete? What interests are served by allowing them to be enforced?

2. What argument can be made in support of reforming (and then enforcing) illegal covenants not to compete? What argument can be made against this practice?

Case Briefing Assignment

11–12. Examine Case A.3 [*AmeriPro Search, Inc. v. Fleming Steel Co.,* 787 A.2d 988 (Sup.Ct.Pa. 2001)] in Appendix A. This case has been excerpted there in great detail. Review and then brief the case, making sure that your brief answers the following questions.

1. What events led to this lawsuit? Did Brauninger (the employment agent) and Kohn (the president of Fleming) agree on how much money AmeriPro would be paid if Fleming hired an engineer recommended by the agency?

2. How did Barracchini (the employee) originally find out about the job opportunity with Fleming Steel in 1993?

3. Who arranged the interview in April 1994, and why did Fleming not hire Barracchini at that time? What about the interview in 1995?

4. What was the trial court's ruling on the question of whether a quasi contract existed?

5. Did the appellate court uphold the lower court's ruling? Why or why not?

Critical-Thinking Legal Question

11–13. You and three co-workers ride to work each day in Julio's automobile, which has a market value of $8,000. One cold morning, the four of you get into the car, but Julio cannot get it started. He yells in anger, "I'll sell this car to anyone for $500!" You drop $500 in his lap. Has a valid contract been formed? Why or why not?

Video Questions

11–14. Go to this text's Web site at http://leet.westbuslaw.com and select "Video Questions." Click on "Chapter 11" and view the video titled *Offer and Acceptance.* Then answer the following questions.

1. In the video, Vinny indicates that he can't sell his car to Oscar for four thousand dollars, and then says, "maybe five . . . ." Discuss whether Vinny has made an offer or a counteroffer.

2. Oscar then says to Vinny, "Okay, I'll take it. But you gotta let me pay you four thousand now and the other thousand in two weeks." According to the chapter, do Oscar and Vinny have an agreement? Why or why not?

3. When Maria later says to Vinny, "I'll take it," has she accepted an offer? Why or why not?

INTERACTING WITH THE INTERNET

For updated links to resources available on the Web, as well as a variety of other materials, visit this text's Web site at

http://leet.westbuslaw.com

The 'Lectric Law Library provides information on contract law, including a definition of a contract, the elements required for a contract, and so on. Go to

http://www.lectlaw.com

Then go to the Laypeople's Law Lounge and scroll down to Contracts.

To find recent cases on contract law decided by the United States Supreme Court and the federal appellate courts, access Cornell University's School of Law site at

http://www.law.cornell.edu/topics/contracts.html

If you are interested in reading the first "Sunday law" in colonial America and learning about some of the punishments meted out in those days for failing to obey such laws, go to

http://www.natreformassn.org/statesman/99/charactr.html

To learn what kinds of clauses are included in typical contracts for certain goods and services, you can explore the collection of contract forms made available by FindLaw at

http://contracts.corporate.findlaw.com/index.html

The following URL will take you to an article that provides information on covenants not to compete:

http://www.frb-law.com/covenants.htm

To learn more about the current debate over online gambling regulation, go to Web site of the Interactive Gaming Council at the following URL and browse through the articles under "News" and "Press Releases":

http://www.igcouncil.org

Employers may inadvertently form an implied employment contract with an employee by making certain statements or promises in employee handbooks. The following URL will take you to an article exploring this topic in BusinessWeekOnline's *Legal Survival Guide For Employers:*

http://businessweek.findlaw.com/employmentbook/HFCHP8_i.html

Although advertisements are generally viewed as invitations to negotiate, not as offers to form a contract, sometimes advertisements are construed as offers. For a case evaluating a claim that an ad constituted an offer, go to

**http://www.law.pitt.edu/madison/contracts/supplement/
leonard_v_pepsico.htm**

ONLINE LEGAL RESEARCH EXERCISES

Go to **http://leet.westbuslaw.com**, the Web site that accompanies this text. Select "Interactive Study Center," and then click on "Chapter 11." There you will find the following Internet research exercises that you can perform to learn more about topics covered in this chapter.

Activity 11–1:   HISTORICAL PERSPECTIVE—Contracts in Ancient Mesopotamia
Activity 11–2:   MANAGEMENT PERSPECTIVE—Implied Employment Contracts
Activity 11–3:   INTERNATIONAL PERSPECTIVE—Contract Consideration in Canada

BEFORE THE TEST

Go to **http://leet. westbuslaw.com**, the Web site that accompanies this text. Select "Interactive Quizzes." You will find at least twenty interactive questions relating to this chapter.

Westlaw® Campus

If your textbook provided for a subscription to Westlaw® Campus, or if you have otherwise purchased access to the Westlaw Campus database, you can access any of the cases presented or cited in this chapter by using your Westlaw Campus account.

CHAPTER 12

Contract Defenses, Discharge, and Remedies

CONTENTS

CHAPTER OBJECTIVES

After reading this chapter, you should be able to answer the following questions:

1. What defenses can be raised against the enforceability of an otherwise valid contract?

2. What contracts must be in writing to be enforceable?

3. How are contractual obligations discharged?

4. What are the different types of damages that may be available on the breach of a contract?

5. What equitable remedies may be granted by a court, and in what circumstances will they be granted?

As the Athenian political leader Solon indicated centuries ago, a contract will not be broken so long as "it is to the advantage of both" parties not to break it. Normally, the reason a person enters into a contract with another is to secure an advantage, and parties usually perform their contractual obligations to enjoy the advantages gained through contracts. Sometimes, however, a party may decide that he or she does not want to, or cannot, perform as promised. When this happens, the party might claim that the contract should not be enforced because he or she did not genuinely assent to its terms. If the contract was oral, the party may assert that even though the contract may be valid (meet all of the requirements for a valid contract specified in Chapter 11), it is nonetheless unenforceable because the contract is one that is required by law to be in writing. Essentially, these types of claims are defenses to contract enforceability—a topic that we examine in this chapter.

> **"Men keep their engagements when it is to the advantage of both not to break them."**
>
> Solon, sixth century B.C.E.
> (Athenian legal reformer)

BREACH OF CONTRACT
The failure, without legal excuse, of a promisor to perform the obligations of a contract.

Alternatively, when it is no longer advantageous for a party to fulfill his or her contractual obligations, the contract may be breached. A **breach of contract** occurs when a party fails to perform part or all of the required duties under a contract. Once a party fails to perform or performs inadequately, the other party—the nonbreaching party—can choose one or more of several remedies. As discussed in Chapter 1, courts distinguish between *remedies at law* and *remedies in equity,* or equitable remedies. Today, the remedy at law is normally money damages. Equitable remedies include rescission and restitution, specific performance, and reformation.

Bear in mind that parties usually fulfill their contractual promises and thus *discharge* their obligations under the contract. In this chapter, after discussing the defenses to contract formation or enforceability, we look at the ways in which contracts can be discharged. We then examine the remedies available to nonbreaching parties when contracts are breached.

DEFENSES TO CONTRACT ENFORCEABILITY

A contract has been entered into by two parties, each with full legal capacity and for a legal purpose. The contract is also supported by consideration. Nonetheless, the contract may be unenforceable if the parties have not genuinely assented to the terms. Lack of genuine assent is a defense to the enforcement of a contract.

A contract that is otherwise valid may also be unenforceable if it is not in the proper form. For example, if a contract is required by law to be in writing, and there is no written evidence of the contract, it may not be enforceable.

Genuineness of Assent

Genuineness of assent may be lacking because of mistake, misrepresentation, undue influence, or duress. Generally, a party who demonstrates that he or she did not genuinely assent to the terms of a contract can choose either to carry out the contract or to rescind (cancel) it and thus avoid the entire transaction.

Mistakes Generally, courts distinguish between *mistakes as to judgment of market value or conditions* and *mistakes as to fact.* Only the latter normally have legal significance.

● **EXAMPLE 1** Suppose that Jud Wheeler contracts to buy ten acres of land because he believes that he can resell the land at a profit to Bart. Can Jud escape his contractual obligations if it later turns out that he was mistaken? Not likely. Jud's overestimation of the value of the land or of Bart's interest in it is an ordinary risk of business for which a court will not normally provide relief. Now suppose that Jud purchases a painting of a landscape from Roth's Gallery. Both Jud and Roth believe that the painting is by the artist Van Gogh. Jud later discovers that the painting is a very clever fake. Because neither Jud nor Roth was aware of this fact when they made their deal, Jud can rescind the contract and recover the purchase price of the painting.●

Mistakes occur in two forms—*unilateral* and *bilateral (mutual)*. A unilateral mistake is made by only one of the contracting parties; a mutual mistake is made by both.

Unilateral Mistakes. A unilateral mistake involves some *material fact*—that is, a fact important to the subject matter of the contract. In general, a unilateral mistake does not afford the mistaken party any right to relief from the contract. In other words, the contract normally is enforceable.[1] ● **EXAMPLE 2** Ellen intends to sell her motor home for $17,500. When she learns that Chin is interested in buying a used motor home, she faxes him an offer to sell her vehicle to him, but when typing the fax, she mistakenly keys in the price of $15,700. Chin writes back, accepting Ellen's offer. Even though Ellen intended to sell her motor home for $17,500, she has made a unilateral mistake and is bound by contract to sell the vehicle to Chin for $15,700.●

Mutual Mistakes. When both parties are mistaken about the same material fact, normally the contract can be rescinded by either party.[2] Note that, as with unilateral mistakes, the mistake must be about a *material fact* (one that is important and central to the contract). If, instead, a mutual mistake concerns the later market value or quality of the object of the contract, the contract normally can be enforced by either party. This rule is based on the theory that both parties assume certain risks when they enter into a contract. Without this rule, almost any party who did not receive what he or she considered a fair bargain could argue bilateral mistake. In essence, this would make adequacy of consideration a factor in determining whether a contract existed, and as discussed previously, the courts normally do not inquire into the adequacy of the consideration.

A word or term in a contract may be subject to more than one reasonable interpretation. In that situation, if the parties to the contract attach materially different meanings to the term, their mutual misunderstanding may allow the contract to be rescinded, or canceled.

The classic case on bilateral mistake is *Raffles v. Wichelhaus,*[3] which was decided by an English court in 1864. The defendant, Wichelhaus, paid for a shipment of Surat cotton from the plaintiff, Raffles, "to arrive 'Peerless' from Bombay." Wichelhaus expected the goods to be shipped on the *Peerless,* a ship sailing from Bombay, India, in October. Raffles expected to ship the goods on a different *Peerless,* which sailed from Bombay in December. When the goods arrived and Raffles tried to deliver them, Wichelhaus refused to accept them. The court held for Wichelhaus, concluding that no mutual assent existed because the parties had attached materially different meanings to an essential term of the written contract (the ship that was to transport the goods).

BE CAREFUL What a party to a contract knows or should know can determine whether the contract is enforceable.

"*Mistakes are the inevitable lot of mankind.*"

SIR GEORGE JESSEL, 1824–1883
(English jurist)

---

1. *The Restatement (Second) of Contracts,* Section 153, liberalizes the general rule to take into account the modern trend of allowing avoidance in some circumstances even though only one party has been mistaken.
2. *Restatement (Second) of Contracts,* Section 152.
3. 159 Eng.Rep. 375 (1864).

ETHICAL ISSUE

Does industry custom affect the court's determination of mutual mistake?

In many situations, when the parties' intentions are not entirely clear from the words of the contract, the courts will look at industry custom for evidence of what the parties probably meant. What happens when both parties intended to agree to something different from what they actually agreed to in the contract? That was the issue in one case in which a property owner (the lessor) had signed a ninety-nine-year lease that gave the party leasing the property (the lessee) an option to purchase. Thirty years later, the lessee sold its interest to another party, who exercised the option to purchase the property. The lessor then discovered an error in the wording of the contract: the contract read "year" although the parties had meant to say "lease year" in the section of the contract giving the method of computing the purchase price. The "year" method of computation led to a much lower purchase price than the "lease year" method.

The lessor offered evidence that the price computation method used in the contract was the result of a mutual mistake and went against industry custom. The trial court agreed, noting that the current lessee should have been aware of the mistake because the customary method of computing income capitalization uses a lease year. The appellate court reversed, however, stating that "evidence of custom, however well established, cannot prevail against the unambiguous words of an express contract." Thus, when a contract is free from ambiguities on its face, the court may not consider evidence of industry custom.[4]

"It was beautiful and simple as all truly great swindles are."

O. HENRY, 1862–1910
(American author)

Fraudulent Misrepresentation Although fraud is a tort, the presence of fraud also affects the genuineness of the innocent party's consent to a contract. When an innocent party consents to a contract induced by fraud, the contract usually can be avoided, because he or she has not *voluntarily* consented to the terms. Normally, the innocent party can either rescind (cancel) the contract and be restored to his or her original position or enforce the contract and seek damages for injuries resulting from the fraud.

Typically, there are three elements of fraud:

1. A misrepresentation of a material fact must occur.
2. There must be an intent to deceive.
3. The innocent party must justifiably rely on the misrepresentation.

Additionally, to collect damages, a party must have been injured as a result of the misrepresentation.

Ordinarily, neither party to a contract has a duty to come forward and disclose facts, and a contract normally will not be set aside because certain pertinent information has not been volunteered. Generally, however, if a *serious* defect or a *serious* potential problem is known to the seller but cannot reasonably be suspected to be known by the buyer, the seller may have a duty to speak.

REMEMBER To collect damages in almost any lawsuit, there must be some sort of injury.

4. *North Grand Mall v. Grand Center*, 278 F.3d 854 (8th Cir. 2002).

A duty to disclose information may also arise in an employment context when the employer either misrepresents or conceals information from a prospective employee during the hiring process. For a further discussion of this issue, see this chapter's *Inside the Legal Environment* feature on the next page.

Innocent Misrepresentation Misrepresentation may also be innocently made. If a person makes a statement that he or she believes to be true but that actually misrepresents material facts, *innocent misrepresentation,* not fraud, has occurred. In this situation, the aggrieved party can rescind (cancel) the contract but usually cannot seek damages. ● EXAMPLE 3 Parris tells Roberta that a tract of land contains 250 acres. Parris does not know that the tract contains only 215 acres and is thus mistaken. Roberta is induced by the statement to form a contract to purchase the land. Even though the misrepresentation is innocent, Roberta can avoid the contract if the misrepresentation is material.●

Undue Influence Undue influence arises from relationships in which one party can greatly influence another party, thus overcoming that party's free will. Minors and elderly people, for example, are often under the influence of guardians. If a guardian induces a young or elderly *ward* (a person placed by a court under the care of a guardian) to enter into a contract that benefits the guardian, the guardian may have exerted undue influence.

CONTRAST Even when there is no undue influence, a minor can avoid a contract.

Undue influence can arise from a number of confidential relationships or relationships founded on trust, including attorney-client, physician-patient, guardian-ward, parent-child, husband-wife, and trustee-beneficiary relationships. The essential feature of undue influence is that the party being taken advantage of does not, in reality, exercise free will in entering into a contract. A contract entered into under excessive or undue influence lacks genuine assent and is therefore voidable.[5]

Duress Assent to the terms of a contract is not genuine if one of the parties is *forced* into the agreement. Forcing a party to enter into a contract because of the fear created by threats is legally defined as *duress.*[6] In addition, blackmail or extortion to induce consent to a contract constitutes duress. Duress is both a defense to the enforcement of a contract and a ground for rescission, or cancellation, of a contract. Therefore, a party who signs a contract under duress can choose to carry out the contract or to avoid the entire transaction. (The wronged party usually has this choice in cases in which assent is not real or genuine.)

The Statute of Frauds—Requirement of a Writing

A commonly used defense to the enforceability of an oral contract is that it is required to be in writing. Today, almost every state has a statute that stipulates what types of contracts must be in writing or at least evidenced by a legally sufficient memorandum. In this text, we refer to such statutes as the **Statute of Frauds.** The primary purpose of the statute is to ensure that there is reliable evidence of the existence and terms of certain classes of contracts deemed historically to be important or complex.

STATUTE OF FRAUDS
A state statute under which certain types of contracts must be in writing to be enforceable.

5. *Restatement (Second) of Contracts,* Section 177.
6. *Restatement (Second) of Contracts,* Sections 174 and 175.

INSIDE THE LEGAL ENVIRONMENT

Misrepresentation in the Employment Context

Given the increasing number of bankruptcies in our economy, there has been a trend among employers to misrepresent the financial status of their companies during the hiring process. Although sometimes these misrepresentations have been willful, at other times they have been unintentional. After all, many job interviewers may themselves be unaware that their own firms are having financial problems.

The Courts React

Increasingly, courts are reacting negatively to what appears to be fraudulent misrepresentation about a company's financial health during hiring interviews. In one case, a group of men were offered jobs at the El-Jay Division of Cedarapids, Inc. During each of the interviews, the applicants asked about El-Jay's future and were told that business was growing, sales were up, and the future looked promising. In reality, Cedarapids's management had already planned to close the El-Jay facility. Each applicant quit his present job or passed up other employment opportunities, moved with his family to the new

work site, and signed an at-will employment agreement.

When El-Jay closed soon after the men started their new jobs, they sued Cedarapids, alleging, in part, fraudulent misrepresentation, based on the statements made to them during their job interviews. The trial court granted summary judgment in favor of Cedarapids. The appellate court, however, concluded that the case should go to trial because there was sufficient evidence to support a finding of fraud. In the court's view, El-Jay could be held liable for either failing to disclose material facts or making representations that were misleading because they were in the nature of "half-truth."[a]

The Trend Continues

In a subsequent case, Philip McConkey, a former New York Giants professional football player, worked as an insurance broker for Ross & Company. While McConkey was working for Ross, representatives of Alexander & Alexander Services, Inc. (A&A), a brokerage firm, offered him a position with their company. McConkey was definitely interested in the offer, but he had already heard rumors

that A&A was going to be acquired by another firm. Consequently, during the negotiations that followed, he asked about a possible takeover of the company. He was assured on several occasions that A&A absolutely was *not* going to be sold to another firm.

McConkey then left his position at Ross and joined A&A. Several months later, A&A was acquired by Aon Corporation, and a short time after that, McConkey was fired. Subsequently, he learned that negotiations to sell the firm to Aon were under way long before he was hired.

McConkey sued both companies, alleging that he had been fraudulently induced to leave his former position. The court agreed, concluding that McConkey had reasonably relied on A&A's misrepresentations regarding the status of the company. The court awarded McConkey over $6 million in damages. The decision was affirmed on appeal.[b]

FOR CRITICAL ANALYSIS

What are some of the ways that a firm can entice qualified job applicants to come to work for it even when the firm's financial future is in doubt?

---

a. *Meade v. Cedarapids, Inc.,* 164 F.3d 1218 (9th Cir. 1999).

b. *McConkey v. Aon Corporation,* 804 A.2d 572 (N.J.Super.A.D. 2002).

Contracts Involving Transfers of Interests in Land Land is real property, which includes not only land but all physical objects that are permanently attached to the soil, such as buildings, plants, trees, and the soil itself. Under the Statute of Frauds, a contract involving the transfer of an interest in land, to be enforceable, must be evidenced by a writing.[7] ● EXAMPLE 4 If Carol contracts orally to sell Seaside Shelter to Axel but later decides not to sell, Axel cannot enforce the contract. Similarly, if Axel refuses to close the deal, Carol cannot force Axel to pay for the land by bringing a lawsuit. The Statute of Frauds is a *defense* to the enforcement of this type of oral contract.●

A contract for the sale of land ordinarily involves the entire interest in the real property, including buildings, growing crops, vegetation, minerals, timber, and anything else affixed to the land. Therefore, a *fixture* (personal property so affixed or so used as to become a part of the realty) is treated as real property.

The Statute of Frauds requires written contracts not just for the sale of land but also for the transfer of other interests in land, such as mortgages and long-term leases.

The One-Year Rule Contracts that cannot, *by their own terms,* be performed within one year from the day after the contract is formed must be in writing to be enforceable. Because disputes over such contracts are unlikely to occur until some time after the contracts are made, resolution of these disputes is difficult unless the contract terms have been put in writing. The one-year period begins to run *the day after the contract is made.* Exhibit 12–1 illustrates the one-year rule. (Note that under the 2003 amendments to Article 2 of the Uniform Commercial Code, contracts for the sale of goods are not subject to this common law rule.)

The test for determining whether an oral contract is enforceable under the one-year rule of the statute is not whether the agreement is *likely* to be performed within one year from the date of contract formation but whether performance within a year is *possible.* When performance of a contract is objectively impossible during the one-year period, the oral contract will be unenforceable.

---

7. In some states, the contract will be enforced, however, if each party admits to the existence of the oral contract in court or admits to its existence during discovery before trial (see Chapter 4).

EXHIBIT 12–1 THE ONE-YEAR RULE

A contract falls under the Statute of Frauds (must be in writing to be enforceable) if it cannot possibly be performed within one year from the day after it was formed.

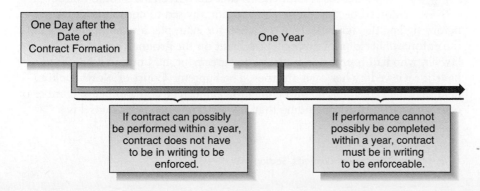

● EXAMPLE 5 Suppose that Bankers Life orally contracts to loan $40,000 to Janet Lawrence "as long as Lawrence and Associates operates its financial consulting firm in Omaha, Nebraska." The contract does not fall within the Statute of Frauds—that is, no writing is required—because Lawrence and Associates could go out of business in one year or less. In this event, the contract would be fully performed within one year.●

COLLATERAL PROMISE
A secondary promise that is ancillary (subsidiary) to a principal transaction or primary contractual relationship, such as a promise made by one person to pay the debts of another if the latter fails to perform. A collateral promise normally must be in writing to be enforceable.

Collateral Promises A **collateral promise,** or secondary promise, is one that is ancillary (subsidiary) to a principal transaction or primary contractual relationship. In other words, a collateral promise is one made by a third party to assume the debts or obligations of a primary party to a contract if that party does not perform. Any collateral promise of this nature falls under the Statute of Frauds and therefore must be in writing to be enforceable.

There is an exception. An oral promise to answer for the debt of another is covered by the Statute of Frauds *unless* the guarantor's main purpose in accepting secondary liability is to secure a personal benefit. Under the "main purpose" rule, this type of contract need not be in writing.[8] The assumption is that a court can infer from the circumstances of a case whether the "leading objective" of the promisor was to secure a personal benefit and thus, in effect, to answer for his or her own debt.

Promises Made in Consideration of Marriage A unilateral promise to pay a sum of money or to give property in consideration of a promise to marry must be in writing. If Mr. Baumann promises to pay Joe Villard $10,000 if Villard promises to marry Baumann's daughter, the promise must be in writing. The same rule applies to **prenuptial agreements**—agreements made before marriage (also called *antenuptial agreements*) that define each partner's ownership rights in the other partner's property. For example, a prospective wife may wish to limit the amount her prospective husband could obtain if the marriage ended in divorce. Prenuptial agreements made in consideration of marriage must be in writing to be enforceable.

PRENUPTIAL AGREEMENT
An agreement made before marriage that defines each partner's ownership rights in the other partner's property. Prenuptial agreements must be in writing to be enforceable.

ETHICAL ISSUE

Should prenuptial agreements be enforced if one party did not have advice of counsel?

Cases occasionally come before the courts in which a party to a prenuptial agreement claims that the agreement should not be enforced because he or she was not advised to consult an attorney before signing the agreement. In one case, for example, a woman challenged the enforceability of a prenuptial agreement on the ground that her husband's lawyer, who had been hired to draft the agreement, had not advised her to have it reviewed by her own attorney. The Supreme Court of North Dakota held that the agreement might be unenforceable. The court joined a number of other jurisdictions in concluding that advice of independent counsel is a

---

8. *Restatement (Second) of Contracts,* Section 116.

significant factor in determining whether a party signed a prenuptial agreement voluntarily.[9]

It is not the only factor, however. In a California case, a wife alleged that she had not signed a prenuptial agreement knowingly or voluntarily on the ground that her husband's attorney, who had drafted the agreement, had not advised her to obtain independent counsel and had not informed her that by signing the agreement she would forfeit certain property rights. Nevertheless, the court held that the agreement was enforceable. The evidence indicated that the woman had agreed to the terms of the contract and that she had had an opportunity to obtain counsel but had failed to do so.[10]

Contracts for the Sale of Goods The Uniform Commercial Code (UCC) contains several Statute of Frauds provisions that require written evidence of a contract. Section 2–201 contains the major provision, which generally requires a writing or memorandum for the sale of goods priced at $500 or more. (Note that under the 2003 amendments to Article 2 of the UCC, this amount has been raised to $5,000.) A writing that will satisfy the UCC requirement need only state the quantity term; other terms agreed on need not be stated "accurately" in the writing, as long as they adequately reflect both parties' intentions. The contract will not be enforceable, however, for any quantity greater than that set forth in the writing. In addition, the writing must be signed by the person against whom enforcement is sought. Beyond these two requirements, the writing need not designate the buyer or the seller, the terms of payment, or the price.

Exceptions to the Statute of Frauds Exceptions to the applicability of the Statute of Frauds are made in certain situations. We describe those situations here.

Partial Performance. In cases involving contracts relating to the transfer of interests in land, if the purchaser has paid part of the price, taken possession, and made permanent improvements to the property, and if the parties cannot be returned to their status quo prior to the contract, a court may grant *specific performance* (performance of the contract according to its precise terms). Whether the courts will enforce an oral contract for an interest in land when partial performance has taken place is usually determined by the degree of injury that would be suffered if the court chose *not* to enforce the oral contract. In some states, mere reliance on certain types of oral contracts is enough to remove them from the Statute of Frauds.

Under the UCC, an oral contract is enforceable to the extent that a seller accepts payment or a buyer accepts delivery of the goods [UCC 2–201(3)(c)].
● EXAMPLE 6 If Ajax Corporation ordered by telephone twenty crates of bleach from Cloney, Inc., and repudiated the contract after ten crates had been delivered and accepted, Cloney could enforce the contract to the extent of the ten crates accepted by Ajax.●

9. *Estate of Lutz,* 563 N.W.2d 90 (N.Dak. 1997).
10. See, for example, *In re Marriage of Bonds,* 24 Cal.4th 1, 5 P.3d 815, 99 Cal.Rptr.2d 252 (2000).

INTERNATIONAL PERSPECTIVE

The Statute of Frauds

As you will read later in this chapter, the United Nations Convention on Contracts for the International Sale of Goods (CISG) provides rules that govern international sales contracts between countries that have ratified the convention, or agreement. Article 11 of the CISG does not incorporate any Statute of Frauds provisions. Rather, it states that a "contract for sale need not be concluded in or evidenced by writing and is not subject to any other requirements as to form."

Article 11 accords with the legal customs of most nations, in which contracts no longer need to meet certain formal or writing requirements to be enforceable. Ironically, even England, the nation that created the original Statute of Frauds in 1677, has repealed all of it except the provisions relating to collateral promises and to transfers of interests in land. Many other countries that once had such statutes have also repealed all or parts of them. Civil law countries, such as France, never have required certain types of contracts to be in writing.

FOR CRITICAL ANALYSIS

If there were no Statute of Frauds and if a dispute arose concerning an oral agreement, how would the parties substantiate their respective positions?

In the following case, a dispute arose over irrigation water rights. The question was whether oral agreements for the rights were outside the Statute of Frauds because the agreements had been partially performed by the parties who claimed that the rights should be theirs.

CASE 12.1   Spears v. Warr

Supreme Court of Utah, 2002.
2002 UT 24,
44 P.3d 742.
http://www.utcourts.gov/courts/sup[a]

BACKGROUND AND FACTS

Edward and Hazel Warr bought approximately 110 acres of land in Tooele County, Utah, to sell in five-acre parcels as the Rocky Top Subdivision beginning in 1986. The Warrs also owned an interest in water from Rose Spring that they planned to use to irrigate the subdivision. During negotiations with prospective buyers, the Warrs represented that water rights were included in the price of the lots. The deeds conveying title to the lots did not convey water rights, however. The new owners repeatedly asked why water was not yet being provided. The Warrs responded that they intended to provide water as soon as possible. Eventually, the Warrs began installing a pipeline to channel water to the lots. Some of the owners helped pay for, and participated in, the installation of the pipe. In 1994, the Warrs asked the owners to pay $2,500 to $5,000 each for the water rights. The owners refused, contending that they had already paid. Melvin Spears and other owners filed a suit in a Utah state court against the Warrs, demanding that they convey (transfer) the water rights. The court ruled in the plaintiffs' favor. The Warrs appealed to the Utah Supreme Court, insisting in part that the Statute of Frauds barred enforcement of the alleged oral contracts for water.

---

a. In the "Supreme Court Opinions By Date" row, click on "2002." From the list of results, scroll to the name of the case and click on it to access the opinion. The Utah state courts maintain this Web site.

CASE 12.1—Continued

IN THE WORDS
OF THE COURT . . .

WILKINS, Justice.

* * * *

Generally, a conveyance [transfer] of real property is within the statute of frauds and unenforceable absent a writing. However, *the doctrine of part performance allows a court of equity to enforce an oral agreement, if it has been partially performed, notwithstanding the statute of frauds.* * * * [Emphasis added.]

* * * *

The standard for sufficient partial performance in Utah is as follows:

[1] the oral contract and its terms must be clear and definite; [2] the acts done in performance of the contract must be equally clear and definite; and [3] the acts must be in reliance on the contract. Such acts in reliance must be such that (a) they would not have been performed had the contract not existed, and (b) the failure to perform on the part of the promisor would result in fraud on the performer who relied, since damages would be inadequate. * * *

In the instant case [the case before the court], we conclude that the plaintiffs' performance removed the oral agreements from the statute of frauds. First, the oral contract and its terms are clear and definite. The trial court determined that "[t]he inclusion of irrigation water in the purchase price of the plaintiffs' lots was a basis of the bargain [to purchase the lots]." * * * [T]he trial court expressly noted, "The terms of the oral contracts were clear and definite, and Plaintiffs undertook acts of part performance which removed the oral contracts from the statute of frauds." The trial court further noted that "[t]here is also overwhelming independent evidence of the oral contracts in * * * the representations made by the Warrs in their dealings with the Tooele Planning Commission * * * ."

Second, the acts done in performance of the contract are equally clear and definite. The trial court found that the parties paid money for the irrigation water at the time they paid for their lots. Payment of * * * consideration for the irrigation water rights constitutes performance of the plaintiffs' contractual obligation.

Third, the plaintiffs' acts were done in reliance on the contract. The plaintiffs paid for the irrigation water rights in reliance on the Warrs' representation that deeds to the water rights would be delivered. Payment of funds for the water rights would not have been made had the oral agreements not existed. Moreover, failure by the Warrs to perform their obligation would result in fraud on the plaintiffs who paid for the water rights.

DECISION AND REMEDY The Utah Supreme Court affirmed the trial court's conclusion that the plaintiffs paid for the water rights at the time they paid for the lots and that the parties orally agreed that the water rights would be transferred after the land transaction. These oral contracts were outside the Statute of Frauds, based on the doctrine of partial performance.

FOR CRITICAL ANALYSIS—Social Consideration *Suppose that the trial court had* not *found that the inclusion of the water rights in the purchase price went to the "basis of the bargain." Would this have affected the outcome of this case? Explain.*

Admissions. In some states, if a party against whom enforcement of an oral contract is sought "admits" in pleadings, testimony, or otherwise in court proceedings that a contract for sale was made, the contract will be enforceable.[11] A contract subject to the UCC will be enforceable, but only to the extent of the quantity admitted [UCC 2–201(3)(b)]. Thus, in Example 6 on page 373, if the president of Ajax Corporation admits under oath that an oral agreement was made with Cloney, Inc., for twenty crates of bleach, the agreement will be enforceable to that extent.

Promissory Estoppel. In some states, an oral contract that would otherwise be unenforceable under the Statute of Frauds may be enforced under the doctrine of promissory estoppel, or detrimental reliance. If a promisor makes a promise on which the promisee justifiably relies to his or her detriment, a court may *estop* (prevent) the promisor from denying that a contract exists. Section 139 of the *Restatement (Second) of Contracts* provides that in these circumstances, an oral promise can be enforceable notwithstanding the Statute of Frauds if the reliance was foreseeable to the person making the promise and if injustice can be avoided only by enforcing the promise.

Special Exceptions under the UCC. Special exceptions to the applicability of the Statute of Frauds apply to sales contracts. Oral contracts for customized goods may be enforced in certain circumstances. Oral contracts *between merchants* that have been confirmed in writing may also be enforceable.

THE PAROL EVIDENCE RULE

PAROL EVIDENCE RULE
A substantive rule of contracts, as well as a procedural rule of evidence, under which a court will not receive into evidence the parties' prior negotiations, prior agreements, or contemporaneous oral agreements if that evidence contradicts or varies the terms of the parties' written contract.

A written contract is ordinarily assumed to be the complete embodiment of the parties' agreement. This assumption underlies the **parol evidence rule,** which prohibits the introduction at trial of evidence of the parties' prior negotiations, prior agreements, or contemporaneous oral agreements if that evidence contradicts or varies the terms of written contracts. Because of the rigidity of the parol evidence rule, however, courts make several exceptions:

1. Evidence of a *subsequent modification* of a written contract can be introduced in court. Keep in mind that the oral modifications may not be enforceable if they come under the Statute of Frauds—for example, if they increase the price of the goods for sale to $500 or more or increase the term for performance to more than one year. Also, oral modifications will not be enforceable if the original contract provides that any modification must be in writing.
2. Oral evidence can be introduced in all cases to show that the contract was voidable or void (for example, induced by mistake, fraud, or misrepresentation).
3. When the terms of a written contract are ambiguous, evidence is admissible to show the meaning of the terms.
4. Evidence is admissible when the written contract is incomplete in that it lacks one or more of the essential terms. The courts allow evidence to "fill in the gaps" in the contract.

---

11. *Restatement (Second) of Contracts,* Section 133. Under the 2003 amendments to the UCC, any admission under oath, including one *not* made in court, will allow the contract to be enforced.

5. Under the UCC, evidence can be introduced to explain or supplement a written contract by showing a prior dealing, course of performance, or usage of trade. When buyers and sellers deal with each other over extended periods of time, certain customary practices develop. These practices are often overlooked in the writing of the contract, so courts allow the introduction of evidence to show how the parties have acted in the past. Usage of trade—practices and customs generally followed in a particular industry—also can shed light on the meaning of certain contract provisions, and thus evidence of trade usage may be admissible.

6. The parol evidence rule does not apply if the existence of the entire written contract is subject to an orally agreed-on condition. Proof of the condition does not alter or modify the written terms but affects the *enforceability* of the written contract. ● **EXAMPLE 7** Jelek agrees to purchase Armand's car for $4,000, but only if Jelek's mechanic, Frank, inspects the car and approves of the purchase. Armand agrees to this condition, but because he is leaving town for the weekend and Jelek wants to use the car (if he buys it) before Armand returns, Jelek drafts a contract of sale, and they both sign it. Frank, the mechanic, does not approve of the purchase, and when Jelek does not buy the car, Armand sues him, alleging that he breached the contract. In this case, Jelek's oral agreement did not alter or modify the terms of the written agreement but concerned whether the contract existed at all. Therefore, the parol evidence rule does not apply.●

7. When an *obvious* or *gross* clerical (or typographical) error exists that clearly would not represent the agreement of the parties, parol evidence is admissible to correct the error. ● **EXAMPLE 8** Sharon agrees to lease 1,000 square feet of office space at the current monthly rate of $3 per square foot from Stone Enterprises. The signed written lease provides for a monthly lease payment of $300 rather than the $3,000 agreed to by the parties. Because the error is obvious, Stone Enterprises would be allowed to admit parol evidence to correct the mistake.●

As the following case illustrates, a court will not apply any of these exceptions merely when a party's "subjective expectations [are] thwarted by a bad bargain."

CASE 12.2 **APJ Associates, Inc. v. North American Philips Corp.**

United States Court of Appeals, Sixth Circuit, 2003. 317 F.3d 610. **http://pacer.ca6.uscourts.gov/ opinions/main.php**[a]

COMPANY PROFILE *Royal Philips Electronics of the Netherlands (**http://www.philips.com**) is one of the world's largest electronics companies. Royal makes and markets color television sets, lighting, electric shavers, medical diagnostic imaging and patient monitoring equipment, and other products. Royal Philips employs over 185,000 persons in more than sixty countries through a variety of subsidiaries, including North American Philips Corporation (Philips), a microprocessor supplier that makes electronic components for automobile cruise control systems.*

BACKGROUND AND FACTS Philips wanted to become a supplier to General Motors Corporation (GMC) and hired APJ Associates, Inc., to develop a business relationship between Philips and GMC. APJ and Philips signed a contract that provided, "Either

---

a. This is a page within the Web site of the U.S. Court of Appeals for the Sixth Circuit. In the left-hand column, click on "Opinions Search." In the "Short Title contains" box, type "APJ" and click "Submit Query." In the "Opinion" box corresponding to the name of the case, click on the number to access the opinion.

(continued)

CASE 12.2—Continued

party may terminate the agreement for its convenience upon at least thirty (30) days prior written notice," with no commissions to be paid on posttermination sales. The contract also stated that it "constitutes the entire Agreement between the parties * * * and supersedes and replaces all prior or contemporaneous agreements, written and verbal." The parties signed three subsequent one-year contracts with the same clauses. Each time, Jim Alexander, APJ's president,

objected, but Philips refused to make any changes. After GMC chose Philips to develop a cruise control module, Philips gave APJ notice that it was terminating their contract and sent APJ a check for $2,649.43. APJ filed a suit in a federal district court against Philips, seeking commissions on future sales. The court issued a summary judgment in Philips's favor. APJ appealed to the U.S. Court of Appeals for the Sixth Circuit.

IN THE WORDS OF THE COURT . . .

BERTELSMAN, District Judge.

* * * *

[APJ] contends * * * that extrinsic evidence is necessary to interpret the terms of the agreements between the parties, and that the district court committed error by holding that the written documents constituted the entire agreement.

* * * *[A] court may not consider extrinsic evidence where the terms of the agreement are clear and unambiguous.* Here, the terms of all four agreements are neither unclear nor inconsistent. The much-discussed thirty-day termination clause, included over Alexander's repeated objections and ratified in the three subsequent agreements, does not indicate any question as to whether the relationship could be terminated at the will of either party. The very fact that Alexander protested the clause every year shows that he was only too well aware of its implications. Since Philips continually refused to make any modification to that term, and since [APJ] continued to sign the contract, *it may not supplant those agreements with evidence of [Philips representatives'] contemporaneous assurances of a long-term relationship.* [Emphasis added.]

* * * Even though the firm may have had an expectation that the manufacturer would not terminate the contract for convenience, the express terms of the contract allowed [Phillips] to do so. * * * [T]he termination clause in this case is unambiguous as a matter of law.

Nor do the provisions for the payment of commissions introduce any ambiguity in the agreement upon which [APJ] can base its claims. The written agreements unequivocally bar the payment of any post-termination commissions. [APJ's] assertion that the oral statement [of a Philips representative that Philips's policy was] "long-term sales equal long-term commissions" constitutes "the essential terms of the contract" is not enough to establish that the written agreements must be interpreted in light of such parol evidence.

Furthermore, each agreement contained an integration clause. * * * *[A]n integration clause in a written contract conclusively establishes that the parties intended the written contract to be the complete expression of their agreement, and the parol evidence rule bars the use of extrinsic evidence to contradict the terms of a written contract intended to be the final and complete expression of the contracting parties' agreement.* [APJ] must therefore be held to the express terms of the agreements it executed. [Emphasis added.]

DECISION AND REMEDY The U.S. Court of Appeals for the Sixth Circuit affirmed the judgment of the lower court. APJ was bound to the written terms of the contracts that it signed because those terms were clear and unambiguous.

FOR CRITICAL ANALYSIS—Social Consideration *Could promissory estoppel serve as a basis for awarding commissions on future sales to APJ?*

CONTRACT DISCHARGE

As mentioned earlier, normally parties perform their contractual duties. Indeed, the most common way to **discharge,** or terminate, one's contractual duties is by the performance of those duties. The duty to perform under a contract may be *conditioned* on the occurrence or nonoccurrence of a certain event, or the duty may be *absolute.* In addition to performance, there are numerous other ways in which a contract can be discharged, including discharge by agreement of the parties and discharge based on impossibility of performance.

Discharge by Performance

The contract comes to an end when both parties fulfill their respective duties by performance of the acts they have promised. Performance can also be accomplished by tender. **Tender** is an unconditional offer to perform by a person who is ready, willing, and able to do so. Therefore, a seller who places goods at the disposal of a buyer has tendered delivery and can demand payment according to the terms of the agreement. A buyer who offers to pay for goods has tendered payment and can demand delivery of the goods. Once performance has been tendered, the party making the tender has done everything possible to carry out the terms of the contract. If the other party then refuses to perform, the party making the tender can consider the duty discharged and sue for breach of contract.

Complete versus Substantial Performance   Normally, conditions expressly stated in the contract must fully occur in all aspects for *complete performance* (strict performance) of the contract to occur. Any deviation breaches the contract and discharges the other party's obligations to perform. Although in most contracts the parties fully discharge their obligations by complete performance, sometimes a party fails to fulfill all of the duties or completes the duties in a manner contrary to the terms of the contract. The issue then arises as to whether the performance was nonetheless sufficiently substantial to discharge the contractual obligations.

To qualify as *substantial performance,* the performance must not vary greatly from the performance promised in the contract, and it must create substantially the same benefits as those promised in the contract. If performance is substantial, the other party's duty to perform remains absolute (less damages, if any, for the minor deviations).[12]

Performance to the Satisfaction of Another   When the subject matter of the contract is personal, a contract to be performed to the satisfaction of one of the parties is conditioned, and performance must actually satisfy that party. ● EXAMPLE 9 Contracts for portraits, works of art, and tailoring are considered personal. Therefore, only the personal satisfaction of the party fulfills the condition—unless a jury finds the party is expressing dissatisfaction only to avoid payment or otherwise is not acting in good faith.●

DISCHARGE
The termination of an obligation. In contract law, discharge occurs when the parties have fully performed their contractual obligations or when events, conduct of the parties, or operation of the law releases the parties from performance.

PERFORMANCE
In contract law, the fulfillment of one's duties arising under a contract with another; the normal way of discharging one's contractual obligations.

TENDER
An unconditional offer to perform an obligation by a person who is ready, willing, and able to do so.

> "The law is not exact upon the subject, but leaves it open to a good man's judgment."
>
> HUGO GROTIUS, 1583–1645
> (Dutch jurist, political leader, and theologian)

---

12. For a classic case on substantial performance, see *Jacob & Youngs, Inc. v. Kent,* 230 N.Y. 239, 129 N.E. 889 (1921).

Material Breach of Contract When a breach of contract is *material*[13]—that is, when performance is not deemed substantial—the nonbreaching party is excused from the performance of contractual duties and has a cause of action to sue for damages caused by the breach. If the breach is *minor* (not material), the nonbreaching party's duty to perform can sometimes be suspended until the breach is remedied, but the duty is not entirely excused. Once the minor breach is cured, the nonbreaching party must resume performance of the contractual obligations undertaken.

A breach entitles the nonbreaching party to sue for damages, but only a material breach discharges the nonbreaching party from the contract. The policy underlying these rules is that contracts should go forward when only minor problems occur, but contracts should be terminated if major problems arise.[14]

Anticipatory Repudiation of a Contract Before either party to a contract has a duty to perform, one of the parties may refuse to perform his or her contractual obligations. This is called **anticipatory repudiation.**[15] When anticipatory repudiation occurs, it is treated as a material breach of contract, and the nonbreaching party is permitted to bring an action for damages immediately, even though the scheduled time for performance under the contract may still be in the future.[16] Until the nonbreaching party treats this early repudiation as a breach, however, the breaching party can retract his or her anticipatory repudiation by proper notice and restore the parties to their original obligations.

There are two reasons for treating an anticipatory repudiation as a present, material breach. First, the nonbreaching party should not be required to remain ready and willing to perform when the other party has already repudiated the contract. Second, the nonbreaching party should have the opportunity to seek a similar contract elsewhere and should have the duty to do so to minimize his or her loss.

Quite often, an anticipatory repudiation occurs when a sharp fluctuation in market prices creates a situation in which performance of the contract would be extremely unfavorable to one of the parties. ● **EXAMPLE 10** Shasta Manufacturing Company contracts to manufacture and sell 100,000 personal computers to New Age, Inc., a computer retailer with 500 outlet stores. Delivery is to be made eight months from the date of the contract. One month later, three suppliers of computer parts raise their prices to Shasta. Because of these higher prices, Shasta stands to lose $500,000 if it sells the computers to New Age at the contract price. Shasta writes to New Age, informing New Age that it cannot deliver the 100,000 computers at the agreed-on contract price. Even though you might sympathize with Shasta, its letter is an anticipatory repudiation of the contract, allowing New Age the option of treating the repudiation as a material breach and proceeding immediately to pursue remedies, even though the actual contract delivery date is still seven months away.●

---

13. *Restatement (Second) of Contracts,* Section 241.
14. See UCC 2–612, which provides that an installment contract for the sale of goods is breached only when one or more nonconforming installments *substantially impairs* the value of the *whole* contract.
15. *Restatement (Second) of Contracts,* Section 253, and UCC 2–610.
16. The doctrine of anticipatory repudiation first arose in the landmark case of *Hochster v. De La Tour,* 2 Ellis and Blackburn Reports 678 (1853), when the English court recognized the delay and expense inherent in a rule requiring a nonbreaching party to wait until the time of performance before suing on an anticipatory repudiation.

ANTICIPATORY REPUDIATION
An assertion or action by a party indicating that he or she will not perform an obligation that the party is contractually obligated to perform at a future time.

REMEMBER The risks that prices will fluctuate and values will change are ordinary business risks for which the law does not provide relief.

Performance of a Sales Contract In the performance of a sales contract, the basic obligation of the seller is to transfer and deliver conforming goods. The basic obligation of the buyer is to accept and pay for conforming goods in accordance with the contract [UCC 2–301]. Overall performance of a sales contract is controlled by the agreement between the parties. When the contract is unclear and disputes arise, the courts look to the UCC.

Discharge by Agreement

Any contract can be discharged by the agreement of the parties. The agreement can be contained in the original contract, or the parties can form a new contract for the express purpose of discharging the original contract.

> "Agreement makes law."
> (LEGAL MAXIM)

Discharge by Rescission The process in which the parties cancel the contract and are returned to the positions they occupied prior to the contract's formation is known as **rescission.** For *mutual rescission* to take place, the parties must make another agreement that also satisfies the legal requirements for a contract—there must be an *offer,* an *acceptance,* and *consideration.* Ordinarily, if the parties agree to rescind the original contract, their promises *not* to perform those acts promised in the original contract will be legal consideration for the second contract.

Mutual rescission can occur in this manner when the original contract is executory on both sides (that is, neither party has completed performance). The agreement to rescind an executory contract is generally enforceable, even if it is made orally and even if the original agreement was in writing.[17] When one party has fully performed, however, an agreement to rescind the original contract is not usually enforceable. Because the performing party has received no consideration for the promise to call off the original bargain, additional consideration is necessary. Under UCC 2–209(1), however, no consideration is needed to modify a contract for a sale of goods.

RESCISSION
A remedy whereby a contract is canceled and the parties are returned to the positions they occupied before the contract was made; may be effected through the mutual consent of the parties, by their conduct, or by court decree.

Discharge by Novation The process of **novation** substitutes a third party for one of the original parties. Essentially, the parties to the original contract and one or more new parties all get together and agree to the substitution. The requirements of a novation are as follows:

1. The existence of a previous, valid obligation.
2. Agreement by all of the parties to a new contract.
3. The extinguishing of the old obligation (discharge of the prior party).
4. A new, valid contract.

NOVATION
The substitution, by agreement, of a new contract for an old one, with the rights under the old one being terminated. Typically, there is a substitution of a new person who is responsible for the contract and the removal of the original party's rights and duties under the contract.

Discharge by Accord and Satisfaction In an *accord and satisfaction,* the parties agree to accept performance different from the performance originally promised. An *accord* is defined as an executory contract (one that has not yet been performed) to perform some act in order to satisfy an existing contractual duty that is not yet discharged.[18] A *satisfaction* is the performance of the

---

17. Agreements to rescind contracts involving transfers of realty, however, must be evidenced by a writing. Another exception has to do with the sale of goods under the UCC, when the sales contract requires written rescission.
18. *Restatement (Second) of Contracts,* Section 281.

accord agreement. An *accord* and its *satisfaction* discharge the original contractual obligation.

When Performance Is Impossible

IMPOSSIBILITY OF PERFORMANCE
A doctrine under which a party to a contract is relieved of his or her duty to perform when performance becomes impossible or totally impracticable (through no fault of either party).

After a contract has been made, performance may become impossible in an objective sense. This is known as **impossibility of performance** and may discharge a contract.[19] *Objective impossibility* ("It can't be done") must be distinguished from *subjective impossibility* ("I'm sorry, I simply can't do it"). Examples of subjective impossibility include contracts in which goods cannot be delivered on time because of a freight car shortage and contracts in which money cannot be paid on time because the bank is closed. In effect, the nonperforming party is saying, "It is impossible for *me* to perform," not "It is impossible for *anyone* to perform." Accordingly, such excuses do not discharge a contract, and the nonperforming party is normally held in breach of contract.

> "Law is a practical matter."
> ROSCOE POUND, 1870–1964
> (American jurist)

Commercial Impracticability The discharge of contractual obligations based on impossibility of performance may occur when performance becomes *commercially impracticable*—that is, much more difficult or expensive than anticipated. In such situations, courts may excuse parties from their performance obligations under the doctrine of *commercial impracticability*. For someone to invoke this doctrine successfully, however, the anticipated performance must become extremely difficult or costly. The added burden of performing not only must be extreme but also *must not have been known by the parties when the contract was made.*

In the following case, a party to a contract for a sale of land argued that the contract should be rescinded because a possible spread of pollution and the potential liability involved made the sale impossible or impracticable.

---

19. *Restatement (Second) of Contracts,* Section 261.

CASE 12.3   Cape-France Enterprises v. Estate of Peed

Supreme Court of Montana, 2001.
305 Mont. 513,
29 P.3d 1011,
2001 MT 139.

BACKGROUND AND FACTS

Cape-France Enterprises owns real property in Bozeman, Montana. In 1994, Lola Peed and her granddaughter Marthe Moore entered into an agreement with Cape-France to buy five acres of the land on which to build a motel or hotel. To complete the sale, the state required the land to be surveyed, subdivided, and rezoned. To subdivide the property, the state required a well to be drilled and the water to be tested. The parties were aware of underground pollution in Bozeman but believed Cape-France's property to be unaffected. Montana's Department of

Environmental Quality, Water Quality Division (DEQ), however, feared that the water under the land was contaminated. The DEQ warned in letters to Cape-France that if there was pollution, drilling a well could exacerbate the problem, treatment of the water would be extensive, and Cape-France would be liable for the cost. When Peed and Moore would not agree to share the risk, Cape-France filed a suit in a Montana state court against Moore and Peed's estate (Peed had since died), seeking to rescind their contract in part on the ground of impossibility or impracticability. The court granted a summary judgment in Cape-France's favor. The defendants appealed to the Montana Supreme Court.

CASE 12.3—Continued

IN THE WORDS OF THE COURT . . .

Justice *JAMES C. NELSON* delivered the Opinion of the Court.

* * * *

* * * [T]he doctrine of impossibility is a valid defense not only when performance is impossible, but also when supervening circumstances make performance impracticable. * * *

* * * [A]n act is impracticable when it can only be done at an excessive, unreasonable and unbargained-for cost. *While the doctrine of impossibility or impracticability is not set in stone, it is applied by courts where, aside from the object of the contract being unlawful, the public policy underlying the strict enforcement of contracts is outweighed by the senselessness of requiring performance.* [Emphasis added.]

The doctrine is applicable under the facts in the case at bar. * * * It is undisputed that after the agreement was executed, the state and local regulatory authorities required the completion of water drilling and testing. The parties discussed the situation. Cape-France was unwilling to assume large risks related to this new, unknown and unexpected situation. Peed-Moore was unwilling to [share the risks to a degree] satisfactory to Cape-France. Contamination, if it exists or occurs by reason of well-drilling, could expose Cape-France as landowners to financial liability of an unquantifiable nature. * * *

Peed and Moore argue that the contract should not be rescinded on the basis of impossibility because it is not impossible to drill the well. They point to the [DEQ] letters as evidence that the well could be drilled and that there is no proof that there would be actual groundwater contamination where they would drill. However, Peed and Moore do not argue, and cannot argue, that there is no groundwater contamination, nor can they say that there will not be any in the future. Unfortunately, the only way to determine whether there is and, if so, the extent of groundwater contamination is to drill a well. And that is the precise activity that may exacerbate the contamination problem, to both parties' substantial and unbargained-for economic detriment. Indeed, it is clear that Peed and Moore are unwilling or unable to share in these economic risks.

Moreover, as already noted, while impossibility or impracticability is a high standard, the application of this doctrine is not limited to cases of literal impossibility. Here, the potential for substantial and unbargained-for damage involved in performing the contract is not only of an economic nature. Just as importantly, environmental degradation with consequences extending well beyond the parties' land sale is also a real possibility.

DECISION AND REMEDY The Montana Supreme Court affirmed the judgment of the lower court. The state supreme court agreed that rescission of this contract was appropriate, on the ground of impossibility or impracticability, because Cape-France would otherwise be forced to expose itself to substantial and unbargained-for economic risks, to expose the public to potential health risks, and to expose the environment to possible degradation.

FOR CRITICAL ANALYSIS—Social Consideration *The Montana state constitution requires that "the State and each person shall maintain and improve a clean and healthful environment in Montana." In light of this clause, what is another basis on which the contract in this case might be rescinded?*

Temporary Impossibility An occurrence or event that makes performance temporarily impossible operates to *suspend* performance until the impossibility ceases. Then, ordinarily, the parties must perform the contract as originally planned. If, however, the lapse of time and the change in circumstances surrounding the contract make it substantially more burdensome for the parties to perform the promised acts, the contract is discharged.

The leading case on the subject, *Autry v. Republic Productions,*[20] involved an actor who was drafted into the army in 1942. Being drafted rendered the actor's contract temporarily impossible to perform, and it was suspended until the end of the war. When the actor got out of the army, the value of the dollar had so changed that performance of the contract would have been substantially burdensome to him. Therefore, the contract was discharged.

DAMAGES

A breach of contract entitles the nonbreaching party to sue for money damages. As you read in Chapter 8, damages are designed to compensate a party for harm suffered as a result of another's wrongful act. In the context of contract law, damages are designed to compensate the nonbreaching party for the loss of the bargain. Often, courts say that innocent parties are to be placed in the position they would have occupied had the contract been fully performed.[21]

Types of Damages

There are basically four kinds of damages: compensatory, consequential, punitive, and nominal damages.

Compensatory Damages As discussed in Chapter 8, *compensatory damages* compensate an injured party for injuries or damages actually sustained by that party. The nonbreaching party must prove that the actual damages arose directly from the loss of the bargain caused by the breach of contract. The amount of compensatory damages is the difference between the value of the breaching party's promised performance under the contract and the value of his or her actual performance. This amount is reduced by any loss that the injured party has avoided, however.

REMEMBER The terms of a contract must be sufficiently definite for a court to determine the amount of damages to award.

● EXAMPLE 11 Suppose that you contract with Marinot Industries to perform certain personal services exclusively for Marinot during August for a payment of $3,500. Marinot cancels the contract and is in breach. You are able to find another job during August but can only earn $1,000. You normally can sue Marinot for breach and recover $2,500 as compensatory damages. You may also recover from Marinot the amount you spent to find the other job.● Expenses or costs that are caused directly by a breach of contract—such as those incurred to obtain performance from another source—are *incidental damages*.

The measurement of compensatory damages varies by type of contract. Certain types of contracts deserve special mention—contracts for the sale of goods, contracts for the sale of land, and construction contracts.

---

20. 30 Cal.2d 144, 180 P.2d 888 (1947).
21. *Restatement (Second) of Contracts,* Section 347; and UCC 1–106(1).

Sale of Goods. In a contract for the sale of goods, the usual measure of compensatory damages is an amount equal to the difference between the contract price and the market price.[22] • **EXAMPLE 12** Suppose that MediQuick Laboratories contracts with Cal Computer Industries to purchase ten model X-15 computer work stations for $4,000 each. If Cal Computer fails to deliver the ten work stations, and the current market price of the work stations is $4,500, MediQuick's measure of damages is $5,000 (10 × $500). • In cases in which the buyer breaches and the seller has not yet produced the goods, compensatory damages normally equal the lost profits on the sale, not the difference between the contract price and the market price.

Sale of Land. The measure of damages in a contract for the sale of land is ordinarily the same as it is for contracts involving the sale of goods—that is, the difference between the contract price and the market price of the land. The majority of states follow this rule regardless of whether it is the buyer or the seller who breaches the contract.

A minority of states, however, follow a different rule when the seller breaches the contract and the breach is not deliberate. An example of a nondeliberate breach of a contract to sell land occurs when a previously unknown easement (a right of use over the property of another) is discovered and renders title to the land unmarketable. (In real property law, *title* means the right to own property or the evidence of that right.) In such a situation, these states allow the prospective purchaser to recover any down payment plus any expenses incurred (such as fees for title searches or attorneys). This minority rule effectively places a purchaser in the position that he or she occupied prior to the contract of sale.

Construction Contracts. With construction contracts, the measure of damages often varies depending on which party breaches and at what stage the breach occurs. See Exhibit 12–2 for illustrations.

---

22. That is, the difference between the contract price and the market price at the time and place at which the goods were to be delivered or tendered. See UCC 2–708 and 2–713.

EXHIBIT 12–2   MEASUREMENT OF DAMAGES—BREACH
                    OF CONSTRUCTION CONTRACTS

PARTY IN BREACH	TIME OF BREACH	MEASUREMENT OF DAMAGES
Owner	Before construction begins	Profits (contract price less cost of materials and labor)
Owner	After construction begins	Profits plus costs incurred up to time of breach
Owner	After construction is completed	Contract price
Contractor	Before construction is completed	Generally, all costs incurred by owner to complete construction

What factors influence the measure of damages on the breach of a construction contract?

CONSEQUENTIAL DAMAGES
Special damages that compensate for a loss that is not direct or immediate (for example, lost profits). The special damages must have been reasonably foreseeable at the time the breach or injury occurred in order for the plaintiff to collect them.

NOTE A seller who does not wish to take on the risk of consequential damages can limit the buyer's remedies.

"The duty to keep a contract at common law means a prediction that you must pay damages if you do not keep it— and nothing else."

OLIVER WENDELL HOLMES, JR.,
1841–1935
(Associate justice of the United States
Supreme Court, 1902–1932)

Consequential Damages Foreseeable damages that result from a party's breach of contract are referred to as **consequential damages,** or *special damages.* Consequential damages differ from compensatory damages in that they are caused by special circumstances beyond the contract itself. When a seller does not deliver goods, *knowing* that a buyer is planning to resell those goods immediately, consequential damages are awarded for the loss of profits from the planned resale. ● **EXAMPLE 13** Gilmore contracts to have a specific item shipped to her—one that she desperately needs to repair her printing press. In contracting with the shipper, Gilmore tells him that she must receive the item by Monday or she will not be able to print her paper and will lose $1,750. If the shipper is late, Gilmore normally can recover the consequential damages caused by the delay (that is, the $1,750 in losses).●

For a nonbreaching party to recover consequential damages, the breaching party must know (or have reason to know) that special circumstances will cause the nonbreaching party to suffer an additional loss. This rule was enunciated in *Hadley v. Baxendale,* a case decided in England in 1854 and presented in this chapter's *Landmark in the Legal Environment* feature. When damages are awarded, compensation is given only for those injuries that the defendant *could reasonably have foreseen* as a probable result of the usual course of events following a breach. If the injury complained of is outside the usual and foreseeable course of events, the plaintiff must show specifically that the defendant had reason to know the facts and foresee the injury.

Punitive Damages Recall from Chapter 8 that *punitive damages* are designed to punish a wrongdoer and set an example to deter similar conduct in the future. Punitive damages, which are also referred to as *exemplary damages,* are generally not recoverable in an action for breach of contract. Such damages have no legitimate place in contract law because they are, in essence,

LANDMARK IN THE LEGAL ENVIRONMENT

Hadley v. Baxendale (1854)

A landmark case in establishing the rule that notice of special ("consequential") circumstances must be given if consequential damages are to be recovered is *Hadley v. Baxendale*,[a] decided in 1854.

CASE BACKGROUND   This case involved a broken crankshaft used in a flour mill run by the Hadley family in Gloucester, England. The crankshaft attached to the steam engine in the mill broke, and the shaft had to be sent to a foundry located in Greenwich so that a new shaft could be made to fit the other parts of the engine.

The Hadleys hired Baxendale, a common carrier, to transport the shaft from Gloucester to Greenwich. Baxendale received payment in advance and promised to deliver the shaft the following day. It was not delivered for several days, however. As a consequence, the mill was closed during those days because the Hadleys had no extra crankshaft on hand to use. The Hadleys sued Baxendale to recover the profits they lost during that time. Baxendale contended that the loss of profits was "too remote."

In the mid-1800s, it was common knowledge that large mills, such as that run by the Hadleys, normally had more than one crankshaft in case the main one broke and had to be repaired, as happened in this case. It is against this background that the parties argued their respective positions on whether the damages resulting from loss of profits while the crankshaft was out for repair were "too remote" to be recoverable.

THE ISSUE BEFORE THE COURT AND THE COURT'S RULING   The crucial issue before the court was whether the Hadleys had informed the carrier, Baxendale, of the special circumstances surrounding the crankshaft's repair, particularly that the mill would have to shut down while the crankshaft was being repaired. If Baxendale had been notified of this circumstance at the time the contract was formed, then the remedy for breaching the contract would have been the amount of damages that would reasonably follow from the breach—including the Hadleys' lost profits.

In the court's opinion, however, the only circumstances communicated by the Hadleys to Baxendale at the time the contract was made were that the item to be transported was a broken crankshaft of a mill and that the Hadleys were the owners and operators of that mill. The court concluded that these circumstances did not reasonably indicate that the mill would have to stop operations if the delivery of the crankshaft was delayed.

Application to Today's World

Today, the rule enunciated by the court in this case still applies. When damages are awarded, compensation is given only for those injuries that the defendant could reasonably have foreseen as a probable result of the usual course of events following a breach. If the injury complained of is outside the usual and foreseeable course of events, the plaintiff must show specifically that the defendant had reason to know the facts and foresee the injury. This is true with respect to contracts in the online environment as well. For example, suppose that a Web merchant loses business (and profits) because of a computer system's failure. If the failure was caused by malfunctioning software, the merchant may sue to recover the lost profits from the software maker if these consequential damages were foreseeable.

---

a. 9 Exch. 341, 156 Eng.Rep. 145 (1854).

penalties, and a breach of contract is not unlawful in a criminal sense. A contract is simply a civil relationship between the parties. The law may compensate one party for the loss of the bargain—no more and no less.

In a few situations, a person's actions can cause both a breach of contract and a tort. For example, the parties can establish by contract a certain reasonable standard or duty of care. Failure to live up to that standard is a breach of contract, and the act itself may constitute negligence. An intentional tort (such as fraud) may also be tied to a breach of contract. In such a situation, it is possible for the nonbreaching party to recover punitive damages for the tort in addition to compensatory and consequential damages for the breach of contract.

Nominal Damages Damages that are awarded to an innocent party when only a technical injury is involved and no actual damage (no financial loss) has been suffered are called **nominal damages**. Nominal damage awards are often small, such as one dollar, but they do establish that the defendant acted wrongfully.

● EXAMPLE 14 Suppose that Parrott contracts to buy potatoes at fifty cents a pound from Lentz. Lentz breaches the contract and does not deliver the potatoes. Meanwhile, the price of potatoes falls. Parrott is able to buy them in the open market at half the price he agreed to pay Lentz. Parrott is clearly better off because of Lentz's breach. Thus, in a suit for breach of contract, Parrott may be awarded only nominal damages for the technical injury he sustained, as no monetary loss was involved.● Most lawsuits for nominal damages are brought as a matter of principle under the theory that a breach has occurred and some damages must be imposed regardless of actual loss.

NOMINAL DAMAGES
A small monetary award (often one dollar) granted to a plaintiff when no actual damage was suffered.

Mitigation of Damages

In most situations, when a breach of contract occurs, the injured party is held to a duty to mitigate, or reduce, the damages that he or she suffers. Under this doctrine of **mitigation of damages**, the required action depends on the nature of the situation. For example, in the majority of states, wrongfully terminated employees have a duty to mitigate damages suffered by their employers' breach. The damages they will be awarded are their salaries less the incomes they would have received in similar jobs obtained by reasonable means. It is the employer's burden to prove the existence of such jobs and to prove that the employee could have been hired. An employee is, of course, under no duty to take a job that is not of the same type and rank.

MITIGATION OF DAMAGES
A rule requiring a plaintiff to have done whatever was reasonable to minimize the damages caused by the defendant.

Liquidated Damages versus Penalties

A **liquidated damages** provision in a contract specifies that a certain amount of money is to be paid in the event of a future default or breach of contract. (*Liquidated* means determined, settled, or fixed.) Liquidated damages differ from penalties. A **penalty** specifies a certain amount to be paid in the event of a default or breach of contract and is designed to penalize the breaching party. Liquidated damages provisions normally are enforceable; penalty provisions are not. This is also the rule under the Uniform Commercial Code [UCC 2–718(1)].

To determine whether a particular provision is for liquidated damages or for a penalty, the court must answer two questions: First, at the time the contract was formed, was it difficult to estimate the potential damages that would be incurred if the contract was not performed on time? Second, was the amount set as damages a reasonable estimate of those potential damages and

LIQUIDATED DAMAGES
An amount, stipulated in the contract, that the parties to a contract believe to be a reasonable estimation of the damages that will occur in the event of a breach.

PENALTY
A sum inserted into a contract, not as a measure of compensation for its breach but rather as punishment for a default. The agreement as to the amount will not be enforced, and recovery will be limited to actual damages.

not excessive?[23] If the answers to both questions are yes, the provision will be enforced. If either answer is no, the provision will normally not be enforced. In a construction contract, it is difficult to estimate the amount of damages that might be caused by a delay in completing construction, so liquidated damages clauses are often used.

The court in the following case answered the liquidated damages questions in the context of a provision in an agreement for the lease of a hotel.

---

23. *Restatement (Second) of Contracts,* Section 356(1).

CASE 12.4 Green Park Inn, Inc. v. Moore

North Carolina Court of Appeals, 2002.
562 S.E.2d 53.
http://www.aoc.state.nc.us/www/
public/html/opinions.htm[a]

COMPANY PROFILE *Green Park Inn (**http://www.greenparkinn.com**) is one of the oldest hotels in the United States. Established in 1882 and listed on the National Register of Historic Places, it is located in the Blue Ridge Mountains near Blowing Rock, North Carolina. Eminent guests have included Annie Oakley, Herbert Hoover, Eleanor Roosevelt, Margaret Mitchell, Calvin Coolidge, and John D. Rockefeller. Green Park Inn is a full-service, first class hotel and restaurant.*

BACKGROUND AND FACTS Allen and Pat McCain own Green Park Inn, Inc., which operates the Green Park Inn. In 1996, they leased the inn to GMAFCO, LLC, which is owned by Gary and Gail Moore. The lease agreement provided that, in case of a default by GMAFCO, Green Park, Inc., would be entitled to $500,000 as "liquidated damages." GMAFCO defaulted on the February 2000 rent. Green Park Inn, Inc., gave GMAFCO an opportunity to cure the default, but GMAFCO made no further payments and returned possession of the property to the lessor. When Green Park Inn, Inc., sought the "liquidated damages," the Moores refused to pay. Green Park Inn, Inc., filed a suit in a North Carolina state court against the Moores, GMAFCO, and their bank to obtain the $500,000. The defendants contended in part that the lease clause requiring payment of "liquidated damages" was an unenforceable penalty provision. The court ordered the defendants to pay Green Park Inn, Inc. The defendants appealed to a state intermediate appellate court.

IN THE WORDS OF THE COURT . . .

HUDSON, Judge.

* * * *

The parties agreed to the following in the liquidated damages clause of the Lease Agreement:

> Allen and Pat McCain, the only two shareholders of lessor, have actively worked in the day to day operation of the hotel for the past fourteen years, and have steadily built up the clientele, reputation and physical plant of the hotel, and, correspondingly, the revenues/profits of the hotel. In addition, Allen and Pat McCain are 64 and 55 years old respectively, and that both retired from the business after this lease was agreed to. The McCains have retired to Florida, and would have to relocate back to Blowing Rock for extended periods of time if they are forced out of retirement to take over operation of the hotel. The parties agree to the following items which will be included in lessor's damages:

> (a) restoration of the physical plant;

---

a. In the "Court of Appeals Opinions" section, click on "2002." On the next page, scroll to the "2 April 2002" section and click on the name of the case to access the opinion. The North Carolina Appellate Division Reporter maintains this Web site.

(continued)

CASE 12.4—Continued

(b) lost lease payments owed to lessor which will not be paid because of lessee's breach with due consideration having been given to lessor's obligation to mitigate damages;

(c) harm to the reputation of the hotel, which will have to be remedied by lessor;

(d) interruption of business damages caused by the necessity of lessor having to hire new employees to recommence operations.

While some of the items listed in the liquidated damages provision are not indefinite or uncertain, others, such as the harm to the hotel's reputation or the cost to the McCains of being forced out of retirement, clearly would have been difficult to ascertain at the time the Lease Agreement was signed. * * *

Whether a liquidated damages amount is a reasonable estimate of the damages that would likely result from a default is a question of fact. * * * [McCain] stated that, after he and his wife were forced out of retirement and back to Blowing Rock to operate the hotel, "[t]he estimate of $500,000.00 as the fair and reasonable estimate to measure the damages suffered by us in the event of default has proven to be just that fair and reasonable." Additionally, the Lease Agreement states that "[t]he parties have agreed that the sum of Five Hundred Thousand Dollars ($500,000.00) represents a fair and reasonable estimate and measure of the damages to be suffered by lessor in the event of default by lessee." Defendants have proffered [offered] no evidence to show the liquidated damages amount was unreasonable. [Emphasis added.]

DECISION AND REMEDY The state intermediate appellate court affirmed the decision of the lower court. The lease provision satisfied the two-part test for liquidated damages. The amount of the damages would have been difficult to determine at the time that the lease was signed, and the estimate of the damages was reasonable.

FOR CRITICAL ANALYSIS—Economic Consideration *If the lease had specified $3 million in damages, would the result in this case have been different? If so, in what way?*

EQUITABLE REMEDIES

When the remedy at law (money damages) is inadequate, a court may grant a remedy in equity, or equitable remedy, such as one of the remedies discussed here.

Rescission and Restitution

When fraud, mistake, duress, or failure of consideration is present, rescission is available. The failure of one party to perform under a contract entitles the other party to rescind (cancel, or undo) the contract.[24] The rescinding party must give prompt notice to the breaching party. Furthermore, both parties must make **restitution** to each other by returning goods, property, or money previously conveyed.[25] If the goods or property can be restored *in specie*—that

RESTITUTION
An equitable remedy under which a person is restored to his or her original position prior to loss or injury, or placed in the position he or she would have been in had the breach not occurred.

---

24. The rescission discussed here refers to *unilateral* rescission, in which only one party wants to undo the contract. In *mutual* rescission, both parties agree to undo the contract. Mutual rescission discharges the contract; unilateral rescission is generally available as a remedy for breach of contract.
25. *Restatement (Second) of Contracts,* Section 370.

is, if they can be returned—they must be. If the goods or property have been consumed, restitution must be made in an equivalent amount of money. Essentially, restitution refers to the recapture of a benefit conferred on the defendant through which the defendant has been unjustly enriched.

● EXAMPLE 15 Andrea pays $10,000 to Miles in return for Miles's promise to design a house for her. The next day Miles calls Andrea and tells her that he has taken a position with a large architectural firm in another state and cannot design the house. Andrea decides to hire another architect that afternoon. Andrea can obtain restitution of $10,000, because she conferred an unjust benefit of $10,000 on Miles. ●

Specific Performance

The equitable remedy of **specific performance** calls for the performance of the act promised in the contract. This remedy is often attractive to a nonbreaching party, because it provides the exact bargain promised in the contract. It also avoids some of the problems inherent in a suit for money damages. First, the nonbreaching party need not worry about collecting the judgment.[26] Second, the nonbreaching party need not look around for another contract. Third, the actual performance may be more valuable than the money damages. Although the equitable remedy of specific performance is often preferable to other remedies, normally it is not granted unless the party's legal remedy (money damages) is inadequate.[27]

For example, contracts for the sale of goods that are readily available on the market rarely qualify for specific performance. Money damages ordinarily are adequate in such situations, because substantially identical goods can be bought or sold in the market. If the goods are unique, however, a court of equity will decree specific performance. For example, paintings, sculptures, and rare books and coins are often unique, and money damages will not enable a buyer to obtain substantially identical substitutes in the market. The same principle applies to contracts relating to sales of land or interests in land, because each parcel of land is unique by legal description.

Courts normally refuse to grant specific performance of contracts for personal services. Sometimes the remedy at law may be adequate if substantially identical services are available from other persons (as with lawn-mowing services). Even for individually tailored personal-service contracts, courts are very hesitant to order specific performance by a party, because public policy strongly discourages involuntary servitude.[28] Moreover, the courts do not want to monitor a personal-service contract. For example, if you contract with

SPECIFIC PERFORMANCE
An equitable remedy requiring exactly the performance that was specified in a contract; usually granted only when money damages would be an inadequate remedy and the subject matter of the contract is unique (for example, real property).

"Specific performance is a remedy of grace and not a matter of right, and the test of whether or not it should be granted depends on the particular circumstances of each case."
GEORGE BUSHNELL, 1887–1965
(American jurist)

---

26. Courts dispose of cases, after trials, by entering judgments. A judgment may order the losing party to pay money damages to the winning party. Collection of judgments, however, poses problems—such as when the judgment debtor is insolvent (cannot pay his or her bills when they become due) or has only a small net worth, or when the debtor's assets cannot be seized, under exemption laws, by a creditor to satisfy a debt (see Chapter 15).
27. *Restatement (Second) of Contracts,* Section 359.
28. The Thirteenth Amendment to the U.S. Constitution prohibits involuntary servitude, but negative injunctions (that is, prohibiting rather than ordering certain conduct) are possible. Thus, you may not be able to compel a person to perform under a personal-service contract, but you may be able to restrain that person from engaging in similar contracts with others for a period of time.

A collection of antique coins and other artifacts. When is specific performance the appropriate remedy for a breach of contract?

a brain surgeon to perform brain surgery on you and the surgeon refuses to perform, the court would not compel (and you certainly would not want) the surgeon to perform under these circumstances. There is no way the court can assure appropriate performance in such a situation.[29]

Reformation

When the parties have imperfectly expressed their agreement in writing, the equitable remedy of *reformation* allows the contract to be rewritten to reflect the parties' true intentions. This remedy applies most often when fraud or mutual mistake (for example, a clerical error) has occurred. If Keshan contracts to buy a certain piece of equipment from Shelley but the written contract refers to a different piece of equipment, a mutual mistake has occurred. Accordingly, a court could reform the contract so that the writing conforms to the parties' original intention as to which piece of equipment is being sold.

Two other examples deserve mention. The first involves two parties who have made a binding oral contract. They further agree to reduce the oral contract to writing, but in doing so, they make an error in stating the terms. Universally, the courts allow into evidence the correct terms of the oral contract, thereby reforming the written contract.

The second example has to do with written covenants not to compete, which were discussed in Chapter 11. If a covenant not to compete is for a valid and legitimate purpose (such as the sale of a business), but the area or time restraints of the covenant are unreasonable, some courts reform the restraints

---

29. Similarly, courts often refuse to order specific performance of construction contracts, because courts are not set up to operate as construction supervisors or engineers.

by making them reasonable and enforce the entire contract as reformed. Other courts throw the entire restrictive covenant out as illegal.

Recovery Based on Quasi Contract

Recall from Chapter 11 that a quasi contract is not a true contract but a fictional contract that is imposed on the parties to obtain justice and prevent unfair enrichment. Hence, a quasi contract becomes an equitable basis for relief. Generally, when one party confers a benefit on another, justice requires that the party receiving the benefit pay a reasonable value for it so as not to be unjustly enriched at the other party's expense.

Quasi-contractual recovery is useful when one party has *partially* performed under a contract that is unenforceable. It can be an alternative to suing for damages, and it allows the party to recover the reasonable value of the partial performance. For quasi-contractual recovery to occur, the party seeking recovery must show the following:

DON'T FORGET The function of a quasi contract is to impose a legal obligation on parties who made no actual promises.

1. A benefit was conferred on the other party.
2. The party conferring the benefit did so with the expectation of being paid.
3. The party seeking recovery did not act as a volunteer in conferring the benefit.
4. Retaining the benefit without paying for it would result in an unjust enrichment of the party receiving the benefit.

● **EXAMPLE 16** Suppose that Ericson contracts to build two oil derricks for Petro Industries. The derricks are to be built over a period of three years, but the parties do not create a written contract. Enforcement of the contract will therefore be barred by the one-year rule of the Statute of Frauds, discussed earlier in this chapter. Ericson completes one derrick, and then Petro Industries informs him that it will not pay for the derrick. Ericson can sue in quasi contract because (1) a benefit (one oil derrick) has been conferred on Petro Industries, (2) Ericson conferred the benefit (built the derrick) expecting to be paid, (3) Ericson did not volunteer to build the derrick but built it under an unenforceable oral contract, and (4) allowing Petro Industries to retain the derrick without paying would enrich the company unjustly. Therefore, Ericson should be able to recover the reasonable value of the oil derrick (under the theory of *quantum meruit*[30]—"as much as he deserves"). The reasonable value is ordinarily equal to the fair market value. ●

ELECTION OF REMEDIES

In many cases, a nonbreaching party has several remedies available. Because the remedies may be inconsistent with one another, the common law of contracts requires the party to choose which remedy to pursue. This is called *election of remedies*. The purpose of the doctrine of election of remedies is to prevent double recovery. ● **EXAMPLE 17** Suppose that Jefferson agrees to sell his land to Adams. Then Jefferson changes his mind and repudiates the contract. Adams can sue for compensatory damages or for specific performance. If she receives damages as a result of the breach, she should not also be granted

---

30. Pronounced *kwahn*-tuhm *mehr*-oo-wuht.

Which remedy a plaintiff elects depends on the subject of the contract, the defenses of the breaching party, the advantages that might be gained in terms of tactics against the defendant, and what the plaintiff can prove with respect to the remedy sought.

specific performance of the sales contract, because that would mean she would end up with both the land and damages, which would be unfair. In effect, she would recover twice for the same breach of contract. The doctrine of election of remedies requires Adams to choose the remedy she wants, and it eliminates any possibility of double recovery.•

Unfortunately, the doctrine has been applied in a rigid and technical manner, leading to some harsh results. • **EXAMPLE 18** Suppose that Wilson is fraudulently induced to buy a parcel of land for $150,000. He spends an additional $10,000 moving onto the land and then discovers the fraud. Instead of suing for damages, Wilson sues to rescind the contract. The court allows Wilson to recover only the purchase price of $150,000. The court denies recovery of the additional $10,000 because the seller, Martin, did not receive the $10,000 and is therefore not required to reimburse Wilson for his moving expenses. So Wilson suffers a net loss of $10,000 on the transaction. If Wilson had elected to sue for damages instead of seeking the remedy of rescission and restitution, he could have recovered the $10,000 as well as the $150,000.• Because of the harsh results of the doctrine of election of remedies, the Uniform Commercial Code (UCC) expressly rejects it. Remedies under the UCC are essentially *cumulative* in nature, as will be discussed next.

REMEDIES FOR BREACH OF A SALES CONTRACT

Sometimes circumstances make it difficult for a person to carry out the performance promised in a contract, in which case the contract may be breached. When breach occurs, the aggrieved party looks for remedies. These remedies range from retaining the goods to requiring the breaching party's performance under the contract. The general purpose of these remedies is to put the aggrieved party "in as good a position as if the other party had fully performed." As just mentioned, remedies under the UCC are *cumulative* in nature; in other words, an innocent party to a breached sales or lease contract is not limited to one, exclusive remedy. (Of course, a party still may not recover twice for the same harm.)

Remedies of the Seller

A buyer breaches a sales contract by any of the following actions: (1) wrongfully rejecting tender of the goods, (2) wrongfully revoking acceptance of the goods, (3) failing to make payment on or before delivery of the goods, or (4) repudiating the contract. On the buyer's breach, the seller is afforded several distinct remedies under the UCC. These include the right to stop or withhold delivery of the goods and the right to recover damages or to recover the purchase price of the goods.

Remedies of the Buyer

A seller breaches a sales contract by failing to deliver conforming goods or repudiating the contract prior to delivery. On the breach, the buyer has a choice of several remedies under the UCC. These remedies include the right to

reject nonconforming or improperly delivered goods; to *cover* (that is, to buy the goods elsewhere and recover from the seller the extra cost of obtaining the substitute goods); to recover damages; and, in certain circumstances, to obtain specific performance of the contract.

PROVISIONS LIMITING REMEDIES

A contract may include provisions stating that no damages can be recovered for certain types of breaches or that damages must be limited to a maximum amount. The contract may also provide that the only remedy for breach is replacement, repair, or refund of the purchase price. Provisions stating that no damages can be recovered are called *exculpatory clauses* (see Chapter 11). Provisions that affect the availability of certain remedies are called *limitation-of-liability clauses.*

Whether these contract provisions and clauses will be enforced depends on the type of breach that is excused by the provision. For example, a provision excluding liability for fraudulent or intentional injury will not be enforced. Likewise, a clause excluding liability for illegal acts or violations of law will not be enforced. A clause excluding liability for negligence may be enforced in some cases. When an exculpatory clause for negligence is contained in a contract made between parties who have roughly equal bargaining positions, the clause usually will be enforced.

The UCC provides that in a contract for the sale of goods, remedies can be limited. (See this chapter's *Legal E-nvironment* feature on the following page for a discussion of a limitation-of-liability clause in a licensing agreement accompanying the sale of a software program.)

RECALL Exculpatory clauses are often held unconscionable, depending on the relative bargaining positions of the parties and the importance to the public interest of the business seeking to enforce the clause.

CONTRACTS FOR THE INTERNATIONAL SALE OF GOODS

International sales contracts between firms or individuals located in different countries are governed by the 1980 United Nations Convention on Contracts for the International Sale of Goods (CISG)—if the countries of the parties to the contract have ratified the CISG (and if the parties have not agreed that some other law will govern their contract). As of 2000, fifty-eight countries had ratified or acceded to the CISG, including the United States, Canada, Mexico, some Central and South American countries, and most of the European nations. Essentially, the CISG is to international sales contracts what Article 2 of the UCC is to domestic sales contracts.

Businesspersons must take special care when drafting international sales contracts to avoid problems caused by distance, including language differences and varying national laws. The fold-out exhibit contained within this chapter, which shows an actual international sales contract used by Starbucks Coffee Company, illustrates many of the special terms and clauses that are typically contained in international contracts for the sale of goods. Annotations in the exhibit explain the meaning and significance of specific clauses in the contract. (See Chapter 24 for a discussion of other laws that frame global business transactions.)

International currency. The values of different types of currencies fluctuate. What other variables should a party consider when entering into an international sales contract?

LEGAL *e*-NVIRONMENT

Limitation of Liability Clauses in Software Licenses

Businesses today rely to a significant extent on computer hardware and software to conduct their operations. While this technology simplifies and streamlines business operations, it also poses some hazards. For example, suppose that, due to a software glitch, a construction company's bid for a construction project is $2 million less than it should have been. Clearly, if the company is awarded the project due to the inaccurate bid, the firm stands to incur a significant loss. This was essentially the problem facing the M. A. Mortenson Company, a nationwide construction contractor, when a bug in a software program that it used to submit bids for construction work caused a bid to be significantly lower than it should have been.

The Problem Facing the M. A. Mortenson Company

The M. A. Mortenson Company purchased software from Timberline Software Corporation. The software analyzed construction project requirements and bid information from subcontractors and found the lowest-cost combination of subcontractors to do the work. The software was distributed subject to a license set forth on the outside of each disk's pouch and on the inside cover of the instruction manuals. The first screen that appeared each time the program was used also referred to the license, which included a limitation on Timberline's liability arising from use of the software. After using the software to prepare a bid, Mortenson discovered that the bid was $1.95 million less than it should have been. The software clearly had a bug, and Timberline was aware of this problem. In fact, Timberline had already provided a newer version of the software to some of its other customers.

Was the Limitation-of-Liability Clause a Part of the Contract?

Mortenson sued Timberline, alleging that the limitation on Timberline's liability was not a part of the parties' contract. Timberline filed a motion for summary judgment, which the court granted. Mortenson fared no better in its appeal—ultimately, to the Washington State Supreme Court. That court held that the terms of the license were part of the contract between Mortenson and Timberline, and that Mortenson's use of the software constituted its assent to the agreement, including the limitation-of-liability clause in the license. The court stated that "as the license was part of the contract between Mortenson and Timberline, its terms are enforceable."

The court noted that the parties had dealt with each other for years, and that the terms of the license, which were similar to those used throughout the software industry, were set forth in several locations. In other words, Mortenson had to accept that it had no legal recourse against Timberline because of the limitation-of-liability clause in the licensing agreement.[a]

FOR CRITICAL ANALYSIS

Is it fair to hold that a business firm is bound by an agreement to limit liability when the firm did not intend to be bound by such an agreement? Why or why not?

---

a. *M. A. Mortenson Co. v. Timberline Software Corp.,* 140 Wash.2d 568, 998 P.2d 305 (2000).

KEY TERMS

Sample Sales Contract for Purchase of Green Coffee

Starbucks Coffee Company was founded in 1971, when it opened its first store in Seattle's Pike Place Market. Today, Starbucks is the leading roaster and retailer of specialty coffee in the world. The company has more than 5,500 stores in twenty-eight countries. Starbucks's chairman and chief global strategist, Howard Schultz, who has been instrumental in the company's expansion, hopes to have 10,000 stores in fifty countries by the end of 2005.

Schultz joined the company in 1982, when Starbucks was still only a small, but highly respected, roaster and retailer of whole-bean and ground coffee. A business trip to Italy opened Schultz's eyes to the rich tradition and popularity of the espresso bar. Espresso drinks became the foundation of his vision for the company, and when Schultz purchased Starbucks in 1987, Starbucks started brewing. In a few years, the company had expanded to numerous locations in the United States and was available in restaurants, hotels, and airports, as well as by mail-order catalogue. In 1992, Starbucks began to sell shares of the company's stock to the public. The price of Starbucks stock initially was $17 per share. The same share of stock today would be worth about $400—a gain of 2,200 percent.

"In the early days, there were only a few members of the financial community who believed in our viability and staying power," says Schultz. No one dreamed that Starbucks would grow from a company that was worth approximately $270 million in 1992 into a company that is worth nearly $10 billion today. With the forward-thinking Schultz at the helm, however, Starbucks blossomed into one of the world's most admired brands. Since opening its first international location in 1996, Starbucks has expanded to 1,200 international locations throughout North America and Europe, as well as in the Middle East and Pacific Rim. Starbucks coffee is now available in supermarkets and online.

In addition to its uncompromising commitment to buying, roasting, and serving only the finest coffees in the world, Starbucks also produces and sells bottled Frappuccino®, a line of premium ice creams, Tazo® Tea, and a line of compact discs.

The company has also given back to the communities in which it operates—sponsoring cultural events, such as jazz and film festivals, and donating money to charities, especially those that benefit children. Starbucks provides funding for education and literacy programs, college scholarship programs, and international relief organizations. Starbucks is also strongly committed to promoting environmentally sound methods of growing coffee and gave $1 million in support to coffee farmers in 2001.

Photo Credit: Jill Doran for Starbucks Coffee

1. This is a co[...]
their princip[...]
subject to th[...]
Goods (CIS[...]
are located i[...]
Commercia[...]

2. Quantity is [...]
court may no[...]

3. Weight per [...]
stated, usa[...]

4. Packaging [...]
shipments a[...]

5. A descriptio[...]
Warranties [...]
9. Internati[...]

6. Under the [...]
not set. See[...]
determinati[...]

7. The terms [...]
be complica[...]
simple, and[...]
ness (for ex[...]
cash, the b[...]

8. *Tender* mea[...]
disposition.[...]
it be ready [...]
warehouse [...]
goods are r[...]

9. The deliver[...]
in breach o[...]
within whic[...]
present pro[...]
pass inspe[...]

10. As part of [...]
when the g[...]
set out in C[...]

11. In some co[...]
some loss [...]
example) o[...]
to which ei[...]

12. Documents[...]
them word [...]
revised, the[...]
incorporate[...]
provisions,[...]

13. In internati[...]
brokers are[...]
commissio[...]

Contract Seller's No.: **504617**
Buyer's No.: **P9264**
Date: **9/11/98**

_____

__Mexican_____ coffee

...ze made of sisal, henequen, jute, burlap, or
...ering of any material properly sewn by hand

...of Buyer and Seller.

_____

...urrency, per __lb._____net, (U.S. Funds)
...redo, TX
(City and State)

_____

...nd governmental regulations have been satisfied,
...). Seller is obliged to give the Buyer two (2)
...owing but not including date of tender.

...Method of Transportation)
...val at __Laredo, TX__
(Country of Importation)

...her with the quantity, description, marks and
...eller's Agent/Broker, to the Buyer or his Agent/
...ater than the fifth business day following arrival
...ally with written confirmation to be sent the

...tract is to be weighed at location named in

...ct is sold on shipping weights. Any loss in
...tender is for account of Seller at contract price.
...days after tender. Weighing expenses, if any, for
_____(Seller or Buyer)
...of Origin and otherwise to comply with laws and
...time of entry, governing marking of import
...y with these regulations to be borne by

...Association of New York City, Inc., in effect on
...oses as a part of this agreement, and together
...addition hereto shall be valid unless signed by the

...reof, which by reference are made a part hereof,
...ules of the Green Coffee Association of New

...MISSION TO BE PAID BY:
eller

__BC Brokerage__
⌐ Broker(s)
...other, such person hereby represents that he is

...nc.

---

14 Arbitration is the settling of a dispute by submitting it to a disinterested party (other than a court) that renders a decision. The procedures and costs can be provided for in an arbitration clause or incorporated through other documents. To enforce an award rendered in an arbitration, the winning party can "enter" (submit) the award in a court "of competent jurisdiction." For a general discussion of arbitration and other forms of dispute resolution (other than courts), see Chapter 3.

15 When goods are imported internationally, they must meet certain import requirements before being released to the buyer. Because of this, buyers frequently want a guaranty clause that covers the goods not admitted into the country and that either requires the seller to replace the goods within a stated time or allows the contract for those goods not admitted to be voided.

16 In the "Claims" clause, the parties agree that the buyer has a certain time within which to reject the goods. The right to reject is a right by law and does not need to be stated in a contract. If the buyer does not exercise the right within the time specified in the contract, the goods will be considered accepted.

17 Many international contracts include definitions of terms so that the parties understand what they mean. Some terms are used in a particular industry in a specific way. Here, the word "chop" refers to a unit of like-grade coffee beans. The buyer has a right to inspect ("sample") the coffee. If the coffee does not conform to the contract, the seller must correct the nonconformity.

18 The "Delivery," "Insurance," and "Freight" clauses, with the "Arrival" clause on page 1, indicate that this is a destination contract. The seller has the obligation to deliver the goods to the destination, not simply deliver them into the hands of a carrier. Under this contract, the destination is a "Bonded Public Warehouse" in a specific location. The seller bears the risk of loss until the goods are delivered at their destination. Typically, the seller will have bought insurance to cover the risk.

19 Delivery terms are commonly placed in all sales contracts. Such terms determine who pays freight and other costs, and, in the absence of an agreement specifying otherwise, who bears the risk of loss. International contracts can use delivery terms as provided under the UCC or can use INCOTERMS, which are published by the International Chamber of Commerce. INCOTERMS differ slightly from UCC terms in legal effect. For example, the INCOTERM "DDP" ("delivered duty paid") requires the seller to arrange shipment, obtain and pay for import or export permits, and get the goods through customs to a named destination.

20 Exported and imported goods are subject to duties, taxes, and other charges imposed by the governments of the countries involved. International contracts spell out who is responsible for these charges.

21 This clause protects a party if the other party should become financially unable to fulfill the obligations under the contract. Thus, if the seller cannot afford to deliver, or the buyer cannot afford to pay, for the stated reasons, the other party can consider the contract breached. This right is subject to "11 USC 365(e)(1)," which refers to a specific provision of the U.S. Bankruptcy Code dealing with executory contracts. Bankruptcy provisions are covered in Chapter 15.

22 In the "Breach or Default of Contract" clause, the parties agreed that the remedies under this contract are the remedies (except for consequential damages) provided by the UCC, as in effect in the state of New York. The amount and "ascertainment" of damages, as well as other disputes about relief, are to be determined by arbitration. Breach of contract and contractual remedies in general are discussed in this chapter. Arbitration is discussed in Chapter 3.

23 Three clauses frequently included in international contracts are omitted here. There is no "choice-of-language" clause designating the official language to be used in interpreting the contract terms. There is no "choice-of-forum" clause designating the place in which disputes will be litigated, except for arbitration (law of New York State). Finally, there is no *force majeure* clause relieving the sellers or buyers from nonperformance due to events beyond their control. See Chapter 24.

TERMS AND CONDITIONS

ARBITRATION: All controversies relating to, in connection with, or arising out of this contract, its modification, making or the authority or obligations of the signatories hereto, and whether involving the principals, agents, brokers, or others who actually subscribe hereto, shall be settled by arbitration in accordance with the "Rules of Arbitration" of the Green Coffee Association of New York City, Inc., as they exist at the time of the arbitration (including provisions as to payment of fees and expenses). Arbitration is the sole remedy hereunder, and it shall be held in accordance with the law of New York State, and judgment of any award may be entered in the courts of that State, or in any other court of competent jurisdiction. All notices or judicial service in reference to arbitration or enforcement shall be deemed given if transmitted as required by the aforesaid rules.

GUARANTEE: (a) If all or any of the coffee is refused admission into the country of importation by reason of any violation of governmental laws or acts, which violation existed at the time the coffee arrived at Bonded-Public Warehouse, seller is required, as to the amount not admitted and as soon as possible, to deliver replacement coffee in conformity to all terms and conditions of this contract, excepting only the Arrival terms, but not later than thirty (30) days after the date of the violation notice. Any payment made and expenses incurred for any coffee denied entry shall be refunded within ten (10) calendar days of denial of entry, and payment shall be made for the replacement delivery in accordance with the terms of this contract. Consequently, if Buyer removes the coffee from the Bonded Public Warehouse, Seller's responsibility as to such portion hereunder ceases.

(b) Contracts containing the overstamp "No Pass-No Sale" on the face of the contract shall be interpreted to mean: If any or all of the coffee is not admitted into the country of Importation in its original condition by reason of failure to meet requirements of the government's laws or Acts, the contract shall be deemed null and void as to that portion of the coffee which is not admitted in its original condition. Any payment made and expenses incurred for any coffee denied entry shall be refunded within ten (10) calendar days of denial of entry.

CONTINGENCY: This contract is not contingent upon any other contract.

CLAIMS: Coffee shall be considered accepted as to quality unless within _fifteen_ (15) calendar days after delivery at Bonded Public Warehouse or within _fifteen_ (15) calendar days after all Government clearances have been received, whichever is later, either:
(a) Claims are settled by the parties hereto, or,
(b) Arbitration proceedings have been filed by one of the parties in accordance with the provisions hereof.
(c) If neither (a) nor (b) has been done in the stated period or if any portion of the coffee has been removed from the Bonded Public Warehouse before representative sealed samples have been drawn by the Green Coffee Association of New York City, Inc., in accordance with its rules, Seller's responsibility for quality claims ceases for that portion so removed.
(d) Any question of quality submitted to arbitration shall be a matter of allowance only, unless otherwise provided in the contract.

DELIVERY: (a) No more than three (3) chops may be tendered for each lot of 250 bags.
(b) Each chop of coffee tendered is to be uniform in grade and appearance. All expense necessary to make coffee uniform shall be for account of seller.
(c) Notice of arrival and/or sampling order constitutes a tender, and must be given not later than the fifth business day following arrival at Bonded Public Warehouse stated on the contract.

INSURANCE: Seller is responsible for any loss or damage, or both, until Delivery and Discharge of coffee at the Bonded Public Warehouse in the Country of Importation.

All Insurance Risks, costs and responsibility are for Seller's Account until Delivery and Discharge of coffee at the Bonded Public Warehouse in the Country of Importation.

Buyer's insurance responsibility begins from the day of importation or from the day of tender, whichever is later.

FREIGHT: Seller to provide and pay for all transportation and related expenses to the Bonded Public Warehouse in the Country of Importation.

EXPORT DUTIES/TAXES: Exporter is to pay all Export taxes, duties or other fees or charges, if any, levied because of exportation.

IMPORT DUTIES/TAXES: Any Duty or Tax whatsoever, imposed by the government or any authority of the Country of Importation, shall be borne by the Importer/Buyer.

INSOLVENCY OR FINANCIAL FAILURE OF BUYER OR SELLER: If, at any time before the contract is fully executed, either party hereto shall meet with creditors because of inability generally to make payment of obligations when due, or shall suspend such payments, fail to meet his general trade obligations in the regular course of business, shall file a petition in bankruptcy or, for an arrangement, shall become insolvent, or commit an act of bankruptcy, then the other party may at his option, expressed in writing, declare the aforesaid to constitute a breach and default of this contract, and may, in addition to other remedies, decline to deliver further or make payment or may sell or purchase for the defaulter's account, and may collect damage for any injury or loss, or shall account for the profit, if any, occasioned by such sale or purchase.

This clause is subject to the provisions of (11 USC 365 (e) 1) if invoked.

BREACH OR DEFAULT OF CONTRACT: In the event either party hereto fails to perform, or breaches or repudiates this agreement, the other party shall subject to the specific provisions of this contract be entitled to the remedies and relief provided for by the Uniform Commercial Code of the State of New York. The computation and ascertainment of damages, or the determination of any other dispute as to relief, shall be made by the arbitrators in accordance with the Arbitration Clause herein.

Consequential damages shall not, however, be allowed.

tract for a sale of coffee to be *imported* internationally. If the parties have
al places of business located in different countries, the contract may be
e United Nations Convention on Contracts for the International Sale of
G)—discussed in this chapter. If the parties' principal places of business
the United States, the contract may be subject to the Uniform
Code (UCC).

one of the most important terms to include in a contract. Without it, a
be able to enforce the contract. See Chapter 11.

nit (bag) can be exactly stated or approximately stated. If it is not so
e of trade in international contracts determines standards of weight.

equirements can be conditions for acceptance and payment. Bulk
e not permitted without the consent of the buyer.

n of the coffee and the "Markings" constitute express warranties.
n contracts for domestic sales of goods are discussed generally in Chapter
nal contracts rely more heavily on descriptions and models or samples.

CC, parties may enter into a valid contract even though the price is
Chapter 11. Under the CISG, a contract must provide for an exact
n of the price.

f payment may take one of two forms: credit or cash. Credit terms can
ted and may involve letters of credit. See Chapter 24. A cash term can be
payment may be by any means acceptable in the ordinary course of busi-
ample, a personal check or a letter of credit). If the seller insists on actual
yer must be given a reasonable time to get it.

ns the seller has placed goods that conform to the contract at the buyer's
This contract requires that the coffee meet all import regulations and that
or pickup by the buyer at a "Bonded Public Warehouse." (A *bonded*
s a place in which goods can be stored without payment of taxes until the
emoved.)

y date is significant because, if it is not met, the buyer may hold the seller
the contract. Under this contract, the seller can be given a "period"
h to deliver the goods, instead of a specific day, which could otherwise
olems. The seller is also given some time to rectify goods that do not
ion (see the "Guarantee" clause on page 2).

proper tender, the seller (or its agent) must inform the buyer (or its agent)
ods have arrived at their destination. The responsibilities of agents are
hapter 16.

tracts, delivered and shipped weights can be important. During shipping,
an be attributed to the type of goods (spoilage of fresh produce, for
to the transportation itself. A seller and buyer can agree on the extent
her of them will bear such losses.

are often incorporated in a contract by reference, because including
for word can make a contract difficult to read. If the document is later
whole contract might have to be reworked. Documents that are typically
d by reference include detailed payment and delivery terms, special
and sets of rules, codes, and standards.

onal sales transactions, and for domestic deals involving certain products,
used to form the contracts. When so used, the brokers are entitled to a

---

OVERLAND COFFEE IMPORT CONTRACT
OF THE
GREEN COFFEE ASSOCIATION
OF
NEW YORK CITY, INC.*
Effective May 9, 1991

SOLD BY: **XYZ CO.**

TO: **Starbucks**

QUANTITY: **Five Hundred** (**500** (Bags) Tons of _____
weighing about **152.117 lbs.** _____ per bag

PACKAGING: Coffee must be packed in clean sound bags of uniform
similar woven material, without inner lining or outer co
and/or machine.
Bulk shipments are allowed if agreed by mutual consen

DESCRIPTION: **High grown Mexican Altura**

PRICE: At ____ **Ten/$10.00 dollars** _____ U. S.
Upon delivery in Bonded Public Warehouse at _____ **La**

PAYMENT: **Cash against warehouse receipts**

Bill and tender to DATE when all import requirements
and coffee delivered or discharged (as per contract term
calendar days free time in Bonded Public Warehouse fo

ARRIVAL: During **December** via **truck**
(Period) (
from **Mexico** _____ for arr
(Country of Exportation)
Partial shipments permitted.

ADVICE OF
ARRIVAL: Advice of arrival with warehouse name and location,
place of entry, must be transmitted directly, or through
Broker. Advice will be given as soon as known but not
at the named warehouse. Such advice may be given ver
same day.

WEIGHTS: (1) DELIVERED WEIGHTS: Coffee covered by this c
tender. Actual tare to be allowed.
(2) SHIPPING WEIGHTS: Coffee covered by this cont
weight exceeding **1/2** percent at location named
(3) Coffee is to be weighed within fifteen (15) calendar
account of _____ **seller**

MARKINGS: Bags to be branded in English with the name of Countr
regulations of the Country of Importation, in effect at th
merchandise. Any expense incurred by failure to comp
Exporter/Seller.

RULINGS: The "Rulings on Coffee Contracts" of the Green Coffee
the date this contract is made, is incorporated for all pu
herewith, constitute the entire contract. No variation or
parties to the contract.
Seller guarantees that the terms printed on the reverse h
are identical with the terms as printed in By-Laws and
York City, Inc., heretofore adopted.
Exceptions to this guarantee are:
ACCEPTED: CO
XYZ Co.
                 Seller
BY_____
                 Agent
Starbucks
                 Buyer
BY_____
                 Agent
When this contract is executed by a person acting for a
fully authorized to commit his principal.

* Reprinted with permission of The Green Coffee Association of New York City,

CHAPTER SUMMARY CONTRACT DEFENSES, DISCHARGE, AND REMEDIES

DEFENSES TO CONTRACT ENFORCEABILITY	
Genuineness of Assent (See pages 366–369.)	1. *Mistakes—* a. Unilateral—Generally, the mistaken party is bound by the contract. b. Bilateral—When both parties are mistaken about the same material fact, such as identity, either party can avoid the contract. If the mistake concerns value or quality, either party can enforce the contract. 2. *Fraudulent or innocent misrepresentation*—When fraud occurs, usually the innocent party can enforce or avoid the contract. For damages, the innocent party must suffer an injury. When innocent misrepresentation occurs, the contract may be rescinded (canceled) but damages are not available. 3. *Undue influence*—Undue influence arises from special relationships, such as fiduciary or confidential relationships, in which one party's free will has been overcome by the undue influence exerted by the other party. Usually, the contract is voidable. 4. *Duress*—Duress is defined as forcing a party to enter a contract under the fear of a threat—for example, the threat of violence or serious economic loss. The party forced to enter the contract can rescind the contract.
The Statute of Frauds and the Parol Evidence Rule (See pages 369–378.)	1. *Statute of Frauds*—The following types of contracts fall under the Statute of Frauds and must be in writing or evidenced by a legally sufficient memorandum to be enforceable: (1) contracts involving transfers of interests in land, (2) contracts the terms of which cannot be performed within one year, (3) collateral promises, (4) promises made in consideration of marriage, and (5) contracts for the sale of goods priced at $500 or more. Exceptions include partial performance, admissions, and promissory estoppel. 2. *Parol evidence rule*—A rule that prohibits the introduction at trial of evidence of the parties' prior negotiations, prior agreements, or contemporaneous oral agreements if that evidence contradicts or varies the terms of written contracts. Because of the rigidity of the parol evidence rule, however, courts make several exceptions.
CONTRACT DISCHARGE	
Performance (See pages 379–381.)	A contract may be discharged by complete (strict) or by substantial performance. In some cases, performance must be to the satisfaction of another. Totally inadequate performance constitutes a material breach of contract. An anticipatory repudiation of a contract allows the other party to sue immediately for breach of contract.
Agreement (See pages 381–382.)	Parties may agree to discharge their contractual obligations in several ways: 1. *By rescission*—The parties mutually agree to rescind (cancel) the contract. 2. *By novation*—A new party is substituted for one of the primary parties to a contract.

(continued)

CHAPTER SUMMARY **CONTRACT DEFENSES, DISCHARGE, AND REMEDIES—Continued**

Agreement—continued	3. *By accord and satisfaction*—The parties agree to render performance different from that originally agreed on.
When Performance Is Impossible (See pages 382–384.)	Parties' obligations under contracts may be discharged by objective impossibility of performance or commercial impracticability of performance.
	THE COMMON REMEDIES AVAILABLE TO THE NONBREACHING PARTY
Damages (See pages 384–390.)	The legal remedy of damages is designed to compensate the nonbreaching party for the loss of the bargain. By awarding money damages, the court tries to place the parties in the positions that they would have occupied had the contract been fully performed. The nonbreaching party frequently has a duty to mitigate (lessen or reduce) the damages incurred as a result of the contract's breach. There are five broad categories of damages:

1. *Compensatory damages*—Damages that compensate the nonbreaching party for injuries actually sustained and proved to have arisen directly from the loss of the bargain resulting from the breach of contract.

   a. In breached contracts for the sale of goods, the usual measure of compensatory damages is an amount equal to the difference between the contract price and the market price.

   b. In breached contracts for the sale of land, the measure of damages is ordinarily the same as in contracts for the sale of goods.

   c. In breached construction contracts, the measure of damages depends on which party breaches and at what stage of construction the breach occurs.

2. *Consequential damages*—Damages resulting from special circumstances beyond the contract itself; the damages flow only from the consequences of a breach. For a party to recover consequential damages, the damages must be the foreseeable result of a breach of contract, and the breaching party must have known at the time the contract was formed that special circumstances existed and that the nonbreaching party would incur additional loss on breach of the contract. Also called *special damages.*

3. *Punitive damages*—Damages awarded to punish the breaching party. Usually not awarded in an action for breach of contract unless a tort is involved.

4. *Nominal damages*—Damages small in amount (such as one dollar) that are awarded when a breach has occurred but no actual damages have been suffered. Awarded only to establish that the defendant acted wrongfully.

5. *Liquidated damages*—Damages that may be specified in a contract as the amount to be paid to the nonbreaching party in the event the contract is later breached. Clauses providing for liquidated damages are enforced if the damages were difficult to estimate at the time the contract was formed and if the amount stipulated is reasonable. If construed to be a penalty, the clause will not be enforced.

CHAPTER SUMMARY CONTRACT DEFENSES, DISCHARGE, AND REMEDIES—Continued

Equitable Remedies (See pages 390–393.)	1. *Rescission and restitution*—A remedy whereby a contract is canceled and the parties are restored to the original positions that they occupied prior to the transaction. Available when fraud, a mistake, duress, or failure of consideration is present. The rescinding party must give prompt notice of the rescission to the breaching party. When a contract is rescinded, both parties must make restitution to each other by returning the goods, property, or money previously conveyed. Restitution prevents the unjust enrichment of the defendant. 2. *Specific performance*—An equitable remedy calling for the performance of the act promised in the contract. Specific performance is only available in special situations—such as those involving contracts for the sale of unique goods or land—and when monetary damages would be an inadequate remedy. Specific performance is not available as a remedy in breached contracts for personal services. 3. *Reformation*—An equitable remedy allowing a contract to be "reformed," or rewritten, to reflect the parties' true intentions. Available when an agreement is imperfectly expressed in writing. 4. *Recovery based on quasi contract*—An equitable theory imposed by the courts to obtain justice and prevent unjust enrichment in a situation in which no enforceable contract exists. The party seeking recovery must show that a benefit was conferred on the other party, the party conferring the benefit did so with the expectation of being paid, the benefit was not volunteered, and retaining the benefit without paying for it would result in the unjust enrichment of the party receiving the benefit.

CONTRACT DOCTRINES RELATING TO REMEDIES

Election of Remedies (See pages 393–394.)	A common law doctrine under which a nonbreaching party must choose one remedy from those available. This doctrine prevents double recovery.
Remedies for Breach of a Sales Contract (See pages 394–395.)	When the buyer breaches a contract for the sale of goods, the seller may stop or withhold delivery of the goods, or recover damages or the purchase price of the goods. When the seller breaches a sales contract, the buyer may reject the goods, recover damages, obtain specific performance, or cover (buy replacement goods) and obtain from the seller the extra cost of the cover.
Provisions Limiting Remedies (See pages 395–396.)	A contract may provide that no damages (or only a limited amount of damages) can be recovered in the event the contract is breached. Clauses excluding liability for fraudulent or intentional injury or for illegal acts cannot be enforced. Clauses excluding liability for negligence may be enforced if both parties hold roughly equal bargaining power. Under the UCC, in contracts for the sale of goods, remedies may be limited.
Contracts for the International Sale of Goods (See page 395.)	International sales contracts are governed by the United Nations Convention on Contracts for the International Sale of Goods (CISG)—if the countries of the parties to the contract have ratified the CISG (and if the parties have not agreed that some other law will govern their contract). Essentially, the CISG is to international sales contracts what Article 2 of the UCC is to domestic sales contracts.

FOR REVIEW

1. What defenses can be raised against the enforceability of an otherwise valid contract?

2. What contracts must be in writing to be enforceable?

3. How are contractual obligations discharged?

4. What are the different types of damages that may be available on the breach of a contract?

5. What equitable remedies may be granted by a court, and in what circumstances will they be granted?

QUESTIONS AND CASE PROBLEMS

12–1. Liquidated Damages. Carnack contracts to sell his house and lot to Willard for $100,000. The terms of the contract call for Willard to pay 10 percent of the purchase price as a deposit toward the purchase price, or as a down payment. The terms further stipulate that should the buyer breach the contract, the deposit will be retained by Carnack as liquidated damages. Willard pays the deposit, but because her expected financing of the $90,000 balance falls through, she breaches the contract. Two weeks later Carnack sells the house and lot to Balkova for $105,000. Willard demands her $10,000 back, but Carnack refuses, claiming that Willard's breach and the contract terms entitle him to keep the deposit. Discuss who is correct.

12–2. Election of Remedies. Perez contracts to buy a new Oldsmobile from Central City Motors, paying $2,000 down and agreeing to make twenty-four monthly payments of $350 each. He takes the car home and, after making one payment, learns that his Oldsmobile has a Chevrolet engine in it rather than the famous Olds Super V-8 engine. Central City never informed Perez of this fact. Perez immediately notifies Central City of his dissatisfaction and returns the car to Central City. Central City accepts the car and returns to Perez the $2,000 down payment plus the one $350 payment. Two weeks later Perez, without a car and feeling angry, files a suit against Central City, seeking damages for breach of warranty and fraud. Discuss the effect of Perez's actions.

12–3. Specific Performance. In which of the following situations might a court grant specific performance as a remedy for the breach of contract?

(a) Tarrington contracts to sell her house and lot to Rainier. Then, on finding another buyer willing to pay a higher purchase price, she refuses to deed the property to Rainier.

(b) Marita contracts to sing and dance in Horace's nightclub for one month, beginning June 1. She then refuses to perform.

(c) Juan contracts to purchase a rare coin from Edmund, who is breaking up his coin collection. At the last minute, Edmund decides to keep his coin collection intact and refuses to deliver the coin to Juan.

(d) There are three shareholders of Astro Computer Corp.: Coase, who owns 48 percent of the stock; De Valle, who owns 48 percent; and Cary, who owns 4 percent. Cary contracts to sell his 4 percent to De Valle but later refuses to transfer the shares to him.

12–4. Measure of Damages. Johnson contracted to lease a house to Fox for $700 a month, beginning October 1. Fox stipulated in the contract that before he moved in, the interior of the house had to be completely repainted. On September 9, Johnson hired Keever to do the required painting for $1,000. He told Keever that the painting had to be finished by October 1 but did not explain why. On September 28, Keever quit for no reason, having completed approximately 80 percent of the work. Johnson then paid Sam $300 to finish the painting, but Sam did not finish until October 4. Fox, when the painting had not been completed as stipulated in his contract with Johnson, leased another home. Johnson found another tenant who would lease the property at $700 a month, beginning October 15. Johnson then sued Keever for breach of contract, claiming damages of $650. This amount included the $300 Johnson paid Sam to finish the painting and $350 for rent for the first half of October, which Johnson had lost as a result of Keever's breach. Johnson had not yet paid Keever anything for Keever's work. Can Johnson collect the $650 from Keever? Explain.

12–5. Measure of Damages. Ben owns and operates a famous candy store. He makes most of the candy sold in the store, and business is particularly heavy during the Christmas season. Ben contracts with Sweet, Inc., to purchase ten thousand pounds of sugar, to be delivered on or before November 15. Ben informs Sweet that this particular order is to be used for the Christmas season business. Because of production problems, the sugar is not tendered to Ben until December 10, at which time Ben refuses the order because it is so late. Ben has been unable to purchase the quantity of sugar needed to meet the Christmas orders and has had to turn down numerous regular customers, some of whom have indicated that they will purchase candy elsewhere in the future. The sugar that Ben has been able to purchase has cost him ten cents per pound above Sweet's price. Ben sues Sweet for breach of contract, claiming as damages the higher price paid for the sugar from others, lost profits from this year's lost Christmas sales, future lost profits from customers who have indicated that they will discontinue doing business with him, and punitive damages for failure to meet the contracted-for delivery date. Sweet claims Ben is limited to compensatory damages only. Discuss who is correct, and why.

12–6. Oral Contract. Robert Pinto, doing business as Pinto Associates, hired Richard MacDonald as an independent contractor in March 1992. The parties orally agreed on the terms of employment, including payment to MacDonald of a share of the company's income, but they did not put anything in writing. In March 1995, MacDonald quit. Pinto then told MacDonald that he was entitled to $9,602.17—25 percent of the difference between the accounts receivable and the accounts payable as of MacDonald's last day. MacDonald disagreed and demanded more than $83,500—25 percent of the revenue from all invoices, less the cost of materials and outside processing, for each of the years that he worked for Pinto. Pinto refused. MacDonald filed a suit in a Connecticut state court against Pinto, alleging breach of contract. In Pinto's response and at the trial, he testified that the parties had an oral contract under which MacDonald was entitled to 25 percent of the difference between accounts receivable and payable as of the date of MacDonald's termination. Did the parties have an enforceable contract? How should the court rule, and why? [*MacDonald v. Pinto,* 62 Conn.App. 317, 771 A.2d 156 (2001)]

Case Problem with Sample Answer

12–7. Mitigation of Damages. Ms. Vuylsteke, a single mother with three children, lived in Portland, Oregon. Cynthia Broan also lived in Oregon until she moved to New York City to open and operate an art gallery. Broan contacted Vuylsteke to manage the gallery under a one-year contract for an annual salary of $72,000. To begin work, Vuylsteke relocated to New York. As part of the move, Vuylsteke transferred custody of her children to her former husband, who lived in London, England. In accepting the job, Vuylsteke also forfeited her husband's alimony and child-support payments, including unpaid amounts of nearly $30,000. Before Vuylsteke started work, Broan repudiated the contract. Unable to find employment for more than an annual salary of $25,000, Vuylsteke moved to London to be near her children. Vuylsteke filed a suit in an Oregon state court against Broan, seeking damages for breach of contract. Should the court hold, as Broan argued, that Vuylsteke did not take reasonable steps to mitigate her damages? Why or why not? [*Vuylsteke v. Broan,* 172 Or.App. 74, 17 P.3d 1072 (2001)]

To view a sample answer for this case problem, go to this book's Web site at http://leet.westbuslaw.com **and click on "Interactive Study Center."**

12–8. Interests in Land. Sierra Bravo, Inc., and Shelby's, Inc., entered into a written "Waste Disposal Agreement"

under which Shelby's allowed Sierra to deposit on Shelby's land waste products, deleterious (harmful) materials, and debris removed by Sierra in the construction of a highway. Later, Shelby's asked Sierra why it had not constructed a waterway and a building pad suitable for a commercial building on the property, as they had orally agreed. Sierra denied any such agreement. Shelby's filed a suit in a Missouri state court against Sierra, alleging breach of contract. Sierra contended that any oral agreement was unenforceable under the Statute of Frauds. Sierra argued that because the right to *remove* minerals from land is considered a contract for the sale of an interest in land to which the Statute of Frauds applies, the Statute of Frauds should apply to the right to *deposit* soil on another person's property. How should the court rule, and why? [*Shelby's, Inc. v. Sierra Bravo, Inc.,* 68 S.W.3d 604 (Mo.App.S.D. 2002)]

12–9. Substantial Performance. Adolf and Ida Krueger contracted with Pisani Construction, Inc., to erect a metal building as an addition to an existing structure. The two structures were to share a common wall, and the frames and panel heights of the new building were to match those of the existing structure. Shortly before completion of the project, however, it was apparent that the roof line of the new building was approximately three inches higher than that of the existing structure. Pisani modified the ridge caps of the buildings to blend the roof lines. The discrepancy had other consequences, however, including misalignment of the gutters and windows of the two buildings, which resulted in an icing problem in the winter. The Kruegers occupied the new structure but refused to make the last payment under the contract. Pisani filed a suit in a Connecticut state court to collect its fee. Did Pisani substantially perform its obligations? Should the Kruegers be ordered to pay? Why or why not? [*Pisani Construction, Inc. v. Krueger,* 68 Conn.App. 361, 791 A.2d 634 (2002)]

12–10. Mitigation of Damages. William West, an engineer, worked for Bechtel Corp., an organization of about 150 engineering and construction companies, which is headquartered in San Francisco, California, and operates worldwide. Except for a two-month period in 1985, Bechtel employed West on long-term assignments or short-term projects for thirty years. In October 1997, West was offered a position on a project with Saudi Arabian Bechtel Co. (SABCO), which West understood would be for two years. In November, however, West was terminated for what he believed was his "age and lack of display of energy." After his return to California, West received numerous offers from Bechtel for work that suited his abilities and met his salary expectations, but he did not accept any of them and did not look for other work. Three months later, he filed a suit in a California state court against Bechtel, alleging in part breach of contract and seeking the salary he would have earned during two years with SABCO. Bechtel responded in part that, even if there had been a breach, West failed to mitigate his damages. Is Bechtel correct? Discuss. [*West v. Bechtel Corp.,* 96 Cal.App.4th 966, 117 Cal.Rptr.2d 647 (1 Dist. 2002)]

A Question of Ethics & Social Responsibility

12–11. Julio Garza was employed by the Texas Animal Health Commission (TAHC) as a health inspector in 1981. His responsibilities included bleeding and tagging cattle, vaccinating and tattooing calves, and working livestock markets. Garza was injured on the job in 1988 and underwent surgery in January 1989. When his paid leave was exhausted, he asked TAHC for light-duty work, specifically the job of tick inspector, but his supervisor refused the request. In September, TAHC notified Garza that he was fired. Garza sued TAHC and others, alleging in part wrongful termination. An important issue before the court was whether Garza had mitigated his damages. The court found that in the seven years between his termination and his trial date, Garza had held only one job—an unpaid job on his parents' ranch. When asked how often he had looked for work during that time, Garza responded that he did not know but that he had looked in "several" places. He had last looked for work three or four months before the trial. That effort was merely an informal inquiry about working on his neighbors' ranch. In view of these facts, consider the following questions. [*Texas Animal Health Commission v. Garza,* 27 S.W.3d 54 (Tex.App.—San Antonio 2000)]

1. The court in this case stated that the "general rule as to mitigation of damages in breach of employment suits is that the discharged employee must use reasonable diligence to mitigate damages by seeking other employment." In your opinion, did Garza fulfill this requirement? If you were the judge, how would you rule in this case?

2. Assume for the moment that Garza was indeed wrongfully terminated. In this situation, would it be fair to Garza to require him to mitigate his damages? Why or why not?

3. Generally, what are the ethical underpinnings of the rule that employees seeking damages for breach of employment contracts must mitigate their damages?

Critical-Thinking Managerial Question

12–12. On Thursday, June 1, you form an oral contract with Jake, who agrees to work for you for one year, beginning on the following Monday, June 5. After Jake has worked for you for three months, you decide that you made a mistake by hiring him and would like to fire him. You tell Jake that you are letting him go, and he reminds you of your oral employment contract. Is your contract with Jake enforceable? Why or why not?

Video Question

12–13. Go to this text's Web site at http://leet.westbuslaw.com and select "Video Questions." Click on "Chapter 12" and view the video titled *Breach and Remedies.* Then answer the following questions.

1. In the video, a carpenter is in the process of constructing shelves to display soda in a grocery store for a sale the next day. The carpenter says that he has an emergency and must quit working on the project and leave. According to the chapter, what is the standard measure of damages for breaching this type of contract?

2. Can Oscar recover consequential damages for the carpenter's breach? Why or why not?

3. If Oscar did not attempt to find anyone else to complete the carpenter's work, would this affect the amount of damages to which Oscar is entitled? Why or why not?

4. List and describe any equitable remedies discussed in the chapter that would be available to Oscar in this scenario.

INTERACTING WITH THE INTERNET

For updated links to resources available on the Web, as well as a variety of other materials, visit this text's Web site at

http://leet.westbuslaw.com

For a discussion of fraudulent misrepresentation, go to the Web site of attorney Owen Katz at

http://www.katzlawoffice.com/misrep.html

For a collection of leading cases involving topics covered in this chapter, go to

http://www.lectlaw.com/files/lws49.htm

The online version of UCC Section 2–201 on the Statute of Frauds includes links to definitions of certain terms used in the section. To access this site, go to

http://www.law.cornell.edu/ucc/2/2-201.html

To read a summary of a case concerning whether the exchange of e-mails satisfied the writing requirements of the Statute of Frauds, go to

http://www.phillipsnizer.com/library/topics/statute_frauds.cfm

The following site offers information on contract law, including breach of contract and remedies:

http://www.law.cornell.edu/topics/contracts.html

ONLINE LEGAL RESEARCH EXERCISES

Go to **http://leet.westbuslaw.com**, the Web site that accompanies this text. Select "Interactive Study Center," and then click on "Chapter 12." There you will find the following Internet research exercises that you can perform to learn more about topics covered in this chapter.

Activity 12–1: HISTORICAL PERSPECTIVE—The English Act for the Prevention of Frauds and Perjuries

Activity 12–2: ECONOMIC PERSPECTIVE—Anticipatory Repudiation

Activity 12–3: MANAGEMENT PERSPECTIVE—Commercial Impracticability

BEFORE THE TEST

Go to **http://leet.westbuslaw.com**, the Web site that accompanies this text. Select "Interactive Quizzes." You will find at least twenty interactive questions relating to this chapter.

Westlaw® Campus

If your textbook provided for a subscription to Westlaw® Campus, or if you have otherwise purchased access to the Westlaw Campus database, you can access any of the cases presented or cited in this chapter by using your Westlaw Campus account.

CHAPTER **13**

E-Contracts

CONTENTS

E-CONTRACT
A contract that is formed
electronically.

CHAPTER OBJECTIVES

*After reading this chapter, you should be able to answer the
following questions:*

1. What are some important clauses to include when making
offers to form electronic contracts, or e-contracts?

2. What are shrink-wrap agreements and click-on agreements?
How have traditional laws been applied to such agreements?
What problems arise in the application of traditional laws to
these agreements?

3. How are electronic signatures used? Are electronic signatures
valid?

4. What is a partnering agreement? What purpose does it serve?

5. What is the Uniform Electronic Transactions Act (UETA)?
What are some of the major provisions of this act?

The basic principles of contract law that were covered in the previous chapters evolved over a long period of time. Certainly, they were formed long before cyberspace and electronic contracting became realities. Therefore, new legal theories, new adaptations of existing laws, and new laws are needed to govern e-contracts, or contracts entered into electronically. To date, however, most courts have adapted traditional contract law principles and, when applicable, provisions of the Uniform Commercial Code (UCC) to cases involving e-contract disputes.

**"The law of toasters,
televisions, and chain saws is
not appropriate for contracts
involving online databases,
artificial intelligence systems,
software, multimedia, and
Internet trade in information."**
Prefatory Note, Uniform Computer
Information Transactions Act

In the first part of this chapter, we look at how traditional laws are being applied to contracts formed online. We then examine some new laws that have been created to apply in situations in which traditional laws governing contracts have sometimes been thought inadequate. For example, traditional laws governing signature and writing requirements are not easily adapted to contracts formed in the online environment. Thus, new laws have been created to address these issues. As the chapter-opening quotation on the previous page indicated, in some ways the law of "toasters, televisions, and chain saws" is simply no longer appropriate to the commercial practices and needs of today.

Additionally, in 2003 the National Conference of Commissioners on Uniform State Laws and the American Legal Institute adopted amendments to the UCC articles that cover the sale and lease of goods (Articles 2 and 2A). Among other things, these amendments updated the UCC to accommodate electronic commerce. We have included Article 2 of the UCC, as well as excerpts from the 2003 amendments to Article 2, in Appendix D.

FORMING CONTRACTS ONLINE

Today, numerous contracts are being formed online. Although the medium through which these sales contracts are generated has changed, the age-old problems attending contract formation have not. Disputes concerning contracts formed online continue to center around contract terms and whether the parties voluntarily assented to those terms.

Note that online contracts may be formed not only for the sale of goods and services but also for the purpose of *licensing*. For example, the "sale" of software generally involves a license, or a right to use the software, rather than the passage of title (ownership rights) from the seller to the buyer. As you read through the following pages, keep in mind that although we typically refer to the offeror and offeree as a *seller* and a *buyer*, in many transactions these parties would be more accurately described as a *licensor* and a *licensee*.

Online Offers

Sellers doing business via the Internet can protect themselves against contract disputes and legal liability by creating offers that clearly spell out the terms that will govern their transactions if the offers are accepted. All important terms should be conspicuous and easily viewed by potential buyers.

An important rule for an offeror to keep in mind is that he or she controls the offer and thus the resulting contract. The seller should therefore anticipate the terms he or she wants to include in a contract and provide for them in the offer. In some instances, a standardized contract form may suffice. At a minimum, the following provisions should be included in an online offer:

- A provision specifying the remedies available to the buyer if the goods turn out to be defective or if the contract is otherwise breached, or broken. Any limitation of remedies should be clearly spelled out.

- A clause that clearly indicates what constitutes the buyer's agreement to the terms of the offer.

- A provision specifying how payment for the goods and of any applicable taxes must be made.

- A statement of the seller's refund and return policies.

- Disclaimers of liability for certain uses of the goods. For example, an online seller of business forms may add a disclaimer that the seller does not accept responsibility for the buyer's reliance on the forms rather than on an attorney's advice.

- How the information gathered about the buyer will be used by the seller.

Dispute-Settlement Provisions   In addition to the above provisions, many online offers include provisions relating to dispute settlement. For example, an arbitration clause might be included, specifying that any dispute arising under the contract will be arbitrated in a specified forum.

Many online contracts also contain a forum-selection clause (indicating the forum, or location, for the resolution of any dispute arising under the contract). As discussed in Chapter 4, significant jurisdictional issues may occur when parties are at a great distance, as they often are when they form contracts via the Internet. A forum-selection clause will help to avert future jurisdictional problems and also help to ensure that the seller will not be required to appear in court in a distant state.

Displaying the Offer   The seller's Web site should include a hypertext link to a page containing the full contract so that potential buyers are made aware of the terms to which they are assenting. The contract generally must be displayed online in a readable format such as a twelve-point typeface. All provisions should be reasonably clear. ● EXAMPLE 1 If a seller is offering certain goods priced according to a complex price schedule, that schedule must be fully provided and explained.●

Indicating How the Offer Can Be Accepted   An online offer should also include some mechanism by which the customer can accept the offer. Typically, online sellers include boxes containing the words "I agree" or "I accept the terms of the offer" that offerees can click on to indicate acceptance. The agreement resulting from such an acceptance is often called a **click-on agreement**.

Online Acceptances

In many ways, click-on agreements are the Internet equivalents of *shrink-wrap agreements* (or *shrink-wrap licenses,* as they are sometimes called). Because similar legal problems have arisen with respect to both shrink-wrap and click-on agreements, we look first at how the law has been applied to shrink-wrap agreements.

A **shrink-wrap agreement** is an agreement whose terms are expressed inside the box in which the goods are packaged. (The term *shrink-wrap* refers to the plastic that covers the box.) Usually, the party who opens the box is told that she or he agrees to the terms by keeping whatever is in the box. Similarly, when the purchaser opens a software package, he or she agrees to abide by the terms of the limited license agreement. ● EXAMPLE 2 John orders a new computer from a national company, which ships the computer to John. Along with the computer, the box contains an agreement setting forth the terms of the sale, including what remedies are available. The document also states that John's retention of the computer for longer than thirty days will be construed as an acceptance of the terms.●

CLICK-ON AGREEMENT
An agreement that arises when a buyer, engaging in a transaction on a computer, indicates his or her assent to be bound by the terms of an offer by clicking on a button that says, for example, "I agree"; sometimes referred to as a *click-on license* or a *click-wrap agreement.*

SHRINK-WRAP AGREEMENT
An agreement whose terms are expressed in a document located inside a box in which goods (usually software) are packaged; sometimes called a *shrink-wrap license.*

INTERNATIONAL PERSPECTIVE

Resolving International Jurisdictional Problems

Given the global nature of e-commerce, jurisdictional problems understandably arise. To address these problems, more than sixty nations, including the United States, have been negotiating an agreement referred to as the Hague Convention on International Jurisdiction and Foreign Judgments in Civil and Commercial Matters. The agreement is intended to create uniform rules governing jurisdiction and enforcement of judgments in cross-border disputes.

The proposed agreement would make more predictable the rules governing jurisdiction in disputes between parties located in different countries. Among other things, nations that are signatory to the convention would be required to recognize judgments rendered in the courts of other countries that had signed the agreement. Special rules would apply to disputes involving consumers.

FOR CRITICAL ANALYSIS

What might result if, because the United States is a signatory to the Hague Convention, U.S. courts are required to enforce foreign judgments that are contrary to U.S. constitutional law?

In most cases, a shrink-wrap agreement is not between a retailer and a buyer but between the manufacturer of the hardware or software and the ultimate buyer-user of the product. The terms generally concern warranties, remedies, and other issues associated with the use of the product.

Shrink-Wrap Agreements—Enforceable Contract Terms Section 2–204 of the Uniform Commercial Code (UCC), the law governing sales contracts, provides that any contract for the sale of goods "may be made in any manner sufficient to show agreement, including conduct by both parties which recognizes the existence of a contract." Thus, a buyer's failure to object to terms contained within a shrink-wrapped software package (or an online offer) may constitute an acceptance of the terms by conduct.[1]

In many cases, the courts have enforced the terms of shrink-wrap agreements in the same way as they have enforced the terms of other contracts. Some courts have reasoned that by including the terms with the product, the seller proposed a contract that the buyer could accept by using the product after having an opportunity to read the terms. Also, it seems practical from a business's point of view to enclose a full statement of the legal terms of a sale with the product rather than to read the statement over the phone, for example, when a buyer calls in an order for the product.

Even when a shrink-wrap agreement would be enforceable in principle, a court may refuse to enforce certain terms for any of the reasons that would render the terms of other contracts unenforceable. The following case illustrates this point.

---

1. For a leading case on this issue, see *ProCD, Inc. v. Zeidenberg,* 86 F.3d 1447 (7th Cir. 1996).

CASE 13.1　People v. Network Associates, Inc.

New York Supreme Court, 2003.
195 Misc.2d 384,
758 N.Y.S.2d 466.

COMPANY PROFILE *Network Associates, Inc. (**http://www.nai.com**), develops and sells software. The company focuses on computer network reliability, security, and speed for businesses, consumers, Internet service providers, and others. Its products include McAfee Security, Sniffer Technologies, and Magic Solutions. Founded in 1989, Network Associates is today based in Santa Clara, California, with offices in thirty-eight countries.*

BACKGROUND AND FACTS Network Associates markets Gauntlet, a software firewall product, over the Internet and at retail locations. Network Associates included on the face of many of its disks, and on its download page on the Internet, a restrictive clause that provided:

Installing this software constitutes acceptance of the terms and conditions of the license agreement in the box. Please read the license agreement before installation. Other rules and regulations of installing the software are: * * * The customer shall not disclose the result of any benchmark test to any third party without Network Associates' prior written approval. * * * The customer will not publish reviews of this product without prior consent from Network Associates.

In July 1999, *Network World Fusion,* an online magazine, published a comparative review of firewall software products, including Network Associates's Gauntlet, without the maker's permission. Network Associates protested. Eliot Spitzer, the attorney general of the state of New York, filed a suit in a New York state court on behalf of "The People of the State of New York" against Network Associates, alleging, among other things, that the restrictive clause constituted fraud.

IN THE WORDS OF THE COURT . . .

MARILYN SHAFER, J. [Judge]
　　* * * *
　　Petitioner argues that the use of words "rules and regulations" in the Restrictive Clause is designed to mislead consumers by leading them to believe that some rules and regulations outside exist under state or federal law prohibiting consumers from publishing reviews and the results of benchmark tests. Petitioner also maintains that the language is deceptive because it may mislead consumers to believe that such clause is enforceable under the lease agreement, when in fact it is not enforceable under the terms of the lease. Petitioner argues that as a result consumers may be deceived into abandoning their right to publish reviews and results of benchmark tests.
　　* * * *
　　* * * *The standard to be used to determine whether a representation is false and deceptive is not whether the actual practice is deceptive, but whether it has the capacity to deceive consumers. * * ** [Emphasis added.]
　　* * * The language of the Restrictive Clause specifically directs consumers to read the license agreement. Because the license agreement * * * states that all of the rights and duties of the parties are contained within that agreement, and does not contain any of the restrictions on publishing reviews and result of benchmark testing, consumers may conclude that those restrictions are not contractual restrictions. Therefore, following respondent's instructions, after reading the license agreement and the Restrictive Clause, consumers may reasonably interpret that the rules and regulations enumerated in the Restrictive Clause exist independent of the license contract and are made and enforced by an entity other than the corporation itself. This language implies that limitations on the publication of reviews do not reflect the

CASE 13.1—Continued

policy of Network Associates, but result from some binding law or other rules and regulations imposed by an entity other than Network Associates. Thus, the Attorney General has made a showing that the language at issue may be deceptive, and as such, the language is not merely unenforceable, but warrants an injunction and the imposition of civil sanctions.

DECISION AND REMEDY The court ordered Network Associates to stop including the restrictive clause on its software. The court also directed the defendant to reveal "the number of instances in which software was sold on discs or through the Internet containing the above-mentioned language in order for the court to determine what, if any, penalties and costs should be ordered."

FOR CRITICAL ANALYSIS—Technological Consideration *Is there an important difference between reading a disputed clause as part of a shrink-wrap agreement and accessing it through a link as part of a click-on agreement?*

Shrink-Wrap Agreements—Proposals for Additional Terms The terms included in shrink-wrap agreements have not always been enforced. One important consideration is whether the parties form their contract before or after the seller communicates the terms of the shrink-wrap agreement to the buyer. If a court finds that the buyer learned of the shrink-wrap terms *after* the parties entered into a contract, the court may conclude that those terms were proposals for additional terms and were not part of the contract unless the buyer expressly agreed to them. This is particularly true when the buyer is a nonmerchant.

Click-On Agreements As described earlier, a click-on agreement arises when a buyer, completing a transaction on a computer, indicates his or her assent to be bound by the terms of an offer by clicking on a button that says, for example, "I agree." The terms may be contained on a Web site through which the buyer is obtaining goods or services, or they may appear on a computer screen when software is loaded. Exhibit 13–1 on the following page shows the language of a click-on agreement that accompanies a package of software made and marketed by Adobe Systems, Inc.

As noted, Article 2 of the UCC provides that acceptance can be made by conduct. The *Restatement (Second) of Contracts,* a compilation of common law contract principles, has a similar provision. It states that parties may agree to a contract "by written or spoken words or by other action or by failure to act."[2] The courts have used these provisions to conclude that a binding contract can be created by conduct, including conduct accepting the terms of a click-on agreement.

---

2. *Restatement (Second) of Contracts,* Section 19.

EXHIBIT 13-1   A CLICK-ON AGREEMENT

This exhibit illustrates an online offer to form a contract. To accept the offer, the user simply scrolls down the page and clicks on the "Accept" box.

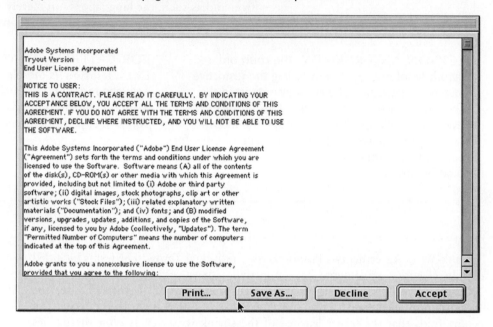

Generally, under the law governing contracts, including sales and lease contracts under the UCC, there is no requirement that all of the terms in a contract must actually have been read by all of the parties to be effective. For example, clicking on a button or box that states "I agree" to certain terms can be enough.

In the following case, the court considered the enforceability of a click-on (click-wrap) agreement under Article 2 of the UCC.

CASE 13.2   i.LAN Systems, Inc. v. NetScout Service Level Corp.

United States District Court,
District of Massachusetts, 2002.
183 F.Supp.2d 328.

COMPANY PROFILE *i.LAN Systems, Inc.*
(**http://www.ilan.com**), *helps companies monitor their computer networks. Based in Los Angeles, California, with a staff that includes approximately forty technicians, i.LAN can troubleshoot network problems almost anywhere in the world. Over the Internet, many problems can be solved remotely using the software tools already built into a network. These tools include software designed and sold by NetScout*

Service Level Corporation, formerly known as NextPoint Networks, Inc.

BACKGROUND AND FACTS A click-wrap provision in the NextPoint software states that the seller's liability is limited to the price paid for the software unless a different term is "specifically accepted by NextPoint in writing." In 1998, i.LAN and NextPoint signed an agreement under which i.LAN agreed to resell the software. In 1999, under a different purchase order, i.LAN bought what it thought was the unlimited right to rent, rather than sell, the software, complete with perpetual upgrades and technical support. When NextPoint dis-

CASE 13.2—Continued

puted this interpretation, i.LAN filed a suit in a federal district court, alleging, among other things, breach of contract. i.LAN sought specific performance (a remedy in which a court orders the breaching party to perform as specified in the contract—see Chapter 12) that included unlimited upgrades and support. The defendant argued that even if the allegation were true, the click-wrap provision limited its liability to the price paid for the software. Both parties filed motions for summary judgment.

IN THE WORDS OF THE COURT . . .

YOUNG, Chief Judge.

Has this happened to you? You plunk down a pretty penny for the latest and greatest software, speed back to your computer, tear open the box, shove the CD-ROM into the computer, click on "install" and, after scrolling past a license agreement which would take at least fifteen minutes to read, find yourself staring at the following dialog box: "I agree." Do you click on the box? You probably do not agree in your heart of hearts, but you click anyway, not about to let some pesky legalese delay the moment for which you've been waiting. *   *   *

*   *   *   *

*   *   * i.LAN's breach of contract claim, if proven, could result in astronomical damages. Recognizing that sellers might want to reduce their exposure to such astronomical damages, the UCC permits *   *   * limitations of liability. NextPoint properly has tried to avail itself of these provisions of the UCC *   *   * . The key question, then, is whether the clickwrap license agreement is enforceable.

*   *   *   *

*   *   * [P]ursuant to UCC 2–204, the analysis is simple: i.LAN manifested assent to the clickwrap license agreement when it clicked on the box stating "I agree," so the agreement is enforceable.[a]

*   *   *   *

*   *   * "[M]oney now, terms later" forms a contract *   *   * when the purchaser receives the box of software, sees the license agreement, and does not return the software. *   *   *

*   *   * "Money now, terms later" is a practical way to form contracts, especially with purchasers of software. If [it is] correct to enforce a shrinkwrap license agreement, where any assent is implicit, then it must also be correct to enforce a clickwrap license agreement, where the assent is explicit. To be sure, *shrinkwrap and clickwrap license agreements share the defect of any standardized contract—they are susceptible to the inclusion of terms that border on the unconscionable—but that is not the issue in this case.* The only issue before the Court is whether clickwrap license agreements are an appropriate way to form contracts, and the Court holds they are. In short, i.LAN explicitly accepted the clickwrap license agreement when it clicked on the box stating "I agree." [Emphasis added.]

DECISION AND REMEDY The court denied the plaintiff's motion for summary judgment and issued a summary judgment in the defendant's favor. The court reasoned that the plaintiff agreed to the click-wrap terms when it clicked on the "I agree" box. Those terms effectively limited the defendant's liability.

FOR CRITICAL ANALYSIS—Social Consideration *If NextPoint's click-wrap provision had permitted specific performance, and the court had entered a judgment in favor of i.LAN, would specific performance have been an appropriate remedy?*

a. Under UCC 2–204, a contract "may be made in any manner sufficient to show agreement, including conduct by both parties which recognizes the existence of such a contract."

Browse-Wrap Terms Like the terms of a click-on agreement, "browse-wrap" terms can occur in a transaction conducted over the Internet. Unlike a click-on agreement, however, **browse-wrap terms** do not require an Internet user to assent to the terms before, say, downloading or using certain software. In other words, a person can install the software without clicking "I agree" to the terms of a license. Offerors of browse-wrap terms generally assert that the terms are binding without the users' active consent.

Critics contend that browse-wrap terms are not enforceable because they do not satisfy the basic elements of contract formation. It has been suggested that to form a valid contract online, a user must at least be presented with the terms before indicating assent.[3] In the case of a browse-wrap term, this would require that a user navigate past it and agree to it before being able to obtain whatever is being granted to the user.

The following case involved the enforceability of a clause in an agreement that the court characterized as a browse-wrap license.

BROWSE-WRAP TERMS
Terms and conditions of use that are presented to an Internet user at the time certain products, such as software, are being downloaded but to which the user need not agree (by clicking "I agree," for example) before being able to install or use the product.

---

3. American Bar Association Committee on the Law of Cyberspace, "Click-Through Agreements: Strategies for Avoiding Disputes on the Validity of Assent" (document presented at the annual American Bar Association meeting in August 2001).

CASE 13.3 Specht v. Netscape Communications Corp.

United States District Court,
Southern District of New York, 2001.
150 F.Supp.2d 585.

BACKGROUND AND FACTS

Netscape Communications Corporation's SmartDownload software makes it easier for users to download files from the Internet without losing progress if they pause to do some other task or their Internet connection is interrupted. Netscape offers SmartDownload free of charge on its Web site to those who indicate, by clicking the mouse in a designated box, that they wish to obtain it. John Gibson clicked in the box and downloaded the software. On the Web site's download page is a reference to a license agreement that is visible only by scrolling to the next screen. Affirmatively indicating assent to the agreement is not required to download the software. The agreement provides that any disputes arising from use of the software are to be submitted to arbitration in California. Believing that SmartDownload transmits private information about its users, Gibson and others filed a suit in a federal district court in New York against Netscape, alleging violations of federal law. Netscape asked the court to order the parties to arbitration in California, according to the license agreement.

IN THE WORDS OF THE COURT . . .

HELLERSTEIN, District Judge.

* * * *

By its terms, Article 2 of the Uniform Commercial Code "applies to transactions in goods." The parties' relationship essentially is that of a seller and a purchaser of goods. Although in this case the product was provided free of charge, the roles are essentially the same as when an individual uses the Internet to purchase software from a company: here, the Plaintiff requested Defendant's product by clicking on an icon marked "Download," and Defendant then tendered the product. Therefore, in determining whether the parties entered into a contract, I look to * * * the Uniform Commercial Code * * *.

* * * *

CASE 13.3—Continued

Unless the Plaintiffs agreed to the License Agreement, they cannot be bound by the arbitration clause *   *   * .

  *   *   *   *

Netscape argues that the mere act of downloading indicates assent. However, *downloading is hardly an unambiguous indication of assent.* The primary purpose of downloading is to obtain a product, not to assent to an agreement. *   *   * Netscape's failure to require users of SmartDownload to indicate assent to its license as a precondition to downloading and using its software is fatal to its argument that a contract has been formed. [Emphasis added.]

Furthermore, *   *   * the individual obtaining SmartDownload is not made aware that he is entering into a contract. SmartDownload is available from Netscape's web site free of charge. Before downloading the software, the user need not view any license agreement terms or even any reference to a license agreement, and need not do anything to manifest assent *   *   * . From the user's vantage point, SmartDownload could be analogized to a free neighborhood newspaper, readily obtained from a sidewalk box or supermarket counter without any exchange with a seller or vender. It is there for the taking.

  *   *   *   *

The case law on software licensing has not eroded the importance of assent in contract formation. *Mutual assent is the bedrock of any agreement to which the law will give force.* Defendants' position, if accepted, would so expand the definition of assent as to render it meaningless. Because the user Plaintiffs did not assent to the license agreement, they are not subject to the arbitration clause *   *   * . [Emphasis added.]

DECISION AND REMEDY The court denied the motion to compel arbitration because the plaintiffs had not assented to the license agreement.

FOR CRITICAL ANALYSIS—Social Consideration *What might be the result in other cases if the court in this case had held that the browse-wrap term was enforceable?*

E-SIGNATURES

In many instances, a contract cannot be enforced unless it is signed by the party against whom enforcement is sought. A significant issue in the context of e-commerce has to do with how electronic signatures, or **e-signatures,** can be created and verified on e-contracts.

In the days when many people could not write, they signed documents with an "X." Then handwritten signatures became common, followed by typed signatures, printed signatures, and, most recently, digital signatures that are transmitted electronically. Throughout the evolution of signature technology, the question of what constitutes a valid signature has arisen again and again, and with good reason—without some consensus on what constitutes a valid signature, little business or legal work could be accomplished. (Technology has also raised other questions relating to signature requirements—see, for example, the question discussed in this chapter's *Legal E-nvironment* feature on the next page.)

E-SIGNATURE
Under the Uniform Electronic Transactions Act, a signature can be any electronic sound, symbol, or process attached to electronically stored information. This definition is intentionally broad in order to give legal effect to acts that people intend to be the equivalent of their written signatures.

LEGAL *e*-NVIRONMENT

E-Mailed Prescription Orders and Signature Requirements

"It is in the nature of things that statutes must at times be applied to situations unforeseen at the time of their enactment." So said a Wisconsin appellate court when trying to apply a state law governing physicians' prescriptions to a program initiated by Walgreen Company. The program enabled physicians to transmit prescription orders to Walgreen pharmacies via e-mail.

The state statute defined a "prescription order" as simply "a written or oral order by a [physician] for a drug or device for a particular patient." If the prescription order was written, it had to be signed. If the order was transmitted to the pharmacist orally—by telephone, for example—it did not, of course, require a signature. The statute, however, said nothing about prescription orders transmitted electronically via e-mail, and therein lay the problem: If e-mailed prescription orders were considered to be in writing, they violated the statutory requirement for written prescriptions because they were not signed. If such prescriptions were deemed to be oral transmissions, there was no violation.

The Pharmacy Board's Position on the Issue

The Wisconsin Pharmacy Examining Board had little trouble concluding that an e-mailed prescription order was analogous to a writing and that Walgreen's program violated the law. The board voiced a number of concerns to the court. One was that if e-mailed prescription orders were permitted, there would be less control over drugs. While pharmacists can recognize a caller's voice over the telephone and thus verify the caller's identity, a computerized communication is more anonymous, creating a danger that the prescription information "will fall into the wrong hands." The board argued that these security considerations should take priority and that the court should bar the use of e-mailed prescription orders.

The Court's Conclusion

The court was not convinced that it should defer to such security concerns. The court concluded that a computer-transmitted prescription was not analogous to a written prescription. Rather, it was more akin to an order transmitted orally by telephone. This, to the court, seemed to be "a more reasonable interpretation than the board's in light of the simple facts of computer transmission: The prescription is put into a computer as text and the message is then electronically transmitted to the pharmacy's terminal, much as a telephone call—or a facsimile—would be." Thus, concluded the court, the use of e-mailed prescription orders did not violate the statute.

The court justified its rather novel conclusion by perhaps equally novel reasoning. The court stated that when a statute must be applied to a situation unforeseen by its drafters, the court must try to determine the "manifest intent" of those lawmakers. The court must examine the "pictures actually drawn by the statutory text" and see if they are "sufficient to cover the new type of situation that the course of events has produced." If the legislature has supplied "sufficient specifications to provide a discernible frame of reference within which the situation now presented quite clearly fits, even though it represents in some degree a new condition of affairs unknown to the lawmakers," the statute may be interpreted accordingly.[a]

FOR CRITICAL ANALYSIS

Suppose that two parties form a contract through the exchange of e-mailed messages. Would this court classify the contract as an oral contract?

a. *Walgreen Co. v. Wisconsin Pharmacy Examining Board,* 217 Wis.2d 290, 577 N.W.2d 387 (Wis.App. 1998).

E-Signature Technologies

Today, numerous technologies allow electronic documents to be signed. These include digital signatures and alternative technologies.

Digital Signatures The most prevalent e-signature technology is the *asymmetric cryptosystem,* which creates a digital signature using two different (asymmetric) cryptographic "keys." With this system, a person attaches a digital signature to a document using a private key, or code. The key has a publicly available counterpart. Anyone with the appropriate software can use the public key to verify that the digital signature was made using the private key. A **cybernotary,** or legally recognized certification authority, issues the key pair, identifies the owner of the keys, and certifies the validity of the public key. The cybernotary also serves as a repository for public keys. Cybernotaries already are available.

CYBERNOTARY
A legally recognized authority that can certify the validity of digital signatures.

Signature Dynamics With another type of signature technology, known as *signature dynamics,* a sender's signature is captured using a stylus and an electronic digitizer pad. A computer program takes the signature's measurements, the sender's identity, the time and date of the signature, and the identity of the hardware. This information is then placed in an encrypted *biometric token* attached to the document being transmitted. To verify the authenticity of the signature, the recipient of the document compares the measurements of the signature with the measurements in the token. When this type of e-signature is used, it is not necessary to have a third party verify the signatory's identity.

Other E-Signature Forms Other forms of e-signatures have been—or are now being—developed as well. For example, some e-signatures use "smart cards." A smart card is a device the size of a credit card that is embedded with code and other data. Like credit and debit cards, this smart card can be inserted into computers to transfer information. Unlike those other cards, however, a smart card can be used to establish a person's identity as validly as a signature on a piece of paper.

In addition, technological innovations now under development will allow an e-signature to be evidenced by an image of a person's retina, fingerprint, or face that is scanned by a computer and then matched to a numeric code. The scanned image and the numeric code are registered with security companies that maintain files on an accessible server that can be used to authenticate a transaction.

State Laws Governing E-Signatures

Most states have laws governing e-signatures. The problem is that state e-signature laws are not uniform. Some states—California is a notable example—provide that many types of documents cannot be signed with e-signatures, while other states are more permissive. Additionally, states differ in the types of e-signatures that they recognize.

In an attempt to create more uniformity among the states, the National Conference of Commissioners on Uniform State Laws promulgated the Uniform Electronic Transactions Act (UETA) in 1999. To date, the UETA has been adopted, at least in part, by more than forty states. The UETA declares, among other things, that a signature may not be denied legal effect or enforceability solely because it is in electronic form. (The 2003 amendments to UCC Article 2 contain a similar provision.)

Federal Law on E-Signatures and E-Documents

In 2000, Congress enacted the Electronic Signatures in Global and National Commerce Act (E-SIGN Act) to provide that no contract, record, or signature may be "denied legal effect" solely because it is in electronic form. In other words, under this law, an electronic signature is as valid as a signature on paper, and an electronic document can be as enforceable as a paper one.

For an electronic signature to be enforceable, the contracting parties must have agreed to use electronic signatures. For an electronic document to be valid, it must be in a form that can be retained and accurately reproduced.

The E-SIGN Act does not apply to all types of documents, however. Contracts and documents that are exempt include court papers, divorce decrees, evictions, foreclosures, health-insurance terminations, prenuptial agreements, and wills. The only agreements governed by the Uniform Commercial Code (UCC) that fall under this law are those covered by Articles 2 and 2A and UCC 1–107 and 1–206.

Despite these limitations, the E-SIGN Act enormously expands the possibilities for contracting online. ● EXAMPLE 3 From a remote location, a businessperson can now open an account with a financial institution, obtain a mortgage or other loan, buy insurance, and purchase real estate over the Internet. Payments and transfers of funds can be done entirely online. Using e-contracts can eliminate the time and costs associated with producing, delivering, signing, and returning paper documents.●

PARTNERING AGREEMENTS

PARTNERING AGREEMENT
An agreement between a seller and a buyer who frequently do business with each other on the terms and conditions that will apply to all subsequently formed electronic contracts.

One way that online sellers and buyers can prevent disputes over signatures in their e-contracts, as well as over the terms and conditions of those contracts, is to form partnering agreements. In a **partnering agreement,** a seller and a buyer who frequently do business with each other agree in advance on the terms and conditions that will apply to all transactions subsequently conducted electronically. The partnering agreement can also establish special access and identification codes to be used by the parties when transacting business electronically.

A partnering agreement reduces the likelihood that disputes will arise under the contract because the buyer and the seller have agreed in advance to the terms and conditions that will accompany each sale. Furthermore, if a dispute does arise, a court or arbitration forum will be able to refer to the partnering agreement when determining the parties' intent with respect to subsequent contracts. Of course, even with a partnering agreement fraud remains a possibility. If an unauthorized person uses a purchaser's designated access number and identification code, it may be some time before the problem is discovered.

THE UNIFORM ELECTRONIC TRANSACTIONS ACT

As noted earlier, the National Conference of Commissioners on Uniform State Laws and the American Law Institute promulgated the Uniform Electronic Transactions Act (UETA) in 1999. The UETA represents one of the first comprehensive efforts to create uniformity and introduce certainty in state laws pertaining to e-commerce.

The primary purpose of the UETA is to remove barriers to e-commerce by giving the same legal effect to electronic records and signatures as is currently given to paper documents and signatures. The UETA defines an *e-signature* as "an electronic sound, symbol, or process attached to or logically associated with a record and executed or adopted by a person with the intent to sign the record."[4] An e-signature includes encrypted digital signatures, names (intended as signatures) at the ends of e-mail messages, and "clicks" on a Web page if the click includes the identification of the person. A **record** is "information that is inscribed on a tangible medium or that is stored in an electronic or other medium and is retrievable in perceivable [visual] form."[5]

The Scope and Applicability of the UETA

The UETA does not create new rules for electronic contracts but rather establishes that records, signatures, and contracts may not be denied enforceability solely due to their electronic form. The UETA does not apply to all writings and signatures but only to electronic records and electronic signatures *relating to a transaction*. A *transaction* is defined as an interaction between two or more people relating to business, commercial, or governmental activities.[6]

The act specifically does not apply to laws governing wills or testamentary trusts, the UCC (other than Articles 2 and 2A), or the Uniform Computer Information Transactions Act (discussed later in this chapter).[7] In addition, the provisions of the UETA allow the states to exclude its application to other areas of law.

As described earlier, Congress passed the E-SIGN Act in 2000, a year after the UETA was presented to the states for adoption. Thus, a significant issue is whether and to what extent the federal E-SIGN Act preempts the UETA as adopted by the states.

The Federal E-SIGN Act and the UETA

The E-SIGN Act refers explicitly to the UETA and provides that if a state has enacted the uniform version of the UETA, it is not preempted by the E-SIGN Act.[8] In other words, if the state has enacted the UETA without modification, state law will govern. The problem is that many states have enacted nonuniform (modified) versions of the UETA, largely for the purpose of excluding other areas of state law from the UETA's terms. The E-SIGN Act specifies that those exclusions will be preempted to the extent that they are inconsistent with the E-SIGN Act's provisions.

The E-SIGN Act, however, explicitly allows the states to enact alternative procedures or requirements for the use or acceptance of electronic records or electronic signatures, *if* certain conditions are met. Generally, the procedures or requirements must be consistent with the provisions of the E-SIGN Act, and the state must not give greater legal status or effect to one specific type of technology. Additionally, if a state has enacted alternative procedures or requirements

RECORD
According to the Uniform Electronic Transactions Act, information that is either inscribed on a tangible medium or stored in an electronic or other medium and that is retrievable.

---

4. UETA 2(8).
5. UETA 2(13).
6. UETA 2(12) and 3.
7. UETA 3(b).
8. 15 U.S.C. Section 7002(2)(A)(i).

after the E-SIGN Act was adopted, the state law must specifically refer to the E-SIGN Act.

Although the E-SIGN Act clearly contains some preemptive language, it is not yet clear exactly how the courts will interpret these provisions. If a state has enacted a modified version of the UETA, a court may find that only a certain provision of that modified version is preempted, or it may find that the entire modified version of the UETA is invalid. Generally, the relationship between the UETA and the E-SIGN Act remains to be clarified by the courts.

Highlights of the UETA

We look next at selected provisions of the UETA. Our discussion is, of course, based on the act's uniform provisions. Keep in mind that the states that have enacted the UETA may have adopted slightly different versions.

The Parties Must Agree to Conduct Transactions Electronically The UETA will not apply to a transaction unless each of the parties has agreed to conduct transactions by electronic means. The agreement need not be explicit, however, and it may be implied by the conduct of the parties and the surrounding circumstances.[9] In the comments that accompany the UETA, the drafters stated that it may be reasonable to infer that a person who gives out a business card with an e-mail address on it has consented to transact business electronically.[10] The party's agreement may also be inferred from a letter or other writing, as well as from some verbal communication. Nothing in the UETA requires that the agreement to conduct transactions electronically be made electronically.

A person who has previously agreed to an electronic transaction can also withdraw his or her consent and refuse to conduct further business electronically. Additionally, the act expressly gives parties the power to vary the UETA's provisions by contract. In other words, *parties can opt out of all or some of the terms of the UETA.* If the parties do not opt out of the terms of the UETA, however, the UETA will govern their electronic transactions.

Attribution In the context of electronic transactions, the term *attribution* refers to the procedures that may be used to ensure that the person sending an electronic record is the same person whose e-signature accompanies the record. Under the UETA, if an electronic record or signature was the act of a particular person, the record or signature may be attributed to that person. If a person types her or his name at the bottom of an e-mail purchase order, that name would qualify as a "signature" and be attributed to the person whose name appeared. Just as in paper contracts, one may use any relevant evidence to prove that the record or signature is or is not the act of the person.[11]

Note that even if an individual's name does not appear on a record (such as in a voice-mail message), the UETA states that the effect of the record is to be determined from the context and surrounding circumstances. In other words, a record may have legal effect even if no one has signed it. For example, a fax

---

9. UETA 5(b).
10. UETA 5, Comment 4B.
11. UETA 9.

that contains a letterhead identifying the sender may, depending on the circumstances, be attributed to that sender.

The UETA does not contain any express provisions about what constitutes fraud or whether an agent (a person who acts on behalf of another—see Chapter 16) is authorized to enter a contract. Under the UETA, other state laws control if any issues relating to agency, authority, forgery, or contract formation arise.

Notarization If a document is required to be notarized under existing state law, the UETA provides that this requirement is satisfied by the electronic signature of a notary public or other person authorized to verify signatures. For example, if a person intends to accept an offer to purchase real estate via e-mail, the requirement is satisfied if a notary public is present to verify the person's identity and affix an electronic signature to the e-mail acceptance.

The Effect of Errors The UETA encourages, but does not require, the use of security procedures (such as encryption) to verify changes to electronic documents and to correct errors. Section 10 of the UETA provides that if the parties have agreed to a security procedure and one party does not detect an error because he or she did not follow the procedure, the conforming party can legally avoid the effect of the change or error. If the parties have not agreed to use a security procedure, then other state laws (including contract law governing mistakes—see Chapter 12) will determine the effect of the error on the parties' agreement.

To avoid the effect of errors, a party must take certain steps. First, the party must promptly notify the other party of the error and of her or his intent not to be bound by the error. Second, the party must take reasonable steps to return any benefit or consideration received. Parties cannot avoid a transaction from which they have benefited. For example, if as a result of the error a party received access to valuable information for which restitution cannot be made, the transaction may be unavoidable. In all other situations in which a change or error occurs in an electronic record (and the parties' agreement does not specifically address errors), the UETA states that the traditional law governing mistakes will control.

Timing Section 15 of the UETA sets forth provisions relating to the sending and receiving of electronic records. These provisions apply unless the parties agree to different terms. Under Section 15, an electronic record is considered *sent* when it is properly directed to the intended recipient in a form readable by the recipient's computer system. Once the electronic record leaves the control of the sender or comes under the control of the recipient, the UETA deems it to have been sent. An electronic record is considered *received* when it enters the recipient's processing system in a readable form—*even if no individual is aware of its receipt.*

Additionally, the UETA provides that, unless otherwise agreed, an electronic record is to be sent from or received at the party's principal place of business. If a party has no place of business, the provision then authorizes the place of sending or receipt to be the party's residence. If a party has multiple places of business, the record should be sent from or received at the location that has the closest relationship to the underlying transaction.

THE UNIFORM COMPUTER INFORMATION TRANSACTIONS ACT

The National Conference of Commissioners on Uniform State Laws (NCCUSL) promulgated the Uniform Computer Information and Transactions Act (UCITA) in 1999. The primary purpose of the UCITA is to validate e-contracts to license or purchase software, or contracts that give access to—or allow the distribution of—computer information.[12] The UCITA is controversial, and only two states (Maryland and Virginia) have adopted it, while four states (Iowa, North Carolina, Vermont, and West Virginia) have passed anti–UCITA provisions. In 2003, the NCCUSL withdrew its support of UCITA. Although the UCITA remains a legal resource, the NCCUSL will no longer seek its adoption by the states, which are thus unlikely to consider it further.

---

12. *Computer information* is "information in an electronic form obtained from or through use of a computer, or that is in digital or an equivalent form capable of being processed by a computer" [UCITA 102(10)].

KEY TERMS

browse-wrap terms   412
click-on agreement   406
cybernotary   415

e-contract   404
e-signature   413
partnering agreement   416

record   417
shrink-wrap agreement   406

CHAPTER SUMMARY   E-CONTRACTS

Online Offers (See pages 405–406.)	The terms of offers made via the Internet should be just as inclusive as the terms of offers made in written (paper) documents. All possible contingencies should be anticipated and provided for in the offer. Because jurisdictional issues frequently arise with online transactions, it is particularly important to include dispute-settlement provisions, as well as a forum-selection clause. The offer should be displayed in such a way as to be easily readable and clear. An online offer should also include some mechanism, such as an "I agree" or "I accept" box, by which the customer can accept the offer.

Online Acceptances
(See pages 406–413.)
	1. *Shrink-wrap agreement—*
	
	   a. Definition—An agreement whose terms are expressed inside a box in which the goods are packaged. The party who opens the box is informed that by keeping the goods, he or she agrees to the terms of the shrink-wrap agreement.
	
	   b. Enforceability—The courts have often enforced shrink-wrap agreements, even if the purchaser-user of the goods did not read the terms of the agreement. A court may deem a shrink-wrap agreement unenforceable, however, if the buyer learns of the shrink-wrap terms *after* the parties entered into the agreement, particularly when the buyer is a nonmerchant.

CHAPTER SUMMARY E-CONTRACTS—Continued

Online Acceptances— continued	2. *Click-on agreement—* a. Definition—An agreement created when a buyer, completing a transaction on a computer, is required to indicate his or her assent to be bound by the terms of an offer by clicking on a button that says, for example, "I agree." The terms of the agreement may appear on a Web site through which the buyer is obtaining goods or services, or they may appear on a computer screen when software is downloaded. b. Enforceability—The courts have enforced click-on agreements, holding that by clicking "I agree," the offeree has indicated acceptance by conduct. In contrast, browse-wrap terms (terms in a license that an Internet user does not have to read prior to downloading a product, such as software) might not be enforced on the ground that the user is not made aware that he or she is entering into a contract.
E-Signatures (See pages 413–416.)	1. *Definition*—The Uniform Electronic Transactions Act (UETA) defines an e-signature as an electronic sound, symbol, or process attached to or logically associated with a record and executed or adopted by a person with the intent to sign the record. 2. *E-signature technologies*—These include the *asymmetric cryptosystem* (which creates a digital signature using cryptographic keys); *signature dynamics* (which involves capturing a sender's signature using a stylus and an electronic digitizer pad); *smart cards* (devices embedded with code and other data); and, probably in the near future, scanned images of retinas, fingerprints, or other physical characteristics linked to numeric codes. 3. *State laws governing e-signatures*—Although most states have laws governing e-signatures, these laws are not uniform. The UETA provides for the validity of e-signatures and may ultimately create more uniformity among the states in this respect. 4. *Federal law on e-signatures and e-documents*—The Electronic Signatures in Global and National Commerce Act (E-SIGN Act) of 2000 gave validity to e-signatures by providing that no contract, record, or signature may be "denied legal effect" solely because it is in an electronic form.
Partnering Agreements (See page 416.)	To reduce the likelihood that disputes will arise under their e-contracts, parties who frequently do business with each other may form a *partnering agreement*. In effect, the parties agree in advance on the terms and conditions that will apply to all transactions subsequently conducted electronically. The agreement can also establish access and identification codes to be used by the parties when transacting business electronically.
The Uniform Electronic Transactions Act (UETA) (See pages 416–419.)	1. *Definition*—A uniform act submitted to the states for adoption. The UETA has been adopted by more than forty states. 2. *Purpose*—To create rules to support the enforcement of e-contracts. Under the UETA, contracts entered into online, as well as other electronic documents, are presumed valid. The UETA does not apply to transactions governed by the UCC or the UCITA (summarized next) or to wills or testamentary trusts.
The Uniform Computer Information Transactions Act (UCITA) (See page 420.)	1. *Definition*—A uniform act submitted to the states for adoption. Only two states have adopted the act. 2. *Purpose*—To validate e-contracts to license or purchase software, or contracts that give access to—or allow the distribution of—computer information.

FOR REVIEW

1. What are some important clauses to include when making offers to form electronic contracts, or e-contracts?
2. What are shrink-wrap agreements and click-on agreements? How have traditional laws been applied to such agreements? What problems arise in the application of traditional laws to these agreements?
3. How are electronic signatures used? Are electronic signatures valid?
4. What is a partnering agreement? What purpose does it serve?
5. What is the Uniform Electronic Transactions Act (UETA)? What are some of the major provisions of this act?

QUESTIONS AND CASE PROBLEMS

13–1. Click-On Agreements. Paul is a financial analyst for King Investments, Inc., a brokerage firm. He uses the Internet to investigate the background and activities of companies that might be good investments for King's customers. While visiting the Web site of Business Research, Inc., Paul sees on his screen a message that reads, "Welcome to businessresearch.com. By visiting our site, you have been entered as a subscriber to our e-publication, *Companies Unlimited.* This publication will be sent to you daily at a cost of $7.50 per week. An invoice will be included with *Companies Unlimited* every four weeks. You may cancel your subscription at any time." Has Paul entered into an enforceable contract to pay for *Companies Unlimited?* Why or why not?

13–2. Click-On Agreements. Anne is a reporter for *Daily Business Journal,* a print publication consulted by investors and other businesspersons. She often uses the Internet to perform research for the articles that she writes for the publication. While visiting the Web site of Cyberspace Investments Corp., Anne reads a pop-up window that states, "Our business newsletter, *E-Commerce Weekly,* is available at a one-year subscription rate of $5 per issue. To subscribe, enter your e-mail address below and click 'Subscribe.' By subscribing, you agree to the terms of the subscriber's agreement. To read this agreement, click 'Agreement.'" Anne enters her e-mail address but does not click on "Agreement" to read the terms. Has Anne entered into an enforceable contract to pay for *E-Commerce Weekly?* Explain.

13–3. Online Acceptance. Bob, a sales representative for Central Computer Co., occasionally uses the Internet to obtain information about his customers and to look for new sales leads. While visiting the Web site of Marketing World, Inc., Bob is presented with an on-screen message that offers, "To improve your ability to make deals, read our monthly online magazine, *Sales Genius,* available at a subscription rate of $15 a month. To subscribe, fill in your name, company name, and e-mail address below, and click 'Yes!' By clicking 'Yes!' you agree to the terms of the subscription con-

tract. To read this contract, click 'Terms.'" Among those terms is a clause that allows Marketing World to charge interest for subscription bills not paid within a certain time. The terms also prohibit subscribers from copying or distributing part or all of *Sales Genius* in any form. Bob subscribes without reading the terms. Marketing World later files a suit against Bob, based on his failure to pay for his subscription. Should the court hold that Bob is obligated to pay interest on the amount? Explain.

13–4. License Agreements. Management Computer Controls, Inc. (MC 2), is a Tennessee corporation in the business of selling software. Charles Perry Construction, Inc., a Florida corporation, entered into two contracts with MC 2 to buy software designed to perform estimating and accounting functions for construction firms. Each contract was printed on a standard order form containing a paragraph that referred to a license agreement. The license agreement included a choice-of-forum and choice-of-law provision: "Agreement is to be interpreted and construed according to the laws of the State of Tennessee. Any action, either by you or MC 2, arising out of this Agreement shall be initiated and prosecuted in the Court of Shelby County, Tennessee, and nowhere else." Each of the software packages arrived with the license agreement affixed to the outside of the box. Additionally, the boxes were sealed with an orange sticker bearing the following warning: "By opening this packet, you indicate your acceptance of the MC 2 license agreement." Alleging that the software was not suitable for use with Windows NT, Perry filed a suit against MC 2 in a Florida state court. MC 2 filed a motion to dismiss the complaint on the ground that the suit should be heard in Tennessee. How should the court rule? Why? [*Management Computer Controls, Inc. v. Charles Perry Construction, Inc.,* 743 So.2d 627 (Fla.App. 1 Dist. 1999)]

13–5. Browse-Wrap Terms. Ticketmaster Corp. operates a Web site that allows customers to buy tickets to concerts, ball games, and other events. On the site's home page are instructions and an index to internal pages (one page per event). Each event page provides basic information (a short description of the event, with the date, time, place, and price) and a description of how to order tickets over the Internet, by telephone, by mail, or in person. The home page contains—if a customer scrolls to the bottom—"terms and conditions" that proscribe, among other things, linking to Ticketmaster's internal pages. A customer need not view these terms to go to an event page. Tickets.Com, Inc., operates a Web site that also publicizes special events. Tickets.Com's site includes links to the internal events pages of Ticketmaster. These links bypass Ticketmaster's home page. Ticketmaster filed a suit in a federal district court against Tickets.Com, alleging in part breach of contract on the ground that Tickets.Com's linking violated Ticketmaster's terms and conditions. Tickets.Com filed a motion to dismiss. Should the court grant the motion? Why or why not? [*Ticketmaster Corp. v. Tickets.Com, Inc.,* 54 U.S.P.Q.2d 1344 (C.D.Cal. 2000)]

13–6. Shrink-Wrap/Click-On Agreements. 1-A Equipment Co. signed a sales order to lease Accware 10 User NT software, which is made and marketed by ICode, Inc. Just above the signature line, the order stated: "Thank you for your order. No returns or refunds will be issued for software license and/or services. All sales are final. Please read the End User License and Service Agreement." The software was delivered in a sealed envelope inside a box. On the outside of the envelope, an "End User Agreement" provided in part, "BY OPENING THIS PACKAGING, CLICKING YOUR ACCEPTANCE OF THE AGREEMENT DURING DOWNLOAD OR INSTALLATION OF THIS PRODUCT, OR BY USING ANY PART OF THIS PRODUCT, YOU AGREE TO BE LEGALLY BOUND BY THE TERMS OF THE AGREEMENT. . . . This agreement will be governed by the laws in force in the Commonwealth of Virginia . . . and exclusive venue for any litigation shall be in Virginia." Later, dissatisfied with the software, 1-A filed a suit in a Massachusetts state court against ICode, alleging breach of contract and misrepresentation. ICode asked the court to dismiss the case on the basis of the "end user agreement." Is the agreement enforceable? Should the court dismiss the suit? Why or why not? [*1-A Equipment Co. v. ICode, Inc.,* 43 UCC Rep.Serv.2d 807 (Mass.Dist. 2000)]

Case Problem with Sample Answer

13–7. Shrink Wrap Agreements. Peerless Wall & Window Coverings, Inc., is a small business in Pennsylvania. To run the cash registers in its stores, manage inventory, and link the stores electronically, in 1994 Peerless installed Point of Sale V6.5 software, produced by Synchronics, Inc., a small corporation in Tennessee that develops and markets business software. Point of Sale V6.5 was written with code that used only a two-digit year field—for example, 1999 was stored as

99. This meant that all dates were interpreted as falling within the twentieth century (2001, stored as 01, would be mistaken for 1901). In other words, Point of Sale V6.5 was not year 2000 (Y2K) compliant. The software was licensed under a shrink-wrap agreement printed on the envelopes containing the disks. The agreement included a clause that, among other things, limited remedies to replacement within ninety days if there was a defect in the disks. "The entire risk as to the quality and performance of the Software is with you." In 1995, Synchronics stopped selling and supporting Point of Sale V6.5. Two years later, Synchronics told Peerless that the software was not Y2K compliant and should be replaced. Peerless sued Synchronics in a federal district court, alleging, in part, breach of contract. Synchronics filed a motion for summary judgment. Who is most likely to bear the cost of replacing the software? Why? [*Peerless Wall & Window Coverings, Inc. v. Synchronics, Inc.,* 85 F.Supp.2d 519 (W.D.Pa. 2000), *aff'd* 234 F.3d 1265 (3d Cir. 2000)]

To view a sample answer for this case problem, go to this book's Web site at http://leet.westbuslaw.com and click on "Interactive Study Center."

13–8. Click-On Agreements. America Online, Inc. (AOL), provided e-mail service to Walter Hughes and other members under a click-on agreement titled "Terms of Service." This agreement consisted of three parts: a "Member Agreement," "Community Guidelines," and a "Privacy Policy." The "Member Agreement" included a forum-selection clause that read, "You expressly agree that exclusive jurisdiction for any claim or dispute with AOL or relating in any way to your membership or your use of AOL resides in the courts of Virginia." When Officer Thomas McMenamon of the Methuen, Massachusetts, Police Department received threatening e-mail sent from an AOL account, he requested and obtained from AOL Hughes's name and other personal information. Hughes filed a suit in a federal district court against AOL, which filed a motion to dismiss on the basis of the forum-selection clause. Considering that the clause was a click-on provision, is it enforceable? Explain. [*Hughes v. McMenamon,* 204 F.Supp.2d 178 (D.Mass. 2002)]

A Question of Ethics & Social Responsibility

13–9. Over the phone, Rich and Enza Hill ordered a computer from Gateway 2000, Inc. Inside the box were the computer and a list of contract terms, which provided that the terms governed the transaction unless the customers returned the computer within thirty days. Among those terms was a clause that required any claims to be submitted to arbitration. The Hills kept the computer for more than thirty days before complaining to Gateway about the computer's components and its performance. When the matter was not resolved to their satisfaction, the Hills filed a suit in a federal district court against Gateway, arguing, among other things, that the computer was defective. Gateway asked the court to enforce the arbitration clause. The Hills claimed that this term was not part of a contract to buy the computer because the list on which it appeared had been in the box and they had not seen the list until after the computer was delivered. In view of these facts, consider the following questions. [*Hill v. Gateway 2000, Inc.,* 105 F.3d 1147 (7th Cir. 1997)]

1. Should the court enforce the arbitration clause in this case? If you were the judge, how would you rule on this issue?
2. In your opinion, do shrink-wrap agreements impose too great a burden on purchasers? Why or why not?

Critical-Thinking Technological Question

13–10. Delta Company buys accounting software from Omega Corporation. On the outside of the software box, on the inside cover of the instruction manual, and on the first screen that appears each time the program is accessed is a license that claims to cover the use of the product. The license also includes a limitation on Omega's liability arising from the use of the software. One year later, Delta discovers that the software has a bug that has imposed on Delta a financial loss. Delta files a suit against Omega. Is the limitation-of-liability clause on the software box enforceable?

INTERACTING WITH THE INTERNET

For updated links to resources available on the Web, as well as a variety of other materials, visit this text's Web site at

http://leet.westbuslaw.com

You can access the UCC, including Article 2, at the Web site of the University of Pennsylvania Law School. Go to

http://www.law.upenn.edu/bll/ulc/ulc.htm

The law firm of Baker & McKenzie offers a summary of the scope and applicability of the E-SIGN Act of 2000 on its Web site. Go to

http://www.bmck.com/ecommerce/E-SIGN_Act.htm

The Web site of the National Conference of Commissioners on Uniform State Laws includes an update of the list of states that have adopted the UETA and the UCITA or considered them for adoption. The site also contains summaries of the acts and "Question and Answer" sections concerning these laws. Go to

http://www.nccusl.org

ONLINE LEGAL RESEARCH EXERCISES

Go to **http://leet.westbuslaw.com**, the Web site that accompanies this text. Select "Interactive Study Center," and then click on "Chapter 13." There you will find the following Internet research exercises that you can perform to learn more about topics covered in this chapter.

Activity 13–1: TECHNOLOGICAL PERSPECTIVE—E-Contract Formation
Activity 13–2: MANAGEMENT PERSPECTIVE—E-Signatures

BEFORE THE TEST

Go to **http://leet.westbuslaw.com**, the Web site that accompanies this text. Select "Interactive Quizzes." You will find at least twenty interactive questions relating to this chapter.

Westlaw® Campus

If your textbook provided for a subscription to Westlaw® Campus, or if you have otherwise purchased access to the Westlaw Campus database, you can access any of the cases presented or cited in this chapter by using your Westlaw Campus account.

CHAPTER **14**

Business Organizations

CONTENTS

CHAPTER OBJECTIVES

After reading this chapter, you should be able to answer the following questions:

1. Which form of business organization is the simplest?

2. What are some advantages and disadvantages of doing business as a partnership or a corporation, respectively?

3. How do limited liability companies and limited liability partnerships differ from traditional corporations and partnerships?

4. What is a franchise? What are the most common types of franchises?

5. What are the rights and duties of the directors and officers of a corporation? What are the rights of shareholders in a corporate enterprise?

M any Americans would agree with Sir Edward Coke's comment in the quotation below that most people, at least, "thirsteth after gaine." Certainly, an entrepreneur's primary motive for undertaking a business enterprise is to make profits. An *entrepreneur* is by definition one who initiates and *assumes the financial risks* of a new enterprise and undertakes to provide or control its management.

One of the questions faced by any entrepreneur who wishes to start up a business is what form of business organization he or she should choose for the business endeavor. In this chapter, we first examine the basic features of the three major traditional business forms—sole proprietorships, partnerships, and corporations. We then look at two relatively new, but significant, business forms: the limited liability company, or LLC, and limited liability partnership, or LLP. The LLC is

> **"[E]veryone thirsteth after gaine."**
> Sir Edward Coke, 1552–1634
> (English jurist and politician)

426

rapidly becoming an attractive alternative to the traditional corporate form. The LLP is a variation of the LLC. We also discuss private franchises. In the final pages of the chapter, we look at the roles, rights, and duties of corporate directors, officers, and shareholders, and at some of the ways in which conflicts among these corporate participants are resolved.

MAJOR TRADITIONAL BUSINESS FORMS

Traditionally, entrepreneurs have used three major forms to structure their business enterprises: the sole proprietorship, the partnership, and the corporation.

Sole Proprietorships

The simplest form of business is a **sole proprietorship.** In this form, the owner is the business; thus, anyone who does business without creating a separate business organization has a sole proprietorship. Sole proprietorships constitute over two-thirds of all American businesses. They are also usually small enterprises—about 1 percent of the sole proprietorships existing in the United States have revenues that exceed $1 million per year. Sole proprietors can own and manage any type of business from an informal, home-office undertaking to a large restaurant or construction firm.

A major advantage of the sole proprietorship is that the proprietor receives all of the profits (because he or she assumes all of the risk). In addition, it is often easier and less costly to start a sole proprietorship than to start any other kind of business, as few legal forms are involved. This type of business organization also entails more flexibility than does a partnership or a corporation. The sole proprietor is free to make any decision he or she wishes to concerning the business—such as whom to hire, when to take a vacation, and what kind

SOLE PROPRIETORSHIP
The simplest form of business, in which the owner is the business; the owner reports business income on his or her personal income tax return and is legally responsible for all debts and obligations incurred by the business.

A manager checks a shipment of the products that his firm sells. Could this be a sole proprietorship?

What are the advantages of operating a bakery as a sole proprietorship?

of business to pursue. A sole proprietor pays only personal income taxes on profits, which are reported as personal income on the proprietor's personal income tax form. Sole proprietors are also allowed to establish certain tax-exempt retirement accounts.[1]

The major disadvantage of the sole proprietorship is that, as sole owner, the proprietor alone bears the burden of any losses or liabilities incurred by the business enterprise. In other words, the sole proprietor has unlimited liability, or legal responsibility, for all obligations incurred in doing business. This unlimited liability is a major factor to be considered in choosing a business form. Another disadvantage is that the proprietor's opportunity to raise capital is limited to personal funds and the funds of those who are willing to make loans. The sole proprietorship also has the disadvantage of lacking continuity on the death of the proprietor. When the owner dies, so does the business—it is automatically dissolved. If the business is transferred to family members or other heirs, a new proprietorship is created.

Partnerships

Traditionally, partnerships have been classified as either general partnerships or limited partnerships. The two forms of partnership differ considerably in regard to legal requirements and the rights and liabilities of partners. We look here at the basic characteristics of each of these forms.

PARTNERSHIP
An agreement by two or more persons to carry on, as co-owners, a business for profit.

General Partnerships A general partnership, or **partnership**, arises from an agreement, express or implied, between two or more persons to carry on a business for profit. Partners are co-owners of a business and have joint control over its operation and the right to share in its profits. No particular form of partnership agreement is necessary for the creation of a partnership, but for practical reasons, the agreement should be in writing. Basically, the partners may agree to almost any terms when establishing the partnership so long as they are not illegal or contrary to public policy.

A partnership is a legal entity only for limited purposes, such as the partnership name and title of ownership and property. A key advantage of the partnership is that the firm itself does not pay federal income taxes, although the firm must file an information return with the Internal Revenue Service (IRS). A partner's profit from the partnership (whether distributed or not) is taxed as individual income to the individual partner. The main disadvantage of the partnership is that the partners are subject to personal liability for partnership obligations. In other words, if the partnership cannot pay its debts, the personal assets of the partners are subject to creditors' claims.

LIMITED PARTNERSHIP
A partnership consisting of one or more general partners (who manage the business and are liable to the full extent of their personal assets for debts of the partnership) and one or more limited partners (who contribute only assets and are liable only up to the amount contributed by them).

Limited Partnerships A special and quite popular form of partnership is the **limited partnership**, which consists of at least one general partner and one or more limited partners. A limited partnership is a creature of statute, because it

---

1. There now exist retirement programs designed for self-employed persons, such as simplified employee pension (SEP) plans, through which a certain percentage of their income can be contributed tax free to the plan, and principal and interest earnings will not be taxed until funds are withdrawn from the plan.

does not come into existence until a *certificate of partnership* is filed with the appropriate state office. A **general partner** assumes responsibility for the management of the partnership and liability for all partnership debts. A **limited partner** has no right to participate in the general management or operation of the partnership and assumes no liability for partnership debts beyond the amount of capital he or she has contributed. Thus, one of the major benefits of becoming a limited partner is this limitation on liability, both with respect to lawsuits brought against the partnership and the amount of funds placed at risk.

Corporations

A third and very widely used type of business organizational form is the **corporation.** Corporations are owned by *shareholders*—those who have purchased ownership shares in the business. A *board of directors,* elected by the shareholders, manages the business. The board of directors normally employs *officers* to oversee day-to-day operations.

The corporation, like the limited partnership, is a creature of statute. The corporation's existence as a legal entity, which can be perpetual, depends generally on state law.

One of the key advantages of the corporate form of business is that the liability of its owners (shareholders) is limited to their investments. The shareholders usually are not personally liable for the obligations of the corporation. Another advantage is that a corporation can raise capital by selling shares of corporate stock to investors. A key disadvantage of the corporate form is that any distributed corporate income is taxed twice. The corporate entity pays taxes on the firm's income, and when income is distributed to shareholders, the shareholders again pay taxes on that income.

S Corporations Some small corporations are able to avoid this double-taxation feature of the corporation by electing to be treated, for tax purposes, as an **S corporation.** Subchapter S of the Internal Revenue Code allows qualifying corporations to be taxed in a way similar to the way a partnership is taxed. In other words, an S corporation is not taxed at the corporate level. As in a partnership, the income is taxed only once—when it is distributed to the shareholder-owners, who pay personal income taxes on their respective shares of the profits.

Qualification Requirements for S Corporations Among the numerous requirements for S corporation status, the following are the most important:

1. The corporation must be a domestic corporation.
2. The corporation must not be a member of an affiliated group of corporations.
3. The shareholders of the corporation must be individuals, estates, or certain trusts. Partnerships and nonqualifying trusts cannot be shareholders. Under specific circumstances, corporations can be shareholders.
4. The corporation must have seventy-five or fewer shareholders.
5. The corporation must have only one class of stock, although not all shareholders need have the same voting rights.
6. No shareholder of the corporation may be a nonresident alien.

GENERAL PARTNER
In a limited partnership, a partner who assumes responsibility for the management of the partnership and liability for all partnership debts.

LIMITED PARTNER
In a limited partnership, a partner who contributes capital to the partnership but has no right to participate in the management and operation of the business. The limited partner assumes no liability for partnership debts beyond the capital contributed.

CORPORATION
A legal entity formed in compliance with statutory requirements. The entity is distinct from its shareholder-owners.

"The art of taxation consists in so plucking the goose as to obtain the largest amount of feathers with the smallest possible amount of hissing."
JEAN BAPTISTE COLBERT, 1619–1683
(French politician and financial reformer)

S CORPORATION
A close business corporation that has met certain requirements as set out by the Internal Revenue Code and thus qualifies for special income tax treatment. Essentially, an S corporation is taxed the same as a partnership, but its owners enjoy the privilege of limited liability.

LIMITED LIABILITY COMPANIES

The two most common forms of business organization selected by two or more persons entering into business together are the partnership and the corporation. As already explained, each form has distinct advantages and disadvantages. For partnerships, the advantage is that partnership income is taxed only once (all income is "passed through" the partnership entity to the partners themselves, who are taxed only as individuals); the disadvantage is the personal liability of the partners. For corporations, the advantage is the limited liability of shareholders; the disadvantage is the double taxation of corporate income. For many entrepreneurs and investors, the ideal business form would combine the tax advantages of the partnership form of business with the limited liability of the corporate enterprise.

The limited partnership and the S corporation partially address these needs. The limited liability of limited partners, however, is conditional: limited liability exists only so long as the limited partner does *not* participate in management. The problem with S corporations is that only small corporations (those with seventy-five or fewer shareholders) may acquire S corporation status. Furthermore, with few exceptions, only *individuals* may be shareholders in an S corporation; partnerships and corporations normally cannot be shareholders. Finally, no nonresident alien can be a shareholder in an S corporation. This means that if, say, a European investor wanted to purchase shares in an S corporation, it would not be permissible.

LIMITED LIABILITY COMPANY (LLC)
A hybrid form of business enterprise that offers the limited liability of the corporation but the tax advantages of a partnership.

Since 1977, an increasing number of states have authorized a new form of business organization called the **limited liability company (LLC).** The LLC is a hybrid form of business enterprise that offers the limited liability of the corporation but the tax advantages of a partnership. The origins and characteristics of this increasingly significant form of business organization are discussed in this chapter's *Landmark in the Legal Environment* feature.

Formation of an LLC

Like the corporation, an LLC must be formed and operated in compliance with state law. About one-fourth of the states specifically require LLCs to have at least two owners, called **members.** In the rest of the states, although some LLC statutes are silent on this issue, one-member LLCs are usually permitted.

MEMBER
The term used to designate a person who has an ownership interest in a limited liability company.

To form an LLC, **articles of organization** must be filed with a central state agency—usually the secretary of state's office. Typically, the articles are required to set forth such information as the name of the business, its principal address, the name and address of a registered agent, the names of the owners, and information on how the LLC will be managed. The business's name must include the words "Limited Liability Company" or the initials "LLC." In addition to filing the articles of organization, a few states require that a notice of the intention to form an LLC be published in a local newspaper.

ARTICLES OF ORGANIZATION
The document filed with a designated state official by which a limited liability company is formed.

Advantages and Disadvantages of LLCs

CONTRAST A partnership must have at least two partners. In many states, an LLC can be created with only one shareholder-member.

A key advantage of the LLC is that the liability of members is limited to the amount of their investments. Another significant advantage is that an LLC with two or more members can choose whether to be taxed as a partnership or a corporation. Unless the LLC indicates that it wishes to be taxed as a cor-

LANDMARK IN THE LEGAL ENVIRONMENT

Limited Liability Company (LLC) Statutes

In 1977, Wyoming became the first state to pass legislation authorizing the creation of a limited liability company (LLC). Although LLCs emerged in the United States only in 1977, they have been in existence for over a century in other areas, including several European and South American nations. The South American *limitada,* for example, is a form of business organization that operates more or less as a partnership but provides limited liability for the owners.

TAXATION OF LLCs In the United States, after Wyoming's adoption of an LLC statute, it still was not known how the Internal Revenue Service (IRS) would treat the LLC for tax purposes. In 1988, however, the IRS ruled that Wyoming LLCs would be taxed as partnerships instead of as corporations, providing that certain requirements were met. Prior to this ruling, only one other state—Florida, in 1982—had authorized LLCs. The 1988 ruling encouraged other states to enact LLC statutes, and in less than a decade, all states had done so.

New IRS rules that went into effect on January 1, 1997, encouraged even more widespread use of LLCs in the business world. These rules provide that any unincorporated business will automatically be taxed as a partnership unless it indicates otherwise on the tax form. The exceptions involve publicly traded companies, companies formed under a state incorporation statute, and certain foreign-owned companies. If a business chooses to be taxed as a corporation, it can indicate this choice by checking a box on the IRS form.

FOREIGN ENTITIES MAY BE LLC MEMBERS Part of the impetus behind the creation of LLCs in this country is that foreign investors are allowed to become LLC members. Generally, in an era increasingly characterized by global business efforts and investments, the LLC offers U.S. firms and potential investors from other countries flexibility and opportunities greater than those available through partnerships or corporations.

Application to Today's World

Once it became clear that LLCs could be taxed as partnerships, the LLC form of business organization was widely adopted. Members could avoid the personal liability associated with the partnership form of business as well as the double taxation of the corporate form of business. Today, LLCs, which not long ago were largely unknown in this country, are a widely used form of business organization.

poration, it is automatically taxed as a partnership by the Internal Revenue Service (IRS). This means that the LLC as an entity pays no taxes; rather, as in a partnership, profits are "passed through" the LLC and paid personally by the members. If LLC members want to reinvest profits in the business, however, rather than distribute the profits to members, they may prefer to be taxed as a corporation if corporate income tax rates are lower than personal tax rates. Part of the attractiveness of the LLC for businesspersons is this flexibility with respect to taxation options. For federal income tax purposes, one-member LLCs are automatically taxed as sole proprietorships unless they indicate that they wish to be taxed as corporations. Still another advantage of the LLC for businesspersons is the flexibility it offers in terms of business operations and management (as will be discussed shortly).

The disadvantages of the LLC are relatively few. Some of the initial disadvantages with respect to uncertainties over how LLCs would be taxed no

REMEMBER A uniform law is a "model" law. It does not become the law of any state until the state legislature adopts it, either in part or in its entirety.

longer exist. The only remaining disadvantage of the LLC is that state statutes are not yet uniform. In an attempt to promote some uniformity among the states with respect to LLC statutes, the National Conference of Commissioners on Uniform State Laws drafted a Uniform Limited Liability Company Act for submission to the states to consider for adoption. Until all of the states have adopted the uniform law, however, an LLC in one state will have to check the rules in the other states in which the firm does business to ensure that it retains its limited liability.

The LLC Operating Agreement

OPERATING AGREEMENT
In a limited liability company, an agreement in which the members set forth the details of how the business will be managed and operated. State statutes typically give the members wide latitude in deciding for themselves the rules that will govern their organization.

The LLC is also a flexible business entity in another important way. In an LLC, the members themselves can decide how to operate the various aspects of the business by forming an **operating agreement.** Operating agreements typically contain provisions relating to management, decision-making procedures, how profits will be divided, the transfer of membership interests, whether the LLC will be dissolved on the death or departure of a member, and other important issues.

Operating agreements need not be in writing, and indeed they need not even be formed for an LLC to exist. Generally, though, LLC members should protect their interests by forming a written operating agreement. As with any business arrangement, disputes may arise over any number of issues. If there is no agreement covering the topic being disputed, such as how profits will be divided, the state LLC statute will govern the outcome. For example, most LLC statutes provide that if the members have not specified how profits will be divided among the members, they will be divided equally. Generally, with respect to issues not covered by an operating agreement or by an LLC statute, the principles of partnership law are applied.

LIMITED LIABILITY PARTNERSHIPS

LIMITED LIABILITY PARTNERSHIP (LLP)
A business organizational form that is similar to the LLC but that is designed more for professionals who normally do business as partners in a partnership. The LLP is a pass-through entity for tax purposes, like the general partnership, but it limits the personal liability of the partners.

The **limited liability partnership** (LLP) is similar to the LLC. The difference between an LLP and an LLC is that the LLP is designed more for professionals who normally do business as partners in a partnership. The major advantage of the LLP is that it allows a partnership to continue as a pass-through entity for tax purposes but limits the personal liability of the partners.

The first state to enact an LLP statute was Texas, in 1991. Other states quickly followed suit, and by 1997, virtually all of the states had enacted LLP statutes.

LLP Formation and Operation

Like LLCs, LLPs must be formed and operated in compliance with state statutes. The appropriate form has to be filed with a central state agency, usually the secretary of state's office, and the business's name must include either "Limited Liability Partnership" or "LLP."

In most states, it is relatively easy to convert a traditional partnership into an LLP because the firm's basic organizational structure remains the same. Additionally, all of the statutory and common law rules governing partnerships still apply (apart from those modified by the LLP statute). Normally, LLP statutes are simply amendments to a state's already existing partnership law.

Advantages of the LLP

The LLP is especially attractive for two categories of businesses: professional services and family businesses. Professional service companies include law firms and accounting firms. Family limited liability partnerships are basically business organizations in which all of the partners are related. Generally, the LLP allows professionals to avoid personal liability for the malpractice of other partners. Although LLP statutes vary from state to state, generally each state statute limits in some way the liability of partners. For example, Delaware law protects each innocent partner from the "debts and obligations of the partnership arising from negligence, wrongful acts, or misconduct." In North Carolina, Texas, and Washington, D.C., the statutes protect innocent partners from obligations arising from "errors, omissions, negligence, incompetence, or malfeasance." Partners in an LLP are liable for their own wrongful acts, however, as well as the wrongful acts of those whom they supervise.

MAJOR BUSINESS FORMS COMPARED

When deciding which form of business organization would be most appropriate, businesspersons normally take several factors into consideration. These factors include ease of creation, the liability of the owners, tax considerations, and the need for capital. Each major form of business organization offers distinct advantages and disadvantages with respect to these and other factors. Exhibit 14–1 on the following two pages summarizes the essential advantages and disadvantages of each of the forms of business organization discussed in this chapter.

PRIVATE FRANCHISES

A **franchise** is defined as any arrangement in which the owner of a trademark, a trade name, or a copyright licenses others to use the trademark, trade name, or copyright in the selling of goods or services. A **franchisee** (a purchaser of a franchise) is generally legally independent of the **franchisor** (the seller of the franchise). At the same time, the franchise is economically dependent on the franchisor's integrated business system. In other words, a franchisee can operate as an independent businessperson but still obtain the advantages of a regional or national organization. Well-known franchises include McDonald's, KFC, and Burger King.

FRANCHISE
Any arrangement in which the owner of a trademark, trade name, or copyright licenses another to use that trademark, trade name, or copyright, under specified conditions or limitations, in the selling of goods and services.

FRANCHISEE
One receiving a license to use another's (the franchisor's) trademark, trade name, or copyright in the sale of goods and services.

FRANCHISOR
One licensing another (the franchisee) to use his or her trademark, trade name, or copyright in the sale of goods or services.

Types of Franchises

Because the franchising industry is so extensive (at least sixty-five types of distinct businesses sell franchises), it is difficult to summarize the many types of franchises that now exist. Generally, though, the majority of franchises fall into one of the following three classifications: distributorships, chain-style business operations, or manufacturing or processing-plant arrangements. We briefly describe these types of franchises here.

Distributorship A *distributorship* arises when a manufacturing concern (franchisor) licenses a dealer (franchisee) to sell its product. Often, a distributorship covers an exclusive territory. An example of this type of franchise is an automobile dealership.

EXHIBIT 14-1   MAJOR BUSINESS FORMS COMPARED

CHARACTERISTIC	SOLE PROPRIETORSHIP	PARTNERSHIP	CORPORATION
Method of Creation	Created at will by owner.	Created by agreement of the parties.	Charter issued by state—created by statutory authorization.
Legal Position	Not a separate entity; owner is the business.	Not a separate legal entity in many states.	Always a legal entity separate and distinct from its owners—a legal fiction for the purposes of owning property and being a party to litigation.
Liability	Unlimited liability.	Unlimited liability.	Limited liability of shareholders—shareholders are not liable for the debts of the corporation.
Duration	Determined by owner; automatically dissolved on owner's death.	Terminated by agreement of the partners, by the death of one or more of the partners, by withdrawal of a partner, by bankruptcy, and so on.	Can have perpetual existence.
Transferability of Interest	Interest can be transferred, but individual's proprietorship then ends.	Although partnership interest can be assigned, assignee does not have full rights of a partner.	Shares of stock can be transferred.
Management	Completely at owner's discretion.	Each general partner has a direct and equal voice in management unless expressly agreed otherwise in the partnership agreement.	Shareholders elect directors, who set policy and appoint officers.
Taxation	Owner pays personal taxes on business income.	Each partner pays pro rata share of income taxes on net profits, whether or not they are distributed.	Double taxation—corporation pays income tax on net profits, with no deduction for dividends, and shareholders pay some income tax on disbursed dividends they receive.
Organizational Fees, Annual License Fees, and Annual Reports	None.	None.	All required.
Transaction of Business in Other States	Generally no limitation.	Generally no limitation.[a]	Normally must qualify to do business and obtain certificate of authority.

a. A few states have enacted statutes requiring that foreign partnerships qualify to do business there.

EXHIBIT 14-1 MAJOR BUSINESS FORMS COMPARED (CONTINUED)

CHARACTERISTIC	LIMITED PARTNERSHIP	LIMITED LIABILITY COMPANY	LIMITED LIABILITY PARTNERSHIP
Method of Creation	Created by agreement to carry on a business for a profit. At least one party must be a general partner and the other(s) limited partner(s). Certificate of limited partnership is filed. Charter must be issued by the state.	Created by an agreement of the owner-members of the company. Articles of organization are filed. Charter must be issued by the state.	Created by agreement of the partners. Certificate of limited liability partnership is filed. Charter must be issued by the state.
Legal Position	Treated as a legal entity.	Treated as a legal entity.	Generally, treated same as a general partnership.
Liability	Unlimited liability of all general partners; limited partners are liable only to the extent of capital contributions.	Member-owners' liability is limited to the amount of capital contributions or investments.	Varies from state to state but usually limits liability of a partner for certain acts committed by other partners.
Duration	By agreement in certificate, or by termination of the last general partner (withdrawal, death, and so on) or last limited partner.	Unless a single-member LLC, can have perpetual existence (same as a corporation).	Terminated by agreement of partners, by death or withdrawal of a partner, or by law (such as bankruptcy).
Transferability of Interest	Interest can be assigned (same as general partnership), but if assignee becomes a member with consent of other partners, certificate must be amended.	Member interests are freely transferable.	Interest can be assigned (same as in a general partnership).
Management	General partners have equal voice or by agreement. Limited partners may not retain limited liability if they actively participate in management.	Member-owners can fully participate in management, or management is selected by member-owners who manage on behalf of the members.	Same as a general partnership.
Taxation	Generally taxed as a partnership.	LLC is not taxed, and members are taxed personally on profits "passed through" the LLC.	Same as a general partnership.
Organizational Fees, Annual License Fees, and Annual Reports	Organizational fee required; usually not others.	Organizational fee required; others vary with states.	Organizational fee required (such as a set amount per partner); usually not others.
Transaction of Business in Other States	Generally, no limitations.	Generally, no limitation but may vary depending on state.	Generally, no limitation, but state laws vary as to formation and limitation of liability.

Chain-Style Business Operation A *chain-style business operation* exists when a franchise operates under a franchisor's trade name and is identified as a member of a select group of dealers that engages in the franchisor's business. Often, the franchisor requires that the franchisee maintain certain standards of operation. In addition, sometimes the franchisee is obligated to deal exclusively with the franchisor to obtain materials and supplies. Examples of this type of franchise are McDonald's and most other fast-food chains.

Manufacturing or Processing-Plant Arrangement A *manufacturing or processing-plant arrangement* exists when the franchisor transmits to the franchisee the essential ingredients or formula to make a particular product. The franchisee then markets the product either at wholesale or at retail in accordance with the franchisor's standards. Examples of this type of franchise are Coca-Cola and other soft-drink bottling companies.

Laws Governing Franchising

Because a franchise relationship is primarily a contractual relationship, it is governed by contract law. If the franchise exists primarily for the sale of products manufactured by the franchisor, the law governing sales contracts as expressed in Article 2 of the Uniform Commercial Code applies (see Chapter 11). Additionally, the federal government and most states have enacted laws governing certain aspects of franchising. Generally, these laws are designed to protect prospective franchisees from dishonest franchisors and to prohibit franchisors from terminating franchises without good cause.

KEEP IN MIND Because a franchise involves the licensing of a trademark, a trade name, or a copyright, the law governing intellectual property may apply in some cases.

Federal Regulation of Franchising Automobile dealership franchisees are protected from automobile manufacturers' bad faith termination of their franchises by the Automobile Dealers' Franchise Act[2]—also known as the Automobile Dealers' Day in Court Act—of 1965. If a manufacturer-franchisor terminates a franchise because of a dealer-franchisee's failure to comply with unreasonable demands (for example, failure to attain an unrealistically high sales quota), the manufacturer may be liable for damages.

Another federal statute is the Petroleum Marketing Practices Act (PMPA)[3] of 1979, which prescribes the grounds and conditions under which a franchisor may terminate or decline to renew a gasoline station franchise. Federal antitrust laws (discussed in Chapter 22), which prohibit certain types of anticompetitive agreements, may also apply in particular circumstances.

In 1979, the Federal Trade Commission (FTC) issued regulations that require franchisors to disclose material facts necessary to a prospective franchisee's making an informed decision concerning the purchase of a franchise.

State Regulation of Franchising State legislation tends to be similar to federal statutes and the FTC regulations. For example, to protect franchisees, a state law might require the disclosure of information that is material to making an informed decision regarding the purchase of a franchise. This could include such information as the actual costs of operation, recurring expenses, and

---

2. 15 U.S.C. Sections 1221 *et seq.*
3. 15 U.S.C. Sections 2801 *et seq.*

profits earned, along with facts substantiating these figures. State deceptive trade practices acts may also prohibit certain types of actions on the part of franchisors.

In response to the need for a uniform franchise law, the National Conference of Commissioners on Uniform State Laws drafted a model law that standardizes the various state franchise regulations. Because the uniform law represents a compromise of so many diverse interests, it has met with little success in being adopted as law by the various states.

A franchisee's claims against a franchisor under a state franchise disclosure law were at issue in the following case.

CASE 14.1   Bixby's Food Systems, Inc. v. McKay

United States District Court,
Northern District of Illinois, 2002.
193 F.Supp.2d 1053.

BACKGROUND AND FACTS In 1994, Phillip and Jan McKay met Ken Miyamoto, the president of Bixby's Food Systems, Inc., a franchisor of bagel restaurants. Miyamoto told the McKays that, among other things, the estimated start-up costs for a Bixby's franchise were between $143,000 and $198,000; that "existing bagel stores were doing annual sales in excess of $1,000,000.00; and that Bixby's franchises would exceed these revenue figures." In April 1995, at a meeting attended by the McKays, Miyamoto said that prospective franchisees had signed

and paid for 340 development agreements when, in fact, no more than 15 had been executed.[a] One week later, the McKays agreed to open a Bixby's store in Geneva, Illinois. Their initial costs, including a lease of space for the store, exceeded $400,000. After opening, their sales ranged from $25,000 to $30,000 per month. After eight months, Bixby's terminated the McKays' franchise agreement for failure to pay certain fees and filed a suit in a federal district court against them for alleged violations of the agreement. The McKays filed a counterclaim against Miyamoto, alleging, in part, violations of the Illinois Franchise Disclosure Act. The McKays filed a motion for summary judgment on these claims.

**IN THE WORDS
OF THE COURT . . .**

NOLAN, United States Magistrate Judge.

*   *   *   *

*   *   * [The Illinois Franchise Disclosure Act (IFDA)] provides that:

[i]n connection with the offer or sale of any franchise made in this State, it is unlawful for any person, directly or indirectly, to *   *   * make any untrue statement of a material fact *   *   * .

The McKays list several untrue statements of material fact made by Miyamoto during the process of the franchise sale [including that] he knew the investment figures [he provided] were false *   *   * but he assured the McKays that the [figures] were accurate *   *   * . The McKays claim that they relied on these *   *   * representations *   *   * .

In addition, the McKays claim that Miyamoto violated [the IFDA] when he represented at the franchisees' April 11, 1995 meeting that Bixby's had 340 executed development agreements *   *   * . The McKays relied on these representations when they executed their franchise agreement *   *   * .

---

a. A *development agreement* gave a prospective franchisee the right to buy a certain number of franchises within a given geographic area.

(continued)

CASE 14.1—Continued

To be actionable under the IFDA, the misrepresentation must be an untrue statement of a material fact. * * *

*A statement expressing an opinion or that relates to future or contingent events rather than to present facts, however, ordinarily does not constitute an actionable misrepresentation * * * .* For example, predictions of future sales or profitability are not considered representations of preexisting material facts. [Emphasis added.]

The McKays have not shown that, contrary to the general rule, Miyamoto's statements about future events, costs, and profitability are actionable misrepresentations under the IFDA, so summary judgment cannot be granted based upon those statements. * * *

The McKays have, however, conclusively shown that in April 1995, Miyamoto falsely claimed that Bixby's had 340 signed and paid-for development agreements when no more than fifteen development agreements had in fact been executed. Miyamoto's untrue statement was material to the McKays' decision to execute the Bixby's franchise agreement a week later. The McKays have demonstrated that there is no genuine dispute that Miyamoto made an untrue statement of a material fact in connection with the offer or sale of any franchise made in this State, and therefore summary judgment should be granted as to the McKays' claim under * * * the IFDA.

DECISION AND REMEDY The court granted the McKays' motion for summary judgment on the claim that Miyamoto violated the Illinois Franchise Disclosure Act when he falsely represented that Bixby's had 340 signed and paid-for development agreements. This was "an untrue statement of a material fact in connection with the offer or sale of any franchise," a violation of state law.

FOR CRITICAL ANALYSIS—Economic Consideration *Generally, what steps can a prospective franchisee take to ensure that a franchisor's statements as to future sales or profitability are reasonable estimates?*

The Franchise Contract

The franchise relationship is defined by a contract between the franchisor and the franchisee. The franchise contract specifies the terms and conditions of the franchise and spells out the rights and duties of the franchisor and the franchisee. If either party fails to perform the contractual duties, that party may be subject to a lawsuit for breach of contract. Generally, the statutory law and case law governing franchising tend to emphasize the importance of good faith and fair dealing in franchise relationships.

Because each type of franchise relationship has its own characteristics, it is difficult to describe the broad range of details a franchising contract may include. We now look at some of the major issues that typically are addressed in a franchise contract.

REMEMBER Unfair contracts between a party with a great amount of bargaining power and another with little power are generally not enforced. This is part of what is called freedom *from* contract.

Payment for the Franchise The franchisee ordinarily pays an initial fee or lump-sum price for the franchise license (the privilege of being granted a franchise). This fee is separate from the various products that the franchisee purchases from or through the franchisor. In some industries, the franchisor relies heavily on the initial sale of the franchise for realizing a profit. In other industries, the continued dealing between the parties brings profit to both. In most situations, the franchisor will receive a stated percentage of the annual sales or annual volume of business done by the franchisee. The franchise agreement may also require the franchisee to pay a percentage of advertising costs and certain administrative expenses.

Business Premises The franchise agreement may specify whether the premises for the business must be leased or purchased outright. In some cases, construction of a building is necessary to meet the terms of the agreement. The agreement usually will specify whether the franchisor supplies equipment and furnishings for the premises or whether this is the responsibility of the franchisee.

Location of the Franchise Typically, the franchisor will determine the territory to be served. Some franchise contracts will give the franchisee exclusive rights, or "territorial rights," to a certain geographical area. Other franchise contracts, while they define the territory allotted to a particular franchise, either specifically state that the franchise is nonexclusive or are silent on the issue of territorial rights.

Many franchise cases involve disputes over territorial rights, and this is one area of franchising in which the implied covenant of good faith and fair dealing often comes into play. ● **EXAMPLE 1** Suppose that a franchisee is not given exclusive territorial rights in the franchise contract, or the contract is silent on the issue. If the franchisor allows a competing franchise to be established nearby, the franchisee may suffer a significant loss in profits. In this situation, a court may hold that the franchisor's actions breached an implied covenant of good faith and fair dealing.●

A particular problem facing franchisees in today's online world is that franchisors may attempt to sell their products themselves via their Web sites. See, for example, the case discussed in the *Legal E-nvironment* feature on page 440.

Business Organization of the Franchisee The business organization of the franchisee is of great concern to the franchisor. Depending on the terms of the franchise agreement, the franchisor may specify particular requirements for the form and capital structure of the business. The franchise agreement may also provide that standards of operation—relating to such aspects of the business as sales quotas, quality, and record keeping—be met by the franchisee. Furthermore, a franchisor may wish to retain stringent control over the training of personnel involved in the operation and over administrative aspects of the business.

Quality Control by the Franchisor Although the day-to-day operation of the franchise business is normally left up to the franchisee, the franchise agreement may provide for the amount of supervision and control agreed on by the parties. When the franchise is a service operation, such as a motel, the contract often provides that the franchisor will establish certain standards for the facility. Typically, the contract will provide that the franchisor is permitted to make periodic inspections to ensure that the standards are being maintained in order to protect the franchise's name and reputation.

As a general rule, the validity of a provision permitting the franchisor to establish and enforce certain quality standards is unquestioned. Because the franchisor has a legitimate interest in maintaining the quality of the product

LEGAL *e*-NVIRONMENT

What Happens to Exclusive Territorial Rights in the Online Environment?

With the growth of inexpensive and easy online marketing, it was inevitable that cyberturf conflicts would eventually arise between franchisors and franchisees. Suppose, for example, that a franchise contract grants to the franchisee exclusive rights to sell the franchised product within a certain territory. What happens if the franchisor then begins to sell the product from its Web site to anyone anywhere in the world, including in the franchisee's territory? Does this constitute a breach of the franchise contract?

Drug Emporium's "Electronic Encroachment"

This issue came before a panel of arbitrators in an American Arbitration Association (AAA) proceeding in 2000. As you learned in Chapter 3, the AAA is a leading provider of arbitration services. The proceeding involved franchise contracts between the Drug Emporium, Inc., and several of its franchisees. The contracts provided that each franchisee had the exclusive right to conduct business in a specific geographic area. The franchisees claimed that the Drug Emporium had breached its contractual obligation to honor their territories by using its Web site to sell directly to customers within the franchisees' territories.

What, Exactly, Is a "Virtual Drugstore"?

One of the first questions the arbitrating panel had to decide was whether a "virtual drugstore" is a

drugstore for purposes of a franchise agreement. The panel had little difficulty in answering the question, stating that "[i]t is not for this panel to divine whether a virtual reality is real or whether it is a phantom." The panel simply noted that the company marketed the site as "the full service online drugstore," that it called the site a drugstore in filings with the Securities and Exchange Commission, and that it advertised the site as "your neighborhood pharmacy."

Ultimately, in what is believed to be the first ruling by a court or arbitrating panel on the issue of electronic encroachment, the arbitrating panel decided in favor of the franchisees. The panel ordered the Drug Emporium to cease marketing its goods from its Web site to potential customers who were physically located within the franchisees' territories.[a]

FOR CRITICAL ANALYSIS

Conflicts such as the one involved in this case can occur not only between franchisors and franchisees but also among competing franchisees. Can franchisees do anything to protect themselves against electronic encroachment by their franchisors or other franchisees?

_____

a. *Emporium Drug Mart, Inc. of Shreveport v. Drug Emporium, Inc.*, No. 71-114-0012600 (American Arbitration Association, September 2, 2000).

BE AWARE Under agency law (see Chapter 16), an employer may be liable for the torts of his or her employees if they occur within the scope of employment, without regard to the personal fault of the employer.

or service to protect its name and reputation, it can exercise greater control in this area than would otherwise be tolerated. Increasingly, however, franchisors are finding that if they exercise too much control over the operations of their franchisees, they may incur liability under agency theory (see Chapter 16) for the acts of their franchisees' employees.

Pricing Arrangements Franchises provide the franchisor with an outlet for the firm's goods and services. Depending on the nature of the business, the franchisor may require the franchisee to purchase certain supplies from the franchisor at an established price.[4] A franchisor who sets the prices at which the franchisee will resell the goods may violate state or federal antitrust laws, or both, however.

Termination of the Franchise The duration of the franchise is a matter to be determined between the parties. Generally, a franchise will start out for a short period, such as a year, so that the franchisee and the franchisor can determine whether they want to stay in business with one another. Usually, the franchise agreement will specify that termination must be "for cause," such as death or disability of the franchisee, insolvency of the franchisee, breach of the franchise agreement, or failure to meet specified sales quotas. Most franchise contracts provide that notice of termination must be given. If no set time for termination is specified, then a reasonable time, with notice, will be implied. A franchisee must be given reasonable time to wind up the business—that is, to do the accounting and return the copyright or trademark or any other property of the franchisor.

Wrongful Termination. Because a franchisor's termination of a franchise often has adverse consequences for the franchisee, much franchise litigation involves claims of wrongful termination. Generally, the termination provisions of contracts are more favorable to the franchisor. This means that the franchisee, who normally invests a substantial amount of time and funds in the franchise operation to make it successful, may receive little or nothing for the business on termination. The franchisor owns the trademark and hence the business.

It is in this area that statutory and case law become important. The federal and state laws discussed earlier attempt, among other things, to protect franchisees from the arbitrary or unfair termination of their franchises by the franchisors. Generally, both statutory and case law emphasize the importance of good faith and fair dealing in terminating a franchise relationship.

The Importance of Good Faith and Fair Dealing. In determining whether a franchisor has acted in good faith when terminating a franchise agreement, the courts generally try to balance the rights of both parties. If a court perceives that a franchisor has arbitrarily or unfairly terminated a franchise, the franchisee will be provided with a remedy for wrongful termination. If a franchisor's decision to terminate a franchise was made in the normal course of the franchisor's business operations, however, and reasonable notice of termination was given to the franchisee, normally a court would not consider such a termination wrongful.

THE NATURE OF THE CORPORATION

The corporation is a creature of statute. Its existence depends generally on state law. Each state has its own body of corporate law, and these laws are not entirely uniform. The Model Business Corporation Act (MBCA) is a codification of modern corporation law that has been influential in the drafting and revision of state corporation statutes. Today, the majority of state statutes are guided by the revised version of the MBCA, known as the Revised Model Business Corporation Act (RMBCA).

"A corporation is an artificial being, invisible, intangible, and existing only in contemplation of law."

JOHN MARSHALL, 1755–1835
(Chief justice of the United States Supreme Court, 1801–1835)

4. Although a franchisor can require franchisees to purchase supplies from it, requiring a franchisee to purchase exclusively from the franchisor may violate federal antitrust laws (see Chapter 22).

A *corporation* can consist of one or more *natural* persons (as opposed to the artificial "person" of the corporation) identified under a common name. The primary document needed to incorporate (that is, form the corporation according to state law) is the **articles of incorporation,** or *corporate charter,* which include such information about the corporation as its functions and the structure of its organization. As soon as a corporation is formed, an organizational meeting is held to adopt **bylaws** (rules for managing the firm) and to elect a board of directors.

The corporation substitutes itself for its shareholders in conducting corporate business and in incurring liability, yet its authority to act and the liability for its actions are separate and apart from the individuals who own it. (In certain limited situations, the "corporate veil" can be pierced; that is, liability for the corporation's obligations can be extended to shareholders—a topic to be discussed later in this chapter.)

Corporate Personnel

Responsibility for the overall management of the corporation is entrusted to a *board of directors,* which is elected by the shareholders. The board of directors hires *corporate officers* and other employees to run the daily business operations of the corporation.

When an individual purchases a share of stock in a corporation, that person becomes a *shareholder* and an owner of the corporation. Unlike the members in a partnership, the body of shareholders can change constantly without affecting the continued existence of the corporation. A shareholder can sue the corporation, and the corporation can sue a shareholder. Additionally, under certain circumstances, a shareholder can sue on behalf of a corporation.

Corporate Taxation

Corporate profits are taxed by state and federal governments. Corporations can do one of two things with corporate profits—retain them or pass them on to shareholders in the form of **dividends.** The corporation receives no tax deduction for dividends distributed to shareholders. Dividends are again taxable (except when they represent distributions of capital) to the shareholder receiving them. This double-taxation feature of the corporation is one of its major disadvantages.

Profits not distributed are retained by the corporation. These **retained earnings,** if invested properly, will yield higher corporate profits in the future and thus normally cause the price of the company's stock to rise. Individual shareholders can then reap the benefits of these retained earnings in the capital gains they receive when they sell their shares.

The consequences of a failure to pay taxes can be severe. Indeed, the state may dissolve a corporation for this reason. Alternatively, corporate status may be suspended until the taxes are paid. In the following case, the state had revoked a corporation's corporate charter because of the corporation's failure to pay certain taxes. The issue before the court was whether a shareholder who had assumed an obligation of the corporation could be held personally liable for the unsatisfactory performance of the contract.

ARTICLES OF INCORPORATION
The document filed with the appropriate governmental agency, usually the secretary of state, when a business is incorporated; state statutes usually prescribe what kind of information must be contained in the articles of incorporation.

BYLAWS
A set of governing rules adopted by a corporation or other association.

DIVIDEND
A distribution to corporate shareholders of corporate profits or income, disbursed in proportion to the number of shares held.

RETAINED EARNINGS
The portion of a corporation's profits that has not been paid out as dividends to shareholders.

CASE 14.2 Bullington v. Palangio

Arkansas Supreme Court, 2001.
345 Ark. 320,
45 S.W.3d 834.
http://courts.state.ar.us/
opinions/opinions.html[a]

BACKGROUND AND FACTS Jerry Bullington, doing business as Bullington Builders, Inc. (BBI), entered into a contract with Helen Palangio for the construction of a new house in Damascus, Arkansas. Bullington signed the contract "Jerry Bullington, d/b/a Bullington Builders, Inc." but did not indicate any official capacity as a corporate officer. BBI had been incorporated in 1993. Its only shareholders were Bullington, who managed the business, and his wife. About one and a half months before Palangio's house was completed, BBI's charter was revoked for failure to pay Arkansas franchise taxes,[b] and it was not reinstated. Bullington finished the house, but Palangio was not satisfied with the work or with Bullington's attempts to address her complaints. More than a year later, Palangio hired another builder to remedy the alleged defects. Palangio then filed a suit in an Arkansas state court against Bullington, alleging, in part, breach of contract and asserting that the corporate entity did not shield him from personal liability. The court held Bullington liable to Palangio for $19,000. Bullington appealed to the Arkansas Supreme Court.

IN THE WORDS OF THE COURT . . .

RAY THORNTON, Justice.

* * * *

* * * [Arkansas Code Section] 26-54-104(a) provides, in relevant part:

(a) Every corporation shall file an annual franchise tax report and pay an annual franchise tax, unless exempted * * * .

Additionally, [Arkansas Code Section] 26-54-111(a) provides:

(a) On or before January 1 of each year, the Secretary of State shall issue a proclamation proclaiming as forfeited the corporate charters * * * of all corporations, both domestic and foreign which, according to his records, are delinquent in the payment of the annual franchise tax for any prior year.

* * * Reading these statutory provisions together, it is clear that *our statutory law imposes an affirmative duty on the corporation to file franchise tax forms and pay the corresponding fees in order to maintain its corporate status.* [Emphasis added.]

In addition to our statutory law, we have well-established case law regarding the issue of whether personal liability attaches for liabilities that arise if a corporate charter * * * is revoked. * * * [T]o exempt any association of persons from personal liability for the debts of a proposed corporation, they must comply fully with the [law] under which the corporation is created[,] and * * * partial compliance with the [law] is not sufficient.

* * * [T]he reasoning behind cases holding officers and stockholders individually liable for obligations that arise during the operation of a corporation when the corporate charter has been revoked for nonpayment of franchise taxes is that they ought not be allowed to avoid personal liability because of their nonfeasance [failure to comply with the law].

* * * *

---

a. In the "Search Cases by Party Name" box, enter "Bullington." In the page showing search results, scroll down the list to "6/21/2001" and click on the case name to access the opinion. The Arkansas judiciary maintains this Web site.
b. A *franchise tax* is an annual tax imposed for the privilege of doing business in a state.

(continued)

CASE 14.2—Continued

In the instant case [the case now before the court], it is undisputed that the corporate charter of Bullington Builders, Inc., was revoked for failure to pay franchise taxes approximately one and one-half months prior to the completion of construction, and the charter was not reinstated. After the corporate charter was revoked, appellant individually assumed the performance of the contract. * * * [W]e hold that appellant was personally liable for any liabilities that resulted from faulty or incomplete performance of the contract, including those arising as breaches of express or implied warranties.

DECISION AND REMEDY The Arkansas Supreme Court affirmed the lower court's judgment, holding Bullington personally liable for the unsatisfactory performance of the contract with Palangio.

FOR CRITICAL ANALYSIS—Economic Consideration *If there had been no express warranties and all implied warranties had been disclaimed, could Bullington have avoided liability?*

Constitutional Rights of Corporations

A corporation is recognized under state and federal law as a "person," and it enjoys many of the same rights and privileges that U.S. citizens enjoy. The Bill of Rights guarantees a person, as a citizen, certain protections, and corporations are considered persons in most instances. Accordingly, a corporation has the same right as a natural person to equal protection of the laws under the Fourteenth Amendment. It has the right of access to the courts as an entity that can sue or be sued. It also has the right of due process before denial of life, liberty, or property, as well as freedom from unreasonable searches and seizures and from double jeopardy.

Under the First Amendment, corporations are entitled to freedom of speech. As we pointed out in Chapter 5, however, commercial speech (such as advertising) and political speech (such as contributions to political causes or candidates) receive significantly less protection than noncommercial speech.

Only the corporation's individual officers and employees possess the Fifth Amendment right against self-incrimination. Additionally, the privileges and immunities clause of the Constitution (Article IV, Section 2) does not protect corporations. This clause requires each state to treat citizens of other states equally with respect to access to courts, travel rights, and so forth.

Torts and Criminal Acts

"Did you expect a corporation to have a conscience, when it has no soul to be damned and no body to be kicked?"
EDWARD THURLOW, 1731–1806
(English jurist)

A corporation is liable for the torts committed by its agents or officers within the course and scope of their employment. This principle applies to a corporation exactly as it applies to the ordinary agency relationships discussed in Chapter 16.

As you learned in Chapter 7, under modern criminal law, a corporation can sometimes be held liable for the criminal acts of its agents and employees, provided the punishment is one that can be applied to the corporation. Corporate criminal prosecutions were at one time relatively rare, but in the past decade they have increased significantly in number. Obviously, corporations cannot be imprisoned, but they can be fined. Of course, corporate directors and officers can be imprisoned, and in recent years, many have faced criminal penalties for their own actions or for the actions of employees under their supervision.

CLASSIFICATION OF CORPORATIONS

The classification of a corporation depends on its purpose, ownership characteristics, and location. A corporation is referred to as a **domestic corporation** by its home state (the state in which it incorporates). A corporation formed in one state but doing business in another is referred to in that other state as a **foreign corporation**. A corporation formed in another country—say, Mexico—but doing business in the United States is referred to in the United States as an **alien corporation**.

A corporation does not have an automatic right to do business in a state other than its state of incorporation. In certain circumstances, it must obtain a *certificate of authority* in any state in which it plans to do business. Once the certificate has been issued, the powers conferred on a corporation by its home state generally can be exercised in the other state.

DOMESTIC CORPORATION
In a given state, a corporation that does business in, and is organized under the law of, that state.

FOREIGN CORPORATION
In a given state, a corporation that does business in the state without being incorporated therein.

ALIEN CORPORATION
A designation in the United States for a corporation formed in another country but doing business in the United States.

CORPORATE MANAGEMENT—SHAREHOLDERS

The acquisition of a share of stock makes a person an owner and shareholder in a corporation. Shareholders thus own the corporation. Although they have no legal title to corporate property, such as buildings and equipment, they do have an *equitable* (ownership) interest in the firm.

As a general rule, shareholders have no responsibility for the daily management of the corporation, although they are ultimately responsible for choosing the board of directors, which does have such control. Ordinarily, corporate officers and other employees owe no direct duty to individual shareholders. Their duty is to the corporation as a whole. A director, however, is in a fiduciary relationship to the corporation and therefore serves the interests of the shareholders. Generally, there is no legal relationship between shareholders and creditors of the corporation. Shareholders can, in fact, be creditors of

BE AWARE Shareholders are not normally agents of their corporation.

BMW automobiles are inspected at a plant in the United States. BMW is classified as an alien corporation. What is the difference between an alien corporation and a foreign corporation?

the corporation and thus have the same rights of recovery against the corporation and thus have the same rights of recovery against the corporation as any other creditor.

In this section, we look at the powers and voting rights of shareholders, which are generally established in the articles of incorporation and under the state's general incorporation law.

Shareholders' Powers

Shareholders must approve fundamental corporate changes before the changes can be effected. Hence, shareholders are empowered to amend the articles of incorporation (charter) and bylaws, approve a merger or the dissolution of the corporation, and approve the sale of all or substantially all of the corporation's assets. Some of these powers are subject to prior board approval.

Directors are elected to (and removed from) the board of directors by a vote of the shareholders. The first board of directors is either named in the articles of incorporation or chosen by the incorporators to serve until the first shareholders' meeting. From that time on, the selection and retention of directors are exclusively shareholder functions.

Directors usually serve their full terms; if they are unsatisfactory, they are simply not reelected. Shareholders have the inherent power, however, to remove a director from office *for cause* (breach of duty or misconduct) by a majority vote.[5] Some state statutes (and some corporate charters) even permit removal of directors *without cause* by the vote of a majority of the holders of outstanding shares entitled to vote.

Shareholders' Meetings

Shareholders' meetings must occur at least annually, and additional, special meetings can be called as needed to take care of urgent matters. Because it is usually not practical for owners of only a few shares of stock of publicly traded corporations to attend shareholders' meetings, such stockholders normally give third parties written authorization to vote their shares at the meeting. This authorization is called a **proxy** (from the Latin *procurare*, "to manage, take care of"). Proxies are often solicited by management, but any person can solicit proxies to concentrate voting power.

Shareholder Voting For shareholders to act during a meeting, a quorum must be present. Generally, a quorum exists when shareholders holding more than 50 percent of the outstanding shares are present. Corporate business matters are presented in the form of *resolutions*, which shareholders vote to approve or disapprove. Some state statutes have set forth specific voting requirements, and corporations' articles or bylaws must abide by these statutory requirements. Some states provide that the unanimous written consent of shareholders is a permissible alternative to holding a shareholders' meeting. Once a quorum is present, a majority vote of the shares represented at the meeting is usually required to pass resolutions.

At times, a greater-than-majority vote will be required either by a statute or by the corporate charter. Extraordinary corporate matters, such as a merger, consolidation, or dissolution of the corporation, require a higher percentage of

PROXY
In corporation law, a written agreement between a stockholder and another under which the stockholder authorizes the other to vote the stockholder's shares in a certain manner.

BE CAREFUL Once a quorum is present, a vote can be taken even if some shareholders leave without casting their votes.

---

5. A director can often demand court review of removal for cause.

the representatives of all corporate shares entitled to vote, not just a majority of those present at that particular meeting.

Cumulative Voting Most states permit or even require shareholders to elect directors by cumulative voting, a method of voting designed to allow minority shareholders representation on the board of directors.[6] When cumulative voting is allowed or required, the number of members of the board to be elected is multiplied by the total number of voting shares. The result equals the number of votes a shareholder has, and this total can be cast for one or more nominees for director. All nominees stand for election at the same time. When cumulative voting is not required either by statute or under the articles, the entire board can be elected by a simple majority of shares at a shareholders' meeting.

● EXAMPLE 2 Suppose that a corporation has 10,000 shares issued and outstanding. One group of shareholders (the minority shareholders) holds only 3,000 shares, and the other group of shareholders (the majority shareholders) holds the other 7,000 shares. Three members of the board are to be elected. The majority shareholders' nominees are Acevedo, Barkley, and Craycik. The minority shareholders' nominee is Drake. Can Drake be elected by the minority shareholders?

If cumulative voting is allowed, the answer is yes. The minority shareholders have 9,000 votes among them (the number of directors to be elected times the number of shares held by the minority shareholders equals 3 times 3,000, which equals 9,000 votes). All of these votes can be cast to elect Drake. The majority shareholders have 21,000 votes (3 times 7,000 equals 21,000 votes), but these votes have to be distributed among their three nominees. The principle of cumulative voting is that no matter how the majority shareholders cast their 21,000 votes, they will not be able to elect all three directors if the minority shareholders cast all of their 9,000 votes for Drake, as illustrated in Exhibit 14–2. ●

6. See, for example, California Corporate Code Section 708. Under RMBCA 7.28, however, no cumulative voting rights exist unless the articles of incorporation so provide.

EXHIBIT 14–2 RESULTS OF CUMULATIVE VOTING

This exhibit illustrates how cumulative voting gives minority shareholders a greater chance of electing a director of their choice. By casting all of their 9,000 votes for one candidate (Drake), the minority shareholders will succeed in electing Drake to the board of directors.

Ballot	Majority Shareholders' Votes			Minority Shareholders' Votes	Directors Elected
	Acevedo	Barkley	Craycik	Drake	
1	10,000	10,000	1,000	9,000	Acevedo/Barkley/Drake
2	9,001	9,000	2,999	9,000	Acevedo/Barkley/Drake
3	6,000	7,000	8,000	9,000	Barkley/Craycik/Drake

CORPORATE MANAGEMENT—DIRECTORS

A corporation typically is governed by a board of directors. Subject to statutory limitations, the number of directors is set forth in the corporation's articles or bylaws.

Election of Directors

The first board of directors is normally appointed by the incorporators on the creation of the corporation, or directors are named by the corporation itself in the articles. The initial board serves until the first annual shareholders' meeting. Subsequent directors are elected by a majority vote of the shareholders.

The term of office for a director is usually one year—from annual meeting to annual meeting. Longer and staggered terms are permissible under most state statutes. A common practice is to elect one-third of the board members each year for a three-year term. In this way, there is greater management continuity.

More than 50 percent of the publicly traded companies in the United States are incorporated under Delaware law.[7] Consequently, decisions of the Delaware courts on questions of corporate law have a wide impact. In the following case, a board increased the number of its members to diminish the effect that subsequently elected directors would have on the board's decisions. This may have been acceptable under the firm's bylaws, but was it valid under Delaware law?

---

7. *Publicly traded* means that the stock of a company can be bought and sold among members of the general public. In contrast, the shares of a *closely held,* or *close, corporation* are often owned by only a few individuals whose right to buy or sell those shares may be restricted, at least initially, to each other.

CASE 14.3   MM Companies, Inc. v. Liquid Audio, Inc.

Delaware Supreme Court, 2003.
813 A.2d 1118.

COMPANY PROFILE *Liquid Audio,
Inc. (http://www.liquidaudio.com), is
a Delaware corporation, with its principal place of
business in Redwood City, California. Liquid Audio provides software and services for the delivery of music
over the Internet. Formed in 1996, Liquid Audio offered
the first digital music-commerce system featuring copy
protection and copyright management, as well as the
first and largest digital music-distribution network.
Liquid Audio's catalogue of secure music downloads is
one of the world's largest.*

BACKGROUND AND FACTS MM Companies,
Inc., a Delaware corporation with its principal place of
business in New York City, owned 7 percent of Liquid
Audio's stock. In October 2001, MM sent a letter to
Liquid Audio's board of directors offering to buy all of
the company's stock for about $3 per share. The board
rejected the offer. Liquid Audio's bylaws provide for a
board of five directors divided into three classes; one
class is elected each year. The next election, at which
two directors would be chosen, was set for September
2002. By mid-August, it appeared that MM's nominees,
Seymour Holtzman and James Mitarotonda, would win
the election. The board amended the bylaws to increase
the number of directors to seven and appointed Judith
Frank and James Somes to fill the new positions. In

CASE 14.3—Continued

September, MM's nominees were elected to the board, but their influence was diminished because there were now seven directors. MM filed a suit in a Delaware state court against Liquid Audio and others, challenging the board's actions. The court ruled in favor of the defendants. MM appealed to the Delaware Supreme Court.

IN THE WORDS OF THE COURT . . .

HOLLAND, Justice:

 *   *   *   *

The most fundamental principles of corporate governance are a function of the allocation of power within a corporation between its stockholders and its board of directors. The stockholders' power is the right to vote on specific matters, in particular, in an election of directors. The power of managing the corporate enterprise is vested in the shareholders' duly elected board representatives. *   *   *

Maintaining a proper balance in the allocation of power between the stockholders' right to elect directors and the board of directors' right to manage the corporation is dependent upon the stockholders' unimpeded right to vote effectively in an election of directors. *   *   * [Emphasis added.]

 *   *   *   *

When the *primary purpose* of a board of directors' [action] is to interfere with or impede the effective exercise of the shareholder franchise in a contested election for directors, the board must first demonstrate a compelling justification for such action as a condition precedent to any judicial consideration of reasonableness and proportionality. *   *   * [S]uch *   *   * actions by a board need not actually prevent the shareholders from attaining any success in seating one or more nominees in a contested election for directors and the election contest need not involve a challenge for outright control of the board of directors. *   *   * [T]he *   *   * actions of the board only need to be taken for the primary purpose of interfering with or impeding the effectiveness of the stockholder vote in a contested election for directors.

 *   *   *   *

 *   *   * [In this case, the directors] amended the bylaws to provide for a board of seven and appointed two additional members of the Board for the primary purpose of diminishing the influence of MM's two nominees *   *   *. That *   *   * action *   *   * compromised the essential role of corporate democracy in maintaining the proper allocation of power between the shareholders and the Board, because that action was taken in the context of a contested election for successor directors. Since the *   *   * Defendants did not demonstrate a compelling justification for that *   *   * action, the bylaw amendment that expanded the size of the Liquid Audio board, and permitted the appointment of two new members on the eve of a contested election, should have been invalidated.

DECISION AND REMEDY The Delaware Supreme Court reversed the judgment of the lower court and remanded the case for further proceedings. The state supreme court concluded that the board's amending the bylaws to increase the number of directors and filling the new positions with appointments was invalid, because the board acted primarily to impede the shareholders' right to vote in an impending election for successor directors.

FOR CRITICAL ANALYSIS—Political Consideration *How could MM's newly elected nominees, or any two directors, affect the decisions of a five-member board?*

Directors' Qualifications and Compensation

Few legal requirements exist concerning directors' qualifications. Only a handful of states impose minimum age and residency requirements. A director is sometimes a shareholder, but this is not a necessary qualification—unless, of course, statutory provisions or corporate articles or bylaws require ownership.

Compensation for directors is ordinarily specified in the corporate articles or bylaws. Because directors have a fiduciary relationship to the shareholders and to the corporation, an express agreement or provision for compensation often is necessary for them to receive money from the funds that they control and for which they have responsibilities.

Board of Directors' Meetings

The board of directors conducts business by holding formal meetings with recorded minutes. The date on which regular meetings are held is usually established in the articles or bylaws or by board resolution, and no further notice is customarily required. Special meetings can be called, with notice sent to all directors.

QUORUM
The number of members of a decision-making body that must be present before business may be transacted.

Quorum requirements can vary among jurisdictions. (A **quorum** is the minimum number of members of a body of officials or other group that must be present in order for business to be validly transacted.) Many states leave decisions regarding quorum requirements to the corporate articles or bylaws. In the absence of specific state statutes, most states provide that a quorum is a majority of the number of directors authorized in the articles or bylaws. Voting is done in person (unlike voting at shareholders' meetings, which can be done by proxy, as discussed earlier in this chapter).[8] The rule is one vote per director. Ordinary matters generally require a simple majority vote; certain extraordinary issues may require a greater-than-majority vote.

ETHICAL ISSUE

Should state corporation laws be changed to allow board of directors' meetings to be held in cyberspace?

Today, the corporation laws of most states—including California, Delaware, New York, and Texas—expressly permit telephone conferences for board of directors' meetings as long as the participants can hear one another. Section 8.20 of the RMBCA also allows directors' meetings to be held by telephone conference. Adapting these laws to provide for meetings via the Internet, however, is difficult. California recently attempted to resolve this problem by permitting board of directors' meetings to be held by electronic video screen communication or similar means, as long as three conditions are satisfied: (1) each participant must be able to communicate with all other participants simultaneously; (2) each participant must be provided with a means of proposing or objecting to specific corporate actions; and (3) the corporation must have a means of verifying that a person participating in the meeting is a director or other person entitled to participate. Whether other states will follow California's lead is not yet known. Clearly, at the heart of the

---

8. Except in Louisiana, which allows a director to vote by proxy under certain circumstances.

decision to use cyberspace for corporate board meetings are two basic concerns: confidentiality and effective communication. Ultimately, it will be up to corporate directors to decide if technology can adequately address these issues.

Directors' Management Responsibilities

Directors have responsibility for all policymaking decisions necessary to the management of corporate affairs. Just as shareholders cannot act individually to bind the corporation, the directors must act as a body in carrying out routine corporate business. One director has one vote, and generally the majority rules. The general areas of responsibility of the board of directors include the following:

1. Declaration and payment of corporate dividends to shareholders.
2. Authorization for major corporate policy decisions—for example, the initiation of proceedings for the sale or lease of corporate assets outside the regular course of business, the determination of new product lines, and the overseeing of major contract negotiations and major management-labor negotiations.
3. Appointment, supervision, and removal of corporate officers and other managerial employees and the determination of their compensation.
4. Financial decisions, such as the issuance of authorized shares and bonds.

   The board of directors can delegate some of its functions to an executive committee or to corporate officers. In doing so, the board is not relieved of its overall responsibility for directing the affairs of the corporation, but corporate officers and managerial personnel are empowered to make decisions relating to ordinary, daily corporate affairs within well-defined guidelines.

Role of Officers and Directors

A director occupies a position of responsibility unlike that of other corporate personnel. Directors are sometimes inappropriately characterized as *agents* (see Chapter 16) because they act on behalf of the corporation. No *individual* director, however, can act as an agent to bind the corporation; and as a group, directors collectively control the corporation in a way that no agent is able to control a principal. Directors are often incorrectly characterized as *trustees* because they occupy positions of trust and control over the corporation. Unlike trustees, however, they do not own or hold title to property for the use and benefit of others.

CONTRAST Shareholders own a corporation and directors make policy decisions, but officers who run the daily business of the corporation often have significant decision-making power.

Officers and Executive Employees   The officers and other executive employees are hired by the board of directors or, in rare instances, by the shareholders. In addition to carrying out the duties articulated in the bylaws, corporate and managerial officers act as agents of the corporation, and the ordinary rules of agency (discussed in Chapter 16) normally apply to their employment. The qualifications required of officers and executive employees are determined at the discretion of the corporation and are included in the articles or bylaws. In most states, a person can hold more than one office and can be both an officer and a director of the corporation.

Fiduciary Duties   Directors and officers have *fiduciary duties* to the corporation, because their relationship with the corporation and its shareholders is

Corporate executives discuss the business of their firm. How do the rights and duties of corporate officers differ from those of corporate directors?

> "It is not the crook in modern business that we fear but the honest man who does not know what he is doing."
>
> OWEN D. YOUNG, 1874–1962
> (American corporate executive and public official)

one of trust and confidence. The fiduciary duties of the directors and officers include the duty of care and the duty of loyalty. The duty of care requires directors and officers to be honest and use prudent business judgment in the conduct of corporate affairs. Directors and officers must carry out their responsibilities in an informed, businesslike manner. The duty of loyalty requires the subordination of the self-interest of the directors and officers to the interest of the corporation. In general, it prohibits directors and officers from using corporate funds or confidential corporate information for personal advantage. Directors and officers can be held liable to the corporation and to the shareholders for breach of either of these duties.

A breach of the duty of loyalty occurs when an officer or director, for his or her personal gain, takes advantage of a business opportunity that is financially within the corporation's reach, is in line with the firm's business, is to the firm's practical advantage, and is one in which the corporation has an interest.

The availability of cash to repay a corporation's debts can represent a "corporate opportunity." Does the use of that cash to repay a loan to a director constitute a "usurping" of that opportunity? That was the question in the following case.

CASE 14.4   In re Cumberland Farms, Inc.

United States Court of Appeals, First Circuit, 2002.
284 F.3d 216.
http://www.ca1.uscourts.gov/opinions/main.php[a]

COMPANY PROFILE *In 1938, Vasilios and Aphrodite Haseotes bought a dairy farm in*

Cumberland, Rhode Island. By 1990, Cumberland Farms, Inc. (**http://www.cumberlandfarms.com** *), a close corporation owned by their six children, owned more than one thousand convenience stores and gas stations, conducted wholesale operations in dairy and other products, owned and managed real estate, and delivered refined petroleum products to gas stations,*

---

a. In the left column, click on "Search." In the "Opinion Number" box, type "01-1344.01A," and click "Submit Query." In the result, click on the "Opinion" number to access the opinion. The U.S. Court of Appeals for the First Circuit maintains this Web site.

CASE 14.4—Continued

including its own. Through these businesses, Cumberland enjoyed a gross annual income of more than $1 billion.

BACKGROUND AND FACTS Demetrios Haseotes became Cumberland's chief executive officer and chairman of its board of directors in 1960. In the 1970s, to ensure Cumberland greater security in its gas supply, Haseotes acquired a refinery in Newfoundland, Canada. Because some states prohibit a company that operates a refinery from selling petroleum products retail, Haseotes chose to own the refinery through his own businesses, including Cumberland Crude Processing, Inc. (CCP). To operate the refinery, CCP borrowed more than $70 million from Cumberland,

under an agreement that required the payment of that loan first. Haseotes also loaned money to CCP. When cash was available, Haseotes had CCP repay $5.75 million to him, without telling the Cumberland board. CCP defaulted on its debt to Cumberland, which filed a bankruptcy petition in 1992. Haseotes filed a claim for $3 million against the firm, which asserted a claim for $5.75 million against him. Cumberland argued that Haseotes breached his duty of loyalty when he had CCP pay its debt to him while ignoring its debt to Cumberland. The court disallowed Haseotes's claim. On appeal, a federal district court affirmed this ruling. Haseotes appealed to the U.S. Court of Appeals for the First Circuit.

IN THE WORDS OF THE COURT . . .

LIPEZ, Circuit Judge.

* * * *

As a member of Cumberland's board of directors, Haseotes owed the corporation a fiduciary duty of loyalty and fair dealing. * * * *[D]irectors must act with absolute fidelity to the corporation and must place their duties to the corporation above every other financial or business obligation.* [Emphasis added.]

The fiduciary duty is especially exacting where the corporation is closely held. In a close corporation like Cumberland, the relationship among the stockholders must be one of trust, confidence and absolute loyalty if the enterprise is to succeed. * * * Disloyalty and self-seeking conduct on the part of any stockholder will engender bickering, corporate stalemates, and, perhaps, efforts to achieve dissolution.

* * * *

* * * When a corporate director learns of an opportunity that could benefit the corporation, she must inform the disinterested shareholders of all the material details of the opportunity so that they may decide whether the corporation can and should take advantage of it. It is inherently unfair for the director to deny the corporation that choice and instead take the opportunity for herself. * * * [T]he nondisclosure of a corporate opportunity is, *in itself,* unfair to a corporation and a breach of fiduciary duty.

* * * *

Here, any funds that became available in CCP provided an opportunity to pay down CCP's * * * debt to Cumberland. That opportunity was more than conceivably advantageous to Cumberland; it was desperately needed. Moreover, * * * [the loan] agreement explicitly required Haseotes to apply any available money toward Cumberland's loan before paying down CCP's debt to himself * * * . Yet, instead of attempting to repay Cumberland's loan, Haseotes had CCP pay more than $5 million on the loan from [him] * * * .

* * * *

* * * In such circumstances, Haseotes was obligated to seek approval from Cumberland's board before acting. * * *

(continued)

CASE 14.4—Continued

* * * *

* * * [Haseotes] argues that disclosure was unnecessary because the other members of Cumberland's board knew that money was available in CCP, and that Haseotes was using it to repay the loan from [him]. * * * [H]owever, * * * Cumberland's directors were not aware of the opportunity for repayment.

DECISION AND REMEDY The U.S. Court of Appeals for the First Circuit affirmed the lower court's judgment. Haseotes breached his duty of loyalty to Cumberland when, without informing Cumberland's board that money had become available in CCP, he had CCP apply the money toward its debt to himself rather than to its debt to Cumberland.

FOR CRITICAL ANALYSIS—Ethical Consideration *If Cumberland's board did, in fact, know that money was available in CCP and that Haseotes was using the money to pay his loan first, would Haseotes still have breached his duty of loyalty?*

Conflicts of Interest

The duty of loyalty also requires officers and directors to disclose fully to the board of directors any possible conflict of interest that might occur in conducting corporate transactions. The various state statutes contain different standards, but a contract will generally *not* be voidable if it was fair and reasonable to the corporation at the time it was made, if there was a full disclosure of the interest of the officers or directors involved in the transaction, and if the contract was approved by a majority of the disinterested directors or shareholders.

● **EXAMPLE 3** Southwood Corporation needs more office space. Lambert Alden, one of its five directors, owns the building adjoining the corporation's main office building. He negotiates a lease with Southwood for the space, making a full disclosure to Southwood and the other four board directors. The lease arrangement is fair and reasonable, and it is unanimously approved by the corporation's board of directors. In this situation, Alden has not breached his duty of loyalty to the corporation, and the contract is thus valid. The rule is one of reason. If it were otherwise, directors would be prevented from ever giving financial assistance to the corporations they serve.●

The Business Judgment Rule

BUSINESS JUDGMENT RULE
A rule that immunizes corporate management from liability for actions that result in corporate losses or damages if the actions are undertaken in good faith and are within both the power of the corporation and the authority of management to make.

Directors and officers are expected to exercise due care and to use their best judgment in guiding corporate management, but they are not insurers of business success. Honest mistakes of judgment and poor business decisions on their part do not make them liable to the corporation for resulting damages. This is the **business judgment rule.** The rule generally immunizes directors and officers from liability for the consequences of a decision that is within managerial authority, as long as the decision complies with management's fiduciary duties and as long as acting on the decision is within the powers of the corporation. Consequently, if there is a reasonable basis for a business decision, it is unlikely that the court will interfere with that decision, even if the corporation suffers as a result.

To benefit from the rule, directors and officers must act in good faith, in what they consider to be the best interests of the corporation, and with the care that an ordinarily prudent person in a similar position would exercise in similar circumstances. This requires an informed decision, with a rational basis, and with no conflict between the decision maker's personal interest and the interest of the corporation. To be informed, the director or officer must do what is necessary to become informed: attend presentations, ask for information from those who have it, read reports, review other written materials such as contracts—in other words, carefully study a situation and its alternatives.

To be free of conflicting interests, the director must not engage in self-dealing. ● EXAMPLE 4 A director should not oppose a *tender offer* (an offer to purchase shares in the company made by another company directly to the shareholders) that is in the corporation's best interest simply because its acceptance may cost the director her or his position. Similarly, a director should not accept a tender offer with only a moment's consideration based solely on the market price of the corporation's shares. ●

> "All business proceeds on beliefs, or judgments of probabilities, and not on certainties."
> CHARLES ELIOT, 1834–1936
> (American educator and editor)

RIGHTS AND DUTIES OF OFFICERS AND MANAGERS

The rights of corporate officers and other high-level managers are defined by employment contracts, because these persons are employees of the company. Corporate officers normally can be removed by the board of directors at any time with or without cause and regardless of the terms of the employment contracts—although in so doing, the corporation may be liable for breach of contract. The duties of corporate officers are the same as those of directors, because both groups are involved in decision making and are in similar positions of control. Hence, officers are viewed as having the same fiduciary duties of care and loyalty in their conduct of corporate affairs as directors have.

RIGHTS OF SHAREHOLDERS

Shareholders possess numerous rights. A significant right—the right to vote their shares—has already been discussed. We now look at some additional rights of shareholders.

Stock Certificates

A **stock certificate** is a certificate issued by a corporation that evidences ownership of a specified number of shares in the corporation. Stock is intangible personal property, and the ownership right exists independently of the certificate itself. A stock certificate may be lost or destroyed, but ownership is not destroyed with it. A new certificate can be issued to replace one that has been lost or destroyed.[9] Notice of shareholders' meetings, dividends, and operational and financial reports are all distributed according to the recorded ownership listed in the corporation's books, not on the basis of possession of the certificate.

STOCK CERTIFICATE
A certificate issued by a corporation evidencing the ownership of a specified number of shares in the corporation.

---

9. For a lost or destroyed certificate to be reissued, a shareholder normally must furnish an indemnity bond to protect the corporation against potential loss should the original certificate reappear at some future time in the hands of a bona fide purchaser [UCC 8–302, 8–405(2)].

Preemptive Rights

A **preemptive right** is a common law concept under which a preference is given to shareholders over all other purchasers to subscribe to or purchase shares of a *new issue* of stock in proportion to the percentage of total shares they already hold. This allows each shareholder to maintain his or her portion of control, voting power, or financial interest in the corporation. Most statutes either (1) grant preemptive rights but allow them to be negated in the corporation's articles or (2) deny preemptive rights except to the extent that they are granted in the articles. The result is that the articles of incorporation determine the existence and scope of preemptive rights. Generally, preemptive rights apply only to additional, newly issued stock sold for cash, and the preemptive rights must be exercised within a specified time period (usually thirty days).

Dividends

As mentioned earlier in this chapter, a *dividend* is a distribution of corporate profits or income ordered by the directors and paid to the shareholders in proportion to their respective shares in the corporation. Dividends can be paid in cash, property, stock of the corporation that is paying the dividends, or stock of other corporations.[10]

State laws vary, but each state determines the general circumstances and legal requirements under which dividends are paid. State laws also control the sources of revenue to be used; only certain funds are legally available for paying dividends.

Illegal Dividends A dividend paid while the corporation is insolvent is automatically an illegal dividend, and shareholders may be liable for returning the payment to the corporation or its creditors. Furthermore, as just discussed, dividends are generally required by statute to be distributed only from certain authorized corporate accounts. Sometimes dividends are improperly paid from an unauthorized account, or their payment causes the corporation to become insolvent. Generally, in such cases, shareholders must return illegal dividends only if they knew that the dividends were illegal when they received them. Whenever dividends are illegal or improper, the board of directors can be held personally liable for the amount of the payment. When directors can show that a shareholder knew that a dividend was illegal when it was received, however, the directors are entitled to reimbursement from the shareholder.

Directors' Failure to Declare a Dividend When directors fail to declare a dividend, shareholders can ask a court to compel the directors to meet and to declare a dividend. For the shareholders to succeed, they must show that the directors have acted so unreasonably in withholding the dividend that the directors' conduct is an abuse of their discretion.

Often, large money reserves are accumulated for a bona fide purpose, such as expansion, research, or other legitimate corporate goals. The mere fact that sufficient corporate earnings or surplus is available to pay a dividend is not

---

10. Technically, dividends paid in stock are not dividends. They maintain each shareholder's proportional interest in the corporation. On one occasion, a distillery declared and paid a "dividend" in bonded whiskey.

enough to compel directors to distribute funds that, in the board's opinion, should not be paid.[11] The courts are circumspect about interfering with corporate operations and will not compel directors to declare dividends unless abuse of discretion is clearly shown.

Inspection Rights

Shareholders in a corporation enjoy both common law and statutory inspection rights. The shareholder's right of inspection is limited, however, to the inspection and copying of corporate books and records for a *proper purpose*, provided the request is made in advance. The shareholder can inspect in person, or an attorney, agent, accountant, or other type of assistant can do so.

Transfer of Shares

Stock certificates generally are negotiable and freely transferable by indorsement and delivery. Transfer of stock in closely held corporations, however, usually is restricted by the bylaws, by a restriction stamped on the stock certificate, or by a shareholder agreement. The existence of any restrictions on transferability must always be noted on the face of the stock certificate, and these restrictions must be reasonable.

Sometimes, corporations or their shareholders restrict transferability by reserving the option to purchase any shares offered for resale by a shareholder. This **right of first refusal** remains with the corporation or the shareholders for only a specified time or a reasonable time. Variations on the purchase option are possible. For example, a shareholder might be required to offer the shares to other shareholders first or to the corporation first.

RIGHT OF FIRST REFUSAL
The right to purchase personal or real property—such as corporate shares or real estate—before the property is offered for sale to others.

When shares are transferred, a new entry is made in the corporate stock book to indicate the new owner. Until the corporation is notified and the entry is complete, the current record owner has the right to be notified of (and attend) shareholders' meetings, the right to vote the shares, the right to receive dividends, and all other shareholder rights.

Shareholder's Derivative Suit

When those in control of a corporation—the corporate directors—fail to sue in the corporate name to redress a wrong suffered by the corporation, shareholders are permitted to do so "derivatively" in what is known as a **shareholder's derivative suit.** Some wrong must have been done to the corporation, and before a derivative suit can be brought, the shareholders must first state their complaint to the board of directors. Only if the directors fail to solve the problem or take appropriate action can the derivative suit go forward.

SHAREHOLDER'S DERIVATIVE SUIT
A suit brought by a shareholder to enforce a corporate cause of action against a third person.

The right of shareholders to bring a derivative action is especially important when the wrong suffered by the corporation results from the actions of corporate directors or officers. This is because the directors and officers would probably want to prevent any action against themselves.

---

11. A striking exception to this rule was made in *Dodge v. Ford Motor Co.,* 204 Mich. 459, 170 N.W. 668 (1919), when Henry Ford, the president and major stockholder of Ford Motor Company, refused to declare a dividend notwithstanding the firm's large capital surplus. The court, holding that Ford had abused his discretion, ordered the company to declare a dividend.

Derivative Actions in Other Nations

In the United States, during the 1980s and the early 1990s, there was a dramatic increase in the number of shareholder suits brought against directors and officers for alleged breaches of duties. Today, most of the claims brought against directors and officers are those alleged in shareholders' derivative suits. Other nations, however, are more restrictive in regard to the use of such suits. In Germany, for example, there is no provision for derivative litigation, and a corporation's duty to its employees is just as significant as its duty to the shareholder-owners of the company. The United Kingdom has no statute authorizing derivative actions, which are permitted only to challenge directors' actions that the shareholders could not legally ratify. Japan authorizes derivative actions but also permits a company to bring a suit against the shareholder-plaintiff for damages if the action is unsuccessful.

FOR CRITICAL ANALYSIS

Do corporations benefit from shareholders' derivative suits? If so, how?

The shareholder's derivative suit is singular in that those suing are not pursuing rights or benefits for themselves personally but are acting as guardians of the corporate entity. Therefore, any damages recovered by the suit normally go into the corporation's treasury, not to the shareholders personally.

LIABILITY OF SHAREHOLDERS

One of the hallmarks of the corporate organization is that shareholders are not personally liable for the debts of the corporation. If the corporation fails, shareholders can lose their investments, but that is generally the limit of their liability.

Disregarding the Corporate Entity

In some unusual situations, a corporate entity is used by its owners to perpetrate a fraud, circumvent the law, or in some other way accomplish an illegitimate objective. In these cases, the court will ignore the corporate structure and *pierce the corporate veil,* thus exposing the shareholders to personal liability [RMBCA 2.04]. In other words, when the facts show that great injustice would result from the use of a corporation to avoid individual responsibility, a court of equity will look behind the corporate structure to the individual stockholder.

The following are some of the factors that may cause the courts to pierce the corporate veil:

1. A party is tricked or misled into dealing with the corporation rather than the individual.

2. The corporation is set up never to make a profit or always to be insolvent, or it is too "thinly" capitalized—that is, it has insufficient capital at the time it is formed to meet its prospective debts or potential liabilities.

3. Statutory corporate formalities, such as holding required corporation meetings, are not followed.

4. Personal and corporate interests are mixed together, or *commingled*, to the extent that the corporation has no separate identity.

Although they are rare, certain other instances arise where a shareholder can be personally liable. One relates to illegal dividends, which were discussed previously. Two others relate to *stock subscriptions* and *watered stock*, which we discuss here.

Stock-Subscription Agreements

Sometimes stock-subscription agreements—written contracts by which one agrees to buy capital stock of a corporation—exist prior to incorporation. Normally, these agreements are treated as continuing offers and are irrevocable (for up to six months under RMBCA 6.20). Once the corporation has been formed, it can sell shares to shareholder investors. In either situation, once the subscription agreement or stock offer is accepted, a binding contract is formed. Any refusal to pay constitutes a breach resulting in the personal liability of the shareholder.

Shares of stock can be paid for by property or by services rendered instead of cash. They cannot be purchased with promissory notes, however. The general rule is that for **par-value shares** (shares that have a specific face value, or formal cash-in value, written on them, such as one penny or one dollar), the corporation must receive a value at least equal to the par-value amount. For **no-par shares** (shares that have no face value—no specific amount printed on their face), the corporation must receive the value of the shares as determined by the board or the shareholders when the stock was issued.

PAR-VALUE SHARES
Corporate shares that have a specific face value, or formal cash-in value, written on them, such as one dollar.

NO-PAR SHARES
Corporate shares that have no face value—that is, no specific dollar amount is printed on their face.

Watered Stock

When the corporation issues shares for less than the values stated above, the shares are referred to as **watered stock**.[12] Usually, the shareholder who receives watered stock must pay the difference to the corporation (the shareholder is personally liable). In some states, the shareholder who receives watered stock may be liable to creditors of the corporation for unpaid corporate debts.

WATERED STOCK
Shares of stock issued by a corporation for which the corporation receives, as payment, less than the stated value of the shares.

DUTIES OF MAJORITY SHAREHOLDERS

In some cases, a majority shareholder is regarded as having a fiduciary duty to the corporation and to the minority shareholders. This occurs when a single shareholder (or a few shareholders acting in concert) owns a sufficient number

---

12. The phrase *watered stock* was originally used to describe cattle that—kept thirsty during a long drive—were allowed to drink large quantities of water just prior to their sale. The increased weight of the "watered stock" allowed the seller to reap a higher profit.

of shares to exercise *de facto* control over the corporation. In these situations, majority shareholders owe a fiduciary duty to the minority shareholders when they sell their shares, because such a sale would be, in fact, a transfer of control of the corporation.

ETHICAL ISSUE

What if, in a close, family-owned corporation, one family member (shareholder) is treated unfairly by the others?

Small corporations owned by family members often face severe problems when relations among the family members deteriorate. For example, suppose that two sisters and their brother are equal shareholders in a corporation. Each shareholder is both a director and an officer of the corporation. Disagreements over how the corporation should be operated arise, and the two sisters, as the majority on the board of directors, vote to fire the brother from his position as corporate president. Although the brother remains a shareholder and a member of the board, he is deprived of his job (and his salary), which may have important economic consequences. Furthermore, he may be prevented by the corporate articles or by a shareholder agreement from selling his shares and investing his money elsewhere.

What can the brother do? Often, the only option in this kind of situation is to petition a court to dissolve the corporation or force the majority shareholders to buy the minority shareholder's shares. Although courts generally are reluctant to interfere with corporate decisions, they have held, in several cases, that majority shareholders owe a fiduciary duty to minority shareholders. A breach of this duty may cause a court to order the majority shareholders to buy out the minority shareholder's interest in the firm or, as a last resort, to dissolve the corporation.

KEY TERMS

CHAPTER SUMMARY BUSINESS ORGANIZATIONS

Major Traditional Business Forms (See pages 427–429.)	1. *Sole proprietorships*—The simplest form of business; used by anyone who does business without creating an organization. The owner is the business. The owner pays personal income taxes on all profits and is personally liable for all business debts.
	2. *Partnerships*—
	a. *General partnerships*—Created by agreement of the parties; not treated as an entity except for limited purposes. Partners have unlimited liability for partnership debts, and each partner normally has an equal voice in management. Income is "passed through" the partnership to the individual partners, who pay personal taxes on the income.
	b. *Limited partnerships*—Must be formed in compliance with statutory requirements. A limited partnership consists of one or more general partners, who have unlimited liability for partnership losses, and one or more limited partners, who are liable only to the extent of their contributions. Only general partners can participate in management.
	3. *Corporations*—A corporation is formed in compliance with statutory requirements, is a legal entity separate and distinct from its owners, and can have perpetual existence. The shareholder-owners elect directors, who set policy and hire officers to run the day-to-day business of the corporation. Shareholders normally are not personally liable for the debts of the corporation. The corporation pays income tax on net profits; shareholders pay income tax on disbursed dividends.
Limited Liability Companies (LLCs) (See pages 430–432.)	1. *Formation*—Articles of organization must be filed with the appropriate state office—usually the office of the secretary of state—setting forth the name of the business, its principal address, the names of the owners (called *members*), and other relevant information.
	2. *Advantages and disadvantages of the LLC*—Advantages of the LLC include limited liability, the option to be taxed as a partnership or as a corporation, and flexibility in deciding how the business will be managed and operated.
	3. *Operating agreement*—When an LLC is formed, the members decide, in an operating agreement, how the business will be managed and what rules will apply to the organization.
Limited Liability Partnerships (LLPs) (See pages 432–433.)	1. *Formation*—Articles must be filed with the appropriate state agency, usually the secretary of state's office. Typically, an LLP is formed by professionals who work together as partners in a partnership. Under most state LLP statutes, it is relatively easy to convert a traditional partnership into an LLP.
	2. *Liability of partners*—LLP statutes vary, but generally they allow professionals to avoid personal liability for the malpractice of other partners. Partners in an LLP continue to be liable for their own wrongful acts and for the wrongful acts of those whom they supervise.
Private Franchises (See pages 433–441.)	1. *Types of franchises*—
	a. Distributorship (for example, automobile dealerships).
	b. Chain-style operation (for example, fast-food chains).
	c. Manufacturing/processing-plant arrangement (for example, soft-drink bottling companies, such as Coca-Cola).

(continued)

CHAPTER SUMMARY BUSINESS ORGANIZATIONS—Continued

Private Franchises— continued	2. *Laws governing franchising*—Franchises are governed by contract law, occasionally by agency law, and by federal and state statutory and regulatory laws.
	
	3. *The franchise contract*—
	
	   a. Ordinarily requires the franchisee (purchaser) to pay a price for the franchise license.
	
	   b. Specifies the territory to be served by the franchisee's firm.
	
	   c. May require the franchisee to purchase certain supplies from the franchisor at an established price.
	
	   d. May require the franchisee to abide by certain standards of quality relating to the product or service offered but cannot set retail resale prices.
	
	   e. Usually provides for the date and/or conditions of termination of the franchise arrangement. Both federal and state statutes attempt to protect certain franchisees from franchisors who unfairly or arbitrarily terminate franchises.

The Nature of the Corporation (See pages 441–444.)	The corporation is a legal entity distinct from its owners. Formal statutory requirements, which vary somewhat from state to state, must be followed in forming a corporation. The corporation can have perpetual existence or be chartered for a specific period of time. 1. *Corporate personnel*—The shareholders own the corporation. They elect a board of directors to govern the corporation. The board of directors hires corporate officers and other employees to run the daily business of the firm. 2. *Corporate taxation*—The corporation pays income tax on net profits; shareholders pay income tax on the disbursed dividends that they receive from the corporation (double-taxation feature). 3. *Torts and criminal acts*—The corporation is liable for the torts committed by its agents or officers within the course and scope of their employment. In some circumstances, a corporation can be held liable (and be fined) for the criminal acts of its agents and employees. In certain situations, corporate officers may be held personally liable for corporate crimes.
Classification of Corporations (See page 445.)	A corporation is referred to as a *domestic corporation* within its home state (the state in which it incorporates). A corporation is referred to as a *foreign corporation* by any state that is not its home state. A corporation is referred to as an *alien corporation* if it originates in another country but does business in the United States.
Directors and Officers (See pages 448–455.)	1. *Election of directors*—The first board of directors is usually appointed by the incorporators; thereafter, directors are elected by the shareholders. Directors usually serve a one-year term, although longer and staggered terms are permitted under most state statutes. 2. *Directors' qualifications and compensation*—Few qualifications are mandated; a director can be a shareholder but is not required to be. Compensation is usually specified in the corporate articles or bylaws. 3. *Board of directors' meetings*—The board of directors conducts business by holding formal meetings with recorded minutes. The date of regular meetings is usually established in the corporate articles or bylaws; special meetings can be called, with notice sent to all directors. Quorum requirements vary from state to state; usually, a quorum is the majority of the corporate directors. Voting must usually be done in person, and in ordinary matters only a majority vote is required.

CHAPTER SUMMARY BUSINESS ORGANIZATIONS—Continued

Directors and Officers—continued	4. *Directors' management responsibilities*—Directors are responsible for declaring and paying corporate dividends to shareholders; authorizing major corporate decisions; appointing, supervising, and removing corporate officers and other managerial employees; determining employees' compensation; making financial decisions necessary to the management of corporate affairs; and issuing authorized shares and bonds. Directors may delegate some of their responsibilities to executive committees and corporate officers and executives.
	5. *Duties*—Directors are obligated to act in good faith, to use prudent business judgment in the conduct of corporate affairs, and to act in the corporation's best interests. Directors have a fiduciary duty to subordinate their own interests to those of the corporation in matters relating to the corporation. If a director fails to exercise these duties, he or she can be answerable to the corporation and to the shareholders for breaching the duties.
	6. *Business judgment rule*—This rule immunizes a director from liability for a corporate decision as long as the decision was within the powers of the corporation and the authority of the director to make and was an informed, reasonable, and loyal decision.
Shareholders (See pages 445–447 and 455–460.)	1. *Shareholders' meetings*—Shareholders' meetings must occur at least annually; special meetings can be called when necessary. Notice of the date, time, and place of the meeting (and its purpose, if it is specially called) must be sent to shareholders. Shareholders may vote by proxy (authorizing someone else to vote their shares) and may submit proposals to be included in the company's proxy materials sent to shareholders before meetings.
	2. *Shareholder voting*—Shareholder voting requirements and procedures are as follows:
	a. A minimum number of shareholders (a quorum—generally, more than 50 percent of shares held) must be present at a meeting for business to be conducted; resolutions are passed (usually) by simple majority vote.
	b. Cumulative voting may or may not be required or permitted. Cumulative voting gives minority shareholders a better chance to be represented on the board of directors.
	c. A shareholder may appoint a proxy (substitute) to vote his or her shares.
	3. *Shareholders' rights*—Shareholders have numerous rights, which may include the following:
	a. The right to a stock certificate and preemptive rights.
	b. The right to obtain a dividend (at the discretion of the directors).
	c. Voting rights.
	d. The right to inspect the corporate records.
	e. The right to sue on behalf of the corporation (bring a shareholder's derivative suit) when the directors fail to do so.
	4. *Shareholders' liability*—Shareholders may be liable for the retention of illegal dividends, for breach of a stock-subscription agreement, and for the value of watered stock.
	5. *Duties of majority shareholders*—In certain situations, majority shareholders may be regarded as having a fiduciary duty to minority shareholders and will be liable if that duty is breached.

FOR REVIEW

1. Which form of business organization is the simplest?

2. What are some advantages and disadvantages of doing business as a partnership or a corporation, respectively?

3. How do limited liability companies and limited liability partnerships differ from traditional corporations and partnerships?

4. What is a franchise? What are the most common types of franchises?

5. What are the rights and duties of the directors and officers of a corporation? What are the rights of shareholders in a corporate enterprise?

QUESTIONS AND CASE PROBLEMS

14–1. Forms of Business Organization. In each of the following situations, determine whether Georgio's Fashions is a sole proprietorship, a partnership, a limited partnership, or a corporation.

   (a) Georgio's defaults on a payment to supplier Dee Creations. Dee sues Georgio's and each of the owners of Georgio's personally for payment of the debt.

   (b) Georgio's raises $200,000 through the sale of shares of its stock.

   (c) At tax time, Georgio's files a tax return with the IRS and pays taxes on the firm's net profits.

   (d) Georgio's is owned by three persons, two of whom are not allowed to participate in the firm's management.

14–2. Choice of Business Form. Jorge, Marta, and Jocelyn are college graduates, and Jorge has come up with an idea for a new product that he believes could make the three of them very rich. His idea is to manufacture soft-drink dispensers for home use and market them to consumers throughout the Midwest. Jorge's personal experience qualifies him to be both first-line supervisor and general manager of the new firm. Marta is a born salesperson. Jocelyn has little interest in sales or management but would like to invest a large sum of money that she has inherited from her aunt. What factors should Jorge, Marta, and Jocelyn consider in deciding which form of business organization to adopt?

14–3. Rights of Shareholders. Dmitri has acquired one share of common stock of a multimillion-dollar corporation with over 500,000 shareholders. Dmitri's ownership is so small that he is questioning what his rights are as a shareholder. For example, he wants to know whether this one share entitles him to attend and vote at shareholders' meetings, inspect the corporate books, and receive periodic dividends. Discuss Dmitri's rights in these matters.

14–4. Duties of Directors. Overland Corp. is negotiating with Wharton Construction Co. for the renovation of Overland's corporate headquarters. Wharton, the owner of Wharton Construction, is also one of the five members of the board of directors of Overland. The contract terms are standard for this type of contract. Wharton has previously informed two of the other Overland directors of his interest in the construction company. Overland's board approves the contract on a three-to-two vote, with Wharton voting with the majority. Discuss whether this contract is binding on the corporation.

14–5. Business Judgment Rule. Charles Pace and Maria Fuentez were shareholders of Houston Industries, Inc. (HII), and employees of Houston Lighting & Power, a subsidiary of HII, when they lost their jobs because of a company-wide reduction in its work force. Pace, as a shareholder, three times wrote to HII, demanding that the board of directors terminate certain HII directors and officers, and file a suit to recover damages for breach of fiduciary duty. Three times, the directors referred the charges to board committees and an outside law firm, which found that the facts did not support the charges. The board also received input from federal regulatory authorities about the facts behind some of the charges. The board notified Pace that it would refuse his demands. In response, Pace and Fuentez filed a shareholder's derivative suit against Don Jordan and the other HII directors, contending that the board's investigation was inadequate. The defendants moved for summary judgment, arguing that the suit was barred by the business judgment rule. How should the court rule? Why? [*Pace v. Jordan,* 999 S.W.2d 615 (Tex.App.—Houston [1 Dist.] 1999)]

Case Problem with Sample Answer

14–6. Disregarding the Corporate Entity. William Soerries was the sole shareholder of Chickasaw Club, Inc., which operated a popular nightclub of the same name in Columbus, Georgia. Soerries maintained corporate checking accounts, but he paid his employees, suppliers, and entertainers in cash out of the club's proceeds. He owned the property on which the club was located and rented it to the club, but he made the mortgage payments out of the club's proceeds. Soerries often paid corporate expenses out of his personal funds. At 11:45 P.M. on July 31, 1996, eighteen-year-old Aubrey Lynn Pursley, who was already intoxicated, entered the Chickasaw Club. A city ordinance prohibited individuals under the age of twenty-one from entering nightclubs, but Chickasaw employees did not check Pursley's identification. Pursley drank more alcohol and was visibly intoxicated when she left the club at 3:00 A.M. with a beer in her hand. Shortly afterward, Pursley was killed when she lost control of her car and struck a tree. Joseph Dancause, Pursley's stepfather, filed a suit in a Georgia state court against Chickasaw Club, Inc., and Soerries for damages. Can Soerries be held personally liable? If so, on what basis? Explain. [*Soerries v. Dancause,* 546 S.E.2d 356 (Ga.App. 2001)]

To view a sample answer for this case problem, go to this book's Web site at http://leet.westbuslaw.com and click on "Interactive Study Center."

14–7. Inspection Rights. Craig Johnson founded Distributed Solutions, Inc. (DSI), in 1991 to make software and provide consulting services, including payroll services for small companies. Johnson was the sole officer and director and the majority shareholder. Jeffrey Hagen was a minority shareholder. In 1993, Johnson sold DSI's payroll services to himself and a few others and set up Distributed Payroll Solutions, Inc. (DPSI). In 1996, DSI had revenues of $739,034 and assets of $541,168. DSI's revenues in 1997 were $934,532. Within a year, however, all of DSI's assets were sold, and Johnson told Hagen that he was dissolving the firm because, in part, it conducted no business and had no prospects for future business. Hagen asked for corporate records to determine the value of DSI's stock, DSI's financial condition, and "whether unauthorized and oppressive acts had occurred in connection with the operation of the corporation which impacted the value of" the stock. When there was no response, Hagen filed a suit in an Illinois state court against DSI and Johnson, seeking an order to compel the inspection. The defendants filed a motion to dismiss, arguing that Hagen had failed to plead a proper purpose. Should the court grant Hagen's request? Discuss. [*Hagen v. Distributed Solutions, Inc.,* 328 Ill.App.3d 132, 764 N.E.2d 1141, 262 Ill.Dec. 24 (1 Dist. 2002)]

14–8. Franchise Termination. In the automobile industry, luxury-car customers are considered the most demanding segment of the market with respect to customer service. Jaguar Cars, a division of Ford Motor Co., is the exclusive U.S. distributor of Jaguar luxury cars. Jaguar Cars distributes its products through franchised dealers. In April 1999, Dave Ostrem Imports, Inc., an authorized Jaguar dealer in Des Moines, Iowa, contracted to sell its dealership to Midwest Automotive III, LLC. A Jaguar franchise generally cannot be sold without Jaguar Cars's permission. Jaguar Cars asked Midwest Auto to submit three years of customer satisfaction

index (CSI) data for all franchises with which its owners had been associated. CSI data are intended to measure how well dealers treat their customers and satisfy their customers' needs. Jaguar Cars requires above-average CSI ratings for its dealers. Most of Midwest Auto's scores fell below the national average. Jaguar Cars rejected Midwest Auto's application and sought to terminate the franchise, claiming that a transfer of the dealership would be "substantially detrimental" to the distribution of Jaguar vehicles in the community. Is Jaguar Cars's attempt to terminate this franchise reasonable? Why or why not? [*Midwest Automotive III, LLC v. Iowa Department of Transportation,* 646 N.W.2d 417 (Iowa 2002)]

14–9. Torts and Criminal Acts. Greg Allen is an employee, shareholder, director, and the president of Greg Allen Construction Co. In 1996, Daniel and Sondra Estelle hired Allen's firm to renovate a home they owned in Ladoga, Indiana. To finance the cost, they obtained a line of credit from Banc One, Indiana, which required periodic inspections to disburse funds. Allen was on the job every day and supervised all of the work. He designed all of the structural changes, including a floor system for the bedroom over the living room, the floor system of the living room, and the stairway to the second floor. He did all of the electrical, plumbing, and carpentry work and installed all of the windows. He did most of the drywall taping and finishing and most of the painting. The Estelles found much of this work to be unacceptable, and the bank's inspector agreed that it was of poor quality. When Allen failed to act on the Estelles' complaints, they filed a suit in an Indiana state court against Allen Construction and Allen personally, alleging in part that his individual work on the project was negligent. Can both Allen and his corporation be held liable for this tort? Explain. [*Greg Allen Construction Co. v. Estelle,* 762 N.E.2d 760 (Ind.App. 2002)]

A Question of Ethics & Social Responsibility

14–10. In 1990, American Design Properties, Inc. (ADP), leased premises at 8604 Olive Blvd. in St. Louis County, Missouri. Under the lease agreement, ADP had the right to terminate the lease on 120 days' written notice, but it did not have the right to sublease the premises without the lessor's (landowner's) consent. ADP had no bank account, no employees, and no money. ADP had never filed an income tax return or held a directors' or shareholders' meeting. In fact, ADP's only business was to collect and pay the exact amount of rent due under the lease. American Design Group, Inc. (ADG), a wholesale distributor of jewelry and other merchandise, actually occupied 8604 Olive Blvd. J. H. Blum owned ADG and was an officer and director of both ADG and ADP. Blum's husband, Marvin, was an officer of ADG and signed the lease as an officer of ADP. Marvin's former son-in-law, Matthew Smith, was a salaried employee of

ADG, an officer of ADG, and an officer and director of ADP. In 1995, Nusrala Four, Inc. (later known as Real Estate Investors Four, Inc.), purchased the property at 8604 Olive Blvd. and became the lessor. No one told Nusrala that ADG was the occupant of the premises leased by ADP. ADP continued to pay the rent until November 1998, when Smith paid with a check drawn on ADG's account. No more payments were made. On February 26, 1999, Marvin sent Nusrala a note that read, "We have vacated the property at 8604 Olive." Nusrala discovered the property had been damaged and filed a suit in a Missouri state court against ADG and ADP, seeking money for the damage. In view of these facts, consider the following questions. [*Real Estate Investors Four, Inc. v. American Design Group, Inc.,* 46 S.W.3d 51 (Mo.App. E.D. 2001)]

1. Given that ADG had not signed the lease and was not rightfully a sublessee, could ADG be held liable, at least in part, for the damage to the premises? Under what theory might the court ignore the separate corporate identities of ADG and ADP? If you were the judge, how would you rule in this case?
2. Assuming that ADP had few, if any, corporate assets, would it be fair to preclude Nusrala from recovering money for the damage from ADG?
3. Is it ever appropriate for a court to ignore the corporate structure? Why or why not?

Critical-Thinking Managerial Question

14-11. Tim Rodale, one of the directors of First National Bank, fails to attend any board of directors' meetings in five and a half years, never inspects any of the bank's books or records, and generally neglects to supervise the efforts of the bank president and the loan committee. Meanwhile, the bank president makes various improper loans and permits large overdrafts. Can Rodale be held liable to the bank for losses resulting from the unsupervised actions of the bank president and the loan committee? Explain.

Video Question

14-12. Go to this text's Web site at **http://leet.westbuslaw.com** and select "Video Questions." Click on "Chapter 14" and view the video titled *Corporation or LLC: Which Is Better?* Then answer the following questions.

1. Compare the liability that Anna and Caleb would be exposed to as shareholders/owners in a corporation versus being members in a limited liability company (LLC).
2. How are corporations taxed differently than LLCs?
3. Suppose that you were in the position of Anna and Caleb. Would you choose to create a corporation or an LLC? Why?

INTERACTING WITH THE INTERNET

For updated links to resources available on the Web, as well as a variety of other materials, visit this text's Web site at

http://leet.westbuslaw.com

To learn how the U.S. Small Business Administration assists in forming, financing, and operating businesses, go to

http://www.sbaonline.sba.gov

For information on the FTC regulations on franchising, as well as state laws regulating franchising, go to

http://www.ftc.gov/bcp/franchise/netfran.htm

A good source of information on the purchase and sale of franchises is Franchising.org, which is online at

http://www.franchising.org

One of the best sources on the Web for information on corporations, including their directors, is the EDGAR database of the Securities and Exchange Commission (SEC) at

http://www.sec.gov/edgar.shtml

Cornell University's Legal Information Institute has links to state corporation statutes at

http://www.law.cornell.edu/topics/state_statutes.html

ONLINE LEGAL RESEARCH EXERCISES

Go to **http://leet.westbuslaw.com**, the Web site that accompanies this text. Select "Interactive Study Center," and then click on "Chapter 14." There you will find the following Internet research exercises that you can perform to learn more about topics covered in this chapter.

Activity 14–1: ECONOMIC PERSPECTIVE—D&O Insurance
Activity 14–2: MANAGEMENT PERSPECTIVE—Franchises

BEFORE THE TEST

Go to **http://leet.westbuslaw.com**, the Web site that accompanies this text. Select "Interactive Quizzes." You will find at least twenty interactive questions relating to this chapter.

Westlaw® Campus

If your textbook provided for a subscription to Westlaw® Campus, or if you have otherwise purchased access to the Westlaw Campus database, you can access any of the cases presented or cited in this chapter by using your Westlaw Campus account.

CHAPTER **15**

Creditors' Rights and Bankruptcy

CONTENTS

CHAPTER OBJECTIVES

After reading this chapter, you should be able to answer the following questions:

1. What is a prejudgment attachment? What is a writ of execution? How does a creditor use these remedies?

2. What is garnishment? When might a creditor undertake a garnishment proceeding?

3. In a bankruptcy proceeding, what constitutes the debtor's estate in property? What property is exempt from the estate under federal bankruptcy law?

4. What is the difference between an exception to discharge and an objection to discharge?

5. In a Chapter 11 reorganization, what is the role of the debtor in possession?

America's font of practical wisdom, Benjamin Franklin, observed a truth known to all debtors in the quotation below—that creditors do observe "set days and times" and will expect to recover their money on the agreed-on dates. Historically, debtors and their families have been subjected to punishment, including involuntary servitude and imprisonment, for their inability to pay debts. The modern legal system, however, has moved away from a punishment philosophy in dealing with debtors. In fact, many observers say that it has moved too far in the other direction, to the detriment of creditors.

Normally, creditors have no problem collecting the debts owed to them. When disputes arise over the amount owed, however, or when the debtor simply cannot or will not pay, what happens? What remedies are available to creditors when debtors

> **"Creditors are . . . great observers of set days and times."**
> Benjamin Franklin, 1706–1790
> (American diplomat, author, and scientist)

default? In the first part of this chapter, we focus on other laws that assist the debtor and creditor in resolving their disputes without the debtor's having to resort to bankruptcy. The second part of this chapter discusses bankruptcy as a last resort in resolving debtor-creditor problems.

LAWS ASSISTING CREDITORS

Both the common law and statutory laws other than Article 9 of the UCC create various rights and remedies for creditors. We discuss here some of these rights and remedies.

Liens

A *lien* is an encumbrance on (claim against) property to satisfy a debt or protect a claim for the payment of a debt. Creditors' liens include mechanic's, artisan's, innkeeper's, and judicial liens.

Mechanic's Lien When a person contracts for labor, services, or materials to be furnished for the purpose of making improvements on real property (land and things attached to the land, such as buildings and trees—see Chapter 21) but does not immediately pay for the improvements, the creditor can file a **mechanic's lien** on the property. This creates a special type of debtor-creditor relationship in which the real estate itself becomes security for the debt.

• **EXAMPLE 1** A painter agrees to paint a house for a homeowner for an agreed-on price to cover labor and materials. If the homeowner refuses to pay for the work or pays only a portion of the charges, a mechanic's lien against the property can be created. The painter is the lienholder, and the real property is encumbered (burdened) with a mechanic's lien for the amount owed. If the homeowner does not pay the lien, the property can be sold to satisfy the debt. Notice of the foreclosure (the process by which the creditor deprives the debtor of his or her property) and sale must be given to the debtor in advance, however.•

Note that state law governs mechanic's liens. The time period within which a mechanic's lien must be filed is usually 60 to 120 days from the last date labor or materials were provided.

The following case concerned the amount owed under a lien filed by an unpaid subcontractor against a property owner after the primary contractor, whom the owner had paid in advance of the work, went out of business.

> "Creditors: One of a tribe of savages dwelling beyond the Financial Straits and dreaded for their desolating incursions."
>
> AMBROSE BIERCE, 1842–1914
> (American writer)

MECHANIC'S LIEN
A statutory lien on the real property of another, created to ensure payment for work performed and materials furnished in the repair or improvement of real property, such as a building.

CASE 15.1   AEG Holdings, L.L.C. v. Tri-Gem's Builders, Inc.

Superior Court of New Jersey,
Appellate Division, 2002.
347 N.J.Super. 511,
790 A.2d 954.
http://lawlibrary.rutgers.edu/search.shtml[a]

BACKGROUND AND FACTS L & N Enterprises– Hammonton, L.L.C., contracted with Tri-Gem's Builders, Inc., to construct an addition to L & N's commercial building in New Jersey for $198,200. Tri-Gem's hired AEG Holdings, L.L.C., as a subcontractor for some of the work. During the project, L & N paid Tri-Gem's a total of $129,604. Tri-Gem's went out of business, however, without finishing the job and without paying anything to its subcontractor. AEG filed a lien against L & N for $126,717, which was the amount owed to AEG for the work it had performed. AEG then filed a suit in a New

---

a. In the "Find Case by Citation" section, enter "347" in the "Volume" box and "511" in the "Page" box, and select "N.J.Super." as the "Reporter." Click on "Submit Form" to access the opinion. Rutgers University School of Law in Camden, New Jersey, maintains this Web site.

(continued)

CASE 15.1—Continued

Jersey state court for a judgment on the lien. The court awarded AEG the difference between the price of the contract between L & N and Tri-Gem's and the amount that L & N paid to Tri-Gem's ($198,200 minus $129,604, which equals $68,596). L & N appealed to a state inter-mediate appellate court, arguing that Tri-Gem's left the job without completing much work, which meant that L & N would have to hire others to finish the job at a cost exceeding the total original contract price.

IN THE WORDS OF THE COURT . . .

CIANCIA, J.A.D. [Judge, Appellate Division]
  *   *   *   *
  *   *   * Appellant [L & N] argues the rule [under the state lien statute] should be that as long as the property owner has paid the contractor more than the lien claim of the subcontractor, the property owner has no obligation to the subcontractor. In our view, appellant's interpretation of the [statute] runs counter to the legislative policy reflected therein *   *   * .
  *   *   * *Lien statutes are remedial and are designed to guarantee effective security to those who furnish labor or materials used to enhance the value of the property of others,* and, where the terms of the statute reasonably permit, the law should be construed to effect this remedial purpose. [Emphasis added.]
  Appellant's interpretation of the law protects property owners, but it does not protect lien-holding subcontractors. Even with the trial court's decision, AEG is only receiving a little more than half of what it is legitimately owed. If there are multiple subcontractors on a job and, by way of example, each claims an amount equal to ten percent of the total contract price, a property owner would owe nothing to any of them under appellant's interpretation of the [statute] so long as the property owner had paid the contractor more than ten percent of the total price. We are confident that the [state] Legislature never intended such a draconian [extremely harsh] application of the [statute].
  While it is true *   *   * that a property owner should not be made to pay twice, what is meant by that is that the property owner is never subject to liens in an amount greater than the amount unpaid by the owner to its prime con-tractor at the time the lien claim is filed by one claiming a lien through that prime contractor. Appellant points out that a property owner under this interpretation may very well end up paying more for the finished job than the original contract price. The property owner, however, has means to guard against that result. What appears to have happened here is that appellant's payments to Tri-Gem's got ahead of the work actually performed and when Tri-Gem's abandoned the job, L & N had to pay someone else to do the work Tri-Gem's should have done in the first place. That may not be fair to L & N, but leaving an innocent subcon-tractor without any payment is too high a price for correcting the inequity placed upon the property owner. The [state lien statute] does not suggest any such result and, indeed, in our view, suggests that when choosing between two innocent per-sons in these circumstances, it is the lien holder who prevails.

DECISION AND REMEDY The state intermediate appellate court affirmed the judgment in favor of AEG. A property owner who pays a contractor in advance runs the risk of never getting the work that is paid for from that contractor. A subcontractor does not bear the risk of that possibility, however. Thus, a property owner's liability is not reduced by payments made to a contractor that are not earned and due before a sub-contractor's lien is filed.

FOR CRITICAL ANALYSIS—Economic Consideration *What might L & N have done to avoid the financial loss it faced when Tri-Gem's left the job before completing much work on the project?*

Artisan's Lien An **artisan's lien** is a security device created at common law through which a creditor can recover payment from a debtor for labor and materials furnished in the repair or improvement of personal property. • EXAMPLE 2 Cindy leaves her diamond ring at the jeweler's to be repaired and to have her initials engraved on the band. In the absence of an agreement, the jeweler can keep the ring until Cindy pays for the services. Should Cindy fail to pay, the jeweler has a lien on Cindy's ring for the amount of the bill and normally can sell the ring in satisfaction of the lien. •

In contrast to a mechanic's lien, an artisan's lien is *possessory*. The lienholder ordinarily must have retained possession of the property and have expressly or impliedly agreed to provide the services on a cash, not a credit, basis. Usually, the lienholder retains possession of the property. When this occurs, the lien remains in existence as long as the lienholder maintains possession, and the lien is terminated once possession is voluntarily surrendered—unless the surrender is only temporary. If it is a temporary surrender, there must be an agreement that the property will be returned to the lienholder. Even with such an agreement, if a third party obtains rights in that property while it is out of the possession of the lienholder, the lien is lost. The only way that a lienholder can protect a lien and surrender possession at the same time is to record notice of the lien (if state law so permits) in accordance with state lien and recording statutes.

Modern statutes permit the holder of an artisan's lien to foreclose and sell the property subject to the lien to satisfy payment of the debt. As with the mechanic's lien, the holder of an artisan's lien is required to give notice to the owner of the property prior to foreclosure and sale. The sale proceeds are used to pay the debt and the costs of the legal proceedings, and the surplus, if any, is paid to the former owner.

Innkeeper's Lien An **innkeeper's lien** is another security device created at common law. An innkeeper's lien is placed on the baggage of guests for the agreed-on hotel charges that remain unpaid. If no express agreement has been made concerning the amount of those charges, the lien will be for the reasonable value of the accommodations furnished. The innkeeper's lien is terminated either by the guest's payment of the hotel charges or by the innkeeper's surrender of the baggage to the guest, unless the surrender is temporary. Additionally, the lien is terminated by the innkeeper's foreclosure and sale of the property.

Judicial Liens When a debt is past due, a creditor can bring a legal action against the debtor to collect the debt. If the creditor is successful in the action, the court awards the creditor a judgment against the debtor (usually for the amount of the debt plus any interest and legal costs incurred in obtaining the judgment). Frequently, however, the creditor is unable to collect the awarded amount.

To ensure that a judgment in the creditor's favor will be collectible, creditors are permitted to request that certain nonexempt property of the debtor be seized to satisfy the debt. (As will be discussed later in this chapter, under state or federal statutes, certain property is exempt from attachment by creditors.) If the court orders the debtor's property to be seized prior to a judgment in the creditor's favor, the court's order is referred to as a *writ of attachment*. If the court orders the debtor's property to be seized following a judgment in the creditor's favor, the court's order is referred to as a *writ of execution*.

Painters finish the trim on a house. If the homeowner does not pay for the work, what can the painters do to collect what they are owed?

ARTISAN'S LIEN
A possessory lien given to a person who has made improvements and added value to another person's personal property as security for payment for services performed.

INNKEEPER'S LIEN
A possessory lien placed on the luggage of hotel guests for hotel charges that remain unpaid.

Attachment. In the context of judicial liens, **attachment** is a court-ordered seizure and taking into custody of property prior to the securing of a judgment for a past-due debt. Attachment rights are created by state statutes. Attachment is a *prejudgment* remedy because it occurs either at the time of or immediately after the commencement of a lawsuit and before the entry of a final judgment. By statute, to attach before judgment, a creditor must comply with specific restrictions and requirements. The due process clause of the Fourteenth Amendment to the U.S. Constitution limits the courts' power to authorize seizure of a debtor's property without notice to the debtor or a hearing on the facts.

To use attachment as a remedy, the creditor must have an enforceable right to payment of the debt under law and must follow certain procedures. Otherwise, the creditor can be liable for damages for wrongful attachment. She or he must file with the court an *affidavit* (a written or printed statement, made under oath or sworn to) stating that the debtor is in default and stating the statutory grounds under which attachment is sought. The creditor must also post a bond to cover at least court costs, the value of the loss of use of the good suffered by the debtor, and the value of the property attached. When the court is satisfied that all the requirements have been met, it issues a **writ of attachment,** which directs the sheriff or other public officer to seize nonexempt property. If the creditor prevails at trial, the seized property can be sold to satisfy the judgment.

Writ of Execution. If the debtor will not or cannot pay the judgment, the creditor is entitled to go back to the court and obtain a court order directing the sheriff to seize (levy) and sell any of the debtor's nonexempt real or personal property that is within the court's geographic jurisdiction (usually the county in which the courthouse is located). This order is called a **writ of execution.** The proceeds of the sale are used to pay off the judgment, accrued interest, and the costs of the sale. Any excess is paid to the debtor. The debtor can pay the judgment and redeem the nonexempt property any time before the sale takes place. (Because of exemption laws and bankruptcy laws, however, many judgments are virtually uncollectible.)

Garnishment

Garnishment occurs when a creditor is permitted to collect a debt by seizing property of the debtor that is being held by a third party. Typically, a garnishment judgment is served on a debtor's employer so that part of the debtor's usual paycheck will be paid to the creditor. As a result of a garnishment proceeding, the court orders the debtor's employer to turn over a portion of the debtor's wages to pay the debt.

The legal proceeding for a garnishment action is governed by state law, and garnishment operates differently from state to state. According to the laws in some states, the creditor needs to obtain only one order of garnishment, which will then continuously apply to the debtor's weekly wages until the entire debt is paid. In other states, the creditor must go back to court for a separate order of garnishment for each pay period. Garnishment is usually a postjudgment remedy, but it can be a prejudgment remedy with a proper hearing by a court.

Both federal laws and state laws limit the amount of money that can be garnished from a debtor's weekly take-home pay.[1] Federal law provides a framework to protect debtors from suffering unduly when paying judgment debts.[2] State laws also provide dollar exemptions, and these amounts are often larger than those provided by federal law. Under federal law, garnishment of an employee's wages for any one indebtedness cannot be a ground for dismissal of an employee.

In the following case, the issue was whether, for purposes of a garnishment order, an employee's wages included the tips that the employee received directly from her employer's customers.

1. Some states (for example, Texas) do not permit garnishment of wages by private parties except under a child-support order.
2. For example, the federal Consumer Credit Protection Act of 1968, 15 U.S.C. Sections 1601–1693r, provides that a debtor can retain either 75 percent of the disposable earnings per week or the sum equivalent to thirty hours of work paid at federal minimum-wage rates, whichever is greater.

CASE 15.2 Shanks v. Lowe

Court of Appeals of Maryland, 2001.
364 Md. 538,
774 A.3d 411.

BACKGROUND AND FACTS

Laura Shanks won a judgment in a Maryland state court against Susan Lowe for $6,000. Shanks obtained a garnishment order and served it on Lowe's employer, Kibby's Restaurant & Lounge, which was ordered to withhold her attachable wages to pay the judgment and other costs. Exempt, under Maryland statutes, was one of two amounts, whichever was greater: (1) $154.50 multiplied by the number of weeks in which wages due were earned or (2) 75 percent of disposable wages ("the part of wages that remain after deduction of any amount required to be withheld by law").[a] Kibby's responded that Lowe's gross wages averaged $95 per week and that her "disposable income average per week is approx $35–$40," which was less than the allowable exemption of $154.50. Kibby's added that she also earned tips, which Kibby's included in her wages for tax purposes,[b] but claimed that the tips were not wages for garnishment purposes because they were never in Kibby's possession—restaurant patrons paid them directly to Lowe. The court agreed and dismissed the garnishment. Shanks appealed to a state intermediate appellate court, which affirmed the dismissal. Shanks appealed to the Maryland Court of Appeals, the state's highest court.

IN THE WORDS OF THE COURT . . .

WILNER, Judge:

The issue before us is whether tips earned by a waitress (or other person who earns tips) constitute "wages" for purposes of the Maryland wage garnishment law * * * . Principally at issue is whether tips fall within the definition of "wages" in [Maryland Code Section] 15–601(c): "all monetary remuneration paid to any employee for his employment." * * *

* * * * *

* * * Maryland Code [Section] 3–413(1) * * * requires each employer in Maryland to pay its employees the minimum wage required by the

a. See Maryland Code Sections 15–601 through 15–607.
b. For example, in one week, Kibby's reported to the federal and state governments $92.44 in wages due to Lowe and $153.50 in tips, for total taxable wages of $245.94. From that amount, Kibby's deducted $29.25 in federal taxes, $18.82 in Social Security taxes, and $13.87 in state taxes, leaving $30.50 owed to Lowe over the amount of her tips.

(continued)

CASE 15.2—Continued

Federal Fair Labor Standards Act. The term "wage" is defined in [Section] 3–401(e) as "all compensation that is due to an employee for employment" * * * . Section 3–419 takes specific account of tips and, as to any employee who regularly receives more than $30/month in tips, * * * provides, in relevant part, that an employer may include, "as part of the wage of an employee to whom this section applies," an amount that the employer sets to represent the tips of the employee, up to $2.77/hour. This is consistent with the Federal law, which defines a "tipped employee" as an employee engaged in an occupation in which he or she customarily and regularly receives more than $30/month in tips and, in relevant part, calculates the required minimum wage for such an employee as the actual cash wage paid by the employer plus an additional amount on account of tips equal to the difference between that actual cash wage and the minimum wage * * * . Thus, *for purposes of the State and Federal minimum wage laws, tips are regarded as part of wages.* [Emphasis added.]

Significantly, tips are included within the meaning of wages for purposes of the unemployment insurance and workers' compensation laws, each of which provide benefits based on the employee's wages. Were Ms. [Lowe] to file a claim for either unemployment insurance or workers' compensation benefits, any benefits to which she might be entitled would be determined on the basis of the aggregate amounts she received from both Kibby's and its customers.
* * * *

These statutes illustrate a consistent view by the General Assembly [Maryland's legislature] that, in using terms such as "wage" or "wages," it intended to include all forms of remuneration, whether or not paid directly by the employer, except to the extent specifically excluded. When it desired to limit the scope of a statute to the remuneration paid in the form of a salary or other periodic payment by an employer, it made that intent clear.

DECISION AND REMEDY The Maryland Court of Appeals reversed the judgment of the lower court and remanded the case for further proceedings. The state's highest court held that under state law, for purposes of a garnishment order, tips constitute "monetary remuneration paid to any employee for his employment" and are therefore part of the employee's wages.

FOR CRITICAL ANALYSIS—Economic Consideration *From a practical perspective, how can the creditor recover the employee's tips from the employer, given that customers give the tips directly to the employee?*

Creditors' Composition Agreements

CREDITORS' COMPOSITION AGREEMENT
An agreement formed between a debtor and his or her creditors in which the creditors agree to accept a lesser sum than that owed by the debtor in full satisfaction of the debt.

Creditors may contract with the debtor for discharge of the debtor's liquidated debts (debts that are definite, or fixed, in amount) on payment of a sum less than that owed. These agreements are called **creditors' composition agreements,** or simply *composition agreements,* and are usually held to be enforceable.

Mortgage Foreclosure

Mortgage holders have the right to foreclose on mortgaged property in the event of a debtor's default. The usual method of foreclosure is by judicial sale of the property, although the statutory methods of foreclosure vary from state to state. If the proceeds of the foreclosure sale are sufficient to cover both the costs of the foreclosure and the mortgaged debt, the debtor receives any surplus. If the sale proceeds are insufficient to cover the foreclosure costs and the mortgaged debt, however, the **mortgagee** (the creditor-lender) can seek to recover the difference from the **mortgagor** (the debtor) by obtaining a deficiency judgment representing the difference between the mortgaged debt and the amount actually received from the proceeds of the foreclosure sale.

The mortgagee obtains a deficiency judgment in a separate legal action pursued subsequent to the foreclosure action. The deficiency judgment entitles the mortgagee to recover the amount of the deficiency from other property owned by the debtor.

Suretyship and Guaranty

When a third person promises to pay a debt owed by another in the event the debtor does not pay, either a *suretyship* or a *guaranty* relationship is created. Suretyship and guaranty have a long history under the common law and provide creditors with the right to seek payment from the third party if the primary debtor defaults on his or her obligations. Exhibit 15–1 illustrates the relationship between a suretyship or guaranty party and the creditor.

Surety A contract of strict **suretyship** is a promise made by a third person to be responsible for the debtor's obligation. It is an express contract between the **surety** (the third party) and the creditor. The surety in the strictest sense is

MORTGAGEE
Under a mortgage agreement, the creditor who takes a security interest in the debtor's property.

MORTGAGOR
Under a mortgage agreement, the debtor who gives the creditor a security interest in the debtor's property in return for a mortgage loan.

SURETYSHIP
An express contract in which a third party to a debtor-creditor relationship (the surety) promises to be primarily responsible for the debtor's obligation.

SURETY
A person, such as a cosigner on a note, who agrees to be primarily responsible for the debt of another.

EXHIBIT 15–1 SURETYSHIP AND GUARANTY PARTIES

In a suretyship or guaranty arrangement, a third party promises to be responsible for a debtor's obligations. A third party who agrees to be *primarily* liable for the debt (that is, liable even if the principal debtor does not default) is known as a surety; a third party who agrees to be *secondarily* liable for the debt (that is, liable only if the principal debtor defaults) is known as a guarantor. Normally, a promise of guaranty (a collateral, or secondary, promise) must be in writing to be enforceable.

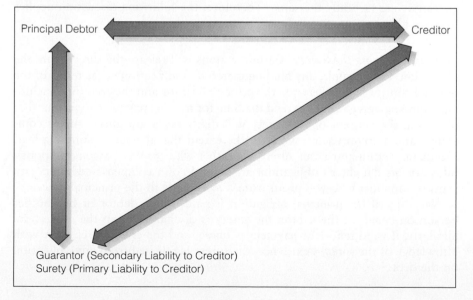

Principal Debtor — Creditor

Guarantor (Secondary Liability to Creditor)
Surety (Primary Liability to Creditor)

primarily liable for the debt of the principal. The creditor need not exhaust all legal remedies against the principal debtor before holding the surety responsible for payment. The creditor can demand payment from the surety from the moment the debt is due.

● **EXAMPLE 3** Robert Delmar wants to borrow money from the bank to buy a used car. Because Robert is still in college, the bank will not lend him the money unless his father, Joseph Delmar, who has dealt with the bank before, will cosign the note (add his signature to the note, thereby becoming a surety and thus jointly liable for payment of the debt). When Joseph Delmar cosigns the note, he becomes primarily liable to the bank. On the note's due date, the bank has the option of seeking payment from either Robert or Joseph Delmar, or both jointly. ●

Guaranty A guaranty contract is similar to a suretyship contract in that it includes a promise to answer for the debt or default of another. With a guaranty arrangement, the **guarantor**—the third person making the guaranty—is *secondarily* liable. The guarantor can be required to pay the obligation *only after the principal debtor defaults,* and default usually takes place only after the creditor has made an attempt to collect from the debtor.

GUARANTOR
A person who agrees to satisfy the debt of another (the debtor) only after the principal debtor defaults; a guarantor's liability is thus secondary.

● **EXAMPLE 4** A small corporation, BX Enterprises, needs to borrow money to meet its payroll. The bank is skeptical about the creditworthiness of BX and requires Dawson, its president, who is a wealthy businessperson and the owner of 70 percent of BX Enterprises, to sign an agreement making himself personally liable for payment if BX does not pay off the loan. As a guarantor of the loan, Dawson cannot be held liable until BX Enterprises is in default. ●

The Statute of Frauds requires that a guaranty contract between the guarantor and the creditor must be in writing to be enforceable unless the *main purpose* exception applies. This exception provides that if the main purpose of the guaranty agreement is to benefit the guarantor, the contract need not be in writing to be enforceable.

Defenses of the Surety and the Guarantor The defenses of the surety and the guarantor are basically the same. Therefore, the following discussion applies to both, although it refers only to the surety.

Actions Releasing the Surety. Certain actions will release the surety from the obligation. For example, any binding material modification in the terms of the original contract made between the principal debtor and the creditor—including a binding agreement to extend the time for making payment—without first obtaining the consent of the surety will discharge a gratuitous surety completely and a compensated surety to the extent that the surety suffers a loss. (An example of a gratuitous surety is a father who agrees to assume responsibility for his daughter's obligation; an example of a compensated surety is a venture capitalist who will profit from a loan made to the principal debtor.)

Naturally, if the principal obligation is paid by the debtor or by another person on behalf of the debtor, the surety is discharged from the obligation. Similarly, if valid tender of payment is made, and the creditor rejects it with knowledge of the surety's existence, the surety is released from any obligation on the debt.

Defenses of the Principal Debtor. Generally, the surety can use any defenses available to a principal debtor to avoid liability on the obligation to the creditor. Defenses available to the principal debtor that the surety *cannot* use include the principal debtor's incapacity or bankruptcy and the statute of limitations. The ability of the surety to assert any defenses the debtor may have against the creditor is the most important concept in suretyship, because most of the defenses available to the surety are also those of the debtor.

Other Defenses. Obviously, a surety may also have his or her own defenses— for example, incapacity or bankruptcy. If the creditor fraudulently induced the surety to guarantee the debt of the debtor, the surety can assert fraud as a defense. In most states, the creditor has a legal duty to inform the surety, prior to the formation of the suretyship contract, of material facts known by the creditor that would substantially increase the surety's risk. Failure to do so is fraud and makes the suretyship obligation voidable. In addition, if a creditor surrenders the collateral to the debtor or impairs the collateral while knowing of the surety and without the surety's consent, the surety is released to the extent of any loss suffered from the creditor's actions. The primary reason for this requirement is to protect the surety who agreed to become obligated only because the debtor's collateral was in the possession of the creditor.

Rights of the Surety and the Guarantor The rights of the surety and the guarantor are basically the same. Therefore, again, the following discussion applies to both.

Subrogation and Reimbursement. When the surety pays the debt owed to the creditor, the surety is entitled to certain rights. First, the surety has the legal **right of subrogation.** Simply stated, this means that any right the creditor had against the debtor now becomes the right of the surety. Included are creditor rights in bankruptcy, rights to collateral possessed by the creditor, and rights to judgments secured by the creditor. In short, the surety now stands in the shoes of the creditor and may pursue any remedies that were available to the creditor against the debtor.

Second, the surety has the **right of reimbursement** from the debtor. Basically, the surety is entitled to receive from the debtor all outlays made on behalf of the suretyship arrangement. Such outlays can include expenses incurred as well as the actual amount of the debt paid to the creditor.

Co-Sureties and the Right of Contribution. In the case of **co-sureties** (two or more sureties on the same obligation owed by the debtor), a surety who pays more than her or his proportionate share on a debtor's default is entitled to recover from the co-sureties the amount paid above the surety's obligation. This is the **right of contribution.** Generally, a co-surety's liability either is determined by agreement or, in the absence of agreement between the co-sureties, can be specified in the suretyship contract itself.

● EXAMPLE 5 Assume that two co-sureties are obligated under a suretyship contract to guarantee the debt of a debtor. Together, the sureties' maximum liability is $25,000. As specified in the suretyship contract, surety A's maximum liability is $15,000, and surety B's is $10,000. The debtor owes $10,000 and is in default. Surety A pays the creditor the entire $10,000. In the absence

RIGHT OF SUBROGATION
The right of a person to stand in the place of (be substituted for) another, giving the substituted party the same legal rights that the original party had.

RIGHT OF REIMBURSEMENT
The legal right of a person to be restored, repaid, or indemnified for costs, expenses, or losses incurred or expended on behalf of another.

CO-SURETY
A joint surety; a person who assumes liability jointly with another surety for the payment of an obligation.

RIGHT OF CONTRIBUTION
The right of a co-surety who pays more than his or her proportionate share on a debtor's default to recover the excess paid from other co-sureties.

of any agreement between the two co-sureties, surety A can recover $4,000 from surety B ($10,000/$25,000 × $10,000 = $4,000).●

LAWS ASSISTING DEBTORS

HOMESTEAD EXEMPTION
A law permitting a debtor to retain the family home, either in its entirety or up to a specified dollar amount, free from the claims of unsecured creditors or trustees in bankruptcy.

The law protects debtors as well as creditors. Certain property of the debtor, for example, is exempt from creditors' actions. Probably the most familiar of these exemptions is the **homestead exemption.** Each state permits the debtor to retain the family home, either in its entirety or up to a specified dollar amount, free from the claims of unsecured creditors or trustees in bankruptcy. The purpose of the homestead exemption is to ensure that the debtor will retain some form of shelter.

●EXAMPLE 6 Suppose that Van Cleave owes Acosta $40,000. The debt is the subject of a lawsuit, and the court awards Acosta a judgment of $40,000 against Van Cleave. Van Cleave's home is valued at $50,000, and the state exemption on homesteads is $25,000. There are no outstanding mortgages or other liens. To satisfy the judgment debt, Van Cleave's family home is sold at public auction for $45,000. The proceeds of the sale are distributed as follows:

1. Van Cleave is given $25,000 as his homestead exemption.
2. Acosta is paid $20,000 toward the judgment debt, leaving a $20,000 deficiency judgment that can be satisfied from any other nonexempt property (personal or real) that Van Cleave may have, if allowed by state law.●

State exemption statutes usually include both real and personal property. Personal property that is most often exempt from satisfaction of judgment debts includes the following:

1. Household furniture up to a specified dollar amount.
2. Clothing and certain personal possessions, such as family pictures or a Bible.

A notice announces the auction of a house. Under what conditions might a creditor not receive full payment from the proceeds of the sale?

Public Notice
By order of the 8th District Court of Alameda, this property will be sold at public

AUCTION
============
Saturday, May 3 - Noon

All bids must be supported by bank certified check for at least 20% of the bid amount. Remainder of bid must be paid with certified check within 48 hours of bid.

3. A vehicle (or vehicles) for transportation (at least up to a specified dollar amount).

4. Certain classified animals, usually livestock but including pets.

5. Equipment that the debtor uses in a business or trade, such as tools or professional instruments, up to a specified dollar amount.

Consumer protection statutes (see Chapter 19) also protect debtors' rights. Of course, bankruptcy laws, which are discussed in the next section, are designed specifically to assist debtors in need of relief from their debts.

BANKRUPTCY AND REORGANIZATION

At one time, debtors who could not pay their debts as they came due faced harsh consequences, including imprisonment and involuntary servitude. Today, in contrast, debtors have numerous rights. Some of these rights have already been mentioned. We now look at another significant right of debtors: the right to petition for bankruptcy relief under federal law.

Bankruptcy law in the United States has two goals—to protect a debtor by giving him or her a fresh start, free from creditors' claims, and to ensure equitable treatment to creditors who are competing for a debtor's assets. Bankruptcy law is federal law, but state laws on secured transactions, liens, judgments, and exemptions also play a role in federal bankruptcy proceedings.

Current bankruptcy law (the Bankruptcy Code, or simply the Code) is based on the Bankruptcy Reform Act of 1978, as amended. By the time you read this text, however, a bankruptcy reform act now before Congress may have been enacted. See this chapter's *Landmark in the Legal Environment* feature on the next two pages for a discussion of the proposed legislation.

> "How often have I been able to trace bankruptcies and insolvencies to some lawsuit, . . . the costs of which have mounted up to large sums."
>
> HENRY PETER BROUGHAM, 1778–1868
> (English politician)

Bankruptcy Courts

Bankruptcy proceedings are held in federal bankruptcy courts. A bankruptcy court's primary function is to hold *core proceedings*[3] dealing with the procedures required to administer the estate of the debtor in bankruptcy. Bankruptcy courts are under the authority of U.S. district courts, and rulings from bankruptcy courts can be appealed to the district courts. Fundamentally, a bankruptcy court performs an administrative function for the district court concerning matters in bankruptcy. A bankruptcy court can conduct a jury trial if the appropriate district court has authorized it and if the parties to the bankruptcy consent to a jury trial.

RECALL Congress regulates the jurisdiction of the federal courts, within the limits set by the Constitution. Congress can expand or reduce the number of federal courts at any time.

Types of Bankruptcy Relief

The Bankruptcy Code, which is contained in Title 11 of the U.S. Code (U.S.C.), is divided into a series of "chapters." Chapters 1, 3, and 5 of the Code include general definitional provisions and provisions governing case administration and procedures, creditors, the debtor, and the estate. These three chapters of the Code apply generally to all types of bankruptcies. The

---

3. *Core proceedings* are procedural functions, such as allowance of claims, decisions on preferences, automatic-stay proceedings, confirmation of bankruptcy plans, discharge of debts, and so on. These terms and procedures are defined and discussed in the following sections of this chapter.

LANDMARK IN THE LEGAL ENVIRONMENT

The Proposed Bankruptcy Reform Act

Article I, Section 8, of the U.S. Constitution gives Congress the power to establish "uniform Laws on the subject of Bankruptcies throughout the United States." Congress has exercised this power since 1800. As mentioned elsewhere, the basis for current bankruptcy law is the Bankruptcy Reform Act of 1978. The 1978 act, referred to since then simply as the Bankruptcy Code, has been amended several times since its passage. If the proposed Bankruptcy Abuse Prevention and Consumer Protection Act of 2003[a] currently before Congress is enacted, as it may be by the time this book is in print, the Bankruptcy Code will undergo another significant overhaul.

PREVENTING ABUSE The proposed legislation is, in part, a response to businesses' concerns about the sharp rise in personal bankruptcy filings. Since 1980, the number of bankruptcy filings per year has climbed from less than 300,000 to over 1.4 million. The perception has been that debtors who were by no means poor were taking advantage of the bankruptcy system to erase debts that they legitimately owed. One of the major goals of the act is to require consumers to pay their debts instead of having those debts discharged in a Chapter 7 (liquidation) bankruptcy proceeding.

To that end, the act calls for a complicated system of "means testing" to prevent debtors who earn more than their state's median family income (in most cases, about $50,000) from filing for Chapter 7 bankruptcy. Essentially, debtors who can afford to repay a certain percentage of their debts over a five-year period will not be able to take advantage of Chapter 7 but instead will have to accept a Chapter 13 repayment plan. The proposed act also requires debtors to participate in financial

a. The provisions of the act discussed in this feature are drawn from H.R. 978, which was issued on March 19, 2003.

LIQUIDATION
The sale of all of the nonexempt assets of a debtor and the distribution of the proceeds to the debtor's creditors. Chapter 7 of the Bankruptcy Code provides for liquidation bankruptcy proceedings.

next five chapters set forth the different types of relief that debtors may seek. Chapter 7 provides for **liquidation** proceedings (the selling of all nonexempt assets and the distribution of the proceeds to the debtor's creditors). Chapter 9 governs the adjustment of the debts of municipalities. Chapter 11 governs reorganizations. Chapter 12 (for family farmers) and Chapter 13 (for individuals) provide for adjustment of the debts of parties with regular income.[4]

In the following pages, we deal first with liquidation proceedings under Chapter 7 of the Code. We then examine the procedures required for Chapter 11 reorganizations and for Chapter 12 and Chapter 13 plans.

CHAPTER 7—LIQUIDATION

Liquidation is the most familiar type of bankruptcy proceeding and is often referred to as an *ordinary,* or *straight, bankruptcy.* Put simply, debtors in straight bankruptcies state their debts and turn their assets over to trustees. The trustees sell the assets and distribute the proceeds to creditors. With cer-

---

4. There are no Chapters 2, 4, 6, 8, or 10 in Title 11. Such "gaps" are not uncommon in the U.S.C. This is because, when a statute is enacted, chapter numbers (or other subdivisional unit numbers) are sometimes reserved for future use. (A gap may also appear if a law has been repealed.)

LANDMARK IN THE LEGAL ENVIRONMENT

The New Bankruptcy Reform Act (Continued)

counseling before filing for bankruptcy.

OTHER KEY PROVISIONS OF THE PROPOSED ACT

Another key provision of the act places limits on the homestead exemptions that exist in six states, among them Florida and Texas. Homestead exemptions in these states allow debtors petitioning for bankruptcy to shield unlimited amounts of equity in their homes from creditors. The new act requires that a home be owned for at least forty months before the exemption can be claimed. If the home is owned for less than forty months, a homeowner can claim only $125,000 as a homestead exemption.

Another provision requires credit-card companies to make expanded disclosures about their interest rates and payment schedules. The act also limits the ability of parents to use the bankruptcy system as a means of avoiding child-support payments.

Additionally, the act increases protections for family farmers and provides more protection for personal information possessed by businesses undergoing bankruptcy. Earlier versions of the proposed act prevented those who have been convicted of violence at abortion-clinic protests from filing for bankruptcy to avoid fines and debts. Although this provision was marginal to the major thrust of the legislation, it nonetheless helped to prevent passage of an earlier version of the act.

Application to Today's World

The Bankruptcy Reform Act of 1978 was widely criticized for making it too easy for debtors to discharge their debts in bankruptcy. Clearly, the new bankruptcy reform legislation addresses this criticism. Although there is general support for bankruptcy reform, some critics warn that the proposed act has gone too far in protecting creditors and in preventing debtors from obtaining bankruptcy relief.

---

tain exceptions, the remaining debts are then **discharged** (extinguished), and the debtors are relieved of the obligation to pay the debts.

Any "person"—defined as including individuals, partnerships, and corporations—may be a debtor under Chapter 7. Railroads, insurance companies, banks, savings and loan associations, investment companies licensed by the Small Business Administration, and credit unions *cannot* be Chapter 7 debtors, however. Other chapters of the Code or other federal or state statutes apply to them. A husband and wife may file jointly for bankruptcy under a single petition.

DISCHARGE
In bankruptcy proceedings, the extinction of the debtor's dischargeable debts.

Filing the Petition

A straight bankruptcy may be commenced by the filing of either a voluntary or an involuntary **petition in bankruptcy**—the document that is filed with a bankruptcy court to initiate bankruptcy proceedings.

Voluntary Bankruptcy A voluntary petition is brought by the debtor, who files official forms designated for that purpose in the bankruptcy court. A **consumer-debtor** (defined as an individual whose debts are primarily consumer debts) who has selected Chapter 7 must state in the petition, at the time of filing, that

PETITION IN BANKRUPTCY
The document that is filed with a bankruptcy court to initiate bankruptcy proceedings. The official forms required for a petition in bankruptcy must be completed accurately, sworn to under oath, and signed by the debtor.

CONSUMER-DEBTOR
An individual whose debts are primarily consumer debts (debts for purchases made primarily for personal or household use).

he or she understands the relief available under other chapters and has chosen to proceed under Chapter 7. If the consumer-debtor is represented by an attorney, the attorney must file an affidavit stating that she or he has informed the debtor of the relief available under each chapter. Any debtor who is liable on a claim held by a creditor can file a voluntary petition. The debtor does not even have to be insolvent to do so.[5] The voluntary petition contains the following schedules:

1. A list of both secured and unsecured creditors, their addresses, and the amount of debt owed to each.
2. A statement of the financial affairs of the debtor.
3. A list of all property owned by the debtor, including property claimed by the debtor to be exempt.
4. A listing of current income and expenses.

The official forms must be completed accurately, sworn to under oath, and signed by the debtor. To conceal assets or knowingly supply false information on these schedules is a crime under the bankruptcy laws. If the voluntary petition for bankruptcy is found to be proper, the filing of the petition will itself constitute an order for relief. An **order for relief** relieves the debtor of the immediate obligation to pay the debts listed in the petition. Once a consumer-debtor's voluntary petition has been filed, the clerk of the court (or person directed) must give the trustee and creditors mailed notice of the order for relief not more than twenty days after the entry of the order.

As mentioned previously, debtors do not have to be insolvent to file for voluntary bankruptcy. Debtors do not have unfettered access to Chapter 7 bankruptcy proceedings, however. Section 707(b) of the Bankruptcy Code allows a bankruptcy court to dismiss a petition for relief under Chapter 7 if the granting of relief would constitute "substantial abuse" of Chapter 7.

● EXAMPLE 7 Howard Rock, a consumer-debtor, petitions for Chapter 7 relief. The court might determine, after evaluating Rock's schedule listing current income and expenses, that he would be able to pay his creditors a reasonable amount from future income. In this situation, the court might conclude that it would be a substantial abuse of Chapter 7 to allow Rock to have his debts completely discharged. The court might dismiss Rock's Chapter 7 petition after a hearing and encourage him to file a repayment plan under Chapter 13 of the Code, if that would substantially increase the likelihood that the creditors would receive payment. ●

Involuntary Bankruptcy An involuntary bankruptcy occurs when the debtor's creditors force the debtor into bankruptcy proceedings. An involuntary case cannot be commenced against a farmer[6] or a charitable institution (or those entities not eligible for Chapter 7 relief—mentioned earlier), however. For an involuntary action to be filed against other debtors, the following requirements must be met: If the debtor has twelve or more creditors, three or more

---

ORDER FOR RELIEF
A court's grant of assistance to a complainant. In bankruptcy proceedings, the order relieves the debtor of the immediate obligation to pay the debts listed in the bankruptcy petition.

---

5. The inability to pay debts as they become due is known as *equitable* insolvency. A *balance-sheet* insolvency, which exists when a debtor's liabilities exceed assets, is not the test. Thus, it is possible for debtors to petition voluntarily for bankruptcy even though their assets far exceed their liabilities. This situation may occur when a debtor's cash flow problems become severe.

6. *Farmers* are defined as persons who receive more than 80 percent of their gross income from farming operations, such as tilling the soil; dairy farming; ranching; or the production or raising of crops, poultry, or livestock. Corporations and partnerships, as well as individuals, can be farmers.

of those creditors having unsecured claims totaling at least $11,625 must join in the petition. If a debtor has fewer than twelve creditors, one or more creditors having a claim of $11,625 may file.

If the debtor challenges the involuntary petition, a hearing will be held, and the debtor's challenge will fail if the bankruptcy court finds either of the following:

1. That the debtor is generally not paying debts as they become due.
2. That a general receiver, custodian, or assignee took possession of, or was appointed to take charge of, substantially all of the debtor's property within 120 days before the filing of the petition.

If the court allows the bankruptcy to proceed, the debtor will be required to supply the same information in the bankruptcy schedules as in a voluntary bankruptcy.

An involuntary petition should not be used as an everyday debt-collection device, and the Code provides penalties for the filing of frivolous (unjustified) petitions against debtors. Judgment may be granted against the petitioning creditors for the costs and attorneys' fees incurred by the debtor in defending against an involuntary petition that is dismissed by the court. If the petition is filed in bad faith, damages can be awarded for injury to the debtor's reputation. Punitive damages may also be awarded.

A store advertises a court-ordered bankruptcy sale. On what basis might a court enter an order for relief in an involuntary bankruptcy proceeding initiated by the store's creditors?

Automatic Stay

The filing of a petition, either voluntary or involuntary, operates as an **automatic stay** on (suspension of) virtually all litigation and other action by creditors against the debtor or the debtor's property. In other words, once a petition is filed, creditors cannot commence or continue most legal actions against the debtor to recover claims or to repossess property in the hands of the debtor. A secured creditor (secured creditors will be discussed later in this chapter), however, may petition the bankruptcy court for relief from the automatic stay in certain circumstances. Additionally, the automatic stay does not apply to paternity, alimony, or family maintenance and support debts.

A creditor's failure to abide by an automatic stay imposed by the filing of a petition can be costly. If a creditor *knowingly* violates the automatic-stay provision (a willful violation), any party injured is entitled to recover actual damages, costs, and attorneys' fees and may also be entitled to recover punitive damages.

Creditors' Meeting and Claims

Within a reasonable time after the order of relief is granted (not less than ten days or more than thirty days), the bankruptcy court must call a meeting of the creditors listed in the schedules filed by the debtor. The bankruptcy judge does not attend this meeting.

Debtor's Presence Required The debtor must attend this meeting (unless excused by the court) and submit to an examination under oath. Failure to appear or the making of false statements under oath may result in the debtor's being denied a discharge of bankruptcy. At the meeting, the trustee ensures that the debtor is advised of the potential consequences of bankruptcy and of his or her ability to file under a different chapter of the Bankruptcy Code.

AUTOMATIC STAY
In bankruptcy proceedings, the suspension of virtually all litigation and other action by creditors against the debtor or the debtor's property. The stay is effective the moment the debtor files a petition in bankruptcy.

BE AWARE A debtor who lies, commits bribery, conceals assets, uses a false name, or makes false claims at a creditors' meeting is subject to a $5,000 fine and up to five years in prison.

Creditors' Claims   In a bankruptcy case in which the debtor has no assets (called a "no-asset case"), creditors are notified of the debtor's petition for bankruptcy but are instructed not to file a claim. In such a situation, the creditors will receive no payment, and most, if not all, of the debtor's debts will be discharged.

If there are sufficient assets to be distributed to creditors, however, each creditor must normally file a *proof of claim* with the bankruptcy court clerk within ninety days of the creditors' meeting to be entitled to receive a portion of the debtor's estate. The proof of claim lists the creditor's name and address, as well as the amount that the creditor asserts is owed to the creditor by the debtor. If a creditor fails to file a proof of claim, the bankruptcy court or trustee may file the proof of claim on the creditor's behalf but is not obligated to do so. If a claim is for a disputed amount, the bankruptcy court will set the value of the claim.

Creditors' claims are automatically allowed unless contested by the trustee, the debtor, or another creditor. The Code, however, does not allow claims for breach of employment contracts or real estate leases for terms longer than one year. These claims are limited to one year's wages or rent, despite the remaining length of either contract in breach.

Property of the Estate

On the commencement of a liquidation proceeding under Chapter 7, an **estate in property** is created. The estate consists of all the debtor's legal and equitable interests in property currently held, wherever located, together with certain jointly owned property, property transferred in transactions voidable by the trustee, proceeds and profits from the property of the estate, and certain after-acquired property. Interests in certain property—such as gifts, inheritances, property settlements (resulting from divorce), or life insurance death proceeds—to which the debtor becomes entitled *within 180 days after filing* may also become part of the estate. Thus, the filing of a bankruptcy petition generally fixes a dividing line: property acquired prior to the filing becomes property of the estate, and property acquired after the filing, except as just noted, remains the debtor's.

Exempted Property

Any individual debtor is entitled to exempt certain property from the property of the estate. The Bankruptcy Code establishes a federal exemption scheme under which the following property is exempt:[7]

1. Up to $17,425 in equity in the debtor's residence and burial plot (the homestead exemption).
2. Interest in a motor vehicle up to $2,775.
3. Interest in household goods and furnishings, wearing apparel, appliances, books, animals, crops, and musical instruments up to $450 in a particular item but limited to $9,300 in total.
4. Interest in jewelry up to $1,150.

---

7. The dollar amounts stated in the Bankruptcy Code were adjusted automatically on April 1, 1998, and will be adjusted every three years thereafter based on changes in the Consumer Price Index. The amounts stated in this chapter are in accordance with those computed on April 1, 2001.

5. Any other property worth up to $925, plus any unused part of the $17,425 homestead exemption up to an amount of $8,725.
6. Interest in any tools of the debtor's trade, up to $1,750.
7. Certain life insurance contracts owned by the debtor.
8. Certain interests in accrued dividends or interests under life insurance contracts owned by the debtor.
9. Professionally prescribed health aids.
10. The right to receive Social Security and certain welfare benefits, alimony and support payments, and certain pension benefits.
11. The right to receive certain personal-injury and other awards, up to $17,425.

Individual states have the power to pass legislation precluding debtors in their states from using the federal exemptions. At least thirty-five states have done this. In those states, debtors may use only state (not federal) exemptions. In the rest of the states, an individual debtor (or husband and wife who file jointly) may choose between the exemptions provided under state law and the federal exemptions. State laws may provide significantly greater protection for debtors than federal law. For example, Florida and Texas traditionally have provided for generous exemptions for homeowners. State laws may also define the property coming within an exemption differently than does the federal law.

The Trustee's Role

Promptly after the order for relief has been entered, an interim, or provisional, trustee is appointed by the **U.S. trustee** (a government official who performs certain administrative tasks that a bankruptcy judge would otherwise have to perform). The interim trustee administers the debtor's estate until the first meeting of creditors, at which time either a permanent trustee is elected or the interim trustee becomes the permanent trustee. Trustees are entitled to compensation for services rendered, plus reimbursement for expenses.

The basic duty of the trustee is to collect the debtor's available estate and reduce it to money for distribution, preserving the interests of both the debtor and unsecured creditors. In other words, the trustee is accountable for administering the debtor's estate. To enable the trustee to accomplish this duty, the Code gives her or him certain powers, stated in both general and specific terms.

Trustee's Powers The trustee has the power to require persons holding the debtor's property at the time the petition is filed to deliver the property to the trustee. To enable the trustee to implement this power, the Code provides that the trustee occupies a position equivalent in rights to that of certain other parties. For example, in some situations, the trustee has the same rights as creditors and can obtain a judicial lien or levy execution on the debtor's property. This means that a trustee has priority over an unperfected secured party to the debtor's property (secured creditors will be discussed shortly). The trustee also has rights equivalent to those of the debtor.

In addition, the trustee has the power to avoid (cancel) certain types of transactions, including those transactions that the debtor could rightfully avoid, *preferences,* certain statutory *liens,* and *fraudulent transfers* by the debtor. Avoidance powers must be exercised within two years of the order for relief (the period runs even if a trustee has not been appointed). These powers of the trustee are discussed in more detail in the following subsections.

U.S. TRUSTEE
A government official who performs certain administrative tasks that a bankruptcy judge would otherwise have to perform.

NOTE Usually, when property is recovered as a preference, the trustee sells it and distributes the proceeds to the debtor's creditors.

Voidable Rights   A trustee steps into the shoes of the debtor. Thus, any reason that a debtor can use to obtain the return of his or her property can be employed by the trustee as well. These grounds for recovery include fraud, duress, incapacity, and mutual mistake.

• **EXAMPLE 8**   Rob sells his boat to Inga. Inga gives Rob a check, knowing that there are insufficient funds in her bank account to cover the check. Inga has committed fraud. Rob has the right to avoid that transfer and recover the boat from Inga. Thus, if Rob petitions for bankruptcy and the court enters an order for relief, the trustee can exercise the same right to recover the boat from Inga.• If the trustee does not take action to enforce one of his or her rights, the debtor in a Chapter 7 bankruptcy will nevertheless be able to enforce that right.[8]

Preferences   A debtor is not permitted to transfer property or to make a payment that favors—or gives a **preference** to—one creditor over others. The trustee is allowed to recover payments made both voluntarily and involuntarily to one creditor in preference over another.

To have made a preferential payment that can be recovered, an *insolvent* debtor generally must have transferred property, for a *preexisting* debt, during the *ninety days* prior to the filing of the petition in bankruptcy. The transfer must give the creditor more than the creditor would have received as a result of the bankruptcy proceedings. The trustee does not have to prove insolvency, as the Code provides that the debtor is presumed to be insolvent during this ninety-day period.

If a preferred creditor has sold the property to an innocent third party, the trustee cannot recover the property from the innocent party. The creditor, however, generally can be held accountable for the value of the property.

Preferences to Insiders.   Sometimes, the creditor receiving the preference is an *insider*—an individual, a partner, a partnership, or an officer or a director of a corporation (or a relative of one of these) who has a close relationship with the debtor. In this situation, the avoidance power of the trustee is extended to transfers made within *one year* before filing; however, the *presumption* of insolvency is confined to the ninety-day period. Therefore, the trustee must prove that the debtor was insolvent at the time of an earlier transfer.

Transfers That Are Not Preferences.   Not all transfers are preferences. To be a preference, the transfer must be made for something other than current consideration. Therefore, most courts generally assume that payment for services rendered within ten to fifteen days prior to the payment of the current consideration is not a preference. If a creditor receives payment in the ordinary course of business, such as payment of last month's telephone bill, the payment cannot be recovered by the trustee in bankruptcy. To be recoverable, a preference must be a transfer for an antecedent (preexisting) debt, such as a year-old printing bill. In addition, the Code permits a consumer-debtor to transfer any property to a creditor up to a total value of $600 without the transfer's constituting a preference. Also, certain other debts, including alimony and child support, are not preferences.

---

8. In a Chapter 11 reorganization (to be discussed later), for which generally no trustee exists, the debtor has the same avoiding powers as a trustee in a Chapter 7 liquidation. In repayment plans under Chapters 12 and 13 (also to be discussed later), a trustee must be appointed.

Liens on Debtor's Property The trustee is permitted to avoid the fixing of certain statutory liens, such as a mechanic's lien, on property of the debtor. Liens that first became effective at the time the bankruptcy petition was filed or the debtor became insolvent are voidable by the trustee. Liens that are not perfected or enforceable against a good faith purchaser on the date of the petition are also voidable.

Fraudulent Transfers The trustee may avoid fraudulent transfers or obligations if they were made within one year of the filing of the petition or if they were made with actual intent to hinder, delay, or defraud a creditor. Transfers made for less than reasonably equivalent consideration are also vulnerable if the debtor thereby became insolvent, was left engaged in business with an unreasonably small amount of capital, or intended to incur debts that would be beyond his or her ability to pay. When a fraudulent transfer is made outside the Code's one-year limit, creditors may seek alternative relief under state laws. State laws often allow creditors to recover for transfers made up to three years prior to the filing of a petition.

Property Distribution

Creditors are either secured or unsecured. A *secured* creditor has a security interest in collateral that secures the debt. An *unsecured* creditor does not have any security interest.

Secured Creditors The Code provides that a consumer-debtor, within thirty days of the filing of a Chapter 7 petition or before the date of the first meeting of the creditors (whichever is first), must file with the clerk a statement of intention with respect to the secured collateral. The statement must indicate whether the debtor will retain the collateral or surrender it to the secured party. Additionally, if applicable, the debtor must specify whether the collateral will be claimed as exempt property and whether the debtor intends to redeem the property or reaffirm the debt secured by the collateral. The trustee is obligated to enforce the debtor's statement within forty-five days after the statement is filed.

If the collateral is surrendered to the secured party, the secured creditor can enforce the security interest either by accepting the property in full satisfaction of the debt or by foreclosing on the collateral and using the proceeds to pay off the debt. Thus, the secured party has priority over unsecured parties to the proceeds from the disposition of the secured collateral. Indeed, the Code provides that if the value of the secured collateral exceeds the secured party's claim, the secured party also has priority to the proceeds in an amount that will cover reasonable fees (including attorneys' fees, if provided for in the security agreement) and costs incurred because of the debtor's default. Any excess over this amount is used by the trustee to satisfy the claims of unsecured creditors. Should the secured collateral be insufficient to cover the secured debt owed, the secured creditor becomes an unsecured creditor for the remainder of the debt.

Unsecured Creditors Bankruptcy law establishes an order or priority for classes of debts owed to *unsecured* creditors, and they are paid in the order of their priority. Each class of debt must be fully paid before the next class is entitled to any of the proceeds—if there are sufficient funds to pay the entire class. If not, the proceeds are distributed *proportionately* to each creditor in the class, and all classes lower in priority on the list receive nothing. The order of priority among classes of unsecured creditors is as follows:

1. Administrative expenses—including court costs, trustee fees, and bankruptcy attorneys' fees.
2. In an involuntary bankruptcy, expenses incurred by the debtor in the ordinary course of business from the date of the filing of the petition up to the appointment of the trustee or the issuance by the court of an order for relief.
3. Unpaid wages, salaries, and commissions earned within ninety days of the filing of the petition, limited to $4,650 per claimant. Any claim in excess of $4,650 is treated as a claim of a general creditor (listed as number 9 below).
4. Unsecured claims for contributions to be made to employee benefit plans, limited to services performed during 180 days prior to the filing of the bankruptcy petition and $4,650 per employee.
5. Claims by farmers and fishers, up to $4,650, against debtor operators of grain storage or fish storage or processing facilities.
6. Consumer deposits of up to $2,100 given to the debtor before the petition was filed in connection with the purchase, lease, or rental of property or the purchase of services that were not received or provided. Any claim in excess of $2,100 is treated as a claim of a general creditor (listed as number 9 below).
7. Paternity, alimony, maintenance, and support debts.
8. Certain taxes and penalties due to government units, such as income and property taxes.
9. Claims of general creditors.
10. Commitments to the Federal Deposit Insurance Corporation, and other organizations, to maintain the capital of an insured depository institution.

If any amount remains after the priority classes of creditors have been satisfied, it is turned over to the debtor.

Discharge

BE AWARE Often, a discharge in bankruptcy—even under Chapter 7—does not free a debtor of *all* of his or her debts.

From the debtor's point of view, the purpose of a liquidation proceeding is to obtain a fresh start through the discharge of debts.[9] Certain debts, however, are not dischargeable in a liquidation proceeding. Also, some debtors may not qualify—because of their conduct—to have all debts discharged in bankruptcy.

Exceptions to Discharge Claims that are not dischargeable under Chapter 7 include the following:

1. Claims for back taxes accruing within three years prior to bankruptcy.
2. Claims for amounts borrowed by the debtor to pay federal taxes.
3. Claims against property or money obtained by the debtor under false pretenses or by false representations.

---

9. Discharges are granted under Chapter 7 only to *individuals,* not to corporations or partnerships. The latter may use Chapter 11, or they may terminate their existence under state law.

4. Claims by creditors who were not notified of the bankruptcy; these claims did not appear on the schedules the debtor was required to file.
5. Claims based on fraud or misuse of funds by the debtor while she or he was acting in a fiduciary capacity or claims involving the debtor's embezzlement or larceny.
6. Alimony, child support, and (with certain exceptions) property settlements.
7. Claims based on willful or malicious conduct by the debtor toward another or the property of another.
8. Certain government fines and penalties.
9. Certain student loans, unless payment of the loans imposes an undue hardship on the debtor and the debtor's dependents.
10. Consumer debts of more than $1,150 for luxury goods or services owed to a single creditor incurred within sixty days of the order for relief. This denial of discharge is a rebuttable presumption (that is, the denial may be challenged by the debtor), however, and any debts reasonably incurred to support the debtor or dependents are not classified as luxuries.
11. Cash advances totaling more than $1,150 that are extensions of open-end consumer credit obtained by the debtor within sixty days of the order for relief. A denial of discharge of these debts is also a rebuttable presumption.
12. Judgments or consent decrees against a debtor as a result of the debtor's operation of a motor vehicle while intoxicated.

ETHICAL ISSUE

Should punitive damages for fraud be dischargeable in bankruptcy?

As stated in item number 5 in the preceding list of exceptions to discharge, claims based on fraud are not dischargeable in bankruptcy. Often, a claim based on fraud consists of damages that were awarded to the creditor by a court in a lawsuit against the debtor for fraud. A question that sometimes comes before the courts is whether punitive damages, as well as actual damages, should be nondischargeable. How this question is answered depends on the way in which a court interprets the language of the Bankruptcy Code with respect to fraud-based claims. Section 523(a)(2)(A) of the Code excepts from discharge in bankruptcy "any debt . . . for money, property, services, or an extension, renewal, or refinancing of credit, to the extent obtained by . . . false pretenses, a false representation, or actual fraud." To resolve conflicting interpretations of this provision by the lower courts, the United States Supreme Court addressed the issue. In making its decision, the Court emphasized that the Bankruptcy Code "has long prohibited debtors from discharging liabilities incurred on account of their fraud, embodying a basic policy animating the Code of affording relief only to an 'honest but unfortunate debtor.'" According to the Court, when read in the historical context of bankruptcy law and other provisions of the current Bankruptcy Code, the relevant provision of the Code should be interpreted to mean that punitive damages for fraud are nondischargeable.[10]

10. *Cohen v. De La Cruz*, 523 U.S. 213, 118 S.Ct. 1212, 140 L.Ed.2d 341 (1998).

In the following case, an employer sought to have a debt to an ex-employee for unpaid commissions discharged in bankruptcy. The question before the court was whether the debt arose from "willful and malicious injury" caused by the debtor's tortious conduct, which would mean that it was not dischargeable.

CASE 15.3	In re Jercich

United States Court of Appeals,
Ninth Circuit, 2001.
238 F.3d 1202.

BACKGROUND AND FACTS In June 1981, James Petralia began to work for George Jercich, Inc., a mortgage company wholly owned and operated by George Jercich. Petralia's primary duty was to obtain investors to fund the home loans. Jercich agreed to pay Petralia a salary plus monthly commissions for loans that were funded through his efforts. When Jercich failed to pay the commissions, Petralia quit and filed a suit in a California state court against Jercich. The court found that Jercich had not paid

Petralia; that Jercich had the clear ability to make the payments to Petralia but chose not to do so; that instead of paying Petralia and other employees, Jercich used the money for personal investments, including a horse ranch; and that Jercich's behavior was willful and deliberate and constituted "substantial oppression." The court ruled in Petralia's favor. Jercich appealed this ruling to a state intermediate appellate court and filed for bankruptcy in a federal bankruptcy court. The state court affirmed the judgment against Jercich, but the bankruptcy court held that the debt was dischargeable. A bankruptcy appellate panel affirmed this holding.[a] Petralia appealed to the U.S. Court of Appeals for the Ninth Circuit.

IN THE WORDS OF THE COURT . . .

T. G. NELSON, Circuit Judge:

* * * * *

* * * [A]lthough * * * an intentional breach of contract generally will not give rise to a nondischargeable debt, *where an intentional breach of contract is accompanied by tortious conduct which results in willful and malicious injury, the resulting debt is excepted from discharge * * *.* [Emphasis added.]

* * * *

In the present case, the state trial court found that Jercich had the "clear ability" to pay Petralia his wages when they were due, but willfully "chose not to" in violation of California law. * * *

Based on these state court findings, we hold that Jercich's nonpayment of wages under the particular circumstances of this case constituted tortious conduct.

* * * *

* * * [T]he willful injury requirement * * * is met when it is shown either that the debtor had a subjective motive to inflict the injury or that the debtor believed that injury was substantially certain to occur as a result of his conduct. We believe that this holding comports with * * * bankruptcy law's fundamental policy of granting discharges only to the honest but unfortunate debtor.

Application of this standard to the state court's factual findings demonstrates that the injury to Petralia was willful. * * *

* * * *

---

a. A *bankruptcy appellate panel,* with the consent of the parties, has jurisdiction to hear appeals from final judgments, orders, and decrees of bankruptcy judges.

CASE 15.3—Continued

A "malicious" injury involves (1) a wrongful act, (2) done intentionally, (3) which necessarily causes injury, and (4) is done without just cause or excuse. In the present case, the state court found Jercich knew he owed Petralia the wages and that injury to Petralia was substantially certain to occur if the wages were not paid; that Jercich had the clear ability to pay Petralia the wages; and that despite his knowledge, Jercich chose not to pay and instead used the money for his own personal benefit. Jercich has pointed to no just cause or excuse for his behavior. Moreover, Jercich's deliberate and willful failure to pay was found by the state trial court to constitute substantial oppression * * * which [under California law] is "despicable conduct that subjects a person to cruel and unjust hardship in conscious disregard of that person's rights." We hold that these state court findings are sufficient to show that the injury inflicted by Jercich was malicious * * * .

DECISION AND REMEDY The U.S. Court of Appeals for the Ninth Circuit reversed the decision of the bankruptcy appellate panel, holding that Jercich's debt to Petralia was not dischargeable.

FOR CRITICAL ANALYSIS—Social Consideration *A fundamental policy of bankruptcy*

law is to give a fresh start only to the "honest but unfortunate debtor." What corollary to this policy is the basis for some of the exceptions to discharge listed previously?

Objections to Discharge In addition to the exceptions to discharge previously listed, the following circumstances (relating to the debtor's conduct and not the debt) will cause a discharge to be denied:

1. The debtor's concealment or destruction of property with the intent to hinder, delay, or defraud a creditor.
2. The debtor's fraudulent concealment or destruction of financial records.
3. The granting of a discharge to the debtor within six years of the filing of the petition.[11]

When a discharge is denied under these circumstances, the assets of the debtor are still distributed to the creditors, but the debtor remains liable for the unpaid portions of all claims.

This chapter's *Inside the Legal Environment* feature on page 492 illustrates how a bankruptcy court may analyze a debtor's intent at the time of making credit-card purchases to determine if the debt is nondischargeable because of fraud.

Effect of Discharge The primary effect of a discharge is to void, or set aside, any judgment on a discharged debt and prohibit any action to collect a discharged debt. A discharge does not affect the liability of a co-debtor.

Revocation of Discharge The Code provides that a debtor's discharge may be revoked. On petition by the trustee or a creditor, the bankruptcy court may, within one year, revoke the discharge decree if it is discovered that the debtor

---

11. A discharge under Chapter 13 of the Code within six years of the filing of the petition does not bar a subsequent Chapter 7 discharge when a good faith Chapter 13 plan paid at least 70 percent of all allowed unsecured claims and was the debtor's "best effort."

Credit-Card Fraud—The Intent Factor

At issue in a number of bankruptcy cases is the following question: When debtors run up credit-card bills, knowing that they lack the ability to pay the bills, have they engaged in fraud? How the courts answer this question is important for both creditors and debtors. If you are in the credit-card business, for example, it would be in your interest to have the court deem that such actions amount to fraud—because if it does, then the debt will not be dischargeable in bankruptcy. Naturally, the debtor would want the court to reach the opposite conclusion.

What the Courts Say

Fraud, of course, requires intent. So a central question in bankruptcy cases confronting this issue is whether a debtor's knowledge of his or her inability to pay a debt, at the time the debt is incurred, equates to intent to defraud. In the past, many lower courts dealing with this debate held that it did. This assumption seems to be changing, however.

Consider a case that came before the Sixth Circuit Court of Appeals. The case involved a woman who had taken $11,600 in cash advances on her credit cards to finance her gambling habit. During bankruptcy proceedings, she testified that she had hoped to repay the debt out of her gambling winnings, even though she realized that there was no reasonable expectation of being able to do this. The court, concluding that there was no fraud because the debtor had *intended* to repay the debt, allowed the debt to be discharged in bankruptcy. According to the court, "To measure a debtor's intention to repay by her ability to do so, without more, would be contrary to one of the main reasons consumers use credit cards: because they often lack the ability to pay in full at the time they desire credit."[a] In an earlier case, another federal appellate court had held similarly, concluding that the "hopeless state of a debtor's financial condition should never

become a substitute for an actual finding of bad faith."[b]

Implications for Creditors

These rulings, while they may be good news for debtors, are not so for creditors. According to attorney Robert Markoff of Chicago, "Creditors are faced with a real uphill battle. If the debtor says she intended to pay, you're pretty much stuck."[c] Note that a provision in the bankruptcy reform bill currently pending in Congress (see this chapter's *Landmark in the Legal Environment* on pages502 480 and 481) addresses this problem by stating that certain debts incurred within ninety days before a bankruptcy petition is filed would be nondischargeable.

FOR CRITICAL ANALYSIS

Debtors could easily claim that they intended to pay their debts, regardless of whether they in fact intended to do so. Does this mean that it is impossible to objectively determine intent to defraud in these types of cases?

a. *In re Rembert,* 141 F.3d 277 (6th Cir. 1998).

b. *In re Anastas,* 94 F.3d 1280 (9th Cir. 1996).
c. As quoted in Jake Halpern, "Credit Cards Easier to Discharge," *Lawyers Weekly USA,* May 4, 1998, p. 19.

was fraudulent or dishonest during the bankruptcy proceedings. The revocation renders the discharge void, allowing creditors not satisfied by the distribution of the debtor's estate to proceed with their claims against the debtor.

Reaffirmation of Debt A debtor may voluntarily agree to pay off a debt—for example, a debt owed to a family member, close friend, or some other party—even though the debt could be discharged in bankruptcy. An agreement to pay a debt dischargeable in bankruptcy is referred to as a *reaffirmation agreement.*

To be enforceable, reaffirmation agreements must be made before a debtor is granted a discharge, and they must be filed with the court. If the debtor is represented by an attorney, court approval is not required if the attorney files a declaration or affidavit stating that (1) the debtor has been fully informed of the consequences of the agreement (and a default under the agreement), (2) the agreement is made voluntarily, and (3) the agreement does not impose undue hardship on the debtor or the debtor's family. If the debtor is not represented by an attorney, court approval is required, and the agreement will be approved only if the court finds that the agreement will result in no undue hardship to the debtor and is in his or her best interest.

The agreement must contain a clear and conspicuous statement advising the debtor that reaffirmation is not required. The debtor can rescind, or cancel, the agreement at any time prior to discharge or within sixty days of filing the agreement, whichever is later. This rescission period must be stated *clearly* and *conspicuously* in the reaffirmation agreement.

CHAPTER 11—REORGANIZATION

The type of bankruptcy proceeding used most commonly by a corporate debtor is the Chapter 11 *reorganization*. In a reorganization, the creditors and the debtor formulate a plan under which the debtor pays a portion of his or her debts and the rest of the debts are discharged. The debtor is allowed to continue in business. Although this type of bankruptcy is commonly a corporate reorganization, any debtor (except a stockbroker or a commodities broker) who is eligible for Chapter 7 relief is eligible for relief under Chapter 11.[12] Railroads are also eligible.

The same principles that govern the filing of a liquidation petition apply to reorganization proceedings. The case may be brought either voluntarily or involuntarily. The same principles govern the entry of the order for relief. The automatic-stay provision is also applicable in reorganizations. This chapter's *Legal E-nvironment* feature on page 494 looks at circumstances involving a failed online business that was petitioned into involuntary bankruptcy under Chapter 11.

A bankruptcy court, after notice and a hearing, may dismiss or suspend all proceedings in a case at any time if dismissal or suspension would better serve the interests of the creditors. The Code also allows a court, after notice and a hearing, to dismiss a case under reorganization "for cause." Cause includes the absence of a reasonable likelihood of rehabilitation, the inability to effect a plan, and an unreasonable delay by the debtor that is prejudicial to (may harm the interests of) creditors.[13] A debtor need not be insolvent to be entitled to Chapter 11 protection.[14]

"Debt rolls a man over and over, binding him hand and foot, and letting him hang upon the fatal mesh until the long-legged interest devours him."

HENRY WARD BEECHER, 1813–1887
(American clergyman, writer, and abolitionist)

Workouts

In some instances, creditors may prefer private, negotiated debt-adjustment agreements, also known as **workouts,** to bankruptcy proceedings. Often, these out-of-court workouts are much more flexible and thus more conducive to a

WORKOUT
An out-of-court agreement between a debtor and his or her creditors in which the parties work out a payment plan or schedule under which the debtor's debts can be discharged.

---

12. *Toibb v. Radloff,* 501 U.S. 157, 111 S.Ct. 2197, 115 L.Ed.2d 145 (1991).
13. See 11 U.S.C. Section 1112(b).
14. *In re Johns-Manville Corp.,* 36 Bankr. 727 (S.D.N.Y. 1984).

LEGAL *e*-NVIRONMENT

Personal Data on the Auction Block

Businesses on the verge of failure, and businesses that have failed, often find themselves in bankruptcy court. In the spring and summer of 2000, with the sudden drop of investors' interest in online businesses, many of those firms filed for bankruptcy.

One problem facing a failed online business is what to do with its customer list. Offline companies (firms not based on the Web) have commonly bought and sold customer lists, which can attract high prices because they include information about customer buying habits, as well as addresses and other personal data. E-commerce companies, however, generally promise not to sell this information to third parties.

What Am I Bid?

Toysmart.com, LLC, had this policy. Toysmart.com was also a failing dot-com. In June 2000, the company's creditors filed a petition for the firm's involuntary bankruptcy under Chapter 11. As part of the process, Toysmart.com filed a motion seeking court approval for the sale of its assets, including its customer list and customer-profile information. The court put off making a judgment on the propriety of the sale until a prospective purchaser appeared. Toysmart.com then placed an ad in the *Wall Street Journal,* offering to sell its customer data to the highest bidder.

TRUSTe, a nonprofit privacy organization that awards seals of approval to Web sites with strict privacy policies, asked the Federal Trade Commission (FTC) about the legality of this auction. The FTC filed a suit in a federal district court against Toysmart.com, alleging violations of the FTC Act and the Children's Online Privacy Protection Act. The controversy swelled because the personal information had been provided, in some instances, by children using the Toysmart.com Web site. More than forty state attorneys general joined the battle against the auction.[a]

Going, Going, Gone

Toysmart.com reached a settlement with the FTC, agreeing, in the event of a sale of substantially all of its assets, to transfer the data to a family-friendly company that would agree to comply with Toysmart.com's privacy policy. When the creditors objected to this proposal, the judge refused to consent to it. Eventually, the creditors agreed to a deal in which Walt Disney Company, one of the owners of Toysmart.com, paid $50,000 to have the data destroyed.

Response to Toysmart.com's case was dramatic. Since the summer of 2000, fewer bankrupt online businesses have tried to sell their customer information. Others have changed their privacy policies to allow such sales. In 2001, TRUSTe issued guidelines on the use of personal information in bankruptcies and other major fundamental changes that occur to Web-based businesses. The guidelines ask that the firms notify customers and offer them the choice to keep their personal data out of a deal (see **http://www.truste.com** for more information).

Finally, the bankruptcy reform bill being considered by Congress at the time of this writing would prohibit the sale of customer information if that sale would violate a privacy policy.

FOR CRITICAL ANALYSIS

What effect might the privacy policy amendment in the bankruptcy reform bill before Congress have on bankrupt online businesses?

---

a. For the court's response to a request by the state of Texas regarding the case, see *Federal Trade Commission v. Toysmart.com, LLC,* 2000 WL 1523287 (D.Mass. 2000).

speedy settlement. Speed is critical because delay is one of the most costly elements in any bankruptcy proceeding. Another advantage of workouts is that they avoid the various administrative costs of bankruptcy proceedings.

Debtor in Possession

On entry of the order for relief, the debtor generally continues to operate her or his business as a **debtor in possession (DIP)**. The court, however, may appoint a trustee (often referred to as a *receiver*) to operate the debtor's business if gross mismanagement of the business is shown or if appointing a trustee is in the best interests of the estate.

DEBTOR IN POSSESSION (DIP)
In Chapter 11 bankruptcy proceedings, a debtor who is allowed to continue in possession of the estate in property (the business) and to continue business operations.

The DIP's role is similar to that of a trustee in a liquidation. The DIP is entitled to avoid preferential payments made to creditors and fraudulent transfers of assets that occurred prior to the filing of the Chapter 11 petition. The DIP has the power to decide whether to cancel or assume obligations under executory contracts (contracts that have not yet been performed) that were made prior to the petition.

ETHICAL ISSUE

Should those who "bankrupt" a firm be allowed to continue to manage the firm as debtors in possession?

Chapter 11 reorganizations have become the target of substantial criticism. One of the arguments against Chapter 11 is that it allows the very managers who "bankrupted" a firm to continue to manage the firm as debtors in possession while the firm is in Chapter 11 proceedings. According to some critics, the main beneficiaries of Chapter 11 corporate reorganizations are not the shareholder-owners of the corporations but attorneys and current management. Basically, these critics argue that reorganizations do not preserve companies' assets because large firms must pay millions of dollars for attorneys and accountants during the reorganization process, which can take years to complete.

Creditors' Committees

As soon as practicable after the entry of the order for relief, a creditors' committee of unsecured creditors is appointed. The committee may consult with the trustee or the DIP concerning the administration of the case or the formulation of the reorganization plan. Additional creditors' committees may be appointed to represent special interest creditors. Orders affecting the estate generally will not be made without either the consent of the committee or a hearing in which the judge hears the position of the committee.

Certain small businesses that do not own or manage real estate can avoid creditors' committees. In these cases, bankruptcy judges may enter orders without a committee's consent.

The Reorganization Plan

A reorganization plan to rehabilitate the debtor is a plan to conserve and administer the debtor's assets in the hope of an eventual return to successful operation and solvency. The plan must be fair and equitable and must do the following:

1. Designate classes of claims and interests.
2. Specify the treatment to be afforded the classes. (The plan must provide the same treatment for each claim in a particular class.)
3. Provide an adequate means for execution.

Filing the Plan Only the debtor may file a plan within the first 120 days after the date of the bankruptcy court's order for relief. If the debtor does not meet the 120-day deadline, however, or if the debtor fails to obtain the required creditor consent (see below) within 180 days, any party may propose a plan. The plan need not provide for full repayment to unsecured creditors. Instead, unsecured creditors receive a percentage of each dollar owed to them by the debtor. If a small-business debtor chooses to avoid creditors' committees, the time for the debtor's filing is shortened to 100 days, and any other party's plan must be filed within 160 days.

Acceptance and Confirmation of the Plan Once the plan has been developed, it is submitted to each class of creditors for acceptance. Normally, each class must accept the plan. A class has accepted the plan when a majority of the creditors, representing two-thirds of the amount of the total claim, vote to approve it. Even when all classes of claims accept the plan, the court may refuse to confirm it if it is not "in the best interests of the creditors." A spouse or child of the debtor can block the plan if it does not provide for payment of his or her claims in cash.

Even if only one class of claims has accepted the plan, the court may still confirm the plan under the Code's so-called **cram-down provision.** In other words, the court may confirm the plan over the objections of a class of creditors. Before the court can exercise this right of cram-down confirmation, it must be demonstrated that the plan "does not discriminate unfairly" against any creditors and that the plan is "fair and equitable."

The plan is binding on confirmation. The debtor is given a reorganization discharge from all claims not protected under the plan. This discharge does not apply to any claims that would be denied discharge under liquidation.

Debtors are allowed considerable freedom under Chapter 11 to do business. But this freedom is not as unlimited as it is outside the bankruptcy process, as the following case illustrates.

CRAM-DOWN PROVISION
A provision of the Bankruptcy Code that allows a court to confirm a debtor's Chapter 11 reorganization plan even though only one class of creditors has accepted it. To exercise the court's right under this provision, the court must demonstrate that the plan does not discriminate unfairly against any creditors and is fair and equitable.

CASE 15.4   In re Beyond.com Corp.

United States Bankruptcy Court,
Northern District of California, 2003.
289 Bankr. 138.

COMPANY PROFILE *Founded in 1994, Beyond.com Corporation principally built,*

hosted, managed, and marketed online stores from its base in Santa Clara, California. Beyond.com's first venture was a retail Web site for computer products. In 2000, the firm began to focus on providing support for other Web merchants, showcasing its clients' e-stores

CASE 15.4—Continued

in an Internet mall. Despite the change in focus, however, Beyond.com was unable to pay its debts, and the company ceased operations.

BACKGROUND AND FACTS In 2002, Beyond.com filed a Chapter 11 petition and a reorganization plan in a federal bankruptcy court. The company also filed a disclosure statement, which set out the details underlying the plan. Among other things, the plan envisioned that the reorganized debtor would "retain all of the rights, powers, and duties of a trustee under the Bankruptcy Code." The plan appointed the debtor's former chief operating officer, John Barratt, "Liquidation Manager." In this capacity, Barratt could dispose of the debtor's property, enter into agreements on the debtor's behalf, file suits against unidentified defendants, and retain and pay advisers and other "professionals." Under most circumstances, none of these actions would be subject to court supervision or limitation. The plan also limited Barratt's personal liability for acts performed in this capacity. The debtor asked the court to approve the disclosure statement, as required before a plan is submitted to creditors.

IN THE WORDS
OF THE COURT . . .

MARILYN MORGAN, Bankruptcy Judge.

*   *   *   *

Conceptually, Beyond.com's plan and disclosure statement is as freewheeling with the Bankruptcy Code *   *   * as Enron's accountants were with the tax laws in the 1990s. There are many reasons why the disclosure statement before the court should not be approved. However, this decision focuses on the requirements of 11 U.S.C. Section 1129(a), specifically Section 1129(a)(1) *   *   *.

*   *   *   *

*   *   * This section provides that the bankruptcy court has the power to confirm a plan only if it complies with applicable provisions of the Bankruptcy Code.

Beyond.com's proposed plan contains numerous provisions that modify the requirements of the Bankruptcy Code. Of greatest concern to the court are those provisions that dramatically reduce notice to creditors of matters that the drafters of the Bankruptcy Code *   *   * considered fundamental to bankruptcy due process. *Notice, after all, is the cornerstone underpinning bankruptcy procedure.* For example, the plan grants the Liquidation Manager the authority under the plan to dispose of property and to engage in agreements without court order or compliance with [Code provisions] *   *   * regarding the abandonment of property of the estate, *   *   * the retention and compensation of professionals, *   *   * [and] *   *   * the sale of property of the estate *   *   * . The modifications to the applicable provisions of [the Code] are not minor, ministerial [administrative] or simply pragmatic. In effect, the plan affords the reorganized debtor the prerogative to comply selectively with the provisions of the Bankruptcy Code *   *   * without judicial supervision. A more cynical view suggests that providing the least notice to the fewest people reduces oversight. Accordingly, the plan fails to satisfy the requirements of Section 1129(a)(1). [Emphasis added.]

*   *   *   *

This plan is not confirmable chiefly because it alters the Bankruptcy Code in derogation of the notice provisions that provide fundamental protections for creditors and because its thrust is to avoid judicial supervision unless it is convenient to the debtor or its professionals. However, the court has a continuing oversight responsibility in liquidation cases that cannot be selectively invoked. In its exuberance rewriting provisions of the Code, the author of the proposed

(continued)

CASE 15.4—Continued

plan overlooked the requirements of Section 1129(a), which provide a framework ensuring the integrity of the system. These defects cannot be cured.

DECISION AND REMEDY The court refused to confirm Beyond.com's disclosure statement and reorganization plan because it undercut the notice requirements and court supervision provisions of the Bankruptcy Code.

FOR CRITICAL ANALYSIS—Social Consideration *How much information should be revealed in a disclosure statement accompanying a reorganization plan?*

CHAPTER 13—REPAYMENT PLAN

NOTE A secured debt is a debt in which a security interest in personal property or fixtures assures payment of the obligation.

Chapter 13 of the Bankruptcy Code provides for the "Adjustment of Debts of an Individual with Regular Income." Individuals (not partnerships or corporations) with regular income who owe fixed unsecured debts of less than $290,525 or fixed secured debts of less than $871,550 may take advantage of bankruptcy repayment plans. This includes salaried employees; individual proprietors; and individuals who live on welfare, Social Security, fixed pensions, or investment income. Many small-business debtors have a choice of filing under either Chapter 11 or Chapter 13. Repayment plans offer several advantages. One advantage is that they are less expensive and less complicated than reorganization or liquidation proceedings.

A Chapter 13 repayment plan can be initiated only by the filing of a voluntary petition by the debtor. Certain liquidation and reorganization cases may be converted to Chapter 13 with the consent of the debtor. A Chapter 13 repayment plan may be converted to a Chapter 7 liquidation at the request of either the debtor or, under certain circumstances, a creditor. A Chapter 13 repayment plan may also be converted to a Chapter 11 reorganization after a hearing. On the filing of a petition under Chapter 13, a trustee must be appointed. The automatic stay previously discussed also takes effect. Although the stay applies to all or part of a consumer debt, it does not apply to any business debt incurred by the debtor.

The Repayment Plan

Shortly after the petition is filed, the debtor must file a repayment plan. This plan may provide either for payment of all obligations in full or for payment of a lesser amount. A plan of rehabilitation by repayment provides for the debtor's future earnings or income to be turned over to the trustee as necessary for execution of the plan. The time for payment under the plan may not exceed three years unless the court approves an extension. The term, with extension, may not exceed five years.

The Code requires the debtor to make "timely" payments, and the trustee is required to ensure that the debtor commences these payments. The debtor must begin making payments under the proposed plan within thirty days after the plan has been filed with the court. If the plan has not been confirmed, the trustee is instructed to retain the payments until the plan is confirmed and then distribute them accordingly. If the plan is denied, the trustee will return the payments to the debtor less any costs. If the debtor fails to make timely payments or to begin payments within the thirty-day period, the court may convert the repayment plan to a liquidation bankruptcy or dismiss the petition.

Confirmation of the Plan After the plan is filed, the court holds a confirmation hearing, at which interested parties may object to the plan. The court will confirm a plan with respect to each claim of a secured creditor under any of the following circumstances:

1. The secured creditors have accepted the plan.
2. The plan provides that creditors retain their claims against the debtor's property, and the value of the property to be distributed to the creditors under the plan is not less than the secured portion of their claims.
3. The debtor surrenders the property securing the claim to the creditors.

Objection to the Plan Unsecured creditors do not have a vote to confirm a repayment plan, but they can object to it. The court can approve a plan over the objection of the trustee or any unsecured creditor only in either of the following situations:

1. The value of the property to be distributed under the plan is at least equal to the amount of the claims.
2. All the debtor's projected disposable income to be received during the three-year plan period will be applied to making payments. Disposable income is all income received less amounts needed to support the debtor and dependents and/or amounts needed to meet ordinary expenses to continue the operation of a business.

Modification of the Plan Prior to the completion of payments, the plan may be modified at the request of the debtor, the trustee, or an unsecured creditor. If any interested party has an objection to the modification, the court must hold a hearing to determine approval or disapproval of the modified plan.

Discharge

After the completion of all payments, the court grants a discharge of all debts provided for by the repayment plan. Except for allowed claims not provided for by the plan, certain long-term debts provided for by the plan, and claims for alimony and child support, all other debts are dischargeable. A discharge of debts under a Chapter 13 repayment plan is sometimes referred to as a "superdischarge." One of the reasons for this is that the law allows a Chapter 13 discharge to include fraudulently incurred debt and claims resulting from malicious or willful injury. Therefore, a discharge under Chapter 13 may be much more beneficial to some debtors than a liquidation discharge under Chapter 7 might be.

Even if the debtor does not complete the plan, a hardship discharge may be granted if failure to complete the plan was due to circumstances beyond the debtor's control and if the value of the property distributed under the plan was greater than creditors would have received in a liquidation proceeding. A discharge can be revoked within one year if it was obtained by fraud.

BE CAREFUL Courts, trustees, and creditors carefully monitor Chapter 13 debtors. If payments are not made, a court can require a debtor to explain why and may allow a creditor to take back her or his property.

CHAPTER 12—FAMILY-FARMER PLAN

The Bankruptcy Code defines a *family farmer*[15] as one whose gross income is at least 50 percent farm dependent and whose debts are at least 80 percent farm related. The total debt must not exceed $1.5 million. A partnership or closely held corporation that is at least 50 percent owned by the farm family can also take advantage of Chapter 12.

The procedure for filing a family-farmer bankruptcy plan is very similar to the procedure for filing a repayment plan under Chapter 13. The farmer-debtor must file a plan not later than ninety days after the order for relief. The filing of the petition acts as an automatic stay against creditors' actions against the estate.

The content of a family-farmer plan is basically the same as that of a Chapter 13 repayment plan. The plan can be modified by the farmer-debtor but, except for cause, must be confirmed or denied within forty-five days of the filing of the plan.

Court confirmation of the plan is the same as for a repayment plan. In summary, the plan must provide for payment of secured debts at the value of the collateral. If the secured debt exceeds the value of the collateral, the remaining debt is unsecured. For unsecured debtors, the plan must be confirmed if either the value of the property to be distributed under the plan equals the amount of the claim or the plan provides that all of the farmer-debtor's disposable income to be received in a three-year period (or longer, by court approval) will be applied to making payments. Completion of payments under the plan discharges all debts provided for by the plan.

A farmer who has already filed a reorganization or repayment plan may convert the plan to a family-farmer plan. The farmer-debtor may also convert a family-farmer plan to a liquidation plan.

---

15. Contrast this definition with the definition of a *farmer* given in footnote 6 on page 482.

KEY TERMS

CHAPTER SUMMARY CREDITORS' RIGHTS AND BANKRUPTCY

REMEDIES AVAILABLE TO CREDITORS	

Liens
(See pages 469–472.)
	1. *Mechanic's lien*—A nonpossessory, filed lien on an owner's real estate for labor, services, or materials furnished to or made on the realty.
	
	2. *Artisan's lien*—A possessory lien on an owner's personal property for labor performed or value added.
	
	3. *Innkeeper's lien*—A possessory lien on a hotel guest's baggage for hotel charges that remain unpaid.
	
	4. *Judicial liens*—
	
	   a. *Attachment*—A court-ordered seizure of property prior to a court's final determination of the creditor's rights to the property. Attachment is available only on the creditor's posting of a bond and strict compliance with the applicable state statutes.
	
	   b. *Writ of execution*—A court order directing the sheriff to seize (levy) and sell a debtor's nonexempt real or personal property to satisfy a court's judgment in the creditor's favor.

Garnishment (See pages 472–474.)	A collection remedy that allows the creditor to attach a debtor's money (such as wages owed or bank accounts) and property that are held by a third person.
Creditors' Composition Agreement (See page 474.)	A contract between a debtor and his or her creditors by which the debtor's debts are discharged by payment of a sum less than the sum that is actually owed.
Mortgage Foreclosure (See pages 474–475.)	On the debtor's default, the entire mortgage debt is due and payable, allowing the creditor to foreclose on the realty by selling it to satisfy the debt.
Suretyship or Guaranty (See pages 475–478.)	Under contract, a third person agrees to be primarily or secondarily liable for the debt owed by the principal debtor. A creditor can turn to this third person for satisfaction of the debt.
LAWS ASSISTING DEBTORS	

Exemptions
(See pages 478–479.)
	Numerous laws, including consumer protection statutes, assist debtors. Additionally, state laws exempt certain types of real and personal property from levy of execution or attachment.
	
	1. *Real property*—Each state permits a debtor to retain the family home, either in its entirety or up to a specified dollar amount, free from the claims of unsecured creditors or trustees in bankruptcy (homestead exemption).
	
	2. *Personal property*—Personal property that is most often exempt from satisfaction of judgment debts includes the following:
	
	   a. Household furniture up to a specified dollar amount.
	
	   b. Clothing and certain personal possessions.
	
	   c. Transportation vehicles up to a specified dollar amount.
	
	   d. Certain classified animals, such as livestock and pets.
	
	   e. Equipment used in a business or trade up to a specified dollar amount.

(continued)

CHAPTER SUMMARY CREDITORS' RIGHTS AND BANKRUPTCY—Continued

BANKRUPTCY—A COMPARISON OF CHAPTERS 7, 11, 12, AND 13

ISSUE	CHAPTER 7	CHAPTER 11	CHAPTERS 12 AND 13
Purpose	Liquidation.	Reorganization.	Adjustment.
Who Can Petition	Debtor (voluntary) or creditors (involuntary).	Debtor (voluntary) or creditors (involuntary).	Debtor (voluntary) only.
Who Can Be a Debtor	Any "person" (including partnerships and corporations) except railroads, insurance companies, banks, savings and loan institutions, investment companies licensed by the Small Business Administration, and credit unions. Farmers and charitable institutions cannot be involuntarily petitioned.	Any debtor eligible for Chapter 7 relief; railroads are also eligible.	*Chapter 12*—Any family farmer (one whose gross income is at least 50 percent farm dependent and whose debts are at least 80 percent farm related) or any partnership or closely held corporation at least 50 percent owned by a farm family, when total debt does not exceed $1.5 million. *Chapter 13*—Any individual (not partnerships or corporations) with regular income who owes fixed unsecured debts of less than $290,525 or fixed secured debts of less than $871,550.
Procedure Leading to Discharge	Nonexempt property is sold with proceeds to be distributed (in order) to priority groups. Dischargeable debts are terminated.	Plan is submitted; if it is approved and followed, debts are discharged.	Plan is submitted and must be approved if the debtor turns over disposable income for a three-year period; if the plan is followed, debts are discharged.
Advantages	On liquidation and distribution, most debts are discharged, and the debtor has an opportunity for a fresh start.	Debtor continues in business. Creditors can either accept the plan, or it can be "crammed down" on them. The plan allows for the reorganization and liquidation of debts over the plan period.	Debtor continues in business or possession of assets. If the plan is approved, most debts are discharged after a three-year period.

FOR REVIEW

1. What is a prejudgment attachment? What is a writ of execution? How does a creditor use these remedies?

2. What is garnishment? When might a creditor undertake a garnishment proceeding?

3. In a bankruptcy proceeding, what constitutes the debtor's estate in property? What property is exempt from the estate under federal bankruptcy law?

4. What is the difference between an exception to discharge and an objection to discharge?

5. In a Chapter 11 reorganization, what is the role of the debtor in possession?

QUESTIONS AND CASE PROBLEMS

15–1. Creditors' Remedies. In what circumstances would a creditor resort to each of the following remedies when trying to collect on a debt?

(a) Mechanic's lien.
(b) Artisan's lien.
(c) Innkeeper's lien.
(d) Writ of attachment.
(e) Writ of execution.
(f) Garnishment.

15–2. Rights of the Surety. Meredith, a farmer, borrowed $5,000 from Farmer's Bank and gave the bank $4,000 in bearer bonds to hold as collateral for the loan. Meredith's neighbor, Peterson, who had known Meredith for years, signed as a surety on the note. Because of a drought, Meredith's harvest that year was only a fraction of what it normally was, and he was forced to default on his payments to Farmer's Bank. The bank did not immediately sell the bonds but instead requested $5,000 from Peterson. Peterson paid the $5,000 and then demanded that the bank give him the $4,000 in securities. Can Peterson enforce this demand? Explain.

15–3. Rights of the Guarantor. Sabrina is a student at Sunnyside University. In need of funds to pay for tuition and books, she attempts to secure a short-term loan from University Bank. The bank agrees to make a loan if Sabrina will have someone financially responsible guarantee the loan payments. Abigail, a well-known businessperson and a friend of Sabrina's family, calls the bank and agrees to pay the loan if Sabrina cannot. Because of Abigail's reputation, the bank makes the loan. Sabrina makes several payments on the loan, but because of illness she is not able to work for one month. She requests that University Bank extend the loan for three months. The bank agrees and raises the interest rate for the extended period. Abigail has not been notified of the extension (and therefore has not consented to it). One month later, Sabrina drops out of school. All attempts to collect from Sabrina have failed. University Bank wants to hold Abigail liable. Will the bank succeed? Explain.

15–4. Creditors' Remedies. Orkin owns a relatively old home valued at $45,000. He notices that the bathtubs and fixtures in both bathrooms are leaking and need to be replaced. He contracts with Pike to replace the bathtubs and fixtures. Pike replaces them and submits her bill of $4,000 to Orkin. Because of financial difficulties, Orkin does not pay the bill. Orkin's only asset is his home, which under state law is exempt up to $40,000 as a homestead. Discuss fully Pike's remedies in this situation.

15–5. Guaranty. In 1988, Jamieson-Chippewa Investment Co. entered into a five-year commercial lease with TDM Pharmacy, Inc., for certain premises in Ellisville, Missouri, on which TDM intended to operate a small drugstore. Dennis and Tereasa McClintock ran the pharmacy business. The lease granted TDM three additional five-year options to renew. The lease was signed by TDM and by the McClintocks individually as guarantors. The lease did not state that the guaranty was continuing. In fact, there were no words of guaranty in the lease other than the single word "Guarantors" on the signature page. In 1993, Dennis McClintock, acting as the president of TDM, exercised TDM's option to renew the lease for one term. Three years later, when the pharmacy failed, TDM defaulted on the lease. Jamieson-Chippewa filed a suit in a Missouri state court against the McClintocks for the rent for the rest of the term, based on their guaranty. The McClintocks filed a motion for summary judgment, contending that they had not guaranteed any rent payments beyond the initial five-year term. How should the court rule? Why? [*Jamieson-Chippewa Investment Co. v. McClintock*, 996 S.W.2d 84 (Mo.App.E.D. 1999)]

15–6. Voidable Preference. The Securities and Exchange Commission (SEC) filed a suit in a federal district court against First Jersey Securities, Inc., and others, alleging fraud in First Jersey's sale of securities (stock). The court ordered the defendants to turn over to the SEC $75 million in illegal profits. This order made the SEC the largest unsecured creditor of First Jersey. First Jersey filed a voluntary petition in a federal bankruptcy court to declare bankruptcy under Chapter 11. On the same day, the debtor transferred 200,001 shares of stock to its law firm, Robinson, St. John, & Wayne (RSW), in payment for services in the SEC suit and the bankruptcy petition. The stock represented essentially all of the debtor's assets. RSW did not find a buyer for the stock for more than two months. The SEC objected to the transfer, contending that it was a voidable preference, and asked that RSW be disqualified from representing the debtor. RSW responded that the transfer was made in the ordinary course of business. Also, asserted RSW, the transfer was not in payment of an "antecedent debt," because the firm had not presented First Jersey with a bill for its services and therefore the debt was not yet past due. Was the stock transfer a voidable preference? Should the court disqualify RSW? Why or why not? [*In re First Jersey Securities, Inc.*, 180 F.3d 504 (3d Cir. 1999)]

Case Problem with Sample Answer

15–7. Discharge in Bankruptcy. Mr. Mallinckrodt received an undergraduate degree from the University of Miami and, in 1995, a graduate degree from Barry University in mental-health counseling. To finance this education, Mallinckrodt borrowed from the Education Resources Institute, Inc., and others. Unable to find a job as a counselor, Mallinckrodt worked as a tennis instructor and coach. (At one time, he had played professional tennis and was ranked among the top eight hundred players in the world.) In 1996, he ruptured his Achilles tendon and was unable to work. After a lengthy rehabilitation, he was employed on a part-time, hourly basis at Horizon Psychological Services, but the work was intermittent and low paying. He continued to work as a tennis instructor and was also a licensed real estate broker but had little income in either field. With monthly income of about $549 after taxes, and expenses of $544, Mallinckrodt filed a bankruptcy petition to discharge his student loan debt, which with interest totaled nearly $73,000. Is this debt dischargeable? Discuss. [*In re Mallinckrodt*, 260 Bankr. 892 (S.D.Fla. 2001)]

To view a sample answer for this case problem, go to this book's Web site at http://leet.westbuslaw.com and click on "Interactive Study Center."

15–8. Garnishment. Susan Guinta is a real estate salesperson. Smythe Cramer Co. obtained in an Ohio state court a garnishment order to attach Guinta's personal earnings. The order was served on Russell Realtors to attach sales commissions that Russell owed to Guinta. Russell objected, arguing that commissions are not personal earnings and are therefore exempt from attachment under a garnishment of personal earnings. An Ohio statute defines *personal earnings* as "money, or any other consideration or thing of value, that is

paid or due to a person in exchange for work, labor, or personal services provided by the person to an employer." An *employer* is "a person who is required to withhold taxes out of payments of personal earnings made to a judgment debtor." Russell does not withhold taxes from its salespersons' commissions. Under a federal statute, *earnings* means "compensation paid or payable for personal services, whether denominated as wages, salary, commission, bonus, or otherwise." Where the federal definition is more restrictive and results in a smaller garnishment, that definition is controlling. Property other than personal earnings may be subject to garnishment without limits. How should the court rule regarding Russell's objection? Why? [*Smythe Cramer Co. v. Guinta*, 762 N.E.2d 1083 (Ohio Mun. 2001)]

15–9. Guaranty. In 1981, in Troy, Ohio, Willis and Mary Jane Ward leased a commercial building to Buckeye Pizza Corp. to operate a pizza parlor. Two years later, Buckeye assigned its interest in the building to Ohio Ltd. In 1985, Ohio sold its pizza business, including its lease of the Wards' building, to NR Dayton Mall, Inc., an Indiana corporation and a subsidiary of Noble Roman's, Inc. As part of the deal, Noble Roman's agreed that it "unconditionally guarantees the performance by N.R. DAYTON MALL, INC., of all its obligations under the . . . Assumption Undertaking." In the "Assumption Undertaking," NR agreed to accept assignment of the Ward lease and to pay Buckeye's and Ohio's expenses if they were sued under it. A dozen years later, NR defaulted on the lease and abandoned the premises. The Wards filed a suit in an Indiana state court against Noble Roman's and others, contending that the firm was liable for NR's default. Noble Roman's argued that it had guaranteed only to indemnify Buckeye and Ohio. The Wards filed a motion for summary judgment. Should the court grant the motion? Explain. [*Noble Roman's, Inc. v. Ward*, 760 N.E.2d 1132 (Ind.App. 2002)]

15–10. Discharge in Bankruptcy. Jon Goulet attended the University of Wisconsin in Eau Claire and Regis University in Denver, Colorado, from which, in 1972, he earned a bachelor's degree in history. Over the next ten years, he worked as a bartender and restaurant manager. In 1984, he became a life insurance agent, and his income ranged from $20,000 to $30,000. In 1989, however, his agent's license was revoked for insurance fraud, and he was arrested for cocaine possession. From 1991 to 1995, Goulet was again at the University of Wisconsin, working toward, but failing to obtain, a master's degree in psychology. To pay for his studies, he took out student loans totaling $76,000. Goulet then returned to bartending and restaurant management and tried real estate sales. His income for the year 2000 was $1,490, and his expenses, excluding a child-support obligation, were $5,904. When the student loans came due, Goulet filed a petition for bankruptcy. On what ground might the loans be dischargeable? Should the court grant a discharge on this ground? Why or why not? [*Goulet v. Educational Credit Management Corp.*, 284 F.3d 773 (7th Cir. 2002)]

15-11. In September 1986, Edward and Debora Davenport pleaded guilty in a Pennsylvania court to welfare fraud and were sentenced to probation for one year. As a condition of their probation, the Davenports were ordered to make monthly restitution payments to the county probation department, which would forward the payments to the Pennsylvania Department of Public Welfare, the victim of the Davenports' fraud. In May 1987, the Davenports filed a petition for Chapter 13 relief and listed the restitution payments among their debts. The bankruptcy court held that the restitution obligation was a dischargeable debt. Ultimately, the United States Supreme Court reviewed the case. The Court noted that under the Bankruptcy Code, a debt is defined as a liability on a claim, and a claim is defined as a right to payment. Because the restitution obligations clearly constituted a right to payment, the Court held that the obligations were dischargeable in bankruptcy. [*Pennsylvania Department of Public Welfare v. Davenport*, 495 U.S. 552, 110 S.Ct. 2126, 109 L.Ed.2d 588 (1990)]

1. Critics of this decision contend that the Court adhered to the letter, but not the spirit, of bankruptcy law in arriving at its conclusion. In what way, if any, did the Court not abide by the "spirit" of bankruptcy law?
2. Do you think that Chapter 13 plans, which allow nearly all types of debts to be discharged, tip the scales of justice too far in favor of debtors?

Critical-Thinking Managerial Question

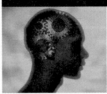

15-12. G&M Trucking borrows money from Middleton Bank to buy two trucks, giving the bank a security interest in the trucks. This interest means that the bank can repossess the trucks if G&M defaults on its payments to the bank. G&M fails to make its monthly payments for two months and files a petition in bankruptcy. Under bankruptcy law, the bank is prevented from repossessing the trucks. The trucks are depreciating at a rate of several hundred dollars a month, however, and will soon be worth much less than the balance due on the loan. Is there anything that the bank can do to protect its investment?

INTERACTING WITH THE INTERNET

For updated links to resources available on the Web, as well as a variety of other materials, visit this text's Web site at

http://leet.westbuslaw.com

The Legal Information Institute at Cornell University offers a collection of law materials concerning debtor-creditor relationships, including federal statutes and recent Supreme Court decisions on this topic, at

http://www.law.cornell.edu/topics/debtor_creditor.html

The U.S. Department of Labor's Web site contains a page on garnishment and employees' rights in relation to garnishment proceedings at

http://www.dol.gov/asp/programs/guide/garnish.htm

The U.S. Bankruptcy Code is online at

http://www4.law.cornell.edu/uscode/11

Another good resource for bankruptcy information is the American Bankruptcy Institute (ABI) at

http://www.abiworld.org

ONLINE LEGAL RESEARCH EXERCISES

Go to **http://leet.westbuslaw.com**, the Web site that accompanies this text. Select "Interactive Study Center," and then click on "Chapter 15." There you will find the following Internet research exercises that you can perform to learn more about topics covered in this chapter.

Activity 15–1: MANAGEMENT PERSPECTIVE—Mechanic's Liens
Activity 15–2: HISTORICAL PERSPECTIVE—Bankruptcy
Activity 15–3: ECONOMIC PERSPECTIVE—Bankruptcy Alternatives

BEFORE THE TEST

Go to **http://leet.westbuslaw.com**, the Web site that accompanies this text. Select "Interactive Quizzes." You will find at least twenty interactive questions relating to this chapter.

Westlaw® Campus

If your textbook provided for a subscription to Westlaw® Campus, or if you have otherwise purchased access to the Westlaw Campus database, you can access any of the cases presented or cited in this chapter by using your Westlaw Campus account.

UNIT THREE   Cumulative Business Hypothetical

Samuel Polson has an idea for a new software application. Polson hires an assistant and invests a considerable amount of his own time and funds developing the application. To develop other software, and to manufacture and market his applications, Polson needs financial capital.

1. Polson borrows $5,000 from his friend Michael Brant. Polson promises to repay Brant the $5,000 in three weeks. Brant, in urgent need of money, borrows $5,000 from his friend Mary Viva and assigns his rights to the $5,000 Polson owes him to Viva in return for the loan. Viva notifies Polson of the assignment. Polson pays Brant the $5,000 on the date stipulated in their contract. Brant refuses to give the money to Viva, and Viva sues Polson. Is Polson obligated to pay Viva $5,000 also? Discuss.

2. Polson learns that a competitor, Trivan, Inc., has already filed for a patent on a nearly identical program and has manufactured and sold the software to some customers. Polson learns from a reliable source that Trivan paid Polson's assistant a substantial sum of money to obtain a copy of the program. What legal recourse does Polson have against Trivan? Discuss fully.

3. While Polson is developing his idea and founding his business, he has no income. He continues to have living expenses, however, as well as payments due on his mortgage, various credit-card debts, and some loans that he took out to pay for his son's college tuition. As his business begins to make money, Polson files for Chapter 7 liquidation to be rid of his personal debts entirely, even though he believes he could probably pay them off over a four-year period if he scrimped and used every cent available to pay his creditors. Are all of Polson's personal debts dischargeable under Chapter 7, including the debts incurred for his son's education? Given the fact that Polson could foreseeably pay off his debts over a four-year period, will the court allow Polson to obtain relief under Chapter 7? Why or why not?

4. Polson is the sole owner of the business and pays no business income taxes. What is the form of Polson's business organization? What other options, in terms of business organizational forms, does Polson have? What are the advantages and disadvantages of each option? If Polson decides to incorporate the business under the name Polson Software, Inc., what steps will he need to take to do so?

CHAPTER 16

Employment Relationships

CONTENTS

AGENCY
A relationship between two parties
in which one party (the agent)
agrees to represent or act for the
other (the principal).

CHAPTER OBJECTIVES

After reading this chapter, you should be able to answer the following questions:

1. What is an agency relationship, and how do agency relationships arise?

2. What is the difference between an employee and an independent contractor?

3. What are the rights and duties of parties to an agency relationship?

4. What federal statutes govern wages and worker health and safety in the workplace? What is the purpose of workers' compensation laws?

5. How does the government provide for income security? What are some issues relating to employee privacy rights?

Employment relationships are agency relationships. Indeed, one of the most common, important, and pervasive legal relationships is that of agency. In an agency relationship between two parties, one of the parties, called the *agent,* agrees to represent or act for the other, called the *principal.* The principal has the right to control the agent's conduct in matters entrusted to the agent, and the agent must exercise his or her powers "for the benefit of the principal only," as Justice Joseph Story indicated in the quotation alongside. By using agents, a principal can conduct multiple business operations simul-

> "[It] is a universal principle in the law of agency that the powers of the agent are to be exercised for the benefit of the principal only, and not of the agent or of third parties."
>
> Joseph Story, 1779–1845
> (Associate justice of the United States
> Supreme Court, 1811–1844)

taneously in various locations. Thus, for example, contracts that bind the principal, such as a corporation or other business firm, can be made at different places with different persons at the same time. Because agency relationships permeate the business world, an understanding of the law of agency is crucial to understanding the legal environment of business.

Also important to the framework of the legal environment of business are employment statutes. For most of this century, the relationship of employer and employee has been the subject of federal and state legislation. Many of these statutes are discussed in the last part of this chapter.

AGENCY RELATIONSHIPS

Section 1(1) of the *Restatement (Second) of Agency*[1] defines *agency* as "the fiduciary relation which results from the manifestation of consent by one person to another that the other shall act in his behalf and subject to his control, and consent by the other so to act." In other words, in a principal-agent relationship, the parties have agreed that the agent will act *on behalf and instead of* the principal in negotiating and transacting business with third persons. The term **fiduciary** is at the heart of agency law. When used as an adjective, as in "fiduciary relationship," it means that the relationship involves trust and confidence.

FIDUCIARY
As an adjective, a relationship founded on trust and confidence.

Agency relationships commonly exist between employers and employees. Agency relationships may sometimes also exist between employers and independent contractors who are hired to perform special tasks or services.

Employer-Employee Relationships

Normally, all employees who deal with third parties are deemed to be agents. ● EXAMPLE 1 A salesperson in a department store is an agent of the store's owner (the principal) and acts on the owner's behalf. Any sale of goods made by the salesperson to a customer is binding on the principal. Similarly, most representations of fact made by the salesperson with respect to the goods sold are binding on the principal.●

Because employees who deal with third parties are normally deemed agents of their employers, agency law and employment law overlap considerably. Agency relationships, though, as will become apparent, can exist outside an employee-employer relationship and thus have a broader reach than employment laws do. Additionally, bear in mind that agency law is based on the common law. In the employment realm, many common law doctrines have been displaced by statutory law and government regulations governing employment relationships.

Employment laws (state and federal) apply only to the employer-employee relationship. Statutes governing Social Security, withholding taxes, workers' compensation, unemployment compensation, workplace safety, employment discrimination, and the like are applicable only if there is employer-employee status. *These laws do not apply to the independent contractor.*

---

1. The *Restatement (Second) of Agency* is an authoritative summary of the law of agency and is often referred to by jurists in their decisions and opinions.

Employer–Independent Contractor Relationships

Independent contractors are not employees, because by definition, those who hire them have no control over the details of their physical performance. Section 2 of the *Restatement (Second) of Agency* defines an **independent contractor** as follows:

> [An independent contractor is] a person who contracts with another to do something for him [or her] but who is not controlled by the other nor subject to the other's right to control with respect to his [or her] physical conduct in the performance of the undertaking. He [or she] may or may not be an agent.

INDEPENDENT CONTRACTOR
One who works for, and receives payment from, an employer but whose working conditions and methods are not controlled by the employer. An independent contractor is not an employee but may be an agent.

Building contractors and subcontractors are independent contractors, and a property owner does not control the acts of either of these professionals. Truck drivers who own their equipment and hire themselves out on a per-job basis are independent contractors, but truck drivers who drive company trucks on a regular basis are usually employees.

The relationship between a person or firm and an independent contractor may or may not involve an agency relationship. ● EXAMPLE 2 An owner of real estate who hires a real estate broker to negotiate a sale of his or her property not only has contracted with an independent contractor (the real estate broker) but also has established an agency relationship for the specific purpose of assisting in the sale of the property.●

Determining Employee Status

A question the courts frequently face in determining liability under agency law is whether a person hired by another to do a job is an employee or an independent contractor. Because employers are normally held liable as principals for the actions taken by their employee-agents within the scope of employment (as will be discussed later in this chapter), the court's decision as to employee versus independent-contractor status can be significant for the parties.

Criteria Used by the Courts In determining whether a worker has the status of an employee or an independent contractor, the courts often consider the following questions:

1. How much control can the employer exercise over the details of the work? (If an employer can exercise considerable control over the details of the work, this indicates employee status.)
2. Is the worker engaged in an occupation or business distinct from that of the employer? (If not, this indicates employee status.)
3. Is the work usually done under the employer's direction or by a specialist without supervision? (If the work is usually done under the employer's direction, this indicates employee status.)
4. Does the employer supply the tools at the place of work? (If so, this indicates employee status.)
5. For how long is the person employed? (If the person is employed for a long period of time, this indicates employee status.)
6. What is the method of payment—by time period or at the completion of the job? (Payment by time period, such as once every two weeks or once a month, indicates employee status.)

7. What degree of skill is required of the worker? (If little skill is required, this may indicate employee status.)

Sometimes, it is advantageous to have employee status—to take advantage of laws protecting employees, for example. At other times, it may be beneficial to have independent-contractor status—for tax purposes, for example, as you will read shortly.

ETHICAL ISSUE

Why should it be left to the courts to determine who is and who is not an independent contractor?

Not surprisingly, many employers prefer to designate certain workers as independent contractors rather than as employees. As long as an employee agrees to be classified as an independent contractor, why should a court interfere in this decision? The answer is, at least in part, that issues of fairness may be involved, and the common law of agency, as developed and applied by the courts, implicitly recognizes these issues. After all, if a worker is an independent contractor, the worker must pay all Social Security taxes, instead of sharing them with his or her employer. Additionally, the worker will not be entitled to employer-provided benefits—such as pension plans, stock option plans, group insurance coverage, and so on—that are available to employees. Furthermore, the worker will not receive the legal protections afforded to employees under such laws as those regulating safety in the workplace and those protecting employees from discrimination. Another consideration is that workers normally lack "bargaining power." Thus, if an employer states that a worker is being hired as an independent contractor, what can the worker do? Generally, in this situation the worker has only two options: he or she must either accept the arrangement or forfeit the job.[2]

Criteria Used by the IRS Often, the criteria for determining employee status are established by a statute or an administrative agency. Businesspersons should be aware that the Internal Revenue Service (IRS) has established its own criteria for determining whether a worker is an independent contractor or an employee. Until 1996 the IRS considered twenty factors in determining a worker's status, but these criteria were abolished in favor of rules that essentially encourage IRS examiners to focus on just one factor—the degree of control the business exercises over the worker.

The IRS tends to scrutinize closely a firm's classification of a worker as an independent contractor rather than an employee because independent contractors can avoid certain tax liabilities by taking advantage of business organizational forms available to small businesses. Even though a firm classifies a worker as an independent contractor, if the IRS decides that the worker should be classified as an employee, the employer will be responsible for paying any applicable Social Security, withholding, and unemployment taxes.

---

2. See the *Question of Ethics and Social Responsibility* at the end of this chapter for a case brought against Microsoft Corporation by workers who were required to be independent contractors instead of employees.

AGENCY FORMATION

Agency relationships normally are consensual; that is, they come about by voluntary consent and agreement between the parties. Generally, the agreement need not be in writing,[3] and consideration is not required. A principal must have contractual capacity, however. A person who cannot legally enter into contracts directly is not allowed to do so indirectly through an agent.

An agency relationship can be created for any legal purpose. An agency relationship that is created for an illegal purpose or that is contrary to public policy is unenforceable. ● EXAMPLE 3 Suppose that Sharp (as principal) contracts with Blesh (as agent) to sell illegal narcotics. This agency relationship is unenforceable, because selling illegal narcotics is a felony and is contrary to public policy.● It is also illegal for medical doctors and other licensed professionals to employ unlicensed agents to perform professional actions.

Generally, there are four ways in which an agency relationship can arise: by agreement of the parties, by ratification, by estoppel, and by operation of law. We look here at each of these possibilities.

Agency by Agreement

Because an agency relationship is, by definition, normally consensual, ordinarily it must be based on an express or implied agreement that the agent will act for the principal and the principal agrees to have the agent so act. An agency agreement can take the form of an express written or oral contract. An agency agreement can also be implied by conduct. ● EXAMPLE 4 A hotel allows only Boris Koontz to park cars, but Boris has no employment contract there. The hotel's manager tells Boris when to work, as well as where and how to park the cars. The hotel's conduct amounts to a manifestation of its willingness to have Boris park its customers' cars, and Boris can infer from the hotel's conduct that he has authority to act as a parking valet. It can be inferred that Boris is an agent for the hotel, his purpose being to provide valet parking services for hotel guests.● In the following case, the court considered whether an agency relationship could be inferred from the conduct of the parties.

---

3. There are two main exceptions to the statement that agency agreements need not be in writing: (1) Whenever agency authority empowers the agent to enter into a contract that the Statute of Frauds requires to be in writing, the agent's authority from the principal must likewise be in writing. (2) A power of attorney, which confers authority to an agent, must be in writing.

CASE 16.1   Acordia of Virginia Insurance Agency, Inc. v. Genito Glenn, L.P.[a]

Supreme Court of Virginia, 2002.
263 Va. 377,
560 S.E.2d 246.
http://www.courts.state.va.us/opin.htm[b]

BACKGROUND AND FACTS
Genito Glenn, Limited Partnership, was the owner of a proposed apartment complex project in Chesterfield County, Virginia. Rather than searching out the best insurance policy itself, Genito arranged with National Housing Corporation (NHC) to procure insurance coverage for the project. NHC contracted with Acordia of Virginia Insurance Agency, Inc., to obtain a policy. The

---

a. *L.P.* is an abbreviation for the term *limited partnership,* a type of business organization. Limited partnerships were discussed in Chapter 14.
b. In the "Supreme Court of Virginia Opinions" section, click on one of the links to access a list of the case names. Scroll down the list to the name of the case and click on the record number to access the opinion. Virginia's Judicial System maintains this Web site.

CASE 16.1—Continued

project's builder used, as ground fill, fly ash, which was defective, resulting in cracks in the buildings' foundations. This compromised the structural integrity of the buildings, which had to be demolished and rebuilt. Genito filed a claim for its loss under what it believed to be its insurance policy. Coverage was denied, however, because Genito had not been named as the insured party. Genito filed a suit in a Virginia state court against Acordia, alleging, in part, negligence in the performance of contractual obligations. Acordia argued that it and Genito were not in privity of contract (were not involved in a direct contractual relationship), a required element of Genito's cause of action. The court ruled that Acordia and Genito were in privity and awarded Genito $1,825,136.54, plus interest. Acordia appealed to the Virginia Supreme Court.

IN THE WORDS OF THE COURT . . .

Opinion by Justice *CYNTHIA D. KINSER.*

* * * *

* * * In the absence of privity, a person cannot be held liable for economic loss damages caused by the negligent performance of a contract.

Genito asserts that when NHC contracted with Acordia to procure a builders risk insurance policy to cover Genito, * * * NHC was acting as Genito's agent, thus creating privity between Genito and Acordia. * * * Acordia argues that evidence of an element necessary to establish a principal-agent relationship, specifically, the right to control, is absent * * * .

* * * [A]gency [is] a fiduciary relationship resulting from one person's manifestation of consent to another person that the other shall act on his behalf and subject to his control, and the other person's manifestation of consent so to act. *While the power of control is an important factor to consider in determining whether an agency relationship exists, agency may be inferred from the conduct of the parties and from the surrounding facts and circumstances.* [Emphasis added.]

* * * *

Applying these principles, we conclude that the facts and circumstances in this case, as well as the parties' conduct, demonstrate that an agency relationship existed between Genito and NHC. Russell W. Johnson, who previously worked as a financial manager at NHC, stated that he contacted Acordia for the purpose of obtaining insurance coverage for several limited partnerships and their respective apartment complex building projects, including the Genito project. Continuing, Johnson testified that he told J. Scott Eckmann, a property casualty insurance broker who was formerly a senior vice president at Acordia, about the various limited partnerships, explained that these partnerships would own the projects, and stressed the necessity that every partnership be protected under the insurance policy. * * *

Eckmann acknowledged that he knew that NHC was acting on behalf of all of the limited partnerships to procure insurance coverage * * * . Eckmann also stated that he delivered the builders risk insurance policy purportedly issued to cover Genito and its apartment complex project to Johnson at NHC. NHC's responsibility for procuring insurance, the manner in which it set about to do so, and the information disclosed by Johnson to Eckmann were consistent with the existence of an agency relationship between NHC and Genito. An agent commonly represents the principal in the creation and performance of contracts with third parties.

DECISION AND REMEDY The Virginia Supreme Court affirmed the lower court's ruling in Genito's favor. NHC acted as Genito's agent in procuring the insurance policy through Acordia, thus establishing the element of privity, which was needed to allow Genito to recover

(continued)

CASE 16.1—Continued

damages for its economic loss resulting from Acordia's negligent performance of its contractual obligations.

FOR CRITICAL ANALYSIS—Social Consideration *Genito sued Acordia under the tort*

theory of negligence. Can you think of any other legal theory on which Genito might have based its action against Acordia? (Hint: Was Genito a third party beneficiary of the contract between NHC and Acordia?)

Agency by Ratification

On occasion, a person who is in fact not an agent (or who is an agent acting outside the scope of his or her authority) may make a contract on behalf of another (a principal). If the principal approves or affirms that contract by word or by action, an agency relationship is created by **ratification.** Ratification is a question of intent, and intent can be expressed by either words or conduct.

RATIFICATION
The act of accepting and giving legal force to an obligation that previously was not enforceable.

Agency by Estoppel

When a principal causes a third person to reasonably believe that another person is his or her agent, and the third person deals with the supposed agent, the principal is "estopped to deny" the agency relationship. In such a situation, the principal's actions create the *appearance* of an agency that does not in fact exist.

● **EXAMPLE 5** Suppose that Andrew accompanies Charles, a seed sales representative, to call on a customer, Steve, the proprietor of the General Seed Store. Andrew has done independent sales work but has never signed an employment agreement with Charles. Charles boasts to Steve that he wishes he had three more assistants "just like Andrew." Steve has reason to believe from Charles's statements that Andrew is an agent for Charles. Steve then places seed orders with Andrew. If Charles does not correct the impression that Andrew is an agent, Charles will be bound to fill the orders just as if Andrew were really Charles's agent. Charles's representation to Steve created the impression that Andrew was Charles's agent and had authority to solicit orders.●

The acts or declarations of a purported *agent* in and of themselves do not create an agency by estoppel. Rather, it is normally the deeds or statements of the *principal* that create an agency by estoppel. ● **EXAMPLE 6** Suppose that Olivia walks into Dru's Dress Boutique and claims to be a sales agent for an exclusive Paris dress designer, Pierre Dumont. Dru has never had business relations with Pierre Dumont. Based on Olivia's claim, however, Dru gives Olivia an order and prepays 15 percent of the sales price. Olivia is not an agent, and the dresses are never delivered. Dru cannot hold Pierre Dumont liable. Olivia's acts and declarations alone do not create an agency by estoppel.●

A proprietor reviews the inventory in her clothing store. Under what circumstances might a clothing importer be considered to act as an agent for the store?

Agency by Operation of Law

There are other situations in which the courts will find an agency relationship in the absence of a formal agreement. This may occur in family relationships. For example, suppose one spouse purchases certain basic necessaries and charges them to the other spouse's charge account. The courts will often rule that the latter is liable for payment for the necessaries, either because of a social policy of promoting the general welfare of the spouse or because of a legal duty to supply necessaries to family members.

Agency by operation of law may also occur in emergency situations, when the agent's failure to act outside the scope of his or her authority would cause the principal substantial loss. If the agent is unable to contact the principal, the courts will often grant this emergency power. For example, a railroad engineer may contract on behalf of his or her employer for medical care for an injured motorist hit by the train.

DUTIES OF AGENTS AND PRINCIPALS

The principal-agent relationship gives rise to duties that govern both parties' conduct. As discussed previously, an agency relationship is *fiduciary*—one of trust. In a fiduciary relationship, each party owes the other the duty to act with the utmost good faith. In general, for every duty of the principal, the agent has a corresponding right, and vice versa.

When one party to the agency relationship violates his or her duty to the other party, the remedies available to the nonbreaching party arise out of contract and tort law. These remedies include monetary damages, termination of the agency relationship, injunction, and required accountings.

> "I am 'in a fiduciary position'—which is always a d_____ uncomfortable position."
> FREDERIC W. MAITLAND, 1850–1906
> (English jurist and historian)

Agent's Duties to the Principal

Generally, the agent owes the principal five duties—performance, notification, loyalty, obedience, and accounting.

Performance An implied condition in every agency contract is the agent's agreement to use reasonable diligence and skill in performing the work. When an agent fails to perform his or her duties entirely, liability for breach of contract normally will result. The degree of skill or care required of an agent is usually that expected of a reasonable person under similar circumstances. Generally, this is interpreted to mean ordinary care. An agent may, however, have represented himself or herself as possessing special skills (such as those that an accountant or attorney possesses). In these situations, the agent is expected to exercise the skill or skills claimed. Failure to do so constitutes a breach of the agent's duty.

Notification There is a maxim in agency law that notice to the agent is notice to the principal. An agent is thus required to notify the principal of all matters that come to his or her attention concerning the subject matter of the agency. This is the duty of notification. The law assumes that the principal knows of any information acquired by the agent that is relevant to the agency—regardless of whether the agent actually passes on this information to the principal.

Loyalty Loyalty is one of the most fundamental duties in a fiduciary relationship. Simply stated, the agent has the duty to act solely for the benefit of his or her principal and not in the interest of the agent or a third party. For example, an agent cannot represent two principals in the same transaction unless both know of the dual capacity and consent to it. The duty of loyalty also means that any information or knowledge acquired through the agency relationship is considered confidential. It would be a breach of loyalty to disclose such information either during the agency relationship or after its termination. Typical examples of confidential information are trade secrets and customer

BE AWARE An agent's disclosure of confidential information could constitute the business tort of misappropriation of trade secrets.

A real estate agent stands by a "For Sale" sign. If this agent knows a buyer who is willing to pay more than the asking price for this property, what duty would the agent breach if he bought the property and then resold it at a profit to the buyer?

lists compiled by the employer-principal. In short, the agent's loyalty must be undivided. The agent's actions must be strictly for the benefit of the principal and must not result in any secret profit for the agent.

● **EXAMPLE 7** Suppose that Ryder contracts with Alton, a real estate agent, to sell Ryder's property. Alton knows that he can find a buyer who will pay substantially more for the property than Ryder is asking. If Alton secretly purchased Ryder's property, however, and then sold it at a profit to another buyer, Alton would breach his duty of loyalty as Ryder's agent. Alton has a duty to act in Ryder's best interests and can only become the purchaser in this situation with Ryder's knowledge and approval.●

Obedience When an agent is acting on behalf of the principal, a duty is imposed on that agent to follow all lawful and clearly stated instructions of the principal. Any deviation from such instructions is a violation of this duty. During emergency situations, however, when the principal cannot be consulted, the agent may deviate from such instructions without violating this duty. Whenever instructions are not clearly stated, the agent can fulfill the duty of obedience by acting in good faith and in a manner reasonable under the circumstances.

Accounting Unless an agent and a principal agree otherwise, the agent has the duty to keep and make available to the principal an account of all property and money received and paid out on behalf of the principal. This includes gifts from third persons in connection with the agency. For example, a gift from a customer to a salesperson for prompt deliveries made by the salesperson's firm, in the absence of a company policy to the contrary, belongs to the firm. The agent has a duty to maintain separate accounts for the principal's funds and for the agent's personal funds, and no intermingling of these accounts is allowed.

ETHICAL ISSUE

What happens when the duty of loyalty conflicts with other duties?

The duty of loyalty to one's employer-principal is a fundamental ethical duty that has been written into law. The duty is rooted in the principle that a person cannot serve two masters at the same time. In an agency relationship, the agent's loyalty must be undivided. There are times, however, when the ethical duty of loyalty may come into conflict with another duty, such as one's duty to society. For example, suppose that one's principal-employer is involved in an illegal activity. Or suppose that this employer is aware that a company product is dangerous but refuses to acknowledge consumer complaints or even act on its own studies showing that the product is defective. In either of these situations, must an agent-employee of the firm keep silent, out of loyalty to his or her employer? Or should the agent-employee disregard the duty of loyalty in these situations and "blow the whistle" on the employer's actions (by reporting them to a government official, for example, or to the press)?

Some scholars have argued that many of the greatest evils in the past twenty-five years have been accomplished in the name of "duty" to the principal.

Principal's Duties to the Agent

The principal also owes certain duties to the agent. These duties relate to compensation, reimbursement and indemnification, cooperation, and safe working conditions.

Compensation In general, when a principal requests certain services from an agent, the agent reasonably expects payment. The principal therefore has a duty to pay the agent for services rendered. For example, when an accountant or an attorney is asked to act as an agent, an agreement to compensate the agent for such service is implied. The principal also has a duty to pay that compensation in a timely manner. Except in a gratuitous agency relationship, in which an agent does not act for money, the principal must pay the agreed-on value for an agent's services. If no amount has been expressly agreed on, then the principal owes the agent the customary compensation for such services.

Reimbursement and Indemnification Whenever an agent disburses sums of money to fulfill the request of the principal or to pay for necessary expenses in the course of a reasonable performance of his or her agency duties, the principal has the duty to reimburse the agent for these payments. Agents cannot recover for expenses incurred by their own misconduct or negligence, however.

Subject to the terms of the agency agreement, the principal has the duty to compensate, or *indemnify*, an agent for liabilities incurred because of authorized and lawful acts and transactions. For example, if the principal fails to perform a contract formed by the agent with a third party and the third party then sues the agent, the principal is obligated to compensate the agent for any costs incurred in defending against the lawsuit. Additionally, the principal must indemnify (pay) the agent for the value of benefits that the agent confers on the principal. The amount of indemnification is usually specified in the agency contract. If it is not, the courts will look to the nature of the business and the type of loss to determine the amount.

Cooperation A principal has a duty to cooperate with the agent and to assist the agent in the agent's performance of his or her duties. The principal must do nothing to prevent such performance. ● EXAMPLE 8 Suppose that Akers (the principal) grants Johnson (the agent) an exclusive territory within which Johnson may sell Akers's products, thus creating an exclusive agency. In this situation, Akers cannot compete with Johnson within that territory—or appoint or allow another agent to so compete—because this would violate the exclusive agency. If Akers did so, he would be exposed to liability for Johnson's lost sales or profits.●

Safe Working Conditions The common law requires the principal to provide safe working premises, equipment, and conditions for all agents and employees. The principal has a duty to inspect working conditions and to warn agents and employees about any unsafe areas. When the agency is one of employment, the employer's liability and the safety standards with which the employer must comply normally are covered by federal and state statutes and regulations.

AGENT'S AUTHORITY

> "The law is not a series of calculating machines where definitions and answers come tumbling out when the right levers are pushed."
>
> WILLIAM O. DOUGLAS, 1898–1980
> (Associate justice of the United States Supreme Court, 1939–1975)

An agent's authority to act can be either *actual* (express or implied) or *apparent*. *Express authority* is authority declared in clear, direct, and definite terms. Express authority can be given orally or in writing. *Implied authority* can be (1) conferred by custom, (2) inferred from the position the agent occupies, or (3) inferred as being reasonably necessary to carry out express authority. ● EXAMPLE 9 Mueller is employed by Al's Supermarket to manage one of its stores. Al's has not expressly stated that Mueller has authority to contract with third persons. In this situation, however, authority to manage a business implies authority to do what is reasonably required (as is customary or can be inferred from a manager's position) to operate the business. Reasonably required actions include creating contracts to hire employees, to buy merchandise and equipment, and to arrange for advertising the products sold in the store.●

Actual authority arises from what the principal manifests *to the agent*. *Apparent authority*, in contrast, exists when the principal, by either words or actions, causes a *third party* reasonably to believe that an agent has authority to act, even though the agent has no express or implied authority. If the third party changes his or her position in reliance on the principal's representations, the principal may be *estopped* from denying that the agent had authority. Note that here, in contrast to agency formation by estoppel, the issue has to do with the apparent authority of an *agent*, not the apparent authority of a person who is in fact not an agent.

LIABILITY IN AGENCY RELATIONSHIPS

Frequently, the issue arises as to which party, the principal or the agent, should be held liable for the contracts formed by the agent or for the torts or crimes committed by the agent. We look here at these aspects of agency law.

BE AWARE An agent who exceeds his or her authority to enter into a contract that the principal does not ratify may be liable to the third party on the ground of misrepresentation.

Liability for Contracts

An important consideration in determining liability for a contract formed by an agent is whether the third party knew the identity of the principal at the time the contract was made. The *Restatement (Second) of Agency*, Section 4, classifies principals as disclosed, partially disclosed, or undisclosed.

DISCLOSED PRINCIPAL
A principal whose identity is known to a third party at the time the agent makes a contract with the third party.

PARTIALLY DISCLOSED PRINCIPAL
A principal whose identity is unknown by a third person, but the third person knows that the agent is or may be acting for a principal at the time the agent and the third person form a contract.

Disclosed or Partially Disclosed Principal A principal whose identity is known to the third party at the time the agent makes the contract is a **disclosed principal.** For example, if an agent signs a contract with a third party for office supplies and indicates his or her status as purchasing agent for the owner of an office supply store, the principal—the store's owner—is fully disclosed. The identity of a **partially disclosed principal** is not known by the third party, but the third party knows that the agent is or may be acting for a principal at the time the contract is made. ● EXAMPLE 10 Sarah has contracted with a real estate agent to sell certain property. She wishes to keep her identity a secret, but the agent can make it perfectly clear to a purchaser of the real estate that the agent is acting in an agency capacity for a principal. In this situation, Sarah is a partially disclosed principal.●

A disclosed or partially disclosed principal is liable to a third party for a contract made by an agent who is acting within the scope of his or her authority. Ordinarily, if the principal is disclosed or partially disclosed, the agent has no contractual liability if the principal or the third party does not perform the contract. If the agent *exceeds* the scope of his or her authority and the principal fails to ratify (affirm) the unauthorized contract, however, the third party cannot hold the principal liable for nonperformance. In such situations, the agent is generally liable unless the third party knew of the agent's lack of authority. The following case illustrates the rules that apply to contracts signed by agents on behalf of fully disclosed principals.

CASE 16.2 McBride v. Taxman Corp.

Appellate Court of Illinois,
First District, 2002.
327 Ill.App.3d 992,
765 N.E.2d 51,
262 Ill.Dec. 225.
http://state.il.us/court/default.htm[a]

BACKGROUND AND FACTS Walgreens Company entered into a lease with Taxman Corporation to operate a drugstore in Kedzie Plaza, a shopping center in Chicago, Illinois, owned by Kedzie Plaza Associates; Taxman was the center's property manager. The lease required the "Landlord" to promptly remove snow and ice from the center's sidewalks. Taxman also signed, on behalf of Kedzie Associates, an agreement with Arctic Snow and Ice Control, Inc., to remove ice and snow from the sidewalks surrounding the Walgreens store. On January 27, 1996, Grace McBride, a Walgreens employee, slipped and fell on snow and ice outside the entrance to the store. McBride filed a suit in an Illinois state court against Taxman and others, alleging, among other things, that Taxman had negligently failed to remove the accumulation of ice and snow.[b] Taxman filed a motion for summary judgment in its favor, which the court granted. McBride appealed to a state intermediate appellate court.

IN THE WORDS OF THE COURT . . .

Justice *CERDA* delivered the opinion of the court.

* * * *

On October 10, 1995, Taxman signed, on behalf of the owner, Arctic's one-page "Snow Removal Proposal & Contract" (although dated August 7, 1995), for the term November 15, 1995, through April 15, 1996, for the shopping center where this Walgreens store was located. * * *

Also on October 10, 1995, Arctic and Taxman signed a multi-page document dated October 3, 1995, that was apparently drafted by Taxman. The document was not given a title but contained several pages of terms concerning snow removal "per contract(s) attached." * * *

* * * *

Plaintiff argues that the contract between Taxman and Arctic created a duty of Taxman to remove ice and snow for the benefit of plaintiff. * * *

* * * *

The Arctic proposal and contract was signed "Kedzie Associates by the Taxman." The Taxman-drafted portion of the contract contained a line above

---

a. On this page, click on "Appellate Court of Illinois." On the next page, in the "Appellate Court Documents" section, click on "Appellate Court Opinions." In the result, in the "Appellate Court" section, click on "2002." On the next page, in the "First District" section, click on "January." Finally, scroll to the bottom of the chart and click on the case name to access the opinion. The state of Illinois maintains this Web site.

b. McBride included in her suit complaints against Walgreens and Kedzie Associates but settled these complaints before trial.

(continued)

CASE 16.2—Continued

the signature of Taxman's director of property management stating "The Taxman Corporation, agent for per contracts attached." The latter document specifically stated that the contract was not an obligation of Taxman and that all liabilities were those of the owner and not Taxman. We conclude that Taxman was the management company for the property owner and entered into the two contracts for snow and ice removal only as the owner's agent.

Taxman did not assume a contractual obligation to remove snow or ice; it merely retained Arctic as a contractor on behalf of the owner.

DECISION AND REMEDY The state intermediate appellate court affirmed the judgment of the lower court. The appellate court held that Taxman entered into the snow removal contracts only as the agent of the owner, whose identity was fully disclosed. As agent for a disclosed principal, Taxman had no liability for the nonperformance of the principal or the third party to the contract.

FOR CRITICAL ANALYSIS—Social Consideration *Suppose that the Arctic contract had not identified Kedzie as the principal. Might the court's decision in this case have been different?*

UNDISCLOSED PRINCIPAL
A principal whose identity is unknown by a third person, and the third person has no knowledge that the agent is acting for a principal at the time the agent and the third person form a contract.

Undisclosed Principal The identity of an **undisclosed principal** is totally unknown to the third party. Furthermore, the third party has no knowledge that the agent is acting in an agency capacity at the time the contract is made. When neither the fact of agency nor the identity of the principal is disclosed, a third party is deemed to be dealing with the agent personally, and the agent is liable as a party to the contract. If an agent has acted within the scope of his or her authority, the undisclosed principal is also liable as a party to the contract, just as if the principal had been fully disclosed at the time the contract was made. Conversely, with some exceptions, the undisclosed principal can hold the third party to the contract.

Liability for Torts and Crimes

Obviously, an agent is liable for his or her own torts and crimes. Whether the principal can also be held liable depends on several factors. A principal may be liable for an agent's torts under the doctrine of *respondeat superior,*[4] a Latin term meaning "let the master respond." This doctrine, which is discussed in this chapter's *Landmark in the Legal Environment* feature, is similar to the theory of strict liability discussed in Chapter 9. The doctrine imposes vicarious (substitute) liability on the employer without regard to the personal fault of the employer for torts committed by an employee in the course or scope of employment.

RESPONDEAT SUPERIOR
In Latin, "Let the master respond." A doctrine under which a principal or an employer is held liable for the wrongful acts committed by agents or employees while acting within the course and scope of their agency or employment.

Liability for Agent's Torts The key to determining whether a principal may be liable for the torts of the agent under the doctrine of *respondeat superior* is whether the torts are committed within the scope of the agency or employment. The *Restatement (Second) of Agency,* Section 229, indicates the factors that courts will consider in determining whether or not a particular act occurred within the course and scope of employment. These factors are as follows:

---

4. Pronounced ree-*spahn*-dee-uht soo-*peer*-ee-your.

LANDMARK IN THE LEGAL ENVIRONMENT

The Doctrine of *Respondeat Superior*

The idea that a master (employer) must respond to third persons for losses negligently caused by the master's servant (employee) first appeared in Lord Holt's opinion in *Jones v. Hart* (1698).[a] By the early nineteenth century, this maxim had been adopted by most courts and was referred to as the doctrine of *respondeat superior*.

THEORIES OF LIABILITY The vicarious (indirect) liability of the master for the acts of the servant has been supported primarily by two theories. The first theory rests on the issue of *control:* the master has control over the acts of the servant and is thus responsible for injuries arising out of such service. The second theory is economic in nature: because the master takes the benefits or profits of the servant's service, he or she should also suffer the losses; moreover, the master is better able than the servant to absorb such losses.

The *control* theory is clearly recognized in the *Restatement (Second) of Agency,* in which the master is defined as "a principal who employs an agent to perform service in his affairs and who controls, or has the right to control, the physical conduct of the other in the performance of the

service." Accordingly, a servant is defined as "an agent employed by a master to perform service in his affairs whose physical conduct in his performance of the service is controlled, or is subject to control, by the master."

LIMITATIONS ON THE EMPLOYER'S LIABILITY There are limitations on the master's liability for the acts of the servant, however. An employer (master) is only responsible for the wrongful conduct of an employee (servant) that occurs in the scope of employment. The criteria used by the courts in determining whether an employee is acting within the scope of employment are set forth in the *Restatement (Second) of Agency*. Generally, the act must be of a kind the servant was employed to do; must have occurred within "authorized time and space limits"; and must have been "activated, at least in part, by a purpose to serve the master."

Application to Today's World

The courts have accepted the doctrine of respondeat superior *for nearly two centuries. This theory of vicarious liability has numerous practical implications in all situations in which a principal-agent (master-servant, employer-employee) relationship exists. Today, the small-town grocer with one clerk and the multinational corporation with thousands of employees are equally subject to the doctrinal demand of "let the master respond."*

a. K.B. 642, 90 Eng. Rep. 1255 (1698).

1. Whether the act was authorized by the employer.
2. The time, place, and purpose of the act.
3. Whether the act was one commonly performed by employees on behalf of their employers.
4. The extent to which the employer's interest was advanced by the act.
5. The extent to which the private interests of the employee were involved.
6. Whether the employer furnished the means or instrumentality (for example, a truck or a machine) by which the injury was inflicted.
7. Whether the employer had reason to know that the employee would perform the act in question and whether the employee had ever done it before.
8. Whether the act involved the commission of a serious crime.

Islamic Law and *Respondeat Superior*

The doctrine of *respondeat superior* is well established in the legal systems of the United States and most Western countries. Middle Eastern countries,

however, do not employ the principle. Islamic law, codified in the *sharia,* holds to a strict principle that responsibility for human actions lies with the individual and cannot be vicariously extended to others. This principle and other concepts of Islamic law are based on the sayings of Mohammed, the

seventh-century prophet and founder of Islam.

FOR CRITICAL ANALYSIS

How would American society be affected if employers could not be held vicariously liable for their employees' torts?

NOTE An agent-employee going to or from work or meals is not usually considered to be within the scope of employment. An agent-employee whose job requires travel, however, is considered to be within the scope of employment for the entire trip, including the return home.

A principal is exposed to tort liability whenever a third person sustains a loss due to the agent's misrepresentation. The principal's liability depends on whether or not the agent was actually or apparently authorized to make representations and whether such representations were made within the scope of the agency. The principal is always directly responsible for an agent's misrepresentation made within the scope of the agent's authority, whether the misrepresentation was made fraudulently or simply by the agent's mistake or oversight.

Liability for Independent Contractor's Torts Generally, the principal is not liable for physical harm caused to a third person by the negligent act of an independent contractor in the performance of the contract. This is because the employer does not have the *right to control* the details of an independent contractor's performance. Exceptions to this rule are made in certain situations, however, as when exceptionally hazardous activities are involved. Examples of such activities include blasting operations, the transportation of highly volatile chemicals, or the use of poisonous gases. In these situations, a principal cannot be shielded from liability merely by using an independent contractor. Strict liability is imposed on the principal as a matter of law and, in some states, by statute.

A truck lies on its side following an accident. If the driver had stopped at a bar during working hours and become inebriated, and this accident was caused by the driver's inebriated state, who would be held responsible for the damage?

Liability for Agent's Crimes An agent is liable for his or her own crimes. A principal or employer is not liable for an agent's crime even if the crime was committed within the scope of authority or employment—unless the principal participated by conspiracy or other action. In some jurisdictions, under specific statutes, a principal may be liable for an agent's violation, in the course and scope of employment, of regulations, such as those governing sanitation, prices, weights, and the sale of liquor.

WAGE-HOUR LAWS

In the 1930s, Congress enacted several laws regulating the wages and working hours of employees. In 1931, Congress passed the Davis-Bacon Act,[5] which requires the payment of "prevailing wages" to employees of contractors and subcontractors working on government construction projects. In 1936, the Walsh-Healey Act[6] was passed. This act requires that a minimum wage, as well as overtime pay of time and a half, be paid to employees of manufacturers or suppliers entering into contracts with agencies of the federal government.

In 1938, Congress passed the Fair Labor Standards Act[7] (FLSA). This act extended wage-hour requirements to cover all employers engaged in interstate commerce or engaged in the production of goods for interstate commerce, plus selected types of businesses. We examine here the FLSA's provisions in regard to child labor, maximum hours, and minimum wages.

Child Labor

The FLSA prohibits oppressive child labor. Children under fourteen years of age are allowed to do certain types of work, such as deliver newspapers, work for their parents, and be employed in the entertainment and (with some exceptions) agricultural areas. Children who are fourteen or fifteen years of age are allowed to work, but not in hazardous occupations. Most states require persons under sixteen years of age to obtain work permits. There are also numerous restrictions on how many hours per day and per week they can work. ● **EXAMPLE 11** Children in this age group cannot work during school hours, for more than three hours on a school day (or eight hours on a nonschool day), for more than eighteen hours during a school week (or forty hours during a nonschool week), or before 7 A.M. or after 7 P.M. (9 P.M. during the summer). ●

Persons between the ages of sixteen and eighteen do not face such restrictions on working times and hours, but they cannot be employed in hazardous jobs or in jobs detrimental to their health and well-being. Persons over the age of eighteen are not affected by any of the above-mentioned restrictions.

Hours and Wages

Under the FLSA, any employee who agrees to work more than forty hours per week must be paid no less than one and a half times his or her regular pay for all hours over forty. Note that the FLSA overtime provisions only apply after an employee has worked more than forty hours per *week*. Thus, employees who work for ten hours a day, four days per week, are not entitled to overtime pay because they do not work more than forty hours a week.

Certain employees are exempt from the overtime provisions of the act. Exempt employees fall into four categories: executives, administrative employees, professional employees, and outside salespersons. Generally, to fall into one of these categories, an employee must earn more than a specified amount of income per week and devote a certain percentage of work time to the performance of specific types of duties, as determined by the FLSA. To qualify as

5. 40 U.S.C. Sections 276a–276a-5.
6. 41 U.S.C. Sections 35–45.
7. 29 U.S.C. Sections 201–260.

Children take a break from their work in a coal mine in the early twentieth century. What restrictions do employers face in employing children today?

MINIMUM WAGE
The lowest wage, either by government regulation or union contract, that an employer may pay an hourly worker.

an outside salesperson, the employee must regularly engage in sales work away from the office and spend no more than 20 percent of work time per week performing duties other than sales.

The FLSA provides that a **minimum wage** of a specified amount (currently, $5.15 per hour) must be paid to employees in covered industries. Congress periodically revises such minimum wages. Under the FLSA, the term *wages* includes the reasonable cost to the employer of furnishing employees with board, lodging, and other facilities if they are customarily furnished by that employer.

Do the FLSA's provisions apply to "telecommuters" and others in the work force who do not perform their jobs in the employer's workplace? For a discussion of this issue and others relating to the "virtual workplace," see this chapter's *Legal E-nvironment* feature.

WORKER HEALTH AND SAFETY

Under the common law, employees injured on the job had to rely on tort law or contract law theories in suits they brought against their employers. Additionally, workers had some recourse under the common law governing agency relationships, which imposes a duty on a principal-employer to provide a safe workplace for his or her agent-employee. Today, numerous state and federal statutes protect employees and their families from the risk of accidental injury, death, or disease resulting from their employment. This section discusses the primary federal statute governing health and safety in the workplace, along with state workers' compensation acts.

The Occupational Safety and Health Act

At the federal level, the primary legislation for employee health and safety protection is the Occupational Safety and Health Act of 1970.[8] Congress passed this act in an attempt to ensure safe and healthful working conditions for practically every employee in the country. The act provides for specific standards that employers must meet, plus a general duty to keep workplaces safe.

Enforcement Agencies Three federal agencies develop and enforce the standards set by the Occupational Safety and Health Act. The Occupational Safety and Health Administration (OSHA) is part of the Department of Labor and has the authority to promulgate standards, make inspections, and enforce the act. OSHA has safety standards governing many workplace details, such as the structural stability of ladders and the requirements for railings. OSHA also establishes standards that protect employees against exposure to substances that may be harmful to their health.

The National Institute for Occupational Safety and Health is part of the Department of Health and Human Services. Its main duty is to conduct research on safety and health problems and to recommend standards for OSHA to adopt. Finally, the Occupational Safety and Health Review Commission is an independent agency set up to handle appeals from actions taken by OSHA administrators.

---

8. 29 U.S.C. Sections 553, 651–678.

LEGAL *e*-NVIRONMENT

Employment Issues in the Virtual Workplace

Over thirty million workers in the United States telecommute, up from fewer than twenty million at the end of the last decade. Between eight and ten million U.S. workers now telecommute full-time—never laying eyes on, or feet in, a physical office building. As often happens, though, a spurt in technology—mainly due to the growth in Internet use—has caused real-world conditions to leap ahead of the law. After all, virtually all state and federal statutes governing employment were drafted when the only workplace was the traditional one.

Overtime and Computer-Related Occupations

Not until the early 1990s did the U.S. Department of Labor issue regulations defining exemptions to the overtime-pay requirements of the Fair Labor Standards Act for employees in computer-related occupations. Under the regulations, these employees can qualify as "professionals" and thus be exempt from these requirements. When an employee falls within this (or any other) exemption to the overtime-pay requirements of the act, the employee is not entitled to be paid time and a half for overtime hours.

The professional exemption does not apply to trainees or to entry-level employees in computer specialties, such as programming and analysis. Individuals operating computers or manufacturing, repairing, or maintaining computer hardware are also *not* included in the professional exemption for overtime pay. Under most circumstances, junior programmers, programmer trainees, data-entry specialists, and computer operators are considered not to have sufficient discretion and independence to qualify as administrative employees. They are, consequently, subject to federal overtime regulations.

Regulating the Safety of At-Home Work Sites

The Occupational Safety and Health Administration (OSHA), which is discussed elsewhere in this chapter, did not issue a formal directive on home-office safety until 2000. At that time, OSHA stated that it would not conduct home-office inspections and would not hold employers liable for their employees' home offices. It also stated that it did not expect employers to inspect the home offices of their telecommuting employees.

Nonetheless, OSHA holds employers responsible for any situation in which hazardous materials or work processes are provided or required to be used in an employee's home office. Additionally, employers must keep OSHA injury and illness records for any work-related injuries and illnesses that occur in home work environments (these records will be discussed further later in this chapter). In contrast, OSHA has not applied these record-keeping requirements to virtual employees working, for example, out of their cars, in hotel rooms, and at airports. At some point in the future, however, OSHA may audit remote work sites and increase record-keeping requirements for employers.

FOR CRITICAL ANALYSIS

Why might telecommuting employees sometimes accept being wrongly classified (and not being paid overtime)?

Procedures and Violations OSHA compliance officers may enter and inspect facilities of any establishment covered by the Occupational Safety and Health Act.[9] Employees may also file complaints of violations. Under the act, an

---

9. In the past, warrantless inspections were conducted. In 1978, however, the United States Supreme Court held that warrantless inspections violated the warrant clause of the Fourth Amendment to the Constitution. See *Marshall v. Barlow's, Inc.,* 436 U.S. 307, 98 S.Ct. 1816, 56 L.Ed.2d 305 (1978).

employer cannot discharge an employee who files a complaint or who, in good faith, refuses to work in a high-risk area if bodily harm or death might result.

Employers with eleven or more employees are required to keep occupational injury and illness records for each employee. Each record must be made available for inspection when requested by an OSHA inspector. Whenever a work-related injury or disease occurs, employers must make reports directly to OSHA. Whenever an employee is killed in a work-related accident or when five or more employees are hospitalized in one accident, the employer must notify the Department of Labor within forty-eight hours. If the company fails to do so, it will be fined. Following the accident, a complete inspection of the premises is mandatory.

Criminal penalties for willful violation of the Occupational Safety and Health Act are limited. Employers may be prosecuted under state laws, however. In other words, the act does not preempt state and local criminal laws.[10]

Workers' Compensation

WORKERS' COMPENSATION LAWS
State statutes establishing an administrative procedure for compensating workers' injuries that arise out of—or in the course of—their employment, regardless of fault.

State **workers' compensation laws** establish an administrative procedure for compensating workers injured on the job. Instead of suing, an injured worker files a claim with the administrative agency or board that administers the local workers' compensation claims.

Covered Employees Most workers' compensation statutes are similar. No state covers all employees. Typically excluded are domestic workers, agricultural workers, temporary employees, and employees of common carriers (companies that provide transportation services to the public). Typically, the statutes cover minors. Usually, the statutes allow employers to purchase insurance from a private insurer or a state fund to pay workers' compensation benefits in the event of a claim. Most states also allow employers to be self-insured—that is, employers who show an ability to pay claims do not need to buy insurance.

Recovery of Benefits In general, the right to recover benefits is predicated wholly on the existence of an employment relationship and the fact that the injury was *accidental* and *occurred on the job or in the course of employment,* regardless of fault. Intentionally inflicted self-injury, for example, would not be considered accidental and hence would not be covered. If an injury occurred while an employee was commuting to or from work, it would not usually be considered to have occurred on the job or in the course of employment and hence would not be covered.

An employee must notify his or her employer promptly (usually within thirty days) of an injury. Generally, an employee also must file a workers' compensation claim with the appropriate state agency or board within a certain period (sixty days to two years) from the time the injury is first noticed, rather than from the time of the accident.

Workers' Compensation versus Litigation An employee's acceptance of workers' compensation benefits bars the employee from suing for injuries caused by

---

10. *Pedraza v. Shell Oil Co.,* 942 F.2d 48 (1st Cir. 1991); cert. denied, *Shell Oil Co. v. Pedraza,* 502 U.S. 1082, 112 S.Ct. 993, 117 L.Ed.2d 154 (1992).

the employer's negligence. By barring lawsuits for negligence, workers' compensation laws also bar employers from raising common law defenses to negligence, such as contributory negligence, assumption of risk, or injury caused by a "fellow servant" (another employee). A worker may sue an employer who *intentionally* injures the worker, however.

INCOME SECURITY

Federal and state governments participate in insurance programs designed to protect employees and their families by covering the financial impact of retirement, disability, death, hospitalization, and unemployment. The key federal law on this subject is the Social Security Act of 1935.[11]

Social Security and Medicare

The Social Security Act provides for old-age (retirement), survivors, and disability insurance. The act is therefore often referred to as OASDI. Both employers and employees must "contribute" under the Federal Insurance Contributions Act (FICA)[12] to help pay for the employees' loss of income on retirement. The basis for the employee's and the employer's contribution is the employee's annual wage base—the maximum amount of the employee's wages that are subject to the tax. The employer withholds the employee's FICA contribution from the employee's wages and then matches this contribution. (In 2003, employers were required to withhold 6.2 percent of each employee's wages, up to a maximum wage base of $87,900, and to match this contribution.)

Retired workers are then eligible to receive monthly payments from the Social Security Administration, which administers the Social Security Act. Social Security benefits are fixed by statute but increase automatically with increases in the cost of living.

Medicare, a health-insurance program, is administered by the Social Security Administration for people sixty-five years of age and older and for some under the age of sixty-five who are disabled. It has two parts, one pertaining to hospital costs and the other to nonhospital medical costs, such as visits to doctors' offices. People who have Medicare hospital insurance can also obtain additional federal medical insurance if they pay small monthly premiums, which increase as the cost of medical care increases. As with Social Security contributions, both the employer and the employee contribute to Medicare. Currently, 2.9 percent of the amount of *all* wages and salaries paid to employees goes toward financing Medicare. Unlike Social Security contributions, there is no cap on the amount of wages subject to the Medicare tax.

One issue that has arisen under FICA and the Federal Unemployment Tax Act (FUTA), discussed later in this chapter, is whether wages should be taxed according to the rates in effect when the wages are owed or the rates in effect when the wages are actually paid. The amounts in dispute can be large, as the following case illustrates.

BE AWARE Social Security currently covers almost all jobs in the United States. Nine out of ten workers contribute to this protection for themselves and their families.

11. 42 U.S.C. Sections 301–1397e.
12. 26 U.S.C. Sections 3101–3125.

CASE 16.3 United States v. Cleveland Indians Baseball Co.

Supreme Court of the United States, 2001.
532 U.S. 200,
121 S.Ct. 1433,
149 L.Ed.2d 401.
http://supct.law.cornell.edu/
supct/cases/historic.htm[a]

HISTORICAL AND ECONOMIC SETTING *In any given year, the amount of FICA and FUTA tax owed depends on two factors: the tax rate and the ceiling on taxable wages (the wage base), which limits the amount of wages subject to tax. The rates and the ceilings increase over time. For example, in 1986, the FICA tax on employees and employers was 5.7 percent on wages up to $42,000; in 1987, it was 5.7 percent on wages up to $43,800; and in 1994, 6.2 percent on wages up to $60,600. The Medicare tax on employees and employers remained constant at 1.45 percent each from 1986 to 1994, but the wage base rose from $42,000 in 1986 to $43,800 in 1987. By 1994, Congress had abolished the ceiling, subjecting all wages to the Medicare tax. In 1986 and 1987, the FUTA tax was 6.0 percent on wages up to $7,000; in 1994, it was 6.2 percent on wages up to $7,000.*

BACKGROUND AND FACTS In 1994, the Major League Baseball Players Association settled a grievance with twenty-six major league baseball teams for conspiring to stop the steep escalation of salaries for free agent players. Several teams agreed to pay a total of $280 million to the players. Under the agreement, the Cleveland Indians Baseball Company owed eight players a total of $610,000 in salary for 1986 and fourteen players a total of $1,457,848 for 1987. The company paid the amounts in 1994. The company also paid taxes on the amounts according to the 1994 rates and ceilings and then applied for a refund of more than $100,000, claiming that the taxes should have been computed according to the 1986 and 1987 rates and ceilings.[b] The Internal Revenue Service (IRS) denied the claim, and the company filed a suit in a federal district court against the federal government. The court ordered a refund of the FICA and FUTA taxes. The government appealed to the U.S. Court of Appeals for the Sixth Circuit, which affirmed the lower court's order. The government appealed to the United States Supreme Court.

IN THE WORDS OF THE COURT . . .

Justice *GINSBURG* delivered the opinion of the Court.

* * * *

The Internal Revenue Service has long maintained regulations interpreting the FICA and FUTA tax provisions. In their current form, the regulations specify that the employer tax "attaches *at the time that the wages are paid* by the employer" and "is computed by applying to the wages paid by the employer the rate in effect *at the time such wages are paid*." Echoing the language in [FICA] and [FUTA], these regulations have continued unchanged in their basic substance since 1940.

Although the regulations, like the statute, do not specifically address backpay, the Internal Revenue Service has consistently interpreted them to require taxation of back wages according to the year the wages are actually paid, regardless of when those wages were earned or should have been paid. We need not decide whether the Revenue Rulings themselves are entitled to deference [high regard]. In this case, the Rulings simply reflect the agency's longstanding interpretation of its own regulations. Because that interpretation is reasonable, it attracts substantial judicial deference. We do not resist according such deference in reviewing an agency's steady interpretation of its own

---

a. In the "Search" box, type "Cleveland Indians," select "all current and historic decisions" and click on "submit." In the result, scroll to the name of the case and click on it to access the opinion. The Legal Information Institute of Cornell Law School in Ithaca, New York, maintains this Web site.

b. All but one of the players had collected wages from the company exceeding the ceilings in 1986 and 1987. Because those players, and the company, paid the maximum amount of employment taxes in 1986 and 1987, allocating the 1994 payments back to those years would mean that they would not owe taxes on the amounts. Treating the back wages as taxable in 1994, however, would mean that they would incur significant tax liability, partly because the company did not pay any of the players any other wages in 1994.

CASE 16.3—Continued

61-year-old regulation implementing a 62-year-old statute. Treasury regulations and interpretations long continued without substantial change, applying to unamended or substantially reenacted statutes, are deemed to have received congressional approval and have the effect of law.

     *   *   *   *

In line with the text and administrative history of the relevant taxation provisions, we hold that, for FICA and FUTA tax purposes, back wages should be attributed to the year in which they are actually paid.

DECISION AND REMEDY The United States Supreme Court held that taxes on wages should be computed using the rates and ceilings that apply in the year when the wages are actually paid, not those in effect in the year when the wages should have been paid. The Court reversed the decision of the lower court.

FOR CRITICAL ANALYSIS—Political Consideration *In this case, the rule applied by the Court disadvantaged the taxpayer; in other cases, it has disadvantaged the government. With that in mind, what was Congress's likely intent regarding the FICA and FUTA tax provisions?*

Private Pension Plans

There has been significant legislation to regulate employee retirement plans set up by employers to supplement Social Security benefits. The major federal act covering these retirement plans is the Employee Retirement Income Security Act (ERISA) of 1974.[13] This act empowers the Labor Management Services Administration of the Department of Labor to enforce its provisions governing employers who have private pension funds for their employees. ERISA does not require an employer to establish a pension plan. When a plan exists, however, ERISA establishes standards for its management.

A key provision of ERISA concerns vesting. **Vesting** gives an employee a legal right to receive pension benefits at some future date when he or she stops working. Before ERISA was enacted, some employees who had worked for companies for as long as thirty years received no pension benefits when their employment terminated, because those benefits had not vested. ERISA establishes complex vesting rules. Generally, however, all employee contributions to pension plans vest immediately, and employee rights to employer pension-plan contributions vest after five years of employment.

VESTING
The creation of an absolute or unconditional right or power.

In an attempt to prevent mismanagement of pension funds, ERISA has established rules on how they must be invested. Pension managers must be cautious in their investments and refrain from investing more than 10 percent of the fund in securities (stocks and bonds) of the employer. ERISA also contains detailed record-keeping and reporting requirements.

Unemployment Insurance

The United States has a system of unemployment insurance in which employers pay into a fund, the proceeds of which are paid out to qualified unemployed workers. The Federal Unemployment Tax Act (FUTA) of 1935[14] created a

WATCH OUT A state government can place a lien on the property of an employer who does not pay unemployment taxes.

---

13. 29 U.S.C. Sections 1001 *et seq.*
14. 26 U.S.C. Sections 3301–3310.

state-administered system that provides unemployment compensation to eligible individuals. The FUTA and state laws require employers that fall under the provisions of the act to pay unemployment taxes at regular intervals.

COBRA

Federal legislation also addresses the issue of health insurance for workers whose jobs have been terminated—and who are thus no longer eligible for group health-insurance plans. The Consolidated Omnibus Budget Reconciliation Act (COBRA) of 1985[15] prohibits, for a certain time period, the elimination of a worker's medical, optical, or dental insurance coverage on the voluntary or involuntary termination of the worker's employment. Employers, with some exceptions, must comply with COBRA if they employ twenty or more workers and provide a benefit plan to those workers. They must inform an employee of COBRA's provisions when a group health plan is established and if that worker faces termination or a reduction of hours that would affect his or her eligibility for coverage under the plan.

The employer is relieved of the responsibility to provide benefit coverage if it completely eliminates its group benefit plan. An employer is also relieved of responsibility when the worker becomes eligible for Medicare, becomes covered under a spouse's health plan, becomes insured under a different plan (with a new employer, for example), or fails to pay the premium. An employer that does not comply with COBRA risks substantial penalties, such as a tax of up to 10 percent of the annual cost of the group plan or $500,000, whichever is less.

FAMILY AND MEDICAL LEAVE

In 1993, Congress passed the Family and Medical Leave Act (FMLA)[16] to allow employees to take time off work for family or medical reasons. A majority of the states also have legislation allowing for a leave from employment for family or medical reasons, and many employers maintain private family-leave plans for their workers.

Coverage and Applicability

The FMLA requires employers who have fifty or more employees to provide employees with up to twelve weeks of unpaid family or medical leave during any twelve-month period. During the employee's leave, the employer must continue the worker's health-care coverage and guarantee employment in the same position or a comparable one when the employee returns to work. An important exception to the FMLA, however, allows the employer to avoid reinstatement of a *key employee*—defined as an employee whose pay falls within the top 10 percent of the firm's work force. Additionally, the act does not apply to employees who have worked less than one year or less than twenty-five hours a week during the previous twelve months.

---

15. 29 U.S.C. Sections 1161–1169.
16. 29 U.S.C. Sections 2601, 2611–2619, 2651–2654.

Generally, an employee may take family leave when he or she wishes to care for a newborn baby, an adopted child, or a foster child.[17] An employee may take medical leave when the employee or the employee's spouse, child, or parent has a "serious health condition" requiring care. For most absences, the employee must demonstrate that the health condition requires continued treatment by a health-care provider and includes a period of incapacity of more than three days. Under regulations issued by the Department of Labor in 1995, however, employees suffering from certain chronic health conditions, such as asthma or diabetes, may take FMLA leave for their own incapacities that require absences of less than three days.

Remedies for Violations

Employers who violate the FMLA may be held liable for damages to compensate employees for unpaid wages (or salary), lost benefits, denied compensation, and actual monetary losses (such as the cost of providing for care) up to an amount equivalent to the employee's wages for twelve weeks. The employer may also be required to reinstate an employee in his or her job or grant a promotion that had been denied. A successful plaintiff is also entitled to court costs; attorneys' fees; and in cases involving bad faith on the part of the employer, double damages.

The FMLA expressly covers private and public (government) employees. Some states argued, and some courts agreed, however, that public employees could not sue their state employers in federal courts to enforce their FMLA rights unless the states consented to be sued.[18] This argument came before the United States Supreme Court in the following case.

---

17. The foster care must be state sanctioned before such an arrangement falls within the coverage of the FMLA.

18. Under the Eleventh Amendment to the U.S. Constitution, a state is immune from suit in a federal court unless the state consents to be sued. As you will read in Chapter 17, the Supreme Court has held that the Eleventh Amendment, as interpreted by the Court, prohibits state employees from suing their employers (state government agencies and representatives) for violations of the federal laws protecting against discrimination based on age and disability—unless the state consents to be sued.

CASE 16.4	Nevada Department of Human Resources v. Hibbs

Supreme Court of the United States, 2003.
__ U.S. __,
123 S.Ct. 1972,
155 L.Ed.2d 953.
**http://supct.law.cornell.edu/
supct/cases/name.htm**[a]

HISTORICAL AND CULTURAL SETTING *At one time, many state laws limited women's employment opportunities and often subjected women to distinctive restrictions, terms, conditions, and benefits for the jobs that they could obtain. These laws were based on the beliefs that a woman is, and should remain, the* center of home and family life, and that a "proper discharge" of a woman's "maternal functions—having in view not merely her own health, but the well-being of the race—justifies legislation to protect her from the greed as well as the passion of man."[b] *Congress enacted Title VII of the Civil Rights Act of 1964, in part, to outlaw gender discrimination in the workplace (employment discrimination generally is discussed in detail in Chapter 17).*

BACKGROUND AND FACTS William Hibbs worked for the Nevada Department of Human

---

a. Scroll to the name of the case and click on it to access the opinion.
b. See, for example, *Muller v. Oregon,* 208 U.S. 412, 28 S.Ct. 324, 52 L.Ed. 551 (1908).

(continued)

CASE 16.4—Continued

Resources. In April 1997, Hibbs asked for time off under the FMLA to care for his sick wife, who was recovering from a car accident and neck surgery. The department granted Hibbs's request, allowing him to use the leave intermittently, as needed, beginning in May. Hibbs did this until August 5, after which he did not return to work. In October, the department told Hibbs that he had exhausted his FMLA leave, that no further leave would be granted, and that he must return to work by November 12. When he did not return, he was discharged. Hibbs filed a suit in a federal district court against the department. The court held that the U.S. Constitution's Eleventh Amendment barred the suit. On Hibbs's appeal, the U.S. Court of Appeals for the Ninth Circuit reversed this holding. The department appealed to the United States Supreme Court.

IN THE WORDS OF THE COURT . . .

Chief Justice *REHNQUIST* delivered the opinion of the Court.

*   *   *   *

[After the enactment of Title VII of the Civil Rights Act of 1964] state gender discrimination did not cease. *   *   * According to evidence that was before Congress when it enacted the FMLA, States continue[d] to rely on invalid gender stereotypes in the employment context, specifically in the administration of leave benefits. *   *   *

*   *   *   *

Congress *   *   * heard testimony that "[p]arental leave for fathers *   *   * is rare. Even *   *   * [w]here child-care leave policies do exist, men, *both in the public and private sectors,* receive notoriously discriminatory treatment in their requests for such leave." Many States offered women extended "maternity" leave that far exceeded the typical 4- to 8-week period of physical disability due to pregnancy and childbirth, but very few States granted men a parallel benefit: Fifteen States provided women up to one year of extended maternity leave, while only four provided men with the same. This and other differential leave policies were not attributable to any differential physical needs of men and women, but rather to the pervasive sex-role stereotype that caring for family members is women's work.

*   *   *   *

*   *   * Because employers continued to regard the family as the woman's domain, they often denied men similar accommodations or discouraged them from taking leave. These mutually reinforcing stereotypes created a self-fulfilling cycle of discrimination that forced women to continue to assume the role of primary family caregiver, and fostered employers' stereotypical views about women's commitment to work and their value as employees. *   *   *

We believe that Congress's chosen remedy, the family-care leave provision of the FMLA, is congruent [corresponds to] and [is] proportional to the targeted violation. *   *   *

By creating an across-the-board, routine employment benefit for all eligible employees, Congress sought to ensure that family-care leave would no longer be stigmatized as an inordinate drain on the workplace caused by female employees, and that employers could not evade leave obligations simply by hiring men. By setting a minimum standard of family leave for *all* eligible employees, irrespective of gender, the FMLA attacks the formerly state-sanctioned stereotype that only women are responsible for family caregiving, thereby reducing employers' incentives to engage in discrimination by basing hiring and promotion decisions on stereotypes.

DECISION AND REMEDY The United States Supreme Court affirmed the lower court's decision, concluding that the FMLA corresponds to and is proportional to the discrimination that Congress intended

CASE 16.4—Continued

the FMLA to address. Thus, the FMLA, which expressly covers public employees, can serve as the basis for a suit against a state employer regardless of whether the state consents to the suit.

FOR CRITICAL ANALYSIS—Cultural Consideration *Can a law foster discrimination even when the law is not obviously discriminatory?*

EMPLOYEE PRIVACY RIGHTS

In the last twenty-five years, concerns about the privacy rights of employees have arisen in response to the sometimes invasive tactics used by employers to monitor and screen workers. Perhaps the greatest privacy concern in today's employment arena has to do with electronic performance monitoring. Clearly, employers need to protect themselves from liability for their employees' online activities. They also have a legitimate interest in monitoring the productivity of their workers. At the same time, employees expect to have a certain zone of privacy in the workplace. Indeed, many lawsuits have involved allegations that employers' intrusive monitoring practices violate employees' privacy rights.

A number of laws protect privacy rights. We look here at laws that apply in the employment context. Recall from Chapter 5 that the U.S. Constitution does not contain a provision that explicitly guarantees a right to privacy. A personal right to privacy, however, has been inferred from other constitutional guarantees provided by the First, Third, Fourth, Fifth, and Ninth Amendments to the Constitution. Tort law (see Chapter 8), state constitutions, and a number of state and federal statutes also provide for privacy rights.

Electronic Monitoring in the Workplace

According to a survey by the American Management Association, more than two-thirds of employers engage in some form of electronic monitoring of their employees. Types of monitoring include reviewing employees' e-mail and computer files, video recording of employee job performance, and recording and reviewing telephone conversations and voice mail.

The Electronic Communications Privacy Act The major statute with which employers must comply is the Electronic Communications Privacy Act (ECPA) of 1986, as amended.[19] This act modified existing federal wiretapping law to cover electronic forms of communication, such as communications via cellular telephones or e-mail. The ECPA prohibits the intentional interception of any wire or electronic communication or the intentional disclosure or use of the information obtained by the interception. Excluded from coverage, however, are any electronic communications through devices that are furnished to the subscriber or user by a provider of wire or electronic communication service and that are being used by the subscriber or user, or by the provider of the service, "in the ordinary course of its business."

This "business-extension exception" to the ECPA permits an employer to monitor employee electronic communications in the ordinary course of business.

---

19. 18 U.S.C. Sections 2510–2521.

It does not, however, allow an employer to monitor employees' *personal* communications. Under another exception to the ECPA, though, an employer may avoid liability under the act if the employees consent to having their electronic communications intercepted by the employer. Thus, an employer may be able to avoid liability under the ECPA by simply requiring employees to sign forms indicating that they consent to such monitoring.

Privacy Expectations and E-Mail Systems In cases brought by employees alleging that their privacy has been invaded by e-mail monitoring, the courts have tended to hold for the employers. This is true even when employees were not informed that their e-mail would be monitored. ● EXAMPLE 12 In a leading case on this issue, the Pillsbury Company promised its employees that it would not read their e-mail or terminate or discipline them based on the content of their e-mail. Despite this promise, Pillsbury intercepted employee Michael Smyth's e-mail, decided that it was unprofessional and inappropriate, and fired him. In Smyth's suit against the company, he claimed that his termination was a violation of the public policy protecting employee privacy rights. The court, however, found no "reasonable expectation of privacy in e-mail communications voluntarily made by an employee to his supervisor over the company e-mail system."[20]●

Other Types of Monitoring

In the interests of public safety and to reduce unnecessary costs, many employers, including the government, require their employees to submit to drug-testing procedures. Other types of monitoring in the workplace have included lie-detector tests, AIDS (acquired immune deficiency syndrome) tests, employment screening procedures, and even genetic screening. These types of testing have often been subject to challenge as violations of employee privacy rights.

State laws relating to the privacy rights of private-sector employees vary from state to state. Some state constitutions may prohibit private employers from testing for drugs, and state statutes may restrict drug testing by private employers in any number of ways. A collective bargaining agreement may also provide protection against drug testing. In some instances, employees have brought an action against the employer for the tort of invasion of privacy (discussed in Chapter 8).

Constitutional limitations apply to the testing of government employees. The Fourth Amendment provides that individuals have the right to be "secure in their persons" against "unreasonable searches and seizures" conducted by government agents. Drug tests have been held constitutional, however, when there was a reasonable basis for suspecting government employees of using drugs. Additionally, when drug use in a particular government job could threaten public safety, testing has been upheld. ● EXAMPLE 13 A Department of Transportation rule that requires employees engaged in oil and gas pipeline operations to submit to random drug testing was upheld, even though the rule did not require that before being tested the individual must have been suspected of drug use. The court held that the government's interest in promoting public safety in the pipeline industry outweighed the employees' privacy interests.[21]●

---

20. *Smyth v. Pillsbury Co.,* 914 F.Supp. 97 (E.D.Pa. 1996).
21. *Electrical Workers Local 1245 v. Skinner,* 913 F.2d 1454 (9th Cir. 1990).

ETHICAL ISSUE

Should employers be allowed to conduct genetic testing?

A serious privacy issue today concerns the genetic testing of employees or prospective employees in an effort to identify individuals who might develop significant health problems in the future. To be sure, this may be beneficial to employers. Employees who are subject to such testing, however, complain that genetic testing is one of the most intrusive types of monitoring that employers can undertake. Although to date only a few cases involving this issue have come before the courts, the courts seem to be siding with the employees on this matter.

In one case, for example, the Lawrence Berkeley Laboratory screened prospective employees for the gene that causes sickle cell anemia, although the applicants were not informed of this. In a lawsuit subsequently brought by the prospective employees, a federal appellate court held that they had a cause of action for violation of their privacy rights.[22] The case was later settled for $2.2 million. In another case, the Equal Employment Opportunity Commission (EEOC), the federal agency in charge of administering laws prohibiting employment discrimination, brought an action against a railroad company that had genetically tested its employees. The EEOC contended that the genetic testing violated the Americans with Disabilities Act of 1990 (discussed in Chapter 17). In 2002, this case was settled out of court, also for $2.2 million.[23]

---

22. *Norman-Bloodsaw v. Lawrence Berkeley Laboratory,* 135 F.3d 1260 (9th Cir. 1998).
23. For a discussion of this settlement, see David Hechler, "Railroad to Pay $2.2 Million over Genetic Testing," *The National Law Journal,* May 13, 2002, p. A22.

KEY TERMS

agency 510	minimum wage 526	undisclosed principal 522
disclosed principal 520	partially disclosed principal 520	vesting 531
fiduciary 511	ratification 516	workers' compensation laws 528
independent contractor 512	*respondeat superior* 522	

CHAPTER SUMMARY EMPLOYMENT RELATIONSHIPS

Agency Relationships (See pages 511–513.)	In a *principal-agent* relationship, an agent acts on behalf of and instead of the principal in dealing with third parties. An employee who deals with third parties is normally an agent. An independent contractor is not an employee, and the employer has no control over the details of physical performance. The independent contractor is not usually an agent.
Agency Formation (See pages 514–517.)	1. *By agreement*—Through express consent (oral or written) or implied by conduct. 2. *By ratification*—The principal, either by act or agreement, ratifies the conduct of an agent who acted outside the scope of authority or the conduct of a person who is in fact not an agent.

(continued)

CHAPTER SUMMARY EMPLOYMENT RELATIONSHIPS—Continued

Agency Formation—continued	3. *By estoppel*—When the principal causes a third person to believe that another person is his or her agent, and the third person deals with the supposed agent in reasonable reliance on the agency's existence, the principal is "estopped to deny" the agency relationship. 4. *By operation of law*—Based on a social duty (such as the need to support family members) or created in emergency situations when the agent is unable to contact the principal.

Duties of Agents and Principals (See pages 517–519.)	1. *Duties of the agent—*
	
	   a. *Performance*—The agent must use reasonable diligence and skill in performing his or her duties or use the special skills that the agent has represented to the principal that the agent possesses.
	
	   b. *Notification*—The agent is required to notify the principal of all matters that come to his or her attention concerning the subject matter of the agency.
	
	   c. *Loyalty*—The agent has a duty to act solely for the benefit of his or her principal and not in the interest of the agent or a third party.
	
	   d. *Obedience*—The agent must follow all lawful and clearly stated instructions of the principal.
	
	   e. *Accounting*—The agent has a duty to make available to the principal records of all property and money received and paid out on behalf of the principal.
	
	2. *Duties of the principal—*
	
	   a. *Compensation*—Except in a gratuitous agency relationship, the principal must pay the agreed-on value (or reasonable value) for an agent's services.
	
	   b. *Reimbursement and indemnification*—The principal must reimburse the agent for all sums of money disbursed at the request of the principal and for all sums of money the agent disburses for necessary expenses in the course of reasonable performance of his or her agency duties.
	
	   c. *Cooperation*—A principal must cooperate with and assist an agent in performing his or her duties.
	
	   d. *Safe working conditions*—A principal must provide safe working conditions for the agent-employee.

Agent's Authority (See page 520.)	1. *Actual authority*—Can be either express or implied. *Express authority* can be oral or in writing. Authorization must be in writing if the agent is to execute a contract that must be in writing. *Implied authority* is authority that is customarily associated with the position of the agent or authority that is deemed necessary for the agent to carry out expressly authorized tasks. 2. *Apparent authority*—Exists when the principal, by word or action, causes a third party reasonably to believe that an agent has authority to act, even though the agent has no express or implied authority.
Liability in Agency Relationships (See pages 520–524.)	1. *Liability for contracts*—If the principal's identity is disclosed or partially disclosed at the time the agent forms a contract with a third party, the principal is liable to the third party under the contract if the agent acted within the scope of his or her authority. If the principal's identity is undisclosed at the time of contract formation, the agent is

CHAPTER SUMMARY EMPLOYMENT RELATIONSHIPS—Continued

Liability In Agency Relationships— continued	personally liable to the third party, but if the agent acted within the scope of authority, the principal is also bound by the contract.
	2. *Liability for agent's torts*—Under the doctrine of *respondeat superior,* the principal is liable for any harm caused to another through the agent's torts if the agent was acting within the scope of his or her employment at the time the harmful act occurred. The principal is also liable for an agent's misrepresentation, whether made knowingly or by mistake.
	3. *Liability for independent contractor's torts*—A principal is not liable for harm caused by an independent contractor's negligence, unless hazardous activities are involved (in which situation the principal is strictly liable for any resulting harm) or other exceptions apply.
	4. *Liability for agent's crimes*—An agent is responsible for his or her own crimes, even if the crimes were committed while the agent was acting within the scope of authority or employment. A principal will be liable for an agent's crime only if the principal participated by conspiracy or other action or (in some jurisdictions) if the agent violated certain government regulations in the course of employment.
Wage-Hour Laws (See pages 524–526.)	1. *Davis-Bacon Act (1931)*—Requires the payment of "prevailing wages" to employees of contractors and subcontractors working on federal government construction projects.
	2. *Walsh-Healey Act (1936)*—Requires that a minimum wage and overtime pay be paid to employees of firms that contract with federal agencies.
	3. *Fair Labor Standards Act (1938)*—Extended wage-hour requirements to cover all employers whose activities affect interstate commerce plus certain businesses. The act has specific requirements in regard to child labor, maximum hours, and minimum wages.
Worker Health and Safety (See pages 525–529.)	1. The Occupational Safety and Health Act of 1970 requires employers to meet specific safety and health standards that are established and enforced by the Occupational Safety and Health Administration (OSHA).
	2. State workers' compensation laws establish an administrative procedure for compensating workers who are injured in accidents that occur on the job, regardless of fault.
Income Security (See pages 529–532.)	1. *Social Security and Medicare*—The Social Security Act of 1935 provides for old-age (retirement), survivors, and disability insurance. Both employers and employees must make contributions under the Federal Insurance Contributions Act (FICA) to help pay for the employees' loss of income on retirement. The Social Security Administration administers Medicare, a health-insurance program for older or disabled persons.
	2. *Private pension plans*—The federal Employee Retirement Income Security Act (ERISA) of 1974 establishes standards for the management of employer-provided pension plans.
	3. *Unemployment insurance*—The Federal Unemployment Tax Act of 1935 created a system that provides unemployment compensation to eligible individuals. Covered employers are taxed to help cover the costs of unemployment compensation.
COBRA (See page 532.)	The Consolidated Omnibus Budget Reconciliation Act (COBRA) of 1985 requires employers to give employees, on termination of employment, the option of continuing their medical, optical, or dental insurance coverage for a certain period.

(continued)

CHAPTER SUMMARY EMPLOYMENT RELATIONSHIPS—Continued

Family and Medical Leave (See pages 532–535.)	The Family and Medical Leave Act (FMLA) of 1993 requires employers with fifty or more employees to provide their employees (except for key employees) with up to twelve weeks of unpaid family or medical leave during any twelve-month period for the following reasons: 1. *Family leave*—May be taken to care for a newborn baby, an adopted child, or a foster child. 2. *Medical leave*—May be taken when the employee or the employee's spouse, child, or parent has a serious health condition requiring care.
Employee Privacy Rights (See pages 535–537.)	A right to privacy has been inferred from guarantees provided by the First, Third, Fourth, Fifth, and Ninth Amendments to the U.S. Constitution. State laws may also provide for privacy rights. Employer practices that have been challenged by employees as invasive of their privacy rights include drug testing, AIDS testing, genetic screening, and performance monitoring.

FOR REVIEW

1. What is an agency relationship, and how do agency relationships arise?
2. What is the difference between an employee and an independent contractor?
3. What are the rights and duties of parties to an agency relationship?
4. What federal statutes govern wages and worker health and safety in the workplace? What is the purpose of workers' compensation laws?
5. How does the government provide for income security? What are some issues relating to employee privacy rights?

QUESTIONS AND CASE PROBLEMS

16–1. Agency Formation. Pete Gaffrey is a well-known, wealthy financier living in the city of Takima. Alan Winter, Gaffrey's friend, tells Til Borge that he (Winter) is Gaffrey's agent for the purchase of rare coins. Winter even shows Borge a local newspaper clipping mentioning Gaffrey's interest in coin collecting. Borge, knowing of Winter's friendship with Gaffrey, contracts with Winter to sell to Gaffrey a rare coin valued at $25,000. Winter takes the coin and disappears with it. On the date of contract payment, Borge seeks to collect from Gaffrey, claiming that Winter's agency made Gaffrey liable. Gaffrey does not deny that Winter was a friend, but he claims that Winter was never his agent. Discuss fully whether an agency was in existence at the time the contract for the rare coin was made.

16–2. Agent's Duties to Principal. Iliana is a traveling sales agent. Iliana not only solicits orders but also delivers the goods and collects payments from her customers. Iliana places all payments in her private checking account and at the end of each month draws sufficient cash from her bank to cover the payments made. Giberson Corp., Iliana's employer, is totally unaware of this procedure. Because of a slowdown

in the economy, Giberson tells all its sales personnel to offer 20 percent discounts on orders. Iliana solicits orders, but she offers only 15 percent discounts, pocketing the extra 5 percent paid by customers. Iliana has not lost any orders by this practice, and she is rated as one of Giberson's top salespersons. Giberson now learns of Iliana's actions. Discuss fully Giberson's rights in this matter.

16–3. Health and Safety Regulations. Denton and Carlo were employed at an appliance plant. Their job required them to do occasional maintenance work while standing on a wire mesh platform twenty feet above the plant floor. Other employees had fallen through the mesh platform, one of whom had been killed by the fall. When Denton and Carlo were asked by their supervisor to do work that would likely require them to walk on the mesh, they refused due to their fear of bodily harm or death. Because of their refusal to do the requested work, the two employees were fired from their jobs. Was their discharge wrongful? If so, under what federal employment law? To what federal agency or department should they turn for assistance?

16–4. Workers' Compensation. Galvin Strang worked for a tractor company in one of its factories. Near his work station there was a conveyor belt that ran through a large industrial oven. Sometimes, the workers would use the oven to heat their meals. Thirty-inch-high flasks containing molds were fixed at regular intervals on the conveyor and were transported into the oven. Strang had to walk between the flasks to get to his work station. One day, the conveyor was not moving, and Strang used the oven to cook a frozen pot pie. As he was removing the pot pie from the oven, the conveyor came on. One of the flasks struck Strang and seriously injured him. Strang sought recovery under the state workers' compensation law. Should he recover? Why or why not?

16–5. Hours and Wages. Richard Ackerman was an advance sales representative and account manager for Coca-Cola Enterprises, Inc. His primary responsibility was to sell Coca-Cola products to grocery stores, convenience stores, and other sales outlets. Coca-Cola also employed merchandisers, who did not sell Coca-Cola products but performed tasks associated with their distribution and promotion, including restocking shelves, filling vending machines, and setting up displays. The account managers, who serviced the smaller accounts themselves, regularly worked between fifty-five and seventy-two hours each week. Coca-Cola paid them a salary, bonuses, and commissions, but it did not pay them—unlike the merchandisers—additional compensation for the overtime. Ackerman and the other account managers filed a suit in a federal district court against Coca-Cola, alleging that they were entitled to overtime compensation. Coca-Cola responded that because of an exemption under the Fair Labor Standards Act, it was not required to pay them overtime. Is Coca-Cola correct? Explain. [*Ackerman v. Coca-Cola Enterprises, Inc.*, 179 F.3d 1260 (10th Cir. 1999)]

Case Problem with Sample Answer

16–6. Performance Monitoring. Patience Oyoyo worked as a claims analyst in the claims management department of Baylor Healthcare Network, Inc. When questions arose about Oyoyo's performance on several occasions, department manager Debbie Outlaw met with Oyoyo to discuss, among other things, Oyoyo's personal use of a business phone. Outlaw reminded Oyoyo that company policy prohibited excessive personal calls and that these would result in the termination of her employment. Outlaw began to monitor Oyoyo's phone usage, noting lengthy outgoing calls on several occasions, including some long-distance calls. Eventually, Outlaw terminated Oyoyo's employment, and Oyoyo filed a suit in a federal district court against Baylor. Oyoyo asserted in part that in monitoring her phone calls, the employer had invaded her privacy. Baylor asked the court to dismiss this claim. In whose favor should the court rule, and why? [*Oyoyo v. Baylor Healthcare Network, Inc.*, __ F.Supp.2d __ (N.D.Tex. 2000)]

To view a sample answer for this case problem, go to this book's Web site at http://leet.westbuslaw.com and click on "Interactive Study Center."

16–7. Agency Formation. Ford Motor Credit Co. is a subsidiary of Ford Motor Co. with its own offices, officers, and directors. Ford Credit buys contracts and leases of automobiles entered into by dealers and consumers. Ford Credit also provides inventory financing for dealers' purchases of Ford and non-Ford vehicles and makes loans to Ford and non-Ford dealers. Dealers and consumers are not required to finance their purchases or leases of Ford vehicles through Ford Credit. Ford Motor is not a party to the agreements between Ford Credit and its customers and does not directly receive any payments under those agreements. Also, Ford Credit is not subject to any agreement with Ford Motor "restricting or conditioning" its ability to finance the dealers' inventories or the consumers' purchases or leases of vehicles. A number of plaintiffs filed a product liability suit in a Missouri state court against Ford Motor. Ford Motor claimed that the court did not have venue. The plaintiffs asserted that Ford Credit, which had an office in the jurisdiction, acted as Ford's "agent for the transaction of its usual and customary business" there. Is Ford Credit an agent of Ford Motor? Discuss. [*State ex rel. Ford Motor Co. v. Bacon*, 63 S.W.3d 641 (Mo. 2002)]

16–8. Liability for Independent Contractor's Torts. Greif Brothers Corp., a steel drum manufacturer, owned and operated a manufacturing plant in Youngstown, Ohio. In 1987, Lowell Wilson, the plant superintendent, hired Youngstown Security Patrol, Inc. (YSP), a security company, to guard Greif property and "deter thieves and vandals." Some YSP security guards, as Wilson knew, carried firearms. Eric Bator, a YSP security guard, was not certified as an armed guard but nevertheless took his gun, in a briefcase, to work. While working at the Greif plant on August 12, 1991, Bator fired his gun at Derrell Pusey, in the belief that Pusey was an intruder. The bullet struck and killed Pusey. Pusey's mother filed a suit in an Ohio state court against Greif and others, alleging in part that her son's death was the result of YSP's negligence, for which Greif was responsible. Greif filed a motion for a directed verdict. What is the plaintiff's best argument that Greif is responsible for YSP's actions? What is Greif's best defense? Explain. [*Pusey v. Bator*, 94 Ohio St.3d 275, 762 N.E.2d 968 (2002)]

A Question of Ethics & Social Responsibility

16–9. In 1990, the Internal Revenue Service (IRS) determined that a number of independent contractors working for Microsoft Corp. were actually employees of the company for tax purposes. The IRS arrived at this conclusion based on the significant control that Microsoft exercised over the independent contractors' work performance. As a result of the IRS's findings, Microsoft was ordered to pay back payroll taxes for hundreds of independent contractors who should have been classified as employees. Rather than contest the ruling, Microsoft required most of the workers in question, as well as a number of its other independent contractors, to become associated with employment agencies and work for Microsoft as temporary workers ("temps") or lose the opportunity to work for Microsoft. Workers who refused to register with employment agencies, as well as some who did register, sued Microsoft. The workers alleged that they were actually employees of the company and, as such, entitled to participate in Microsoft's stock option plan for employees. Microsoft countered that it need not provide such benefits because each of the workers had signed an independent-contractor agreement specifically stating that the worker was responsible for his or her own benefits. In view of these facts, consider the following questions. [*Vizcaino v. U.S. District Court for the Western District of Washington,* 173 F.3d 713 (9th Cir. 1999)]

1. If the decision were up to you, how would you rule in this case? Why?
2. Normally, when a company hires temporary workers from an employment agency, the agency—not the employer—is responsible for paying Social Security taxes and other withholding taxes. Yet the U.S. Court of Appeals for the Ninth Circuit held that being an employee of a temporary employment agency did not preclude the employee from having the status of a common law employee of Microsoft at the same time. Is this fair to the employer? Why or why not?
3. Generally, do you believe that Microsoft was trying to "skirt the law"—and its ethical responsibilities—by requiring its employees to sign up as "temps"?
4. Given that the employees here had signed independent-contractor agreements, was it fair for the court to order Microsoft to allow these employees to participate in its stock option plan?

Critical-Thinking Legal Question

16–10. Emily Anderson, a salesperson for Gold Products, has no authority to collect payments for orders solicited from customers. A customer, Martin Huerta, pays Anderson for an order. Anderson takes the payment to Gold's accountant, who accepts the payment and sends Huerta a receipt. This procedure is followed for other orders by Huerta. One time, however, Anderson absconds with the money. Can Huerta claim that the payment to Anderson was authorized and thus, in effect, a payment to Gold?

INTERACTING WITH THE INTERNET

For updated links to resources available on the Web, as well as a variety of other materials, visit this text's Web site at

http://leet.westbuslaw.com

An excellent source for information on agency law, including court cases involving agency concepts, is the Legal Information Institute (LII) at Cornell University. You can access the LII's Web page on this topic at

http://www.law.cornell.edu/topics/agency.html

The 'Lectric Law Library's Lawcopedia contains a summary of agency laws at

http://www.lectlaw.com/d-a.htm

Scroll down through the A's and select the link to Agent for useful information on this area of the law.

An outstanding Web site for information on employee benefits, including the full text of the FMLA, COBRA, other relevant statutes and case law, and current articles, is BenefitsLink. Go to

http://www.benefitslink.com/index.shtml

The American Federation of Labor–Congress of Industrial Organizations (AFL–CIO) provides links to a broad variety of labor-related resources at

http://www.aflcio.org

The Occupational Safety and Health Administration (OSHA) offers information related to workplace health and safety at

http://www.osha.gov

ONLINE LEGAL RESEARCH EXERCISES

Go to **http://leet.westbuslaw.com**, the Web site that accompanies this text. Select "Interactive Study Center," and then click on "Chapter 16." There you will find the following Internet research exercises that you can perform to learn more about topics covered in this chapter.

Activity 16–1: ECONOMIC PERSPECTIVE—**Employees or Independent Contractors?**

Activity 16–2: MANAGEMENT PERSPECTIVE—**Workplace Monitoring and Surveillance**

BEFORE THE TEST

Go to **http://leet.westbuslaw.com**, the Web site that accompanies this text. Select "Interactive Quizzes." You will find at least twenty interactive questions relating to this chapter.

Westlaw® Campus

If your textbook provided for a subscription to Westlaw® Campus, or if you have otherwise purchased access to the Westlaw Campus database, you can access any of the cases presented or cited in this chapter by using your Westlaw Campus account.

CHAPTER **17**

Equal Employment Opportunities

CHAPTER OBJECTIVES

*After reading this chapter, you should be able to answer the
following questions:*

1. Generally, what kind of conduct is prohibited by Title VII of
the Civil Rights Act of 1964, as amended?

2. What is the difference between disparate-treatment
discrimination and disparate-impact discrimination?

3. What remedies are available under Title VII of the 1964 Civil
Rights Act, as amended?

4. What federal acts prohibit discrimination based on age and
discrimination based on disability?

5. What are three defenses to claims of employment
discrimination?

During the early 1960s, we as a nation focused our attention on the civil rights
of all Americans, including our rights under the Fourteenth Amendment to
the equal protection of the laws. Out of this movement to end racial and other
forms of discrimination grew a body of law protecting workers against discrimination in the workplace. In the past several decades, judicial decisions, administrative agency actions, and legislation have restricted the ability of employers,
and unions as well, to discriminate against workers on the basis of race,
color, religion, national origin, gender,
age, or disability. A class of persons
defined by one or more of these criteria is known as a **protected class.**

Several federal statutes prohibit
discrimination in the employment
context against members of protected classes. The most important

PROTECTED CLASS
A group of persons protected by
specific laws because of the group's
defining characteristics. Under laws
prohibiting employment
discrimination, these characteristics
include race, color, religion, national
origin, gender, age, and disability.

**"Nor shall any state . . . deny
to any person within its
jurisdiction the equal
protection of the laws."**
Fourteenth Amendment to the
U.S. Constitution, July 28, 1868

544

statute is Title VII of the Civil Rights Act of 1964.[1] Title VII prohibits discrimination on the basis of race, color, religion, national origin, and gender at any stage of employment. The Age Discrimination in Employment Act of 1967[2] and the Americans with Disabilities Act of 1990[3] prohibit discrimination on the basis of age and disability, respectively.

The focus of this chapter is on the kinds of discrimination prohibited by these federal statutes. Note, however, that discrimination against employees on the basis of any of these criteria may also violate state human rights statutes or other state laws or public policies prohibiting discrimination.

TITLE VII OF THE CIVIL RIGHTS ACT OF 1964

Title VII of the Civil Rights Act of 1964 and its amendments prohibit **employment discrimination** against employees, job applicants, and union members on the basis of race, color, national origin, religion, and gender at any stage of employment. Title VII applies to employers with fifteen or more employees, labor unions with fifteen or more members, labor unions that operate hiring halls (to which members go regularly to be rationed jobs as they become available), employment agencies, and state and local governing units and agencies. A special section of the act prohibits discrimination in most federal government employment.

EMPLOYMENT DISCRIMINATION
Treating employees or job applicants unequally on the basis of race, color, national origin, religion, gender, age, or disability; prohibited by federal statutes.

The Equal Employment Opportunity Commission

Compliance with Title VII is monitored by the Equal Employment Opportunity Commission (EEOC). A victim of alleged discrimination, before bringing a suit against the employer, must first file a claim with the EEOC. The EEOC may investigate the dispute and attempt to obtain the parties' voluntary consent to an out-of-court settlement. If voluntary agreement cannot be reached, the EEOC may then file a suit against the employer on the employee's behalf. If the EEOC decides not to investigate the claim, the victim can bring her or his own lawsuit against the employer.

The EEOC does not investigate every claim of employment discrimination, regardless of the merits of the claim. Generally, it investigates only "priority cases," such as cases involving retaliatory discharge (which occurs when an employee is fired in retaliation for submitting a claim to the EEOC) and cases involving types of discrimination that are of particular concern to the EEOC.

Types of Discrimination

Title VII of the Civil Rights Act of 1964 prohibits both intentional and unintentional discrimination.

Intentional Discrimination Intentional discrimination by an employer against an employee is known as **disparate-treatment discrimination.** Because intent may sometimes be difficult to prove, courts have established certain procedures

DISPARATE-TREATMENT DISCRIMINATION
A form of employment discrimination that results when an employer intentionally discriminates against employees who are members of protected classes.

---

1. 42 U.S.C. Sections 2000e–2000e-17.
2. 29 U.S.C. Sections 621–634.
3. 42 U.S.C. Sections 12102–12118.

for resolving disparate-treatment cases. Suppose that a woman applies for employment with a construction firm and is rejected. If she sues on the basis of disparate-treatment discrimination in hiring, she must show that (1) she is a member of a protected class, (2) she applied and was qualified for the job in question, (3) she was rejected by the employer, and (4) the employer continued to seek applicants for the position or filled the position with a person not in a protected class.

If the woman can meet these relatively easy requirements, she makes out a *prima facie* case of illegal discrimination. Making out a *prima facie* case of discrimination means that the plaintiff has met her initial burden of proof and will win in the absence of a legally acceptable employer defense (defenses to claims of employment discrimination will be discussed later in this chapter). The burden next shifts to the employer-defendant, who must articulate a legal reason for not hiring the plaintiff. To prevail, the plaintiff must then show that the employer's reason is a *pretext* (not the true reason) and that discriminatory intent actually motivated the employer's decision.

PRIMA FACIE CASE
A case in which the plaintiff has produced sufficient evidence supporting his or her claim that the case can go to a jury; a case in which the evidence is such that the plaintiff will win if the defendant produces no affirmative defense or evidence to disprove it.

Disparate-Impact Discrimination Employers often find it necessary to use interviews and testing procedures to choose from among a large number of applicants for job openings. Minimum educational requirements are also common. Employer practices, such as those involving educational requirements, may have an unintended discriminatory impact on a protected class. **Disparate-impact discrimination** occurs when, as a result of educational or other job requirements or hiring procedures, an employer's work force does not reflect the percentage of nonwhites, women, or members of other protected classes that characterizes qualified individuals in the local labor market. If a person challenging an employment practice having a discriminatory effect can show a connection between the practice and the disparity, he or she makes out a *prima facie* case, and no evidence of discriminatory intent need be shown. Disparate-impact discrimination can also occur when an educational or other job requirement or hiring procedure excludes members of a protected class from an employer's work force at a substantially higher rate than nonmembers, regardless of the racial balance in the employer's work force.

DISPARATE-IMPACT DISCRIMINATION
A form of employment discrimination that results from certain employer practices or procedures that, although not discriminatory on their face, have a discriminatory effect.

Discrimination Based on Race, Color, and National Origin

If a company's standards or policies for selecting or promoting employees have the effect of discriminating against employees or job applicants on the basis of race, color, or national origin, they are illegal unless they have a substantial, demonstrable relationship to realistic qualifications for the job in question (and this exception does not apply to discrimination on the basis of race). Discrimination against these protected classes in regard to employment conditions and benefits is also illegal.

● EXAMPLE 1 In one case, Cynthia McCullough, an African American woman with a college degree, worked at a deli in a grocery store. More than a year later, the owner of the store promoted a white woman to the position of deli manager. The white woman had worked in the deli for just three months, had only a sixth-grade education, and could not calculate prices or read recipes. Although the owner gave various reasons for promoting the white woman instead of McCullough, a federal appellate court held that these reasons were likely just excuses and that the real reason was discriminatory intent.[4]●

Are English-only policies in the workplace a form of national-origin discrimination?

As the U.S. population becomes more multilingual, so does the work force. In response to this development, many employers have instituted English-only policies in their workplaces, particularly in states with large immigrant populations, such as Texas and California. Are English-only policies fair to workers who do not speak English? Do they violate Title VII's prohibition against discrimination on the basis of race or national origin, as workers in a number of lawsuits have alleged? Generally, the courts have shown a fair degree of tolerance with respect to English-only rules, especially when an employer can show that there is a legitimate business reason for the rules, such as improved communication among employees or worker safety. In contrast, the courts tend to regard with suspicion "blanket" English-only policies—policies that require that only English be spoken not only during work time but also on breaks, lunch hours, and the like. For example, a federal district court held that a Texas firm had engaged in disparate-treatment discrimination based on national origin by requiring that only English be spoken in the workplace, including during breaks, except when employees were communicating with customers who could not speak English.[5]

Discrimination Based on Religion

Title VII of the Civil Rights Act of 1964 also prohibits government employers, private employers, and unions from discriminating against persons because of their religion. An employer must reasonably accommodate the religious practices of its employees, unless to do so would cause undue hardship to the employer's business. For example, if an employee's religion prohibits him or her from working on a certain day of the week or at a particular type of job, the employer must make a reasonable attempt to accommodate these religious requirements. Employers must reasonably accommodate an employee's religious belief even if the belief is not based on the tenets or dogma of a particular church, sect, or denomination. The only requirement is that the belief be sincerely held by the employee.[6]

---

4. *McCullough v. Real Foods, Inc.,* 140 F.3d 1123 (8th Cir. 1998). The federal district court had granted summary judgment for the employer in this case. The Eighth Circuit Court of Appeals reversed the district court's decision and remanded the case for trial.

5. *EEOC v. Premier Operator Services, Inc.,* 113 F.Supp.2d 1066 (N.D.Tex. 2000).

6. *Frazee v. Illinois Department of Employment Security,* 489 U.S. 829, 109 S.Ct. 1514, 103 L.Ed.2d 914 (1989).

Discrimination Based on Gender

Under Title VII, as well as other federal acts, employers are forbidden to discriminate against employees on the basis of gender. Employers are prohibited from classifying jobs as male or female and from advertising in help-wanted columns that are designated male or female unless the employer can prove that the gender of the applicant is essential to the job. Furthermore, employers cannot have separate male and female seniority lists.

Generally, to succeed in a suit for gender discrimination, a plaintiff must demonstrate that gender was a determining factor in the employer's decision to hire, fire, or promote her or him. Typically, this involves looking at all of the surrounding circumstances.

The Pregnancy Discrimination Act of 1978,[7] which amended Title VII, expanded the definition of gender discrimination to include discrimination based on pregnancy. Women affected by pregnancy, childbirth, or related medical conditions must be treated—for all employment-related purposes, including the receipt of benefits under employee benefit programs—the same as other persons not so affected but similar in ability to work.

In the following case, the plaintiff charged the defendant with gender discrimination. The plaintiff made out a *prima facie* case, and the defendant presented a nondiscriminatory reason as a defense. Was the defendant's reason a pretext covering a discriminatory motive? That was the question before the court.

---

7. 42 U.S.C. Section 2000e(k).

CASE 17.1   Carey v. Mount Desert Island Hospital

United States Court of Appeals,
First Circuit, 1998.
156 F.3d 31.
http://www.law.emory.edu/1circuit/aug98[a]

COMPANY PROFILE *Mount Desert Island Hospital (MDI) is a forty-nine-bed facility in Bar Harbor, Maine, with a medical staff that specializes in family practice, general surgery, internal medicine, ophthalmology, pathology, and radiology. A consulting staff includes practitioners of other medical specialties. MDI also operates an occupational health service, community health education, and affiliated health centers: Community Health Center in Southwest Harbor; Family Health Center, Women's Health Center, Breast Center, and High Street Health Center in Bar Harbor; and Northeast Harbor Clinic, open seasonally, in Northeast Harbor. MDI is licensed by the state of Maine and fully accredited by the Joint Commission on Accreditation of Healthcare Organizations.*

BACKGROUND AND FACTS Michael Carey was a vice president in charge of the finance department for Mount Desert Island Hospital (MDI). When the position of chief executive officer (CEO) opened up, Carey applied, and his application was endorsed by Dan Hobbs, the acting CEO. At the time, an audit of the finance department revealed some deficiencies, but the auditor concluded that the department was "already attacking the problem." MDI's board offered the CEO post to Leslie Hawkins, a woman, who accepted. Less than a year later, Hawkins fired Carey, giving as reasons the problems cited in the audit and "lack of confidence" in Carey. Carey filed a suit in a federal district court against MDI for gender discrimination in violation of Title VII and other laws. Evidence introduced during the trial included a statement by one female executive that "we have different standards for men and women" with regard to discipline and termination and a statement by another female executive

---

a. This page contains links to opinions of the U.S. Court of Appeals for the First Circuit decided in August 1998. Click on the *Carey* case name to access the opinion. This Web site is maintained by Emory University School of Law in Atlanta, Georgia.

CASE 17.1—Continued

that "it's about time that we get a woman for this [CEO] position." The court awarded Carey more than $300,000 in damages. MDI appealed to the U.S. Court of Appeals for the First Circuit.

IN THE WORDS
OF THE COURT . . .

COFFIN, Senior Circuit Judge.

* * * *

* * * [T]his was a case with much to say on either side, involving the always difficult question of probing the wellsprings of human motivation.

* * *

* * * *

In a case such as this, where a plaintiff must rely on circumstantial as opposed to direct evidence of gender discrimination, the evidence will necessarily be composed of bits and pieces, which may or may not point to an atmosphere of gender discrimination. While an employer should not find itself in jeopardy by reason of occasional stray remarks by ordinary employees, circumstantial evidence of a discriminatory atmosphere at a plaintiff's place of employment is relevant to the question of motive in considering a discrimination claim * * * .

* * * *

* * * [Based on the record, we] hold that there was sufficient evidence to support a finding that deficiencies in Carey's handling of financial controls were not the real reason for his discharge but instead covered an action stemming from gender discrimination.

DECISION AND REMEDY The U.S. Court of Appeals for the First Circuit affirmed the lower court's judgment. The court held that that there was sufficient evidence to support a finding that the reason for Carey's discharge was gender discrimination.

FOR CRITICAL ANALYSIS—Cultural Consideration *Is it possible to fully protect employees from gender discrimination in the workplace?*

Sexual Harassment

Title VII also protects employees against **sexual harassment** in the workplace. Sexual harassment has often been classified as either *quid pro quo* harassment or hostile-environment harassment. *Quid pro quo* is a Latin phrase often translated to mean "something in exchange for something else." *Quid pro quo* harassment occurs when job opportunities, promotions, salary increases, or other benefits are given in return for sexual favors. According to the United States Supreme Court, hostile-environment harassment occurs when "the workplace is permeated with discriminatory intimidation, ridicule, and insult, that is sufficiently severe or pervasive to alter the conditions of the victim's employment and create an abusive working environment."[8]

Generally, the courts apply this Supreme Court guideline on a case-by-case basis. Some courts have held that just one incident of sexually offensive conduct—such as a sexist remark by a co-worker or a photo on an employer's

SEXUAL HARASSMENT
In the employment context, (1) the granting of job promotions or other benefits in return for sexual favors or (2) language or conduct that is so sexually offensive that it creates a hostile working environment.

---

8. *Harris v. Forklift Systems,* 510 U.S. 17, 114 S.Ct. 367, 126 L.Ed.2d 295 (1993).

desk of his bikini-clad wife—can create a hostile environment.[9] At least one court has held that a worker can recover damages under Title VII because *other* persons were sexually harassed in the workplace.[10] According to some employment specialists, employers should assume that hostile-environment harassment has occurred if an employee claims that it has.

Harassment by Supervisors What if an employee is harassed by a manager or supervisor of a large firm, and the firm itself (the employer) is not aware of the harassment? Should the employer be held liable for the harassment nonetheless? For some time, the courts were in disagreement on this issue. Typically, employers were held liable for Title VII violations by their managerial or supervisory personnel in *quid pro quo* harassment cases regardless of whether the employers knew about the harassment. In hostile-environment cases, the majority of courts tended to hold employers liable only if they knew or should have known of the harassment and failed to take prompt remedial action.

Tangible Employment Action. For an employer to be held liable for a supervisor's sexual harassment, the supervisor must have taken a tangible employment action against the employee. A *tangible employment action* is a significant change in employment status, such as firing or failing to promote an employee; reassigning the employee to a position with significantly different responsibilities; or effecting a significant change in employment benefits.

Only a supervisor, or another person acting with the authority of the employer, can cause this sort of injury. A co-worker can sexually harass another employee, and anyone who has regular contact with an employee can inflict psychological injuries by offensive conduct. A co-worker cannot dock another's pay, demote her or him, or set conditions for continued employment, however.

The elements of the definition of tangible employment action were at issue in the following case.

"Justice is better than chivalry if we cannot have both."

ALICE STONE BLACKWELL, 1857–1950
(American suffragist and editor)

---

9. For other examples, see *Radtke v. Everett,* 442 Mich. 368, 501 N.W.2d 155 (1993); and *Nadeau v. Rainbow Rugs, Inc.,* 675 A.2d 973 (Me. 1996).
10. *Leibovitz v. New York City Transit Authority,* 4 F.Supp.2d 144 (E.D.N.Y. 1998).

CASE 17.2   Jin v. Metropolitan Life Insurance Co.

United States Court of Appeals,
Second Circuit, 2002.
310 F.3d 84.
http://www.tourolaw.edu/2ndCircuit[a]

BACKGROUND AND FACTS In 1989, Min Jin began working for Metropolitan Life Insurance Company (MetLife) as a sales agent at the company's "Broadway branch" in Manhattan, New York. In May 1993, Gregory Morabito assumed supervisory duties at the Broadway branch. At the same time, Morabito began to engage in a pattern of conduct toward Jin that included making sexual remarks to her

in the office and calling her at home; offensively touching her buttocks, breasts, and legs at the office when she was making sales calls from her desk and when she was walking clients to the elevator; requiring her to attend weekly private meetings in his locked office during which he would threaten her to force her to engage in sexual acts; and threatening to fire her and physically harm her if she did not accede to his demands. Her later request for disability benefits for the harassment was denied, and MetLife fired her in 1995. Jin filed a suit in a federal district court against MetLife, alleging sexual harassment in violation of Title

---

a. In the left-hand column, click on "Reported Decisions." From the menu, click on "2002." In the list, click on "June." Scroll to the name of the case and click on it to access the opinion.

CASE 17.2—Continued

VII. The court instructed the jury to determine whether Jin was subject to a tangible employment action. When the jury found that she was not, the court ruled in MetLife's favor. Jin appealed to the U.S. Court of Appeals for the Second Circuit.

IN THE WORDS OF THE COURT . . .

FEINBERG, Circuit Judge.

* * * *

* * * In its instructions, the district court utilized what appeared to be an exclusive list of three economic-based harms to define a tangible employment action: "One, unjustifiably refusing to process policies sold by [Jin], or two, unjustifiably causing her disability claim to be denied, or three, unjustifiably firing her." * * * By leading the jury to believe it could consider *only* the three enumerated harms, * * * the district court improperly narrowed the scope of possible tangible employment actions considered by the jury.

* * * *

Jin argues that the jury should have been allowed to consider as a tangible employment action Morabito's use of his supervisory authority to require Jin to submit to weekly sexual abuse.

* * * *

Requiring an employee to engage in unwanted sex acts is one of the most pernicious and oppressive forms of sexual harassment that can occur in the workplace. * * * *It is hardly surprising that this type of conduct* * * * *fits squarely within the definition of "tangible employment action"* * * * . [Emphasis added.]

Here, Jin presented evidence that Morabito ordered her to submit to demeaning sexual acts, explicitly threatened to fire her if she did not submit, and then allowed her to keep her job after she submitted. Essentially, according to Jin, he used his authority to impose on her the added job requirement that she submit to weekly sexual abuse in order to retain her employment.

* * * It was Morabito's empowerment by MetLife as an agent who could make economic decisions affecting employees under his control that enabled him to force Jin to submit to his weekly sexual abuse. * * * Also, that Morabito as a supervisor could require Jin to report to his private office where he could make his threats and carry on his abuses further supports the claim that his empowerment was as the company's agent.

* * * *

* * * When a supervisor makes decisions affecting the terms and conditions of [a] plaintiff's employment based upon her submission to his sexual advances, he uses his authority to effect * * * a significant change in employment status.

DECISION AND REMEDY The U.S. Court of Appeals for the Second Circuit vacated the order of the lower court and remanded the case for a new trial. Because Morabito, as Jin's supervisor, threatened to fire her if she did not submit to sexual acts and then allowed her to keep her job after she submitted, the jury should have been instructed to consider the conditioning of her continued employment on her submission as a possible tangible employment action.

FOR CRITICAL ANAYSIS—Cultural Consideration *Suppose that the roles in this case had been reversed so that the demands had been made by a woman to a man. Would the result have been different?*

Supreme Court Guidelines. In 1998, in two separate cases, the United States Supreme Court issued some significant guidelines relating to the liability of employers for their supervisors' harassment of employees in the workplace. In *Faragher v. City of Boca Raton,*[11] the Court held that an employer (a city) could be held liable for a supervisor's harassment of employees even though the employer was unaware of the behavior. The Court reached this conclusion primarily because, although the city had a written policy against sexual harassment, the policy had not been distributed to city employees. Additionally, the city had not established any procedures that could be followed by employees who felt that they were victims of sexual harassment. In *Burlington Industries, Inc. v. Ellerth,*[12] the Court ruled that a company could be held liable for the harassment of an employee by one of its vice presidents even though the employee suffered no adverse job consequences.

The guidelines set forth in these two cases have been helpful to employers and employees alike. On the one hand, employees benefit by the ruling that employers may be held liable for their supervisors' harassment even though the employers were unaware of the actions and even though the employees suffered no adverse job consequences. On the other hand, the Court made it clear in both decisions that employers have an affirmative defense against liability for their supervisors' harassment of employees if the employers can show that (1) they have taken "reasonable care to prevent and correct promptly any sexually harassing behavior" (by establishing effective harassment policies and complaint procedures, for example) and (2) the employees suing for harassment failed to follow these policies and procedures.

Harassment by Co-Workers Often, employees alleging harassment complain that the actions of co-workers, not supervisors, are responsible for creating a hostile working environment. In such cases, the employee still has a cause of action against the employer. Normally, though, the employer will be held liable only if it knew, or should have known, about the harassment and failed to take immediate remedial action.

Harassment by Nonemployees Employers may also be liable for harassment by *nonemployees* in certain circumstances. ● EXAMPLE 2 If a restaurant owner or manager knows that a certain customer repeatedly harasses a waitress and permits the harassment to continue, the restaurant owner may be liable under Title VII even though the customer is not an employee of the restaurant. The issue turns on the control that the employer exerts over a nonemployee. In one case, an owner of a Pizza Hut franchise was held liable for the harassment of a waitress by two male customers because no steps were taken to prevent the harassment.[13] ●

Same-Gender Harassment The courts have also had to address the issue of whether men who are harassed by other men, and women who are harassed by other women, are protected by laws that prohibit gender-based discrimination in the workplace. For example, what if the male president of a firm demands sexual favors from a male employee? Does this action qualify as

---

11. 524 U.S. 775, 118 S.Ct. 2275, 141 L.Ed.2d 662 (1998).
12. 524 U.S. 742, 118 S.Ct. 2257, 141 L.Ed.2d 633 (1998).
13. *Lockard v. Pizza Hut, Inc.,* 162 F.3d 1062 (10th Cir. 1998).

INTERNATIONAL PERSPECTIVE

Sexual Harassment in Other Nations

The problem of sexual harassment in the workplace is not confined to the United States. Indeed, it is a worldwide problem for female workers. In Egypt, Turkey, Argentina, Brazil, and many other countries, there is no legal protection against any form of employment discrimination. Even in countries that do have laws prohibiting discriminatory employment practices, including gender-based discrimination, those laws often do not specifically include sexual

harassment as a discriminatory practice.

Several countries have attempted to remedy this omission by passing new laws or amending others to explicitly prohibit sexual harassment in the workplace. Japan, for example, has amended its Equal Employment Opportunity Law to include a provision making sexual harassment illegal. Other nations, including Thailand, have passed sexual-harassment laws. The European Union, which some years ago outlawed gender-based discrimination, is considering a proposal that would identify sexual harassment as a form of discrimination. In

the meantime, old traditions die hard. Women's support groups throughout Europe contend that corporations in European countries tend to view sexual harassment with "quiet tolerance." They contrast this attitude with that of most U.S. corporations, which have implemented specific procedures to deal with harassment claims.

FOR CRITICAL ANALYSIS

Why do you think U.S. corporations are more aggressive than European companies in taking steps to prevent sexual harassment in the workplace?

sexual harassment? For some time, the courts were widely split on this issue. In 1998, in *Oncale v. Sundowner Offshore Services, Inc.,*[14] the Supreme Court resolved the issue by holding that Title VII protection extends to situations in which individuals are harassed by members of the same gender.

Online Harassment

Employees' online activities can create a hostile working environment in many ways. Racial jokes, ethnic slurs, and other comments contained in e-mail may become the basis for a claim of hostile-environment harassment or some other form of discrimination. A worker who sees sexually explicit images on a co-worker's computer screen may find the images offensive and claim that they create a hostile working environment. Generally, employers may be able to avoid liability for online harassment if they take prompt remedial action.

● **EXAMPLE 3** In *Daniels v. WorldCom, Inc.,*[15] Angela Daniels, an employee of Robert Half International under contract to WorldCom, Inc., received racially harassing e-mailed jokes from another employee. After receiving the jokes, Daniels complained to WorldCom managers. Shortly afterward, the company issued a warning to the offending employee about the proper use of the e-mail system and held two meetings to discuss company policy on the use of the

---

14. 523 U.S. 75, 118 S.Ct. 998, 140 L.Ed.2d 207 (1998).
15. 1998 WL 91261 (N.D.Tex. 1998).

system. In Daniels's suit against WorldCom for racial discrimination, a federal district court concluded that the employer was not liable for its employee's racially harassing e-mails because the employer took prompt remedial action.●

Generally, employers who want to avoid online harassment in the workplace seem to be caught between the proverbial "rock and a hard place." On the one hand, if they do not take effective steps to curb such harassment, they may face liability for violating Title VII. On the other hand, if they monitor their employees' communications, they may face liability under other laws—for invading their employees' privacy, for example. Additionally, an employee who is fired for misusing the employer's computer system to, say, e-mail pornographic images to co-workers or others may claim that he or she was discharged without just cause (see, for example, the case discussed in this chapter's *Legal E-nvironment* feature). Finally, there are constitutional rights to be considered. In one case, a court held that religious speech that unintentionally creates a hostile environment is constitutionally protected.[16]

Remedies under Title VII

Employer liability under Title VII may be extensive. If the plaintiff successfully proves that unlawful discrimination occurred, he or she may be awarded reinstatement, back pay, retroactive promotions, and damages. Compensatory damages are available only in cases of intentional discrimination. Punitive damages can be recovered against a private employer only if the employer acted with malice or reckless indifference to an individual's rights. The sum of the amount of compensatory and punitive damages is limited by the statute to specific amounts against specific employers, ranging from $50,000 against employers with one hundred or fewer employees to $300,000 against employers with more than five hundred employees.

EQUAL PAY ACT OF 1963

The Equal Pay Act of 1963 was enacted as an amendment to the Fair Labor Standards Act of 1938. Basically, the act prohibits gender-based discrimination in the wages paid for equal work on jobs when their performance requires equal skill, effort, and responsibility under similar conditions. It is job content rather than job description that controls in all cases. Small differences in job content, however, do not justify higher pay for one gender.

To determine whether the Equal Pay Act has been violated, a court will look to the primary duties of the two jobs. The jobs of a barber and a beautician, for example, are considered essentially equal. So, too, are those of a tailor and a seamstress. For the act's equal pay requirements to apply, the male and female employees must work at the same establishment.

A wage differential for equal work is justified if it is shown to be based on (1) seniority, (2) a merit system, (3) a system that pays according to quality or quantity of production, or (4) any factor other than gender. The Equal Pay Act is administered by the EEOC.

---

16. *Meltebeke v. B.O.L.I.,* 903 P.2d 351 (Or. 1995).

LEGAL *e*-NVIRONMENT

E-Mail in the Workplace and "Universal Standards of Behavior"

As mentioned in Chapter 16, many employers today establish and implement policies that specify permissible and impermissible uses of the Internet in the workplace. What if employees who violate such a policy claim that they did not knowingly do so, however? In this situation, if the employer discharges the employees for violating the policy, can the employees successfully claim that they were discharged without just cause, thus entitling them to unemployment compensation? This question came before a Utah appellate court in *Autoliv ASP, Inc. v. Department of Workforce Services.*[a]

Autoliv's Harassment and E-Mail Policies

Autoliv ASP, Inc., a supplier of auto-safety products, gives each of its more than six thousand employees an employee handbook. Among other things, the handbook states that Autoliv will not "tolerate or permit illegal harassment or retaliation of any nature within our workforce." The handbook also states that the use of e-mail "for reasons other than transmittal of business-related information" is prohibited and that violations of company policies can result in any of several disciplinary actions, including termination.

In 1999, Autoliv learned that an employee had received offensive and sexually harassing e-mail from other Autoliv employees. The company immediately investigated and learned that two employees had, on numerous occasions, sent messages containing jokes, photos, and short videos that were sexually explicit and clearly offensive in nature. Shortly thereafter, Autoliv fired the two employees for "improper and unauthorized use of company e-mail." When the employees applied to the state's Department of Workforce Services for

unemployment benefits, a threshold question was whether they had been fired with just cause. If so, they *would not* be entitled to unemployment benefits. If not, they *would* be entitled to the benefits—and Autoliv would ultimately have to pay higher unemployment taxes as a result.

Were the Employees Fired for Just Cause?

Under the relevant state statute, to be fired for just cause employees had to have "knowledge of the conduct which the employer expected." The two employees testified that they had not knowingly engaged in misconduct. Further, if Autoliv had concluded that they were engaging in misconduct, Autoliv should have warned them and allowed them to change their conduct. The state agency agreed, noting that because abuse of the company's e-mail system was common among Autoliv employees, Autoliv should have notified the employees that their misconduct would not be tolerated before firing them. Because Autoliv had not done so, the termination was without just cause.

Autoliv appealed the agency's decision to a state appellate court, asserting on appeal that it was "incomprehensible" for the agency to hold that a worker could be unaware of the dangers of sending sexually offensive materials to co-workers through a company's computer network. The court agreed with Autoliv, stating that "[s]uch materials in the workplace could have subjected the employer to sexual harassment and sex discrimination lawsuits." The court reversed the agency's decision, concluding that "in today's workplace, the e-mail transmission of sexually explicit and offensive jokes, pictures, and videos constitutes a flagrant violation of a universal standard of behavior."

FOR CRITICAL ANALYSIS

If employees are to be held to universal standards of behavior, how can they know what those standards are?

---

a. 29 P.3d 7 (Utah Ct. App. 2001).

ETHICAL ISSUE

Should market forces be considered a factor other than gender in compensation discrimination cases?

Traditionally, one of the defenses employers have raised in discrimination cases brought under the Equal Pay Act has been that their pay determinations were based on the market forces of supply and demand. In other words, if, say, more women than men were available for a particular job at a lower pay rate, the employer could argue that this characteristic of the marketplace was a factor other than gender. Employers have not always succeeded in this defense, and the latest guidelines on compensation discrimination issued by the Equal Employment Opportunity Commission (EEOC) in 2000 may make it even more difficult to do so. Among other things, the guidelines state that "payment of lower wages to women based on an assumption that women are available . . . at lower compensation rates does not qualify as a factor other than sex." The guidelines then state that an employer may cite market factors as a reason for compensation discrimination "only if the employer proves that any compensation disparity is not based on sex." Critics of the guidelines point out that the EEOC's somewhat circular reasoning will make it extremely difficult for employers to cite market factors as a defense at all. Although EEOC compliance guidelines are not legal requirements in themselves, they will no doubt influence case outcomes because the courts normally give deference to the EEOC's interpretations of the law.[17]

DISCRIMINATION BASED ON AGE

Age discrimination is potentially the most widespread form of discrimination, because anyone—regardless of race, color, national origin, or gender—could be a victim at some point in life. The Age Discrimination in Employment Act (ADEA) of 1967, as amended, prohibits employment discrimination on the basis of age against individuals forty years of age or older. An amendment to the act prohibits mandatory retirement for nonmanagerial workers. For the act to apply, an employer must have twenty or more employees, and the employer's business activities must affect interstate commerce.

Procedures under the ADEA

REMEMBER The Fourteenth Amendment prohibits any state from denying any person "the equal protection of the laws." This prohibition applies to the federal government through the due process clause of the Fifth Amendment.

The burden-shifting procedure under the ADEA is similar to that under Title VII. If a plaintiff can establish that she or he (1) was a member of the protected age group, (2) was qualified for the position from which she or he was discharged, and (3) was discharged under circumstances that give rise to an inference of discrimination, the plaintiff has established a *prima facie* case of unlawful age discrimination. The burden then shifts to the employer, who

---

17. You can access the section of the EEOC's Compliance Manual that contains these guidelines at the EEOC's Web site at **http://www.eeoc.gov**. The Web site also contains an "Equal Pay" page that includes information on compensation discrimination laws, as well as descriptions of recent EEOC equal pay cases.

must articulate a legitimate reason for the discrimination. If the plaintiff can prove that the employer's reason is only a pretext and that the plaintiff's age was a determining factor in the employer's decision, the employer will be held liable under the ADEA.

Numerous cases of alleged age discrimination have been brought against employers who, to cut costs, replaced older, higher-salaried employees with younger, lower-salaried workers. Whether a firing is discriminatory or simply part of a rational business decision to prune the company's ranks is not always clear. Companies generally defend a decision to discharge a worker by asserting that the worker could no longer perform his or her duties or that the worker's skills were no longer needed. The employee must prove that the discharge was motivated, at least in part, by age bias. Proof that qualified older employees are generally discharged before younger employees or that co-workers continually made unflattering age-related comments about the discharged worker may be enough. The plaintiff need not prove that he or she was replaced by a person outside the protected class—that is, by a person under the age of forty years.[18] Rather, the issue in all ADEA cases turns on whether age discrimination has, in fact, occurred, regardless of the age of the replacement worker.

State Employees and the ADEA

Under the Eleventh Amendment to the Constitution, as that amendment has often been interpreted by the United States Supreme Court, states are immune from lawsuits brought by private individuals in federal court, unless a state consents to the suit. In a number of cases brought in the late 1990s, state agencies that were sued by state employees for age discrimination sought to have the suits dismissed on this ground.

● EXAMPLE 4 In two Florida cases, professors and librarians contended that their employers—two Florida state universities—denied them salary increases and other benefits because they were getting old and their successors could be hired at lower cost. The universities claimed that as agencies of a sovereign state, they could not be sued in federal court without the state's consent. Because the courts were rendering conflicting opinions in these cases, the United States Supreme Court agreed to address the issue. In *Kimel v. Florida Board of Regents,*[19] decided in early 2000, the Court held that the sovereign immunity granted the states by the Eleventh Amendment precluded suits against them by private parties alleging violations of the ADEA. According to the Court, Congress had exceeded its constitutional authority when it included in the ADEA a provision stating that "all employers," including state employers, were subject to the act.●

DISCRIMINATION BASED ON DISABILITY

The Americans with Disabilities Act (ADA) of 1990 is designed to eliminate discriminatory employment practices that prevent otherwise qualified workers with disabilities from fully participating in the national labor force. Prior to

---

18. *O'Connor v. Consolidated Coin Caterers Corp.,* 517 U.S. 308, 116 S.Ct. 1307, 134 L.Ed.2d 433 (1996).
19. 528 U.S. 62, 120 S.Ct. 631, 145 L.Ed.2d 522 (2000).

Co-workers discuss business matters. Which workers with disabilities are protected from employment discrimination by the Americans with Disabilities Act?

1990, the major federal law providing protection to those with disabilities was the Rehabilitation Act of 1973. That act covered only federal government employees and those employed under federally funded programs. Basically, the ADA requires that employers reasonably accommodate the needs of persons with disabilities unless to do so would cause the employer to suffer an undue hardship. The ADA extends federal protection against disability-based discrimination to all workplaces with fifteen or more workers. Note, though, that the United States Supreme Court has held, as it did with respect to the ADEA, that lawsuits under the ADA cannot be brought against state government employers.[20]

To prevail on a claim under the ADA, a plaintiff must show that he or she (1) has a disability, (2) is otherwise qualified for the employment in question, and (3) was excluded from the employment solely because of the disability. As in Title VII cases, a claim alleging violation of the ADA can be commenced only after the plaintiff has pursued the claim through the EEOC. Plaintiffs can sue for many of the same remedies available under Title VII. They can seek reinstatement, back pay, a limited amount of compensatory and punitive damages (for intentional discrimination), and certain other forms of relief. Repeat violators may be ordered to pay fines of up to $100,000.

The ADA does not apply to very small businesses. Under the ADA, an "employer" is not covered unless its workforce includes "15 or more employees for each working day in each of 20 or more calendar weeks in the current or preceding calendar year." The question in the following case was whether the shareholders and directors of a corporation should be counted as "employees" of the corporation.

---

20. *Board of Trustees of the University of Alabama v. Garrett,* 531 U.S. 356, 121 S.Ct. 955, 148 L.Ed.2d 866 (2001).

CASE 17.3   Clackamas Gastroenterology Associates, P.C. v. Wells[a]

Supreme Court of the United States, 2003.
__ U.S. __,
123 S.Ct. 1673,
155 L.Ed.2d 615.
**http://supct.law.cornell.
edu/supct/index.htm**[b]

BACKGROUND AND FACTS Clackamas Gastroenterology Associates, P.C., a medical clinic in Oregon, employed Deborah Anne Wells as a bookkeeper from 1986 until 1997. After the clinic terminated Wells's employment, she filed a suit in a federal district court against the clinic, alleging discrimination on the basis of disability in violation of the ADA. The clinic asserted that the ADA did not apply to it because it did not have fifteen employees and filed a motion for summary judgment. The court granted the motion, and Wells appealed to the U.S. Court of Appeals for the Ninth Circuit, which reversed the judgment. The clinic appealed to the United States Supreme Court. The question was whether the four physician-shareholders who owned the corporation and constituted its board of directors counted as employees.

**IN THE WORDS
OF THE COURT . . .**

Justice *STEVENS* delivered the opinion of the Court.
*   *   *   *

We have often been asked to construe the meaning of "employee" where the statute containing the term does not helpfully define it. The definition of the term in the ADA simply states that an "employee" is "an individual

---

a. *P.C.* is an abbreviation for *professional corporation,* a form of business organization. See Chapter 14.
b. In the "Search" box, type in "Clackamas." Then select "all current and historic decisions" and click on "Submit." When that page opens, click on the case name to view the opinion.

CASE 17.3—Continued

employed by an employer." That surely qualifies as a mere nominal definition that is completely circular and explains nothing. * * *

* * * [W]hen Congress has used the term "employee" without defining it, we have concluded that Congress intended to describe the conventional master-servant relationship as understood by common-law agency doctrine.

* * * *

* * * *At common law the relevant factors defining the master-servant relationship focus on the master's control over the servant.* * * We think that the common-law element of control is the principal guidepost that should be followed in this case. [Emphasis added.]

This is the position that is advocated by the Equal Employment Opportunity Commission (EEOC), the agency that has special enforcement responsibilities under the ADA and other federal statutes containing similar threshold issues for determining coverage. It argues that a court should examine "whether shareholder-directors operate independently and manage the business or instead are subject to the firm's control." According to the EEOC's view, "[i]f the shareholder-directors operate independently and manage the business, they are proprietors and not employees; if they are subject to the firm's control, they are employees."

* * * *

As the EEOC's standard reflects, an employer is the person, or group of persons, who owns and manages the enterprise. The employer can hire and fire employees, can assign tasks to employees and supervise their performance, and can decide how the profits and losses of the business are to be distributed. The mere fact that a person has a particular title—such as partner, director, or vice president—should not necessarily be used to determine whether he or she is an employee or a proprietor. Nor should the mere existence of a document styled "employment agreement" lead inexorably to the conclusion that either party is an employee. Rather * * * the answer to whether a shareholder-director is an employee depends on all of the incidents of the relationship * * * with no one factor being decisive.

DECISION AND REMEDY The United States Supreme Court reversed the lower court's decision and remanded the case to that court to determine whether the four director-shareholder physicians were employees of the clinic. The Supreme Court endorsed a standard that used "the common-law element of control" as "the principal guidepost" for making that determination.

FOR CRITICAL ANALYSIS—Social Consideration *What factors might be relevant to determining whether an individual controls a business organization or is controlled by it?*

What Is a Disability?

The ADA is broadly drafted to define persons with disabilities as persons with a physical or mental impairment that substantially limits their everyday activities. More specifically, the ADA defines *disability* as "(1) a physical or mental impairment that substantially limits one or more of the major life activities of such individuals; (2) a record of such impairment; or (3) being regarded as having such an impairment."

Health conditions that have been considered disabilities under federal law include blindness, alcoholism, heart disease, cancer, muscular dystrophy, cerebral palsy, paraplegia, diabetes, acquired immune deficiency syndrome (AIDS) and the human immunodeficiency virus (HIV), and morbid obesity (defined as existing when an individual's weight is two times that of the normal person).[21] The ADA excludes from coverage certain conditions, such as kleptomania.

Can a person whose disability can be controlled by medication or a corrective device still qualify for protection under the ADA? Generally, the courts have held that the determination of whether a person is substantially limited in a major life activity is based on how the person functions when taking medication or using corrective devices, not on how the person functions without these measures. Since 1999, the courts have concluded that plaintiffs with such conditions as nearsightedness, diabetes, bipolar disorder, and epilepsy do *not* fall under the ADA's protections if the conditions can be corrected.[22] In effect, these decisions have narrowed the definition of *disability* and thus limited the scope of the ADA. (For other case examples of how the courts have been limiting the applicability of the ADA in recent years, see this chapter's *Inside the Legal Environment* feature.)

Reasonable Accommodation

The ADA does not require that *unqualified* applicants with disabilities be hired or retained. Therefore, employers are not obligated to accommodate the needs of job applicants or employees with disabilities who are not otherwise qualified for the work. If a job applicant or an employee with a disability, with reasonable accommodation, can perform essential job functions, however, the employer must make the accommodation. Required modifications may include installing ramps for a wheelchair, establishing more flexible working hours, creating or modifying job assignments, and creating or improving training materials and procedures.

Employee Preferences Generally, employers should give primary consideration to employees' preferences in deciding what accommodations should be made. What happens if a job applicant or employee does not indicate to the employer how her or his disability can be accommodated so that the employee can perform essential job functions? In this situation, the employer may avoid liability for failing to hire or retain the individual on the ground that the applicant or employee has failed to meet the "otherwise qualified" requirement.[23]

Undue Hardship Employers who do not accommodate the needs of persons with disabilities must demonstrate that the accommodations will cause *undue hardship*. Generally, the law offers no uniform standards for identifying what is an undue hardship other than the imposition of a "significant difficulty or expense" on the employer.

21. *Cook v. Rhode Island Department of Mental Health,* 10 F.3d 17 (1st Cir. 1993).
22. See, for example, *Orr v. Walmart Stores, Inc.,* 297 F.3d 720 (8th Cir. 2002).
23. See, for example, *Beck v. University of Wisconsin Board of Regents,* 75 F.3d 1130 (7th Cir. 1996); and *White v. York International Corp.,* 45 F.3d 357 (10th Cir. 1995).

Narrowing the Definition of *Disability*

The Americans with Disabilities Act (ADA) does not precisely define what constitutes a disability under the act. Thus, deciding which disabilities qualify under the ADA has largely been left to the courts. Clearly, how the courts interpret the act has significant implications for both employers and employees. When a court holds that a person's impairment does not "substantially limit" a major life activity, that person will not be considered to have a disability under the ADA. Employers benefit from such a holding because they will not be required to accommodate persons with similar disabilities. In contrast, of course, individuals suffering from similar disabilities will not be able to obtain the protections afforded by the ADA.

Starting in 1999, the United States Supreme Court has issued a series of decisions narrowing the definition of what constitutes a disability under the act. As mentioned elsewhere in this chapter, one way that the courts have limited the applicability of the ADA is by holding that conditions that can be corrected with medication or special devices do not qualify as disabilities under the act. Here, we look at some other cases that are furthering this trend toward limiting the scope of the ADA.

The *Toyota* Case

In 2002, the Supreme Court further narrowed the scope of the ADA by its broad interpretation of what constitutes a substantially limiting impairment of a major life activity. The case before the Court involved Ella Williams, an employee of Toyota Motor Manufacturing in Kentucky. Williams's use of tools on an engine fabrication assembly line eventually caused pain in her hands, wrist, and arm. For the following two years, she held modified-duty jobs to avoid repetitive physical activity. Nonetheless, she started to experience pain in her neck and shoulders and was finally placed on a no-work-of-any-kind restriction. Toyota then terminated her employment.

The Supreme Court had to decide whether her condition, usually referred to as carpal tunnel syndrome, constituted a disability under the ADA. The Court unanimously held that it did not. The Court stated that although the employee could not perform the manual tasks associated with her job, the condition did not constitute a disability under the ADA because it did not "substantially limit" the major life activity of performing manual tasks. For the fired worker, Williams, to prevail, her carpal tunnel syndrome would have had to be so severe that it prevented or severely restricted activities that were of central importance to her daily life, not just work-related activities.[a]

Further Limiting the Scope of the ADA

In a 2001 case, the Supreme Court also limited the applicability of the ADA by holding that lawsuits under the ADA cannot be brought against state government employers. The Court concluded that states, as sovereigns, are immune from lawsuits brought against them by private parties under the federal ADA.[b] The Court went on to further reduce the reach of the ADA by supporting Equal Employment Opportunity Commission regulations that permit an employer to refuse to hire a person when the job would pose a threat to that person's health.[c]

FOR CRITICAL ANALYSIS

Prior to 1999, the Supreme Court and other federal courts had tended to interpret the ADA's definition of disability expansively, thus enlarging the scope of the act's coverage. Why do you think that the courts have reversed this trend in the last few years?

a. *Toyota Motor Manufacturing, Kentucky, Inc. v. Williams,* 534 U.S. 184, 122 S.Ct. 681, 151 L.Ed.2d 615 (2002).
b. *Board of Trustees of the University of Alabama v. Garrett,* 531 U.S. 356, 121 S.Ct. 955, 148 L.Ed.2d 866 (2001).
c. *Chevron USA, Inc. v. Echazabal,* 536 U.S. 73, 122 S.Ct. 2045, 153 L.Ed.2d 82 (2002).

Usually, the courts decide whether an accommodation constitutes an undue hardship on a case-by-case basis. In one case, the court decided that paying for a parking space near the office for an employee with a disability was not an undue hardship.[24] In another case, the court held that accommodating the request of an employee with diabetes for indefinite leave until his disease was under control would create an undue hardship for the employer because the employer would not know when the employee was returning to work. The court stated that reasonable accommodation under the ADA means accommodation so that the employee can perform the job now or "in the immediate future" rather than at some unspecified distant time.[25]

We now look at some specific requirements of the ADA concerning the extent to which employers must reasonably accommodate the needs of employees with disabilities.

Job Applications and Preemployment Physical Exams Employers must modify their job-application process so that those with disabilities can compete for jobs with those who do not have disabilities. ● **EXAMPLE 5** A job announcement that includes only a phone number would discriminate against potential job applicants with hearing impairments. Thus, the job announcement must also provide an address.●

Employers are restricted in the kinds of questions they can ask on job-application forms and during preemployment interviews. Furthermore, they cannot require persons with disabilities to submit to preemployment physicals unless such exams are required of all other applicants. Employers can condition an offer of employment on the employee's successfully passing a medical examination, but disqualifications must result from the discovery of problems that render the applicant unable to perform the job for which he or she is to be hired.

Dangerous Workers Employers are not required to hire or retain workers who, because of their disabilities, pose a "direct threat to the health or safety" of their co-workers or the public. This danger must be substantial and immediate; it cannot be speculative. In the wake of the AIDS epidemic, many employers have been concerned about hiring or continuing to employ a worker who has AIDS under the assumption that the worker might pose a direct threat to the health or safety of others in the workplace. Courts have generally held, however, that AIDS is not so contagious as to disqualify employees in most jobs. Therefore, employers must reasonably accommodate job applicants or employees who have AIDS or who test positive for HIV, the virus that causes AIDS.

Health-Insurance Plans Workers with disabilities must be given equal access to any health insurance provided to other employees. Employers can exclude from coverage preexisting health conditions and certain types of diagnostic or surgical procedures, however. An employer can also put a limit, or cap, on health-care payments under its particular group health policy—as long as such caps are "applied equally to all insured employees" and do not "discriminate on the basis of disability." Whenever a group health-care plan makes a disability-

DON'T FORGET Preemployment screening procedures must be applied carefully in regard to all job applicants.

---

24. See *Lyons v. Legal Aid Society,* 68 F.3d 1512 (2d Cir. 1995).
25. *Myers v. Hase,* 50 F.3d 278 (4th Cir. 1995).

based distinction in its benefits, the plan violates the ADA. The employer must then be able to justify the distinction by proving one of the following:

1. That limiting coverage of certain ailments is required to keep the plan financially sound.
2. That coverage of certain ailments would cause such a significant increase in premium payments or their equivalent that the plan would be unappealing to a significant number of workers.
3. That the disparate treatment is justified by the risks and costs associated with a particular disability.

The ADA and Substance Abusers Drug addiction is a disability under the ADA because drug addiction is a substantially limiting impairment. Those who are currently using illegal drugs are not protected by the act. The ADA protects only persons with *former* drug addictions—those who have completed a supervised drug-rehabilitation program or are currently in a supervised rehabilitation program. Individuals who have used drugs casually in the past are not protected under the act. They are not considered addicts and therefore do not have a disability (addiction).

People recovering from alcoholism are protected by the ADA. Employers cannot legally discriminate against employees simply because they are suffering from alcoholism and must treat them in the same way they treat other employees. In other words, an employee suffering from alcoholism who comes to work late because she or he was drinking the night before must be disciplined in the same way as employees who come to work late for other reasons. Of course, employers have the right to prohibit the use of alcohol in the workplace and can require that employees not be under the influence of alcohol while working. Employers can also fire or refuse to hire a person suffering from alcoholism if he or she poses a substantial risk of harm either to himself or herself or to others and the risk cannot be reduced by reasonable accommodation.

Hostile-Environment Claims under the ADA

As discussed earlier in this chapter, under Title VII of the Civil Rights Act of 1964, an employee can base certain types of employment-discrimination causes of action on a hostile-environment theory. Using this theory, a worker may be able to sue her or his employer successfully even if the worker was not fired or otherwise discriminated against.

Can a worker file a suit founded on a hostile-environment claim under the ADA? The ADA does not expressly provide for such suits, but some courts have allowed them. Others have assumed that the claim was possible without deciding whether the ADA allowed it.[26] Acts that might form the basis for such a claim would likely consist of conduct that a reasonable person would find offensive enough to change the conditions of the person's employment.

Whether a disabled worker who was harassed by her co-workers could successfully sue her employer for a hostile environment was the issue in the following case.

A discussion occurs at a meeting of Alcoholics Anonymous. Should employers be allowed to discriminate against persons suffering from alcoholism?

26. See, for example, *Steele v. Thiokol Corp.,* 241 F.3d 1248 (10th Cir. 2001).

CASE 17.4   Flowers v. Southern Regional Physician Services, Inc.

United States Court of Appeals,
Fifth Circuit, 2001.
247 F.3d 229.
http://www.ca5.uscourts.gov/oparchdt.cfm[a]

BACKGROUND AND FACTS

Beginning in September 1993, Sandra Flowers worked for Southern Regional Physician Services, Inc., as a medical assistant to Dr. James Osterberger. In March 1995, Margaret Hallmark, Flowers's immediate supervisor, discovered that Flowers was infected with the human immunodeficiency virus (HIV). Suddenly, Flowers, who had received only excellent performance reviews, was the subject of several negative disciplinary reports. Also, in one week, she was required to take four drug tests. Previously, she had been asked to take only one. Hallmark stopped socializing with Flowers, her co-workers began avoiding her, and the president of the hospital refused to shake her hand. In November 1995, after being put on probation twice, Flowers was fired. She filed a suit in a federal district court against Southern Regional under the ADA, arguing in part that she had been subjected to a hostile environment on the basis of her disability. The court entered a judgment in her favor and awarded her $100,000. Southern Regional appealed to the U.S. Court of Appeals for the Fifth Circuit.

IN THE WORDS OF THE COURT . . .

KING, Chief Judge:

*   *   *   *

The ADA provides that no employer covered by the Act "shall discriminate against a qualified individual with a disability because of the disability of such individual in regard to * * * *terms, conditions, and privileges of employment.*" In almost identical fashion, Title VII provides that it is unlawful for an employer "to fail or refuse to hire or to discharge any individual, or otherwise to discriminate against any individual with respect to his compensation, *terms, conditions, or privileges of employment,* because of such individual's race, color, religion, sex, or national origin[.]"

It is evident, after a review of the ADA's language, purpose, and remedial framework, that Congress's intent in enacting the ADA was, *inter alia* [among other things], to eradicate disability-based harassment in the workplace. First, as a matter of statutory interpretation, * * * the [United States] Supreme Court interpreted Title VII, which contains language similar to that in the ADA, to provide a cause of action for harassment which is sufficiently severe or pervasive to alter the conditions of the victim's employment and create an abusive working environment * * * because it affects a term, condition, or privilege of employment. We conclude that the language of Title VII and the ADA dictates a consistent reading of the two statutes. Therefore, following the Supreme Court's interpretation of the language contained in Title VII, we interpret the phrase "terms, conditions, and privileges of employment," as it is used in the ADA, to strike at harassment in the workplace.

Not only are Title VII and the ADA similar in their language, they are also alike in their purposes and remedial structures. *Both Title VII and the ADA are aimed at the same evil—employment discrimination against individuals of certain classes.* Moreover, this court has recognized that the ADA is part of the same broad remedial framework as * * * Title VII, and that all the anti-discrimination acts have been subjected to similar analysis. Furthermore, other courts of appeals have noted the correlation between the two statutes. We con-

---

a. This is the "Opinions Archive by Date Released" page within the Web site of the U.S. Court of Appeals for the Fifth Circuit. Click on "2001." When the link opens, click on "May." When that link opens, click on "May 4." From the list that appears, click on the docket number next to the name of the case to access the opinion.

CASE 17.4—Continued

clude, therefore, that the purposes and remedial frameworks of the two statutes also command our conclusion that the ADA provides a cause of action for disability-based harassment.[Emphasis added.]

DECISION AND REMEDY The U.S. Court of Appeals for the Fifth Circuit held that the right to bring a hostile-environment claim under the ADA can be inferred because the ADA is similar in language, purpose, and "remedial structure" to Title VII. The court added that Flowers was entitled only to nominal dam-

ages, however, because she had not proved that she had actually suffered emotional injury.

FOR CRITICAL ANALYSIS—Political Consideration *What might an employer do to avoid hostile-environment claims under the ADA?*

DEFENSES TO EMPLOYMENT DISCRIMINATION

The first line of defense for an employer charged with employment discrimination is to assert that the plaintiff has failed to meet his or her initial burden of proving that discrimination in fact occurred. As noted, plaintiffs bringing cases under the ADA sometimes find it difficult to meet this initial burden because they must prove that their alleged disabilities are disabilities covered by the ADA. Furthermore, plaintiffs in ADA cases must prove that they were otherwise qualified for the job and that their disabilities were the sole reason they were not hired or were fired.

Once a plaintiff succeeds in proving that discrimination occurred, the burden shifts to the employer to justify the discriminatory practice. Often, employers attempt to justify the discrimination by claiming that it was a result of a business necessity, a bona fide occupational qualification, or a seniority system. In some cases, as noted earlier, an effective antiharassment policy and prompt remedial action when harassment occurs may shield employers from liability under Title VII for sexual harassment.

Business Necessity

An employer may defend against a claim of disparate-impact discrimination by asserting that a practice that has a discriminatory effect is a **business necessity.** ● EXAMPLE 6 If requiring a high school diploma is shown to have a discriminatory effect, an employer might argue that a high school education is necessary for workers to perform the job at the required level of competence. If the employer can demonstrate to the court's satisfaction that there is a definite connection between a high school education and job performance, the employer will succeed in this business necessity defense.●

BUSINESS NECESSITY
A defense to allegations of employment discrimination in which the employer demonstrates that an employment practice that discriminates against members of a protected class is related to job performance.

Bona Fide Occupational Qualification

Another defense applies when discrimination against a protected class is essential to a job—that is, when a particular trait is a **bona fide occupational qualification** (BFOQ). For example, a men's fashion magazine might legitimately hire only male models. Similarly, the Federal Aviation Administration can legitimately impose age limits for airline pilots. Race or color, however, can never be a BFOQ. Generally, courts have restricted the BFOQ defense to instances in which the

BONA FIDE OCCUPATIONAL QUALIFICATION (BFOQ)
Identifiable characteristic reasonably necessary to the normal operation of a particular business. Such characteristics can include gender, national origin, and religion, but not race.

employee's gender is essential to the job. In 1991, the United States Supreme Court held that even a fetal protection policy that was adopted to protect the unborn children of female employees from the harmful effects of exposure to lead was an unacceptable BFOQ.[27]

Seniority Systems

SENIORITY SYSTEM
In regard to employment relationships, a system in which those who have worked longest for the company are first in line for promotions, salary increases, and other benefits and last to be laid off if the work force must be reduced.

An employer with a history of discrimination may have no members of protected classes in upper-level positions. Even if the employer now seeks to be unbiased, it may face a lawsuit in which the plaintiff asks a court to order that minorities be promoted ahead of schedule to compensate for past discrimination. If no present intent to discriminate is shown, however, and promotions and other job benefits are distributed according to a fair **seniority system** (in which workers with more years of service are promoted first and laid off last), the employer can raise this as an affirmative defense against the suit.

After-Acquired Evidence Is No Defense

In some situations, employers have attempted to avoid liability for employment discrimination on the basis of "after-acquired evidence" of an employee's misconduct—that is, evidence of an employee's prior misconduct that is acquired after a lawsuit is under way. ● **EXAMPLE 7** Suppose that an employer fires a worker, and the employee sues the employer for employment discrimination. During pretrial investigation, the employer learns that the employee made material misrepresentations on his or her employment application—misrepresentations that, had the employer known about them, would have served as a ground to fire the individual.● According to the United States Supreme Court, after-acquired evidence of wrongdoing cannot be used to shield an employer entirely from liability for employment discrimination. It can, however, be used to limit the amount of damages for which the employer is liable.[28]

AFFIRMATIVE ACTION

AFFIRMATIVE ACTION
Job-hiring policies that give special consideration to members of protected classes in an effort to overcome present effects of past discrimination.

Federal statutes and regulations providing for equal opportunity in the workplace were designed to reduce or eliminate discriminatory practices with respect to hiring, retaining, and promoting employees. **Affirmative action** programs go a step further and attempt to make up for past patterns of discrimination by giving members of protected classes preferential treatment in hiring or promotion.

Affirmative action policies were first mandated by an executive order issued by President Lyndon Johnson in 1965. All government agencies, including those of state and local governments, were required to implement such policies. Affirmative action requirements were also imposed on companies that contract to do business with the federal government and on institutions that receive federal funds. Because a significant percentage of the nation's employees work for government agencies or for firms that do business with the gov-

---

27. *United Auto Workers v. Johnson Controls, Inc.,* 113 U.S. 158, 111 S.Ct. 1196, 113 L.Ed.2d 158 (1991).
28. *McKennon v. Nashville Banner Publishing Co.,* 513 U.S. 352, 115 S.Ct. 879, 130 L.Ed.2d 852 (1995).

ernment, this presidential executive order has had a profound impact on the American workplace.

Title VII of the Civil Rights Act of 1964 neither requires nor prohibits affirmative action, and thus private companies and organizations that do not do business with the government or receive federal funds have not been required to implement such policies—although many have done so voluntarily. Note, though, that the courts and the Equal Employment Opportunity Commission have sometimes ordered private companies to undertake affirmative action when they found evidence of past discrimination. Labor unions that have been found to discriminate against women or minorities in the past have also been required to establish and follow affirmative action plans.

Challenges to Affirmative Action

Affirmative action programs have caused much controversy, particularly when they result in what is frequently called "reverse discrimination"—discrimination against "majority" workers, such as white males (or discrimination against other minority groups that are not given preferential treatment under a particular affirmative action program). At issue is whether affirmative action programs, because of their inherently discriminatory nature, violate employee rights or the equal protection clause of the Fourteenth Amendment to the U.S. Constitution.

When an affirmative action plan undertaken by a private employer (one that does not do business with the government) is challenged on the basis of reverse discrimination, the court decides the issue under Title VII. Generally, the courts have held that an affirmative action plan is valid if the employer can show that minorities and women have been notably underrepresented in the workplace in the past and that the plan does not unnecessarily restrict the rights of male or nonminority employees. More controversial today is the issue of whether affirmative action plans required by the government (that is, plans undertaken by employers that receive government funds or that do business with the government) violate the equal protection clause of the Fourteenth Amendment to the Constitution.

The *Bakke* Case   An early non–employment-related case addressing this issue, *Regents of the University of California v. Bakke,*[29] involved an affirmative action program implemented by the University of California at Davis. Allan Bakke, who had been turned down for medical school at the Davis campus, sued the university for reverse discrimination after he discovered that his academic record was better than the records of some of the minority applicants who had been admitted to the program.

The United States Supreme Court held that affirmative action programs were subject to intermediate scrutiny. Recall from the discussion of the equal protection clause in Chapter 5 that any law or action evaluated under a standard of intermediate scrutiny, to be constitutionally valid, must be substantially related to important government objectives. Applying this standard, the Court held that the university could give favorable weight to minority applicants as part of a plan to increase minority enrollment so as to achieve a more culturally diverse

---

29. 438 U.S. 265, 98 S.Ct. 2733, 57 L.Ed.2d 750 (1978).

student body. The Court stated, however, that the use of a quota system, in which a certain number of places are explicitly reserved for minority applicants, violated the equal protection clause of the Fourteenth Amendment.

The *Adarand* Case Although the *Bakke* case and later court decisions alleviated the harshness of the quota system, today's courts are going even further in questioning the constitutional validity of affirmative action programs. In 1995, in its landmark decision in *Adarand Constructors, Inc. v. Peña,*[30] the United States Supreme Court held that any federal, state, or local affirmative action program that uses racial or ethnic classifications as the basis for making decisions is subject to strict scrutiny by the courts.

In effect, the Court's ruling in *Adarand* means that an affirmative action program is constitutional only if it attempts to remedy past discrimination and does not make use of quotas or preferences. Furthermore, once such a program has succeeded in the goal of remedying past discrimination, it must be changed or dropped.

Subsequent Court Decisions In 1996, in *Hopwood v. State of Texas,*[31] the Court of Appeals for the Fifth Circuit went beyond the Supreme Court's *Adarand* decision. In the *Hopwood* case, two white law school applicants sued the University of Texas School of Law in Austin, alleging that they were denied admission because of the school's affirmative action program. The program allowed admitting officials to take racial and other factors into consideration when determining which students would be admitted. The court held that the program violated the equal protection clause because it discriminated in favor of minority applicants. In its decision, the court directly challenged the *Bakke* decision by stating that the use of race even as a means of achieving diversity on college campuses "undercuts the Fourteenth Amendment."

In 2003, the United States Supreme Court reviewed two cases involving issues similar to that in the *Hopwood* case. Both cases involved admissions programs at the University of Michigan. In *Gratz v. Bollinger,*[32] two white applicants who were denied undergraduate admission to the university alleged reverse discrimination. The school's policy gave each applicant a score based on a number of factors, including grade point average, standardized test results, and personal achievements. The system *automatically* awarded every "underrepresented" minority (African American, Hispanic, and Native American) applicant twenty points—one-fifth of the points needed to guarantee admission. The Court held that this policy violated the equal protection clause.

In contrast, in *Grutter v. Bollinger,*[33] the Court held that the University of Michigan Law School's admission policy was constitutional. In that case, the Court concluded that "[u]niversities can, however, consider race or ethnicity more flexibly as a 'plus' factor in the context of individualized consideration of each and every applicant." The significant difference between the two

---

30. 515 U.S. 200, 115 S.Ct. 2097, 132 L.Ed.2d 158 (1995).
31. 84 F.3d 720 (5th Cir. 1996).
32. ___U.S.___, 123 S.Ct. 2411, 156 L.Ed.2d 257 (2003).
33. ___U.S.___, 123 S.Ct. 2325, 156 L.Ed.2d 304 (2003).

admissions policies, in the Court's view, was that the law school's approach did not apply a mechanical formula giving "diversity bonuses" based on race or ethnicity.

State Actions

In the meantime, some state governments have been taking action. California and Washington, by voter initiatives in 1996 and 1998, respectively, ended state-government–sponsored affirmative action in those states. Similar movements are currently under way in other state and local areas as well. Additionally, a number of universities have modified their admissions policies to increase opportunities for minority students without directly considering racial or ethnic factors. For example, California has put into effect a "top 4 percent plan." Under this plan, the top 4 percent of students from certain low-performing and predominantly minority high schools are automatically accepted at the Berkeley and Los Angeles campuses of the University of California. Since 1996, Texas has had a similar plan that uses a much higher percentage (top 10 percent).

STATE STATUTES

Although the focus of this chapter has been on federal legislation, most states also have statutes that prohibit employment discrimination. Generally, the kinds of discrimination prohibited under federal legislation are also prohibited by state laws. In addition, state statutes often provide protection for certain individuals who are not covered under federal laws. For example, a New Jersey appellate court has held that anyone over the age of eighteen is entitled to sue for age discrimination under the state law, which specifies no threshold age limit.[34]

Furthermore, state laws prohibiting discrimination may apply to firms with fewer employees than the threshold number required under federal statutes, thus offering protection to a larger number of workers. Even when companies are too small to be covered by state statutes, state courts may uphold employees' rights against discrimination in the workplace for public-policy reasons. Finally, state laws may provide for damages, such as damages for emotional distress, that are not provided for under federal statutes.

---

34. *Bergen Commercial Bank v. Sisler*, 307 N.J.Super. 333, 704 A.2d 1017 (1998).

KEY TERMS

affirmative action   566
bona fide occupational
   qualification (BFOQ)   565
business necessity   565
disparate-impact
   discrimination   546

disparate-treatment
   discrimination   545
employment discrimination   545
prima facie case   546

protected class   544
seniority system   566
sexual harassment   549

CHAPTER SUMMARY **EQUAL EMPLOYMENT OPPORTUNITIES**

Title VII of the Civil Rights Act of 1964 (See pages 545–554.)	Title VII prohibits employment discrimination based on race, color, national origin, religion, or gender. 1. *Procedures*—Employees must file a claim with the Equal Employment Opportunity Commission (EEOC). The EEOC may sue the employer on the employee's behalf; if it does not, the employee may sue the employer directly. 2. *Types of discrimination*—Title VII prohibits both intentional (disparate-treatment) and unintentional (disparate-impact) discrimination. Disparate-impact discrimination occurs when an employer's practice, such as hiring only persons with a certain level of education, has the effect of discriminating against a class of persons protected by Title VII. Title VII also extends to discriminatory practices, such as various forms of harassment, in the online environment. 3. *Remedies for discrimination under Title VII*—If a plaintiff proves that unlawful discrimination occurred, he or she may be awarded reinstatement, back pay, and retroactive promotions. Damages (both compensatory and punitive) may be awarded for intentional discrimination.
Equal Pay Act of 1963 (See pages 554–556.)	The Equal Pay Act of 1963 prohibits gender-based discrimination in the wages paid for equal work on jobs when their performance requires equal skill, effort, and responsibility under similar conditions.
Discrimination Based on Age (See pages 556–557.)	The Age Discrimination in Employment Act (ADEA) of 1967 prohibits employment discrimination on the basis of age against individuals forty years of age or older. Procedures for bringing a case under the ADEA are similar to those for bringing a case under Title VII.
Discrimination Based on Disability (See pages 557–565.)	The Americans with Disabilities Act (ADA) of 1990 prohibits employment discrimination against persons with disabilities who are otherwise qualified to perform the essential functions of the jobs for which they apply. 1. *Procedures and remedies*—To prevail on a claim under the ADA, the plaintiff must show that she or he has a disability, is otherwise qualified for the employment in question, and was excluded from the employment solely because of the disability. Procedures under the ADA are similar to those required in Title VII cases; remedies are also similar to those under Title VII. 2. *Definition of disability*—The ADA defines the term *disability* as a physical or mental impairment that substantially limits one or more major life activities; a record of such impairment; or being regarded as having such an impairment. 3. *Reasonable accommodation*—Employers are required to reasonably accommodate the needs of persons with disabilities. Reasonable accommodations may include altering job-application procedures, modifying the physical work environment, and permitting more flexible work schedules. Employers are not required to provide accommodations if doing so will cause undue hardship. Employers need not hire or retain workers with disabilities who are not qualified for their jobs or who pose a definite threat to health and safety in the workplace.
Defenses to Employment Discrimination (See pages 565–566.)	If a plaintiff proves that employment discrimination occurred, an employer can avoid liability by successfully asserting that the discrimination was required for reasons of business necessity, to meet a bona fide occupational qualification, or to maintain a legitimate seniority system. Evidence of prior employee misconduct acquired after the employee has been fired is not a defense to discrimination.

CHAPTER SUMMARY EQUAL EMPLOYMENT OPPORTUNITIES—Continued

Affirmative Action (See pages 566–569.)	Affirmative action programs attempt to make up for past patterns of discrimination by giving members of protected classes preferential treatment in hiring or promotion. Increasingly, such programs are being strictly scrutinized by the courts, and state-sponsored affirmative action has been banned in California and Washington.
State Statutes (See page 569.)	Generally, the kinds of discrimination prohibited by federal statutes are also prohibited by state laws. State laws may provide for more extensive protection and remedies than federal laws.

FOR REVIEW

1. Generally, what kind of conduct is prohibited by Title VII of the Civil Rights Act of 1964, as amended?
2. What is the difference between disparate-treatment discrimination and disparate-impact discrimination?
3. What remedies are available under Title VII of the 1964 Civil Rights Act, as amended?
4. What federal acts prohibit discrimination based on age and discrimination based on disability?
5. What are three defenses to claims of employment discrimination?

QUESTIONS AND CASE PROBLEMS

17-1. Title VII Violations. Discuss fully whether either of the following actions would constitute a violation of Title VII of the 1964 Civil Rights Act, as amended:

(a) Tennington, Inc., is a consulting firm and has ten employees. These employees travel on consulting jobs in seven states. Tennington has an employment record of hiring only white males.

(b) Novo Films, Inc., is making a film about Africa and needs to employ approximately one hundred extras for this picture. Novo advertises in all major newspapers in southern California for the hiring of these extras. The ad states that only African Americans need apply.

17-2. Discrimination Based on Age. Tavo Jones had worked since 1974 for Westshore Resort, where he maintained golf carts. During the first decade, he received positive job evaluations and numerous merit pay raises. He was promoted to the position of supervisor of golf-cart maintenance at three courses. Then a new employee, Ben Olery, was placed in charge of the golf courses. He demoted Jones, who was over the age of forty, to running only one of the three cart facilities, and he froze Jones's salary indefinitely. Olery also demoted five other men over the age of forty. Another cart facility was placed under the supervision of Blake Blair. Later,

the cart facilities for the three courses were again consolidated, but Blair—not Jones—was put in charge. At the time, Jones was still in his forties, and Blair was in his twenties. Jones overheard Blair say that "we are going to have to do away with these . . . old and senile" men. Jones quit and sued Westshore for employment discrimination. Should he prevail? Explain.

17-3. Discrimination Based on Disability. Ananda Lane is a hearing-impaired repairperson currently employed with the Southwestern Telephone Co. Her job requires her to drive the company truck to remote rural areas in all kinds of weather, to climb telephone poles, to make general repairs to telephone lines, and so on. She has held this position for five years, a full year longer than any other employee, and she is quite competent. Ananda recently applied for a promotion to the position of repair crew coordinator, a position that would require her to be in constant communication with all repairpersons in the field. Southwestern rejected Ananda's application, stating that the company "needs someone in this critical position who can speak and hear clearly, someone who does not suffer from any hearing disability." Ananda says she could easily perform the essentials of the job if Southwestern would provide her with a sign language interpreter. Although Southwestern agrees that Ananda is otherwise qualified for the coordinator position, the company has concluded that the cost of hiring an interpreter would be prohibitive, and therefore it should not be required to accommodate her disability under the Americans with Disabilities Act. Who is correct? Discuss.

17-4. Defenses to Employment Discrimination.
Dorothea O'Driscoll had worked as a quality control inspector for Hercules, Inc., for six years when her employment was terminated in 1986. O'Driscoll, who was over forty years of age, sued Hercules for age discrimination in violation of the Age Discrimination in Employment Act of 1967. While preparing for trial, Hercules learned that O'Driscoll, when she applied for the job, had misrepresented her age, did not disclose a previous employer, falsely represented that she had never applied for work with Hercules before, and falsely stated that she had completed two quarters of study at a technical college. Hercules defended against O'Driscoll's claim of age discrimination by stating that had it known of this misconduct, it would have terminated her employment anyway. What should the court decide? Discuss fully. [*O'Driscoll v. Hercules, Inc.*, 12 F.3d 176 (10th Cir. 1994)]

17-5. Discrimination Based on Disability.
When the University of Maryland Medical System Corp. learned that one of its surgeons was HIV positive, the university offered him transfers to positions that did not involve surgery. The surgeon refused, and the university terminated him. The surgeon filed a suit in a federal district court against the university, alleging in part a violation of the Americans with Disabilities Act. The surgeon claimed that he was otherwise qualified for his former position. What does he have to prove to win his case? Should he be reinstated? [*Doe v. University of Maryland Medical System Corp.*, 50 F.3d 1261 (4th Cir. 1995)]

17-6. Discrimination Based on Race.
Theodore Rosenblatt, a white attorney, worked for the law firm of Bivona & Cohen, P.C. When Bivona & Cohen terminated Rosenblatt's employment, he filed a suit in a federal district court against the firm. Rosenblatt claimed that he had been discharged because he was married to an African American and that a discharge for such a reason violated Title VII and other laws. The firm filed a motion for summary judgment, arguing that he was alleging discrimination against his wife, not himself, and thus did not have standing to sue under Title VII for racial discrimination. Should the court grant or deny the motion? Explain. [*Rosenblatt v. Bivona & Cohen, P.C.*, 946 F.Supp. 298 (S.D.N.Y. 1996)]

17-7. Religious Discrimination.
Mary Tiano, a devout Roman Catholic, worked for Dillard Department Stores, Inc. (Dillard's), in Phoenix, Arizona. Dillard's considered Tiano a productive employee because her sales exceeded $200,000 a year. At the time, the store gave its managers the discretion to grant unpaid leave to employees but prohibited vacations or leave during the holiday season—October through December.

Tiano felt that she had a "calling" to go on a "pilgrimage" in October 1988 to Medjugorje, Yugoslavia, where some persons claimed to have had visions of the Virgin Mary. The Catholic Church had not designated the site an official pilgrimage site, the visions were not expected to be stronger in October, and tours were available at other times. The store managers denied Tiano's request for leave, but she had a nonrefundable ticket and left anyway. Dillard's terminated her employment. For a year, Tiano searched for a new job, and she did not attain the level of her Dillard's salary for four years. She filed a suit in a federal district court against Dillard's, alleging religious discrimination in violation of Title VII. Can Tiano establish a *prima facie* case of religious discrimination? Explain. [*Tiano v. Dillard Department Stores, Inc.*, 139 F.3d 679 (9th Cir. 1998)]

17-8. Discrimination Based on Disability.
Vaughn Murphy has hypertension (high blood pressure). Unmedicated, his blood pressure is approximately 250/160. With medication, however, he can function normally and engage in the same activities as anyone else. In 1994, United Parcel Service, Inc. (UPS), hired Murphy to be a mechanic, a position that required him to drive commercial motor vehicles. To get the job, Murphy had to comply with a U.S. Department of Transportation (DOT) regulation that a driver have "no current clinical diagnosis of high blood pressure likely to interfere with his/her ability to operate a commercial vehicle safely." At the time, Murphy's blood pressure was measured at 186/124 (which is extremely high), but he was erroneously certified and started work. Within a month, the error was discovered, and he was fired. Murphy obtained another mechanic's job—one that did not require DOT certification—and filed a suit in a federal district court against UPS, claiming discrimination under the Americans with Disabilities Act. UPS filed a motion for summary judgment. Should the court grant UPS's motion? Explain. [*Murphy v. United Parcel Service, Inc.*, 527 U.S. 516, 119 S.Ct. 2133, 144 L.Ed.2d 484 (1999)]

Case Problem with Sample Answer

17-9. Discrimination Based on Disability.
PGA Tour, Inc., sponsors professional golf tournaments. A player can enter in several ways, but the most common method is to successfully compete in a three-stage qualifying tournament known as the Q-School. Anyone can enter the Q-School by submitting two letters of recommendation and paying $3,000 to cover greens fees and the cost of a golf cart. The use of a cart is permitted during the first two stages but is prohibited during the third stage. The rules governing the events include the "Rules of Golf," which apply at all levels of amateur and professional golf and do not prohibit the use of golf carts, and the

"hard card," which applies specifically to the PGA tour and requires the players to walk the course during most of a tournament. Casey Martin is a talented golfer with a degenerative circulatory disorder that prevents him from walking extended distances. Martin entered the Q-School and asked for permission to use a cart during the third stage. PGA refused. Martin filed a suit in a federal district court against PGA, alleging a violation of the Americans with Disabilities Act. Is a golf cart in these circumstances a reasonable accommodation under the ADA? Why or why not? [*PGA Tour, Inc. v. Martin*, 531 U.S. 1049, 121 S.Ct. 1879, 149 L.Ed.2d 904 (2001)]

To view a sample answer for this case problem, go to this book's Web site at http://leet.westbuslaw.com and click on "Interactive Study Center."

17–10. Discrimination Based on Race. The hiring policy of Phillips Community College of the University of Arkansas (PCCUA) is to conduct an internal search for qualified applicants before advertising outside the college. Steven Jones, the university's chancellor, can determine the application and appointment process for vacant positions, however, and is the ultimate authority in hiring decisions. Howard Lockridge, an African American, was the chair of PCCUA's Technical and Industrial Department. Between 1988 and 1998, Lockridge applied for several different positions, some of which were unadvertised, some of which were unfilled for years, and some of which were filled with less qualified persons from outside the college. In 1998, when Jones advertised an opening for the position of dean of Industrial Technology and Workforce Development, Lockridge did not apply for the job. Jones hired Tracy McGraw, a white male. Lockridge filed a suit in a federal district court against the university under Title VII. The university filed a motion for summary judgment in its favor. What are the elements of a *prima facie* case of disparate-treatment discrimination? Can Lockridge pass this test, or should the court issue a judgment in the university's favor? Explain. [*Lockridge v. Board of Trustees of the University of Arkansas*, 294 F.3d 1010 (8th Cir. 2002)]

A Question of Ethics & Social Responsibility

17–11. Luz Long and three other Hispanic employees (the plaintiffs) worked as bank tellers for the Culmore branch of the First Union Corp. of Virginia. The plaintiffs often conversed with one another in Spanish, their native language. In 1992, the Culmore branch manager adopted an English-only policy, which required all employees to speak English during working hours unless they needed to speak another language to assist customers. The plaintiffs refused to cooperate with the new policy and were eventually fired. In a

suit against the bank, the plaintiffs alleged that the English-only policy discriminated against them on the basis of their national origin. The court granted the bank's motion for summary judgment, concluding that "[t]here is nothing in Title VII which . . . provides that an employee has a right to speak his or her native tongue while on the job." [*Long v. First Union Corp. of Virginia*, 894 F.Supp. 933 (E.D.Va. 1995)]

1. The bank argued that the policy was implemented in response to complaints made by fellow employees that the Spanish-speaking employees were creating a hostile environment by speaking Spanish among themselves in the presence of other employees. From an ethical perspective, is this a sufficient reason to institute an English-only policy?

2. Is it ever ethically justifiable for employers to deny bilingual employees the opportunity to speak their native language while on the job?

3. Might there be situations in which English-only policies are necessary to promote worker health and safety?

Case Briefing Assignment

17–12. Examine Case A.4 [*Sutton v. United Airlines, Inc.*, 527 U.S. 471, 119 S.Ct. 2139, 144 L.Ed.2d 450 (1999)] in Appendix A. This case has been excerpted there in great detail. Review and then brief the case, making sure that your brief answers the following questions.

1. For what jobs were the plaintiffs applying, and what disability did the plaintiffs claim they had?

2. Did United Airlines refuse to interview the plaintiffs? Did United reject all applicants with less than perfect vision?

3. What did the lower court hold regarding the plaintiffs' claims of disability-based discrimination?

4. Did the Supreme Court conclude that the plaintiffs were not disabled under the terms of the ADA? Why or why not?

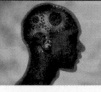

Critical-Thinking Managerial Question

17–13. A fifty-four-year-old plant manager who earned approximately $25.00 per hour was temporarily laid off when the plant was closed for the winter. When spring came, the manager was replaced by a forty-three-year-old worker who earned approximately $14.00 an hour. The older manager, who had worked for the company for twenty-seven years, was given no opportunity to accept a lower wage rate or otherwise accommodate the firm's need to reduce costs. Did this dismissal violate the Age Discrimination in Employment Act? Why or why not?

Video Question

17–14. Go to this text's Web site at http://leet.westbuslaw.com and select "Video Questions." Click on "Chapter 17" and view the video titled *Age Discrimination*. Then answer the following questions.

1. What would Jake have to show about Herman's auto dealership for the Age Discrimination and Employment Act (ADEA) to apply?

2. Suppose that after Herman tells Jake that the position is filled, but they will keep his name on file, Jake leaves and does not get hired. Would Jake have a cause of action for age discrimination? What would he have to prove to maintain an action?

3. In the video, Herman eventually admits to Jake that he thinks Jake is too old for the position. Then, when he finds out more about Jake's previous experience, he hires him. Can Jake sue Herman for these statements even though he was hired?

4. Herman tells Jake that he will "work him like a dog." If, after a few months, Herman decides that Jake is not working hard enough and fires him, can Jake establish a *prima facie* case of age discrimination under the ADEA?

INTERACTING WITH THE INTERNET

For updated links to resources available on the Web, as well as a variety of other materials, visit this text's Web site at

http://leet.westbuslaw.com

The law firm of Arent Fox posts articles on current issues in the area of employment law, including sexual harassment, on its Web site at

http://www.arentfox.com

An abundance of helpful information on disability-based discrimination, including the text of the Americans with Disabilities Act of 1990, can be found at the following Web site:

http://www.jan.wvu.edu/links/adalinks.htm

An excellent source for information on various forms of employment discrimination is the Equal Employment Opportunity Commission's Web site at

http://www.eeoc.gov

ONLINE LEGAL RESEARCH EXERCISES

Go to **http://leet.westbuslaw.com**, the Web site that accompanies this text. Select "Interactive Study Center," and then click on "Chapter 17." There you will find the following Internet research exercises that you can perform to learn more about topics covered in this chapter.

Activity 17–1: SOCIAL PERSPECTIVE—**Americans with Disabilities**
Activity 17–2: MANAGEMENT PERSPECTIVE—**Equal Employment Opportunity**
Activity 17–3: CULTURAL PERSPECTIVE—**Religious and National-Origin Discrimination**

BEFORE THE TEST

Go to **http://leet.westbuslaw.com**, the Web site that accompanies this text. Select "Interactive Quizzes." You will find at least twenty interactive questions relating to this chapter.

Westlaw® Campus

If your textbook provided for a subscription to Westlaw® Campus, or if you have otherwise purchased access to the Westlaw Campus database, you can access any of the cases presented or cited in this chapter by using your Westlaw Campus account.

CHAPTER 18

Labor-Management Relations

CONTENTS

CHAPTER OBJECTIVES

After reading this chapter, you should be able to answer the following questions:

1. What federal statutes govern labor unions and collective bargaining?

2. How does the way in which a union election is conducted protect the rights of employees and employers?

3. What type of strikes are illegal?

4. What activities are prohibited as unfair employer practices?

5. What are the rights of nonunion employees?

Through the first half of the nineteenth century, most Americans were self-employed, often in agriculture. For those who were employed by others, the employers generally set the terms of employment. The nature of employment changed with the growth of the industrial revolution, which had begun about 1760. Fewer Americans were self-employed. Terms of employment were sometimes set through bargaining between employees and employers. Most industrial enterprises were in their infancies, however, and to encourage their development, the government gave employers considerable freedom to hire, fire, and determine other employment standards in response to changing conditions in the marketplace.

With increasing industrialization, the size of workplaces and the number of workplace hazards increased. Workers came to believe that to counter the power and freedom of their employers and to protect themselves, they needed to organize into unions. Employers discouraged—sometimes forcibly—collective activities such as

> "Experience has proved that protection by law of the right of employees to organize and bargain collectively . . . promotes the flow of commerce."
>
> National Labor Relations Act of 1935, Section 1

unions. In support of unionization, Congress enacted such legislation as the Railway Labor Act of 1926.[1] These laws were often restricted to particular industries. Beginning in 1932, Congress enacted a number of statutes that increased employees' rights in general. As the quotation on the previous page indicates, at the heart of these rights is the right to join unions and engage in collective bargaining with management to negotiate working conditions, salaries, and benefits for a group of workers.

This chapter describes the development of labor law and legal recognition of the right to form unions. The laws that govern the management-union relationship are set forth in historical perspective. Then we discuss the process of unionizing a company, the collective bargaining required of a unionized employer, the "industrial war" of strikes and lockouts that may result if bargaining fails, and the labor practices that are considered unfair under federal law.

An employer's rules. How do federal labor laws influence the adoption of such rules?

FEDERAL LABOR LAW

Federal labor laws governing union-employer relations have developed considerably since the first law was enacted in 1932. Initially, the laws were concerned with protecting the rights and interests of workers. Subsequent legislation placed some restraints on unions and granted rights to employers. This section summarizes the four major federal labor law statutes.

Norris-LaGuardia Act

Congress protected peaceful strikes, picketing, and boycotts in 1932 in the Norris-LaGuardia Act.[2] The statute restricted federal courts in their power to issue injunctions against unions engaged in peaceful strikes. The act also provided that contracts limiting an employee's right to join a union are unlawful. Such contracts are known as **yellow dog contracts.** (In the early part of the twentieth century, "yellow dog" meant "coward.") In effect, this act declared a national policy permitting employees to organize.

In the following case, a union threatened to picket an employer unless the employer agreed to subcontract work only to subcontractors who employed the union's members. The court had to decide whether, under the Norris-LaGuardia Act, it could issue an injunction to restrain the union from picketing.

YELLOW DOG CONTRACT
An agreement under which an employee promises his or her employer, as a condition of employment, not to join a union.

---

1. 45 U.S.C. Sections 151–188.
2. 29 U.S.C. Sections 101–115.

| **CASE 18.1** | Burlington Northern Santa Fe Railway Co. v. International Brotherhood of Teamsters Local 174 |

United States Court of Appeals, Ninth Circuit, 2000.
203 F.3d 703.
http://www.ca9.uscourts.gov[a]

BACKGROUND AND FACTS Burlington Northern and Santa Fe Railway Company operates a hub in Seattle, Washington. Burlington terminated a subcontract with Eagle Systems, Inc., for loading and

---

a. In the left column, click on "Opinions." On the page that opens, click on "2000." In the expanded list, click on "February." In that list, scroll to the name of the case ("BURLINGTON NORTHERN V IBET") and click on it to access the opinion.

(continued)

CASE 18.1—Continued

unloading services at the Seattle hub and transferred the work to another subcontractor, Parsec, Inc. As a consequence, fifty-three Eagle employees lost their jobs. International Brotherhood of Teamsters Local 174 represented the Eagle employees who had been laid off, as well as the employees of other subcontractors who worked under subcontracts with Burlington. Local 174 did not represent the Parsec employees, however. The union was afraid that Burlington's use of other subcontractors who did not employ Local 174's members would cause "substantial economic costs and personal hardship." The union asked Burlington to persuade Parsec to hire the former Eagle employees. Burlington refused. Local 174 asked Burlington to

agree not to subcontract in the future any loading and unloading services to any subcontractor whose employees were not represented by Local 174. The union threatened to picket in support of this demand. Burlington filed a suit in a federal district court against Local 174, alleging violations of federal labor law, among other things, and seeking an injunction. The court granted the injunction, restraining Local 174 from "[c]alling, ordering, authorizing, encouraging, inducing, approving, continuing, starting, suffering, permitting or carrying out any strike, picket or work stoppage" at Burlington's facilities. The union appealed to the U.S. Court of Appeals for the Ninth Circuit.

IN THE WORDS OF THE COURT . . .

PREGERSON, Circuit Judge.

* * * *

The Norris-LaGuardia Act deprives federal courts of jurisdiction to issue an injunction to restrain peaceful picketing in "any case involving or growing out of any labor dispute." Norris-LaGuardia defines the term "labor dispute" as

> any controversy concerning terms or conditions of employment, or concerning the association or representation of persons in negotiating, fixing, maintaining, changing, or seeking to arrange terms or conditions of employment, regardless of whether or not the disputants stand in the proximate relation of employer and employee.

We hold that a dispute between a union and a client company (here, Burlington Northern) over whether the client company's subcontractors must employ that union's members is a Norris-LaGuardia labor dispute. Thus, * * * the district court had no power to enjoin Local 174 from picketing Burlington Northern.

* * * *

* * * *The [United States] Supreme Court has consistently characterized Norris-LaGuardia's definition of "labor dispute" as "broad."* Equally expansive is the test that the Supreme Court fashioned for determining whether a particular controversy is a labor dispute. Simply, "the employer-employee relationship [must be at] the matrix of the controversy." [Emphasis added.]

It is clear that "the matrix" of Local 174's dispute with Burlington Northern is "the employer-employee relationship." Members of Local 174 lost their jobs because Burlington Northern transferred their work to a subcontractor who did not rehire them and who signed a collective bargaining agreement with a different union. Local 174 feared that Burlington Northern would terminate other subcontracts under which its members worked, leading to more job losses and causing wages and working conditions to deteriorate. Local 174 asked Burlington Northern to guarantee that this process would not occur, but Burlington Northern refused. In short, this dispute is about who will perform work at Burlington Northern's Seattle hub, which union will represent the employees of Burlington Northern's subcontractors, and what will be the terms of their employment.

CASE 18.1—Continued

DECISION AND REMEDY The U.S. Court of Appeals for the Ninth Circuit vacated the lower court's order and remanded with instructions to dismiss the case. The court could not issue an injunction to block Local 174's picketing because the disagreement between Burlington and Local 174 was a "labor dispute" within the meaning of the Norris-LaGuardia Act. Under that act, a federal court cannot issue an injunction to block peaceful picketing that is part of a labor dispute.

FOR CRITICAL ANALYSIS—Social Consideration *Generally, how would the relationship between labor and management be affected if unions did not have the right to picket?*

National Labor Relations Act

The National Labor Relations Act of 1935 (NLRA),[3] also called the Wagner Act, established the right of employees to form unions, the right of those unions to engage in collective bargaining (negotiate contracts for their members), and the right to strike. The act also created the National Labor Relations Board (NLRB) to oversee union elections and to prevent employers from engaging in unfair labor union activities and unfair labor practices. Details of the NLRA are provided in this chapter's *Landmark in the Legal Environment* feature on the following page.

To be protected under the NLRA, an individual must be an "employee," as that term is defined in the statute.[4] Courts have long held that job applicants fall within the definition (otherwise, the NLRA's ban on discrimination in regard to hiring would mean nothing). The United States Supreme Court has held that an individual can be a company's "employee" even if, at the same time, a union pays the individual to organize the company.[5]

Labor-Management Relations Act

The Labor-Management Relations Act of 1947 (LMRA, or Taft-Hartley Act)[6] was passed to proscribe certain union practices. The Taft-Hartley Act contained provisions protecting employers as well as employees. The act was bitterly opposed by organized labor groups. It provided a detailed list of unfair labor activities that unions as well as management were now forbidden to practice. In addition, the law gave the president the authority to intervene in labor disputes and delay strikes that would "imperil the national health or safety."

An important provision of the LMRA concerned the **closed shop**—a firm that requires union membership of its workers as a condition of obtaining employment. Closed shops were made illegal under the Taft-Hartley Act. The act preserved the legality of the **union shop,** which does not require membership as a prerequisite for employment but can, and usually does, require that workers join the recognized union after a specified amount of time on the job. The act also allowed individual states to pass their own **right-to-work laws**—

CLOSED SHOP
A firm that requires union membership by its workers as a condition of employment. The closed shop was made illegal by the Labor-Management Relations Act of 1947.

UNION SHOP
A place of employment in which all workers, once employed, must become union members within a specified period of time as a condition of their continued employment.

RIGHT-TO-WORK LAW
A state law providing that employees are not to be required to join a union as a condition of obtaining or retaining employment.

---

3. 29 U.S.C. Sections 151–169.
4. 29 U.S.C. Section 152(3).
5. *NLRB v. Town & Country Electric, Inc.,* 516 U.S. 85, 116 S.Ct. 450, 133 L.Ed. 2d 371 (1995).
6. 29 U.S.C. Sections 141, 504.

LANDMARK IN THE LEGAL ENVIRONMENT

The National Labor Relations Act (1935)

The National Labor Relations Act of 1935 is often referred to as the Wagner Act because it was sponsored by Senator Robert Wagner. (Appendix E presents excerpts from the National Labor Relations Act.) During the 1930s, Wagner sponsored several pieces of legislation, particularly in the field of labor law. Until the early 1930s, employers had been free to establish the terms and conditions of employment. Collective activities by employees, such as participation in unions, were discouraged by employers. In 1934, when Wagner introduced the bill subsequently enacted as the National Labor Relations Act (NLRA), he saw it as a vehicle through which the disparate balance of power between employers and employees could be corrected.

Section 1 of the NLRA justifies the act under the commerce clause of the Constitution. Section 1 states that unequal bargaining power between employees and employers leads to economic instability, and refusals of employers to bargain collectively lead to strikes. These disturbances impede the flow of interstate commerce. It is declared to be the policy of the United States, under the authority given to the federal government under the commerce clause, to ensure the free flow of commerce by encouraging collective bargaining and unionization.

PURPOSES OF THE NLRA The pervading purpose of the NLRA was to protect interstate commerce by securing for employees the rights established by Section 7 of the act: to organize, to bargain collectively through representatives of their own choosing, and to engage in concerted activities for that and other purposes. In Section 8, the act specifically defined a number of employer practices as unfair to labor:

1. Interference with the efforts of employees to form, join, or assist labor organizations or to engage in concerted activities for their mutual aid or protection [Section 8(a)(1)].

2. Domination of a labor organization or contribution of financial or other support to it [Section 8(a)(2)].
3. Discrimination in the hiring or awarding of tenure to employees because of union affiliation [Section 8(a)(3)].
4. Discrimination against employees for filing charges under the act or giving testimony under the act [Section 8(a)(4)].
5. Refusal to bargain collectively with the duly designated representative of the employees [Section 8(a)(5)].

THE CREATION OF THE NLRB Another purpose of the act was to promote fair and just settlements of disputes by peaceful processes and to avoid industrial warfare. The act created the National Labor Relations Board (NLRB) to oversee elections and to prevent employers from engaging in unfair and illegal union activities and unfair labor practices. The board was granted investigatory powers and was authorized to issue and serve complaints against employers in response to employee charges of unfair labor practices. The board was further empowered to issue cease-and-desist orders—which could be enforced by a federal court of appeals if necessary—when violations were found.

Application to Today's World

The NLRA was initially viewed by employers as a drastic piece of legislation, and the act elicited a great deal of opposition. Some even claimed that, by passing the act, Congress had exceeded its authority under the commerce clause. In 1937, however, in National Labor Relations Board v. Jones & Laughlin Steel Corp.,[a] *the United States Supreme Court held that the act and its application were constitutionally valid. Today, the NLRB continues to investigate employees' charges of unfair labor practices and to serve complaints against employers in response to these charges.*

---

a. 301 U.S. 1, 57 S.Ct. 615, 81 L.Ed. 893 (1937).

laws making it illegal for union membership to be required for *continued* employment in any establishment. Thus, union shops are technically illegal in states with right-to-work laws.

Labor-Management Reporting and Disclosure Act

The Labor-Management Reporting and Disclosure Act of 1959 (Landrum-Griffin Act)[7] established an employee bill of rights, as well as reporting requirements for union activities to prevent corruption. The Landrum-Griffin Act strictly regulated internal union business procedures.

Union elections, for example, are regulated by the Landrum-Griffin Act, which requires that regularly scheduled elections of officers occur and that secret ballots be used. Ex-convicts are prohibited from holding union office. Moreover, union officials are made accountable for union property and funds. Members have the right to attend and to participate in union meetings, to nominate officers, and to vote in most union proceedings.

Coverage and Procedures

Coverage of the federal labor laws is broad and extends to all employers whose business activity either involves or affects interstate commerce. Some workers are specifically excluded from these laws. Railroads and airlines are not covered by the NLRA but are covered by a separate act, the Railway Labor Act, which closely parallels the NLRA. Other types of employees, such as agricultural workers and domestic servants, are excluded from the NLRA and have no coverage under separate legislation.

When a union or employee believes that the employer has violated federal labor law (or vice versa), the union or employee files a charge with a regional office of the NLRB. The form for an employee to use to file an unfair labor practice charge against an employer is shown in Exhibit 18–1 on the next page. The charge is investigated, and if it is found worthy, the regional director files a complaint. An administrative law judge (ALJ) initially hears the complaint and rules on it (see Chapter 6). The board reviews the ALJ's findings and decision. If the NLRB finds a violation, it may issue remedial orders (including requiring rehiring of discharged workers). The NLRB decision may be appealed to a U.S. court of appeals.

THE DECISION TO FORM OR SELECT A UNION

The key starting point for labor relations law is the decision by a company's employees to form a union, which is usually referred to in the law as their bargaining representative. Most workplaces have no union, and workers bargain individually with the employer. If the workers decide that they want the added power of collective union representation, they must follow certain steps to have a union certified. Usually, the employer will fight these efforts to unionize.

---

7. 29 U.S.C. Sections 153, 1111.

EXHIBIT 18–1 UNFAIR LABOR PRACTICE COMPLAINT FORM

FORM EXEMPT UNDER 44 U.S.C. 3512

FORM NLRB-501 (11-94)	UNITED STATES OF AMERICA NATIONAL LABOR RELATIONS BOARD **CHARGE AGAINST EMPLOYER**	**DO NOT WRITE IN THIS SPACE**	
		Case	Date Filed

INSTRUCTIONS: File an original and 4 copies of this charge with NLRB Regional Director for the region in which the alleged unfair labor practice occurred or is occurring.

1. EMPLOYER AGAINST WHOM CHARGE IS BROUGHT

a. Name of Employer	b. Number of workers employed

c. Address *(street, city, state, ZIP code)*	d. Employer Representative	e. Telephone No.
		Fax No.

f. Type of Establishment *(factory, mine, wholesaler, etc.)*	g. Identify Principal Product or Service

h. The above-named employer has engaged in and is engaging in unfair labor practices within the meaning of section 8(a), subsections (1) and *(list subsections)* _____ of the National Labor Relations Act. and these unfair labor practices are unfair practices affecting commerce within the meaning of the Act.

2. Basis of the Charge *(set forth a clear and concise statement of the facts constituting the alleged unfair labor practices)*

By the above and other acts, the above-named employer has interfered with, restrained, and coerced employees in the exercise of the rights guaranteed in Section 7 of the Act

3. Full name of party filing charge *(if labor organization, give full name, including local name and number)*

4a. Address *(street and number, city, state, and ZIP code)*	4b. Telephone No.
	Fax No.

5. Full name of national or international labor organization of which it is an affiliate or constituent unit *(to be filled in when charge is filed by a labor organization)*

6. DECLARATION

I declare that I have read the above charge and that the statements are true to the best of my knowledge and belief.

By _____   _____
     (signature of representative or person making charge)   *(Title, if any)*

Address _____   _____   _____
                                                                                            (Telephone No.)   *(Date)*

WILLFUL FALSE STATEMENTS ON THIS CHARGE CAN BE PUNISHED BY FINE AND IMPRISONMENT (U.S. CODE, TITLE 18, SECTION 1001)

Preliminary Organizing

Suppose that a national union, such as the Communications Workers of America (CWA), wants to organize workers who produce semiconductor chips. The union would visit the manufacturing plant of a company—SemiCo in this example. If some SemiCo workers are interested in joining the union, they must begin organizing. An essential part of the process is to decide exactly which workers will be covered in the planned union. Will all manufacturing workers be covered or just those engaged in a single step in the manufacturing process?

The first step in forming a union is to get the relevant workers to sign **authorization cards.** These cards usually state that the worker desires to have a certain union, such as the CWA, represent the work force. If those in favor of the union can obtain authorization cards from a majority of workers, they may present the cards to the employer and ask the employer, SemiCo, to recognize the union formally. SemiCo is not required to do so, however.

More frequently, authorization cards are obtained to justify an election among workers for unionization. If SemiCo refuses to recognize the union based on authorization cards, an election is necessary to determine whether unionization has majority support among the workers. After the unionizers obtain authorization cards from at least 30 percent of the workers to be represented, the unionizers present these cards to the NLRB regional office with a petition for an election.

This 30 percent support is generally considered a sufficient showing of interest to justify an election on union representation. Union backers are not required to employ authorization cards but generally must have some evidence that at least 30 percent of the relevant work force supports a union or an election on unionization.

AUTHORIZATION CARD
A card signed by an employee that gives a union permission to act on his or her behalf in negotiations with management once a majority of the employees has signed such cards.

Appropriate Bargaining Unit

The NLRB considers the employees' petition as a basis for calling an election. In addition to a sufficient showing of interest in unionization, the proposed union must represent an **appropriate bargaining unit.**

Not every group of workers can form together into a single union. One key requirement of an appropriate bargaining unit is a *mutuality of interest* among all the workers to be represented. Groups of workers with significantly conflicting interests may not be represented in a single union.

Job Similarity One factor in determining the mutuality of interest is the *similarity of the jobs* of all the workers to be unionized. The NLRB considers factors such as similar levels of skill and qualifications, similar levels of wages and benefits, and similar working conditions. If represented workers have vastly different working conditions, they are unlikely to have the mutuality of interest necessary to bargain as a single unit with their employer.

One issue of job similarity has involved companies that employ both general industrial workers and craft workers (those with specialized skills, such as electricians). On many occasions, the NLRB has found that industrial and craft workers should be represented by different unions, although this is not an absolute rule.

Work Site Proximity A second important factor in determining the appropriate bargaining unit is *geographical.* If workers at only a single manufacturing

APPROPRIATE BARGAINING UNIT
A designation based on job duties, skill levels, and so on, of the proper entity that should be covered by a collective bargaining agreement.

plant are to be unionized, the geographical factor is not a problem. Even if the workers desire to join a national union, such as the CWA, they can join together in a single "local" division of that union. Geographical disparity may become a problem if a union is attempting to join workers at many different manufacturing sites together into a single union.

Nonmanagement Employees A third factor to be considered is the rule against unionization of *management* employees. The labor laws differentiate between labor and management and preclude members of management from being part of a union. There is no clear-cut definition of management, but supervisors are considered management and may not be included in worker unions. A supervisor is an individual who has the discretionary authority, as a representative of the employer, to make decisions such as hiring, suspending, promoting, firing, or disciplining other workers.[8] Professional employees, including legal and medical personnel, may be considered labor rather than management.

Moving toward Certification

A union, then, becomes certified through a procedure that begins with petitioning the NLRB. The proposed union must present authorization cards or other evidence showing an employee interest level of at least 30 percent. The organization must also show that the proposed union represents an appropriate bargaining unit. If the workers are under the NLRA's jurisdiction and if no other union has been certified within the past twelve months for these workers, the NLRB will schedule an election.

UNION ELECTION

Labor law provides for an election to determine whether employees choose to be represented by a union and, if so, which union. The NLRB supervises this election, ensuring secret voting and voter eligibility. The election is usually held about a month after the NLRB orders the vote (although it may be much longer, if management disputes the composition of an appropriate bargaining unit). If the election is a fair one, and if the proposed union receives majority support, the board certifies the union as the bargaining representative. Otherwise, the board will not certify the union.

Sometimes, a plant with an existing union may attempt to *decertify* the union (de-unionize). Although this action may be encouraged by management, it must be conducted by the employees. This action also requires a petition to the NLRB, with a showing of 30 percent employee support and no certification within the past year. The NLRB may grant this petition and call for a decertification election.

Union Election Campaign

Union organizers may campaign among workers to solicit votes for unionization. Considerable litigation has arisen over the rights of workers and outside union supporters to conduct such campaigns.

---

8. *Waldau v. Merit Systems Protection Board,* 19 F.3d 1395 (Fed.Cir. 1994).

The Employer's Right to Limit Campaign Activities The employer retains great control over any activities, including unionization campaigns, that take place on company property and on company time. Employers may lawfully use this authority to limit the campaign activities of union supporters. • EXAMPLE 1 Management may prohibit all solicitations and distribution of pamphlets on company property as long as it has a legitimate business reason for doing so (such as to ensure safety or to prevent interference with business). The employer may also reasonably limit the places where solicitation occurs (for example, limit it to the lunchroom), limit the times during which solicitation can take place, and prohibit all outsiders from access to the workplace. All these actions are lawful. •

Suppose that a union seeks to organize clerks at a department store. Courts have reasoned that an employer can prohibit all solicitation in areas of the store open to the public. Union campaign activities in these circumstances could seriously interfere with the store's business.

Restrictions on Management There are some legal restrictions on management regulation of union solicitation. The key restriction is the *nondiscrimination* rule. An employer may prohibit all solicitation during work time or in certain places but may not selectively prohibit union solicitation during work hours. If the employer permits political candidates to campaign on the employer's premises, for example, it also must permit union solicitation.[9] Additionally, companies cannot prevent union-related solicitation in work areas as long as the activity is conducted outside working hours—during lunch hours or coffee breaks, for example.

ETHICAL ISSUE

Is an employer's e-mail system a "work area"?

An emerging issue has to do with whether employers, if they allow employees to use company-owned e-mail systems for nonbusiness purposes, must permit employees to use e-mail to exchange messages related to unionization or union activities. In the few cases involving this issue, the NLRB has ruled that, in these circumstances, employees can use e-mail for communicating union-related messages. Suppose, however, that a company's policy prohibits employees from using e-mail for nonbusiness purposes. Given that employees are permitted to engage in union-related solicitation in work areas as long as they are on a break from work, should they also be able to use their employer's e-mail system while on a break? Is an e-mail system a "work area"? To date, the NLRB has not ruled on this question, which clearly involves issues of fairness—for both employers and employees. Even if the NLRB were to decide that an employer's e-mail system is a work area, questions would remain. For example, what if an employee sends a union-related e-mail message while on a break but the employee receiving it, without knowing its contents, opens it during working hours? Can anything be done to prevent this kind of situation from occurring?

---

9. *Nonemployee* union organizers do not have the right to trespass on an employer's property to organize employees, however. See *Lechmere, Inc. v. NLRB,* 502 U.S. 527, 112 S.Ct. 841, 117 L.Ed.2d 79 (1992).

Workers' Rights and Obligations Workers have a right to some reasonable opportunity to campaign. ● EXAMPLE 2 The United States Supreme Court held that employees have a right to distribute a pro-union newsletter in nonworking areas on the employer's property during nonworking time. In this case, management had the burden of showing some material harm from this action and could not do so.[10]●

Like an employer, a union and its supporters may not engage in unfair labor practices during a union election campaign. In the following case, the court considered the impact of a union proponent's allegedly unfair labor practice on the outcome of an election.

---

10. *Eastex, Inc. v. NLRB,* 437 U.S. 556, 98 S.Ct. 2505, 57 L.Ed.2d 428 (1978).

CASE 18.2   Associated Rubber Co. v. National Labor Relations Board

United States Court of Appeals,
Eleventh Circuit, 2002.
296 F.3d 1055.
http://www.law.emory.edu/11circuit[a]

BACKGROUND AND FACTS
Associated Rubber Company owns three rubber-production plants in Tallapoosa, Georgia. In June 1999, the United Steelworkers of America, AFL-CIO-CLC, filed a petition with the National Labor Relations Board (NLRB), seeking an election to obtain certification as the collective bargaining representative of maintenance workers, truck drivers, and mechanics employed at Associated Rubber's plants. During the election campaign, Leroy Brown, an Associated Rubber employee and a union supporter, threatened Tim Spears, an employee and a union opponent. Three days before

the election, Brown speeded up the rate at which heavy, scalding batches of rubber compound were mixed and sent to Spears. Barely able to handle the speed, Spears told his foreman that if the union won the election, he would quit his job out of fear the incident would be repeated. Other employees were aware of Brown's threat and the "Banbury incident" (Banbury was the brand name of the compound mixer). The union won the election by a vote of 53 to 50. Associated Rubber filed an objection on the basis of Brown's conduct. The NLRB concluded that the election was not tainted, certified the union, and ordered Associated Rubber to bargain. Associated Rubber appealed the order to the U.S. Court of Appeals for the Eleventh Circuit.

**IN THE WORDS
OF THE COURT . . .**

CARNES, Circuit Judge:
        *   *   *   *

When the union itself engages in objectionable misconduct, the Board will overturn the election if the conduct interfered with the employees' exercise of free choice to such an extent that it materially affected the results of the election. If, however, a third party engages in misconduct, the party objecting to the election has the burden of showing that the misconduct was so aggravated as to create a general atmosphere of fear and reprisal rendering a free election impossible. * * * [Emphasis added.]
        *   *   *   *

Applying these legal standards to the record in this case convinces us that the Board's conclusion that the Banbury mixer incident did not warrant overturning the election should itself be overturned. To begin with, the record shows that Brown accelerated the mixer in retaliation for Spears' refusal to accept union literature. Brown threatened to make Spears "pay" for refusing

---

a. In the "Listing by Month of Decision" section, in the "2002" row, click on "July." In the result, click on the name of the case to access the opinion. Emory University School of Law in Atlanta, Georgia, maintains this Web site.

CASE 18.2—Continued

to accept union literature, and he did so. Seven or eight days after the threat, and as the election drew near, Brown accelerated the Banbury mixer during Spears' shift as mill operator, causing the hot 450-pound batches of rubber compound to drop at a faster rate, a rate that made things more difficult and more dangerous than would have been the case but for Brown's malicious behavior. * * *

* * * *

* * * No employee ought to be subjected to any increased danger because of his position in a union certification election, and an increased risk of injury can itself be enough to have a chilling effect on the employees' right to freely decide whether they wish to be represented by a union.

* * * *

Importantly, the incident occurred only three days before the election took place. That fact makes the incident worse and increases the impact it had on the election. * * *

* * * *

In sum, the fact that Spears was threatened and then retaliated against in a way that placed him in personal danger would reasonably create fear in the minds of employees who were voting in the certification election. Although there apparently is no evidence that Spears' own vote was affected, at least seven people, including Spears, knew of the incident and connected it to Brown's earlier threat, and the election results turned on two votes.

DECISION AND REMEDY The U.S. Court of Appeals for the Eleventh Circuit set aside the NLRB's order. The court held that given the seriousness of the incident, the degree to which news of it was disseminated before the election, its proximity to the election, and the closeness of the vote, the NLRB should have ordered a new election.

FOR CRITICAL ANALYSIS—Social Consideration *If Brown's conduct in the "Banbury incident" had been motivated by something other than his support for the union and Spears's refusal to accept union literature, would the result in this case have been different?*

Management Election Campaign

Management may also campaign among its workers against the union (or for decertification of an existing union). Campaign tactics, however, are carefully monitored and regulated by the NLRB. Otherwise, the economic power of management might allow coercion of the workers.

Management still has many advantages in the campaign. For example, management is allowed to call all workers together during work time and make a speech against unionization. Management need not give the union supporters an equal opportunity for rebuttal. The NLRB does restrict what management may say in such a speech, however.

No Threats In campaigning against the union, the employer may not make threats of reprisals if employees vote to unionize. ● **EXAMPLE 3** A supervisor may not state, "If the union wins, you'll all be fired." This would be a threat. Even if an employer says, "Our competitor's plant in town unionized, and half the workers lost their jobs," the NLRB might consider this to be a veiled threat and therefore unfair. ●

"Laboratory Conditions" Obviously, union election campaigns are not like national political campaigns, in which a political party can make almost any claim. The NLRB tries to maintain "laboratory conditions" for a fair election that is unaffected by pressure. In establishing such conditions, the board considers the totality of circumstances in the campaign. The NLRB is especially strict about promises (or threats) made by the employer at the last minute, immediately before the election, because the union lacks an opportunity to respond effectively to these last-minute statements.

There is even a specific rule that prohibits an employer from making any election speech on company time, to massed assemblies of workers, within twenty-four hours of the time for voting. Such last-minute speeches are permitted only if employees attend voluntarily and on their own time.[11]

The employer is also prohibited from taking actions that might intimidate its workers. Employers may not undertake certain types of surveillance of workers or even create the impression of observing workers to identify union sympathizers. Management also is limited in its ability to question individual workers about their positions on unionization. These actions are deemed to contain implicit threats.

NLRB Options If the employer issues threats or engages in other unfair labor practices and then wins the election, the NLRB may invalidate the results. The NLRB may certify the union, even though it lost the election, and direct the employer to recognize the union as the employees' exclusive bargaining representative. Alternatively, the NLRB may ask a court to order a new election.

COLLECTIVE BARGAINING

COLLECTIVE BARGAINING
The process by which labor and management negotiate the terms and conditions of employment, including working hours and workplace conditions.

If a fair election is held and the union wins, the NLRB will certify the union as the *exclusive bargaining representative* of the workers polled. Unions may provide a variety of services to their members, but the central legal right of a union is to serve as the sole representative of the group of workers in bargaining with the employer over the workers' rights.

The concept of bargaining is at the heart of the federal labor laws. When a union is officially recognized, it may make a demand to bargain with the employer. The union then sits at the table opposite the representatives of management to negotiate contracts for its workers. The terms of employment that result from the negotiations apply to all workers in the bargaining unit, even those who do not choose to belong to the union. This process is known as **collective bargaining.** Such bargaining is like most other business negotiations, and each side uses its economic power to pressure or persuade the other side to grant concessions.

Bargaining is a somewhat vague term. Bargaining does not mean that either side must give in to demands or even that the sides must always compromise. It does mean that a demand must be taken seriously and considered as part of a package to be negotiated. Most important, both sides must bargain in "good faith."

---

11. Political party–like electioneering on behalf of a union, on the day of a union election, however, has been held acceptable and does not invalidate the election. See *Overnite Transportation Co. v. NLRB,* 104 F.3d 109 (7th Cir. 1997).

INTERNATIONAL PERSPECTIVE

Union Rights in Great Britain

A British union that has been recognized by an employer for collective bargaining purposes has certain rights. These rights include the right to receive information related to collective bargaining issues, the right to time off, the right to appoint a representative to handle safety matters, and the right to be consulted before an employer relocates its place of business.

FOR CRITICAL ANALYSIS

Do you think employees have rights that should apply in all countries around the world under all circumstances?

Subjects of Bargaining

A common issue in collective bargaining concerns the subjects over which the parties can bargain. The law makes certain subjects mandatory for collective bargaining. These topics cannot be "taken off the table" unilaterally but must be discussed and bargained over.

Terms and Conditions of Employment The NLRA provides that employers may bargain with workers over wages, hours of work, and other terms and conditions of employment. These are broad terms that cover many employment issues. Suppose that a union wants a contract provision granting all workers four weeks of paid vacation. The company need not give in to this demand but must at least consider it and bargain over it.

Many other employment issues are also considered appropriate subjects for collective bargaining. These include safety rules, insurance coverage, pension and other employee benefit plans, procedures for employee discipline, procedures for employee grievances against the company, and even the price of food sold in the company cafeteria.

A few subjects are illegal in collective bargaining. Management need not bargain over a provision that would be illegal if included in a contract. Thus, if a union presents a demand for **featherbedding** (the hiring of unnecessary excess workers) or for an unlawful closed shop, management need not respond to these demands.

Closing or Relocating a Plant Management need not bargain with a union over the decision to close a particular facility. Similarly, management need not bargain over a decision to relocate a plant if the move involves a basic change in the nature of the employer's operation.[12] Management may, however, choose to bargain over such decisions to obtain concessions on other bargaining subjects.

Management must bargain over the economic consequences of such decisions, though. Thus, issues such as **severance pay** (compensation for the

"I see an America where the workers are really free and through their great unions . . . can take their proper place in the council tables with the owners and managers of business."

FRANKLIN D. ROOSEVELT,
1882–1945
(Thirty-second president
of the United States, 1932–1945)

FEATHERBEDDING
A requirement that more workers be employed to do a particular job than are actually needed.

SEVERANCE PAY
Funds in excess of normal wages or salaries paid to an employee on termination of his or her employment with a company.

---

12. *Dubuque Packing Co.,* 303 N.L.R.B. No. 386 (1991).

termination of employment) in the event of a plant shutdown are appropriate for collective bargaining. Also, if a relocation does *not* involve a basic change in the nature of an operation, management must bargain over the decision unless it can show (1) that the work performed at the new location varies significantly from the work performed at the former plant; (2) that the work performed at the former plant is to be discontinued entirely and not moved to the new location; (3) that the move involves a change in the scope and direction of the enterprise; (4) that labor costs were not a factor in the decision; or (5) that even if labor costs were a factor, the union could not have offered concessions that would have changed the decision to relocate.

Privacy Issues Employee privacy rights were discussed in Chapter 16. Are these rights, and their potential or real violations, appropriate subjects for collective bargaining? The NLRB has determined that physical examinations, requirements for drug or alcohol testing, and polygraph (lie-detector) testing are mandatory subjects of bargaining. The question in the following case was whether the use of hidden surveillance cameras could also be bargained over.

CASE 18.3   National Steel Corp. v. NLRB

United States Court of Appeals, Seventh Circuit, 2003.
324 F.3d 928.
http://laws.findlaw.com/7th/952521.html[a]

BACKGROUND AND FACTS
National Steel Corporation operates a plant in Granite City, Illinois, where it employs approximately three thousand employees, who are represented by ten different unions and covered by seven different collective bargaining agreements. National Steel uses over one hundred video cameras in plain view to monitor areas of the plant and periodically employs hidden cameras to investigate suspected misconduct. In February 1999,

National Steel installed a hidden camera to discover who was using a manager's office when the manager was not at work. The camera revealed a union member using the office to make long-distance phone calls. When National Steel discharged the employee, the union asked the company about other hidden cameras and indicated that it wanted to bargain over their use. National Steel refused to supply the information. The union filed a charge with the NLRB, which ordered National Steel to provide the information and bargain over the use of the cameras. National Steel appealed to the U.S. Court of Appeals for the Seventh Circuit.

IN THE WORDS OF THE COURT . . .

WILLIAMS, Circuit Judge.
* * * *
The [National Labor Relations] Board determined * * * that the use of hidden surveillance cameras is a mandatory subject of collective bargaining because it found the installation and use of such cameras "analogous to physical examinations, drug/alcohol testing requirements, and polygraph testing, all of which the Board has found to be mandatory subjects of bargaining." It found that hidden cameras are focused primarily on the "working environment" that employees experience on a daily basis and are used to expose misconduct or violations of the law by employees or others. The Board held that such changes in an employer's methods have "serious implications for its employees' job security." The Board found that the use of such devices "is not entrepreneurial in character [and] is not fundamental to the basic direction of the enterprise." We

---
a. This is a page within the Web site maintained by FindLaw (now a part of West Group).

CASE 18.3—Continued

find the Board's legal conclusion * * * objectively reasonable and wholly supported. * * *

* * * According to National Steel, requiring it to bargain over hidden surveillance cameras, especially as to their locations precludes an employer from meaningfully using such devices because bargaining itself will compromise the secrecy that is required for them to be effective. * * *

* * * [T]he Board acknowledged an employer's need for secrecy if hidden surveillance cameras are to serve a purpose. The Board's order to National Steel preserves those managerial interests while also honoring the union's collective bargaining rights. It only requires National Steel to negotiate with the unions over the company's installation and use of hidden surveillance cameras and * * * does not dictate how the legitimate interests of the parties are to be accommodated in the process. The Board's order does not mandate an outcome of negotiations, nor does it make any suggestion that National Steel must yield any prerogatives, other than yielding the right to proceed exclusive of consultation with the union. * * * *Here, the Board's order is consistent with the [National Labor Relations] Act's requirement that parties resolve their differences through good-faith bargaining;* it simply directs National Steel to initiate an accommodation process, and to provide assertedly confidential information in accord with whatever accommodation the parties agree upon (such as a confidentiality agreement * * *). The Board's order does not eliminate National Steel's management right to use hidden cameras and it seeks to preserve the level of confidentiality necessary to allow for the continued effective use of such devices. [Emphasis added.]

DECISION AND REMEDY The U.S. Court of Appeals for the Seventh Circuit upheld the NLRB's order to National Steel to bargain over the use of hidden surveillance cameras in the workplace. The court emphasized that this order did not prohibit their use, but only made that use a subject of collective bargaining.

FOR CRITICAL ANALYSIS—Social Consideration *Can an employer's interests ever justify the use of hidden video cameras in the workplace?*

Good Faith Bargaining

Parties engaged in collective bargaining often claim that the other side is not bargaining in good faith, as required by labor law. Although good faith is a matter of subjective intent, a party's actions are used to evaluate the finding of good or bad faith in bargaining. Obviously, the employer must be willing to meet with union representatives. Excessive delaying tactics may be proof of bad faith, as is insistence on obviously unreasonable contract terms. Suppose that a company makes a single overall contract offer on a "take-it-or-leave-it" basis and refuses to consider modifications of individual terms. This also is considered bad faith in bargaining.

While bargaining is going on, management may not make unilateral changes in important working conditions, such as wages or hours of employment. These changes must be bargained over. Once bargaining reaches an impasse, management may make such unilateral changes. The law also includes an exception permitting unilateral changes in cases of business necessity. A series of decisions have found other actions to constitute bad faith in bargaining, including the following:

- Engaging in a campaign among workers to undermine the union.
- Constantly shifting positions on disputed contract terms.
- Sending bargainers who lack authority to commit the company to a contract.

If an employer (or a union) refuses to bargain in good faith without justification, it has committed an unfair labor practice, and the other party may petition the NLRB for an order requiring good faith bargaining. Except in extreme cases, the NLRB does not have authority to require a party to accede to any specific contract terms. The NLRB may require a party to reimburse the other side for its litigation expenses.

STRIKES

When extensive collective bargaining has been conducted and the parties still cannot agree, an impasse has been reached. The union may call a strike against the employer to pressure it into making concessions. A *strike* occurs when the unionized workers leave their jobs and refuse to work. The workers also typically picket the plant, standing outside the facility with signs that complain of management's unfairness.

A strike is an extreme action. Striking workers lose their right to be paid. Management loses production and may lose customers, whose orders cannot be filled. Labor law regulates the circumstances and conduct of strikes. Most strikes are "economic strikes," which are initiated because the union wants a better contract. A union may also strike when the employer has engaged in unfair labor practices.

The right to strike is guaranteed by the NLRA, within limits, and strike activities, such as picketing, are protected by the free speech guarantee of the First Amendment to the Constitution. Nonworkers have a right to participate in picketing an employer. The NLRA also gives workers the right to refuse to cross a picket line of fellow workers who are engaged in a lawful strike. Not all strikes are lawful, however.

Illegal Strikes

An otherwise lawful strike may become illegal because of the conduct of the strikers. Violent strikes (including the threat of violence) are illegal. The use of violence against management employees or substitute workers is illegal. Certain forms of "massed picketing" are also illegal. If the strikers form a barrier and deny management or other nonunion workers access to the plant, the strike is illegal. Similarly, "sit-down" strikes, in which employees simply stay in the plant without working, are illegal.

SECONDARY BOYCOTT
A union's refusal to work for, purchase from, or handle the products of a secondary employer, with whom the union has no dispute, for the purpose of forcing that employer to stop doing business with the primary employer, with whom the union has a labor dispute.

Secondary Boycotts A strike directed against someone other than the strikers' employer, such as the companies that sell materials to the employer, is a **secondary boycott.** Suppose that the unionized workers of SemiCo (our hypothetical semiconductor company) go out on strike. To increase their economic leverage, the workers picket the leading suppliers and customers of SemiCo in an attempt to hurt the company's business. SemiCo is considered the primary

Striking workers picket to publicize their labor dispute. Why is the right to strike important to unions?

employer, and its suppliers and customers are considered secondary employers. Picketing of the suppliers or customers is a secondary boycott, which was made illegal by the Taft-Hartley Act.

Common Situs Picketing. A controversy may arise in a strike when both the primary employer and a secondary employer occupy the same job site. In this case, it may be difficult to distinguish between lawful picketing of the primary employer and an unlawful strike against a secondary employer. The law permits a union to picket a site occupied by both primary and secondary employers, an act called **common situs picketing.** If evidence indicates that the strike is directed against the secondary employer, however, it may become illegal. • EXAMPLE 4 If a union sends a threatening letter to the secondary employer about the strike, that fact may show that the picketing includes an illegal secondary boycott.•

COMMON SITUS PICKETING
The illegal picketing of a primary employer's site by workers who are involved in a labor dispute with a secondary employer.

Hot-Cargo Agreements. In what is called a **hot-cargo agreement,** employers voluntarily agree with unions not to handle, use, or deal in goods produced by nonunion employees of other firms. This particular type of secondary boycott was *not* made illegal by the Taft-Hartley Act, because that act only prevented unions from inducing *employees* to strike or otherwise act to force employers not to handle these goods. The Landrum-Griffin Act addressed this problem:

HOT-CARGO AGREEMENT
An agreement in which employers voluntarily agree with unions not to handle, use, or deal in goods produced by nonunion employees of other firms; a type of secondary boycott explicitly prohibited by the Labor-Management Reporting and Disclosure Act of 1959.

> It shall be [an] unfair labor practice for any labor organization and any employer to enter into any contract or any agreement . . . whereby such employer . . . agrees to refrain from handling, using, selling, transporting or otherwise dealing in any of the products of any other employer, or to cease doing business with any other person.

Hot-cargo agreements are therefore illegal. Parties injured by an illegal hot-cargo agreement or other secondary boycott may sue the union for damages.

A union may legally urge consumer boycotts of the primary employer, even at the site of a secondary employer. • **EXAMPLE 5** Suppose that a union is on strike against SemiCo, which manufactures semiconductors that are bought by Intellect, Inc., a distributor of electronic components. Intellect sells SemiCo's semiconductors to computer manufacturers. The striking workers can urge the manufacturers not to buy SemiCo's products. The workers cannot urge a total boycott of Intellect, as that would constitute a secondary boycott.•

Wildcat Strikes   A **wildcat strike** occurs when a group of workers, perhaps dissatisfied with a union's representation, calls its own strike. The union is the exclusive bargaining representative of a group of workers, and only the union can call a strike. A wildcat strike, unauthorized by the certified union, is illegal.

   • **EXAMPLE 6** In one case, several concrete workers left their jobs because it was raining and went on "strike." The court found the strike illegal because it was not preceded by a demand on the employer for action and because the employer had made shelter available for the workers and paid them for waiting time.•

WILDCAT STRIKE
A strike that is not authorized by the union that ordinarily represents the striking employees.

Strikes That Threaten National Health or Safety   The law also places some restrictions on strikes that threaten national health or safety. The law does not prohibit such strikes, nor does it require the settlement of labor disputes that threaten the national welfare. The Taft-Hartley Act simply provides time to encourage the settlement of these disputes, called the "cooling-off period."

   One of the most controversial aspects of the Taft-Hartley Act was the establishment of this **eighty-day cooling-off period**—a provision allowing federal courts to issue injunctions against strikes that would create a national emergency. The president of the United States can obtain a court injunction that will last for eighty days, and presidents have occasionally used this provision. During these eighty days, the president and other government officials can work with the employer and the union to produce a settlement and avoid a strike that may cause a national emergency.

EIGHTY-DAY COOLING-OFF PERIOD
A provision of the Taft-Hartley Act that allows federal courts to issue injunctions against strikes that might create a national emergency.

Strikes That Contravene No-Strike Clauses   A strike may also be illegal if it contravenes a **no-strike clause.** The previous collective bargaining agreement between a union and an employer may have contained a clause in which the union agreed not to strike (a no-strike clause). The law permits the employer to enforce this no-strike clause and obtain an injunction against the strike in some circumstances.

   The Supreme Court held that a no-strike clause could be enforced with an injunction if the contract contained a clause providing for arbitration of unresolved disputes.[13] The Court held that the arbitration clause was an effective substitute for the right to strike. In the absence of an applicable arbitration provision, however, an employer cannot enjoin (forbid) a strike, even if the contract contains a no-strike clause.

NO-STRIKE CLAUSE
Provision in a collective bargaining agreement that states that the employees will not strike for any reason and labor disputes will be resolved by arbitration.

Replacement Workers

Suppose that SemiCo's workers go out on strike. SemiCo is not required to shut down its operations but may find substitute workers to replace the strikers, if possible. These substitute workers are often called "scabs" by union

---

13. *Boys Markets, Inc. v. Retail Clerks Local 770*, 398 U.S. 235, 90 S.Ct. 1583, 26 L.Ed.2d 199 (1970).

supporters. An employer may even give the replacement workers permanent positions with the company.

In the 1930s and 1940s, strikes were powerful in part because employers often had difficulty finding trained replacements to keep their businesses running during strikes. Since the illegal air traffic controller strike in 1981, when President Ronald Reagan successfully hired replacement workers, employers have increasingly used this strategy, with considerable success. ● EXAMPLE 7 Even the National Football League (NFL), when struck by the players in 1987, found replacements to play for the NFL teams. Although some scoffed at the ability of the replacement players, the tactic was largely successful for management, as the strike was called off after only three weeks.● An employer can even use an employment agency to recruit replacement workers.[14]

Rights of Strikers after the Strike

An important issue concerns the rights of strikers after the strike ends. In a typical economic strike over working conditions, the strikers have no right to return to their jobs. If satisfactory replacement workers have been found, the strikers may find themselves out of work. The law does prohibit the employer from discriminating against former strikers. Even if the employer fires all the strikers and retains all the replacement workers, former strikers must be rehired to fill any new vacancies. Former strikers who are rehired retain their seniority rights.

Different rules apply when a union strikes because the employer has engaged in unfair labor practices. If an employer is discriminating against a union's workers, they may go out on an unfair labor practice strike. Furthermore, an economic strike may become an unfair labor practice strike if the employer refuses to bargain in good faith. In the case of an unfair labor practice strike, the employer may still hire replacements but must give the strikers back their jobs once the strike is over. An employer may, however, refuse to rehire unfair labor practice strikers if the strike was deemed unlawful or if there is simply no longer any work for them to do.

LOCKOUTS

Lockouts are the employer's counterpart to the worker's right to strike. A **lockout** occurs when the employer shuts down to prevent employees from working. Lockouts are usually used when the employer believes that a strike is imminent.

Lockouts may be a legal employer response. ● EXAMPLE 8 In the leading Supreme Court case on this issue, a union and an employer had reached a stalemate in collective bargaining. The employer feared that the union would delay a strike until the busy season and thereby cause the employer to suffer more greatly from the strike. The employer called a lockout before the busy season to deny the union this leverage, and the Supreme Court held that this action was legal.[15]●

LOCKOUT
The closing of a plant to employees by an employer to gain leverage in collective bargaining negotiations.

---

14. *Professional Staff Nurses Association v. Dimensions Health Corp.*, 110 Md.App. 270, 677 A.2d 87 (1996).
15. *American Ship Building Co. v. NLRB*, 380 U.S. 300, 85 S.Ct. 955, 13 L.Ed.2d 855 (1965).

Some lockouts are illegal, however. An employer may not use its lockout weapon as a tool to break the union and pressure employees into decertification. Consequently, an employer must show some economic justification for instituting a lockout.

UNFAIR LABOR PRACTICES

The preceding sections have discussed unfair labor practices involved in the significant acts of union elections, collective bargaining, and strikes. Many unfair labor practices may occur within the normal working relationship as well. The most important of these practices are discussed below. Exhibit 18–2 lists the basic unfair labor practices.

Employer's Refusal to Recognize the Union and to Negotiate

As noted above, once a union has been certified as the exclusive representative of a bargaining unit, an employer must recognize and bargain in good faith with the union over issues affecting all employees who are within the bargaining unit. Failure to do so is an unfair labor practice. Because the National Labor Relations Act embraces a policy of majority rule, certification of the union as the bargaining unit's representative binds *all* of the employees in that bargaining unit. Thus, the union must fairly represent all the members of the bargaining unit.

Presumption of Employee Support Certification does not mean that a union will continue indefinitely as the exclusive representative of the bargaining unit. If the union loses the majority support of those it represents, an employer is not obligated to continue recognition of, or negotiation with, the union. As a practical matter, a newly elected representative needs time to establish itself among the workers and to begin to formulate and implement its programs. Therefore, as a matter of labor policy, a union is immune from attack by employers and from repudiation by the employees for a period of one year after certification. During this period, it is *presumed* that the union enjoys

EXHIBIT 18–2   BASIC UNFAIR LABOR PRACTICES

Employers *It is unfair to . . .*	Unions *It is unfair to . . .*
1. Refuse to recognize a union and refuse to bargain in good faith.	1. Refuse to bargain in good faith.
2. Interfere with, restrain, or coerce employees in their efforts to form a union and bargain collectively.	2. Picket to coerce unionization without the support of a majority of the employees.
3. Dominate a union.	3. Demand the hiring of unnecessary excess workers.
4. Discriminate against union workers.	4. Discriminate against nonunion workers.
5. Agree to participate in a secondary boycott.	5. Agree to participate in a secondary boycott.
6. Punish employees for engaging in concerted activity.	6. Engage in an illegal strike.
	7. Charge excessive membership fees.

majority support among the employees; the employer cannot refuse to deal with the union as the employees' exclusive representative, even if the employees prefer not to be represented by that union.

Beyond the one-year period, the presumption of majority support continues, but it is *rebuttable*. An employer may rebut (attempt to refute) the presumption with objective evidence that a majority of employees do not wish to be represented by the union. If the evidence is sufficient to support a *good faith belief* that the union no longer enjoys majority support among the employees, the employer may refuse to continue to recognize and negotiate with the union.[16]

Questions of Majority Support A delicate question arises during a strike in which an employer hires replacement workers. Specifically, should it be *assumed* that the replacement workers do not support the union? If they do not, and if as a result the union no longer has majority support, the employer need not continue negotiating with the union.

Another question arises when two companies merge or consolidate, when one company buys the assets or stock of another, or when, under any other circumstances, one employer steps into the shoes of another. Is a collective bargaining agreement between a union and a predecessor employer binding on the union and the successor employer? This was the issue in the following case.

---

16. An employer cannot agree to a collective bargaining agreement and later refuse to abide by it, however, on the ground of a good faith belief that the union did not have majority support when the agreement was negotiated. See *Auciello Iron Works, Inc. v. NLRB,* 517 U.S. 781, 116 S.Ct. 1754, 135 L.Ed.2d 64 (1996).

CASE 18.4 Canteen Corp. v. NLRB

United States Court of Appeals,
Seventh Circuit, 1997.
103 F.3d 1355.
http://www.ca7.uscourts.gov[a]

BACKGROUND AND FACTS The food service employees at the Medical College of Wisconsin were represented by the Hotel Employees and Restaurant Employees Union. When Canteen Corporation took over the food service, it agreed to negotiate a new contract with the union. Meanwhile, without informing the union, Canteen told the employ- ees that their wages would be cut 20 to 25 percent. The employees resigned. Canteen then recruited employees from other sources and refused to negotiate with the union on the ground that it no longer represented the employees. The union filed an unfair labor practice charge with the National Labor Relations Board (NLRB). The NLRB ordered Canteen to reinstate the employees at their previous wage rates until a new contract could be negotiated. Canteen asked the U.S. Court of Appeals for the Seventh Circuit to review the order.

IN THE WORDS
OF THE COURT . . .

RIPPLE, Circuit Judge.

*   *   *   *

*   *   * A new employer must consult with the union when it is clear that the employer intends to hire the employees of its predecessor as the initial workforce. *   *   *

*   *   *   *

---

a. This page provides access to some of the opinions of the U.S. Court of Appeals for the Seventh Circuit, which maintains this Web site. In the left column, click on "Judicial Opinions." When that page opens, in the box under "Last Name or Corporation," enter "Canteen," select "Begins," and click "Search for Person." From the results, click on docket number "95-2736" next to the case name to access the opinion.

(continued)

CASE 18.4—Continued

* * * The totality of Canteen's conduct demonstrated that it was perfectly clear that Canteen planned to retain the predecessor employees.
* * *

* * * Canteen's intention to retain the * * * employees was backed by an expectation so strong that it neglected to take serious steps to recruit from other sources until it was informed that they had rejected job offers.

* * * Canteen intended from the outset to hire all of the predecessor employees and did not mention in [its] discussions [with the union] the possibility of any other changes in its initial terms and conditions of employment.

DECISION AND REMEDY The U.S. Court of Appeals for the Seventh Circuit ordered that the NLRB's order be enforced. The employer was required to reinstate the employees at their previous wage rates until a new contract could be negotiated.

FOR CRITICAL ANALYSIS—Social Consideration *Why should an employer be forced to honor a collective bargaining agreement between a union and the employer's predecessor?*

Employer's Interference in Union Activities

The NLRA declares it to be an unfair labor practice for an employer to interfere with, restrain, or coerce employees in the exercise of their rights to form a union and bargain collectively. Unlawful employer interference may take a variety of forms.

Courts have found it an unfair labor practice for an employer to make threats that may interfere with an employee's decision to join a union. Even asking employees about their views on the union may be considered coercive. Employees responding to such questioning must be able to remain anonymous and must receive assurances against employer reprisals. Employers also may not prohibit certain forms of union activity in the workplace. If an employee has a grievance with the company, the employer cannot prevent the union's participation in support of the employee, for example.

If an employer has unlawfully interfered with the operation of a union, the NLRB or a reviewing court may issue a cease-and-desist order halting the practice. The company typically is required to post the order on a bulletin board and renounce its past unlawful conduct.

Employer's Domination of Union

In the early days of unionization, employers fought back by forming employer-sponsored unions to represent employees. These "company unions" were seldom more than the puppets of management. The NLRA outlawed company unions and any other form of employer domination of workers' unions.

A number of acts are considered unfair labor practices under the law against employer domination. For example, an employer can have no say in which employees belong to the union or which employees serve as union officers. Nor may supervisors or other management personnel participate in union meetings.

Company actions that support a union may be considered improper potential domination. For this reason, a company cannot give union workers pay for time spent on union activities, because this is considered undue support for the union. The company may not provide financial aid to a union and may not solicit workers to join a union.

Employer's Discrimination against Union Employees

The NLRA prohibits employers from discriminating against workers because they are union officers or are otherwise associated with a union. When workers must be laid off, the company cannot consider union participation as a criterion for deciding whom to fire.

The provisions prohibiting discrimination also apply to hiring decisions.
● EXAMPLE 9 Suppose that certain employees of SemiCo are represented by a union, but the company is attempting to weaken the union's strength. The company is prohibited from requiring potential new hires to guarantee that they will not join the union.●

Discriminatory punishment of union members or officers can be difficult to prove. The company will claim to have good reasons for its action. The NLRB has specified a series of factors to be considered in determining whether an action had an unlawful, discriminatory motivation. These include giving inconsistent reasons for the action, applying rules inconsistently and more strictly against union members, failing to give an expected warning prior to discharge or other discipline, and acting contrary to worker seniority.

The decision to close a facility cannot be made with a discriminatory motive. If a company has several facilities and only one is unionized, the company cannot shut down the union plant simply because of the union. The company could shut down the union plant if it were demonstrably less efficient than the other facilities, however.

Union's Unfair Labor Practices

Certain union activities are declared to be unfair labor practices by the Taft-Hartley Act. Secondary boycotts, discussed above, are one such union unfair labor practice.

Coercion Another significant union unfair labor practice is coercion or restraint on an employee's decision to participate in or refrain from participating in union activities. Obviously, it is unlawful for a union to threaten an employee or a family with violence for failure to join the union. The law's prohibition includes economic coercion as well. Suppose that a union official declares, "We have a lot of power here; you had better join the union, or you may lose your job." This threat is an unfair labor practice.

The NLRA provides unions with the authority to regulate their own internal affairs, which includes disciplining union members. This discipline cannot be used in an improperly coercive fashion, however. The union may expel an employee from membership but may not fine or otherwise discipline a worker.

Discrimination Another significant union unfair labor practice is discrimination. A union may not discriminate against workers because they refuse to join. This provision also prohibits a union from using its influence to cause an employer to discriminate against workers who refuse to join the union. A union cannot force an employer to deny promotions to workers who fail to join the union.

Other Unfair Practices Other union unfair labor practices include featherbedding (discussed earlier in this chapter), participation in picketing to coerce unionization without majority employee support, and refusal to engage in good faith bargaining with employer representatives.

Unions are allowed to bargain for certain "union security clauses" in contracts. Although closed shops are illegal, a union can bargain for a provision that requires workers to contribute to the union within thirty days after they are hired. This is typically called an *agency shop,* or *union shop, clause.*

The union shop clause can compel workers to begin paying dues to the certified union but cannot require the worker to "join" the union. Dues payment can be required to prevent workers from taking the benefits of union bargaining without contributing to the union's efforts. The clause cannot require workers to contribute their efforts to the union, however, or to go out on strike.

Even a requirement of dues payment has its limits. Excessive initiation fees or dues may be illegal. Unions often use their revenues to contribute to causes or to lobby politicians. A nonunion employee subject to a union shop clause who must pay dues cannot be required to contribute to this sort of union expenditure.

RIGHTS OF NONUNION EMPLOYEES

Most labor law involves the formation of unions and associated rights. Even nonunion employees have some similar rights, however. Most workers do not belong to unions, so this issue is significant. The NLRA protects concerted employee action, for example, and does not limit its protection to certified unions.

Concerted Activity

CONCERTED ACTION
Action by employees, such as a strike or picketing, with the purpose of furthering their bargaining demands or other mutual interests.

Data from the NLRB indicate that growing numbers of nonunion employees are challenging employer barriers to their **concerted action.** Protected concerted action is that taken by employees for their mutual benefit regarding wages, hours, or terms and conditions of employment.

Even an action by a single employee may be protected concerted activity, if that action is taken for the benefit of other employees and if the employee has at least discussed the action with other approving workers. If only a single worker engages in a protest or walkout, the employer will not be liable for an unfair labor practice if it fires the worker unless the employer is aware that this protest or walkout is concerted activity taken with the assent of other workers.

Safety

A common circumstance for nonunion activity is concern over workplace safety. The Labor-Management Relations Act authorizes an employee to walk off the job if he or she has a good faith belief that the working conditions are abnormally dangerous. The employer cannot lawfully discharge the employee under these conditions.

● EXAMPLE 10 Suppose that Knight Company operates a plant building mobile homes. A large ventilation fan at the plant blows dust and abrasive materials into the faces of workers. The workers have complained, but Knight Company has done nothing. The workers finally refuse to work until the fan is modified, and Knight fires them. The NLRB will find that the walkout is a protected activity and can command Knight to rehire the workers with back pay.●

To be protected under federal labor law, a safety walkout must be *concerted* activity. If a single worker walks out over a safety complaint, other workers must be affected by the safety issue for the walkout to be protected under the LMRA.

Employee Committees

Personnel specialists note that worker problems are often attributable to a lack of communication between labor and management. In a nonunion work force, a company may wish to create some institution to communicate with workers and act together with them to improve workplace conditions. This institution, generally called an **employee committee,** is composed of representatives from both management and labor. The committee meets periodically and has some authority to create rules. The committee gives employees a forum to voice their dissatisfaction with certain conditions and gives management a conduit to inform workers fully of policy decisions.

EMPLOYEE COMMITTEE
A committee created by an employer and composed of representatives of management and nonunion employees to act together to improve workplace conditions.

The creation of an employee committee may be entirely motivated by good intentions on the company's part and may serve the interests of workers as well as management. Nevertheless, employee committees are fraught with potential problems under federal labor laws, and management must be aware of these difficulties. The central problem with employee committees is that they may become the functional equivalent of unions dominated by management, in violation of the NLRA. Thus, these committees cannot perform union functions. ● EXAMPLE 11   The employee representatives on such a committee should not present a package of proposals on wages and terms of employment, because this is the role of a union negotiating committee.●

KEY TERMS

CHAPTER SUMMARY **LABOR-MANAGEMENT RELATIONS**

Federal Labor Law (See pages 577–581.)	1. *Norris-LaGuardia Act of 1932*—Extended legal protection to peaceful strikes, picketing, and boycotts. Restricted the power of the courts to issue injunctions against unions engaged in peaceful strikes.
	2. *National Labor Relations Act of 1935 (Wagner Act)*—Established the rights of employees to engage in collective bargaining and to strike. Created the National Labor Relations Board (NLRB) to oversee union elections and prevent employers from engaging in unfair labor practices (such as refusing to recognize and negotiate with a certified union or interfering in union activities).
	3. *Labor-Management Relations Act of 1947 (Taft-Hartley Act)*—Extended to employers protections already enjoyed by employees. Provided a list of activities prohibited to unions (secondary boycotts, use of coercion or discrimination to influence employees' decisions to participate or refrain from union activities) and allowed employers to propagandize against unions before any NLRB election. Prohibited closed shops (which require that all workers belong to a union as a condition of employment), allowed states to pass right-to-work laws, and provided for an eighty-day cooling-off period.
	4. *Labor-Management Reporting and Disclosure Act of 1959 (Landrum-Griffin Act)*— Regulated internal union business procedures and union elections. Imposed restrictions on the types of persons who may serve as union officers and outlawed hot-cargo agreements.
Union Organizing (See pages 581–588.)	1. *Authorization cards*—Before beginning an organizing effort, a union will attempt to assess worker support for unionization by obtaining signed authorization cards from the employees. It can then ask the employer to recognize the union, or it can submit the cards with a petition to the National Labor Relations Board.
	2. *Appropriate bargaining unit*—In determining whether workers constitute an appropriate bargaining unit, the NLRB will consider whether the skills, tasks, and jobs of the workers are sufficiently similar so that they can all be adequately served by a single negotiating position.
	3. *Union election campaign*—The NLRB is charged with monitoring union elections. During an election campaign, an employer may legally limit union activities as long as it can offer legitimate business justifications for those limitations. In regulating the union's presence on the business premises, the employer must treat the union in the same way it would treat any other entity having on-site contact with its workers. The NLRB is particularly sensitive to any threats in an employer's communications to workers, such as declarations that a union victory will result in the closing of the plant. The NLRB will also closely monitor sudden policy changes regarding compensation, hours, or working conditions that the employer makes before the election.
	4. *Union certification*—Certification by the NLRB means that the union is the exclusive representative of a bargaining unit and that the employer must recognize the union and bargain in good faith with it over issues affecting all employees who are within the bargaining unit.
Collective Bargaining (See pages 588–592.)	Once a union is elected, its representatives will engage in collective bargaining with the employer. Topics such as wages, hours of work, and other conditions of employment are discussed during collective bargaining sessions. Some demands, such as a demand for featherbedding or for a closed shop, are illegal. If the parties reach an impasse, the union may call a strike against the employer to bring additional economic pressure to bear. This is one way in which the union can offset management's superior bargaining power.

CHAPTER SUMMARY   LABOR-MANAGEMENT RELATIONS—Continued

Strikes and Lockouts (See pages 592–596.)	1. *Right to strike*—The right to strike is protected by the U.S. Constitution. During a strike, an employer is no longer obligated to pay union members, and union members are no longer required to show up for work. 2. *Secondary boycott*—Strikers are not permitted to engage in a secondary boycott by picketing the suppliers of an employer. Similarly, striking employees are not permitted to coerce the employer's customers into agreeing not to do business with it. 3. *Wildcat strike*—A wildcat strike occurs when a small group of union members engages in a strike against the employer without the permission of the union. 4. *Replacement workers*—An employer may hire permanent replacement employees in the event of an economic strike. If the strike is called by the union to protest the employer's unwillingness to engage in good faith negotiations, then the employer must rehire the striking workers after the strike is settled, even if it has since replaced them with other workers. 5. *Lockouts*—Employers may respond to threatened employee strikes by shutting down the plant altogether to prevent employees from working. Lockouts are used when the employer believes a strike is imminent.
Unfair Labor Practices (See pages 596–600.)	1. An employer's refusal to recognize or negotiate with the union, interference in union activities, domination of the union, and discrimination against union employees. 2. A union's coercive actions against employees, discrimination against nonunion members, featherbedding, and other practices.
Rights of Nonunion Employees (See pages 600–601.)	The National Labor Relations Act protects concerted action on the part of nonunion employees. Protected concerted action includes walkouts and other activities regarding wages, hours, workplace safety, or other terms or conditions of employment.

FOR REVIEW

1. What federal statutes govern labor unions and collective bargaining?
2. How does the way in which a union election is conducted protect the rights of employees and employers?
3. What type of strikes are illegal?
4. What activities are prohibited as unfair employer practices?
5. What are the rights of nonunion employees?

QUESTIONS AND CASE PROBLEMS

18–1. Preliminary Organizing. A group of employees at the Briarwood Furniture Company's manufacturing plant were interested in joining a union. A representative of the American Federation of Labor and Congress of Industrial Organizations (AFL-CIO) told the group that her union was prepared to represent the workers and suggested that the group members begin organizing by obtaining authorization cards from their fellow employees. After obtaining 252 authorization cards from among Briarwood's 500 nonman-

agement employees, the organizers requested that the company recognize the AFL-CIO as the official representative of the employees. The company refused. Has the company violated federal labor laws? What should the organizers do?

18–2. Appropriate Bargaining Unit. The Briarwood Furniture Company, discussed in the preceding problem, employs 400 unskilled workers and 100 skilled workers in its plant. The unskilled workers operate the industrial machinery used in processing Briarwood's line of standardized plastic office furniture. The skilled workers, who work in an entirely separate part of the plant, are experienced artisans who craft Briarwood's line of expensive wood furniture products. Do you see any problems with a single union's representing all the workers at the Briarwood plant? Explain. Would your answers to Problem 18–1 change if you knew that 51 of the authorization cards had been signed by the skilled workers, with the remainder signed by the unskilled workers?

18–3. Unfair Labor Practices. Suppose that Consolidated Stores is undergoing a unionization campaign. Prior to the election, management says that the union is unnecessary to protect workers. Management also provides bonuses and wage increases to the workers during this period. The employees reject the union. Union organizers protest that the wage increases during the election campaign unfairly prejudiced the vote. Should these wage increases be regarded as an unfair labor practice? Discuss.

18–4. Unfair Labor Practices. SimpCo was engaged in ongoing negotiations over a new labor contract with the union representing the company's employees. As the deadline for expiration of the old labor contract drew near, several employees who were active in union activities were disciplined for being late to work. The union claimed that other employees had not been dealt with as harshly and that the company was discriminating on the basis of union activity. When the negotiations failed to prove fruitful and the old contract expired, the union called a strike. The company claimed the action was an economic strike to press the union's demands for higher wages. The union contended the action was an unfair labor practice strike because of the alleged discrimination. What importance does the distinction have for the striking workers and the company?

18–5. Secondary Boycotts. For many years, grapefruit was shipped to Japan from Fort Pierce and Port Canaveral, Florida. In 1990, Coastal Stevedoring Co. in Fort Pierce and Port Canaveral Stevedoring, Ltd., in Port Canaveral— nonunion firms—were engaged in a labor dispute with the International Longshoremen's Association (ILA). The ILA asked the National Council of Dockworkers' Unions of Japan to prevent Japanese shippers from using nonunion stevedores in Florida, and the council warned Japanese firms that their workers would not unload fruit loaded in the United States by nonunion labor. The threat caused all citrus shipments from Florida to Japan to go through Tampa, where they were loaded by stevedores represented by the ILA. Coastal, Canaveral, and others complained to the National Labor Relations Board (NLRB), alleging that the ILA's request of the Japanese unions was an illegal secondary boycott. How should the NLRB rule? [*International Longshoremen's Association, AFL-CIO*, 313 N.L.R.B. No. 53 (1993)]

18–6. Unfair Labor Practices. The Teamsters Union represented twenty-seven employees of Curtin Matheson

Scientific, Inc. When a collective bargaining agreement between the union and the company expired, the company made an offer for a new agreement, which the union rejected. The company locked out the twenty-seven employees, and the union began an economic strike. The company hired replacement workers. When the union ended its strike and offered to accept the company's earlier offer, the company refused. The company also refused to bargain further, asserting doubt that the union was supported by a majority of the employees. The union sought help from the National Labor Relations Board (NLRB), which refused to presume that the replacement workers did not support the union. On the company's appeal, a court overturned the NLRB's ruling. The union appealed to the United States Supreme Court. How should the Court rule? [*NLRB v. Curtin Matheson Scientific, Inc.*, 494 U.S. 775, 110 S.Ct. 1542, 108 L.Ed.2d 801 (1990)]

18–7. Good Faith Bargaining. American Commercial Barge Line Co. was an affiliation made up of a number of barge and towing companies. The Seafarers International Union of North America (SIU) represented workers for Inland Tugs (IT), a separate corporate division of American Commercial Barge Line. When SIU and IT began negotiating a new collective bargaining agreement, SIU demanded that the bargaining unit include all the employees of American Commercial Barge Line. SIU also demanded that any contract include a pledge by other American Commercial Barge Line companies to continue their contributions to SIU funds, which provided for union activities. Unable to agree on these issues, the parties continued to meet for several years. Meanwhile, on the basis of an employee poll, IT changed its system of calculating wages. SIU filed a complaint with the NLRB, claiming that these changes were an unfair labor practice. IT responded that SIU was not bargaining in good faith. How should the NLRB rule? Explain. [*Inland Tugs, A Division of American Commercial Barge Line Co. v. NLRB*, 918 F.2d 1299 (7th Cir. 1990)]

Case Problem with Sample Answer

18–8. Union Recognition. The International Association of Machinists and Aerospace Workers was certified as the exclusive representative of a unit of employees of F & A Food Sales, Inc. The employees were associated with F & A's trucking operations. The parties negotiated a collective bargaining agreement (CBA) that recognized the union as the employees' representative and reserved F & A's right to subcontract work as the company deemed necessary. Five months after negotiating the CBA, F & A subcontracted the services performed by the unit to Ryder Dedicated Logistics, Inc. Ryder operated from the same facility, used the same trucks, and employed substantially the same employees as had F & A. The union did not represent the workers while Ryder employed them. Seventeen months later, Ryder terminated the subcontract, and F & A resumed its own trucking operations with the same facility, the same trucks, and many of the same employees. The union asserted its right to represent the employees under the CBA. F & A refused to recognize the union. The union filed a charge of unfair labor practice with the NLRB. Is the CBA still in effect? Is the union still the representative of this unit of employees? Explain. [*National Labor Relations Board v. F & A Food Sales, Inc.*, 202 F.3d 1258 (10th Cir. 2000)]

To view a sample answer for this case problem, go to this book's Web site at http://leet.westbuslaw.com and click on "Interactive Study Center."

18–9. Unfair Labor Practice. The New York Department of Education's e-mail policy prohibits the use of the e-mail system for unofficial purposes, except that officials of the New York Public Employees Federation (PEF), the union representing state employees, can use the system for some limited communications, including the scheduling of union meetings and activities. In 1998, Michael Darcy, an elected PEF official, began sending mass, union-related e-mails to employees, including a summary of a union delegates' convention, a union newsletter, a criticism of proposed state legislation, and a criticism of the state governor and the Governor's Office of Employee Relations. Richard Cate, the Department's chief operating officer, met with Darcy and reiterated the Department's e-mail policy. When Darcy refused to stop his use of the e-mail system, Cate terminated his access to it. Darcy filed a complaint with the New York Public Employment Relations Board, alleging an unfair labor practice. Do the circumstances support Cate's action? Why or why not? [*Benson v. Cuevas*, 293 A.D.2d 927, 741 N.Y.S.2d 310 (3 Dept. 2002)]

ter, daughter, and daughter-in-law. In 1987, Chizmar's relatives and four other staff members designated the Oil, Chemical, and Atomic Workers International Union as their bargaining representative. Chizmar was not involved, but when Monte was notified that his office was unionizing, he told Chizmar that someone else could do her job for "$20,000 less" and fired her. He told another employee that one of his reasons for firing Chizmar was that he "was not going to put up with any union bullsh—." During negotiations with the union, Monte said that he planned to "get rid of the whole family." Chizmar's family complained to the National Labor Relations Board (NLRB) that the firing was an unfair labor practice. The NLRB agreed and ordered that Chizmar be reinstated with back pay. Kenrich appealed. In view of these facts, consider the following questions. [*Kenrich Petrochemicals, Inc. v. NLRB*, 907 F.2d 400 (3d Cir. 1990)]

1. The National Labor Relations Act does not protect supervisors who engage in union activities. Should the appellate court affirm the NLRB's order nonetheless?

2. If the appellate court does not affirm the NLRB's order, what message will be sent to the supervisors and employees of Kenrich?

3. Is there anything Kenrich could (legally) do to avoid the unionization of its employees? Would it be ethical to counter the wishes of the employees to unionize?

Critical-Thinking Legal Question

18–11. Suppose that a disaffected union member feels that the union is no longer providing proper representation for employees and starts a campaign to decertify the union. In these circumstances, what can the union do?

A Question of Ethics & Social Responsibility

18–10. Salvatore Monte was president of Kenrich Petrochemicals, Inc. Helen Chizmar had been Kenrich's office manager since 1963. Among the staff that Chizmar supervised were her sis-

INTERACTING WITH THE INTERNET

For updated links to resources available on the Web, as well as a variety of other materials, visit this text's Web site at

http://leet.westbuslaw.com

The American Federation of Labor–Congress of Industrial Organizations (AFL–CIO) provides links to a broad variety of labor-related resources at

http://www.aflcio.org

The National Labor Relations Board is online at the following URL:

http://www.nlrb.gov

ONLINE LEGAL RESEARCH EXERCISES

Go to **http://leet.westbuslaw.com**, the Web site that accompanies this text. Select "Interactive Study Center," and then click on "Chapter 18." There you will find the following Internet research exercises that you can perform to learn more about topics covered in this chapter.

Activity 18–1: MANAGEMENT PERSPECTIVE—The National Labor Relations Board
Activity 18–2: HISTORICAL PERSPECTIVE—Labor Unions and Labor Law

BEFORE THE TEST

Go to **http://leet.westbuslaw.com**, the Web site that accompanies this text. Select "Interactive Quizzes." You will find at least twenty interactive questions relating to this chapter.

Westlaw® Campus

If your textbook provided for a subscription to Westlaw® Campus, or if you have otherwise purchased access to the Westlaw Campus database, you can access any of the cases presented or cited in this chapter by using your Westlaw Campus account.

UNIT FOUR Cumulative Business Hypothetical

Falwell Motors, Inc., is a large corporation that manufactures automobile batteries.

1. One of Falwell's salespersons, Loren, puts in long hours every week. He spends most of his time away from the office generating sales. Less than 10 percent of his work time is devoted to other duties. Usually, he receives a substantial bonus at the end of each year from his employer, and Loren now relies on this supplement to his annual salary and commission. One year, the employer does not give any of its employees year-end bonuses. Loren calculates the number of hours he had worked during the year beyond the required forty hours a week. Then he tells Falwell's president that if he is not paid for these overtime hours, he will sue the company for the overtime pay he has "earned." Falwell's president tells Loren that Falwell is not obligated to pay Loren overtime because Loren is a salesperson. What federal statute governs this dispute? Under this statute, is Falwell required to pay Loren for the "overtime hours"? Why or why not?

2. One day Barry, one of the salespersons, anxious to make a sale, intentionally quotes a price to a customer that is $500 lower than Falwell has authorized for that particular product. The customer purchases the product at the quoted price. When Falwell learns of the deal, it claims that it is not legally bound to the sales contract because it did not authorize Barry to sell the product at that price. Is Falwell bound by the contract? Discuss fully.

3. One day Gina, a Falwell employee, suffered a serious burn when she accidentally spilled some acid on her hand. The accident occurred because another employee, who was suspected of using illegal drugs, carelessly bumped into her. The hand required a series of skin grafting operations before it healed sufficiently to allow Gina to return to work. Gina wants to obtain compensation for her lost wages and medical expenses. Can she do so? If so, how?

4. After Gina's injury, Falwell decides to conduct random drug tests on all of its employees. Several employees claim that the testing violates their privacy rights. If the dispute is litigated, what factors will the court consider in deciding whether the random drug testing is legally permissible?

5. Aretha, a Falwell employee, is disgusted by the sexually offensive behavior of several male employees. She has complained to her supervisor on several occasions about the offensive behavior, but the supervisor merely laughs at her concerns. Aretha decides to bring a legal action against the company for sexual harassment. Does Aretha's complaint concern *quid pro quo* harassment or hostile-environment harassment? What federal statute protects employees from sexual harassment? What remedies are available under that statute? What procedures must Aretha follow in pursuing her legal action?

CHAPTER 19

Consumer Protection

CONTENTS

CHAPTER OBJECTIVES

After reading this chapter, you should be able to answer the following questions:

1. When will advertising be deemed deceptive?

2. What special rules apply to telephone solicitation?

3. What is Regulation Z, and to what type of transactions does it apply?

4. How does the Federal Food, Drug and Cosmetic Act protect consumers?

5. What are the major federal statutes providing for consumer protection in credit transactions?

The public interest that Justice William O. Douglas refers to in the quotation below was evident during the 1960s and 1970s in what has come to be known as the consumer movement. Some have labeled the 1960s and 1970s the age of the consumer because so much legislation was passed to protect consumers against purportedly unsafe products and unfair practices of sellers. Since the 1980s, the impetus driving the consumer movement has lessened, to a great extent because so many of its goals have been achieved. *Consumer law* consists of all of the statutes, administrative agency rules, and judicial decisions that serve to protect the interests of consumers.

In this chapter, we examine some of the sources and some of the major issues of consumer protection. Sources of consumer protection exist at all levels of government. At the federal level, a number of laws have been passed to define the duties of sellers

> "Subject to specific constitutional limitations, when the legislature has spoken, the public interest has been declared in terms well nigh conclusive."
>
> William O. Douglas, 1898–1980
> (Associate justice of the United States Supreme Court, 1939–1975)

and the rights of consumers. Exhibit 19–1 shows selected areas of consumer law that are regulated by statutes. Federal administrative agencies, such as the Federal Trade Commission (FTC), also provide an important source of consumer protection. Nearly every agency and department of the federal government has an office of consumer affairs, and most states have one or more such offices, including the offices of state attorneys general, to assist consumers.

Because of the wide variation among state consumer protection laws, our primary focus here will be on federal legislation—specifically, on legislation governing deceptive advertising, telemarketing and electronic advertising, labeling and packaging, sales, health protection, product safety, and credit protection. Realize, though, that state laws often provide more sweeping and significant protections for the consumer than do federal laws. The chapter concludes with a discussion of state consumer protection laws.

DECEPTIVE ADVERTISING

One of the earliest—and still one of the most important—federal consumer protection laws is the Federal Trade Commission Act of 1914.[1] The act created the FTC to carry out the broadly stated goal of preventing unfair and deceptive trade practices, including deceptive advertising, within the meaning of Section 5 of the act.

Defining Deceptive Advertising

Generally, **deceptive advertising** occurs if a reasonable consumer would be misled by the advertising claim. Vague generalities and obvious exaggerations are permissible. These claims are known as *puffing*. Recall from Chapter 8

DECEPTIVE ADVERTISING
Advertising that misleads consumers, either by making unjustified claims concerning a product's performance or by omitting a material fact concerning the product's composition or performance.

---

1. 15 U.S.C. Sections 41–58.

EXHIBIT 19–1 SELECTED AREAS OF CONSUMER LAW REGULATED BY STATUTES

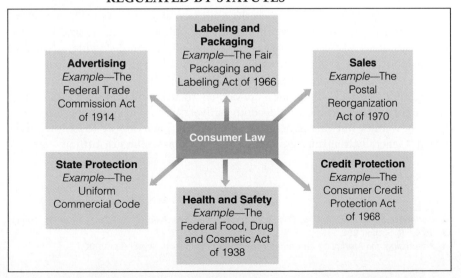

Labeling and Packaging
Example—The Fair Packaging and Labeling Act of 1966

Advertising
Example—The Federal Trade Commission Act of 1914

Sales
Example—The Postal Reorganization Act of 1970

Consumer Law

State Protection
Example—The Uniform Commercial Code

Health and Safety
Example—The Federal Food, Drug and Cosmetic Act of 1938

Credit Protection
Example—The Consumer Credit Protection Act of 1968

that puffing, or puffery, consists of statements about a product that a reasonable person would not believe to be true. When a claim takes on the appearance of literal authenticity, however, problems may arise. Advertising that would *appear* to be based on factual evidence but that in fact is scientifically untrue will be deemed deceptive. A classic example is provided by a 1944 case in which the claim that a skin cream would restore youthful qualities to aged skin was deemed deceptive.[2]

Some advertisements contain "half-truths," meaning that the information presented is true but incomplete and leads consumers to a false conclusion. ● **EXAMPLE 1** The makers of Campbell's soups advertised that most Campbell's soups were low in fat and cholesterol and thus were helpful in fighting heart disease. What the ad did not say was that Campbell's soups are high in sodium, and high-sodium diets may increase the risk of heart disease. The FTC ruled that Campbell's claims were thus deceptive.● Advertising that contains an endorsement by a celebrity may be deemed deceptive if the celebrity actually makes no use of the product.

Bait-and-Switch Advertising

BAIT-AND-SWITCH ADVERTISING
Advertising a product at a very attractive price (the "bait") and then, once the consumer is in the store, saying that the advertised product either is not available or is of poor quality; the customer is then urged to purchase ("switched" to) a more expensive item.

The FTC has promulgated rules to govern specific forms of advertising. One important rule is contained in the FTC's Guides on Bait Advertising.[3] The rule is designed to prohibit what is referred to as **bait-and-switch advertising**—that is, advertising a very low price for a particular item that will likely be unavailable to the consumer, who will then be encouraged to purchase a more expensive item. The low price is the "bait" to lure the consumer into the store. The salesperson is instructed to "switch" the consumer to a different item. According to the FTC guidelines, bait-and-switch advertising occurs if the seller refuses to show the advertised item, fails to have reasonable quantities of it available, neglects to promise to deliver the advertised item within a reasonable time, or discourages employees from selling the item.

Online Deceptive Advertising

Deceptive advertising can occur in the online environment as well. For several years, the FTC has been active in monitoring online advertising and has identified hundreds of Web sites that have made false or deceptive advertising claims concerning products ranging from medical treatments for various diseases to exercise equipment and weight loss products.

In 2000, the FTC issued new guidelines to help online businesses comply with existing laws prohibiting deceptive advertising.[4] The guidelines do not set forth new rules but rather describe how existing laws apply to online advertising. Generally, the rules emphasize that all ads—online or offline—must be

---

2. *Charles of the Ritz Distributing Corp. v. Federal Trade Commission,* 143 F.2d 676 (2d Cir. 1944).
3. 16 C.F.R. Section 288.
4. *Advertising and Marketing on the Internet: Rules of the Road,* September 2000.

truthful and not misleading and that any claims made in any ads must be substantiated. Additionally, ads cannot be unfair, defined in the guidelines as "caus[ing] or . . . likely to cause substantial consumer injury that consumers could not reasonably avoid and that is not outweighed by the benefit to consumers or competition."

The guidelines also call for "clear and conspicuous" disclosure of any qualifying or limiting information. The FTC suggests that advertisers should assume that consumers will not read an entire Web page. Therefore, to satisfy the "clear and conspicuous" requirement, advertisers should place the disclosure as close as possible to the claim being qualified or include the disclosure within the claim itself. If such placement is not feasible, the next-best placement is on a section of the page to which a consumer can easily scroll. Generally, hyperlinks to a disclosure are recommended only for lengthy disclosures or for disclosures that must be repeated in a variety of locations on the Web page.

FTC Actions against Deceptive Advertising

The FTC receives complaints from many sources, including competitors of alleged violators, consumers, consumer organizations, trade associations, Better Business Bureaus, government organizations, and state and local officials. If enough consumers complain and the complaints are widespread, the FTC will investigate the problem and perhaps take action. If, after its investigations, the FTC believes that a given advertisement is unfair or deceptive, it drafts a formal complaint, which it sends to the alleged offender. The company may agree to settle the complaint without further proceedings.

If the company does not agree to settle the complaint, the FTC can conduct a hearing—which is similar to a trial—in which the company can present its defense. The hearing is held before an administrative law judge (ALJ) instead of a federal district court judge (see the discussion of administrative law in Chapter 6). If the FTC succeeds in proving that an advertisement is unfair or deceptive, it usually issues a **cease-and-desist order** requiring that the challenged advertising be stopped. It might also impose a sanction known as **counteradvertising** by requiring the company to advertise anew—in print, on radio, and on television—to inform the public about the earlier misinformation.

When an ALJ rules against a company, the company can appeal to the full commission. The FTC commissioners listen to the parties' arguments and may uphold, modify, or reverse the ALJ's decision. If the commission rules against a company, the company can appeal the FTC's order through judicial channels, but a reviewing court generally accords great weight to the FTC's judgment. This is because the court recognizes that the FTC, as the administrative agency that deals continually with such claims, is often in a better position than the courts to determine when a practice is deceptive within the meaning of the Federal Trade Commission Act.

In the following case, the FTC contended that a business firm and its owner misrepresented the profit their customers could expect to earn from phone-card dispensing machines, in violation of the Federal Trade Commission Act.

CEASE-AND-DESIST ORDER
An administrative or judicial order prohibiting a person or business firm from conducting activities that an agency or court has deemed illegal.

COUNTERADVERTISING
Advertising undertaken pursuant to a Federal Trade Commission order for the purpose of correcting earlier false claims that were made about a product.

CASE 19.1 Federal Trade Commission v. Tashman

United States Court of Appeals,
Eleventh Circuit, 2003.
318 F.3d 1273.
**http://law.emory.edu/
11circuit/11casearch.html**[a]

BACKGROUND AND FACTS Stephen Tashman sold machines that dispense phone cards, and the cards that go in them, through his Telecard Dispensing Corporation (TDC). TDC's ads asked, "Do you really want to make more money—an additional twenty-five to thirty-five thousand dollars a year or more, possibly a lot more, and only work three to five hours per week? With a very small investment you can make $600 to $700 a week or more—maybe a lot more—working as little as five hours a week." TDC claimed that its "locators" put machines in public places experiencing a traffic flow of at least five hundred persons per day, 2 percent of whom were likely to buy the cards, and that the machines could be "expected" to pay for themselves in about six months. The FTC filed a suit in a federal district court against Tashman and his firm, alleging, in part, violations of the Federal Trade Commission Act. During the trial, the FTC revealed that TDC had no basis for its claims. Many locations did not have foot traffic at a rate of five hundred people per day, and the 2 percent figure was completely made up. Most customers who bought machines did not recoup their original investments. Despite these findings, the court entered a judgment in the defendants' favor. The FTC appealed to the U.S. Court of Appeals for the Eleventh Circuit.

**IN THE WORDS
OF THE COURT . . .**

TJOFLAT, Circuit Judge:

*　*　*　*

To establish liability under [the Federal Trade Commission Act], the FTC must establish that (1) there was a representation; (2) the representation was likely to mislead customers acting reasonably under the circumstances, and (3) the representation was material. The defendants concede that the first and third elements have been established; they dispute only the second element. The undisputed evidence shows, however, that TDC had no basis for the representations it made. *　*　* One searches in vain for the district court's analysis on whether particular assertions were likely to mislead. In its findings of fact and conclusions of law, for example, the court jumped from a correct recitation of the legal standard to a discussion of irrelevant points such as the fact that the business was "new" and the fact that "migrant workers" might buy the cards, leading the court to conclude that "[i]t was therefore up to the potential customers to weigh the risks and profit potential, and to follow up their investment with the hard work and business savvy necessary to make the venture successful and profitable." With regard to the second point, no one doubts the utility of phone cards or claims that the product is a scam; all that is at issue are the statements made by the defendants. As for the first point, *there is no "new business" immunity from the Federal Trade Commission Act. Indeed, it is precisely in the context of a new venture that investors are unlikely to have their own data.* In the "new business" setting, investors are the most vulnerable to the representations and purported "expertise" of those in the business of selling novel business opportunities. Finally, *caveat emptor* ["buyer beware"] is simply not the law, and the district court's conclusion to the contrary is incorrect. [Emphasis added.]

The district court even seemed to concede that misrepresentations were made. In its findings of fact and conclusions of law, it held that "reasonable potential customers would not have believed that they could make tens of

---

a. In the "Enter Keyword(s)" box, type "Tashman," and click on "Search" to access the opinion. This is a page within a Web site maintained by Emory University School of Law in Atlanta, Georgia.

CASE 19.1—Continued

thousands of dollars while working only three to four hours per week." The [Federal Trade Commission Act] does not have an "extravagant claim" defense. * * *

In short, the record contains overwhelming evidence that misrepresentations were made and that reasonable consumers were likely to (and, in fact, did) rely on those statements. Rather than analyzing those statements, the court focused on a few satisfied customers, the utility of the product being sold, and why the government ought not protect consumers from what it perceived as a lack of "hard work" and "walking around common sense." The district court's legal conclusions are incorrect.

DECISION AND REMEDY The U.S. Court of Appeals for the Eleventh Circuit vacated the judgment of the lower court and remanded the case for the entry of a judgment in favor of the FTC. The defendants made misleading material statements on which reasonable consumers "were likely to (and, in fact, did) rely." The appellate court ordered the lower court to determine an appropriate remedy, including damages and an injunction.

FOR CRITICAL ANALYSIS—Social Consideration *What prevents the prosecution in cases such as this from being based on the inflated perceptions of the profit potential of a legitimate business opportunity on the part of a small percentage of disgruntled customers?*

TELEMARKETING AND ELECTRONIC ADVERTISING

The pervasive use of the telephone to market goods and services to homes and businesses led to the passage in 1991 of the Telephone Consumer Protection Act (TCPA).[5] The act prohibits telephone solicitation using an automatic telephone dialing system or a prerecorded voice. In addition, most states have laws regulating telephone solicitation. The TCPA also makes it illegal to transmit ads via fax without first obtaining the recipient's permission. (Similar issues have arisen with respect to junk e-mail, called "spam"—see Chapter 8.) The act is enforced by the Federal Communications Commission and also provides for a private right of action.

REMEMBER Changes in technology often require changes in the law.

The Telemarketing and Consumer Fraud and Abuse Prevention Act[6] of 1994 directed the FTC to establish rules governing telemarketing and to bring actions against fraudulent telemarketers. The FTC's Telemarketing Sales Rule[7] of 1995 requires a telemarketer, before making a sales pitch, to inform the recipient that the call is a sales call and to identify the seller's name and the product being sold. The rule makes it illegal for telemarketers to misrepresent information. Additionally, telemarketers must inform the people they call of the total cost of the goods being sold, any restrictions on obtaining or using the goods, and whether a sale will be considered final and nonrefundable. A telemarketer must also remove a consumer's name from its list of potential contacts if the customer so requests.

In 2003, the FTC established the National Do Not Call Registry. Any telemarketer who calls a number on the registry after October 1, 2003, will face

5. 47 U.S.C. Sections 227 *et seq.*
6. 15 U.S.C. Sections 6101–6108.
7. 16 C.F.R. Sections 310.1–310.8.

fines of up to $11,000 per call. Charities and political campaigns are exempt, however, as are any enterprises with which the consumer has an actual business relationship.

The following case involved telemarketers engaged in allegedly deceptive advertising.

CASE 19.2 Federal Trade Commission v. Growth Plus International Marketing, Inc.

United States District Court,
Northern District of Illinois, 2001.
___F.Supp.2d ___.

BACKGROUND AND FACTS A group of Canadian corporations and individuals engaged in a telemarketing enterprise to sell Canadian lottery packages to consumers in the United States. What the telemarketers did not tell the consumers was that the sales were illegal. In fact, the sellers claimed that they were authorized to make the sales. They also misrepresented the buyers' chances of winning and used high-pressure sales tactics. The corporations included Growth Plus International Marketing, Inc. The Federal Trade Commission (FTC) filed a suit in a federal district court against Growth Plus and the others, alleging deceptive advertising. The FTC asked the court for, among other things, a preliminary injunction.

IN THE WORDS OF THE COURT . . .

ASPEN, Acting Chief District J. [Judge]

*   *   *   *

*   *   * When the [Federal Trade] Commission seeks an injunction, the "public interest" test applies, which involves two factors: (a) the likelihood that the Commission will ultimately succeed on the merits, and (b) the balance of the equities. *   *   *

*   *   *   *

*   *   * The [evidence at this point establishes] a strong case that the defendants were guilty of numerous misrepresentations or omissions. For example, (a) the defendants told customers that it was legal for them to sell the lottery tickets in the United States, when it was not; (b) the defendants told customers that they were authorized by the Canadian government to sell lottery tickets, when in fact they were not; (c) the defendants represented to consumers that they had a good chance of winning the lottery because they would be playing with a large pool of people, without disclosing that the odds of winning were roughly 1 in 14 million. This information that was misrepresented or concealed plainly was material to the consumers' decisions to purchase the tickets: The knowledge that the sale of the tickets was illegal under federal law and that the "good chance" of winning was in fact a 1 in 14 million shot certainly are the types of information that would likely affect the decision of whether to participate in the lottery. And, in fact, the Commission has provided sworn statements from several consumers indicating that they would not have purchased the lottery tickets had they known that the sales of tickets were illegal.

*   *   * For these same reasons, the Commission has made a strong case that it will likely prevail on the merits of its claim that defendants have violated the *Telemarketing Sales Rule, which prohibits sellers and telemarketers from making false or misleading statements to induce persons to acquire goods or services.* [Emphasis added.]

CASE 19.2—Continued

   *   *   * Turning to the balance of the equities, the Court notes that although private equities may be considered, public equities receive far greater weight. In this case, the balance of equities weighs heavily in favor of the issuance of preliminary injunctive relief. There is a strong public interest in an immediate halt to illegal sale of lottery tickets accomplished through the use of misleading devices. By contrast, the Court perceives very little private interest in the continuance of such sales pending further proceedings in the case *   *   * .

DECISION AND REMEDY The court granted the FTC's request for a preliminary injunction. The court concluded that the FTC had made a strong case against the defendants, whose misrepresentations had misled consumers.

FOR CRITICAL ANALYSIS—Technological Consideration *Would the result in this case likely have been different if the defendants had offered the Canadian lottery tickets for sale only on the Internet?*

LABELING AND PACKAGING

In addition to broadly restricting advertising, a number of federal and state laws deal specifically with the information given on labels and packages. The restrictions are designed to provide accurate information about the product and to warn about possible dangers from its use or misuse. In general, labels must be accurate—that is, they must use words as the words are understood by the ordinary consumer. For example, a box of cereal cannot be labeled "giant" if it would exaggerate the amount of cereal contained in the box. In some instances, labels must specify the raw materials used in the product, such as the percentage of cotton, nylon, or other fibers used in a garment. In other instances, the products must carry a warning. Cigarette packages and advertising, for example, must include one of several warnings about the health hazards associated with smoking.[8]

   Federal laws regulating the labeling and packaging of products include the Fair Packaging and Labeling Act of 1966,[9] which requires that products carry

8. 15 U.S.C. Sections 1331 *et seq.*
9. 15 U.S.C. Sections 4401–4408.

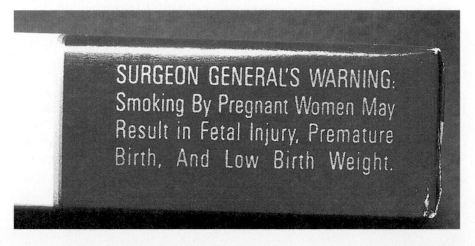

A warning appears on a package of cigarettes, as required by federal law. Why is Congress concerned with protecting consumers against purportedly unsafe products?

labels that identify (1) the product; (2) the net quantity of the contents, as well as the quantity of servings, if the number of servings is stated; (3) the manufacturer; and (4) the packager or distributor. The act also provides that requirements may be added concerning descriptions on packages, savings claims, ingredients in nonfood products, and standards for the partial filling of packages. Labels of food products must give nutrition information, including fat content and type. These restrictions are enforced by the Department of Health and Human Services, as well as the FTC. The Nutrition Labeling and Education Act of 1990 requires standard nutrition facts (including fat content) on food labels; regulates the use of such terms as *fresh* and *low fat;* and, subject to the federal Food and Drug Administration's approval, authorizes certain health claims.

The Comprehensive Smokeless Tobacco Health Education Act of 1986[10] requires that producers, packagers, and importers of smokeless tobacco label their product with one of several warnings about the health hazards associated with the use of smokeless tobacco; the warnings are similar to those contained on cigarette packages. Other federal laws regulating the labeling of products include the Wool Products Labeling Act of 1939,[11] the Fur Products Labeling Act of 1951,[12] and the Flammable Fabrics Act of 1953.[13]

SALES

A number of statutes that protect the consumer in sales transactions concern the disclosure of certain terms in sales and provide rules governing home or door-to-door sales, mail-order transactions, referral sales, and unsolicited merchandise. The Federal Reserve Board of Governors, for example, has issued **Regulation Z,** which governs credit provisions associated with sales contracts, and numerous states have passed laws governing the remedies available to consumers in home sales. Furthermore, states have provided a number of consumer protection measures, such as implied warranties, through the adoption of the Uniform Commercial Code. In some states, the Uniform Consumer Credit Code's requirements, including disclosure requirements, also protect consumers in credit transactions.

REGULATION Z
A set of rules promulgated by the Federal Reserve Board to implement the provisions of the Truth-in-Lending Act.

Door-to-Door Sales

The laws of most states single out door-to-door sales for special treatment, in part because of the nature of the sales transaction. Repeat purchases are less likely than in stores, so the seller has less incentive to cultivate the goodwill of the purchaser. Furthermore, the seller is unlikely to present alternative products and their prices. Thus, a number of states have passed **"cooling-off" laws** that permit the buyers of goods sold door to door to cancel their contracts within a specified period of time, usually two to three days after the sale.

An FTC regulation also requires sellers to give consumers three days to cancel any door-to-door sale. Because this rule applies in addition to the relevant state statutes, consumers receive the benefits of both. In addition, the FTC rule

"COOLING-OFF" LAWS
Laws that allow buyers a period of time, such as three days, in which to cancel door-to-door sales contracts.

---

10. 15 U.S.C. Sections 1451 *et seq.*
11. 15 U.S.C. Section 68.
12. 15 U.S.C. Section 69.
13. 15 U.S.C. Section 1191.

requires that consumers be notified in Spanish of this right if the oral negotiations for the sale were in that language.

Telephone and Mail-Order Sales

Sales made by telephone and mail order are the greatest source of complaints to the nation's Better Business Bureaus. Many mail-order houses are far removed from the buyers who purchase from them, thus making it more difficult for a consumer to bring a complaint against a seller.

To a certain extent, consumers are protected under federal laws prohibiting mail fraud, which were discussed in Chapter 7, and under state consumer protection laws that parallel and supplement the federal laws. In addition, the Postal Reorganization Act of 1970[14] provides that unsolicited merchandise sent by U.S. mail can be retained, used, discarded, or disposed of in any manner the recipient deems appropriate, without the recipient's incurring any obligation to the sender.

The FTC Mail or Telephone Order Merchandise Rule of 1993, which amended the FTC Mail Order Rule of 1975,[15] provides specific protections for consumers who purchase goods via phone lines or through the mails. The 1993 rule, which became effective in March 1994, extended the 1975 rule to include sales in which orders are transmitted using computers, fax machines, or some similar means involving telephone lines. Among other things, the rule requires mail-order merchants to ship orders within the time promised in their catalogues or advertisements, to notify consumers when orders cannot be shipped on time, and to issue a refund within a specified period of time when a consumer cancels an order.

Online Sales

In recent years, the Internet has become a vehicle for a wide variety of business-to-consumer sales transactions. Most mail-order houses now have a Web presence, and consumers can purchase from other Web sites an increasing array of goods, ranging from airline tickets to books to xylophones. Protecting consumers from fraudulent and deceptive sales practices conducted via the Internet has proved to be a challenging task. Nonetheless, the FTC and other federal agencies have brought a number of enforcement actions against those who perpetrate online fraud. Additionally, certain criminal laws, such as the federal statute prohibiting wire fraud, apply to online transactions.

Some states have amended their consumer protection statutes to cover Internet transactions as well. For example, the California legislature revised its Business and Professional Code to include transactions conducted over the Internet or by "any other electronic means of communication." Previously, that code covered only telephone, mail-order catalogue, radio, and television sales. Now any entity selling over the Internet in California must create an explicit on-screen notice indicating its refund and return policies, where its business is physically located, its legal name, and a number of other details. Various states are also setting up information sites to help consumers protect themselves.

---

14. 39 U.S.C. Section 3009.
15. 16 C.F.R. Sections 435.1–435.2.

HEALTH AND SAFETY PROTECTION

Laws discussed earlier regarding the labeling and packaging of products go a long way toward promoting consumer health and safety. There is a significant distinction, however, between regulating the information dispensed about a product and regulating the content of the product. The classic example is tobacco products. Producers of tobacco products are required to warn consumers about the hazards associated with the use of their products. As yet, however, the sale of tobacco products has not been significantly restricted, despite their obvious hazards. We now examine various laws that regulate the actual products made available to consumers.

Food and Drugs

The first federal legislation regulating food and drugs was enacted in 1906 as the Pure Food and Drugs Act.[16] That law, as amended in 1938, exists now as the Federal Food, Drug and Cosmetic Act (FFDCA).[17] The act protects consumers against adulterated and misbranded foods and drugs. More recent amendments to the act added other substantive and procedural requirements. In its present form, the act establishes food standards, specifies safe levels of potentially hazardous food additives, and sets classifications of food and food advertising.

BE AWARE The Food and Drug Administration is authorized to obtain, among other things, orders for the recall and seizure of certain products.

Most of these statutory requirements are monitored and enforced by the Food and Drug Administration (FDA). Under an extensive set of procedures established by the FDA, drugs must be shown to be effective as well as safe before they can be marketed to the public, and the use of some food additives suspected of being carcinogenic is prohibited. A 1975 amendment to the FFDCA[18] authorizes the FDA to regulate medical devices, such as pacemakers and other health devices and equipment, and to withdraw from the market any such device that is mislabeled.

Consumer Product Safety

Consumer product-safety legislation began in 1953 with the enactment of the Flammable Fabrics Act, which prohibits the sale of highly flammable clothing and materials. Over the next two decades, Congress enacted legislation regarding the design or composition of specific classes of products. Then, in 1972, Congress, by enacting the Consumer Product Safety Act,[19] created a comprehensive scheme of regulation over matters concerning consumer safety. The act also established far-reaching authority over consumer safety by creating the Consumer Product Safety Commission (CPSC). The CPSC's role includes administering other product-safety legislation, such as the Child Protection and Toy Safety Act of 1969,[20] the Federal Hazardous Substances Act of 1960,[21] and the Flammable Fabrics Act.

---

16. 21 U.S.C. Sections 1–5, 7–15.
17. 21 U.S.C. Section 301.
18. 21 U.S.C. Sections 360(c) *et seq.*
19. 15 U.S.C. Section 2051.
20. 15 U.S.C. Section 1262(e).
21. 15 U.S.C. Sections 1261–1273.

The CPSC's Authority The CPSC conducts research on the safety of individual products, and it maintains a clearinghouse on the risks associated with various consumer products. The Consumer Product Safety Act authorizes the CPSC to set standards for consumer products and to ban the manufacture and sale of any product that the commission deems to be potentially hazardous to consumers. The CPSC also has authority to remove from the market any products it believes to be imminently hazardous and to require manufacturers to report on any products already sold or intended for sale if the products have proved to be hazardous. The CPSC's authority is sufficiently broad to allow it to ban not only products it deems hazardous but any product that it considers to pose an "unreasonable risk" to the consumer. Products banned by the CPSC include various types of fireworks, cribs, and toys, as well as many products containing asbestos or vinyl chloride.

Notification Requirements The Consumer Product Safety Act requires the distributors of consumer products to notify immediately the CPSC on receipt of information that a product "contains a defect which . . . creates a substantial risk to the public" or "an unreasonable risk of serious injury or death." The following case illustrates the consequences of failing to fulfill this requirement.

CASE 19.3 United States v. Mirama Enterprises, Inc.

United States District Court,
Southern District of California, 2002.
185 F.Supp.2d 1148.

COMPANY PROFILE *Mirama Enterprises, Inc., began operations in 1996 and today does business as Aroma Housewares Company from its headquarters in San Diego, California. Aroma imports a variety of electric kitchen appliances from China and Taiwan and distributes them to retailers in the United States and abroad. From early 1996 until early 1998, Aroma distributed to a variety of retail outlets in the United States a juice extractor, or juicer, which extracts the juice from fruits and vegetables. Semco, which is headquartered in Taiwan, manufactured the juicer.*

BACKGROUND AND FACTS In early January 1998, Aroma received a complaint from a consumer whose juicer had broken. In February, consumer Richard

Norton wrote Aroma to report that his juicer had shattered. In capital letters, Norton stated that the juicer

SUDDENLY EXPLODED, THROWING WITH GREAT VIOLENCE PIECES OF THE CLEAR PLASTIC COVER AND SHREDS OF THE RAZOR-SHARP SEPARATOR SCREEN AS FAR AS EIGHT FEET IN MY KITCHEN. * * *

Over the next months, twenty-three complaints about exploding juicers, some of which caused injuries, were made by consumers, including Jan Griffin, who added, "I feel that this juicer should be recalled, as it is very unsafe. The injuries that I suffered could have been a lot worse." In August, consumer Sylvia Mendoza filed a suit against Aroma, alleging injuries caused by a shattering juicer. On November 16, Aroma filed a report with the CPSC, which recalled the juicer on June 30, 1999. The federal government filed a suit against Mirama, seeking damages for its alleged failure to notify the CPSC of the danger earlier. The government filed a motion for summary judgment.

IN THE WORDS OF THE COURT . . . *KEEP,* District Judge.
                                    * * * *
    [The] reporting requirement was imposed upon consumer product manufacturers to protect the public health and safety—the sooner the [Consumer Product Safety] Commission knows of a potential problem, the sooner it can

(continued)

CASE 19.3—Continued

investigate and take necessary action. This notification requirement was statutorily imposed upon manufacturers * * * because they are often the first to receive information about hazardous consumer products. * * *

The thrust of the Act is clearly for firms to quickly inform the Commission as soon as they might "reasonably believe" that their product, through defect or otherwise, poses a significant threat to consumers. Upon receipt of "first information," a company is required to report *within 24 hours* to the Commission. Companies are advised that they should not await complete or accurate risk estimates before reporting * * * . While a firm may investigate to determine whether the information is reportable, a firm should not take more than 10 days unless it can demonstrate that such additional time is reasonable. * * * [Emphasis added.]

* * * The issue is whether, prior to [its reporting] date, Aroma received information which "reasonably supported" the conclusion that the juicer either * * * contained a "defect" which created a "substantial product hazard," such that it "created a substantial risk to the public," or created an "unreasonable risk of serious injury or death."

* * * *

The Court finds that Aroma was in receipt of overwhelming evidence such that a reasonable person could conclude that the juicer contained a defect which created a substantial risk to the public. The Court will not set forth again the litany of phone calls and letters with which scared, angry, and often injured consumers bombarded the company. The Court finds particularly noteworthy, however, several items in particular. * * * [I]n a period of approximately only one month, Aroma received three telephone calls and two letters recounting exploding juicers, flying pieces of razor-sharp metal, and one emergency room visit. Hence, by at least early March, Aroma had enough information for a reasonable person to conclude that the juicer contained a defect, whether in the actual unit or in the instructions and warnings, that created a substantial risk to the public.

DECISION AND REMEDY The court granted the plaintiff's motion for summary judgment. The defendant had sufficient knowledge from consumer complaints that the juicer contained "a defect which . . . creates a substantial risk to the public" to report to the CPSC as early as March 1998.

FOR CRITICAL ANALYSIS—Social Consideration *Under what legal theory might the consumers who were injured by the exploding juicers sue the manufacturer for damages?*

CREDIT PROTECTION

Because of the extensive use of credit by American consumers, credit protection is one of the most important areas regulated by consumer protection legislation. One of the most significant statutes regulating the credit and credit-card industry is the Truth-in-Lending Act (TILA), the name commonly given to Title 1 of the Consumer Credit Protection Act (CCPA),[22] which was passed by Congress in 1968.

---

22. 15 U.S.C. Sections 1601–1693r. The act was amended in 1980 by the Truth-in-Lending Simplification and Reform Act.

Truth in Lending

The TILA is basically a *disclosure law.* It is administered by the Federal Reserve Board and requires sellers and lenders to disclose credit terms and loan terms so that individuals can shop around for the best financing arrangements. TILA requirements apply only to persons who, in the ordinary course of business, lend funds, sell on credit, or arrange for the extension of credit. Thus, sales or loans made between two consumers do not come under the protection of the act. Additionally, only debtors who are natural persons (as opposed to the artificial "person" of a corporation) are protected by this law; other legal entities are not.

The disclosure requirements are found in Regulation Z, which, as mentioned earlier in this chapter, was promulgated by the Federal Reserve Board. If the contracting parties are subject to the TILA, the requirements of Regulation Z apply to any transaction involving an installment sales contract in which payment is to be made in more than four installments. Transactions subject to Regulation Z typically include installment loans, retail and installment sales, car loans, home-improvement loans, and certain real estate loans if the amount of financing is less than $25,000.

Under the provisions of the TILA, all the terms of a credit instrument must be clearly and conspicuously disclosed. With some exceptions, the TILA provides for contract rescission (cancellation) if a creditor fails to follow exactly the procedures required by the act.

NOTE The Federal Reserve Board is part of the Federal Reserve System, which influences the lending and investing activities of commercial banks and the cost and availability of credit.

ETHICAL ISSUE

Should consumer protection laws be strictly enforced when consumers abuse these laws?

Generally, the courts strictly enforce the TILA, as well as other consumer protection laws. This is true even in cases in which consumers have obviously taken unfair advantage of the TILA's requirements to avoid genuine obligations that they voluntarily assumed. For example, under the TILA, borrowers are allowed three business days to rescind, without penalty, a consumer loan that uses their principal dwelling as security. The lender must state specifically the last day on which the borrower can rescind the agreement. If the lender inadvertently fails to do so, the borrower can rescind the loan within three years after it was made. Suppose that, on this basis alone, a consumer decides to rescind a loan within the three-year period. Is this fair to the lender? Perhaps not. The courts, though, balance this potential for abuse against the overall benefit that consumers gain from strict compliance requirements. In essence, the TILA is a "strict liability" statute, as are most consumer protection laws. In other words, intention normally is irrelevant in determining whether a consumer protection statute has been violated.

Equal Credit Opportunity In 1974, Congress enacted, as an amendment to the TILA, the Equal Credit Opportunity Act (ECOA).[23] The ECOA prohibits the denial of credit solely on the basis of race, religion, national origin, color,

---

23. 15 U.S.C. Section 1643.

gender, marital status, or age. The act also prohibits credit discrimination on the basis of whether an individual receives certain forms of income, such as public-assistance benefits.

Under the ECOA, a creditor cannot require the signature of an applicant's spouse, other than as a joint applicant, on a credit instrument if the applicant qualifies under the creditor's standards of creditworthiness for the amount and terms of the credit request. Creditors are permitted to ask for any information from a credit applicant except information that would be used for the type of discrimination covered in the act or its amendments.

Credit-Card Rules The TILA also contains provisions regarding credit cards. One provision limits the liability of a cardholder to $50 per card for unauthorized charges made before the creditor is notified that the card has been lost. Another provision prohibits a credit-card company from billing a consumer for any unauthorized charges if the credit card was improperly issued by the company. ● **EXAMPLE 2** Suppose that a consumer receives an unsolicited credit card in the mail and the card is later stolen and used by the thief to make purchases. In this situation, the consumer to whom the card was sent will not be liable for the unauthorized charges.●

Further provisions of the act concern billing disputes related to credit-card purchases. If a debtor thinks that an error has occurred in billing or wishes to withhold payment for a faulty product purchased by credit card, the act outlines specific procedures for both the consumer and the credit-card company in settling the dispute.

Consumer Leases The Consumer Leasing Act (CLA) of 1988[24] amended the TILA to provide protection for consumers who lease automobiles and other goods. The CLA applies to those who lease or arrange to lease consumer goods in the ordinary course of their business. The act applies only if the goods are priced at $25,000 or less and if the lease term exceeds four months. The CLA and its implementing regulation, Regulation M,[25] require lessors to disclose in writing all of the material terms of the lease.

Fair Credit Reporting

In 1970, to protect consumers against inaccurate credit reporting, Congress enacted the Fair Credit Reporting Act (FCRA).[26] The act provides that consumer credit reporting agencies can issue credit reports only for specified purposes, including the extension of credit, the issuance of insurance policies, compliance with a court order, and compliance with a consumer's request for a copy of his or her own credit report. The act further provides that any time a consumer is denied credit or insurance on the basis of the consumer's credit report, or is charged more than others ordinarily would be for credit or insurance, the consumer must be notified of that fact and of the name and address of the credit reporting agency that issued the credit report.

Under the act, consumers can request the source of any information being given out by a credit agency, as well as the identity of anyone who has received

---

24. 15 U.S.C. Sections 1667–1667e.
25. 12 C.F.R. Part 213.
26. 15 U.S.C. Sections 1681 *et seq.*

an agency's report. Consumers are also permitted to have access to the information contained about them in a credit reporting agency's files. If a consumer discovers that a credit reporting agency's files contain inaccurate information about the consumer's credit standing, the agency, on the consumer's written request, must investigate the matter and delete any unverifiable or erroneous information within a reasonable period of time.

Fair Debt-Collection Practices

In 1977, Congress enacted the Fair Debt Collection Practices Act (FDCPA)[27] in an attempt to curb what were perceived to be abuses by collection agencies. The act applies only to specialized debt-collection agencies that, usually for a percentage of the amount owed, regularly attempt to collect debts on behalf of someone else. Creditors who attempt to collect debts are not covered by the act unless, by misrepresenting themselves to debtors, they cause the debtors to believe they are collection agencies.

Requirements under the Act The act explicitly prohibits a collection agency from using any of the following tactics:

1. Contacting the debtor at the debtor's place of employment if the debtor's employer objects.
2. Contacting the debtor at inconvenient or unusual times (for example, calling the debtor at three o'clock in the morning) or at any time if the debtor is being represented by an attorney.
3. Contacting third parties other than the debtor's parents, spouse, or financial adviser about payment of a debt unless a court authorizes such action.
4. Using harassment or intimidation (for example, using abusive language or threatening violence) or employing false and misleading information (for example, posing as a police officer).
5. Communicating with the debtor at any time after receiving notice that the debtor is refusing to pay the debt, except to advise the debtor of further action to be taken by the collection agency.

The FDCPA also requires collection agencies to include a "validation notice" whenever they initially contact a debtor for payment of a debt or within five days of that initial contact. The notice must state that the debtor has thirty days within which to dispute the debt and to request a written verification, or validation, of the debt from the collection agency. The debtor's request for debt validation must be in writing.

Enforcement of the Act The enforcement of the FDCPA is primarily the responsibility of the Federal Trade Commission. The FDCPA provides that a debt collector who fails to comply with the act is liable for actual damages, plus additional damages not to exceed $1,000[28] and attorneys' fees.

Cases brought under the FDCPA often raise questions as to who qualifies as a debt collector or debt-collecting agency subject to the act. For example, for several years it was not clear whether attorneys who attempted to collect

---

27. 15 U.S.C. Section 1692.
28. According to the U.S. Court of Appeals for the Sixth Circuit, the $1,000 limit on damages applies to each lawsuit, not to each violation. See *Wright v. Finance Service of Norwalk, Inc.,* 22 F.3d 647 (6th Cir. 1994).

debts owed to their clients were subject to the FDCPA's provisions. In 1995, the United States Supreme Court addressed this issue to resolve conflicting opinions in the lower courts. The Court held that an attorney who regularly tries to obtain payment of consumer debts through legal proceedings meets the FDCPA's definition of *debt collector.*[29]

Another question that sometimes arises in FDCPA litigation is what, exactly, constitutes a debt. In the following case, the court considered whether a dishonored check constituted a debt within the meaning of the FDCPA.

---

29. *Heintz v. Jenkins,* 514 U.S. 291, 115 S.Ct. 1489, 131 L.Ed.2d 395 (1995).

CASE 19.4   Snow v. Jesse L. Riddle, P.C.

United States Court of Appeals,
Tenth Circuit, 1998.
143 F.3d 1350.
http://www.kscourts.org/ca10[a]

BACKGROUND AND FACTS At a Circle-K store, Alan Snow paid for merchandise with his personal check in the amount of $23.12. Circle-K deposited the check at its bank, but the check was dishonored because of insufficient funds. Circle-K sent the returned check to its attorney, Jesse L. Riddle, P.C., for collection. In a letter to Snow, Riddle wrote that "the

check amount, along with a service fee of $15, must be paid within seven (7) days of this notice. If it is not paid, . . . [a] suit [will] be filed." Snow paid the check and then filed a suit in a federal district court against Riddle. Snow alleged in part that Riddle's letter violated the FDCPA because it did not contain a validation notice. Riddle filed a motion to dismiss on the ground that the FDCPA does not cover a dishonored check because it is not an "offer or extension of credit." The court granted the motion, and Snow appealed to the U.S. Court of Appeals for the Tenth Circuit.

IN THE WORDS OF THE COURT . . .

McWILLIAMS, Senior Circuit Judge.

* * * *

[The FDCPA] provides as follows:

* * * Abusive debt collection practices contribute to the number of personal bankruptcies, to marital instability, to the loss of jobs, and to invasions of individual privacy. * * * It is the purpose of [the FDCPA] to eliminate abusive debt collection practices by debt collectors * * *.

* * * *

* * * [A] payment obligation arising from a dishonored check create[s] a "debt" triggering the protections of the [FDCPA].* * * *[A]n offer or extension of credit is not required for a payment obligation to constitute a "debt" under the [FDCPA].* * * [Emphasis added.]*

* * * *

* * * Under the "plain meaning" test, it would seem to us that a "debt" is created where one obtains goods and gives a dishonored check in return therefor.

DECISION AND REMEDY The U.S. Court of Appeals for the Tenth Circuit reversed the decision of the lower court and remanded the case. The appellate court held that a dishonored check constitutes a debt within the meaning of the FDCPA.

FOR CRITICAL ANALYSIS—Political Consideration *Should those who write bad checks to pay for consumer goods or services be protected by the FDCPA?*

---

a. This page contains links to opinions of the U.S. Court of Appeals for the Tenth Circuit. In the first paragraph, click on "plaintiff/defendant case name." When the page opens, scroll down the list of cases and click on the *Snow* case name to access the opinion. This Web site is maintained by the Washburn University School of Law.

LEGAL *e*-NVIRONMENT

Is an Internet Ad a "Writing"?

Many statutes that require a statement or agreement to be in writing do not define specifically what *in writing* means. Traditionally, this has not posed many problems. In the online environment, however, unique questions arise. For example, among the twenty-one practices that "constitute unfair methods of competition and unfair or deceptive acts or practices" under Pennsylvania's Unfair Trade Practices and Consumer Protection Law (UTPCPL) is a breach of written warranty. What if a warranty is made via the Internet? Is it a written warranty?

The Claims against the Quigley Corporation

This question arose in a case brought by a class of plaintiffs who had purchased Cold-Eeze zinc lozenges. The manufacturer of the lozenges, the Quigley Corporation, had stated in ads transmitted via radio, television, and the Internet that Cold-Eeze contained a "patented formula clinically proven to reduce the severity and duration of common cold symptoms." In their suit against Quigley, the plaintiffs claimed that the company had engaged in deceptive advertising because the lozenges did not lessen the severity or duration of the common cold. In all, the plaintiffs alleged that Quigley had engaged in five practices that violated the UTPCPL: deceptive marketing of goods, marketing of altered goods, "bait" advertising, breach of written warranty, and fraud.

Quigley contended that there could be no breach of written warranty because the ads were not in writing. The Pennsylvania state court hearing the case agreed that the radio and TV ads were not in writing, but what about the Internet ads?

Were the Internet Ads in Writing?

In making its decision, the court considered the purpose of the UTPCPL as well as definitions of the term *writing* given in various dictionaries. The court concluded that a seller gives a buyer "a written guarantee or warranty under [the UTPCPL] if the seller intentionally sets forth the guarantee or warranty in letters, words, or the equivalent on a physical medium and gives the guarantee to the buyer in that form." The court further concluded that a "physical medium" was one that was "visible." Applying this definition to the facts of the case, the court decided that the Internet ad was in writing because "[t]he defendant intentionally set forth its Internet ad in letters and words on a visible medium—buyers' computer screens linked to the Internet."[a]

FOR CRITICAL ANALYSIS

Was Quigley's statement about Cold-Eeze an express warranty or an implied warranty?

---

a. *Tesauro v. The Quigley Corp.,* No. 00080111 (Pennsylvania Court of Common Pleas for Philadelphia County, April 9, 2001). For a summary of this unpublished opinion, see "Pennsylvania Court Defines 'Writing' for Consumer Fraud Purposes," *The Internet Newsletter,* May 2001, p. 9.

STATE CONSUMER PROTECTION LAWS

Thus far, our primary focus has been on federal legislation. As mentioned, however, state laws often provide more extensive protections for consumers than do federal laws. The warranty and unconscionability provisions of the Uniform Commercial Code (discussed in Chapters 9 and 11) offer important protections for consumers against unfair practices on the part of sellers. Far less widely adopted than the UCC is the Uniform Consumer Credit Code, which has provisions concerning truth in lending, maximum credit ceilings, door-to-door sales, fine-print clauses, and other practices affecting consumer transactions.

Virtually all states have specific consumer protection acts, often titled "deceptive trade practices acts." Although state consumer protection statutes vary widely in their provisions, a common thread runs through most of them. Typically, these laws are directed at sellers' deceptive practices, such as providing false or misleading information to consumers. An example of the broad protection such legislation may provide is the Texas Deceptive Trade Practices Act of 1973, which forbids a seller from selling to a buyer anything that the buyer does not need or cannot afford. (For another example, see this chapter's *Legal E-nvironment* feature on the preceding page.)

KEY TERMS

bait-and-switch advertising 612	"cooling-off" laws 618	deceptive advertising 611
cease-and-desist order 613	counteradvertising 613	Regulation Z 618

CHAPTER SUMMARY CONSUMER PROTECTION

Deceptive Advertising (See pages 611–615.)	1. *Definition of deceptive advertising*—Generally, an advertising claim will be deemed deceptive if it would mislead a reasonable consumer.
	
	 2. *Bait-and-switch advertising*—The FTC prohibits advertising a lower-priced product (the "bait") when the intention is not to sell the advertised product but to lure consumers into the store and convince them to buy a higher-priced product (the "switch").
	
	 3. *Online deceptive advertising*—The FTC has issued guidelines to help online businesses comply with existing laws prohibiting deceptive advertising. The guidelines do not set forth new rules but rather describe how existing laws apply to online advertising.
	
	 4. *FTC actions against deceptive advertising*—
	
	     a. Cease-and-desist orders—Requiring the advertiser to stop the challenged advertising.
	
	     b. Counteradvertising—Requiring the advertiser to advertise to correct the earlier misinformation.

Telemarketing and Electronic Advertising (See pages 615–617.)	The Telephone Consumer Protection Act of 1991 prohibits telephone solicitation using an automatic telephone dialing system or a prerecorded voice, as well as the transmission of advertising materials via fax without the recipient's permission to do so. In 2003, the FTC established the National Do Not Call Registry.
Labeling and Packaging (See pages 617–618.)	Manufacturers must comply with labeling and packaging requirements for their specific products. In general, all labels must be accurate and not misleading.
Sales (See pages 618–619.)	1. *Door-to-door sales*—The FTC requires all door-to-door sellers to give consumers three days (a "cooling-off" period) to cancel any sale. States provide for similar protection. 2. *Telephone and mail-order sales*—Federal and state statutes and regulations govern certain practices of sellers who solicit over the telephone or through the mails and prohibit the use of the mails to defraud individuals. 3. *Online sales*—Increasingly, the Internet is being used to conduct business-to-consumer transactions. Consumers are protected to some extent under both state and federal laws against fraudulent and deceptive online sales practices.

CHAPTER SUMMARY CONSUMER PROTECTION—Continued

Health and Safety Protection (See pages 620–622.)	1. *Food and drugs*—The Federal Food, Drug and Cosmetic Act of 1938, as amended, protects consumers against adulterated and misbranded foods and drugs. The act establishes food standards, specifies safe levels of potentially hazardous food additives, and sets classifications of food and food advertising.
	2. *Consumer product safety*—The Consumer Product Safety Act of 1972 seeks to protect consumers from risk of injury from hazardous products. The Consumer Product Safety Commission has the power to remove products that are deemed imminently hazardous from the market and to ban the manufacture and sale of hazardous products.
Credit Protection (See pages 622–626.)	1. *Consumer Credit Protection Act, Title I (Truth-in-Lending Act, or TILA)*—A disclosure law that requires sellers and lenders to disclose credit terms and loan terms in certain transactions, including retail and installment sales and loans, car loans, home-improvement loans, and specific real estate loans. Additionally, the TILA provides for the following:
	a. Equal credit opportunity—Creditors are prohibited from discriminating on the basis of race, religion, marital status, gender, and so on.
	b. Credit-card protection—Liability of cardholders for unauthorized charges is limited to $50, providing notice requirements are met; consumers are not liable for unauthorized charges made on unsolicited credit cards. Procedures for resolving billing disputes are set forth.
	c. Consumer leases—The Consumer Leasing Act (CLA) of 1988 amended the TILA to protect consumers who lease automobiles and other goods priced at $25,000 or less if the lease term exceeds four months.
	2. *Fair Credit Reporting Act*—Entitles consumers to request verification of the accuracy of a credit report and to have unverified or false information removed from their files.
	3. *Fair Debt Collection Practices Act*—Prohibits debt collectors from using unfair debt-collection practices, such as contacting the debtor at his or her place of employment (if the employer objects) or at unreasonable times, contacting third parties about the debt, harassing the debtor, and so on.
State Consumer Protection Laws (See pages 627–628.)	State laws often provide for greater consumer protection against deceptive trade practices than do federal laws. In addition, the warranty and unconscionability provisions of the Uniform Commercial Code protect consumers against sellers' deceptive practices. The Uniform Consumer Credit Code, which has not been widely adopted by the states, provides credit protection for consumers.

FOR REVIEW

1. When will advertising be deemed deceptive?
2. What special rules apply to telephone solicitation?
3. What is Regulation Z, and to what type of transactions does it apply?
4. How does the Federal Food, Drug and Cosmetic Act protect consumers?
5. What are the major federal statutes providing for consumer protection in credit transactions?

QUESTIONS AND CASE PROBLEMS

19–1. Unsolicited Merchandise. Andrew, a resident of California, received a flyer in the U.S. mail announcing a new line of regional cookbooks distributed by the Every-Kind Cookbook Co. Andrew was not interested and threw the flyer away. Two days later, Andrew received in the mail an introductory cookbook entitled *Inner Mongolian Regional Cookbook,* as announced in the flyer, on a "trial basis" from Every-Kind. Andrew was not interested but did not go to the trouble to return the cookbook. Every-Kind demanded payment of $20.95 for the *Inner Mongolian Regional Cookbook.* Discuss whether Andrew can be required to pay for the cookbook.

19–2. Sales. On June 28, a sales representative for Renowned Books called on the Guevaras at their home. After listening to a very persuasive sales pitch, the Guevaras agreed in writing to purchase a twenty-volume set of historical encyclopedias from Renowned Books for a total price of $299. An initial down payment of $35 was required, with the remainder of the price to be paid in monthly payments over a one-year period. Two days later, the Guevaras, having second thoughts about the purchase, contacted the book company and stated that they had decided to rescind the contract. Renowned Books said this would be impossible. Has Renowned Books violated any consumer law by not allowing the Guevaras to rescind their contract? Explain.

19–3. Credit Protection. Maria Ochoa receives two new credit cards on May 1. She has solicited one of them from Midtown Department Store, and the other arrives unsolicited from High-Flying Airlines. During the month of May, Ochoa makes numerous credit-card purchases from Midtown Department Store, but she does not use the High-Flying Airlines card. On May 31, a burglar breaks into Ochoa's home and steals both credit cards, along with other items. Ochoa notifies the Midtown Department Store of the theft on June 2, but she fails to notify High-Flying Airlines. Using the Midtown credit card, the burglar makes a $500 purchase on June 1 and a $200 purchase on June 3. The burglar then charges a vacation flight on the High-Flying Airlines card for $1,000 on June 5. Ochoa receives the bills for these charges and refuses to pay them. Discuss Ochoa's liability in these situations.

19–4. Deceptive Advertising. Thompson Medical Co. marketed a new cream, called Aspercreme, which was supposed to help people with arthritis and others suffering from minor aches. Aspercreme contained no aspirin. Thompson's television advertisements stated that the product provided "the strong relief of aspirin right where you hurt" and showed the announcer holding up aspirin tablets, as well as a tube of Aspercreme. The Federal Trade Commission held that the advertisements were misleading because they led consumers to believe that Aspercreme contained aspirin. Thompson

Medical Co. appealed this decision and argued that the advertisements never actually stated that its product contained aspirin. How should the court rule? Discuss. [*Thompson Medical Co. v. Federal Trade Commission,* 791 F.2d 189 (D.C. Cir. 1986)]

19–5. Equal Credit Opportunity. The Riggs National Bank of Washington, D.C., loaned more than $11 million to Samuel Linch and Albert Randolph. To obtain the loan, Linch and Randolph provided personal financial statements. Linch's statement included substantial assets that he owned jointly with his wife, Marcia. As a condition of the loan, Riggs required that Marcia, as well as Samuel and Albert, sign a personal guaranty for repayment. When the borrowers defaulted, Riggs filed a suit in a federal district court to recover its funds, based on the personal guaranties. The court ruled against the borrowers, who appealed. On what basis might the borrowers argue that Riggs had violated the Equal Credit Opportunity Act? [*Riggs National Bank of Washington, D.C. v. Linch,* 36 F.3d 370 (4th Cir. 1994)]

19–6. Debt Collection. Equifax A.R.S., a debt-collection agency, sent Donna Russell a notice about one of her debts. The front of the notice stated that "[i]f you do not dispute this claim (see reverse side) and wish to pay it within the next 10 days we will not post this collection to your file." The reverse side set out Russell's rights under the Fair Debt Collection Practices Act (FDCPA), including the right to take thirty days to decide whether to contest the claim. Russell filed a suit in a federal district court against Equifax. The court ruled against Russell, who appealed. On what basis might Russell argue that Equifax had violated the FDCPA? [*Russell v. Equifax A.R.S.,* 74 F.3d 30 (2d Cir. 1996)]

19–7. Debt Collection. Rancho Santa Margarita Recreation and Landscape Corp., a condominium association, attempted unsuccessfully to collect an assessment fee from Andrew Ladick. The association referred the matter to the law offices of Gerald J. Van Gemert. Van Gemert sent Ladick a letter demanding payment of the fee. The letter did not include a Fair Debt Collection Practices Act (FDCPA) validation notice, nor did it disclose that Van Gemert was attempting to collect a debt and that any information obtained would be used for that purpose. Ladick filed a suit in a federal district court against Van Gemert and his office, alleging violations of the FDCPA. Van Gemert filed a motion for summary judgment on the ground that the assessment was not a debt, as defined by the FDCPA; he argued, in part, that Ladick's obligation had not arisen out of a transaction, as required by the FDCPA definition. Will the court agree with Van Gemert? Why or why not? [*Ladick v. Van Gemert,* 146 F.3d 1205 (10th Cir. 1998)]

19–8. Debt Collection. Gloria Mahon incurred a bill of $279.70 for medical services rendered by Dr. Larry Bowen. For more than two years, Bowen sent monthly billing statements to the Mahons at their home address (where they had lived for forty-five years). Getting no response, Bowen assigned the collection of the account to Credit Bureau of Placer County, Inc. Credit Bureau uses computerized collection tracking and filing software, known as Columbia Ultimate Business Systems (CUBS). CUBS automatically generates standardized collection notices and acts as an electronic filing system for each account, recording all collection activities, including which notices are sent to whom and on what date. Credit Bureau employees monitor the activity, routinely noting whether an envelope is returned undelivered. Credit Bureau mailed three CUBS–generated notices to the Mahons. According to Credit Bureau's records, the notices were not returned, and the Mahons did not respond. Credit Bureau reported the Mahons' account as delinquent. The Mahons filed a suit in a federal district court against Credit Bureau, alleging in part that the agency had failed to send a validation notice, as required by the Fair Debt Collection Practices Act. Credit Bureau filed a motion for summary judgment. Should a notice be considered sent only if a debtor acknowledges its receipt? Why or why not? [*Mahon v. Credit Bureau of Placer County, Inc.,* 171 F.3d 1197 (9th Cir. 1999)]

19–10. Fair Credit Reporting Act. Source One Associates, Inc., is based in Poughquag, New York. Peter Easton, Source One's president, is responsible for its daily operations. Between 1995 and 1997, Source One received requests from persons in Massachusetts seeking financial information about individuals and businesses. To obtain this information, Easton first obtained the targeted individuals' credit reports through Equifax Consumer Information Services by claiming the reports would be used only in connection with credit transactions involving the consumers. From the reports, Easton identified financial institutions at which the targeted individuals held accounts and then called the institutions to learn the account balances by impersonating either officers of the institutions or the account holders. The information was then provided to Source One's customers for a fee. Easton did not know why the customers wanted the information. The state ("Commonwealth") of Massachusetts filed a suit in a Massachusetts state court against Source One and Easton, alleging, among other things, violations of the Fair Credit Reporting Act (FCRA). Did the defendants violate the FCRA? Explain. [*Commonwealth v. Source One Associates, Inc.,* 436 Mass. 118, 763 N.E.2d 42 (2002)]

Case Problem with Sample Answer

19–9. Fair Debt Collection. CrossCheck, Inc., provides check-authorization services to retail merchants. When a customer presents a check, the merchant contacts CrossCheck, which estimates the probability that the check will clear the bank. If the probability is within an acceptable statistical range, CrossCheck notifies the merchant. If the check is dishonored, the merchant sends it to CrossCheck, which pays it. CrossCheck then attempts to redeposit it. If this fails, CrossCheck takes further steps to collect the amount. CrossCheck attempts to collect on more than two thousand checks per year and spends $2 million on these efforts, which involve about 7 percent of its employees and 6 percent of its total expenses. William Winterstein took his truck to C&P Auto Service Center, Inc., for a tune-up and paid for the service with a check. C&P contacted CrossCheck and, on its recommendation, accepted the check. When the check was dishonored, C&P mailed it to CrossCheck, which reimbursed C&P and sent a letter to Winterstein requesting payment. Winterstein filed a suit in a federal district court against CrossCheck, asserting that the letter violated the Fair Debt Collection Practices Act. CrossCheck filed a motion for summary judgment. On what ground might the court grant the motion? Explain. [*Winterstein v. CrossCheck, Inc.,* 149 F.Supp.2d 466 (N.D.Ill. 2001)]

To view a sample answer for this case problem, go to this book's Web site at http://leet.westbuslaw.com and click on "Interactive Study Center."

A Question of Ethics & Social Responsibility

19–11. Renee Purtle bought a 1986 Chevrolet Blazer from Eldridge Auto Sales, Inc. To finance the purchase through Eldridge, Purtle filled out a credit application on which she misrepresented her employment status. Based on the misrepresentation, Eldridge extended credit. In the credit contract, Eldridge did not disclose the finance charge, the annual percentage rate, or the total sales price or use the term *amount financed,* as the Truth-in-Lending Act (TILA) and its regulations require. Purtle defaulted on the loan, and Eldridge repossessed the vehicle. Purtle filed a suit in a federal district court against Eldridge, alleging violations of the TILA. The court awarded Purtle $1,000 in damages, plus attorneys' fees and costs. Eldridge appealed, arguing in part that Purtle was not entitled to damages because she had committed fraud on her credit application. Considering these facts, answer the following questions. [*Purtle v. Eldridge Auto Sales, Inc.,* 91 F.3d 797 (6th Cir. 1996)]

1. How will the appellate court rule in this case? Why?
2. The trial court awarded Purtle money damages for the car dealer's violation of the TILA even though Purtle had lied about her job on the credit application. Do you think it is fair for the court to reward a plaintiff who has committed fraud? What should the court do?
3. The plaintiff in this case also defaulted on the loan. Generally, should a person who defaults on a loan be prohibited from suing the creditor for violating the TILA? Why or why not?

Critical-Thinking Ethical Question

19–12. As discussed in the text, many states have enacted laws that go even further than federal law to protect the interests of consumers. These laws vary tremendously from state to state. Generally, do you think it is fair that citizens of one state receive more protection than citizens of another state? What about fairness to sellers, who may be prohibited from engaging in a practice in one state that is perfectly legal in another? Should all consumer protection statutes be federally legislated? Why or why not?

Video Question

19–13. Go to this text's Web site at http://leet.westbuslaw.com and select "Video Questions." Click on "Chapter 19" and view the video titled *Advertising Communication Law: Bait and Switch.* Then answer the following questions.

1. Is the auto dealership's advertisement for the truck in the video deceptive? Why or why not?
2. Is the advertisement for the truck an offer to which the dealership is bound? Does it matter if Betty detrimentally relied on the advertisement?
3. Is Tony committed to buying Betty's trade-in truck for three thousand dollars because that is what he told her over the phone?

INTERACTING WITH THE INTERNET

For updated links to resources available on the Web, as well as a variety of other materials, visit this text's Web site at

http://leet.westbuslaw.com

A government-sponsored Web site that contains reports on consumer issues, including issues relating to online deceptive advertising and other forms of online fraud, can be accessed at

http://www.consumer.gov

The FTC's Web site offers extensive information on consumer protection laws, consumer problems, enforcement issues, and other topics relevant to consumer law. Go to

http://www.ftc.gov

To learn more about the FTC's "cooling-off" rule, you can access it directly by going to the following URL:

http://www.ftc.gov/bcp/conline/pubs/buying/cooling.htm

ONLINE LEGAL RESEARCH EXERCISES

Go to **http://leet.westbuslaw.com**, the Web site that accompanies this text. Select "Interactive Study Center," and then click on "Chapter 19." There you will find the following Internet research exercises that you can perform to learn more about topics covered in this chapter.

Activity 19–1: HISTORICAL PERSPECTIVE—The Food and Drug Administration
Activity 19–2: MANAGEMENT PERSPECTIVE—Internet Advertising and Marketing

BEFORE THE TEST

Go to **http://leet.westbuslaw.com**, the Web site that accompanies this text. Select "Interactive Quizzes." You will find at least twenty interactive questions relating to this chapter.

Westlaw® Campus

If your textbook provided for a subscription to Westlaw® Campus, or if you have otherwise purchased access to the Westlaw Campus database, you can access any of the cases presented or cited in this chapter by using your Westlaw Campus account.

CHAPTER **20**

Protecting the Environment

CONTENTS

CHAPTER OBJECTIVES

After reading this chapter, you should be able to answer the following questions:

1. Under what common law theories can polluters be held liable?

2. What is an environmental impact statement, and who must file one?

3. What does the Environmental Protection Agency do?

4. What major federal statutes regulate air and water pollution?

5. What is Superfund? To what categories of persons does liability under Superfund extend?

Concern over the degradation of the environment has increased over time in response to the environmental effects of population growth, urbanization, and industrialization. Although we may at times try to ignore our connection to nature, as Rachel Carson indicates in the quotation below, most of us realize that our survival, to a large extent, depends on the preservation of our environment. Environmental protection is not without a price, however. For many businesses, the costs of complying with environmental regulations are high, and for some they are too high. A constant tension exists between the desirability of increasing profits and productivity and the need to protect the environment.

In this chapter, we discuss laws and regulations designed to protect and preserve our environmental resources. Environmental law consists of statutes passed by federal, state, and local governments and regulations issued by administrative agencies. Before examining statutory and regulatory laws, however, we look at the remedies available under the common law.

"Man, however much he may like to pretend the contrary, is part of nature."

Rachel Carson, 1907–1964
(American writer and conservationist)

COMMON LAW ACTIONS

Common law remedies against environmental pollution originated centuries ago in England. Those responsible for operations that created dirt, smoke, noxious odors, noise, or toxic substances were sometimes held liable under common law theories of nuisance or negligence. Today, injured individuals continue to rely on the common law to obtain damages and injunctions against business polluters.

Nuisance

Under the common law doctrine of **nuisance,** persons can be held liable if they use their property in a way that unreasonably interferes with others' rights to use or enjoy their own property. In these situations, the courts commonly balance the equities between the harm caused by the pollution and the costs of stopping it.

Courts have often denied injunctive relief on the ground that the hardships that would be imposed on the polluter and on the community are greater than the hardships suffered by the plaintiff. ● EXAMPLE 1 A factory that causes neighboring landowners to suffer from smoke, dirt, and vibrations may be left in operation if it is the core of a local economy. The injured parties may be awarded only money damages. These damages may include compensation for the decrease in the value of their property that results from the factory's operation.●

Property owners may be given relief from pollution in situations in which they can identify a distinct harm separate from that affecting the general public. This is referred to as a "private nuisance." Under the common law, citizens were denied standing (access to the courts—see Chapter 4) unless they had suffered a harm distinct from the harm suffered by the public at large. Some states still require this. An action to abate a "public nuisance" can be brought by a public authority (such as a state's attorney general), however.

Negligence and Strict Liability

An injured party can sue a business polluter in tort under the negligence and strict liability theories discussed in Chapters 8 and 9. The basis for a negligence action is the business's alleged failure to use reasonable care toward the party, whose injury was foreseeable and was caused by the lack of reasonable care. For example, employees might sue an employer whose failure to use proper pollution controls contaminated the air and caused the employees to suffer respiratory illnesses. A developing area of tort law involves *toxic torts*—actions against toxic polluters.

Businesses that engage in ultrahazardous activities—such as the transportation of radioactive materials—are strictly liable for whatever injuries the activities cause. In a strict liability action, the injured party does not need to prove that the business failed to exercise reasonable care.

NUISANCE
A common law doctrine under which persons can be held liable for using their property in a way that unreasonably interferes with others' rights to use or enjoy their own property.

"A nuisance may be merely a right thing in the wrong place, like a pig in the parlor instead of the barnyard."
GEORGE SUTHERLAND, 1862–1942
(Associate justice of the United States Supreme Court, 1922–1938)

STATE AND LOCAL REGULATION

Many states regulate the amount of pollutants a business can release into the environment. Thus, for example, even when state zoning laws permit a business's proposed development, the proposal may have to be altered to change the development's impact on the environment. State laws may restrict a business's discharge of chemicals into the air or water or regulate its disposal of toxic wastes. States may also regulate the disposal or recycling of other wastes, including glass, metal, and plastic containers and paper. Additionally, states may restrict emissions from motor vehicles.

City, county, and other local governments control some aspects of the environment. For instance, local zoning laws (see Chapter 21) control some land use. These laws may be designed to inhibit or direct the growth of cities and suburbs or to protect the natural environment. In the interest of safeguarding the environment, these laws may prohibit certain land uses. An ongoing controversy concerns whether landowners should be compensated when restrictions are placed on the use of their property for the purpose of protecting the environment. For a discussion of this issue, see this chapter's *Inside the Legal Environment* feature.

Other aspects of the environment may be subject to local regulation for other reasons. Methods of waste and garbage removal and disposal, for example, can have a substantial impact on a community. The appearance of buildings and other structures, including advertising signs and billboards, may affect traffic safety, property values, or local aesthetics. Noise generated by a business or its customers may be annoying, disruptive, or damaging to neighbors. The location and condition of parks, streets, and other publicly used land subject to local control have an impact on the environment and can also affect business.

FEDERAL REGULATION

Congress has enacted a number of statutes to control the impact of human activities on the environment. Some of these have been passed to improve the quality of air and water. Some of them specifically regulate toxic chemicals, including pesticides, herbicides, and hazardous wastes.

Environmental Regulatory Agencies

Much of the body of federal law governing business activities consists of the regulations issued and enforced by administrative agencies. The most well known of the agencies regulating environmental law is the Environmental Protection Agency (EPA), which was created in 1970 to coordinate federal environmental responsibilities. Other federal agencies with authority to regulate specific environmental matters include the Department of the Interior, the Department of Defense, the Department of Labor, the Food and Drug Administration, and the Nuclear Regulatory Commission. These regulatory agencies—and all other agencies of the federal government—must take environmental factors into consideration when making significant decisions.

Most federal environmental laws provide that citizens can sue to enforce environmental regulations if government agencies fail to do so—or can sue to protest agency enforcement actions if they believe these actions go too far. Typically, a threshold hurdle in such suits is meeting the requirements for standing to sue.

ENVIRONMENTAL IMPACT STATEMENT (EIS)
A statement required by the National Environmental Policy Act for any major federal action that will significantly affect the quality of the environment. The statement must analyze the action's impact on the environment and explore alternative actions that might be taken.

Assessing the Environmental Impact of Agency Actions

The National Environmental Policy Act (NEPA) of 1969[1] requires that for every major federal action that significantly affects the quality of the environment, an **environmental impact statement (EIS)** must be prepared. An action qualifies as major if it involves a substantial commitment of resources (monetary or

---

1. 42 U.S.C. Sections 4321–4370d.

INSIDE THE LEGAL ENVIRONMENT

Environmental Takings

As you will read in Chapter 21, the Fifth Amendment to the U.S. Constitution gives the government the power to "take" private property for public use. The Fifth Amendment attaches an important condition to this power, however: when private land is taken for public use, the landowner must be given "just compensation." An ongoing legal controversy involves whether environmental regulations that limit private property owners' uses of their property constitute a "taking" of private property in the public interest. If so, the property owners should receive the just compensation guaranteed under the Fifth Amendment. In some cases, the courts have held for the property owners on this issue.[a] In others, however, the courts have sided with government regulators.

The *Tahoe* Case

In 2002, a case came before the United States Supreme Court in which property owners alleged that their property had been "temporarily taken" by environmental regulations. The case, *Tahoe-Sierra Preservation Council v. Tahoe Regional Planning Agency*,[b] involved an attempt to curb pollution and the growth of algae in Lake Tahoe, on the California-Nevada border. In 1981, the Tahoe Regional Planning Agency issued a temporary moratorium (suspension) on the construction of residential housing in areas around the lake that were the most susceptible to further environmental damage. The moratorium was extended over the next several years until 1987 when it was replaced by a "revised plan," which is still in effect.

Most of the affected property owners were older couples who had purchased their lots decades earlier and had planned to build retirement homes along the lake. The moratorium, however, allowed no exceptions and prohibited any land use whatsoever. The regulations were so stringent that some owners were even forbidden to enter onto their own land without the agency's permission. Ultimately, the owners sued the agency, claiming that a regulatory taking had occurred. Even if the taking was only temporary, the regulations had forced the owners to give up all reasonable use of their land, economically and personally, for a period of time, and they deserved to be compensated for this deprivation.

The Supreme Court Sides with the Regulators

When the case came before the United States Supreme Court, the Court sided with the regulators. The Court held that the agency's actions had not deprived the owners of their property for too long a time, and thus no taking had occurred. How long is too long? The Court said no categorical rule could be stated; the answer always depends on "the facts presented."

FOR CRITICAL ANALYSIS

Private property owners complain that they alone should not have to bear the costs of environmental preservation, given that all members of the public reap the benefits. Should private landowners be compensated when their land is essentially "taken" for public use by environmental regulations?

a. See, for example, *City of Monterey v. Del Monte Dunes at Monterey, Ltd.,* 526 U.S. 687, 119 S.Ct. 1624, 143 L.Ed.2d 882 (1999), excerpts from which are presented in Appendix A.

b. 535 U.S 302, 122 S.Ct. 1465, 152 L.Ed.2d 517 (2002).

otherwise). An action is federal if a federal agency has the power to control it. Construction by a private developer of a ski resort on federal land, for example, may require an EIS. Building or operating a nuclear plant, which requires a federal permit, or constructing a dam as part of a federal project requires an EIS. If an agency decides that an EIS is unnecessary, it must issue a statement supporting this conclusion.

An EIS must analyze (1) the impact on the environment that the action will have, (2) any adverse effects on the environment and alternative actions that might be taken, and (3) irreversible effects the action might generate. EISs have become instruments for private citizens, consumer interest groups, businesses, and others to challenge federal agency actions on the basis that the actions improperly threaten the environment.

The question in the following case was whether the U.S. Department of Transportation (DOT) acted "arbitrarily and capriciously" in failing to prepare an EIS before issuing final regulations that permitted Mexico-based "motor carriers" to operate within the United States. The regulations were important to U.S. compliance with its treaty obligations under the North American Free Trade Agreement (NAFTA). Labor unions representing U.S. truck drivers, and other organizations, challenged the DOT's action.

CASE 20.1   Public Citizen v. Department of Transportation

United States Court of Appeals,
Ninth Circuit, 2003.
316 F.3d 1002.

HISTORICAL AND
INTERNATIONAL SETTING *In 1992, the United States, Canada, and Mexico signed NAFTA to establish a free trade zone encompassing those nations. Environmental concerns dominated the debate over NAFTA in the United States. After the parties negotiated a second treaty, the North American Agreement on Environmental Cooperation, in 1993, Congress passed the North American Free Trade Agreement Implementation Act. In that act, Congress made clear that NAFTA cannot be construed "to amend or modify any law of the United States * * * regarding * * * the protection of the environment."*[a] *NAFTA became effective in 1994.*

BACKGROUND AND FACTS Foreign trucks are permitted to enter the United States only if they are

authorized to do so. The DOT is generally required to grant permission to any carrier that is willing and able to comply with certain statutes and regulations. In 2002, the Federal Motor Carrier Safety Administration (FMCSA), an agency within the DOT, proposed "Application and Safety Rules" to permit complying trucks based in Mexico to operate in the United States beyond specified border zones. After soliciting public comments on the proposed rules, the DOT determined that an EIS was not required. The DOT concluded that the rules would not significantly affect the quality of the environment, and issued a statement—an "Environmental Assessment" (EA)—to support this conclusion and an order to implement the rules. Public Citizen, and other environmental and labor organizations, petitioned the U.S. Court of Appeals for the Ninth Circuit for a review of this order, asserting that the agency failed to examine adequately the environmental consequences.

IN THE WORDS
OF THE COURT . . .

WARDLAW, Circuit Judge:
* * * *

The Council on Environmental Quality ("CEQ"), a body established by NEPA, has issued regulations implementing NEPA. * * *
* * * *

---

a. 19 U.S.C. Section 3312(a)(2).

CASE 20.1—Continued

The CEQ regulations explain that [a] proposed federal action must be analyzed with regard to several contexts—national, regional, and local—as well as by looking at the short- and long-term effects of the proposed action. Measured against this standard, DOT's EA is woefully inadequate. The EA calculates likely emissions increases if the Application and Safety Rules are implemented. It dismisses those increases as insignificant, however, because they are "very small relative to national levels of emissions." It does not conduct any analysis regarding whether these increases may be localized in certain areas near the Mexican border, including such likely destinations as Southern California or Texas.

 * * * The law requires DOT to consider the most likely localities to be affected by increased Mexican truck traffic and to perform more localized analyses for these areas. Indeed, comments submitted to FMCSA * * * analyzed publicly available government data to predict, not surprisingly, that major cities near the Mexican border would likely suffer the greatest environmental impact as a result of the regulations. The fact that commenters [those who made comments on the proposed rule during the rulemaking process] performed such an analysis does not indicate that their analysis was correct, but rather that it was possible to conduct such an analysis. DOT's failure to do so indicates that it did not take a sufficiently "hard look" at the environmental effects of its actions or at the public comments it received.

Furthermore, DOT failed to address adequately the long-term effects of its actions. In conducting its EA, DOT limited its analysis to the environmental impact of Mexican trucks in the year 2002. This is anomalous in itself, considering that the regulations were scheduled to become effective only as of May 3, 2002. More significantly, the EA offered no projections of the increase (or decrease) in Mexican truck traffic after 2002, though the regulations were certainly expected to continue in effect beyond the end of [2002] * * * .

 * * * *

Once again, DOT received this very criticism in public comments during its rulemaking process. The commenters used available government data to estimate future increases in Mexican truck traffic after 2002. This alone should have prompted DOT to conduct a long-term analysis, as required by the CEQ regulations, or at the very least, to convincingly * * * explain its absence.

DECISION AND REMEDY The U.S. Court of Appeals for the Ninth Circuit found that the "Application and Safety Rules" were major federal actions that could significantly affect the environment, and held that the DOT acted arbitrarily and capriciously in concluding that it did not need to prepare an EIS for the regulations. The court remanded the matter to the DOT for the agency to prepare an EIS.

FOR CRITICAL ANALYSIS—Political Consideration *When state environmental regulations are stricter than those of the federal government, should a federal agency consider whether its proposed action might violate the state rules?*

Agency Decision Making and Wildlife Preservation

Other federal laws also require that environmental values be considered in agency decision making. Among the most important of these laws are those that have been enacted to protect fish and wildlife. Under the Fish and Wildlife

Coordination Act of 1958,[2] federal agencies proposing to approve the impounding or diversion of a stream's waters must consult with the Fish and Wildlife Service with a view to preventing the loss of fish and wildlife resources.

Also important is the Endangered Species Act of 1973.[3] This act requires all federal agencies to take steps to ensure that their actions "do not jeopardize the continued existence of endangered species" or the habitat of an endangered species. An action may jeopardize the continued existence of a species if it sets in motion a chain of events that reduces the chances that the species will survive.

AIR POLLUTION

Federal involvement with air pollution goes back to the 1950s, when Congress authorized funds for air-pollution research. In 1963, the federal government passed the Clean Air Act,[4] which focused on multistate air pollution and provided assistance to states. Various amendments, particularly in 1970, 1977, and 1990, strengthened the government's authority to regulate the quality of air.

Mobile Sources of Pollution

Regulations governing air pollution from automobiles and other mobile sources specify pollution standards and establish time schedules for meeting the standards. For example, under the 1990 amendments to the Clean Air Act, automobile manufacturers were required to cut new automobiles' exhaust emissions of nitrogen oxide by 60 percent and of other pollutants by 35 percent by 1998. Regulations in effect for 2004 model cars call for nitrogen oxide tailpipe emissions to be cut by nearly 10 percent by 2007. For the first time, sport utility vehicles (SUVs) and light trucks will be required to meet the same standards as automobiles.

Service stations are also subject to environmental regulations. The 1990 amendments required service stations to sell gasoline with a higher oxygen content in forty-one cities that experienced carbon monoxide pollution in the winter. Service stations in the most polluted urban areas, including Los Angeles and eight other cities, were required to sell even cleaner burning gasoline.

The EPA attempts to update pollution-control standards when new scientific information becomes available. In light of evidence that very small particles (2.5 microns, or millionths of a meter) of soot affect health as significantly as larger particles, the EPA issued new particulate standards for motor vehicle exhaust systems and other sources of pollution. The EPA also instituted a more rigorous standard for ozone, which is formed when sunlight combines with pollutants from cars and other sources. Ozone is a major component of smog.

A factory releases effluents (waste products) into the atmosphere. On what basis might affected residents file a suit to obtain relief from any damages caused by pollution?

---

2. 16 U.S.C. Sections 661–666c.
3. 16 U.S.C. Sections 1531–1544.
4. 42 U.S.C. Sections 7401 *et seq.*

Should the costs of EPA regulations be weighed against their prospective benefits?

In setting standards governing air quality, traditionally the EPA has not been required to take costs into account. Rather, the emphasis has been on the benefits. For example, when the EPA issued its new rules on particulate matter and ozone, the head of the EPA claimed that the new standards would save 15,000 lives a year. Given that the EPA values a human life at $5 million, the agency calculated that the lives saved and medical expenses avoided by the stricter standards would amount to $100 billion a year in benefits. Nothing was said about the costs of implementing these rules, however.

Environmental groups tend to downplay these costs and to value potential lives saved very highly. In contrast, business groups, particularly those affected adversely by strict air standards, think that the EPA should factor in these costs. In 2000, the debate over this issue was resolved by the United States Supreme Court. In the case, a number of business groups had challenged the EPA's stricter air-quality standards, claiming that the EPA had exceeded its authority under the Clean Air Act by issuing the regulations. The groups also claimed that the EPA had to take economic costs into account when developing new regulations. The Court, however, held that the EPA had not exceeded its authority under the Clean Air Act and confirmed that the EPA need not take economic costs into account when creating new rules.[5]

Stationary Sources of Pollution

The Clean Air Act authorizes the EPA to establish air-quality standards for stationary sources of pollution (such as manufacturing plants), but the primary responsibility for implementing these standards rests with state and local governments. The EPA sets primary and secondary levels of ambient standards—that is, maximum levels of certain pollutants—and the states formulate plans to achieve those standards. These plans are to provide for the attainment of primary standards within a specified time and secondary standards within a reasonable time. For economic, political, and technological reasons, however, the deadlines are often subject to change.

Different standards apply to sources of pollution in clean areas and sources in polluted ones. Different standards also apply to existing sources of pollution and major new sources. Major new sources include existing sources modified by changes in methods of operation that increase emissions. Standards for major sources require use of the *maximum achievable control technology,* or MACT, to reduce emissions from the combustion of fossil fuels (coal and oil). The EPA issues guidelines as to what equipment meets this standard.

Under the 1990 amendments to the Clean Air Act, 110 of the oldest coal-burning power plants in the United States had to cut their emissions of sulfur

5. *Whitman v. American Trucking Associations,* 531 U.S. 457, 121 S.Ct. 903, 149 L.Ed.2d 1 (2000).

dioxide by 40 percent by the year 2001 to reduce acid rain. Utilities are granted "credits" allowing them to emit certain amounts of sulfur dioxide, and those that emit less than the allowed amounts can sell their credits to other polluters. Controls on other factories and businesses are intended to reduce ground-level ozone pollution in ninety-six cities to healthful levels by 2005 (except Los Angeles, which has until 2010). The amendments also required an end to the production of chlorofluorocarbons, carbon tetrachloride, and methyl chloroform, which are used in air conditioning, refrigeration, and insulation and linked to depletion of the ozone layer in the upper atmosphere.

The relationship between the Clean Air Act's 1990 amendments and a New York state law was at issue in the following case.

CASE 20.2   Clean Air Markets Group v. Pataki

United States District Court,
Northern District of New York, 2002.
194 F.Supp.2d 147.

HISTORICAL AND ENVIRONMENTAL SETTING
Acid rain allegedly has negative effects on water, forests, human health, and buildings and other structures and has long been recognized as an environmental problem. Acid rain consists of atmospheric sulfates and nitrates, which are formed from sulfur dioxide (SO$_2$) and nitrogen oxides (NOx). These substances are emitted as by-products of the combustion of fossil fuels, most notably during the generation of electricity. Emissions originating in fourteen midwestern, eastern, and southern states contribute significantly to acid rain in New York. These high-contributing states are referred to as "Upwind States."

BACKGROUND AND FACTS
By 1999, it was clear to some scientists that SO$_2$ emissions at the rates

permitted by the Clean Air Act would not permit the environmental restoration of parts of the state of New York. Additional reductions in SO$_2$ emissions would be required. George Pataki, the governor of New York, ordered New York utilities to cut SO$_2$ emissions to half of the amount permitted by the Clean Air Act by January 2, 2007. By doing this, the New York utilities would have additional SO$_2$ credits to sell. In May 2000, the New York state legislature enacted the Air Pollution Mitigation Law (APML), which stipulated that most sums received for the sale or trade of SO$_2$ allowances to a polluter in an Upwind State would be forfeited to the New York Public Service Commission (PSC), which regulates New York utilities. This effectively lowered the market value of credits originating with New York utilities. Clean Air Markets Group (CAMG) filed a suit in a federal district court against Pataki and others, claiming in part that the APML was preempted under the U.S. Constitution's supremacy clause.[a] All parties filed motions for summary judgment.

IN THE WORDS OF THE COURT . . .

HURD, District Judge.

*   *   *   *

*   *   * [The APML] creates an obstacle to the accomplishment and execution of the full purposes and objectives of Congress. [The Clean Air Act] provides that SO$_2$ allowances "may be transferred among designated representatives of the owners or operators of [covered units (utilities)] and *any* other person who holds such allowances." [The APML's] restrictions on transferring allowances to units in the Upwind States is contrary to the federal provision that allowances be tradeable to *any* other person. Additionally, Congress considered geographically restricted allowance transfers and rejected it. The EPA,

---

a. As explained in Chapter 5, if federal law has not supplanted a whole field of state law, state law is preempted to the extent that it actually conflicts with federal law. A conflict between state and federal law occurs when compliance with both is physically impossible or when the state law is an obstacle to accomplishing the objective of federal law.

CASE 20.2—Continued

in setting regulations to implement [the Clean Air Act], also considered geographically restricted allowance trading and rejected it * * * . *The rejection of a regionally restricted allowance trading system illustrates the Congressional objective of having a nationwide trading market for SO$_2$ allowances. New York's regional restrictions on SO$_2$ allowance trading by New York units are an obstacle to the execution of that objective.* [Emphasis added.]

Pataki argues that the Air Pollution Mitigation Law * * * imposes a more stringent requirement for air pollution control or abatement, as expressly permitted. However, * * * the Air Pollution Mitigation Law sets no emissions requirements. It sets no requirements for air pollution control or abatement at all. Rather, the New York law is a state regulation of federally allocated SO$_2$ allowances. Further, it is a restriction on the nationwide trading system for which the Clean Air Act provides. It is insufficient to merely say that it imposes requirements for air pollution control, or that the goal is air pollution control or abatement. New York's Air Pollution Mitigation Law is preempted because it interferes with the Clean Air Act's method for achieving the goal of air pollution control: a cap and nationwide SO$_2$ allowance trading system.

In addition to interfering with the nationwide trading of SO$_2$ allowances, the Air Pollution Mitigation Law would result in decreased availability of SO$_2$ allowances in the Upwind States. Restricted availability of SO$_2$ allowances could indirectly reduce emissions in the Upwind States. No doubt that the New York legislators had this in mind when the Air Pollution Mitigation Law was enacted. However, the Clean Air Act permits restrictions on emissions by a state in that state, but it does not permit one state to control emissions in another state. Thus, the inevitable result of laws such as New York's Air Pollution Mitigation Law would be the indirect regulation of allowance trading and emissions in other states, which could not be done directly.

DECISION AND REMEDY The court granted the CAMG's motion for summary judgment, holding that New York's Air Pollution Mitigation Law is preempted, under the supremacy clause, by the Clean Air Act because it interferes with that law's methods for achieving air-pollution control. The court enjoined the enforcement of the state law.

FOR CRITICAL ANALYSIS—Environmental Consideration *Suppose that the APML also provided for a subsidy to those who claimed that the value of their pollution credits had been reduced. Would this have affected the outcome of the case?*

Hazardous Air Pollutants

Hazardous air pollutants are those likely to cause death or serious irreversible or incapacitating illness. In all, 189 of these pollutants have been identified, including asbestos, benzene, beryllium, cadmium, mercury, and vinyl chloride. These pollutants may cause cancer as well as neurological and reproductive damage. They are emitted from stationary sources by a variety of business activities, including smelting, dry cleaning, house painting, and commercial baking. Instead of establishing specific emissions standards for each hazardous air pollutant, the 1990 amendments to the Clean Air Act require industry to use pollution-control equipment that represents the maximum achievable control technology (MACT).

In 1996, the EPA issued a rule to regulate hazardous air pollutants emitted by landfills. The rule requires landfills constructed after May 30, 1991, that emit more than a specified amount of pollutants to install landfill gas collection and control systems. The rule also requires the states to impose the same requirements on landfills constructed before May 30, 1991, if they accepted waste after November 8, 1987.[6]

Violations of the Clean Air Act

For violations of emission limits under the Clean Air Act, the EPA can assess civil penalties of up to $25,000 per day. Additional fines of up to $5,000 per day can be assessed for other violations, such as failing to maintain the required records. To penalize those who find it more cost effective to violate the act than to comply with it, the EPA is authorized to obtain a penalty equal to the violator's economic benefits from noncompliance. Persons who provide information about violators may be paid up to $10,000. Private citizens can also sue violators.

Those who knowingly violate the act may be subject to criminal penalties, including fines of up to $1 million and imprisonment for up to two years (for false statements or failures to report violations). Corporate officers are among those who may be subject to these penalties.

WATER AND NOISE POLLUTION

Water pollution stems mostly from industrial, municipal, and agricultural sources. Pollutants entering streams, lakes, and oceans include organic wastes, heated water, sediments from soil run-off, nutrients (including detergents, fertilizers, and human and animal wastes), and toxic chemicals and other hazardous substances. We look here at laws and regulations governing water pollution.

> " Among the treasures of our land is water—fast becoming our most valuable, most prized, most critical resource. "
>
> DWIGHT D. EISENHOWER, 1890–1969
> (Thirty-fourth president of the United States, 1953–1961)

Navigable Waters

Federal regulations governing the pollution of water can be traced back to the Rivers and Harbors Appropriations Act of 1899.[7] These regulations required a permit for discharging or depositing refuse in navigable waterways. In 1948, Congress passed the Federal Water Pollution Control Act (FWPCA),[8] but its regulatory system and enforcement powers proved to be inadequate.

In 1972, amendments to the FWPCA—known as the Clean Water Act—established the following goals: (1) make waters safe for swimming, (2) protect fish and wildlife, and (3) eliminate the discharge of pollutants into the water. The amendments set specific time schedules, which were extended by amendment in 1977 and by the Water Quality Act of 1987.[9] Under these schedules, the EPA establishes limits on discharges of various types of pollutants based on the technology available for controlling them. The 1972

---

6. 40 C.F.R. Sections 60.750–759.
7. 33 U.S.C. Sections 401–418.
8. 33 U.S.C. Sections 1251–1387.
9. This act amended 33 U.S.C. Section 1251.

amendments also require municipal and industrial polluters to apply for permits before discharging wastes into navigable waters.

Under the act, violators are subject to a variety of civil and criminal penalties. Civil penalties for each violation range from $10,000 per day to as much as $25,000 per day or per violation. Criminal penalties range from a fine of $2,500 per day and imprisonment for up to one year (for negligent violations) to a fine of $1 million and fifteen years' imprisonment (for persons who knowingly violate and endanger another person). Injunctive relief and damages can also be imposed. The polluting party can be required to clean up the pollution or pay for the cost of doing so.

Wetlands

The Clean Water Act prohibits the filling or dredging of **wetlands** unless a permit is obtained from the Army Corps of Engineers. The EPA defines *wetlands* as "those areas that are inundated or saturated by surface or ground water at a frequency and duration sufficient to support, and that under normal circumstances do support, a prevalence of vegetation typically adapted for life in saturated soil conditions." In recent years, the broad interpretation of what constitutes a wetland subject to the regulatory authority of the federal government has generated substantial controversy.

● **EXAMPLE 2** Perhaps one of the most controversial regulations was the migratory-bird rule issued by the Army Corps of Engineers. Under this rule, all bodies of water that could affect interstate commerce, including seasonal ponds or waters "used or suitable for use by migratory birds" that fly over state borders, were navigable waters subject to federal regulation as wetlands under the Clean Water Act. In 2001, after years of controversy, the United States Supreme Court struck down the rule. The case involved a group of communities in the Chicago suburbs that wanted to build a landfill in a tract of land northwest of Chicago that had once been used as a strip mine. Over time, areas that had once been pits in the mine became ponds used by a variety of migratory birds. State and local agencies approved the project, but the Army Corps of Engineers, claiming that the shallow ponds formed a habitat for migratory birds, refused to grant a permit for the landfill. A lawsuit followed, and when the case reached the Supreme Court, the Court held that the Army Corps of Engineers had exceeded its authority under the Clean Water Act. The Court stated that it was not prepared to hold that isolated and seasonal ponds, puddles, and "prairie potholes" become "navigable waters of the United States" simply because they serve as a habitat for migratory birds.[10] ●

Drinking Water

Another statute governing water pollution is the Safe Drinking Water Act of 1974.[11] This act requires the EPA to set maximum levels for pollutants in public water systems. Public water system operators must come as close as possible to meeting the EPA's standards by using the best available technology that is economically and technologically feasible. The EPA is particularly concerned

WETLANDS
Water-saturated areas of land that support specific types of vegetation. Under the Clean Water Act, wetlands are protected areas that cannot be filled in or dredged by private contractors or parties without a permit.

---

10. *Solid Waste Agency of Northern Cook County v. U.S. Army Corps of Engineers,* 531 U.S. 159, 121 S.Ct. 675, 148 L.Ed.2d 576 (2001).
11. 42 U.S.C. Sections 300f to 300j-25.

about contamination from underground sources. Pesticides and wastes leaked from landfills or disposed of in underground injection wells are among the more than two hundred pollutants known to exist in groundwater used for drinking in at least thirty-four states. The act was amended in 1996 to give the EPA more flexibility in setting regulatory standards.

Ocean Dumping

The Marine Protection, Research, and Sanctuaries Act of 1972[12] (popularly known as the Ocean Dumping Act), as amended in 1983, regulates the transporting and dumping of material into ocean waters. It prohibits entirely the ocean dumping of radiological, chemical, and biological warfare agents and high-level radioactive waste. A violation of any provision may result in a civil penalty of $50,000, and a knowing violation is a criminal offense that may result in a $50,000 fine, imprisonment for not more than a year, or both. An injunction may also be imposed.

Oil Spills

In 1989, the supertanker *Exxon Valdez* caused the worst oil spill in North American history in the waters of Alaska's Prince William Sound. A quarter of a million barrels of crude oil—more than ten million gallons—leaked out of the ship's broken hull. In response to the *Exxon Valdez* disaster, Congress passed the Oil Pollution Act of 1990.[13] Any onshore or offshore oil facility, oil shipper, vessel owner, or vessel operator that discharges oil into navigable waters or onto an adjoining shore may be liable for clean-up costs, as well as damages.

The act provides for civil penalties of $1,000 per barrel spilled or $25,000 for each day of the violation. The party held responsible for the clean-up costs can bring a civil suit, however, for contribution from other potentially liable parties. The act also created a $1 billion oil clean-up and economic compensation fund and decreed that by the year 2011, oil tankers using U.S. ports must be double hulled to limit the severity of accidental spills.

Noise Pollution

Regulations concerning noise pollution include the Noise Control Act of 1972.[14] This act directed the EPA to establish noise-emission standards—for example, for railroad noise emissions. The standards must be achievable by the best available technology, and they must be economically within reason. Violations of provisions of the Noise Control Act can result in penalties of not more than $50,000 per day and imprisonment for not more than two years.

"All property in this country is held under the implied obligation that the owner's use of it shall not be injurious to the community."

JOHN HARLAN, 1899–1971
(Associate justice of the United States Supreme Court, 1955–1971)

---

12. 16 U.S.C. Sections 1401–1445.
13. 33 U.S.C. Sections 2701–2761.
14. 42 U.S.C. Sections 4901–4918.

TOXIC CHEMICALS

Originally, most environmental clean-up efforts were directed toward reducing smog and making water safe for fishing and swimming. Over time, some scientists argued that chemicals released into the environment in relatively small amounts could also pose a threat to human life and health. Control of these toxic chemicals has become an important part of environmental law.

Pesticides and Herbicides

The federal statute regulating pesticides and herbicides is the Federal Insecticide, Fungicide, and Rodenticide Act (FIFRA) of 1947.[15] Under FIFRA, pesticides and herbicides must be (1) registered before they can be sold, (2) certified and used only for approved applications, and (3) used in limited quantities when applied to food crops. If a substance is identified as harmful, the EPA can cancel its registration after a hearing. If the harm is imminent, the EPA can suspend registration pending the hearing. The EPA, or state officers or employees, can also inspect factories in which these chemicals are manufactured.

Under 1996 amendments to FIFRA, for a pesticide to remain on the market, there must be "reasonable certainty of no harm" to people from exposure to the pesticide.[16] This means that there must be no more than a one-in-a-million risk to people of developing cancer from exposure in any way, including eating food that contains residues from the pesticide. Pesticide residues are in nearly all fruits and vegetables and processed foods. Under the 1996 amendments, the EPA must distribute to grocery stores brochures on high-risk pesticides that are in food, and the stores must display these brochures for consumers.

Violations of FIFRA It is a violation of FIFRA to sell a pesticide or herbicide that is unregistered, a pesticide or herbicide with a registration that has been canceled or suspended, or a pesticide or herbicide with a false or misleading label. For example, it is an offense to sell a substance that is adulterated (that has a chemical strength different from the concentration declared on the label). It is also an offense to destroy or deface any labeling required under the act. The act's labeling requirements include directions for the use of the pesticide or herbicide, warnings to protect human health and the environment, a statement of treatment in case of poisoning, and a list of the ingredients.

Penalties for Violations Penalties for registrants and producers for violating FIFRA include imprisonment for up to one year and a fine of no more than $50,000. Penalties for commercial dealers include imprisonment for up to one year and a fine of no more than $25,000. Farmers and other private users of pesticides or herbicides who violate the act are subject to a $1,000 fine and imprisonment for up to thirty days.

---

15. 7 U.S.C. Sections 135–136y.
16. 21 U.S.C. Section 346a.

Toxic Substances

The first comprehensive law covering toxic substances was the Toxic Substances Control Act of 1976.[17] The act was passed to regulate chemicals and chemical compounds that are known to be toxic—such as asbestos and polychlorinated biphenyls, popularly known as PCBs—and to institute investigation of any possible harmful effects from new chemical compounds. The regulations authorize the EPA to require that manufacturers, processors, and other organizations planning to use chemicals first determine their effects on human health and the environment. The EPA can regulate substances that may pose an imminent hazard or an unreasonable risk of injury to health or the environment. The EPA may require special labeling, limit the use of a substance, set production quotas, or prohibit the use of a substance altogether.

HAZARDOUS WASTE DISPOSAL

Some industrial, agricultural, and household wastes pose more serious threats than others. If not properly disposed of, these toxic chemicals may present a substantial danger to human health and the environment. In particular, if released into the environment, they may contaminate public drinking water resources.

Resource Conservation and Recovery Act

In 1976, Congress passed the Resource Conservation and Recovery Act (RCRA)[18] in reaction to ever-increasing concern over the effects of hazardous waste materials on the environment. The RCRA required the EPA to establish regulations to monitor and control hazardous waste disposal and to determine which forms of solid waste should be considered hazardous and thus subject to regulation. The EPA has promulgated various technical requirements for storage and treatment of hazardous waste by certain types of facilities. The act also requires all producers of hazardous waste materials to label and package properly any hazardous waste to be transported.

Amendments to the RCRA The RCRA was amended in 1984 and 1986 to add several new regulatory requirements to those already monitored and enforced by the EPA. The amendments had two basic aims. One was to decrease the use of land containment in the disposal of hazardous waste. The other was to require compliance with the act by some generators of hazardous waste—such as those generating less than 1,000 kilograms (2,200 pounds) a month—that had previously been excluded from regulation under the RCRA.

Penalties under the RCRA Under the RCRA, a company can be assessed a civil penalty based on the seriousness of the violation, the probability of harm, and the extent to which the violation deviates from RCRA requirements. The assessment can be up to $25,000 for each day of violation.[19] Criminal penalties include fines of up to $50,000 for each day of violation, imprisonment for up to

---

17. 15 U.S.C. Sections 2601–2692.
18. 42 U.S.C. Sections 6901 *et seq.*
19. 42 U.S.C. Section 6928(a).

two years (in most instances), or both.[20] In addition, if a person knowingly violates the RCRA requirements and endangers the life of another, he or she may be imprisoned for up to fifteen years and fined up to $250,000.[21] Criminal fines and the time of imprisonment can also be doubled for repeat offenders.

The following case involved a conviction under the criminal provisions of the RCRA. The defendant questioned whether the federal government has the authority to enforce those provisions, considering that the EPA has authorized the states to manage hazardous waste programs under the RCRA.

---

20. 42 U.S.C. Section 6928(d).
21. 42 U.S.C. Section 6928(e).

CASE 20.3   **United States v. Elias**

United States Court of Appeals,
Ninth Circuit, 2001.
269 F.3d 1003.

BACKGROUND AND FACTS

Allen Elias was the owner of Evergreen Resources, Inc., a fertilizer company in Idaho, when he decided to transfer sulfuric acid from two railroad cars into a stationary 25,000-gallon tank. Elias had used the tank in his previous business to store by-products of a cyanide leaching process. At the bottom of the thirty-six-foot-long, eleven-foot-high tank were one to two tons of cyanide-laced sludge, hardened and more than a foot deep. Elias ordered four employees, including Scott Dominguez, to enter the tank and wash the sludge out.

Elias did not provide any safety equipment. Forty-five minutes after entering the tank, wearing only his regular work clothes, Dominguez collapsed. The treating physician concluded that the cause was cyanide poisoning. A federal grand jury charged Elias with, among other things, storing or disposing of hazardous waste without a permit while knowingly placing others in imminent danger of death or serious bodily injury in violation of the RCRA. Elias was convicted, sentenced to seventeen years in prison, and ordered to pay $6.3 million in restitution to Dominguez.[a] Elias appealed to the U.S. Court of Appeals for the Ninth Circuit, arguing in part that Idaho's EPA–authorized hazardous waste program displaced the federal program, leaving no federal crimes and no federal jurisdiction.

IN THE WORDS OF THE COURT . . .

T. G. NELSON, Circuit Judge:

*   *   *   *

*   *   * [42 U.S.C. Section 6926 of the RCRA], which governs "Authorized State hazardous waste programs," provides in relevant part:

> Any State which seeks to administer and enforce a hazardous waste program pursuant to this subchapter may *   *   * submit to the [EPA] an application *   *   * . [If the EPA approves the program,] [s]uch State is authorized to carry out such program in lieu of the Federal program *   *   * .

*   *   *   *

*   *   * The linchpin [central element] of [Elias's] argument *   *   * is that the term "program" in Section 6926 incorporates the exclusive responsibility to enforce criminal provisions penalizing the disposal of hazardous wastes. *   *   *

*   *   * *[T]he EPA [does] not interpret RCRA to cede exclusive enforcement authority to states and *   *   * if the EPA's interpretation of Section 6926's "in lieu of" provision is reasonable, we must defer to the agency's interpretation*

---

a. To date, this is the harshest prison term imposed for an environmental crime in the United States.

(continued)

CASE 20.3—Continued

even if the agency could also have reached another reasonable interpretation, or even if we would have reached a different result had we construed the statute initially. *   *   * [T]he EPA's interpretation [is] reasonable because we [can] discern no clear congressional intent that Section 6926 be read to disable the EPA from issuing orders *   *   * wherever an authorized state hazardous waste program operates "in lieu of the Federal program" and because the EPA's conclusion that its power to issue orders *   *   * survives in those states where an authorized state program is operating is plainly consistent with a straightforward reading of the [RCRA]. [Emphasis added.]

*   *   *   *

Legislative history also supports the EPA's contention that RCRA's criminal enforcement provisions are meant to apply within states having authorized programs *   *   * : Prior to the 1984 RCRA Amendments—when, as today, RCRA provided for state programs which, when federally approved, would be carried out "in lieu" of the federal program, and which authorized the state to issue and enforce permits—the [criminal provision] was worded so as to apply in so many words to violations both of federal and state permitting programs.

*   *   *

The 1984 amendments increased the applicable criminal penalties and simply substituted "under this subchapter" for the references to the specific subsections under which permits, federal and state, may be granted. *   *   * [This language] did not, therefore, in any way narrow the scope of federal criminal jurisdiction. Nor did the legislative record hint at any intention by Congress to narrow the scope of federal criminal jurisdiction. To the contrary, Congress manifested its desire to retain a strong federal presence. Had Congress intended to impose a hitherto unknown limitation upon the scope of its laws criminalizing permit violations, its intentions would surely have been manifested *   *   * .

For these reasons, we conclude that, under RCRA, the federal government retains *   *   * its criminal *   *   * enforcement powers.

DECISION AND REMEDY The U.S. Court of Appeals for the Ninth Circuit affirmed the judgment of the lower court. The appellate court held that the EPA's authorization of Idaho's hazardous waste program did not deprive the federal government of its enforcement authority under the RCRA. The court also upheld Elias's prison sentence. It remanded the case to strike the restitution order, however, because Elias's offense "is

one of the few for which Congress has not sanctioned the imposition of restitution."

FOR CRITICAL ANALYSIS—Political Consideration *In light of the court's reasoning in this case, what authority do states with federally approved hazardous waste programs have under the RCRA?*

Superfund

In 1980, Congress passed the Comprehensive Environmental Response, Compensation, and Liability Act (CERCLA),[22] commonly known as Superfund, to regulate the clean-up of leaking hazardous waste–disposal sites. A special federal fund was created for that purpose. Because of its impact on the

---

22. 42 U.S.C. Sections 9601–9675.

business community, the act is presented as this chapter's *Landmark in the Legal Environment* feature on page 653.

Potentially Responsible Parties under Superfund Superfund provides that when a release or a threatened release of hazardous chemicals from a site occurs, the EPA can clean up the site and recover the cost of the clean-up from the following persons: (1) the person who generated the wastes disposed of at the site, (2) the person who transported the wastes to the site, (3) the person who owned or operated the site at the time of the disposal, or (4) the current owner or operator. A person falling within one of these categories is referred to as a **potentially responsible party (PRP)**. In the following case, the issue was the meaning of *disposal* as that term is used in the provision of CERCLA that lists PRPs.

POTENTIALLY RESPONSIBLE PARTY (PRP)
A party liable for the costs of cleaning up a hazardous waste–disposal site under the Comprehensive Environmental Response, Compensation, and Liability Act (CERCLA). Any person who generated the hazardous waste, transported it, owned or operated the waste site at the time of disposal, or currently owns or operates the site may be responsible for some or all of the clean-up costs.

CASE 20.4 Carson Harbor Village, Ltd. v. Unocal Corp.

United States Court of Appeals, Ninth Circuit, 2001.
270 F.3d 863.

BACKGROUND AND FACTS
Beginning in 1945, Unocal Corporation leased property in Carson, California, and used it for petroleum production, operating oil wells, pipelines, aboveground storage tanks, and production facilities. Carson Harbor Village Mobile Home Park, a general partnership controlled by Richard Braley and Walker Smith, owned a mobile home park on seventy acres of the property from 1977 until 1983, when Carson Harbor Village, Ltd., took over the park. An undeveloped wetlands area covered nearly seventeen acres of the site. In 1993,

Carson Harbor discovered hazardous substances in the wetlands area. An investigation revealed that the materials were by-products of petroleum production and had been on the property for several decades before its development as a mobile home park. The material and surrounding soils contained elevated levels of total petroleum hydrocarbons (TPH) and lead. Carson Harbor paid $285,000 for their removal and then filed a suit in a federal district court against the partnership and others under CERCLA, seeking in part to recover the removal cost plus damages. The partnership filed a motion for summary judgment, which the court granted. Carson Harbor appealed to the U.S. Court of Appeals for the Ninth Circuit.

IN THE WORDS OF THE COURT . . .

MCKEOWN, Circuit Judge:

     *   *   *   *

CERCLA defines "disposal" *   *   * with reference to the definition of "disposal" in RCRA, which in turn defines "disposal" as follows:

> The term "disposal" means the discharge, deposit, injection, dumping, spilling, leaking, or placing of any solid waste or hazardous waste into or on any land or water so that such solid waste or hazardous waste or any constituent thereof may enter the environment or be emitted into the air or discharged into any waters, including ground waters.

Under this definition, for the Partnership Defendants to be PRPs, there must have been a "discharge, deposit, injection, dumping, spilling, leaking, or placing" of contaminants on the property during their ownership.

     *   *   *   *

Examining the facts of this case, we hold that the gradual passive migration of contamination through the soil that allegedly took place during the Partnership Defendants' ownership was not a "discharge, deposit, injection,

(continued)

CASE 20.4—Continued

dumping, spilling, leaking, or placing" and, therefore, was not a "disposal" within the meaning of [CERCLA]. The contamination on the property included tar-like and slag materials. The tar-like material was highly viscous and uniform, without any breaks or stratification. The slag material had a vesicular structure and was more porous and rigid than the tar-like material. There was some evidence that the tar-like material moved through the soil and that lead and/or TPH may have moved from that material into the soil. If we try to characterize this passive soil migration in plain English, a number of words come to mind, including gradual "spreading," "migration," "seeping," "oozing," and possibly "leaching." But certainly none of those words fits within the plain and common meaning of "discharge, * * * injection, dumping, * * * or placing." *Although these words generally connote active conduct, even if we were to infuse passive meanings, these words simply do not describe the passive migration that occurred here.* Nor can the gradual spread here be characterized as a "deposit," because there was neither a deposit by someone, nor does the term deposit encompass the gradual spread of contaminants. The term "spilling" is likewise inapposite. Nothing spilled out of or over anything. Unlike the spilling of a barrel or the spilling over of a holding pond, movement of the tar-like and slag materials was not a spill. [Emphasis added.]

Of the terms defining "disposal," the only one that might remotely describe the passive soil migration here is "leaking." But under the plain and common meaning of the word, we conclude that there was no "leaking." The circumstances here are not like that of the leaking barrel or underground storage tank envisioned by Congress, or a vessel or some other container that would connote "leaking." Therefore, there was no "disposal," and the Partnership Defendants are not PRPs. On this basis, we affirm the district court's grant of summary judgment to the Partnership Defendants on the CERCLA claim.

DECISION AND REMEDY The U.S. Court of Appeals for the Ninth Circuit affirmed the judgment of the lower court. The appellate court held that the partnership was not liable as a PRP. The passive migration of the contaminants through the soil during the partnership's ownership of the site was not a *disposal* as that term is used in CERCLA.

FOR CRITICAL ANALYSIS—Social Consideration *Why not interpret the term* disposal *to include all subsoil passive migration of hazardous substances and thus hold any owner of contaminated property liable for the cost of its clean-up?*

Joint and Several Liability under Superfund Liability under Superfund is usually joint and several—that is, a person who generated *only a fraction of the hazardous waste* disposed of at the site may nevertheless be liable for *all* of the clean-up costs. CERCLA authorizes a party who has incurred clean-up costs to bring a "contribution action" against any other person who is liable or potentially liable for a percentage of the costs.

GLOBAL ENVIRONMENTAL ISSUES

Pollution does not respect geographic borders. Indeed, one of the reasons that the federal government became involved in environmental protection was that state regulation alone could not solve the problem of air or water pollution. Pollutants generated in one state moved in the air and water to other states.

LANDMARK IN THE LEGAL ENVIRONMENT

Superfund

The origins of the Comprehensive Environmental Response, Compensation, and Liability Act (CERCLA) of 1980, which is commonly referred to as Superfund, can be traced to drafts that the Environmental Protection Agency (EPA) started to circulate in 1978.

DUMP SITES ARE "TICKING TIME BOMBS"
EPA officials emphasized the political necessity of new legislation by pointing to what they considered "ticking time bombs"—dump sites around the country that were ready to explode and injure the public with toxic fumes.

The popular press was also running prominent stories about hazardous waste dump sites at the time. The New York Love Canal disaster first made headlines in 1978. Residents in the area complained about health problems, contaminated sludge oozing into their basements, and chemical "volcanoes" erupting in their yards as a result of the approximately 21,000 tons of chemicals that Hooker Chemical had dumped into the canal from 1942 to 1953. By the middle of May 1980, the Love Canal situation was making the national news virtually every day, and it remained in the headlines for a month.

CERCLA—ITS PURPOSE AND PRIMARY ELEMENTS
The basic purpose of CERCLA, which was amended in 1986 by the Superfund Amendments and Reauthorization Act, is to regulate the clean-up of leaking hazardous waste–disposal sites. The act has four primary elements:

- It established an information-gathering and analysis system that allows federal and state governments to characterize chemical dump sites and to develop priorities for appropriate action.

- It authorized the EPA to respond to hazardous substance emergencies and to clean up a leaking site directly through contractors or through cooperative agreements with the states if the persons responsible for the problem fail to clean up the site.

- It created a Hazardous Substance Response Trust Fund (Superfund) to pay for the clean-up of hazardous sites. Monies for the fund are obtained through taxes on certain businesses, such as those processing or producing petroleum.

- It allowed the government to recover the cost of clean-up from the persons who were (even remotely) responsible for hazardous substance releases.

Application to Today's World

The provisions of CERCLA profoundly affect today's businesses and business decision making. Virtually any business decision relating to the purchase and sale of property, for example, requires an analysis of previous activities on the property to determine whether those activities resulted in contamination. Additionally, to avoid violating CERCLA, owners and managers of manufacturing plants must be extremely cautious in arranging for the removal and disposal of any hazardous waste materials. Unless Congress significantly changes CERCLA and the way in which it is implemented, businesses will continue to face potentially extensive liability for violations under this act.

Neither does pollution respect national borders. Environmental issues, perhaps more than any others, bring home to everyone the fact that the world today is truly a global community. What one country does or does not do with respect to environmental preservation may be felt by citizens in countries thousands of miles distant.

Cross-Border Pollution

One issue that has come to the fore in recent years is **cross-border pollution.** On numerous occasions, beaches in San Diego, California, have been closed because of pollution originating in Mexico. Canada has complained for years about air pollution in that nation caused by sulfuric acid generated by coal-burning power plants in the United States. Examples similar to these can be found everywhere in the world. Countries have made various attempts to reduce cross-border pollution, through treaties or other agreements, but it remains a challenging issue for virtually all nations.

Global Warming

Another challenging—and controversial—issue is potential global warming. The fear is that emissions, largely from combustion of fossil fuels, will remain in the atmosphere and create a "greenhouse effect" by preventing heat from radiating outward. Concerns over this problem have led to many attempts to force all world polluters to "clean up their acts." For example, leaders of 160 nations have already agreed to reduce greenhouse emissions in their respective countries. They did this when they created the Kyoto Protocol, which was drawn up at a world summit meeting held in Kyoto, Japan, in 1997. The Kyoto Protocol, which is often referred to as the global warming treaty, established different rates of reduction in greenhouse emissions for different countries or regions. Most nations, however, including the United States, will not meet the treaty's objectives. Indeed, the Bush administration told the world in early 2001 that the treaty was a dead letter because it did not address the problem of curbing greenhouse gases from most of the developing world. In 2003, Russian president Vladimir Putin did the same.

Is Economic Development the Answer?

Economists have shown that economic development is the quickest way to reduce pollution worldwide. This is because after a nation reaches a certain per capita income level, the more economic growth the nation experiences, the lower its pollution output. This occurs because richer nations have the resources to pay for pollution reduction. For example, the United States pollutes much less per unit of output than do developing nations—because we are willing to pay for pollution abatement.

KEY TERMS

CHAPTER SUMMARY PROTECTING THE ENVIRONMENT

Common Law Actions (See page 635.)	1. *Nuisance*—A common law doctrine under which actions against pollution-causing activities can be brought. An individual can bring an action only if he or she suffers a harm separate and distinct from that of the general public. 2. *Negligence and strict liability*—Parties can recover damages for injuries sustained as a result of a firm's pollution-causing activities if it can be demonstrated that the harm was a foreseeable result of the firm's failure to exercise reasonable care (negligence); businesses engaging in ultrahazardous activities are liable for whatever injuries the activities cause, regardless of whether the firms exercise reasonable care.
State and Local Regulation (See pages 635–636.)	Activities affecting the environment are controlled at the local and state levels through regulations relating to land use, the disposal and recycling of garbage and waste, and pollution-causing activities in general.

Federal Regulation (See pages 636–652.)	1. *Environmental protection agencies*—The most well known of the agencies regulating environmental law is the federal Environmental Protection Agency (EPA), which was created in 1970 to coordinate federal environmental programs. The EPA administers most federal environmental policies and statutes.
	
	2. *Assessing environmental impact*—The National Environmental Policy Act of 1969 imposes environmental responsibilities on all federal agencies and requires the preparation of an environmental impact statement (EIS) for every major federal action. An EIS must analyze the action's impact on the environment, its adverse effects and possible alternatives, and its irreversible effects on environmental quality.
	
	3. *Important areas regulated by the federal government*—Important areas regulated by the federal government include the following:
	
	  a. Air pollution—Regulated under the authority of the Clean Air Act of 1963 and its amendments, particularly those of 1970, 1977, and 1990.
	
	  b. Water pollution—Regulated under the authority of the Rivers and Harbors Appropriation Act of 1899, as amended, and the Federal Water Pollution Control Act of 1948, as amended by the Clean Water Act of 1972.
	
	  c. Noise pollution—Regulated by the Noise Control Act of 1972.
	
	  d. Toxic chemicals and hazardous waste—Pesticides and herbicides, toxic substances, and hazardous waste are regulated under the authority of the Federal Insecticide, Fungicide, and Rodenticide Act of 1947, the Toxic Substances Control Act of 1976, and the Resource Conservation and Recovery Act of 1976, respectively. The Comprehensive Environmental Response, Compensation, and Liability Act (CERCLA) of 1980, as amended, regulates the clean-up of hazardous waste–disposal sites.

Global Environmental Issues (See pages 652–654.)	Pollution does not respect geographic borders, and environmental problems are pressing in today's global community. Two major problems that nations are addressing today are cross-border pollution and global warming.

FOR REVIEW

1. Under what common law theories can polluters be held liable?
2. What is an environmental impact statement, and who must file one?
3. What does the Environmental Protection Agency do?
4. What major federal statutes regulate air and water pollution?
5. What is Superfund? To what categories of persons does liability under Superfund extend?

QUESTIONS AND CASE PROBLEMS

20–1. Clean Air Act. Current scientific knowledge indicates that there is no safe level of exposure to a cancer-causing agent. In theory, even one molecule of such a substance has the potential for causing cancer. Section 112 of the Clean Air Act requires that all cancer-causing substances be regulated to ensure a margin of safety. Some environmental groups have argued that all emissions of such substances must be eliminated if a margin of safety is to be reached. Such a total elimination would likely shut down many major U.S. industries. Should the Environmental Protection Agency totally eliminate all emissions of cancer-causing chemicals? Discuss.

20–2. Water Pollution. Fruitade, Inc., is a processor of a soft drink called Freshen Up. Fruitade uses returnable bottles and employs a special acid to clean its bottles for further beverage processing. The acid is diluted with water and then allowed to pass into a navigable stream. Fruitade crushes its broken bottles and also throws the crushed glass into the stream. Discuss fully any environmental laws that Fruitade has violated.

20–3. Common Law Actions. Moonbay is a home-building corporation that primarily develops retirement communities. Farmtex owns a number of feedlots in Sunny Valley. Moonbay purchased 20,000 acres of farmland in the same area and began building and selling homes on this acreage. In the meantime, Farmtex continued to expand its feedlot business, and eventually only 500 feet separated the two operations. Because of the odor and flies from the feedlots, Moonbay found it difficult to sell the homes in its development. Moonbay wants to enjoin Farmtex from operating its feedlots in the vicinity of the retirement home development. Under what common law theory would Moonbay file this action? Has Farmtex violated any federal environmental laws? Discuss.

20–4. Hazardous Waste. Asarco, Inc., had a copper smelter at Ruston, Washington. As part of its operations, Asarco produced a by-product called slag, a hard, rocklike substance. Industrial Mineral Products (IMP) sold the slag for Asarco to Louisiana-Pacific Corp. and other businesses, which used the slag as ballast to stabilize the ground at log-sorting yards in the Tacoma, Washington, area. About nine months after IMP

stopped selling the slag, it sold substantially all of its assets to L-Bar Products, Inc. Government agencies later discovered that the slag reacted with the acidic wood waste in the log-sorting yards, causing heavy metals from the slag to leach into the groundwater and soil. Louisiana-Pacific and the Port of Tacoma sued Asarco under the Comprehensive Environmental Response, Compensation, and Liability Act (CERCLA), claiming that Asarco was liable for clean-up costs. Asarco brought a third party claim against L-Bar as corporate successor to IMP. L-Bar moved for summary judgment, claiming that it was not the successor to IMP and could not be liable under CERCLA for IMP's actions. Will the court agree with L-Bar? Discuss fully. [*Louisiana-Pacific Corp. v. Asarco, Inc.,* 909 F.2d 1260 (9th Cir. 1990)]

20–5. Toxic Chemicals. The EPA canceled the registration of the pesticide diazinon for use on golf courses and sod farms because of concern about the effects of diazinon on birds. The Federal Insecticide, Fungicide, and Rodenticide Act authorizes cancellation of the registration of products that "generally cause unreasonable adverse effects on the environment." The statute further defines "unreasonable adverse effects on the environment" to mean "any unreasonable risk to man or the environment, taking into account the . . . costs and benefits." Thus, in determining whether a pesticide should continue to be used, it is necessary to balance the risks and benefits of its use. Does this mean that a judge must find that the pesticide kills birds more often than not to prohibit the pesticide's use, or is it sufficient to find that the use of the pesticide results in recurrent bird kills? [*Ciba-Geigy Corp. v. Environmental Protection Agency,* 874 F.2d 277 (5th Cir. 1989)]

20–6. Water Pollution. Taylor Bay Protective Association is a nonprofit corporation established for the purpose of restoring and improving the water quality of Taylor Bay. Local water districts began operating a flood control project in the area. As part of the project, a pumping station was developed. Testimony at trial revealed that the pumps were operated contrary to the instructions provided in the operation and maintenance manual. The pumps acted as vacuums, sucking up silt and depositing the silt in Taylor Bay. Thus, the project resulted in sedimentation and turbidity problems in the downstream watercourse of Taylor Bay. The association sued the local water districts, alleging that the pumping operations created a nuisance. Do the pumping operations qualify as a common law nuisance? Who should be responsible for the clean-up costs? Discuss both questions fully. [*Taylor Bay Protective Association v. Environmental Protection Agency,* 884 F.2d 1073 (8th Cir. 1989)]

20–7. Nuisance. Portland General Electric Co. maintained a turbine facility. Nearby residents complained that the facility emitted low-frequency sound waves that caused them to suffer loss of sleep, emotional distress, and mental strain. Consequently, these residents sued the company, claiming that it was creating a nuisance. The defendant contended that the plaintiffs had suffered no special harm. The district court dismissed the plaintiffs' complaint, and the plaintiffs appealed the decision. Should the appellate court affirm the dismissal? Explain. [*Frady v. Portland General Electric Co.,* 55 Or.App. 344, 637 P.2d 1345 (1981)]

20–8. Clean Water Act. Attique Ahmad owned the Spin-N-Market, a convenience store and gas station. The gas pumps were fed by underground tanks, one of which had a leak at its top that allowed water to enter. Ahmad emptied the tank by pumping its contents into a storm drain and a sewer system. Through the storm drain, gasoline flowed into a creek, forcing the city to clean the water. Through the sewer system, gasoline flowed into a sewage treatment plant, forcing the city to evacuate the plant and two nearby schools. Ahmad was charged with discharging a pollutant without a permit, which is a criminal violation of the Clean Water Act. The act provides that a person who "knowingly violates" the act commits a felony. Ahmad claimed that he had believed he was discharging only water. Did Ahmad commit a felony? Why or why not? Discuss fully. [*U.S. v. Ahmad,* 101 F.3d 386 (5th Cir. 1996)]

Case Problem with Sample Answer

20–9. Environmental Impact Statement. Greers Ferry Lake is in Arkansas, and its shoreline is under the management of the U.S. Army Corps of Engineers, which is part of the U.S. Department of Defense (DOD). The Corps's 2000 Shoreline Management Plan (SMP) rezoned numerous areas along the lake, authorized the Corps to issue permits for the construction of new boat docks in the rezoned areas, increased by 300 percent the area around habitable structures that could be cleared of vegetation, and instituted a Wildlife Enhancement Permit to allow limited modifications of the shoreline. In relation to the SMP's adoption, the Corps issued a Finding of No Significant Impact, which declared that no environmental impact statement (EIS) was necessary. The Corps issued thirty-two boat dock construction permits under the SMP before Save Greers Ferry Lake, Inc., filed a suit in a

federal district court against the DOD, asking the court to, among other things, stop the Corps from acting under the SMP and order it to prepare an EIS. What are the requirements for an EIS? Is an EIS needed in this case? Explain. [*Save Greers Ferry Lake, Inc. v. Department of Defense,* 255 F.3d 498 (8th Cir. 2001)]

To view a sample answer for this case problem, go to this book's Web site at http://leet.westbuslaw.com **and click on "Interactive Study Center."**

20–10. CERCLA. Beginning in 1926, Marietta Dyestuffs Co. operated an industrial facility in Marietta, Ohio, to make dyes and other chemicals. In 1944, Dyestuffs became part of American Home Products Corp. (AHP), which sold the Marietta facility to American Cyanamid Co. in 1946. In 1950, AHP sold the rest of the Dyestuffs assets and all of its stock to Goodrich Co., which immediately liquidated the acquired corporation. Goodrich continued to operate the dissolved corporation's business, however. Cyanamid continued to make chemicals at the Marietta facility, and in 1993, it created Cytec Industries, Inc., which expressly assumed all environmental liabilities associated with Cyanamid's ownership and operation of the facility. Cytec spent nearly $25 million on clean-up costs and filed a suit in a federal district court against Goodrich to recover, under CERCLA, a portion of the costs attributable to the clean-up of hazardous wastes that may have been discarded at the site between 1926 and 1946. Cytec filed a motion for summary judgment in its favor. Should the court grant Cytec's motion? Explain. [*Cytec Industries, Inc. v. B. F. Goodrich Co.,* 196 F.Supp.2d 644 (S.D. Ohio 2002)]

A Question of Ethics & Social Responsibility

20–11. The Endangered Species Act of 1973 makes it unlawful for any person to "take" endangered or threatened species. The act defines *take* to mean "harass, harm, pursue," "wound," or "kill." The secretary of the interior (Bruce Babbitt) issued a regulation that further defined *harm* to include "significant habitat modification or degradation where it actually kills or injures wildlife." A group of businesses and individuals involved in the timber industry brought an action against the secretary of the interior and others. The group complained that the application of the "harm" regulation to the red-cockaded woodpecker and the northern spotted owl had injured the group economically by preventing logging operations (habitat modification) in Pacific Northwest forests containing these species. The group challenged the regulation's validity, contending that Congress had not intended the word *take* to include habitat modification. The case ultimately reached the United States Supreme Court, which held that the secretary had reasonably construed Congress's intent when he defined *harm* to include habitat modification. [*Babbitt v. Sweet Home Chapter of Communities for a Great Oregon,* 515 U.S. 687, 115 S.Ct. 2407, 132 L.Ed.2d 597 (1995)]

1. Traditionally, the term *take* has been used to refer to the capture or killing of wildlife, usually for private gain. Is the secretary's regulation prohibiting habitat modification consistent with this definition?
2. One of the issues in this case was whether Congress intended to protect existing generations of species or future generations. How do the terms *take* and *habitat modification* relate to this issue?
3. Three dissenting Supreme Court justices contended that construing the act as prohibiting habitat modification "imposes unfairness to the point of financial ruin—not just upon the rich, but upon the simplest farmer who finds his land conscripted to national zoological use." Should private parties be required to bear the burden of preserving habitats for wildlife?

4. Generally, should the economic welfare of private parties be taken into consideration in the creation and application of environmental statutes and regulations?

Critical-Thinking Economic Question

20-12. Standard Landfill, Inc., owns and operates a landfill site at which hazardous wastes are disposed. National Chemical Corp. generates waste disposed of at the site. When the Environmental Protection Agency (EPA) discovers that waste at Standard's site is being disposed of improperly and has contaminated the soil, the EPA cleans up the site and files suit in a federal district court to recover the costs from Standard and National. Can either or both of these companies be held liable for the clean-up costs?

INTERACTING WITH THE INTERNET

For updated links to resources available on the Web, as well as a variety of other materials, visit this text's Web site at

http://leet.westbuslaw.com

For information on the EPA's standards, guidelines, and regulations, go to the EPA's Web site at

http://www.epa.gov

To learn about the RCRA's "buy-recycled" requirements and other steps that the federal government has taken toward "greening the environment," go to

http://www.epa.gov/cpg

The Law Library of the Indiana University School of Law provides numerous links to online environmental law sources. Go to

http://www.law.indiana.edu/lib/index.html

ONLINE LEGAL RESEARCH EXERCISES

Go to **http://leet.westbuslaw.com**, the Web site that accompanies this text. Select "Interactive Study Center," and then click on "Chapter 20." There you will find the following Internet research exercises that you can perform to learn more about topics covered in this chapter.

Activity 20–1: HISTORICAL PERSPECTIVE—**Nuisance Law**
Activity 20–2: MANAGEMENT PERSPECTIVE—**Complying with Environmental Regulations**
Activity 20–3: ETHICAL PERSPECTIVE—**Environmental Justice**

BEFORE THE TEST

Go to **http://leet.westbuslaw.com**, the Web site that accompanies this text. Select "Interactive Quizzes." You will find at least twenty interactive questions relating to this chapter.

Westlaw® Campus

If your textbook provided for a subscription to Westlaw® Campus, or if you have otherwise purchased access to the Westlaw Campus database, you can access any of the cases presented or cited in this chapter by using your Westlaw Campus account.

CHAPTER **21**

Land-Use Control and Real Property

CHAPTER OBJECTIVES

*After reading this chapter, you should be able to answer the
following questions:*

1. What are the different types of ownership interests in real
property?

2. How can ownership interests in real property be transferred?

3. What is a leasehold estate, and how does it arise?

4. What are the respective duties of the landlord and tenant
concerning the use and maintenance of leased property?

5. What limitations may be imposed on the rights of property
owners?

From earliest times, property has provided a means for survival. Primitive
peoples lived off the fruits of the land, eating the vegetation and wildlife.
Later, as the wildlife was domesticated and the vegetation cultivated, property
provided pasturage and farmland. In the twelfth and thirteenth centuries, the
power of feudal lords was determined by the amount of land that they held;
the more land they held, the more powerful they were. After the age of feu-
dalism passed, property continued to be an indicator of family wealth and
social position. In the Western world, the protection of an individual's right to
his or her property has become, in the words of Jean-Jacques Rousseau quoted
below, one of the "most sacred of all the rights of citizenship."

In this chapter, we first examine closely the nature of real property. We then
look at the various ways in which real property can be owned and at how
ownership rights in real property are
transferred from one person to
another. We also include a discussion
of leased property and landlord-
tenant relationships. The chapter concludes with a discussion of how the
use of land is controlled.

> **"The right of property is the
> most sacred of all the rights
> of citizenship."**
>
> Jean-Jacques Rousseau, 1712–1778
> (French writer and philosopher)

THE NATURE OF REAL PROPERTY

Real property consists of land and the buildings, plants, and trees that it contains. Real property also includes subsurface and air rights, as well as personal property that has become permanently attached to real property. Whereas personal property is movable, real property—also called *real estate* or *realty*—is immovable.

Land

Land includes the soil on the surface of the earth and the natural or artificial structures that are attached to it. It further includes all the waters contained on or under the surface and much, but not necessarily all, of the airspace above it. The exterior boundaries of land extend down to the center of the earth and up to the farthest reaches of the atmosphere (subject to certain qualifications).

Air and Subsurface Rights

The owner of real property has relatively exclusive rights to the airspace above the land, as well as to the soil and minerals underneath it.

Air Rights Early cases involving air rights dealt with matters such as the right to run a telephone wire across a person's property when the wire did not touch any of the property[1] and whether a bullet shot over a person's land constituted trespass.[2] Today, disputes concerning air rights may involve the right of commercial and private planes to fly over property and the right of individuals and

---

1. *Butler v. Frontier Telephone Co.,* 186 N.Y. 486, 79 N.E. 716 (1906).
2. *Herrin v. Sutherland,* 74 Mont. 587, 241 P. 328 (1925).

A plane flies low over a residential area. Are the property owners' rights violated by such a low-flying plane?

governments to seed clouds and produce rain artificially. Flights over private land do not normally violate the property owners' rights unless the flights are low and frequent enough to cause a direct interference with the enjoyment and use of the land.[3] Leaning walls or buildings and projecting eave spouts or roofs may also violate the air rights of an adjoining property owner.

Subsurface Rights In many states, the owner of the surface of a piece of land is not the owner of the subsurface, and hence the land ownership may be separated. Subsurface rights can be extremely valuable, as these rights include the ownership of minerals and, in most states, oil and natural gas. Water rights are also extremely valuable, especially in the West. When the ownership is separated into surface and subsurface rights, each owner can pass title to what he or she owns without the consent of the other owner. Each owner has the right to use the land owned, and in some cases a conflict arises between a surface owner's use and the subsurface owner's need to extract minerals, oil, and natural gas. When this occurs, one party's interest may become subservient to that of the other party, either by statute or case decision.

Significant limitations on either air rights or subsurface rights normally have to be indicated on the deed transferring title at the time of purchase. (Deeds and the types of warranties they contain are discussed later in this chapter.)

Plant Life and Vegetation

Plant life, both natural and cultivated, is also considered to be real property. In many instances, the natural vegetation, such as trees, adds greatly to the value of the realty. When a parcel of land is sold and the land has growing crops on it, the sale includes the crops, unless otherwise specified in the sales contract. When crops are sold by themselves, however, they are considered to be personal property or goods. Consequently, the sale of crops is a sale of goods, and therefore it is governed by the Uniform Commercial Code rather than by real property law.[4]

Fixtures

Certain personal property can become so closely associated with the real property to which it is attached that the law views it as real property. Such property is known as a **fixture**—a thing *affixed* to realty, meaning it is attached to it by roots; embedded in it; permanently situated on it; or permanently attached by means of cement, plaster, bolts, nails, or screws. The fixture can be physically attached to real property, be attached to another fixture, or even be without any actual physical attachment to the land (such as a statue). As long as the owner intends the property to be a fixture, normally it will be a fixture.

Fixtures are included in the sale of land if the sales contract does not provide otherwise. The sale of a house includes the land and the house and the garage on the land, as well as the cabinets, plumbing, and windows. Because these are permanently affixed to the property, they are considered to be a part of it. Unless otherwise agreed, however, the curtains and throw rugs are not included. Items such as drapes and window-unit air conditioners are difficult

BE AWARE If, during an excavation, a subsurface owner causes the land to subside, he or she may be liable to the owner of the surface.

FIXTURE
A thing that was once personal property but that has become attached to real property in such a way that it takes on the characteristics of real property and becomes part of that real property.

---

3. *United States v. Causby,* 328 U.S. 256, 66 S.Ct. 1062, 90 L.Ed. 1206 (1946).
4. See UCC 2–107(2).

to classify. Thus, a contract for the sale of a house or commercial realty should indicate which items of this sort are included in the sale to avoid disputes.

At issue in the following case was whether an agricultural irrigation system qualified as a fixture.

CASE 21.1 In re Sand & Sage Farm & Ranch, Inc.

United States Bankruptcy Court, District of Kansas, 2001. 266 Bankr. 507.

BACKGROUND AND FACTS In 1988, Randolf and Sandra Ardery bought an eighty-acre tract in Edwards County, Kansas. On the land was an eight-tower center-pivot irrigation system. The system consisted of an underground well and pump connected to a pipe that ran to the pivot, where the water line was attached to a further system of pipes and sprinklers suspended from the towers, extending over the land in a circular fashion. The system's engine and gearhead were bolted to a concrete slab above the pump and well and were attached to the pipe. To

secure a loan to buy the land, the Arderys granted to Farmers State Bank a mortgage that covered "all buildings, improvements, and fixtures." In 1996, the Arderys, and their firm Sand & Sage Farm & Ranch, Inc., granted Ag Services of America a security interest in the farm's equipment. Nothing in the security agreement or financing statement referred to fixtures.[a] In 2000, the Arderys and Sand & Sage filed for bankruptcy in a federal bankruptcy court and asked for permission to sell the land, with the irrigation system, to Bohn Enterprises, Limited Partnership. Ag Services claimed that it had priority to the proceeds covering the value of the irrigation system. The bank responded that it had priority because the system was a fixture.

IN THE WORDS OF THE COURT . . .

ROBERT E. NUGENT, Bankruptcy Judge.

* * * *

* * * [There is] a three-step judicial test for determining whether personalty attached to real estate is legally a fixture. Paraphrased, the steps are:

(i) how firmly the goods are attached or the ease of their removal (annexation);
(ii) the relationship of the parties involved (intent); and
(iii) how operation of the goods is related to the use of the land (adaptation).

Of the three factors, intent is the controlling factor and is deduced largely from the property-owner's acts and the surrounding circumstances. [Emphasis added.]

* * * *

* * * [The irrigation system] is firmly attached to the realty. The irrigation pipes are connected to the center pivot which is bolted to a cement slab in the center of the irrigation property and connected to the underground well and pump by wires and pipes. Further, the system is not easily removable. The towers must be disassembled in sections and transported separately, and disassembly and removal of the engine, gearhead and pump would be time-consuming and require the assistance of experienced people. It would also be expensive * * * .

The relationships between the parties involved in each transaction also suggest the shared intent that the irrigation system be a fixture. In 1988, * * * Ardery [bought the land] with the irrigation system included. Ardery, in turn,

---

a. A *security interest* is a creditor's interest in certain property of the debtor (called *collateral*). The security interest is created by a security agreement to secure a debt or obligation owed by the debtor to the creditor.

(continued)

CASE 21.1—Continued

mortgaged the land, and the fixtures, to the Bank [whose officer] testified that he considered the conveyance of the mortgage to include the system as that was the Bank's custom and practice in Edwards County. Ardery and Bohn clearly intend the system to pass with the land in the sale now before the Court. * * *

The irrigation system is suitably adapted to the land. There can be little dispute concerning the need for pivot irrigation in the semi-arid conditions of southwestern Kansas. All witnesses agreed, and it is well within this Court's common experience, that irrigated units of land are substantially more productive of crops than dryland acres. This alone demonstrates the relation between the operation of the goods and use of the land.

DECISION AND REMEDY The court concluded that the system was a fixture. The bank was entitled to the proceeds from its sale.

FOR CRITICAL ANALYSIS—Social Consideration *How can a court objectively determine whether someone did or did not intend an item to be a fixture?*

OWNERSHIP OF REAL PROPERTY

> "Few . . . men own their property. The property owns them."
>
> ROBERT G. INGERSOLL, 1833–1899
> (American politician and lecturer)

Ownership of property is an abstract concept that cannot exist independently of the legal system. No one can actually possess or *hold* a piece of land, the air above it, the earth below it, and all the water contained on it. The legal system therefore recognizes certain rights and duties that constitute ownership interests in real property.

Property ownership is often viewed as a bundle of rights. One who possesses the entire bundle of rights is said to hold the property in *fee simple*, which is the most complete form of ownership. When only some of the rights in the bundle are transferred to another person, the effect is to limit the ownership rights of both the one transferring the rights and the one receiving them.

Ownership in Fee Simple

FEE SIMPLE ABSOLUTE
An ownership interest in land in which the owner has the greatest possible aggregation of rights, privileges, and power. Ownership in fee simple absolute is limited absolutely to a person and his or her heirs.

CONVEYANCE
The transfer of a title to land from one person to another by deed; a document (such as a deed) by which an interest in land is transferred from one person to another.

FEE SIMPLE DEFEASIBLE
An ownership interest in real property that can be taken away (by the prior grantor) on the occurrence or nonoccurrence of a specified event.

The most common type of property ownership today is the fee simple. Generally, the term *fee simple* is used to designate a **fee simple absolute,** in which the owner has the greatest possible aggregation of rights, privileges, and power. The fee simple is limited absolutely to a person and his or her heirs and is assigned forever without limitation or condition. The rights that accompany a fee simple include the right to use the land for whatever purpose the owner sees fit, subject to laws that prevent the owner from unreasonably interfering with another person's land and subject to applicable zoning laws. Furthermore, the owner has the rights of *exclusive* possession and use of the property. A fee simple is potentially infinite in duration and can be disposed of by deed or by will (by selling or giving away). When there is no will, the fee simple passes to the owner's legal heirs.

Ownership in fee simple may become limited whenever a **conveyance,** or transfer of real property, is made to another party *conditionally*. When this occurs, the fee simple is known as a **fee simple defeasible** (the word *defeasible* means "capable of being terminated or annulled"). ● **EXAMPLE 1** A conveyance "to A and his heirs as long as the land is used for charitable purposes" creates a fee simple defeasible, because ownership of the property is conditioned on the land's being used for charitable purposes. The original owner retains a *partial* ownership interest, because if the specified condition does not occur (if the land ceases to be used for charitable purposes), then the land reverts, or returns, to the original owner. If the original owner is not living at the time, the land passes to his or her heirs.•

Life Estates

A **life estate** is an estate that lasts for the life of some specified individual. A conveyance "to A for his life" creates a life estate.[5] In a life estate, the life tenant has fewer rights of ownership than the holder of a fee simple defeasible, because the rights necessarily cease to exist on the life tenant's death.

The life tenant has the right to use the land, provided that he or she commits no waste (injury to the land). In other words, the life tenant cannot injure the land in a manner that would adversely affect its value. The life tenant can use the land to harvest crops or, if mines and oil wells are already on the land, can extract minerals and oil from it, but the life tenant cannot exploit the land by creating new wells or mines. The life tenant is entitled to any rents or royalties generated by the realty and has other rights, such as the right to mortgage or lease the life estate. These cannot extend beyond the life of the tenant, however. In addition, with few exceptions, the owner of a life estate has an exclusive right to possession during his or her life.

Along with these rights, the life tenant also has some duties—to keep the property in repair and to pay property taxes. In short, the owner of the life estate has the same rights as a fee simple owner except that he or she must maintain the value of the property during his or her tenancy, less the decrease in value resulting from the normal use of the property allowed by the life tenancy.

LIFE ESTATE
An interest in land that exists only for the duration of the life of some person, usually the holder of the estate.

Future Interests

When an owner in fee simple absolute conveys the estate conditionally to another (such as with a fee simple defeasible) or for a limited period of time (such as with a life estate), the original owner still retains an interest in the land. The owner retains the right to repossess ownership of the land if the conditions of the fee simple defeasible are not met or when the life of the life-estate holder ends. The interest in the property that the owner retains (or transfers to another) is called a **future interest,** because if it arises, it will only arise in the future.

If the owner retains ownership of the future interest, the future interest is described as a **reversionary interest,** because the property will revert to the original owner if the condition specified in a fee simple defeasible fails or when a life tenant dies. If, however, the owner of the future interest transfers ownership rights in that future interest to another, the future interest is described as a **remainder.** For example, a conveyance "to A for life, then to B" creates a life estate for A and a remainder (future interest) for B. An **executory interest** is a type of future interest very similar to a remainder, the difference being that an executory interest does not take effect immediately on the expiration of another interest, such as a life estate. For example, a conveyance "to A and his

FUTURE INTEREST
An interest in real property in which the holder does not possess the property but may possess it in the future.

REVERSIONARY INTEREST
A future interest in property retained by the original owner.

REMAINDER
A future interest in property held by a person other than the original owner.

EXECUTORY INTEREST
A future interest, held by a person other than the one granting the interest, that begins after the termination of the preceding estate.

---

5. A less common type of life estate is created by the conveyance "to A for the life of B." This is known as an estate *pur autre vie,* or an estate for the duration of the life of another.

(or her) heirs, as long as the premises are used for charitable purposes, and if not so used for charitable purposes, then to B" creates an executory interest in the property for B.

Nonpossessory Interests

In contrast to the types of property interests just described, some interests in land do not include any rights to possess the property. These interests are thus known as *nonpossessory interests*. Three forms of nonpossessory interests are easements, profits, and licenses.

An **easement** is the right of a person to make limited use of another person's real property without taking anything from the property. An easement, for example, can be the right to travel over another's property. In contrast, a **profit**[6] is the right to go onto land in possession of another and take away some part of the land itself or some product of the land. If Akmed, the owner of Sandy View, gives Carmen the right to go there and remove all the sand and gravel that she needs for her cement business, Carmen has a profit.

A **license** is the revocable right of a person to come onto another person's land. It is a personal privilege that arises from the consent of the owner of the land and that can be revoked by the owner. A ticket to attend a movie at a theater is an example of a license. ● **EXAMPLE 2** Assume that a Broadway theater owner issues to Carla a ticket to see a play. If Carla is refused entry into the theater because she is improperly dressed, she has no right to force her way into the theater. The ticket is only a revocable license, not a conveyance of an interest in property.●

EASEMENT
A nonpossessory right to use another's property in a manner established by either express or implied agreement.

PROFIT
In real property law, the right to enter on and remove things from the property of another (for example, the right to enter onto a person's land and remove sand and gravel therefrom).

LICENSE
A revocable right or privilege of a person to come on another person's land.

TRANSFER OF OWNERSHIP

Ownership of real property can pass from one person to another in a number of ways. Commonly, ownership interests in land are transferred by sale, in which case the terms of the transfer are specified in a real estate sales contract. When real property is sold or transferred as a gift, title to the property is conveyed by means of a **deed**—the instrument of conveyance of real property. We look here at transfers of real property by deed, as well as some other ways in which ownership rights in real property can be transferred.

DEED
A document by which title to property (usually real property) is passed.

Deeds

A valid deed must contain the following elements:

1. The names of the buyer (grantee) and seller (grantor).
2. Words evidencing an intent to convey the property (for example, "I hereby bargain, sell, grant, or give").
3. A legally sufficient description of the land.
4. The grantor's (and, sometimes, the spouse's) signature.

Additionally, to be valid, a deed must be delivered to the person to whom the property is being conveyed or to his or her agent.

---

6. The term *profit,* as used here, does not refer to the "profits" made by a business firm. Rather, it means a gain or an advantage.

Warranty Deeds Different types of deeds provide different degrees of protection against defects of title. A **warranty deed** warrants the greatest number of things and thus provides the greatest protection for the buyer, or grantee. In most states, special language is required to make a deed a general warranty deed; normally, the deed must include a written promise to protect the buyer against all claims of ownership of the property. A sample warranty deed is shown in Exhibit 21–1 on page 668. Warranty deeds commonly include a number of *covenants,* or promises, that the grantor makes to the grantee.

A *covenant of seisin*[7] and a *covenant of the right to convey* warrant that the seller has title to the estate that the deed describes and the power to convey the estate, respectively. The covenant of seisin specifically assures the buyer that the seller has the property in the purported quantity and quality. A *covenant against encumbrances* is a covenant that the property being sold or conveyed is not subject to any outstanding rights or interests that will diminish the value of the land, except as explicitly stated. Examples of common encumbrances include mortgages, liens, profits, easements, and private deed restrictions on the use of the land.

A *covenant of quiet enjoyment* guarantees that the buyer will not be disturbed in his or her possession of the land by the seller or any third persons.
● EXAMPLE 3 Assume that Julio sells a two-acre lot and office building by warranty deed. Subsequently, a third person shows better title than Julio had and proceeds to evict the buyer. Here, the covenant of quiet enjoyment has been breached, and the buyer can sue to recover the purchase price of the land plus any other damages incurred as a result of the eviction.●

Quitclaim Deeds A **quitclaim deed** offers the least amount of protection against defects in the title. Basically, a quitclaim deed conveys to the buyer whatever interest the seller had; so, if the seller had no interest, then the buyer receives no interest. Quitclaim deeds are often used when the seller is uncertain as to the extent of his or her rights in the property.

Recording Statutes Every jurisdiction has **recording statutes,** which allow deeds to be recorded. Recording a deed gives notice to the public that a certain person is now the owner of a particular parcel of real estate. Thus, prospective buyers can check the public records to see whether there have been earlier transactions creating interests or rights in specific parcels of real property. Placing everyone on notice as to the identity of the true owner is intended to prevent the previous owners from fraudulently conveying the land to other purchasers. Deeds are recorded in the county in which the property is located. Many state statutes require that the grantor sign the deed in the presence of two witnesses before it can be recorded.

Will or Inheritance

Property that is transferred on an owner's death is passed either by will or by state inheritance laws. If the owner of land dies with a will, the land passes in accordance with the terms of the will. If the owner dies without a will, state inheritance statutes prescribe how and to whom the property will pass.

WARRANTY DEED
A deed in which the seller assures (warrants to) the buyer that the grantor has title to the property conveyed in the deed, that there are no encumbrances on the property other than what the seller has represented, and that the buyer will enjoy quiet possession of the property; a deed that provides the greatest amount of protection for the grantee.

QUITCLAIM DEED
A deed intended to pass any title, interest, or claim that the seller may have in the property but not warranting that such title is valid. A quitclaim deed offers the least amount of protection against defects in the title.

RECORDING STATUTES
Statutes that allow deeds, mortgages, and other real property transactions to be recorded so as to provide notice to future purchasers or creditors of an existing claim on the property.

---

7. Pronounced *see*-zuhn.

EXHIBIT 21-1   A SAMPLE WARRANTY DEED

Date: May 31, 2005

Grantor: GAYLORD A. JENTZ AND WIFE, JOANN H. JENTZ

Grantor's Mailing Address (including county):
    4106 North Loop Drive
    Austin, Travis County, Texas

Grantee: DAVID F. FRIEND AND WIFE, JOAN E. FRIEND AS JOINT TENANTS
        WITH RIGHT OF SURVIVORSHIP
Grantee's Mailing Address (including county):
    5929 Fuller Drive
    Austin, Travis County, Texas

Consideration:
For and in consideration of the sum of Ten and No/100 Dollars ($10.00) and other
valuable consideration to the undersigned paid by the grantees herein named, the
receipt of which is hereby acknowledged, and for which no lien is retained, either
express or implied.

Property (including any improvements):
Lot 23, Block "A", Northwest Hills, Green Acres Addition, Phase 4, Travis County,
Texas, according to the map or plat of record in volume 22, pages 331-336 of the
Plat Records of Travis County, Texas.

Reservations from and Exceptions to Conveyance and Warranty:

This conveyance with its warranty is expressly made subject to the following:

Easements and restrictions of record in Volume 7863, Page 53, Volume 8430,
Page 35, Volume 8133, Page 152 of the Real Property Record of Travis County,
Texas; Volume 22, Pages 335-339, of the Plat Records of Travis County, Texas;
and to any other restrictions and easements affecting said property which are
of record in Travis County, Texas.

   Grantor, for the consideration and subject to the reservations from and exceptions to conveyance and
warranty, grants, sells, and conveys to Grantee the property, together with all and singular the rights and
appurtenances thereto in any wise belonging, to have and hold it to Grantee, Grantee's heirs, executors,
administrators, successors, or assigns forever.   Grantor binds Grantor and Grantor's heirs, executors,
administrators, and successors to warrant and forever defend all and singular the property to Grantee and
Grantee's heirs, executors, administrators, successors, and assigns against every person whomsoever lawfully
claiming or to claim the same or any part thereof, except as to the reservations from and exceptions to
conveyance and warranty.

   When the context requires, singular nouns and pronouns include the plural.

                                            BY: _____
                                                Gaylord A. Jentz

                                            BY: _____
                                                JoAnn H. Jentz

                        (Acknowledgment)

STATE OF TEXAS
COUNTY OF TRAVIS

     This instrument was acknowledged before me on the 31st day of May, 2005

                                _____
                                Notary Public.State of Texas
                                Notary's name (printed) Rosemary Potter

        Notary Seal
                                Notary's commission expires: 5/31/2008

Adverse Possession

Adverse possession is a means of obtaining title to land without delivery of a deed. Essentially, when one person possesses the property of another for a certain statutory period of time (three to thirty years, with ten years being most common), that person, called the *adverse possessor,* acquires title to the land and cannot be removed from it by the original owner. The adverse possessor is vested with a perfect title just as if there had been a conveyance by deed.

For property to be held adversely, four elements must be satisfied:

1. Possession must be actual and exclusive; that is, the possessor must take sole physical occupancy of the property.

2. The possession must be open, visible, and notorious, not secret or clandestine. The possessor must occupy the land for all the world to see.

3. Possession must be continuous and peaceable for the required period of time. This requirement means that the possessor must not be interrupted in the occupancy by the true owner or by the courts.

4. Possession must be hostile and adverse. In other words, the possessor must claim the property as against the whole world. He or she cannot be living on the property with the permission of the owner.

ADVERSE POSSESSION
The acquisition of title to real property by occupying it openly, without the consent of the owner, for a period of time specified by a state statute. The occupation must be actual, open, notorious, exclusive, and in opposition to all others, including the owner.

ETHICAL ISSUE

What public policies underlie the doctrine of adverse possession?

There are a number of public-policy reasons for the adverse possession doctrine. One reason is that it furthers society's interest in resolving boundary disputes in as fair a manner as possible. For example, suppose that a couple mistakenly assumes that they own a certain strip of land by their driveway. They plant grass and shrubs in the area, and maintain the property over the years. The shrubs contribute to the beauty of their lot and to the value of the property. Some thirty years later, their neighbors have a survey taken, and the results show that the strip of property actually belongs to them. In this situation, the couple could claim that they owned the property by adverse possession, and a court would likely agree.

The doctrine of adverse possession thus helps to determine ownership rights when title to property is in question. The doctrine also furthers the policies of rewarding possessors for putting land to productive use, keeping land in the stream of commerce, and not rewarding owners who sit on their rights too long.

LEASE
In real property law, a contract by which the owner of real property (the landlord, or lessor) grants to a person (the tenant, or lessee) an exclusive right to use and possess the property, usually for a specified period of time, in return for rent or some other form of payment.

LEASEHOLD ESTATES

Often, real property is used by those who do not own it. A **lease** is a contract by which the owner of real property (the landlord, or lessor) grants to a person (the tenant, or lessee) an exclusive right to use and possess the property, usually for a specified period of time, in return for rent or some other form of payment. Property in the possession of a tenant is referred to as a **leasehold estate.**

LEASEHOLD ESTATE
An estate in realty held by a tenant under a lease. In every leasehold estate, the tenant has a qualified right to possess and/or use the land.

The respective rights and duties of the landlord and tenant that arise under a lease agreement will be discussed shortly. Here we look at the types of leasehold estates, or tenancies, that can be created when real property is leased.

Tenancy for Years

A **tenancy for years** is created by an express contract by which property is leased for a specified period of time, such as a day, a month, a year, or a period of years. For example, signing a one-year lease to occupy an apartment creates a tenancy for years. At the end of the period specified in the lease, the lease ends (without notice), and possession of the apartment returns to the lessor. If the tenant dies during the period of the lease, the lease interest passes to the tenant's heirs as personal property. Often, leases include renewal or extension provisions.

Periodic Tenancy

A **periodic tenancy** is created by a lease that does not specify how long it is to last but does specify that rent is to be paid at certain intervals. This type of tenancy is automatically renewed for another rental period unless properly terminated. For example, a periodic tenancy is created by a lease that states, "Rent is due on the tenth day of every month." This provision creates a tenancy from month to month. This type of tenancy can also extend from week to week or from year to year.

Under the common law, to terminate a periodic tenancy, the landlord or tenant must give at least one period's notice to the other party. If the tenancy extends from month to month, for example, one month's notice must be given prior to the last month's rent payment. State statutes may require a different period for notice of termination in a periodic tenancy, however.

Tenancy at Will

Suppose that a landlord rents an apartment to a tenant "for as long as both agree." In such a situation, the tenant receives a leasehold estate known as a **tenancy at will.** Under the common law, either party can terminate the tenancy without notice (that is, "at will"). This type of estate usually arises when a tenant who has been under a tenancy for years retains possession after the termination date of that tenancy with the landlord's consent. Before the tenancy has been converted into a periodic tenancy (by the periodic payment of rent), it is a tenancy at will, terminable by either party without notice. Once the tenancy is treated as a periodic tenancy, termination notice must conform to the one already discussed for that type of tenancy. The death of either party or the voluntary commission of waste by the tenant will terminate a tenancy at will.

Tenancy at Sufferance

The mere possession of land without right is called a **tenancy at sufferance.** It is not a true tenancy. A tenancy at sufferance is not an estate, because it is created when a tenant *wrongfully* retains possession of property. Whenever a tenancy for years, periodic tenancy, or tenancy at will ends and the tenant continues to retain possession of the premises without the owner's permission, a tenancy at sufferance is created. When a tenancy at sufferance arises, the owner can immediately evict the tenant.

LANDLORD-TENANT RELATIONSHIPS

In the past several decades, landlord-tenant relationships have become much more complex than they were before, as has the law governing them. Generally, the law has come to apply contract doctrines, such as those providing for implied warranties and unconscionability, to the landlord-tenant relationship. Increasingly, landlord-tenant relationships have become subject to specific state and local statutes and ordinances as well. In 1972, in an effort to create more uniformity in the law governing landlord-tenant relationships, the National Conference of Commissioners on Uniform State Laws issued the Uniform Residential Landlord and Tenant Act (URLTA). We look now at how a landlord-tenant relationship is created and at the respective rights and duties of landlords and tenants.

Creating the Landlord-Tenant Relationship

A landlord-tenant relationship is established by a lease contract. As mentioned, a lease contract arises when a property owner (landlord) agrees to give another party (the tenant) the exclusive right to possess the property—usually for a price and for a specified term. (For some examples of how Internet companies are redefining leasing requirements, see this chapter's *Legal E-nvironment* feature on page 672.)

Form of the Lease A lease contract may be oral or written. Under the common law, an oral lease is valid. As with most oral contracts, however, a party who seeks to enforce an oral lease may have difficulty proving its existence. In most states, statutes mandate that leases be in writing for some tenancies (such as those exceeding one year). To ensure the validity of a lease agreement, it should therefore be in writing and do the following:

1. Express an intent to establish the relationship.
2. Provide for the transfer of the property's possession to the tenant at the beginning of the term.
3. Provide for the landlord's reversionary interest, which entitles the property owner to retake possession at the end of the term.
4. Describe the property—for example, give its street address.
5. Indicate the length of the term, the amount of the rent, and how and when it is to be paid.

Legal Requirements State or local law often dictates permissible lease terms. For example, a statute or ordinance might prohibit the leasing of a structure that is in a certain physical condition or is not in compliance with local building codes. Similarly, a statute may prohibit the leasing of property for a particular purpose. For instance, a state law might prohibit gambling houses. Thus, if a landlord and tenant intend that the leased premises be used only to house an illegal betting operation, their lease is unenforceable.

A property owner cannot legally discriminate against prospective tenants on the basis of race, color, national origin, religion, gender, or disability.

NOTE Sound business practice dictates that a lease for commercial property should be written carefully and clearly define the parties' rights and obligations.

LEGAL *e*-NVIRONMENT

Leasing Requirements in a Cyber Age

Traditionally, entrepreneurs who sought to lease premises for their businesses were interested primarily in one thing—location. A warehouser, for example, would want to lease a building easily accessible by carriers, such as trucks. A retailer would want to lease premises that were easily accessible by prospective customers and that offered a reasonable amount of safety for these "business invitees." A professional would want to lease space in a conveniently located office building. Details of the leasing agreement—such as which party would pay for utilities, repairs, and the like—were important, of course, but location was usually a primary factor in the decision to lease specific premises. In today's world of e-commerce, however, Internet companies are redefining leasing needs—needs that must be addressed in lease contracts.

Access to Telecommunications Services

Foremost among the needs of any company selling its products or services online is access to high-capacity fiber-optic cable and phone lines. Thus, access to telecommunications services, not location, is often the primary consideration in deciding where to lease property. In fact, access requirements often lead Internet start-up companies to lease premises in areas that in other respects would be unfavorable.

For example, the best access to telecommunications systems is often in older, downtown areas that are near central phone company distribution centers, not in the newer areas of a city.

Flexibility, Added Security, and Financing

Physical access needs also differ for online companies because they often operate on a 24/7 (twenty-four-hours-a-day, seven-days-a-week) schedule. This means that the tenant must have access to the premises at any hour of the day during every day of the week, and parking must also be available on the same basis. Because employees may be coming and going during the middle of the night, extra security guards may be required to escort employees to and from their cars.

A relatively new development involves using equity ownership in a new Internet company as a bargaining tool when negotiating lease terms. For example, during the dot.com boom of the late 1990s and early 2000s, a start-up company could offer to transfer company stock or stock options to the landlord in return for a reduced rent.

FOR CRITICAL ANALYSIS

If you were a landlord, what factors would you consider when deciding whether to accept stock in a new Internet company in return for a reduced rental payment?

Similarly, a tenant cannot legally promise to do something counter to laws prohibiting discrimination. A tenant, for example, cannot legally promise to do business only with members of a particular race. The public policy underlying these prohibitions is to treat all people equally.

Rights and Duties

The rights and duties of landlords and tenants generally pertain to four broad areas of concern—the possession, use, and maintenance of leased property and, of course, rent.

Possession Possession involves both the obligation of the landlord to deliver possession to the tenant at the beginning of the lease term and the right of the tenant to obtain possession and retain it until the lease expires.

The covenant of quiet enjoyment mentioned previously also applies to leased premises. Under this covenant, the landlord promises that during the lease term, neither the landlord nor anyone having a superior title to the property will disturb the tenant's use and enjoyment of the property. This covenant forms the essence of the landlord-tenant relationship, and if it is breached, the tenant can terminate the lease and sue for damages.

If the landlord deprives the tenant of the tenant's possession of the leased property or interferes with the tenant's use or enjoyment of it, an eviction occurs. An **eviction** occurs, for example, when the landlord changes the lock and refuses to give the tenant a new key. A **constructive eviction** occurs when the landlord wrongfully performs or fails to perform any of the undertakings the lease requires, thereby making the tenant's further use and enjoyment of the property exceedingly difficult or impossible. Examples of constructive eviction include a landlord's failure to provide heat in the winter, light, or other essential utilities.

EVICTION
A landlord's act of depriving a tenant of possession of the leased premises.

CONSTRUCTIVE EVICTION
A form of eviction that occurs when a landlord fails to perform adequately any of the undertakings (such as providing heat in the winter) required by the lease, thereby making the tenant's further use and enjoyment of the property exceedingly difficult or impossible.

Use and Maintenance of the Premises If the parties do not limit by agreement the uses to which the property may be put, the tenant may make any use of it, as long as the use is legal and reasonably relates to the purpose for which the property is adapted or ordinarily used and does not injure the landlord's interest.

The tenant is responsible for any damages to the premises that he or she causes, intentionally or negligently, and the tenant may be held liable for the cost of returning the property to the physical condition it was in at the lease's inception. Unless the parties have agreed otherwise, the tenant is not responsible for ordinary wear and tear and the property's consequent depreciation in value.

Usually, the landlord must comply with state statutes and city ordinances that delineate specific standards for the construction and maintenance of buildings. Typically, these codes contain structural requirements common to the construction, wiring, and plumbing of residential and commercial buildings. In some jurisdictions, landlords of residential property are required by statute to maintain the premises in good repair.

Implied Warranty of Habitability The **implied warranty of habitability** requires a landlord who leases residential property to deliver the premises to the tenant in a habitable condition—that is, in a condition that is safe and suitable for people to live in—at the beginning of a lease term and to maintain them in that condition for the lease's duration. Some state legislatures have enacted this warranty into law. In other jurisdictions, courts have based the warranty on the existence of a landlord's statutory duty to keep leased premises in good repair, or they have simply applied it as a matter of public policy.

IMPLIED WARRANTY OF HABITABILITY
An implied promise by a landlord that rented residential premises are fit for human habitation—that is, in a condition that is safe and suitable for people to live in.

Generally, this warranty applies to major, or *substantial,* physical defects that the landlord knows or should know about and has had a reasonable time to repair—for example, a large hole in the roof. An unattractive or annoying feature, such as a crack in the wall, may be unpleasant, but unless the crack is a structural defect or affects the residence's heating capabilities, it is probably not sufficiently substantial to make the place uninhabitable.

At issue in the following case was whether the lack of a smoke detector constituted a violation of a statutory requirement that rental property be "in reasonable repair and fit for human habitation."

CASE 21.2   Schiernbeck v. Davis

United States Court of Appeals,
Eighth Circuit, 1998.
143 F.3d 434.
http://laws.findlaw.com/8th[a]

HISTORICAL AND TECHNOLOGICAL SETTING

Different smoke detectors come with a variety of capabilities. Some can detect flames with little smoke and can detect even "smokeless" fires. Other devices include strobe lights for alerting the hearing impaired, fixtures for lighting darkened areas, "hush" buttons for nuisance alarms, and buttons for testing the functions. A basic, battery-operated smoke detector, with an alarm only, can cost as little as $6. Certain states require the installation of smoke detectors on property offered for rent. A missing smoke detector in residential rental property is a violation of some local building codes. Not every jurisdiction requires their use, however.

BACKGROUND AND FACTS   Linda Schiernbeck rented a house from Clark and Rosa Davis. A month after moving into the house, Schiernbeck noticed a discolored circular area where, she determined, a smoke detector had previously been attached to the wall. Schiernbeck later claimed that she told Clark Davis about the missing detector. Davis did not remember the conversation. He admitted, however, that he gave Schiernbeck a detector, which she denied. At any rate, when a fire in the house severely injured Schiernbeck, she filed a suit in a federal district court against the Davises, alleging negligence and breach of contract for failing to provide a detector. The Davises filed a motion for summary judgment, arguing that they had no duty to install a detector in a rental house. The court ruled in the Davises' favor, and Schiernbeck appealed to the U.S. Court of Appeals for the Eighth Circuit.

IN THE WORDS OF THE COURT . . .

WATERS, District Judge.

*   *   *   *

*   *   * South Dakota Codified Laws Section 43-32-8 requires that the lessor keep the leased premises "in reasonable repair and fit for human habitation *   *   * ." We do not believe that equipping the leased premises with a smoke detector constitutes keeping the premises in "reasonable repair." *   *   * [T]he accepted dictionary definition [of "repair" is:] "To restore to a sound or good state after decay, injury, dilapidation, or partial destruction." Schiernbeck cites an additional part of the dictionary's definition which states *   *   * "to supply *   *   * that which is lost or destroyed" to include replacing a missing smoke detector in the definition of repair. We conclude, however, that when reading the entire definition, the term "repair" does not encompass replacing a missing smoke detector.

*   *   *   *

In addition, we do not believe that the Davises were required to replace the smoke detector in order to make the rental house "fit for human habitation." *   *   * Clearly, unstable stairs create a place that is unfit for human habitation, as does a lack of running water, heat, or electricity. We do not believe, however, that a lessor *   *   * is required to equip his or her residential premises with smoke detectors, fire extinguishers, carbon monoxide detectors, etc. in order to make the leased premises "fit for human habitation."

---

a. This Web site is maintained by FindLaw (now a part of West Group). This page provides access to some of the opinions of the U.S. Court of Appeals for the Eighth Circuit. In the "Search" box, type "97-3431" and click "Search" to access the *Schiernbeck* opinion.

CASE 21.2—Continued

DECISION AND REMEDY The U.S. Court of Appeals for the Eighth Circuit held that a landlord's statutory duty to keep rental premises "in reasonable repair and fit for human habitation" does not include installing a smoke detector. The court affirmed the lower court's judgment.

FOR CRITICAL ANALYSIS—Ethical Consideration *What is a landlord's ethical duty with respect to keeping rental premises "fit for human habitation"?*

Rent *Rent* is the tenant's payment to the landlord for the tenant's occupancy or use of the landlord's real property. Generally, the tenant must pay the rent even if he or she refuses to occupy the property or moves out, as long as the refusal or the move is unjustifiable and the lease is in force.

Under the common law, destruction by fire or flood of a building leased by a tenant did not relieve the tenant of the obligation to pay rent and did not permit the termination of the lease. Today, however, state statutes have altered the common law rule. If the building burns down, apartment dwellers in most states are not continuously liable to the landlord for the payment of rent.

In some situations, such as when a landlord breaches the implied warranty of habitability, a tenant is allowed to withhold rent as a remedy. When rent withholding is authorized under a statute (sometimes referred to as a "rent-strike" statute), the tenant must usually put the amount withheld into an *escrow account*. This account is held in the name of the depositor (in this case, the tenant) and an *escrow agent* (in this case, usually the court or a government agency), and the funds are returnable to the depositor if the third person (in this case, the landlord) fails to fulfill the escrow condition. Generally, the tenant may withhold an amount equal to the amount by which the defect rendering the premises unlivable reduces the property's rental value. How much that is may be determined in different ways, and the tenant who withholds more than is legally permissible is liable to the landlord for the excessive amount withheld.

NOTE Options that may be available to a tenant on a landlord's breach of the implied warranty of habitability include repairing the defect and deducting the amount from the rent, canceling the lease, and suing for damages.

Transferring Rights to Leased Property

Either the landlord or the tenant may wish to transfer his or her rights to the leased property during the term of the lease.

Transferring the Landlord's Interest Just as any other real property owner can sell, give away, or otherwise transfer his or her property, so can a landlord—who is, of course, the leased property's owner. If complete title to the leased property is transferred, the tenant becomes the tenant of the new owner. The new owner may collect subsequent rent but must abide by the terms of the existing lease agreement.

Transferring the Tenant's Interest The tenant's transfer of his or her entire interest in the leased property to a third person is an *assignment of the lease*. A lease assignment is an agreement to transfer all rights, title, and interest in the lease to the assignee. It is a complete transfer. Many leases require that the assignment have the landlord's written consent, and an assignment that lacks consent can be avoided (nullified) by the landlord. A landlord who knowingly accepts rent from the assignee, however, will be held to have waived the requirement. An assignment does not terminate a tenant's liabilities under a lease agreement, however, because the tenant may assign rights but not duties. Thus, even though the assignee of the lease is required to pay rent, the original tenant is not released from the contractual obligation to pay the rent if the assignee fails to do so.

The tenant's transfer of all or part of the premises for a period shorter than the lease term is a **sublease**. The same restrictions that apply to an assignment of the tenant's interest in leased property apply to a sublease. ● EXAMPLE 4 A student, Derek, leases an apartment for a two-year period. Although Derek had planned on attending summer school, he is offered a job in Europe for the summer months and accepts. Because he does not wish to pay three months' rent for an unoccupied apartment, Derek subleases the apartment to Singleton, who becomes a sublessee. (Derek may have to obtain his landlord's consent for this sublease if the lease requires it.) Singleton is bound by the same terms of the lease as Derek, but as in a lease assignment, Derek remains liable for the obligations under the lease if Singleton fails to fulfill them. ●

SUBLEASE
A lease executed by the lessee of real estate to a third person, conveying the same interest that the lessee enjoys but for a shorter term than that held by the lessee.

LAND-USE CONTROL

Property owners—even those who possess the entire bundle of rights set out earlier in this chapter—cannot do with their property whatever they wish. The rights of every property owner are subject to certain conditions and limitations.

There are three sources of land-use control. First, the law of torts (see Chapter 8) places on the owners of land obligations to protect the interests of individuals who come on the land and the interests of the owners of nearby land. Second, landowners may agree with others to restrict or limit the use of their property. Such agreements may "run with the land" when ownership is transferred to others. Thus, one who acquires real property with actual or *constructive* (imputed by law) notice of a restriction may be bound by an earlier, voluntary agreement to which he or she was not a party.

Third, controls are imposed by the government. Land use is subject to regulation by the state within whose political boundaries the land is located. Most states authorize control over land use through various planning boards and zoning authorities at a city or county level. The federal government does not engage in land-use control under normal circumstances, except with respect to federally owned land.[8] The federal government does influence state and local regulation, however, through the allocation of federal funds. Stipulations on land use may be a condition to the states' receiving such funds.

Sources of Public Control

The states' power to control the use of land through legislation is derived from their *police power* and the doctrine of *eminent domain*. Under their police power, state governments enact legislation that promotes the health, safety,

---

8. Federal (and state) laws concerning environmental matters such as air and water quality, the protection of endangered species, and the preservation of natural wetlands are also a source of land-use control. Some of these laws were discussed in Chapter 20.

and welfare of their citizens. This legislation includes land-use controls. The power of **eminent domain** is the government's authority to take private property for public use or purpose without the owner's consent. Typically, this is accomplished through a judicial proceeding to obtain title to the land.

Police Power

As an exercise of its police power,[9] a state can regulate the use of land within its jurisdiction. A few states control land use at the state level. Hawaii, for instance, employs a statewide land-use classification scheme. Some states have a land-permit process that operates in conjunction with local control. Florida, for example, uses such a scheme in certain areas of "critical environmental concern" to permit or prohibit development on the basis of available roads, sewers, and so on. Vermont also utilizes a statewide land-permit program.

Usually, however, a state authorizes its city or county governments to regulate the use of land within their local jurisdictions. A state confers this power through *enabling legislation*. Enabling legislation normally requires local governments to devise *general plans* before imposing other land-use controls. Enabling acts also typically authorize local bodies to enact *zoning laws* to regulate the use of land and the types of and specifications for structures. Local planning boards may regulate the development of subdivisions, in which private developers subdivide tracts of land and construct commercial or residential units for resale to others. Local governments may also enact growth-management ordinances to control development in their jurisdictions.

Government Plans Most states require that land-use laws follow a local government's general plan. A **general plan** is a comprehensive, long-term scheme dealing with the physical development, and in some cases redevelopment, of a city or community. It addresses such concerns as types of housing, protection of natural resources, provision of public facilities and transportation, and other issues related to land use. A plan indicates the direction of growth in a community and the contributions that private developers must make toward providing public facilities, such as roads. If a proposed use is not authorized by the general plan, the plan may be amended to permit the use. (A plan may also be amended to preclude a proposed use.)

Even when a proposed use complies with a general plan, it may not be allowed. Most jurisdictions have requirements in addition to those in the general plan. These requirements are then included in *specific plans*—also called special, area, or community plans. Specific plans typically pertain to only a portion of a jurisdiction's area. For example, a specific plan may concern a downtown area subject to redevelopment efforts, an area with special environmental concerns, or an area with increased public transportation needs arising from population growth.

Zoning Laws In addition to complying with a general plan and any specific plans, a particular land use must comply with zoning laws. The term **zoning** refers to the dividing of an area into districts to which specific land-use regulations apply. A typical zoning law consists of a zoning map and a zoning

EMINENT DOMAIN
The power of a government to take land for public use from private citizens for just compensation.

GENERAL PLAN
A comprehensive document that local jurisdictions are often required by state law to devise and implement as a precursor to specific land-use regulations.

ZONING
The division of a city by legislative regulation into districts and the application in each district of regulations having to do with structural and architectural designs of buildings and prescribing the use to which buildings within designated districts may be put.

9. As pointed out in Chapter 5, the police power of a state encompasses the right to regulate private activities to protect or promote the public order, health, safety, morals, and general welfare.

ordinance. The zoning map indicates the characteristics of each parcel of land within an area and divides that area into districts. The zoning ordinance specifies the restrictions on land use within those districts.

Zoning ordinances generally include two types of restrictions. One type pertains to the kind of land use—such as commercial versus residential—to which property within a particular district may be put. The second type dictates the engineering features and architectural design of structures built within that district.

Use Restrictions. Districts are typically zoned for residential, commercial, industrial, or agricultural use. Each district may be further subdivided for degree or intensity of use. For example, a residential district may be subdivided to permit a certain number of apartment buildings and a specific number of units in each building. Commercial and industrial districts are often zoned to permit *heavy* or *light* activity. Heavy activity might include the operation of large factories. Light activity might encompass the operation of professional office buildings or small retail shops. Zoning that specifies the use to which property may be put is referred to as **use zoning.**

Structural Restrictions. Restrictions known as *bulk regulations* cover such details as minimum floor-space requirements and minimum lot-size restrictions. For example, a particular district's minimum floor-space requirements might specify that a one-story building contain a minimum of 1,240 square feet of floor space, and minimum lot-size restrictions might mandate that each single-family dwelling be built on a lot that is at least one acre in size. Referred to collectively as **bulk zoning,** these regulations also dictate *setback* (the distance between a building and a street, sidewalk, or other boundary) and the height of buildings, with different requirements for buildings in different areas.

Restrictions related to structure may also be concerned with such matters as architectural control, the overall appearance of a community, and the preservation of historic buildings. An ordinance may require that all proposed construction be approved by a design review board composed of local architects. A community may restrict the size and placement of outdoor advertising, such as billboards and business signs. A property owner may be prohibited from tearing down or remodeling a historic landmark or building. In challenges against these types of restrictions, the courts have generally upheld the regulations.

Variances. A **zoning variance** allows property to be used or structures to be built in some way that varies from the restrictions of a zoning ordinance. ● EXAMPLE 5 A variance may exempt property from a use restriction to allow, for example, a bakery shop in a residential area. Or a variance may exempt a building from a height restriction so that, for example, a two-story house can be built in a district in which houses are otherwise limited to one floor.● Some jurisdictions do not permit variances from use restrictions.

Variances are normally granted by local adjustment boards. In general, a property owner must meet three criteria to obtain a variance:

1. The owner must find it impossible to realize a reasonable return on the land as currently zoned.
2. The adverse effect of the zoning ordinance must be particular to the party seeking the variance and not have a similar effect on other owners in the same zone.

USE ZONING
Zoning classifications within a particular municipality that may be distinguished based on the uses to which the land is to be put.

BULK ZONING
Zoning regulations that restrict the amount of structural coverage on a particular parcel of land.

ZONING VARIANCE
The granting of permission by a municipality or other public board to a landowner to use his or her property in a way that does not strictly conform with the zoning regulations so as to avoid causing the landowner undue hardship.

3. Granting the variance must not substantially alter the essential character of the zoned area.

Perhaps the most important of these criteria is whether the variance would substantially alter the character of the area. Courts are more lenient about the other requirements when reviewing decisions of adjustment boards.

In contrast to a "use" provision, an "area" restriction regulates the area, height, density, setback, or sideline attributes of a building or other development on a piece of property. For example, an area provision may dictate the distance between buildings. In the following case, a builder sought a variance from an area provision.

CASE 21.3 Richard Roeser Professional Builder, Inc. v. Anne Arundel County

Maryland Court of Appeals, 2002.
386 Md. 294,
793 A.2d 545.
http://www.courts.state.md.us/search[a]

HISTORICAL AND ECONOMIC SETTING *For decades, it has been a common practice in most states for a buyer to contract to buy property subject to the condition that the contract will be consummated (will become binding) only if a local zoning board grants a variance to permit development of the property. Although it has been argued that this practice constitutes a "self-created" hardship for the buyer, the courts have generally approved requests for variances in such circumstances.*[b]

BACKGROUND AND FACTS In 1999, with a certain project in mind, Richard Roeser Professional Builder, Inc. (RRPB), contracted to buy two lots near

Annapolis, Maryland, in Anne Arundel County, for $62,000. Part of one of the lots was adjacent to wetlands. County "Critical Area" zoning provisions required a setback "buffer zone" between wetlands and any development on the property. At the time, RRPB knew that variances from the provisions would be required to build the firm's project on the lot. RRPB applied for those variances, but the county zoning board denied the request on the ground that "[t]he conditions surrounding the Petitioners' request for a variance have been self-created." RRPB filed a suit in a Maryland state court against the county. The court rejected the board's decision. The board appealed to a state intermediate appellate court, which reversed the judgment of the lower court and directed it to reinstate the decision of the board. RRPB appealed to the Maryland Court of Appeals, the state's highest court.

IN THE WORDS OF THE COURT . . . *CATHELL*, Judge.

* * * *

* * * [Z]oning constitutes restrictions on land, not on title. Both the Maryland Declaration of Rights and the Fifth Amendment of the United States Constitution guarantee rights to property owners. Property owners start out with the unrestricted right to use their land as they see fit. Under the common law, those rights are limited only by a restriction as to uses that create traditional nuisances. * * * [H]owever, * * * reasonable regulation is constitutional. That said, it must, nonetheless, be recognized that *regulation of land, including zoning regulations, are limitations on the full exercise of a property owner's constitutional rights as well as his or her rights under the common law.* [Emphasis added.]

---

a. In the "Search in:" box, select "Court of Appeals." In the "For:" box, type "Roeser," and click on "Search." In the result, click on the icon to access the opinion. The Maryland Judiciary maintains this Web site.
b. See, for example, *Myron v. City of Plymouth*, 562 N.W.2d 21 (Minn.App. 1997).

(continued)

CASE 21.3—Continued

* * * [W]e must not forget the underlying principle that * * * zoning ordinances are in derogation of [deviate from] the common law right to so use private property as to realize its highest utility, and while they should be liberally construed to accomplish their plain purpose and intent, they should not be extended by implication to cases not clearly within the scope of the purpose and intent manifest in their language. In that respect, reasonable zoning limitations are always directed to the property, itself, and its uses and structures, not to the completely separate matter of title to property, which is another whole field of law. In zoning, it is the property that is regulated, not the title.

In Maryland, when title is transferred, it takes with it all the encumbrances and burdens that attach to title; but it also takes with it all the benefits and rights inherent in ownership. If a predecessor in title was subject to a claim that he had created his own hardship, that burden, for variance purposes, passes with the title. But, at the same time, if the prior owner has not self-created a hardship, a self-created hardship is not immaculately conceived merely because the new owner obtains title.

DECISION AND REMEDY The Maryland Court of Appeals reversed the judgment of the lower court and remanded the case for further proceedings. The Maryland Court of Appeals held that RRPB's purchase of the property, with notice that it was subject to restrictions, including a "Critical Area" buffer zone for wetlands under county zoning provisions, was not a self-created hardship that precluded RRPB from receiving a variance.

FOR CRITICAL ANALYSIS—Social Consideration *Why should it matter whether a hardship was "self-created" when determining whether a variance should be granted?*

Subdivision Regulations When subdividing a parcel of land into smaller plots, a private developer must comply not only with local zoning ordinances but also with local subdivision regulations. Subdivision regulations are different from zoning ordinances, although they may be administered by the same local agencies that oversee the zoning process. In the design of a subdivision, the local authorities may demand, for example, the allocation of space for a public park or school or may require a developer to construct streets to accommodate a specific level of traffic.

Growth-Management Ordinances To prevent population growth from racing ahead of the community's ability to provide necessary public services, local authorities may enact a growth-management ordinance to limit, for example, the number of residential building permits. A property owner may thus be precluded from constructing a residential building on his or her property even if the area is zoned for the use and the proposed structure complies with all other requirements. A growth-management ordinance may prohibit the issuance of residential building permits for a specific period of time, until the occurrence of a specific event (such as a decline in the total number of residents in the community), or on the basis of the availability of necessary public services (such as the capacity for drainage in the area or the proximity of hospitals and police stations).

Limitations on the Exercise of Police Power The government's exercise of its police power to regulate the use of land is limited in at least three ways. Two of these limitations arise under the Fourteenth Amendment to the Constitution. The third limitation arises under the Fifth Amendment and requires that, under certain circumstances, the government must compensate an owner who is deprived of the use of his or her property.

Due Process and Equal Protection. A government cannot regulate the use of land in a way that violates either the due process clause or the equal protection clause of the Fourteenth Amendment. A government may be deemed to violate the due process clause if it acts arbitrarily or unreasonably. Thus, there must be a *rational basis* for classifications that are imposed on property. Any classification that is reasonably related to the health or general welfare of the public is deemed to have a rational basis.

Under the equal protection clause, land-use controls cannot be discriminatory. A zoning ordinance is discriminatory if it affects one parcel of land in a way in which it does not affect surrounding parcels and if there is no rational basis for the difference. For example, classifying a single parcel in a way that does not accord with a general plan is discriminatory. Similarly, a zoning ordinance cannot be racially discriminatory. ● EXAMPLE 6 A community may not zone itself to exclude all low-income housing if the intention is to exclude minorities.●

As explained in Chapter 5, substantive due process focuses on the substance of governmental action. In the following case, a local zoning board delayed action on a business's proposal to build and operate a multiplex theater complex. The issue before the court was whether a new standard should be applied in a substantive due process challenge to this delay.

CASE 21.4   **United Artists Theatre Circuit, Inc. v. Township of Warrington, Pennsylvania**

United States Court of Appeals,
Third Circuit, 2003.
316 F.3d 392.

BACKGROUND AND FACTS In January 1996, United Artists Theatre Circuit, Inc. (UA), an owner and operator of movie theaters, obtained preliminary approval from the board of supervisors of Warrington Township, Pennsylvania, to build a multiplex theater. The board subsequently changed its approval to require UA to acquire an easement for a left-turn lane and install a signal before construction could begin. UA filed a suit against the township in a Pennsylvania state court, which ultimately ruled that the new requirement was unlawful. Meanwhile, in January 1997, Regal

Cinema proposed a competing theater. Because the market could support only one theater, the project that was approved first was likely to be the only one built. The board asked each party to pay an annual "impact" fee of $100,000. Regal agreed. UA refused. The board granted final approval to the Regal proposal in May, but tabled its vote on UA's proposal three times before granting final approval in September. UA filed a suit in a federal district court against the township and each supervisor, claiming in part violations of substantive due process. The defendants filed motions for summary judgment, which the court denied, concluding that each supervisor had an "improper motive" in delaying approval of UA's proposal. The defendants appealed to the U.S. Court of Appeals for the Third Circuit.

IN THE WORDS
OF THE COURT . . .

ALITO, Circuit Judge:
         * * * *

In *County of Sacramento v. Lewis,*[a] the [United States] Supreme Court explained the standard that applies when a plaintiff alleges that an action

---

a. 523 U.S. 833, 118 S.Ct. 1708, 140 L.Ed.2d 1043 (1998).

(continued)

CASE 21.4—Continued

taken by an executive branch official violated substantive due process. * * * The Court observed that *"the core of the concept" of due process is "protection against arbitrary action" and that "only the most egregious official conduct can be said to be arbitrary in the constitutional sense." * * * [T]he cognizable level of executive abuse of power [is] that which shocks the conscience * * *.* [Emphasis added.]

* * * *

* * * United Artists maintains that this case is not governed by the "shocks the conscience" standard, but by the less demanding "improper motive" test that * * * was * * * applied by our court in a line of land use cases. In these cases, we held that a municipal land use decision violates substantive due process if it was made for any reason unrelated to the merits or with any improper motive.

* * * *

[But] we see no reason why the present case should be exempted from the *Lewis* shocks-the-conscience test simply because the case concerns a land use dispute. * * * Since [the *Lewis* case,] our court has applied the "shocks the conscience" standard in a variety of contexts. There is no reason why land use cases should be treated differently. We thus hold that, in light of *Lewis,* [the "improper motive" test that we applied in previous cases is] no longer good law.

* * * *

Application of the "shocks the conscience" standard in this context also prevents us from being cast in the role of a zoning board of appeals. * * * [E]very appeal by a disappointed developer from an adverse ruling of the local planning board involves some claim of abuse of legal authority, but it is not enough simply to give these state law claims constitutional labels such as "due process" or "equal protection" in order to raise a substantial federal question * * *. Land use decisions are matters of local concern, and such disputes should not be transformed into substantive due process claims based only on allegations that government officials acted with improper motives.

DECISION AND REMEDY The U.S. Court of Appeals for the Third Circuit vacated the lower court's judgment and remanded the case for reconsideration of the defendants' motions for summary judgment under the "shocks the conscience" test.

FOR CRITICAL ANALYSIS—Social Consideration *Are there significant differences between an "improper motives" standard and a "shocks the conscience" test?*

Just Compensation. Under the Fifth Amendment, private property may not be taken for a public purpose without the payment of just compensation.[10] If government restrictions on a landowner's property rights are overly burdensome, the regulation may be deemed a taking. A *taking* occurs when a regulation denies an owner the ability to use his or her property for any reasonable income-producing or private purpose for which it is suited. This requires the government to pay the owner.

---

10. Although the Fifth Amendment pertains to actions taken by the federal government, the Fourteenth Amendment has been interpreted as extending this limitation to state actions.

A view of the ocean from a public park. If this had once been private property, why would the government have been prohibited from taking it for public use without paying the owner?

● **EXAMPLE 7** Suppose that Perez purchases a large tract of land with the intent to subdivide and develop it into residential properties. At the time of the purchase, there are no zoning laws restricting use of the land. After Perez has taken significant steps to develop the property, the county attempts to zone the tract for use as "public parkland only." If this prohibits Perez from developing any of the land, normally it will be deemed a taking. If the county does not fairly compensate Perez, the regulation will be held unconstitutional and void.●

The distinction between an ordinance that merely restricts land use and an outright taking is crucial. A restriction is simply an exercise of the state's police power; even though it limits a property owner's land use, the owner generally need not be compensated for the limitation. If an ordinance or other government action completely deprives an owner of use or benefit of property or constitutes an outright governmental taking of property, however, the owner must be compensated.

The United States Supreme Court has held that restrictions do not constitute a taking of an owner's property if they "substantially advance legitimate state interests" and do not "den[y] an owner economically viable use of his land."[11] It is not clear, however, exactly what constitutes a "legitimate state interest" or when particular restrictions "substantially advance" that interest. Furthermore, the term "economically viable use" has not yet been clearly defined.

Eminent Domain

As noted above, governments have an inherent power to take property for public use or purpose without the consent of the owner. This is the power of eminent domain, and it is very important in the public control of land use.

Every property owner holds his or her interest in land subject to a superior interest. Just as in medieval England the king was the ultimate landowner, so

"[A] strong public desire to improve the public condition is not enough to warrant achieving the desire by a shorter cut than . . . paying for the change."
OLIVER WENDELL HOLMES, JR.,
1841–1935
(Associate justice of the United States Supreme Court, 1902–1932)

---

11. *Agins v. Tiburon,* 447 U.S. 255, 100 S.Ct. 2138, 65 L.Ed.2d 106 (1980).

INSIDE THE LEGAL ENVIRONMENT

Takings for Private Developments

Government takings of private property for public use are often controversial. This is understandable, given that landowners whose property is taken may have a substantial interest at stake in condemnation proceedings. For example, suppose that you own a thriving business and that part of the reason for the business's profitability is its location. You learn that your city is planning to condemn the property in order to create new on-off ramps to a nearby freeway. Although the city's purpose in condemning the property may be rational and in the public interest, you believe

that your business will suffer by having to move elsewhere.

Many people who have found themselves in just this situation have learned that they can do little about it. Their property will be taken, provided that the government's purpose in condemning the property is rational, the public will benefit from the action, and the property owners are given "just compensation."

Private or Public Use

For some time, state and local governments have been using the power of eminent domain to transfer property to private developers. Government officials claim that this use of eminent domain helps attract private

developers and businesses that provide jobs and increase tax revenues, thus revitalizing communities. Eminent domain is also commonly being employed to encourage redevelopment—in blighted areas of a city, for example. When eminent domain is used in this way, essentially one group of private owners is replaced by another group of private owners.

Takings for private development or redevelopment have sometimes been challenged on the ground that the property is not being taken for "public" use, as required by the U.S. Constitution. In these cases, the courts have generally focused on whether the proposed use of the land is genuinely in the public interest or is mainly to further private interests.

in the United States the government retains an ultimate ownership right in all land. This right, known as eminent domain, is sometimes referred to as the *condemnation power* of the government to take land for public use. It gives to the government a right to acquire possession of real property in the manner directed by the Constitution and the laws of the state whenever the public interest requires it. Property may not be taken for private benefit, but only for public use. (For a discussion of a current controversy involving the purpose of takings, see this chapter's *Inside the Legal Environment* feature.)

• EXAMPLE 8 When a new public highway is to be built, the government must decide where to build it and how much land to condemn. After the government determines that a particular parcel of land is necessary for public use, it brings a judicial proceeding to obtain title to the land.•

Under the Fifth Amendment, although the government may take land for public use, it must pay fair and just compensation for it. Thus, in the previous highway example, after the proceeding to obtain title to the land, there is a second proceeding in which the court determines the *fair value* of the land. Fair value is usually approximately equal to market value.

INSIDE THE LEGAL ENVIRONMENT

Takings for Private Developments (Continued)

The Tide May Be Turning

By and large, the courts have supported the government agencies in these cases, although a series of cases in recent years indicates that this pattern may be changing. Consider a case decided by the Illinois Supreme Court in 2002. It involved an Illinois state agency that had issued bonds and lent the proceeds of the bonds to Gateway International Motorsports Corporation. The purpose of the loan was to finance the development of a sports facility (a racetrack) in the region. The racetrack flourished, and soon Gateway needed more parking space. The state agency then condemned a parcel of property adjacent to the racetrack for Gateway to use for additional parking.

The owner of the adjacent property challenged the taking, contending that it was for private, not public, use. Ultimately, the Illinois Supreme Court sided with the property owner. According to the court, the power of eminent domain is to be "exercised with restraint, not abandon," and it was "a violation of the constitutional public use limitation for a government agency to take unoffending property in order to convey it for the expansion of parking of another private business."[a] Other courts in the early 2000s have reached similar conclusions in cases involving takings for purposes that are not clearly in the public interest.[b]

FOR CRITICAL ANALYSIS

Do you agree with the argument that if state and local governments could not use their condemnation power to improve, say, inner-city areas through redevelopment, society would suffer in the long run? Even if you do agree, do you believe that the Fifth Amendment permits such takings?

a. *Southwestern Illinois Development Authority v. National City Environmental, L.L.C.,* 199 Ill.2d 225, 768 N.E.2d 1, 263 Ill.Dec. 241 (2002).
b. See, for example, *99 Cents Only Stores v. Lancaster Redevelopment Agency,* 2001 WL 811050 (C.D.Cal. 2001).

KEY TERMS

CHAPTER SUMMARY LAND-USE CONTROL AND REAL PROPERTY

The Nature of Real Property (See pages 661–664.)	Real property (also called real estate or realty) is immovable. It includes land, subsurface and air rights, plant life and vegetation, and fixtures.
Ownership of Real Property (See pages 664–666.)	1. *Fee simple absolute*—The most complete form of ownership. 2. *Fee simple defeasible*—Ownership in fee simple that can end if a specified event or condition occurs. 3. *Life estate*—An estate that lasts for the life of a specified individual; ownership rights in a life estate are subject to the rights of the future-interest holder. 4. *Future interest*—A residuary interest not granted by the grantor in conveying an estate to another for life, for a specified period of time, or on the condition that a specific event does or does not occur. The grantor may retain the residuary interest (which is then called a reversionary interest) or transfer ownership rights in the future interest to another (the interest is then referred to as a remainder). 5. *Nonpossessory interest*—An interest that involves the right to use real property but not to possess it. Easements, profits, and licenses are nonpossessory interests.
Transfer of Ownership (See pages 666–669.)	1. *By deed*—When real property is sold or transferred as a gift, title to the property is conveyed by means of a deed. A deed must meet specific legal requirements. A *warranty deed* warrants the most extensive protection against defects of title. A *quitclaim deed* conveys to the grantee whatever interest the grantor had; it warrants less than any other deed. A deed may be recorded in the manner prescribed by *recording statutes* in the appropriate jurisdiction to give third parties notice of the owner's interest. 2. *By will or inheritance*—If the owner dies after having made a valid will, the land passes as specified in the will. If the owner dies without having made a will, the heirs inherit according to state inheritance statutes. 3. *By adverse possession*—When a person possesses the property of another for a statutory period of time (three to thirty years, with ten years being the most common), that person acquires title to the property, provided the possession is actual and exclusive, open and visible, continuous and peaceable, and hostile and adverse (without the permission of the owner).
Leasehold Estates (See pages 669–671.)	A leasehold estate is an interest in real property that is held only for a limited period of time, as specified in the lease agreement. Types of tenancies relating to leased property include the following: 1. *Tenancy for years*—Tenancy for a period of time stated by express contract. 2. *Periodic tenancy*—Tenancy for a period determined by the frequency of rent payments; automatically renewed unless proper notice is given. 3. *Tenancy at will*—Tenancy for as long as both parties agree; no notice of termination is required. 4. *Tenancy at sufferance*—Possession of land without legal right.
Landlord-Tenant Relationships (See pages 671–676.)	1. *Lease agreement*—The landlord-tenant relationship is created by a lease agreement. State or local laws may dictate whether the lease must be in writing and what lease terms are permissible. 2. *Rights and duties*—The rights and duties that arise under a lease agreement generally pertain to the following areas: a. Possession—The tenant has an exclusive right to possess the leased premises, which must be available to the tenant at the agreed-on time. Under the covenant of quiet

CHAPTER SUMMARY **LAND-USE CONTROL AND REAL PROPERTY—Continued**

Landlord-Tenant Relationships— continued	enjoyment, the landlord promises that during the lease term neither the landlord nor anyone having superior title to the property will disturb the tenant's use and enjoyment of the property.
	b. Use and maintenance of the premises—Unless the parties agree otherwise, the tenant may make any legal use of the property. The tenant is responsible for any damage that he or she causes. The landlord must comply with laws that set specific standards for the maintenance of real property. The implied warranty of habitability requires that a landlord furnish and maintain residential premises in a habitable condition (that is, in a condition safe and suitable for human life).
	c. Rent—The tenant must pay the rent as long as the lease is in force, unless the tenant justifiably refuses to occupy the property or withholds the rent because of the landlord's failure to maintain the premises properly.
	3. *Transferring rights to leased property—*
	a. If the landlord transfers complete title to the leased property, the tenant becomes the tenant of the new owner. The new owner may then collect the rent but must abide by the existing lease.
	b. Generally, tenants may assign their rights (but not their duties) under a lease contract to a third person. Tenants may also sublease leased property to a third person, but the original tenant is not relieved of any obligations to the landlord under the lease. In either case, the landlord's consent may be required.
Land-Use Control— Private Control (See page 676.)	1. *The law of torts—*Owners are obligated to protect the interests of those who come on the land and those who own nearby land.
	2. *Private agreements—*Owners may agree with others to limit the use of their property.
Land-Use Control— Government Police Power (See pages 677–683.)	1. *Government plans—*Most states require that local land-use laws follow a general plan.
	2. *Zoning laws—*Laws that divide an area into districts to which specific land-use regulations apply. Districts may be zoned for residential, commercial, industrial, or agricultural use. Within all districts there may be minimum lot-size requirements, structural restrictions, and other bulk zoning regulations. A variance allows for the use of property in ways that vary from the restrictions.
	3. *Subdivision regulations—*Laws directing the dedication of specific plots of land to specific uses within a subdivision.
	4. *Growth-management ordinances—*Limits on, for example, the number of residential building permits.
	5. *Limits on the police power:*
	a. Due process and equal protection—Land-use controls cannot be arbitrary, unreasonable, or discriminatory.
	b. Just compensation—Private property taken for a public purpose requires payment of just compensation. "Taking" for a public purpose includes enacting overly burdensome regulations.
Land-Use Control— Eminent Domain (See pages 683–685.)	1. *Condemnation power—*Governments have the inherent power to take property for public use without the consent of the owner.
	2. *Limits on the power of eminent domain—*Private property taken for a public purpose requires payment of just compensation.

FOR REVIEW

1. What are the different types of ownership interests in real property?

2. How can ownership interests in real property be transferred?

3. What is a leasehold estate, and how does it arise?

4. What are the respective duties of the landlord and tenant concerning the use and maintenance of leased property?

5. What limitations may be imposed on the rights of property owners?

QUESTIONS AND CASE PROBLEMS

21–1. Tenant's Rights and Responsibilities. You are a student in college and plan to attend classes for nine months. You sign a twelve-month lease for an apartment. Discuss fully each of the following situations.

(a) You have a summer job in another town and wish to assign the balance of your lease (three months) to a fellow student who will be attending summer school. Can you do so?

(b) You are graduating in May. The lease will have three months remaining. Can you terminate the lease without liability by giving a thirty-day notice to the landlord?

21–2. Property Ownership. Antonio is the owner of a lakeside house and lot. He deeds the house and lot "to my wife, Angela, for life, then to my son, Charles." Given these facts, answer the following questions:

(a) Does Antonio have any ownership interest in the lakeside house after making these transfers? Explain.

(b) What is Angela's interest called? Is there any limitation on her rights to use the property as she wishes?

(c) What is Charles's interest called? Why?

21–3. Property Ownership. Lorenz was a wanderer twenty-two years ago. At that time, he decided to settle down on an unoccupied, three-acre parcel of land that he did not own. People in the area indicated to him that they had no idea who owned the property. Lorenz built a house on the land, got married, and raised three children while living there. He fenced in the land, placed a gate with a sign above it that read "Lorenz's Homestead," and had trespassers removed. Lorenz is now confronted by Joe Reese, who has a deed in his name as owner of the property. Reese, claiming ownership of the land, orders Lorenz and his family off the property. Discuss who has the better "title" to the property.

21–4. Deeds. Wiley and Gemma are neighbors. Wiley's lot is extremely large, and his present and future use of it will not involve the entire area. Gemma wants to build a single-car garage and driveway along the present lot boundary. Because of ordinances requiring buildings to be set back fifteen feet from an adjoining property line, and because of the placement of her existing structures, Gemma cannot build the

garage. Gemma contracts to purchase ten feet of Wiley's property along their boundary line for $3,000. Wiley is willing to sell but will give Gemma only a quitclaim deed, whereas Gemma wants a warranty deed. Discuss the differences between these deeds as they would affect the rights of the parties if the title to this ten feet of land later proved to be defective.

21–5. Subdivision Regulations. Suppose that as a condition of a developer's receiving approval for constructing a new residential community, the local authorities insist that the developer dedicate, or set aside, land for a new hospital. The hospital would serve not only the proposed residential community but also the rest of the city. If the developer challenges the condition in court, under what standard might the court invalidate the condition?

21–6. Warranty of Habitability. Three-year-old Nkenge Lynch fell from the window of her third-floor apartment and suffered serious and permanent injuries. There were no window stops or guards on the window. The use of window stops, even if installed, is optional with the tenant. Stanley James owned the apartment building. Zsa Zsa Kinsey, Nkenge's mother, filed a suit on Nkenge's behalf in a Massachusetts state court against James, alleging in part a breach of an implied warranty of habitability. The plaintiff did not argue that the absence of stops or guards made the apartment unfit for human habitation but that their absence "endangered and materially impaired her health and safety," and therefore the failure to install them was a breach of warranty. Should the court rule that the absence of window stops breached a warranty of habitability? Should the court mandate that landlords provide window guards? Why or why not? [*Lynch v. James*, 44 Mass.App.Ct. 448, 692 N.E.2d 81 (1998)]

21–7. Eminent Domain. The state of Indiana, through its department of transportation, planned to improve U.S. Highway 41 in Parke County, Indiana. To accomplish the improvement, Indiana sought to obtain from Thomas Collom approximately half an acre of his property abutting the east side of the highway and offered him $4,495 for it. When Collom refused to sell, the state filed a suit in an Indiana state court against Collom to obtain the property.

Collom denied that his half acre was necessary for the improvement that the state wanted to make to the highway. He asserted that the state did not need his land because the highway would curve west, away from his property, and no drainage ditch was necessary given the existing water flow in the area. The state argued that this was not an appropriate response because a determination of the need for a taking was the responsibility of the state, not the owner of the property that the state was trying to take. In whose favor should the court rule, and why? [*State of Indiana v. Collom,* 720 N.E.2d 737 (Ind.App. 1999)]

Case Problem with Sample Answer

21-8. Security Deposits. Jennifer Tribble leased an apartment from Spring Isle II, a limited partnership. The written lease agreement provided that if Tribble was forced to move because of a job transfer or because she accepted a new job, she could vacate on sixty days' notice and owe only an extra two months' rent plus no more than a $650 rerenting fee. The initial term was for one year, and the parties renewed the lease for a second one-year term. The security deposit was $900. State law allowed a landlord to withhold a security deposit for the nonpayment of rent but required timely notice stating valid reasons for the withholding or the tenant would be entitled to twice the amount of the deposit as damages. One month into the second term, Tribble notified Spring Isle in writing that she had accepted a new job and would move out within a week. She paid the extra rent required by the lease, but not the rerental fee, and vacated the apartment. Spring Isle wrote her a letter stating that it was keeping the entire security deposit until the apartment was rerented or the lease term ended, whichever came first. Spring Isle later filed a suit in a Wisconsin state court against Tribble, claiming that she owed, among other things, additional rent to cover the period until the apartment's rerental and the costs of rerenting. Tribble responded that withholding the security deposit was improper and she was entitled to "any penalties." Does Tribble owe Spring Isle anything? Does Spring Isle owe Tribble anything? Explain. [*Spring Isle II v. Tribble,* 610 N.W.2d 229 (Wis.App. 2000)]

To view a sample answer for this case problem, go to this book's Web site at http://leet.westbuslaw.com and click on "Interactive Study Center."

21-9. Easements. In 1988, Gary Dubin began leasing property from Robert Chesebrough at 26011 Bouquet Canyon Road in Los Angeles County, California, to operate Alert Auto, a vehicle repair shop. There was a narrow driveway on one side of the premises, but blocking the widest means of access were crash posts on the adjacent unoccupied property, which Chesebrough also owned. The lease did not mention a means of access, but Dubin's primary customers were to be

large trucks and motor homes, which could reach Alert Auto only over the wide driveway. Chesebrough had the posts removed. After his death, the Robert Newhall Chesebrough Trust became the owner of both properties, which Wespac Management Group, Inc., managed. In 2000, Wespac reinstalled the posts. Dubin filed a suit in a California state court against the Trust and others, alleging that he had an easement, which the posts were obstructing, and sought damages and an injunction. The defendants denied the existence of any easement. Does Dubin have an easement? If so, how was it created? Explain. [*Dubin v. Robert Newhall Chesebrough Trust,* 96 Cal.App.4th 465, 116 Cal.Rptr.2d 872 (2 Dist. 2002)]

21-10. Commercial Lease Terms. Metropolitan Life Insurance Co. leased space in its Trail Plaza Shopping Center in Florida to Winn-Dixie Stores, Inc., to operate a supermarket. Under the lease, the landlord agreed not to permit "any [other] property located within the shopping center to be used for or occupied by any business dealing in or which shall keep in stock or sell for off-premises consumption any staple or fancy groceries" in more than "500 square feet of sales area." In 1999, Metropolitan leased 22,000 square feet of space in Trail Plaza to 99 Cent Stuff-Trail Plaza, LLC, under a lease that prohibited it from selling "groceries" in more than 500 square feet of "sales area." Shortly after 99 Cent Stuff opened, it began selling food and other products, including soap, matches, and paper napkins. Alleging that these sales violated the parties' leases, Winn-Dixie filed a suit in a Florida state court against 99 Cent Stuff and others. The defendants argued in part that the groceries provision covered only food and the 500-square-foot restriction included only shelf space, not store aisles. How should these lease terms be interpreted? Should the court grant an injunction in Winn-Dixie's favor? Explain. [*Winn-Dixie Stores, Inc. v. 99 Cent Stuff-Trail Plaza, LLC,* 811 So.2d 719 (Fla.App. 3 Dist. 2002)]

A Question of Ethics & Social Responsibility

21-11. John and Terry Hoffius own property in Jackson, Michigan, which they rent. Kristal McCready and Keith Kerr responded to the Hoffiuses' ad about the property. The Hoffiuses refused to rent to McCready and Kerr, however, when they learned that the two were single and intended to live together. John Hoffius told all prospective tenants that unmarried cohabitation violated his religious beliefs. McCready and others filed a suit in a Michigan state court against the Hoffiuses. They alleged in part that the Hoffiuses' actions violated the plaintiffs' civil rights under a state law that prohibits discrimination on the basis of "marital status." The Hoffiuses responded in part that forcing them to rent to unmarried couples in violation of the Hoffiuses' religious beliefs would be unconstitutional. [*McCready v. Hoffius,* 586 N.W.2d 723 (Mich. 1998)]

1. Was it the plaintiffs' "marital status" or their conduct to which the defendants objected? Did the defendants violate the plaintiffs' civil rights? Explain.

2. Should a court, in the interest of preventing discrimination in housing, compel a landlord to violate his or her conscience? In other words, whose rights should prevail in this case? Why?

3. Is there an objective rule that determines when civil rights or religious freedom, or any two similarly important principles, should prevail? If so, what is it? If not, should there be?

Case Briefing Assignment

21–12. Examine Case A.5 [*City of Monterey v. Del Monte Dunes at Monterey*, 526 U.S. 687, 119 S.Ct. 1624, 143 L.Ed.2d 882 (1999)] in Appendix A. This case has been excerpted there in great detail. Review and then brief the case, making sure that your brief answers the following questions.

1. What actions of the city of Monterey led to this lawsuit?

2. Why did Del Monte Dunes claim that the city of Monterey had taken its property?

3. What did the trial court decide in this case?

4. What primary issue is in dispute before the Supreme Court?

5. What was the question that the jury was asked to determine and that the Court considered to be "essentially fact-bound"?

Critical-Thinking Legal Question

21–13. Garza Construction Co. erects a silo (a grain storage facility) on Reeve's ranch. Garza also lends Reeve the money to pay for the silo under an agreement providing that the silo is not to become part of the land until Reeve completes the loan payments. Before the silo is paid for, Metropolitan State Bank, the mortgage holder on Reeve's land, forecloses on the property. Metropolitan contends that the silo is a fixture to the realty and that the bank is therefore entitled to the proceeds from its sale. Garza argues that the silo is personal property and that the proceeds should therefore go to Garza. Is the silo a fixture? Why or why not?

INTERACTING WITH THE INTERNET

For updated links to resources available on the Web, as well as a variety of other materials, visit this text's Web site at

http://leet.westbuslaw.com

Information on the buying and financing of homes, as well as the full text of the Real Estate Settlement Procedures Act, is online at

http://www.hud.gov/buying

For links to numerous sources relating to real property, go to

http://www.findlaw.com/01topics/index.html

and click on "Property Law & Real Estate."

For information on condemnation procedures and rules under one state's (California's) law, go to

http://www.eminentdomainlaw.net/propertyguide.html

For answers to frequently asked questions on Veterans Administration home loans, go to

http://www.homeloans.va.gov

ONLINE LEGAL RESEARCH EXERCISES

Go to **http://leet.westbuslaw.com**, the Web site that accompanies this text. Select "Interactive Study Center," and then click on "Chapter 21." There you will find the following Internet research exercises that you can perform to learn more about topics covered in this chapter.

Activity 21–1: ECONOMIC PERSPECTIVE—**Eminent Domain**
Activity 21–2: MANAGEMENT PERSPECTIVE—**Fair Housing**

BEFORE THE TEST

Go to **http://leet.westbuslaw.com**, the Web site that accompanies this text. Select "Interactive Quizzes." You will find at least twenty interactive questions relating to this chapter.

Westlaw® Campus

If your textbook provided for a subscription to Westlaw® Campus, or if you have otherwise purchased access to the Westlaw Campus database, you can access any of the cases presented or cited in this chapter by using your Westlaw Campus account.

CHAPTER 22

Promoting Competition

CONTENTS

CHAPTER OBJECTIVES

After reading this chapter, you should be able to answer the following questions:

1. What is a monopoly? What is market power? How do these concepts relate to each other?

2. What type of activity is prohibited by Section 1 of the Sherman Act? What type of activity is prohibited by Section 2 of the Sherman Act?

3. What are the four major provisions of the Clayton Act, and what types of activities do these provisions prohibit?

4. What agencies of the federal government enforce the federal antitrust laws?

5. What are four activities that are exempt from the antitrust laws?

Today's antitrust laws are the direct descendants of common law actions intended to limit *restraints on trade*—agreements between firms that have the effect of reducing competition in the marketplace. Such actions date to the fifteenth century in England. In America, concern over monopolistic practices arose following the Civil War with the growth of large corporate enterprises and their attempts to reduce or eliminate competition. In an attempt to thwart competition, they legally tied themselves together in business trusts. *Business trusts* are forms of business organization in which trustees hold title to property for the benefit of others. The most powerful of these trusts, the Standard Oil trust, is examined in this chapter's *Landmark in the Legal Environment* feature on page 694.

"Free competition is worth more to society than it costs."
Oliver Wendell Holmes, Jr., 1841–1935
(Associate justice of the United States Supreme Court, 1902–1932)

Many states attempted to control such monopolistic behavior by enacting statutes outlawing the use of trusts. That is why all of the laws that regulate economic competition today are referred to as **antitrust laws.** At the national level, Congress passed the Sherman Antitrust Act in 1890. In 1914, Congress passed the Clayton Act and the Federal Trade Commission Act to further curb anticompetitive and unfair business practices. Since their passage, the 1914 acts have been amended by Congress to broaden and strengthen their coverage.

This chapter examines these major antitrust statutes, focusing particularly on the Sherman Act and the Clayton Act, as amended, and the types of activities prohibited by those acts. Remember in reading this chapter that the basis of antitrust legislation is the desire to foster competition. Antitrust legislation was initially created—and continues to be enforced—because of our belief that competition leads to lower prices, generates more product information, and results in a better distribution of wealth between consumers and producers. As Oliver Wendell Holmes, Jr., stated in the chapter-opening quotation on the previous page, free competition is worth more to our society than the cost we pay for it. The cost is, of course, government regulation of business behavior.

ANTITRUST LAWS
Laws designed to protect trade and commerce from restraints, monopolies, price fixing, and price discrimination.

THE SHERMAN ANTITRUST ACT

In 1890, Congress passed "An Act to Protect Trade and Commerce against Unlawful Restraints and Monopolies"—commonly known as the Sherman Antitrust Act or, more simply, the Sherman Act. The Sherman Act was and remains one of the government's most powerful weapons in the struggle to maintain a competitive economy. Because of the act's significance, we examine its passage in this chapter's *Landmark in the Legal Environment* feature on page 694.

Major Provisions of the Sherman Act

Sections 1 and 2 contain the main provisions of the Sherman Act:

1: Every contract, combination in the form of trust or otherwise, or conspiracy, in restraint of trade or commerce among the several States, or with foreign nations, is hereby declared to be illegal [and is a felony punishable by fine and/or imprisonment].

2: Every person who shall monopolize, or attempt to monopolize, or combine or conspire with any other person or persons, to monopolize any part of the trade or commerce among the several States, or with foreign nations, shall be deemed guilty of a felony [that is similarly punishable].

These two sections of the Sherman Act are quite different. Violation of Section 1 requires two or more persons, as a person cannot contract or combine or conspire alone. Thus, the essence of the illegal activity is *the act of joining together.* Section 2 applies both to several people who have joined together and to individual persons because it specifies "[e]very person who . . . ." Thus, unilateral conduct can result in a violation of Section 2.

The cases brought to court under Section 1 of the Sherman Act differ from those brought under Section 2. Section 1 cases are often concerned with finding an agreement (written or oral) that leads to a restraint of trade. Section 2 cases deal with the structure of a monopoly that already exists in the marketplace. The term **monopoly** is generally used to describe a market in which

"As a charter of freedom, the [Sherman] Act has a generality and adaptability comparable to that found to be desirable in constitutional provisions."
CHARLES EVANS HUGHES, 1862–1948
(Chief justice of the United States Supreme Court, 1930–1941)

MONOPOLY
A term generally used to describe a market in which there is a single seller or a limited number of sellers.

LANDMARK IN THE LEGAL ENVIRONMENT

The Sherman Antitrust Act of 1890

The author of the Sherman Antitrust Act of 1890, Senator John Sherman, was the brother of the famed Civil War general William Tecumseh Sherman and a recognized financial authority. Sherman had been concerned for years with the diminishing competition within American industry and the emergence of monopolies, such as the Standard Oil trust.

THE STANDARD OIL TRUST By 1890, the Standard Oil trust had become the foremost petroleum refining and marketing combination in the United States. Streamlined, integrated, and centrally and efficiently controlled, its monopoly over the industry could not be disputed. Standard Oil controlled 90 percent of the U.S. market for refined petroleum products, and small manufacturers were incapable of competing with such an industrial leviathan.

The increasing consolidation occurring in American industry, and particularly the Standard Oil trust, did not escape the attention of the American public. In March 1881, Henry Demarest Lloyd, a young journalist from Chicago, published an article in the *Atlantic Monthly* entitled "The Story of a Great Monopoly," which discussed the success of the Standard Oil Company. The article brought to the public's attention for the first time the fact that the petroleum industry in America was dominated by one firm—Standard Oil. Lloyd's article, which was so popular that the issue was reprinted six times, marked the beginning of the American public's growing awareness of, and concern over, the growth of monopolies.

THE PASSAGE OF THE SHERMAN ANTITRUST ACT The common law regarding trade regulation was not always consistent. Certainly, it was not very familiar to the legislators of the Fifty-first Congress of the United States. The public concern over large business integrations and trusts was familiar, however. In 1888, in 1889, and again in 1890, Senator Sherman introduced in Congress bills designed to destroy the large combinations of capital that were, he felt, creating a lack of balance within the nation's economy. Sherman told Congress that the Sherman Act "does not announce a new principle of law, but applies old and well-recognized principles of the common law."[a] In 1890, the bill was enacted into law.

In the pages that follow, we look closely at the major provisions of this act. Generally, the act prohibits business combinations and conspiracies that restrain trade and commerce, as well as certain monopolistic practices.

Application to Today's World

The Sherman Antitrust Act remains very relevant to today's world. The widely publicized monopolization case brought by the U.S. Department of Justice and a number of state attorneys general against Microsoft Corporation in 2001 is just one example of the relevance of the Sherman Act to modern business developments and practices. (This case is presented later in this chapter as Case 22.4.)

a. 21 Congressional Record 2456 (1890).

MONOPOLY POWER
The ability of a monopoly to dictate what takes place in a given market.

MARKET POWER
The power of a firm to control the market price of its product. A monopoly has the greatest degree of market power.

there is a single seller or a limited number of sellers. Whereas Section 1 focuses on agreements that are restrictive—that is, agreements that have a wrongful purpose—Section 2 looks at the so-called misuse of **monopoly power** in the marketplace. Monopoly power exists when a firm has an extremely great amount of **market power**—the power to affect the market price of its product. We return to a discussion of these two sections of the Sherman Act after we look at the act's jurisdictional requirements.

Jurisdictional Requirements

Because Congress can regulate only interstate commerce, the Sherman Act applies solely to restraints that affect interstate commerce. As discussed in Chapter 5, courts have construed the meaning of *interstate commerce* broadly, bringing even local activities within the regulatory power of the national government. In regard to the Sherman Act, courts have generally held that any activity that substantially affects interstate commerce is covered by the act. The Sherman Act also extends to nationals abroad who are engaged in activities that have an effect on U.S. foreign commerce. (The extraterritorial application of U.S. antitrust laws will be discussed in this chapter's *International Perspective* feature on page 711, as well as in Chapter 24.)

SECTION 1 OF THE SHERMAN ACT

The underlying assumption of Section 1 of the Sherman Act is that society's welfare is harmed if rival firms are permitted to join in an agreement that consolidates their market power or otherwise restrains competition. The types of trade restraints that Section 1 of the Sherman Act prohibits generally fall into two broad categories: *horizontal restraints* and *vertical restraints,* both of which are discussed shortly.

Per Se Violations versus the Rule of Reason

Some restraints are so blatantly and substantially anticompetitive that they are deemed *per se* violations—illegal *per se* (on their face, or inherently)—under Section 1. Other agreements, however, even though they result in enhanced market power, do not *unreasonably* restrain trade. Under what is called the **rule of reason,** anticompetitive agreements that allegedly violate Section 1 of the Sherman Act are analyzed with the view that they may, in fact, constitute reasonable restraints on trade.

The need for a rule-of-reason analysis of some agreements in restraint of trade is obvious—if the rule of reason had not been developed, virtually any business agreement could conceivably be held to violate the Sherman Act. Justice Louis Brandeis effectively phrased this sentiment in *Chicago Board of Trade v. United States,* a case decided in 1918:

> Every agreement concerning trade, every regulation of trade, restrains. To bind, to restrain, is of their very essence. The true test of legality is whether the restraint imposed is such as merely regulates and perhaps thereby promotes competition or whether it is such as may suppress or even destroy competition.[1]

When analyzing an alleged Section 1 violation under the rule of reason, a court will consider several factors. These factors include the purpose of the agreement, the parties' power to implement the agreement to achieve that purpose, and the effect or potential effect of the agreement on competition. Yet another factor that a court might consider is whether the parties could have relied on less restrictive means to achieve their purpose.

PER SE VIOLATION
A type of anticompetitive agreement—such as a horizontal price-fixing agreement—that is considered to be so injurious to the public that there is no need to determine whether it actually injures market competition; rather, it is in itself (*per se*) a violation of the Sherman Act.

RULE OF REASON
A test by which a court balances the positive effects (such as economic efficiency) of an agreement against its potentially anticompetitive effects. In antitrust litigation, many practices are analyzed under the rule of reason.

---

1. 246 U.S. 231, 38 S.Ct. 242, 62 L.Ed. 683 (1918).

Section 1—Horizontal Restraints

HORIZONTAL RESTRAINT
Any agreement that in some way restrains competition between rival firms competing in the same market.

The term **horizontal restraint** is encountered frequently in antitrust law. A horizontal restraint is any agreement that in some way restrains competition between rival firms competing in the same market. In the following subsections, we look at several types of horizontal restraints.

Price Fixing Any agreement between or among competitors to fix prices constitutes a *per se* violation of Section 1. Perhaps the definitive case regarding **price-fixing agreements** remains the 1940 case of *United States v. Socony-Vacuum Oil Co.*[2] In that case, a group of independent oil producers in Texas and Louisiana were caught between falling demand due to the Great Depression of the 1930s and increasing supply from newly discovered oil fields in the region. In response to these conditions, a group of major refining companies agreed to buy "distress" gasoline (excess supplies) from the independents so as to dispose of it in an "orderly manner." Although there was no explicit agreement as to price, it was clear that the purpose of the agreement was to limit the supply of gasoline on the market and thereby raise prices.

PRICE-FIXING AGREEMENT
An agreement between or among competitors to fix the prices of products or services at a certain level.

The United States Supreme Court recognized the dangerous effects that such an agreement could have on open and free competition. The Court held that the asserted reasonableness of a price-fixing agreement is never a defense; any agreement that restricts output or artificially fixes price is a *per se* violation of Section 1. The rationale of the *per se* rule was best stated in what is now the most famous portion of the Court's opinion—footnote 59. In that footnote, Justice William O. Douglas compared a freely functioning price system to a body's central nervous system, condemning price-fixing agreements as threats to "the central nervous system of the economy."

The joint use of market data by competitors can make a market more efficient and benefit consumers. Fixing the price that a participant pays for that data, however, may make the market less competitive and innovative. Whether this is a violation of antitrust law was the question in the following case.

---

2. 310 U.S. 150, 60 S.Ct. 811, 84 L.Ed.2d 1129 (1940).

CASE 22.1   Freeman v. San Diego Association of Realtors

United States Court of Appeals,
Ninth Circuit, 2003.
322 F.3d 1133.

HISTORICAL AND ECONOMIC

SETTING *Real estate professionals (agents) share information about properties on the market with the help of a computerized database known as a multiple listing service (MLS). Agents who subscribe to an MLS can peruse the listings of other subscribers and post their own. Operating an MLS involves more than maintaining a database, however. Someone must enroll new subscribers, bill and collect payments, ensure that postings comply with guidelines, and provide staff to answer subscribers' questions. These support services are part of the cost of delivering an MLS.*

BACKGROUND AND FACTS At one time, twelve MLSs served San Diego County, California. Different real estate trade associations, including the San Diego Association of Realtors (SDAR), operated the MLSs to cover various regions of the county. Individual associations' costs varied widely, depending on the support services and the number of subscribers, but each association set its prices independently. In 1992, the associations formed Sandicor, a new corporation, to maintain a single MLS encompassing the entire county. Each association agreed to provide support services for a fixed price and to charge uniform subscription fees. For the associations whose costs exceeded the agreed-on price, Sandicor returned a portion of the fees to cover the difference. Arleen Freeman, and other agents who

CASE 22.1—Continued

subscribed to Sandicor's MLS, filed a suit in a federal district court against SDAR and others, claiming that by fixing support prices, the defendants violated Section 1 of the Sherman Act. The court issued a summary judgment in the defendants' favor. Both sides appealed to the U.S. Court of Appeals for the Ninth Circuit.

IN THE WORDS OF THE COURT . . .

KOZINSKI, Circuit Judge:

Competition is the mainspring of a capitalist economy. Sometimes, however, cooperation can make markets more efficient; setting industry standards and pooling market data are two examples of arrangements that often benefit consumers. Antitrust laws acknowledge these benefits, but still treat the arrangements with skepticism, for *seemingly benign agreements may conceal highly anticompetitive schemes.* * * * [Emphasis added.]

* * * *

* * * No antitrust violation is more abominated than the agreement to fix prices. With few exceptions, price-fixing agreements are unlawful *per se* under the Sherman Act and * * * no showing of so-called competitive abuses or evils which those agreements were designed to eliminate or alleviate may be interposed as a defense. The dispositive [decisive] question generally is not whether any price fixing was justified, but simply whether it occurred.

* * * Prior to 1992, the associations made independent decisions about how to price their support services * * * . When they decided to form a countywide database, they * * * set a fixed, uniform fee that they would receive for providing support services. * * * They admit that they fixed the fee in order to ensure that financially weaker associations would make more money than under a competitive regime * * * .

* * * *

[The defendants] claim that price fixing was justified to convince the smaller associations [with the higher costs] to join the countywide MLS. * * *

* * * *

* * * Firms cannot fix prices as a mere *quid pro quo* [something in return for something else] for providing consumers with better products. Antitrust law presumes that competitive markets offer sufficient incentives and resources for innovation, and that *cartel pricing leads not to a dedication of newfound wealth to the public good but to complacency and stagnation.* [Emphasis added.]

* * * *

Stripped to its essentials, defendants' argument is that some of the firms they wanted to include in the joint venture were so inefficient that they could survive only under cartel pricing. Defendants' concern for the weakest among them has a quaint * * * charm to it, but we find it hard to square with the competitive philosophy of our antitrust laws. Inefficiency is precisely what the market aims to weed out. The Sherman Act, to put it bluntly, contemplates some roadkill on the turnpike to Efficiencyville.

DECISION AND REMEDY The U.S. Court of Appeals for the Ninth Circuit concluded that the defendants violated Section 1 of the Sherman Act by fixing support fees. The court reversed the lower court's judgment on this issue and remanded the case for the entry of a summary judgment in favor of the plaintiffs.

FOR CRITICAL ANALYSIS—Economic Consideration *Could the defendants have maintained a comprehensive MLS without fixing prices?*

GROUP BOYCOTT
The refusal to deal with a particular person or firm by a group of competitors.

Group Boycotts A **group boycott** is an agreement by two or more competitors to boycott, or refuse to deal with, a particular person or firm. Such group boycotts have been held to constitute *per se* violations of Section 1 of the Sherman Act. Section 1 has been violated if it can be demonstrated that the boycott or joint refusal to deal was undertaken with the intention of eliminating competition or preventing entry into a given market. Some boycotts, such as group boycotts against a supplier for political reasons, may be protected under the First Amendment right to freedom of expression, however.

The issue in the following case was whether a *single* buyer's decision to buy from one supplier rather than another should be considered a group boycott.

CASE 22.2   NYNEX Corp. v. Discon, Inc.

Supreme Court of the United States, 1998.
525 U.S. 128,
119 S.Ct. 493,
142 L.Ed.2d 510.
**http://supct.law.cornell.edu/
supct/index.html**[a]

BACKGROUND AND FACTS NYNEX Corporation owns New York Telephone Company (NYTel), which provides telephone service to most of New York. NYTel has a monopoly on phone service in the areas that it serves. NYNEX also owns NYNEX Material Enterprises. Material Enterprises obtains removal services for NYTel. These services consist of salvaging and disposing of obsolete equipment. Material Enterprises, which had been using the services of Discon, Inc., switched its business to AT&T Technologies, Inc., which supplied the removal services at inflated prices. Material Enterprises charged the inflated prices to NYTel, which passed the

charges on to its customers. Material Enterprises later received secret rebates of the excessive charges from AT&T. (Essentially, Material Enterprises and NYNEX used NYTel's monopoly to obtain increased revenues.) When the scheme was uncovered, NYTel agreed to refund over $35 million to its customers. Discon, Inc., filed a suit in a federal district court against NYNEX and others, alleging, among other things, that as part of their scheme, the defendants had conspired to eliminate Discon from the market in favor of AT&T, because Discon had refused to participate in the rebate conspiracy. Discon contended that this was an illegal group boycott. The defendants filed a motion to dismiss, which the court granted. Discon appealed to the U.S. Court of Appeals for the Second Circuit, which reversed the lower court's judgment and held that the treatment of Discon could be an illegal group boycott. The defendants appealed to the United States Supreme Court.

**IN THE WORDS
OF THE COURT . . .**

Justice *BREYER* delivered the opinion of the Court.

*   *   *   *

*   *   * [T]he specific legal question before us is whether an antitrust court considering an agreement by a buyer to purchase goods or services from one supplier rather than another should (after examining the buyer's reasons or justifications) apply the *per se* rule if it finds no legitimate business reason for that purchasing decision. We conclude no boycott-related *per se* rule applies and that *the plaintiff here must allege and prove harm, not just to a single competitor, but to the competitive process, i.e., to competition itself.* [Emphasis added.]

Our conclusion rests in large part upon precedent, for precedent limits the *per se* rule in the boycott context to cases involving horizontal agreements among direct competitors. *   *   *

---

a. In the "Search" box, enter the name of the case and then select "all current and historic decisions" and click on "submit." On the page that opens, scroll to the case name and click on it. When that page opens, choose the format in which you want to view the opinion and click on its link to access it. This database is part of a site maintained by the Legal Information Institute at Cornell Law School.

CASE 22.2—Continued

* * * [In a previous case] this Court * * * held that a "vertical restraint is not illegal *per se* unless it includes some agreement on price or price levels." This precedent makes the *per se* rule inapplicable, for the case before us concerns only a vertical agreement and a vertical restraint, a restraint that takes the form of depriving a supplier of a potential customer.

Nor have we found any special feature of this case that could distinguish it from the precedent * * * . We concede Discon's claim that the petitioners' behavior hurt consumers by raising telephone service rates. But that consumer injury naturally flowed not so much from a less competitive market for removal services, as from the exercise of market power that is lawfully in the hands of a monopolist, namely, New York Telephone, combined with a deception worked upon the regulatory agency that prevented the agency from controlling New York Telephone's exercise of its monopoly power.

To apply the *per se* rule here—where the buyer's decision, though not made for competitive reasons, composes part of a regulatory fraud—would transform cases involving business behavior that is improper for various reasons, say, cases involving nepotism or personal pique, into treble-damages antitrust cases. And that *per se* rule would discourage firms from changing suppliers—even where the competitive process itself does not suffer harm.

The freedom to switch suppliers lies close to the heart of the competitive process that the antitrust laws seek to encourage. At the same time, other laws, for example, "unfair competition" laws, business tort laws, or regulatory laws, provide remedies for various competitive practices thought to be offensive to proper standards of business morality. Thus, this Court has refused to apply *per se* reasoning in cases involving that kind of activity. [Emphasis added.]

DECISION AND REMEDY The Supreme Court vacated the decision of the U.S. Court of Appeals for the Second Circuit and remanded the case for further proceedings. A choice by a single buyer to buy from one supplier rather than another is not subject to the *per se* group boycott rule, even if there is no legitimate business reason for that buyer's purchasing decision.

FOR CRITICAL ANALYSIS—Social Consideration *Could Discon have succeeded in a suit against NYNEX and the others under any other legal theory? Explain.*

Horizontal Market Division It is a *per se* violation of Section 1 of the Sherman Act for competitors to divide up territories or customers. ● EXAMPLE 1 Manufacturers A, B, and C compete against each other in the states of Kansas, Nebraska, and Iowa. By agreement, A sells products only in Kansas; B sells only in Nebraska; and C sells only in Iowa. This concerted action not only reduces marketing costs but also allows all three (assuming there is no other competition) to raise the price of the goods sold in their respective states. The same violation would take place if A, B, and C simply agreed that A would sell only to institutional purchasers (such as school districts, universities, state agencies and departments, and municipalities) in all three states, B only to wholesalers, and C only to retailers.●

Trade Associations Businesses in the same general industry or profession frequently organize trade associations to pursue common interests. A trade association's activities may include facilitating exchanges of information, representing members' business interests before governmental bodies, conducting advertising campaigns, and setting regulatory standards to govern the industry or profession.

Generally, the rule of reason is applied to many of these horizontal actions. If a court finds that a trade association practice or agreement that restrains trade is sufficiently beneficial both to the association and to the public, it may deem the restraint reasonable. Other trade association agreements may have such substantially anticompetitive effects that the court will consider them to be in violation of Section 1 of the Sherman Act. ● **EXAMPLE 2** In *National Society of Professional Engineers v. United States,*[3] it was held that the society's code of ethics—which prohibited members from discussing prices with a potential customer until after the customer had chosen an engineer—was a Section 1 violation. The United States Supreme Court found that this ban on competitive bidding was "nothing less than a frontal assault on the basic policy of the Sherman Act." ●

Joint Ventures Joint ventures undertaken by competitors are also subject to antitrust laws. A *joint venture* is an undertaking by two or more individuals or firms for a specific purpose. If a joint venture does not involve price fixing or market divisions, the agreement will be analyzed under the rule of reason. Whether the venture will then be upheld under Section 1 depends on an overall assessment of the purposes of the venture, a strict analysis of the potential benefits relative to the likely harms, and—in some cases—an assessment of whether there are less restrictive alternatives for achieving the same goals.[4]

Section 1—Vertical Restraints

A **vertical restraint** of trade results from an agreement between firms at different levels in the manufacturing and distribution process. In contrast to horizontal relationships, which occur at the same level of operation, vertical relationships encompass the entire chain of production: the purchase of inventory, basic manufacturing, distribution to wholesalers, and eventual sale of a product at the retail level. For some products, these distinct phases may be carried out by different firms. If a single firm carries out two or more of the phases involved in bringing a product to the final consumer, the firm is considered to be a **vertically integrated firm.**

Even though firms operating at different functional levels are not in direct competition with one another, they are in competition with other firms. Thus, agreements between firms standing in a vertical relationship do significantly affect competition.

Territorial or Customer Restrictions In arranging for the distribution of its product, a manufacturing firm often wishes to insulate dealers from direct competition with other dealers selling the product. To this end, it may institute territorial restrictions, or it may attempt to prohibit wholesalers or retailers from reselling the product to certain classes of buyers, such as competing retailers. There may be legitimate, procompetitive reasons for imposing such

3. 453 U.S. 679, 98 S.Ct. 1355, 55 L.Ed.2d 637 (1978).
4. See, for example, *United States v. Morgan,* 118 F.Supp. 621 (S.D.N.Y. 1953). This case is often cited as a classic example of how to judge joint ventures under the rule of reason.

territorial or customer restrictions. ● EXAMPLE 3 A computer manufacturer may wish to prevent a dealer from cutting costs and undercutting rivals by providing computers without promotion or customer service, while relying on nearby dealers to provide these services.●

Vertical territorial and customer restrictions are judged under a rule of reason. In *United States v. Arnold, Schwinn & Co.*,[5] a case decided in 1967, the Supreme Court held that vertical territorial and customer restrictions were *per se* violations of Section 1 of the Sherman Act. Ten years later, however, in *Continental T.V., Inc. v. GTE Sylvania, Inc.*,[6] the Court overturned the *Schwinn* decision and held that such vertical restrictions should be judged under the rule of reason. The *Continental* case marked a definite shift from rigid characterization of these kinds of vertical restraints to a more flexible, economic analysis of the restraints under the rule of reason.

Resale Price Maintenance Agreements An agreement between a manufacturer and a distributor or retailer in which the manufacturer specifies what the retail prices of its products must be is referred to as a **resale price maintenance agreement.** This type of agreement may violate Section 1 of the Sherman Act.

In a 1968 case, *Albrecht v. Herald Co.*,[7] the United States Supreme Court held that these vertical price-fixing agreements constituted *per se* violations of Section 1 of the Sherman Act. In the following case, which involved an agreement that set a maximum price for the resale of products supplied by a wholesaler to a dealer, the Supreme Court reevaluated its approach in the *Albrecht* case. At issue was whether such price-fixing arrangements should continue to be deemed *per se* violations of Section 1 of the Sherman Act or whether the rule of reason should be applied.

RESALE PRICE MAINTENANCE AGREEMENT
An agreement between a manufacturer and a retailer in which the manufacturer specifies what the retail price of its products must be.

---

5. 388 U.S. 365, 87 S.Ct. 1856, 18 L.Ed.2d 1249 (1967).
6. 433 U.S. 36, 97 S.Ct. 2549, 53 L.Ed.2d 568 (1977).
7. 390 U.S. 145, 88 S.Ct. 869, 19 L.Ed.2d 998 (1968).

A retail store displays a well-known designer's clothing. Is an agreement between the manufacturer and an independent retailer to sell the clothing at a certain minimum price considered a violation of the Sherman Act?

CASE 22.3   State Oil Co. v. Khan

Supreme Court of the United States, 1997.
522 U.S. 3,
118 S.Ct. 275,
139 L.Ed.2d 199.
http://www.findlaw.com/
casecode/supreme.html[a]

BACKGROUND AND FACTS Barkat Khan leased a gas station under a contract with State Oil Company, which also agreed to supply gas to Khan for resale. Under the contract, State Oil would set a suggested retail price and sell gas to Khan for 3.25 cents per gallon less than that price. Khan could sell the gas at a higher price, but he would then be required to pay State Oil the difference (which would equal the entire profit Khan realized from raising the price). Khan failed to pay some of the rent due under the lease, and State Oil terminated the contract. Khan filed a suit in a federal district court against State Oil, alleging, among other things, price fixing in violation of the Sherman Act. The trial court granted summary judgment for State Oil. Khan appealed. The U.S. Court of Appeals for the Seventh Circuit reversed this judgment, and State Oil appealed to the United States Supreme Court.

**IN THE WORDS
OF THE COURT . . .**

Justice *O'CONNOR* delivered the opinion of the Court.

* * * * *

* * * Our analysis is * * * guided by our general view that the primary purpose of the antitrust laws is to protect interbrand competition. * * * [C]ondemnation of practices resulting in lower prices to consumers is especially costly because cutting prices in order to increase business often is the very essence of competition.

* * * *[W]e find it difficult to maintain that vertically-imposed maximum prices could harm consumers or competition to the extent necessary to justify their per se invalidation.* * * * [Emphasis added.]

* * * * *

* * * [T]he *per se* rule * * * could in fact exacerbate [make worse] problems related to the unrestrained exercise of market power by monopolist-dealers. Indeed, both courts and antitrust scholars have noted that [the *per se*] rule may actually harm consumers and manufacturers. * * *

* * * * *

* * * [V]ertical maximum price fixing, like the majority of commercial arrangements subject to the antitrust laws, should be evaluated under the rule of reason. In our view, rule-of-reason analysis can effectively identify those situations in which vertical maximum price fixing amounts to anticompetitive conduct.

DECISION AND REMEDY The United States Supreme Court vacated the decision of the appellate court and remanded the case. The Supreme Court held that vertical price fixing is not a *per se* violation of the Sherman Act but should be evaluated under the rule of reason.

FOR CRITICAL ANALYSIS—Economic Consideration *Should all "commercial arrangements subject to the antitrust laws" be evaluated under the rule of reason?*

---

a. This page, which is included in a Web site maintained by FindLaw (now a part of West Group), contains links to opinions of the United States Supreme Court. In the "Party Name Search" box, type "Khan," and then click on "Search." When the results appear, click on the case name to access the opinion.

Refusals to Deal As discussed previously, joint refusals to deal (group boycotts) are subject to close scrutiny under Section 1 of the Sherman Act. A single manufacturer acting unilaterally, however, is generally free to deal, or not to deal, with whomever it wishes. In vertical arrangements, even though a manufacturer cannot set retail prices for its products, it can refuse to deal with retailers or dealers that cut prices to levels substantially below the manufacturer's suggested retail prices. In *United States v. Colgate & Co.*,[8] for example, the United States Supreme Court held that a manufacturer's advance announcement that it would not sell to price cutters was not a violation of the Sherman Act.

In some instances, however, a unilateral refusal to deal will violate antitrust laws. These instances involve offenses proscribed under Section 2 of the Sherman Act and occur only if (1) the firm refusing to deal has—or is likely to acquire—monopoly power and (2) the refusal is likely to have an anticompetitive effect on a particular market.

SECTION 2 OF THE SHERMAN ACT

Section 1 of the Sherman Act proscribes certain concerted, or joint, activities that restrain trade. In contrast, Section 2 condemns "every person who shall monopolize, or attempt to monopolize." Two distinct types of behavior are subject to sanction under Section 2: *monopolization* and *attempts to monopolize*. A tactic that may be involved in either offense is **predatory pricing**. Predatory pricing involves an attempt by one firm to drive its competitors from the market by selling its product at prices substantially *below* the normal costs of production; once the competitors are eliminated, the firm will attempt to recapture its losses and go on to earn higher profits by driving prices up far above their competitive levels.

PREDATORY PRICING
The pricing of a product below cost with the intent to drive competitors out of the market.

Monopolization

In *United States v. Grinnell Corp.*,[9] the United States Supreme Court defined the offense of **monopolization** as involving two elements: "(1) the possession of monopoly power in the relevant market and (2) the willful acquisition or maintenance of the power as distinguished from growth or development as a consequence of a superior product, business acumen, or historic accident." A violation of Section 2 requires that both these elements—monopoly power and an intent to monopolize—be established.

MONOPOLIZATION
The possession of monopoly power in the relevant market and the willful acquisition or maintenance of that power, as distinguished from growth or development as a consequence of a superior product, business acumen, or historic accident.

Monopoly Power The Sherman Act does not define *monopoly*. In economic parlance, monopoly refers to control by a single entity. It is well established in antitrust law, however, that a firm may be a monopolist even though it is not the sole seller in a market. Additionally, size alone does not determine whether a firm is a monopoly. For example, a "mom and pop" grocery located in an isolated desert town is a monopolist if it is the only grocery serving that particular market. Size in relation to the market is what matters because monopoly involves the power to affect prices and output.

---

8. 250 U.S. 300, 39 S.Ct. 465, 63 L.Ed. 992 (1919).
9. 384 U.S. 563, 86 S.Ct. 1698, 16 L.Ed.2d 778 (1966).

MARKET-SHARE TEST
The primary measure of monopoly power. A firm's market share is the percentage of a market that the firm controls.

Market Power. *Monopoly power,* as mentioned earlier in this chapter, exists when a firm has an extremely great amount of market power. If a firm has sufficient market power to control prices and exclude competition, that firm has monopoly power. As difficult as it is to define market power precisely, it is even more difficult to measure it. Courts often use the so-called **market-share test**[10]—a firm's percentage share of the "relevant market"—in determining the extent of the firm's market power. A firm may be considered to have monopoly power if its share of the relevant market is 70 percent or more. This is merely a rule of thumb, however; it is not a binding principle of law. In some cases, a smaller share may be held to constitute monopoly power.[11]

Relevant Market. The relevant market consists of two elements: (1) a relevant product market and (2) a relevant geographic market. What should the relevant product market include? No doubt, it must include all products that, although produced by different firms, have identical attributes, such as sugar. Products that are not identical, however, may sometimes be substituted for one another. Coffee may be substituted for tea, for example. In defining the relevant product market, the key issue is the degree of interchangeability between products. If one product is a sufficient substitute for another, the two products are considered to be part of the same product market.

The second component of the relevant market is the geographic boundaries of the market. For products that are sold nationwide, the geographic boundaries of the market encompass the entire United States. If a producer and its competitors sell in only a limited area (one in which customers have no access to other sources of the product), the geographic market is limited to that area. A national firm may thus compete in several distinct areas and have monopoly power in one area but not in another.

> "A rule of such a nature as to bring all trade or traffic into the hands of one company, or one person, and to exclude all others, is illegal."
>
> SIR EDWARD COKE, 1552–1634
> (English jurist and legal scholar)

The Intent Requirement Monopoly power, in and of itself, does not constitute the offense of monopolization under Section 2 of the Sherman Act. The offense also requires an *intent* to monopolize. A dominant market share may be the result of business acumen or the development of a superior product. It may simply be the result of historic accident. In these situations, the acquisition of monopoly power is not an antitrust violation. Indeed, it would be contrary to society's interest to condemn every firm that acquired a position of power because it was well managed, was efficient, and marketed a product desired by consumers.

If, however, a firm possesses market power as a result of carrying out some purposeful act to acquire or maintain that power through anticompetitive means, it is in violation of Section 2. In most monopolization cases, intent may be inferred from evidence that the firm had monopoly power and engaged in anticompetitive behavior.

The following case included an allegation of a violation of Section 2 of the Sherman Act.

KEEP IN MIND Section 2 of the Sherman Act essentially condemns the act of monopolizing, not the possession of monopoly power.

---

10. Other measures of market power have been devised, but the market-share test is the most widely used.

11. This standard was first articulated by Judge Learned Hand in *United States v. Aluminum Co. of America,* 148 F.2d 416 (2d Cir. 1945). A 90 percent share was held to be clear evidence of monopoly power. Anything less than 64 percent, said Judge Hand, made monopoly power doubtful, and anything less than 30 percent was clearly not monopoly power.

CASE 22.4 United States v. Microsoft Corp.

United States Court of Appeals,
District of Columbia Circuit, 2001.
253 F.3d 34.
http://www.cadc.uscourts.gov[a]

HISTORICAL AND TECHNOLOGICAL SETTING *In 1981, Microsoft Corporation released the first version of its Microsoft Disk Operating System (MS-DOS). When International Business Machines Corporation (IBM) selected MS-DOS for preinstallation on its first generation of personal computers (PCs), Microsoft's product became the dominant operating system for Intel-compatible PCs.*[b] *In 1985, Microsoft began shipping a software package called Windows. Although originally a user interface on top of MS-DOS, Windows took on more operating-system functionality over time. Throughout the 1990s, Microsoft's share of the market for Intel-compatible operating systems was more than 90 percent.*

BACKGROUND AND FACTS In 1994, Netscape Communications Corporation began marketing Navigator, the first popular graphical Internet browser. Navigator worked with Java, a technology developed by Sun Microsystems, Inc. Java technology enabled applications to run on a variety of platforms, which meant that users did not need Windows. Microsoft perceived a threat to its dominance of the operating-system market and developed a competing browser, Internet Explorer (Explorer). Microsoft then began to require computer makers who wanted to install Windows to also install Explorer and exclude Navigator. Meanwhile, Microsoft commingled browser code and other code in Windows so that deleting files containing Explorer would cripple the operating system. Microsoft offered to promote and pay Internet service providers (ISPs) to distribute Explorer and exclude Navigator. Microsoft also developed its own Java code and deceived many independent software sellers into believing that this code would help in designing cross-platform applications when, in fact, it would run only on Windows. The U.S. Department of Justice and a number of state attorneys general filed a suit in a federal district court against Microsoft, alleging, in part, monopolization in violation of Section 2 of the Sherman Act. The court ruled against Microsoft.[c] Microsoft appealed to the U.S. Court of Appeals for the District of Columbia Circuit.

IN THE WORDS OF THE COURT . . .

PER CURIAM:

* * * *

* * * Claiming that software competition is uniquely "dynamic," [Microsoft] suggests * * * that monopoly power in the software industry should be proven directly, that is, by examining a company's actual behavior to determine if it reveals the existence of monopoly power. * * *

* * * *

* * * Microsoft's pattern of exclusionary conduct could only be rational if the firm knew that it possessed monopoly power. It is to that conduct that we now turn.

* * * *

* * * [P]rovisions in Microsoft's agreements licensing Windows to [computer makers] * * * reduce usage share of Netscape's browser and, hence, protect Microsoft's operating system monopoly. * * *

* * * *

---

a. On this page, in the left column, click on "Opinions." In the section headed "Please select from the following menu to find opinions by date of issue," choose "June" from the "Month" menu, select "2001" from the "Year" menu, and click on "Go!" From the result, scroll to the name of the case and click on the docket number to access the opinion. The U.S. Court of Appeals for the District of Columbia Circuit maintains this Web site.

b. An *Intel-compatible PC* is designed to function with Intel Corporation's 80×86/Pentium families of microprocessors or with compatible microprocessors.

c. The district court ordered, among other things, a structural reorganization of Microsoft, including a separation of its operating-system and applications businesses. See *United States v. Microsoft,* 97 F.Supp.2d 59 (D.D.C. 2000).

(continued)

CASE 22.4—Continued

Therefore, Microsoft's efforts to gain market share in one market (browsers) served to meet the threat to Microsoft's monopoly in another market (operating systems) by keeping rival browsers from gaining the critical mass of users necessary to attract developer attention away from Windows as the platform for software development. * * *

* * * *

* * * [W]e conclude that [Microsoft's] commingling [of browser and non-browser code] has an anticompetitive effect; * * * the commingling deters [computer makers] from pre-installing rival browsers, thereby reducing the rivals' usage share and, hence, developers' interest in rivals' [Application Programming Interfaces (APIs)] as an alternative to the API set exposed by Microsoft's operating system.

* * * *

* * * By ensuring that the majority of all [ISP] subscribers are offered [Internet Explorer] either as the default browser or as the only browser, Microsoft's deals with the [ISPs] clearly have a significant effect in preserving its monopoly * * * .

* * * *

* * * Microsoft's exclusive deals with the [Independent Software Vendors] had a substantial effect in further foreclosing rival browsers from the market * * * .

DECISION AND REMEDY The U.S. Court of Appeals for the District of Columbia Circuit affirmed the part of the lower court's opinion holding that Microsoft did possess and maintain monopoly power in the market for Intel-compatible operating systems. The appellate court reversed other holdings of the lower court, however, and remanded the case for a reconsideration of the appropriate remedy.

FOR CRITICAL ANALYSIS—Technological Consideration *How might the passage of time between certain conduct and the outcome of litigation affect judicial rulings that apply to technological product markets?*

COMMENT *The appellate court also concluded that the trial court judge's remarks (to members of the press*

and others during the trial) "would give a reasonable, informed observer cause to question his impartiality in ordering the company split in two." The appellate court cited this bias as its reason for reversing the order to break up Microsoft and remanding the case to a different trial court judge to reconsider what penalty would be appropriate. Microsoft appealed to the United States Supreme Court, but the Court declined to hear the case. Essentially, the appellate court opened the door to a much lighter penalty for Microsoft. Since then, the Department of Justice and several of the state attorneys general who brought the suit agreed with Microsoft to settle the case. On November 1, 2002, a federal trial judge approved the settlement. Generally, the settlement gives consumers more choice and allows Microsoft's rivals more flexibility to offer competing software features on computers running Windows.

Attempts to Monopolize

ATTEMPTED MONOPOLIZATION
Any actions by a firm to eliminate competition and gain monopoly power.

Section 2 also prohibits **attempted monopolization** of a market. Any action challenged as an attempt to monopolize must have been specifically intended to exclude competitors and garner monopoly power. In addition, the attempt must have had a "dangerous" probability of success—only serious threats of monopolization are condemned as violations. The probability cannot be dangerous unless the alleged offender possesses some degree of market power.

ETHICAL ISSUE

Are we destined for more monopolies in the future?

Knowledge and information form the building blocks of the so-called new economy. Some observers believe that the nature of this new economy means that we will see an increasing number of monopolies similar to Microsoft. Consider that the basis for all antitrust law is that monopoly leads to restricted output and hence higher prices for consumers. That is how a monopolist maximizes profits relative to a competitive firm. In a knowledge-based sector, however, increasing output often leads to reduced prices (because the long-run average costs decrease when output is increased). This is exactly what Microsoft has done over the years—increased its output, which has led to lower prices for operating systems and applications, especially when corrected for inflation.

This may mean that antitrust authorities will have to have a greater tolerance for knowledge-based monopolies to allow them to benefit from economies of scale. After all, the ultimate beneficiary of such economies of scale is the consumer. In the early 1900s, economist Joseph Schumpeter argued in favor of allowing monopolies. According to his theory of "creative destruction," monopolies stimulate innovation and economic growth because firms that capture monopoly profits have a greater incentive to innovate. Those that do not survive—the firms that are "destroyed"—leave room for more efficient firms, ones that will survive.

THE CLAYTON ACT

In 1914, Congress attempted to strengthen federal antitrust laws by enacting the Clayton Act. The Clayton Act was aimed at specific anticompetitive and monopolistic practices that the Sherman Act did not cover. The substantive provisions of the act deal with four distinct forms of business behavior, which are declared illegal but not criminal. With regard to each of the four provisions, the act's prohibitions are qualified by the general condition that the behavior is illegal only if it substantially tends to lessen competition or tends to create monopoly power. The major offenses under the Clayton Act are set out in Sections 2, 3, 7, and 8 of the act.

> "The commerce of the world is conducted by the strong, and usually it operates against the weak."
>
> HENRY WARD BEECHER, 1813–1887
> (American abolitionist leader)

Section 2—Price Discrimination

Section 2 of the Clayton Act prohibits **price discrimination**, which occurs when a seller charges different prices to competitive buyers for identical goods. Because businesses frequently circumvented Section 2 of the act, Congress strengthened this section by amending it with the passage of the Robinson-Patman Act in 1936.

As amended, Section 2 prohibits price discrimination that cannot be justified by differences in production costs or transportation expenses or by cost differences due to other reasons. To violate Section 2, the seller must be engaged in interstate commerce, and the effect of the price discrimination must be to substantially lessen competition or create a competitive injury. Under Section 2, as amended, a seller is prohibited from reducing a price to one buyer

PRICE DISCRIMINATION
Setting prices in such a way that two competing buyers pay two different prices for identical products or services.

below the price charged to that buyer's competitor. Even offering goods to different customers at the same price but with different delivery arrangements may violate Section 2 in some circumstances.[12]

An exception is made if the seller can justify the price reduction by demonstrating that the lower price was charged temporarily and in good faith to meet another seller's equally low price to the buyer's competitor. To be predatory, a seller's pricing policies must also include a reasonable prospect that the seller will recoup its losses.[13]

Section 3—Exclusionary Practices

Under Section 3 of the Clayton Act, sellers or lessors cannot sell or lease goods "on the condition, agreement or understanding that the . . . purchaser or lessee thereof shall not use or deal in the goods . . . of a competitor or competitors of the seller." In effect, this section prohibits two types of vertical agreements involving exclusionary practices—exclusive-dealing contracts and tying arrangements.

EXCLUSIVE-DEALING CONTRACT
An agreement under which a seller forbids a buyer to purchase products from the seller's competitors.

Exclusive-Dealing Contracts A contract under which a seller forbids a buyer to purchase products from the seller's competitors is called an **exclusive-dealing contract.** A seller is prohibited from making an exclusive-dealing contract under Section 3 if the effect of the contract is "to substantially lessen competition or tend to create a monopoly."

● EXAMPLE 4 In *Standard Oil Co. of California v. United States*,[14] a leading case decided by the United States Supreme Court in 1949, the then-largest gasoline seller in the nation made exclusive-dealing contracts with independent stations in seven western states. The contracts involved 16 percent of all retail outlets, whose sales were approximately 7 percent of all retail sales in that market. The Court noted that the seven largest gasoline suppliers all used exclusive-dealing contracts with their independent retailers and together controlled 65 percent of the market. Looking at market conditions after the arrangements were instituted, the Court found that market shares were extremely stable and entry into the market was apparently restricted. Thus, the Court held that Section 3 of the Clayton Act had been violated because competition was "foreclosed in a substantial share" of the relevant market.●

TYING ARRANGEMENT
An agreement between a buyer and a seller under which the buyer of a specific product or service becomes obligated to purchase additional products or services from the seller.

Tying Arrangements When a seller conditions the sale of a product (the tying product) on the buyer's agreement to purchase another product (the tied product) produced or distributed by the same seller, a **tying arrangement,** or *tie-in sales agreement*, results. The legality of a tie-in agreement depends on many factors, particularly the purpose of the agreement and the agreement's likely effect on competition in the relevant markets (the market for the tying product and the market for the tied product).

● EXAMPLE 5 In 1936, the United States Supreme Court held that International Business Machines and Remington Rand had violated Section 3 of the Clayton

---

12. *Bell v. Fur Breeders Agricultural Cooperative,* 3 F.Supp.2d 1241 (D.Utah 1998).
13. See, for example, *Brooke Group, Ltd. v. Brown & Williamson Tobacco Corp.,* 509 U.S. 209, 113 S.Ct. 2578, 125 L.Ed.2d 168 (1993), in which the Supreme Court held that a seller's price-cutting policies could not be predatory "[g]iven the market's realities"—the size of the seller's market share, the expanding output by other sellers, and additional factors.
14. 337 U.S. 293, 69 S.Ct. 1051, 93 L.Ed. 1371 (1949).

Act by requiring the purchase of their own machine cards (the tied product) as a condition to the leasing of their tabulation machines (the tying product). Because only these two firms sold completely automated tabulation machines, the Court concluded that each possessed market power sufficient to "substantially lessen competition" through the tying arrangements.[15] ●

Section 3 of the Clayton Act has been held to apply only to commodities, not to services. Tying arrangements, however, can also be considered agreements that restrain trade in violation of Section 1 of the Sherman Act. Thus, cases involving tying arrangements of services have been brought under Section 1 of the Sherman Act. Traditionally, the courts have held tying arrangements challenged under the Sherman Act to be illegal *per se*. In recent years, however, courts have shown a willingness to look at factors that are important in a rule-of-reason analysis.

Section 7—Mergers

Under Section 7 of the Clayton Act, a person or business organization cannot hold stock and/or assets in another entity "where the effect . . . may be to substantially lessen competition." Section 7 is the statutory authority for preventing mergers or acquisitions that could result in monopoly power or a substantial lessening of competition in the marketplace. Section 7 applies to three specific types of mergers: horizontal mergers, vertical mergers, and conglomerate mergers. We discuss each type of merger in the following subsections.

A crucial consideration in most merger cases is the **market concentration** of a product or business. Determining market concentration involves allocating percentage market shares among the various companies in the relevant market. When a small number of companies share a large part of the market, the market is concentrated. For example, if the four largest grocery stores in Chicago accounted for 80 percent of all retail food sales, the market clearly would be concentrated in those four firms. Competition, however, is not necessarily diminished solely as a result of market concentration, and other factors will be considered in determining whether a merger will violate Section 7. One factor of particular importance in evaluating the effects of a merger is whether the merger will make it more difficult for potential competitors to enter the relevant market.

Horizontal Mergers Mergers between firms that compete with each other in the same market are called **horizontal mergers.** If a horizontal merger creates an entity with anything other than a small percentage market share, the merger will be presumed illegal. This is because the United States Supreme Court has held that Congress, in amending Section 7 of the Clayton Act in 1950, intended to prevent mergers that increase market concentration.[16] When analyzing the legality of a horizontal merger, the courts also consider three other factors: overall concentration of the relevant product market, the relevant market's history of tending toward concentration, and whether the apparent design of the merger is to establish market power or to restrict competition.

> "Combinations are no less unlawful because they have not as yet resulted in restraint."
> HUGO L. BLACK, 1886–1971
> (Associate justice of the United States Supreme Court, 1937–1971)

MARKET CONCENTRATION
The degree to which a small number of firms control a large percentage of a relevant market area.

HORIZONTAL MERGER
A merger between two firms that are competing in the same market.

---

15. *International Business Machines Corp. v. United States,* 298 U.S. 131, 56 S.Ct. 701, 80 L.Ed. 1085 (1936).
16. *Brown Shoe v. United States,* 370 U.S. 294, 82 S.Ct. 1502, 8 L.Ed.2d 510 (1962).

The Federal Trade Commission and the U.S. Department of Justice have established guidelines indicating which mergers will be challenged. Under the guidelines, the first factor to be considered is the degree of concentration in the relevant market. Other factors include the ease of entry into the relevant market, economic efficiency, the financial condition of the merging firms, the nature and price of the product or products involved, and so on. If a firm is a leading one—having a share of at least 35 percent and twice that of the next leading firm—any merger with a firm having as little as a 1 percent share will probably be challenged.

VERTICAL MERGER
The acquisition by a company at one level in a marketing chain of a company at a higher or lower level in the chain (such as its supplier or retailer).

Vertical Mergers A **vertical merger** occurs when a company at one stage of production acquires a company at a higher or lower stage of production in the same marketing chain. An example of a vertical merger occurs when a company merges with one of its suppliers or retailers. Courts in the past have focused almost exclusively on *foreclosure* in assessing vertical mergers. Foreclosure occurs when competitors of one of the merging firms lose opportunities to sell to or buy from the other firm.

• EXAMPLE 6 In *United States v. E. I. du Pont de Nemours & Co.,*[17] du Pont was challenged for acquiring a considerable amount of General Motors (GM) stock. In holding that the transaction was illegal, the United States Supreme Court noted that the stock acquisition would enable du Pont to prevent other sellers of fabrics and finishes from selling to GM, which then accounted for 50 percent of all auto fabric and finishes purchases.•

Today, whether a vertical merger will be deemed illegal generally depends on several factors, including market concentration, barriers to entry into the market, and the apparent intent of the merging parties. Mergers that do not prevent competitors of either merging firm from competing in a segment of the market will not be condemned as foreclosing competition and are legal.

CONGLOMERATE MERGER
A merger between unrelated firms that are neither competitors nor customers or suppliers of each other.

Conglomerate Mergers There are three general types of **conglomerate mergers:** market-extension, product-extension, and diversification mergers. A market-extension merger occurs when a firm seeks to sell its product in a new market by merging with a firm already established in that market. A product-extension merger occurs when a firm seeks to add a closely related product to its existing line by merging with a firm already producing that product. For example, a manufacturer might seek to extend its line of household products to include floor wax by acquiring a leading manufacturer of floor wax. Diversification occurs when a firm merges with another firm that offers a product or service wholly unrelated to the first firm's existing activities. An example of a diversification merger is an automobile manufacturer's acquisition of a motel chain.

Although in a conglomerate merger no firm is removed from the marketplace, conglomerate mergers can be challenged under Section 7 of the Clayton Act. In deciding whether the act has been violated, the courts usually evaluate (1) whether the merger will allow the acquiring firm to shift assets and revenue to the acquired firm to potentially drive out businesses that compete with the acquired firm and (2) whether the merger creates a barrier, keeping other firms from entering the relevant market.

---

17. 353 U.S. 586, 77 S.Ct. 872, 1 L.Ed.2d 1057 (1957).

The Extraterritorial Application of Antitrust Laws

As mentioned earlier in this chapter, the reach of U.S. antitrust laws extends beyond the territorial borders of the United States. The U.S. government (the Department of Justice or the Federal Trade Commission) and private parties can bring an action against a foreign party that has violated Section 1 of the Sherman Act. The Federal Trade Commission Act can also be applied to foreign trade. In addition, foreign mergers, if Section 7 of the Clayton Act applies, can be brought within the jurisdiction of U.S. courts. Before U.S. courts will exercise jurisdiction and apply antitrust laws to actions occurring in other countries, however, normally it must be shown that the alleged violation had a substantial effect on U.S. commerce. (See Chapter 24 for a further discussion of the extraterritorial application of U.S. antitrust laws.)

In the past, companies usually had to be concerned only with U.S. antitrust laws. Today, however, many countries have adopted antitrust laws. The European Union has antitrust provisions that are broadly analogous to Sections 1 and 2 of the Sherman Act, as well as laws governing mergers. Japanese antitrust laws prohibit unfair trade practices, monopolization, and restrictions that unreasonably restrain trade. Several nations in Southeast Asia, including Vietnam, Indonesia, and Malaysia, have either enacted statutes protecting competition or are considering them for adoption. Argentina, Peru, Brazil, Chile, and several other Latin American countries have adopted modern antitrust laws as well. Most of the antitrust laws apply extraterritorially, as U.S. antitrust laws do. This means that a U.S. company may be subject to another nation's antitrust laws if the company's conduct has a substantial effect on that nation's commerce.

FOR CRITICAL ANALYSIS

Do antitrust laws place too great a burden on commerce in the global marketplace?

Section 8—Interlocking Directorates

Section 8 of the Clayton Act deals with *interlocking directorates*—that is, the practice of having individuals serve as directors on the boards of two or more competing companies simultaneously. Specifically, no person can be a director in two or more competing corporations at the same time if either of the corporations has capital, surplus, or undivided profits amounting to more than $18,919,000 or competitive sales of $1,891,900 or more. The threshold amounts are adjusted each year by the Federal Trade Commission. (The amounts given here are those announced in 2003.)

THE FEDERAL TRADE COMMISSION ACT

The Federal Trade Commission Act was enacted in 1914, the same year the Clayton Act was written into law. Section 5 is the sole substantive provision of the act. It provides, in part, as follows: "Unfair methods of competition in or affecting commerce, and unfair or deceptive acts or practices in or affecting commerce are hereby declared illegal." Section 5 condemns all forms of anticompetitive behavior that are not covered under other federal antitrust laws. The act also created the Federal Trade Commission to implement the act's provisions.

CONTRAST Section 5 of the Federal Trade Commission Act is broader than the other antitrust laws. It covers virtually all anticompetitive behavior, including conduct that does not violate either the Sherman Act or the Clayton Act.

ENFORCEMENT OF ANTITRUST LAWS

DIVESTITURE
The act of selling one or more of a company's divisions, such as a subsidiary or plant; often mandated by the courts in merger or monopolization cases.

The federal agencies that enforce the federal antitrust laws are the U.S. Department of Justice (DOJ) and the Federal Trade Commission (FTC). The DOJ can prosecute violations of the Sherman Act as either criminal or civil violations. Violations of the Clayton Act are not crimes, and the DOJ can enforce that statute only through civil proceedings. The various remedies that the DOJ has asked the courts to impose include **divestiture** (making a company give up one or more of its operating functions) and dissolution. The DOJ might force a group of meat packers, for example, to divest itself of control or ownership of butcher shops.

The FTC also enforces the Clayton Act (but not the Sherman Act). In addition, it has sole authority to enforce violations of Section 5 of the Federal Trade Commission Act. FTC actions are effected through administrative orders, but if a firm violates an FTC order, the FTC can seek court sanctions for the violation.

Private Actions

A private party can sue for damages and attorneys' fees under Section 4 of the Clayton Act if the party is injured as a result of a violation of any of the federal antitrust laws, except Section 5 of the Federal Trade Commission Act. In some instances, private parties can also seek injunctive relief to prevent antitrust violations. The courts have determined that the ability to sue depends on the directness of the injury suffered by the would-be plaintiff. Thus, a person wishing to sue under the Sherman Act must prove (1) that the antitrust violation either caused or was a substantial factor in causing the injury that was suffered and (2) that the unlawful actions of the accused party affected business activities of the plaintiff that were protected by the antitrust laws.

Treble Damages

In recent years, more than 90 percent of all antitrust actions have been brought by private plaintiffs. One reason for this is that successful plaintiffs can recover *treble damages*—three times the damages that they have suffered as a result of the violation. Such recoveries by private plaintiffs for antitrust violations have been rationalized as encouraging people to act as "private attorneys general" who will vigorously pursue antitrust violators on their own initiative.

EXEMPTIONS FROM ANTITRUST LAWS

There are many legislative and constitutional limitations on antitrust enforcement. Most statutory and judicially created exemptions to the antitrust laws apply to the following areas or activities:

1. *Labor.* Section 6 of the Clayton Act generally permits labor unions to organize and bargain without violating antitrust laws. Section 20 of the Clayton Act specifies that strikes and other labor activities are not violations of any law of the United States. A union can lose its exemption, however, if it combines with a nonlabor group rather than acting simply in its own self-interest.

2. *Agricultural associations and fisheries.* Section 6 of the Clayton Act (along with the Capper-Volstead Act of 1922) exempts agricultural cooperatives from the antitrust laws. The Fisheries Cooperative Marketing Act of 1976 exempts from antitrust legislation individuals in the fishing industry who collectively catch, produce, and prepare for market their products. Both

exemptions allow members of such co-ops to combine and set prices for a particular product but do not allow them to engage in exclusionary practices or restraints of trade directed at competitors.

3. *Insurance.* The McCarran-Ferguson Act of 1945 exempts the insurance business from the antitrust laws whenever state regulation exists. This exemption does not cover boycotts, coercion, or intimidation on the part of insurance companies.

4. *Foreign trade.* Under the provisions of the 1918 Webb-Pomerene Act, American exporters can engage in cooperative activity to compete with similar foreign associations. This type of cooperative activity cannot, however, restrain trade within the United States or injure other American exporters. The Export Trading Company Act of 1982 broadened the Webb-Pomerene Act by permitting the Department of Justice to certify properly qualified export trading companies. Any activity within the scope described by the certificate is exempt from public prosecution under the antitrust laws.

5. *Professional baseball.* In 1922, the United States Supreme Court held that professional baseball was not within the reach of federal antitrust laws because it did not involve "interstate commerce."[18] Some of the effects of this decision, however, were modified by the Curt Flood Act of 1998.

6. *Oil marketing.* The 1935 Interstate Oil Compact allows states to determine quotas on oil that will be marketed in interstate commerce.

7. *Cooperative research and production.* Cooperative research among small-business firms is exempt under the Small Business Act of 1958, as amended. Research or production of a product, process, or service by joint ventures consisting of competitors is exempt under special federal legislation, including the National Cooperative Research Act of 1984 and the National Cooperative Production Amendments of 1993.

8. *Joint efforts by businesspersons to obtain legislative or executive action.* This exemption is often referred to as the *Noerr-Pennington* doctrine.[19] It allows, for example, DVD producers to jointly lobby Congress to change the copyright laws without being held liable for attempting to restrain trade. Though selfish rather than purely public-minded conduct is permitted, there is an exception: an action will not be protected if the action clearly is "objectively baseless in the sense that no reasonable [person] could reasonably expect success on the merits" and is an attempt to make anticompetitive use of government processes.[20]

9. *Other exemptions.* Other activities exempt from antitrust laws include activities approved by the president in furtherance of the defense of our nation (under the Defense Production Act of 1950, as amended); state actions, when the state policy is clearly articulated and the policy is actively supervised by the state;[21] and activities of regulated industries (such as the communication and banking industries) when federal commissions, boards, or agencies (such as the Federal Communications Commission and the Federal Maritime Commission) have primary regulatory authority.

NOTE State actions include the regulation of public utilities, whose rates may be set by the states in which they do business.

---

18. *Federal Baseball Club of Baltimore, Inc. v. National League of Professional Baseball Clubs,* 259 U.S. 200, 42 S.Ct. 465, 66 L.Ed. 898 (1922).

19. See *United Mine Workers of America v. Pennington,* 381 U.S. 657, 85 S.Ct. 1585, 14 L.Ed.2d 626 (1965); and *Eastern Railroad Presidents Conference v. Noerr Motor Freight, Inc.,* 365 U.S. 127, 81 S.Ct. 523, 5 L.Ed.2d 464 (1961).

20. *Professional Real Estate Investors, Inc. v. Columbia Pictures Industries, Inc.,* 508 U.S. 49, 113 S.Ct. 1920, 123 L.Ed.2d 611 (1993).

21. See *Parker v. Brown,* 347 U.S. 341, 63 S.Ct. 307, 87 L.Ed. 315 (1943).

KEY TERMS

antitrust law   693
attempted monopolization   706
conglomerate merger   710
divestiture   712
exclusive-dealing contract   708
group boycott   698
horizontal merger   709
horizontal restraint   696
market concentration   709

market power   694
market-share test   704
monopolization   703
monopoly   693
monopoly power   694
per se violation   695
predatory pricing   703
price discrimination   707
price-fixing agreement   696

resale price maintenance
   agreement   701
rule of reason   695
tying arrangement   708
vertical merger   710
vertical restraint   700
vertically integrated firm   700

CHAPTER SUMMARY   PROMOTING COMPETITION

Sherman Antitrust Act (1890) (See pages 693–707.)	1. *Major provisions*—
	a. Section 1—Prohibits contracts, combinations, and conspiracies in restraint of trade.
	(1) Horizontal restraints subject to Section 1 include price-fixing agreements, group boycotts (joint refusals to deal), horizontal market division, trade association agreements, and joint ventures.
	(2) Vertical restraints subject to Section 1 include territorial or customer restrictions, resale price maintenance agreements, and refusals to deal.
	b. Section 2—Prohibits monopolies and attempts to monopolize.
	2. *Jurisdictional requirements*—The Sherman Act applies only to activities that have a significant impact on interstate commerce.
	3. *Interpretative rules*—
	a. *Per se* rule—Applied to restraints on trade that are so inherently anticompetitive that they cannot be justified and are deemed illegal as a matter of law.
	b. Rule of reason—Applied when an anticompetitive agreement may be justified by legitimate benefits. Under the rule of reason, the lawfulness of a trade restraint will be determined by the purpose and effects of the restraint.
Clayton Act (1914) (See pages 707–711.)	The major provisions are as follows:
	1. *Section 2*—As amended in 1936 by the Robinson-Patman Act, prohibits price discrimination that substantially lessens competition and prohibits a seller engaged in interstate commerce from selling to two or more buyers goods of similar grade and quality at different prices when the result is a substantial lessening of competition or the creation of a competitive injury.
	2. *Section 3*—Prohibits exclusionary practices, such as exclusive-dealing contracts and tying arrangements, when the effect may be to substantially lessen competition.
	3. *Section 7*—Prohibits mergers when the effect may be to substantially lessen competition or to tend to create a monopoly.
	a. Horizontal merger—The acquisition by merger or consolidation of a competing firm engaged in the same relevant market. Will be unlawful only if a merger results in the

CHAPTER SUMMARY PROMOTING COMPETITION—Continued

Clayton Act (1914)—continued	merging firms' holding a disproportionate share of the market, resulting in a substantial lessening of competition, and if the merger does not enhance consumer welfare by increasing efficiency of production or marketing. b. Vertical merger—The acquisition by a seller of one of its buyers or vice versa. Will be unlawful if the merger prevents competitors of either merging firm from competing in a segment of the market that otherwise would be open to them, resulting in a substantial lessening of competition. c. Conglomerate merger—The acquisition of a noncompeting business. 4. *Section 8*—Prohibits interlocking directorates.
Federal Trade Commission Act (1914) (See page 711.)	Prohibits unfair methods of competition; established and defined the powers of the Federal Trade Commission.
Enforcement of Antitrust Laws (See page 712.)	Antitrust laws are enforced by the Department of Justice, by the Federal Trade Commission, and in some cases by private parties, who may be awarded treble damages and attorneys' fees.
Exemptions from Antitrust Laws (See pages 712–713.)	1. Labor unions (under Section 6 of the Clayton Act of 1914). 2. Agricultural associations and fisheries (under Section 6 of the Clayton Act of 1914, the Capper-Volstead Act of 1922, and the Fisheries Cooperative Marketing Act of 1976). 3. Insurance—when state regulation exists (under the McCarran-Ferguson Act of 1945). 4. Export trading companies (under the Webb-Pomerene Act of 1918 and the Export Trading Company Act of 1982). 5. Professional baseball (by a 1922 judicial decision, modified by a 1998 federal statute). 6. Oil marketing (under the Interstate Oil Compact of 1935). 7. Cooperative research and production (under various acts, including the Small Business Administration Act of 1958, as amended; the National Cooperative Research Act of 1984; and the National Cooperative Production Amendments of 1993). 8. Joint efforts by businesspersons to obtain legislative or executive action (under the *Noerr-Pennington* doctrine). 9. Other activities, including certain national defense actions, state actions, and actions of certain regulated industries.

FOR REVIEW

1. What is a monopoly? What is market power? How do these concepts relate to each other?
2. What type of activity is prohibited by Section 1 of the Sherman Act? What type of activity is prohibited by Section 2 of the Sherman Act?
3. What are the four major provisions of the Clayton Act, and what types of activities do these provisions prohibit?
4. What agencies of the federal government enforce the federal antitrust laws?
5. What are four activities that are exempt from the antitrust laws?

QUESTIONS AND CASE PROBLEMS

22–1. Sherman Act. An agreement that is blatantly and substantially anticompetitive is deemed a *per se* violation of Section 1 of the Sherman Act. Under what rule is an agreement analyzed if it appears to be anticompetitive but is not a *per se* violation? In making this analysis, what factors will a court consider?

22–2. Antitrust Laws. Allitron, Inc., and Donovan, Ltd., are interstate competitors selling similar appliances, principally in the states of Indiana, Kentucky, Illinois, and Ohio. Allitron and Donovan agree that Allitron will no longer sell in Ohio and Indiana and that Donovan will no longer sell in Kentucky and Illinois. Have Allitron and Donovan violated any antitrust law? If so, which law? Explain.

22–3. Antitrust Laws. The partnership of Alvaredo and Parish is engaged in the oil-wellhead service industry in the states of New Mexico and Colorado. The firm currently has about 40 percent of the market for this service. Webb Corp. competes with the Alvaredo-Parish partnership in the same state area. Webb has approximately 35 percent of the market. Alvaredo and Parish acquire the stock and assets of Webb Corp. Do the antitrust laws prohibit the type of action undertaken by Alvaredo and Parish? Discuss fully.

22–4. Horizontal Restraints. Jorge's Appliance Corp. was a new retail seller of appliances in Sunrise City. Because of its innovative sales techniques and financing, Jorge's caused the appliance department of No-Glow Department Store to lose a substantial number of sales. No-Glow, a large chain store with a great deal of buying power, told a number of appliance manufacturers that if they continued to sell to Jorge's, No-Glow would discontinue its large volume of purchases from them. The manufacturers immediately stopped selling appliances to Jorge's. Jorge's filed suit against No-Glow and the manufacturers, claiming that their actions constituted an antitrust violation. No-Glow and the manufacturers were able to prove that Jorge's was a small retailer with a limited portion of the market. They claimed that because the relevant market was not substantially affected, they were not guilty of restraint of trade. Discuss fully whether there was an antitrust violation.

22–5. Exclusionary Practices. Instant Foto Corp. is a manufacturer of photography film. At present, Instant Foto has approximately 50 percent of the market. Instant Foto advertises that the purchase price for its film includes photo processing by Instant Foto Corp. Instant Foto claims that its film processing is specially designed to improve the quality of photos taken with Instant Foto film. Is Instant Foto's combination of film purchase and film processing an antitrust violation? Explain.

22–6. Antitrust Laws. Great Western Directories, Inc. (GW), is an independent publisher of telephone directory Yellow Pages. GW buys information for its listings from Southwestern Bell Telephone Co. (SBT). Southwestern Bell Corp. owns SBT and Southwestern Bell Yellow Pages (SBYP), which publishes a directory in competition with GW. In June 1988, in some markets, SBT raised the price for its listing information, and SBYP lowered the price for advertising in its Yellow Pages. GW feared that these companies would do the same thing in other local markets, making it too expensive for GW to compete in those markets. Because of this fear, GW left one market and declined to compete in another. Consequently, SBYP had a monopoly in those markets. GW and another independent publisher filed a suit in a federal district court against Southwestern Bell Corp. What antitrust law, if any, did Southwestern Bell Corp. violate? Should the independent companies be entitled to damages? [*Great Western Directories, Inc. v. Southwestern Bell Telephone Co.*, 74 F.3d 613 (5th Cir. 1996)]

22–7. Restraint of Trade. The National Collegiate Athletic Association (NCAA) coordinates the intercollegiate athletic programs of its members by issuing rules and setting standards governing, among other things, the coaching staffs. The NCAA set up a cost reduction committee to consider ways to cut the costs of intercollegiate athletics while maintaining competition. The committee included financial aid personnel, intercollegiate athletic administrators, college presidents, university faculty members, and a university chancellor. It was felt that "only a collaborative effort could reduce costs while maintaining a level playing field." The committee proposed a rule to restrict the annual compensation of certain coaches to $16,000. The NCAA adopted the rule. Basketball coaches affected by the rule filed a suit in a federal district court against the NCAA, alleging a violation of Section 1 of the Sherman Antitrust Act. Is the rule a *per se* violation of the Sherman Act, or should it be evaluated under the rule of reason? If it is subject to the rule of reason, is it an illegal restraint of trade? Discuss fully. [*Law v. National Collegiate Athletic Association*, 134 F.3d 1010 (10th Cir. 1998)]

22–8. Tying Arrangement. Public Interest Corp. (PIC) owned and operated the television station WTMV-TV in Lakeland, Florida. MCA Television, Ltd., owns and licenses syndicated television programs. The parties entered into a licensing contract with respect to several television shows. MCA conditioned the license on PIC's agreeing to take another show, *Harry and the Hendersons*. PIC agreed to this arrangement, although it would not have chosen to license *Harry* if it had not had to do so to secure the licenses for the other shows. More than two years into the contract, a dispute arose over PIC's payments, and negotiations failed to resolve the dispute. In a letter, MCA suspended PIC's broadcast rights for all of its shows and stated that "[a]ny telecasts of MCA programming by WTMV-TV . . . will be deemed unauthorized and shall constitute an infringement of MCA's copyrights." PIC nonetheless continued broadcasting MCA's programs, with the exception of *Harry*. MCA filed a suit in a federal district court against PIC, alleging breach of contract and copyright infringement. PIC filed a counterclaim, contending in part that MCA's deal was an illegal tying arrangement. Is PIC correct? Explain. [*MCA Television, Ltd. v. Public Interest Corp.*, 171 F.3d 1265 (11th Cir. 1999)]

Case Problem with Sample Answer

22–9. Attempted Monopolization. In 1995, to make personal computers (PCs) easier to use, Intel Corp. and other companies developed a standard, called the universal serial bus (USB) specification, to enable the easy attachment of peripherals (printers and other hardware) to PCs. Intel and others formed the Universal Serial Bus Implementers Forum (USB-IF) to promote USB technology and products. Intel, however, makes relatively few USB products and does not make any USB interconnect devices. Multivideo Labs, Inc. (MVL), designed and distributed active extension cables (AECs) to connect peripheral devices to each other or to a PC. The AECs were not USB compliant, a fact that Intel employees told other USB-IF members. Asserting that this caused a "general cooling of the market" for AECs, MVL filed a suit in a federal district court against Intel, claiming in part attempted monopolization in violation of the Sherman Act. Intel filed a motion for summary judgment. How should the court rule, and why? [*Multivideo Labs, Inc. v. Intel Corp.*, __ F.Supp.2d __ (S.D.N.Y. 2000)]

To view a sample answer for this case problem, go to this book's Web site at http://leet.westbuslaw.com and click on "Interactive Study Center."

22–10. Monopolization. Moist snuff is a smokeless tobacco product sold in small round cans from racks, which include point-of-sale (POS) ads. POS ads are critical because tobacco advertising is restricted and the number of people who use smokeless tobacco products is relatively small. In the moist snuff market in the United States, there are only four competitors, including U.S. Tobacco Co. and its affiliates (USTC) and Conwood Co. In 1990, USTC, which held 87 percent of the market, began to convince major retailers, including Wal-Mart Stores, Inc., to use USTC's "exclusive racks" to display its products and those of all other snuff makers. USTC agents would then destroy competitors' racks. USTC also began to provide retailers with false sales data to convince them to maintain its poor-selling items and drop competitors' less expensive products. Conwood's Wal-Mart market share fell from 12 percent to 6.5 percent. In stores in which USTC did not have rack exclusivity, however,

Conwood's market share increased to 25 percent. Conwood filed a suit in a federal district court against USTC, alleging in part that USTC used its monopoly power to exclude competitors from the moist snuff market. Should the court rule in Conwood's favor? What is USTC's best defense? Discuss. [*Conwood Co., L.P. v. U.S. Tobacco Co.*, 290 F.3d 768 (6th Cir. 2002)]

A Question of Ethics & Social Responsibility

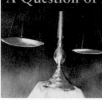

22–11. A group of lawyers in the District of Columbia regularly acted as court-appointed attorneys for indigent defendants in District of Columbia criminal cases. At a meeting of the Superior Court Trial Lawyers Association (SCTLA), the attorneys agreed to stop providing this representation until the district increased their compensation. Their subsequent boycott had a severe impact on the district's criminal justice system, and the District of Columbia gave in to the lawyers' demands for higher pay. After the lawyers had returned to work, the Federal Trade Commission filed a complaint against the SCTLA and four of its officers and, after an investigation, ruled that the SCTLA's activities constituted an illegal group boycott in violation of antitrust laws. [*Federal Trade Commission v. Superior Court Trial Lawyers Association*, 493 U.S. 411, 110 S.Ct. 768, 107 L.Ed.2d 851 (1990)]

1. The SCTLA obviously was aware of the negative impact its decision would have on the district's criminal justice system. Given this fact, do you think the lawyers behaved ethically?

2. On appeal, the SCTLA claimed that its boycott was undertaken to publicize the fact that the attorneys were underpaid and that the boycott thus constituted an expression protected by the First Amendment. Do you agree with this argument?

3. Labor unions have the right to strike when negotiations between labor and management fail to result in agreement. Is it fair to prohibit members of the SCTLA from "striking" against their employer, the District of Columbia, simply because the SCTLA is a professional organization and not a labor union?

Critical-Thinking Technological Question

22–12. Alpha, Inc., manufactures computer hardware and provides repair service for the hardware. Alpha also makes and markets software and support for those who use the software, but the company refuses to provide software support to those who do not purchase its hardware service. Is Alpha's practice a tying arrangement? Discuss.

INTERACTING WITH THE INTERNET

For updated links to resources available on the Web, as well as a variety of other materials, visit this text's Web site at

http://leet.westbuslaw.com

You can access the Antitrust Division of the U.S. Department of Justice online at

http://www.usdoj.gov/atr.index.html

To see the American Bar Association's Web page on antitrust law, go to

http://www.abanet.org/antitrust

The Federal Trade Commission offers an abundance of information on antitrust law, including "A Plain English Guide to Antitrust Laws," at

http://www.ftc.gov/ftc/antitrust.htm

ONLINE LEGAL RESEARCH EXERCISES

Go to **http://leet.westbuslaw.com**, the Web site that accompanies this text. Select "Interactive Study Center," and then click on "Chapter 22." There you will find the following Internet research exercises that you can perform to learn more about topics covered in this chapter.

Activity 22–1: HISTORICAL PERSPECTIVE—The Standard Oil Trust
Activity 22–2: MANAGEMENT PERSPECTIVE—Avoiding Antitrust Problems

BEFORE THE TEST

Go to **http://leet.westbuslaw.com**, the Web site that accompanies this text. Select "Interactive Quizzes." You will find at least twenty interactive questions relating to this chapter.

Westlaw® Campus

If your textbook provided for a subscription to Westlaw® Campus, or if you have otherwise purchased access to the Westlaw Campus database, you can access any of the cases presented or cited in this chapter by using your Westlaw Campus account.

CHAPTER 23

Investor Protection and Online Securities Offerings

CHAPTER OBJECTIVES

After reading this chapter, you should be able to answer the following questions:

1. What is meant by the term *securities?*

2. What are the two major statutes regulating the securities industry? When was the Securities and Exchange Commission created, and what are its major purposes and functions?

3. What is insider trading? Why is it prohibited?

4. What are some of the features of state securities laws?

5. How are securities laws being applied in the online environment?

SECURITY
Generally, a stock certificate, bond, note, debenture, warrant, or other document given as evidence of an ownership interest in a corporation or as a promise of repayment by a corporation.

The stock market crash of October 29, 1929, and the ensuing economic depression caused the public to focus on the importance of securities markets for the economic well-being of the nation. Congress was pressured to regulate securities trading, and the result was the Securities Act of 1933[1] and the Securities Exchange Act of 1934.[2] Both acts were designed to provide investors with more information to help them make buying and selling decisions about **securities**—generally defined as any documents evidencing corporate ownership (stock) or debts (bonds)—and to prohibit deceptive, unfair, and manipulative practices in the purchase and sale of securities.

> "It shall be unlawful for any person in the offer or sale of any security . . . to engage in any transaction, practice, or course of business which operates or would operate as a fraud or deceit upon the purchaser."
>
> Securities Act of 1933, Section 17

---

1. 15 U.S.C. Sections 77a–77aa.
2. 15 U.S.C. Sections 78a–78mm.

Today, the sale and transfer of securities are heavily regulated by federal and state statutes and by government agencies.

This chapter discusses the nature of federal securities regulation and its effect on the business world. The federal administrative agency that regulates securities transactions is the Securities and Exchange Commission (SEC). Because of its importance, we examine the origin and functions of the SEC in this chapter's *Landmark in the Legal Environment* feature on page 722 and 723. We discuss the Sarbanes-Oxley Act, which was passed by Congress in 2002 and which will have a significant impact on certain types of securities transactions. We then examine the major traditional laws governing securities offerings and trading. The online world has brought some dramatic changes to securities offerings and regulation. In the concluding pages of this chapter, we look at how securities laws are being adapted to the online environment.

THE SARBANES-OXLEY ACT OF 2002

In 2002, following a series of corporate scandals that included misleading audits by accounting firms, Congress passed the Sarbanes-Oxley Act.[3] (We discussed some of the scandals that led to the passage of the act in Chapter 2.) Some regard this act as one of the most significant modifications of securities regulation since the 1930s. Generally, the act attempts to increase corporate accountability by imposing stricter disclosure requirements and harsher penalties for violations of securities laws. Among other things, the act requires chief corporate executives to take responsibility for the accuracy of financial statements and reports that are filed with the SEC. Chief executive officers and chief financial officers personally must certify that the statements and reports are accurate and complete.

Additionally, the new rules require that certain financial and stock-transaction reports must be filed with the SEC earlier than was required under the previous rules. The act also mandates SEC oversight over a new entity, called the Public Company Accounting Oversight Board, that will regulate and oversee public accounting firms. Other provisions of the act create new private civil actions and expand the SEC's remedies in administrative and civil actions.

Because of the importance of this act for corporate leaders and for those dealing with securities transactions, we present some of the act's key provisions relating to corporate accountability in Exhibit 23–1.

SECURITIES ACT OF 1933

The Securities Act of 1933 was designed to prohibit various forms of fraud and to stabilize the securities industry by requiring that all relevant information concerning the issuance of securities be made available to the investing public. Essentially, the purpose of this act is to require disclosure.

---

3. H.R. 3762. This act was signed by President George W. Bush on July 30, 2002, and became effective on August 29, 2002.

EXHIBIT 23-1 SOME KEY PROVISIONS OF THE SARBANES-OXLEY ACT
OF 2002 RELATING TO CORPORATE ACCOUNTABILITY

Certification Requirements—Under Section 906 of the Sarbanes-Oxley Act, the chief executive officers (CEOs) and chief financial officers (CFOs) of most major companies listed on public stock exchanges must now certify financial statements that are filed with the SEC. For virtually all filed financial reports, CEOs and CFOs have to certify that such reports "fully comply" with SEC requirements and that all of the information reported "fairly represents in all material respects, the financial conditions and results of operations of the issuer." Under Section 302 of the act, CEOs and CFOs of reporting companies are required to certify, for each quarterly and annual filing with the SEC, the following:

- That a signing officer reviewed the report.
- That to the best of the signing officer's knowledge, the report contains no untrue statements of material fact and does not omit statements of material fact.
- That the signing officer or officers have established an internal control system designed to ensure discovery of material information that should be in the report.
- That the signing officer disclosed to the auditors any significant deficiencies in the internal control system.

Loans to Directors and Officers—To prevent companies from making loans to corporate officers and later forgiving those loans (to the detriment of shareholders), the Sarbanes-Oxley Act included a provision targeting this practice. Section 402 of the act prohibits any reporting company, as well as any private company that is filing an initial public offering, from extending, renewing, arranging, or maintaining personal loans to directors and executive officers. There are some exceptions under the act for certain consumer and housing loans.

Protection for Whistleblowers—The Sarbanes-Oxley Act also offers protection for "whistleblowers"—those employees who report ("blow the whistle" on) wrongdoing by their employers. Section 806 of the act prohibits publicly traded companies from discharging, demoting, suspending, threatening, harassing, or otherwise discriminating against an employee who provides information to the government or assists in any government investigation regarding conduct that the employee reasonably believes constitutes a violation of securities laws.

Blackout Periods—Rules established under Section 306 of the act prohibit certain types of securities transactions during "blackout periods"—periods during which the issuer's ability to purchase, sell, or otherwise transfer funds in individual account plans (such as pension funds) is suspended.

Enhanced Penalties—

- *Violations of Section 906 Certification Requirements*—A CEO or CFO who certifies a financial report or statement to be filed with the SEC knowing that the report or statement does not fulfill all of the requirements of Section 906 will be subject to criminal penalties up to $1 million in fines, up to ten years in prison, or both. Moreover, if a CEO or CFO "willfully" certifies a report knowing that it does not comport with all of the requirements of Section 906, the penalty can extend to up to $5 million in fines, twenty years in prison, or both.
- *Violations of the Securities Exchange Act of 1934*—Penalties for securities fraud under the Securities Exchange Act of 1934 were also increased (see the discussion of these penalties later in this chapter).
- *Destruction or Alteration of Documents*—The act provides that anyone who alters, destroys, or conceals documents or otherwise obstructs or impedes any official proceeding will be subject to fines, imprisonment for up to twenty years, or both.
- *Other Forms of White-Collar Crime*—The act also stiffened the criminal penalties for violations of federal mail and wire fraud laws (see Chapter 7) and the Employment Retirement Income Security Act of 1974 (see Chapter 16). The act orders the U.S. Sentencing Commission (discussed in Chapter 7) to revise the sentencing guidelines for white-collar crimes to conform with the provisions of the Sarbanes-Oxley Act.

Statute of Limitations for Securities Fraud—Section 804 of the act provides that a private right of action for securities fraud may be brought no later than two years after the discovery of the violation or five years after the violation, whichever is earlier.

LANDMARK IN THE LEGAL ENVIRONMENT

The Securities and Exchange Commission

In 1931, the Senate passed a resolution calling for an extensive investigation of securities trading. The investigation led, ultimately, to the passage by Congress of the Securities Act of 1933, which is also known as the *truth-in-securities* bill. In the following year, Congress passed the Securities Exchange Act. This 1934 act created the Securities and Exchange Commission (SEC).

MAJOR RESPONSIBILITIES OF THE SEC

The SEC was created as an independent regulatory agency whose function was to administer the 1933 and 1934 acts. Its major responsibilities in this respect are as follows:

- Requiring disclosure of facts concerning offerings of securities listed on national securities exchanges and of certain securities traded over the counter.
- Regulating the trade in securities on the national and regional securities exchanges and in the over-the-counter markets.
- Investigating securities fraud.

- Regulating the activities of securities brokers, dealers, and investment advisers and requiring their registration.
- Supervising the activities of mutual funds.
- Recommending administrative sanctions, injunctive remedies, and criminal prosecution against those who violate securities laws. (The SEC can bring enforcement actions for civil violations of federal securities laws. The Fraud Section of the Criminal Division of the Department of Justice prosecutes criminal violations.)

THE SEC'S EXPANDING REGULATORY POWERS

Since its creation, the SEC's regulatory functions have gradually been increased by legislation granting it authority in different areas. For example, to further curb securities fraud, the Securities Enforcement Remedies and Penny Stock Reform Act of 1990[a] amended existing securities laws to allow SEC administrative law judges to hear many more types of securities violation cases; the SEC's enforcement options were greatly expanded as well. The act also provides that courts can bar

---

a. 15 U.S.C. Section 77g.

What Is a Security?

Section 2(1) of the Securities Act states that *securities* include the following:

> [A]ny note, stock, treasury stock, bond, debenture, evidence of indebtedness, certificate of interest or participation in any profit-sharing agreement, collateral-trust certificate, preorganization certificate or subscription, transferable share, investment contract, voting-trust certificate, certificate of deposit for a security, fractional undivided interest in oil, gas, or other mineral rights, or, in general, any interest or instrument commonly known as a "security," or any certificate of interest or participation in, temporary or interim certificate for, receipt for, guarantee of, or warrant or right to subscribe to or purchase, any of the foregoing.[4]

---

4. 15 U.S.C. Section 77b(1). Amendments in 1982 added stock options.

LANDMARK IN THE LEGAL ENVIRONMENT

The Securities and Exchange Commission (Continued)

persons who have engaged in securities fraud from serving as officers and directors of publicly held corporations. The Securities Acts Amendments of 1990 authorized the SEC to seek sanctions against those who violate foreign securities laws.[b] Under the Market Reform Act of 1990, the SEC can suspend trading in securities in the event that prices rise and fall excessively in a short period of time.[c]

The National Securities Markets Improvement Act of 1996 expanded the power of the SEC to exempt persons, securities, and transactions from the requirements of the securities laws.[d] (This part of the act is also known as the Capital Markets Efficiency Act.) In addition, the act limited the authority of the states to regulate certain securities transactions, as well as particular investment advisory firms.[e]

As you read on page 720, the Sarbanes-Oxley Act of 2002 represents a sweeping revision of federal securities laws. Among other things, this act further expanded the authority of the SEC by directing the agency to issue new rules relating to corporate disclosure requirements and by creating an SEC oversight board.

Application to Today's World

Congress and the SEC are now attempting to streamline the regulatory process to make it more efficient and more relevant to today's securities trading practices, including those occurring in the online environment. As the number and types of online securities frauds increase, the SEC is trying to keep pace by expanding its online fraud division. It has created an automated surveillance system for online stock fraud. This system, which is constantly being updated, scans the Internet for words and phrases commonly used by fraud perpetrators, such as "get rich quick!" The SEC has been criticized for privacy violations, but it continues to pursue its efforts through its Office of Internet Enforcement, the so-called Cyberforce. Several hundred employees work in this division.

b. 15 U.S.C. Section 78a.
c. 15 U.S.C. Section 78i(h).
d. 15 U.S.C. Sections 77z-3, 78mm.
e. 15 U.S.C. Section 80b-3a.

Generally, the courts have interpreted the Securities Act's definition of what constitutes a security,[5] when it is not obvious that the transaction or device is one of the securities listed above, to include investment contracts. An *investment contract* is any transaction in which a person (1) invests (2) in a common enterprise (3) reasonably expecting profits (4) derived *primarily* or *substantially* from others' managerial or entrepreneurial efforts.[6]

We usually think of securities in their most common forms—stocks and bonds issued by corporations. Securities can take many forms, however, and have been held to include whiskey, cosmetics, worms, and cemetery lots, as well as investment contracts in condominiums, franchises, limited partnerships, and mineral rights.

In the following case, the question was whether sales of pay phones and agreements to service the phones constituted sales of securities.

5. See 15 U.S.C. Section 77b(a)(1).
6. *SEC v. W. J. Howey Co.*, 328 U.S. 293, 66 S.Ct. 1100, 90 L.Ed. 1244 (1946).

CASE 23.1 SEC v. Alpha Telcom, Inc.

United States District Court,
District of Oregon, 2002.
187 F.Supp.2d 1250.

BACKGROUND AND FACTS Paul Rubera started Alpha Telcom, Inc., in 1986 to sell, install, and maintain phones and business systems in Grants Pass, Oregon. In 1997, Alpha began to sell pay phones to buyers, most of whom also entered into service agreements with Alpha. Most of these buyers selected a "Level Four Service Agreement," which required Alpha to select a location for a phone, install it, obtain all licenses, maintain and clean the phone, pay the bills, and collect the revenue. Buyers were guaranteed—and were paid—a 14 percent return on the amount of their purchase. The pay-phone program was presented and promoted through American Telecommunications Company (ATC), Alpha's marketing subsidiary. From July 1998 through June 2001, Alpha's expenses for the program were $21,798,000, while revenues were $21,698,000. Despite the loss, Alpha paid investors approximately $17.9 million. To make these payments, Alpha borrowed money from ATC. Alpha filed for bankruptcy in August 2001. The Securities and Exchange Commission (SEC) filed a suit in a federal district court against Alpha and Rubera, alleging violations of the Securities Act of 1933. The defendants argued that the pay-phone program did not involve sales of securities.

IN THE WORDS OF THE COURT . . .

PANNER, District Judge.

*   *   *   *

*   *   * *An investment contract involves: (1) an investment of money; (2) in a common enterprise; (3) with the expectation of profits to be derived from the efforts of others.* *   *   * [Emphasis added.]

*   *   *   *

The first element *   *   * is met. The investors make cash investments with the expectation of receiving profits.

*   *   *   *

The second element of the *   *   * test can be satisfied by the existence of either vertical commonality or horizontal commonality. Vertical commonality is the dependence of the investors' fortunes on the success or expertise of the promoter. Horizontal commonality is the pooling of investor funds and interests. *   *   *

Vertical commonality clearly exists. Investors relied on the expertise of Alpha to negotiate and lease sites for the phones, to establish service lines for the phones, and to make all business decisions related to the operation of the phones. Alpha also serviced and maintained the phones, which was important to these investors who had no expertise in the workings of telephones and no desire to maintain or service the phones. *   *   *

Horizontal commonality also exists. ATC loaned money to Alpha. *   *   * [I]t was clearly used, at least in part, to make payments to existing investors. ATC's only source of revenue was money from new investors. As a result, new investor money was being used to pay returns to existing investors. Other evidence of horizontal commonality exists in that Alpha did not pay its investors according to the revenue generated by individual pay phones. Investors would receive their 14 percent return *   *   * regardless of whether their particular phone actually generated that much money *   *   *.

*   *   *   *

The issue for [the third] element is whether the efforts made by those other than the investor are the undeniably significant ones, those essential managerial efforts which affect the failure or success of the enterprise. *   *   *

CASE 23.1—Continued   * * * [N]inety percent of investors chose Alpha as the service provider. * * * [T]hese investors had no expertise or interest in the operation of pay telephones. Alpha was ultimately responsible for those essential managerial efforts [that] affect the failure or success of the enterprise, and the investors retained no control over the business.

DECISION AND REMEDY The court concluded that the pay-phone program was a security because it involved (1) an investment of money, (2) in a common enterprise, (3) with the expectation of profits to be derived from the efforts of others. The court issued an injunction to prohibit further violations of the Securities Act of 1933 and ordered Rubera to disgorge profits of more than $3.7 million, plus interest.

FOR CRITICAL ANALYSIS—Social Consideration *The court also noted that 90 percent of the investors chose Alpha as their service provider. Does this fact have any bearing on the question of whether the pay-phone program was an investment contract?*

Registration Statement

Section 5 of the Securities Act of 1933 broadly provides that if a security does not qualify for an exemption, that security must be *registered* before it is offered to the public either through the mails or through any facility of interstate commerce, including securities exchanges. Issuing corporations must file a *registration statement* with the SEC. Investors must be provided with a *prospectus* that describes the security being sold, the issuing corporation, and the investment or risk attaching to the security. In principle, the registration statement and the prospectus supply sufficient information to enable unsophisticated investors to evaluate the financial risk involved.

DON'T FORGET The purpose of the Securities Act of 1933 is disclosure—the SEC does not consider whether a security is worth the investment price.

Contents of the Registration Statement The registration statement must include the following:

1. A description of the significant provisions of the security offered for sale, including the relationship between that security and the other capital securities of the registrant. Also, the corporation must disclose how it intends to use the proceeds of the sale.
2. A description of the registrant's properties and business.
3. A description of the management of the registrant and its security holdings, remuneration, and other benefits, including pensions and stock options. Any interests of directors or officers in any material transactions with the corporation must be disclosed.
4. A financial statement certified by an independent public accounting firm.
5. A description of pending lawsuits.

Those who register securities offerings with the SEC should realize that as of 1998, the SEC requires certain documents, or portions of documents, to be written in "plain English."

Other Requirements Before filing the registration statement and the prospectus with the SEC, the corporation is allowed to obtain an *underwriter*—a company that agrees to purchase the new issue of securities for resale to the public. There is a twenty-day waiting period (which can be accelerated by the SEC)

A registration statement discusses a security that is being offered to the public. What are the major contents of a registration statement?

after registration before the securities can be sold. During this period, oral offers between interested investors and the issuing corporation concerning the purchase and sale of the proposed securities may take place, and very limited written advertising is allowed. At this time, the so-called **red herring** prospectus may be distributed. It gets its name from the red legend printed across it stating that the registration has been filed but has not become effective.

After the waiting period, the registered securities can be legally bought and sold. Written advertising is allowed in the form of a **tombstone ad,** so named because historically the format resembled a tombstone. Such ads simply tell the investor where and how to obtain a prospectus. Normally, any other type of advertising is prohibited.

RED HERRING
A preliminary prospectus that can be distributed to potential investors after the registration statement (for a securities offering) has been filed with the Securities and Exchange Commission. The name derives from the red legend printed across the prospectus stating that the registration has been filed but has not become effective.

TOMBSTONE AD
An advertisement, historically in a format resembling a tombstone, of a securities offering. The ad informs potential investors of where and how they can obtain a prospectus.

Exempt Securities

A number of specific securities are exempt from the registration requirements of the Securities Act of 1933. These securities—which can also generally be resold without being registered—include the following:[7]

1. All bank securities sold prior to July 27, 1933.
2. Commercial paper (such as negotiable instruments), if the maturity date does not exceed nine months.
3. Securities of charitable organizations.
4. Securities resulting from a corporate reorganization issued for exchange with the issuer's existing security holders and certificates issued by trustees, receivers, or debtors in possession under the bankruptcy laws (bankruptcy laws were discussed in Chapter 15).
5. Securities issued exclusively for exchange with the issuer's existing security holders, provided no commission is paid (for example, stock dividends and stock splits).
6. Securities issued to finance the acquisition of railroad equipment.
7. Any insurance, endowment, or annuity contract issued by a state-regulated insurance company.
8. Government-issued securities.
9. Securities issued by banks, savings and loan associations, farmers' cooperatives, and similar institutions subject to supervision by governmental authorities.
10. In consideration of the "small amount involved,"[8] an issuer's offer of up to $5 million in securities in any twelve-month period.

BE AWARE The issuer of an exempt security does not have to disclose the same information that other issuers do.

For the last exemption, under Regulation A,[9] the issuer must file with the SEC a notice of the issue and an offering circular, which must also be provided to investors before the sale. This is a much simpler and less expensive process than the procedures associated with full registration. Companies are allowed to "test the waters" for potential interest before preparing the offering circular. To *test the waters* means to determine potential interest without actually selling any securities or requiring any commitment on the part of those who are interested. In addition, small-business issuers (companies with less than $25 million in annual revenues and less than $25 million in outstanding voting stock) can

7. 15 U.S.C. Section 77c.
8. 15 U.S.C. Section 77c(b).
9. 17 C.F.R. Sections 230.251–230.263.

use an integrated registration and reporting system that is simpler than the full registration system.

Exhibit 23–2 summarizes the securities and the transactions (discussed next) that are exempt from the registration requirements under the Securities Act of 1933 and SEC regulations.

Exempt Transactions

An issuer of securities that are not exempt under one of the ten categories listed in the previous subsection can avoid the high cost and complicated procedures associated with registration by taking advantage of certain transaction exemptions. These exemptions are very broad, and thus many sales occur without registration. Because there is some overlap in the coverage of the exemptions, an offering may qualify for more than one.

Small Offerings—Regulation D The SEC's Regulation D contains four separate exemptions from registration requirements for limited offers (offers that either involve a small amount of money or are made in a limited manner).

EXHIBIT 23–2 EXEMPTIONS UNDER THE 1933 SECURITIES ACT

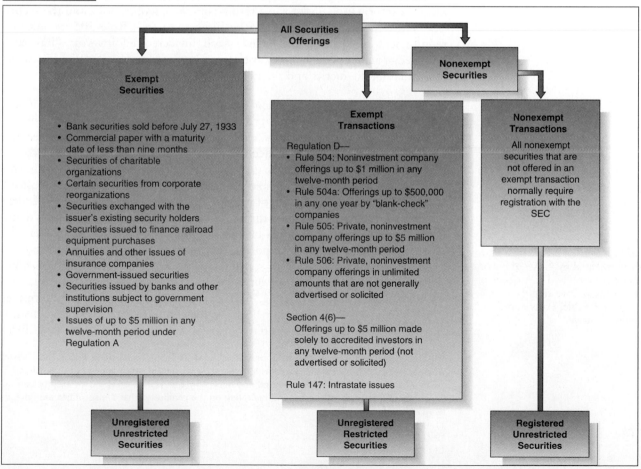

Rule 504. Noninvestment company offerings up to $1 million in any twelve-month period are exempt. In contrast to investment companies (discussed later in this chapter), noninvestment companies are firms that are not engaged primarily in the business of investing or trading in securities.

Rule 504a. Offerings up to $500,000 in any one year by so-called blank-check companies—companies with no specific business plans except to locate and acquire currently unknown businesses or opportunities—are exempt if no general solicitation or advertising is used, if the SEC is notified of the sales, and if precaution is taken against nonexempt, unregistered resales.[10] The limits on advertising and unregistered resales do not apply if the offering is made solely in states that provide for registration and disclosure and the securities are sold in compliance with those provisions.[11]

Rule 505. Private, noninvestment company offerings up to $5 million in any twelve-month period are exempt, regardless of the number of **accredited investors** (banks, insurance companies, investment companies, the issuer's executive officers and directors, and persons whose income or net worth exceeds certain limits), so long as there are no more than thirty-five unaccredited investors; no general solicitation or advertising is used; the SEC is notified of the sales; and precaution is taken against nonexempt, unregistered resales. If the sale involves *any* unaccredited investors, *all* investors must be given material information about the offering company, its business, and the securities before the sale. Unlike Rule 506 (discussed next), Rule 505 includes no requirement that the issuer believe each unaccredited investor "has such knowledge and experience in financial and business matters that he is capable of evaluating the merits and the risks of the prospective investment."[12]

Rule 506. Private, noninvestment company offerings that are not generally solicited or advertised are exempt in unlimited amounts if the SEC is notified of the sales; precaution is taken against nonexempt, unregistered resales; and the issuer believes that each unaccredited investor has sufficient knowledge or experience in financial matters to be capable of evaluating the investment's merits and risks. There can be no more than thirty-five unaccredited investors, although an unlimited number of accredited investors can participate. If there are *any* unaccredited investors, the issuer must provide to *all* purchasers material information about itself, its business, and the securities before the sale.[13]

This is perhaps the most important exemption to those firms that want to raise funds through the sale of securities without registering them. It is often referred to as the *private placement* exemption because it exempts "transactions not involving any public offering."[14] This provision applies to private offerings to a limited number of persons who are sufficiently sophisticated and in a sufficiently strong bargaining position to be able to assume the risk of the investment

---

ACCREDITED INVESTOR
In the context of securities offerings, a "sophisticated" investor, such as a bank, an insurance company, an investment company, an executive officer or director of the issuing company, or any person whose income or net worth exceeds certain limits.

KEEP IN MIND An investor can be sophisticated by virtue of his or her education and experience or by virtue of investing through a knowledgeable, experienced representative.

---

10. Precautions to be taken against nonexempt, unregistered resales include asking the investor whether he or she is buying the securities for others; before the sale, disclosing to each purchaser in writing that the securities are unregistered and thus cannot be resold, except in an exempt transaction, without first being registered; and indicating on the certificates that the securities are unregistered and restricted.
11. 17 C.F.R. Section 230.504a.
12. 17 C.F.R. Section 230.505.
13. 17 C.F.R. Section 230.506.
14. 15 U.S.C. Section 77d(2).

(and who thus have no need for federal registration protection). It applies as well to private offerings to similarly situated institutional investors.

Small Offerings—Section 4(6) Under Section 4(6) of the Securities Act of 1933, an offer made *solely* to accredited investors is exempt if its amount is not more than $5 million. Any number of accredited investors can participate, but no unaccredited investors can do so. No general solicitation or advertising can be used; the SEC must be notified of all sales; and precaution must be taken against nonexempt, unregistered resales. Precaution is necessary because these are *restricted* securities and can be resold only by registration or in an exempt transaction.[15] (The securities purchased and sold by most people who deal in stock are called, in contrast, *unrestricted* securities.)

Intrastate Issues—Rule 147 Also exempt are intrastate transactions involving purely local offerings.[16] This exemption applies to most offerings that are restricted to residents of the state in which the issuing company is organized and doing business. For nine months after the last sale, virtually no resales can be made to nonresidents, and precautions must be taken against this possibility. These offerings remain subject to applicable laws in the state of issue.

Resales Most securities can be resold without registration (although some resales may be subject to restrictions, as discussed above in connection with specific exemptions). The Securities Act of 1933 provides exemptions for resales by most persons other than issuers or underwriters. The average investor who sells shares of stock does not have to file a registration statement with the SEC. Resales of restricted securities acquired under Rule 504a, Rule 505, Rule 506, or Section 4(6), however, trigger the registration requirements unless the party selling them complies with Rule 144 or Rule 144A. These rules are sometimes referred to as "safe harbors."

Rule 144. Rule 144 exempts restricted securities from registration on resale if there is adequate current public information about the issuer, if the person selling the securities has owned them for at least one year, if they are sold in certain limited amounts in unsolicited brokers' transactions, and if the SEC is given notice of the resale.[17] "Adequate current public information" consists of the reports that certain companies are required to file under the Securities Exchange Act of 1934. A person who has owned the securities for at least three years is subject to none of these requirements, unless the person is an affiliate. An *affiliate* is one who controls, is controlled by, or is in common control with the issuer. Sales of *nonrestricted* securities by an affiliate are also subject to the requirements for an exemption under Rule 144 (except that the affiliate need not have owned the securities for at least two years).

CONTRAST Securities do not have to be held for two years to be exempt from registration on a resale under Rule 144A, as they do under Rule 144.

Rule 144A. Securities that at the time of issue are not of the same class as securities listed on a national securities exchange or quoted in a U.S. automated interdealer quotation system can be resold under Rule 144A.[18] They can be sold only to a qualified institutional buyer (an institution, such as an insurance

---

15. 15 U.S.C. Section 77d(6).
16. 15 U.S.C. Section 77c(a)(11); 17 C.F.R. Section 230.147.
17. 17 C.F.R. Section 230.144.
18. 17 C.F.R. Section 230.144A.

company, an investment company, or a bank, that owns and invests at least $100 million in securities). The seller must take reasonable steps to ensure that the buyer knows that the seller is relying on the exemption under Rule 144A. A sample restricted stock certificate is shown in Exhibit 23–3.

Violations of the 1933 Act

As mentioned, the SEC has the power to investigate and bring civil enforcement actions against companies that violate federal securities laws, including the Securities Act of 1933. Criminal violations are prosecuted by the Department of Justice. Violators can be penalized by fines of up to $10,000, imprisonment for up to five years, or both. Private parties can also bring suits against those who violate federal securities laws. Those who purchase securities and suffer harm as a result of false or omitted statements or other violations can sue in federal court to recover their losses and other damages.

SECURITIES EXCHANGE ACT OF 1934

The Securities Exchange Act of 1934 provides for the regulation and registration of securities exchanges, brokers, dealers, and national securities associations, such as the National Association of Securities Dealers (NASD). The SEC

EXHIBIT 23–3 A SAMPLE RESTRICTED STOCK CERTIFICATE

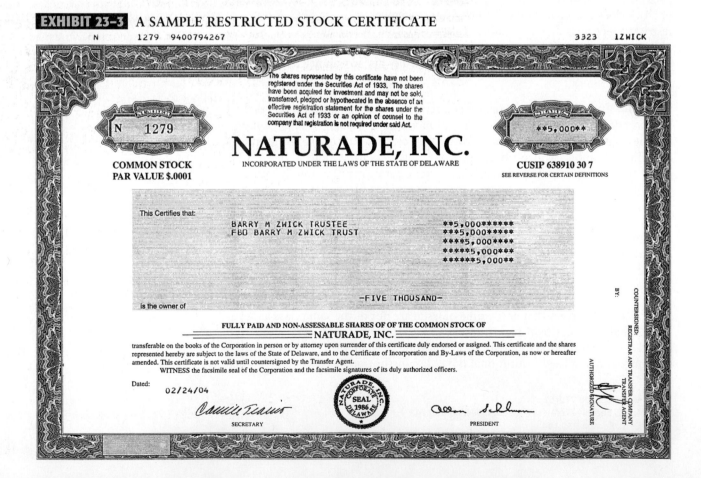

regulates the markets in which securities are traded by maintaining a continuous disclosure system for all corporations with securities on the securities exchanges and for companies that have assets in excess of $10 million and five hundred or more shareholders. These corporations are referred to as Section 12 companies because they are required to file with the exchange a registration application for their securities under Section 12 of the 1934 act.

The act also regulates proxy solicitation for voting (discussed in Chapter 14) and allows the SEC to engage in market surveillance to regulate undesirable market practices such as fraud, market manipulation, and misrepresentation.

Section 10(b), SEC Rule 10b-5, and Insider Trading

Section 10(b) is one of the most important sections of the Securities Exchange Act of 1934. This section proscribes the use of "any manipulative or deceptive device or contrivance in contravention of such rules and regulations as the [SEC] may prescribe." Among the rules that the SEC has promulgated pursuant to the 1934 act is **SEC Rule 10b-5,** which prohibits the commission of fraud in connection with the purchase or sale of any security.

One of the major goals of Section 10(b) and SEC Rule 10b-5 is to prevent so-called **insider trading.** Because of their positions, corporate directors and officers often obtain advance inside information that can affect the future market value of the corporate stock. Obviously, their positions give them a trading advantage over the general public and shareholders. The 1934 Securities Exchange Act defines inside information and extends liability to officers and directors for taking advantage of such information in their personal transactions when they know that it is unavailable to the persons with whom they are dealing. Furthermore, Section 10(b) and SEC Rule 10b-5 cover not only corporate officers, directors, and majority shareholders but also any other persons having access to or receiving information of a nonpublic nature on which trading is based.

E*Trade displays its home page. Online trading through a firm such as E*Trade does not involve personal contact with a broker. Does this mean that online trading is unregulated?

SEC RULE 10b-5
A rule of the Securities and Exchange Commission that makes it unlawful, in connection with the purchase or sale of any security, to make any untrue statement of a material fact or to omit a material fact if such omission causes the statement to be misleading.

INSIDER TRADING
The purchase or sale of securities on the basis of information that has not been made available to the public.

ETHICAL ISSUE

Should liability under SEC Rule 10b-5 arise from the mere possession of inside information by a person trading in securities?

Suppose that an investor has a plan to trade certain stocks but then, before the trade is actually carried out, comes into possession of inside information relating to that stock. If the investor goes ahead with the trading strategy, should he or she be held liable for violating SEC Rule 10b-5? After all, the investor did not intend to defraud or deceive anyone; he or she simply intended to implement a preexisting financial strategy. For some time, the courts differed in their approach to this question, which clearly has both ethical and legal implications. Some courts concluded that for liability under SEC Rule 10b-5 to arise, an investor had to *use* the inside information in his or her possession.[19] Other courts held that merely *possessing* inside information about certain stocks, while trading in those stocks, was enough to establish liability

---

19. See, for example, *United States v. Smith,* 155 F.3d 1051 (9th Cir. 1998).

Home-decorating authority Martha Stewart leaves a U.S. district court in New York in November 2003. She was charged with insider trading after she sold shares of stock in ImClone Systems in 2001, just one day before a negative decision from the Food and Drug Administration sent the stock price plummeting. Prosecutors contend that she acted on a tip from an insider; Stewart denies that she did so. What securities law prohibits insider trading?

> " Anyone who says businessmen deal only in facts, not fiction, has never read old five-year projections. "
>
> MALCOLM FORBES, 1919–1990
> (American publisher)

under SEC Rule 10b-5.[20] To clarify this issue, the SEC adopted a new rule, Rule 10b5-1.[21] Generally, the rule allows corporate insiders to engage in prearranged or certain other securities transactions without being subject to liability under SEC Rule 10b-5. In other words, a corporate insider is now permitted to buy or sell stock without having to worry about liability if she or he, *after* deciding to buy or sell a stock, learns inside information relating to that stock.

Disclosure Requirements under SEC Rule 10b-5 Any material omission or misrepresentation of material facts in connection with the purchase or sale of a security may violate not only Section 11 of the Securities Act of 1933 but also the antifraud provisions of Section 10(b) and SEC Rule 10b-5 of the 1934 act. The key to liability (which can be civil or criminal) under Section 10(b) and SEC Rule 10b-5 is whether the information is *material*.

Examples of Material Facts Calling for Disclosure. The following are some examples of material facts calling for disclosure under the rule:

1. A new ore discovery.
2. Fraudulent trading in the company stock by a broker-dealer.
3. A dividend change (whether up or down).
4. A contract for the sale of corporate assets.
5. A new discovery (process or product).
6. A significant change in the firm's financial condition.

Note that none of these facts, in itself, is *automatically* a material fact. Rather, it will be regarded as a material fact if it is significant enough that it will likely affect an investor's decision as to whether to purchase or sell certain securities.

The following is one of the landmark cases interpreting SEC Rule 10b-5. The SEC sued Texas Gulf Sulphur Company for issuing a misleading press release. The release underestimated the magnitude and the value of a mineral discovery. The SEC also sued several of Texas Gulf Sulphur's directors, officers, and employees under SEC Rule 10b-5 for purchasing large amounts of the corporate stock prior to the announcement of the corporation's rich ore discovery.

---

20. See, for example, *United States v. Teicher*, 987 F.2d 112 (2d Cir. 1993).
21. 65 F.R. 51716 (August 24, 2000).

LANDMARK AND CLASSIC CASES

CASE 23.2   SEC v. Texas Gulf Sulphur Co.

United States Court of Appeals, Second Circuit, 1968.
401 F.2d 833.

HISTORICAL AND ENVIRONMENTAL SETTING *No court has ever held that every buyer or seller is entitled to all of the information relating to all of the circumstances in*

every stock transaction. By the mid-1950s, however, significant understatement of the value of the assets of a company had been held to be materially misleading.[a] In 1957, the Texas Gulf Sulphur Company (TGS) began exploring for minerals in eastern Canada. In March 1959, aerial geophysical surveys were conducted over more than fifteen thousand square miles of the area. The operations revealed numerous and

a. *Speed v. Transamerica Corp.*, 99 F.Supp. 808 (D.Del. 1951).

CASE 23.2—Continued

extraordinary variations in the conductivity of the rock, which indicated a remarkable concentration of commercially exploitable minerals. One site of such variations was near Timmins, Ontario. On October 29 and 30, 1963, a ground survey of the site near Timmins indicated a need to drill for further evaluation.

BACKGROUND AND FACTS The Texas Gulf Sulphur Company drilled a hole on November 12, 1963, that appeared to yield a core with an exceedingly high mineral content. TGS kept secret the results of the core sample. Officers and employees of the company made substantial purchases of TGS's stock or accepted stock options after learning of the ore discovery, even though further drilling was necessary to establish whether there was enough ore to be mined commer-

cially. On April 11, 1964, an unauthorized report of the mineral find appeared in the newspapers. On the following day, April 12, TGS issued a press release that played down the discovery and stated that it was too early to tell whether the ore finding would be a significant one. Later on, TGS announced a strike of at least twenty-five million tons of ore, substantially driving up the price of TGS stock. The SEC brought suit in a federal district court against the officers and employees of TGS for violating the insider-trading prohibition of SEC Rule 10b-5. The officers and employees argued that the prohibition did not apply. They reasoned that the information on which they had traded was not material, as the mine had not been commercially proved. The court held that most of the defendants had not violated SEC Rule 10b-5, and the SEC appealed.

IN THE WORDS OF THE COURT . . .

WATERMAN, Circuit Judge.

* * * *

* * * [W]hether facts are material within Rule 10b-5 when the facts relate to a particular event and are undisclosed by those persons who are knowledgeable thereof will depend at any given time upon a balancing of both the indicated probability that the event will occur and the anticipated magnitude of the event in light of the totality of the company activity. Here, * * * knowledge of the possibility, which surely was more than marginal, of the existence of a mine of the vast magnitude indicated by the remarkably rich drill core located rather close to the surface (suggesting mineability by the less expensive openpit method) within the confines of a large anomaly (suggesting an extensive region of mineralization) might well have affected the price of TGS stock and would certainly have been an important fact to a reasonable * * * investor in deciding whether he should buy, sell, or hold. After all, this first drill core was "unusually good and * * * excited the interest and speculation of those who knew about it."

* * * *

* * * [A] major factor in determining whether the * * * discovery was a material fact is the importance attached to the drilling results by those who knew about it. * * * [T]he timing by those who knew of it of their stock purchases and their purchases of *short-term* calls [rights to buy shares at a specified price within a specified time period]—purchases in some cases by individuals who had never before purchased calls or even TGS stock— virtually compels the inference that the insiders were influenced by the drilling results. [Emphasis added.]

* * * *

We hold, therefore, that all transactions in TGS stock or calls by individuals apprised of the drilling results * * * were made in violation of Rule 10b-5.

DECISION AND REMEDY The federal appellate court reversed the lower court's decision and remanded the case to the trial court. The employees and officers had violated SEC Rule 10b-5's prohibition

against insider trading, even though they did not know the full extent and profit potential of the mine at the time they purchased the stock.

(continued)

CASE 23.2—Continued

COMMENT *This landmark case affirmed the principle that the test of whether information is material, for SEC Rule 10b-5 purposes, is whether it would affect the judgment of reasonable investors. The corporate insiders' purchases of stock and stock options (rights to* *purchase stock) indicated that they were influenced by the drilling results and that the information about the drilling results was material. The courts continue to cite this case when applying SEC Rule 10b-5 to cases of alleged insider trading.*

The Private Securities Litigation Reform Act of 1995. Ironically, one of the effects of SEC Rule 10b-5 was to deter disclosure of forward-looking information. ● EXAMPLE 1 A company announces that its projected earnings in a certain time period will be X amount. It turns out that the forecast is wrong. The earnings are in fact much lower, and the price of the company's stock is affected—negatively. The shareholders then bring a class-action suit against the company, alleging that the directors violated SEC Rule 10b-5 by disclosing misleading financial information.●

In an attempt to rectify this problem and promote disclosure, Congress passed the Private Securities Litigation Reform Act of 1995. Among other things, the act provides a "safe harbor" for publicly held companies that make forward-looking statements, such as financial forecasts. Those who make such statements are protected against federal liability for securities fraud as long as the statements are accompanied by "meaningful cautionary statements identifying important factors that could cause actual results to differ materially from those in the forward-looking statement."[22]

After the 1995 act was passed, a number of securities class-action suits were filed in state courts to skirt the requirements of the 1995 federal act. In response to this problem, Congress passed the Securities Litigation Uniform Standards Act of 1998. The act placed stringent limits on the ability of plaintiffs to bring class-action suits in state courts against firms whose securities are traded on national stock exchanges. Exceptions were made to preserve certain suits brought under state law affecting the conduct of corporate officers with respect to specific corporate actions, including tender offers.

Applicability of SEC Rule 10b-5 SEC Rule 10b-5 applies in virtually all cases concerning the trading of securities, whether on organized exchanges, in over-the-counter markets, or in private transactions. The rule covers, among other things, notes, bonds, agreements to form a corporation, and joint-venture agreements. Generally, it covers just about any form of security. It is immaterial whether a firm has securities registered under the 1933 act for the 1934 act to apply.

Although SEC Rule 10b-5 is applicable only when the requisites of federal jurisdiction—such as the use of the mails, of stock exchange facilities, or of any instrumentality of interstate commerce—are present, virtually no commercial transaction can be completed without such contact. In addition, the states have corporate securities laws, many of which include provisions similar to SEC Rule 10b-5.

---

22. 15 U.S.C. Sections 77z-2, 78u-5.

ETHICAL ISSUE

Should insider trading be legal?

SEC Rule 10b-5 has broad applicability. As will be discussed shortly, the rule covers not only corporate insiders but even "outsiders"—those who receive and trade on tips received from insiders. Investigating and prosecuting violations of SEC Rule 10b-5 is costly, both for the government and for those accused of insider trading. Some people doubt that such extensive regulation is necessary and even contend that insider trading should be legal. Would there be any benefit from the legalization of insider trading? To evaluate this question, review the facts in *SEC v. Texas Gulf Sulphur Co.* (Case 23.2 in this chapter). If insider trading had been legal, the discovery of the ore sample would probably have caused many more company insiders to purchase stock. Consequently, the price of Texas Gulf's stock would have increased fairly quickly. These increases presumably would have attracted the attention of outside investors, who would have learned sooner that something positive had happened to the company and would thus have had the opportunity to purchase the stock. The higher demand for the stock would have more quickly translated into higher prices for the stock and hence, perhaps, a more efficient capital market.

Outsiders and SEC Rule 10b-5 The traditional insider-trading case involves true insiders—corporate officers, directors, and majority shareholders who have access to (and trade on) inside information. Increasingly, liability under Section 10(b) of the 1934 act and SEC Rule 10b-5 has been extended to include certain "outsiders"—those persons who trade on inside information acquired indirectly. Two theories have been developed under which outsiders can be held liable for insider trading: the *tipper/tippee theory* and the *misappropriation theory.*

Tipper/Tippee Theory. Anyone who acquires inside information as a result of a corporate insider's breach of his or her fiduciary duty can be liable under SEC Rule 10b-5. This liability extends to **tippees** (those who receive "tips" from insiders) and even remote tippees (tippees of tippees).

TIPPEE
A person who receives inside information.

The key to liability under this theory is that the inside information must be obtained as a result of someone's breach of a fiduciary duty to the corporation whose shares are involved in the trading. Liability arises when there is a breach of a duty not to disclose inside information, the disclosure is made in exchange for personal benefit, and the tippee knows of this breach (or should know of it) and benefits from it.[23]

Misappropriation Theory. Liability for insider trading can also be established under the misappropriation theory. This theory holds that if an individual wrongfully obtains (misappropriates) inside information and trades on it for her or his personal gain, then the individual should be held liable because, in essence, the individual stole information rightfully belonging to another.

---

23. See, for example, *Chiarella v. United States,* 445 U.S. 222, 100 S.Ct. 1108, 63 L.Ed.2d 348 (1980); and *Dirks v. SEC,* 463 U.S. 646, 103 S.Ct. 3255, 77 L.Ed.2d 911 (1983).

The misappropriation theory has been controversial because it significantly extends the reach of SEC Rule 10b-5 to outsiders who would not ordinarily be deemed fiduciaries of the corporations in whose stock they trade. The United States Supreme Court, however, has held that liability under SEC Rule 10b-5 can be based on the misappropriation theory.[24]

Insider Reporting and Trading—Section 16(b)

Officers, directors, and certain large stockholders[25] of Section 12 corporations (corporations that are required to file with the exchange a registration application for their securities under Section 12 of the 1934 act) must file reports with the SEC concerning their ownership and trading of the corporations' securities.[26] To discourage such insiders from using nonpublic information about their companies for their personal benefit in the stock market, Section 16(b) of the 1934 act provides for the recapture by the corporation of all profits realized by an insider on any purchase and sale or sale and purchase of the corporation's stock within any six-month period.[27] It is irrelevant whether the insider actually uses inside information; all such short-swing profits must be returned to the corporation.

Section 16(b) applies not only to stock but to warrants, options, and securities convertible into stock. In addition, the courts have fashioned complex rules for determining profits. Corporate insiders are wise to seek specialized counsel prior to trading in the corporation's stock. Exhibit 23–4 compares the effects of SEC Rule 10b-5 and Section 16(b).

Proxy Statements

Section 14(a) of the Securities Exchange Act of 1934 regulates the solicitation of proxies from shareholders of Section 12 companies. The SEC regulates the content of proxy statements. As discussed in Chapter 14, a proxy statement is a statement that is sent to shareholders by corporate officials who are requesting authority to vote on behalf of the shareholders in a particular election on specified issues. Whoever solicits a proxy must fully and accurately disclose in the proxy statement all of the facts that are pertinent to the matter on which the shareholders are to vote. SEC Rule 14a-9 is similar to the antifraud provisions of SEC Rule 10b-5. Remedies for violations are extensive; they range from injunctions that prevent a vote from being taken to monetary damages.

Violations of the 1934 Act

As already mentioned, violations of Section 10(b) of the Securities Exchange Act of 1934 and SEC Rule 10b-5 include insider trading. This is a criminal offense, with criminal penalties. Violators of these laws may also be subject to civil lia-

---

24. *United States v. O'Hagan,* 521 U.S. 642, 117 S.Ct. 2199, 138 L.Ed.2d 724 (1997).
25. Those stockholders owning 10 percent of the class of equity securities registered under Section 12 of the 1934 act.
26. 15 U.S.C. Section 78*l*.
27. When a decline is predicted in the market for a particular stock, a trader can realize profits by "selling short"—selling borrowed shares at the current price and repurchasing later at a lower price to cover the "short sale."

EXHIBIT 23-4   COMPARISON OF COVERAGE, APPLICATION, AND LIABILITIES
UNDER SEC RULE 10b-5 AND SECTION 16(b)

AREA OF COMPARISON	SEC RULE 10b-5	SECTION 16(b)
What is the subject matter of the transaction?	Any security (does not have to be registered).	Any security (does not have to be registered).
What transactions are covered?	Purchase or sale.	Short-swing purchase and sale or short-swing sale and purchase.
Who is subject to liability?	Virtually anyone with inside information under a duty to disclose—including officers, directors, controlling stockholders, and tippees.	Officers, directors, and certain 10 percent stockholders.
Is omission or misrepresentation necessary for liability?	Yes.	No.
Are there any exempt transactions?	No.	Yes, there are a variety of exemptions.
Is direct dealing with the party necessary?	No.	No.
Who can bring an action?	A person transacting with an insider, the SEC, or a purchaser or seller damaged by a wrongful act.	A corporation or a shareholder by derivative action.

bility. For any sanctions to be imposed, however, there must be *scienter*—the violator must have had an intent to defraud or knowledge of his or her misconduct. *Scienter* can be proved by a showing that a defendant made false statements or wrongfully failed to disclose material facts.

Violations of Section 16(b) include the sale by insiders of stock acquired less than six months before the sale. These violations are subject to civil sanctions. Liability under Section 16(b) is strict liability. *Scienter* is not required.

In the following case, investors charged a corporation with violating Section 10(b) and SEC Rule 10b-5. The question before the court was whether the investors had alleged sufficient facts to indicate *scienter*.

CASE 23.3   In re MCI Worldcom, Inc., Securities Litigation

United States District Court,
Eastern District of New York, 2000.
93 F.Supp.2d 276.

BACKGROUND AND FACTS In early 1999, MCI Worldcom, Inc., began negotiating to buy SkyTel Communications, Inc., then a leading provider of wireless messaging services. When investors heard rumors of the deal, the price of SkyTel stock rose 12 percent. On the morning of May 25, an Internet news service, the Company Sleuth, reported that MCI had registered "skytelworldcom.com" as an Internet domain name.[a] SkyTel's stock price rose 16 percent before noon. At noon, Barbara Gibson, an MCI spokesperson and senior manager of corporate communication, told the media that the name registration had been done by an employee acting alone and "was

---

a. It is common for business firms to register domain names before their actual use to protect them from cybersquatters—see Chapter 10.

(continued)

CASE 23.3—Continued

not an indication of official company intention." Immediately following Gibson's statement, SkyTel's stock price fell below the previous day's price. On May 28, MCI announced that it would buy all of SkyTel's stock for $1.3 billion. Paul Curnin and other investors who had sold the stock between May 25 and 28 filed a suit in a federal district court against MCI, alleging violations of Section 10(b) and SEC Rule 10b-5. MCI filed a motion to dismiss.

IN THE WORDS
OF THE COURT . . .

GLASSER, District Judge.

*   *   *   *

*   *   * [A] plaintiff can plead [*scienter*] in one of two ways: (1) by identifying circumstances indicating conscious or reckless behavior by the defendant, or (2) by alleging facts showing a motive to commit fraud and a clear opportunity to do so. *   *   *

*   *   *   *

To show motive, plaintiffs must show concrete benefits to a defendant that could be realized by one or more of the false statements and wrongful nondisclosures alleged. *   *   * Plaintiffs assert that MCI was motivated to artificially deflate the price of SkyTel stock in order to help ensure that the acquisition price would not have to be increased. It also did so to make the intended takeover [of SkyTel] more attractive and at a higher premium than if SkyTel's stock price had remained higher because of the merger rumors reignited by the news stories reporting on the registration of the skytelworldcom.com domain name. [Emphasis added.]

*   *   *   *

In response, defendant asserts that plaintiffs fail to allege that Gibson had any knowledge of the confidential merger negotiations, and that such knowledge cannot be assumed or conclusorily [positively] asserted. MCI argues that if Gibson is not alleged to have had any knowledge of the confidential merger negotiations, opportunity has not been sufficiently alleged. *   *   * [I]t is reasonable to assume, [however, that] the official MCI spokesperson, the Senior Manager of Corporation Communications at MCI, did know of an impending merger which was announced three days later.

*   *   *   *

*   *   * Defendant argues that its alleged motive is insufficient as a matter of law because the alleged fraud did not entail any "concrete" economic benefit to MCI and, therefore, it was not in MCI's economic interests to deflate the price of SkyTel shares.

*   *   * [B]eing able to acquire a company for a significantly reduced price is a sufficient economic benefit to satisfy the motive requirement for *scienter.*

*   *   *

*   *   *   *

Plaintiffs have also alleged facts that constitute strong circumstantial evidence of conscious misbehavior or recklessness by MCI. *   *   * [T]hree days prior to the announcement of the merger, MCI's official corporate spokesperson falsely denied any "official company intention" regarding the registration of a domain name that was an obvious combination of MCI's and SkyTel's names. The [investors] understood the denial to mean there would be no takeover, as evidenced by the drop in SkyTel's price. *   *   * [I]t was MCI itself that registered the domain name, and not, as Ms. Gibson suggested, an MCI employee acting alone.

CASE 23.3—Continued

DECISION AND REMEDY The court denied the motion to dismiss. The investors had successfully alleged *scienter* through motive and opportunity, as well as through facts from which an inference of conscious misbehavior or recklessness could be drawn.

FOR CRITICAL ANALYSIS—Technological Consideration *What effect has the Internet had on the opportunity to commit violations of the securities laws, as well as to avoid such violations?*

Criminal Penalties For violations of Section 10(b) and Rule 10b-5, an individual may be fined up to $5 million, imprisoned for up to twenty years, or both. A partnership or a corporation may be fined up to $25 million.[28]

Civil Sanctions The Insider Trading Sanctions Act of 1984 permits the SEC to bring suit in a federal district court against anyone violating or aiding in a violation of the 1934 act or SEC rules by purchasing or selling a security while in the possession of material nonpublic information.[29] The violation must occur on or through the facilities of a national securities exchange or from or through a broker or dealer. Transactions pursuant to a public offering by an issuer of securities are excepted. The court can assess as a penalty as much as triple the profit gained or the loss avoided by the guilty party. Profit or loss is defined as "the difference between the purchase or sale price of the security and the value of that security as measured by the trading price of the security at a reasonable period of time after public dissemination of the nonpublic information."[30]

The Insider Trading and Securities Fraud Enforcement Act of 1988 enlarged the class of persons subject to civil liability for insider-trading violations. This act also gave the SEC authority to award **bounty payments** (rewards given by government officials for acts beneficial to the state) to persons providing information leading to the prosecution of insider-trading violations.[31]

> **BOUNTY PAYMENT**
> A reward given to a person or persons who perform a certain service—such as informing legal authorities of illegal actions.

Private parties can also sue violators of Section 10(b) and Rule 10b-5 (as they did in Case 23.3). A private party can obtain rescission of a contract to buy securities or damages to the extent of the violator's illegal profits. Those found liable have a right to seek contribution from those who share responsibility for the violations, including accountants, attorneys, and corporations.[32] For violations of Section 16(b), a corporation can bring an action to recover the short-swing profits.

THE REGULATION OF INVESTMENT COMPANIES

Investment companies, and mutual funds in particular, grew rapidly after World War II. **Investment companies** act on behalf of many smaller shareholders/owners by buying a large portfolio of securities and managing that portfolio

> **INVESTMENT COMPANY**
> A company that acts on behalf of many smaller shareholders by buying a large portfolio of securities and professionally managing that portfolio.

---

28. These numbers reflect the increased penalties under the Sarbanes-Oxley Act of 2002. Under Section 807 of the act, for a willful violation of the 1934 act the violator may, in addition to being subject to a fine, be imprisoned for up to twenty-five years.

29. 15 U.S.C. Section 78u(d)(2)(A).

30. 15 U.S.C. Section 78u(d)(2)(C).

31. 15 U.S.C. Section 78u-1.

32. Note that a private cause of action under Section 10(b) and SEC Rule 10b-5 cannot be brought against accountants, attorneys, and others who "aid and abet" violations of the act. Only the SEC can bring actions against so-called aiders and abettors. See *SEC v. Fehn*, 97 F.3d 1276 (9th Cir. 1996).

professionally. A **mutual fund** is a specific type of investment company that continually buys or sells to investors shares of ownership in a portfolio. Such companies are regulated by the Investment Company Act of 1940,[33] which provides for SEC regulation of their activities. The 1940 act was expanded by the Investment Company Act Amendments of 1970. Further minor changes were made in the Securities Acts Amendments of 1975. The National Securities Markets Improvement Act of 1996 increased the SEC's authority to regulate investment companies by limiting virtually all of the authority of the states to regulate these enterprises.

MUTUAL FUND
A type of investment company that continually buys and sells to investors shares of ownership in a portfolio.

Definition of an Investment Company

For the purposes of the act, an *investment company* is defined as any entity that (1) "is . . . engaged primarily . . . in the business of investing, reinvesting, or trading in securities" or (2) is engaged in such business and more than 40 percent of the company's assets consist of investment securities. Excluded from coverage by the act are banks, insurance companies, savings and loan associations, finance companies, oil and gas drilling firms, charitable foundations, tax-exempt pension funds, and other special types of institutions, such as closely held corporations.

Registration and Reporting Requirements

The 1940 act requires that every investment company register with the SEC by filing a notification of registration. Each year, registered investment companies must file reports with the SEC. To safeguard company assets, all securities must be held in the custody of a bank or stock exchange member, and that bank or stock exchange member must follow strict procedures established by the SEC.

Restrictions on Investment Companies

The 1940 act also imposes restrictions on the activities of investment companies and persons connected with them. For example, investment companies are not allowed to purchase securities on the margin (pay only part of the total price, borrowing the rest), sell short (sell shares not yet owned), or participate in joint trading accounts. Additionally, no dividends may be paid from any source other than accumulated, undistributed net income.

STATE SECURITIES LAWS

BE AWARE Federal securities laws do not take priority over state securities laws.

Today, all states have their own corporate securities laws, or "blue sky laws," that regulate the offer and sale of securities within individual state borders. (The phrase *blue sky laws* dates to a 1917 decision by the United States Supreme Court in which the Court declared that the purpose of such laws was to prevent "speculative schemes which have no more basis than so many feet of 'blue sky.'")[34] Article 8 of the Uniform Commercial Code, which has been adopted by all of the states, also imposes various requirements relating to the

---

33. 15 U.S.C. Sections 80a-1 to 80a-64.
34. *Hall v. Geiger-Jones Co.,* 242 U.S. 539, 37 S.Ct. 217, 61 L.Ed. 480 (1917).

purchase and sale of securities. State securities laws apply mainly to intrastate transactions. Since the adoption of the 1933 and 1934 federal securities acts, the state and federal governments have regulated securities concurrently. Issuers must comply with both federal and state securities laws, and exemptions from federal law are not exemptions from state laws.

There are differences in philosophy among state statutes, but certain features are common to all state blue sky laws. Typically, state laws have disclosure requirements and antifraud provisions, many of which are patterned after Section 10(b) of the Securities Exchange Act of 1934 and SEC Rule 10b-5. State laws also provide for the registration or qualification of securities offered or issued for sale within the state and impose disclosure requirements. Unless an applicable exemption from registration is found, issuers must register or qualify their stock with the appropriate state official, often called a *corporations commissioner*. Additionally, most state securities laws regulate securities brokers and dealers. The Uniform Securities Act, which has been adopted in part by several states, was drafted to be acceptable to states with differing regulatory philosophies.

ONLINE SECURITIES OFFERINGS AND DISCLOSURES

The Spring Street Brewing Company, headquartered in New York, made history when it became the first company to attempt to sell securities via the Internet. Through its online *initial public offering* (IPO), which ended in early 1996, Spring Street raised about $1.6 million—without having to pay any commissions to brokers or underwriters. The offering was made pursuant to Regulation A, which, as mentioned earlier in this chapter, allows small-business issuers to use a simplified registration procedure.

Such online IPOs are particularly attractive to small companies and start-up ventures that may find it difficult to raise capital from institutional investors or through underwriters. By making the offering online under Regulation A, the company can avoid both commissions and the costly and time-consuming filings required for a traditional IPO under federal and state law.

Clearly, technological advances have affected the securities industry—and securities law—just as they have affected other areas of the law. Corporations are now using the Internet to communicate information to the SEC, shareholders, potential investors, and others. Indeed, as you will read shortly, the SEC has changed or modified a number of its rules to encourage online filings of securities documents, including prospectuses.

Investors, in turn, can now use the Internet to access information that can help them make informed decisions. The SEC's EDGAR (Electronic Data Gathering, Analysis, and Retrieval) database includes IPOs, proxy statements, annual corporate reports, registration statements, and other documents that have been filed with the commission. These and other developments have brought about what one scholar calls a "near-revolution" in the way securities are issued and traded.[35]

What if there is a discrepancy between a graph in a printed prospectus and the description of that graph in the electronic version of the prospectus filed with the SEC via the EDGAR database? Is the accompanying registration statement invalid? Those were questions in the following case.

---

35. Robert A. Prentice, "The Future of Corporate Disclosure: The Internet, Securities Fraud, and Rule 10b-5," 47 *Emory Law Journal* 1 (Winter 1998).

CASE 23.4   DeMaria v. Andersen

United States Court of Appeals,
Second Circuit, 2003.
318 F.3d 170.
http://laws.findlaw.com/2nd/017505.html[a]

BACKGROUND AND FACTS

Bankrate, Inc., produces, syndicates, and publishes financial information on the Internet. In March 1999, in anticipation of an IPO, Bankrate, which was then known as ILife.com, Inc., filed a registration statement and a prospectus with the SEC via the EDGAR database. ILife.com also distributed a printed version of the prospectus to the public. Due to an apparently inadvertent error, the EDGAR prospectus inaccurately summarized a bar graph that appeared in the printed prospectus. The graph reported online publishing revenue and losses, but the summary incorrectly identified the losses as revenue and did not mention losses. The SEC declared the statement effective for an IPO of 3.5 million shares at $13 per share. Three days later, the stock closed at $10.50 per share. By August, the stock was trading at about $0.67 per share. Brian DeMaria and other investors filed a suit in a federal district court against William Andersen, an ILife.com officer, and others, arguing that because of the inaccurate summary, the securities in the IPO were "unregistered," and thus were sold in violation of the Securities Act of 1933. The court dismissed this claim. The plaintiffs appealed to the U.S. Court of Appeals for the Second Circuit.

**IN THE WORDS
OF THE COURT . . .**

JOHN M. WALKER, JR., Chief Judge.
         *   *   *   *

Section 12 of the 1933 Act provides that "[a]ny person who *   *   * offers or sells a security in violation of [Section 5] *   *   * shall be liable *   *   * to the person purchasing such security from him." Section 5, in turn, states that "[u]nless a registration statement is in effect as to a security, it shall be unlawful" to sell or carry such security through interstate commerce *   *   *.
         *   *   *   *

We reject plaintiffs' argument because it rests on an erroneous interpretation of the regulations pertaining to SEC filings. [SEC] Rule 304[b] provides the rules and regulations for preparing EDGAR filings that include graphic, image or audio material as follows:

(a) If a filer includes graphic, image or audio material in a document delivered to investors and others that cannot be reproduced in an electronic filing, the electronically filed version of that document shall include a fair and accurate narrative description, tabular representation or transcript of the omitted material *   *   *.
(b)(1) The graphic, image and audio material in the version of a document delivered to investors and others shall be deemed part of the electronic filing and subject to the liability and anti-fraud provisions of the federal securities laws. *   *   *

*   *   * Plaintiffs contend that *   *   * subsection (b) of Rule 304 is applicable only "*if* and *when* Rule 304(a) has been satisfied."
In its *amicus* brief,[c] the SEC asserts that

[t]he "fair and accurate" requirement of Section 304(a) is not a precondition to a Printed Prospectus being "deemed part of" the EDGAR registration statement under Rule 304(b)(1). The two subsections operate independently, and nothing

---

a. This is a page within the FindLaw Web site.
b. 17 C.F.R. Section 232.304.
c. A brief (a document containing a legal argument supporting a desired outcome in a particular case) filed by a third party, or *amicus curiae* (Latin for "friend of the court"), who is not directly involved in the litigation but who has an interest in the outcome of the case.

CASE 23.4—Continued

in the rule makes compliance with Section 304(a) a predicate condition to Section 304(b)(1).

* * * [A]s the SEC explains, the purpose of Rule 304(b) is simply "to assure that the graphic material is subject to civil liability that relates to false or misleading statements in the registration statement." In light of this purpose, plaintiffs' assertion that Rule 304(b) liability is contingent upon satisfaction of Rule 304(a)'s "fair and accurate" requirement makes no sense.

We are bound by the SEC's interpretations of its regulations * * * unless they are plainly erroneous or inconsistent with the regulations. Because that deferential standard is easily met here, we adopt the SEC's position, which is dispositive of plaintiffs' * * * claim.

DECISION AND REMEDY The U.S. Court of Appeals for the Second Circuit affirmed the lower court's dismissal of the plaintiffs' claim. Under the SEC's rules, the graph in the printed prospectus was considered part of the EDGAR prospectus and registration statement. Because the printed prospectus conformed to the statement, the sale of the securities was not "unregistered."

FOR CRITICAL ANALYSIS—Social Consideration *Does deeming a printed prospectus to be part of a registration statement completely absolve those who sign the statement from any liability under the securities laws?*

Regulations Governing Online Securities Offerings

One of the early questions posed by online offerings was whether the delivery of securities *information* via the Internet met the requirements of the 1933 Securities Act, which traditionally were applied to the delivery of paper documents. In an interpretative release issued in 1995, the SEC stated that "[t]he use of electronic media should be at least an equal alternative to the use of paper-based media" and that anything that can be delivered in paper form under the current securities laws might also be delivered in electronic form.[36] For example, a prospectus in downloadable form will meet SEC requirements.

Basically, there has been no change in the substantive law of disclosure; only the delivery vehicle has changed. When the Internet is used for delivery of a prospectus, the same rules apply as for the delivery of a paper prospectus. These rules are as follows:

1. *Timely and adequate notice of the delivery of information is required.* Hosting a prospectus on a Web site does not constitute adequate notice, but separate e-mails or even postcards will satisfy the SEC's notice requirements.
2. *The online communication system must be easily accessible.* This is very simple to do today because virtually anyone interested in purchasing securities has access to the Web.
3. *Some evidence of delivery must be created.* This requirement is relatively easy to satisfy. Those making online offerings can require an e-mail return receipt verification of any materials sent electronically.

36. "Use of Electronic Media for Delivery Purposes," Securities Act Release No. 33-7233 (October 6, 1995). The rules governing the use of electronic transmissions for delivery purposes were subsequently confirmed in Securities Act Release No. 33-7289 (May 9, 1996) and expanded in Securities Act Release No. 33-7856 (April 28, 2000).

Once these three requirements have been satisfied, the prospectus has been successfully delivered.

Potential Liability Created by Online Offering Materials

All printed prospectuses indicate that only the information given in the prospectuses can be used in making an investment decision in the securities offered. The same wording, of course, appears on Web-based offerings. Those who create such Web-based offerings may be tempted, however, to go one step further. They may include hyperlinks to other sites that have analyzed the future prospects of the company, the products and services sold by the company, or the offering itself. To avoid potential liability, however, online offerors (the entities making the offerings) need to exercise caution when including such hyperlinks.

● EXAMPLE 2 Suppose that a hyperlink goes to an analyst's Web page on which the company making the offering is heavily touted. Further suppose that after the IPO, the stock price falls. By including the hyperlink on its Web site, the offering company is impliedly supporting the information presented on the linked page. In such a situation, the company may be liable under federal securities laws.[37]●

Potential problems may also occur with some Regulation D offerings, if the offeror places the offering circular on its Web site for general consumption by anybody on the Internet. Because Regulation D offerings are private placements, general solicitation is restricted. If anyone can have access to the offering circular on the Web, the Regulation D exemption may be disqualified.

Online Securities Offerings by Foreign Companies

Online securities offerings by foreign companies may also present problems. Traditionally, foreign companies have not been able to offer new shares to the U.S. public without first registering them with the SEC. Today, however, anybody in the world can offer shares of stock worldwide via the Web.

The SEC asks that foreign issuers on the Internet implement measures to warn U.S. investors. For example, a foreign company offering shares of stock on the Internet must include a disclaimer on its Web site stating that it has not gone through the registration procedure in the United States. If the SEC believes that a Web site's offering of foreign securities has been targeted at U.S. residents, it will pursue that company in an attempt to require it to register in the United States.[38]

ONLINE SECURITIES FRAUD

The Internet, of course, has also been used to commit fraud. A major problem facing the SEC today is how to enforce the antifraud provisions of the securities laws in the online environment. In 1999, in the first cases involving illegal

---

37. See, for example, *In re Syntex Corp. Securities Litigation,* 95 F.3d. 922 (9th Cir. 1996).
38. International Series Release No. 1125 (March 23, 1998).

online securities offerings, the SEC filed suit against three individuals for illegally offering securities on an Internet auction site.[39] In essence, all three indicated that their companies would go public soon and attempted to sell unregistered securities via the Web auction site. All of these actions were in violation of Sections 5, 17(a)(1), and 17(a)(3) of the 1933 Securities Act. Since then, the SEC has brought a variety of Internet-related fraud cases, including cases involving investment scams and the manipulation of stock prices in Internet chat rooms.

Investment Scams

An ongoing problem for the SEC is how to curb investment scams. One fraudulent investment scheme involved twenty thousand investors, who lost, in all, more than $3 million. Some cases have involved false claims about the earnings potential of home-business programs, such as the claim that one could "earn $4,000 or more each month." Others have concerned claims of "guaranteed credit repair."

Using Chat Rooms to Manipulate Stock Prices

"Pumping and dumping" occurs when a person who has purchased a particular stock heavily promotes ("pumps up") that stock—thereby creating a great demand for it and driving up its price—and then sells ("dumps") it. The practice of pumping up a stock and then dumping it is quite old. In the online world, however, the process can occur much more quickly and efficiently.

● **EXAMPLE 3** The most famous case in this area involved Jonathan Lebed, a fifteen-year-old stock trader and Internet user from New Jersey. Lebed was the first minor ever charged with securities fraud by the SEC, but he is unlikely to be the last. The SEC charged that Lebed bought thinly traded stocks. After purchasing a stock, he would flood stock-related chat rooms, particularly at Yahoo!'s finance boards, with messages touting the stock's virtues. He used numerous false names so that no one would know that a single person was posting the messages. He would say that the stock was the most "undervalued stock in history" and that its price would jump by 1,000 percent "very soon." When other investors would buy the stock, the price would go up quickly, and Lebed would sell out. The SEC forced the teenager to repay almost $300,000 in gains plus interest. He was allowed, however, to keep about $500,000 of the profits he made trading small-company stocks that he also touted on the Internet.●

The SEC has been bringing an increasing number of cases against those who manipulate stock prices in this way. Consider that in 1995, such fraud resulted in only six SEC cases. By 2004, the SEC had brought more than two hundred actions against online perpetrators of fraudulent stock-price manipulation. (Stock prices can also be affected by negative statements about a company and its officers. See, for example, the case discussed in this chapter's *Legal E-nvironment* feature on the following page.)

---

39. *In re Davis,* SEC Administrative File No. 3-10080 (October 20, 1999); *In re Haas,* SEC Administrative File No. 3-10081 (October 20, 1999); *In re Sitaras,* SEC Administrative File No. 3-10082 (October 20, 1999).

LEGAL *e*-NVIRONMENT

Fact versus Opinion

The SEC typically claims that fraud occurs when a false statement of fact is made. Many statements about stock, however—such as "this stock is headed for $20"—are simply opinions. Opinions can never be labeled true or false at the time they are made; otherwise, they would not be opinions. As long as a person has a "genuine belief" that such an opinion is true, then presumably no fraud is involved. Thus, a defense often raised in cases involving allegedly untrue statements made on the Internet is that the statements were simply statements of opinion, not statements of fact.

In determining whether a statement is one of fact or opinion, a court will normally consider a number of factors. By way of illustration, consider a case brought by Global Telemedia International, Inc. (GTMI), against a number of "John Does" who had posted messages in online chat rooms.

The Problem Facing GTMI

In March 2000, GTMI's stock was trading at $4.70 per share. That month, persons using various aliases began to post messages in the GTMI chat room on the Raging Bull Web site. (Raging Bull is a financial service Web site that organizes chat rooms dedicated to publicly traded companies.) The messages were critical of GTMI and its officers. Over the next six months, GTMI's stock price decreased significantly—by October, the stock was closing at $0.25 a share. GTMI and its officers sued those who had posted the messages, most of whom were listed as "John Does" in the suit. In the suit, GTMI alleged, among other things, defamation (see Chapter 8).

Distinguishing between Fact and Opinion

The court noted that defamation of a publicly traded company requires a "false statement of fact made with malice that caused damage." The defendants (those who had posted the messages)

asserted that their online statements were not actionable because they were statements of opinion, not statements of fact. Ultimately, the court agreed with the defendants. In making its decision, the court looked at the "totality of the circumstances," including the context and format of the statements, as well as the expectations of the audience in that particular situation.

Here, said the court, the context and format strongly suggested that the postings constituted opinion, not fact. "The statements were posted anonymously in . . . an Internet chat room in which about 1,000 messages a week are posted about GTMI. . . . They were part of an ongoing, freewheeling and highly animated exchange about GTMI and its turbulent history. At least several participants in addition to Defendants were repeat posters . . . ." The court went on to stress that the postings were "full of hyperbole, invective, shorthand phrases and language not generally found in fact-based documents, such as corporate press releases or SEC filings." In sum, concluded the court, the statements were not statements of fact but statements of opinion. As such, they were not defamatory.[a]

FOR CRITICAL ANALYSIS

Why didn't GTMI sue the Web site operator, Raging Bull, instead of—or in addition to—the "John Does"?

---

a. *Global Telemedia International, Inc. v. Does*, 132 F.Supp.2d 1261 (C.D.Cal. 2001).

KEY TERMS

accredited investor   728

bounty payment   739

insider trading   731

investment company   739

mutual fund   740

red herring   726

SEC Rule 10b-5   731

security   719

tippee   735

tombstone ad   726

CHAPTER SUMMARY   INVESTOR PROTECTION AND ONLINE SECURITIES OFFERINGS

The Sarbanes-Oxley Act of 2002 (See pages 720, 721.)	Attempts to increase corporate accountability by imposing stricter disclosure requirements and harsher penalties for violations of securities laws.
Securities Act of 1933 (See pages 720–730.)	Prohibits fraud and stabilizes the securities industry by requiring disclosure of all essential information relating to the issuance of stocks to the investing public. 1. *Registration requirements*—Securities, unless exempt, must be registered with the SEC before being offered to the public through the mails or any facility of interstate commerce (including securities exchanges). The *registration statement* must include detailed financial information about the issuing corporation; the intended use of the proceeds of the securities being issued; and certain disclosures, such as interests of directors or officers and pending lawsuits. 2. *Prospectus*—A *prospectus* must be provided to investors, describing the security being sold, the issuing corporation, and the risk attaching to the security. 3. *Exemptions*—The SEC has exempted certain offerings from the requirements of the Securities Act of 1933. Exemptions are determined on the basis of the size of the issue, whether the offering is private or public, and whether advertising is involved. Exemptions are summarized in Exhibit 23–2.

Securities Exchange Act of 1934 (See pages 730–739.)	Provides for the regulation and registration of securities exchanges, brokers, dealers, and national securities associations (such as the NASD). Maintains a continuous disclosure system for all corporations with securities on the securities exchanges and for those companies that have assets in excess of $5 million and five hundred or more shareholders (Section 12 companies).
	
	 1. *SEC Rule 10b-5 [under Section 10(b) of the 1934 act]*—
	
	    a. Applies to insider trading by corporate officers, directors, majority shareholders, and any persons receiving information not available to the public who base their trading on this information.
	
	    b. Liability for violation can be civil or criminal.
	
	    c. Failing to disclose material facts that must be disclosed under this rule constitutes a violation.
	
	    d. Applies in virtually all cases concerning the trading of securities—a firm does not have to have its securities registered under the 1933 act for the 1934 act to apply.
	
	    e. Liability of "outsiders" can be based on the tipper/tippee or the misappropriation theory.

(continued)

CHAPTER SUMMARY **INVESTOR PROTECTION AND ONLINE SECURITIES OFFERINGS—Continued**

Securities Exchange Act of 1934— continued	f. Applies only when the requisites of federal jurisdiction (such as use of the mails, stock exchange facilities, or any facility of interstate commerce) are present.
	2. *Insider trading [under Section 16(b) of the 1934 act]*—To prevent corporate officers and directors from taking advantage of inside information (information not available to the investing public), the 1934 act requires officers, directors, and shareholders owning 10 percent or more of the issued stock of a corporation to turn over to the corporation all short-term profits (called short-swing profits) realized from the purchase and sale or sale and purchase of corporate stock within any six-month period.
	3. *Proxies [under Section 14(a) of the 1934 act]*—The SEC regulates the content of proxy statements sent to shareholders by corporate managers of Section 12 companies who are requesting authority to vote on behalf of the shareholders in a particular election on specified issues. Section 14(a) is essentially a disclosure law, with provisions similar to the antifraud provisions of SEC Rule 10b-5.
The Regulation of Investment Companies (See pages 739–740.)	The Investment Company Act of 1940 provides for SEC regulation of investment company activities. It was altered and expanded by the amendments of 1970 and 1975.
State Securities Laws (See pages 740–741.)	All states have corporate securities laws *(blue sky laws)* that regulate the offer and sale of securities within state borders; these laws are designed to prevent "speculative schemes which have no more basis than so many feet of 'blue sky.' " States regulate securities concurrently with the federal government.
Online Securities Offerings and Disclosures (See pages 741–744.)	In 1995, the SEC announced that anything that can be delivered in paper form under current securities laws may also be delivered in electronic form. Generally, when the Internet is used for the delivery of a prospectus, the same rules apply as for the delivery of a paper prospectus. When securities offerings are made online, the offerors should be careful that any hyperlinked materials do not mislead investors. Caution should also be used in making certain Regulation D offerings for which general solicitation is restricted.
Online Securities Fraud (See pages 744–746.)	A major problem facing the SEC today is how to enforce the antifraud provisions of the securities laws in the online environment. Internet-related forms of securities fraud include the manipulation of stock prices in online chat rooms and illegal securities offerings.

FOR REVIEW

1. What is meant by the term *securities*?
2. What are the two major statutes regulating the securities industry? When was the Securities and Exchange Commission created, and what are its major purposes and functions?
3. What is insider trading? Why is it prohibited?
4. What are some of the features of state securities laws?
5. How are securities laws being applied in the online environment?

QUESTIONS AND CASE PROBLEMS

23–1. Registration Requirements. Langley Brothers, Inc., a corporation incorporated and doing business in Kansas, decides to sell no-par common stock worth $1 million to the public. The stock will be sold only within the state of Kansas. Joseph Langley, the chairman of the board, says the offering need not be registered with the Securities and Exchange Commission. His brother, Harry, disagrees. Who is right? Explain.

23–2. Registration Requirements. Huron Corp. has 300,000 common shares outstanding. The owners of these shares live in several different states. Huron decides to split the 300,000 shares two for one. Will Huron Corp. have to file a registration statement and prospectus on the 300,000 new shares to be issued as a result of the split? Explain.

23–3. SEC Rule 10b-5. In early 1985, FMC Corp. made plans to buy some of its own stock as part of a restructuring of its balance statement. Unknown to FMC management, the brokerage firm FMC employed—Goldman, Sachs & Co.—disclosed information on the stock purchase that found its way to Ivan Boesky. FMC was one of the seven major corporations in whose stock Boesky allegedly traded using inside information. Boesky made purchases of FMC's stock between February 18 and February 21, 1986, and between March 12 and April 4, 1986. Boesky's purchases amounted to a substantial portion of the total volume of FMC stock traded during these periods. The price of FMC stock increased from $71.25 on February 20, 1986, to $97.00 on April 25, 1986. As a result, FMC paid substantially more for the repurchase of its own stock than anticipated. When FMC discovered Boesky's knowledge of its recapitalization plan, FMC sued Boesky for the excess price it had paid—approximately $220 million. Discuss whether FMC should recover under Section 10(b) of the Securities Exchange Act and SEC Rule 10b-5. [*In re Ivan F. Boesky Securities Litigation*, 36 F.3d 255 (2d Cir. 1994)]

23–4. SEC Rule 10b-5. Louis Ferraro was the chairman and president of Anacomp, Inc. In June 1988, Ferraro told his good friend Michael Maio that Anacomp was negotiating a tender offer for stock in Xidex Corp. Maio passed on the information to Patricia Ladavac, a friend of both Ferraro and Maio. Maio and Ladavac immediately purchased shares in Xidex stock. On the day that the tender offer was announced—an announcement that caused the price of Xidex shares to increase—Maio and Ladavac sold their Xidex stock and made substantial profits (Maio made $211,000 from the transactions, and Ladavac gained $78,750). The Securities and Exchange Commission (SEC) brought an action against the three individuals, alleging that they had violated, among other laws, SEC Rule 10b-5. Maio and Ladavac claimed that they had done nothing illegal. They argued that they had no fiduciary duty either to Anacomp or

to Xidex and therefore had no duty to disclose any information in their possession or to abstain from trading in the stock of those corporations. Had Maio and Ladavac violated SEC Rule 10b-5? Discuss fully. [*SEC v. Maio,* 51 F.3d 623 (7th Cir. 1995)]

23–5. Definition of a Security. Life Partners, Inc. (LPI), facilitates the sale of life insurance policies owned by persons suffering from AIDS (acquired immune deficiency syndrome) to investors at a discount. The investors pay LPI, and LPI pays the policyholders. Typically, a policyholder, in turn, assigns the policy to LPI, which also obtains the right to make LPI's president the beneficiary of the policy. On the policyholder's death, LPI receives the proceeds of the policy and pays the investor. In this way, the terminally ill sellers secure much-needed income in the final years of life, when employment is unlikely and medical bills are often staggering. The Securities and Exchange Commission (SEC) sought to enjoin (prevent) LPI from engaging in further transactions on the ground that the investment contracts were securities, which LPI had failed to register with the SEC in violation of securities laws. Do the investment contracts meet the definition of a security discussed in this chapter? Discuss fully. [*SEC v. Life Partners, Inc.,* 87 F.3d 536 (D.C.Cir. 1996)]

23–6. Section 10(b). Joseph Jett worked for Kidder, Peabody & Co., a financial services firm owned by General Electric Co. (GE). Over a three-year period, Jett allegedly engaged in a scheme to generate false profits at Kidder, Peabody to increase his performance-based bonuses. When the scheme was discovered, Daniel Chill and other GE shareholders who had bought stock in the previous year filed a suit in a federal district court against GE. The shareholders alleged that GE had engaged in securities fraud in violation of Section 10(b). They claimed that GE's interest in justifying its investment in Kidder, Peabody gave GE "a motive to willfully blind itself to facts casting doubt on Kidder's purported profitability." On what basis might the court dismiss the shareholders' complaint? Discuss fully. [*Chill v. General Electric Co.,* 101 F.3d 263 (2d Cir. 1996)]

23–7. SEC Rule 10b-5. Grand Metropolitan PLC (Grand Met) planned to make a tender offer as part of an attempted takeover of the Pillsbury Co. Grand Met hired Robert Falbo, an independent contractor, to complete electrical work as part of security renovations to its offices to prevent leaks of information concerning the planned tender offer. Falbo was given a master key to access the executive offices. When an executive secretary told Falbo that a takeover was brewing, he used his key to access the offices and eavesdrop on conversations; in this way, he learned that Pillsbury was the target. Falbo bought thousands of shares of Pillsbury stock for less than $40 per share. Within two months, Grand Met made an offer for all outstanding Pillsbury stock at $60 per share and ultimately paid up to $66 per share. Falbo made over $165,000 in profit. The Securities and Exchange Commission (SEC) filed a suit in a federal district court against Falbo and others for alleged violations of, among other things, SEC Rule 10b-5. Under what theory might Falbo be liable? Do the circumstances of this case meet all of the requirements for liability under that theory? Explain. [*SEC v. Falbo*, 14 F.Supp.2d 508 (S.D.N.Y. 1998)]

23–8. Definition of a Security. In 1997, Scott and Sabrina Levine formed Friendly Power Co. (FPC) and Friendly Power Franchise Co. (FPC-Franchise). FPC obtained a license to operate as a utility company in California. FPC granted FPC-Franchise the right to pay commissions to "operators" who converted residential customers to FPC. Each operator paid for a "franchise"—a geographic area determined by such factors as the number of households and competition from other utilities. In exchange for 50 percent of FPC's net profits on sales to residential customers in its territory, each franchise was required to maintain a 5 percent market share of power customers in that territory. Franchises were sold to telemarketing firms, which solicited customers. The telemarketers sold interests in each franchise to between fifty and ninety-four "partners," each of whom invested money. FPC began supplying electricity to its customers in May 1998. Less than three months later, the Securities and Exchange Commission (SEC) filed a suit in a federal district court against the Levines and others, alleging that the "franchises" were unregistered securities offered for sale to the public in violation of the Securities Act of 1933. What is the definition of a security? Should the court rule in favor of the SEC? Why or why not? [*SEC v. Friendly Power Co., LLC*, 49 F.Supp.2d 1363 (S.D.Fla. 1999)]

and others who had bought the stock filed a suit in a federal district court against the firm's officers, alleging violations of the Securities Exchange Act of 1934. The defendants responded, in part, that any alleged misrepresentations were not material and asked the court to dismiss the suit. How should the court rule, and why? [*In re 2TheMart.com, Inc. Securities Litigation*, 114 F.Supp.2d 955 (C.D.Cal. 2000)]

To view a sample answer for this case problem, go to this book's Web site at http://leet.westbuslaw.com and click on "Interactive Study Center."

23–10. Insider Reporting and Trading. Ronald Bleakney, an officer at Natural Microsystems Corp. (NMC), a Section 12 corporation, directed NMC sales in North America, South America, and Europe. In November 1998, Bleakney sold more than 7,500 shares of NMC stock. The following March, Bleakney resigned from the firm, and the next month, he bought more than 20,000 shares of its stock. NMC provided some guidance to employees concerning the rules of insider trading, and with regard to Bleakney's transactions, the corporation said nothing about potential liability. Richard Morales, an NMC shareholder, filed a suit against NMC and Bleakney to compel recovery, under Section 16(b) of the Securities Exchange Act of 1934, of Bleakney's profits from the purchase and sale of his shares. (When Morales died, his executor Deborah Donoghue became the plaintiff.) Bleakney argued that he should not be liable because he relied on NMC's advice. Should the court order Bleakney to disgorge his profits? Explain. [*Donoghue v. Natural Microsystems Corp.*, 198 F.Supp.2d 487 (S.D.N.Y. 2002)]

A Question of Ethics & Social Responsibility

23–11. Susan Waldbaum was a niece of the president and controlling shareholder of Waldbaum, Inc. Susan's mother (the president's sister) told Susan that the company was going to be sold at a favorable price and that a tender offer was soon to be made. She told Susan not to tell anyone except her husband, Keith Loeb, about the sale. (Loeb did not work for the company and was never brought into the family's inner circle, in which family members discussed confidential business information.) The next day, Susan told her husband of the sale and cautioned him not to tell anyone because "it could possibly ruin the sale." The day after he learned of the sale, Loeb told Robert Chestman, his broker, about the sale, and Chestman purchased shares of the company for both Loeb and himself. Chestman was later convicted by a jury of, among other things, trading on misappropriated inside information in violation of SEC Rule 10b-5. [*United States v. Chestman*, 947 F.2d 551 (2d Cir. 1991)]

1. On appeal, the central question was whether Chestman had acquired the inside information about

Case Problem with Sample Answer

23–9. Violations of the 1934 Act. 2TheMart.com, Inc., was conceived in January 1999 to launch an auction Web site to compete with eBay, Inc. On January 19, 2TheMart announced that its Web site was in the "final development" stages and was expected to be active by the end of July as a "preeminent" auction site. The company also said it had "retained the services of leading Web site design and architecture consultants to design and construct" the site. Based on the announcement, investors rushed to buy 2TheMart's stock, causing a rapid increase in the price. On February 3, 2TheMart entered into an agreement with IBM to take preliminary steps to plan the site. Three weeks later, 2TheMart announced that the site was "currently in final development." On June 1, 2TheMart signed a contract with IBM to design, build, and test the site, with a target delivery date of October 8. When 2TheMart's site did not debut as announced, Mary Harrington

the tender offer as a result of an insider's breach of a fiduciary duty. Could Loeb—the "tipper" in this case—be considered an insider?

2. If Loeb was not an insider, did he owe any fiduciary (legal) duty to his wife or his wife's family to keep the information confidential? Would it be fair of the court to impose such a legal duty on Loeb?

Critical-Thinking Ethical Question

23-12. Do you think that the tipper/tippee and misappropriation theories extend liability under SEC Rule 10b-5 too far? Why or why not?

Video Question

23-13. Go to this text's Web site at http://leet.westbuslaw.com and select "Video Questions." Click on "Chapter 23" and view the video titled *Mergers and Acquisitions.* Then answer the following questions.

1. Analyze whether the purchase of Onyx Advertising is a material fact that the Quigley Company had a duty to disclose under SEC Rule 10b-5.

2. Does it matter whether Quigley personally knew about or authorized the company spokesperson's statements? Why or why not?

3. Which case discussed in the chapter presented issues that are very similar to those presented in the video? Under the holding of that case, would Onyx Advertising be able to maintain a suit against the Quigley Company for violation of SEC Rule 10b-5?

4. Who else might be able to bring a suit against the Quigley Company for insider trading under SEC Rule 10b-5?

INTERACTING WITH THE INTERNET

For updated links to resources available on the Web, as well as a variety of other materials, visit this text's Web site at

http://leet.westbuslaw.com

To access the SEC's EDGAR database, go to

http://www.sec.gov/edgar.shtml

To access a user-friendly version of the EDGAR database, go to

http://www.freeedgar.com

The Center for Corporate Law at the University of Cincinnati College of Law examines all of the acts discussed in this chapter. Go to

http://www.law.uc.edu/CCL

To find the Securities Act of 1933, go to

http://www.law.uc.edu/CCL/33Act/index.html

To examine the Securities Exchange Act of 1934, go to

http://www.law.uc.edu/CCL/34Act/index.html

For information on investor protection and securities fraud, including answers to frequently asked questions on the topic of securities fraud, go to

http://www.securitieslaw.com

ONLINE LEGAL RESEARCH EXERCISES

Go to **http://leet.westbuslaw.com**, the Web site that accompanies this text. Select "Interactive Study Center," and then click on "Chapter 23." There you will find the following Internet research exercises that you can perform to learn more about topics covered in this chapter.

Activity 23–1: TECHNOLOGICAL PERSPECTIVE—Electronic Delivery
Activity 23–2: MANAGEMENT PERSPECTIVE—The SEC's Role

BEFORE THE TEST

Go to **http://leet.westbuslaw.com**, the Web site that accompanies this text. Select "Interactive Quizzes." You will find at least twenty interactive questions relating to this chapter.

Westlaw® Campus

If your textbook provided for a subscription to Westlaw® Campus, or if you have otherwise purchased access to the Westlaw Campus database, you can access any of the cases presented or cited in this chapter by using your Westlaw Campus account.

UNIT FIVE   Cumulative Business Hypothetical

Falwell Motors, Inc., is a large corporation that manufactures automobile batteries.

1. The Federal Trade Commission (FTC) learns that one of the retail stores that sells Falwell's batteries engages in deceptive advertising practices. What actions can the FTC take against the retailer?

2. For years, Falwell has shipped the toxic waste created by its manufacturing process to a waste-disposal site in the next county. The waste site has become contaminated by leakage from toxic waste containers delivered to the site by other manufacturers. Can Falwell be held liable for clean-up costs, even though its containers were not the ones that leaked? If so, what is the extent of its liability?

3. Falwell faces stiff competition from Alchem, Inc., another battery manufacturer. To acquire control over Alchem, Falwell makes a tender offer to Alchem's shareholders. If Falwell succeeds in its attempt and Alchem is merged into Falwell, will the merger violate any antitrust laws? Suppose the merger falls through. The vice president of Falwell's battery division and the president of Alchem agree to divide up the market between them, so they will not have to compete for customers. In this agreement legal? Explain.

4. One of Falwell's employees learns that Falwell is contemplating a takeover of a rival. The employee tells her husband about the possibility. The husband calls their broker, who purchases shares in the target corporation for the employee and her husband, as well as for himself. Has the employee violated any securities law? Has her husband? Has the broker? Explain.

CHAPTER 24

The Regulation of International Transactions

CONTENTS

CHAPTER OBJECTIVES

After reading this chapter, you should be able to answer the following questions:

1. What is the principle of comity, and why do courts deciding disputes involving a foreign law or judicial decree apply this principle?

2. What is the act of state doctrine? In what circumstances is this doctrine applied?

3. Under the Foreign Sovereign Immunities Act of 1976, on what bases might a foreign state be considered subject to the jurisdiction of U.S. courts?

4. In what circumstances will U.S. antitrust laws be applied extraterritorially?

5. Do U.S. laws prohibiting employment discrimination apply in all circumstances to U.S. employees working for U.S. employers abroad?

Since ancient times, independent peoples and nations have traded their goods and wares with one another. In other words, international business transactions are not unique to the modern world—people have always found that they could benefit from exchanging goods with others, as suggested by President Woodrow Wilson's statement in the quotation alongside. What is new in our time is that, particularly since World War II, business has become increasingly global in scope. It is not uncommon, for example, for a U.S. corporation to have investments or manufacturing

> **"Our interests are those of the open door—a door of friendship and mutual advantage. This is the only door we care to enter."**
>
> Woodrow Wilson, 1856–1924
> (Twenty-eighth president of the United States, 1913–1921)

plants in a foreign country or for a foreign corporation to have operations in the United States.

Transacting business on an international level is considerably different from transacting business within the boundaries of just one nation. Buyers and sellers face far greater risks in the international marketplace than they do in a domestic context because the laws governing these transactions are more complex and uncertain. For example, the Uniform Commercial Code will govern many disputes that arise between U.S. buyers and sellers of goods unless they have provided otherwise in their contracts. What happens, however, if a U.S. buyer breaches a contract formed with a British seller? What law will govern the dispute—British or American? What if an investor owns substantial assets in a developing nation and the government of that nation decides to nationalize (take ownership of) the property? What recourse does the investor have against the actions of a foreign government? Questions such as these, which normally do not arise in a domestic context, can become critical in international business dealings.

Because the exchange of goods, services, and ideas on a global level is now a common activity, the student of business law should be familiar with the laws pertaining to international business transactions. In this chapter, we first examine the legal context of international business transactions. We then look at some selected areas relating to business activities in a global context, including international sales contracts, letters of credit, and investment protection. We conclude the chapter with a discussion of the application of certain U.S. laws in a transnational setting.

INTERNATIONAL PRINCIPLES AND DOCTRINES

In Chapter 1, we defined *international law* as a body of written and unwritten laws that are observed by otherwise independent nations and that govern the acts of individuals as well as states. We also discussed in that chapter the major sources of international law, including international customs, treaties among nations, and international organizations and conferences. Here, we look at some other legal principles and doctrines that have evolved over time and that the courts of various nations have employed—to a greater or lesser extent—to resolve or reduce conflicts that involve a foreign element. The three important legal principles and doctrines discussed in the following sections are based primarily on courtesy and respect and are applied in the interests of maintaining harmonious relations among nations.

The Principle of Comity

Under what is known as the principle of **comity**, one nation will defer and give effect to the laws and judicial decrees of another country, as long as those laws and judicial decrees are consistent with the law and public policy of the accommodating nation. This recognition is based primarily on courtesy and respect.

● EXAMPLE 1 Assume that a Swedish seller and an American buyer have formed a contract, which the buyer breaches. The seller sues the buyer in a Swedish court, which awards damages. The buyer's assets, however, are in the United States and cannot be reached unless the judgment is enforced by a U.S. court of law. In this situation, if it is determined that the procedures and laws

COMITY
The principle by which one nation defers and gives effect to the laws and judicial decrees of another nation.

applied in the Swedish court were consistent with U.S. national law and policy, a court in the United States will likely defer to (and enforce) the foreign court's judgment.●

The Act of State Doctrine

ACT OF STATE DOCTRINE
A doctrine that provides that the judicial branch of one country will not examine the validity of public acts committed by a recognized foreign government within its own territory.

The **act of state doctrine** is a judicially created doctrine that provides that the judicial branch of one country will not examine the validity of public acts committed by a recognized foreign government within its own territory. This doctrine is premised on the theory that the judicial branch should not "pass upon the validity of foreign acts when to do so would vex the harmony of our international relations with that foreign nation."[1]

The act of state doctrine can have important consequences for individuals and firms doing business with, and investing in, other countries. For example, this doctrine is frequently employed in cases involving expropriation or confiscation. **Expropriation** occurs when a government seizes a privately owned business or privately owned goods for a proper public purpose and awards just compensation. When a government seizes private property for an illegal purpose or without just compensation, the taking is referred to as a **confiscation.** The line between these two forms of taking is sometimes blurred because of differing interpretations of what is illegal and what constitutes just compensation.

EXPROPRIATION
The seizure by a government of a privately owned business or personal property for a proper public purpose and with just compensation.

CONFISCATION
A government's taking of a privately owned business or personal property without a proper public purpose or an award of just compensation.

●**EXAMPLE 2** Tim Flaherty, an American businessperson, owns a mine in Brazil. The government of Brazil seizes the mine for public use and claims that the profits that Tim has realized from the mine in preceding years constitute just compensation. Tim disagrees, but the act of state doctrine may prevent Tim's recovery in a U.S. court.●

When applicable, both the act of state doctrine and the doctrine of sovereign immunity (to be discussed next) tend to immunize foreign governments from the jurisdiction of U.S. courts. This means that firms or individuals who own property overseas often have little legal protection against government actions in the countries in which they operate.

The Doctrine of Sovereign Immunity

SOVEREIGN IMMUNITY
A doctrine that immunizes foreign nations from the jurisdiction of U.S. courts when certain conditions are satisfied.

Under certain conditions, the doctrine of **sovereign immunity** immunizes (protects) foreign nations from the jurisdiction of U.S. courts. In 1976, Congress codified this rule in the Foreign Sovereign Immunities Act (FSIA). The FSIA exclusively governs the circumstances in which an action can be brought in the United States against a foreign nation, including attempts to attach a foreign nation's property.

Section 1605 of the FSIA sets forth the major exceptions to the jurisdictional immunity of a foreign state or country. A foreign state is not immune from the jurisdiction of U.S. courts when the state has "waived its immunity either explicitly or by implication" or when the action is "based upon a commercial activity carried on in the United States by the foreign state."[2]

The question frequently arises as to whether an entity falls within the category of a foreign state. The question of what is a commercial activity has also been the subject of dispute. Under Section 1603 of the FSIA, a *foreign state* is

---

1. *Libra Bank, Ltd. v. Banco Nacional de Costa Rica, S.A.,* 570 F.Supp. 870 (S.D.N.Y. 1983).
2. 28 U.S.C. Section 1605(a)(1), (2).

defined to include both a political subdivision of a foreign state and an instrumentality (such as a government-owned business, bank, or other entity) of a foreign state. A *commercial activity* is broadly defined under Section 1603 to mean a commercial activity that is carried out by a foreign state within the United States. The act, however, does not define the particulars of what constitutes a commercial activity. Rather, it is left up to the courts to decide whether a particular activity is governmental or commercial in nature.

Is a corporation an "instrumentality" of a foreign state if the state owns less than a majority of the corporation's stock? That was the question in the following case.

CASE 24.1 Dole Food Co. v. Patrickson

Supreme Court of the United States, 2003.
__ U.S. __,
123 S.Ct. 1655,
155 L.Ed.2d 643.
**http://supct.law.cornell.edu/
supct/search/search.html**[a]

COMPANY PROFILE *Dole Food Company
(http://www.dole.com) was founded in Hawaii in
1851. Dole is the world's largest producer and seller of
fresh fruit, fresh vegetables, and fresh-cut flowers, and
markets a growing line of packaged foods. The firm
does business in more than 90 countries, employing
globally more than 33,000 full-time permanent
employees and 24,000 full-time seasonal or temporary
employees.*

BACKGROUND AND FACTS In 1997, Gerardo
Patrickson and other farm workers who toiled in banana

fields in Costa Rica, Ecuador, Guatemala, and Panama
filed a suit in a Hawaii state court against Dole Food
Company and others, seeking damages for injuries from
exposure to dibromochloropropane, a chemical used as
an agricultural pesticide. Dole impleaded[b] two Israeli
firms—Dead Sea Bromine Company and Bromine
Compounds, Limited (the Dead Sea companies)—that
allegedly made the pesticides. The Dead Sea companies
asked a federal district court to hear the suit on the
ground that they were instrumentalities of a foreign
state as defined in the FSIA. The court denied this
request, but held that it had jurisdiction on other
grounds and dismissed the suit. The workers appealed
to the U.S. Court of Appeals for the Ninth Circuit, which
reversed the dismissal but agreed that the Dead Sea
companies were not instrumentalities of a foreign state
as defined in the FSIA. The Dead Sea companies
appealed to the United States Supreme Court.

**IN THE WORDS
OF THE COURT . . .**

Justice *KENNEDY* delivered the opinion of the Court.

* * * *

The State of Israel did not have direct ownership of shares in either of the Dead Sea Companies at any time pertinent to this suit. Rather, these companies were, at various times, separated from the State of Israel by one or more intermediate corporate tiers. For example, from 1984–1985, Israel wholly owned a company called Israeli Chemicals, Ltd.; which owned a majority of shares in another company called Dead Sea Works, Ltd.; which owned a majority of shares in Dead Sea Bromine Co., Ltd.; which owned a majority of shares in Bromine Compounds, Ltd.

* * * *

* * * The Dead Sea Companies urge us to ignore corporate formalities and use the colloquial sense of that term. They ask whether, in common parlance,

---

a. In the "Search for" box, enter the name of the case. Highlight the "All decisions" icon and then click on "Search." Scroll to the name of the case and click on it to access the opinion.
b. In this context, *implead* means to bring a new party into an action on the ground that the new party is, or may be, liable to the party who brings him or her in, for all or part of the claim.

(continued)

CASE 24.1—Continued

Israel would be said to own the Dead Sea Companies. We reject this analysis. * * * It is evident from the [FSIA's] text that Congress was aware of settled principles of corporate law and legislated within that context. The language of [Section] 1603(b)(2) refers to ownership of "shares," showing that Congress intended statutory coverage to turn on formal corporate ownership. Likewise, [Section] 1603(b)(1), another component of the definition of instrumentality, refers to a "separate legal person, corporate or otherwise." In light of these *indicia* [indications] that Congress had corporate formalities in mind, we assess whether Israel owned shares in the Dead Sea Companies as a matter of corporate law, irrespective of whether [the state of] Israel could be said to have owned the Dead Sea Companies in everyday parlance.

A basic tenet of American corporate law is that the corporation and its shareholders are distinct entities. An individual shareholder, by virtue of his ownership of shares, does not own the corporation's assets and, as a result, does not own subsidiary corporations in which the corporation holds an interest. * * * The fact that the shareholder is a foreign state does not change the analysis. [Emphasis added.]

Applying these principles, it follows that Israel did not own a majority of shares in the Dead Sea Companies. The State of Israel owned a majority of shares, at various times, in companies one or more corporate tiers above the Dead Sea Companies, but at no time did Israel own a majority of shares in the Dead Sea Companies. Those companies were subsidiaries of other corporations.

DECISION AND REMEDY The United States Supreme Court affirmed the lower court's ruling that a corporation is an instrumentality of a foreign state under the FSIA only if the foreign state itself—not an entity owned by the state—directly owns a majority of the corporation's shares.

FOR CRITICAL ANALYSIS—Social Consideration *Should the Court have "pierced the corporate veil" to hold that the Dead Sea companies were instrumentalities of the state under the FSIA?*

DOING BUSINESS INTERNATIONALLY

EXPORT
To sell products to buyers located in other countries.

A U.S. domestic firm can engage in international business transactions in a number of ways. The simplest way is to seek out foreign markets for domestically produced products or services. In other words, U.S. firms can look abroad for **export** markets for their goods and services.

Alternatively, a U.S. firm can establish foreign production facilities so as to be closer to the foreign market or markets in which its products are sold. The advantages may include lower labor costs, fewer government regulations, and lower taxes and trade barriers. A domestic firm can obtain revenues by licensing its technology to an existing foreign company. Yet another way to expand abroad is by selling franchises to overseas entities. The presence of McDonald's, Burger King, and KFC franchises throughout the world attests to the popularity of franchising.

Exporting

Most U.S. companies make their initial foray into international business through exporting. Exporting can take two forms: direct exporting and indirect exporting. In *direct exporting,* a U.S. company signs a sales contract with a foreign purchaser that provides for the conditions of shipment and payment for the goods. (How payments are made in international transactions is discussed later in this chapter.) If sufficient business develops in a foreign country, a U.S. corporation may set up a specialized marketing organization that, for example, sells directly to consumers in that country. Such *indirect exporting* can be undertaken through a foreign agent or a foreign distributor.

Foreign Agent When a U.S. firm desires a limited involvement in an international market, it will typically establish an *agency relationship* with a foreign firm. In an agency relationship (discussed in Chapter 16), one person (the agent) agrees to act on behalf of another (the principal). The foreign agent is thereby empowered to enter into contracts in the agent's country on behalf of the U.S. principal.

Foreign Distributor When a substantial market exists in a foreign country, a U.S. firm may wish to appoint a distributor located in that country. The U.S. firm and the distributor enter into a **distribution agreement,** which is a contract between the seller and the distributor setting out the terms and conditions of the distributorship—for example, price, currency of payment, availability of supplies, and method of payment. The terms and conditions primarily involve contract law. Disputes concerning distribution agreements may involve jurisdictional or other issues (discussed in detail later in this chapter). In addition, some **exclusive distributorships**—in which distributors agree to distribute only the sellers' goods—have raised antitrust problems.

DISTRIBUTION AGREEMENT
A contract between a seller and a distributor of the seller's products setting out the terms and conditions of the distributorship.

EXCLUSIVE DISTRIBUTORSHIP
A distributorship in which the seller and the distributor of the seller's products agree that the distributor has the exclusive right to distribute the seller's products in a certain geographic area.

Manufacturing Abroad

An alternative to exporting is the establishment of foreign manufacturing facilities. Typically, U.S. firms establish manufacturing plants abroad if they believe that by doing so they will reduce costs—particularly for labor, shipping, and raw materials—and thereby be able to compete more effectively in foreign markets. Apple Computer, IBM, General Motors, and Ford are some of the many U.S. companies that have established manufacturing facilities abroad. Foreign firms have done the same in the United States. Sony, Nissan, and other Japanese manufacturers have established U.S. plants to avoid import duties that the U.S. Congress may impose on Japanese products entering this country.

An American firm can manufacture goods in other countries in several ways. They include licensing and franchising, as well as investing in a wholly owned subsidiary or a joint venture.

Licensing As discussed in Chapter 10, it is possible for U.S. firms to license their technologies to foreign manufacturers. **Technology licensing** may involve a process innovation that lowers the cost of production or a product innovation that generates a superior product. Technology licensing may be an attractive alternative to establishing foreign production facilities, particularly if the process or product innovation has been patented, because the patent protects—at least to some extent—against the possibility that the innovation might be pirated. Like any licensing agreement, a licensing agreement with a foreign-based firm calls for a payment of royalties on some basis—such as so many cents per unit produced or a certain percentage of profits from units sold in a particular geographic territory.

TECHNOLOGY LICENSING
Allowing another to use and profit from intellectual property (patents, copyrights, trademarks, innovative products or processes, and so on) for consideration. In the context of international business transactions, technology licensing is sometimes an attractive alternative to the establishment of foreign production facilities.

Franchising Franchising is a well-known form of licensing. Recall from Chapter 14 that a franchise is an arrangement in which the owner of a trademark, trade name, or copyright (the franchisor) licenses another (the franchisee) to use the trademark, trade name, or copyright—under certain conditions or limitations—in the selling of goods or services in exchange for a fee, usually based on a percentage of gross or net sales. Examples of international franchises include McDonald's, Coca-Cola, Holiday Inn, Avis, and Hertz.

Investing in a Wholly Owned Subsidiary or a Joint Venture Another way to expand into a foreign market is to establish a wholly owned subsidiary firm in a foreign country. A European subsidiary would likely take the form of a *société anonyme* (S.A.), which is similar to a U.S. corporation. In German-speaking nations, it would be called an *Aktiengesellschaft* (A.G.). When a wholly owned subsidiary is established, the parent company, which remains in the United States, retains complete ownership of all the facilities in the foreign country, as well as complete authority and control over all phases of the operation.

    A U.S. firm can also expand into international markets through a joint venture. In a joint venture, the U.S. company owns only part of the operation; the rest is owned either by local owners in the foreign country or by another foreign entity. In a joint venture, all of the firms involved share responsibilities, as well as profits and liabilities.

COMMERCIAL CONTRACTS IN AN INTERNATIONAL SETTING

> "Commerce is the great equalizer. We exchange ideas when we exchange fabrics."
>
> R. G. INGERSOLL, 1833–1899
> (American lawyer and orator)

NOTE The interpretation of the words in a contract can be a matter of dispute even when both parties communicate in the same language.

CHOICE-OF-LANGUAGE CLAUSE
A clause in a contract designating the official language by which the contract will be interpreted in the event of a future disagreement over the contract's terms.

Like all other commercial contracts, an international contract should be in writing. For an example of an actual international sales contract, refer back to the fold-out contract in Chapter 12.

    Language and legal differences among nations can create special problems for parties to international contracts when disputes arise. It is possible to avoid these problems by including in a contract special provisions designating the official language of the contract, the legal forum (court or place) in which disputes under the contract will be settled, and the substantive law that will be applied in settling any disputes. Parties to international contracts should also indicate in their contracts what acts or events will excuse the parties from performance under the contract and whether disputes under the contract will be arbitrated or litigated (see Chapter 3 for a discussion of arbitration clauses).

Choice of Language

A deal struck between a U.S. company and a company in another country frequently involves two languages. Typically, many phrases in one language are not readily translatable into another. Consequently, the complex contractual terms involved may not be understood by one party in the other party's language. To make sure that no disputes arise out of this language problem, an international sales contract should have a **choice-of-language clause** designating the official language by which the contract will be interpreted in the event of disagreement.

Choice of Forum

When several countries are involved, litigation may be pursued in courts in different nations. There are no universally accepted rules as to which court has jurisdiction over particular subject matter or parties to a dispute. Consequently,

INTERNATIONAL PERSPECTIVE

Language Requirements in France

In 1995, France implemented a law making the use of the French language mandatory in certain legal documents. Documents relating to securities offerings, such as prospectuses, for example, must be written in French. So must instruction manuals and warranties for goods and services offered for sale in France. Additionally, all agreements entered into with French state or local authorities, with entities controlled by state or local authorities, and with private entities carrying out a public service (such as providing electricity or other utilities) must be written in French. The law has posed problems for some businesspersons because certain legal terms and phrases in documents governed by, say, U.S. or English law have no equivalent terms and phrases in the French legal system.

FOR CRITICAL ANALYSIS

How might language differences affect the meaning of certain terms or phrases in an international contract?

parties to an international transaction should always include in the contract a **forum-selection clause** indicating what court, jurisdiction, or tribunal will decide any disputes arising under the contract. It is especially important to indicate the specific court that will have jurisdiction. The forum does not necessarily have to be within the geographic boundaries of the home nation of either party. The following case involved a question about the application of a forum-selection clause.

FORUM-SELECTION CLAUSE
A provision in a contract designating the court, jurisdiction, or tribunal that will decide any disputes arising under the contract.

CASE 24.2 Garware Polyester, Ltd. v. Intermax Trading Corp.

United States District Court,
Southern District of New York, 2001.
__ F.Supp.2d __.

BACKGROUND AND FACTS

Garware Polyester, Ltd., based in Mumbai, India, develops and makes plastics and high-tech polyester film. In 1987, Intermax Trading Corporation, based in New York, became Garware's North American sales agent. Over the next decade, the parties executed four written agreements, collectively referred to as the Agency Agreements. Each agreement provided, "The courts at Bombay [India] alone will have jurisdiction to try out suits in respect of any claim or dispute arising out of or under this agreement or in any way relating to the same." Intermax sold Garware products on a commis-

sion basis. In some transactions, Intermax arranged for customers to order products directly from Garware. In other transactions, Intermax sold Garware products through warehouse sales; Intermax bought products from Garware, warehoused them in the United States, and resold them. When Intermax fell behind in its payments, Garware filed a suit in a U.S. federal district court to collect on the unpaid invoices. Garware argued that the forum-selection clause did not apply to the invoices in dispute because they involved the warehouse sales, which, Garware claimed, were not part of, and did not relate to, the Agency Agreements.

(continued)

CASE 24.2—Continued

IN THE WORDS
OF THE COURT . . .

CHIN, D.J. [District Judge]
*   *   *   *
*   *   * [F]orum selection clauses eliminate uncertainty in international commerce and insure that the parties are not unexpectedly subjected to hostile forums and laws. Moreover, international comity dictates that American courts enforce these sorts of clauses out of respect for the integrity and respect of foreign tribunals. *The presumptive validity of forum selection clauses may only be overcome by a strong showing that the clause is unreasonable under the circumstances.* [Emphasis added.]
*   *   *   *
*   *   * A forum selection clause should not be defeated by artful pleading of claims not based on the contract containing the clause if those claims grow out of the contractual relationship, or if the gist of those claims is a breach of that relationship. *   *   *

Here, the "gist" of Garware's claim is a breach of the Agency Agreements. The warehouse sales in question were made by Intermax for the purpose of selling Garware product in the contractually defined territory. The Agency Agreements specifically relate to Intermax's role as Garware's "selling agents for promoting sales of GARFILM *   *   * in the United States of America *   *   * ." Thus, if these sales are not squarely within the scope of the Agency Agreements, they are, at the very least, related to the Agreements. Further, the parties' course of dealing supports the conclusion that the parties themselves believed the Agency Agreements included warehouse sales: as required by the Agreements, Garware paid commissions to Intermax on these sales.

DECISION AND REMEDY The court held that each of the Agency Agreements contained a valid and enforceable forum-selection clause, which applied to this suit. The court dismissed the case for improper venue.

FOR CRITICAL ANALYSIS—Social Consideration *Could the parties in this case have expressly waived the application of the forum-selection clause?*

Choice of Law

CHOICE-OF-LAW CLAUSE
A clause in a contract designating the law (such as the law of a particular state or nation) that will govern the contract.

A contractual provision designating the applicable law—such as the law of Germany or England or California—is called a **choice-of-law clause.** Every international contract typically includes a choice-of-law clause. At common law (and in European civil law systems), parties are allowed to choose the law that will govern their contractual relationship provided that the law chosen is the law of a jurisdiction that has a substantial relationship to the parties and to the international business transaction.

Under Section 1–105 of the Uniform Commercial Code, parties may choose the law that will govern the contract as long as the choice is "reasonable." Article 6 of the United Nations Convention on Contracts for the International Sale of Goods, however, imposes no limitation on the parties' choice of what law will govern the contract. The 1986 Hague Convention on the Law Applicable to Contracts for the International Sale of Goods—often referred to as the Choice-of-Law Convention—allows unlimited autonomy in the choice

INTERNATIONAL PERSPECTIVE

Arbitration versus Litigation

One of the reasons many businesspersons find it advantageous to include arbitration clauses in their international contracts is that arbitration awards are usually easier to enforce than court judgments. The United Nations Convention on the Recognition and Enforcement of Foreign Arbitral Awards, often referred to as the New York Convention, provides for the enforcement of arbitration awards in those countries (nearly one hundred, including the United States) that have signed the convention. In contrast, the enforcement of court judgments normally depends on the principle of comity and bilateral agreements providing for such enforcement. How the principle of comity is applied varies from one nation to another, and many countries have not signed bilateral agreements agreeing to enforce judgments rendered in U.S. courts. Furthermore, even a U.S. court may not enforce a foreign court's judgment if it conflicts with U.S. laws or policies. For example, a U.S. federal appellate court refused to enforce the judgment of a British court in a libel case. The court pointed out that the judgment was contrary to the public policy of the United States generally, which "favors a much broader and more protective freedom of the press than [has] ever been provided for under English law."[a]

FOR CRITICAL ANALYSIS

What might be some other advantages of arbitrating disputes involving international transactions? Are there any disadvantages?

a. *Telnikoff v. Matusevitch,* 159 F.3d 636

of law. The Hague Convention indicates that whenever a choice of law is not specified in a contract, the governing law is that of the country in which the seller's place of business is located.

Force Majeure Clause

Every contract, particularly those involving international transactions, should have a *force majeure* clause. *Force majeure* is a French term meaning "impossible or irresistible force"—sometimes loosely identified as "an act of God." In international business contracts, *force majeure* clauses commonly stipulate that in addition to acts of God, a number of other eventualities (such as governmental orders or regulations, embargoes, or shortages of materials) may excuse a party from liability for nonperformance.

FORCE MAJEURE CLAUSE
A provision in a contract stipulating that certain unforeseen events—such as war, political upheavals, acts of God, or other events—will excuse a party from liability for nonperformance of contractual obligations.

MAKING PAYMENT ON INTERNATIONAL TRANSACTIONS

Currency differences among nations and the geographic distance among parties to international sales contracts add a degree of complexity to international sales that does not exist in the domestic market. Because international contracts involve greater financial risks, special care should be taken in drafting these contracts to specify both the currency in which payment is to be made and the method of payment.

Monetary Systems

Although our national currency, the U.S. dollar, is one of the primary forms of international currency, any U.S. firm undertaking business transactions abroad must be prepared to deal with one or more other currencies. After all, just as a U.S. firm wants to be paid in U.S. dollars for goods and services sold abroad, so, too, does a Japanese firm want to be paid in Japanese yen for goods and services sold outside Japan. Both firms therefore must rely on the convertibility of currencies.

Foreign Exchange Markets Currencies are convertible when they can be freely exchanged for one another at some specified market rate in a **foreign exchange market**. Foreign exchange markets comprise a worldwide system for the buying and selling of foreign currencies. At any point in time, the foreign exchange rate is set by the forces of supply and demand in unrestricted foreign exchange markets. The foreign exchange rate is simply the price of a unit of one country's currency in terms of another country's currency. For example, if today's exchange rate is one hundred Japanese yen for one dollar, that means that anybody with one hundred yen can obtain one dollar, and vice versa.

Correspondent Banking Frequently, a U.S. company can deal directly with its domestic bank, which will take care of the international fund-transfer problem. Commercial banks sometimes have **correspondent banks** in other countries. Correspondent banking is a major means of transferring funds internationally.

● **EXAMPLE 3** Suppose that a customer of Citibank wishes to pay a bill in euros to a company in Paris. Citibank can draw a bank check payable in euros on its account in Crédit Lyonnais, a Paris correspondent bank, and then send the check to the French company to which its customer owes the funds. Alternatively, Citibank's customer can request a wire transfer of the funds to the French company. Citibank instructs Crédit Lyonnais by wire to pay the necessary amount in euros.●

The Clearinghouse Interbank Payment System (CHIPS) handles about 90 percent of both national and international interbank transfers of U.S. funds. In addition, the Society for Worldwide International Financial Telecommunications (SWIFT) is a communication system that provides banks with messages concerning transactions.

Letters of Credit

Because buyers and sellers engaged in international business transactions are frequently separated by thousands of miles, special precautions are often taken to ensure performance under the contract. Sellers want to avoid delivering goods for which they might not be paid. Buyers desire the assurance that sellers will not be paid until there is evidence that the goods have been shipped. Thus, **letters of credit** are frequently used to facilitate international business transactions.

In a simple letter-of-credit transaction, the issuer (a bank) agrees to issue a letter of credit and to ascertain whether the *beneficiary* (seller) performs certain acts. In return, the *account party* (buyer) promises to reimburse the issuer for the amount paid to the beneficiary. The transaction may also involve an *advising bank* that transmits information and a *paying bank* that expedites

FOREIGN EXCHANGE MARKET
Part of a worldwide system in which foreign currencies are bought and sold.

CORRESPONDENT BANK
A bank in which another bank has an account for the purpose of facilitating fund transfers.

LETTER OF CREDIT
A written instrument, usually issued by a bank on behalf of a customer or other person, in which the issuer promises to honor drafts or other demands for payment by third persons in accordance with the terms of the instrument.

payment under the letter of credit. Exhibit 24–1 summarizes the "life cycle" of a letter of credit.

Under a letter of credit, the issuer is bound to pay the beneficiary (seller) when the beneficiary has complied with the terms and conditions of the letter of credit. The beneficiary looks to the issuer, not to the account party (buyer), when it presents the documents required by the letter of credit. Typically, the letter of credit will require that the beneficiary deliver to the issuing bank a *bill of lading* to prove that shipment has been made. Letters of credit assure beneficiaries (sellers) of payment while at the same time assuring account parties (buyers) that payment will not be made until the beneficiaries have complied with the terms and conditions of the letter of credit.

The Value of a Letter of Credit The basic principle behind letters of credit is that payment is made against the documents presented by the beneficiary and not against the facts that the documents purport to reflect. Thus, in a letter-of-credit transaction, the issuer does not police the underlying contract; a letter of credit is independent of the underlying contract between the buyer and the seller. Eliminating the need for banks (issuers) to inquire into whether or not actual conditions have been satisfied greatly reduces the costs of letters of credit. Moreover, the use of letters of credit protects both buyers and sellers.

DON'T FORGET A letter of credit is independent of the underlying contract between the buyer and the seller.

Compliance with a Letter of Credit A letter-of-credit transaction generally involves at least three separate and distinct contracts: the contract between the account party (buyer) and the beneficiary (seller); the contract between the issuer (bank) and the account party (buyer); and, finally, the letter of credit itself, which involves the issuer (bank) and the beneficiary (seller). These contracts are separate and distinct. As already mentioned, the issuer's obligations under the letter of credit do not concern the underlying contract between the buyer and the seller. Rather, it is the issuer's duty to ascertain whether the documents presented by the beneficiary (seller) comply with the terms of the letter of credit.

EXHIBIT 24–1 THE "LIFE CYCLE" OF A LETTER OF CREDIT

Although the letter of credit appears quite complex at first, it is not difficult to understand. This cycle merely involves the exchange of documents (and money) through intermediaries. The following steps depict the letter-of-credit procurement cycle.

Step 1: The buyer and seller agree on the terms of sale. The sales contract dictates that a letter of credit is to be used to finance the transaction.

Step 2: The buyer completes an application for a letter of credit and forwards it to his or her bank, which will issue the letter of credit.

Step 3: The issuing (buyer's) bank then forwards the letter of credit to a correspondent bank in the seller's country.

Step 4: The correspondent bank relays the letter of credit to the seller.

Step 5: Having received assurance of payment, the seller makes the necessary shipping arrangements.

Step 6: The seller prepares the documents required under the letter of credit and delivers them to the correspondent bank.

Step 7: The correspondent bank examines the documents. If it finds them in order, it sends them to the issuing bank and pays the seller in accordance with the terms of the letter of credit.

Step 8: The issuing bank, having received the documents, examines them. If they are in order, the issuing bank will charge the buyer's account and send the documents on to the buyer or his or her customs broker. The issuing bank also will reimburse the correspondent bank.

Step 9: The buyer or broker receives the documents and picks up the merchandise from the shipper (carrier).

Source: National Association of Purchasing Management.

If the documents presented by the beneficiary comply with the terms of the letter of credit, the issuer (bank) must honor the letter of credit. Sometimes, however, it is difficult to determine exactly what a letter of credit demands. Moreover, the courts are divided as to whether *strict* or *substantial* compliance with the terms of a letter of credit is required. Traditionally, courts insisted on strict compliance, but in recent years, some courts have moved to a standard of *reasonable* compliance. If the issuing bank refuses to pay the seller (beneficiary) even though the seller has complied with all the requirements of the letter of credit, the seller can bring an action to enforce payment.

REGULATION OF SPECIFIC BUSINESS ACTIVITIES

Doing business abroad can affect the economies, foreign policy, domestic politics, and other national interests of the countries involved. For this reason, nations impose laws to restrict or facilitate international business. Controls may also be imposed by international agreement. We discuss here how different types of international activities are regulated.

Investing

Investing in foreign nations involves a risk that the foreign government may take possession of the investment property. Expropriation, as already mentioned, occurs when property is taken and the owner is paid just compensation for what is taken. Expropriation does not violate generally observed principles of international law. In contrast, international legal principles are violated when property is confiscated. Confiscation, as discussed earlier, occurs when property is taken and no (or inadequate) compensation is paid. Few remedies are available for confiscation of property by a foreign government. Claims are often resolved by lump-sum settlements after negotiations between the United States and the taking nation.

To counter the deterrent effect that the possibility of confiscation may have on potential investors, many countries guarantee that foreign investors will be compensated if their property is taken. A guaranty can take the form of national constitutional or statutory laws or provisions in international treaties. As further protection for foreign investments, some countries provide insurance for their citizens' investments abroad.

Export Restrictions and Incentives

The U.S. Constitution provides in Article I, Section 9, that "No Tax or Duty shall be laid on Articles exported from any State." Thus, Congress cannot impose any export taxes. Congress can, however, use a variety of other devices to control exports. Congress can set export quotas on various items, such as grain being sold abroad. Under the Export Administration Act of 1979,[3] restrictions can be imposed on the flow of technologically advanced products and technical data.

Devices to stimulate exports and thereby aid domestic businesses include export incentives and subsidies. The Revenue Act of 1971,[4] for example, gave tax benefits to firms marketing their products overseas through certain foreign

NOTE Most countries restrict exports for the same reasons: to protect national security, to further foreign policy objectives, to prevent the spread of nuclear weapons, and to preserve scarce commodities.

---

3. 50 U.S.C. Sections 2401–2420.
4. 26 U.S.C. Sections 991–994.

sales corporations; income produced by the exports was exempt from tax. Under the Export Trading Company Act of 1982,[5] U.S. banks are encouraged to invest in export trading companies, which are formed when exporting firms join together to export a line of goods. The Export-Import Bank of the United States provides financial assistance, consisting primarily of credit guaranties given to commercial banks that in turn lend funds to U.S. exporting companies.

Import Restrictions

All nations have restrictions on imports, and the United States is no exception. Restrictions include strict prohibitions, quotas, and tariffs. Under the Trading with the Enemy Act of 1917,[6] for example, no goods may be imported from nations that have been designated enemies of the United States. Other laws prohibit the importation of illegal drugs and agricultural products that pose dangers to domestic crops or animals.

Quotas and Tariffs Quotas are limits on the amounts of goods that can be imported. Tariffs are taxes on imports. A tariff is usually a percentage of the value of the import, but it can be a flat rate per unit (for example, per barrel of oil). Tariffs raise the prices of goods, which causes some consumers to purchase less expensive, domestically manufactured goods.

Dumping The United States has specific laws directed at what it sees as unfair international trade practices. **Dumping,** for example, is the sale of imported goods at "less than fair value." Fair value is usually determined by the price of those goods in the exporting country. Foreign firms that engage in dumping in the United States hope to undersell U.S. businesses to obtain a larger share of the U.S. market. To prevent this, an extra tariff—known as an *antidumping duty*—may be assessed on the imports.

Minimizing Trade Barriers Restrictions on imports are also known as *trade barriers*. The elimination of trade barriers is seen by many as essential to the world's economic well-being. Most of the world's leading trade nations are members of the World Trade Organization (WTO), which was established in 1995. To minimize trade barriers among nations, each member country of the WTO is required to grant **most-favored-nation status** to other member countries. This means each member is obligated to treat other members at least as well as it does the country that receives its most favorable treatment with regard to imports or exports. (To prevent confusion, in 1998 the status was renamed *normal trade relations* status, or NTR.)

Various regional trade agreements and associations also help to minimize trade barriers between nations. The European Union (EU), for example, attempts to minimize or remove barriers to trade among European member countries. Another important regional trade agreement is the North American Free Trade Agreement (NAFTA). NAFTA, which became effective on January 1, 1994, created a regional trading unit consisting of Mexico, the United States, and Canada. The primary goal of NAFTA is to eliminate tariffs among these three countries on substantially all goods over a period of fifteen to twenty years.

> "The notion dies hard that in some sort of way exports are patriotic but imports are immoral."
>
> LORD HARLECH
> (DAVID ORMSLEY GORE),
> 1918–1985
> (English writer)

DUMPING
The selling of goods in a foreign country at a price below the price charged for the same goods in the domestic market.

MOST-FAVORED-NATION STATUS
A status granted in an international treaty by a provision stating that the citizens of the contracting nations may enjoy the privileges accorded by either party to citizens of the most favored nations. Generally, most-favored-nation clauses are designed to establish equality of international treatment.

---

5. 15 U.S.C. Sections 4001, 4003.
6. 12 U.S.C. Section 95a.

Bribing Foreign Officials

Giving cash or in-kind benefits to foreign government officials to obtain business contracts and other favors is often considered normal practice. To combat such bribery by representatives of U.S. corporations, Congress enacted the Foreign Corrupt Practices Act in 1977.[7] This act and its implications for American businesspersons engaged in international business transactions were discussed in detail in the *Landmark in the Legal Environment* feature in Chapter 2.

U.S. LAWS IN A GLOBAL CONTEXT

The internationalization of business raises questions concerning the extraterritorial effect of a nation's laws—that is, the effect of the country's laws outside its boundaries. To what extent do U.S. domestic laws affect other nations' businesses? To what extent are U.S. enterprises affected by domestic laws when doing business abroad? Here, we discuss these questions in the context of U.S. antitrust law. We also look at the extraterritorial application of U.S. laws prohibiting employment discrimination.

U.S. Antitrust Laws

U.S. antitrust laws (discussed in Chapter 22) have a wide application. They may *subject* persons in foreign nations to their provisions, as well as *protect* foreign consumers and competitors from violations committed by U.S. citizens. Consequently, *foreign persons,* a term that by definition includes foreign governments, can sue under U.S. antitrust laws in U.S. courts.

Section 1 of the Sherman Act provides for the extraterritorial effect of the U.S. antitrust laws. The United States is a major proponent of free competition in the global economy, and thus any conspiracy that has a *substantial effect* on U.S. commerce is within the reach of the Sherman Act. The violation may even occur outside the United States, and foreign governments as well as persons can be sued for violations of U.S. antitrust laws.

Before U.S. courts will exercise jurisdiction and apply antitrust laws, it must be shown that the alleged violation had a substantial effect on U.S. commerce. U.S. jurisdiction is automatically invoked, however, when a *per se* violation occurs.[8] An example of a *per se* violation is a price-fixing contract. • EXAMPLE 4 If a domestic firm joins a foreign cartel to control the production, price, or distribution of goods, and this cartel has a *substantial restraining effect* on U.S. commerce, a *per se* violation may exist. Hence, both the domestic firm and the foreign cartel can be sued for violation of the U.S. antitrust laws. Likewise, if foreign firms doing business in the United States enter into a price-fixing or other anticompetitive agreement to control a portion of U.S. markets, a *per se* violation may exist. •

In the following case, the court considered whether a criminal prosecution under the Sherman Act could be based on price-fixing activities that took place entirely outside the United States but had a substantial effect in this country.

---

7. 15 U.S.C. Sections 78m–78ff.

8. Certain types of restrictive contracts, such as price-fixing agreements, are deemed inherently anti-competitive and thus in restraint of trade as a matter of law. When such a restrictive contract is entered into, there is said to be a *per se* violation of the antitrust laws. See Chapter 22.

CASE 24.3 United States v. Nippon Paper Industries Co.

United States Court of Appeals,
First Circuit, 1997.
109 F.3d 1.

COMPANY PROFILE *In 1993, two Japanese paper companies merged to form Nippon Paper Industries Company. Nippon makes paper and paper products, operating tree plantations and lumber mills in Australia and Chile. In thirteen other countries, Nippon engages in import and export activities in the chemicals, cosmetics, food, and pharmaceuticals industries. Paper production, however, accounts for about three-quarters of the company's sales. In the late 1980s and early 1990s, one of Nippon's predecessors sold thermal fax paper for use in fax machines and medical printing equipment. In 1990, North American thermal fax paper sales by Japanese firms accounted for $120 million, of which $6 million went to Nippon's predecessor.*

BACKGROUND AND FACTS A federal grand jury issued a criminal indictment against Nippon Paper Industries Company (NPI) and others, charging the defendants with agreeing to fix the price of thermal fax paper throughout North America. The indictment alleged that the meetings to reach the agreement had occurred entirely in Japan but that the defendants had sold the paper through subsidiaries in the United States at above-normal prices. The indictment stated that these activities had had a substantial adverse effect on commerce in the United States and had unreasonably restrained trade in violation of Section 1 of the Sherman Act. NPI filed a motion to dismiss the indictment. The court granted the motion, declaring that a criminal antitrust prosecution could not be based on wholly extraterritorial conduct. The government appealed.

IN THE WORDS OF THE COURT . . .

SELYA, Circuit Judge.

* * * *

* * * [C]ivil antitrust actions predicated on wholly foreign conduct which has an intended and substantial effect in the United States come within Section One's jurisdictional reach. * * *

* * * *

* * * [I]n both criminal and civil cases, the claim that Section One applies extraterritorially is based on the same language in the same section of the same statute * * *.

* * * It is a fundamental interpretive principle that identical words or terms used in different parts of the same act are intended to have the same meaning. * * * It follows, therefore, that if the language upon which the indictment rests were the same as the language upon which civil liability rests but appeared in a different section of the Sherman Act, or in a different part of the same section, we would * * * construe the two iterations [statements] of the language identically. Where, as here, the tie binds more tightly—that is, the text under consideration is not merely a duplicate appearing somewhere else in the statute, but is the original phrase in the original setting— * * * the case for reading the language in a [consistent] manner * * * is irresistible.

DECISION AND REMEDY The U.S. Court of Appeals for the First Circuit reversed the decision of the lower court. The criminal indictment under the Sherman Act would not be dismissed simply because the actions on which it was based occurred outside the United States.

FOR CRITICAL ANALYSIS—Economic Consideration *Why should the United States apply its antitrust laws to business firms owned by citizens or the government of another nation?*

Discrimination Laws

As explained in Chapter 17, federal laws in the United States prohibit discrimination on the basis of race, color, national origin, religion, gender, age, and disability. These laws, as they affect employment relationships, generally apply extraterritorially. Since 1984, for example, the Age Discrimination in Employment Act of 1967 has covered U.S. employees working abroad for U.S. employers. The Americans with Disabilities Act of 1990, which requires employers to accommodate the needs of workers with disabilities, also applies to U.S. nationals working abroad for U.S. firms.

For some time, it was uncertain whether the major U.S. law regulating discriminatory practices in the workplace, Title VII of the Civil Rights Act of 1964, applied extraterritorially. The Civil Rights Act of 1991 addressed this issue. The act provides that Title VII applies extraterritorially to all U.S. employees working for U.S. employers abroad. Generally, U.S. employers must abide by U.S. discrimination laws unless to do so would violate the laws of the country where their workplaces are located. This "foreign laws exception" allows employers to avoid being subjected to conflicting laws.

KEY TERMS

act of state doctrine   758

choice-of-language clause   762

choice-of-law clause   764

comity   757

confiscation   758

correspondent bank   766

distribution agreement   761

dumping   769

exclusive distributorship   761

export   760

expropriation   758

force majeure clause   765

foreign exchange market   766

forum-selection clause   763

letter of credit   766

most-favored-nation status   769

sovereign immunity   758

technology licensing   761

CHAPTER SUMMARY   THE REGULATION OF INTERNATIONAL TRANSACTIONS

International Principles and Doctrines (See pages 757–760.)	1. *The principle of comity*—Under this principle, nations give effect to the laws and judicial decrees of other nations for reasons of courtesy and international harmony. 2. *The act of state doctrine*—A doctrine under which American courts avoid passing judgment on the validity of public acts committed by a recognized foreign government within its own territory. 3. *The doctrine of sovereign immunity*—When certain conditions are satisfied, foreign nations are immune from U.S. jurisdiction under the Foreign Sovereign Immunities Act of 1976. Exceptions are made (a) when a foreign state has "waived its immunity either explicitly or by implication" or (b) when the action is "based upon a commercial activity carried on in the United States by the foreign state."
Doing Business Internationally (See pages 760–762.)	Ways in which U.S. domestic firms engage in international business transactions include (a) exporting, which may involve foreign agents or distributors, and (b) manufacturing abroad through licensing arrangements, franchising operations, wholly owned subsidiaries, or joint ventures.

CHAPTER SUMMARY THE REGULATION OF INTERNATIONAL TRANSACTIONS—Continued

Commercial Contracts in an International Setting (See pages 762–765.)	International business contracts often include choice-of-language, forum-selection, and choice-of-law clauses to reduce the uncertainties associated with interpreting the language of the agreements and dealing with legal differences. Most domestic and international contracts include *force majeure* clauses. They commonly stipulate that certain events, such as floods, fire, accidents, labor strikes, and shortages, may excuse a party from liability for nonperformance.
Making Payment on International Transactions (See pages 765–768.)	1. *Currency conversion*—Because nations have different monetary systems, payment on international contracts requires currency conversion at a rate specified in a foreign exchange market. 2. *Correspondent banking*—Correspondent banks facilitate the transfer of funds from a buyer in one country to a seller in another. 3. *Letters of credit*—Letters of credit facilitate international transactions by ensuring payment to sellers and assuring buyers that payment will not be made until the sellers have complied with the terms of the letters of credit. Typically, compliance occurs when a bill of lading is delivered to the issuing bank.
Regulation of Specific Business Activities (See pages 768–770.)	In the interests of their economies, foreign policies, domestic policies, or other national priorities, nations impose laws that restrict or facilitate international business. Such laws regulate foreign investments; exporting and importing activities; and, in the United States, the bribery of foreign officials to obtain favorable contracts. The World Trade Organization attempts to minimize trade barriers among nations, as do regional trade agreements and associations, including the European Union and the North American Free Trade Agreement.
U.S. Laws in a Global Context (See pages 770–772.)	1. *Antitrust laws*—U.S. antitrust laws may be applied beyond the borders of the United States. Any conspiracy that has a substantial effect on commerce within the United States may be subject to the Sherman Act, even if the violation occurs outside the United States. 2. *Discrimination laws*—The major U.S. laws prohibiting employment discrimination, including Title VII of the Civil Rights Act of 1964, the Age Discrimination in Employment Act of 1967, and the Americans with Disabilities Act of 1990, cover U.S. employees working abroad for U.S. firms—*unless* to apply the U.S. laws would violate the laws of the host country.

FOR REVIEW

1. What is the principle of comity, and why do courts deciding disputes involving a foreign law or judicial decree apply this principle?
2. What is the act of state doctrine? In what circumstances is this doctrine applied?
3. Under the Foreign Sovereign Immunities Act of 1976, on what bases might a foreign state be considered subject to the jurisdiction of U.S. courts?
4. In what circumstances will U.S. antitrust laws be applied extraterritorially?
5. Do U.S. laws prohibiting employment discrimination apply in all circumstances to U.S. employees working for U.S. employers abroad?

QUESTIONS AND CASE PROBLEMS

24–1. Letters of Credit. James Reynolds entered into an agreement to purchase dental supplies from Tooth-Tech, Inc. Reynolds also secured a letter of credit from Central Bank to pay for the supplies. Tooth-Tech placed sixty crates of dental supplies onboard a freighter and received in return the invoices required under the letter of credit. The purchaser, Reynolds, subsequently learned that Tooth-Tech, Inc., had filled the sixty crates with rubbish, not dental supplies. Given that an issuer's obligation under a letter of credit is independent of the underlying contract between the buyer and the seller, would the issuer be required to pay the seller in this situation? Explain.

24–2. Letters of Credit. The Swiss Credit Bank issued a letter of credit in favor of Antex Industries to cover the sale of 92,000 electronic integrated circuits manufactured by Electronic Arrays. The letter of credit specified that the chips would be transported to Tokyo by ship. Antex shipped the circuits by air. Payment on the letter of credit was dishonored because the shipment by air did not fulfill the precise terms of the letter of credit. Should a court compel payment? Explain. [*Board of Trade of San Francisco v. Swiss Credit Bank,* 728 F.2d 1241 (9th Cir. 1984)]

24–3. Antitrust Claims. Billy Lamb and Carmon Willis (the plaintiffs) were tobacco growers in Kentucky. Phillip Morris, Inc., and B.A.T. Industries, PLC, routinely purchased tobacco not only from Kentucky growers but also from producers in several foreign countries. In 1982, subsidiaries of Phillip Morris and B.A.T. (the defendants) entered into an agreement with La Fundacion Del Niño (the Children's Foundation) of Caracas, Venezuela, headed by the wife of the president of Venezuela. The agreement provided that the two subsidiaries would donate a total of approximately $12.5 million to the Children's Foundation, and in exchange, the subsidiaries would obtain price controls on Venezuelan tobacco, elimination of controls on retail cigarette prices in Venezuela, tax deductions for the donations, and assurances that existing tax rates applicable to tobacco companies would not be increased. The plaintiffs brought an action, alleging that the Venezuelan arrangement was an inducement designed to restrain trade in violation of U.S. antitrust laws. Such an arrangement, the plaintiffs contended, would result in the artificial depression of tobacco prices to the detriment of domestic tobacco growers, while ensuring lucrative retail prices for tobacco products sold abroad. The trial court held that the plaintiffs' claim was barred by the act of state doctrine. What will result on appeal? Discuss. [*Lamb v. Phillip Morris, Inc.,* 915 F.2d 1024 (6th Cir. 1990)]

24–4. Forum-Selection Clauses. Royal Bed and Spring Co., a Puerto Rican distributor of furniture products, entered into an exclusive distributorship agreement with Famossul Industria e Comercio de Moveis Ltda., a Brazilian manufacturer of furniture products. Under the terms of the contract, Royal Bed was to distribute in Puerto Rico the furniture products manufactured by Famossul in Brazil. The contract contained choice-of-forum and choice-of-law clauses, which designated the judicial district of Curitiba, State of Paraná, Brazil, as the judicial forum and the Brazilian Civil Code as the law to be applied in the event of any dispute. Famossul terminated the exclusive distributorship and suspended the shipment of goods without just cause. Under Puerto Rican law, forum-selection clauses providing for foreign venues are not enforced as a matter of public policy. In what jurisdiction should Royal Bed bring suit? Discuss fully. [*Royal Bed and Spring Co. v. Famossul Industria e Comercio de Moveis Ltda.,* 906 F.2d 45 (5th Cir. 1990)]

24–5. Discrimination Claims. Radio Free Europe and Radio Liberty (RFE/RL), a U.S. corporation doing business in Germany, employs more than three hundred U.S. citizens at its principal place of business in Munich, Germany. The concept of mandatory retirement is deeply embedded in German labor policy, and a contract formed in 1982 between RFE/RL and a German labor union contained a clause that required workers to be retired when they reached the age of sixty-five. When William Mahoney and other American employees (the plaintiffs) reached the age of sixty-five, RFE/RL terminated their employment as required under its contract with the labor union. The plaintiffs sued RFE/RL for discriminating against them on the basis of age, in violation of the Age Discrimination in Employment Act of 1967. Will the plaintiffs succeed in their suit? Discuss fully. [*Mahoney v. RFE/RL, Inc.,* 47 F.3d 447 (D.C. Cir. 1995)]

24–6. Sovereign Immunity. Reed International Trading Corp., a New York corporation, agreed to sell down jackets to Alink, a Russian business. Alink referred Reed to the Bank for Foreign and Economic Affairs of the Russian Federation for payment and gave Reed a letter of credit payable in New York. When Reed tried to collect, the bank refused to pay. Reed (and others) filed a suit in a federal district court against the bank (and others). The bank qualified as a "sovereign" under the Foreign Sovereign Immunities Act and thus claimed in part that it was immune from suit in U.S. courts. On what basis might the court hold that the bank was not immune? Explain. [*Reed International Trading Corp. v. Donau Bank, A.G.,* 866 F.Supp. 750 (S.D.N.Y. 1994)]

24–7. Sovereign Immunity. Nuovo Pignone, Inc., is an Italian company that designs and manufactures turbine systems. Nuovo sold a turbine system to Cabinda Gulf Oil Co. (CABGOC). The system was manufactured, tested, and inspected in Italy, then sent to Louisiana for mounting on a platform by CABGOC's contractor. Nuovo sent a representative to consult on the mounting. The platform went to a CABGOC site off the coast of West Africa. Marcus Pere, an instrument technician at the site, was killed when a turbine within the system exploded. Pere's widow filed a suit in a U.S. federal district court against Nuovo and others. Nuovo claimed sovereign immunity on the ground that its majority shareholder at the time of the explosion was Ente Nazionale Idrocaburi, which was created by the government of Italy to lead its oil and gas exploration and development. Is Nuovo exempt from suit under the doctrine of sovereign immunity? Is it subject to suit under the "commercial activity" exception? Why or why not? [*Pere v. Nuovo Pignone, Inc.,* 150 F.3d 477 (5th Cir. 1998)]

24–8. Dumping. In response to a petition filed on behalf of the U.S. pineapple industry, the U.S. Commerce Department initiated an investigation of canned pineapple imported from Thailand. The investigation concerned Thai producers of the canned fruit, including the Thai Pineapple Public Co. The Thai producers also turned out products, such as pineapple juice and juice concentrate, outside the scope of the investigation. These products use separate parts of the same fresh pineapple, so they share raw material costs. To determine fair value and antidumping duties, the Commerce Department had to calculate the Thai producers' cost of production and, in so doing, had to allocate a portion of the shared fruit costs to the canned fruit. These allocations were based on the producers' own financial records, which were consistent with Thai generally accepted accounting principles. The result was a determination that more than 90 percent of the canned fruit sales were below the cost of production. The producers filed a suit in the U.S. Court of International Trade against the federal government, challenging this allocation. The producers argued that their records did not reflect actual production costs, which instead should be based on the weight of fresh fruit used to make the products. Did the Commerce Department act reasonably in determining the cost of production? Why or why not? [*The Thai Pineapple Public Co. v. United States,* 187 F.3d 1362 (Fed.Cir. 1999)]

Case Problem with Sample Answer

24–9. Sovereign Immunity. Tonoga, Ltd., doing business as Taconic Plastics, Ltd., is a manufacturer incorporated in Ireland with its principal place of business in New York. In 1997, Taconic entered into a contract with a German construction company to supply special material for a tent project designed to shelter religious pilgrims visiting holy sites in Saudi Arabia. Most of the material was made in, and shipped from, New York. The company did not pay Taconic and eventually filed for bankruptcy. Another German firm, Werner Voss Architects and Engineers, acting as an agent for the government of Saudi Arabia, guaranteed the payments due Taconic to induce it to complete the project. When Taconic received all but the final payment, the firm filed a

suit in a federal district court against the government of Saudi Arabia, claiming a breach of the guaranty and seeking to collect, in part, about $3 million. The defendant filed a motion to dismiss based, in part, on the doctrine of sovereign immunity. Under what circumstances does this doctrine apply? What are its exceptions? Should this suit be dismissed under the "commercial activity" exception? Explain. [*Tonoga, Ltd. v. Ministry of Public Works and Housing of Kingdom of Saudi Arabia,* 135 F.Supp.2d 350 (N.D.N.Y. 2001)]

To view a sample answer for this case problem, go to this book's Web site at http://leet.westbuslaw.com and click on "Interactive Study Center."

24–10. Import Control. In 1996, the International Trade Administration (ITA) of the U.S. Department of Commerce assessed antidumping duties against Koyo Seiko Co., NTN Corp., and other companies, on certain tapered roller bearings and their components imported from Japan. In assessing these duties, the ITA requested information from the makers about their home market sales. NTN responded in part that its figures should not include many sample and small-quantity sales, which were made to enable customers to decide whether to buy the products. NTN provided no evidence to support this assertion, however. In calculating the fair market value of the bearings in Japan, the ITA determined, among other things, that sample and small-quantity sales were within the makers' ordinary course of trade. Koyo and others appealed these assessments to the U.S. Court of International Trade. NTN objected in part to the ITA's inclusion of sample and small-quantity sales. On what basis should the ITA make such determinations? Should the court order the ITA to recalculate its assessment on the basis of NTN's objection? Explain. [*Koyo Seiko Co. v. United States,* 186 F.Supp.2d 1332 (CIT [Court of International Trade] 2002)]

A Question of Ethics & Social Responsibility

24–11. Ronald Riley, an American citizen, and Council of Lloyd's, a British insurance corporation with its principal place of business in London, entered into an agreement in 1980 that allowed Riley to underwrite insurance through Lloyd's. The agreement provided that if any dispute arose between Lloyd's and Riley, the courts of England would have exclusive jurisdiction, and the laws of England would apply. Over the next decade, some of the parties insured under policies that Riley underwrote experienced large losses, for which they filed claims. Instead of paying his share of the claims, Riley filed a lawsuit in a U.S. district court against Lloyd's and its managers and directors (all British citizens or entities), seeking, among other things, rescission of the 1980 agreement. Riley alleged that the defendants had violated the Securities Act of 1933, the Securities Exchange Act of 1934, and Rule 10b-5. The defendants asked the court to enforce the forum-selection clause in the agreement. Riley argued that if the clause was enforced, he would be deprived of his rights under the U.S. securities laws. The court held that the parties were to resolve their dispute in England. [*Riley v. Kingsley Underwriting Agencies, Ltd.,* 969 F.2d 953 (10th Cir. 1992)]

1. Did the court's decision fairly balance the rights of the parties? How would you argue in support of the court's decision in this case? How would you argue against it?
2. Should the fact that an international transaction may be subject to laws and remedies different from or less favorable than those of the United States be a valid basis for denying enforcement of forum-selection and choice-of-law clauses?
3. All parties to this litigation other than Riley were British. Should this fact be considered by the court in deciding this case?

Case Briefing Assignment

24–12. Examine Case A.6 [*Trans-Orient Marine Corp. v. Star Trading & Marine, Inc.,* 731 F.Supp. 619 (S.D.N.Y. 1990)] in Appendix A. The case has been excerpted there in great detail. Review and then brief the case, making sure that you include answers to the following questions in your brief.

1. What specific circumstances led to this lawsuit?
2. What was the central international legal issue addressed by the court?
3. How did the court distinguish a "succession of state" from a "succession of government," and what was the effect of the distinction on executory contracts of the state?

4. What "seminal decision" on this issue was referred to by the court? On what other cases did the court rely in its reasoning?

Critical-Thinking Legal Question

24–13. Business cartels and monopolies that are legal in some countries may engage in practices that violate U.S. antitrust laws. In view of this fact, what are some of the implications of applying U.S. antitrust laws extraterritorially?

Video Question

24–14. Go to this text's Web site at **http://leet.westbuslaw.com** and select "Video Questions." Click on "Chapter 24" and view the video titled *International: Letter of Credit.* Then answer the following questions.

1. Do banks always require the same documents to be presented in letter-of-credit transactions? If not, who dictates what documents will be required in the letter of credit?
2. At what point does the seller receive payment in a letter-of-credit transaction?
3. What assurances does a letter of credit provide to the buyer and to the seller involved in the transaction?

INTERACTING WITH THE INTERNET

For updated links to resources available on the Web, as well as a variety of other materials, visit this text's Web site at

http://leet.westbuslaw.com

FindLaw, which is now a part of West Group, includes an extensive array of links to international doctrines and treaties, as well as to the laws of other nations, on its Web site. Go to

http://www.findlaw.com

and click on "Foreign and International Law."

To learn more about what is involved in exporting goods to other countries, go to the state of New Mexico's Web page on "How to Export" at

http://www.edd.state.nm.us/TRADE/HOWTO/howto.htm

For information on the legal requirements of doing business in other nations, a good source is the Internet Law Library's collection of laws of other nations. You can access this source at

http://www.lawguru.com/ilawlib/index.html

ONLINE LEGAL RESEARCH EXERCISES

Go to **http://leet.westbuslaw.com**, the Web site that accompanies this text. Select "Interactive Study Center," and then click on "Chapter 24." There you will find the following Internet research exercises that you can perform to learn more about topics covered in this chapter.

Activity 24–1: INTERNATIONAL PERSPECTIVE—The World Trade Organization
Activity 24–2: MANAGEMENT PERSPECTIVE—Overseas Business Opportunities

BEFORE THE TEST

Go to **http://leet.westbuslaw.com**, the Web site that accompanies this text. Select "Interactive Quizzes." You will find at least twenty interactive questions relating to this chapter.

Westlaw® Campus

If your textbook provided for a subscription to Westlaw® Campus, or if you have otherwise purchased access to the Westlaw Campus database, you can access any of the cases presented or cited in this chapter by using your Westlaw Campus account.

UNIT SIX   Cumulative Business Hypothetical

Macrotech, Inc., makes an innovative computer chip on which the firm obtains a patent and markets under the trademarked brand name "Flash."

1. Macrotech wants to sell the Flash chip to Nitron, Ltd., in Pacifica, a foreign country. Macrotech is concerned, however, that after an initial purchase, Nitron will duplicate the chip, pirate it, and sell the pirated version to computer manufacturers in Pacifica. To avoid this situation, Macrotech could establish its own manufacturing facility in Pacifica, but it does not want to do this. How can Macrotech, without establishing a manufacturing facility in Pacifica, protect against Flash being pirated by Nitron?

2. A representative of Pixel, S.A., in Raretania, a foreign country, contacts Macrotech, says that Pixel may be interested in buying a quantity of the Flash chips, and asks for a demonstration and a list of prices. Before Pixel makes a buy, Macrotech learns that there is a proposal in Congress to tax certain exports, including products such as Flash. Macrotech also learns of a proposal to impose restrictions on the export of Flash and similar products. Which of these proposals is most likely to be implemented, and why? If Congress wanted to stimulate, rather than restrict, the export of Flash, what steps might it take to do so?

3. Quaro Corp. and Selecta Corp., which are manufacturers in Techuan, a foreign country, make products that compete with the Flash chip. When Quaro and Selecta products seem to flood the U.S. market at low prices, Macrotech believes that its competitors have conspired to fix their prices. Can Macrotech file a suit against Quaro and Selecta in a U.S. court? If Quaro thought Macrotech was conspiring with other firms against it, could Quaro file a suit against Macrotech in a U.S. court? What could the U.S. government do if it found that Quaro and Selecta were selling their products in U.S. markets at "less than fair value"?

Briefing Cases and Analyzing Case Problems

HOW TO BRIEF A CASE

To fully understand the law with respect to business, you need to be able to read and understand court decisions. To make this task easier, you can use a method of case analysis that is called *briefing*. There is a fairly standard procedure that you can follow when you "brief" any court case. You must first read the case opinion carefully. When you feel you understand the case, you can prepare a brief of it.

Format of the Brief

Although the format of the brief may vary, typically it will present the essentials of the case under headings such as those listed below.

1. **Citation.** Give the full citation for the case, including the name of the case, the date it was decided, and the court that decided it.

2. **Facts.** Briefly indicate (a) the reasons for the lawsuit; (b) the identity and arguments of the plaintiff(s) and defendant(s), respectively; and (c) the lower court's decision—if appropriate.

3. **Issue.** Concisely phrase, in the form of a question, the essential issue before the court. (If more than one issue is involved, you may have two—or even more—questions here.)

4. **Decision.** Indicate here—with a "yes" or "no," if possible—the court's answer to the question (or questions) in the *Issue* section above.

5. **Reason.** Summarize as briefly as possible the reasons given by the court for its decision (or decisions) and the case or statutory law relied on by the court in arriving at its decision.

Briefed Sample Court Case

When you prepare your brief, be sure that you include all of the important facts. As a guide to how to brief a case, we include here a briefed version of the sample court case that was presented in the appendix to Chapter 1 in Exhibit 1A–3.

WILLIAMS v. DOMINION TECHNOLOGY PARTNERS, L.L.C.
Virginia Supreme Court, 2003.
576 S.E.2d 752.

FACTS Dominion Technology Partners, L.L.C., is an employment firm. When Stihl, Inc., a power-tool manufacturing firm, sought a computer consultant to oversee the installation of a new software package on computer systems at Stihl's facilities in Virginia, Dominion recruited Donald Williams as a candidate. Dominion offered Williams an at-will employment contract, which he accepted. In January 1999, Stihl contracted with Dominion to employ Williams for three months. After the installation was complete, Stihl retained Williams in a support and maintenance role for an indefinite period on a monthly basis. More than a year later, Williams indicated that he would prefer to work under a direct agreement with Stihl. In March 2000, Williams resigned as Dominion's employee. In May, Dominion learned that Williams had continued working at Stihl. Dominion filed a suit in a Virginia state court against Williams, alleging breach of fiduciary duty, among other things. The court entered a judgment in Dominion's favor. Williams appealed to the Virginia Supreme Court.

ISSUE Did Williams breach a duty of loyalty to Dominion?

DECISION No. The Virginia Supreme Court reversed the judgment of the lower court and entered a judgment in Williams's favor. The state supreme court held that "an employee has the right to make arrangements during his employment to compete with his employer after resigning his post" unless there is a contract stating otherwise.

REASON The court recognized that an employee "owes a fiduciary duty of loyalty to his employer during his employment. Subsumed within this general duty of loyalty is the more specific duty that the employee not compete with his employer during his employment." The court explained, however, "[T]hat particular conduct of an employee caused harm to his employer does not establish that the conduct breached any duty to the employer. This is so because the law will not provide relief to every disgruntled player in the rough-and-tumble world comprising the competitive marketplace." Without a contract limiting Williams's actions, "it cannot be said that Williams's conduct to safeguard his own interests was either disloyal or unfair to Dominion. * * * [B]y providing reasonable notice of his intent to resign his post * * * , Williams allowed Dominion to receive all the benefits for which it had bargained."

Review of Briefed Sample Court Case

Here we provide a review of the briefed version to indicate the kind of information that is contained in each section.

Citation The name of the case is *Williams v. Dominion Technology Partners, L.L.C.* Williams is the petitioner; Dominion is the respondent. The Virginia Supreme Court decided this case in 2003. The citation states that this case can be found in volume 576 of the *South Eastern Reporter, Second Series,* on page 752.

Facts The *Facts* section identifies the petitioner and the respondent, describes the events leading up to this suit, the alle-

gations made by the respondent in the initial suit, and (because this case is an appellate court decision) the lower court's rulings and the party appealing those rulings. The appellant's contention on appeal is also sometimes included here.

Issue The *Issue* section presents the central issue (or issues) decided by the Court. In this case, the Virginia Supreme Court reviews the lower court's conclusion that an employee breached a duty of loyalty to an employer. The relevant law includes principles of contract and employment law.

Decision The *Decision* section includes the court's decision on the issue before it. The decision reflects the opinion of the majority of the judges or justices hearing the case. Decisions by appellate courts are frequently phrased in reference to the lower court's decision; that is, the appellate court may "affirm" the lower court's ruling or "reverse" it. Here, the state supreme court determined that in the absence of a contract to the contrary, an employee can arrange during employment to compete with his or her employer after resigning. The court reversed the lower court's judgment on this point and entered a judgment in the petitioner's favor.

Reason The *Reason* section includes references to the relevant laws and legal principles that were applied in coming to a conclusion in the case before the court. The relevant law here consisted of contract and employment law principles relating to an employee's duty of loyalty to an employer. This section also explains the court's application of the law to the facts in the case.

HOW TO ANALYZE CASE PROBLEMS

In addition to learning how to brief cases, students of business law also find it helpful to know how to analyze case problems. Part of the study of business law usually involves analyzing case problems, such as those included in this text at the end of each chapter.

For each case problem in this book, we provide the relevant background and facts of the lawsuit and the issue before the court. When you are assigned one of these problems, your job will be to determine how the court should decide the issue, and why. In other words, you will need to engage in legal analysis and reasoning. Here we offer some suggestions on how to make this task less daunting. We begin by presenting a sample problem:

> While Janet Lawson, a famous pianist, was shopping in Quality Market, she slipped and fell on a wet floor in one of the aisles. The floor had recently been mopped by one of the store's employees, but there were no signs warning customers that the floor in that area was wet. As a result of the fall, Lawson injured her right arm and was unable to perform piano concerts for the next six months. Had she been able to

perform the scheduled concerts, she would have earned approximately $60,000 over that period of time. Lawson sued Quality Market for this amount, plus another $10,000 in medical expenses. She claimed that the store's failure to warn customers of the wet floor constituted negligence and therefore the market was liable for her injuries. Will the court agree with Lawson? Discuss.

Understand the Facts

This may sound obvious, but before you can analyze or apply the relevant law to a specific set of facts, you must clearly understand those facts. In other words, you should read through the case problem carefully and more than once, if necessary, to make sure you understand the identity of the plaintiff(s) and defendant(s) in the case and the progression of events that led to the lawsuit.

In the sample case just given, the identity of the parties is fairly obvious. Janet Lawson is the one bringing the suit; therefore, she is the plaintiff. Quality Market, against whom she is bringing the suit, is the defendant. Some of the case problems you work on may have multiple plaintiffs or defendants. Often, it is helpful to use abbreviations for the parties. To indicate a reference to a plaintiff, for example, the *pi* symbol—π—is often used, and a defendant is denoted by a *delta*—Δ—a triangle.

The events leading to the lawsuit are also fairly straightforward. Lawson slipped and fell on a wet floor, and she contends that Quality Market should be liable for her injuries because it was negligent in not posting a sign warning customers of the wet floor.

When you are working on case problems, realize that the facts should be accepted as they are given. For example, in our sample problem, it should be accepted that the floor was wet and that there was no sign. In other words, avoid making conjectures, such as "Maybe the floor wasn't too wet," or "Maybe an employee was getting a sign to put up," or "Maybe someone stole the sign." Questioning the facts as they are presented only adds confusion to your analysis.

Legal Analysis and Reasoning

Once you understand the facts given in the case problem, you can begin to analyze the case. The IRAC method is a helpful tool to use in the legal analysis and reasoning process. IRAC is an acronym for Issue, Rule, Application, Conclusion. Applying this method to our sample problem would involve the following steps:

1. First, you need to decide what legal **issue** is involved in the case. In our sample case, the basic issue is whether Quality Market's failure to warn customers of the wet floor constituted negligence. As discussed in Chapter 8, negligence is a *tort*—a civil wrong. In a tort lawsuit, the plaintiff seeks to be compensated for another's wrongful act. A defendant will be deemed negligent if he or she breached a duty of care owed to the plaintiff and the breach of that duty caused the plaintiff to suffer harm.

2. Once you have identified the issue, the next step is to determine what **rule of law** applies to the issue. To make this determination, you will want to review carefully the text of the chapter in which the problem appears to find the relevant rule of law. Our sample case involves the tort of negligence, covered in Chapter 8. The applicable rule

of law is the tort law principle that business owners owe a duty to exercise reasonable care to protect their customers ("business invitees"). Reasonable care, in this context, includes either removing—or warning customers of—*foreseeable* risks about which the owner *knew* or *should have known*. Business owners need not warn customers of "open and obvious" risks, however. If a business owner breaches this duty of care (fails to exercise the appropriate degree of care toward customers), and the breach of duty causes a customer to be injured, the business owner will be liable to the customer for the customer's injuries.

3. The next—and usually the most difficult—step in analyzing case problems is the **application** of the relevant rule of law to the specific facts of the case you are studying. In our sample problem, applying the tort law principle just discussed presents few difficulties. An employee of the store had mopped the floor in the aisle where Lawson slipped and fell, but no sign was present indicating that the floor was wet. That a customer might fall on a wet floor is clearly a foreseeable risk. Therefore, the failure to warn customers about the wet floor was a breach of the duty of care owed by the business owner to the store's customers.

4. Once you have completed step 3 in the IRAC method, you should be ready to draw your **conclusion.** In our sample case, Quality Market is liable to Lawson for her injuries, because the market's breach of its duty of care caused Lawson's injuries.

The fact patterns in the case problems presented in this text are not always as simple as those presented in our sample problem. Often, for example, there may be more than one plaintiff or defendant. There also may be more than one issue involved in a case and more than one applicable rule of law. Furthermore, in some case problems the facts may indicate that the general rule of law should not apply. For example, suppose a store employee advised Lawson not to walk on the floor in the aisle because it was wet, but Lawson decided to walk on it anyway. This fact could alter the outcome of the case because the store could then raise the defense of assumption of risk (see Chapter 8). Nonetheless, a careful review of the chapter should always provide you with the knowledge you need to analyze the problem thoroughly and arrive at accurate conclusions.

SELECTED CASES FOR BRIEFING

In the remaining pages of this appendix, we present excerpts from the court opinions referred to in *Case Briefing Assignments.* Court opinions can run from a few pages to hundreds of pages in length. For reasons of space, only the essen-

tial parts of the opinions are presented in the cases that follow. A series of three asterisks indicates that a portion of the text—other than citations and footnotes—has been omitted. Four asterisks indicate the omission of at least one paragraph.

CASE A.1

Reference: Problem 3–11

RODRIGUEZ DE QUIJAS v.
SHEARSON/AMERICAN EXPRESS, INC.
United States Supreme Court, 1989.
490 U.S. 477,
109 S.Ct. 1917,
104 L.Ed.2d 526.

KENNEDY, Justice.

The question here is whether a predispute agreement to arbitrate claims under the Securities Act of 1933 is unenforceable, requiring resolution of the claims only in a judicial forum.

I

Petitioners are individuals who invested about $400,000 in securities. They signed a standard customer agreement with the broker, which included a clause stating that the parties agreed to settle any controversies "relating to [the] accounts" through binding arbitration that complies with specified procedures. The agreement to arbitrate these controversies is unqualified, unless it is found to be unenforceable under federal or state law. * * * The investments turned sour, and petitioners eventually sued respondent and its broker-agent in charge of the accounts, alleging that their money was lost in unauthorized and fraudulent transactions. In their complaint they pleaded various violations of federal and state law, including claims under § [Section] 12(2) of the Securities Act of 1933, * * * and claims under three sections of the Securities Exchange Act of 1934.

The District Court ordered all the claims to be submitted to arbitration except for those raised under § 12(2) of the Securities Act. It held that the latter claims must proceed in the court action under our clear holding on the point in *Wilko v. Swan,* 346 U.S. 427, 74 S.Ct. 182, 98 L.Ed. 168 (1953). The District Court reaffirmed its ruling upon reconsideration, and also entered a default judgment against the broker, who is no longer in the case. The Court of Appeals reversed, concluding that the arbitration agreement is enforceable because this Court's subsequent decisions have reduced *Wilko* to "obsolescence." * * *

II

The *Wilko* case, decided in 1953, required the Court to determine whether an agreement to arbitrate future controversies constitutes a binding stipulation "to waive compliance with any provision" of the Securities Act, which is nullified by § 14 of the Act. * * * The Court considered the language, purposes, and legislative history of the Securities Act, and concluded that the agreement to arbitrate was void under § 14. But the decision was a difficult one in view of the competing legislative policy embodied in the Arbitration Act, which the Court described as "not easily reconcilable," and which strongly favors the enforcement of agreements to arbitrate as a means of securing "prompt, economical and adequate solution of controversies." * * *

It has been recognized that *Wilko* was not obviously correct, for "the language prohibiting waiver of 'compliance with any provision of this title' could easily have been read to relate to substantive provisions of the Act without including the remedy provisions." * * * The Court did not read the language this way in *Wilko,* however, and gave two reasons. First, the Court rejected the argument that "arbitration is merely a form of trial to be used in lieu of a trial at law." * * * The Court found instead that § 14 does not permit waiver of "the right to select the judicial forum" in favor of arbitration, * * * because "arbitration lacks the certainty of a suit at law under the Act to enforce [the buyer's] rights," * * *. Second, the Court concluded that the Securities Act was intended to protect buyers of securities, who often do not deal at arm's length and on equal terms with sellers, by offering them "a wider choice of courts and venue" than is enjoyed by participants in other business transactions, making "the right to select the judicial forum" a particularly valuable feature of the Securities Act. * * *

* * * The shift in the Court's views on arbitration away from those adopted in *Wilko* is shown by the flat statement in [a prior case]: "By agreeing to arbitrate a statutory claim, a party does not forgo the substantive rights afforded by the statute; it only submits to their resolution in an arbitral, rather than a judicial, forum." * * * To the extent that *Wilko* rested on suspicion of arbitration as a method of weakening the protections afforded in the substantive law to would-be complainants, it has fallen far out of step with our current strong endorsement of the federal statutes favoring this method of resolving disputes.

Once the outmoded presumption of disfavoring arbitration proceedings is set to one side, it becomes clear that the right to select the judicial forum and the wider choice of courts are not such essential features of the Securities Act that § 14 is properly construed to bar any waiver of these provisions. Nor are they so critical that they cannot be waived under the rationale that the Securities Act was intended to place buyers of securities on an equal footing with sellers. *Wilko* identified two different kinds of provisions in the Securities Act that would advance this objective. Some are substantive, such as placing on the seller the burden of proving lack of scienter when a buyer alleges fraud. * * * Others are procedural. The specific procedural improvements highlighted in *Wilko* are the statute's broad venue provisions in the federal courts; the existence of nationwide service of process in the federal courts; the extinction of the amount-in-controversy requirement that had applied to fraud suits when they were brought in federal courts under diversity jurisdiction rather than as a federal cause of action; and the grant of concurrent jurisdiction in the state and federal courts without possibility of removal.

There is no sound basis for construing the prohibition in § 14 on waiving "compliance with any provision" of the Securities Act to apply to these procedural provisions. Although the first three measures do facilitate suits by buyers of securities, the grant of concurrent jurisdiction constitutes explicit authorization for complainants to waive those protections by filing suit in state court without possibility of removal to federal court. These measures, moreover, are present in other federal statutes which have not been interpreted to prohibit enforcement of predispute agreements to arbitrate. * * * [T]he party opposing arbitration carries the burden of showing that Congress intended in a separate statute to preclude a waiver of judicial remedies, or that such a waiver of judicial remedies inherently conflicts with the underlying purposes of that other statute. * * * But as Justice Frankfurter said in dissent in *Wilko*, so it is true in this case: "There is nothing in the record before us, nor in the facts of which we can take judicial notice, to indicate that the arbitral system . . . would not afford the plaintiff the rights to which he is entitled." * * *

The language quoted above from § 2 of the Arbitration Act also allows the courts to give relief where the party opposing arbitration presents "well-supported claims that the agreement to arbitrate resulted from the sort of fraud or overwhelming economic power that would provide grounds 'for the revocation of any contract.'" * * * This avenue of relief is in harmony with the Securities Act's concern to protect buyers of securities by removing "the disadvantages under which buyers labor" in their dealings with sellers. * * *

III

We now conclude that *Wilko* was incorrectly decided and is inconsistent with the prevailing uniform construction of other federal statutes governing arbitration agreements in the setting of business transactions. Although we are normally and properly reluctant to overturn our decisions construing statutes, we have done so to achieve a uniform interpretation of similar statutory language * * * and to correct a seriously erroneous interpretation of statutory language that would undermine congressional policy as expressed in other legislation. * * * Both purposes would be served here by overruling the *Wilko* decision. In this case, for example, petitioners' claims under the 1934 Act were subjected to arbitration, while their claim under the 1933 Act was not permitted to go to arbitration, but was required to proceed in court. That result makes little sense for similar claims, based on similar facts, which are supposed to arise within a single federal regulatory scheme. In addition, the inconsistency * * * undermines the essential rationale for a harmonious construction of the two statutes, which is to discourage litigants from manipulating their allegations merely to cast their claims under one of the securities laws rather than another. For all of these reasons, therefore, we overrule the decision in *Wilko*.

The judgment of the Court of Appeals is
AFFIRMED.

CASE A.2

Reference: Problem 5–11

AUSTIN v. BERRYMAN
United States Court of Appeals,
Fourth Circuit, 1989.
878 F.2d 786.

MURNAGHAN, Circuit Judge:

We have before us for *en banc* [by the whole court] reconsideration an appeal taken from an action successfully brought by Barbara Austin in the United States District Court for the Western District of Virginia against the Virginia Employment Commission, challenging a denial of unemployment compensation benefits. * * * In brief, Austin charged, *inter alia* [among other things], that the denial of her claim for unemployment benefits, based on a Virginia statute specifically precluding such benefits for any individual who voluntarily quits work to join his or her spouse in a new location, was an unconstitutional infringement upon the incidents of marriage protected by the Fourteenth Amendment and an unconstitutional burden on her First Amendment right to the free exercise of her religion. Her religion happened to command that she follow her spouse wherever he might go and the sincerity of her religious belief was not questioned. The district court found in Austin's favor and awarded injunctive relief and retroactive benefits.

On appeal, Judge Sprouse, writing for a panel majority, found that the denial of benefits did not implicate Austin's

Fourteenth Amendment rights, but that it did unconstitutionally burden Austin's right to the free exercise of her religion. The panel also found, however, that any award of retroactive benefits was barred by the Eleventh Amendment. One panel member concurred with the panel majority as to the Fourteenth and Eleventh Amendment issues, but dissented as to the existence of a free exercise violation. The panel opinion now, of course, has been vacated by a grant of rehearing *en banc*.

After careful consideration of the additional arguments proffered by both sides, the Court, *en banc*, is convinced that the panel majority correctly concluded that denying Austin unemployment benefits did not infringe upon fundamental marital rights protected by the Fourteenth Amendment. To this extent, we adopt the majority panel opinion. We also find, however, that the denial of benefits did not unconstitutionally burden Austin's First Amendment right to the free exercise of her religion. We are persuaded that the views expressed on the First Amendment, free exercise of religion claim in the opinion dissenting in part from the panel majority are correct, and we hereby adopt that opinion as that of the *en banc* court. As we find that Austin is not entitled to any relief, we need not address whether the Eleventh Amendment bars an award of retroactive benefits.

The decisive consideration, as we see it, is that the proximate cause of Austin's unemployment is geographic distance, not her religious beliefs. There is no conflict between the circumstances of work and Austin's religious precepts. Austin's religious beliefs do not "require" her "to refrain from the work in question." Austin is unable to work simply because she is now too far removed from her employer to make it practical. In striking contrast, if one, for genuine religious beliefs, moves to a new residence in order to continue to live with a spouse, and that residence is not geographically so removed as to preclude regular attendance at the worksite, no unemployment, and hence no unemployment benefits, will arise. That amounts to proof that extent of geographical non-propinquity, not religious belief, led to Austin's disqualification for unemployment benefits.

Austin voluntarily decided to quit her job and join her spouse in a new geographic location 150 miles away.

Virginia has stated that every individual who follows such a course, no matter what the reason, religious or non-religious, is disqualified for unemployment benefits. To craft judicially a statutory exception only for those individuals who profess Austin's religious convictions, particularly in the absence of a direct conflict between a given employment practice and a religious belief, would, in our view, result in a subsidy to members of a particular religious belief, impermissible under the Establishment Clause.

Accordingly, the judgment of the district court is REVERSED.

CASE A.3   Reference: Problem 11–12.

AMERIPRO SEARCH, INC. v. FLEMING STEEL CO.
Superior Court of Pennsylvania, 2001.
787 A. 2D 988.

DEL SOLE, President Judge

Fleming Steel Company ("Fleming") appeals from the judgment entered against it, and in favor of AmeriPro Search, Inc. ("AmeriPro"). Upon review, we reverse.

* * * AmeriPro is an employment referral firm that places professional employees with interested employers. Fleming is a steel fabricator. In May of 1993, Elaine Brauninger, an agent of AmeriPro, contacted Fleming and inquired about Fleming's need for professional employees. * * * Fleming was seeking an employee with an engineering background. * * * Ms. Brauninger was advised that [she] would have to speak to Seth Kohn, president of Fleming, who alone made all decisions relating to employment and salaries.

* * * Ms. Brauninger advised Mr. Kohn that if her services were accepted she would be entitled to a fee equal to 30% of the candidate's first year's salary. Mr. Kohn did not agree because he believed the fee to be too high. Mr. Kohn told Ms. Brauninger that the fee would be as determined by him and AmeriPro only after an agreement to hire a candidate was made. Ms. Brauninger agreed and told Mr. Kohn that she would work with him on the amount of the fee.

One of the candidates referred to Fleming was Dominic Barracchini. Ms. Brauninger had contacted Mr. Barracchini in November of 1993 to determine whether Mr. Barracchini would be interested in a position at Fleming. * * * Despite Mr. Barracchini's statement of interest, an interview could not be arranged with Fleming and Mr. Barracchini took employment with [another] company. In April of 1994, Ms. Brauninger again contacted Mr. Barracchini and informed him that she could arrange for an interview with Fleming. Mr. Kohn interviewed Mr. Barracchini on April 8, 1994. Fleming did not hire Mr. Barracchini because Mr. Barracchini's salary request was too high.

* * * [In February of 1995,] Mr. Barracchini called Ms. Brauninger to inquire whether Fleming was still trying to fill the position for which he had previously interviewed. Ms. Brauninger never got back to Mr. Barracchini regarding his inquiry. Mr. Barracchini then contacted Fleming on his own. * * * Fleming hired Mr. Barracchini as an engineer on June 19, 1995.

On September 6, 1995, AmeriPro sent an invoice to Fleming claiming entitlement to $14,400.00 for placement of Mr. Barracchini with Fleming. Fleming refused to pay * * *.

* * * * *

The trial court determined that there was no express contract formed in this case. * * * The trial court did, however, find that there was a contract implied in law, or a quasi-contract, in this case. It was on this basis that the trial court ordered Fleming to pay AmeriPro the fee for placement of Barracchini.

* * * *

A quasi-contract imposes a duty, not as a result of any agreement, whether express or implied, but in spite of the absence of an agreement, when one party receives unjust enrichment at the expense of another. In determining if the doctrine applies, we focus not on the intention of the parties, but rather on whether the defendant has been unjustly enriched. * * * The most significant element of the doctrine is whether the enrichment of the defendant is unjust * * *.

We cannot find that Fleming was unjustly enriched in this case. Mr. Barracchini was referred to Fleming and the first interview was arranged by AmeriPro. Fleming did not hire Mr. Barracchini at that time because the candidate's salary requirements were too high. Approximately ten months after Mr. Barracchini's initial interview with Fleming, he was laid off from Montage. He contacted Ms. Brauninger to inquire about the job at Fleming and whether it was still open. Ms. Brauninger never responded to Mr. Barracchini's inquiry. As a result, Mr. Barracchini contacted Fleming directly to determine whether the position for which he had previously interviewed was still available. * * * After interviewing Mr. Barracchini in June of 1995, Fleming hired him.

The events leading to the hiring of Mr. Barracchini were separate from any actions taken by Ms. Brauninger and AmeriPro on his behalf. While it is true that AmeriPro and

Brauninger first introduced Barracchini to Fleming and the available position, that connection was broken when Fleming refused to hire Barracchini after the interview in April of 1994. * * * Mr. Barracchini's subsequent independent interaction with Mr. Kohn, which led to his actual employment by Fleming, was removed from previous actions taken by AmeriPro on his behalf.

While it may be argued that Fleming received a benefit from AmeriPro because Barracchini would not have known about the position at Fleming without the initial interaction involving AmeriPro, the doctrine of quasi-contract does not apply simply because the defendant may have benefited as a result of the actions of the plaintiff. Regardless of any benefit Fleming received by AmeriPro's action of first introducing Mr. Barracchini to Fleming, the enrichment of Fleming was not unjust. Mr. Barracchini approached Fleming the second time on his own and the two parties came to an agreement regarding Mr. Barracchini's employment without any involvement by AmeriPro. Fleming did nothing to wrongly secure the benefit of Mr. Barracchini's employment. * * * Because Fleming was not unjustly enriched, we find that there was no quasi-contract, or contract implied in law. Thus, Fleming owes AmeriPro nothing in restitution.

Judgment reversed. * * *

CASE A.4

Reference: Problem 17–12

SUTTON v. UNITED AIRLINES, INC.
Supreme Court of the United States, 1999.
527 U.S. 471,
119 S.Ct. 2139,
144 L.Ed.2d 450.

Justice *O'CONNOR* delivered the opinion of the Court.
* * * *

Petitioners [Karen and Kimberly Sutton] are twin sisters, both of whom have severe myopia. Each petitioner's uncorrected visual acuity is 20/200 or worse in her right eye and 20/400 or worse in her left eye, but with the use of corrective lenses, each * * * has vision that is 20/20 or better. Consequently, without corrective lenses, each effectively cannot see to conduct numerous activities such as driving a vehicle, watching television or shopping in public stores, but with corrective measures, such as glasses or contact lenses, both function identically to individuals without a similar impairment.

In 1992, petitioners applied to respondent [United Airlines, Inc.,] for employment as commercial airline pilots. They met respondent's basic age, education, experience, and Federal Aviation Administration certification qualifications. After submitting their applications for employment, both petitioners were invited by respondent to an interview and to flight simulator tests. Both were told during their interviews, however, that a mistake had been made in inviting them to interview because petitioners did not meet respondent's minimum vision requirement, which was uncorrected visual acuity of 20/100 or better. Due to their failure to meet this requirement, petitioners' interviews were terminated, and neither was offered a pilot position.

In light of respondent's proffered [offered] reason for rejecting them, petitioners filed a charge of disability discrimination under the [Americans with Disabilities Act of 1990 (ADA)] with the Equal Employment Opportunity Commission (EEOC). After receiving a right to sue letter, petitioners filed suit in the United States District Court for the District of Colorado, alleging that respondent had discriminated against them "on the basis of their disability, or because [respondent] regarded [petitioners] as having a disability" in violation of the ADA. Specifically, petitioners alleged that due to their severe myopia they actually have a substantially limiting impairment or are regarded as having such an impairment and are thus disabled under the Act.

The District Court dismissed petitioners' complaint for failure to state a claim upon which relief could be granted. * * * [T]he Court of Appeals for the Tenth Circuit affirmed the District Court's judgment. * * * We granted *certiorari* * * * .

* * * *

* * * The Act defines a "disability" as "a physical or mental impairment that *substantially limits* one or more of the major life activities" of an individual. [Emphasis added.] Because the phrase "substantially limits" appears in the Act in the present indicative verb form, we think the language is properly read as requiring that a person be presently—not potentially or hypothetically—substantially limited in order to demonstrate a disability. A "disability" exists only where an impairment "substantially limits" a major life activity, not where it "might," "could," or "would" be substantially limiting if mitigating measures were not taken. A person whose physical or mental impairment is corrected by medication or other measures does not have an impairment that presently "substantially limits" a major life activity. To be sure, a person whose physical or mental impairment is corrected by mitigating measures still has an impairment, but if the impairment is corrected it does not "substantially limi[t]" a major life activity.

* * * *

* * * The use of a corrective device does not, by itself, relieve one's disability. Rather, one has a disability under [the ADA] if, notwithstanding the use of a corrective device, that individual is substantially limited in a major life activity. For example, individuals who use prosthetic limbs or wheelchairs may be mobile and capable of functioning in society but still be disabled because of a substantial limitation on their ability to walk or run. The same may be true of individuals who take medicine to lessen the symptoms of an impairment so that they can function but nevertheless remain substantially limited. Alternatively, one whose high blood pressure is "cured" by medication may be regarded as disabled by a covered

entity, and thus disabled under [the ADA]. The use or nonuse of a corrective device does not determine whether an individual is disabled; that determination depends on whether the limitations an individual with an impairment actually faces are in fact substantially limiting.

Applying this reading of the Act to the case at hand, we conclude that the Court of Appeals correctly resolved the issue of disability in respondent's favor. As noted above, petitioners allege that with corrective measures, their visual acuity is 20/20 and that they "function identically to individuals without a similar impairment." In addition, petitioners concede that they "do not argue that the use of corrective lenses in itself demonstrates a substantially limiting impairment." Accordingly, because we decide that disability under the Act is to be determined with reference to corrective measures, we agree with the [lower] courts * * * that petitioners have not stated a claim that they are substantially limited in any major life activity.

* * * *

Our conclusion that petitioners have failed to state a claim that they are actually disabled under [the ADA's] disability definition does not end our inquiry. * * * [The ADA] provides that having a disability includes "being regarded as having a physical or mental impairment that substantially limits one or more of the major life activities of such individual." There are two apparent ways in which individuals may fall within this statutory definition: (1) a covered entity mistakenly believes that a person has a physical impairment that substantially limits one or more major life activities, or (2) a covered entity mistakenly believes that an actual, non-limiting impairment substantially limits one or more major life activities. In both cases, it is necessary that a covered entity entertain misperceptions about the individual—it must believe either that one has a substantially limiting impairment that one does not have or that one has a substantially limiting impairment when, in fact, the impair-

ment is not so limiting. These misperceptions often result from stereotypic assumptions not truly indicative of * * * individual ability.

* * * *

* * * By its terms, the ADA allows employers to prefer some physical attributes over others and to establish physical criteria. An employer runs afoul of the ADA when it makes an employment decision based on a physical or mental impairment, real or imagined, that is regarded as substantially limiting a major life activity. * * *

* * * The EEOC has codified regulations interpreting the term "substantially limits" * * * to mean "[u]nable to perform" or "[s]ignificantly restricted." When the major life activity under consideration is that of working, the statutory phrase "substantially limits" requires, at a minimum, that plaintiffs allege they are unable to work in a broad class of jobs. * * * The inability to perform a single, particular job does not constitute a substantial limitation in the major life activity of working.

* * * *

* * * [P]etitioners have failed to allege adequately that their poor eyesight is regarded as an impairment that substantially limits them in the major life activity of working. They allege only that respondent regards their poor vision as precluding them from holding positions as a "global airline pilot." Because the position of global airline pilot is a single job, this allegation does not support the claim that respondent regards petitioners as having a *substantially limiting* impairment. Indeed, there are a number of other positions utilizing petitioners' skills, such as regional pilot and pilot instructor to name a few, that are available to them. * * *

* * * *

For these reasons, the judgment of the Court of Appeals for the Tenth Circuit is affirmed.

It is so ordered.

CASE A.5

Reference: Problem 21–12

CITY OF MONTEREY v. DEL MONTE DUNES AT MONTEREY
United States Supreme Court, 1999.
526 U.S. 687,
119 S.Ct. 1624,
143 L.Ed.2d 882.

Justice *KENNEDY* delivered the opinion of the Court.

This case began with attempts by respondent Del Monte Dunes and its predecessor in interest to develop a parcel of land within the jurisdiction of the petitioner, the city of Monterey. The city, in a series of repeated rejections, denied proposals to develop the property, each time imposing more rigorous demands on the developers. Del Monte Dunes brought suit in the United States District Court for the

Northern District of California, under Rev. Stat. [Section] 1979, 42 U.S.C. [Section] 1983. After protracted litigation, the case was submitted to the jury on Del Monte Dunes' theory that the city effected a regulatory taking or otherwise injured the property by unlawful acts, without paying compensation or providing an adequate postdeprivation remedy for the loss. The jury found for Del Monte Dunes, and the Court of Appeals affirmed.

* * * The controlling question is whether * * * the matter was properly submitted to the jury.

* * * *

* * * [I]n suits sounding in tort for money damages [suits brought not for the recovery of things, such as land or goods, but for damages only], questions of liability were [historically] decided by the jury, rather than the judge, in most cases. * * *

* * * *

In *Williamson County Regional Planning Commission v. Hamilton Bank of Johnson City,* 473 U.S. 172, 105 S.Ct. 3108, 87 L.Ed.2d 126 (1985), we * * * review[ed] a regulatory takings case in which the plaintiff landowner sued a county planning commission in federal court for money damages * * * . Whether the commission had denied the plaintiff all economically viable use of the property had been submitted to the jury. Although the Court did not consider the point, it assumed the propriety of this procedure.

* * * *

In actions at law predominantly factual issues are in most cases allocated to the jury. The allocation rests on a firm historical foundation and serves to preserve the right to a jury's resolution of the ultimate dispute.

Almost from the inception of our regulatory takings doctrine, we have held that whether a regulation of property goes so far that there must be an exercise of eminent domain and compensation to sustain the act * * * depends upon the particular facts. Consistent with this understanding, we have described determinations of liability in regulatory takings cases as essentially * * * factual inquiries, requiring complex factual assessments of the purposes and economic effects of government actions.

In accordance with these pronouncements, we hold that the issue whether a landowner has been deprived of all eco-

nomically viable use of his property is a predominantly factual question. As our implied acknowledgment of the procedure in *Williamson* suggests, in actions at law otherwise within the purview of the Seventh Amendment, this question is for the jury.

The jury's role in determining whether a land-use decision substantially advances legitimate public interests within the meaning of our regulatory takings doctrine presents a more difficult question. Although our cases make clear that this inquiry involves an essential factual component, it no doubt has a legal aspect as well, and is probably best understood as a mixed question of fact and law.

In this case, the narrow question submitted to the jury was whether, when viewed in light of the context and protracted history of the development application process, the city's decision to reject a particular development plan bore a reasonable relationship to its proffered justifications. As the [U.S. Court of Appeals for the Ninth Circuit] recognized, this question was "essentially fact-bound [in] nature." Under these circumstances, we hold that it was proper to submit this narrow, factbound question to the jury.

* * * *

* * * [T]he judgment of the Court of Appeals is affirmed.

CASE A.6   *Reference: Problem 24–12*

**TRANS-ORIENT MARINE CORP. v.
STAR TRADING & MARINE, INC.**
United States District Court,
Southern District of New York, 1990.
731 F.Supp. 619.

WILLIAM C. CONNER, District Judge:

Defendant Republic of the Sudan moves this Court to dismiss the complaint for failure to state a claim or for summary judgment. It claims that the new Republic of the Sudan, as successor state, is not liable for the alleged breach of a five-year exclusive agency contract entered into by the prior sovereign state of Sudan. Defendant further asserts that a fundamental change in circumstances relieves it of any prior contractual obligations.

FACTS   Plaintiff's cause of action for breach of contract arises from an alleged five-year exclusive agency agreement to represent the Sudan in the United States P.L. 480 program [an agricultural trade development and assistance program]. The alleged October 14, 1983 agreement was effective from October 1, 1984 through September 30, 1989. In April 1985, a military coup deposed the then head of state, declaring a state of emergency and suspending the constitution. A twelve-month transitional military regime followed, which was then replaced by a civilian coalition government. The

name of the state was changed from the Sudan to the Republic of Sudan. In June 1989, there was another military coup in which the present military regime overthrew the former civilian administration and suspended the constitution. Both parties agree that the Republic of the Sudan is a foreign sovereign state.

On January 3 and 4, 1985, the then Sudanese government sent letters advising plaintiff that a new agent, CIDCO, had been appointed to handle the contracts under P.L. 480 and that CIDCO would select the shipping agent. This alleged termination of the then-executory contract did not provide the one-year termination notice required under the original contract. Since January 1985, the Sudan has awarded CIDCO a continuing series of contracts to handle the wheat and wheat flour transportation under P.L. 480, in alleged violation of plaintiff's exclusive agency contract. No additional facts are relevant to the present motion.

DISCUSSION   The present Sudanese government asserts that it is not liable for the contractual obligations of the prior sovereign, pointing to the two military coups of 1985 and 1989 to sustain its position that both the 1985 military regime and the present administration are successor states and that there has been a fundamental change in circumstances. Plaintiff contends that neither the 1985 regime nor the present regime is a successor state but that they represent mere changes in government which do not relieve the present regime from the prior government's contractual obligations.

Plaintiff further argues that even if either regime is a successor state, they have ratified the prior government's contract. For the following reasons, summary judgment is denied.

Whether a new administration may terminate the executory portions of its predecessor's contracts is based on the succession of state theory. International law sharply distinguishes the succession of state, which may create a discontinuity of statehood, from a succession of government, which leaves statehood unaffected. It is generally accepted that a change in government, regime or ideology has no effect on that state's international rights and obligations because the state continues to exist despite the change. *   *   *

However, where one sovereign succeeds another, and a new state is created, the rights and obligations of the successor state are affected. The rule with regard to contracts with private foreign individuals involves a balancing of competing interests. While the successor state is permitted to terminate existing contracts originally executed by the former sovereign and the private party, the successor state is liable to that party only for any amount due him as of the date of the change of sovereignty. But if the contract is totally executory, the successor state is released from the contract.

The Restatement of Foreign Relations Law describes a successor state to include: a state that wholly absorbs another state, that takes over part of the territory of another state, that becomes independent of another state of which it had formed a part, or that arises because of the dismemberment of the state of which it had been a part.

Careful study of defendant's submission reveals that the state of Sudan has not (1) wholly absorbed or been wholly absorbed by another state; (2) partly taken over or been partly taken over by another state; (3) become independent from another state of which it had formed a part; or (4) arisen out of dismemberment of a state of which it had been a part since the date of plaintiff's contract. Under the Restatement's definition, the state of Sudan has remained the same entity since its independence in 1956. Defendant's own exhibit in support of its motion substantiates that only a change in government was effected by the two military coups *   *   *.

Accordingly, the only changes in the Sudan since its independence in 1956 have been in the government, with seven distinct successive administrations. But there has been only one state.

Defendant unpersuasively emphasizes various aspects of the relevant transitions to reflect the creation of a new state: that the transitions resulted by way of military coups as opposed to routine, constitutional processes, the re-naming of the nation, the suspension of the constitution, the closing of the borders and the declaration of a state of emergency. Treatises, as well as applicable case law, demonstrate that such features do not effect a succession of state. *   *   *

Furthermore, the Restatement's comparative chart in a Recognition of States section illustrates that a change in government by armed force or fraud, as well as institution of another regime following a civil war, leaves "no question of the existence of the state." It offers as contemporary examples of mere changes in government: Pinochet's 1973 ouster of Allende in Chile, Franco's 1936–39 takeover of Spain, and the Communist revolution in China.

The seminal decision on the distinction between a succession of state versus a change in government is the U.S. Supreme Court decision in *The Sapphire*. In *The Sapphire*, the Supreme Court considered whether a lawsuit begun by the French Emperor, Napoleon III, was abated by the overthrow of the Emperor during the course of litigation. In holding that the action was not extinguished, the Supreme Court stated that, "on the [Emperor's] deposition the sovereignty does not change, but merely the person or persons in whom it resides. . . . A change in such representative works no change in the national sovereignty or its rights."

*   *   *   *

*   *   * In *United States v. National City Bank of New York*, the district court held the post-revolutionary State of Russia liable on the treasury notes of the pre-revolutionary state. Similarly, in *Jackson v. People's Republic of China*, the district court determined that the People's Republic, as successor government to the Imperial Chinese Government, was successor to its obligations, specifically, payment of principal due on the prior government-issued bonds. The law is clear that the obligations of a state are unaffected by a mere change in government. It is of no consequence that the Sudan allegedly breached an executory contract. The distinction between executed and executory contracts only applies where there has been a succession of state. The military coups of 1985 and 1989 did not effect a succession of state of the Sudan but merely changed the state's governing body, leaving the state's obligations undisturbed.

Defendant's alternative claim that a fundamental change of circumstances has occurred since October, 1983 relieving it of any prior contractual obligations is unsubstantiated. Defendant presents no explanation as to what "circumstances constituted an essential basis of the consent of the parties to be bound by the agreement" or what changes have "radically transform[ed] the extent of obligations still to be performed under the agreement." Having failed to demonstrate a fundamental change in circumstances, the present government is therefore contractually obligated to plaintiff under the October 14, 1983 five-year extension of agency contract if its predecessor indeed breached that agreement.

CONCLUSION For the reasons discussed above, summary judgment is denied.

SO ORDERED.

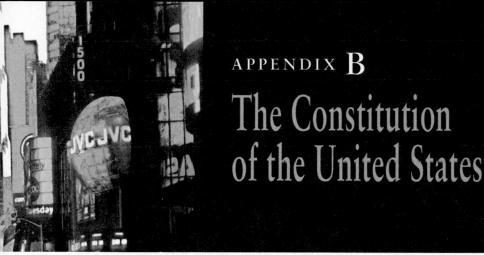

The Constitution of the United States

Note: You can access the full text of the Constitution online by going to **http://memory.loc.gov/const/const.html**. This is a page within the THOMAS Web site, which the U.S. Library of Congress maintains. To read the Bill of Rights or other amendments to the U.S. Constitution, click on the link at the top of the page.

PREAMBLE

We the People of the United States, in Order to form a more perfect Union, establish Justice, insure domestic Tranquility, provide for the common defence, promote the general Welfare, and secure the Blessings of Liberty to ourselves and our Posterity, do ordain and establish this Constitution for the United States of America.

ARTICLE I

Section 1. All legislative Powers herein granted shall be vested in a Congress of the United States, which shall consist of a Senate and House of Representatives.

Section 2. The House of Representatives shall be composed of Members chosen every second Year by the People of the several States, and the Electors in each State shall have the Qualifications requisite for Electors of the most numerous Branch of the State Legislature.

No Person shall be a Representative who shall not have attained to the Age of twenty five Years, and been seven Years a Citizen of the United States, and who shall not, when elected, be an Inhabitant of that State in which he shall be chosen.

Representatives and direct Taxes shall be apportioned among the several States which may be included within this Union, according to their respective Numbers, which shall be determined by adding to the whole Number of free Persons, including those bound to Service for a Term of Years, and excluding Indians not taxed, three fifths of all other Persons. The actual Enumeration shall be made within three Years after the first Meeting of the Congress of the United States, and within every subsequent Term of ten Years, in such Manner as they shall by Law direct. The Number of Representatives shall not exceed one for every thirty Thousand, but each State shall have at Least one Representative; and until such enumeration shall be made,

the State of New Hampshire shall be entitled to chuse three, Massachusetts eight, Rhode Island and Providence Plantations one, Connecticut five, New York six, New Jersey four, Pennsylvania eight, Delaware one, Maryland six, Virginia ten, North Carolina five, South Carolina five, and Georgia three.

When vacancies happen in the Representation from any State, the Executive Authority thereof shall issue Writs of Election to fill such Vacancies.

The House of Representatives shall chuse their Speaker and other Officers; and shall have the sole Power of Impeachment.

Section 3. The Senate of the United States shall be composed of two Senators from each State, chosen by the Legislature thereof, for six Years; and each Senator shall have one Vote.

Immediately after they shall be assembled in Consequence of the first Election, they shall be divided as equally as may be into three Classes. The Seats of the Senators of the first Class shall be vacated at the Expiration of the second Year, of the second Class at the Expiration of the fourth Year, and of the third Class at the Expiration of the sixth Year, so that one third may be chosen every second Year; and if Vacancies happen by Resignation, or otherwise, during the Recess of the Legislature of any State, the Executive thereof may make temporary Appointments until the next Meeting of the Legislature, which shall then fill such Vacancies.

No Person shall be a Senator who shall not have attained to the Age of thirty Years, and been nine Years a Citizen of the United States, and who shall not, when elected, be an Inhabitant of that State for which he shall be chosen.

The Vice President of the United States shall be President of the Senate, but shall have no Vote, unless they be equally divided.

The Senate shall chuse their other Officers, and also a President pro tempore, in the Absence of the Vice President, or when he shall exercise the Office of President of the United States.

The Senate shall have the sole Power to try all Impeachments. When sitting for that Purpose, they shall be on Oath or Affirmation. When the President of the United States is tried, the Chief Justice shall preside: And no Person shall be convicted without the Concurrence of two thirds of the Members present.

Judgment in Cases of Impeachment shall not extend further than to removal from Office, and disqualification to hold and enjoy any Office of honor, Trust, or Profit under the United States: but the Party convicted shall nevertheless be liable and subject to Indictment, Trial, Judgment, and Punishment, according to Law.

Section 4.   The Times, Places and Manner of holding Elections for Senators and Representatives, shall be prescribed in each State by the Legislature thereof; but the Congress may at any time by Law make or alter such Regulations, except as to the Places of chusing Senators.

The Congress shall assemble at least once in every Year, and such Meeting shall be on the first Monday in December, unless they shall by Law appoint a different Day.

Section 5.   Each House shall be the Judge of the Elections, Returns, and Qualifications of its own Members, and a Majority of each shall constitute a Quorum to do Business; but a smaller Number may adjourn from day to day, and may be authorized to compel the Attendance of absent Members, in such Manner, and under such Penalties as each House may provide.

Each House may determine the Rules of its Proceedings, punish its Members for disorderly Behavior, and, with the Concurrence of two thirds, expel a Member.

Each House shall keep a Journal of its Proceedings, and from time to time publish the same, excepting such Parts as may in their Judgment require Secrecy; and the Yeas and Nays of the Members of either House on any question shall, at the Desire of one fifth of those Present, be entered on the Journal.

Neither House, during the Session of Congress, shall, without the Consent of the other, adjourn for more than three days, nor to any other Place than that in which the two Houses shall be sitting.

Section 6.   The Senators and Representatives shall receive a Compensation for their Services, to be ascertained by Law, and paid out of the Treasury of the United States. They shall in all Cases, except Treason, Felony and Breach of the Peace, be privileged from Arrest during their Attendance at the Session of their respective Houses, and in going to and returning from the same; and for any Speech or Debate in either House, they shall not be questioned in any other Place.

No Senator or Representative shall, during the Time for which he was elected, be appointed to any civil Office under the Authority of the United States, which shall have been created, or the Emoluments whereof shall have been increased during such time; and no Person holding any Office under the United States, shall be a Member of either House during his Continuance in Office.

Section 7.   All Bills for raising Revenue shall originate in the House of Representatives; but the Senate may propose or concur with Amendments as on other Bills.

Every Bill which shall have passed the House of Representatives and the Senate, shall, before it become a Law, be presented to the President of the United States; If he approve he shall sign it, but if not he shall return it, with his Objections to the House in which it shall have originated, who shall enter the Objections at large on their Journal, and proceed to reconsider it. If after such Reconsideration two thirds of that House shall agree to pass the Bill, it shall be sent together with the Objections, to the other House, by which it shall likewise be reconsidered, and if approved by two thirds of that House, it shall become a Law. But in all such Cases the Votes of both Houses shall be determined by Yeas and Nays, and the Names of the Persons voting for and against the Bill shall be entered on the Journal of each House respectively. If any Bill shall not be returned by the President within ten Days (Sundays excepted) after it shall have been presented to him, the Same shall be a Law, in like Manner as if he had signed it, unless the Congress by their Adjournment prevent its Return in which Case it shall not be a Law.

Every Order, Resolution, or Vote, to which the Concurrence of the Senate and House of Representatives may be necessary (except on a question of Adjournment) shall be presented to the President of the United States; and before the Same shall take Effect, shall be approved by him, or being disapproved by him, shall be repassed by two thirds of the Senate and House of Representatives, according to the Rules and Limitations prescribed in the Case of a Bill.

Section 8.   The Congress shall have Power To lay and collect Taxes, Duties, Imposts and Excises, to pay the Debts and provide for the common Defence and general Welfare of the United States; but all Duties, Imposts and Excises shall be uniform throughout the United States;

To borrow Money on the credit of the United States;

To regulate Commerce with foreign Nations, and among the several States, and with the Indian Tribes;

To establish an uniform Rule of Naturalization, and uniform Laws on the subject of Bankruptcies throughout the United States;

To coin Money, regulate the Value thereof, and of foreign Coin, and fix the Standard of Weights and Measures;

To provide for the Punishment of counterfeiting the Securities and current Coin of the United States;

To establish Post Offices and post Roads;

To promote the Progress of Science and useful Arts, by securing for limited Times to Authors and Inventors the exclusive Right to their respective Writings and Discoveries;

To constitute Tribunals inferior to the supreme Court;

To define and punish Piracies and Felonies committed on the high Seas, and Offenses against the Law of Nations;

To declare War, grant Letters of Marque and Reprisal, and make Rules concerning Captures on Land and Water;

To raise and support Armies, but no Appropriation of Money to that Use shall be for a longer Term than two Years;

To provide and maintain a Navy;

To make Rules for the Government and Regulation of the land and naval Forces;

To provide for calling forth the Militia to execute the Laws of the Union, suppress Insurrections and repel Invasions;

To provide for organizing, arming, and disciplining, the Militia, and for governing such Part of them as may be employed in the Service of the United States, reserving to the States respectively, the Appointment of the Officers, and the Authority of training the Militia according to the discipline prescribed by Congress;

To exercise exclusive Legislation in all Cases whatsoever, over such District (not exceeding ten Miles square) as may, by Cession of particular States, and the Acceptance of Congress, become the Seat of the Government of the United States, and to exercise like Authority over all Places purchased by the Consent of the Legislature of the State in which the Same shall be, for the Erection of Forts, Magazines, Arsenals, dock-Yards, and other needful Buildings;—And

To make all Laws which shall be necessary and proper for carrying into Execution the foregoing Powers, and all other Powers vested by this Constitution in the Government of the United States, or in any Department or Officer thereof.

Section 9. The Migration or Importation of such Persons as any of the States now existing shall think proper to admit, shall not be prohibited by the Congress prior to the Year one thousand eight hundred and eight, but a Tax or duty may be imposed on such Importation, not exceeding ten dollars for each Person.

The privilege of the Writ of Habeas Corpus shall not be suspended, unless when in Cases of Rebellion or Invasion the public Safety may require it.

No Bill of Attainder or ex post facto Law shall be passed.

No Capitation, or other direct, Tax shall be laid, unless in Proportion to the Census or Enumeration herein before directed to be taken.

No Tax or Duty shall be laid on Articles exported from any State.

No Preference shall be given by any Regulation of Commerce or Revenue to the Ports of one State over those of another: nor shall Vessels bound to, or from, one State be obliged to enter, clear, or pay Duties in another.

No Money shall be drawn from the Treasury, but in Consequence of Appropriations made by Law; and a regular Statement and Account of the Receipts and Expenditures of all public Money shall be published from time to time.

No Title of Nobility shall be granted by the United States: And no Person holding any Office of Profit or Trust under them, shall, without the Consent of the Congress, accept of any present, Emolument, Office, or Title, of any kind whatever, from any King, Prince, or foreign State.

Section 10. No State shall enter into any Treaty, Alliance, or Confederation; grant Letters of Marque and Reprisal; coin Money; emit Bills of Credit; make any Thing but gold and silver Coin a Tender in Payment of Debts; pass any Bill of Attainder, ex post facto Law, or Law impairing the Obligation of Contracts, or grant any Title of Nobility.

No State shall, without the Consent of the Congress, lay any Imposts or Duties on Imports or Exports, except what may be absolutely necessary for executing its inspection Laws: and the net Produce of all Duties and Imposts, laid by any State on Imports or Exports, shall be for the Use of the Treasury of the United States; and all such Laws shall be subject to the Revision and Controul of the Congress.

No State shall, without the Consent of Congress, lay any Duty of Tonnage, keep Troops, or Ships of War in time of Peace, enter into any Agreement or Compact with another State, or with a foreign Power, or engage in War, unless actually invaded, or in such imminent Danger as will not admit of delay.

ARTICLE II

Section 1. The executive Power shall be vested in a President of the United States of America. He shall hold his Office during the Term of four Years, and, together with the Vice President, chosen for the same Term, be elected, as follows:

Each State shall appoint, in such Manner as the Legislature thereof may direct, a Number of Electors, equal to the whole Number of Senators and Representatives to which the State may be entitled in the Congress; but no Senator or Representative, or Person holding an Office of Trust or Profit under the United States, shall be appointed an Elector.

The Electors shall meet in their respective States, and vote by Ballot for two Persons, of whom one at least shall not be an Inhabitant of the same State with themselves. And they shall make a List of all the Persons voted for, and of the Number of Votes for each; which List they shall sign and certify, and transmit sealed to the Seat of the Government of the United States, directed to the President of the Senate. The President of the Senate shall, in the Presence of the Senate and House of Representatives, open all the Certificates, and the Votes shall then be counted. The Person having the greatest Number of Votes shall be the President, if such Number be a Majority of the whole Number of Electors appointed; and if there be more than one who have such Majority, and have an equal Number of Votes, then the House of Representatives shall immediately chuse by Ballot one of them for President; and if no Person have a Majority, then from the five highest on the List the said House shall in like Manner chuse the President. But in chusing the President, the Votes shall be taken by States, the Representation from each State having one Vote; A quorum for this Purpose shall consist of a Member or Members from two thirds of the States, and a Majority of all the States shall be necessary to a Choice. In every Case, after the Choice of the President, the Person having the greater Number of Votes of the Electors shall be the Vice President. But if there should remain two or more who have equal Votes, the Senate shall chuse from them by Ballot the Vice President.

The Congress may determine the Time of chusing the Electors, and the Day on which they shall give their Votes; which Day shall be the same throughout the United States.

No person except a natural born Citizen, or a Citizen of the United States, at the time of the Adoption of this Constitution, shall be eligible to the Office of President; neither shall any Person be eligible to that Office who shall not have attained to the Age of thirty five Years, and been fourteen Years a Resident within the United States.

In Case of the Removal of the President from Office, or of his Death, Resignation or Inability to discharge the Powers and Duties of the said Office, the same shall devolve on the Vice President, and the Congress may by Law provide for the Case of Removal, Death, Resignation or Inability, both of the President and Vice President, declaring what Officer shall then act as President, and such Officer shall act accordingly, until the Disability be removed, or a President shall be elected.

The President shall, at stated Times, receive for his Services, a Compensation, which shall neither be increased nor diminished during the Period for which he shall have been elected, and he shall not receive within that Period any other Emolument from the United States, or any of them.

Before he enter on the Execution of his Office, he shall take the following Oath or Affirmation: "I do solemnly swear (or affirm) that I will faithfully execute the Office of President of the United States, and will to the best of my Ability, preserve, protect and defend the Constitution of the United States."

Section 2.　The President shall be Commander in Chief of the Army and Navy of the United States, and of the Militia of the several States, when called into the actual Service of the United States; he may require the Opinion, in writing, of the principal Officer in each of the executive Departments, upon any Subject relating to the Duties of their respective Offices, and he shall have Power to grant Reprieves and Pardons for Offenses against the United States, except in Cases of Impeachment.

He shall have Power, by and with the Advice and Consent of the Senate to make Treaties, provided two thirds of the Senators present concur; and he shall nominate, and by and with the Advice and Consent of the Senate, shall appoint Ambassadors, other public Ministers and Consuls, Judges of the supreme Court, and all other Officers of the United States, whose Appointments are not herein otherwise provided for, and which shall be established by Law; but the Congress may by Law vest the Appointment of such inferior Officers, as they think proper, in the President alone, in the Courts of Law, or in the Heads of Departments.

The President shall have Power to fill up all Vacancies that may happen during the Recess of the Senate, by granting Commissions which shall expire at the End of their next Session.

Section 3.　He shall from time to time give to the Congress Information of the State of the Union, and recommend to their Consideration such Measures as he shall judge necessary and expedient; he may, on extraordinary Occasions, convene both Houses, or either of them, and in Case of Disagreement between them, with Respect to the Time of Adjournment, he may adjourn them to such Time as he shall think proper; he shall receive Ambassadors and other public Ministers; he shall take Care that the Laws be faithfully executed, and shall Commission all the Officers of the United States.

Section 4.　The President, Vice President and all civil Officers of the United States, shall be removed from Office on Impeachment for, and Convictionof, Treason, Bribery, or other high Crimes and Misdemeanors.

ARTICLE III

Section 1.　The judicial Power of the United States, shall be vested in one supreme Court, and in such inferior Courts as the Congress may from time to time ordain and establish. The Judges, both of the supreme and inferior Courts, shall hold their Offices during good Behaviour, and shall, at stated Times, receive for their Services a Compensation, which shall not be diminished during their Continuance in Office.

Section 2.　The judicial Power shall extend to all Cases, in Law and Equity, arising under this Constitution, the Laws of the United States, and Treaties made, or which shall be made, under their Authority;—to all Cases affecting Ambassadors, other public Ministers and Consuls;—to all Cases of admiralty and maritime Jurisdiction;—to Controversies to which the United States shall be a Party;—to Controversies between two or more States;—between a State and Citizens of another State;—between Citizens of different States;—between Citizens of the same State claiming Lands under Grants of different States, and between a State, or the Citizens thereof, and foreign States, Citizens or Subjects.

In all Cases affecting Ambassadors, other public Ministers and Consuls, and those in which a State shall be a Party, the supreme Court shall have original Jurisdiction. In all the other Cases before mentioned, the supreme Court shall have appellate Jurisdiction, both as to Law and Fact, with such Exceptions, and under such Regulations as the Congress shall make.

The Trial of all Crimes, except in Cases of Impeachment, shall be by Jury; and such Trial shall be held in the State where the said Crimes shall have been committed; but when not committed within any State, the Trial shall be at such Place or Places as the Congress may by Law have directed.

Section 3.　Treason against the United States, shall consist only in levying War against them, or, in adhering to their Enemies, giving them Aid and Comfort. No Person shall be convicted of Treason unless on the Testimony of two Witnesses to the same overt Act, or on Confession in open Court.

The Congress shall have Power to declare the Punishment of Treason, but no Attainder of Treason shall work Corruption of Blood, or Forfeiture except during the Life of the Person attainted.

ARTICLE IV

Section 1.   Full Faith and Credit shall be given in each State to the public Acts, Records, and judicial Proceedings of every other State. And the Congress may by general Laws prescribe the Manner in which such Acts, Records and Proceedings shall be proved, and the Effect thereof.

Section 2.   The Citizens of each State shall be entitled to all Privileges and Immunities of Citizens in the several States.

A Person charged in any State with Treason, Felony, or other Crime, who shall flee from Justice, and be found in another State, shall on Demand of the executive Authority of the State from which he fled, be delivered up, to be removed to the State having Jurisdiction of the Crime.

No Person held to Service or Labour in one State, under the Laws thereof, escaping into another, shall, in Consequence of any Law or Regulation therein, be discharged from such Service or Labour, but shall be delivered up on Claim of the Party to whom such Service or Labour may be due.

Section 3.   New States may be admitted by the Congress into this Union; but no new State shall be formed or erected within the Jurisdiction of any other State; nor any State be formed by the Junction of two or more States, or Parts of States, without the Consent of the Legislatures of the States concerned as well as of the Congress.

The Congress shall have Power to dispose of and make all needful Rules and Regulations respecting the Territory or other Property belonging to the United States; and nothing in this Constitution shall be so construed as to Prejudice any Claims of the United States, or of any particular State.

Section 4.   The United States shall guarantee to every State in this Union a Republican Form of Government, and shall protect each of them against Invasion; and on Application of the Legislature, or of the Executive (when the Legislature cannot be convened) against domestic Violence.

ARTICLE V

The Congress, whenever two thirds of both Houses shall deem it necessary, shall propose Amendments to this Constitution, or, on the Application of the Legislatures of two thirds of the several States, shall call a Convention for proposing Amendments, which, in either Case, shall be valid to all Intents and Purposes, as part of this Constitution, when ratified by the Legislatures of three fourths of the several States, or by Conventions in three fourths thereof, as the one or the other Mode of Ratification may be proposed by the Congress; Provided that no Amendment which may be made prior to the Year One thousand eight hundred and eight shall in any Manner affect the first and fourth Clauses in the Ninth Section of the first Article; and that no State, without its Consent, shall be deprived of its equal Suffrage in the Senate.

ARTICLE VI

All Debts contracted and Engagements entered into, before the Adoption of this Constitution shall be as valid against the United States under this Constitution, as under the Confederation.

This Constitution, and the Laws of the United States which shall be made in Pursuance thereof; and all Treaties made, or which shall be made, under the Authority of the United States, shall be the supreme Law of the Land; and the Judges in every State shall be bound thereby, any Thing in the Constitution or Laws of any State to the Contrary notwithstanding.

The Senators and Representatives before mentioned, and the Members of the several State Legislatures, and all executive and judicial Officers, both of the United States and of the several States, shall be bound by Oath or Affirmation, to support this Constitution; but no religious Test shall ever be required as a Qualification to any Office or public Trust under the United States.

ARTICLE VII

The Ratification of the Conventions of nine States shall be sufficient for the Establishment of this Constitution between the States so ratifying the Same.

AMENDMENT I [1791]

Congress shall make no law respecting an establishment of religion, or prohibiting the free exercise thereof; or abridging the freedom of speech, or of the press; or the right of the people peaceably to assembly, and to petition the Government for a redress of grievances.

AMENDMENT II [1791]

A well regulated Militia, being necessary to the security of a free State, the right of the people to keep and bear Arms, shall not be infringed.

AMENDMENT III [1791]

No Soldier shall, in time of peace be quartered in any house, without the consent of the Owner, nor in time of war, but in a manner to be prescribed by law.

AMENDMENT IV [1791]

The right of the people to be secure in their persons, houses, papers, and effects, against unreasonable searches and seizures, shall not be violated, and no Warrants shall issue, but upon probable cause, supported by Oath or affirmation, and particularly describing the place to be searched, and the persons or things to be seized.

AMENDMENT V [1791]

No person shall be held to answer for a capital, or otherwise infamous crime, unless on a presentment or indictment of a Grand Jury, except in cases arising in the land or naval forces, or in the Militia, when in actual service in time of War or public danger; nor shall any person be subject for the same offence to be twice put in jeopardy of life or limb; nor shall be compelled in any criminal case to be a witness against himself, nor be deprived of life, liberty, or property, without due process of law; nor shall private property be taken for public use, without just compensation.

Amendment VI [1791]

In all criminal prosecutions, the accused shall enjoy the right to a speedy and public trial, by an impartial jury of the State and district wherein the crime shall have been committed, which district shall have been previously ascertained by law, and to be informed of the nature and cause of the accusation; to be confronted with the witnesses against him; to have compulsory process for obtaining witnesses in his favor, and to have the Assistance of Counsel for his defence.

Amendment VII [1791]

In Suits at common law, where the value in controversy shall exceed twenty dollars, the right of trial by jury shall be preserved, and no fact tried by jury, shall be otherwise re-examined in any Court of the United States, than according to the rules of the common law.

Amendment VIII [1791]

Excessive bail shall not be required, nor excessive fines imposed, nor cruel and unusual punishments inflicted.

Amendment IX [1791]

The enumeration in the Constitution, of certain rights, shall not be construed to deny or disparage others retained by the people.

Amendment X [1791]

The powers not delegated to the United States by the Constitution, nor prohibited by it to the States, are reserved to the States respectively, or to the people.

Amendment XI [1798]

The Judicial power of the United States shall not be construed to extend to any suit in law or equity, commenced or prosecuted against one of the United States by Citizens of another State, or by Citizens or Subjects of any Foreign State.

Amendment XII [1804]

The Electors shall meet in their respective states, and vote by ballot for President and Vice-President, one of whom, at least, shall not be an inhabitant of the same state with themselves; they shall name in their ballots the person voted for as President, and in distinct ballots the person voted for as Vice-President, and they shall make distinct lists of all persons voted for as President, and of all persons voted for as Vice-President, and of the number of votes for each, which lists they shall sign and certify, and transmit sealed to the seat of the government of the United States, directed to the President of the Senate;—The President of the Senate shall, in the presence of the Senate and House of Representatives, open all the certificates and the votes shall then be counted;—The person having the greatest number of votes for President, shall be the President, if such number be a majority of the whole number of Electors appointed; and if no person have such majority, then from the persons having the highest numbers not exceeding three on the list of those voted for as President, the House of Representatives shall choose immediately, by ballot, the President. But in choosing the President, the votes shall be taken by states, the representation from each state having one vote; a quorum for this purpose shall consist of a member or members from two-thirds of the states, and a majority of all states shall be necessary to a choice. And if the House of Representatives shall not choose a President whenever the right of choice shall devolve upon them, before the fourth day of March next following, then the Vice-President shall act as President, as in the case of the death or other constitutional disability of the President.—The person having the greatest number of votes as Vice-President, shall be the Vice-President, if such number be a majority of the whole number of Electors appointed, and if no person have a majority, then from the two highest numbers on the list, the Senate shall choose the Vice-President; a quorum for the purpose shall consist of two-thirds of the whole number of Senators, and a majority of the whole number shall be necessary to a choice. But no person constitutionally ineligible to the office of President shall be eligible to that of Vice-President of the United States.

Amendment XIII [1865]

Section 1.   Neither slavery nor involuntary servitude, except as a punishment for crime whereof the party shall have been duly convicted, shall exist within the United States, or any place subject to their jurisdiction.

Section 2.   Congress shall have power to enforce this article by appropriate legislation.

Amendment XIV [1868]

Section 1.   All persons born or naturalized in the United States, and subject to the jurisdiction thereof, are citizens of the United States and of the State wherein they reside. No State shall make or enforce any law which shall abridge the privileges or immunities of citizens of the United States; nor shall any State deprive any person of life, liberty, or property, without due process of law; nor deny to any person within its jurisdiction the equal protection of the laws.

Section 2.   Representatives shall be apportioned among the several States according to their respective numbers, counting the whole number of persons in each State, excluding Indians not taxed. But when the right to vote at any election for the choice of electors for President and Vice President of the United States, Representatives in Congress, the Executive and Judicial officers of a State, or the members of the Legislature thereof, is denied to any of the male inhabitants of such State, being twenty-one years of age, and citizens of the United States, or in any way abridged, except for participation in rebellion, or other crime, the basis of representation therein shall be reduced in the proportion which the number of such male citizens shall bear to the whole number of male citizens twenty-one years of age in such State.

Section 3.   No person shall be a Senator or Representative in Congress, or elector of President and Vice President, or hold any office, civil or military, under the United States, or under any State, who having previously taken an oath, as a member of Congress, or as an officer of the United States, or as a member of any State legislature, or as an executive or judicial officer of any State, to support the Constitution of the United States, shall have engaged in insurrection or rebellion against the same, or given aid or comfort to the enemies thereof. But Congress may by a vote of two-thirds of each House, remove such disability.

Section 4. The validity of the public debt of the United States, authorized by law, including debts incurred for payment of pensions and bounties for services in suppressing insurrection or rebellion, shall not be questioned. But neither the United States nor any State shall assume or pay any debt or obligation incurred in aid of insurrection or rebellion against the United States, or any claim for the loss or emancipation of any slave; but all such debts, obligations and claims shall be held illegal and void.

Section 5. The Congress shall have power to enforce, by appropriate legislation, the provisions of this article.

AMENDMENT XV [1870]

Section 1. The right of citizens of the United States to vote shall not be denied or abridged by the United States or by any State on account of race, color, or previous condition of servitude.

Section 2. The Congress shall have power to enforce this article by appropriate legislation.

AMENDMENT XVI [1913]

The Congress shall have power to lay and collect taxes on incomes, from whatever source derived, without apportionment among the several States, and without regard to any census or enumeration.

AMENDMENT XVII [1913]

Section 1. The Senate of the United States shall be composed of two Senators from each State, elected by the people thereof, for six years; and each Senator shall have one vote. The electors in each State shall have the qualifications requisite for electors of the most numerous branch of the State legislatures.

Section 2. When vacancies happen in the representation of any State in the Senate, the executive authority of such State shall issue writs of election to fill such vacancies: Provided, That the legislature of any State may empower the executive thereof to make temporary appointments until the people fill the vacancies by election as the legislature may direct.

Section 3. This amendment shall not be so construed as to affect the election or term of any Senator chosen before it becomes valid as part of the Constitution.

AMENDMENT XVIII [1919]

Section 1. After one year from the ratification of this article the manufacture, sale, or transportation of intoxicating liquors within, the importation thereof into, or the exportation thereof from the United States and all territory subject to the jurisdiction thereof for beverage purposes is hereby prohibited.

Section 2. The Congress and the several States shall have concurrent power to enforce this article by appropriate legislation.

Section 3. This article shall be inoperative unless it shall have been ratified as an amendment to the Constitution by the legislatures of the several States, as provided in the Constitution, within seven years from the date of the submission hereof to the States by the Congress.

AMENDMENT XIX [1920]

Section 1. The right of citizens of the United States to vote shall not be denied or abridged by the United States or by any State on account of sex.

Section 2. Congress shall have power to enforce this article by appropriate legislation.

AMENDMENT XX [1933]

Section 1. The terms of the President and Vice President shall end at noon on the 20th day of January, and the terms of Senators and Representatives at noon on the 3d day of January, of the years in which such terms would have ended if this article had not been ratified; and the terms of their successors shall then begin.

Section 2. The Congress shall assemble at least once in every year, and such meeting shall begin at noon on the 3d day of January, unless they shall by law appoint a different day.

Section 3. If, at the time fixed for the beginning of the term of the President, the President elect shall have died, the Vice President elect shall become President. If the President shall not have been chosen before the time fixed for the beginning of his term, or if the President elect shall have failed to qualify, then the Vice President elect shall act as President until a President shall have qualified; and the Congress may by law provide for the case wherein neither a President elect nor a Vice President elect shall have qualified, declaring who shall then act as President, or the manner in which one who is to act shall be selected, and such person shall act accordingly until a President or Vice President shall have qualified.

Section 4. The Congress may by law provide for the case of the death of any of the persons from whom the House of Representatives may choose a President whenever the right of choice shall have devolved upon them, and for the case of the death of any of the persons from whom the Senate may choose a Vice President whenever the right of choice shall have devolved upon them.

Section 5. Sections 1 and 2 shall take effect on the 15th day of October following the ratification of this article.

Section 6. This article shall be inoperative unless it shall have been ratified as an amendment to the Constitution by the legislatures of three-fourths of the several States within seven years from the date of its submission.

AMENDMENT XXI [1933]

Section 1. The eighteenth article of amendment to the Constitution of the United States is hereby repealed.

Section 2. The transportation or importation into any State, Territory, or possession of the United States for delivery or use therein of intoxicating liquors, in violation of the laws thereof, is hereby prohibited.

Section 3. This article shall be inoperative unless it shall have been ratified as an amendment to the Constitution by conventions in the several States, as provided in the Constitution, within seven years from the date of the submission hereof to the States by the Congress.

AMENDMENT XXII [1951]

Section 1. No person shall be elected to the office of the President more than twice, and no person who has held the office of President, or acted as President, for more than two years of a term to which some other person was elected President shall be elected to the office of President more than once. But this Article shall not apply to any person holding the office of President when this Article was proposed by the Congress, and shall not prevent any person who may be holding the office of President, or acting as President, during the term within which this Article becomes operative from holding the office of President or acting as President during the remainder of such term.

Section 2. This article shall be inoperative unless it shall have been ratified as an amendment to the Constitution by the legislatures of three-fourths of the several States within seven years from the date of its submission to the States by the Congress.

AMENDMENT XXIII [1961]

Section 1. The District constituting the seat of Government of the United States shall appoint in such manner as the Congress may direct:

A number of electors of President and Vice President equal to the whole number of Senators and Representatives in Congress to which the District would be entitled if it were a State, but in no event more than the least populous state; they shall be in addition to those appointed by the states, but they shall be considered, for the purposes of the election of President and Vice President, to be electors appointed by a state; and they shall meet in the District and perform such duties as provided by the twelfth article of amendment.

Section 2. The Congress shall have power to enforce this article by appropriate legislation.

AMENDMENT XXIV [1964]

Section 1. The right of citizens of the United States to vote in any primary or other election for President or Vice President, for electors for President or Vice President, or for Senator or Representative in Congress, shall not be denied or abridged by the United States, or any State by reason of failure to pay any poll tax or other tax.

Section 2. The Congress shall have power to enforce this article by appropriate legislation.

AMENDMENT XXV [1967]

Section 1. In case of the removal of the President from office or of his death or resignation, the Vice President shall become President.

Section 2. Whenever there is a vacancy in the office of the Vice President, the President shall nominate a Vice President who shall take office upon confirmation by a majority vote of both Houses of Congress.

Section 3. Whenever the President transmits to the President pro tempore of the Senate and the Speaker of the House of Representatives his written declaration that he is unable to discharge the powers and duties of his office, and until he transmits to them a written declaration to the contrary, such powers and duties shall be discharged by the Vice President as Acting President.

Section 4. Whenever the Vice President and a majority of either the principal officers of the executive departments or of such other body as Congress may by law provide, transmit to the President pro tempore of the Senate and the Speaker of the House of Representatives their written declaration that the President is unable to discharge the powers and duties of his office, the Vice President shall immediately assume the powers and duties of the office as Acting President.

Thereafter, when the President transmits to the President pro tempore of the Senate and the Speaker of the House of Representatives his written declaration that no inability exists, he shall resume the powers and duties of his office unless the Vice President and a majority of either the principal officers of the executive department or of such other body as Congress may by law provide, transmit within four days to the President pro tempore of the Senate and the Speaker of the House of Representatives their written declaration that the President is unable to discharge the powers and duties of his office. Thereupon Congress shall decide the issue, assembling within forty-eight hours for that purpose if not in session. If the Congress, within twenty-one days after receipt of the latter written declaration, or, if Congress is not in session, within twenty-one days after Congress is required to assemble, determines by two-thirds vote of both Houses that the President is unable to discharge the powers and duties of his office, the Vice President shall continue to discharge the same as Acting President; otherwise, the President shall resume the powers and duties of his office.

AMENDMENT XXVI [1971]

Section 1. The right of citizens of the United States, who are eighteen years of age or older, to vote shall not be denied or abridged by the United States or by any State on account of age.

Section 2. The Congress shall have power to enforce this article by appropriate legislation.

AMENDMENT XXVII [1992]

No law, varying the compensation for the services of the Senators and Representatives, shall take effect, until an election of Representatives shall have intervened.

APPENDIX C

The Adminstrative Procedure Act of 1946 (Excerpts)

Note: You can access the full text of the Administrative Procedure Act online by going to **http://uscode.house.gov/usc.htm**. In the "Title" box, type "5," and in the "Section" box, type a relevant section number (such as "551"). Click on "Search," and in the list of "documents found," click on the citation to access the text of the statute. The Office of the Law Revision Council of the U.S. House of Representatives maintains this Web site.

Section 551. Definitions

For the purpose of this subchapter—

* * * *

(4) "rule" means the whole or a part of an agency statement of general or particular applicability and future effect designed to implement, interpret, or prescribe law or policy or describing the organization, procedure, or practice requirements of an agency and includes the approval or prescription for the future of rates, wages, corporate or financial structures or reorganizations thereof, prices, facilities, appliances, services or allowances therefor or of valuations, costs, or accounting, or practices bearing on any of the foregoing[.]

* * * *

Section 552. Public Information; Agency Rules, Opinions, Orders, Records, and Proceedings

(a) Each agency shall make available to the public information as follows:

(1) Each agency shall separately state and currently publish in the Federal Register for the guidance of the public—

(A) descriptions of its central and field organization and the established places at which, the employees * * * from whom, and the methods whereby, the public may obtain information, make submittals or requests, or obtain decisions;

* * * *

(C) rules of procedure, descriptions of forms available or the places at which forms may be obtained, and instructions as to the scope and contents of all papers, reports, or examinations;

(D) substantive rules of general applicability adopted as authorized by law, and statements of general policy or interpretations of general applicability formulated and adopted by the agency[.]

* * *

* * * *

Section 552b. Open Meetings

* * * *

(j) Each agency subject to the requirements of this section shall annually report to Congress regarding its compliance with such requirements, including a tabulation of the total number of agency meetings open to the public, the total number of meetings closed to the public, the reasons for closing such meetings, and a description of any litigation brought against the agency under this section, including any costs assessed against the agency in such litigation * * *.

* * * *

Section 553. Rule Making

* * * *

(b) General notice of proposed rule making shall be published in the Federal Register, unless persons subject thereto are named and either personally served or otherwise have actual notice thereof in accordance with law. * * *

(c) After notice required by this section, the agency shall give interested persons an opportunity to participate in the rule making through submission of written data, views, or arguments with or without opportunity for oral presentation. * * *

* * * *

Section 554. Adjudications

* * * *

(b) Persons entitled to notice of an agency hearing shall be timely informed of—

(1) the time, place, and nature of the hearing;

(2) the legal authority and jurisdiction under which the hearing is to be held; and

(3) the matters of fact and law asserted.

* * * *

(c) The agency shall give all interested parties opportunity for—

(1) the submission and consideration of facts, arguments, offers of settlement, or proposals of adjustment when time, the nature of the proceeding, and the public interest permit; and

(2) to the extent that the parties are unable so to determine a controversy by consent, hearing and decision on notice * * *.

* * * *

Section 555. Ancillary Matters

* * * *

(c) Process, requirement of a report, inspection, or other investigative act or demand may not be issued, made, or enforced except as authorized by law. A person compelled to submit data or evidence is entitled to retain or, on payment of lawfully prescribed costs, procure a copy or transcript thereof, except that in a nonpublic investigatory proceeding the witness may for good cause be limited to inspection of the official transcript of his testimony.

* * * *

(e) Prompt notice shall be given of the denial in whole or in part of a written application, petition, or other request of an interested person made in connection with any agency proceeding. * * *

Section 556. Hearings; Presiding Employees; Powers and Duties; Burden of Proof; Evidence; Record as Basis of Decision

* * * *

(b) There shall preside at the taking of evidence—

(1) the agency;

(2) one or more members of the body which comprises the agency; or

(3) one or more administrative law judges * * *.

* * * *

(c) Subject to published rules of the agency and within its powers, employees presiding at hearings may—

(1) administer oaths and affirmations;

(2) issue subpoenas authorized by law;

(3) rule on offers of proof and receive relevant evidence;

(4) take depositions or have depositions taken when the ends of justice would be served;

(5) regulate the course of the hearing;

(6) hold conferences for the settlement or simplification of the issues by consent of the parties or by the use of alternative means of dispute resolution as provided in subchapter IV of this chapter;

(7) inform the parties as to the availability of one or more alternative means of dispute resolution, and encourage use of such methods;

* * * *

(9) dispose of procedural requests or similar matters;

(10) make or recommend decisions in accordance with * * * this title; and

(11) take other action authorized by agency rule consistent with this subchapter.

* * * *

Section 702. Right of Review

A person suffering legal wrong because of agency action * * * is entitled to judicial review thereof. An action in a court of the United States seeking relief other than money damages and stating a claim that an agency or an officer or employee thereof acted or failed to act in an official capacity or under color of legal authority shall not be dismissed nor relief therein be denied on the ground that it is against the United States or that the United States is an indispensable party. The United States may be named as a defendant in any such action, and a judgment or decree may be entered against the United States: Provided, [t]hat any mandatory or injunctive decree shall specify the [f]ederal officer or officers (by name or by title), and their successors in office, personally responsible for compliance. * * *

* * * *

Section 704. Actions Reviewable

Agency action made reviewable by statute and final agency action for which there is no other adequate remedy in a court are subject to judicial review. A preliminary, procedural, or intermediate agency action or ruling not directly reviewable is subject to review on the review of the final agency action.

Note: You can access the full text of Article 2 of the Uniform Commercial Code online at **http://www.leg.state.mn.us/ leg/statutes.asp**. In the "Retrieve a section:" box, type "336" and the section number of an appropriate UCC provision (such as "2-101"). Click on "GO" to access the text, which is Minnesota's version of the statute. The Office of the Revisor of Statutes of the State of Minnesota maintains this Web site. (The 2003 amendments to UCC Article 2 are not as yet available on the Web.)

Article 2
SALES

Part 1 Short Title, General Construction and Subject Matter

§ 2–101. Short Title.

This Article shall be known and may be cited as Uniform Commercial Code—Sales.

§ 2–102. Scope; Certain Security and Other Transactions Excluded From This Article.

Unless the context otherwise requires, this Article applies to transactions in goods; it does not apply to any transaction which although in the form of an unconditional contract to sell or present sale is intended to operate only as a security transaction nor does this Article impair or repeal any statute regulating sales to consumers, farmers or other specified classes of buyers.

§ 2–103. Definitions and Index of Definitions.

(1) In this Article unless the context otherwise requires

(a) "Buyer" means a person who buys or contracts to buy goods.

(b) "Good faith" in the case of a merchant means honesty in fact and the observance of reasonable commercial standards of fair dealing in the trade.

(c) "Receipt" of goods means taking physical possession of them.

(d) "Seller" means a person who sells or contracts to sell goods.

(2) Other definitions applying to this Article or to specified Parts thereof, and the sections in which they appear are:

"Acceptance". Section 2–606.
"Banker's credit". Section 2–325.
"Between merchants". Section 2–104.
"Cancellation". Section 2–106(4).
"Commercial unit". Section 2–105.
"Confirmed credit". Section 2–325.
"Conforming to contract". Section 2–106.
"Contract for sale". Section 2–106.
"Cover". Section 2–712.
"Entrusting". Section 2–403.
"Financing agency". Section 2–104.
"Future goods". Section 2–105.
"Goods". Section 2–105.
"Identification". Section 2–501.
"Installment contract". Section 2–612.
"Letter of Credit". Section 2–325.
"Lot". Section 2–105.
"Merchant". Section 2–104.
"Overseas". Section 2–323.
"Person in position of seller". Section 2–707.
"Present sale". Section 2–106.
"Sale". Section 2–106.
"Sale on approval". Section 2–326.
"Sale or return". Section 2–326.
"Termination". Section 2–106.

(3) The following definitions in other Articles apply to this Article:

"Check". Section 3–104.
"Consignee". Section 7–102.
"Consignor". Section 7–102.
"Consumer goods". Section 9–109.
"Dishonor". Section 3–507.
"Draft". Section 3–104.

(4) In addition Article 1 contains general definitions and principles of construction and interpretation applicable throughout this Article.

As amended in 1994 and 1999.

§ 2–104. Definitions: "Merchant"; "Between Merchants"; "Financing Agency".

(1) "Merchant" means a person who deals in goods of the kind or otherwise by his occupation holds himself out as having knowledge or skill peculiar to the practices or goods involved in the transaction or to whom such knowledge or skill may be attributed by his employment of an agent or broker or other intermediary who by his occupation holds himself out as having such knowledge or skill.

(2) "Financing agency" means a bank, finance company or other person who in the ordinary course of business makes advances against goods or documents of title or who by arrangement with either the seller or the buyer intervenes in ordinary course to make or collect payment due or claimed under the contract for sale, as by purchasing or paying the seller's draft or making advances against it or by merely taking it for collection whether or not documents of title accompany the draft. "Financing agency" includes also a bank or other person who similarly intervenes between persons who are in the position of seller and buyer in respect to the goods (Section 2–707).

(3) "Between merchants" means in any transaction with respect to which both parties are chargeable with the knowledge or skill of merchants.

§ 2–105. Definitions: Transferability; "Goods"; "Future" Goods; "Lot"; "Commercial Unit".

(1) "Goods" means all things (including specially manufactured goods) which are movable at the time of identification to the contract for sale other than the money in which the price is to be paid, investment securities (Article 8) and things in action. "Goods" also includes the unborn young of animals and growing crops and other identified things attached to realty as described in the section on goods to be severed from realty (Section 2–107).

(2) Goods must be both existing and identified before any interest in them can pass. Goods which are not both existing and identified are "future" goods. A purported present sale of future goods or of any interest therein operates as a contract to sell.

(3) There may be a sale of a part interest in existing identified goods.

(4) An undivided share in an identified bulk of fungible goods is sufficiently identified to be sold although the quantity of the bulk is not determined. Any agreed proportion of such a bulk or any quantity thereof agreed upon by number, weight or other measure may to the extent of the seller's interest in the bulk be sold to the buyer who then becomes an owner in common.

(5) "Lot" means a parcel or a single article which is the subject matter of a separate sale or delivery, whether or not it is sufficient to perform the contract.

(6) "Commercial unit" means such a unit of goods as by commercial usage is a single whole for purposes of sale and division of which materially impairs its character or value on the market or in use. A commercial unit may be a single article (as a machine) or a set of articles (as a suite of furniture or an assortment of sizes) or a quantity (as a bale, gross, or carload) or any other unit treated in use or in the relevant market as a single whole.

§ 2–106. Definitions: "Contract"; "Agreement"; "Contract for Sale"; "Sale"; "Present Sale"; "Conforming" to Contract; "Termination"; "Cancellation".

(1) In this Article unless the context otherwise requires "contract" and "agreement" are limited to those relating to the present or future sale of goods. "Contract for sale" includes both a present sale of goods and a contract to sell goods at a future time. A "sale" consists in the passing of title from the seller to the buyer for a price (Section 2–401). A "present sale" means a sale which is accomplished by the making of the contract.

(2) Goods or conduct including any part of a performance are "conforming" or conform to the contract when they are in accordance with the obligations under the contract.

(3) "Termination" occurs when either party pursuant to a power created by agreement or law puts an end to the contract otherwise than for its breach. On "termination" all obligations which are still executory on both sides are discharged but any right based on prior breach or performance survives.

(4) "Cancellation" occurs when either party puts an end to the contract for breach by the other and its effect is the same as that of "termination" except that the cancelling party also retains any remedy for breach of the whole contract or any unperformed balance.

§ 2–107. Goods to Be Severed From Realty: Recording.

(1) A contract for the sale of minerals or the like (including oil and gas) or a structure or its materials to be removed from realty is a contract for the sale of goods within this Article if they are to be severed by the seller but until severance a purported present sale thereof which is not effective as a transfer of an interest in land is effective only as a contract to sell.

(2) A contract for the sale apart from the land of growing crops or other things attached to realty and capable of severance without material harm thereto but not described in subsection (1) or of timber to be cut is a contract for the sale of goods within this Article whether the subject matter is to be severed by the buyer or by the seller even though it forms part of the realty at the time of contracting, and the parties can by identification effect a present sale before severance.

(3) The provisions of this section are subject to any third party rights provided by the law relating to realty records, and the contract for sale may be executed and recorded as a document transferring an interest in land and shall then constitute notice to third parties of the buyer's rights under the contract for sale.

As amended in 1972.

Part 2 Form, Formation and Readjustment of Contract

§ 2–201. Formal Requirements; Statute of Frauds.

(1) Except as otherwise provided in this section a contract for the sale of goods for the price of $500 or more is not enforceable by way of action or defense unless there is some writing sufficient to indicate that a contract for sale has been made between the parties and signed by the party against whom enforcement is sought or by his authorized agent or broker. A writing is not insufficient because it omits or incorrectly states a term agreed upon but the contract is not enforceable under this paragraph beyond the quantity of goods shown in such writing.

(2) Between merchants if within a reasonable time a writing in confirmation of the contract and sufficient against the sender is received and the party receiving it has reason to know its contents, its satisfies the requirements of subsection (1) against such party unless written notice of objection to its contents is given within ten days after it is received.

(3) A contract which does not satisfy the requirements of subsection (1) but which is valid in other respects is enforceable

   (a) if the goods are to be specially manufactured for the buyer and are not suitable for sale to others in the ordinary course of the seller's business and the seller, before notice of repudiation is received and under circumstances which reasonably indicate that the goods are for the buyer, has made either a substantial beginning of their manufacture or commitments for their procurement; or

   (b) if the party against whom enforcement is sought admits in his pleading, testimony or otherwise in court that a contract for sale was made, but the contract is not enforceable under this provision beyond the quantity of goods admitted; or

   (c) with respect to goods for which payment has been made and accepted or which have been received and accepted (Sec. 2–606).

§ 2–202. Final Written Expression: Parol or Extrinsic Evidence.

Terms with respect to which the confirmatory memoranda of the parties agree or which are otherwise set forth in a writing intended by the parties as a final expression of their agreement with respect to such terms as are included therein may not be contradicted by evidence of any prior agreement or of a contemporaneous oral agreement but may be explained or supplemented

   (a) by course of dealing or usage of trade (Section 1–205) or by course of performance (Section 2–208); and

   (b) by evidence of consistent additional terms unless the court finds the writing to have been intended also as a complete and exclusive statement of the terms of the agreement.

§ 2–203. Seals Inoperative.

The affixing of a seal to a writing evidencing a contract for sale or an offer to buy or sell goods does not constitute the writing a sealed instrument and the law with respect to sealed instruments does not apply to such a contract or offer.

§ 2–204. Formation in General.

(1) A contract for sale of goods may be made in any manner sufficient to show agreement, including conduct by both parties which recognizes the existence of such a contract.

(2) An agreement sufficient to constitute a contract for sale may be found even though the moment of its making is undetermined.

(3) Even though one or more terms are left open a contract for sale does not fail for indefiniteness if the parties have intended to make a contract and there is a reasonably certain basis for giving an appropriate remedy.

§ 2–205. Firm Offers.

An offer by a merchant to buy or sell goods in a signed writing which by its terms gives assurance that it will be held open is not revocable, for lack of consideration, during the time stated or if no time is stated for a reasonable time, but in no event may such period of irrevocability exceed three months; but any such term of assurance on a form supplied by the offeree must be separately signed by the offeror.

§ 2–206. Offer and Acceptance in Formation of Contract.

(1) Unless other unambiguously indicated by the language or circumstances

   (a) an offer to make a contract shall be construed as inviting acceptance in any manner and by any medium reasonable in the circumstances;

   (b) an order or other offer to buy goods for prompt or current shipment shall be construed as inviting acceptance either by a prompt promise to ship or by the prompt or current shipment of conforming or nonconforming goods, but such a shipment of non-conforming goods does not constitute an acceptance if the seller seasonably notifies the buyer that the shipment is offered only as an accommodation to the buyer.

(2) Where the beginning of a requested performance is a reasonable mode of acceptance an offeror who is not notified of acceptance within a reasonable time may treat the offer as having lapsed before acceptance.

§ 2–207. Additional Terms in Acceptance or Confirmation.

(1) A definite and seasonable expression of acceptance or a written confirmation which is sent within a reasonable time operates as an acceptance even though it states terms additional to or different from those offered or agreed upon, unless acceptance is expressly made conditional on assent to the additional or different terms.

(2) The additional terms are to be construed as proposals for addition to the contract. Between merchants such terms become part of the contract unless:

(a) the offer expressly limits acceptance to the terms of the offer;

(b) they materially alter it; or

(c) notification of objection to them has already been given or is given within a reasonable time after notice of them is received.

(3) Conduct by both parties which recognizes the existence of a contract is sufficient to establish a contract for sale although the writings of the parties do not otherwise establish a contract. In such case the terms of the particular contract consist of those terms on which the writings of the parties agree, together with any supplementary terms incorporated under any other provisions of this Act.

§ 2–208. Course of Performance or Practical Construction.

(1) Where the contract for sale involves repeated occasions for performance by either party with knowledge of the nature of the performance and opportunity for objection to it by the other, any course of performance accepted or acquiesced in without objection shall be relevant to determine the meaning of the agreement.

(2) The express terms of the agreement and any such course of performance, as well as any course of dealing and usage of trade, shall be construed whenever reasonable as consistent with each other; but when such construction is unreasonable, express terms shall control course of performance and course of performance shall control both course of dealing and usage of trade (Section 1–205).

(3) Subject to the provisions of the next section on modification and waiver, such course of performance shall be relevant to show a waiver or modification of any term inconsistent with such course of performance.

§ 2–209. Modification, Rescission and Waiver.

(1) An agreement modifying a contract within this Article needs no consideration to be binding.

(2) A signed agreement which excludes modification or rescission except by a signed writing cannot be otherwise modified or rescinded, but except as between merchants such a requirement on a form supplied by the merchant must be separately signed by the other party.

(3) The requirements of the statute of frauds section of this Article (Section 2–201) must be satisfied if the contract as modified is within its provisions.

(4) Although an attempt at modification or rescission does not satisfy the requirements of subsection (2) or (3) it can operate as a waiver.

(5) A party who has made a waiver affecting an executory portion of the contract may retract the waiver by reasonable notification received by the other party that strict performance will be required of any term waived, unless the retraction would be unjust in view of a material change of position in reliance on the waiver.

§ 2–210. Delegation of Performance; Assignment of Rights.

(1) A party may perform his duty through a delegate unless otherwise agreed or unless the other party has a substantial interest in having his original promisor perform or control the acts required by the contract. No delegation of performance relieves the party delegating of any duty to perform or any liability for breach.

(2) Except as otherwise provided in Section 9–406, unless otherwise agreed, all rights of either seller or buyer can be assigned except where the assignment would materially change the duty of the other party, or increase materially the burden or risk imposed on him by his contract, or impair materially his chance of obtaining return performance. A right to damages for breach of the whole contract or a right arising out of the assignor's due performance of his entire obligation can be assigned despite agreement otherwise.

(3) The creation, attachment, perfection, or enforcement of a security interest in the seller's interest under a contract is not a transfer that materially changes the duty of or increases materially the burden or risk imposed on the buyer or impairs materially the buyer's chance of obtaining return performance within the purview of subsection (2) unless, and then only to the extent that, enforcement actually results in a delegation of material performance of the seller. Even in that event, the creation, attachment, perfection, and enforcement of the security interest remain effective, but (i) the seller is liable to the buyer for damages caused by the delegation to the extent that the damages could not reasonably by prevented by the buyer, and (ii) a court having jurisdiction may grant other appropriate relief, including cancellation of the contract for sale or an injunction against enforcement of the security interest or consummation of the enforcement.

(4) Unless the circumstnaces indicate the contrary a prohibition of assignment of "the contract" is to be construed as barring only the delegation to the assigness of the assignor's performance.

(5) An assignment of "the contract" or of "all my rights under the contract" or an assignment in similar general terms is an assignment of rights and unless the language or the circumstances (as in an assignment for security) indicate the contrary,

it is a delegation of performance of the duties of the assignor and its acceptance by the assignee constitutes a promise by him to perform those duties. This promise is enforceable by either the assignor or the other party to the original contract.

(6) The other party may treat any assignment which delegates performance as creating reasonable grounds for insecurity and may without prejudice to his rights against the assignor demand assurances from the assignee (Section 2–609).

As amended in 1999.

Part 3 General Obligation and Construction of Contract

§ 2–301. General Obligations of Parties.

The obligation of the seller is to transfer and deliver and that of the buyer is to accept and pay in accordance with the contract.

§ 2–302. Unconscionable Contract or Clause.

(1) If the court as a matter of law finds the contract or any clause of the contract to have been unconscionable at the time it was made the court may refuse to enforce the contract, or it may enforce the remainder of the contract without the unconscionable clause, or it may so limit the application of any unconscionable clause as to avoid any unconscionable result.

(2) When it is claimed or appears to the court that the contract or any clause thereof may be unconscionable the parties shall be afforded a reasonable opportunity to present evidence as to its commercial setting, purpose and effect to aid the court in making the determination.

§ 2–303. Allocations or Division of Risks.

Where this Article allocates a risk or a burden as between the parties "unless otherwise agreed", the agreement may not only shift the allocation but may also divide the risk or burden.

§ 2–304. Price Payable in Money, Goods, Realty, or Otherwise.

(1) The price can be made payable in money or otherwise. If it is payable in whole or in part in goods each party is a seller of the goods which he is to transfer.

(2) Even though all or part of the price is payable in an interest in realty the transfer of the goods and the seller's obligations with reference to them are subject to this Article, but not the transfer of the interest in realty or the transferor's obligations in connection therewith.

§ 2–305. Open Price Term.

(1) The parties if they so intend can conclude a contract for sale even though the price is not settled. In such a case the price is a reasonable price at the time for delivery if

    (a) nothing is said as to price; or

    (b) the price is left to be agreed by the parties and they fail to agree; or

    (c) the price is to be fixed in terms of some agreed market or other standard as set or recorded by a third person or agency and it is not so set or recorded.

(2) A price to be fixed by the seller or by the buyer means a price for him to fix in good faith.

(3) When a price left to be fixed otherwise than by agreement of the parties fails to be fixed through fault of one party the other may at his option treat the contract as cancelled or himself fix a reasonable price.

(4) Where, however, the parties intend not to be bound unless the price be fixed or agreed and it is not fixed or agreed there is no contract. In such a case the buyer must return any goods already received or if unable so to do must pay their reasonable value at the time of delivery and the seller must return any portion of the price paid on account.

§ 2–306. Output, Requirements and Exclusive Dealings.

(1) A term which measures the quantity by the output of the seller or the requirements of the buyer means such actual output or requirements as may occur in good faith, except that no quantity unreasonably disproportionate to any stated estimate or in the absence of a stated estimate to any normal or otherwise comparable prior output or requirements may be tendered or demanded.

(2) A lawful agreement by either the seller or the buyer for exclusive dealing in the kind of goods concerned imposes unless otherwise agreed an obligation by the seller to use best efforts to supply the goods and by the buyer to use best efforts to promote their sale.

§ 2–307. Delivery in Single Lot or Several Lots.

Unless otherwise agreed all goods called for by a contract for sale must be tendered in a single delivery and payment is due only on such tender but where the circumstances give either party the right to make or demand delivery in lots the price if it can be apportioned may be demanded for each lot.

§ 2–308. Absence of Specified Place for Delivery.

Unless otherwise agreed

    (a) the place for delivery of goods is the seller's place of business or if he has none his residence; but

    (b) in a contract for sale of identified goods which to the knowledge of the parties at the time of contracting are in some other place, that place is the place for their delivery; and

    (c) documents of title may be delivered through customary banking channels.

§ 2–309. Absence of Specific Time Provisions; Notice of Termination.

(1) The time for shipment or delivery or any other action under a contract if not provided in this Article or agreed upon shall be a reasonable time.

(2) Where the contract provides for successive performances but is indefinite in duration it is valid for a reasonable time but unless otherwise agreed may be terminated at any time by either party.

(3) Termination of a contract by one party except on the happening of an agreed event requires that reasonable notification be received by the other party and an agreement dispensing with notification is invalid if its operation would be unconscionable.

§ 2–310. Open Time for Payment or Running of Credit; Authority to Ship Under Reservation.

Unless otherwise agreed

(a) payment is due at the time and place at which the buyer is to receive the goods even though the place of shipment is the place of delivery; and

(b) if the seller is authorized to send the goods he may ship them under reservation, and may tender the documents of title, but the buyer may inspect the goods after their arrival before payment is due unless such inspection is inconsistent with the terms of the contract (Section 2–513); and

(c) if delivery is authorized and made by way of documents of title otherwise than by subsection (b) then payment is due at the time and place at which the buyer is to receive the documents regardless of where the goods are to be received; and

(d) where the seller is required or authorized to ship the goods on credit the credit period runs from the time of shipment but post-dating the invoice or delaying its dispatch will correspondingly delay the starting of the credit period.

§ 2–311. Options and Cooperation Respecting Performance.

(1) An agreement for sale which is otherwise sufficiently definite (subsection (3) of Section 2–204) to be a contract is not made invalid by the fact that it leaves particulars of performance to be specified by one of the parties. Any such specification must be made in good faith and within limits set by commercial reasonableness.

(2) Unless otherwise agreed specifications relating to assortment of the goods are at the buyer's option and except as otherwise provided in subsections (1)(c) and (3) of Section 2–319 specifications or arrangements relating to shipment are at the seller's option.

(3) Where such specification would materially affect the other party's performance but is not seasonably made or where one party's cooperation is necessary to the agreed performance of the other but is not seasonably forthcoming, the other party in addition to all other remedies

(a) is excused for any resulting delay in his own performance; and

(b) may also either proceed to perform in any reasonable manner or after the time for a material part of his own performance treat the failure to specify or to cooperate as a breach by failure to deliver or accept the goods.

§ 2–312. Warranty of Title and Against Infringement; Buyer's Obligation Against Infringement.

(1) Subject to subsection (2) there is in a contract for sale a warranty by the seller that

(a) the title conveyed shall be good, and its transfer rightful; and

(b) the goods shall be delivered free from any security interest or other lien or encumbrance of which the buyer at the time of contracting has no knowledge.

(2) A warranty under subsection (1) will be excluded or modified only by specific language or by circumstances which give the buyer reason to know that the person selling does not claim title in himself or that he is purporting to sell only such right or title as he or a third person may have.

(3) Unless otherwise agreed a seller who is a merchant regularly dealing in goods of the kind warrants that the goods shall be delivered free of the rightful claim of any third person by way of infringement or the like but a buyer who furnishes specifications to the seller must hold the seller harmless against any such claim which arises out of compliance with the specifications.

§ 2–313. Express Warranties by Affirmation, Promise, Description, Sample.

(1) Express warranties by the seller are created as follows:

(a) Any affirmation of fact or promise made by the seller to the buyer which relates to the goods and becomes part of the basis of the bargain creates an express warranty that the goods shall conform to the affirmation or promise.

(b) Any description of the goods which is made part of the basis of the bargain creates an express warranty that the goods shall conform to the description.

(c) Any sample or model which is made part of the basis of the bargain creates an express warranty that the whole of the goods shall conform to the sample or model.

(2) It is not necessary to the creation of an express warranty that the seller use formal words such as "warrant" or "guarantee" or that he have a specific intention to make a warranty, but an affirmation merely of the value of the goods or a statement purporting to be merely the seller's opinion or commendation of the goods does not create a warranty.

§ 2–314. Implied Warranty: Merchantability; Usage of Trade.

(1) Unless excluded or modified (Section 2–316), a warranty that the goods shall be merchantable is implied in a contract

for their sale if the seller is a merchant with respect to goods of that kind. Under this section the serving for value of food or drink to be consumed either on the premises or elsewhere is a sale.

(2) Goods to be merchantable must be at least such as

(a) pass without objection in the trade under the contract description; and

(b) in the case of fungible goods, are of fair average quality within the description; and

(c) are fit for the ordinary purposes for which such goods are used; and

(d) run, within the variations permitted by the agreement, of even kind, quality and quantity within each unit and among all units involved; and

(e) are adequately contained, packaged, and labeled as the agreement may require; and

(f) conform to the promises or affirmations of fact made on the container or label if any.

(3) Unless excluded or modified (Section 2–316) other implied warranties may arise from course of dealing or usage of trade.

§ 2–315. Implied Warranty: Fitness for Particular Purpose.

Where the seller at the time of contracting has reason to know any particular purpose for which the goods are required and that the buyer is relying on the seller's skill or judgment to select or furnish suitable goods, there is unless excluded or modified under the next section an implied warranty that the goods shall be fit for such purpose.

§ 2–316. Exclusion or Modification of Warranties.

(1) Words or conduct relevant to the creation of an express warranty and words or conduct tending to negate or limit warranty shall be construed wherever reasonable as consistent with each other; but subject to the provisions of this Article on parol or extrinsic evidence (Section 2–202) negation or limitation is inoperative to the extent that such construction is unreasonable.

(2) Subject to subsection (3), to exclude or modify the implied warranty of merchantability or any part of it the language must mention merchantability and in case of a writing must be conspicuous, and to exclude or modify any implied warranty of fitness the exclusion must be by a writing and conspicuous. Language to exclude all implied warranties of fitness is sufficient if it states, for example, that "There are no warranties which extend beyond the description on the face hereof."

(3) Notwithstanding subsection (2)

(a) unless the circumstances indicate otherwise, all implied warranties are excluded by expressions like "as is", "with all faults" or other language which in common understanding calls the buyer's attention to the exclusion of warranties and makes plain that there is no implied warranty; and

(b) when the buyer before entering into the contract has examined the goods or the sample or model as fully as he desired or has refused to examine the goods there is no implied warranty with regard to defects which an examination ought in the circumstances to have revealed to him; and

(c) an implied warranty can also be excluded or modified by course of dealing or course of performance or usage of trade.

(4) Remedies for breach of warranty can be limited in accordance with the provisions of this Article on liquidation or limitation of damages and on contractual modification of remedy (Sections 2–718 and 2–719).

§ 2–317. Cumulation and Conflict of Warranties Express or Implied.

Warranties whether express or implied shall be construed as consistent with each other and as cumulative, but if such construction is unreasonable the intention of the parties shall determine which warranty is dominant. In ascertaining that intention the following rules apply:

(a) Exact or technical specifications displace an inconsistent sample or model or general language of description.

(b) A sample from an existing bulk displaces inconsistent general language of description.

(c) Express warranties displace inconsistent implied warranties other than an implied warranty of fitness for a particular purpose.

§ 2–318. Third Party Beneficiaries of Warranties Express or Implied.

Note: If this Act is introduced in the Congress of the United States this section should be omitted. (States to select one alternative.)

Alternative A

A seller's warranty whether express or implied extends to any natural person who is in the family or household of his buyer or who is a guest in his home if it is reasonable to expect that such person may use, consume or be affected by the goods and who is injured in person by breach of the warranty. A seller may not exclude or limit the operation of this section.

Alternative B

A seller's warranty whether express or implied extends to any natural person who may reasonably be expected to use, consume or be affected by the goods and who is injured in person by breach of the warranty. A seller may not exclude or limit the operation of this section.

Alternative C

A seller's warranty whether express or implied extends to any person who may reasonably be expected to use, consume or be affected by the goods and who is injured by breach of the warranty. A seller may not exclude or limit the operation of this section with respect to injury to the person of an individual to whom the warranty extends.

As amended 1966.

§ 2–319. F.O.B. and F.A.S. Terms.

(1) Unless otherwise agreed the term F.O.B. (which means "free on board") at a named place, even though used only in connection with the stated price, is a delivery term under which

    (a) when the term is F.O.B. the place of shipment, the seller must at that place ship the goods in the manner provided in this Article (Section 2–504) and bear the expense and risk of putting them into the possession of the carrier; or

    (b) when the term is F.O.B. the place of destination, the seller must at his own expense and risk transport the goods to that place and there tender delivery of them in the manner provided in this Article (Section 2–503);

    (c) when under either (a) or (b) the term is also F.O.B. vessel, car or other vehicle, the seller must in addition at his own expense and risk load the goods on board. If the term is F.O.B. vessel the buyer must name the vessel and in an appropriate case the seller must comply with the provisions of this Article on the form of bill of lading (Section 2–323).

(2) Unless otherwise agreed the term F.A.S. vessel (which means "free alongside") at a named port, even though used only in connection with the stated price, is a delivery term under which the seller must

    (a) at his own expense and risk deliver the goods alongside the vessel in the manner usual in that port or on a dock designated and provided by the buyer; and

    (b) obtain and tender a receipt for the goods in exchange for which the carrier is under a duty to issue a bill of lading.

(3) Unless otherwise agreed in any case falling within subsection (1)(a) or (c) or subsection (2) the buyer must seasonably give any needed instructions for making delivery, including when the term is F.A.S. or F.O.B. the loading berth of the vessel and in an appropriate case its name and sailing date. The seller may treat the failure of needed instructions as a failure of cooperation under this Article (Section 2–311). He may also at his option move the goods in any reasonable manner preparatory to delivery or shipment.

(4) Under the term F.O.B. vessel or F.A.S. unless otherwise agreed the buyer must make payment against tender of the required documents and the seller may not tender nor the buyer demand delivery of the goods in substitution for the documents.

§ 2–320. C.I.F. and C. & F. Terms.

(1) The term C.I.F. means that the price includes in a lump sum the cost of the goods and the insurance and freight to the named destination. The term C. & F. or C.F. means that the price so includes cost and freight to the named destination.

(2) Unless otherwise agreed and even though used only in connection with the stated price and destination, the term C.I.F. destination or its equivalent requires the seller at his own expense and risk to

    (a) put the goods into the possession of a carrier at the port for shipment and obtain a negotiable bill or bills of lading covering the entire transportation to the named destination; and

    (b) load the goods and obtain a receipt from the carrier (which may be contained in the bill of lading) showing that the freight has been paid or provided for; and

    (c) obtain a policy or certificate of insurance, including any war risk insurance, of a kind and on terms then current at the port of shipment in the usual amount, in the currency of the contract, shown to cover the same goods covered by the bill of lading and providing for payment of loss to the order of the buyer or for the account of whom it may concern; but the seller may add to the price the amount of the premium for any such war risk insurance; and

    (d) prepare an invoice of the goods and procure any other documents required to effect shipment or to comply with the contract; and

    (e) forward and tender with commercial promptness all the documents in due form and with any indorsement necessary to perfect the buyer's rights.

(3) Unless otherwise agreed the term C. & F. or its equivalent has the same effect and imposes upon the seller the same obligations and risks as a C.I.F. term except the obligation as to insurance.

(4) Under the term C.I.F. or C. & F. unless otherwise agreed the buyer must make payment against tender of the required documents and the seller may not tender nor the buyer demand delivery of the goods in substitution for the documents.

§ 2–321. C.I.F. or C. & F.: "Net Landed Weights"; "Payment on Arrival"; Warranty of Condition on Arrival.

Under a contract containing a term C.I.F. or C. & F.

(1) Where the price is based on or is to be adjusted according to "net landed weights", "delivered weights", "out turn" quantity or quality or the like, unless otherwise agreed the seller must reasonably estimate the price. The payment due on tender of the documents called for by the contract is the amount so estimated, but after final adjustment of the price a settlement must be made with commercial promptness.

(2) An agreement described in subsection (1) or any warranty of quality or condition of the goods on arrival places upon the seller the risk of ordinary deterioration, shrinkage and the like in transportation but has no effect on the place or time of identification to the contract for sale or delivery or on the passing of the risk of loss.

(3) Unless otherwise agreed where the contract provides for payment on or after arrival of the goods the seller must before payment allow such preliminary inspection as is feasible; but if the goods are lost delivery of the documents and payment are due when the goods should have arrived.

§ 2–322. Delivery "Ex-Ship".

(1) Unless otherwise agreed a term for delivery of goods "ex-ship" (which means from the carrying vessel) or in equivalent language is not restricted to a particular ship and requires delivery from a ship which has reached a place at the named port of destination where goods of the kind are usually discharged.

(2) Under such a term unless otherwise agreed

(a) the seller must discharge all liens arising out of the carriage and furnish the buyer with a direction which puts the carrier under a duty to deliver the goods; and

(b) the risk of loss does not pass to the buyer until the goods leave the ship's tackle or are otherwise properly unloaded.

§ 2–323. Form of Bill of Lading Required in Overseas Shipment; "Overseas".

(1) Where the contract contemplates overseas shipment and contains a term C.I.F. or C. & F. or F.O.B. vessel, the seller unless otherwise agreed must obtain a negotiable bill of lading stating that the goods have been loaded on board or, in the case of a term C.I.F. or C. & F., received for shipment.

(2) Where in a case within subsection (1) a bill of lading has been issued in a set of parts, unless otherwise agreed if the documents are not to be sent from abroad the buyer may demand tender of the full set; otherwise only one part of the bill of lading need be tendered. Even if the agreement expressly requires a full set

(a) due tender of a single part is acceptable within the provisions of this Article on cure of improper delivery (subsection (1) of Section 2–508); and

(b) even though the full set is demanded, if the documents are sent from abroad the person tendering an incomplete set may nevertheless require payment upon furnishing an indemnity which the buyer in good faith deems adequate.

(3) A shipment by water or by air or a contract contemplating such shipment is "overseas" insofar as by usage of trade or agreement it is subject to the commercial, financing or shipping practices characteristic of international deep water commerce.

§ 2–324. "No Arrival, No Sale" Term.

Under a term "no arrival, no sale" or terms of like meaning, unless otherwise agreed,

(a) the seller must properly ship conforming goods and if they arrive by any means he must tender them on arrival but he assumes no obligation that the goods will arrive unless he has caused the non-arrival; and

(b) where without fault of the seller the goods are in part lost or have so deteriorated as no longer to conform to the contract or arrive after the contract time, the buyer may proceed as if there had been casualty to identified goods (Section 2–613).

§ 2–325. "Letter of Credit" Term; "Confirmed Credit".

(1) Failure of the buyer seasonably to furnish an agreed letter of credit is a breach of the contract for sale.

(2) The delivery to seller of a proper letter of credit suspends the buyer's obligation to pay. If the letter of credit is dishonored, the seller may on seasonable notification to the buyer require payment directly from him.

(3) Unless otherwise agreed the term "letter of credit" or "banker's credit" in a contract for sale means an irrevocable credit issued by a financing agency of good repute and, where the shipment is overseas, of good international repute. The term "confirmed credit" means that the credit must also carry the direct obligation of such an agency which does business in the seller's financial market.

§ 2–326. Sale on Approval and Sale or Return; Rights of Creditors.

(1) Unless otherwise agreed, if delivered goods may be returned by the buyer even though they conform to the contract, the transaction is

(a) a "sale on approval" if the goods are delivered primarily for use, and

(b) a "sale or return" if the goods are delivered primarily for resale.

(2) Goods held on approval are not subject to the claims of the buyer's creditors until acceptance; goods held on sale or return are subject to such claims while in the buyer's possession.

(3) Any "or return" term of a contract for sale is to be treated as a separate contract for sale within the statute of frauds section of this Article (Section 2–201) and as contradicting the sale aspect of the contract within the provisions of this Article or on parol or extrinsic evidence (Section 2–202).

As amended in 1999.

§ 2–327. Special Incidents of Sale on Approval and Sale or Return.

(1) Under a sale on approval unless otherwise agreed

(a) although the goods are identified to the contract the risk of loss and the title do not pass to the buyer until acceptance; and

(b) use of the goods consistent with the purpose of trial is not acceptance but failure seasonably to notify the seller of election to return the goods is acceptance, and if the goods conform to the contract acceptance of any part is acceptance of the whole; and

(c) after due notification of election to return, the return is at the seller's risk and expense but a merchant buyer must follow any reasonable instructions.

(2) Under a sale or return unless otherwise agreed

(a) the option to return extends to the whole or any commercial unit of the goods while in substantially their original condition, but must be exercised seasonably; and

(b) the return is at the buyer's risk and expense.

§ 2–328. Sale by Auction.

(1) In a sale by auction if goods are put up in lots each lot is the subject of a separate sale.

(2) A sale by auction is complete when the auctioneer so announces by the fall of the hammer or in other customary manner. Where a bid is made while the hammer is falling in acceptance of a prior bid the auctioneer may in his discretion reopen the bidding or declare the goods sold under the bid on which the hammer was falling.

(3) Such a sale is with reserve unless the goods are in explicit terms put up without reserve. In an auction with reserve the auctioneer may withdraw the goods at any time until he announces completion of the sale. In an auction without reserve, after the auctioneer calls for bids on an article or lot, that article or lot cannot be withdrawn unless no bid is made within a reasonable time. In either case a bidder may retract his bid until the auctioneer's announcement of completion of the sale, but a bidder's retraction does not revive any previous bid.

(4) If the auctioneer knowingly receives a bid on the seller's behalf or the seller makes or procures such as bid, and notice has not been given that liberty for such bidding is reserved, the buyer may at his option avoid the sale or take the goods at the price of the last good faith bid prior to the completion of the sale. This subsection shall not apply to any bid at a forced sale.

Part 4 Title, Creditors and Good Faith Purchasers

§ 2–401. Passing of Title; Reservation for Security; Limited Application of This Section.

Each provision of this Article with regard to the rights, obligations and remedies of the seller, the buyer, purchasers or other third parties applies irrespective of title to the goods except where the provision refers to such title. Insofar as situations are not covered by the other provisions of this Article and matters concerning title became material the following rules apply:

(1) Title to goods cannot pass under a contract for sale prior to their identification to the contract (Section 2–501), and unless otherwise explicitly agreed the buyer acquires by their identification a special property as limited by this Act. Any retention or reservation by the seller of the title (property) in goods shipped or delivered to the buyer is limited in effect to a reservation of a security interest. Subject to these provisions and to the provisions of the Article on Secured Transactions (Article 9), title to goods passes from the seller to the buyer in any manner and on any conditions explicitly agreed on by the parties.

(2) Unless otherwise explicitly agreed title passes to the buyer at the time and place at which the seller completes his performance with reference to the physical delivery of the goods, despite any reservation of a security interest and even though a document of title is to be delivered at a different time or place; and in particular and despite any reservation of a security interest by the bill of lading

(a) if the contract requires or authorizes the seller to send the goods to the buyer but does not require him to deliver them at destination, title passes to the buyer at the time and place of shipment; but

(b) if the contract requires delivery at destination, title passes on tender there.

(3) Unless otherwise explicitly agreed where delivery is to be made without moving the goods,

(a) if the seller is to deliver a document of title, title passes at the time when and the place where he delivers such documents; or

(b) if the goods are at the time of contracting already identified and no documents are to be delivered, title passes at the time and place of contracting.

(4) A rejection or other refusal by the buyer to receive or retain the goods, whether or not justified, or a justified revocation of acceptance revests title to the goods in the seller. Such revesting occurs by operation of law and is not a "sale".

§ 2–402. Rights of Seller's Creditors Against Sold Goods.

(1) Except as provided in subsections (2) and (3), rights of unsecured creditors of the seller with respect to goods which have been identified to a contract for sale are subject to the buyer's rights to recover the goods under this Article (Sections 2–502 and 2–716).

(2) A creditor of the seller may treat a sale or an identification of goods to a contract for sale as void if as against him a retention of possession by the seller is fraudulent under any rule of law of the state where the goods are situated, except that retention of possession in good faith and current course of trade by a merchant-seller for a commercially reasonable time after a sale or identification is not fraudulent.

(3) Nothing in this Article shall be deemed to impair the rights of creditors of the seller

(a) under the provisions of the Article on Secured Transactions (Article 9); or

(b) where identification to the contract or delivery is made not in current course of trade but in satisfaction of or as security for a pre-existing claim for money, security or the like and is made under circumstances which under any rule of law of the state where the goods are situated would apart from this Article constitute the transaction a fraudulent transfer or voidable preference.

§ 2–403. Power to Transfer; Good Faith Purchase of Goods; "Entrusting".

(1) A purchaser of goods acquires all title which his transferor had or had power to transfer except that a purchaser of a limited interest acquires rights only to the extent of the interest purchased. A person with voidable title has power to transfer a good title to a good faith purchaser for value. When goods have been delivered under a transaction of purchase the purchaser has such power even though

(a) the transferor was deceived as to the identity of the purchaser, or

(b) the delivery was in exchange for a check which is later dishonored, or

(c) it was agreed that the transaction was to be a "cash sale", or

(d) the delivery was procured through fraud punishable as larcenous under the criminal law.

(2) Any entrusting of possession of goods to a merchant who deals in goods of that kind gives him power to transfer all rights of the entruster to a buyer in ordinary course of business.

(3) "Entrusting" includes any delivery and any acquiescence in retention of possession regardless of any condition expressed between the parties to the delivery or acquiescence and regardless of whether the procurement of the entrusting or the possessor's disposition of the goods have been such as to be larcenous under the criminal law.

(4) The rights of other purchasers of goods and of lien creditors are governed by the Articles on Secured Transactions (Article 9), Bulk Transfers (Article 6) and Documents of Title (Article 7).
As amended in 1988.

Part 5 Performance

§ 2–501. Insurable Interest in Goods; Manner of Identification of Goods.

(1) The buyer obtains a special property and an insurable interest in goods by identification of existing goods as goods to which the contract refers even though the goods so identified are non-conforming and he has an option to return or reject them. Such identification can be made at any time and in any manner explicitly agreed to by the parties. In the absence of explicit agreement identification occurs

(a) when the contract is made if it is for the sale of goods already existing and identified;

(b) if the contract is for the sale of future goods other than those described in paragraph (c), when goods are shipped, marked or otherwise designated by the seller as goods to which the contract refers;

(c) when the crops are planted or otherwise become growing crops or the young are conceived if the contract is for the sale of unborn young to be born within twelve months after contracting or for the sale of crops to be harvested within twelve months or the next normal harvest season after contracting whichever is longer.

(2) The seller retains an insurable interest in goods so long as title to or any security interest in the goods remains in him and where the identification is by the seller alone he may until default or insolvency or notification to the buyer that the identification is final substitute other goods for those identified.

(3) Nothing in this section impairs any insurable interest recognized under any other statute or rule of law.

§ 2–502. Buyer's Right to Goods on Seller's Insolvency.

(1) Subject to subsections (2) and (3) and even though the goods have not been shipped a buyer who has paid a part or all of the price of goods in which he has a special property under the provisions of the immediately preceding section may on making and keeping good a tender of any unpaid portion of their price recover them from the seller if:

(a) in the case of goods bought for personal, family, or household purposes, the seller repudiates or fails to deliver as required by the contract; or

(b) in all cases, the seller becomes insolvent within ten days after receipt of the first installment on their price.

(2) The buyer's right to recover the goods under subsection (1)(a) vests upon acquisition of a special property, even if the seller had not then repudiated or failed to deliver.

(3) If the identification creating his special property has been made by the buyer he acquires the right to recover the goods only if they conform to the contract for sale.
As amended in 1999.

§ 2–503. Manner of Seller's Tender of Delivery.

(1) Tender of delivery requires that the seller put and hold conforming goods at the buyer's disposition and give the buyer any notification reasonably necessary to enable him to take delivery. The manner, time and place for tender are determined by the agreement and this Article, and in particular

(a) tender must be at a reasonable hour, and if it is of goods they must be kept available for the period reasonably necessary to enable the buyer to take possession; but

(b) unless otherwise agreed the buyer must furnish facilities reasonably suited to the receipt of the goods.

(2) Where the case is within the next section respecting shipment tender requires that the seller comply with its provisions.

(3) Where the seller is required to deliver at a particular destination tender requires that he comply with subsection (1) and also in any appropriate case tender documents as described in subsections (4) and (5) of this section.

(4) Where goods are in the possession of a bailee and are to be delivered without being moved

(a) tender requires that the seller either tender a negotiable document of title covering such goods or procure acknowledgment by the bailee of the buyer's right to possession of the goods; but

(b) tender to the buyer of a non-negotiable document of title or of a written direction to the bailee to deliver is sufficient tender unless the buyer seasonably objects, and receipt by the bailee of notification of the buyer's rights fixes those rights as against the bailee and all third persons; but risk of loss of the goods and of any failure by the bailee to honor the non-negotiable document of title or to obey the direction remains on the seller until the buyer has had a reasonable time to present the document or direction, and a refusal by the bailee to honor the document or to obey the direction defeats the tender.

(5) Where the contract requires the seller to deliver documents

(a) he must tender all such documents in correct form, except as provided in this Article with respect to bills of lading in a set (subsection (2) of Section 2–323); and

(b) tender through customary banking channels is sufficient and dishonor of a draft accompanying the documents constitutes non-acceptance or rejection.

§ 2–504. Shipment by Seller.

Where the seller is required or authorized to send the goods to the buyer and the contract does not require him to deliver them at a particular destination, then unless otherwise agreed he must

(a) put the goods in the possession of such a carrier and make such a contract for their transportation as may be reasonable having regard to the nature of the goods and other circumstances of the case; and

(b) obtain and promptly deliver or tender in due form any document necessary to enable the buyer to obtain possession of the goods or otherwise required by the agreement or by usage of trade; and

(c) promptly notify the buyer of the shipment.

Failure to notify the buyer under paragraph (c) or to make a proper contract under paragraph (a) is a ground for rejection only if material delay or loss ensues.

§ 2–505. Seller's Shipment under Reservation.

(1) Where the seller has identified goods to the contract by or before shipment:

(a) his procurement of a negotiable bill of lading to his own order or otherwise reserves in him a security interest in the goods. His procurement of the bill to the order of a financing agency or of the buyer indicates in addi-

tion only the seller's expectation of transferring that interest to the person named.

(b) a non-negotiable bill of lading to himself or his nominee reserves possession of the goods as security but except in a case of conditional delivery (subsection (2) of Section 2–507) a non-negotiable bill of lading naming the buyer as consignee reserves no security interest even though the seller retains possession of the bill of lading.

(2) When shipment by the seller with reservation of a security interest is in violation of the contract for sale it constitutes an improper contract for transportation within the preceding section but impairs neither the rights given to the buyer by shipment and identification of the goods to the contract nor the seller's powers as a holder of a negotiable document.

§ 2–506. Rights of Financing Agency.

(1) A financing agency by paying or purchasing for value a draft which relates to a shipment of goods acquires to the extent of the payment or purchase and in addition to its own rights under the draft and any document of title securing it any rights of the shipper in the goods including the right to stop delivery and the shipper's right to have the draft honored by the buyer.

(2) The right to reimbursement of a financing agency which has in good faith honored or purchased the draft under commitment to or authority from the buyer is not impaired by subsequent discovery of defects with reference to any relevant document which was apparently regular on its face.

§ 2–507. Effect of Seller's Tender; Delivery on Condition.

(1) Tender of delivery is a condition to the buyer's duty to accept the goods and, unless otherwise agreed, to his duty to pay for them. Tender entitles the seller to acceptance of the goods and to payment according to the contract.

(2) Where payment is due and demanded on the delivery to the buyer of goods or documents of title, his right as against the seller to retain or dispose of them is conditional upon his making the payment due.

§ 2–508. Cure by Seller of Improper Tender or Delivery; Replacement.

(1) Where any tender or delivery by the seller is rejected because non-conforming and the time for performance has not yet expired, the seller may seasonably notify the buyer of his intention to cure and may then within the contract time make a conforming delivery.

(2) Where the buyer rejects a non-conforming tender which the seller had reasonable grounds to believe would be acceptable with or without money allowance the seller may if he seasonably notifies the buyer have a further reasonable time to substitute a conforming tender.

§ 2–509. Risk of Loss in the Absence of Breach.

(1) Where the contract requires or authorizes the seller to ship the goods by carrier

(a) if it does not require him to deliver them at a particular destination, the risk of loss passes to the buyer when the goods are duly delivered to the carrier even though the shipment is under reservation (Section 2–505); but

(b) if it does require him to deliver them at a particular destination and the goods are there duly tendered while in the possession of the carrier, the risk of loss passes to the buyer when the goods are there duly so tendered as to enable the buyer to take delivery.

(2) Where the goods are held by a bailee to be delivered without being moved, the risk of loss passes to the buyer

(a) on his receipt of a negotiable document of title covering the goods; or

(b) on acknowledgment by the bailee of the buyer's right to possession of the goods; or

(c) after his receipt of a non-negotiable document of title or other written direction to deliver, as provided in subsection (4)(b) of Section 2–503.

(3) In any case not within subsection (1) or (2), the risk of loss passes to the buyer on his receipt of the goods if the seller is a merchant; otherwise the risk passes to the buyer on tender of delivery.

(4) The provisions of this section are subject to contrary agreement of the parties and to the provisions of this Article on sale on approval (Section 2–327) and on effect of breach on risk of loss (Section 2–510).

§ 2–510. Effect of Breach on Risk of Loss.

(1) Where a tender or delivery of goods so fails to conform to the contract as to give a right of rejection the risk of their loss remains on the seller until cure or acceptance.

(2) Where the buyer rightfully revokes acceptance he may to the extent of any deficiency in his effective insurance coverage treat the risk of loss as having rested on the seller from the beginning.

(3) Where the buyer as to conforming goods already identified to the contract for sale repudiates or is otherwise in breach before risk of their loss has passed to him, the seller may to the extent of any deficiency in his effective insurance coverage treat the risk of loss as resting on the buyer for a commercially reasonable time.

§ 2–511. Tender of Payment by Buyer; Payment by Check.

(1) Unless otherwise agreed tender of payment is a condition to the seller's duty to tender and complete any delivery.

(2) Tender of payment is sufficient when made by any means or in any manner current in the ordinary course of business unless the seller demands payment in legal tender and gives any extension of time reasonably necessary to procure it.

(3) Subject to the provisions of this Act on the effect of an instrument on an obligation (Section 3–310), payment by check is conditional and is defeated as between the parties by dishonor of the check on due presentment.

As amended in 1994.

§ 2–512. Payment by Buyer Before Inspection.

(1) Where the contract requires payment before inspection non-conformity of the goods does not excuse the buyer from so making payment unless

(a) the non-conformity appears without inspection; or

(b) despite tender of the required documents the circumstances would justify injunction against honor under this Act (Section 5–109(b)).

(2) Payment pursuant to subsection (1) does not constitute an acceptance of goods or impair the buyer's right to inspect or any of his remedies.

As amended in 1995.

§ 2–513. Buyer's Right to Inspection of Goods.

(1) Unless otherwise agreed and subject to subsection (3), where goods are tendered or delivered or identified to the contract for sale, the buyer has a right before payment or acceptance to inspect them at any reasonable place and time and in any reasonable manner. When the seller is required or authorized to send the goods to the buyer, the inspection may be after their arrival.

(2) Expenses of inspection must be borne by the buyer but may be recovered from the seller if the goods do not conform and are rejected.

(3) Unless otherwise agreed and subject to the provisions of this Article on C.I.F. contracts (subsection (3) of Section 2–321), the buyer is not entitled to inspect the goods before payment of the price when the contract provides

(a) for delivery "C.O.D." or on other like terms; or

(b) for payment against documents of title, except where such payment is due only after the goods are to become available for inspection.

(4) A place or method of inspection fixed by the parties is presumed to be exclusive but unless otherwise expressly agreed it does not postpone identification or shift the place for delivery or for passing the risk of loss. If compliance becomes impossible, inspection shall be as provided in this section unless the place or method fixed was clearly intended as an indispensable condition failure of which avoids the contract.

§ 2–514. When Documents Deliverable on Acceptance; When on Payment.

Unless otherwise agreed documents against which a draft is drawn are to be delivered to the drawee on acceptance of the draft if it is payable more than three days after presentment; otherwise, only on payment.

§ 2–515. Preserving Evidence of Goods in Dispute.

In furtherance of the adjustment of any claim or dispute

(a) either party on reasonable notification to the other and for the purpose of ascertaining the facts and preserving evidence has the right to inspect, test and sample the goods including such of them as may be in the possession or control of the other; and

(b) the parties may agree to a third party inspection or survey to determine the conformity or condition of the goods and may agree that the findings shall be binding upon them in any subsequent litigation or adjustment.

Part 6 Breach, Repudiation and Excuse

§ 2–601. Buyer's Rights on Improper Delivery.

Subject to the provisions of this Article on breach in installment contracts (Section 2–612) and unless otherwise agreed under the sections on contractual limitations of remedy (Sections 2–718 and 2–719), if the goods or the tender of delivery fail in any respect to conform to the contract, the buyer may

(a) reject the whole; or

(b) accept the whole; or

(c) accept any commercial unit or units and reject the rest.

§ 2–602. Manner and Effect of Rightful Rejection.

(1) Rejection of goods must be within a reasonable time after their delivery or tender. It is ineffective unless the buyer seasonably notifies the seller.

(2) Subject to the provisions of the two following sections on rejected goods (Sections 2–603 and 2–604),

(a) after rejection any exercise of ownership by the buyer with respect to any commercial unit is wrongful as against the seller; and

(b) if the buyer has before rejection taken physical possession of goods in which he does not have a security interest under the provisions of this Article (subsection (3) of Section 2–711), he is under a duty after rejection to hold them with reasonable care at the seller's disposition for a time sufficient to permit the seller to remove them; but

(c) the buyer has no further obligations with regard to goods rightfully rejected.

(3) The seller's rights with respect to goods wrongfully rejected are governed by the provisions of this Article on Seller's remedies in general (Section 2–703).

§ 2–603. Merchant Buyer's Duties as to Rightfully Rejected Goods.

(1) Subject to any security interest in the buyer (subsection (3) of Section 2–711), when the seller has no agent or place of business at the market of rejection a merchant buyer is under a duty after rejection of goods in his possession or control to follow any reasonable instructions received from the seller with respect to the goods and in the absence of such instructions to make reasonable efforts to sell them for the seller's account if they are perishable or threaten to

decline in value speedily. Instructions are not reasonable if on demand indemnity for expenses is not forthcoming.

(2) When the buyer sells goods under subsection (1), he is entitled to reimbursement from the seller or out of the proceeds for reasonable expenses of caring for and selling them, and if the expenses include no selling commission then to such commission as is usual in the trade or if there is none to a reasonable sum not exceeding ten per cent on the gross proceeds.

(3) In complying with this section the buyer is held only to good faith and good faith conduct hereunder is neither acceptance nor conversion nor the basis of an action for damages.

§ 2–604. Buyer's Options as to Salvage of Rightfully Rejected Goods.

Subject to the provisions of the immediately preceding section on perishables if the seller gives no instructions within a reasonable time after notification of rejection the buyer may store the rejected goods for the seller's account or reship them to him or resell them for the seller's account with reimbursement as provided in the preceding section. Such action is not acceptance or conversion.

§ 2–605. Waiver of Buyer's Objections by Failure to Particularize.

(1) The buyer's failure to state in connection with rejection a particular defect which is ascertainable by reasonable inspection precludes him from relying on the unstated defect to justify rejection or to establish breach

(a) where the seller could have cured it if stated seasonably; or

(b) between merchants when the seller has after rejection made a request in writing for a full and final written statement of all defects on which the buyer proposes to rely.

(2) Payment against documents made without reservation of rights precludes recovery of the payment for defects apparent on the face of the documents.

§ 2–606. What Constitutes Acceptance of Goods.

(1) Acceptance of goods occurs when the buyer

(a) after a reasonable opportunity to inspect the goods signifies to the seller that the goods are conforming or that he will take or retain them in spite of their nonconformity; or

(b) fails to make an effective rejection (subsection (1) of Section 2–602), but such acceptance does not occur until the buyer has had a reasonable opportunity to inspect them; or

(c) does any act inconsistent with the seller's ownership; but if such act is wrongful as against the seller it is an acceptance only if ratified by him.

(2) Acceptance of a part of any commercial unit is acceptance of that entire unit.

§ 2–607. Effect of Acceptance; Notice of Breach; Burden of Establishing Breach After Acceptance; Notice of Claim or Litigation to Person Answerable Over.

(1) The buyer must pay at the contract rate for any goods accepted.

(2) Acceptance of goods by the buyer precludes rejection of the goods accepted and if made with knowledge of a non-conformity cannot be revoked because of it unless the acceptance was on the reasonable assumption that the non-conformity would be seasonably cured but acceptance does not of itself impair any other remedy provided by this Article for non-conformity.

(3) Where a tender has been accepted

(a) the buyer must within a reasonable time after he discovers or should have discovered any breach notify the seller of breach or be barred from any remedy; and

(b) if the claim is one for infringement or the like (subsection (3) of Section 2–312) and the buyer is sued as a result of such a breach he must so notify the seller within a reasonable time after he receives notice of the litigation or be barred from any remedy over for liability established by the litigation.

(4) The burden is on the buyer to establish any breach with respect to the goods accepted.

(5) Where the buyer is sued for breach of a warranty or other obligation for which his seller is answerable over

(a) he may give his seller written notice of the litigation. If the notice states that the seller may come in and defend and that if the seller does not do so he will be bound in any action against him by his buyer by any determination of fact common to the two litigations, then unless the seller after seasonable receipt of the notice does come in and defend he is so bound.

(b) if the claim is one for infringement or the like (subsection (3) of Section 2–312) the original seller may demand in writing that his buyer turn over to him control of the litigation including settlement or else be barred from any remedy over and if he also agrees to bear all expense and to satisfy any adverse judgment, then unless the buyer after seasonable receipt of the demand does turn over control the buyer is so barred.

(6) The provisions of subsections (3), (4) and (5) apply to any obligation of a buyer to hold the seller harmless against infringement or the like (subsection (3) of Section 2–312).

§ 2–608. Revocation of Acceptance in Whole or in Part.

(1) The buyer may revoke his acceptance of a lot or commercial unit whose non-conformity substantially impairs its value to him if he has accepted it

(a) on the reasonable assumption that its nonconformity would be cured and it has not been seasonably cured; or

(b) without discovery of such non-conformity if his acceptance was reasonably induced either by the diffi-

culty of discovery before acceptance or by the seller's assurances.

(2) Revocation of acceptance must occur within a reasonable time after the buyer discovers or should have discovered the ground for it and before any substantial change in condition of the goods which is not caused by their own defects. It is not effective until the buyer notifies the seller of it.

(3) A buyer who so revokes has the same rights and duties with regard to the goods involved as if he had rejected them.

§ 2–609. Right to Adequate Assurance of Performance.

(1) A contract for sale imposes an obligation on each party that the other's expectation of receiving due performance will not be impaired. When reasonable grounds for insecurity arise with respect to the performance of either party the other may in writing demand adequate assurance of due performance and until he receives such assurance may if commercially reasonable suspend any performance for which he has not already received the agreed return.

(2) Between merchants the reasonableness of grounds for insecurity and the adequacy of any assurance offered shall be determined according to commercial standards.

(3) Acceptance of any improper delivery or payment does not prejudice the party's right to demand adequate assurance of future performance.

(4) After receipt of a justified demand failure to provide within a reasonable time not exceeding thirty days such assurance of due performance as is adequate under the circumstances of the particular case is a repudiation of the contract.

§ 2–610. Anticipatory Repudiation.

When either party repudiates the contract with respect to a performance not yet due the loss of which will substantially impair the value of the contract to the other, the aggrieved party may

(a) for a commercially reasonable time await performance by the repudiating party; or

(b) resort to any remedy for breach (Section 2–703 or Section 2–711), even though he has notified the repudiating party that he would await the latter's performance and has urged retraction; and

(c) in either case suspend his own performance or proceed in accordance with the provisions of this Article on the seller's right to identify goods to the contract notwithstanding breach or to salvage unfinished goods (Section 2–704).

§ 2–611. Retraction of Anticipatory Repudiation.

(1) Until the repudiating party's next performance is due he can retract his repudiation unless the aggrieved party has since the repudiation cancelled or materially changed his position or otherwise indicated that he considers the repudiation final.

(2) Retraction may be by any method which clearly indicates to the aggrieved party that the repudiating party intends to

perform, but must include any assurance justifiably demanded under the provisions of this Article (Section 2–609).

(3) Retraction reinstates the repudiating party's rights under the contract with due excuse and allowance to the aggrieved party for any delay occasioned by the repudiation.

§ 2–612. "Installment Contract"; Breach.

(1) An "installment contract" is one which requires or authorizes the delivery of goods in separate lots to be separately accepted, even though the contract contains a clause "each delivery is a separate contract" or its equivalent.

(2) The buyer may reject any installment which is nonconforming if the non-conformity substantially impairs the value of that installment and cannot be cured or if the non-conformity is a defect in the required documents; but if the non-conformity does not fall within subsection (3) and the seller gives adequate assurance of its cure the buyer must accept that installment.

(3) Whenever non-conformity or default with respect to one or more installments substantially impairs the value of the whole contract there is a breach of the whole. But the aggrieved party reinstates the contract if he accepts a non-conforming installment without seasonably notifying of cancellation or if he brings an action with respect only to past installments or demands performance as to future installments.

§ 2–613. Casualty to Identified Goods.

Where the contract requires for its performance goods identified when the contract is made, and the goods suffer casualty without fault of either party before the risk of loss passes to the buyer, or in a proper case under a "no arrival, no sale" term (Section 2–324) then

(a) if the loss is total the contract is avoided; and

(b) if the loss is partial or the goods have so deteriorated as no longer to conform to the contract the buyer may nevertheless demand inspection and at his option either treat the contract as voided or accept the goods with due allowance from the contract price for the deterioration or the deficiency in quantity but without further right against the seller.

§ 2–614. Substituted Performance.

(1) Where without fault of either party the agreed berthing, loading, or unloading facilities fail or an agreed type of carrier becomes unavailable or the agreed manner of delivery otherwise becomes commercially impracticable but a commercially reasonable substitute is available, such substitute performance must be tendered and accepted.

(2) If the agreed means or manner of payment fails because of domestic or foreign governmental regulation, the seller may withhold or stop delivery unless the buyer provides a means or manner of payment which is commercially a substantial equivalent. If delivery has already been taken, payment by the means or in the manner provided by the

regulation discharges the buyer's obligation unless the regulation is discriminatory, oppressive or predatory.

§ 2–615. Excuse by Failure of Presupposed Conditions.

Except so far as a seller may have assumed a greater obligation and subject to the preceding section on substituted performance:

(a) Delay in delivery or non-delivery in whole or in part by a seller who complies with paragraphs (b) and (c) is not a breach of his duty under a contract for sale if performance as agreed has been made impracticable by the occurrence of a contingency the nonoccurrence of which was a basic assumption on which the contract was made or by compliance in good faith with any applicable foreign or domestic governmental regulation or order whether or not it later proves to be invalid.

(b) Where the causes mentioned in paragraph (a) affect only a part of the seller's capacity to perform, he must allocate production and deliveries among his customers but may at his option include regular customers not then under contract as well as his own requirements for further manufacture. He may so allocate in any manner which is fair and reasonable.

(c) The seller must notify the buyer seasonably that there will be delay or non-delivery and, when allocation is required under paragraph (b), of the estimated quota thus made available for the buyer.

§ 2–616. Procedure on Notice Claiming Excuse.

(1) Where the buyer receives notification of a material or indefinite delay or an allocation justified under the preceding section he may by written notification to the seller as to any delivery concerned, and where the prospective deficiency substantially impairs the value of the whole contract under the provisions of this Article relating to breach of installment contracts (Section 2–612), then also as to the whole,

(a) terminate and thereby discharge any unexecuted portion of the contract; or

(b) modify the contract by agreeing to take his available quota in substitution.

(2) If after receipt of such notification from the seller the buyer fails so to modify the contract within a reasonable time not exceeding thirty days the contract lapses with respect to any deliveries affected.

(3) The provisions of this section may not be negated by agreement except in so far as the seller has assumed a greater obligation under the preceding section.

Part 7 Remedies

§ 2–701. Remedies for Breach of Collateral Contracts Not Impaired.

Remedies for breach of any obligation or promise collateral or ancillary to a contract for sale are not impaired by the provisions of this Article.

§ 2–702. Seller's Remedies on Discovery of Buyer's Insolvency.

(1) Where the seller discovers the buyer to be insolvent he may refuse delivery except for cash including payment for all goods theretofore delivered under the contract, and stop delivery under this Article (Section 2–705).

(2) Where the seller discovers that the buyer has received goods on credit while insolvent he may reclaim the goods upon demand made within ten days after the receipt, but if misrepresentation of solvency has been made to the particular seller in writing within three months before delivery the ten day limitation does not apply. Except as provided in this subsection the seller may not base a right to reclaim goods on the buyer's fraudulent or innocent misrepresentation of solvency or of intent to pay.

(3) The seller's right to reclaim under subsection (2) is subject to the rights of a buyer in ordinary course or other good faith purchaser under this Article (Section 2–403). Successful reclamation of goods excludes all other remedies with respect to them.

§ 2–703. Seller's Remedies in General.

Where the buyer wrongfully rejects or revokes acceptance of goods or fails to make a payment due on or before delivery or repudiates with respect to a part or the whole, then with respect to any goods directly affected and, if the breach is of the whole contract (Section 2–612), then also with respect to the whole undelivered balance, the aggrieved seller may

    (a) withhold delivery of such goods;

    (b) stop delivery by any bailee as hereafter provided (Section 2–705);

    (c) proceed under the next section respecting goods still unidentified to the contract;

    (d) resell and recover damages as hereafter provided (Section 2–706);

    (e) recover damages for non-acceptance (Section 2–708) or in a proper case the price (Section 2–709);

    (f) cancel.

§ 2–704. Seller's Right to Identify Goods to the Contract Notwithstanding Breach or to Salvage Unfinished Goods.

(1) An aggrieved seller under the preceding section may

    (a) identify to the contract conforming goods not already identified if at the time he learned of the breach they are in his possession or control;

    (b) treat as the subject of resale goods which have demonstrably been intended for the particular contract even though those goods are unfinished.

(2) Where the goods are unfinished an aggrieved seller may in the exercise of reasonable commercial judgment for the purposes of avoiding loss and of effective realization either complete the manufacture and wholly identify the goods to the contract or cease manufacture and resell for scrap or salvage value or proceed in any other reasonable manner.

§ 2–705. Seller's Stoppage of Delivery in Transit or Otherwise.

(1) The seller may stop delivery of goods in the possession of a carrier or other bailee when he discovers the buyer to be insolvent (Section 2–702) and may stop delivery of carload, truckload, planeload or larger shipments of express or freight when the buyer repudiates or fails to make a payment due before delivery or if for any other reason the seller has a right to withhold or reclaim the goods.

(2) As against such buyer the seller may stop delivery until

    (a) receipt of the goods by the buyer; or

    (b) acknowledgment to the buyer by any bailee of the goods except a carrier that the bailee holds the goods for the buyer; or

    (c) such acknowledgment to the buyer by a carrier by reshipment or as warehouseman; or

    (d) negotiation to the buyer of any negotiable document of title covering the goods.

(3) (a) To stop delivery the seller must so notify as to enable the bailee by reasonable diligence to prevent delivery of the goods.

    (b) After such notification the bailee must hold and deliver the goods according to the directions of the seller but the seller is liable to the bailee for any ensuing charges or damages.

    (c) If a negotiable document of title has been issued for goods the bailee is not obliged to obey a notification to stop until surrender of the document.

    (d) A carrier who has issued a non-negotiable bill of lading is not obliged to obey a notification to stop received from a person other than the consignor.

§ 2–706. Seller's Resale Including Contract for Resale.

(1) Under the conditions stated in Section 2–703 on seller's remedies, the seller may resell the goods concerned or the undelivered balance thereof. Where the resale is made in good faith and in a commercially reasonable manner the seller may recover the difference between the resale price and the contract price together with any incidental damages allowed under the provisions of this Article (Section 2–710), but less expenses saved in consequence of the buyer's breach.

(2) Except as otherwise provided in subsection (3) or unless otherwise agreed resale may be at public or private sale including sale by way of one or more contracts to sell or of identification to an existing contract of the seller. Sale may be as a unit or in parcels and at any time and place and on any terms but every aspect of the sale including the method, manner, time, place and terms must be commercially reasonable. The resale must be reasonably identified as referring to the broken contract, but it is not necessary that the goods be in existence or that any or all of them have been identified to the contract before the breach.

(3) Where the resale is at private sale the seller must give the buyer reasonable notification of his intention to resell.

(4) Where the resale is at public sale

(a) only identified goods can be sold except where there is a recognized market for a public sale of futures in goods of the kind; and

(b) it must be made at a usual place or market for public sale if one is reasonably available and except in the case of goods which are perishable or threaten to decline in value speedily the seller must give the buyer reasonable notice of the time and place of the resale; and

(c) if the goods are not to be within the view of those attending the sale the notification of sale must state the place where the goods are located and provide for their reasonable inspection by prospective bidders; and

(d) the seller may buy.

(5) A purchaser who buys in good faith at a resale takes the goods free of any rights of the original buyer even though the seller fails to comply with one or more of the requirements of this section.

(6) The seller is not accountable to the buyer for any profit made on any resale. A person in the position of a seller (Section 2–707) or a buyer who has rightfully rejected or justifiably revoked acceptance must account for any excess over the amount of his security interest, as hereinafter defined (subsection (3) of Section 2–711).

§ 2–707. "Person in the Position of a Seller".

(1) A "person in the position of a seller" includes as against a principal an agent who has paid or become responsible for the price of goods on behalf of his principal or anyone who otherwise holds a security interest or other right in goods similar to that of a seller.

(2) A person in the position of a seller may as provided in this Article withhold or stopF delivery (Section 2–705) and resell (Section 2–706) and recover incidental damages (Section 2–710).

§ 2–708. Seller's Damages for Non-Acceptance or Repudiation.

(1) Subject to subsection (2) and to the provisions of this Article with respect to proof of market price (Section 2–723), the measure of damages for non-acceptance or repudiation by the buyer is the difference between the market price at the time and place for tender and the unpaid contract price together with any incidental damages provided in this Article (Section 2–710), but less expenses saved in consequence of the buyer's breach.

(2) If the measure of damages provided in subsection (1) is inadequate to put the seller in as good a position as performance would have done then the measure of damages is the profit (including reasonable overhead) which the seller would have made from full performance by the buyer, together with any incidental damages provided in this Article (Section 2–710), due allowance for costs reasonably incurred and due credit for payments or proceeds of resale.

§ 2–709. Action for the Price.

(1) When the buyer fails to pay the price as it becomes due the seller may recover, together with any incidental damages under the next section, the price

(a) of goods accepted or of conforming goods lost or damaged within a commercially reasonable time after risk of their loss has passed to the buyer; and

(b) of goods identified to the contract if the seller is unable after reasonable effort to resell them at a reasonable price or the circumstances reasonably indicate that such effort will be unavailing.

(2) Where the seller sues for the price he must hold for the buyer any goods which have been identified to the contract and are still in his control except that if resale becomes possible he may resell them at any time prior to the collection of the judgment. The net proceeds of any such resale must be credited to the buyer and payment of the judgment entitles him to any goods not resold.

(3) After the buyer has wrongfully rejected or revoked acceptance of the goods or has failed to make a payment due or has repudiated (Section 2–610), a seller who is held not entitled to the price under this section shall nevertheless be awarded damages for non-acceptance under the preceding section.

§ 2–710. Seller's Incidental Damages.

Incidental damages to an aggrieved seller include any commercially reasonable charges, expenses or commissions incurred in stopping delivery, in the transportation, care and custody of goods after the buyer's breach, in connection with return or resale of the goods or otherwise resulting from the breach.

§ 2–711. Buyer's Remedies in General; Buyer's Security Interest in Rejected Goods.

(1) Where the seller fails to make delivery or repudiates or the buyer rightfully rejects or justifiably revokes acceptance then with respect to any goods involved, and with respect to the whole if the breach goes to the whole contract (Section 2–612), the buyer may cancel and whether or not he has done so may in addition to recovering so much of the price as has been paid

(a) "cover" and have damages under the next section as to all the goods affected whether or not they have been identified to the contract; or

(b) recover damages for non-delivery as provided in this Article (Section 2–713).

(2) Where the seller fails to deliver or repudiates the buyer may also

(a) if the goods have been identified recover them as provided in this Article (Section 2–502); or

(b) in a proper case obtain specific performance or replevy the goods as provided in this Article (Section 2–716).

(3) On rightful rejection or justifiable revocation of acceptance a buyer has a security interest in goods in his possession

or control for any payments made on their price and any expenses reasonably incurred in their inspection, receipt, transportation, care and custody and may hold such goods and resell them in like manner as an aggrieved seller (Section 2–706)

§ 2–712. "Cover"; Buyer's Procurement of Substitute Goods.

(1) After a breach within the preceding section the buyer may "cover" by making in good faith and without unreasonable delay any reasonable purchase of or contract to purchase goods in substitution for those due from the seller.

(2) The buyer may recover from the seller as damages the difference between the cost of cover and the contract price together with any incidental or consequential damages as hereinafter defined (Section 2–715), but less expenses saved in consequence of the seller's breach.

(3) Failure of the buyer to effect cover within this section does not bar him from any other remedy.

§ 2–713. Buyer's Damages for Non-Delivery or Repudiation.

(1) Subject to the provisions of this Article with respect to proof of market price (Section 2–723), the measure of damages for non-delivery or repudiation by the seller is the difference between the market price at the time when the buyer learned of the breach and the contract price together with any incidental and consequential damages provided in this Article (Section 2–715), but less expenses saved in consequence of the seller's breach.

(2) Market price is to be determined as of the place for tender or, in cases of rejection after arrival or revocation of acceptance, as of the place of arrival.

§ 2–714. Buyer's Damages for Breach in Regard to Accepted Goods.

(1) Where the buyer has accepted goods and given notification (subsection (3) of Section 2–607) he may recover as damages for any non-conformity of tender the loss resulting in the ordinary course of events from the seller's breach as determined in any manner which is reasonable.

(2) The measure of damages for breach of warranty is the difference at the time and place of acceptance between the value of the goods accepted and the value they would have had if they had been as warranted, unless special circumstances show proximate damages of a different amount.

(3) In a proper case any incidental and consequential damages under the next section may also be recovered.

§ 2–715. Buyer's Incidental and Consequential Damages.

(1) Incidental damages resulting from the seller's breach include expenses reasonably incurred in inspection, receipt, transportation and care and custody of goods rightfully rejected, any commercially reasonable charges, expenses or commissions in connection with effecting cover and any other reasonable expense incident to the delay or other breach.

(2) Consequential damages resulting from the seller's breach include

(a) any loss resulting from general or particular requirements and needs of which the seller at the time of contracting had reason to know and which could not reasonably be prevented by cover or otherwise; and

(b) injury to person or property proximately resulting from any breach of warranty.

§ 2–716. Buyer's Right to Specific Performance or Replevin.

(1) Specific performance may be decreed where the goods are unique or in other proper circumstances.

(2) The decree for specific performance may include such terms and conditions as to payment of the price, damages, or other relief as the court may deem just.

(3) The buyer has a right of replevin for goods identified to the contract if after reasonable effort he is unable to effect cover for such goods or the circumstances reasonably indicate that such effort will be unavailing or if the goods have been shipped under reservation and satisfaction of the security interest in them has been made or tendered. In the case of goods bought for personal, family, or household purposes, the buyer's right of replevin vests upon acquisition of a special property, even if the seller had not then repudiated or failed to deliver.

As amended in 1999.

§ 2–717. Deduction of Damages From the Price.

The buyer on notifying the seller of his intention to do so may deduct all or any part of the damages resulting from any breach of the contract from any part of the price still due under the same contract.

§ 2–718. Liquidation or Limitation of Damages; Deposits.

(1) Damages for breach by either party may be liquidated in the agreement but only at an amount which is reasonable in the light of the anticipated or actual harm caused by the breach, the difficulties of proof of loss, and the inconvenience or nonfeasibility of otherwise obtaining an adequate remedy. A term fixing unreasonably large liquidated damages is void as a penalty.

(2) Where the seller justifiably withholds delivery of goods because of the buyer's breach, the buyer is entitled to restitution of any amount by which the sum of his payments exceeds

(a) the amount to which the seller is entitled by virtue of terms liquidating the seller's damages in accordance with subsection (1), or

(b) in the absence of such terms, twenty per cent of the value of the total performance for which the buyer is obligated under the contract or $500, whichever is smaller.

(3) The buyer's right to restitution under subsection (2) is subject to offset to the extent that the seller establishes

(a) a right to recover damages under the provisions of this Article other than subsection (1), and

(b) the amount or value of any benefits received by the buyer directly or indirectly by reason of the contract.

(4) Where a seller has received payment in goods their reasonable value or the proceeds of their resale shall be treated as payments for the purposes of subsection (2); but if the seller has notice of the buyer's breach before reselling goods received in part performance, his resale is subject to the conditions laid down in this Article on resale by an aggrieved seller (Section 2–706).

§ 2–719. Contractual Modification or Limitation of Remedy.

(1) Subject to the provisions of subsections (2) and (3) of this section and of the preceding section on liquidation and limitation of damages,

(a) the agreement may provide for remedies in addition to or in substitution for those provided in this Article and may limit or alter the measure of damages recoverable under this Article, as by limiting the buyer's remedies to return of the goods and repayment of the price or to repair and replacement of nonconforming goods or parts; and

(b) resort to a remedy as provided is optional unless the remedy is expressly agreed to be exclusive, in which case it is the sole remedy.

(2) Where circumstances cause an exclusive or limited remedy to fail of its essential purpose, remedy may be had as provided in this Act.

(3) Consequential damages may be limited or excluded unless the limitation or exclusion is unconscionable. Limitation of consequential damages for injury to the person in the case of consumer goods is prima facie unconscionable but limitation of damages where the loss is commercial is not.

§ 2–720. Effect of "Cancellation" or "Rescission" on Claims for Antecedent Breach.

Unless the contrary intention clearly appears, expressions of "cancellation" or "rescission" of the contract or the like shall not be construed as a renunciation or discharge of any claim in damages for an antecedent breach.

§ 2–721. Remedies for Fraud.

Remedies for material misrepresentation or fraud include all remedies available under this Article for non-fraudulent breach. Neither rescission or a claim for rescission of the contract for sale nor rejection or return of the goods shall bar or be deemed inconsistent with a claim for damages or other remedy.

§ 2–722. Who Can Sue Third Parties for Injury to Goods.

Where a third party so deals with goods which have been identified to a contract for sale as to cause actionable injury to a party to that contract

(a) a right of action against the third party is in either party to the contract for sale who has title to or a security interest or a special property or an insurable interest in the goods; and if the goods have been destroyed or converted a right of action is also in the party who either bore the risk of loss under the contract for sale or has since the injury assumed that risk as against the other;

(b) if at the time of the injury the party plaintiff did not bear the risk of loss as against the other party to the contract for sale and there is no arrangement between them for disposition of the recovery, his suit or settlement is, subject to his own interest, as a fiduciary for the other party to the contract;

(c) either party may with the consent of the other sue for the benefit of whom it may concern.

§ 2–723. Proof of Market Price: Time and Place.

(1) If an action based on anticipatory repudiation comes to trial before the time for performance with respect to some or all of the goods, any damages based on market price (Section 2–708 or Section 2–713) shall be determined according to the price of such goods prevailing at the time when the aggrieved party learned of the repudiation.

(2) If evidence of a price prevailing at the times or places described in this Article is not readily available the price prevailing within any reasonable time before or after the time described or at any other place which in commercial judgment or under usage of trade would serve as a reasonable substitute for the one described may be used, making any proper allowance for the cost of transporting the goods to or from such other place.

(3) Evidence of a relevant price prevailing at a time or place other than the one described in this Article offered by one party is not admissible unless and until he has given the other party such notice as the court finds sufficient to prevent unfair surprise.

§ 2–724. Admissibility of Market Quotations.

Whenever the prevailing price or value of any goods regularly bought and sold in any established commodity market is in issue, reports in official publications or trade journals or in newspapers or periodicals of general circulation published as the reports of such market shall be admissible in evidence. The circumstances of the preparation of such a report may be shown to affect its weight but not its admissibility.

§ 2–725. Statute of Limitations in Contracts for Sale.

(1) An action for breach of any contract for sale must be commenced within four years after the cause of action has accrued. By the original agreement the parties may reduce the period of limitation to not less than one year but may not extend it.

(2) A cause of action accrues when the breach occurs, regardless of the aggrieved party's lack of knowledge of the breach. A breach of warranty occurs when tender of delivery is made, except that where a warranty explicitly extends to future performance of the goods and discovery of the breach must await the time of such performance the cause of action accrues when the breach is or should have been discovered.

(3) Where an action commenced within the time limited by subsection (1) is so terminated as to leave available a remedy by another action for the same breach such other action may be commenced after the expiration of the time limited and within six months after the termination of the first action unless the termination resulted from voluntary discontinuance or from dismissal for failure or neglect to prosecute.

(4) This section does not alter the law on tolling of the statute of limitations nor does it apply to causes of action which have accrued before this Act becomes effective.

Article 2 Amendments (Excerpts)[1]

Part 1 Short Title, General Construction and Subject Matter

* * * *

§ 2–103. Definitions and Index of Definitions.

(1) In this article unless the context otherwise requires

* * * *

(b) "Conspicuous", with reference to a term, means so written, displayed, or presented that a reasonable person against which it is to operate ought to have noticed it. A term in an electronic record intended to evoke a response by an electronic agent is conspicuous if it is presented in a form that would enable a reasonably configured electronic agent to take it into account or react to it without review of the record by an individual. Whether a term is "conspicuous" or not is a decision for the court. Conspicuous terms include the following:

(i) for a person:

(A) a heading in capitals equal to or greater in size than the surrounding text, or in contrasting type, font, or color to the surrounding text of the same or lesser size and;

(B) language in the body of a record or display in larger type than the surrounding text, or in contrasting type, font, or color to the surrounding text of the same size, or set off from surrounding text of the same size by symbols or other marks that call attention to the language; and

(ii) for a person or an electronic agent, a term that is so placed in a record or display that the person or electronic agent cannot proceed without taking action with respect to the particular term.

(c) "Consumer" means an individual who buys or contracts to buy goods that, at the time of contracting, are intended by the individual to be used primarily for personal, family, or household purposes.

(d) "Consumer contract" means a contract between a merchant seller and a consumer.

* * * *

(j) "Good faith" means honesty in fact and the observance of reasonable commercial standards of fair dealing.

(k) "Goods" means all things that are movable at the time of identification to a contract for sale. The term includes future goods, specially manufactured goods, the unborn young of animals, growing crops, and other identified things attached to realty as described in Section 2–107. The term does not include information, the money in which the price is to be paid, investment securities under Article 8, the subject matter of foreign exchange transactions, and choses in action.

* * * *

(m) "Record" means information that is inscribed on a tangible medium or that is stored in an electronic or other medium and is retrievable in perceivable form.

(n) "Remedial promise" means a promise by the seller to repair or replace the goods or to refund all or part of the price upon the happening of a specified event.

* * * *

(p) "Sign" means, with present intent to authenticate or adopt a record,

(i) to execute or adopt a tangible symbol; or

(ii) to attach to or logically associate with the record an electronic sound, symbol, or process.

* * * *

Part 2 Form, Formation, Terms and Readjustment of Contract; Electronic Contracting

§ 2–201. Formal Requirements; Statute of Frauds.

(1) A contract for the sale of goods for the price of $5,000 or more is not enforceable by way of action or defense unless there is some record sufficient to indicate that a contract for sale has been made between the parties and signed by the party against which enforcement is sought or by the party's authorized agent or broker. A record is not insufficient because it omits or incorrectly states a term agreed upon but the contract is not enforceable under this subsection beyond the quantity of goods shown in the record.

(2) Between merchants if within a reasonable time a record in confirmation of the contract and sufficient against the sender is received and the party receiving it has reason to know its contents, it satisfies the requirements of subsection (1) against the recipient unless notice of objection to its contents is given in a record within 10 days after it is received.

---

1. Additions and new wording are underlined. What follows represents only selected changes made by the 2003 amendments. Although the National Conference of Commissioners on Uniform State Laws and the American Law Institute approved the amendments in May of 2003, as of this writing, they have not as yet been adopted by any state.

(3) A contract which does not satisfy the requirements of subsection (1) but which is valid in other respects is enforceable

(a) if the goods are to be specially manufactured for the buyer and are not suitable for sale to others in the ordinary course of the seller's business and the seller, before notice of repudiation is received and under circumstances which reasonably indicate that the goods are for the buyer, has made either a substantial beginning of their manufacture or commitments for their procurement; or

(b) if the party against which enforcement is sought admits in the party's pleading, or in the party's testimony or otherwise under oath that a contract for sale was made, but the contract is not enforceable under this paragraph beyond the quantity of goods admitted; or

(c) with respect to goods for which payment has been made and accepted or which have been received and accepted (Sec. 2–606).

(4) A contract that is enforceable under this section is not rendered unenforceable merely because it is not capable of being performed within one year or any other applicable period after its making.

*   *   *   *

§ 2–207. Terms of Contract; Effect of Confirmation.

Subject to Section 2–202, if (i) conduct by both parties recognizes the existence of a contract although their records do not otherwise establish a contract, (ii) a contract is formed by an offer and acceptance, or (iii) a contract formed in any manner is confirmed by a record that contains terms additional to or different from those in the contract being confirmed, the terms of the contract, are:

(a) terms that appear in the records of both parties;

(b) terms, whether in a record or not, to which both parties agree; and

(c) terms supplied or incorporated under any provision of this Act.

*   *   *   *

Part 3 General Obligation and Construction of Contract

*   *   *   *

§ 2–312. Warranty of Title and Against Infringement; Buyer's Obligation Against Infringement.

(1) Subject to subsection (3) there is in a contract for sale a warranty by the seller that

(a) the title conveyed shall be, good and its transfer rightful and shall not, unreasonably expose the buyer to litigation because of any colorable claim to or interest in the goods; and

(b) the goods shall be delivered free from any security interest or other lien or encumbrance of which the buyer at the time of contracting has no knowledge.

(2) Unless otherwise agreed a seller that is a merchant regularly dealing in goods of the kind warrants that the goods shall be delivered free of the rightful claim of any third person by way of infringement or the like but a buyer that furnishes specifications to the seller must hold the seller harmless against any such claim that arises out of compliance with the specifications.

(3) A warranty under this section may be disclaimed or modified only by specific language or by circumstances that give the buyer reason to know that the seller does not claim title, that the seller is purporting to sell only the right or title as the seller or a third person may have, or that the seller is selling subject to any claims of infringement or the like.

§ 2–313. Express Warranties by Affirmation, Promise, Description, Sample; Remedial Promise.

(1) In this section, "immediate buyer" means a buyer that enters into a contract with the seller.

*   *   *   *

(4) Any remedial promise made by the seller to the immediate buyer creates an obligation that the promise will be performed upon the happening of the specified event.

§ 2–313A. Obligation to Remote Purchaser Created by Record Packaged with or Accompanying Goods.

(1) In this section:

(a) "Immediate buyer" means a buyer that enters into a contract with the seller.

(b) "Remote purchaser" means a person that buys or leases goods from an immediate buyer or other person in the normal chain of distribution.

(2) This section applies only to new goods and goods sold or leased as new goods in a transaction of purchase in the normal chain of distribution.

(3) If in a record packaged with or accompanying the goods the seller makes an affirmation of fact or promise that relates to the goods, provides a description that relates to the goods, or makes a remedial promise, and the seller reasonably expects the record to be, and the record is, furnished to the remote purchaser, the seller has an obligation to the remote purchaser that:

(a) the goods will conform to the affirmation of fact, promise or description unless a reasonable person in the position of the remote purchaser would not believe that the affirmation of fact, promise or description created an obligation; and

(b) the seller will perform the remedial promise.

(4) It is not necessary to the creation of an obligation under this section that the seller use formal words such as "warrant" or "guarantee" or that the seller have a specific intention to undertake an obligation, but an affirmation merely of the

value of the goods or a statement purporting to be merely the seller's opinion or commendation of the goods does not create an obligation.

(5) The following rules apply to the remedies for breach of an obligation created under this section:

(a) The seller may modify or limit the remedies available to the remote purchaser if the modification or limitation is furnished to the remote purchaser no later than the time of purchase or if the modification or limitation is contained in the record that contains the affirmation of fact, promise or description.

(b) Subject to a modification or limitation of remedy, a seller in breach is liable for incidental or consequential damages under Section 2–715, but not for lost profits.

(c) The remote purchaser may recover as damages for breach of a seller's obligation arising under subsection (2) the loss resulting in the ordinary course of events as determined in any reasonable manner.

(5) An obligation that is not a remedial promise is breached if the goods did not conform to the affirmation of fact, promise or description creating the obligation when the goods left the seller's control.

§ 2–313B. Obligation to Remote Purchaser Created by Communication to the Public.

(1) In this section:

(a) "Immediate buyer" means a buyer that enters into a contract with the seller.

(b) "Remote purchaser" means a person that buys or leases goods from an immediate buyer or other person in the normal chain of distribution.

(2) This section applies only to new goods and goods sold or leased as new goods in a transaction of purchase in the normal chain of distribution.

(3) If in an advertisement or a similar communication to the public a seller makes an affirmation of fact or promise that relates to the goods, provides a description that relates to the goods, or makes a remedial promise, and the remote purchaser enters into a transaction of purchase with knowledge of and with the expectation that the goods will conform to the affirmation of fact, promise, or description, or that the seller will perform the remedial promise, the seller has an obligation to the remote purchaser that:

(a) the goods will conform to the affirmation of fact, promise or description unless a reasonable person in the position of the remote purchaser would not believe that the affirmation of fact, promise or description created an obligation; and

(b) the seller will perform the remedial promise.

(4) It is not necessary to the creation of an obligation under this section that the seller use formal words such as "warrant" or "guarantee" or that the seller have a specific inten-

tion to undertake an obligation, but an affirmation merely of the value of the goods or a statement purporting to be merely the seller's opinion or commendation of the goods does not create an obligation.

(5) The following rules apply to the remedies for breach of an obligation created under this section:

(a) The seller may modify or limit the remedies available to the remote purchaser if the modification or limitation is furnished to the remote purchaser no later than the time of purchase. The modification or limitation may be furnished as part of the communication that contains the affirmation of fact, promise or description.

(b) Subject to a modification or limitation of remedy, a seller in breach is liable for incidental or consequential damages under Section 2–715, but not for lost profits.

(c) The remote purchaser may recover as damages for breach of a seller's obligation arising under subsection (2) the loss resulting in the ordinary course of events as determined in any reasonable manner.

(6) An obligation that is not a remedial promise is breached if the goods did not conform to the affirmation of fact, promise or description creating the obligation when the goods left the seller's control.

*   *   *   *

§ 2–316. Exclusion or Modification of Warranties.
*   *   *   *

(2) Subject to subsection (3), to exclude or modify the implied warranty of merchantability or any part of it in a consumer contract the language must be in a record, be conspicuous, and state "The seller undertakes no responsibility for the quality of the goods except as otherwise provided in this contract," and in any other contract the language must mention merchantability and in case of a record must be conspicuous. Subject to subsection (3), to exclude or modify the implied warranty of fitness the exclusion must be in a record and be conspicuous. Language to exclude all implied warranties of fitness in a consumer contract must state "The seller assumes no responsibility that the goods will be fit for any particular purpose for which you may be buying these goods, except as otherwise provided in the contract," and in any other contract the language is sufficient if it states, for example, that "There are no warranties that extend beyond the description on the face hereof." Language that satisfies the requirements of this subsection for the exclusion and modification of a warranty in a consumer contract also satisfies the requirements for any other contract.

(3) Notwithstanding subsection (2):

(a) unless the circumstances indicate otherwise, all implied warranties are excluded by expressions like "as is", "with all faults" or other language which in common understanding calls the buyer's attention to the exclusion of warranties, makes plain that there is no implied warranty, and in a consumer contract evidenced by a record is set forth conspicuously in the record; and

(b) when the buyer before entering into the contract has examined the goods or the sample or model as fully as desired or has refused to examine the goods after a demand by the seller there is no implied warranty with regard to defects which an examination ought in the circumstances to have revealed to the buyer; and

(c) an implied warranty can also be excluded or modified by course of dealing or course of performance or usage of trade.

*   *   *   *

§ 2–318. Third Party Beneficiaries of Warranties and Obligations.

(1) In this section:

(a) "Immediate buyer" means a buyer that enters into a contract with the seller.

(b) "Remote purchaser" means a person that buys or leases goods from an immediate buyer or other person in the normal chain of distribution.

Alternative A to subsection (2)

(2) A seller's warranty to an immediate buyer, whether express or implied, a seller's remedial promise to an immediate buyer, or a seller's obligation to a remote purchaser under Section 2–313A or 2–313B extends to any natural person who is in the family or household of the immediate buyer or the remote purchaser or who is a guest in the home of either if it is reasonable to expect that the person may use, consume or be affected by the goods and who is injured in person by breach of the warranty, remedial promise or obligation. A seller may not exclude or limit the operation of this section.

Alternative B to subsection (2)

(2) A seller's warranty to an immediate buyer, whether express or implied, a seller's remedial promise to an immediate buyer, or a seller's obligation to a remote purchaser under Section 2–313A or 2–313B extends to any natural person who may reasonably be expected to use, consume or be affected by the goods and who is injured in person by breach of the warranty, remedial promise or obligation. A seller may not exclude or limit the operation of this section.

Alternative C to subsection (2)

(2) A seller's warranty to an immediate buyer, whether express or implied, a seller's remedial promise to an immediate buyer, or a seller's obligation to a remote purchaser under Section 2–313A or 2–313B extends to any person that may reasonably be expected to use, consume or be affected by the goods and that is injured by breach of the warranty,

remedial promise or obligation. A seller may not exclude or limit the operation of this section with respect to injury to the person of an individual to whom the warranty, remedial promise or obligation extends.

*   *   *   *

Part 5 Performance

*   *   *   *

§ 2–502. Buyer's Right to Goods on Seller's Insolvency.

(1) Subject to subsections (2) and (3) and even though the goods have not been shipped a buyer that has paid a part or all of the price of goods in which the buyer has a special property under the provisions of the immediately preceding section may on making and keeping good a tender of any unpaid portion of their price recover them from the seller if:

(a) in the case of goods bought by a consumer, the seller repudiates or fails to deliver as required by the contract; or

(b) in all cases, the seller becomes insolvent within ten days after receipt of the first installment on their price.

(2) The buyer's right to recover the goods under subsection (1) vests upon acquisition of a special property, even if the seller had not then repudiated or failed to deliver.

(3) If the identification creating the special property has been made by the buyer, the buyer acquires the right to recover the goods only if they conform to the contract for sale.

*   *   *   *

§ 2–508. Cure by Seller of Improper Tender or Delivery; Replacement.

(1) Where the buyer rejects goods or a tender of delivery under Section 2–601 or 2–612 or, except in a consumer contract, justifiably revokes acceptance under Section 2–608(1)(b) and the agreed time for performance has not expired, a seller that has performed in good faith, upon seasonable notice to the buyer and at the seller's own expense, may cure the breach of contract by making a conforming tender of delivery within the agreed time. The seller shall compensate the buyer for all of the buyer's reasonable expenses caused by the seller's breach of contract and subsequent cure.

(2) Where the buyer rejects goods or a tender of delivery under Section 2–601 or 2–612 or except in a consumer contract justifiably revokes acceptance under Section 2–608(1)(b) and the agreed time for performance has expired, a seller that has performed in good faith, upon seasonable notice to the buyer and at the seller's own expense, may cure the breach of contract, if the cure is appropriate and timely under the circumstances, by making a tender of conforming goods. The seller shall compensate the buyer for all of the buyer's reasonable expenses caused by the seller's breach of contract and subsequent cure.

§ 2–509. Risk of Loss in the Absence of Breach.

(1) Where the contract requires or authorizes the seller to ship the goods by carrier

   (a) if it does not require <u>the seller</u> to deliver them at a particular destination, the risk of loss passes to the buyer when the goods are delivered to the carrier even though the shipment is under reservation (Section 2–505); but

   (b) if it does require <u>the seller</u> to deliver them at a particular destination and the goods are there tendered while in the possession of the carrier, the risk of loss passes to the buyer when the goods are there so tendered as to enable the buyer to take delivery.

(2) Where the goods are held by a bailee to be delivered without being moved, the risk of loss passes to the buyer

   (a) on <u>the buyer's</u> receipt of a negotiable document of title covering the goods; or

   (b) on acknowledgment by the bailee <u>to the buyer</u> of the buyer's right to possession of the goods; or

   (c) after <u>the buyer's</u> receipt of a non-negotiable document of title or other direction to deliver <u>in a record,</u> as provided in subsection (4)(b) of Section 2–503.

(3) In any case not within subsection (1) or (2), the risk of loss passes to the buyer on <u>the buyer's</u> receipt of the goods.

(4) The provisions of this section are subject to contrary agreement of the parties and to the provisions of this Article on sale on approval (Section 2–327) and on effect of breach on risk of loss (Section 2–510).

* * * *

§ 2–513. Buyer's Right to Inspection of Goods.

* * * *

(3) Unless otherwise agreed, the buyer is not entitled to inspect the goods before payment of the price when the contract provides

   (a) for delivery <u>on terms that under applicable course of performance, course of dealing, or usage of trade are interpreted to preclude inspection before payment;</u> or

   (b) for payment against documents of title, except where such payment is due only after the goods are to become available for inspection.

* * * *

Part 6 Breach, Repudiation and Excuse

* * * *

§ 2–605. Waiver of Buyer's Objections by Failure to Particularize.

(1) The buyer's failure to state in connection with rejection a particular defect <u>or in connection with revocation of acceptance a defect that justifies revocation</u> precludes <u>the buyer</u> from relying on the unstated defect to justify rejection or <u>revocation of acceptance if the defect is ascertainable by reasonable inspection</u>

   (a) where the seller <u>had a right to cure the defect and</u> could have cured it if stated seasonably; or

   (b) between merchants when the seller has after rejection made a request in <u>a record for a full and</u> final statement <u>in record form</u> of all defects on which the buyer proposes to rely.

(2) <u>A buyer's payment</u> against documents <u>tendered to the buyer</u> made without reservation of rights precludes recovery of the payment for defects apparent on the face of the documents.

* * * *

§ 2–607. Effect of Acceptance; Notice of Breach; Burden of Establishing Breach After Acceptance; Notice of Claim or Litigation to Person Answerable Over.

* * * *

(3) Where a tender has been accepted

   (a) the buyer must within a reasonable time after <u>the buyer</u> discovers or should have discovered any breach notify the seller. <u>However, failure to give timely notice bars the buyer from a remedy only to the extent that the seller is prejudiced by the failure</u> and

   (b) if the claim is one for infringement or the like (subsection (3) of Section 2–312) and the buyer is sued as a result of such a breach <u>the buyer</u> must so notify the seller within a reasonable time after <u>the buyer</u> receives notice of the litigation or be barred from any remedy over for liability established by the litigation.

* * * *

§ 2–608. Revocation of Acceptance in Whole or in Part.

* * * *

(4) <u>If a buyer uses the goods after a rightful rejection or justifiable revocation of acceptance, the following rules apply:</u>

   (a) <u>Any use by the buyer which is unreasonable under the circumstances is wrongful as against the seller and is an acceptance only if ratified by the seller.</u>

   (b) <u>Any use of the goods which is reasonable under the circumstances is not wrongful as against the seller and is not an acceptance, but in an appropriate case the buyer shall be obligated to the seller for the value of the use to the buyer.</u>

* * * *

§ 2–612. "Installment Contract"; Breach.

* * * *

(2) The buyer may reject any installment which is non-conforming if the non-conformity substantially impairs the

value of that installment to the buyer or if the non-conformity is a defect in the required documents; but if the non-conformity does not fall within subsection (3) and the seller gives adequate assurance of its cure the buyer must accept that installment.

(3) Whenever non-conformity or default with respect to one or more installments substantially impairs the value of the whole contract there is a breach of the whole. But the aggrieved party reinstates the contract if the party accepts a non-conforming installment without seasonably notifying of cancellation or if the party brings an action with respect only to past installments or demands performance as to future installments.

*   *   *   *

Part 7 Remedies

§ 2–702. Seller's Remedies on Discovery of Buyer's Insolvency.

*   *   *   *

(2) Where the seller discovers that the buyer has received goods on credit while insolvent the seller may reclaim the goods upon demand made within a reasonable time after the buyer's receipt of the goods. Except as provided in this sub-section the seller may not base a right to reclaim goods on the buyer's fraudulent or innocent misrepresentation of solvency or of intent to pay.

*   *   *   *

§ 2–703. Seller's Remedies in General.

(1) A breach of contract by the buyer includes the buyer's wrongful rejection or wrongful attempt to revoke acceptance of goods, wrongful failure to perform a contractual obliga-tion, failure to make a payment when due, and repudiation.

(2) If the buyer is in breach of contract the seller, to the extent provided for by this Act or other law, may:

(a) withhold delivery of the goods:

(b) stop delivery of the goods under Section 2–705;

(c) proceed under Section 2–704 with respect to goods unidentified to the contract or unfinished;

(d) reclaim the goods under Section 2–507(2) or 2–702(2);

(e) require payment directly from the buyer under Section 2–325(c);

(f) cancel;

(g) resell and recover damages under Section 2–706;

(h) recover damages for nonacceptance or repudiation under Section 2–708(1);

(i) recover lost profits under Section 2–708(2);

(j) recover the price under Section 2–709;

(k) obtain specific performance under Section 2–716;

(l) recover liquidated damages under Section 2–718;

(m) in other cases, recover damages in any manner that is reasonable under the circumstances.

(3) If a buyer becomes insolvent, the seller may:

(a) withhold delivery under Section 2–702(1);

(b) stop delivery of the goods under Section 2–705;

(c) reclaim the goods under Section 2–702(2).

*   *   *   *

§ 2–705. Seller's Stoppage of Delivery in Transit or Otherwise.

(1) The seller may stop delivery of goods in the possession of a carrier or other bailee when the seller discovers the buyer to be insolvent (Section 2–702) or when the buyer repudiates or fails to make a payment due before delivery or if for any other reason the seller has a right to withhold or reclaim the goods.

*   *   *   *

§ 2–706. Seller's Resale Including Contract for Resale.

(1) In an appropriate case involving breach by the buyer, the seller may resell the goods concerned or the undelivered bal-ance thereof. Where the resale is made in good faith and in a commercially reasonable manner the seller may recover the difference between the contract price and the resale price together with any incidental or consequential damages allowed under the provisions of this Article (Section 2–710), but less expenses saved in consequence of the buyer's breach.

*   *   *   *

§ 2–708. Seller's Damages for Non-Acceptance or Repudiation.

(1) Subject to subsection (2) and to the provisions of this Article with respect to proof of market price (Section 2–723)

(a) the measure of damages for non-acceptance by the buyer is the difference between the contract price and the market price at the time and place for tender together with any incidental or consequential damages provided in this Article (Section 2–710), but less expenses saved in consequence of the buyer's breach; and

(b) the measure of damages for repudiation by the buyer is the difference between the contract price and the mar-ket price at the place for tender at the expiration of a commercially reasonable time after the seller learned of the repudiation, but no later than the time stated in para-graph (a), together with any incidental or consequential damages provided in this Article (Section 2–710), but less expenses saved in consequence of the buyer's breach.

(2) If the measure of damages provided in subsection (1) or in Section 2–706 is inadequate to put the seller in as good a position as performance would have done then the measure of damages is the profit (including reasonable overhead) which the seller would have made from full performance by the buyer, together with any incidental or consequential damages provided in this Article (Section 2–710).

§ 2–709. Action for the Price.

(1) When the buyer fails to pay the price as it becomes due the seller may recover, together with any incidental or consequential damages under the next section, the price

(a) of goods accepted or of conforming goods lost or damaged within a commercially reasonable time after risk of their loss has passed to the buyer; and

(b) of goods identified to the contract if the seller is unable after reasonable effort to resell them at a reasonable price or the circumstances reasonably indicate that such effort will be unavailing.

* * * *

§ 2–710. Seller's Incidental and Consequential Damages.

(1) Incidental damages to an aggrieved seller include any commercially reasonable charges, expenses or commissions incurred in stopping delivery, in the transportation, care and custody of goods after the buyer's breach, in connection with return or resale of the goods or otherwise resulting from the breach.

(2) Consequential damages resulting from the buyer's breach include any loss resulting from general or particular requirements and needs of which the buyer at the time of contracting had reason to know and which could not reasonably be prevented by resale or otherwise.

(3) In a consumer contract, a seller may not recover consequential damages from a consumer.

* * * *

§ 2–711. Buyer's Remedies in General; Buyer's Security Interest in Rejected Goods.

(1) A breach of contract by the seller includes the seller's wrongful failure to deliver or to perform a contractual obligation, making of a nonconforming tender of delivery or performance, and repudiation.

(2) If a seller is in breach of contract under subsection (1) the buyer, to the extent provided for by this Act or other law, may:

(a) in the case of rightful cancellation, rightful rejection or justifiable revocation of acceptance recover so much of the price as has been paid;

(b) deduct damages from any part of the price still due under Section 2–717;

(c) cancel;

(d) cover and have damages under Section 2–712 as to all goods affected whether or not they have been identified to the contract;

(e) recover damages for non-delivery or repudiation under Section 2–713;

(f) recover damages for breach with regard to accepted goods or breach with regard to a remedial promise under Section 2–714;

(g) recover identified goods under Section 2–502;

(h) obtain specific performance or obtain the goods by replevin or similar remedy under Section 7–716;

(i) recover liquidated damages under Section 2–718;

(j) in other cases, recover damages in any manner that is reasonable under the circumstances.

(3) On rightful rejection or justifiable revocation of acceptance a buyer has a security interest in goods in the buyer's possession or control for any payments made on their price and any expenses reasonably incurred in their inspection, receipt, transportation, care and custody and may hold such goods and resell them in like manner as an aggrieved seller (Section 2–706).

* * * *

§ 2–713. Buyer's Damages for Non-Delivery or Repudiation.

(1) Subject to the provisions of this Article with respect to proof of market price (Section 2–723), if the seller wrongfully fails to deliver or repudiates or the buyer rightfully rejects or justifiably revokes acceptance

(a) the measure of damages in the case of wrongful failure to deliver by the seller or rightful rejection or justifiable revocation of acceptance by the buyer is the difference between the market price at the time for tender under the contract and the contract price together with any incidental or consequential damages provided in this Article (Section 2–715), but less expenses saved in consequence of the seller's breach; and

(b) the measure of damages for repudiation by the seller is the difference between the market price at the expiration of a commercially reasonable time after the buyer learned of the repudiation, but no later than the time stated in paragraph (a), and the contract price together with any incidental or consequential damages provided in this Article (Section 2–715), less expenses saved in consequence of the seller's breach.

* * * *

§ 2–725. Statute of Limitations in Contracts for Sale.

(1) Except as otherwise provided in this section, an action for breach of any contract for sale must be commenced

within the later of four years after the right of action has accrued under subsection (2) or (3) or one year after the breach was or should have been discovered, but no longer than five years after the right of action accrued. By the original agreement the parties may reduce the period of limitation to not less than one year but may not extend it. However, in a consumer contract, the period of limitation may not be reduced.

(2) Except as otherwise provided in subsection (3), the following rules apply:

(a) Except as otherwise provided in this subsection, a right of action for breach of a contract accrues when the breach occurs, even if the aggrieved party did not have knowledge of the breach.

(b) For breach of a contract by repudiation, a right of action accrues at the earlier of when the aggrieved party elects to treat the repudiation as a breach or when a commercially reasonable time for awaiting performance has expired.

(c) For breach of a remedial promise, a right of action accrues when the remedial promise is not performed when performance is due.

(d) In an action by a buyer against a person that is answerable over to the buyer for a claim asserted against the buyer, the buyer's right of action against the person answerable over accrues at the time the claim was originally asserted against the buyer.

(3) If a breach of a warranty arising under Section 2–312, 2–313(2), 2–314, or 2–315, or a breach of an obligation, other than a remedial promise, arising under Section 2–313A or 2–313B, is claimed the following rules apply:

(a) Except as otherwise provided in paragraph (c), a right of action for breach of a warranty arising under Section 2–313(2), 2–314 or 2–315 accrues when the seller has tendered delivery to the immediate buyer, as defined in Section 2–313, and has completed performance of any agreed installation or assembly of the goods.

(b) Except as otherwise provided in paragraph (c), a right of action for breach of an obligation other than a remedial promise arising under Section 2–313A or 2–313B accrues when the remote purchaser, as defined in sections 2–313A and 2–313B, receives the goods.

(c) Where a warranty arising under Section 2–313(2) or an obligation, other than a remedial promise, arising under 2–313A or 2–313B explicitly extends to future performance of the goods and discovery of the breach must await the time for performance the right of action accrues when the immediate buyer as defined in Section 2–313 or the remote purchaser as defined in Sections 2–313A and 2–313B discovers or should have discovered the breach.

(d) A right of action for breach of warranty arising under Section 2–312 accrues when the aggrieved party discovers or should have discovered the breach. However, an action for breach of the warranty of non-infringement may not be commenced more than six years after tender of delivery of the goods to the aggrieved party.

*   *   *   *

APPENDIX E

The National Labor Relations Act of 1935 (Excerpts)

Note: You can access the full text of the National Labor Relations Act of 1935 online at **http://uscode.house.gov/usc.htm**. The official citation to this act includes 29 U.S.C. Sections 151–169. In the "Title" box, type "29," and in the "Section" box, type a relevant section number (such as, for example, "151"). Click on "Search." In the list of "documents found," click on the citation to access the text of the statute.

§ 157. Right of Employees as to Organization, Collective Bargaining, etc.

Employees shall have the right to self-organization, to form, join, or assist labor organizations, to bargain collectively through representatives of their own choosing, and to engage in other concerted activities for the purpose of collective bargaining or other mutual aid or protection, and shall also have the right to refrain from any or all of such activities except to the extent that such right may be affected by an agreement requiring membership in a labor organization as a condition of employment as authorized in section 158(a)(3) of this title.

§ 158. Unfair Labor Practices

(a) Unfair labor practices for an employer

It shall be an unfair labor practice for an employer—

(1) to interfere with, restrain, or coerce employees in the exercise of the rights guaranteed in section 157 of this title;

(2) to dominate or interfere with the formation or administration of any labor organization or contribute financial or other support to it: Provided, [t]hat subject to rules and regulations made and published by the Board pursuant to section 156 of this title, an employer shall not be prohibited from permitting employees to confer with him during working hours without loss of time or pay;

(3) by discrimination in regard to hire or tenure of employment or any term or condition of employment to encourage or discourage membership in any labor organization: Provided, [t]hat nothing in this subchapter, or in any other statute of the United States, shall preclude an employer from making an agreement with a labor organization (not established, maintained, or assisted by any action defined in this subsection as an unfair labor practice) to require as a condition of employment membership therein on or after the thirtieth day following the beginning of such employment or the effective date of such agreement, whichever is the later, (i) if such labor organization is the representative of the employees as provided in section 159(a) of this title, in the appropriate collective-bargaining unit covered by such agreement when made, and (ii) unless following an election held as provided in section 159(e) of this title within one year preceding the effective date of such agreement, the Board shall have certified that at least a majority of the employees eligible to vote in such election have voted to rescind the authority of such labor organization to make such an agreement: Provided further, [t]hat no employer shall justify any discrimination against an employee for nonmembership in a labor organization (A) if he has reasonable grounds for believing that such membership was not available to the employee on the same terms and conditions generally applicable to other members, or (B) if he has reasonable grounds for believing that membership was denied or terminated for reasons other than the failure of the employee to tender the periodic dues and the initiation fees uniformly required as a condition of acquiring or retaining membership;

(4) to discharge or otherwise discriminate against an employee because he has filed charges or given testimony under this subchapter;

(5) to refuse to bargain collectively with the representatives of his employees, subject to the provisions of section 159(a) of this title.

(b) Unfair labor practices by labor organization

It shall be an unfair labor practice for a labor organization or its agents—

(1) to restrain or coerce (A) employees in the exercise of the rights guaranteed in section 157 of this title: Provided, [t]hat this paragraph shall not impair the right of a labor organization to prescribe its own rules with respect to the acquisition or retention of membership therein; or (B) an employer in the selection of his representatives for the purposes of collective bargaining or the adjustment of grievances;

(2) to cause or attempt to cause an employer to discriminate against an employee in violation of subsection (a)(3) of this section or to discriminate against an employee with respect to whom membership in such organization has been denied or terminated on some ground other than his failure to tender the periodic dues and the initiation fees uniformly required as a condition of acquiring or retaining membership;

(3) to refuse to bargain collectively with an employer, provided it is the representative of his employees subject to the provisions of section 159(a) of this title;

(4) (i) to engage in, or to induce or encourage any individual employed by any person engaged in commerce or in an industry affecting commerce to engage in, a strike or a refusal in the course of his employment to use, manufacture, process, transport, or otherwise handle or work on any goods, articles, materials, or commodities or to perform any services; or (ii) to threaten, coerce, or restrain any person engaged in commerce or in an industry affecting commerce[.] * * *

(5) to require of employees covered by an agreement authorized under subsection (a)(3) of this section the payment, as a condition precedent to becoming a member of such organization, of a fee in an amount which the Board finds excessive or discriminatory under all the circumstances. In making such a finding, the Board shall consider, among other relevant factors, the practices and customs of labor organizations in the particular industry, and the wages currently paid to the employees affected;

(6) to cause or attempt to cause an employer to pay or deliver or agree to pay or deliver any money or other thing of value, in the nature of an exaction, for services which are not performed or not to be performed; and

(7) to picket or cause to be picketed, or threaten to picket or cause to be picketed, any employer where an object thereof is forcing or requiring an employer to recognize or bargain with a labor organization as the representative of his employees, or forcing or requiring the employees of an employer to accept or select such labor organization as their collective bargaining representative[.] * * *

(c) Expression of views without threat of reprisal or force or promise of benefit

The expressing of any views, argument, or opinion, or the dissemination thereof, whether in written, printed, graphic, or visual form, shall not constitute or be evidence of an unfair labor practice under any of the provisions of this subchapter, if such expression contains no threat of reprisal or force or promise of benefit.

(d) Obligation to bargain collectively

For the purposes of this section, to bargain collectively is the performance of the mutual obligation of the employer and the representative of the employees to meet at reasonable times and confer in good faith with respect to wages, hours, and other terms and conditions of employment, or the negotiation of an agreement, or any question arising thereunder, and the execution of a written contract incorporating any agreement reached if requested by either party, but such obligation does not compel either party to agree to a proposal or require the making of a concession: Provided, [t]hat where there is in effect a collective-bargaining contract covering employees in an industry affecting commerce, the duty to bargain collectively shall also mean that no party to such contract shall terminate or modify such contract, unless the party desiring such termination or modification—

(1) serves a written notice upon the other party to the contract of the proposed termination or modification sixty days prior to the expiration date thereof, or in the event such contract contains no expiration date, sixty days prior to the time it is proposed to make such termination or modification;

(2) offers to meet and confer with the other party for the purpose of negotiating a new contract or a contract containing the proposed modifications;

(3) notifies the Federal Mediation and Conciliation Service within thirty days after such notice of the existence of a dispute, and simultaneously therewith notifies any State or Territorial agency established to mediate and conciliate disputes within the State or Territory where the dispute occurred, provided no agreement has been reached by that time; and

(4) continues in full force and effect, without resorting to strike or lock-out, all the terms and conditions of the existing contract for a period of sixty days after such notice is given or until the expiration date of such contract, whichever occurs later[.] * * *

APPENDIX F

The Sherman Act of 1890 (Excerpts)

Note: You can access the full text of the Sherman Act of 1890 online at **http://uscode.house.gov/usc.htm**. In the "Title" box, type "15," and in the "Section" box, type a relevant section number (such as, for example, "1"). Click on "Search." In the list of "documents found," scroll to the citation with the appropriate title (such as, in this example, "Sec. 1. Trusts, etc., in restraint of trade illegal; penalty"). Click on the citation to access the text of the statute.

Section 1. Every contract, combination in the form of trust or otherwise, or conspiracy, in restraint of trade or commerce among the several States, or with foreign nations, is declared to be illegal. Every person who shall make any contract or engage in any combination or conspiracy hereby declared to be illegal shall be deemed guilty of a felony, and, on conviction thereof, shall be punished by fine not exceeding $10,000,000 if a corporation, or, if any other person, $350,000, or by imprisonment not exceeding three years, or by both said punishments, in the discretion of the court.

Section 2. Every person who shall monopolize, or attempt to monopolize, or combine or conspire with any other person or persons, to monopolize any part of the trade or commerce among the several States, or with foreign nations, shall be deemed guilty of a felony, and, on conviction thereof, shall be punished by fine not exceeding $10,000,000 if a corporation, or, if any other person, $350,000, or by imprisonment not exceeding three years, or by both said punishments, in the discretion of the court.

Section 3. Every contract, combination in form of trust or otherwise, or conspiracy, in restraint of trade or commerce in any Territory of the United States or of the District of Columbia, or in restraint of trade or commerce between any such Territory and another, or between any such Territory or Territories and any State or States or the District of Columbia, or with foreign nations, or between the District of Columbia and any State or States or foreign nations, is

declared illegal. Every person who shall make any such contract or engage in any such combination or conspiracy, shall be deemed guilty of a felony, and, on conviction thereof, shall be punished by fine not exceeding $10,000,000 if a corporation, or, if any other person, $350,000, or by imprisonment not exceeding three years, or by both said punishments, in the discretion of the court.

* * * *

Section 7. Every combination, conspiracy, trust, agreement, or contract is declared to be contrary to public policy, illegal, and void when the same is made by or between two or more persons or corporations, either of whom, as agent or principal, is engaged in importing any article from any foreign country into the United States, and when such combination, conspiracy, trust, agreement, or contract is intended to operate in restraint of lawful trade, or free competition in lawful trade or commerce, or to increase the market price in any part of the United States of any article or articles imported or intended to be imported into the United States, or of any manufacture into which such imported article enters or is intended to enter. Every person who shall be engaged in the importation of goods or any commodity from any foreign country in violation of this section, or who shall combine or conspire with another to violate the same, is guilty of a misdemeanor, and on conviction thereof in any court of the United States such person shall be fined in a sum not less than $100 and not exceeding $5,000, and shall be further punished by imprisonment, in the discretion of the court, for a term not less than three months nor exceeding twelve months.

Section 8. The word "person", or "persons", wherever used in sections 1 to 7 of this title shall be deemed to include corporations and associations existing under or authorized by the laws of either the United States, the laws of any of the Territories, the laws of any State, or the laws of any foreign country.

APPENDIX G

The Clayton Act of 1914 (Excerpts)

Note: You can access the full text of the Clayton Act of 1914 online at **http://uscode.house.gov/usc.htm**. In the "Title" box, type "15," and in the "Section" box, type a relevant section number (such as, for example, "12"). Click on "Search." In the list of "documents found," click on the citation with the appropriate title (such as, in this example, "Sec. 12. Definitions; short title") to access the text of the statute.

Section 3. That it shall be unlawful for any person engaged in commerce, in the course of such commerce, to lease or make a sale or contract for sale of goods, wares, merchandise, machinery, supplies, or other commodities, whether patented or unpatented, for use, consumption, or resale within the United States or * * * other place under the jurisdiction of the United States, or fix a price charged therefor, or discount from, or rebate upon, such price, on the condition, agreement, or understanding that the lessee or purchaser thereof shall not use or deal in the goods, wares, merchandise, machinery, supplies, or other commodities of a competitor or competitors of the lessor or seller, where the effect of such lease, sale, or contract for sale or such condition, agreement, or understanding may be to substantially lessen competition to tend to create a monopoly in any line of commerce.

Section 4. That any person who shall be injured in his business or property by reason of anything forbidden in the antitrust laws may sue therefor in any district court of the United States in the district in which the defendant resides or is found, or has an agent, without respect to the amount in controversy, and shall recover threefold the damages by him sustained, and the cost of suit, including a reasonable attorney's fee.

Section 4A. Whenever the United States is hereafter injured in its business or property by reason of anything forbidden in the antitrust laws it may sue therefor in the United States district court for the district in which the defendant resides or is found or has an agent, without respect to the amount in controversy, and shall recover actual damages by it sustained and the cost of suit.

Section 4B. Any action to enforce any cause of action under sections 4 or 4A shall be forever barred unless commenced within four years after the cause of action accrued. No cause of action barred under existing law on the effective date of this act shall be revived by this Act.

* * * *

Section 6. That the labor of a human being is not a commodity or article of commerce. Nothing contained in the antitrust laws shall be construed to forbid the existence and operation of labor, agricultural or horticultural organizations, instituted for the purposes of mutual help, and not having capital stock or conducted for profit, or to forbid or restrain individual members of such organizations from lawfully carrying out the legitimate objects thereof; nor shall such organizations or the members thereof, be held or construed to be illegal combinations or conspiracies in restraint of trade, under the antitrust laws.

Section 7. That no person engaged in commerce shall acquire, directly or indirectly, the whole or any part of the stock or other share capital and no corporation subject to the jurisdiction of the Federal Trade Commission shall acquire the whole or any part of the assets of another corporation engaged also in commerce, where in any line of commerce in any section of the country, the effect of such acquisition may be substantially to lessen competition, or to tend to create a monopoly.

No person shall acquire, directly or indirectly, the whole or any part of the stock or other share capital and no corporation subject to the jurisdiction of the Federal Trade Commission shall acquire the whole or any part of the assets of one or more corporations engaged in commerce, where in any line of commerce in any section of the country, the effect of such acquisition, of such stocks or assets, or of the use of such stock by the voting or granting of proxies or otherwise, may be substantially to lessen competition, or to tend to create a monopoly.

This section shall not apply to persons purchasing such stock solely for investment and not using the same by voting or otherwise to bring about, or in attempting to bring about, the substantial lessening of competition * * * .

Section 8. * * * No person at the same time shall be a director in any two or more corporations any one of which has capital, surplus, and undivided profits aggregating more than $1,000,000 engaged in whole or in part in commerce, * * * if such corporations are or shall have been theretofore, by virtue of their business and location of operation, competitors, so that the elimination of competition by agreement between them would constitute a violation of any of the provisions of the antitrust laws. * * *

The Federal Trade Commission Act of 1914 (Excerpts)

Note: You can access the full text of the Federal Trade Commission Act of 1914 online at **http://uscode.house.gov/ usc.htm**. In the "Title" box, type "15," and in the "Section" box, type a relevant section number (such as, for example, "45"). Click on "Search." In the list of "documents found," click on the citation to access the text of the statute.

Section 5.

(a)(1) Unfair methods of competition in or affecting commerce, and unfair or deceptive acts or practices in or affecting commerce, are hereby declared unlawful.

(2) The Commission is hereby empowered and directed to prevent persons, partnerships, or corporations from using unfair methods of competition in or affecting commerce and unfair or deceptive acts or practices in or affecting commerce.

(1) Any person, partnership, or corporation who violates an order of the Commission after it has become final, and while such order is in effect, shall forfeit and pay to the United States a civil penalty of not more than $10,000 for each violation, which shall accrue to the United States and may be recovered in a civil action brought by the Attorney General of the United States. Each separate violation of such an order shall be a separate offense, except that in the case of a violation through continuing failure to obey or neglect to obey a final order of the Commission, each day of continuance of such failure or neglect shall be deemed a separate offense. In such actions, the United States district courts are empowered to grant mandatory injunctions and such other and further equitable relief as they deem appropriate in the enforcement of such final orders of the Commission.

APPENDIX I

The Securities Act of 1933 (Excerpts)

Note: You can access the full text of the Securities Act of 1933 online at **http://uscode.house.gov/usc.htm**. In the "Title" box, type "15," and in the "Section" box, type a relevant section number (such as, for example, "77b"). Click on "Search." In the list of "documents found," click on the citation to access the text of the statute.

Definitions

Section 2. When used in this title, unless the context requires—

(1) The term "security" means any note, stock, treasury stock, bond, debenture, evidence of indebtedness, certificate of interest or participation in any profit-sharing agreement, collateral-trust certificate, preorganization certificate or subscription, transferable share, investment contract, voting-trust certificate, certificate of deposit for a security, fractional undivided interest in oil, gas, or other mineral rights, any put, call, straddle, option, or privilege on any security, certificate of deposit, or group or index of securities (including any interest therein or based on the value thereof), or any put, call, straddle, option, or privilege entered into on a national securities exchange relating to foreign currency, or, in general, any interest or participation in, temporary or interim certificate for, receipt for, guarantee of, or warrant or right to subscribe to or purchase, any of the foregoing.

Exempted Securities

Section 3. (a) Except as hereinafter expressly provided the provisions of this title shall not apply to any of the following classes of securities:

* * * *

(2) Any security issued or guaranteed by the United States or any territory thereof, or by the District of Columbia, or by any State of the United States, or by any political subdivision of a State or Territory, or by any public instrumentality of one or more States or Territories, or by any person controlled or supervised by and acting as an instrumentality of the Government of the United States pursuant to authority granted by the Congress of the United States; or any certificate of deposit for any of the foregoing; or any security issued or guaranteed by any bank; or any security issued by or representing an interest in or a direct obligation of a Federal Reserve Bank. * * *

(3) Any note, draft, bill of exchange, or banker's acceptance which arises out of a current transaction or the proceeds of which have been or are to be used for current transactions, and which has a maturity at the time of issuance of not exceeding nine months, exclusive of days of grace, or any renewal thereof the maturity of which is likewise limited;

(4) Any security issued by a person organized and operated exclusively for religious, educational, benevolent, fraternal, charitable, or reformatory purposes and not for pecuniary profit, and no part of the net earnings of which inures to the benefit of any person, private stockholder, or individual;

* * * *

(11) Any security which is a part of an issue offered and sold only to persons resident within a single State or Territory, where the issuer of such security is a person resident and doing business within, or, if a corporation, incorporated by and doing business within, such State or Territory.

(b) The Commission may from time to time by its rules and regulations and subject to such terms and conditions as may be described therein, add any class of securities to the securities exempted as provided in this section, if it finds that the enforcement of this title with respect to such securities is not necessary in the public interest and for the protection of investors by reason of the small amount involved or the limited character of the public offering; but no issue of securities shall be exempted under this subsection where the aggregate amount at which such issue is offered to the public exceeds $5,000,000.

Exempted Transactions

Section 4. The provisions of section 5 shall not apply to—

(1) transactions by any person other than an issuer, underwriter, or dealer.

(2) transactions by an issuer not involving any public offering.

(3) transactions by a dealer (including an underwriter no longer acting as an underwriter in respect of the security involved in such transactions), except—

(A) transactions taking place prior to the expiration of forty days after the first date upon which the security was bona fide offered to the public by the issuer or by or through an underwriter.

(B)   transactions in a security as to which a registration statement has been filed taking place prior to the expiration of forty days after the effective date of such registration statement or prior to the expiration of forty days after the first date upon which the security was bona fide offered to the public by the issuer or by or through an underwriter after such effective date, whichever is later (excluding in the computation of such forty days any time during which a stop order issued under section 8 is in effect as to the security), or such shorter period as the Commission may specify by rules and regulations or order, and

(C)   transactions as to the securities constituting the whole or a part of an unsold allotment to or subscription by such dealer as a participant in the distribution of such securities by the issuer or by or through an underwriter.

With respect to transactions referred to in clause (B), if securities of the issuer have not previously been sold pursuant to an earlier effective registration statement the applicable period, instead of forty days, shall be ninety days, or such shorter period as the Commission may specify by rules and regulations or order.

(4) brokers' transactions, executed upon customers' orders on any exchange or in the over-the-counter market but not the solicitation of such orders.

*   *   *   *

(6) transactions involving offers or sales by an issuer solely to one or more accredited investors, if the aggregate offering price of an issue of securities offered in reliance on this paragraph does not exceed the amount allowed under Section 3(b) of this title, if there is no advertising or public solicitation in connection with the transaction by the issuer or anyone acting on the issuer's behalf, and if the issuer files such notice with the Commission as the Commission shall prescribe.

Prohibitions Relating to Interstate Commerce and the Mails

Section 5. (a) Unless a registration statement is in effect as to a security, it shall be unlawful for any person, directly or indirectly—

(1) to make use of any means or instruments of transportation or communication in interstate commerce or of the mails to sell such security through the use or medium of any prospectus or otherwise; or

(2) to carry or cause to be carried through the mails or in interstate commerce, by any means or instruments of transportation, any such security for the purpose of sale or for delivery after sale.

(b) It shall be unlawful for any person, directly or indirectly—

(1) to make use of any means or instruments of transportation or communication in interstate commerce or of the mails to carry or transmit any prospectus relating to any security with respect to which a registration statement has been filed under this title, unless such prospectus meets the requirements of section 10, or

(2) to carry or to cause to be carried through the mails or in interstate commerce any such security for the purpose of sale or for delivery after sale, unless accompanied or preceded by a prospectus that meets the requirements of subsection (a) of section 10.

(c) It shall be unlawful for any person, directly, or indirectly, to make use of any means or instruments of transportation or communication in interstate commerce or of the mails to offer to sell or offer to buy through the use or medium of any prospectus or otherwise any security, unless a registration statement has been filed as to such security, or while the registration statement is the subject of a refusal order or stop order or (prior to the effective date of the registration statement) any public proceeding of examination under section 8.

APPENDIX J

The Securities Exchange Act of 1934 (Excerpts)

Note: You can access the full text of the Securities Exchange Act of 1934 online at **http://uscode.house.gov/usc.htm**. In the "Title" box, type "15," and in the "Section" box, type a relevant section number (such as, for example, "78b"). Click on "Search." In the list of "documents found," click on the citation to access the text of the statute.

Definitions and Application of Title

Section 3. (a) When used in this title, unless the context otherwise requires—

* * * *

(4) The term "broker" means any person engaged in the business of effecting transactions in securities for the account of others, but does not include a bank.

(5) The term "dealer" means any person engaged in the business of buying and selling securities for his own account, through a broker or otherwise, but does not include a bank, or any person insofar as he buys or sells securities for his own account, either individually or in some fiduciary capacity, but not as part of a regular business.

* * * *

(7) The term "director" means any director of a corporation or any person performing similar functions with respect to any organization, whether incorporated or unincorporated.

(8) The term "issuer" means any person who issues or proposes to issue any security; except that with respect to certificates of deposit for securities, voting-trust certificates, or collateral-trust certificates, or with respect to certificates of interest or shares in an unincorporated investment trust not having a board of directors or the fixed, restricted manage-

ment, or unit type, the term "issuer" means the person or persons performing the acts and assuming the duties of depositor or manager pursuant to the provisions of the trust or other agreement or instrument under which such securities are issued; and except that with respect to equipment-trust certificates or like securities, the term "issuer" means the person by whom the equipment or property is, or is to be, used.

(9) The term "person" means a natural person, company, government, or political subdivision, agency, or instrumentality of a government.

Regulation of the Use of Manipulative and Deceptive Devices

Section 10. It shall be unlawful for any person, directly or indirectly, by the use of any means or instrumentality of interstate commerce or of the mails, or of any facility of any national securities exchange—

(a) To effect a short sale, or to use or employ any stop-loss order in connection with the purchase or sale, of any security registered on a national securities exchange, in contravention of such rules and regulations as the Commission may prescribe as necessary or appropriate in the public interest or for the protection of investors.

(b) To use or employ, in connection with the purchase or sale of any security registered on a national securities exchange or any security not so registered, any manipulative or deceptive device or contrivance in contravention of such rules and regulations as the Commission may prescribe as necessary or appropriate in the public interest or for the protection of investors.

APPENDIX K

The Digital Millennium Copyright Act of 1998 (Excerpts)

Note: You can access the full text of the Digital Millennium Copyright Act of 1998 online at **http://uscode.house.gov/usc.htm**. In the "Title" box, type "17," and in the "Section" box, type a relevant section number (such as "1201"). Click on "Search." In the list of "documents found," click on the citation to access the text of the statute.

Sec. 1201. Circumvention of copyright protection systems

(a) VIOLATIONS REGARDING CIRCUMVENTION OF TECHNOLOGICAL MEASURES—(1)(A) No person shall circumvent a technological measure that effectively controls access to a work protected under this title. * * *

* * * * *

(b) ADDITIONAL VIOLATIONS—(1) No person shall manufacture, import, offer to the public, provide, or otherwise traffic in any technology, product, service, device, component, or part thereof, that—

(A) is primarily designed or produced for the purpose of circumventing protection afforded by a technological measure that effectively protects a right of a copyright owner under this title in a work or a portion thereof;

(B) has only limited commercially significant purpose or use other than to circumvent protection afforded by a technological measure that effectively protects a right of a copyright owner under this title in a work or a portion thereof; or

(C) is marketed by that person or another acting in concert with that person with that person's knowledge for use in circumventing protection afforded by a technological measure that effectively protects a right of a copyright owner under this title in a work or a portion thereof.

* * * * *

Sec. 1202. Integrity of copyright management information

(a) FALSE COPYRIGHT MANAGEMENT INFORMATION—No person shall knowingly and with the intent to induce, enable, facilitate, or conceal infringement—

(1) provide copyright management information that is false, or

(2) distribute or import for distribution copyright management information that is false.

(b) REMOVAL OR ALTERATION OF COPYRIGHT MANAGEMENT INFORMATION—No person shall, without the authority of the copyright owner or the law—

(1) intentionally remove or alter any copyright management information,

(2) distribute or import for distribution copyright management information knowing that the copyright management information has been removed or altered without authority of the copyright owner or the law, or

(3) distribute, import for distribution, or publicly perform works, copies of works, or phonorecords, knowing that copyright management information has been removed or altered without authority of the copyright owner or the law, knowing, or, with respect to civil remedies under section 1203, having reasonable grounds to know, that it will induce, enable, facilitate, or conceal an infringement of any right under this title.

(c) DEFINITION—As used in this section, the term "copyright management information" means any of the following information conveyed in connection with copies or phonorecords of a work or performances or displays of a work, including in digital form, except that such term does not include any personally identifying information about a user of a work or of a copy, phonorecord, performance, or display of a work:

(1) The title and other information identifying the work, including the information set forth on a notice of copyright.

(2) The name of, and other identifying information about, the author of a work.

(3) The name of, and other identifying information about, the copyright owner of the work, including the information set forth in a notice of copyright.

(4) With the exception of public performances of works by radio and television broadcast stations, the name of, and other identifying information about, a performer whose performance is fixed in a work other than an audiovisual work.

(5) With the exception of public performances of works by radio and television broadcast stations, in the case of an audiovisual work, the name of, and other identifying information about, a writer, performer, or director who is credited in the audiovisual work.

(6) Terms and conditions for use of the work.

(7) Identifying numbers or symbols referring to such information or links to such information.

(8) Such other information as the Register of Copyrights may prescribe by regulation, except that the Register of Copyrights may not require the provision of any information concerning the user of a copyrighted work.

* * * *

Sec. 512. Limitations on liability relating to material online

(a) TRANSITORY DIGITAL NETWORK COMMUNICATIONS—A service provider shall not be liable for monetary relief, or, except as provided in subsection (j), for injunctive or other equitable relief, for infringement of copyright by reason of the provider's transmitting, routing, or providing connections for, material through a system or network controlled or operated by or for the service provider, or by reason of the intermediate and transient storage of that material in the course of such transmitting, routing, or providing connections, if—

(1) the transmission of the material was initiated by or at the direction of a person other than the service provider;

(2) the transmission, routing, provision of connections, or storage is carried out through an automatic technical process without selection of the material by the service provider;

(3) the service provider does not select the recipients of the material except as an automatic response to the request of another person;

(4) no copy of the material made by the service provider in the course of such intermediate or transient storage is maintained on the system or network in a manner ordinarily accessible to anyone other than anticipated recipients, and no such copy is maintained on the system or network in a manner ordinarily accessible to such anticipated recipients for a longer period than is reasonably necessary for the transmission, routing, or provision of connections; and

(5) the material is transmitted through the system or network without modification of its content.

APPENDIX L

The Electronic Signatures in Global and National Commerce Act of 2000 (Excerpts)

Note: You can access the full text of the Electronic Signatures in Global and National Commerce Act of 2000 online at **http://uscode.house.gov/usc.htm**. In the "Title" box, type "15," and in the "Section" box, type a relevant section number (such as "7001"). Click on "Search." In the list of "documents found," click on the citation to access the text of the statute.

SEC. 101. GENERAL RULE OF VALIDITY.

(a) IN GENERAL—Notwithstanding any statute, regulation, or other rule of law (other than this title and title II), with respect to any transaction in or affecting interstate or foreign commerce—

(1) a signature, contract, or other record relating to such transaction may not be denied legal effect, validity, or enforceability solely because it is in electronic form; and

(2) a contract relating to such transaction may not be denied legal effect, validity, or enforceability solely because an electronic signature or electronic record was used in its formation.

*   *   *   *

(d) RETENTION OF CONTRACTS AND RECORDS—

(1) ACCURACY AND ACCESSIBILITY—If a statute, regulation, or other rule of law requires that a contract or other record relating to a transaction in or affecting interstate or foreign commerce be retained, that requirement is met by retaining an electronic record of the information in the contract or other record that—

(A) accurately reflects the information set forth in the contract or other record; and

(B) remains accessible to all persons who are entitled to access by statute, regulation, or rule of law, for the period required by such statute, regulation, or rule of law, in a form that is capable of being accurately reproduced for later reference, whether by transmission, printing, or otherwise.

(2) EXCEPTION—A requirement to retain a contract or other record in accordance with paragraph (1) does not apply to any information whose sole purpose is to enable the contract or other record to be sent, communicated, or received.

(3) ORIGINALS—If a statute, regulation, or other rule of law requires a contract or other record relating to a transaction in or affecting interstate or foreign commerce to be provided, available, or retained in its original form, or provides consequences if the contract or other record is not provided, available, or retained in its original form, that statute, regulation, or rule of law is satisfied by an electronic record that complies with paragraph (1).

(4) CHECKS—If a statute, regulation, or other rule of law requires the retention of a check, that requirement is satisfied by retention of an electronic record of the information on the front and back of the check in accordance with paragraph (1).

*   *   *   *

(g) NOTARIZATION AND ACKNOWLEDGMENT—If a statute, regulation, or other rule of law requires a signature or record relating to a transaction in or affecting interstate or foreign commerce to be notarized, acknowledged, verified, or made under oath, that requirement is satisfied if the electronic signature of the person authorized to perform those acts, together with all other information required to be included by other applicable statute, regulation, or rule of law, is attached to or logically associated with the signature or record.

(h) ELECTRONIC AGENTS—A contract or other record relating to a transaction in or affecting interstate or foreign commerce may not be denied legal effect, validity, or enforceability solely because its formation, creation, or delivery involved the action of one or more electronic agents so long as the action of any such electronic agent is legally attributable to the person to be bound.

(i) INSURANCE—It is the specific intent of the Congress that this title and title II apply to the business of insurance.

(j) INSURANCE AGENTS AND BROKERS—An insurance agent or broker acting under the direction of a party that enters into a contract by means of an electronic record or electronic signature may not be held liable for any deficiency in the electronic procedures agreed to by the parties under that contract if—

(1) the agent or broker has not engaged in negligent, reckless, or intentional tortious conduct;

(2) the agent or broker was not involved in the development or establishment of such electronic procedures; and

(3) the agent or broker did not deviate from such procedures.

*   *   *   *

SEC. 103. SPECIFIC EXCEPTIONS.

(a) EXCEPTED REQUIREMENTS—The provisions of section 101 shall not apply to a contract or other record to the extent it is governed by—

(1) a statute, regulation, or other rule of law governing the creation and execution of wills, codicils, or testamentary trusts;

(2) a State statute, regulation, or other rule of law governing adoption, divorce, or other matters of family law; or

(3) the Uniform Commercial Code, as in effect in any State, other than sections 1–107 and 1–206 and Articles 2 and 2A.

(b) ADDITIONAL EXCEPTIONS—The provisions of section 101 shall not apply to—

(1) court orders or notices, or official court documents (including briefs, pleadings, and other writings) required to be executed in connection with court proceedings;

(2) any notice of—

(A) the cancellation or termination of utility services (including water, heat, and power);

(B) default, acceleration, repossession, foreclosure, or eviction, or the right to cure, under a credit agreement secured by, or a rental agreement for, a primary residence of an individual;

(C) the cancellation or termination of health insurance or benefits or life insurance benefits (excluding annuities); or

(D) recall of a product, or material failure of a product, that risks endangering health or safety; or

(3) any document required to accompany any transportation or handling of hazardous materials, pesticides, or other toxic or dangerous materials.

APPENDIX M

The Uniform Electronic Transactions Act (Excerpts)

Note: You can access the full text of the Uniform Electronic Transactions Act online at **http://www.law.upenn.edu/bll/ulc/fnact99/1990s/ueta99.htm**. This is a page within the Web site of the University of Pennsylvania Law School, which provides drafts of uniform and model acts in association with the National Conference of Commissioners on Uniform State Laws.

*　*　*　*

Section 5. USE OF ELECTRONIC RECORDS AND ELECTRONIC SIGNATURES; VARIATION BY AGREEMENT.

(a) This [Act] does not require a record or signature to be created, generated, sent, communicated, received, stored, or otherwise processed or used by electronic means or in electronic form.

(b) This [Act] applies only to transactions between parties each of which has agreed to conduct transactions by electronic means. Whether the parties agree to conduct a transaction by electronic means is determined from the context and surrounding circumstances, including the parties' conduct.

(c) A party that agrees to conduct a transaction by electronic means may refuse to conduct other transactions by electronic means. The right granted by this subsection may not be waived by agreement.

(d) Except as otherwise provided in this [Act], the effect of any of its provisions may be varied by agreement. The presence in certain provisions of this [Act] of the words "unless otherwise agreed," or words of similar import, does not imply that the effect of other provisions may not be varied by agreement.

(e) Whether an electronic record or electronic signature has legal consequences is determined by this [Act] and other applicable law.

Section 6. CONSTRUCTION AND APPLICATION. This [Act] must be construed and applied:

(1) to facilitate electronic transactions consistent with other applicable law; (2) to be consistent with reasonable practices concerning electronic transactions and with the continued expansion of those practices; and

(3) to effectuate its general purpose to make uniform the law with respect to the subject of this [Act] among States enacting it.

Section 7. LEGAL RECOGNITION OF ELECTRONIC RECORDS, ELECTRONIC SIGNATURES, AND ELECTRONIC CONTRACTS.

(a) A record or signature may not be denied legal effect or enforceability solely because it is in electronic form.

(b) A contract may not be denied legal effect or enforceability solely because an electronic record was used in its formation.

(c) If a law requires a record to be in writing, an electronic record satisfies the law.

(d) If a law requires a signature, an electronic signature satisfies the law.

*　*　*　*

Section 10. EFFECT OF CHANGE OR ERROR. If a change or error in an electronic record occurs in a transmission between parties to a transaction, the following rules apply:

(1) If the parties have agreed to use a security procedure to detect changes or errors and one party has conformed to the procedure, but the other party has not, and the nonconforming party would have detected the change or error had that party also conformed, the conforming party may avoid the effect of the changed or erroneous electronic record.

(2) In an automated transaction involving an individual, the individual may avoid the effect of an electronic record that resulted from an error made by the individual in dealing with the electronic agent of another person if the electronic agent did not provide an opportunity for the prevention or correction of the error and, at the time the individual learns of the error, the individual:

(A) promptly notifies the other person of the error and that the individual did not intend to be bound by the electronic record received by the other person;

(B) takes reasonable steps, including steps that conform to the other person's reasonable instructions, to return to the other person or, if instructed by the other person, to destroy the consideration received, if any, as a result of the erroneous electronic record; and

(C) has not used or received any benefit or value from the consideration, if any, received from the other person.

(3) If neither paragraph (1) nor paragraph (2) applies, the change or error has the effect provided by other law, including the law of mistake, and the parties' contract, if any.

(4) Paragraphs (2) and (3) may not be varied by agreement.

Spanish Equivalents for Important Legal Terms in English

Abandoned property: bienes abandonados
Acceptance: aceptación; consentimiento; acuerdo
Acceptor: aceptante
Accession: toma de posesión; aumento; accesión
Accommodation indorser: avalista de favor
Accommodation party: firmante de favor
Accord: acuerdo; convenio; arregio
Accord and satisfaction: transacción ejecutada
Act of state doctrine: doctrina de acto de gobierno
Administrative law: derecho administrativo
Administrative process: procedimiento o metódo administrativo
Administrator: administrador (-a)
Adverse possession: posesión de hecho susceptible de proscripción adquisitiva
Affirmative action: acción afirmativa
Affirmative defense: defensa afirmativa
After-acquired property: bienes adquiridos con posterioridad a un hecho dado
Agency: mandato; agencia
Agent: mandatorio; agente; representante
Agreement: convenio; acuerdo; contrato
Alien corporation: empresa extranjera
Allonge: hojas adicionales de endosos
Answer: contestación de la demande; alegato
Anticipatory repudiation: anuncio previo de las partes de su imposibilidad de cumplir con el contrato
Appeal: apelación; recurso de apelación
Appellate jurisdiction: jurisdicción de apelaciones
Appraisal right: derecho de valuación

Arbitration: arbitraje
Arson: incendio intencional
Articles of partnership: contrato social
Artisan's lien: derecho de retención que ejerce al artesano
Assault: asalto; ataque; agresión
Assignment of rights: transmisión; transferencia; cesión
Assumption of risk: no resarcimiento por exposición voluntaria al peligro
Attachment: auto judicial que autoriza el embargo; embargo

Bailee: depositario
Bailment: depósito; constitución en depósito
Bailor: depositante
Bankruptcy trustee: síndico de la quiebra
Battery: agresión; física
Bearer: portador; tenedor
Bearer instrument: documento al portador
Bequest or legacy: legado (de bienes muebles)
Bilateral contract: contrato bilateral
Bill of lading: conocimiento de embarque; carta de porte
Bill of Rights: declaración de derechos
Binder: póliza de seguro provisoria; recibo de pago a cuenta del precio
Blank indorsement: endoso en blanco
Blue sky laws: leyes reguladoras del comercio bursátil
Bond: título de crédito; garantía; caución
Bond indenture: contrato de emisión de bonos; contrato del ampréstito
Breach of contract: incumplimiento de contrato
Brief: escrito; resumen; informe
Burglary: violación de domicilio
Business judgment rule: regla de juicio comercial
Business tort: agravio comercial

Case law: ley de casos; derecho casuístico
Cashier's check: cheque de caja
Causation in fact: causalidad en realidad
Cease-and-desist order: orden para cesar y desistir
Certificate of deposit: certificado de depósito
Certified check: cheque certificado
Charitable trust: fideicomiso para fines benéficos
Chattel: bien mueble
Check: cheque
Chose in action: derecho inmaterial; derecho de acción
Civil law: derecho civil
Close corporation: sociedad de un solo accionista o de un grupo restringido de accionistas
Closed shop: taller agremiado (emplea solamente a miembros de un gremio)
Closing argument: argumento al final
Codicil: codicilo
Collateral: garantía; bien objeto de la garantía real
Comity: cortesía; cortesía entre naciones
Commercial paper: instrumentos negociables; documentos a valores commerciales
Common law: derecho consuetudinario; derecho común; ley común
Common stock: acción ordinaria
Comparative negligence: negligencia comparada
Compensatory damages: daños y perjuicios reales o compensatorios
Concurrent conditions: condiciones concurrentes
Concurrent jurisdiction: competencia concurrente de varios tribunales para entender en una misma causa
Concurring opinion: opinión concurrente

Condition: condición
Condition precedent: condición suspensiva
Condition subsequent: condición resolutoria
Confiscation: confiscación
Confusion: confusión; fusión
Conglomerate merger: fusión de firmas que operan en distintos mercados
Consent decree: acuerdo entre las partes aprobado por un tribunal
Consequential damages: daños y perjuicios indirectos
Consideration: consideración; motivo; contraprestación
Consolidation: consolidación
Constructive delivery: entrega simbólica
Constructive trust: fideicomiso creado por aplicación de la ley
Consumer protection law: ley para proteger el consumidor
Contract: contrato
Contract under seal: contrato formal o sellado
Contributory negligence: negligencia de la parte actora
Conversion: usurpación; conversión de valores
Copyright: derecho de autor
Corporation: sociedad anónima; corporación; persona juridica
Co-sureties: cogarantes
Counterclaim: reconvención; contrademanda
Counteroffer: contraoferta
Course of dealing: curso de transacciones
Course of performance: curso de cumplimiento
Covenant: pacto; garantía; contrato
Covenant not to sue: pacto or contrato a no demandar
Covenant of quiet enjoyment: garantía del uso y goce pacífico del inmueble
Creditors' composition agreement: concordato preventivo
Crime: crimen; delito; contravención
Criminal law: derecho penal
Cross-examination: contrainterrogatorio
Cure: cura; cuidado; derecho de remediar un vicio contractual
Customs receipts: recibos de derechos aduaneros

Damages: daños; indemnización por daños y perjuicios
Debit card: tarjeta de débito
Debtor: deudor

Debt securities: seguridades de deuda
Deceptive advertising: publicidad engañosa
Deed: escritura; título; acta translativa de domino
Defamation: difamación
Delegation of duties: delegación de obligaciones
Demand deposit: depósito a la vista
Depositions: declaración de un testigo fuera del tribunal
Devise: legado; deposición testamentaria (bienes inmuebles)
Directed verdict: veredicto según orden del juez y sin participación activa del jurado
Direct examination: interrogatorio directo; primer interrogatorio
Disaffirmance: repudiación; renuncia; anulación
Discharge: descargo; liberación; cumplimiento
Disclosed principal: mandante revelado
Discovery: descubrimiento; producción de la prueba
Dissenting opinion: opinión disidente
Dissolution: disolución; terminación
Diversity of citizenship: competencia de los tribunales federales para entender en causas cuyas partes intervinientes son cuidadanos de distintos estados
Divestiture: extinción premature de derechos reales
Dividend: dividendo
Docket: orden del día; lista de causas pendientes
Domestic corporation: sociedad local
Draft: orden de pago; letrade cambio
Drawee: girado; beneficiario
Drawer: librador
Duress: coacción; violencia

Easement: servidumbre
Embezzlement: desfalco; malversación
Eminent domain: poder de expropiación
Employment discrimination: discriminación en el empleo
Entrepreneur: empresario
Environmental law: ley ambiental
Equal dignity rule: regla de dignidad egual
Equity security: tipo de participación en una sociedad
Estate: propiedad; patrimonio; derecho
Estop: impedir; prevenir
Ethical issue: cuestión ética
Exclusive jurisdiction: competencia exclusiva

Exculpatory clause: cláusula eximente
Executed contract: contrato ejecutado
Execution: ejecución; cumplimiento
Executor: albacea
Executory contract: contrato aún no completamente consumado
Executory interest: derecho futuro
Express contract: contrato expreso
Expropriation: expropriación

Federal question: caso federal
Fee simple: pleno dominio; dominio absoluto
Fee simple absolute: dominio absoluto
Fee simple defeasible: dominio sujeta a una condición resolutoria
Felony: crimen; delito grave
Fictitious payee: beneficiario ficticio
Fiduciary: fiduciaro
Firm offer: oferta en firme
Fixture: inmueble por destino, incorporación a anexación
Floating lien: gravamen continuado
Foreign corporation: sociedad extranjera; U.S. sociedad constituída en otro estado
Forgery: falso; falsificación
Formal contract: contrato formal
Franchise: privilegio; franquicia; concesión
Franchisee: persona que recibe una concesión
Franchisor: persona que vende una concesión
Fraud: fraude; dolo; engaño
Future interest: bien futuro

Garnishment: embargo de derechos
General partner: socio comanditario
General warranty deed: escritura translativa de domino con garantía de título
Gift: donación
Gift *causa mortis:* donación por causa de muerte
Gift *inter vivos:* donación entre vivos
Good faith: buena fe
Good faith purchaser: comprador de buena fe

Holder: tenedor por contraprestación
Holder in due course: tenedor legítimo
Holographic will: testamento ológrafico
Homestead exemption laws: leyes que exceptúan las casas de familia de ejecución por duedas generales
Horizontal merger: fusión horizontal

Identification: identificación

Implied-in-fact contract: contrato implícito en realidad
Implied warranty: guarantía implícita
Implied warranty of merchantability: garantía implícita de vendibilidad
Impossibility of performance: imposibilidad de cumplir un contrato
Imposter: imposter
Incidental beneficiary: beneficiario incidental; beneficiario secundario
Incidental damages: daños incidentales
Indictment: auto de acusación; acusación
Indorsee: endorsatario
Indorsement: endoso
Indorser: endosante
Informal contract: contrato no formal; contrato verbal
Information: acusación hecha por el ministerio público
Injunction: mandamiento; orden de no innovar
Innkeeper's lien: derecho de retención que ejerce el posadero
Installment contract: contrato de pago en cuotas
Insurable interest: interés asegurable
Intended beneficiary: beneficiario destinado
Intentional tort: agravio; cuasi-delito intencional
International law: derecho internacional
Interrogatories: preguntas escritas sometidas por una parte a la otra o a un testigo
Inter vivos **trust:** fideicomiso entre vivos
Intestacy laws: leyes de la condición de morir intestado
Intestate: intestado
Investment company: compañia de inversiones
Issue: emisión

Joint tenancy: derechos conjuntos en un bien inmueble en favor del beneficiario sobreviviente
Judgment *n.o.v.*: juicio no obstante veredicto
Judgment rate of interest: interés de juicio
Judicial process: acto de procedimiento; proceso jurídico
Judicial review: revisión judicial
Jurisdiction: jurisdicción

Larceny: robo; hurto
Law: derecho; ley; jurisprudencia
Lease: contrato de locación; contrato de alquiler

Leasehold estate: bienes forales
Legal rate of interest: interés legal
Legatee: legatario
Letter of credit: carta de crédito
Levy: embargo; comiso
Libel: libelo; difamación escrita
Life estate: usufructo
Limited partner: comanditario
Limited partnership: sociedad en comandita
Liquidation: liquidación; realización
Lost property: objetos perdidos

Majority opinion: opinión de la mayoría
Maker: persona que realiza u ordena; librador
Mechanic's lien: gravamen de constructor
Mediation: mediación; intervención
Merger: fusión
Mirror image rule: fallo de reflejo
Misdemeanor: infracción; contravención
Mislaid property: bienes extraviados
Mitigation of damages: reducción de daños
Mortgage: hypoteca
Motion to dismiss: excepción parentoria
Mutual fund: fondo mutual

Negotiable instrument: instrumento negociable
Negotiation: negociación
Nominal damages: daños y perjuicios nominales
Novation: novación
Nuncupative will: testamento nuncupativo

Objective theory of contracts: teoria objetiva de contratos
Offer: oferta
Offeree: persona que recibe una oferta
Offeror: oferente
Order instrument: instrumento o documento a la orden
Original jurisdiction: jurisdicción de primera instancia
Output contract: contrato de producción

Parol evidence rule: regla relativa a la prueba oral
Partially disclosed principal: mandante revelado en parte
Partnership: sociedad colectiva; asociación; asociación de participación
Past consideration: causa o contraprestación anterior

Patent: patente; privilegio
Pattern or practice: muestra o práctica
Payee: beneficiario de un pago
Penalty: pena; penalidad
Per capita: por cabeza
Perfection: perfeción
Performance: cumplimiento; ejecución
Personal defenses: excepciones personales
Personal property: bienes muebles
Per stirpes: por estirpe
Plea bargaining: regateo por un alegato
Pleadings: alegatos
Pledge: prenda
Police powers: poders de policia y de prevención del crimen
Policy: póliza
Positive law: derecho positivo; ley positiva
Possibility of reverter: posibilidad de reversión
Precedent: precedente
Preemptive right: derecho de prelación
Preferred stock: acciones preferidas
Premium: recompensa; prima
Presentment warranty: garantía de presentación
Price discrimination: discriminación en los precios
Principal: mandante; principal
Privity: nexo jurídico
Privity of contract: relación contractual
Probable cause: causa probable
Probate: verificación; verificación del testamento
Probate court: tribunal de sucesiones y tutelas
Proceeds: resultados; ingresos
Profit: beneficio; utilidad; lucro
Promise: promesa
Promisee: beneficiario de una promesa
Promisor: promtente
Promissory estoppel: impedimento promisorio
Promissory note: pagaré; nota de pago
Promoter: promotor; fundador
Proximate cause: causa inmediata o próxima
Proxy: apoderado; poder
Punitive, or exemplary, damages: daños y perjuicios punitivos o ejemplares

Qualified indorsement: endoso con reservas
Quasi contract: contrato tácito o implícito
Quitclaim deed: acto de transferencia de una propiedad por finiquito, pero sin ninguna garantía sobre la validez del título transferido

Ratification: ratificación
Real property: bienes inmuebles
Reasonable doubt: duda razonable
Rebuttal: refutación
Recognizance: promesa; compromiso; reconocimiento
Recording statutes: leyes estatales sobre registros oficiales
Redress: reparacíon
Reformation: rectificación; reforma; corrección
Rejoinder: dúplica; contrarréplica
Release: liberación; renuncia a un derecho
Remainder: substitución; reversión
Remedy: recurso; remedio; reparación
Replevin: acción reivindicatoria; reivindicación
Reply: réplica
Requirements contract: contrato de suministro
Rescission: rescisión
Res judicata: cosa juzgada; res judicata
Respondeat superior: responsabilidad del mandante o del maestro
Restitution: restitución
Restrictive indorsement: endoso restrictivo
Resulting trust: fideicomiso implícito
Reversion: reversión; sustitución
Revocation: revocación; derogación
Right of contribution: derecho de contribución
Right of reimbursement: derecho de reembolso
Right of subrogation: derecho de subrogación
Right-to-work law: ley de libertad de trabajo
Robbery: robo
Rule 10b-5: Regla 10b-5

Sale: venta; contrato de compreventa
Sale on approval: venta a ensayo; venta sujeta a la aprobación del comprador
Sale or return: venta con derecho de devolución
Sales contract: contrato de compraventa; boleto de compraventa
Satisfaction: satisfacción; pago
Scienter: a sabiendas
S corporation: S corporación
Secured party: acreedor garantizado
Secured transaction: transacción garantizada
Securities: volares; titulos; seguridades
Security agreement: convenio de seguridad

Security interest: interés en un bien dado en garantía que permite a quien lo detenta venderlo en caso de incumplimiento
Service mark: marca de identificación de servicios
Shareholder's derivative suit: acción judicial entablada por un accionista en nombre de la sociedad
Signature: firma; rúbrica
Slander: difamación oral; calumnia
Sovereign immunity: immunidad soberana
Special indorsement: endoso especial; endoso a la orden de una person en particular
Specific performance: ejecución precisa, según los términos del contrato
Spendthrift trust: fideicomiso para pródigos
Stale check: cheque vencido
Stare decisis: acatar las decisiones, observar los precedentes
Statutory law: derecho estatutario; derecho legislado; derecho escrito
Stock: acciones
Stock warrant: certificado para la compra de acciones
Stop-payment order: orden de suspensión del pago de un cheque dada por el librador del mismo
Strict liability: responsabilidad unconditional
Summary judgment: fallo sumario

Tangible property: bienes corpóreos
Tenancy at will: inguilino por tiempo indeterminado (según la voluntad del propietario)
Tenancy by sufferance: posesión por tolerancia
Tenancy by the entirety: locación conyugal conjunta
Tenancy for years: inguilino por un término fijo
Tenancy in common: specie de copropiedad indivisa
Tender: oferta de pago; oferta de ejecución
Testamentary trust: fideicomiso testamentario
Testator: testador (-a)
Third party beneficiary contract: contrato para el beneficio del tercero-beneficiario
Tort: agravio; cuasi-delito
Totten trust: fideicomiso creado por un depósito bancario
Trade acceptance: letra de cambio aceptada
Trademark: marca registrada

Trade name: nombre comercial; razón social
Traveler's check: cheque del viajero
Trespass to land: ingreso no authorizado a las tierras de otro
Trespass to personal property: violación de los derechos posesorios de un tercero con respecto a bienes muebles
Trust: fideicomiso; trust

Ultra vires: ultra vires; fuera de la facultad (de una sociedad anónima)
Unanimous opinion: opinión unámine
Unconscionable contract or clause: contrato leonino; cláusula leonino
Underwriter: subscriptor; asegurador
Unenforceable contract: contrato que no se puede hacer cumplir
Unilateral contract: contrato unilateral
Union shop: taller agremiado; empresa en la que todos los empleados son miembros del gremio o sindicato
Universal defenses: defensas legitimas o legales
Usage of trade: uso comercial
Usury: usura

Valid contract: contrato válido
Venue: lugar; sede del proceso
Vertical merger: fusión vertical de empresas
Voidable contract: contrato anulable
Void contract: contrato nulo; contrato inválido, sin fuerza legal
Voir dire: examen preliminar de un testigo a jurado por el tribunal para determinar su competencia
Voting trust: fideicomiso para ejercer el derecho de voto

Waiver: renuncia; abandono
Warranty of habitability: garantía de habitabilidad
Watered stock: acciones diluídos; capital inflado
White-collar crime: crimen administrativo
Writ of attachment: mandamiento de ejecución; mandamiento de embargo
Writ of *certiorari*: auto de avocación; auto de certiorari
Writ of execution: auto ejecutivo; mandamiento de ejecutión
Writ of mandamus: auto de mandamus; mandamiento; orden judicial

Glossary

A

Acceptance • A voluntary act by the offeree that shows assent, or agreement, to the terms of an offer; may consist of words or conduct.

Accredited investor • In the context of securities offerings, a "sophisticated" investor, such as a bank, an insurance company, an investment company, an executive officer or director of the issuing company, or any person whose income or net worth exceeds certain limits.

Act of state doctrine • A doctrine that provides that the judicial branch of one country will not examine the validity of public acts committed by a recognized foreign government within its own territory.

Actionable • Capable of serving as the basis of a lawsuit. An actionable claim can be pursued in a lawsuit or other court action.

Actual malice • Real and demonstrable evil intent. In a defamation suit, a statement made about a public figure normally must be made with actual malice (with either knowledge of its falsity or a reckless disregard of the truth) for liability to be incurred.

Adhesion contract • A standard-form contract, such as that between a large retailer and a consumer, in which the stronger party dictates the terms.

Adjudication • The act of rendering a judicial decision. In the administrative process, the proceeding in which an administrative law judge hears and decides on issues that arise when an administrative agency charges a person or a firm with violating a law or regulation enforced by the agency.

Administrative agency • A federal or state government agency established to perform a specific function. Administrative agencies are authorized by legislative acts to make and enforce rules to administer and enforce the acts.

Administrative law • The body of law created by administrative agencies (in the form of rules, regulations, orders, and decisions) in order to carry out their duties and responsibilities.

Administrative law judge (ALJ) • One who presides over an administrative agency hearing and who has the power to administer oaths, take testimony, rule on questions of evidence, and make determinations of fact.

Administrative process • The procedure used by administrative agencies in the administration of law.

Adverse possession • The acquisition of title to real property by occupying it openly, without the consent of the owner, for a period of time specified by a state statute. The occupation must be actual, open, notorious, exclusive, and in opposition to all others, including the owner.

Affirmative action • Job-hiring and admissions policies that give special consideration to members of protected classes in an effort to overcome present effects of past discrimination.

Agency • A relationship between two parties in which one party (the agent) agrees to represent or act for the other (the principal).

Agreement • A meeting of two or more minds in regard to the terms of a contract; usually broken down into two events—an offer by one party to form a contract, and an acceptance of the offer by the person to whom the offer is made.

Alien corporation • A designation in the United States for a corporation formed in another country but doing business in the United States.

Alienation • A term used to define the process of transferring land out of one's possession (thus "alienating" the land from oneself).

Alternative dispute resolution (ADR) • The resolution of disputes in ways other than those involved in the traditional judicial process. Negotiation, mediation, and arbitration are forms of ADR.

Answer • Procedurally, a defendant's response to the plaintiff's complaint.

Anticipatory repudiation • An assertion or action by a party indicating that he or she will not perform an obligation that the party is contractually obligated to perform at a future time.

Antitrust laws • Laws designed to protect trade and commerce from restraints, monopolies, price fixing, and price discrimination.

Appropriate bargaining unit • A designation based on job duties, skill levels, and so on, of the proper entity that should be covered by a collective bargaining agreement.

Appropriation • In tort law, the use by one person of another person's name, likeness, or other identifying characteristic without permission and for the benefit of the user.

Arbitration • The settling of a dispute by submitting it to a disinterested third party (other than a court), who renders a decision. The decision may or may not be legally binding.

Arbitrator • A disinterested party who, by prior agreement of the parties submitting their dispute to arbitration, has the power to resolve the dispute and (generally) bind the parties.

Arson • The intentional burning of another's dwelling. Today, arson statutes have been extended to cover any real property regardless of ownership and the destruction of property by other means—for example, by explosion.

Articles of incorporation • The document filed with the appropriate governmental agency, usually the secretary of state, when a business is incorporated; state statutes usually prescribe what kind of information must be contained in the articles of incorporation.

Articles of organization • The document filed with a designated state official by which a limited liability company is formed.

Artisan's lien • A possessory lien given to a person who has made improvements and added value to another person's personal property as security for payment for services performed.

Assault • Any word or action intended to make another person fearful of immediate physical harm; a reasonably believable threat.

Assignment • The act of transferring to another all or part of one's rights arising under a contract.

Assumption of risk • A doctrine whereby a plaintiff may not recover for injuries or damages suffered from risks he or she knew of and voluntarily assumed.

Attachment • In the context of judicial liens, a court-ordered seizure and taking into custody of property prior to the securing of a judgment for a past-due debt.

Attempted monopolization • Any actions by a firm to eliminate competition and gain monopoly power.

Attorney • A person who has received a law degree and has been licensed by one or more states to practice law.

Attorney-client privilege • Protected communications between an attorney and client made for the purpose of furnishing or obtaining professional legal advice or assistance. Courts and other government institutions cannot require disclosure of the communications.

Authorization card • A card signed by an employee that gives a union permission to act on his or her behalf in negotiations with management once a majority of the employees has signed such cards.

Automatic stay • In bankruptcy proceedings, the suspension of virtually all litigation and other action by creditors against the debtor or the debtor's property. The stay is effective the moment the debtor files a petition in bankruptcy.

Award • In the context of arbitration, the arbitrator's decision. In the context of litigation, the amount of money awarded to a plaintiff in a civil lawsuit as damages.

B

Bait-and-switch advertising • Advertising a product at a very attractive price (the "bait") and then, once the consumer is in the store, saying that the advertised product either is not available or is of poor quality; the customer is then urged to purchase ("switched" to) a more expensive item.

Bankruptcy court • A federal court of limited jurisdiction that handles only bankruptcy proceedings. Bankruptcy proceedings are governed by federal bankruptcy law.

Battery • The unprivileged, intentional touching of another.

Beyond a reasonable doubt • The standard of proof used in criminal cases. If there is any reasonable doubt that a criminal defendant committed the crime with which she or he has been charged, then the verdict must be "not guilty."

Bilateral contract • A type of contract that arises when a promise is given in exchange for a return promise.

Bill of rights • The first ten amendments to the U.S. Constitution.

Binding authority • Any source of law that a court must follow when deciding a case. Binding authorities include constitutions, statutes, and regulations that govern the issue being decided, as well as court decisions that are controlling precedents within the jurisdiction.

Blue laws • State or local laws that prohibit the performance of certain types of commercial activities on Sunday.

Bona fide occupational qualification (BFOQ) • Identifiable characteristic reasonably necessary to the normal operation of a particular business. Such characteristics can include gender, national origin, and religion, but not race or color.

Bounty payment • A reward given to a person or persons who perform a certain service—such as informing legal authorities of illegal actions.

Breach of contract • The failure, without legal excuse, of a promisor to perform the obligations of a contract.

Brief • A formal legal document submitted by the attorney for the appellant or the appellee (in answer to the appellant's brief) to an appellate court when a case is appealed. The appellant's brief outlines the facts and issues of the case, the judge's rulings or jury's findings that should be reversed or modified, the applicable law, and the arguments on the client's behalf.

Browse-wrap terms • Terms and conditions of use that are presented to an Internet user at the time certain products, such as software, are being downloaded but to which the user need not agree (by clicking "I agree," for example) before being able to install or use the product.

Bulk zoning • Zoning regulations that restrict the amount of structural coverage on a particular parcel of land.

Bureaucracy • The organizational structure, consisting of government bureaus and agencies, through which the government implements and enforces the laws.

Burglary • The unlawful entry or breaking into a building with the intent to commit a felony. (Some state statutes expand this to include the intent to commit any crime.)

Business ethics • Ethics in a business context; a consensus of what constitutes right or wrong behavior in the world of business and the application of moral principles to situations that arise in a business setting.

Business invitee • A person, such as a customer or a client, who is invited onto business premises by the owner of those premises for business purposes.

Business judgment rule • A rule that immunizes corporate management from liability for actions that result in corporate losses or damages if the actions are undertaken in good faith and are within both the power of the corporation and the authority of management to make.

Business necessity • A defense to allegations of employment discrimination in which the employer demonstrates that an employment practice that discriminates against members of a protected class is related to job performance.

Business tort • The wrongful interference with another's business rights.

Bylaws • A set of governing rules adopted by a corporation or other association.

C

Case law • The rules of law announced in court decisions. Case law includes the aggregate of reported cases that interpret judicial precedents, statutes, regulations, and constitutional provisions.

Categorical imperative • A concept developed by the philosopher Immanuel Kant as an ethical guideline for behavior. In deciding whether an action is right or wrong, or desirable or undesirable, a person should evaluate the action in terms of what would happen if everybody else in the same situation, or category, acted the same way.

Causation in fact • An act or omission without which an event would not have occurred.

Cease-and-desist order • An administrative or judicial order prohibiting a person or business firm from conducting activities that an agency or court has deemed illegal.

Checks and balances • The national government is composed of three separate branches: the executive, the legislative, and the judicial branches. Each branch of the government exercises a check on the actions of the others.

Choice-of-language clause • A clause in a contract designating the official language by which the contract will be interpreted in the event of a future disagreement over the contract's terms.

Choice-of-law clause • A clause in a contract designating the law (such as the law of a particular state or nation) that will govern the contract.

Citation • A reference to a publication in which a legal authority—such as a statute or a court decision—or other source can be found.

Civil law • The branch of law dealing with the definition and enforcement of all private or public rights, as opposed to criminal matters.

Civil law system • A system of law derived from that of the Roman Empire and based on a code rather than case law; the predominant system of law in the nations of continental Europe and the nations that were once their colonies. In the United States, Louisiana, because of its historical ties to France, has in part a civil law system.

Click-on agreement • An agreement that arises when a buyer, engaging in a transaction on a computer, indicates his or her assent to be bound by the terms of an offer by clicking on a button that says, for example, "I agree"; sometimes referred to as a *click-on license* or a *click-wrap agreement.*

Closed shop • A firm that requires union membership by its workers as a condition of employment. The closed shop was made illegal by the Labor-Management Relations Act of 1947.

Collateral promise • A secondary promise that is ancillary (subsidiary) to a principal transaction or primary contractual relationship, such as a promise made by one person to pay the debts of another if the latter fails to perform. A collateral promise normally must be in writing to be enforceable.

Collective bargaining • The process by which labor and management negotiate the terms and conditions of employment, including working hours and workplace conditions.

Comity • The principle by which one nation defers and gives effect to the laws and judicial decrees of another nation.

Commerce clause • The provision in Article I, Section 8, of the U.S. Constitution that gives Congress the power to regulate interstate commerce.

Common law • That body of law developed from custom or judicial decisions in English and U.S. courts, not attributable to a legislature.

Common situs picketing • The illegal picketing of a primary employer's site by workers who are involved in a labor dispute with a secondary employer.

Comparative negligence • A theory in tort law under which the liability for injuries resulting from negligent acts is shared by all persons who were guilty of negligence (including the injured party), on the basis of each person's proportionate carelessness.

Compensatory damages • A money award equivalent to the actual value of injuries or damages sustained by the aggrieved party.

Complaint • The pleading made by a plaintiff alleging wrongdoing on the part of the defendant; the document that, when filed with a court, initiates a lawsuit.

Computer crime • Any act that is directed against computers and computer parts, that uses computers as instruments of crime, or that involves computers and constitutes abuse.

Concerted action • Action by employees, such as a strike or picketing, with the purpose of furthering their bargaining demands or other mutual interests.

Conciliation • A form of alternative dispute resolution in which the parties reach an agreement themselves with the help of a neutral third party, called a conciliator, who facilitates the negotiations.

Concurrent jurisdiction • Jurisdiction that exists when two different courts have the power to hear a case. For example, some cases can be heard in a federal or a state court.

Confiscation • A government's taking of a privately owned business or personal property without a proper public purpose or an award of just compensation.

Conglomerate merger • A merger between unrelated firms that are neither competitors nor customers or suppliers of each other.

Consent • The voluntary agreement to a proposition or an act of another; a concurrence of wills.

Consequential damages • Special damages that compensate for a loss that is not direct or immediate (for example, lost profits). The special damages must have been reasonably foreseeable at the time the breach or injury occurred in order for the plaintiff to collect them.

Consideration • Generally, the value given in return for a promise. The consideration, which must be present to make the contract legally binding, must be something of legally sufficient value and bargained for.

Constitutional law • Law based on the U.S. Constitution and the constitutions of the various states.

Constructive eviction • A form of eviction that occurs when a landlord fails to perform adequately any of the undertakings (such as providing heat in the winter) required by the lease, thereby making the tenant's further use and enjoyment of the property exceedingly difficult or impossible.

Consumer-debtor • An individual whose debts are primarily consumer debts (debts for purchases made primarily for personal or household use).

Contract • An agreement that can be enforced in court; formed by two or more parties who agree to perform or to refrain from performing some act now or in the future.

Contractual capacity • The threshold mental capacity required by the law for a party who enters into a contract to be bound by that contract.

Contributory negligence • A theory in tort law under which a complaining party's own negligence contributed to or caused his or her injuries. Contributory negligence is an absolute bar to recovery in a minority of jurisdictions.

Conversion • The act of wrongfully taking or retaining possession of a person's personal property and placing it in the service of another.

Conveyance • The transfer of a title to land from one person to another by deed; a document (such as a deed) by which an interest in land is transferred from one person to another.

"Cooling-off" laws • Laws that allow buyers a period of time, such as three days, in which to cancel door-to-door sales contracts.

Copyright • The exclusive right of authors to publish, print, or sell an intellectual production for a statutory period of time. A copyright has the same monopolistic nature as a patent or trademark, but it differs in that it applies exclusively to works of art, works of literature, and other works of authorship (including computer programs).

Corporate social responsibility • The concept that corporations can and should act ethically and be accountable to society for their actions.

Corporation • A legal entity formed in compliance with statutory requirements. The entity is distinct from its shareholder-owners.

Correspondent bank • A bank in which another bank has an account for the purpose of facilitating fund transfers.

Cost-benefit analysis • A decision-making technique that involves weighing the costs of a given action against the benefits of that action.

Co-surety • A joint surety; a person who assumes liability jointly with another surety for the payment of an obligation.

Counteradvertising • Advertising undertaken pursuant to a Federal Trade Commission order for the purpose of correcting earlier false claims that were made about a product.

Counterclaim • A claim made by a defendant in a civil lawsuit against the plaintiff. In effect, the defendant is suing the plaintiff.

Counteroffer • An offeree's response to an offer in which the offeree rejects the original offer and at the same time makes a new offer.

Cram-down provision • A provision of the Bankruptcy Code that allows a court to confirm a debtor's Chapter 11 reorganization plan even though only one class of creditors has accepted it. To exercise the court's right under this provision, the court must demonstrate that the plan does not discriminate unfairly against any creditors and is fair and equitable.

Creditors' composition agreement • An agreement formed between a debtor and his or her creditors in which the creditors agree to accept a lesser sum than that owed by the debtor in full satisfaction of the debt.

Crime • A wrong against society proclaimed in a statute and punishable by society through fines and/or imprisonment—and, in some cases, death.

Criminal law • Law that defines and governs actions that constitute crimes. Generally, criminal law has to do with wrongful actions committed against society for which society demands redress.

Cross-border pollution • Pollution across national boundaries; air and water degradation in one nation resulting from pollution-causing activities in a neighboring country.

Cyber crime • A crime that occurs online, in the virtual community of the Internet, as opposed to the physical world.

Cyber mark • A trademark in cyberspace.

Cyber stalker • A person who commits the crime of stalking in cyberspace. Generally, stalking consists of harassing a person and putting that person in reasonable fear for his or her safety or the safety of his or her immediate family.

Cyber terrorist • A hacker whose purpose is to exploit a target computer to create a serious impact, such as corrupting a program to sabotage a business.

Cyber tort • A tort committed via the Internet.

Cyberlaw • An informal term used to refer to all laws governing electronic communications and transactions, particularly those conducted via the Internet.

Cybernotary • A legally recognized authority that can certify the validity of digital signatures.

Cybersquatting • An act that occurs when a person registers a domain name that is the same as, or confusingly similar to, the

trademark of another and offers to sell the domain name back to the trademark owner.

Damages • Money sought as a remedy for a breach of contract or for a tortious act.

Debtor in possession (DIP) • In Chapter 11 bankruptcy proceedings, a debtor who is allowed to continue in possession of the estate in property (the business) and to continue business operations.

Deceptive advertising • Advertising that misleads consumers, either by making unjustified claims concerning a product's performance or by omitting a material fact concerning the product's composition or performance.

Deed • A document by which title to property (usually real property) is passed.

Defamation • Anything published or publicly spoken that causes injury to another's good name, reputation, or character.

Default judgment • A judgment entered by a court against a defendant who has failed to appear in court to answer or defend against the plaintiff's claim.

Defendant • One against whom a lawsuit is brought; the accused person in a criminal proceeding.

Defense • That which a defendant offers and alleges in an action or suit as a reason why the plaintiff should not recover or establish what he or she seeks.

Delegation doctrine • A doctrine based on Article I, Sections 1 and 8, of the U.S. Constitution, which have been construed to allow Congress to delegate some of its power to make and implement laws to administrative agencies.

Delegation of duties • The act of transferring to another all or part of one's duties arising under a contract.

Deposition • The testimony of a party to a lawsuit or a witness taken under oath before a trial.

Disaffirmance • The legal avoidance, or setting aside, of a contractual obligation.

Discharge • The termination of an obligation. In contract law, discharge occurs when the parties have fully performed their contractual obligations or when events, conduct of the parties, or operation of the law releases the parties from performance. In bankruptcy proceedings, discharge refers to the extinction of the debtor's dischargeable debts.

Disclosed principal • A principal whose identity is known to a third party at the time the agent makes a contract with the third party.

Discovery • A phase in the litigation process during which the opposing parties may obtain information from each other and from third parties prior to trial.

Disparagement of property • An economically injurious false statement made about another's product or property; includes the torts of slander of quality and slander of title.

Disparate-impact discrimination • A form of employment discrimination that results from certain employer practices or procedures that, although not discriminatory on their face, have a discriminatory effect.

Disparate-treatment discrimination • A form of employment discrimination that results when an employer intentionally discriminates against employees who are members of protected classes.

Distributed network • A network that can be used by persons located (distributed) around the country or the globe to share computer files.

Distribution agreement • A contract between a seller and a distributor of the seller's products setting out the terms and conditions of the distributorship.

Diversity of citizenship • Under Article III, Section 2, of the Constitution, a basis for federal district court jurisdiction over a lawsuit between (1) citizens of different states, (2) a foreign country and citizens of a state or of different states, or (3) citizens of a state and citizens or subjects of a foreign country. The amount in controversy must be more than $75,000 before a federal district court can take jurisdiction in such cases.

Divestiture • The act of selling one or more of a company's divisions, such as a subsidiary or plant; often mandated by the courts in merger or monopolization cases.

Dividend • A distribution to corporate shareholders of corporate profits or income, disbursed in proportion to the number of shares held.

Docket • The list of cases entered on a court's calendar and thus scheduled to be heard by the court.

Domain name • The core part of an Internet address, such as "westlaw.com." The top level (the part of the name to the right of the period) represents the type of entity that operates the site ("com" is an abbreviation for "commercial"). The second level (the part of the name to the left of the period) is chosen by the entity.

Domestic corporation • In a given state, a corporation that does business in, and is organized under the law of, that state.

Double jeopardy • A situation occurring when a person is tried twice for the same criminal offense; prohibited by the Fifth Amendment to the Constitution.

Dram shop act • A state statute that imposes liability on tavern owners and bartenders for injuries resulting from accidents caused by intoxicated persons when the sellers or servers of alcoholic drinks contributed to the intoxication.

Due process clause • The provisions of the Fifth and Fourteenth Amendments to the Constitution that guarantee that no person shall be deprived of life, liberty, or property without due process of law. Similar clauses are found in most state constitutions.

Dumping • The selling of goods in a foreign country at a price below the price charged for the same goods in the domestic market.

Duress • Unlawful pressure brought to bear on a person, causing the person to perform an act that she or he would not otherwise have performed.

Duty of care • The duty of all persons, as established by tort law, to exercise a reasonable amount of care in their dealings with others. Failure to exercise due care, which is normally determined by the "reasonable person standard," constitutes the tort of negligence.

E

Early neutral case evaluation • A form of alternative dispute resolution in which a neutral third party evaluates the strengths and weaknesses of the disputing parties' positions; the evaluator's opinion forms the basis for negotiating a settlement.

Easement • A nonpossessory right to use another's property in a manner established by either express or implied agreement.

E-contract • A contract that is formed electronically.

Eighty-day cooling-off period • A provision of the Taft-Hartley Act that allows federal courts to issue injunctions against strikes that might create a national emergency.

Embezzlement • The fraudulent appropriation of funds or other property by a person to whom such items have been entrusted.

Eminent domain • The power of a government to take land for public use from private citizens for just compensation.

Employee committee • A committee created by an employer and composed of representatives of management and nonunion employees to act together to improve workplace conditions.

Employment discrimination • Treating employees or job applicants unequally on the basis of race, color, national origin, religion, gender, age, or disability; prohibited by federal statutes.

Enabling legislation • Statutes enacted by Congress that authorize the creation of an administrative agency and specify the name, composition, purpose, functions, and powers of the agency being created.

Entrapment • In criminal law, a defense in which the defendant claims that he or she was induced by a public official—usually an undercover agent or police officer—to commit a crime that he or she would otherwise not have committed.

Entrepreneur • One who initiates and assumes the financial risks of a new enterprise and undertakes to provide or control its management.

Environmental impact statement (EIS) • A statement required by the National Environmental Policy Act for any major federal action that will significantly affect the quality of the environment. The statement must analyze the action's impact on the environment and explore alternative actions that might be taken.

Equal protection clause • The provision in the Fourteenth Amendment to the Constitution that guarantees that no state will "deny to any person within its jurisdiction the equal protection of the laws." This clause mandates that the state governments treat similarly situated individuals in a similar manner.

Equitable principles and maxims • General propositions or principles of law that have to do with fairness (equity).

Establishment clause • The provision in the First Amendment to the Constitution that prohibits Congress from creating any law "respecting an establishment of religion."

Estate in property • In bankruptcy proceedings, all of the debtor's legal and equitable interests in property currently held, wherever located, together with certain jointly owned property, property transferred in transactions voidable by the trustee, proceeds and profits from the property of the estate, and certain property interests to which the debtor becomes entitled within 180 days after filing for bankruptcy.

Ethics • Moral principles and values applied to social behavior.

Eviction • A landlord's act of depriving a tenant of possession of the leased premises.

Exclusionary rule • In criminal procedure, a rule under which any evidence that is obtained in violation of the accused's constitutional rights guaranteed by the Fourth, Fifth, and Sixth Amendments, as well as any evidence derived from illegally obtained evidence, will not be admissible in court.

Exclusive distributorship • A distributorship in which the seller and the distributor of the seller's products agree that the distributor has the exclusive right to distribute the seller's products in a certain geographic area.

Exclusive-dealing contract • An agreement under which a seller forbids a buyer to purchase products from the seller's competitors.

Exclusive jurisdiction • Jurisdiction that exists when a case can be heard only in a particular court or type of court.

Exculpatory clause • A clause that releases the contractual party from liability in the event of a monetary or physical injury, no matter who is at fault.

Executed contract • A contract that has been completely performed by both parties.

Executive agency • An administrative agency within the executive branch of government. At the federal level, executive agencies are those within the cabinet departments.

Executory contract • A contract that has not as yet been fully performed.

Executory interest • A future interest, held by a person other than the grantor, that begins after the termination of the preceding estate.

Export • To sell products to buyers located in other countries.

Express contract • A contract in which the terms of the agreement are fully and explicitly stated in words, oral or written.

Express warranty • A promise, ancillary to an underlying sales agreement, that is included in the written or oral terms of the sales agreement under which the promisor assures the quality, description, or performance of the goods.

Expropriation • The seizure by a government of a privately owned business or personal property for a proper public purpose and with just compensation.

F

Featherbedding • A requirement that more workers be employed to do a particular job than are actually needed.

Federal form of government • A system of government in which the states form a union and the sovereign power is divided between a central government and the member states.

Federal question • A question that pertains to the U.S. Constitution, acts of Congress, or treaties. A federal question provides a basis for federal jurisdiction.

Fee simple absolute • An ownership interest in land in which the owner has the greatest possible aggregation of rights, privileges, and power. Ownership in fee simple absolute is limited absolutely to a person and his or her heirs.

Fee simple defeasible • An ownership interest in real property that can be taken away (by the prior grantor) on the occurrence or nonoccurrence of a specified event.

Felony • A crime—such as arson, murder, rape, or robbery—that carries the most severe sanctions, which range from one year in a state or federal prison to the death penalty.

Fiduciary • As a noun, a person having a duty created by his or her undertaking to act primarily for another's benefit in matters connected with the undertaking. As an adjective, a relationship founded on trust and confidence.

Filtering software • A computer program that includes a pattern through which data are passed. When designed to block access to certain Web sites, the pattern blocks the retrieval of a site whose address or key words are on a list within the program.

Final order • The final decision of an administrative agency on an issue. If no appeal is taken, or if the case is not reviewed or considered anew by the agency commission, the administrative law judge's initial order becomes the final order of the agency.

Fixture • A thing that was once personal property but that has become attached to real property in such a way that it takes on the characteristics of real property and becomes part of that real property.

Force majeure clause • A provision in a contract stipulating that certain unforeseen events—such as war, political upheavals, acts of God, or other events—will excuse a party from liability for nonperformance of contractual obligations.

Foreign corporation • In a given state, a corporation that does business in the state without being incorporated therein.

Foreign exchange market • Part of a worldwide system in which foreign currencies are bought and sold.

Forgery • The fraudulent making or altering of any writing in a way that changes the legal rights and liabilities of another.

Forum-selection clause • A provision in a contract designating the court, jurisdiction, or tribunal that will decide any disputes arising under the contract.

Franchise • Any arrangement in which the owner of a trademark, trade name, or copyright licenses another to use that trademark, trade name, or copyright, under specified conditions or limitations, in the selling of goods and services.

Franchisee • One receiving a license to use another's (the franchisor's) trademark, trade name, or copyright in the sale of goods and services.

Franchisor • One licensing another (the franchisee) to use his or her trademark, trade name, or copyright in the sale of goods or services.

Fraudulent misrepresentation • Any misrepresentation, either by misstatement or by omission of a material fact, knowingly made with the intention of deceiving another and on which a reasonable person would and does rely to his or her detriment.

Free exercise clause • The provision in the First Amendment to the Constitution that prohibits Congress from making any law "prohibiting the free exercise" of religion.

Future interest • An interest in real property that is not at present possessory but will or may become possessory in the future.

G

Garnishment • A legal process used by a creditor to collect a debt by seizing property of the debtor (such as wages) that is being held by a third party (such as the debtor's employer).

General partner • In a limited partnership, a partner who assumes responsibility for the management of the partnership and liability for all partnership debts.

General plan • A comprehensive document that local jurisdictions are often required by state law to devise and implement as a precursor to specific land-use regulations.

Good Samaritan statute • A state statute stipulating that persons who rescue or provide emergency services to others in peril—unless they do so recklessly, thus causing further harm—cannot be sued for negligence.

Grand jury • A group of citizens called to decide, after hearing the state's evidence, whether a reasonable basis (probable cause) exists for believing that a crime has been committed and whether a trial ought to be held. Grand juries usually include more jurors than ordinary trial juries.

Group boycott • The refusal to deal with a particular person or firm by a group of competitors.

Guarantor • A person who agrees to satisfy the debt of another (the debtor) only after the principal debtor defaults; a guarantor's liability is thus secondary.

H

Hacker • A person who uses one computer to break into another.

Historical school • A school of legal thought that emphasizes the evolutionary process of law and that looks to the past to discover what the principles of contemporary law should be.

Homestead exemption • A law permitting a debtor to retain the family home, either in its entirety or up to a specified dollar amount, free from the claims of unsecured creditors or trustees in bankruptcy.

Horizontal merger • A merger between two firms that are competing in the same market.

Horizontal restraint • Any agreement that in some way restrains competition between rival firms competing in the same market.

Hot-cargo agreement • An agreement in which employers voluntarily agree with unions not to handle, use, or deal in goods produced by nonunion employees of other firms; a type of secondary boycott explicitly prohibited by the Labor-Management Reporting and Disclosure Act of 1959.

I

Identity theft • The theft of another's identifying information—such as name, date of birth, and Social Security number—and the use of the information to access the victim's financial resources.

Implied-in-fact contract • A contract formed in whole or in part from the conduct of the parties (as opposed to an express contract).

Implied warranty of fitness for a particular purpose • A presumed promise made by a merchant seller of goods that the goods are fit for the particular purpose for which the buyer will use the goods. The seller must know the buyer's purpose and be aware that the buyer is relying on the seller's skill and judgment to select suitable goods.

Implied warranty of habitability • An implied promise by a landlord that rented residential premises are fit for human habitation—that is, in a condition that is safe and suitable for people to live in.

Implied warranty of merchantability • A presumed promise by a merchant seller of goods that the goods are reasonably fit for the general purpose for which they are sold, are correctly packaged and labeled, and are of proper quality.

Impossibility of performance • A doctrine under which a party to a contract is relieved of his or her duty to perform when performance becomes impossible or totally impracticable (through no fault of either party).

Incidental beneficiary • A third party who incidentally benefits from a contract but whose benefit was not the reason the contract was formed; an incidental beneficiary has no rights in a contract and cannot sue to have the contract enforced.

Independent contractor • One who works for, and receives payment from, an employer but whose working conditions and methods are not controlled by the employer. An independent contractor is not an employee but may be an agent.

Independent regulatory agency • An administrative agency that is considered part of the government's executive branch but is not under the direction of the president. Independent agency officials cannot be removed without cause.

Indictment • The formal written accusation of a crime, made by a grand jury and presented to a court for prosecution against the accused person.

Information • A formal accusation or complaint made by a government prosecutor without a grand jury indictment.

Initial order • In the context of administrative law, an agency's disposition in a matter other than a rulemaking. An administrative law judge's initial order becomes final unless it is appealed.

Innkeeper's lien • A possessory lien placed on the luggage of hotel guests for hotel charges that remain unpaid.

Insider trading • The purchase or sale of securities on the basis of inside information (information that has not been made available to the public).

Intellectual property • Property resulting from intellectual, creative processes.

Intended beneficiary • A third party for whose benefit a contract is formed; an intended beneficiary can sue the promisor if such a contract is breached.

Intentional tort • A wrongful act knowingly committed.

International law • The law that governs relations among nations. National laws, customs, treaties, and international conferences and organizations are generally considered to be the most important sources of international law.

Interrogatories • A series of written questions for which written answers are prepared, usually with the assistance of the party's attorney, and then signed under oath by a party to a lawsuit.

Investment company • A company that acts on behalf of many smaller shareholders by buying a large portfolio of securities and professionally managing that portfolio.

J

Judicial process • The procedures relating to, or connected with, the administration of justice through the judicial system.

Judicial review • The process by which a court decides on the constitutionality of legislative enactments and actions of the executive branch.

Jurisdiction • The authority of a court to hear and decide a specific action.

Jurisprudence • The science or philosophy of law.

Justiciable controversy • A controversy that is not hypothetical or academic but real and substantial; a requirement that must be satisfied before a court will hear a case.

L

Larceny • The wrongful taking and carrying away of another person's personal property with the intent to permanently deprive the owner of the property. Some states classify larceny as either grand or petit, depending on the property's value.

Law • A body of enforceable rules governing relationships among individuals and between individuals and their society.

Lease • A contract by which the owner of property (the lessor) grants to a person (the lessee) an exclusive right to use and possess the property, usually for a specified period of time, in return for rent or some other form of payment.

Leasehold estate • An estate in realty held by a tenant under a lease. In every leasehold estate, the tenant has a qualified right to possess and/or use the land.

Legal positivism • A school of legal thought centered on the assumption that there is no law higher than the laws created by the government. Laws must be obeyed, even if they are unjust, to prevent anarchy.

Legal realism • A school of legal thought of the 1920s and 1930s that generally advocated a less abstract and more realistic approach to the law, an approach that takes into account customary practices and the circumstances in which transactions take place. The school left a lasting imprint on American jurisprudence.

Legislative rule • An administrative agency rule that carries the same weight as a congressionally enacted statute.

Letter of credit • A written instrument, usually issued by a bank on behalf of a customer or other person, in which the issuer promises to honor drafts or other demands for payment by third persons in accordance with the terms of the instrument.

Libel • Defamation in writing or other permanent form (such as a digital recording) having the quality of permanence.

License • A revocable right or privilege of a person to come on another person's land.

Life estate • An interest in land that exists only for the duration of the life of some person, usually the holder of the estate.

Limited liability company (LLC) • A hybrid form of business enterprise that offers the limited liability of the corporation but the tax advantages of a partnership.

Limited liability partnership (LLP) • A business organizational form that is similar to the LLC but that is designed more for professionals who normally do business as partners in a partnership. The LLP is a pass-through entity for tax purposes, like the general partnership, but it limits the personal liability of the partners.

Limited partner • In a limited partnership, a partner who contributes capital to the partnership but has no right to participate in the management and operation of the business. The limited partner assumes no liability for partnership debts beyond the capital contributed.

Limited partnership • A partnership consisting of one or more general partners (who manage the business and are liable to the full extent of their personal assets for debts of the partnership) and one or more limited partners (who contribute only assets and are liable only up to the amount contributed by them).

Liquidated damages • An amount, stipulated in the contract, that the parties to a contract believe to be a reasonable estimation of the damages that will occur in the event of a breach.

Liquidation • The sale of all of the nonexempt assets of a debtor and the distribution of the proceeds to the debtor's creditors. Chapter 7 of the Bankruptcy Code provides for liquidation bankruptcy proceedings.

Litigant • A party to a lawsuit.

Litigation • The process of resolving a dispute through the court system.

Lockout • The closing of a plant to employees by an employer to gain leverage in collective bargaining negotiations.

Long arm statute • A state statute that permits a state to obtain personal jurisdiction over nonresident defendants. A defendant must have certain "minimum contacts" with that state for the statute to apply.

M

Mailbox rule • A rule providing that an acceptance of an offer becomes effective on dispatch (on being placed in a mailbox), if mail is, expressly or impliedly, an authorized means of communication of acceptance to the offeror.

Malpractice • Professional misconduct or lack of the requisite degree of skill as a professional. Negligence—the failure to exercise due care—on the part of a professional, such as a physician, is commonly referred to as malpractice.

Market concentration • The degree to which a small number of firms control a large percentage of a relevant market area.

Market power • The power of a firm to control the market price of its product. A monopoly has the greatest degree of market power.

Market-share test • The primary measure of monopoly power. A firm's market share is the percentage of a market that the firm controls.

Mechanic's lien • A statutory lien on the real property of another, created to ensure payment for work performed and materials furnished in the repair or improvement of real property, such as a building.

Mediation • A method of settling disputes outside of court by using the services of a neutral third party, called a mediator. The mediator acts as a communicating agent between the parties and suggests ways in which the parties can resolve their dispute.

Mediator • A person who attempts to reconcile the differences between two or more parties.

Member • The term used to designate a person who has an ownership interest in a limited liability company.

Meta tag • A key word in a document that can serve as an index reference to the document. On the Web, search engines return results based, in part, on the tags in Web documents.

Minimum wage The lowest wage, either by government regulation or union contract, that an employer may pay an hourly worker.

Mini-trial A private proceeding in which each party to a dispute argues its position before the other side and vice versa. A neutral third party may be present and act as an adviser if the parties fail to reach an agreement.

Mirror image rule • A common law rule that requires, for a valid contractual agreement, that the terms of the offeree's acceptance adhere exactly to the terms of the offeror's offer.

Misdemeanor • A lesser crime than a felony, punishable by a fine or incarceration in jail for up to one year.

Mitigation of damages • A rule requiring a plaintiff to have done whatever was reasonable to minimize the damages caused by the defendant.

Money laundering • Falsely reporting income that has been obtained through criminal activity as income obtained through a legitimate business enterprise—in effect, "laundering" the "dirty money."

Monopolization • The possession of monopoly power in the relevant market and the willful acquisition or maintenance of that power, as distinguished from growth or development as a consequence of a superior product, business acumen, or historic accident.

Monopoly • A term generally used to describe a market in which there is a single seller or a limited number of sellers.

Monopoly power • The ability of a monopoly to dictate what takes place in a given market.

Moral minimum • The minimum degree of ethical behavior expected of a business firm, which is usually defined as compliance with the law.

Mortgagee • Under a mortgage agreement, the creditor who takes a security interest in the debtor's property.

Mortgagor • Under a mortgage agreement, the debtor who gives the creditor a security interest in the debtor's property in return for a mortgage loan.

Most-favored-nation status • A status granted in an international treaty by a provision stating that the citizens of the contracting nations may enjoy the privileges accorded by either party to citizens of the most favored nations. Generally, most-favored-nation clauses are designed to establish equality of international treatment.

Motion for a directed verdict • In a jury trial, a motion for the judge to take the decision out of the hands of the jury and direct a verdict for the party who filed the motion on the ground that the other party has not produced sufficient evidence to support her or his claim.

Motion for a new trial • A motion asserting that the trial was so fundamentally flawed (because of error, newly discovered evidence, prejudice, or other reason) that a new trial is necessary to prevent a miscarriage of justice.

Motion for judgment *n.o.v.* • A motion requesting the court to grant judgment in favor of the party making the motion on the ground that the jury verdict against him or her was unreasonable and erroneous.

Motion for judgment on the pleadings • A motion by either party to a lawsuit at the close of the pleadings requesting the court to decide the issue solely on the pleadings without proceeding to trial. The motion will be granted only if no facts are in dispute.

Motion for summary judgment • A motion requesting the court to enter a judgment without proceeding to trial. The motion can be based on evidence outside the pleadings and will be granted only if no facts are in dispute.

Motion to dismiss • A pleading in which a defendant asserts that the plaintiff's claim fails to state a cause of action (that is, has no basis in law) or that there are other grounds on which a suit should be dismissed.

Mutual fund • A type of investment company that continually buys and sells to investors shares of ownership in a portfolio.

N

National law • Law that pertains to a particular nation (as opposed to international law).

Natural law • The belief that government and the legal system should reflect universal moral and ethical principles that are inherent in human nature. The natural law school is the oldest and one of the most significant schools of legal thought.

Necessaries • Necessities required for life, such as food, shelter, clothing, and medical attention; may include whatever is believed to be necessary to maintain a person's standard of living or financial and social status.

Negligence *per se* • An action or failure to act in violation of a statutory requirement.

Negligence • The failure to exercise the standard of care that a reasonable person would exercise in similar circumstances.

Negotiation • In regard to dispute settlement, a process in which parties, with or without attorneys to represent them, attempt to settle their dispute without going to court.

Nominal damages • A small monetary award (often one dollar) granted to a plaintiff when no actual damage was suffered.

No-par shares • Corporate shares that have no face value—that is, no specific dollar amount is printed on their face.

No-strike clause • A provision in a collective bargaining agreement that states that the employees will not strike for any reason and that labor disputes will be resolved by arbitration.

Notice-and-comment rulemaking • A procedure in agency rulemaking that requires (1) notice, (2) opportunity for comment, and (3) a published draft of the final rule.

Novation • The substitution, by agreement, of a new contract for an old one, with the rights under the old one being terminated. Typically, there is a substitution of a new person who is responsible for the contract and the removal of the original party's rights and duties under the contract.

Nuisance • A common law doctrine under which persons can be held liable for using their property in a way that unreasonably interferes with others' rights to use or enjoy their own property.

O

Offer • A promise or commitment to perform or refrain from performing some specified act in the future.

Offeree • A person to whom an offer is made.

Offeror • A person who makes an offer.

Online dispute resolution (ODR) • The resolution of disputes with the assistance of organizations that offer dispute-resolution services via the Internet.

Operating agreement • In a limited liability company, an agreement in which the members set forth the details of how the business will be managed and operated. State statutes typically give the members wide latitude in deciding for themselves the rules that will govern their organization.

Optimum profits • The amount of profits that a business can make and still act ethically, as opposed to maximum profits, defined as the amount of profits a firm can make if it is willing to disregard ethical concerns.

Order for relief • A court's grant of assistance to a complainant. In bankruptcy proceedings, the order relieves the debtor of the immediate obligation to pay the debts listed in the bankruptcy petition.

P

Parol evidence rule • A substantive rule of contracts, as well as a procedural rule of evidence, under which a court will not receive into evidence the parties' prior negotiations, prior agreements, or contemporaneous oral agreements if that evidence contradicts or varies the terms of the parties' written contract.

Partially disclosed principal • A principal whose identity is unknown by a third person, but the third person knows that the agent is or may be acting for a principal at the time the agent and the third person form a contract.

Partnering agreement • An agreement between a seller and a buyer who frequently do business with each other on the terms and conditions that will apply to all subsequently formed electronic contracts.

Partnership • An agreement by two or more persons to carry on, as co-owners, a business for profit.

Par-value shares • Corporate shares that have a specific face value, or formal cash-in value, written on them, such as one dollar.

Past consideration • An act done before the contract is made, which ordinarily, by itself, cannot be consideration for a later promise to pay for the act.

Patent • A government grant that gives an inventor the exclusive right or privilege to make, use, or sell his or her invention for a limited time period.

Peer-to-peer (P2P) networking • A technology that allows Internet users to access files on other users' computers.

Penalty • A sum inserted into a contract, not as a measure of compensation for its breach but rather as punishment for a default. The agreement as to the amount will not be enforced, and recovery will be limited to actual damages.

Per se violation A type of anticompetitive agreement—such as a horizontal price-fixing agreement—that is considered to be so injurious to the public that there is no need to determine whether it actually injures market competition; rather, it is in itself (*per se*) a violation of the Sherman Act.

Performance • In contract law, the fulfillment of one's duties arising under a contract with another; the normal way of discharging one's contractual obligations.

Periodic tenancy • A lease interest in land for an indefinite period involving payment of rent at fixed intervals, such as week to week, month to month, or year to year.

Persuasive authority • Any legal authority or source of law that a court may look to for guidance but on which it need not rely in making its decision. Persuasive authorities include cases from other jurisdictions and secondary sources of law.

Petition in bankruptcy • The document that is filed with a bankruptcy court to initiate bankruptcy proceedings. The official forms required for a petition in bankruptcy must be completed accurately, sworn to under oath, and signed by the debtor.

Petty offense • In criminal law, the least serious kind of criminal offense, such as a traffic or building-code violation.

Plaintiff • One who initiates a lawsuit.

Plea bargain • A negotiated agreement between a criminal defendant and the prosecutor in a criminal case that usually involves the defendant's pleading guilty to a lesser offense in return for a lighter sentence.

Pleadings • Statements made by the plaintiff and the defendant in a lawsuit that detail the facts, charges, and defenses involved in the litigation; the complaint and answer are part of the pleadings.

Police powers • Powers possessed by states as part of their inherent sovereignty. These powers may be exercised to protect or promote the public order, health, safety, morals, and general welfare.

Positive law • The body of conventional, or written, law of a particular society at a particular point in time.

Precedent • A court decision that furnishes an example or authority for deciding subsequent cases involving identical or similar facts.

Predatory behavior • Business behavior that is undertaken with the intention of unlawfully driving competitors out of the market.

Predatory pricing • The pricing of a product below cost with the intent to drive competitors out of the market.

Preemption • A doctrine under which certain federal laws preempt, or take precedence over, conflicting state or local laws.

Preemptive rights • Rights held by shareholders that entitle them to purchase newly issued shares of a corporation's stock, equal in percentage to shares presently held, before the stock is offered to any outside buyers. Preemptive rights enable shareholders to maintain their proportionate ownership and voice in the corporation.

Preference • In bankruptcy proceedings, property transfers or payments made by the debtor that favor (give preference to) one creditor over others. The bankruptcy trustee is allowed to recover payments made both voluntarily and involuntarily to one creditor in preference over another.

Prenuptial agreement • An agreement made before marriage that defines each partner's ownership rights in the other partner's property. Prenuptial agreements must be in writing to be enforceable.

Preventive law • The law that an attorney practices when he or she plays the role of an adviser for a client, spotting possible legal problems and suggesting preventive measures before the problems harm the client.

Price discrimination • Setting prices in such a way that two competing buyers pay two different prices for identical products or services.

Price-fixing agreement • An agreement between competitors to fix the prices of products or services at a certain level.

Prima facie case • A case in which the plaintiff has produced sufficient evidence supporting his or her claim that the case can go to a jury; a case in which the evidence is such that the plaintiff will win if the defendant produces no affirmative defense or evidence to disprove it.

Primary source of law • A document that establishes the law on a particular issue, such as a constitution, a statute, an administrative rule, or a court decision.

Principle of rights • The principle that human beings have certain fundamental rights (to life, freedom, and the pursuit of happiness, for example). Those who adhere to this "rights theory" believe that a key factor in determining whether a business decision is ethical is how that decision affects the rights of various groups. These groups include the firm's owners, its employees, the consumers of its products or services, its suppliers, the community in which it does business, and society as a whole.

Privilege • In tort law, the ability to act contrary to another person's right without that person's having legal redress for such acts. Privilege may be raised as a defense to defamation.

Probable cause • Reasonable grounds for believing that a person should be arrested or searched.

Probate court • A state court of limited jurisdiction that conducts proceedings relating to the settlement of a deceased person's estate.

Procedural law • Law that establishes the methods of enforcing the rights established by substantive law.

Product liability • The legal liability of manufacturers, sellers, and lessors of goods to consumers, users, and bystanders for injuries or damages that are caused by the goods.

Profit • In real property law, the right to enter onto and remove things from the property of another (for example, the right to enter onto a person's land and remove sand and gravel therefrom).

Promisee • A person to whom a promise is made.

Promisor • A person who makes a promise.

Promissory estoppel • A doctrine that applies when a promisor makes a clear and definite promise on which the promisee justifiably relies; such a promise is binding if justice will be better served by the enforcement of the promise.

Protected class • A group of persons protected by specific laws because of the group's defining characteristics. Under laws prohibiting employment discrimination, these characteristics include race, color, religion, national origin, gender, age, and disability.

Proximate cause • Legal cause; exists when the connection between an act and an injury is strong enough to justify imposing liability.

Proxy • In corporation law, a written agreement between a stockholder and another under which the stockholder authorizes the other to vote the stockholder's shares in a certain manner.

Public policy • A government policy based on widely held societal values and (usually) expressed or implied in laws or regulations.

Puffery • A salesperson's exaggerated claims concerning the quality of items offered for sale. Such claims involve opinions rather than facts and are not considered to be legally binding promises or warranties.

Punitive damages • Money damages that may be awarded to a plaintiff to punish the defendant and deter future similar conduct.

Q

Quasi contract • A fictional contract imposed on parties by a court in the interests of fairness and justice; usually, quasi contracts are imposed to avoid the unjust enrichment of one party at the expense of another.

Quitclaim deed • A deed intended to pass any title, interest, or claim that the grantor may have in the property but not warranting that such title is valid. A quitclaim deed offers the least amount of protection against defects in the title.

Quorum • The number of members of a decision-making body that must be present before business may be transacted.

R

Ratification • The act of accepting and giving legal force to an obligation that previously was not enforceable.

Reasonable person standard • The standard of behavior expected of a hypothetical "reasonable person." The standard against which negligence is measured and that must be observed to avoid liability for negligence.

Record • According to the Uniform Electronic Transactions Act, information that is either inscribed on a tangible medium or stored in an electronic or other medium and that is retrievable.

Recording statutes • Statutes that allow deeds, mortgages, and other real property transactions to be recorded so as to provide notice to future purchasers or creditors of an existing claim on the property.

Red herring • A preliminary prospectus that can be distributed to potential investors after the registration statement (for a securities offering) has been filed with the Securities and Exchange Commission. The name derives from the red legend printed across the prospectus stating that the registration has been filed but has not become effective.

Regulation Z • A set of rules promulgated by the Federal Reserve Board to implement the provisions of the Truth-in-Lending Act.

Remainder • A future interest in property held by a person other than the original owner.

Remedy • The relief given to an innocent party to enforce a right or compensate for the violation of a right.

Reply • Procedurally, a plaintiff's response to a defendant's answer.

Res ipsa loquitur • A doctrine under which negligence may be inferred simply because an event occurred, if it is the type of event that would not occur in the absence of negligence. Literally, the term means "the facts speak for themselves."

Resale price maintenance agreement • An agreement between a manufacturer and a retailer in which the manufacturer specifies what the retail price of its products must be.

Rescission • A remedy whereby a contract is canceled and the parties are returned to the positions they occupied before the contract was made; may be effected through the mutual consent of the parties, by their conduct, or by court decree.

Respondeat superior • In Latin, "Let the master respond." A doctrine under which a principal or an employer is held liable for the wrongful acts committed by agents or employees while acting within the course and scope of their agency or employment.

Restitution • An equitable remedy under which a person is restored to his or her original position prior to loss or injury, or placed in the position he or she would have been in had the breach not occurred.

Retained earnings • The portion of a corporation's profits that has not been paid out as dividends to shareholders.

Reversionary interest • A future interest in property retained by the original owner.

Revocation • In contract law, the withdrawal of an offer by an offeror; unless the offer is irrevocable, it can be revoked at any time prior to acceptance without liability.

Right of contribution • The right of a co-surety who pays more than his or her proportionate share on a debtor's default to recover the excess paid from other co-sureties.

Right of first refusal • The right to purchase personal or real property—such as corporate shares or real estate—before the property is offered for sale to others.'

Right of reimbursement • The legal right of a person to be restored, repaid, or indemnified for costs, expenses, or losses incurred or expended on behalf of another.

Right of subrogation • The right of a person to stand in the place of (be substituted for) another, giving the substituted party the same legal rights that the original party had.

Right-to-work law • A state law providing that employees are not to be required to join a union as a condition of obtaining or retaining employment.

Robbery • The act of forcefully and unlawfully taking personal property of any value from another; force or intimidation is usually necessary for an act of theft to be considered a robbery.

Rule of four • A rule of the United States Supreme Court under which the Court will not issue a writ of *certiorari* unless at least four justices approve of the decision to issue the writ.

Rule of reason • A test by which a court balances the positive effects (such as economic efficiency) of an agreement against its potentially anticompetitive effects. In antitrust litigation, many practices are analyzed under the rule of reason.

Rulemaking • The actions undertaken by administrative agencies when formally adopting new regulations or amending old ones. Under the Administrative Procedure Act, rulemaking includes notifying the public of proposed rules or changes and receiving and considering the public's comments.

S

S corporation • A close business corporation that has met certain requirements as set out by the Internal Revenue Code and thus qualifies for special income tax treatment. Essentially, an S corporation is taxed the same as a partnership, but its owners enjoy the privilege of limited liability.

Sales contract • A contract for the sale of goods under which the ownership of goods is transferred from a seller to a buyer for a price.

Search warrant • An order granted by a public authority, such as a judge, that authorizes law enforcement personnel to search particular premises or property.

SEC Rule 10b-5 • A rule of the Securities and Exchange Commission that makes it unlawful, in connection with the purchase or sale of any security, to make any untrue statement of a material fact or to omit a material fact if such omission causes the statement to be misleading.

Secondary boycott • A union's refusal to work for, purchase from, or handle the products of a secondary employer, with whom the union has no dispute, for the purpose of forcing that employer to stop doing business with the primary employer, with whom the union has a labor dispute.

Secondary source of law • A publication that summarizes or interprets the law, such as a legal encyclopedia, a legal treatise, or an article in a law review.

Security • Generally, a stock certificate, bond, note, debenture, warrant, or other document given as evidence of an ownership interest in a corporation or as a promise of repayment by a corporation.

Self-defense • The legally recognized privilege to protect oneself or one's property against injury by another. The privilege of self-defense protects only acts that are reasonably necessary to protect oneself, one's property, or another person.

Self-incrimination • The giving of testimony that may subject the testifier to criminal prosecution. The Fifth Amendment to the Constitution protects against self-incrimination by providing that no person "shall be compelled in any criminal case to be a witness against himself."

Seniority system • In regard to employment relationships, a system in which those who have worked longest for the company are first in line for promotions, salary increases, and other benefits and last to be laid off if the work force must be reduced.

Service mark • A mark used in the sale or advertising of services to distinguish the services of one person or company from those of others.

Severance pay • Funds in excess of normal wages or salaries paid to an employee on termination of his or her employment with a company.

Sexual harassment • In the employment context, (1) the granting of job promotions or other benefits in return for sexual favors or (2) language or conduct that is so sexually offensive that it creates a hostile working environment.

Shareholder's derivative suit • A suit brought by a shareholder to enforce a corporate cause of action against a third person.

Shrink-wrap agreement • An agreement whose terms are expressed in a document located inside a box in which goods (usually software) are packaged; sometimes called a *shrink-wrap license.*

Slander • Defamation in oral form.

Slander of quality (trade libel) • The publication of false information about another's product, alleging that it is not what its seller claims.

Slander of title • The publication of a statement that denies or casts doubt on another's legal ownership of any property, causing financial loss to that property's owner.

Small claims court • A special court in which parties may litigate small claims (such as $5,000 or less). Attorneys are not required in small claims courts and, in some states, are not allowed to represent the parties.

Sociological school • A school of legal thought that views the law as a tool for promoting justice in society.

Sole proprietorship • The simplest form of business, in which the owner is the business; the owner reports business income on his or her personal income tax return and is legally responsible for all debts and obligations incurred by the business.

Sovereign immunity • A doctrine that immunizes foreign nations from the jurisdiction of U.S. courts when certain conditions are satisfied.

Spam • Bulk, unsolicited ("junk") e-mail.

Specific performance • An equitable remedy requiring exactly the performance that was specified in a contract; usually granted only when money damages would be an inadequate remedy and the subject matter of the contract is unique (for example, real property).

Standing to sue • The requirement that an individual must have a sufficient stake in a controversy before he or she can bring a lawsuit. The plaintiff must demonstrate that he or she has been either injured or threatened with injury.

Stare decisis • A common law doctrine under which judges are obligated to follow the precedents established in prior decisions.

Statute of Frauds • A state statute under which certain types of contracts must be in writing to be enforceable.

Statutes of repose • Laws that place time limits on some claims so that defendants will not be vulnerable to lawsuits indefinitely.

Statutory law • The body of law enacted by legislative bodies (as opposed to constitutional law, administrative law, or case law).

Stock certificate • A certificate issued by a corporation evidencing the ownership of a specified number of shares in the corporation.

Strict liability • Liability regardless of fault. In tort law, strict liability is imposed on a merchant who introduces into commerce a good that is unreasonably dangerous when in a defective condition.

Sublease • A lease executed by the lessee of real estate to a third person, conveying the same interest that the lessee enjoys but for a shorter term than that held by the lessee.

Submission • An agreement by two or more parties to refer any disputes they may have under their contract to a disinterested third party, such as an arbitrator, who has the power to render a binding decision.

Substantive law • Law that defines, describes, regulates, and creates legal rights and obligations.

Summary jury trial • A method of settling disputes in which a trial is held, but the jury's verdict is not binding. The verdict acts only as a guide to both sides in reaching an agreement during the mandatory negotiations that immediately follow the summary jury trial.

Summons • A document informing a defendant that a legal action has been commenced against him or her and that the defendant must appear in court on a certain date to answer the plaintiff's complaint. The document is delivered by a sheriff or any other person so authorized.

Supremacy clause • The provision in Article VI of the Constitution that provides that the Constitution, laws, and treaties of the United States are "the supreme Law of the Land." Under this clause, state and local laws that directly conflict with federal law will be rendered invalid.

Surety • A person, such as a cosigner on a note, who agrees to be primarily responsible for the debt of another.

Suretyship • An express contract in which a third party to a debtor-creditor relationship (the surety) promises to be primarily responsible for the debtor's obligation.

Symbolic speech • Nonverbal expressions of beliefs. Symbolic speech, which includes gestures, movements, and articles of clothing, is given substantial protection by the courts.

T

Technology licensing • Allowing another to use and profit from intellectual property (patents, copyrights, trademarks, innovative products or processes, and so on) for consideration. In the context of international business transactions, technology licensing is sometimes an attractive alternative to the establishment of foreign production facilities.

Tenancy at sufferance • A type of tenancy under which one who, after rightfully being in possession of leased premises, continues (wrongfully) to occupy the property after the lease has been terminated. The tenant has no rights to possess the property and occupies it only because the person entitled to evict the tenant has not done so.

Tenancy at will • A type of tenancy under which either party can terminate the tenancy without notice; usually arises when a tenant who has been under a tenancy for years retains possession, with the landlord's consent, after the tenancy for years has terminated.

Tenancy for years • A type of tenancy under which property is leased for a specified period of time, such as a month, a year, or a period of years.

Tender • An unconditional offer to perform an obligation by a person who is ready, willing, and able to do so.

Third party beneficiary • One for whose benefit a promise is made in a contract but who is not a party to the contract.

Tippee • A person who receives inside information.

Tombstone ad • An advertisement, historically in a format resembling a tombstone, of a securities offering. The ad informs potential investors of where and how they can obtain a prospectus.

Tort • A civil wrong not arising from a breach of contract. A breach of a legal duty that proximately causes harm or injury to another.

Tortfeasor • One who commits a tort.

Trade dress • The image and overall appearance of a product—for example, the distinctive decor, menu, layout, and style of service of a particular restaurant. Basically, trade dress is subject to the same protection as trademarks.

Trade name • A term that is used to indicate part or all of a business's name and that is directly related to the business's reputation and goodwill. Trade names are protected under the common law (and under trademark law, if the name is the same as the firm's trademarked property).

Trade secrets • Information or processes that give a business an advantage over competitors who do not know the information or processes.

Trademark • A distinctive mark, motto, device, or emblem that a manufacturer stamps, prints, or otherwise affixes to the goods it produces so that they can be identified on the market and their origins made known. Once a trademark is established (under the common law or through registration), the owner is entitled to its exclusive use.

Trespass to land • The entry onto, above, or below the surface of land owned by another without the owner's permission or legal authorization.

Trespass to personal property • The unlawful taking or harming of another's personal property; interference with another's right to the exclusive possession of his or her personal property.

Tying arrangement • An agreement between a buyer and a seller under which the buyer of a specific product or service becomes obligated to purchase additional products or services from the seller.

U

U.S. trustee • A government official who performs certain administrative tasks that a bankruptcy judge would otherwise have to perform.

Unconscionable contract (or Unconscionable clause) • A contract or clause that is void on the basis of public policy because one party, as a result of his or her disproportionate bargaining power, is forced to accept terms that are unfairly burdensome and that unfairly benefit the dominating party.

Undisclosed principal • A principal whose identity is unknown by a third person, and the third person has no knowledge that the agent is acting for a principal at the time the agent and the third person form a contract.

Unenforceable contract • A valid contract rendered unenforceable by some statute or law.

Unilateral contract • A contract that results when an offer can only be accepted by the offeree's performance.

Union shop • A place of employment in which all workers, once employed, must become union members within a specified period of time as a condition of their continued employment.

Unreasonably dangerous product • A product that is defective to the point of threatening a consumer's health and safety. A product will be considered unreasonably dangerous if it is dangerous beyond the expectation of the ordinary consumer or if a less dangerous alternative was economically feasible for the manufacturer but the manufacturer failed to produce it.

Use zoning • Zoning classifications within a particular municipality that may be distinguished based on the uses to which the land is to be put.

Usury • Charging an illegal rate of interest.

Utilitarianism • An approach to ethical reasoning that evaluates behavior not on the basis of any absolute ethical or moral values but on the basis of the consequences of that behavior for those who will be affected by it. In utilitarian reasoning, a "good" decision is one that results in the greatest good for the greatest number of people affected by the decision.

V

Valid contract • A contract that results when elements necessary for contract formation (agreement, consideration, legal purpose, and contractual capacity) are present.

Venue • The geographic district in which an action is tried and from which the jury is selected.

Verdict • A formal decision made by a jury.

Vertical merger • The acquisition by a company at one level in a marketing chain of a company at a higher or lower level in the chain (such as its supplier or retailer).

Vertical restraint • Any restraint on trade created by agreements between firms at different levels in the manufacturing and distribution process.

Vertically integrated firm • A firm that carries out two or more functional phases (manufacture, distribution, retailing, and so on) of a product.

Vesting • The creation of an absolute or unconditional right or power.

Void contract • A contract having no legal force or binding effect.

Voidable contract • A contract that may be legally avoided (canceled, or annulled) at the option of one of the parties.

Voir dire • Old French verbs that mean, "to speak the truth." In jury trials, the phrase refers to the process in which the attorneys question prospective jurors to determine whether they are biased or have any connection with a party to the action or with a prospective witness.

W

Warranty deed • A deed in which the seller assures (warrants to) the buyer that the seller has title to the property conveyed in the deed, that there are no encumbrances on the property other than what the seller has represented, and that the buyer will enjoy quiet possession of the property; a deed that provides the greatest amount of protection for the buyer.

Watered stock • Shares of stock issued by a corporation for which the corporation receives, as payment, less than the stated value of the shares.

Wetlands • Water-saturated areas of land that support specific types of vegetation. Under the Clean Water Act, wetlands are protected areas that cannot be filled in or dredged by private contractors or parties without a permit.

White-collar crime • Nonviolent crime committed by individuals or corporations to obtain a personal or business advantage.

Wildcat strike • A strike that is not authorized by the union that ordinarily represents the striking employees.

Workers' compensation laws • State statutes establishing an administrative procedure for compensating workers' injuries that arise out of—or in the course of—their employment, regardless of fault.

Workout • An out-of-court agreement between a debtor and his or her creditors in which the parties work out a payment plan or schedule under which the debtor's debts can be discharged.

Writ of attachment • A court's order, prior to a trial to collect a debt, directing the sheriff or other officer to seize nonexempt property of the debtor. If the creditor prevails at trial, the seized property can be sold to satisfy the judgment.

Writ of *certiorari* • A writ from a higher court asking the lower court for the record of a case.

Writ of execution • A court's order, after a judgment has been entered against the debtor, directing the sheriff to seize (levy) and sell any of the debtor's nonexempt real or personal property. The proceeds of the sale are used to pay off the judgment, accrued interest, and costs of the sale; any surplus is paid to the debtor.

Y

Yellow dog contract • An agreement under which an employee promises his or her employer, as a condition of employment, not to join a union.

Z

Zoning • The division of a city by legislative regulation into districts and the application in each district of regulations having to do with structural and architectural designs of buildings and prescribing the use to which buildings within designated districts may be put.

Zoning variance • The granting of permission by a municipality or other public board to a landowner to use his or her property in a way that does not strictly conform with the zoning regulations so as to avoid causing the landowner undue hardship.

Table of Cases

Note: The titles of cases presented within the text of the chapters are in boldface.

Index

Photo Credits

7 © Michael Evans, Sygma   10 From the Painting by Benjamin Ferrers, National Portrait Gallery, Photo: Corbis-Bettmann   32 © PhotoDisc   45 Ron Edmonds, AP Photo   65 Jeff Greenberg, PhotoEdit   67 © PhotoDisc   72 © Tom McCathy, PhotoEdit   82 Steven Senne, AP Photo   102 © Bettmann   115 Alburquerque Journal, Mark Holm, AP Photo   117 © Richard Strauss, Smithsonian Institution, Collection of the Supreme Court of the United States   128 Courtesy of the Michigan Governor's Office   144 Sabina Louise Pierce, AP Photo   149 © Chris Brown, Stock Boston   150 Ben Margot, AP Photo   205 Marta Lavandier, AP Photo   206 Steve Ueckert, Pool, AP Photo   213 © Michael Newman, PhotoEdit   221 NYPD, AP Photo   245 © Frederick D. Bodlin, Stock Boston   257 Paul Thompson, Image State   276 © Steve Leonard, Black Star   295 © Mike Mazzaschi, Stock Boston   296 Chris Kasson, AP Photo   297 By Authors   327 PhotoDisc   330 © Ron Chapple, FPG   332 © Billy E. Barnes, PhotoEdit   338 © PhotoDisc   345 © Michael Newman, PhotoEdit   349 © M. Borchi, Photo Researchers   386 © PhotoDisc   392 © Elizabeth Simpson, FPG   382 ©PhotoDisc   427 © Jim Erickson, The Stock Market   428 © PhotoDisc   445 © McIntyre, Photo Researchers   452 © PhotoDisc   471 © Myrleen Ferguson, PhotoEdit   478 © Tony Freeman, PhotoEdit   516 © Comstock   518 © Amy C. Etra, PhotoEdit   524 © Michael Newman, PhotoEdit   525 © The Library of Congress   558 Maria De Kord, Image State   562 © John Boykin, PhotoEdit   577 © Deborah Davis, PhotoEdit   593 © Jonathan Nourok, PhotoEdit   617 Robert Brenner, PhotoDisc   640 PhotoDisc   661 © Jonathan Nourok, PhotoEdit   683 © PhotoDisc   701 © John Coletti, Stock Boston   725 © David Young-Wolff, PhotoEdit   732 Hayden Roger Celestin EPA-Photo

Chapter-Ending Pedagogy

- Key Terms (with appropriate page references).
- Chapter Summary (in graphic format with page references).
- For Review (a series of brief review questions).
- Questions and Case Problems (includes hypotheticals as well as problems based on actual cases).
- A Question of Ethics and Social Responsibility.

- Case Briefing Assignment (in selected chapters; instructs students to brief cases contained in Appendix A).
- For Critical Analysis.
- Interacting with the Internet.
- Online Legal Research Exercises.
- Before the Test.
- Video Question (in selected chapters).

Unit-Ending Pedagogy

CUMULATIVE BUSINESS HYPOTHETICAL Each unit concludes with a section that introduces a hypothetical business firm and then asks a series of questions about how the law applies to the various actions taken by the firm. The questions cover many of the legal topics discussed throughout the unit. This feature can be found on the Following pages:

- The Foundations 1
- The Public Environment 136
- The Private Environment 233
- The Employment Environment 509
- The Regulatory Environment 609
- The International Environment 755

APPENDICES